Hering's Dictionary of Classical and Modern Cookery

Hering's Dictionary of Classical and Modern Cookery

HERING'S DICTIONARY OF CLASSICAL AND MODERN COOKERY

and
Practical Reference Manual
for the
Hotel, Restaurant and Catering Trade

Brief recipes,
professional knowledge concerning wine,
cocktails and other drinks,
menu knowledge and table service

Vocabulary in English, French, German,
Italian and Spanish

9th English Edition
by
WALTER BICKEL

VIRTUE & COMPANY LIMITED
LONDON, DUBLIN and COULSDON

Edited, revised and translated by Walter Bickel
Title of original publication:
„Lexikon der Küche" by Richard Hering

ISBN 3-8057-0281-7

English Language Edition, Distributed by Virtue & Company Limited,
25 Breakfield, Coulsdon, Surrey, United Kingdom.

Offsetprinting and bookbinding:
Brühlsche Universitätsdruckerei, Giessen (Germany)

Preface

I have long admired Hering's Dictionary of Classical and Modern Cookery as a most workmanlike distillation of the literature of professional cookery into portable form. "Gastronomy is the reasoned comprehension of everything connected with the nourishment of man", wrote Brillat-Savarin. It is this Dictionary's distinction that so much of what the professional chef and restaurateur needs to know of such a vast subject can be found within its pages.

But not only have I admired the Dictionary, but for many years have known and respected Walter Bickel, its editor, a true scholar-chef, who has not merely preserved the best of Hering's work on classical recipes but has kept the dictionary up to date as an equally authentic guide to modern practise.

Richard Hering's Dictionary was, when it appeared almost seventy years ago, a modest little book of less than 1000 abbreviated recipes in repertory style. Its author could hardly have realised that his lexicon was destined to endure for edition to edition into the now substantial repertory of over 16 000 professional recipe summaries and itself to achieve the status of a culinary classic. Much of this reputation is due to the solid work in post-war years of its distinguished editor, Mr. Walter Bickel, himself the author of many books and articles on gastronomical themes, has skilfully kept up to date and improved this famous dictionary.

The original author, Richard Hering, was chef the cuisine of Vienna's Hotel Metropole. Walter Bickel, too, is a former chef of the greatest distinction. Following a long experience in London from apprenticeship at the old Restaurant Frascati, he held appointments both in England's provinces as well as further experience in its capital, at the Trocadero and Clariges. He was for 4 years chef at the German Embassy in Paris and was directeur de cuisine of the German Pavillon during the World Exhibition, 1937. One-time chef at the court of Roumania, he was also catering director of Ashinger and Kempinski which before the war was the largest catering concern on the continent.

To his task of editing Hering's Dictionary, therefore, Walter Bickel has for many years brought an unique knowledge of French cuisine and the English, German and French languages. However, his width of interest has brought additional features to the Dictionary's repertory including professional information about drinks, table service and also a 5 language vocabulary. Just as importantly, Walter Bickel, has brought to his task scholarly interest, an orderly mind and a deep knowledge of and respect for culinary tradition, history and literature. The result is that this new edition of Hering's Dictionary of Classical and Modern Cookery remains an unique guide to gastronomy, both traditional and modern. It is destined to renew the success it has for so long richly deserved.

John Fuller

Formerly Professor of Hotel Management and Director The Scottish Hotel School, University of Strathclyde, Glasgow, and formerly Visiting Professor, Michigan State University, U. S. A.

Introduction

This is no cookery book in the usual sense of the word but a most comprehensive gastronomic encyclopedia and reference work for employers and employees in the catering trade. For the chef who knows the fundamental basics of cookery, this "chefs reminder" will certainly prove to be a most valuable help, and for hoteliers, restaurateurs and the waiting personel a reliable guide through all the classical, modern, international and regional dishes occurring in finer Hotel and Restaurant kitchens. All readers will derive lasting benefits from the articles on service, wine and professional knowledge, menu-making, carving and the glossary of kitchen terms and expressions.

The curtailed recipes in this book cover everything in cookery and are based on the original recipes of master chefs from all over the world. Wherever there has been a doubt about the authencity of a dish or where two or more versions differ, all versions are given, obsolete recipes have been discarded.

Walter Bickel

HOW TO USE THIS BOOK

All recipes are concisely presented in encyclopedic order. The English name is given first followed by the French name. Cross-references have been used only when it is felt that they are necessary.

To facilitate the finding of any recipe or culinary term there are three complete indexes. The first covers all recipes, culinary terms and information of interest in English; the second is a complete guide to all recipes in French and the third an index of the regional dishes of many countries.

Table of Contents

Hors-d'oeuvre

Appetizers Side dishes		Savouries, Savories
Hors-d'oeuvre	French	Savouries
Vorspeisen	German	Würzbissen
Antipasti	Italian	Saporitos
Entradas	Spanish	Bocado-saproso

Appetizers or side dishes ought to be small, dainty and toothsome. The idea is that one should nibble at a few but refrain from making a meal of them. As the French word "Hors-d'oeuvre" indicates they are something outside of the main edifice of the meal, especially cold appetizers. Cold appetizers are usually served as a first course; assorted appetizers for luncheon and rich hors-d'oeuvre such a lobster, goose liver patty or parfait, chilled melon, caviar, oysters etc. at dinner parties. If lobster or goose liver patty etc. is presented as an appetizer it must not be served again as part of another dish or as a garnish during the meal. As a rule hot side dishes are served after the soup and help to reinforce a meal in the role of a light entrée.

What counts above all is the presentation of these dishes. They must be attractive and original and ought to be served on immaculate silver plate and glistening crystal dishes or very fine china.

Very small side dishes such as smoked fish, cheese, tiny broiled sausages, scampi etc. stuck on sticks or skewers help to stimulate the appetite and may be served as appetizers for cocktail parties.

Savouries or savories are sharp fancy tidbits very often made of cheese and usually served in Great Britain after the ice cream or at the end of the meal. In other countries many of these savouries are served as an appetizer and cheese soufflés, tartlets etc. instead of a sweet at gentlemen's luncheons.

A

Aceto-dolce: Italian sweet sour fruit-pickles with mustard seeds and vegetables in white wine and honey.

Achards: East Indian commercial pickles consisting of melon, knob celery, bamboo, radishes, nuts, cucumbers, Indian corn and mushrooms in spiced vinegar.

Agoursi: see Ogourzi.

Alligator Pear Cocktail: see Avocado Cocktail.

Allumettes: see puff pastry sticks.

Almonds, Salted: Amandes salées: scald, peel and roast almonds lightly sprinkled with salt and oil.

Anchovies, Deviled: Anchovis à la diable: fresh anchovies boned, lightly spread with mustard, sprinkled with cayenne, dipped in egg and breadcrumbs, deep fried, dressed on toast.

Anchovies, Fried: Anchois frits: Fillets dipped in frying batter, fried in deep fat, dressed with fried parsley and lemon.

— **with Green Peppers:** Anchois aux poivrons: fillets of anchovies arranged criss-cross on glass dish, garnished with shredded green peppers, chopped hard boiled eggs, capers and chopped parsley.

— **Marinated:** Anchois marinées: fresh anchovies, fried, marinated for 24 hours with oil, vinegar, pepper, sliced root vegetables and spices, served cold; toast separately.

— **Modern Style:** à la moderne: fillets of anchovies rolled round olives stuffed with fish purée in French dressing with chopped fine herbs.

— **Norvegian: Kilkis:** Commercial product.

Anchovy Fillets: Filets d'anchois: Marinated in oil, dressed criss-cross on glass dish.

— **Paste, Provençale:** Purée d'anchois à la provençale, also Tapenade: Anchovies crushed with ripe olives, garlic, thyme and bay leaves, seasoned with mustard and Worcestershire sauce, strained, mixed with oil and brandy, filled in jars, covered with oil; spread for toast or canapes.

— **Puffs, Swedish:** Petits choux à la suédoise: Small puffs of unsweetened cream puff paste, baked, when cold filled with minced anchovy fillets, mixed with butter and hard egg yolks strained through a sieve and creamed, glazed with aspic jelly, sprinkled with chopped hard boiled egg and truffles, decorated with a slice of boiled lobster.

— **Rings:** Rings filled with capers preserved in oil; commercial product.

— **Tartlets:** Tartelettes d'anchois: puffpaste tartlets filled with anchovy paste or marinated anchovies, garnished with hard boiled egg, capers, tarragon and chervil.

— **Toast:** Pain grillé aux anchois: toast spread with butter, seasoned with mustard powder and Cayenne pepper, anchovy fillets criss-cross on top, garnished with chopped hard boiled egg, chopped parsley and lemon.

Angels on Horseback: see oysters English Style.

Anguille: see Eel.

Antipasti: I. An Italian commercial combination of preserved sardines, tuna, pickles, capers, anchovies, olives, artichoke bottoms etc. preserved in oil.
II. Artichoke bottoms, cauliflower, carrots, celery, green peppers, egg-plant, tunafish etc. Broil peppers and egg plant, cook vegetables, marinate in stone jar with salt, bay leaves, garlic, nutmeg, pepper, oil and tarragon vinegar.

Appetizer, Livonian: Livländer Vorschmack: diced desalted herrings mixed with butter, egg yolks, pepper, paprika and stiffly beaten egg whites, baked in flat baking pan, cut in pieces, served hot. (Russian)

— **Russian:** see Zakouski.

Appetizers, Greek: Hors-d'oeuvre à la grecque: consist of preparations à la grecque such as artichoke bottoms, celery, mushrooms, button onions etc. which see.

— **Swedish:** Appétissants à la suédoise: dainty open face sandwiches of rye bread spread with anchovy or other butter, topped with herring, anchovies, smoked salmon, eggs, lobster, raw oysters, hard boiled eggs, ham, hard sausage etc., decorated attractively.

Apples, Californian: Pommes à la californienne: apples, peeled and hollowed out, stuffed with salad of chicken and celery, lid put on and decorated with green butter.

Artichoke Bottoms with Cauliflower: Fonds d'artichauts à la Dubarry: fill cold marinated bottoms with cauliflower sprigs, boiled, marinated and covered with mayonnaise.

— — **Dieppe Style:** à la dieppoise: filled with mussels and shrimps mixed with mayonnaise sauce.

— — **Garnished:** garnis: cooked, marinated in oil and lemon juice, filled with tuna fish, vegetable or asparagus salad etc.

— — **Greek Style:** à la grecque: prepared the same way as artichokes.

— — **in Oil:** à la l'huile: cooked in oil and lemon juice with chopped onions, served cold.

— — **President Style:** à la président: stuffed with purée of chicken blended with mayonnaise, garnished with slices of hard boiled egg and truffle, glazed with aspic jelly.

Artichokes, Devilled: Artichauts à la diable: cut small artichokes in quarters, parboil, season highly, dip in frying batter, fry and sprinkle with salt mixed with cayenne.

— **Greek Style:** à la grecque: cut small artichokes in quarters, scald, cook in white wine, vinegar, oil condimented with fennel, onions, celery, coriander, bayleaves and thyme, serve cold in their liquor.

— **Oriental Style:** Artichauts à l'orientale: small artichokes, hollowed out, stuffed with bread crumbs mixed with chopped mint, salt, pepper and garlic, stewed in oil and lemon juice, served cold.

Aspic, Italian Chicken: Aspic de volaille à l'italienne: moulds lined with aspic, decorated with truffles, filled with tiny strips of roast chicken, smoked ox tongue and truffles, filled with aspic, chilled, turned out, dressed on Italian salad, served with remoulade sauce.

— **Lobster:** Aspic de homard: mould lined with aspic, decorated with truffle, hard boiled egg white etc., filled with lobster salad, chilled, turned out and served with chopped aspic.

— **Metropole:** slices of boned and skinned sterlet, poached in white wine and fish stock, when cold garnished with a slice of tomato, halved hard boiled eggs filled with caviar with a crayfish tail on top, glazed with aspic jelly made of fish stock clarified with raw egg white and pressed caviar. (Russian)

— **Shrimp:** Aspic de crevettes: mould lined with aspic jelly, decorated with small shrimps and truffles, froth of shrimps in center, filled with aspic, chilled, turned out, adorned with aspic jelly.

— **Tsars Style:** Aspic du tsar: same as Metropole but served with grated horseradish, mixed with salt, vinegar, pinch of sugar and whipped cream. (Russian)

Attereaux: see skewers.

Avocado Cocktail: dice avocados and serve chilled, covered with cocktail sauce made of tomato catsup, Worcestershire sauce, lemon juice and thick cream, seasoned with paprika.

B

Bananas Cumberland: Bananes à la Cumberland: bananas sliced thin, mixed with Cumberland sauce, chopped pistachios sprinkled on top; served cold.

— **Pickled:** Condiment de bananes: boil sugar, vinegar and peppercorns tied in a bag, drain liquor, mix with chopped green peppers, boil, pour over bananas and let them marinate a week.

Barquettes: small boat shaped moulds, lined with puff or short paste, rice or semolina, baked, filled with salpicon, purée, salads etc., served hot or cold.

— **Aurora:** boats of unsweetened short paste filled with Italian salad bound with mayonnaise mixed with tomato purée.

— **with Caviar:** à la russe: puff paste boats filled with caviar, springled with chopped chives.

— **Danish:** à la danoise: small pieces of cucumber, boat-shaped, hollowed out, cooked, stuffed with purée of smoked salmon, smoked herring and hard boiled egg, sprinkled with grated horseradish.

— **Indian:** à l'indienne: lined with rice, filled with purée of chicken and chopped ham, seasoned with curry, garnished with slices of hard boiled egg and chopped parsley.

— **Lobster:** à l'américaine: boats baked of yeast dough, hollowed out, filled with diced lobster in American sauce (which see), covered with lobster mousse, baked.

— **Mirabeau:** puff pastry boats filled with chopped egg, mixed with anchovy butter, garnished with anchovy fillets.

— **Norma:** boats of baked yeast dough, hollowed out, filled with salad of tuna fish, garnished with caviar, slices of hard boiled egg, lemon and chopped chives.

— **Northern Style:** à la nordique: boats of yeast dough, hollowed out, filled with diced chicken in mayonnaise, garnished with asparagus tips and truffles.

— **Oyster:** de huîtres: boats lined with puff paste, baked, filled with oysters in cream sauce, sprinkled with grated parmesan cheese, browned.

— **with Soft Roes:** baked boats of yeast dough hollowed out, filled with poached soft roe in cream sauce, sprinkled with grated Parmesan, browned.

— **Varsovian:** à la varsovienne: boats of yeast dough, baked, hollowed out, filled with salad of chopped beets, pickles and hard boiled eggs, garnished with caviar.

Beef, Potted: beef paste preserved in cans or jars, used as spread for canapes or sandwiches.

— **Smoked Brisket of:** Hamburger Rauchfleisch; smoked brisket, boiled, when cold cut in thin slices, served with horseradish. (German)

Beefsteak à la tartare: see Tartar Steak.

Bengalines of Woodcock: Bengalines de bécasse: small moulds lined with mousse of woodcock, filled with small slices of roast woodcock breast, covered with mousse, chilled, turned out, coated with brown game chaudfroid sauce, sprinkled with chopped truffles.

Beurrecks: see Turkish cheese sticks.

Blinis: see Russian pancakes.

Blinzes: see Cheese Blinzes, Jewish.

Boars Head, Stuffed: head boned, stuffed with forcemeat mixed with diced oxtongue, goose liver, truffles and pistachios, tied in a cloth, boiled, cooled, decorated with imitation tusks, eyes etc., garnished with aspic jelly, served with Cumberland sauce.

Brochettes: see skewers.

C

Cabbage, Stuffed: Chou farci: parboiled leaves of white cabbage, stuffed with parboiled rice, mixed with chopped onions, diced tomatoes and green peppers, shaped into small heads, braised, marinated with oil and vinegar, served cold.

Caisse: Caisse or Cassolette: small container, round, sometimes square, in silver, paper or crockery or baked of batter, not more than 2½ inches in diameter, used for hot food, A cassolette is a caisse with a handle. See also main dishes.

— **Beet root:** Caisse de betteraves: large cubes of boiled beet root, hollowed out, marinated in vinegar, filled with diced pickled cucumber, hard boiled eggs, capers, anchovies and chopped herbs, seasoned with oil vinegar and mustard.

— **Cardinal:** Caisses à la cardinal: diced lobster and truffles, bound with Béchamel sauce, mixed with lobster butter, filled in china cases, sprinkled with grated cheese and browned.

— **Casanova:** caisse of batter filled with strips of cooked knob celery, truffles and hard boiled egg, bound with mayonnaise sauce.

— **Mascotte:** small china cases filled with Rachel salad (which see) with strips of chicken, garnished with asparagus tips and truffles.

Calf's Brains Italian Style: Cervelle de veau à l'italienne: cooked in white wine, when cold, jellied with aspic mixed with chopped herbs.

— **Brains, Marinated:** Cervelle de veau marinée: cooked, when cold marinated with salt, pepper, vinegar and oil.

— **Brains Robert:** Slice and alternate with cooked slices of knob celery, cover with mayonnaise, seasoned with mustard.

— **Brains in Shells:** Cervelle de veau en coquilles: cold, marinated slices, filled in shells, covered with mayonnaise sauce, sprinkled with herbs, chopped hard boiled eggs and capers.

— **Brains Vinaigrette:** Cervelle de veau vinaigrette: brains cooked, cold slices on lettuce, vinaigrette dressing with chopped herbs poured over.

— **Feet:** Pieds de veau: see main dishes.

— **Foot Salad:** Salade des pieds de veau: cooked boned, cut, in fine strips, marinated with French dressing, bound with green mayonnaise, served on lettuce leaves, garnished with slices of hard boiled egg and capers.

Camembert Fritters: Camembert frit: cut in cubes, breadcrumbed, fried in hot fat, seasoned with salt mixed with a dash of Cayenne pepper (Savory).

Canapés: dainty slices of bread, square, round, oval or rectangular, usually, toasted, nicely garnished and decorated.

Canapés

— **Admirals:** à l'amiral: oval slices, spread with shrimp butter, topped with shrimps' tails sprinkled with lobster coral.

— **Alberta:** cut in squares, spread with anchovy butter, smoked salmon strips criss-cross on top, decorated with red beets and maitre d'hotel butter.

— **Alladin:** Cut slices in half moons, toast, spread with purée of stockfish, garnish with chutney.

— **Alsatian:** à l'alsacienne: rounds of buttered toast, slice of goose liver parfait on top, garnished with slice of truffle, glazed with Madeira aspic jelly.

— **Anchovy:** aux anchois: squares or rectangles of buttered toast, covered with chopped hard boiled egg, anchovy fillets criss-cross on top.

— **Andalusian:** à l'andalouse: spread with butter, shrimps, anchovy fillets and chopped green peppers on top, covered with mayonnaise, sprinkled with chopped truffles.

— **Bagration:** spread of chopped lettuce, lobster, anchovies, olives and beetroot, mixed with mayonnaise.

— **Basle:** à la bâloise: squares of toast, spread with white purée of onion, thin slice of Swiss cheese on top baked, served hot.

— **Bayonese:** à la bayonnaise: squares of toast, topped with chopped ham, bound with thick Madeira sauce, sprinkled with grated cheese, browned, served hot.

— **Beef Marrow:** à la moelle: toasted ovals, spread with plain butter, poached slices of beef marrow, seasoned with salt and paprika on top, sprinkled with chopped parsley, served hot.

— **Bernese:** à la bernoise: fried squares, topped with chopped ham, bound with cream sauce, covered with a thin slice of Swiss cheese, browned, served hot.

— **Bresse Style:** à la bressane: squares of toast, covered with slice of fried ham, topped with fried chicken livers and grilled mushrooms, brown butter poured over, served hot.

— **Bristol:** squares oft toast, covered with slice of fried ham, topped with slices of poached beef marrow and a grilled mushroom, sprinkled with chopped parsley, served hot.

— **Capuchin:** à la capucine: rye bread spread with mayonnaise, one half topped with chopped hard boiled egg yolks, the other half with caviar, a small shrimp in the center.

— **Cardinal:** round, spread with mayonnaise, slice of lobster on top, garnished with slice of truffle, glazed with aspic jelly.

— **Chicken:** de volaille: toast, round or oval, topped with chopped chicken, mixed with butter, seasoned with salt and pepper.

— **Coquelin:** spread with anchovy purée mixed with grated cheese and butter, garnished with anchovy butter, gherkins and capers.

— **Crayfish:** aux écrevisses: spread with crayfish butter, topped with small crayfish tails, glazed with aspic jelly.

— **Danish:** à la danoise: squares of rye bread, spread with radish butter, strips of smoked salmon and herrings and caviar on top.

Canapés

— **Derby:** ham spread, mixed with chopped pickled walnuts.

— **Diana:** à la Diane: rectangles of buttered toast, covered with slice of grilled bacon, topped with fried chicken livers, served hot.

— **Dutch:** à l'hollandaise: round pieces of toast, topped with scrambled eggs, mixed with smoked haddock, served hot.

— **French:** à la française: rectangles, spread with anchovy butter, topped with a sardine, coated with remoulade sauce, sprinkled with chopped parsley.

— **Game:** de gibier: rounds of buttered toast, spread with purée of game blended with chopped mushrooms and truffles, served hot.

— **Gourmets:** toasted ovals, spread with goose liver butter, thin slice of chicken breast on top, glazed with Madeira jelly, adorned with chopped truffles.

— **Harlequin:** à l'arlequin: slices of different cuts, spread with various butter compositions, topped with chopped ham, ox tongue, hard boiled egg yolks and whites, smoked salmon, garnished with slices of truffle, chopped lobster coral etc.

— **Hungarian:** à la hongroise: rounds of plain bread, buttered, spread with purée of chicken, topped with chopped sweet red peppers.

— **Imperial:** à l'impériale: round, spread with butter, slice of goose liver patty on top, adorned with slice of truffle, glazed with Port jelly.

— **Indian:** à l'indienne: spread with chopped hard boiled egg yolks, mixed with butter and curry powder, topped with chopped mango chutney.

— **Ivanhoe:** Round pieces of toast spread with purée of smoked haddock, a grilled mushroom on top, served hot.

— **Lobster:** de homard: squares, spread with purée of butter, slice of lobster in center, adorned with mayonnaise sprinkled with chopped lobster coral or chopped hard boiled eggs.

— **Lothringian:** à la lorraine: square slices, spread with butter, topped with chopped chicken and smoked ox tongue, garnished with aspic jelly.

— **Lucca:** Oval slices, spread with butter, topped with caviar, a raw oyster in the center.

— **Lucille:** Cut in ovals, mustard butter spread, chopped smoked tongue and a thin slice of chicken breast on top.

— **Lucullus:** Rounds of toast, spread with chopped beef (tartare), a raw oyster in the center, adorned with caviar, half a slice of lemon on one side.

— **Mexican:** à la mexicaine: spread with plain butter, topped with chopped sardines and anchovy fillets, garnished with round slice of hard boiled egg with chopped red peppers in center.

— **Monte-Carlo:** toast spread with purée of goose liver patty, chopped hard boiled egg on top.

— **Mushroom:** aux champignons: rounds of buttered toast, topped with large grilled mushroom, served hot.

— **Norvegian:** à la norvégienne: rectangles of rye bread, spread with butter topped with strips of anchovy fillets, garnished with horseradish butter.

Canapés

— **Otéro:** rounds of toast, spread with plain butter, topped with caviar, a raw oyster placed in center, adorned with remoulade sauce.

— **Ox Tongue:** à l'écarlate: spread of mustard butter, topped with slices of smoked ox tongue, garnished with aspic jelly.

— **Oyster:** aux huîtres: rounds of toast, spread with butter, breaded fried oyster on top, served hot.

— **Princess:** à la princesse: rounds of toast, spread with plain butter, topped with chopped chicken, garnished with strips of anchovy fillets and a round slice of hard boiled egg, sprinkled with chopped chives.

— **à la réforme:** Spread of anchovy butter, topped with mixture of chopped smoked tongue, hard boiled egg and gherkins, adorned with aspic jelly.

— **Shrimp:** aux crevettes: spread with shrimp butter, topped, with shrimp tails, glazed with aspic jelly.

— **Spring:** à la printanière: plain white bread, spread with parsley butter, covered with chopped watercress, garnished with slices of hard boiled egg.

— **Soft Roe:** aux laitances: spread with plain butter, poached marinated soft roes of herring or carp on top.

— **Strassburg:** à la strassbourgoise: fried rounds of white bread, covered with small round slice of fried apple, topped with sauted slice of fresh goose liver, covered with a second slice of apple, served hot.

— **Sultans:** à la sultane: spread with anchovy butter, covered with diced lobster, topped with chopped lettuce and red peppers mixed with mayonnaise.

— **Tartar:** squares or rectangles of rye bread, spread with butter, topped with chopped lean beef, seasoned with salt and pepper, chopped onions and chopped gherkins on each side.

— **Tunny:** au thon: spread of mashed canned tunny fish, garnished with chopped aspic jelly.

— **Turbigo:** spread with plain butter, topped with chopped shrimps, cooked knob celery and pickles mixed with thick cold tomato sauce.

— **Windsor:** spread of chicken purée, mixed with chopped ham, smoked tongue and mustard powder, adorned with slices of gherkins and capers.

Cappone magro: seafood salad and mayonnaise, garnished with shredded chicken and sliced truffles. (Italian)

Carcass, Chicken: Carcasse de volaille: carcass of roast chicken, spread with mustard, sprinkled with cayenne pepper and grilled (Savoury).

Cardoons, Greek Style: Cardon à la grecque: cook in water with lemon juice, oil, thyme, bay leaves, fennel, peppercorns and tomatoes, serve cold in the broth.

Caroline: an éclair of unsweetened cream puff paste, stuffed with purée of fish, shellfish, meat, goose liver or game etc., coated with chaudfroid sauce matching the stuffing, glazed with aspic jelly.

Carp, Marinated: Carpe en marinade: pieces of carp poached in water with vinegar, shredded vegetables and spices, served cold in the jellied stock.

Cauliflower Salad: Salade de choux-fleurs: parboiled, when cold marinated with salt, pepper, oil, vinegar and mustard powder, served very cold, sprinkled with chopped herbs.

Caviar: The salted roe of various large sturgeons. Serve in glass dish on crushed ice on a napkin, for the finest service on carved and decorated iceblock with two cavities, one above, in which the dish or can with caviar is placed and one below for electric lights, to illuminate the ice. Caviar is served with lemon, toast and butter.

— **Andalusian:** Caviar à l'andalouse: hollow a middle sized boiled onion, fill with mixture of caviar, chopped hard boiled egg, bread crumbs, butter and pepper, bake, serve on toast with anchovy butter.

— **and Blini:** Caviar au blinis: caviar served with blini (which see), melted butter and thick sour cream.

— **Cannelons:** Cannelons au caviar: tubes of puff paste filled with caviar.

— **Malossol:** the grey mildly salted roe of the Beluga, the largest fish of the sturgeon family.

— **Pressed:** Caviar pressé: diced, marinated with French dressing and chopped onions, served very cold.

— **Rolls, Russian:** Petits pains de caviar à la russe: small rolls of rich yeast dough (brioches), cut in half, toasted, filled with caviar mixed with chopped onions and chives.

— **Salad:** Salade de caviar: usually made of carp or salmon caviar (Keta caviar), finely mashed with onions, seasoned with pepper and lemon juice, mixed with oil like mayonnaise, garnished with sliced tomatoes and black olives, served very cold (Roumanian)

— **Salmon** (Keta Caviar): Caviar de Namur: jellow caviar of salmon served with lemon.

— **Sticks:** Bâtons de caviar: small strips of puff paste, baked when cold, cut open and filled with caviar.

— **Tartlets:** Tartelettes au caviar: puff paste tartlet shells, filled with caviar, covered with mayonnaise, decorated with strips of anchovy fillets, glazed with aspic jelly.

Celery: Céleri en branches: Tender stalks cut lengthwise in four, served raw with salt as appetizer or with cheese.

— **Housewife Style:** Célery à la bonne femme: raw celery cut in slices, mixed with sliced potatoes and mayonnaise, seasoned with mustard powder.

— **Stuffed:** mashed Roquefort cheese, mixed with butter and cream, seasoned with Worcestershire sauce and paprika, piped into stalks of raw celery, served on lettuce and ice.

Cervelat: cervelas: cut in thin slices and garnished with parsley.

Chartreuse of Goose Liver: Chartreuse de foie gras: line mould with aspic jelly, arrange various cold vegetables symmetrically on sides, fill centre with cubes of goose liver patty, seal with aspic, chill, unmould and garnish with aspic.

— **of Quail:** Chartreuse de cailles: line mould with aspic jelly, arrange fancy vegetables as above, place quail larded with truffles and pistachios in centre, seal with aspic jelly, chill, unmould and serve on vegetable salad.

Chaudfroid Beaulieu: de faisan à la Beaulieu: small moulds lined with aspic jelly, decorated with truffle and hard boiled egg-white, when set lined with brown game chaudfroid sauce, filled with mousse of pheasant, mixed with purée of goose liver patty, covered with aspic jelly, chilled and turned out in small tartlets of puff paste.

Chaudfroid of Fieldfare: de grives à la gastronome: mould lined first with aspic jelly, decorated, coated with brown chaudfroid sauce, filled with roast cold fieldfare and aspic jelly, chilled, turned out on salad of shredded celery in mayonnaise sauce.

— **Oyster:** Chaudfroid d'huîtres: small mould lined with aspic jelly, filled with raw oysters, covered with pink chaudfroid sauce, chilled, turned out on toast, garnished with shredded lettuce.

— **of Partridge Prince Leopold:** slices of roast partridge breasts, coated with partridge mousse mixed with purée of goose liver patty, covered with brown chaudfroid sauce, sprinkled with chopped boiled ham and truffles, glazed with aspic jelly. Center of dish filled with salad of artichoke bottoms, truffles and champignons in mayonnaise, seasoned with mustard and Worcestershire sauce, decorated with truffle balls and rings of stuffed olives.

Cheese Blinzes, Jewish: Crêpes au fromage à la juive: sifted flour beaten with eggs, milk and very little oil, seasoned with salt and sugar, very small round pancakes baked with this batter, filled with creamed butter mixed with egg-yolks, cottage and cream cheese, seasoned with salt and sugar, chopped lemon and orange peels added.

— **Custard:** Crème de fromage: Parmesan cheese boiled in milk, seasoned with pepper, salt and paprika, thickened with egg yolks, filled in small pudding moulds, poached, chilled and served very cold.

— **Fritters, Polish:** Nalesnikis: mix cottage cheese with butter, egg yolks and cream, season, spread between two layers of thin pancakes, cut in squares, dip in frying batter and bake in deep fat. (Polish)

— **and Onions, Swiss Style:** see Käserösti.

— **Paillettes:** Paillettes de fromage: cheese straws cut very thin.

— **Puffs:** Choux au fromage: small unsweetened cream puffs baked, filled with soufflé mixture, baked slowly until filling is done, served hot. (Savory)

— **Puffs, Swiss:** Perles suisses: unsweetened cream puff paste, mixed with chopped Swiss cheese, seasoned with cayenne, baked, served hot. (Savory)

— **Soufflé Brillat-Savarin:** Soufflé de fromage Brillat-Savarin: thick cream sauce mixed with grated Swiss and Parmesan cheese, seasoned with cayenne pepper, nutmeg and salt, mixed with egg yolks, stiffly whipped egg whites folded in, poured in soufflé, dish greased with butter and baked in hot oven.

— **Soufflé, Italian:** Soufflé de fromage à l'italienne: Same as other cheese soufflés but exclusively with Parmesan cheese.

— **Soufflé, Lyonese:** à la lyonnaise: same as Brillat-Savarin but mixed with diced truffles cooked in white wine.

— **Straws:** Pailles au fromage: Dough of flour, milk, butter, grated cheese, seasoned with salt, pepper and paprika, rolled out thin, cut in thin strips and baked. (Savory)

— **Talmouse:** Talmouse de fromage: fill center of puff paste, squares, 4 × 4, with cheese soufflé and chopped Swiss cheese, eggwash and fold, brush outside with egg, bake and serve hot.

Cheese
— **Tartlets:** Ramequins: small unsweetened cream puffs, mixed with grated parmesan and diced Swiss cheese, topped with small slice of Swiss cheese and baked. (Savory)
— **Turnover:** See cheese talmouse.
— **Waffles:** Gaufrettes au fromage: puff paste mixed with grated Swiss or Parmesan cheese, cut in strips and baked.

Chicken Legs (Drum Sticks), Stuffed: Jambonneaux de volaille: stuffed with forcemeat, cooked in stock, when cold coated with brown chaudfroid sauce, glazed with aspic jelly, garnished with aspic.
— **Livers:** Foies de volaille: See main dishes.
— **Potted:** chicken paste preserved in cans or jars, used as spread for canapés or sandwiches.

Ciernikis: cottage cheese, mixed with butter and flour, seasoned with salt, pepper and nutmeg, dough rolled and cut in squares, boiled drained, sprinkled with grated cheese and covered with bread crumbs browned in butter. (Polish)

Cockscombs Demidow: Crètes de coq D: boil cocks' combs in white stock, split, fill with goose liver paste, coat with Villeroy sauce, breadcrumb and fry.

Cocktail Appetizers: sliced lobster, crayfish tails, shrimps, bearded mussels, tunny fish, bearded oysters etc., filled in glasses, covered with cocktail sauce, garnished ad libitum, served very cold.
— **Clam:** cold chopped clams served in glass covered with cocktail sauce.
— **Fruit Juice:** glass half filled with crushed ice, fruit juice such as orange, grapefruit, pine apple etc., pure or mixed with lemon juice, and spiced syrup poured over and served at once.
— **Lobster:** Cocktail de homard: diced boiled lobster filled in glasses covered with cocktail sauce, served with lemon slices.
— **Oyster:** Cocktail d'huîtres: served on half shell, glass with cocktail sauce placed in center of group.
— **Shrimp:** de crevettes: parboiled shrimps, served cold in glasses, topped with cocktail sauce, served with lemon slice.
— **Sauce:** composition of catsup, chili sauce, grated horseradish, chopped green or red peppers, Tabasco, Worcestershire sauce, herbs etc., used for seafood cocktails, oysters etc.

Cods tongues: Langues de cabillaud: cooked in white wine with onions, herbs, spice and small mushrooms, served chilled in their liquor.

Columbines: Colombines: semolina cooked in stock, mixed with egg yolks and grated cheese; line small tartlet moulds with the mixture, fill with purée or some very fine ragout, cover with mixture, sprinkle with bread crumbs and cheese, bake and serve hot.

Condés: see puff paste sticks with cheese.

Cornets, Alsatian: Cornets à l'alsacienne: cones of noodle dough egged and breadcrumbed, baked, filled with purée of goose liver.
— **Ham:** Cornets de jambon: smoked ham shaped into cones, filled with grated horseradish mixed with unsweetened whipped cream flavored with paprika and lemon juice.

Cornets
— **Northern Ham:** Cornets de jambon à la nordique: boiled ham twisted to cones, filled with French salad, decorated with truffle slices, glazed with jelly, garnished with aspic jelly.
Coulibiac: see Fish Pie, Russian.
Crab Croquettes: Croquettes de crabe: crabmeat thickened with cream sauce and egg yolks, shaped, breadcrumbed, fried.
— **Merry Widow:** crabmeat dressed on lettuce leaves, garnished with asparagus tips, covered with mayonnaise.
— **Salad:** Salade de crabe: crabmeat, tomatoes and diced celery, decorated with anchovy fillets, capers and hard boiled eggs, French dressing.
— **Stuffed:** crabmeat mixed with chopped fried onions, seasoned with mustard and Worcestershire sauce, filled in shells, covered with Béchamel sauce, sprinkled with grated cheese and gratinated.
Crabmeat Cocktail Ravigote: diced chilled crabmeat, served in cocktail glasses with ravigote sauce instead of cocktail sauce.
— **Croquettes, Cold:** crabmeat mixed with mayonnaise, stiffened with aspic jelly, shaped to croquettes, rolled in chopped hard boiled eggs and parsley.
— **Ravigote:** crabmeat mixed with fine slices of celery and ravigote sauce, dressed in shells, sprinkled with capers and adorned with julienne of lettuce.
Crayfish Froth in Champagne: Mousse d'écrevisses au champagne: sauté crayfish in butter with mirepoix and fine herbs, simmer with tomatoes and seasoning in champagne, break meat out of tails and claws, pound, strain, mix with cream sauce, the reduced stock, aspic jelly and whipped cream, fill in small soufflé casseroles or ramekins, chill, garnish with crayfish tails, truffle slices and aspic jelly.
— **Tails Vinaigrette:** Queues d'écrevisses à la vinaigrette: cold crayfish tails, marinated with vinaigrette sauce.
— **Zephyr:** Zephyr d'écrevisses: mousse of crayfish paste, cream sauce, crayfish butter and seasoning, mixed with aspic jelly and whipped cream, filled in small moulds decorated with truffles and chilled.
Creams, Shaped: Crèmes moulées: purée of fish, shellfish, meat, game or poultry, mixed with aspic jelly and whipped, unsweetened cream, seasoned, filled in small moulds lined with aspic jelly and decorated, sealed with aspic jelly, chilled, turned out and garnished with aspic jelly.
Crépinettes: see main dishes.
Cromesquis: see main dishes.
Croquettes: see main dishes.
Croustades: see main dishes.
Crusts: Croûtes: thick slices of white bread cut round, in squares or triangles, center hollowed out to receive filling, fried in butter, served hot or cold.
— **Charles V.:** filled with poached soft carps roe, covered with cheese soufflé and baked.
— **English:** Croûtes à l'anglaise: filled with fishpaste, seasoned with Worcestershire sauce, mixed with butter, garnished with strips of fish.
— **Epicurean:** à l'épicurienne: filled with chopped spinach, hard boiled eggs, anchovies and capers.

Crusts

— **Eureka:** filled with mushroom soufflé mixture, garnished with anchovy fillets.

— **Goose Liver:** au foie gras: filled with purée of goose liver patty, served cold.

— **Gourmet:** du gourmet: rye bread, broiled ham, covered with slice of Swiss cheese sprinkled with cayenne pepper, browned.

— **Indian:** à l'indienne: filled with curried rice mixed with diced hard boiled eggs, shrimps, chutney and parsley.

— **Mephisto:** filled with poached carps roe, covered with sauce piquante.

— **Mirabeau:** spread of anchovy butter and garnish of anchovy fillets; served cold or hot.

— **Norwegian:** à la norvégienne: spread with anchovy paste, filled with diced truffles, hard boiled eggs and smoked salmon, chopped chives sprinkled on top.

— **with Ox Marrow:** à la moelle: slices of poached ox marrow, truffle slice, covered with Bordelaise sauce, sprinkled with chopped chives.

— **Polish:** à la polonaise: filled with chopped roast hare mixed with chopped anchovies and hard boiled egg yolks, seasoned and bound with brown sauce.

— **Romanow:** filled with purée of tunafish, sprinkled with chopped pistachios.

— **Rosamond:** filled with diced tomato salad, garnished with anchovy fillets and slices of hard boiled eggs; served cold.

— **Spanish:** à l'espagnole: spread with anchovy butter, filled with hard boiled eggs and anchovy fillets, bound with tartar sauce, garnished with olives, served cold.

— **Tsarina:** à la czarine: spread with cold onion purée mixed with anchovy paste, filled with caviar.

— **Tunny Fish:** filled with purée of tunny fish, garnished with shrimp tails and caviar.

Cucumber Salad: Salade de concombres: peeled down from stem, sliced thin, sprinkled with salt, left for while, water pressed out, dressed on lettuce leaves, French dressing poured over.

— **Salad in Mayonnaise Sauce:** Salade de concombres à la mayonnaise: as above but covered with mayonnaise.

Cucumbers, Danish: Concombres à la danoise: thick slices, hollowed out, filled with purée of salmon mixed with dices of marinated herrings and hard boiled egg, sprinkled with grated horse radish.

— **Stuffed:** Concombres farcis: thick slices peeled, hollowed out, parboiled, marinated, stuffed with purée of fish, hashed meat, salad of fish, meat or poultry etc.

— **Swedish:** à la suédoise: filled with herring salad.

Cutlet, Lobster, Moldavian: Côtelette de homard moldavienne: cutlet mould lined with aspic jelly, decorated with truffle, filled with lobster froth, sealed with aspic, turned out and served on Russian salad.

— **Lobster, Parisian Style:** à la parisienne: cutlet mould lined with aspic jelly, decorated with pistachios, filled with purée of lobster mixed with butter and well seasoned, chilled, served on forcemeat of cooked lobster mixed with chopped truffles, pistachio and lobster butter, garnished with crayfish tails.

Cutlet

— **Salmon:** Côtelette de saumon: salmon paste mixed with butter and seasoned or purée mixed with aspic and unsweetened whipped cream, filled in small cutlet moulds lined with aspic jelly or chaudfroid sauce.

— **Salmon, Italian:** à l'italienne: salmon paste mixed with butter and tomato purée, filled in mould lined with tomato-chaudfroid sauce, decorated with truffle, dressed on Italian salad, sprinkled with chopped pistachios.

— **Salmon, Ostend Style:** à l'ostendaise: filled in mould lined with aspic jelly, decorated with slices of truffle and oysters, served with shrimp salad.

— **Salmon, Russian:** de saumon à la russe: mould lined with white chaudfroid sauce mixed with caviar, filled with salmon froth, turned out on Russian salad.

— **Salmon with Vegetable Salad:** Côtelette des saumon Vert-pré: filled in moulds lined with green chaudfroid sauce, dressed on vegetable salad, garnished with aspic jelly.

— **Sturgeon:** Côtelette d'esturgeon: cut in cutlet shaped slices, poached, when cold glazed with aspic jelly and decorated, dressed on Russian salad.

D

Darioles, Gaulish Style: Darioles à la gauloise: small moulds lined with aspic jelly, filled with diced cocks' combs, kidneys, truffles and mushrooms in mayonnaise sauce, covered with jelly, turned out when set.

— **Princess Style:** Darioles à la princesse: moulds lined with purée of green peas mixed with egg, filled with diced sweetbreads, truffles and mushrooms in thick suprême sauce, topped with purée, poached, turned out; suprême sauce.

— **Regina:** lined with fish forcemeat with chopped mushrooms, filled with salpicon of soft roe and crayfish, poached served with crayfish sauce.

D'Artois Appetizer: Dartois or D'Artois: thin sheet of puff paste, coated with force meat, covered with some fine ragoût, covered with another sheet of puff paste, egg washed, baked, cut in slices and served hot.

Devils on Horseback: prunes wrapped in strips of bacon, fastened on skewers or toothpicks, broiled, seasoned with cayenne, served on toast. (Savoury)

Diablotins: cream puff paste mixed with grated parmesan, highly spiced, shaped to small dumplings, boiled, sprinkled with grated cheese and browned.

Dominoes: cold fish, meat or poultry, covered with a purée made of the same meat or goose liver patty, cut into dominos, coated with chaudfroid sauce, garnished with black dots of truffles in imitation of domino stones, glazed with jelly.

Duchesses: small cream puffs, stuffed with different kinds of purées, coated with chaudfroid sauce, glazed with aspic jelly.

— **Sultan Style:** à la sultane: stuffed with chicken purée with chopped pistachios, coated with chicken chaudfroid sauce, sprinkled with chopped pistachios.

— **Nantua:** stuffed with purée of crayfish, coated with cold jellied Nantua sauce.

E

Eclairs: Sticks of cream puff paste; piped on baking sheets, baked, emptied and stuffed with liver paste, fish or chicken paste, etc., covered with chaudfroid sauce and glazed with jelly. Eclair appetizers should not be longer than about three inches.

— **with Anchovies:** aux anchois: stuffed with purée of white fish mixed with purée of anchovies, glazed with aspic jelly.

— **with Caviar:** au caviar: stuffed with caviar.

— **Karoly:** stuffed with purée of woodcock, coated with brown chaudfroid sauce, glazed with jelly, decorated with truffles.

— **Rossini:** stuffed with purée of goose liver patty mixed with chopped truffles, coated with brown chaudfroid sauce, glazed with jelly.

Eel Italian Style: Anguille à l'italienne: first grilled, then marinated in hot acidulated wine stock flavored with aromatic herbs and spices.

— **Smoked:** Anguille fumée: cut in pieces, skinned, served on chopped jelly or lettuce leaves with toast and butter.

— **in White Wine:** Anguille au vin blanc: cooked in white wine with aromatic herbs and served in the jellified stock.

Egg Salad: Salade d'oeufs: hard boiled eggs, cut in slices, dressed on lettuce leaves, seasoned with salt, pepper, vinegar and oil, sprinkled with chopped chervil.

Egg-plant Greek Style: Aubergines à la grecque: small egg-plants cut lengthwise, cooked in white wine, oil, water, lemon, juice, fennel, celery, thyme, garlic and button onions, served cold with their liquor.

— — **Nimes Style:** Aubergines à la nîmoise: cut in halves, salted, baked in oil, topped with chopped red peppers and diced tomatoes, cooked in oil with lemon juice, garlic and herbs, served cold.

— — **Roumanian Style:** Aubergines à la roumaine: cut top off for lid of small egg-plants, hollow out, stuff with blanched rice, chopped tomatoes and the flesh of the egg-plant, season, put lid on and cook in oil, tomato purée, lemon juice and aromatic herbs. Serve cold in their liquor with a slice of lemon on top.

Eggs in Nests: Nids à la Chartres: thick oval slices of bread, hollowed out, fried, when cold stuffed with imitation eggs made of goose liver patty, glazed with aspic jelly, sprinkled with chopped hard boiled eggs and truffles.

— **Stuffed:** Oeufs farcis: see eggs.

Emmenthal Cheese, Fried: cut in slices, seasoned with paprika, dipped in egg and bread crumbs, deep fried (Savory).

Endives Greek Style: Endives à la grecque: braised, macerated in oil, lemon juice, crushed garlic, spices and tomatoes, served cold.

Escabecia: any kind of small fish, turned in flour, fried in oil, marinated in hot oil, vinegar, water, sliced onions and carrots, crushed garlic, bay leaves and spices for 24 hours, served cold (Spanish).

F

Fennel Knobs Greek Style: Pieds de fenouil à la grecque: parboil and prepare the same way as artichokes Greek style, which see.

— — **Italian Style:** Pieds de fenouil à l'italienne: parboiled, cooked in oil and white wine with chopped onions and tomatoes, sliced mushrooms, parsley and thyme, served cold in their liquor.

— — **Roumanian Style:** Pieds de fenouil à la roumaine: parboiled, cooked with sunflower oil, lemon juice, water, peppercorns, thyme, bay leaves and chopped tomatoes, served cold in their liquor with slices of lemon.

Figs, Fresh: Figues: fresh ripe green or blue figs, served cold on vine leaves with pepper and butter.

Finnan Haddie (Smoked Haddock) on Toast: poached, flaked, dressed on toast, melted butter on top.

Fish Pie, Russian: Coulibiac: fish pie, chiefly salmon or sturgeon, with kascha, chopped vesiga, hard boiled eggs and fine herbs baked in light yeast dough.

— **Salad:** Salade de poisson: fish, flaked, dressed on lettuce leaves, covered with tartar sauce, garnished with quarters of hard boiled eggs, slices of potatoes, beetroots and pickles.

Fondants: very small pear shaped croquettes made of purée of fish, meat, fowl, game etc., bread crumbed and baked in deep fat.

— **Pheasant:** de faisan: purée of pheasant and chicken livers bound with thick Madeira sauce.

— **Goose Liver:** de foie gras: purée of goose liver and truffles bound with thick Madeira sauce.

Fondue à la neuchâteloise: rub baking dish with garlic, dissolve diced Emmenthal cheese in white wine, butter, pepper, cayenne and kirsch; serve with large cubes of white bread. (Swiss)

Fowl Legs (Drum Sticks), Stuffed: Ballotines de volaille: boned, stuffed with forcemeat, simmered in chicken stock, when cold coated with white chaudfroid sauce, decorated with truffle, glazed with aspic jelly, garnished with asparagus tips and aspic.

Fritters: Beignets: raw or precooked food, dipped in frying batter and fried in deep fat.
See also main dishes.

— **Artichoke:** Beignets d'artichauts: precooked artichoke bottoms marinated in lemon juice, salt and oil, dipped in frying batter and fried.

— **Brain:** de cervelle: precooked calf's brains, sliced, marinated, dipped in frying batter, fried served with tomato sauce.

— **Cheese:** de fromage: diced camembert, mixed with thick cream sauce, egg yolks and paprika, shaped, breadcrumbed, fried and served with fried parsley. (Savory)

— **Cheese, Neapolitain:** à la napolitaine: corn meal cooked in chicken broth, mixed with butter and grated parmesan cheese, poured on greased baking-tin, when cold spread with cheese soufflé mixture, covered with another sheet of paste, cut round or in squares and baked.

Fritters
— **Swiss Cheese:** de fromage à la suisse: grated Emmenthal cheese mixed with bread crumbs, egg yolks, milk and paprika, when cold cut round, egg washed and baked.
Frivolities: Frivolités: small dainty appetizers, such as boats or tartlets, cream puffs or éclairs, stuffed with purée of fish, crayfish, lobster, chicken, game, goose livers patty etc., and small creams of fish, meat, game or poultry etc. in decorated moulds set in aspic jelly.
Frogs' legs in Aurora Sauce: Nymphes à l'aurore: poached in white wine, covered with fish-chaudfroid sauce colored with tomato purée and seasoned with paprika, set in champagne jelly.
— — **in Jelly:** Nymphes ballerines: poached in white wine, coated with green chaudfroid sauce, glazed with jelly, dressed on lettuce leaves, garnished with diced jelly.
— — **Lyonese Style:** Grenouilles à la lyonnaise: sauted in butter with onions, fine herbs and lemon juice; served hot.

G

Galantine: a fine boneless sort of meat loaf in skin, served cold, decorated and jellied.
— **Bankers Style:** Galantine à la financière: galantine of game cut in slices, garnished with lobster salad, marinated artichoke bottoms, truffles, pickles and marinated mushrooms.
— **of Chicken:** Galantine de volaille: skin and bone bird carefully, spread out skin, stuff with chicken and veal forcemeat, fillets of chicken breast, goose liver, salt pork, beef tongue, truffles and pistachios, roll together, tie in napkin and poach slowly in white stock. Cool in stock, remove cloth, cover with white chaudfroid sauce, decorate and glaze with aspic jelly.
— **of Pheasant:** Galantine de faisan: prepared the same way as galantine of chicken.
— **of Wild Boar:** Galantine de marcassin: young wild boar carefully cleaned and boned, skin spread out on a cloth, stuffed with forcemeat of pork and veal, mixed with diced ox tongue, salt pork, pistachios, truffles and hard boiled eggs, tied in a cloth, poached slowly, cooled in the stock, served cold glaced and garnished with aspic jelly.
Galettes Briardes: small round flat cakes made of Brie cheese, eggs and nutmeg, eggwashed and baked (Savory).
Gänseweißsauer: cut goose in small pieces, simmer with pot herbs until tender, dress in baking or other dish, when cold pour over the clarified, jellied stock (German).
Gherkins: Cornichons: small prickly cucumbers preserved in vinegar.
Gondoles à la Duse: peeled and hollowed out apples poached in white wine, served cold, filled with salad of smoked salmon, celery and green peppers in mayonnaise.
Goby: Nonats: the small "fry" of a Mediterranean goby, parboiled, marinated with vinegar, oil and chopped herbs, dressed with diced tomatoes, artichoke bottom and beet roots, adorned with slices of hard boiled eggs.
— **Russian Style:** Goujons à la russe: poached in white wine and stock, when cold covered with mayonnaise sauce, sprinkled with chopped parsley.

Golden Buck: I. poached eggs on toast covered with Welsh rarebit cheese; II. thin tenderloin (fillet of beef) sautéd on toast, prepared the same way. (Savory)

Goosebreast, Smoked: Poitrine d'oie fumée: cut in thin slices, garnished with aspic jelly and parsley.

Goose Liver Froth: Mousse de foie gras: goose liver paste mixed with unsweetened whipped cream, jellied, filled in decorated mould, chilled and served with aspic.

— — **Froth Northern Style:** thick oval slices of bread, scooped out slightly, fried, stuffed domewise with goose liver froth, coated with white chaudfroid sauce, decorated with truffle, jellied, served with Muscovite salad and Cumberland sauce.

— — **in Jelly:** Foie gras en gelée: poached in stock with wine when cold placed in mould and covered with aspic jelly flavored with Madeira, Marsala, Sherry or Port.

— — **Medallions:** Médaillons de foie gras: base of toast cut round, covered with purée of goose liver patty, sprinkled with chopped truffles.

— — **Parfait Lucullus:** Parfait de foie gras Lucullus: tick slices of truffled goose liver parfait, cut in halves, placed upright in long oval mould and covered with Madeira jelly; when cold cut in slices with jelly on both sides.

— — **Patty Russian Style:** Pâte de foie gras à la russe: pyramid of patty scooped out with a spoon, placed in the centre of a glass dish, surrounded with tiny puff pastry patties filled with caviar.

— — **Patty Truffled:** Pâte de foie gras truffée: scooped out with spoon, garnished with aspic jelly, served with toast and butter.

— — **Queen Style:** Parfait de foie gras à la reine: small round slices coated with chicken chaudfroid sauce, decorated with truffles, glazed and garnished with aspic jelly.

Gorgonzola, Fried: Gorgonzola frit: small cubes of Gorgonzola cheese, wrapped in thin slices of bacon, dipped in batter and fried (Savory).

H

Ham: Jambon: see main dishes.

— **Bayonne:** raw, cut in thin slices, garnished with aspic jelly.

— **Froth Nancy Style:** Mousse de jambon à la nancéenne: raw ham pounded in mortar with goose liver patty, strained, mixed with egg whites and whipped unsweetened cream, filled in moulds garnished with sliced truffles, slices of goose liver and strips of ham, poached in bain-marie.

— **Kipferl:** Schinkenkipferl: Dough of baked, mashed potatoes, flour, yeast, eggs, yolks and milk, rolled out thin, center filled with chopped boiled ham mixed with butter, egg yolks and grated parmesan, shaped into crescents, egg-washed and baked, served hot or cold (Austrian).

— **Parma:** de Parme: raw, cut into thin slices, garnished with parsley or aspic jelly.

— **Potted:** ham paste, preserved in cans or jars, used as spread for canapés or sandwiches etc.

— **Prague:** Jambon de Prague: boiled, served cold cut in thin slices, garnished with aspic jelly and grated horseradish.

Ham

— **Snow:** Neige de jambon: minced ham, mixed with chopped parsley, chervil, thyme, basil, mustard, eggs, egg yolk and milk, filled in moulds lined with bread crumbs, poached, turned out, covered entirely with stiffly whipped egg whites, mixed with chopped ham, seasoned with salt and pepper, baked.

— **Westphalian:** de Westphalie: raw, cut in thin slices and garnished with aspic jelly or turned in cornucopias and stuffed with creamed horseradish or fine vegetable salad.

— **York:** de York: cut in thin slices garnished with parsley.

Hamburger Rauchfleisch: see Beef smoked brisket of.

Hazelnuts, Spiced: Noisettes diablées, roast, remove husks, sprinkle with oil, salt and cayenne pepper (Savory).

Helianti: Hélianthe: scraped, put in water with lemon juice, boiled, when cold cut in slices mixed with chopped radishes, gherkins and capers, bound with mayonnaise sauce with sour cream and mustard powder.

Herring, Bismarck: fillets of lightly salted herrings boiled in wine pickle, served with strips of carrots and pickled cucumbers, slices of onions and a few drops of the pickle.

— **Cakes, Livonian:** Pain de hareng à la livonienne: fillets of salt herrings, desalted in milk, chopped fine, mixed with egg yolks, bread crumbs and unsweetened whipped cream, fried in small pans.

— **Dieppe Style:** Harengs à la dieppoise: fresh herrings, cleaned, boiled in white wine and water with sliced carrots and onions, thyme, bayleaves, peppercorns and salt, served cold in the stock.

— **Esthonian Style:** à l'esthonienne: desalted chopped salt herrings, mixed with butter, breadcrumbs and sour cream, fried in small pans.

— **with French Beans:** Hareng aux haricots verts: fillets of salt herrings, desalted, marinated with vinegar, oil and pepper, served with salad of French beans.

— **Marinated:** Harengs marinés: desalt herrings for several days, marinate in wine vinegar, with sliced lemons, bayleaves, black peppercorns, mustard, seeds and spices for two days; crushed and strained milt, blended with heavy sour cream added to herrings, filled in stone jar and kept for a few days before serving.

— **Matjes:** Hareng vierge: immature female herring.

— **Pickled Smoked:** Hareng fumé mariné: fillets of smoked herring soaked in milk with seasoning, served with mayonnaise with chopped challots, chervil and pickles.

— **Salad, Russian:** Salade de hareng à la russe: alternate fillets of herring with red beets, sliced hard boiled eggs and capers, cover with vinaigrette sauce mixed with grated horseradish.

— **Salad, Welsh:** Salade de hareng à la galloise: desalted herring, hard boiled eggs, knob celery, carrots, apples and potatoes, diced, mixed with capers and chopped anchovies, bound with mayonnaise sauce, dressed in glass dish alternated with fillets of anchovies, desalted fillets of herrings, smoked herrings and smoked eel, garnished with radishes, hard boiled eggs and cornets of smoked salmon.

Herring
— **Smoked:** Hareng fumé.
— **Smoked, Livonian:** Hareng fumé à la livonienne: alternate fillets of smoked herrings with sliced potatoes, sliced apples and chopped chervil, tarragon and fennel, dress with pepper, oil and vinegar.
— **Smoked, Russian:** Hareng fumé à la russe:
A. fillets of smoked herrings alternated with slices of boiled potatoes, seasoned with vinegar and oil, sprinkled with chopped challots, parsley and chervil.
B. fillets of smoked herrings alternated with sliced red beets, seasoned with vinegar, and oil, garnished with chopped yolks and whites of hard boiled egg, capers and chopped parsley.

Hors-d'oeuvre à la grecque: see Greek Appetizer.
— — **à la russe:** see Zakouski.
— — **à la suédoise:** see Appetizers, Swedish.
— — **varié:** mixed appetizers or side dishes.

Huîtres: see Oysters.

I

Illustrierte Salzgurke: Garnished Pickled Cucumber: slices of pickled cucumber, dressed alternately with slices of Emmenthal cheese and anchovy fillets, garnished with ham cornets filled with capers and halved hard boiled eggs filled with caviar. (German).

K

Knob Celery, (Celeriac) Marinated: Céleri-rave mariné: parboiled, cut in strips, marinated with vinegar, oil, salt and mustard powder.
— — **Greek Style:** à la grecque: cut in cubes, mixed with cubed apples and button onions cooked in spiced vinegar, white wine and oil, mixed with diced tomatoes, served in the liquor.

Käserösti: Slices of white bread covered with chopped Swiss cheese, soaked in milk, baked in baking dish, chopped fried onions on top. (Swiss)

Kilkis: see anchovies, Norvegian.

L

Lamprey in Oil: Lamproie à l'huile: Commercial product.

Leeks Greek Style: Poireaux à la grecque: prepared the same way as artichokes.
— **Russian Style:** à la russe: boil, cool and marinate small pieces, cut in half, stuff with caviar, chopped eggs and horseradish.
— **Vinaigrette:** Poireaux à la vinaigrette: slice and boil, serve cold with vinaigrette sauce poured over.

Lettuce Genoa Style: Laitue à la genoise: lettuce leaves, stuffed with chopped hard boiled eggs and anchovy fillets, bound with mayonnaise sauce, sprinkled with chopped red beets, capers and parsley.

— **Indian Style:** Laitue à l'indienne: lettuce leaves, stuffed with diced lobster and anchovy fillets bound with mayonnaise sauce seasoned with curry powder.

Livländer Vorschmack: see Appetizer, Livonian.

Lobster: Homard: see fish course.

— **Froth:** Mousse de homard: cold paste of boiled lobster, seasoned with salt, cayenne pepper and brandy, mixed with aspic jelly and unsweetened whipped cream, filled in small moulds lined with jelly and decorated with truffle, white of hard boiled eggs etc., chilled, turned out and garnished with cubes of aspic jelly.

— **Spiny:** Langouste: see fish course.

Long Island Buck: dissolve Cheddar cheese in beer, season with paprika and Worcestershire sauce, mix with egg yolks, pour over toast, bake in baking dish, serve hot. (Savory)

M

Macedoine of Vegetables, Marinated: Macédoine de legumes marinées: cauliflower, French beans, artichokes and red or green peppers, cut uniformly, green peas, button onions and gherkins blanched, all covered with hot mild vinegar and mustard seed, marinated for a week, served cold.

Mackerel in Jelly: Maquereau en gelée: Commercial product.

— **in Oil:** Maquereau à l'huile: Commercial product.

— **Smoked:** Maquereau fumé: Commercial product.

Mango: fruit of an Indian tree, sold in pickled or preserved state.

Marrow Bones: Os à la moelle: split bones, poach and serve hot.

Marrow, Small Vegetable: Courgette.

Marrow, Vegetable, Greek Style: à la grecque: proceed as for artichokes Greek style.

— — **Marinated:** Courgettes au verjus: cooked in water and vinegar, marinated in juice of unripe green grapes with thyme, bay leaves and coriander.

— — **Roman Style:** à la romaine: parboiled slices, marinated in French dressing, dipped in frying batter, fried, served with tomato sauce.

— — **Roumanian Style:** à la roumaine: stuffed with pilaf rice mixed with diced green peppers and tomato purée, seasoned with paprika, simmered in oil, lemon juice and tomatoes, served cold.

Mayonnaise, Chicken: Mayonnaise de volaille: cold chicken picked from bones, skinned, cut in strips, marinated with oil, vinegar, salt and pepper, dressed on shredded lettuce, covered with mayonnaise, garnished with hard boiled eggs, pickles, capers and red beets or aspic jelly.

— **Fish:** Mayonnaise de poisson: fish boiled, picked clean from bones and skin, flaked, cooled, dressed on shredded lettuce, covered with mayonnaise, garnished with anchovy fillets, capers, olives and hard boiled eggs.

Mazagran: various fine minces, baked between two sheets of duchesse potatoes (which see), cut in different shapes and served hot.

Medallion, Westphalian: à la westphalienne: base of buttered toast cut oval, oval slice of Westphalian ham, garnished with green butter and sliced pickles.

Melon, Iced: Melon frappé: Cantaloupe or Honey-Dew melons cut in thick slices, seeds removed, served on crushed ice, sugar and powdered ginger served separately, May also be eaten with salt and pepper.

— **with ham:** au jambon de Parme: Cantaloup or Honey-Dew melon, cut in sections, seeds removed, placed on crushed ice; thin slices of Parma ham served separately.

— **with Wine, Chilled:** Melon frappé au vin: cut off top for lid, remove seeds, fill with Sherry, Madeira or Port wine, put lid on, chill.

Mortadella: a smoked Italian sausage sliced very thin, cut in half or quartered and served on chopped jelly or lettuce leaves.

Mousse: Froth: a light, fluffy preparation of fish, shellfish, meat, poultry or game etc., made of purée strained through a sieve, seasoned, mixed with cream or velouté sauce, aspic and whipped unsweetened cream, filled in decorated moulds lined with aspic jelly.

Mushrooms, Deviled: à la diable: sauted in butter, seasoned with lemon juice and Cayenne.

— **in Glass Bell:** sous cloche: trimmed, seasoned with salt and pepper, stuffed with herb butter, dressed on fried bread in glass-covered dish, cooked in oven and served in same dish.

— **Marinated:** Cèpes marinés: parboiled, marinated in hot vinegar and oil, seasoned with garlic, thyme, fennel, bay-leaves, parley roots, coriander, salt and pepper, served cold.

— **Stuffed:** Champignons farcis: large fried mushrooms stuffed with purée of tunny fish, covered with French dressing.

Mussels French Style: à la française: precooked, marinated, bound with mayonnaise seasoned with mustard, pepper and chopped herbs.

— **Marinated:** Moules marinées: precooked mussels, marinated in oil, vinegar, pepper, mustard powder, served very cold.

Mustard Gherkins: Cornichons à la moutarde: Commercial product.

N

Nalesnikis: see cheese fritters, Polish.

Nuts, Marinated: Cerneaux au verjus: fresh nut kernels, marinated in the fresh juice of green grapes, served with a pinch of salt and chopped chervil.

Nymphes à l'aurore: see frogs legs in Aurora sauce.

— **ballerines:** see frogs legs in jelly.

O

Ogourzi: Russian cucumbers, cut in slices, salted, dried, blended with sour cream and sprinkled with chopped dill.

Okra American Style: Gombos à l'américaine: stewed in oil with diced tomatoes, garlic, lemon juice and spices, served chilled with their liquor.

Olive-Nut Sandwiches: Buttered toast, topped with blanched chopped nuts, chopped olives and mayonnaise.

— **Paste Provençal:** Purée d'olives à la provençale: pound pitted ripe olives with anchovies, thyme, bayleaves, garlic, mustard and Worcestershire sauce, strain, dilute with brandy and oil, season with pepper and keep in stone jar for future use covered with oil. Spread for canapes or stuffing for leeks, tomatoes or olives.

Olives Queen Style: à la reine: large olives pitted, stuffed with anchovy paste, mixed with chopped pickles and hard boiled eggs.

— **Stuffed:** Olives farcies: usually stuffed with pimiento and marketed according to size.

— **Stuffed, Alsatian:** Olives à l'alsacienne: pitted olives, stuffed with goose liver purée mixed with chopped ham.

Ox Cheek: Museau de boeuf.

— **Cheek Salad:** Salade de museau de boeuf: mouth and palate of beef, scalded, cooked with herbs, pickled with French dressing. Also marketed.

— **Palate:** Palais de boeuf: boiled, cleaned, trimmed, cut in strips, marinated in vinaigrette sauce, served cold.

— **Tongue, Smoked:** served cold, garnished with aspic and horseradish.

Oyster: F.: huître; G.: Auster; I. ostriche; S. ostras. Many edible varieties: European, American, Australian, Japanese and South African. Opened with special knife or machine, served cold on ice with lemon, thin slices of white or rye bread and butter. Oysters are eaten raw, semi or fully cooked and should not be overdone. Served as appetizer cold or warm and also used as a garnish for fish and other dishes.

Oysters American Style: à l'américaine: poached, filled in half shell, covered with American sauce.

— **Baltimore:** dressed on half shell greased with butter, sprinkled with mixture of breadcrumbs, grated cheese and chopped parsley, melted butter dropped on top, baked in the oven.

— **Belleclaire:** fried, dressed on buttered toast covered with a slice of fried ham and slices of fried mushrooms.

— **Borchardt:** raw bearded oysters, dressed on slices of tomatoes, surrounded with a cordon of caviar.

— **Broiled Oysters and Bacon:** en brochette: oysters wrapped in bacon, alternated on skewers with mushrooms, dipped in egg and breadcrumbs, broiled and served with Maître d'hôtel butter.

— **Burgundy Style:** à la bourguignonne: dressed on half shell, coated with snail butter, sprinkled with breadcrumbs, a little melted butter dropped on top and glazed.

— **Californian Style:** à la californienne: coated with flour, slightly fried in butter, covered with diced stewed tomatoes and green peppers mixed with a little demiglace.

— **in Cases:** en caisses: poached in own juice and white wine, liquor boiled down, mixed with cream sauce, egg yolks and the stiffly beaten eggwhites, seasoned with Cayenne pepper, filled in small containers of fireproof china, glass or earthenware, baked in oven.

Oysters

— **and Caviar:** au caviar: tiny puff pastry tartlets half filled with caviar, a bearded raw oyster on top, seasoned with a drop of lemon juice and a pinch of Cayenne pepper.

— **Cocktail:** American system: served chilled on half shell with grated horseradish, small crackers, Tabasco and cocktail sauce. European system: served in glass covered with cocktail sauce, lemon slice stuck in the glass.

— **Creole:** seasoned, rolled in crushed crackers, fried in butter, served on toast coated with Creole sauce.

— **Delmonico:** poached, coated with cream sauce thickened with egg yolks and flavored with lemon juice.

— **Deviled:** à la diable: same as on skewers, but breadcrumbs mixed with mustard powder and a pinch of Cayenne pepper, devil sauce served separately.

— **Dubarry:** poached in own juice, filled in baked, scooped out potatoes, covered with cream sauce, sprinkled with grated cheese and glazed.

— **Dutch Style:** à la hollandaise: baking dish greased with butter, filled with asparagus tips and slices of poached ox marrow, topped with poached oysters, seasoned with Cayenne pepper and lemon juice, sprinkled with bread crumbs, melted butter poured over and baked.

— **in Egg Sauce:** à la poulette: poached, mixed with button mushrooms and poulette sauce flavored with the oyster liquor.

— **English Style:** à l'anglaise: wrapped in bacon, fixed on skewers, broiled, dressed on buttered toast. Usually called "Angels on horseback".

— **Favorite Style:** à la favorite: filled in half shell, a slice of lemon on top, covered with cream sauce, sprinkled with grated cheese, glazed and served hot.

— **Florence:** à la florentine: poached, dressed on half shell on plain spinach sweated in butter, coated with cheese sauce, sprinkled with grated cheese and glazed.

— **Fricassee:** en fricassée: poached oysters, mixed with button mushrooms, veal forcemeat dumplings, slices of sweetbread and velouté sauce flavored with oyster juice, thickened with egg yolks and cream.

— **Fried:** frites: dipped in egg and breadcrumbs, fried in deep fat, served with lemon and fried parsley; Tartare sauce separately.

— **Fritters:** Beignets d'huîtres: poached, dipped in frying batter, deep fried, served with fried parsley and lemon.

— **on Half Shell:** au naturel: dressed on half shell on crushed ice, thin slices of Graham or rye bread, butter and pepper or vinaigrette sauce or small crackers, grated horseradish and Tabasco sauce served separately as desired.

— **Louis:** dressed in half shell, covered with breadcrumbs mixed with chopped shallots and paprika, melted butter dropped on top, baked in the oven.

— **Louise:** mixed with fried slices of yellow boletus, coated with cream sauce finished with lobster butter, seasoned with Cayenne pepper, baked in the oven.

— **Louisiana:** placed in baking dish alternately with crackers, diced tomatoes and okra, sprinkled with grated cheese and baked in the oven.

Oysters

— **Manhattan:** filled in half shell, coated with chopped bacon, green and red peppers, mushrooms, herbs and onions, baked in the oven.

— **Marinated:** marinées: raw bearded oysters, marinated in vinegar, oil, pepper, chopped herbs and hard boiled eggs.

— **Marshal Style:** à la maréchale: poached, dipped in frying batter, deep fried, dressed on lemon slices, garnished with fried parsley.

— **Mornay:** poached, dressed in shell, coated with cheese sauce, sprinkled with grated cheese, melted butter dropped on top and glazed.

— **Newburgh:** poached in Newburgh sauce, served in chafing dish with toast.

— **Pan Roast:** pan broiled on top of hot stove, sautéd with butter, chopped red and green peppers and fine herbs, served on toast.

— **Patties:** oysters in cream or poulette sauce, filled in small puffpaste patties.

— **Pickled:** preboiled stock of white wine, vinegar, sliced onions, carrots, knob celery and peppercorns, strained, poured hot over bearded oysters, oysters served chilled in part of the stock sprinkled with chopped parsley.

— **Pie:** Pâté d'huîtres: pike forcemeat mixed with chopped oysters, mushrooms, lemon-peel, nutmeg and herbs, filled in pie dish alternately with oysters, crayfish tails, mushrooms and carp roes, covered with puff pastry, decorated and baked; oyster sauce served separately.

— **Pompadour:** poached, filled in half shell, coated with Dutch sauce mixed with chopped truffles.

— **in Puff pastry Shell:** Vol-au-vent d'huîtres: shell filled with poached oysters, mushrooms, truffles, crayfish tails and fish forcemeat dumplings in crayfish sauce.

— **Scalloped:** placed in fireproof dish on cracker meal, covered with unsweetened custard, seasoned with salt and Cayenne pepper and cracker meal, melted butter dropped on top and baked.

— **on Skewers:** en brochette: wrapped in thin slices of bacon, fixed on skewers alternated with mushroom caps, dipped in egg and breadcrumbs, broiled, served with herb butter.

— **Soufflé:** Soufflé d'huîtres: poached oysters filled in soufflé dish, covered with forcemeat of fish and oysters, mixed with egg yolks and stiffly whippened egg whites, seasoned with Cayenne pepper and baked.

— **Stew:** poached lightly with butter in own juice with pinch of salt and Cayenne pepper, mixed with hot milk or half cream and milk, crackers served separately.

— **Valparaiso:** raw oysters, placed in baking dish, covered with chopped mushrooms and celery, coated with cream sauce and glazed in the oven.

— **Victor:** dressed on half shell, coated with mixture of chopped mushrooms, nuts, parsley, salt, pepper and butter, baked in the oven.

— **Victor Hugo:** dressed on half shell, coated with a mixture of grated horseradish, grated Parmesan cheese, breadcrumbs and butter, baked in the oven.

Oysters
— **Villeroi:** poached, when cold dipped in Villeroi sauce, egged and breadcrumbed, deep fried, garnished with fried parsley, tomato sauce served separately.
— **Virginia:** wrapped in thin slices of ham, dipped in egg and breadcrumbs and deep fried.
— **Wladimir:** poached, dressed on half shell, coated with suprême sauce, sprinkled with grated cheese and white breadcrumbs, melted butter dropped on top and glazed.

P

Palm Shoot Salad: Salade de coeurs de palmier: cooked shoots mixed with mayonnaise flavored with Madeira and truffle juice, sprinkled with chopped truffles.
Pancakes with caviar: Crêpes au caviar: cold caviar, placed between two very small, thin unsweetened pancakes, served with lemon.
— **Northern Style:** Crêpes à la nordique: very thin unsweetened pancakes filled with caviar, rolled, cut in slices and served cold.
— **Romanow:** very thin pancakes, filled with caviar, garnished with chopped parsley, onions and fennel, on lettuce leaves and sliced lemons.
— **Russian:** Blini à la russe: batter of half wheat and half buckwheat flour, milk, yeast and egg yolks, stiffly beaten whites of eggs and whipped cream, seasoned with salt, sometimes mixed with chopped hard boiled eggs and chopped herring, baked on griddle or in small skillets.
— **Russian, with Caviar:** Blini au caviar: griddle cakes made of half wheat and half buckwheat flour with yeast, milk and melted butter, stacked with caviar spread between them, covered with thick sour cream (Russian).
Patties: Pâtes: see main dishes.
— **Small:** Petits Pâtés: see main dishes.
— **Russian:** Piroguis: see main dishes.
Pellmenes, Sibirian: Pellmènes à la sibirienne: kind of small raviolis, stuffed with chopped roast hazel-hen and ham, seasoned with salt, pepper, nutmeg and chopped parsley, bound with thick brown sauce, boiled, drained and served with melted butter.
Peppers Greek Style: Poivrons à la grecque: prepared the same way as artichokes.
— **Marinated:** Poivrons marinés: parboiled, skinned, cut in strips, marinated with vinegar and oil.
— **Roumanian Style:** à la roumaine: stuffed with half cooked rice, mixed with diced tomatoes and chopped onions, braised with fried sliced onions, oil, lemon juice and tomato sauce, served cold with a slice of lemon on top.
— **Stuffed:** see mains dishes.
— **Sweet:** Poivrons doux.
Piccalilli: Pickles in mustard, a commercial product.
Pickles, Mixed: gherkins, onions, cauliflowers, cucumbers and chilis preserved in vinegar.
Pigs' Trotters: (Pigs' Feet) Pieds de porc: see main dishes.
Pim Olas: green olives stuffed with pimientos; commercial product.
Pimientos: Piments: remove seeds, boil, cut in strips, marinate in vinegar, oil and salt.

Pimientos
— **Algerian Style:** à l'algérienne: blanched, skinned, cut in strips, marinated and dressed with onion rings.
— **Greek Style:** à la grecque: blanch, skin, cut in strips and prepare the same way as artichokes.
Pistachios, Salted: scald, peel, toast and salt, add drop of gum instead of oil to give lustre and make salt adhere.
Plovers Eggs Swedish Style: Oeufs de vanneau à la suédoise: boil hard for fifteen minutes, chill, wrap in slices of smoked salmon, serve in ring of vegetable salad set in aspic jelly.
Potatoes, Ardennes Style: Pommes à l'ardennaise: baked potatoes, cut top off for lid, hollowed out, filled with potato purée mixed with egg yolks, butter, chopped ham, mushrooms, parsley and grated parmesan cheese, seasoned with salt, pepper and nutmeg, sprinkled with cheese and baked.
Poutargue or Provencal Pressed Caviar: Caviar à la provençale: the pressed roe of mullets, cut in slices, marinated in oil, lemon juice, pepper and chopped onions.
Puff pastry Patties, Small: Bouchés: see main dishes.
Puff pastry Sticks: Allumettes: puff pastry spread with cheese, lobster, goose liver or other paste, cut in strips and baked.
— — — **with Anchovies:** Allumettes d'anchois: spread of fish forcemeat mixed with anchovy paste, garnished with fillets of anchovies and baked.
— — — **Caprice:** Allumettes Caprice: chicken spread, mixed with chopped smoked ox tongue and truffles.
— — — **with Cheese:** Allumettes au fromage: spread of thick Béchamel sauce mixed with grated parmesan cheese, seasoned with cayenne, sprinkled with grated cheese and baked.
— — — **with Cheese Soufflé:** Feuilletés au parmesan: strips of puff pastry, covered with parmesan soufflé and baked.
— — — **with Crayfish:** Allumettes d'écrevisses: spread of crayfish forcemeat, mixed with chopped pistachios.
— — — **with Salmon:** Allumettes au saumon: spread with salmon forcemeat, garnished with small strips of smoked salmon.

Q

Quiche Lorraine: Tart or tartlet of puff or unsweetened short pastry, lined with bacon, filled with small thin slices of Swiss cheese, covered with custard made of egg yolks, milk and cream, seasoned with salt and nutmeg, baked, served hot.

R

Radishes: Radis: Red or white, eaten raw with butter as relish or with salt and in salads.
— **Black:** Radis noirs: peeled, cut in thin slices, salted, water poured off after a while, seasoned with vinegar, pepper and oil.
Rarebit, Buck: Poached egg on toast, placed in baking dish, covered with Cheddar cheese dissolved in beer, seasoned with mustard and pepper, browned quickly.

Rarebit
— **Oyster:** poach oysters, place on toast, cover with melted cheese flavored with oyster juice and mixed with egg yolks and bake (Savoury).
— **Vanderbilt:** toast spread with anchovy butter, topped with chopped hard boiled eggs, covered with melted Cheddar cheese.

Rastegais: small patties of yeast dough filled with salmon, rice, chopped hard boiled eggs, butter and chopped parsley, served hot (Russian).

Red Beets, Beet-roots: Betteraves.
— **Pickled:** baked or boiled, peeled, sliced, marinated in vinegar, sliced onions, horseradish, bay leaves, peppercorns and sugar for a while before using.
— **Salad of:** Salad de betteraves: pickled beets cut in strips, seasoned with chopped onions, pepper, mustard powder, lemon juice, and thick cream.

Red Mullets Oriental Style: Rougets à l'orientale small red mullets, poached in white wine with shallots, bay leaves, thyme, fennel, celery, parsley roots, pepper corns, coriander and saffron, served cold in a part of the strained stock.

Rilettes: highly seasoned mince of cooked chopped pork, marketed in jars.

Rissoles: crescents of puff paste, filled with minced meat or fish, fried in deep fat.
— **Bresse Style:** à la bressane: filled with minced chicken livers and mushrooms, bound with thick mushroom sauce.
— **Lucy:** filled with minced sprats, mixed with Roquefort cheese.
— **Norman:** à la normande: filled with diced mussels, oysters and shrimps, cohered with Norman sauce.
— **with Shrimps:** à la Joinville: filled with minced shrimps, truffles and mushrooms bound with Norman sauce.
— **Vegetable:** à la bouquetière: stuffed with chopped vegetables and asparagus tips, bound with thick cream sauce.
— **Victoria:** filled with minced lobster and truffles, bound with Norman sauce.

Roast Beef on Toast, Creamed: slice of roast beef, warmed up in cream sauce, served on toast, covered with cream sauce.

Roquefort, Fried: Roquefort frit: squares wrapped in bacon, dipped in frying batter, fried. (Savoury).

S

Salads: Salades: for fish and meat salads see also main dishes and fish course.
— **First Course:** fresh fruit diced, marinated in French dressing and served on lettuce, e. g:

Salad Melon, Grape and Orange: orange segments, grapes and diced melon, dressed on lettuce leaves, French dressing.
— **Orange, Banana and Cherry:** pitted fresh cherries, green peppers and orange segments dressed on lettuce, French dressing.
— **Orange, Tomato and Pepper:** sliced tomatoes, rings of green peppers and orange segments dressel on lettuce, sprinkled with chopped onions, French dressing.

Salad Alexander: shredded ham, sliced cooked mushrooms, strips of knob celery, red beets, raw apples and endives, marinated in vinegar, oil and salt, bound with mayonnaise, garnished with slices of red beets and potatoes.

— **Bagration:** strips of chicken breast, celery, sliced artichoke bottoms and macaroni cut in small pieces, marinated, bound with mayonnaise, dressed dome shaped on glass dish, garnished with truffles, ox tongue, hard boiled egg whites and egg yolks and parsley.

— **Beef:** de boeuf: slices of cold boiled beef, potatoes, pickled cucumbers and onions, diced tomatoes and hard boiled eggs, mustard dressing, sprinkled with chopped parsley.

— **Brjanski:** roast venison and calf's head, cut in strips sliced pickled cucumbers, raw apples and hard boiled eggs, dressed in bunches; creamed mustard mayonnaise served separately (Russian).

— **Café Anglais:** precooked morels, truffles and shrimps dressed with mayonnaise.

— **Danitcheff:** slices of knob celery, artichoke bottoms, potatoes, truffles and asparagus tips in mayonnaise with chopped chervil.

— **Dumas:** mussels poached in white wine, cooked truffles and potatoes, diced, French dressing.

— **Empire:** arrange separately: small slices of poached sturgeon, asparagus tips, green peas, sliced tomatoes and fresh cucumbers, diced artichoke bottoms, green beans and cauliflower buds, French dressing (Russian).

— **Francillon:** sliced potatoes, marinated in Chablis wine and half as much sliced truffles and bearded mussels in French dressing.

— **Grand Duchess:** Salade grande-duchesse: vegetable salad mixed and garnished with strips of fillets of sole, fillets of anchovies, shrimps and pickled cucumber, French dressing.

— **Imperial:** à l'impériale: shredded chicken, asparagus tips, and green beans arranged on lettuce, garnished truffle slices, French dressing (Russian).

— **Italian:** à l'italienne: diced carrots, turnips, potatoes, tomatoes, green beans, anchovy fillets, hard boiled eggs, pitted olives and capers in mayonnaise with chopped fine herbs.

— **Monastic:** monastique: marinate and arrange separately poached sturgeon, raw saurkraut, button onions, sliced dill pickles, sliced potatoes and green onions, sprinkle with chopped dill; French dressing.

— **Monte Carlo:** arrange separately in bunches, shredded partridges, tomatoes, diced calf's head, sliced celery and artichoke bottoms, French dressing.

— **Northern:** à la nordique: arrange separately: strips of boiled beef, celery, knob celery, sliced onions, green beans, diced tomatoes and pitted olives, mustard dressing.

— **Olivier:** dress in shape of a cupola diced potatoes, pickled cucumbers and shredded lettuce, bound with mayonnaise, flavored with Kabul sauce, and garnish with slices of hazelhen, pickled cucumbers, fresh cucumbers, tomatoes, truffles and hard boiled eggs and crayfish tails. (Russian)

Salad

— **Paillard:** poached flaked sturgeon, sliced pickled cucumbers, potatoes and hard boiled eggs in mayonnaise flavored with Kabul sauce, garnished with small slices of poached sturgeon, fresh cucumbers, potatoes and shredded lettuce.

— **Princess:** à la princesse: broiled shredded veal kidneys, asparagus tips, celery, red peppers and cucumber slices arranged on lettuce, mustard dressing.

— **Russian Fish:** de yerchi: mould lined with aspic jelly, filled with poached slices of yerchi (pope, ruffe, a sort of fresh water perch) and vegetable salad, turned out and garnished with crayfish tails (Russian)

— **Shrimp:** de crevettes: line small moulds with aspic jelly, fill with shrimps mixed with anchovy fillets, capers and chopped pickled cucumbers in mayonnaise.

— **Swedish:** Salade suédoise: small slices of boiled beef, potatoes, red beets, apples, anchovy fillets, herrings fillets in small pieces, pickles and capers, seasoned with vinegar, oil, mustard powder, paprika and salt, garnished with raw oysters, anchovy fillets, red beets and quarters of hard boiled eggs.

— **Sylvia:** arrange separately: shredded partridge, beets, green beans, green asparagus and tomatoes; mustard dressing.

— **Tomato:** de tomates: scald and peel ripe tomatoes, cut in slices, French dressing and Worcestershire sauce, sprinkle with chopped parsley.

Salami: sausages of various kinds, Hungarian, Italian or Gotha, cut in thin slices.

Salmon, Marinated: Saumon mariné: poach salmon steak in white wine with tomatoes, mushrooms, sliced pickles, green olives, paprika and salt, chill, serve in the stock.

— **Potted:** salmon paste preserved in cans or jars, used principally as spread for canapes or sandwiches etc.

— **Smoked:** Saumon fumé: cut in very thin slices, served flat on chopped aspic jelly, lettuce or toast or turned in small cornucopias and filled with vegetable or other fine salads or horseradish cream.

Salsify (Oyster plant), Marinated: Salsifis mariné: cut in pieces, boiled, marinated with salt, pepper, vinegar and oil, served well chilled.

— **Greek Style:** à la grecque: parboil and prepare the same way as for artichokes Greek style.

Sandwich: sandwich consists of two very thin slices of bread, butter and filling usually cut square, oblong or in triangles.

— **Bookmaker:** thin fillet steak (tenderloin), rare, cold, spread with English mustard and grated horseradish, placed between two slices of buttered toast, wrapped in blotting paper, lightly pressed, served without the paper.

— **Chicken:** white meat of boiled or roast chicken, sliced or chopped, between two slices of bread lightly buttered, cut diagonally.

— **Club:** slice of toast, buttered, covered with shredded lettuce in mayonnaise, chopped chicken and Westphalian ham arranged in layers, topped with a second slice of buttered toast.

— **Restaurant:** sliced cold roast fillet of beef (tenderloin), ham, ox tongue and anchovy fillets, arranged in layers between two slices of bread slightly buttered.

Sardines, Broiled: broiled, served on buttered toast.
- **with Cheese:** Sardines au parmesan: hot sardines on toast, covered with parmesan soufflé preparation and baked.
- **Deviled:** broiled, dressed on toast spread with mustard butter, sprinkled with cayenne.
- **Hungarian:** sardines crushed, mixed with chopped onions and paprika, spread on bread.
- **in Oil:** Commercial product usually served in the open tin with butter.
- **Rarebit:** hot sardines on toast, covered with dissolved cheese as for Welsh Rarebit.
- **in Tomato Sauce:** Sardines à la sauce tomate: Commercial product.
- **Vinaigrette:** à la vinaigrette: skinned and served with vinaigrette sauce.

Sausage, Marinated: Saucissons à l'huile: sliced cervelat, marinated in French dressing with chopped onions.
- **Viennese:** Saucissons de Vienne: heat up in boiling water, serve with grated horseradish, mustard, saurkraut or goulash sauce.

Sausages, Assorted: Saucissons divers: a variety of sausages, sliced and garnished with lettuce, pickles, tomatoes, hard boiled eggs and aspic jelly.
- **Small:** Andouilles: see main dishes.

Scotch Woodcock: anchovy fillets on toast covered with scrambled eggs, coated with melted cheese, baked, anchovy fillets on top.

Seafood: Fruits de mer: all sorts of shellfish, bivalves, molluscs and other marine delicacies served hot or cold.

Sea Hedgehog: Oursin: see fish course.

Sheep's Trotters: Pieds de mouton: see main dishes.

Shrimps, Devilled: Crevettes à la diable: shrimps dipped in egg and breadcrumbs, fried and seasoned with salt and Cayenne pepper.
- **Doria:** Crevettes à la Doria: marinated tomato halves, filled with shrimp salad, garnished with marinated slices of fresh cucumber.
- **Fried:** Crevettes frites: breadcrumbed, fried in deep fat, dressed on fried parsley.
- **Modern Style:** à la moderne: shrimps bound with mayonnaise, filled in glass, garnished with whole shrimps, slices of hard boiled egg and lemon.
- **Newest Style:** à la fin de siècle: half a lemon adorned with whole shrimps and garnished with parsley.

Shrimp Patties: Petits pains de crevettes: shrimps pounded together with olives, gherkins and chutney, mixed with eggs and cream, seasoned with salt and Cayenne pepper, filled in small moulds lined with bread crumbs, poached in bainmarie, served hot with shrimp sauce.

Shrimp Salad: Salade de crevettes: diced shrimps and celery, bound with mayonnaise, garnished with hard boiled eggs, fillets of anchovies and capers.

Sigui, Smoked: Lavaret fumé: a sort of smoked Russian char or grayling.

Skewers: Attereaux, Brochettes: any kind of food cooked on spits of silver or wood, about 6 inches long. See main dishes.

Smörgas-Bord: Swedish Appetizers: all sorts of Swedish open sandwiches, salads, smoked and pickled fish, cold cuts etc., various kinds of breads and crackers, eaten before dinner with a glass of Aquavit.

Soft Roe: Laitance: soft roes of herrings or carp, poached in butter and white wine or lemon juice, more often fried in butter, served on toast or in fancy "boats" of puff pastry or as garnish.

Soft Roes, Deviled: Laitances à la diable: fried, seasoned with cayenne pepper, served on hot buttered toast.

— — **Hungarian Style:** small puff pastry boats, filled with buttered noodles, poached soft roes of carp on top, covered with paprika sauce and dusted with paprika.

Soufflé, Cheese: de fromage: dissolve cheese, mix with milk and flour, season with salt, paprika and Worcestershire sauce, add egg yolks while mixture is hot, fold in egg whites beaten stiff, fill in ramekins and bake in hot oven.

— **Lobster:** Soufflé de homard: well seasoned forcemeat of lobster, blended with cream sauce and egg yolks, egg whites beaten stiffly folded in, baked in ramekins or small casseroles.

— **Oyster:** Soufflé d'huîtres: Prepare forcemeat of fish and oysters with egg white, mix in thick cream, season, fill in small casseroles with a raw oyster in the center, poach in oven.

— **Russian Herring:** Soufflé de hareng à la russe: forcemeat of desalted salt herrings, mixed with mashed potatoes and egg yolks, seasoned, egg whites stiffly beaten folded in, baked.

— **Small:** Petites souffleées: The basis of hot unsweetened souffleées is either a paste or purée of fish, meat, fowl, game or cheese etc., mixed with sauce and egg yolks, the stiffly beaten egg whites incorporated in the purée. They are usually served in small silver casseroles, cocottes or ramekins.

— **Tunny Fish:** de thon: mix purée of canned tunny fish with cream sauce, butter, cream, egg yolks and egg whites beaten stiff, fill in small casseroles and bake.

Sprats: Esprots: skin and serve on lettuce leaves or marinate in vinegar and oil.

Sterlet Aspic: cold, slices of poached sterlet, decorated with hard egg white and tarragon, glazed with aspic jelly, dressed on Russian salad, served with Russian mayonnaise (Russian).

T

Tartar Steak: Beefsteak à la tartare: ball off raw chopped tenderloin with a raw egg yolk on top in an indention, garnished with chopped onions, herbs, pickles and capers.

Tartlets, Finnan Haddie: Tartelettes à l'aigrefin fumé: filled with smoked flaked haddock in curry sauce.

— **Marquise:** moulds lined with puff pastry, filled with chopped Swiss cheese, covered with cheese sauce seasoned with Cayenne, baked, served hot. (Savory)

— **Romanow:** puff pastry shells, lined with anchovy butter, filled with caviar, garnished with smoked salmon.

Tartlets, Scotch: filled with purée of smoked haddock, bound with white sauce.
— **Tosca:** puff pastry tartlets, filled with salpicon of crayfish in lobster sauce, covered with cheese soufflé, baked.

Tomato Jelly: Gelée de tomates: raw tomato paste mixed with chopped onions, salt, pepper, pinch of sugar and gelatine, filled in small moulds, chilled, cut in slices, dressed on lettuce leaves, garnished with slices of hard boiled eggs and mayonnaise.
— **Surprise:** en surprise.
A: Stuffed with caviar, raw oyster on top, covered with lid.
B: Stuffed with diced knob celery in mayonnaise, covered with lid, dressed on lettuce leaf.

Tomatoes, Stuffed, Antiboise: Tomates farcies à l'antiboise: tomatoes, peeled, top cut off, centre hollowed out, stuffed with tunny salad, hard boiled eggs, herbs and mayonnaise.
— **Stuffed, Astor:** stuffed with thick purée of tomatoes mixed with unsweetened whipped cream, seasoned with paprika, garnished with whipped cream.
— **Bristol:** stuffed with chicken salad, ox tongue, celery and mustard mayonnaise, sprinkled with chopped truffle, adorned with dots of whipped, unsweetened cream.
— **Genoise Style:** à la genoise: tomato slices garnished with strips of green peppers, decorated with anchovy fillets, seasoned with pepper, vinegar and oil.
— **Hotel Plaza:** half tomatoes, dressed on lettuce leaves, stuffed with sardine purée mixed with tomato catchup, decorated with a ring of green peppers and a slice of stuffed olives.
— **Lucullus:** stuffed with chopped chicken, hard boiled eggs, celery, anchovy fillets, capers and olives in mayonnaise, sprinkled with chopped truffles, garnished with fresh hazelnut kernels.
— **Marinated:** Tomates marinées: seasoned with salt and pepper, marinated in oil and vinegar or lemon juice.
— **Mirabeau:** stuffed with chopped celery, truffles and anchovy fillets in mayonnaise decorated with anchovy fillets.
— **Monaco Style:** à la monégasque: tomatoes hollowed out, marinated, stuffed with chopped tunny mixed with hard boiled eggs, chopped onions and chives.
— **Nana:** stuffed with chopped chicken and chopped nut kernels in mayonnaise, dressed on lettuce, covered with mayonnaise.
— **Northern Style:** à la nordique: stuffed with caviar, slice of hard boiled egg on top, garnished with anchovy fillets, adorned with tartar sauce.
— **Stuffed with Oysters:** farcies aux huîtres: stuffed with poached oysters in cold poulette sauce with cream and lemon juice.
— **Parisian Style:** à la parisienne: slices of marinated tomatoes dressed on lettuce leaves, topped with diced parboiled knob celery mixed with chopped anchovy fillets, chervil, chives and shallots in French dressing.
— **Polish Style:** à la polonaise: stuffed with very fine herring salad in mayonnaise.
— **Rivoli:** stuffed with tomato froth, garnished with a cold poached cockscomb.

Tomatoes
— **Roumanian Style:** à la roumaine: stuffed with pilaw rice, mixed with diced tomatoes and green peppers, simmered in oil and lemon juice, served cold with a slice of peeled lemon on top.
— **Waldersee:** stuffed with purée of goose liver patty.
— **Waldorf:** filled with diced apple salad, celery and mayonnaise, sprinkled with chopped nuts.

Trout Salad: Salade de truite: fillets of poached trout, dressed on lettuce leaves, seasoned with salt, pepper, vinegar and oil, covered with ravigote sauce.

Tunny, Tunnyfish, also Tuna: Thon: marketed fresh or canned in oil.
— **Greek Style:** Thon à la grecque: slices of fresh tunny, poached in court bouillon of onions, garlic, carrots, spices, salt, oil and lemon juice, cooled and served in the stock.
— **Marinette:** slices of canned tunny dressed on tomato slices, garnished with potato salad and pickled button onions.
— **in Oil:** à l'huile: canned slices of tunny marinated in oil, seasoned, dressed on lettuce, garnished with sliced tomatoes and cucumbers.
— **Salad:** en salade: canned or fresh tunny, flaked with chopped chervil, parsley and shallots, French dressing.

Turkish Cheese Sticks: Beurrecks: chopped Emmenthal cheese mixed with hot cream sauce, seasoned with Cayenne, spread out to cool, shaped in form of small cigars, rolled in thin strips of noodle dough, dipped in egg and breadcrumbs and fried in deep fat.

V

Varenikis: see vegetable and farinaceous dishes.
Vatrouschkis: see vegetable and farinaceous dishes.
Victoria Rolls: Petits pains Victoria: small round rolls made of rich yeast dough, hollowed out and filled with chopped lobster in mayonnaise, goose liver patty, purée of chicken etc.

W

Watermelon: Pastèque: chilled, cut in slices, served on crushed ice.
Welsh Rarebit or Rabbit: Cheddar cheese dissolved in beer or ale, seasoned with Cayenne pepper, mustard powder and Worcestershire sauce, poured over hot toast (Savory).

Y

Yellow Boletus, Marinated: Gribuis: parboiled, marinated with vinegar, oil, salt, garlic, bay leaves and peppercorns, served cold in their stock (Russian).

Z

Zakouski: Russian Appetizers: serve in glass or china dishes each sort separately: radishes, anchovy fillets, oysters, caviar, smoked sturgeon, smoked salmon, sardines, small marinated fish, sausage, cheese, yeast dough patties filled with meat or fish etc. Lay Zakouski table in separate room and serve vodka and other spirits at the same time.

Sauces and Gravies

French: Sauces — Italian: Salse
German: Saucen — Spanish: Salsas

Good fonds and sauces are the foundation of fine cuisine. Their preparation is considered the most important business in every large kitchen. Sauces are invariably made from basic stocks that should be carefully treated and well seasoned. Very often they are finished off with egg yolks, cream, fresh butter and wine, many of them are garnished with mushrooms, truffles, oysters, shredded vegetables and other ingredients. It should be the aim of every sauce cook to adapt his sauces to the character of the dish he is serving. With suitable ingredients an experienced sauce cook can prepare an astounding variety of sauces suitable for every dish.

Stocks

Simple Brown Stock: Fond brun, Jus: Beef and veal bones and trimmings and mirepoix browned in fat, plain bouillon or water added, boiled slowly for 5 — 6 hours, seasoned lightly and strained.

White Stock: Fond blanc: Blanched veal bones and trimmings, a bunch of herbs, a larded onion and mushroom waste, water added, boiled slowly for about 3 hours and strained.

White Poultry Stock: Fond de volaille: Made like white stock from cooking fowls or by cooking veal bones with poultry waste.

Fish Stock: Fond de poisson: see fish course.

Simple Gravy: Jus de viande: The natural juices of roast meat deglazed with a little brown stock if desired.

Brown Veal Gravy: Jus de veau: Blanched veal bones and knuckles browned together with mirepoix, covered with white stock, boiled slowly for 4 — 5 hours, skimmed carefully and strained.

Thick Veal Gravy: Jus de veau lié: Brown veal gravy boiled down to the desired consistency, lightly thickened with arrow-root or corn starch and strained.

Concentrated Brown Stock, Meat Glaze: Glace de viande: Brown stock reduced by slow boiling to a glue-like consistency when warm, tough like rubber when cold. Poultry and fish glaze are made the same way with the respective stocks.

Basic Sauces

Simple Brown Sauce, Spanish Sauce: Espagnole: Brown roux with brown stock, browned mirepoix, a few peppercorns and a bunch of herbs consisting of parsley sprigs, thym, rosemary and a bayleaf added, boiled slowly for 10 to 12 hours, carefully skimmed and degreased, strained.

Finished Brown Sauce: Demi-glace: Spanish sauce refined by adding brown veal gravy, fresh tomatoes or tomato purée, mushroom waste and ham parings, boiled down slowly to the desired consistency, carefully skimmed and degreased, strained.

Tomato Sauce: Sauce tomate: mirepoix and diced bacon waste browned in butter, squeezed out tomatoes or tomato purée added, simmered together in the oven, sprinkled with flour, plain stock, a little garlic, a few peppercorns, a bunch of herbs, salt and a pinch of sugar added, boiled slowly for 1 — 1,1/2 hours, strained, improved with a few flakes of butter.

Velvet Sauce: Velouté:

1. **Veal Velouté: Velouté de veau:** white roux covered with white stock, boiled slowly for 1,1/2 hours, seasoned, strained.
2. **Chicken Velouté:** Velouté de volaille: prepared like veal velouté with chicken or poultry stock.
3. **Fish Velouté:** Velouté de poisson: prepared like veal velouté with fish stock.
4. **Vegetable Velouté:** Velouté de légumes: prepared like veal velouté with vegetable stock.

German Sauce: Sauce allemande: Veal velouté with additional strengthening, white and mushroom stock, seasoned with white pepper and lemon juice, beaten egg yolks added, reduced to the desired consistency, stirring with a spatula all the time, strained through an etamine cloth.

White Poultry or Supreme Sauce: Sauce suprême: 5 parts poultry and 1 part mushroom stock, reduced, chicken velouté and fresh cream added, boiled down to the desired consistency, seasoned, strained and beaten with a little butter.

White Sauce or Béchamel: White roux with milk and a larded onion added, boiled slowly for 1 hour, seasoned with salt, white pepper and a little grated nutmeg, strained, if possible improved with cream.

Dutch or Hollandaise Sauce: Sauce hollandaise: equal parts of vinegar and water and a pinch of white pepper boiled down (so called reduction), egg yolks added and whipped to a creamy foam with an egg whisk in water bath. Pulled aside and luke warm melted butter or soft flaky butter beaten in carefully, seasoned with salt, Cayenne pepper and lemon juice, strained through a cloth. Dutch sauce must be kept luke warm only or it will curdle.

A

aux Abatis see giblet.

Admiral: sauce amiral: white wine sauce with chopped shallots and grated lemon peel, anchovy butter added, garnished with capers.

Aegir: Dutch sauce flavored with mustard powder.

African: africaine: demi-glace seasoned with Cayenne pepper, flavored with Madeira, garnished with onion rings and diced truffles.

Aigre-doux: see sweet-sour.

à l'Ail: see garlic.

aux Airelles: see cranberry.

Albert: English butter sauce mixed with grated horseradish, seasoned with English mustard, vinegar and sugar.

Albuféra: suprême sauce finished with meat glaze and pimento butter.
Alcide: white wine sauce with chopped sweated shallots and grated horseradish.
Alexandra: suprême sauce with truffle extract.
Alexandra: (cold) mayonnaise prepared with sieved yolks of hardboiled eggs, seasoned with English mustard, mixed with chopped chervil.
Algerian: algérienne: tomato sauce garnished with strips of green or red peppers.
Allemande: see German.
Alliance: reduction of white wine, a little tarragon vinegar and white pepper, mixed with egg yolks, beaten until thick, melted butter added, seasoned with lemon juice and Cayenne, garnished with chopped chervil.
Alsacienne: see Alsatian.
Alsatian: alsacienne (cold): boiled calf's brain pounded in the mortar with onions, strained, seasoned with salt, pepper, mustard, vinegar and lemon juice, beaten with oil.
Ambassadress: ambassadrice: suprême sauce blended with chicken purée, finished off with whipped cream.
Américaine: see American.
American: américaine: lobster shells prepared like lobster American style (q. v.) pounded in the mortar, rubbed through a sieve, mixed with fish velouté, beaten up with butter, highly seasoned.
American (cold): mayonnaise blended with lobster purée, seasoned with mustard.
Anchovy: aux anchois: I. white wine sauce beaten with anchovy butter. II. Normandy sauce beaten with anchovy butter, garnished with diced anchovy fillets. III. butter sauce seasoned with anchovy essence.
Ancienne: see ancient.
Ancient: ancienne: Dutch sauce garnished with chopped gherkins, mushrooms and truffles.
Andalusian: andalouse: mayonnaise blended with tomato purée, garnished with diced sweet peppers.
à l'Aneth: see dill.
Antibe: antiboise: mayonnaise blended with tomato purée, finished off with anchovy paste and chopped tarragon.
Antin: Madeira sauce garnished with chopped shallots, boiled down in white wine, chopped mushrooms, truffles and fine herbs.
Apfelkren: apple and horseradish sauce: grated raw apples mixed with grated horseradish, seasoned with vinegar, sugar and paprika, moistened with white wine. (Austrian)
Apple and horseradish: aux pommes et raifort: apple sauce mixed with grated horseradish, seasoned with lemon juice and Cayenne pepper.
Apple: sauce aux pommes: apple purée slightly sweetened and flavored with cinnamon.
Archevêque: see arch-bishop.
Arch-bishop: archevêque: herb sauce garnished with capers.
Arch-duke: archiduc: suprême sauce finished off with reduced champagne.
Archiduc: see arch-duke.
Arlesian: arlesienne: Béarnaise sauce colored with tomato purée, finished off with anchovy paste, garnished with diced tomatoes.

Aromatic: aromate: I. a decoction of thyme, sweet basil, sage, majoram, chives, tarragon and withe wine reduced, filled up with demi-glace, strained, garnished with chopped tarragon and chervil.
II. veal velouté with a reduced decoction of majoram, sage, sweet basil, chives, shallots, peppercorns, thyme and white wine, strained, mixed with chopped chervil.
Artois: meat glace beaten with crayfish and herb butter.
Aurora: aurore: I. veal velouté colored with tomato purée, slightly buttered.
II. fish velouté colored with tomato purée slightly buttered.
Avignon: avignonnaise: cream sauce flavored with garlic, mixed with grated Parmesan and chopped parsley, bound with egg yolks.

B

Banquière: see banker.
Banker's: Banquière: suprême sauce colored with tomato purée, blended with veal glaze and butter, flavored with Madeira.
Barbecue: indeterminable sharp sauce prepared in different ways, for instance: tomato purée mixed with meat gravy, catchup, grated horseradish, smoke juice, garlic and onion juice, seasoned with salt, mustard powder, Chili powder, paprika, sugar and Cayenne pepper, flavored with tarragon vinegar, A 1 and Worcestershire sauce.
Bastard, Pale: bâtarde blonde: Bastard sauce prepared with fish fumet.
Bâtarde: see bastard and butter sauce.
Bavarian: bavaroise: Dutch sauce, creamed, beaten with crayfish butter, garnished with diced crayfish tails.
Bavaroise: see Bavarian.
Béarnaise: chopped shallots, white pepper, tarragon and salt boiled down in wine vinegar, allowed to cool, egg yolks added, whipped to a thick foam in a water bath, melted butter beaten in, seasoned with Cayenne pepper, strained, mixed with chopped tarragon and chervil.
Beauharnais: Béarnaise sauce without chopped chervil and tarragon, blended with tarragon purée.
Béchamel: white roux moistened with milk, seasoned with salt, a larded onion added, boiled, strained. May be improved with cream.
Beefsteak: a commercial sauce, ready bottled.
Berchoux: German sauce, cream added, herb butter beaten in.
Bercy: I. chopped shallots sweated in butter, moistened with 1/2 white wine and 1/2 fish fumet, reduced, fish velouté added, butter beaten in, mixed with chopped parsley. (for fish)
II. chopped shallots and white pepper, moistened with white wine, reduced, meat glaze added, butter beaten in, garnished with diced blanched beef marrow and chopped parsley. (for grilled meat)
au Beurre: see butter sauce.
Beurre noir: see black butter.
Bigarade: sugar burned to caramel, moistened with orange and lemon juice, boiled down, duck stock and demi-glace added, garnished with julienne of orange and lemon peel.

Black Butter: beurre noir: butter darkly browned, a few drops of vinegar added.

Boatman's: canotière: same as bastard sauce, but prepared with fish stock.

Bonnefoy: prepared like Bordeaux sauce but with white wine, garnished with diced blanched beef marrow and chopped parsley.

Bordeaux: bordelaise: chopped shallots, thyme, bay leaf and white pepper, moistened with red wine, boiled down, demi-glace added, boiled, strained, beaten with butter. For meat dishes garnished with blanched, diced beef marrow and a little chopped parsley.

Bordelaise: see Bordeaux.

Bourguignonne: see Burgundy.

Brantôme: cream sauce boiled down with white wine and oyster liquor, crayfish butter beaten in, seasoned with Cayenne pepper, garnished with grated truffles.

Bread Sauce au pain à l'anglaise: milk boiled with onion, grated white bread added, boiled for 5 minutes, onion removed, seasoned with salt, nutmeg and Cayenne, finished off with cream and butter.

Bresse: bressanne: Spanish sauce flavored with Madeira and orange juice, seasoned with Cayenne, finished off with purée of sautéd chicken livers.

Breton: bretonne: I. lightly fried chopped onions moistened with white wine, reduced, demi-glace, tomato purée and garlic added, cooked, strained, beaten with butter garnished with chopped parsley.
II. white wine sauce finished off with cream and butter, julienne of mushrooms, leeks, celery and onions, sweated in butter, added.

Broglie: demi-glace boiled down with mushroom stock, beaten with butter, flavored with Madeira, garnished with diced fried ham.

Bulgarian: bulgare: thick cold tomato sauce mixed with mayonnaise, garnished with diced cooked knob celery.

Burgundy: à la bourguignonne: chopped shallots, parsley sprigs, thyme, bay leaf and mushroom waste moistened with red wine, boiled down partly, thickened with butterpaste, strained, beaten with butter, seasoned with Cayenne.

Butter (Bastard Sauce): bâtarde: white roux moistened with water, cooked, bound with egg yolks, buttered and creamed, seasoned with lemon juice, strained.

— **Parisian:** creamed butter mixed with chopped shallots, chopped parsley and tarragon, a little sage, chopped anchovy fillets, mustard, lemon juice, salt, paprika and Worcestershire sauce.

— **English:** au beurre à l'anglaise: bastard sauce without liaison.

Byron: red wine, seasoned, boiled up, thickened with arrowroot, beaten with butter, garnished with short truffle strips.

C

Californian: californienne: (cold) thick cream mixed with tomato catchup, seasoned with Worcestershire sauce, tabasco, paprika and lemon juice.

Cambridge: hard boiled egg yolks, anchovies, capers, dill and tarragon rubbed through a sieve, oil beaten in as for mayonnaise, seasoned with mustard, vinegar and Cayenne pepper, finished off with chopped parsley.

Camerani: demi-glace, flavored with Madeira, mixed with chopped truffles.

Canotière: see boatman's sauce.

Caper: aux câpres: I. English butter sauce flavored with lemon juice, garnished with capers.
II. bastard sauce garnished with capers.
III. demi-glace garnished with capers.

Cardinal: Béchamel sauce finished off with fish fumet, truffle extract and lobster coulis, seasoned with Cayenne pepper.

Carignan: demi-glace finished off with duck and truffle extract, flavored with Malaga wine.

Casanova: mayonnaise mixed with chopped hard boiled egg yolks, tarragon and truffles.

Castelan: castellane: demi-glace with meat glaze and butter, garnished with finely diced sweet peppers and ham, flavored with Madeira.

Catalonian: catalane: demi-glace seasoned with mustard, garlic and Cayenne pepper, flavored with Madeira, garnished with chopped fried onions.

Catsup, Catchup, Ketchup: an East Indian pickle, made of tomatoes, green walnuts or mushrooms, highly spiced. Commercial product in bottles.

Cavalier: cavalière: demi-glace mixed with tomato purée, seasoned with mustard and tarragon vinegar, garnished with capers and chopped gherkins.

Caviar: Dutch sauce with caviar added before serving, served luke warm.

Celery: au céleri: celery cooked in white stock with a larded onion, stock reduced, celery rubbed through a sieve and mixed with cream sauce, finished off with a little of the stock.

aux Cèpes: see yellow boletus.

Chambord: salmon heads and parings sweated in butter with mirepoix, thyme, bay leaf and parsley sprigs, moistened with red wine, boiled down, filled up with demi-glace, cooked, strained, beaten with butter and anchovy paste.

Champagne: au champagne: I. demi-glace boiled down with champagne, flavored with a little cognac.
II. reduced champagne, mixed with egg yolks and beaten with butter as in Dutch sauce.

aux Champignons: see mushroom.

Chantilly: I. mayonnaise seasoned with lemon juice, unsweetened whipped cream added at the last minute.
II. Dutch sauce, unsweetened whipped cream added before serving.

Charcutière: see pork-butcher.

Chartres: demi-glace flavored with tarragon, garnished with chopped tarragon.

Chasseur: see hunter.

Chateaubriand: a decoction of chopped shallots, thyme, bay leaf, mushroom peels and white wine, reduced, strained, meat glaze added, beaten with butter, finished off with chopped parsley and tarragon.

Chaudfroid, Blond: blonde: same as white with a little liquid meat glaze added.

Chaudfroid

— **Brown:** brune: demi-glace blended with truffle extract and aspic jelly, flavored with Madeira; for game demi-glace boiled down with game trimmings or game extract.

— **Green:** verte, velouté beaten with green herb purée blended with cream and aspic jelly; may also be colored with spinach maté.

— **Pink:** rosée: veal or fish or chicken velouté colored with tomato purée or for fish dishes beaten with crayfish or lobster butter, blended with aspic jelly and cream.

— **Tomato:** tomatée: white chaudfroid sauce mixed with bright red tomato paste.

— **White:** chaudfroid blanche: veal or fish velouté blended with aspic jelly and cream.

Cheese: Mornay: Béchamel sauce beaten with butter, mixed with grated Parmesan and Swiss cheese. May be bound with egg yolks before butter is added.

Cherbourg: cream sauce beaten with crayfish butter, garnished with crayfish tails.

Cherry: dried morellos cooked with red wine, water, cinnamon, lemon peel and a little sugar, thickened with browned breadcrumbs, rubbed through a sieve, seasoned with lemon juice, garnished with pitted morellos. Specially for wild boar.

Chevreuil: mirepoix and game or venison leavings lightly fried in butter, moistened with red wine, boiled down, filled up with pepper sauce, cooked, strained, seasoned with Cayenne pepper and a pinch of sugar.

Chief Ranger: grand veneur: pepper sauce with game extract, finished off with red currant jelly and cream.

Chili: Commercial bottled sauce made of pounded red and green chili peppers, salt, tomatoes, onions, sugar, vinegar and spices etc. highly flavored.

Chive: civette: suprême sauce beaten with crayfish butter, garnished with chopped chives.
II. veal velouté, garnished with chopped chives.
III. (cold) Schnittlauch Sauce: mashed hard-boiled egg yolks mixed with white bread soaked in milk, strained, seasoned with vinegar, mixed with chopped chives. (Austrian)

Choron: Béarnaise sauce mixed with a little bright red tomato purée.

Chutney: Commercial condiment, bottled, made of ginger, mangoes, cucumbers, tamarind pulp, fried apples, beet and lemon juice, vinegar, garlic, chilis, spices etc., highly flavored.

au Citron: see lemon.

Clam: aux clovisses: fish velouté made partly with clam stock, seasoned with lemon juice, beaten with a little butter, garnished with chopped clams.

Cocktail: composition of tomato-catsup, grated horseradish, chili sauce, Worcestershire sauce, tabasco, chopped green peppers and herbs.

Colbert: meat or poultry glaze beaten with butter, seasoned with lemon juice, garnished with chopped parsley and tarragon.

Cordelier: see Franciscan.

Countess: comtesse: fish velouté beaten with anchovy butter, seasoned with lemon juice.

Cranberry: aux airelles: boiled in little water, rubbed through a sieve, slightly sweetened.
Crayfish: écrevisses: Dutch or white wine sauce beaten with crayfish butter.
Cream: crème: Béchamel sauce finished off with plenty of cream.
Cream: crème (cold): whipped cream mixed with grated horseradish, seasoned with vinegar, salt and sugar.
— **French:** fleurette: thick Dutch sauce blended with thin cream.
— **German:** meat or game gravy boiled down with sour cream, seasoned with paprika and lemon juice.
Créole: tomato sauce with a decoction of garlic, onions and white wine, seasoned with Cayenne pepper, garnished with strips of red peppers.
Cucumber: aux concombres: veal velouté flavored with aniseed, garnished with julienne or small slices of pickled cucumbers and chopped parsley.
Cumberland: (cold): red currant jelly, rubbed through a sieve, flavored with Port, orange juice, mustard, ginger powder and Cayenne pepper, garnished with blanched chopped shallots and juilenne of orange and lemon peel.
Curry: I. chopped onions sweated in butter, with curry powder, moistened with coconut milk, fish or veal velouté added, cooked, finished off with cream.
II. chopped onions and apples lightly fried in butter, sprinkled with curry powder, moistened with coconut milk, thick veal gravy or demi-glace added, boiled down, garnished with chopped mangoes.
Cussy: demi-glace mixed with poultry glaze flavored with Madeira.
Czech: tchèque: mayonnaise mixed with cold cream sauce.

D

Danish: danoise: cream sauce blended with chicken purée and mushroom extract mixed with chopped herbs.
Danoise: see Danish.
Daumont: Dutch sauce with oyster liquor, seasoned with lemon juice, garnished with diced mushrooms, truffles and oysters.
Demi-deuil: see half-mourning.
Demidoff: Madeira sauce garnished with sliced truffles.
Demi-glace: basic Spanish sauce boiled down with strong brown veal stock, flavored with a little Madeira.
Devil: diable: I. decotion of chopped shallots, white pepper, half white wine and half vinegar, moistened with demi-glace, strained, garnished with chopped fine herbs.
II. decoction of chopped shallots and white pepper in vinegar, demi-glace and tomato purée added, strained, seasoned with Harvey sauce and Cayenne pepper.
Devonshire: German sauce garnished with diced red tongue.
Diable: see devil.
Diana: Diane: pepper sauce finished off with cream, garnished with diced hard boiled egg whites and truffles.
Dieppe: dieppoise: fish velouté blended with shrimp butter.
Dill: à l'aneth: veal velouté or Béchamel seasoned with lemon juice, mixed with chopped dill. For fish prepared with fish velouté.

Diplomate: Normandy sauce blended with lobster butter, garnished with dices of truffles and lobster.

Divine: Dutch sauce blended with poultry glaze, finished off with whipped cream.

Duchess: duchesse: cream sauce beaten with a little butter and cream, garnished with chopped red tongue and mushrooms.

Dunant: Dutch sauce blended with truffle essence, beaten with langoustine butter, finished off at the last minute with whipped unsweetened cream.

Dutch: hollandaise: see basic sauces.

Duxelles: chopped onions and shallots sweated in butter, moistened with white wine, reduced, filled up with half tomato and half demi-glace, mixed with plenty of chopped mushrooms fried in butter and chopped parsley and boiled for a while.

E

Ecossaise: see Scotch sauce.

Ecrevisses: see crayfish.

Egg-sauce: aux oeufs: I. Dutch sauce garnished with diced hard-boiled eggs.
II. melted butter seasoned with salt, pepper and lemon juice, mixed with diced hard-boiled eggs and chopped parsley.
III. English egg-sauce: English butter sauce garnished with diced hard-boiled eggs.

Eglantine: see rose-hip.

Empress': impératrice: German sauce with truffle and chicken extract, finished off with whipped cream.

English Bread Sauce: see bread.

Epicurean: épicurienne: I. bastard sauce blended with mushroom catsup, seasoned with Cayenne pepper and vinegar.
II. (cold) mayonnaise blended with cucumber purée and anchovy paste, flavored with chutney.

Espagnole: see Spanish.

Esterhazy: chopped onions fried in butter, moistened with white wine, boiled down, mixed with demi-glace, meat glaze and sour cream, boiled up, seasoned with paprika, garnished with strips of carrots and knob celery lightly simmered in butter.

Etretat: German sauce with fish fumet and tomato purée, garnished with oysters and mushrooms.

F

Felix: demi-glace beaten with lobster butter, seasoned with lemon juice.

Fennel: au fenouil: English butter sauce garnished with cooked finely diced fennel.

au Fenouil: see fennel.

Fermière: see tenant.

Financier's: financière: demi-glace flavored with truffle extract.

Finnish: finnoise: chicken velouté seasoned with paprika, garnished with strips of green peppers and chopped herbs.
Fisher's: pêcheurs (cold): shrimp purée beaten with oil seasoned with salt, pepper and wine vinegar.
Flamande: see Flemish.
Flemish: flamande: I. butter sauce seasoned with mustard and lemon juice, chopped parsley added.
II. melted butter seasoned with French mustard and lemon juice, chopped parsley added.
Fleurette: see cream sauce, French.
Forester's: forestière: demi-glace garnished with sliced sautéd mushrooms flavored with Sherry.
Foyot: Béarnaise sauce blended with meat glaze.
Française: see French.
Francis I.: François I.: white wine sauce beaten with butter, garnished with diced tomatoes and mushrooms.
Francis Joseph: François Joseph: chief ranger's sauce with reduced champagne.
Franciscan: cordelier: Madeira sauce blended with goose liver purée, garnished with sliced truffles.
French: française: Béarnaise sauce blended with fish glaze and tomato purée.

G

Garibaldi: demi-glace seasoned with mustard, Cayenne pepper and garlic, beaten with a little anchovy butter.
Garlic: à l'ail: demi-glace strongly flavored with garlic, beaten with a little butter.
Garlic (cold): aïoli, ailloli: crushed garlic mixed with mashed hard-boiled eggs, mashed fresh boiled potatoes, salt, pepper and lemon juice, beaten with oil as for mayonnaise.
— **Turkish:** à l'ail à la turque: crushed garlic mixed with white bread soaked in milk, rubbed through a sieve, egg yolks and vinegar added, beaten with oil as for mayonnaise.
Gascon: gasconne: veal velouté with a reduction of herbs in white wine, beaten with a little anchovy butter.
Gastronomer's: gastronome: demi-glace blended with reduction of champagne, seasoned with Cayenne pepper, meat glaze added, flavored with Madeira.
General: général: demi-glace boiled up with lemon juice, tarragon vinegar, garlic and finely chopped orange peel, flavored with Sherry.
Geneva: génevoise: chopped salmon heads and parings sweated in butter with mirepoix, moistened with red wine, boiled down, demi-glace, seasoning and bunch of herbs added, boiled down to a strong sauce, strained, flavored with anchovy essence, beaten with butter.
Génevoise: see Geneva.
Genoa: génoise (cold): mayonnaise blended with purée of pistachios, herbs and almonds, seasoned with lemon juice.
Génoise: see Genoa.
German: allemande: veal velouté boiled down with white wine and mushroom essence, seasoned with lemon juice, bound with egg yolks.

Giblet: aux abatis: giblets sautéd with chopped onions, sprinkled with flour, browned, moistened with brown poultry stock or water, seasoned, cooked, strained, flavored with Sherry, garnished with the diced gizzards and diced sautéd livers.

Gipsy: Zingara: demi-glace with tomato purée, seasoned with Cayenne pepper, flavored with Madeira, garnished with julienne of mushrooms, truffles, ham and ox tongue.

Girondin: Dutch sauce seasoned with mustard.

Gloucester (cold): mayonnaise with sour cream, seasoned with Worcestershire sauce and English mustard, garnished with chopped fennel.

Godard: reduction of white wine with mirepoix and chopped ham, mixed with demi-glace and mushroom stock, boiled down and strained.

Golfin: white wine sauce garnished with strips of gherkins and red tongue.

Gooseberry: groseilles: I. slightly sweetened purée of green gooseberries.
II. green unripe gooseberries blanched, cooked in white wine with a little sugar, mixed with bastard sauce.

Gourmet: red wine sauce boiled up with fish fumet, blended with lobster butter, garnished with diced lobster and truffles.

Grand-veneur: see chief ranger.

Grandville: white wine sauce garnished with diced truffles, mushrooms and shrimps.

Grape, Polish: white roux mixed with white stock and grape juice, boiled up, strained.

Gratin: chopped shallots boiled down with white wine, dry duxelles and demi-glace added (if for fish a little fish fumet), boiled up, finished off with chopped parsley

Green: verte: mayonnaise mixed with a purée of blanched herbs.

Gribiche (cold): hardboiled egg yolks beaten with vinegar and oil as for mayonnaise, seasoned with mustard, garnished with chopped gherkins, capers, parsley, tarragon, chives and julienne of hard-boiled egg whites.

Groseilles: see gooseberry.

H

Hachée: see hash.

Half-mourning: demi-deuil: chicken or veal velouté flavored with truffle essence, garnished with sliced truffles.

Harvey: commercial sauce obtainable in bottles.

Hash: hachée: chopped shallots and onions lightly fried in butter, moistened with a little vinegar, boiled down, demi-glace and tomato purée added, when done mixed with dry duxelles, chopped parsley, ham and small capers.

Havre: havraise: white wine sauce boiled down with mussel stock, garnished with mussels and shrimps.

Hazelnut: noisettes: Dutch sauce blended with purée of grilled hazelnuts.

Henry IV.: Henri IV.: Béarnaise sauce mixed with liquid meat glaze.

Herb: aux fines herbes I. infusion of tarragon, chervil, chives, parsley and chopped shallots, strained, mixed with demiglace, garnished with chopped herbs.
II.white wine sauce mixed with chopped herbs, beaten with herb butter.

Herb Butter: beurre maître d'hôtel: fresh butter kneaded with chopped parsley, pepper and lemon juice.

Hollandaise: see Dutch.

Holstein: cream sauce with reduction of fish stock and white wine, seasoned with nutmeg, bound with egg yolk.

Homard: see lobster.

Homely: bourgeoise: demi-glace seasoned with tarragon vinegar and mustard.

Hongroise: see Hungarian.

Horseradish: raifort: I. German sauce mixed with sour cream and grated horseradish, seasoned with a little vinegar and Cayenne pepper.
II. hot cream with white breadcrumbs and horseradish stirred in.
III. (cold) grated horseradish seasoned with salt, pepper and lemon juice, thick cream added.
IV. Béchamel sauce boiled up with a little beef stock grated horseradish added, seasoned with vinegar and Cayenne pepper.
V. grated horseradish boiled up with a little beef stock, demi-glace added, seasoned with mustard and vinegar.

— **Cream, Chilled:** Crème de raifort glacée: I. whipped cream mixed with grated horseradish, seasoned with lemon juice and Cayenne pepper, chilled.
II. whipped cream mixed with grated horseradish and grated orange peel, flavored with orange juice and frozen.
II. grated horseradish and apple purée mixed with whipped cream, seasoned with sugar and lemon juice, frozen. Suitable for boiled beef, cold meat and game dishes.

Housekeeper's: ménagère: chopped onions fried in butter, sprinkled with flour, moistened with beef stock, boiled, mixed with chopped anchovies and parsley, seasoned with lemon juice.

Housewife's: bonne-femme: chopped shallots sweated in butter, moistened with fish stock, boiled, bound with egg yolks and cream, seasoned with lemon juice.

Hungarian: I. hongroise: white wine sauce mixed with liquid veal glaze and sour cream, seasoned with paprika.
II. chopped onions and diced salt pork sautéd in lard, demi-glace and sour cream added, boiled, seasoned with paprika.
III. chopped onions and diced salt pork slightly browned in lard sprinkled with flour, sour cream and meat glaze added. boiled, seasoned with paprika.

Hunter: chasseur: sliced mushrooms and chopped shallots sautéd in butter, moistened with white wine, boiled down, demi-glace added, beaten with a little butter and finished off with chopped parsley.

Hussar: hussarde: chopped shallots and onions sweated in butter, moistened with white wine, boiled down, demiglace, tomato purée, raw ham, garlic and bunch of herbs added, all boiled together, strained, garnished with grated horseradish, finely diced ham and chopped parsley.

I

Indian: indienne: I. German sauce flavored with curry powder. II. chopped onions and apples fried in butter, sprinkled with flour, browned, curry powder added, moistened with beef stock, boiled to a thick strong sauce, finished off with coconut milk and cream.
III. (cold) mayonnaise mixed with purée of baked apples, seasoned with curry powder, chutney and mushroom catsup.

Isigny: Dutch sauce mixed with very thick cream.

Italian: italienne: I. duxelles sauce with finely diced ham and chopped parsley added.
II. (cold) boiled calf's brain rubbed through a sieve, mixed with egg yolks, seasoned, beaten up with vinegar and oil as for mayonnaise.

Ivory: ivoire: veal velouté blended with meat glaze.

J

Juniper Berry: au genièvre: I. chopped ham and onions sweated in butter, crushed juniper berries and red wine added, boiled down, mixed with demi-glace, boiled, strained.
II. game bones and trimmings, chopped onions, carrots and salt pork slightly browned in butter, moistened with red wine, crushed juniper berries added, boiled down, demi-glace and game essence added, boiled, strained.

K

Kabul: commercial Russian sauce obtainable in bottles, used for flavoring salads and sauces.

Kidney: aux rognons: Madeira sauce garnished at the last minute with finely diced calf's kidneys and chopped shallots sautéd in butter.

L

Laguipierre: bastard sauce mixed with fish glaze, seasoned with lemon juice.

Lapin: see rabbit.

Lapostole: apricot purée boiled up with grated orange peel, sugar and white wine, strained, flavored with orange juice and Grand-Marnier liquor, garnished with blanched julienne of orange peel. (Special sauce for soufflés)

Lavallière: demi-glace with game essence and sour cream, garnished with truffle julienne and chopped tarragon.

with Leaves: aux peluches: Dutch sauce garnished with blanched tarragon, parsley and chervil leaves.

Leclerc: demi-glace boiled down with mushroom stock and white wine, seasoned with mustard and Cayenne pepper.

Ledoyen: roasted trimmings of game birds sautéd in butter, boiled up with pepper sauce, orange marmelade added, strained, seasoned with English mustard and lemon juice, beaten with butter, flavored with Sherry.

Leek: aux poireaux: chopped leeks sweated in butter, cooked with cream sauce, seasoned with Cayenne pepper, garnished with julienne of leeks.

Leghorn: à la livournaise (cold): oil and vinegar, seasoned with pepper and nutmeg, mixed with chopped hard-boiled egg yolks, chopped parsley and anchovy paste.

Lemon: au citron: I. creamed butter seasoned with grated lemon peel, lemon juice and Cayenne pepper, mixed with chopped parsley.
II. Dutch sauce mixed with grated lemon peel, seasoned with lemon juice.

Lithuanian: lithuanienne: Colbert sauce mixed with fried breadcrumbs and chopped herbs.

Livonian: livonienne: I. demi-glace with sour cream, beaten with butter, garnished with shredded fennel.
II. fish velouté, beaten with butter, garnished with julienne of truffles, carrots and chopped parsley.

Livournaise: see Leghorn.

Lobster: homard: I. Normandy sauce beaten with lobster purée.
II. fish velouté beaten with lobster butter, garnished with diced lobster.

Lombard: Dutch sauce with chopped mushrooms and parsley.

Lyonese: lyonnaise: I. chopped onions, fried in butter, moistened with half white wine and half vinegar, boiled down, demi-glace added.
II. veal velouté or Béchamel sauce with chopped onions boiled down in white wine, a little garlic and chopped herbs.

M

Madeira: madère: demi-glace flavored strongly with Madeira before serving.

Madère: see Madeira.

Magenta: Béarnaise sauce mixed with diced tomatoes and chopped herbs.

Maillot: Madeira sauce with reduction of shallots in white wine, seasoned with Cayenne pepper, garnished with chopped hard-boiled egg yolks.

Maintenon: cream sauce mixed with white onion purée, a little garlic and grated Parmesan, seasoned with Cayenne pepper.

Maître d'hôtel: see herb butter.

Malaga: demi-glace with a reduction of chopped shallots in white wine, seasoned with Cayennne pepper, flavored with Malaga wine and lemon juice.

Maltese: maltaise: Dutch sauce with grated orange peel, flavored with blood orange juice.

Mandelkren: horseradish sauce with almonds: I. cream sauce with almond milk, boiled up with grated horseradish, seasoned and strained.
II. (cold) pounded almonds mixed with egg yolks and grated horseradish, seasoned with salt and sugar, beaten with oil and vinegar (as for mayonnaise). (Austrian)

Marengo: hunter sauce flavored with garlic, garnished with sliced sautéd mushrooms.

Marguery: Dutch sauce mixed with oyster liquor, garnished with poached bearded oysters.

Marigny: demi-glace boiled up with tomato purée, mushroom stock and white wine, garnished with sliced mushrooms and pitted olives.

Mariner's: marinière: Bercy sauce with reduced mussel stock, beaten with butter, garnished with bearded mussels.

Marly: creamed veal velouté beaten with butter, seasoned with Cayenne pepper, garnished with chopped mushrooms.

Marquise: Dutch sauce with caviar added at the last minute.
Marrow: moelle: prepared like Bordeaux sauce but with white wine, garnished with diced blanched beef marrow and chopped parsley.
Marseille (cold): mayonnaise mixed with purée of sea-urchins.
Marshal: maréchale: German sauce boiled up with mushroom stock, garnished with chopped mushrooms.
Maximilian: Dutch sauce blended with anchovy essence.
Mayonnaise: raw egg yolks mixed with seasoning and a little vinegar, slightly warmed oil stirred in gradually until the mixture is thick, a few drops of vinegar added now and then to prevent mayonnaise from getting too thick; a few drops of boiling water added at the last minute will prevent curdling.
— **Hamburg Style:** à la hambourgeoise: mayonnaise seasoned with mustard, grated lemon peel and an pinch of sugar, flavored with Madeira.
— **Jellied:** mayonnaise collée: 1 part liquid aspic jelly added to 2 parts mayonnaise.
— **Russian:** mayonnaise à la russe: mayonnaise prepared with tarragon vinegar, grated horseradish and a little luke warm aspic jelly added.
Médici: Béarnaise sauce with tomato purée and a reduction of red wine.
Melba: **I.** Savoury sauce invented by Escoffier, bottled commercially.
II. Newburgh sauce beaten with lobster butter, garnished with oyster crabs.
Menthe: see mint.
Mexican: mexicaine: mayonnaise flavored with anchovy essence or paste, garnished with chopped red and green peppers.
Milanese: milanaise: **I.** German sauce mixed with tomato purée, garnished with diced tomatoes and pine-kernels.
II. demi-glace mixed with tomato purée and meat glaze, flavored with garlic, garnished with julienne of mushrooms sautéd in butter.
Mint: menthe: fresh chopped mint leaves soaked in very mild wine vinegar, slightly sweetened, heated for a short time, strained, garnished with fresh chopped mint leaves, served cold with roast mutton.
— **Jelly:** gelée à la menthe: cold mint sauce slightly thickened with gelatine, coloured green with spinach maté.
Mirabeau: German sauce flavored with garlic, beaten with herb butter.
Miroton: demi-glace mixed with tomato purée, seasoned with mustard, garnished with onion rings fried in butter.
Moelle: see marrow.
Montebello: mixture of half Béarnaise and half thick tomato sauce.
Montigny: Veal velouté colored with tomato purée, a little meat glaze and chopped herbs added.
Morel: aux morilles: German sauce with sliced braised morels added.
Mornay: see cheese sauce.
Mousquetaire: see musketeer.
Mousseline: Dutch sauce blended with whipped cream before serving.
Moutarde: see mustard.

Muscovite: moscovite: pepper sauce with an infusion of juniper berries, garnished with sliced almonds or pine-kernels and raisins, flavored with Marsala.

Mushroom: aux champignons: I. demi-glace boiled down with mushroom stock, garnished with small fluted mushroom caps.
I. German sauce boiled down with mushroom stock, garnished with sliced cooked mushrooms.

Musketeer: mousquetaire: I. provencal sauce with chopped tarragon and herbs.
II. (cold) mayonnaise with a reduction of chopped shallots in white wine and chopped chives, seasoned with Cayenne pepper.

Mussel: aux moules: I. Normandy sauce with reduced mussel stock, garnished with bearded mussels.
II. Dutch sauce with reduced mussel stock, garnished with bearded mussels.

Mustard: moutarde: I. white butter, cream or Dutch sauce seasoned with mustard.
II. (cold) mayonnaise seasoned with mustard.

N

Nantua: Béchamel boiled down with cream, beaten with crayfish butter, garnished with small crayfish tails.

Naples: napolitaine: I. very fine mirepoix boiled down with Marsala and diced tomatoes, boiled up with demi-glace, beaten with a little butter.
II. lemon juice and oil mixed with crushed garlic, chopped parsley, salt and pepper.

Napolitaine: see Naples.

Navarese: navarraise: tomato sauce flavored with garlic, garnished with chopped herbs.

Nevernese: nivernaise: German sauce garnished with tiny carrot and turnip balls simmered in butter.

Newburgh: I. raw sliced lobster sautéd in butter and paprika seasoned, sprinkled with cognac and set alight, moistened with cream and fish fumet, boiled, lobster, taken out, the pounded shells added, cooked, strained, whipped up with lobster butter, flavored with Sherry.
II. sliced cooked lobster sautéd in butter, seasoned, moistened with Sherry and thick cream, boiled down, lobster taken out, sauce thickened with egg yolks and cream.

Noisettes: see hazelnut.

Nora: pepper sauce blended with cranberry purée, seasoned with lemon juice and Worcestershire sauce.

Normandy: normande: fish velouté boiled up with fish fumet, mushroom stock and oyster liquor, bound with egg yolks and cream, beaten with butter.

Norwegian: norvegienne: mashed hardboiled egg yolks seasoned with mustard and vinegar, stirred up with oil as for mayonnaise.

O

Oberskren: cream sauce mixed with grated horseradish, seasoned with paprika, pinch of sugar and salt, finished off with thick cream. (Austrian)

aux Oeufs: see egg-sauce.

Olive: aux olives: demi-glace flavored with Sherry, garnished with pitted blanched olives.
Omega: Dutch sauce garnished with shredded chervil.
Onion, Brown: onions à brun: I. chopped onions browned in butter, boiled down in white wine, demi-glace added, seasoned with salt, pepper, sugar, vinegar and mustard, strained.
II. demi-glace mixed with onion purée, seasoned with paprika, beaten with butter.
— **English:** sliced onions cooked in milk, seasoned with salt, pepper and nutmeg, strained, mixed with cream sauce prepared with a part of the onion stock.
— **Viennese:** Wiener Zwiebelsauce: chopped onions and garlic browned in lard, mixed with brown roux, filled up with beef stock, boiled, seasoned with salt and a pinch of sugar. (Austrian)
— **White:** oignons à blanc Soubise: sliced onions lightly fried in butter, Béchamel sauce added, cooked, strained, seasoned with Cayenne pepper, mellowed with cream.
Orange: 1. demi-glace flavored with orange and lemon juice, garnished with julienne of orange peel.
— 2. red currant jelly mixed with orange peel rubbed on sugar, chopped blanched shallots, mustard, Port and Cayenne pepper, garnished with blanched orange julienne.
Oriental: orientale: creamed American sauce flavored with curry.
Orléans: fish velouté boiled up with white wine and mushroom stock, beaten with crayfish butter, seasoned with Cayenne pepper.
Oscar: highly flavored commercially bottled sauce.
à l'oseille: see sorrel.
Oyster: aux huîtres: I. Normandy sauce with oyster liquor, seasoned with lemon juice, garnished with poached bearded oysters.
II. Béchamel sauce with oyster liquor, garnished with poached, bearded oysters.
— **Brown:** aux huîtres à brun: demi-glace flavored with oyster liquor, garnished with poached bearded oysters.

P

Pain à l'anglaise: see bread sauce.
Palermo: I. palermitaine: crushed garlic mixed with egg yolks and lemon juice, beaten with oil like mayonnaise, seasoned with Cayenne pepper.
II. demi-glace boiled up with red wine, beaten with shallot butter, garnished with blanched orange julienne.
Paloise: see Pau.
Paprika: I. sliced onions fried in butter, heavily sprinkled with paprika, moistened with sour cream and veal glaze, boiled down, beaten with butter.
II. chopped onions sweated in butter, heavily sprinkled with paprika, moistened with white wine, reduced, mixed with veal velouté and cream.
Parisian: parisienne: demi-glace with a reduction of chopped shallots in white wine and meat glaze, seasoned with lemon juice.
Parsley: persil: fish or veal velouté garnished with chopped parsley.

Parsley, English: au persil à l'anglaise: English butter sauce with an infusion of parsley leaves, garnished with chopped, blanched parsley.
For fish take fish velouté and prepare the same way.

Pau: paloise: same as Béarnaise sauce but prepared with mint instead of tarragon.

Paul Bert: mixture of half white wine and half Béarnaise sauce with a little tomato purée.

Pauvre-homme: see poor man.

aux Peluches: see with leaves.

Pepper: poivrade ordinaire: mirepoix sweated in butter; crushed peppercorns, vinegar and white wine added, reduced, filled up with demi-glace, boiled down, strained, mellowed with butter.

— **for game:** poivrade pour gibier: same as above, but boiled up with game trimmings fried in butter and improved with game essence.

— **English:** poivrade à l'anglaise: pepper sauce blended with a little red currant jelly.

Périgord or Périgourdine: demi-glace with truffle essence, garnished with chopped truffles.

au Persil: see parsley.

Piccalilli: I. Dutch sauce mixed with chopped mustard pickles.
II. demi-glace flavored with anchovy essence, mixed with a reduction of chopped onions in wine vinegar, English mustard and chopped pickles.

aux Pignons: see with pine-kernels.

Piment: demi-glace garnished with julienne of sweet peppers.

with Pine-kernels: aux pignons: sour-sweet pepper sauce mixed with chopped pine-kernels.

Piquant: piquante: reduction of chopped shallots in half white wine and half vinegar, filled up with demi-glace, strained, seasoned with Cayenne pepper, garnished with chopped gherkins, parsley, tarragon and chervil.

aux Poireaux: see with leeks.

Poivrade: see pepper.

Polignac: white wine sauce improved with cream, garnished with thick julienne of mushrooms.

Polish: polonaise: I. veal velouté mixed with sour cream, grated horseradish and chopped fennel, seasoned with lemon juice.
II. demi-glace with a reduction of red wine, seasoned with sugar and vinegar, garnished with blanched slivered almonds and raisins.

aux Pommes: see apple sauce.

Pompadour: white wine sauce beaten with crayfish butter, garnished with truffle julienne, diced crayfish tails, chopped tarragon and chervil.

Pondicherry veal velouté colored with tomato purée, seasoned with curry powder.

Poor Man's: pauvre-homme: demi-glace with chopped shallots, parsley and chives and browned breadcrumbs.

Pork-butcher: charcutière: Robert sauce mixed with gherkin strips.

Port: au Porto: demi-glace flavored with Port at serving.

— **English:** au Porto à l'anglaise: reduction of chopped shallots and thyme in Port, chopped orange and lemon peel and juice added, boiled down, strained, filled up with thick veal gravy, seasoned with Cayenne pepper.

au Porto: see Portwine.

Portuguese: chopped onions sweated in butter, diced tomatoes, light tomato sauce, liquid meat glace and a little garlic added, boiled up, seasoned, finished off with chopped parsley.

Poulette: German sauce blended with mushroom essence, seasoned with lemon juice, finished off with chopped parsley.

Pretty Girl: jolie-fille: suprême sauce garnished with chopped hard-boiled egg yolks and parsley.

Prince: princière: white wine sauce beaten with crayfish butter, garnished with diced crayfish tails and truffle strips.

Princess: cream sauce with mushroom and chicken essence, improved with cream.

Provencal: provençale: diced tomatoes sautéd in hot oil, chopped parsley, garlic, salt, pepper and pinch of sugar added, cooked.

Q

Queen: à la reine: suprême sauce blended with whipped cream, garnished with strips of chicken breast.

R

Rabbit: lapin: rabbit liver sautéd in butter, rubbed through a sieve, reduction of chopped shallots in wine vinegar, thyme and chopped parsley added, filled up with demi-glace or thick veal gravy, flavored with Sherry.

Rachel: Béarnaise sauce blended with demi-glace, garnished with diced tomatoes.

Ravigote: I. reduction of half white wine and half tarragon vinegar, mixed with veal velouté, beaten with shallot butter, garnished with chopped chervil, tarragon and chives.
II. oil and vinegar mixed with chopped capers, onions, parsley, tarragon and chervil, seasoned with salt and pepper.

Raifort: see horseradish.

Raisin: aux raisins: white roux mixed with white stock and white wine, cooked, seasoned with sugar and salt, garnished with blanched slivered almonds and seedless raisins.

Red Wine: au vin rouge: I. reduction of chopped shallots in red wine, fish glaze added, beaten with butter, seasoned with Cayenne pepper and a few drops of anchovy essence.
II. chopped shallots and mirepoix sweated in butter, red wine added, boiled down, filled up with demi-glace, strained, beaten with butter.

Reform: réforme: pepper sauce, garnished with julienne of truffles, hard-boiled egg whites, mushrooms, ox tongue and gherkins.

Regency: régence: I. reduction of mirepoix and truffle peels in Rhine wine, demi-glace added, boiled up, strained.
II. Normandy sauce with a reduction of mushroom and truffle peels in Rhine wine, finished off with truffle essence.
III. suprême sauce with reduction of truffle and mushroom peels in Rhine wine.

Reine, à la: see Queen.
Remoulade: mayonnaise seasoned with mustard and anchovy essence, garnished with chopped capers, gherkins, tarragon and chervil.
Rich: riche: Normandy sauce with truffle essence, beaten with lobster butter, garnished with diced truffles.
Richelieu: I. tomato sauce blended with liquid meat glaze, garnished with diced tomatoes.
II. demi-glace with a reduction of white wine, fish fumet and truffle essence, flavored with Madeira.
Robert: chopped onions lightly fried in butter, moistened with white wine and vinegar, boiled down, demi-glace added, seasoned with pepper, finished off with mustard.
Roebuck: chevreuil: I. venison parings sweated in butter with mirepoix, moistened with red wine, boiled down, pepper sauce added, strained, seasoned with Cayenne pepper and pinch of sugar.
II. diced ham and onions sautéd in butter, vinegar added, reduced, boiled up with demi-glace, flavored with Portwine and red currant jelly.
aux Rognons: see kidney.
Roman: romaine: sugar burnt to caramel, dissolved in a little vinegar, demi-glace and game stock added, garnished with sultanas, black currants and pine-kernels.
Roosevelt: tomato sauce blended with a little apple purée, garnished with blanched julienne of lemon peel.
Rose Hip: églantine: purée of rose hips cooked in white wine slightly- sweetened, seasoned with lemon juice.
Rouenese: rouennaise: Bordeaux sauce with a reduction of chopped shallots in red wine, finished off with purée of raw duck livers, seasoned highly with Cayenne pepper and lemon juice.
Rougemont: mayonnaise sauce seasoned with mustard, garnished with chopped tarragon.
Rubens: reduction of mirepoix in white wine and fish fumet, strained, beaten with egg yolks and butter as in Dutch sauce, finished off with crayfish coulis and anchovy essence.
Ruby: rubis: I. ripe tomatoes rubbed through a sieve, the water strained off, the purée beaten with vinegar and oil as for mayonnaise, seasoned with salt and sugar.
II. thick veal gravy blended with liquid veal glaze, seasoned with Portwine and juice of blood oranges. (Specially for feather game.)
Russian: russe: velouté blended with sour cream, mixed with grated horseradish, seasoned with tarragon vinegar.

S

Sage: à la sauge: demi-glace with an infusion of sage in white wine and chopped sage.
Sailor: matelote: reduction of red wine and fish stock with mushroom peels, demi-glace added, strained, beaten with butter, seasoned with Cayenne pepper.
Salmis: mirepoix and game trimmings fried in butter, moistened with red or white wine, boiled down, demi-glace added, cooked for 40 minutes, strained, finished off with game essence and a little butter.

Saxon: saxonne: white butter sauce with a reduction of chopped shallots in white wine and fish stock, seasoned with mustard and lemon juice.

Scotch: écossaise: I. light Béchamel sauce mixed with hard-boiled egg yolks rubbed through a sieve and sliced hard-boiled egg whites.
II. cream sauce, garnished with brunoise of carrots, turnips, knob celery, onions and green beans simmered in butter and white stock.

Sevilla: sevillane: velouté blended with tomato purée and purée of sweet red peppers.

Sherry: Xérès: demi-glace flavored with Sherry.

Shrimp: aux crevettes: fish velouté beaten with shrimp butter, garnished with shrimps.

— **English:** aux crevettes à l'anglaise: butter sauce beaten with shrimp butter, seasoned with anchovy essence, garnished with shrimp tails.

Sicilian: sicilienne: demi-glace boiled down with game stock, flavored with Marsala, garnished with fried onion rings.

Smitane: see sour cream sauce.

Soja, Soy: commercial sauce made from fermented soy beans with salt and spices; marketed in bottles.

Solferino: liquid meat glaze beaten with herb and shallot butter, finished off with tomato essence, seasoned with Cayenne pepper and lemon juice.

Sorrel: à l'oseille: demi-glace garnished with shredded sorrel simmered in butter.

— **Austrian:** Sauerampfer-Sauce: white butter sauce garnished with shredded sorrel. (Austrian)

Soubise: see white onion sauce.

Souchet: white wine sauce, garnished with julienne of carrots, leeks and celery cooked in butter and fish stock.

Sour cream: smitane: chopped onions sweated in butter, moistened with white wine, boiled down, sour cream added, boiled, strained, seasoned with Kabul sauce.

— **Grape:** au verjus: demi-glace boiled down with the juice of sour (unripe) grapes, beaten with butter, flavored with Sherry.

Souwaroff: Béarnaise sauce blended with liquid meat glaze, garnished with truffle strips.

Spanish: espagnole (cold): mayonnaise seasoned with garlic, mustard and paprika, garnished with finely diced ham.

Spring: printanière: veal velouté beaten with herb butter, garnished with finely diced spring vegetables.

St. Cloud: tomato sauce with chopped tarragon.

St. Malo: white wine sauce with a reduction of chopped shallots in white wine, seasoned with mustard and anchovy paste.

St. Menehould: cream sauce mixed with a little liquid meat glaze, garnished with chopped mushrooms and parsley.

Steward's: maître d'hôtel: butter sauce seasoned with lemon juice, garnished with chopped parsley.

Stragotte: salmi sauce mixed with tomato purée, flavored with Madeira.

Suédoise: see Swedish.

Sultan: sultane: demi-glace boiled down with game stock, flavored with Portwine, garnished with sultanas.

Supreme: suprême: poultry velouté boiled down with chicken and mushroom essence and cream, strained, beaten with butter.

Swedish: suédoise (cold): apple purée cooked in white wine, mixed with thick mayonnaise and grated horseradish.

Sweet Sauces: see sweets.

Sweet-Sour: aigre-doux: I. German sauce mixed with red currant jelly, seasoned with lemon juice.
II. demi-glace with game essence, mixed with red currant jelly, seasoned with vinegar.

Sylvia: Dutch sauce with an infusion of tarragon leaves, garnished with chopped tarragon.

T

Tabasco: commercial pepper sauce, made of ripe tabasco peppers infused in vinegar, in small bottles with squirt top.

Taratar: blanched hazelnuts, almonds or pine-kernels pounded in the mortar with garlic, mixed with white bread soaked in milk, beaten with oil as for mayonnaise, seasoned with salt and vinegar or lemon juice. (Turkish)

Tarragon, Brown: estragon à brun: reduction of chopped shallots in white wine mixed with demi-glace, garnished with chopped tarragon.

— **White:** estragon à blanc: suprême or German sauce beaten with butter, garnished with chopped tarragon.

Tartar (cold): mayonnaise prepared with hard-boiled egg yolks, garnished with onions and chives chopped very fine.

Tenant: fermière: very small half-moon shaped slices of carrots, knob celery and turnips and shredded leeks simmered in butter, mixed with creamed veal velouté or white wine sauce according to use.

Terebiye: eggs mixed with cold water and flour, beaten with lemon juice and vegetable stock. Special sauce for dolmas, egg-plants and courgettes. (Turkish)

Tomato, Austrian: Paradeissauce: mirepoix and chopped onions lightly fried in butter, chopped tomatoes and white stock added, boiled, thickened with white roux, strained, seasoned with salt, sugar and vinegar. (Austrian)

— **Gravy:** jus tomaté: veal gravy flavored with tomato purée.

— **Italian:** salsa di pomodoro: chopped onions, diced salt pork and garlic sweated in oil, mixed with chopped tomatoes, seasoned with salt, pepper, parsley and sweet basil, boiled, strained. (Italian)

Toulouse: German sauce boiled down with mushroom and truffle stock.

Trianon (cold): mayonnaise mixed with tomato purée and white onion purée, garnished with chopped gherkins and red peppers.

Truffle: aux truffes: demi-glace boiled down with truffle essence, flavored with Madeira, garnished with diced or chopped truffles.

Turtle: tortue: demi-glace with a little tomato purée and an infusion of turtle herbs in white wine, finished off with truffle essence and Cayenne pepper, flavored with Madeira.

Tyrolian: tyrolienne: I. same as Béarnaise sauce, but prepared with olive oil instead of butter.
II. mayonnaise mixed with bright red tomato purée.

U

Unequalled: nonpareille: I. Dutch sauce beaten with crayfish butter, garnished with diced crayfish tails, mushrooms and truffles.
II. Dutch sauce blended with lobster butter, garnished with diced lobster.

Uzés: Dutch sauce beaten with anchovy paste, flavored with Madeira.

V

Valentine (cold): mayonnaise seasoned with mustard, mixed with grated horseradish and chopped tarragon.

Valeria: red wine sauce seasoned with mustard, mixed with grated horseradish and chopped chervil.

Valois: same as Foyot.

Veal Gravy, Thick: jus de veau lié: brown veal gravy thickened with arrowroot.

Venison: venaison: I. pepper sauce mixed with red currant jelly, blended with cream.
II. demi-glace boiled down with game essence, seasoned with Cayenne pepper, beaten with butter.
III. same as chief-ranger sauce.

Venetian: vénetienne: white wine sauce with a reduction of chopped shallots, tarragon and chervil in vinegar, strained, beaten with green herb butter, garnished with chopped tarragon and chervil.

Verdi (cold): mayonnaise colored with spinach green, mixed with sour cream, garnished with chopped pickles and chives.

au Verjus: see sour grape.

Vernet: cream sauce beaten with herb butter, garnished with chopped truffles, gherkins and hard-boiled egg whites.

Véron: 1 part Normandy sauce mixed with 3 parts Tyrolian sauce, finnished off with liquid veal glaze and anchovy essence.

Verte: see green.

Victoria: lobster sauce, garnished with diced lobster and truffles.

Village: villageoise: veal velouté blended with white onion purée, boiled down with veal stock and mushroom essence, bound with egg yolks and cream, beaten with butter.

Villeroi: German sauce boiled down with truffle and ham essence until thick enough to cover fish, meat or any other preparation à la Villeroi.
— **with Onion Purée:** Villeroy Soubisée: plain Villeroy sauce with onion purée and sometimes chopped truffles added.
— **with Tomato Purée:** Villeroy tomatée: plain Villeroy sauce with very thick and red tomato purée added.

Vincent (cold): green herb mayonnaise mixed with the same amount of tartar sauce.

au Vin Rouge: see red wine sauce.

Vinaigrette: mixture of vinegar and oil, seasoned with salt and pepper, garnished with chopped parsley, chervil, chives, tarragon, onions and capers.

Virgin: vierge: cream sauce blended with artichoke purée, finished off with whipped cream.

W

Warsawian: varsovienne: cream sauce mixed with horseradish, flavored with orange juice.

Watercress: au cresson: veal velouté beaten with watercress purée, garnished with capers.

Waterfish: Dutch sauce, garnished with strips of parsley roots, carrots and grated orange peel, simmered in stock of freshwater fish, finished off with the boiled-down stock.

White: blanche: milk, thickened with butter-paste, seasoned with salt, pepper and lemon juice.

— **Friars:** à la carmélite: Burgundy sauce garnished with julienne of lean ham and glazed button onions.

— **Wine:** vin blanc: I. fish velouté bound with egg yolks, beaten with butter.

II. fish fumet and white wine boiled down, bound with egg yolks, beaten with butter as for Dutch sauce.

III. Dutch sauce with a reduction of fish fumet and white wine.

IV. fish fumet and white wine boiled down to glaze, beaten with butter.

Wiener Zwiebelsauce: see onion sauce, Viennese.

Wine-merchant: marchand de vin: chopped shallots boiled down in red wine, filled up with demi-glace, boiled, strained, beaten with butter.

Wladimir: suprême sauce blended with liquid meat glaze.

Worcestershire: commercial sauce made of soy beans, vinegar, onion, lime, tamarind juice and spices, obtainable in bottles for table use.

Y

Yellow Boletus: aux cèpes: veal or fish velouté improved with cream, garnished with small thin slices of yellow boletus simmered in butter.

Yorkshire: demi-glace blended with red currant jelly, flavored with Portwine, garnished with blanched julienne of orange peel.

Z

Zingara: see gipsy.

Zouave: demi-glace mixed with tomato purée, seasoned with mustard and garlic, garnished with chopped tarragon.

Soups

Clear Soups		Thick Soups
Consommés	French	Potages, Potages liés
Klare Suppen, Fleischbrühen	German	Gebundene Suppen
Brodi	Italian	Zuppe
Sopas claras	Spanish	Sopas spessas

National, Regional, Miscellaneous, Cold, Fruit and Wine Soups

If no appetizers are served soups are usually taken at the beginning of a meal. Fine wholesome soups can be made in a great many varieties but only with good basic soup stocks; they require imagination, skill and patient labor. Indispensable in the making of good soups are white, brown, fish and game stock, milk, the careful selection of all ingredients, slow boiling, careful skimming and degreasing and proper straining. Double beef broth (Consommé) ought to be clear in the first instance and not clarified twice, each clarification meaning loss of strength.
Most purée soups may be transformed into cream or velvet soups if rice, potatoes, lentils or toast are replaced by cream sauce (Béchamel) or velvet sauce (velouté).
Nearly every soup can be readily indentified under one of the following designations.

CLASSIFICATION

1. Clear Soups — Consommés

Beef Broth, Simple: Consommé blanc, simple: plain clear soup made of beef, beef bones, vegetables, herbs and spices, boiled slowly for 5 hours, strained, not clarified.

Fish Broth, Simple: Consommé de poisson, simple: plain clear soup of fish bones, trimmings, leeks, celery, parsley, mushroom trimmings, herbs and peppercorns, not clarified.

Game Broth, Simple: Consommé de gibier, simple: bones and trimmings of game or venison, browned with mirepoix, cooked slowly with herbs and spices, strained, not clarified.

Beef Broth, Double: Consommé de boeuf, Consommé: plain beef broth strengthened and clarified with chopped beef and vegetables, strained, golden, clear, ready for garnish.

Chicken Broth, Double: Consommé de volaille: simple beef or chicken broth, strengthened and clarified with chopped beef and vegetables, browned, trimmings and chicken carcass, added, strained, golden, clear, ready for garnish.

Fish Broth, Double: Consommé de poisson: simple fish broth, strengthened and clarified with chopped white fish meat, leeks, herbs, seasoning and white wine added, strained, clear, ready for garnish.

Game Broth, Double: Consommé de gibier: simple game broth, strengthened and clarified with chopped venison, browned bones and trimmings of game, herbs, fungi, spices and a few crushed juniper berries added, strained, golden, clear, ready for garnish.

Consommé double: double beef, chicken, fish or game broth with additional strength and seasoning, strained, golden, clear, ready for garnish.

2. Thick Soups — Potages liés

a) Purée Soups — Potages purées

1. **Vegetable soups:** Purées de légumes: vegetables, cut in slices, sweated in butter, sliced potatoes, rice, lentils or toast added as thickening, cooked with plain beef, fish, chicken or game stock, seasoned, rubbed through a sieve, mellowed with butter.
2. **Poultry Soups:** Purées de volaille: poultry and rice, cooked in white beef, veal or chicken stock, meat pounded with the rice, mixed with the stock, rubbed through a sieve, reheated, seasoned, mellowed with butter.
3. **Game Soups:** Purées de gibier: roast game or venison, cooked with lentils in plain game stock, seasoned, meat boned, pounded with the lentils in a mortar, mixed with the stock, rubbed through a sieve, reheated, mellowed with butter.

b) Cream Soups — Potages crèmes

Foundation: white roux and milk (Béchamel), additioned with vegetable, meat, fish or game purée which characterize the soup, mixed with white stock, thickened with cream.

1. **Fish Cream Soup:** Crème de poisson: boned fish sweated in butter, simmered with light cream sauce (Béchamel), rubbed through a sieve, mixed with fish stock, bound with cream.
2. **Chicken Cream Soup:** Crème de volaille: chicken boiled in plain stock, boned, meat pounded, simmered with cream sauce, seasoned, mixed with the stock, rubbed through a sieve, thickened with cream.
3. **Vegetable Cream Soup:** Crème de légumes: purée of vegetables, simmered in cream sauce, mixed with white stock, rubbed through a sieve, thickened with cream.

c) Velvet Soups — Potages veloutés

Foundation: white roux, diluted with veal, chicken broth or fish stock; fish, meat, chicken or game purée added to characterize the soup, which is then cooked, seasoned, strained, and thickened with egg yolks and cream.

1. **Velvet Fish Soup:** Velouté de poisson: boned fish sweated in butter, cooked with fish veloutè, seasoned, rubbed through a sieve, mixed with fish stock, bound with egg yolks and cream.
2. **Velvet Chicken Soup:** Velouté de volaille: chicken purée, blended with velouté of chicken, seasoned, rubbed through a sieve, mixed with simple chicken broth, bound with egg yolks and cream.
3. **Velvet Vegetable Soup:** Velouté de légumes: purée of vegetables, simmered in velouté sauce, seasoned, rubbed through a sieve, mixed with white stock, bound with egg yolks and cream.

Abbreviations: C. = Consommé; Cr. = Crème; Pr. = Purée; P. = Potage; V. = Velouté.

Clear Soups

A

Adèle: Chicken consommé with peas, pearls of carrots and chicken quenelles.

Adelina Patti: Chicken consommé with peas, pearls of carrots and cubes of royal (egg custard) with chestnut purée.

Admirals Style: à l'amiral: Fish consommé with fish quenelles, diced lobster, mushrooms and rice.

African: à l'africaine: Beef consommé with rice, diced artichoke bottoms, and tiny puffs of cream puff paste seasoned with curry powder.

Albion I: Fish consommé slightly thickened with tapioca, garnished with lobster quenelles and strips of truffles.

Albion II: Chicken consommé garnished with shredded truffles, asparagus tips, chicken and goose liver quenelles and cocks' combs.

Alexandra: Chicken consommé slightly thickened with tapioca, garnished with shredded lettuce, chicken quenelles and strips of white chicken meat.

Alsatian: à l'alsacienne: Chicken consommé garnished with sauerkraut stewed in beef broth and small raviolis stuffed with goose liver forcemeat.

Ambassadors: à l'ambassadeur: Strong chicken consommé, garnished with purée of truffles royal cut in small round slices, diced mushrooms and white chicken meat.

Ambassadress Style: à l'ambassadrice: Chicken consommé with dices of white chicken meat, mushrooms and royal in three colours: truffles, tomatoes and peas.

American Chicken Soup: C. de volaille à l'américaine: Clear chicken broth with rice, crushed peeled tomatoes and cubes of chicken meat.

Andalusian: à l'andalouse: Chicken consommé garnished with cubes of tomato royal, rice, strips of ham and pancake mixture poured into the broth through a colander.

— **Ham Broth:** C. de jambon à l'andalouse: Beef broth strongly flavored with ham, garnished with rice and cubes of royal with tomato purée.

— **Noodle Soup:** C. aux nouilles à l'andalouse: Beef consommé flavored with tomato, garnished with vermicelli and cubes of cooked ham.

with Angels' Hair: aux cheveux d'anges: Beef consommé with especially fine vermicelli cooked in the broth.

Anglers Soup: Soupe des pêcheurs: Strong fish consommé garnished with mussels, peas and diced tomatoes.

Anjou: Game consommé garnished with asparagus tips, rice and game quenelles.

Aremberg Beef Broth: d'Aremberg: Beef consommé with peas, pearls of carrots, turnips and truffles, chervil.

— **Chicken Broth:** de volaille à l'Aremberg: Chicken consommé garnished with pearls of carrots, turnips and truffles, chicken quenelles, asparagus royal in round slices.

Artagnan: Beef consommé strongly flavoured with essence of heathcock, garnished with strips of heathcock meat and peas.

Aulagnier: Beef consommé garnished with peas and strips of cabbage.

Aurora: à l'aurore: Beef consommé flavored with tomato juice, slightly thickened with tapioca, garnished with strips of white chicken meat.

B

Balmoral: Clear mockturtle soup garnished with diced calf's foot and veal quenelles.

Baron Brisse: Beef consommé garnished with rice and cubes of royal in three colours: cream, spinach and truffle.

with Baked Peas: aux pois frits: Beef consommé garnished with unsweetened pancake mixture strained through a colander in hot deep fat and fried.

Béhague: Chicken consommé with poached egg and chervil.

Benevent: Beef consommé flavored with tomato, garnished with strips of ox tongue, ox palate and cooked macaroni.

Berchoux: Game consommé, garnished with cubes of quail and chestnut royal, diced mushrooms and truffles.

Berny: Beef consommé slightly thickened with tapioca, garnished with dauphine potatoes, mixed with chopped almonds and truffles made into tiny balls and fried.

Birds' Nests Soup: Rich beef consommé flavored with turtle herbs and Madeira wine, garnished with the cleaned boiled and shredded edible nests of the East Indian Salangane swallow.

Bismarck: Strong beef consommé slightly thickened with arrow root, flavored with Port, garnished with diced mushrooms and Cheddar cheese.

Boïeldieu: Chicken consommé garnished with small foie gras quenelles, chicken quenelles and truffle quenelles.

Bonaparte: Chicken consommé garnished with chicken quenelles.

Bourbon: Chicken consommé slightly thickened with tapioca, garnished with fancy chicken quenelles with goose liver, decorated with three truffle lilies, and chervil.

Bourdalou: Chicken consommé garnished with four different kinds of royal: tomato, green asparagus, chicken and carrots.

Braganza: Beef consommé garnished with Nizam pearls (a kind of sago), very small pearls of cucumber and royal in four colours.

Brasilian: à la brésilienne: Beef consommé garnished with vegetable julienne, strips of pimiento and rice.

with Bread Crusts: aux croûtes à l'ancienne: Beef consommé with small rounds of fried bread, slightly hollowed out, filled with thick vegetable purée, sprinkled with grated cheese, browned in oven and served separately.

Breton: à la bretonne: Beef consommé garnished with strips of leek, knob celery, mushrooms and shredded chervil.

Briand: Chicken consommé garnished with dices of chicken, ham and veal and shredded chervil.

Brides C.: C. Petite-mariée: Chicken consommé garnished with purée of chicken royal with almond milk and chervil shreds.

Brieux: Chicken consommé slightly thickened with sago, garnished with truffle pearls and green and black royal, pistachio and truffle, cut in round slices.

Brighton: Beef consommé flavored with Sherry, garnished with veal quenelles, strips of cooked calf's head and julienne of vegetables.

Brillat-Savarin: Chicken consommé flavored with celery, slightly thickened with arrow-root, garnished with strips of truffles, mushrooms and carrots.

Britannia: Chicken consommé garnished with foie gras quenelles, asparagus tips, strips of truffles and tomato royal cut in triangular shapes.

British: Fish consommé garnished with neatly cut strips of truffles and cubes of lobster royal.

Brunoise: Rich beef consommé garnished with braised finely diced carrots, leeks turnips, celery, onions and French beans peas and chervil.

— **Royal:** Same as above but with cubes of cream royal.

Butchers: à la bouchère: Strong beef consommé garnished with small braised balls of cabbage and blanched beef marrow.

C

Camerani: Beef consommé garnished with braised diced carrots, celery and leeks as well as cooked broken spaghetti; grated parmesan cheese is served extra.

Camino: Unsweetened pancake dough mixed with grated Parmesan cheese strained through a colander into boiling beef consommé.

Cancalais: Rich fish consommé slightly thickened with tapioca, garnished with poached oysters, strips of fillets of soles and whiting quenelles.

Capuchins: à la capucine: Chicken consommé garnished with shredded lettuce and spinach; profiterolles filled with chicken purée served separately.

Cardinal: Fish consommé flavored with lobster, garnished with lobster quenelles.

Carême: Rich chicken and veal consommé garnished with round slices of carrots and turnips, shredded lettuce and asparagus tips.

Carlton: Rich beef consommé garnished with cubes of cream royal, quenelles and tiny crisp puffs of unsweetened cream puff paste mixed with grated cheese.

Carmelite: Fish consommé slightly thickened with arrowroot, garnished with cubes of fish forcemeat and rice.

Carmen: Beef consommé flavored with tomato juice and red peppers, garnished with rice, strips of green peppers and shredded chervil.

Carolina: à la caroline: Chicken consommé garnished with rice, cubes of almond milk royal and shredded chervil.

Castellane: Game consommé flavored with essence of woodcock, garnished with strips of woodcock and creamed woodcock and lentil royal.

Catalonian: à la catalane: Beef consommé garnished with rice, diced poached tomatoes and strips of green peppers.

Caux Style: à la cauchoise: Beef consommé garnished with slices of braised vegetables and diced cooked bacon and lamb.

Cavour: Chicken consommé garnished with green peas, cooked broken macaroni and baked "peas" (unsweetened pancake mixture strained through a coarse colander into hot fat and fried).

with Celery Essence: Beef consommé flavored with celery.

Celestine: Beef or chicken consommé garnished with strips of thin unsweetened pancakes mixed with chopped chervil.

Chancelors: à la chancelière: Beef consommé garnished with round slices of pea royal, strips of white chicken meat, truffles and mushrooms.

Charivari: Beef consommé garnished with strips of braised carrots, turnips, knob celery, onions and cabbage.

Charley: Beef consommé thickened with tapioca, garnished with asparagus tips, poached eggs and shredded chervil.

Charolaise: Clear oxtail soup garnished with small braised onions, pearls of carrots, small pieces of oxtail and very small stuffed cabbage leaves shaped into balls.

Charterhouse: à la chartreuse: Beef consommé slightly thickened with tapioca, garnished with poached diced tomatoes and tiny raviolis, stuffed with spinach purée, goose liver and with mushrooms mixed with chicken forcemeat.

Châtelaine: Chicken consommé thickened with tapioca, garnished with royal of onion and artichoke purée cut in cubes, and chicken quenelles stuffed with chestnut purée.

with Cheese Croûtons: aux diablotins: Chicken consommé with devilled cheese croûtons sprinkled with Cayenne pepper.

Cherburg: Cherbourg: Beef consommé flavored with Madeira wine, garnished with strips of truffles and mushrooms, ham quenelles and poached eggs.

Chevreuse: Chicken consommé garnished with slices of chicken royal and semolina royal and short strips of white chicken meat and truffles.

with Chicken Puffs: aux profiterolles: Beef consommé served with very small crisp puffs of cream puff paste filled with chicken purée.

with Chickens Wings: aux ailerons: Chicken consommé garnished with stuffed chicken wings simmered in chicken broth.

Choiseul: Beef consommé garnished with fancy-cut cream royal and asparagus tips.

Christopher Columbus: Christoph Colomb: Chicken consommé flavored with tomatoes, slightly thickened with tapioca, garnished with cubes of tomato royal and chicken quenelles.

Cincinnati: Chicken consommé garnished with pearls of carrots, turnips, potatoes and profiterolles stuffed with chicken purée.

Claremont: Beef consommé garnished with fried onion rings and round slices of cream royal.

Cleopatra: Cléopâtre: Chicken consommé garnished with diced tomatoes.

Clothilde: Beef consommé garnished with button onions cooked in broth.

Colbert: Beef consommé garnished with pearls of spring root vegetables and poached eggs.

Colombine: Chicken consommé garnished with pearls of carrots and turnips, strips of pigeon meat and poached pigeons eggs.

Countess: Comtesse: Chicken consommé thickened with tapioca, garnished with asparagus royal, chicken quenelles decorated with truffles to imitate a countess' crown and shredded lettuce.

Croûte-au-Pot: Rich beef consommé garnished with neatly cut vegetables cooked in the soup and diced beef; shortly before serving, crusts of toasted French bread placed on top; usually served in earthenware or fire proof china pot.

Cussy: Game consommé garnished with partridge quenelles, cubes of chestnut and partridge royal and strips of truffles, flavored with Sherry and Cognac shortly before serving.

Cyrano: Duck consommé; quenelles of duck forcemeat half a teaspoonful size, cooked, covered with suprême sauce, sprinkled with cheese and gratinated in the oven, are served extra.

Czarevitch: Tsarevitch: Game consommé flavored with Sherry, garnished with hazel-hen quenelles and strips of truffles.

Czarina: Tsarine: Beef consommé flavored with fennel, garnished with diced cooked vesiga.

Czech: à la tchèque: Chicken consommé garnished with diced chicken meat, tomatoes, peas and thin strips of unsweetened pancakes.

D

Danish: à la danoise: Wild duck consommé flavored with Marsala wine, garnished with game quenelles and diced mushrooms

Dante: Chicken consommé flavored with pigeon essence, garnished with strips of truffles and ox tongue and quenelles coloured with saffron.

d'Assas: Chicken consommé garnished with very small balls of stuffed lettuce and carrot royal cut in cubes.

Daudet: Chicken consommé garnished with cubes of chicken and ham royal, lobster quenelles and strips of knob celery.

Daumont: Beef consommé thickened with tapioca, garnished with rice, strips of beef palate and mushrooms.

Delavergne: Chicken consommé garnished with cubes of royal, asparagus tips and very small soft boiled eggs.

Delriche: Chicken consommé garnished with vermicelli, blanched slices of beef marrow and croûtons.

Demidow: Chicken consommé garnished with pearls of carrots, turnips and truffles, chicken quenelles with chopped fine herbs and shredded chervil.

Deslignac: Beef consommé garnished with round slices of royal, small stuffed lettuce balls and shredded chervil.

Diana: à la Diane: Partridge consommé garnished with game quenelles, truffle slices cut in half moon shapes, flavored with Sherry.

Dijon Style: à la dijonaise: Chicken consommé thickened with tapioca, garnished with game quenelles and strips of ox tongue.

Diplomate: Chicken consommé garnished with cooked chicken forcemeat cut in round slices and truffle rings.

Diva: Chicken consommé garnished with large chicken quenelles decorated with truffles and cubes of lobster royal.

Divette: Chicken consommé garnished with round slices of crayfish royal, fish quenelles and truffle pearls.

Dolores: Chicken consommé garnished with strips of white chicken meat and saffron rice.

Dom Miguel: Game consommé garnished with game quenelles and cubes of cream royal.

Don Carlos: Beef consommé garnished with cubes of royal, diced poached tomatoes, rice and shredded chervil.

Doria: Chicken consommé garnished with oval shaped pieces of cucumber, chicken quenelles, fried pearls of cheese cream puff paste and shredded chervil.

Douglas: Chicken consommé garnished with diced artichoke bottoms, asparagus tips and cubes of braised sweetbread.

Dounou: Chicken consommé flavored with turtle herbs, thickened with tapioca, garnished with chicken quenelles, diced artichoke bottoms and truffles; tiny puff paste patties filled with chicken purée served extra.

Dubarry: Beef consommé slightly thickened with tapioca, garnished with cubes of cauliflower royal and cauliflower buds.

Dubourg: Chicken consommé garnished with rice, cubes of chicken royal and shredded chervil.

Duchess: à la duchesse: Chicken consommé garnished with shredded lettuce, sago and cubes of plain royal.

Dufferin: Fish consommé, slightly curried, garnished with curried fish quenelles, rice and strips of sole fillets.

Dumesnil: Beef consommé garnished with vegetable julienne, sliced blanched beef marrow and shredded chervil.

Dumont: Beef consommé garnished with strips of cabbage, ox tongue and mushrooms.

Dupré: Chicken consommé garnished with pearls of carrots and turnips, quenelles and croûtons.

Duse: Chicken consommé garnished with pearl shaped chicken quenelles flavored with tomato, poached tortelinni and fancy shaped noodles.

E

Easter: à la pascale: Chicken consommé garnished with peas, cubes of carrots and turnips royal, sprinkled with chopped fennel green.

Edward VII.: Edouard VII.: Chicken consommé slightly flavored with curry, garnished with rice, tiny puff paste patties filled with chicken purée served extra.

Egyptian: à l'égyptienne: Mutton broth flavored with saffron, garnished with rice, diced aubergines and okra.

Elisabeth: Beef consommé garnished with strips of leeks, vermicelli and diced artichoke bottoms; grated cheese served separately.

Emanuel: Chicken consommé with grated Parmesan cheese, garnished with pieces of spaghetti, strips of chicken meat and cubes of tomato royal.

Epicurean: des épicuriens: Chicken consommé garnished with shredded, blanched almonds and shredded chervil.

F

Farmer Style: à la fermière: Beef consommé garnished with strips of root vegetables and diced potatoes.

Farmer's Wife Style: à la belle fermière: Rich beef consommé garnished with strips of cabbage, diced green beans and small squares of cooked noodles.

Favorite: Chicken consommé slightly thickened with tapioca, garnished with small potato balls, strips of artichoke bottoms and mushrooms and chervil.

Federal: Chicken consommé seasoned with Cayenne pepper, garnished with sliced truffles and cubes of plain royal.

Flemish: à la flamande: Beef consommé garnished with sprouts royal, peas and shredded chervil.

Fleury: Chicken consommé garnished with small, flat round chicken quenelles and peas.

Floreal: à la floréale: Chicken consommé garnished with carrots and turnips cut in shape of marguerites, peas, asparagus tips and quenelles with pistachios cut into imitation leaves and chervil.

Florence Style: à la florentine: Chicken consommé with three sorts of quenelles: with chopped ox tongue, red, with chopped chicken meat, white, and purée of spinach, green.

Flower Girl Style: à la bouquetière: Beef consommé garnished with peas, diced French beans, asparagus tips and balls or small cubes of carrots and turnips.

Francatelli: Chicken consommé garnished with chicken royal, goose liver quenelles, cockscombs and kidneys.

Francforter: à la francfortoise: Beef consommé flavored with juniper berries, strips of red cabbage boiled in beef broth, slices of Frankfurter sausage; grated cheese served separately.

Francillon: Ring of chicken forcemeat piped on soup plates, a very small raw egg placed in the center, slightly poached in the oven, hot chicken consommé poured over.

Franklin: Beef consommé garnished with balls of carrots and turnips, profiterolles and cubes of royal with vegetable purée.

French: à la française: Chicken consommé garnished with shredded lettuce, chicken quenelles and chervil.

Frou-frou: Chicken consommé garnished with pearls of carrots, tiny crisp profiterolles and shredded chervil.

G

Gabrielle: Chicken consommé with egg yolks garnished with cubes of chicken royal and diced crayfish tails.

Garibaldi: Beef consommé with diced poached tomatoes and strips of spaghetti.

Gaul Style: à la galloise or gauloise: Chicken consommé garnished with cockscombs and kidneys and ham royal in cubes.

George Sand: Fish consommé garnished with fish quenelles with crayfish butter, cooked diced morels and carps soft roes on small fried croûtons served separately.

Germaine: Chicken consommé garnished with chicken quenelles, cubes of pea royal and chervil.

German: à l'allemande: Beef consommé garnished with strips of boiled red cabbage and slices of Frankfurter.

Germinal: Beef consommé flavored with tarragon, garnished with peas, diced French beans, asparagus tips and quenelles containing chopped tarragon and chervil.

with Giblets: aux abatis: Chicken consommé with giblets cut in small pieces and diced braised root vegetables.

Gipsies: à la zingara: Chicken consommé garnished with three different sorts of royal.

Girondine: Beef consommé garnished with cubes of ham royal and strips of carrots.

Gouffé: Chicken consommé thickened with tapioca, garnished with strips of chicken meat, ox tongue, truffles and hard boiled egg yolks strained through a sieve.

Gourmet: du gourmet: Chicken consommé garnished with diced game meat, goose liver and ox tongue, small round slices of poached chicken forcemeat and shredded pistachios.

Grand Duchess: à la grande duchesse: Chicken consommé garnished with strips of chicken meat, ox tongue, asparagus tips and chicken quenelles.

Green Meadow: Vert-pré: Beef consommé thickened with tapioca, garnished with asparagus tips, diced French beans, sorrel and shredded lettuce.

with Green Vegetables: à la vermandoise: Beef consommé thickened with tapioca, garnished with peas, asparagus tips, diced French beans, shredded lettuce and sorrel.

Grenade: Beef consommé garnished with ham royal cut grenade shape, diced poached tomatoes and chervil.

Grimaldi: Beef consommé flavored with tomatoes, garnished with tomato royal and strips of knob celery.

Gutenberg: Beef consommé garnished with asparagus tips, peas, diced mushrooms and braised root vegetables and slices of Frankfurt sausage.

H

Harlequin: à l'arlequin: Beef consommé garnished with vermicelli and quenelles in three colors: yellow, green and red.

House-wifes Style: à la bonne femme: Beef consommé garnished with diced potatoes cooked in broth, strips of leek and carrots and croûtons.

Hunters Style: Chasseur: Game consommé flavored with Port, garnished with strips of mushrooms and chervil; small puffs of cream puff paste stuffed with purée of partridge served separately.

I

Imperial: à l'impériale: Chicken consommé slightly thickened with tapioca, garnished with small round slices of poached chicken forcemeat, slices of cockscombs and kidneys, small bright green peas and chervil.

Indian: à l'indienne: Chicken consommé flavored with curry powder, garnished with cubes of coconut royal and rice.

Irish Duck C.: à l'irlandaise: Duck consommé garnished with duck quenelles, braised diced root vegetables and strips of cabbage cooked in broth.

Irma: Beef consommé garnished with curried quenelles and strips of mushrooms.

Isoline: Chicken consommé garnished with chicken quenelles stuffed with asparagus purée, strips of mushrooms, chicken meat and truffles.

Italian: à l'italienne: Beef consommé garnished with: cubes of spinach and tomato royal, and macaroni cooked in broth and cut in very small pieces; grated Parmesan cheese served separately.

with Italian Paste: aux pâtes d'Italie: Beef consommé garnished with small noodles of different shapes.

J

Jacobine: Beef consommé garnished with diced carrots, green beans, trunips, truffles and peas.

Jacqueline: Chicken consommé garnished with braised, fancy cut carrots, pastilles of cream royal, peas, asparagus tips, rice and chervil.

Jellied Madrilene: Madrilène en gelée: Madrid consommé with additional strength, lightly jellied when cold.

Jellied with Wine: en gelée au vin: Rich chicken consommé flavored with Madeira, Sherry, Marsala, Malvasier etc. served slightly jellied.

Jenny Lind: Game consommé flavored with quails, garnished with quail breasts and diced mushrooms.

Jockey Club: Chicken consommé garnished with rounds of carrots and pea and chicken royal.

Johore: Chicken consommé flavored with curry, garnished with strips of chicken meat, rice and curried royal.

Juanita: Chicken consommé garnished with cubes of cream of rice royal, diced poached tomatoes and sieved hard egg yolks.

Judic: Rich chicken consommé garnished with truffle rings, rosette shaped chicken quenelles and very small braised lettuces, usually served separately.

Julia: Chicken consommé thickened with tapioca, garnished with cubes of royal and small crisp profiterolles.

Julienne: Beef consommé garnished with root vegetables cut in small strips and braised, peas and chervil.

Juliette: Chicken consommé garnished with small round chicken quenelles, cubes of spinach royal and strips of hard-boiled egg whites.

K

Kings: des rois: Chicken consommé with quail flavor, garnished with quail quenelles, quail breasts, asparagus tips and truffle pearls.

Kléber: Beef consommé garnished with peas, diced knob celery, goose liver quenelles and chervil.

L

Ladies Delight: Délice de dames: Rich chicken consommé flavored with celery, garnished with thin strips of celery, hard-boiled egg whites and diced tomatoes, served slightly jellied.

Lady Morgan: Fish consommé flavored with oysters, garnished with crayfish quenelles, strips of truffles, mushrooms, fillets of sole and bearded oysters.

Labourdane: Duck consommé garnished with cauliflower buds, cubes of pea royal, royal with duck purée and shredded chervil.

Laffite: Chicken consommé flavored with Madeira wine, garnished with strips of cockscombs and kidneys, mushrooms and truffles, cucumber pearls and small pitted olives.

Lagrandière: Chicken consommé garnished with strips of chicken meat and crisp profiterolles filled with purée of artichoke bottoms.

Laguipierre: Game consommé garnished with game royal and poached pigeons eggs.

with Leeks: aux poireaux: Beef consommé flavored with leeks, strips of leek and chervil.

Leo XIII: Beef and veal consommé garnished with royal cut in papal tiara and cross shapes.

Lesseps: Beef consommé garnished with cubes of calf's brain royal and chervil.

with Lettuce: aux laitues: Beef consommé garnished with shredded lettuce.

Lille Style: à la lilloise: Rich beef consommé flavored with tarragon and chervil, garnished with strips of truffles, mushrooms and roasted almonds.

Little Duke: Petit-duc: Beef consommé thickened with tapioca, garnished with strips of chicken meat, truffles and chervil.

Londonderry: Beef consommé thickened with tapioca, garnished with quenelles and cubes of calf's head, flavored with Madeira wine.

London Style: à la londonienne: Rich beef consommé flavored with turtle herbs garnished with cubes of calf's head and rice.

Longchamps: Beef consommé garnished with fine noodles, strips of sorrel and shredded chervil.

Lord Chesterfield: Rich beef consommé flavored with turtle herbs, Cayenne pepper and Sherry wine, garnished with chicken, crayfish and truffle quenelles.

Lorette: Chicken consommé spiced with paprika, garnished with asparagus tips, strips of truffles, chervil; tiny balls of Lorette potatoes served separately.

with Love Apples, Jellied: en gelée aux pommes d'amour: Rich chicken consommé flavored with tomato juice and Marsala wine, served jellied.

Lucullus: Beef consommé garnished with cauliflower buds, pearls of carrots and turnips, and three different sorts of quenelles, red, white and yellow.

M

with Macaroni: au macaroni: Beef consommé garnished with macaroni cut in small pieces, grated parmesan cheese served separately.

Macdonald: Rich beef consommé garnished with raviolis stuffed with spinach, brain royal and diced cucumbers.

with Macédoine: Beef consommé garnished with diced, braised vegetables.

Maecenas: à la mécène: Chicken consommé garnished with diced knob celery, game quenelles and chicken royal.

Madrid Style: à la madrilène: Rich chicken consommé flavored with tomato and red peppers, garnished with diced poached tomatoes, served cold.

Magdalena: à la madeleine: Chicken consommé garnished with cubes of celery, shredded lettuce, almond shaped chicken quenelles; crisp profiterolles served separately.

Magenta: Chicken consommé thickened with arrowroot, garnished with truffle quenelles, strips of mushrooms, truffles and diced tomatoes.

Mancelle: Game consommé garnished with very small poached chestnuts and cubes of game royal.

Maria: Chicken consommé slightly thickened with tapioca, garnished with cubes of purée of haricot beans royal, pearls of carrots and turnips, peas and lozenges of French beans.

Marie Louise: Chicken consommé garnished with cubes of plain royal and peas.

Margot: Chicken consommé garnished with two sorts of quenelles: chicken and chicken mixed with spinach purée.

Marigny: Chicken consommé garnished with chicken quenelles, peas, strips of cucumber and chervil.

Marly: Chicken consommé garnished with strips of leek, celery, chicken, shredded lettuce, chervil and cheese croûtons.

Marquise: Beef consommé highly flavored with celery, garnished with slices of blanched calf's marrow and chicken quenelles mixed with finely chopped hazelnuts.

with Marrow: à la moelle: Rich beef consommé garnished with slices of blanched beef marrow; fried croûtons served separately.

Martinière: Chicken consommé garnished with slices of stuffed, braised cabbage, peas, chervil and square shaped diablotins.

Mary Stuart: Marie Stuart: Beef consommé garnished with chicken quenelles decorated with truffles, thickened with tapioca.

Meat Pot, Small: Petite Marmite: Rich beef consommé garnished with nicely cut pot vegetables and small pieces of boiled beef, usually served in individual earthen soup pots; fried slices of French bread with blanched beef marrow served separately.

— — **Kisseleff:** Petite Marmite Kisseleff: Beef broth, not clarified, garnished with diced calf's foot, chicken, turnips, carrots and knob celery, shredded lettuce, cabbage and leeks.

Médicis: Beef consommé slightly thickened with tapioca, garnished with purée of peas and purée of carrots royal and shredded sorrel.

Meissonier: Beef consommé garnished with diced artichoke bottoms and tomatoes, peas and chervil.

Mercédès: Beef consommé flavored with Sherry wine, garnished with rings of pimentoes and stars of cockscombs.

Messaline: Chicken consommé flavored with tomato, garnished with cocks' kidneys, strips of pimentoes and rice.

Metternich: Pheasant consommé garnished with strips of pheasant meat and cubes of artichoke-bottom royal.

Mignon: Fish consommé garnished with fish quenelles, truffle pearls and shrimps.

Mikado: Chicken consommé strongly flavored with tomatoes, garnished with diced white chicken meat and tomatoes.

Milanese: à la milanaise: Chicken consommé garnished with small pieces of macaroni mixed with Béchamel, dipped in bread crumbs and fried; grated Parmesan cheese served separately.

Mimosa: Chicken consommé garnished with royal in different colors: with purée of carrots, peas, cream and purée of hard-boiled egg yolks.

Mireille: Chicken consommé garnished with slices of poached chicken forcemeat with purée of tomatoes and saffron rice.

Mirette: Beef consommé garnished with chicken quenelles, shredded lettuce and chervil; cheese straws served separately.

Mock-turtle, Clear: Fausse tortue claire: Rich beef consommé flavored with turtle herbs, celery, mushrooms, Madeira wine and Cayenne pepper, garnished with diced calf's head and quenelles.

— — **Sovereigns Style:** Rich beef consommé flavored with turtle herbs, celery, mushrooms, Cayenne pepper and Madeira wine, garnished with chicken quenelles, asparagus tips and diced calf's head.

Mogador: Chicken consommé thickened with tapioca, garnished with goose liver royal and white chicken meat, ox tongue and truffles cut in shape of lozenges.

Moldavian: à la moldave: Fish consommé with pickled cucumber brine flavored with Madeira wine, garnished with strips of mushrooms, diced sturgeons' meat and vesiga, and peeled, sliced lemon.

Molière: Rich beef consommé garnished with small dumplings made of fried bread crumbs, chopped shallots, parsley and eggs; blanched marrow on toast served separately.

Monaco: Chicken consommé garnished with pea-shaped truffles, carrots and turnips and very crisp profiterolles.

Mona Lisa: Rich beef consommé garnished with chicken quenelles and peas.

Monselet: Beef consommé garnished with strips of ox tongue, slices of poached beef marrow, peas, chervil and fried croûtons.

Monte-Carlo: Chicken consommé garnished with pea-shaped chicken quenelles, shredded lettuce and chervil; hazelnut sized, very crisp profiterolles served separately.

Montesquieu: Beef consommé garnished with strips of chicken meat, ham and mushrooms and cauliflower buds.

Montmorency: Chicken consommé thickened with tapioca, garnished with asparagus tips, chicken quenelles, rice and chervil.

Montmort: Chicken consommé garnished with half-moon shaped slices of carrots and turnips, poached chicken forcemeat mixed with chopped truffles and ox tongue, cut in small round pieces; cubes of cream and of purée of pea royal, asparagus tips and chervil added.

with Mussels: Strong fish consommé flavored with mussel juice, garnished with small poached and bearded mussels and fried croûtons.

Murillo: Chicken consommé garnished with very thin noodles, diced tomatoes and chervil.

Murillo: Fish consommé flavored with tomato, garnished with fish quenelles.

N

Nansen: Rich beef consommé slightly flavored with vodka; very small caviar canapes served separately.

Nantaise: Chicken consommé garnished with peas, pearl barley and strips of chicken meat.

Naples Style: à la napolitaine: Beef consommé flavored with tomato juice, garnished with strips of ham and knob celery, macaroni cut in small pieces and chervil; grated Parmesan cheese served separately.

Napoleon: Chicken consommé garnished with triangular shaped raviolis stuffed with purée of goose liver.

Navarin: Beef consommé garnished with cubes of pea royal, small crayfish tails and chopped, blanched parsley.

Nelson: Fish consommé slightly thickened with arrowroot, garnished with rice; small profiterolles stuffed with hashed lobster American styles served separately.

Nemours: Chicken consommé thickened with tapioca, garnished with carrots royal, mixed with finely diced vegetables, Japan pearls and strips of truffles.

Nesselrode: Game consommé with hazel-hen flavor, garnished with chestnut royal, strips of hazel-hen and diced mushrooms.

New York Style: à la new yorkaise: Beef consommé garnished with game quenelles, cubes of onion royal and tomato royal and chervil.

Nice Style: à la niçoise: Chicken consommé garnished with cubes of tomato and green bean royal, diced potatoes and shredded chervil.

Nilson: Chicken consommé thickened with tapioca, garnished with three sorts of quenelles: chicken and chopped ham, chicken and chopped truffles, chicken and chopped chives, peas and chervil.

Ninon: Chicken consommé garnished with pearls of carrots, turnips and truffles; tiny tartlets of chicken forcemeat stuffed with hashed chicken, decorated with truffle star served separately.

Nivernaise: Beef consommé garnished with pearls of carrots and turnips, cubes of onion royal and chervil.

Noailles: Chicken consommé garnished with strips of ox tongue and chicken, cubes of artichoke bottom royal and chervil.

O

Old Fashioned Soup: à l'ancienne: Beef consommé, garnished with dry slices of French bread coated with the vegetables used for the soup, mashed and sprinkled with grated cheese, gratinated in the tureen in which the soup is served.

— — **French Soup:** Croûte-au-pot à l'ancienne: Beef consommé garnished with cubes of chicken and beef cooked with the broth, diced pot vegetables, served with slices of fried French bread with poached beef marrow.

Olga: Beef consommé flavored with Port garnished with strips of truffles, leek, carrots and knob celery.

Oriental: à l'orientale: Mutton consommé flavored with tomato juice and saffron, garnished with rice, brain royal cut in shape of half moons and hard-boiled egg yolks strained through a sieve.

Orleans: à l'orléanaise: Beef consommé garnished with chicory royal, diced French beans, flageolets and chervil.

Orléans: à la d'Orléans: Chicken consommé thickened with tapioca, garnished with cubes of cream, tomato and spinach royal and chervil.

Orsay: à la d'Orsay: Chicken consommé garnished with poached yolks, pigeon quenelles, strips of pigeon meat and chervil.

Ostend Style: à l'ostendaise: Rich fish consommé flavored with oyster liquor, garnished with poached bearded oysters.

Oxtail: de queues de boeuf: Rich beef consommé flavored with herbs and Sherry, garnished with small pieces of oxtail and diced root vegetables.

with Oyster Raviolis: Oysters poached in white wine, diced, mixed with fish forcemeat, seasoned, stuffed in tiny rounds of noodle dough, poached and served in strong fish consommé.

P

Palermo: à la palermitaine: Chicken consommé garnished with pieces of spaghetti, cubes of tomato royal and diced chicken meat, grated Parmesan cheese served separately.

Palestine: Beef consommé garnished with pearls of carrots and turnips, peas and diced beans.

Palestro: Beef consommé garnished with strips of root vegetables, shredded lettuce, rice and cubes of tomato royal.

with Pancakes: Fanchonette: Chicken consommé garnished with small round pieces of pancake stuffed with chicken purée and chopped truffles.

Parisian: à la parisienne: chicken consommé garnished with cubes of royal with minced root vegetables, braised, diced vegetables and chervil.

Patti: Chicken consommé thickened with tapioca, garnished with diced artichoke bottoms and truffles.

with Pearl Barley: à l'orge perlé: Beef consommé garnished with pearl barley cooked in broth.

Perfect: Parfait: Chicken consommé thickened with tapioca, flavored with Madeira, garnished with cubes of royal.

Peter the Great: Pierre le Grand: Beef consommé garnished with strips of celery and turnips, shredded lettuce and tarragon.

Petite Marmite: See Meat Pot, Small.

Petrarch: Pétrarque: Beef consommé garnished with shredded leeks, grilled pistachios and diablotins.

Pheasant: de faisan: Pheasant consommé garnished with strips of pheasant meat and croûtons.

Picard: à la picarde: Beef consommé garnished with shredded leeks and croûtons.

Piedmontese: à la piémontaise: Beef consommé flavored with saffron, garnished with rice, diced ham, Piedmont truffles and diced tomatoes; grated cheese served separately.

Pilaw Soup, Turkish: de mouton à la turque: Mutton consommé garnished with rice cooked in fat mutton broth.

Pojarsky: Chicken consommé with hazel-hen flavor; small hazel-hen or chicken cutlets à la Pojarsky served separately.

Polignac: Beef consommé garnished with cooked chicken forcemeat with chopped truffles and ox tongue in small round pieces.

Polignac: Fish consommé garnished with lobster quenelles and diced mushrooms.

Polish: à la polonaise: Chicken consommé garnished with unsweetened pancakes coated with chicken forcemeat, rolled up, cooked and cut in slices.

Pondicherry: Mutton broth flavored with curry, garnished with rice and strips of unsweetened pancakes filled with mutton hash.

Portuguese: à la portugaise: Rich beef consommé strongly flavored with tomato juice, spiced with Cayenne pepper, served cold in cups.

Portuguese: Beef consommé flavored with tomato juice, garnished with diced tomatoes and rice.

Potemkin: Rich fish consommé clarified with pounded press caviar and white wine, garnished with asparagus tips and strips of carrot and celery.

Prince Nicolai: Chicken consommé flavored with tomato juice and red peppers, garnished with diced red peppers, celery and small crayfish tails.

Prince of Wales: Prince de Galles: Chicken consommé garnished with asparagus tips and truffled chicken quenelles.

Princess': à la princesse: Chicken consommé garnished with pearl barley, cubes of pea royal and strips of white chicken meat.

Princess Alice: Chicken consommé thickened with tapioca, garnished with shredded lettuce, strips of artichoke bottoms and chicken meat.

Q

Queens: à la reine: Chicken consommé slightly thickened with tapioca, garnished with cubes of chicken royal and strips of white chicken meat.

R

Rabelais: Game consommé garnished with strips of celery and truffled lark quenelles, flavored before serving with Vouvray wine.

Rachel: Chicken consommé thickened with tapioca, garnished with strips of artichoke bottoms; beef marrow on toast served separately.

Rabelais: Game consommé flavored with truffles and larks, garnished with celery strips and lark quenelles with chopped truffles.

Rampolla: Fish consommé flavored with crayfish and Rhenish wine (hock), garnished with strips of eelpout, crayfish tails, oysters and diced mushrooms.

Raphael: Beef consommé garnished with cubes of knob celery.

Raspail: Rich beef consommé garnished with chicken quenelles and asparagus tips.

with Raviolis: aux raviolis: Beef consommé garnished with very small raviolis stuffed with spinach or some other purée.

Récamier: Chicken consommé garnished with sago, truffle balls and chicken quenelles.

Réjane: Chicken consommé flavored with chervil, garnished with confetti-shaped carrot royal, filbert and cream royal and raw eggs strained through a colander into the soup.

Rembrand: Chicken consommé garnished with cubes of pea royal and diced white chicken meat.

Remusat: Beef consommé garnished with quenelles mixed with tomato purée, spinach purée, diced root vegetables and chervil.

Renaissance: Chicken consommé garnished with balls of spring vegetables, cubes of fine herbs royal and chervil.

Rich: à la riche: Rich chicken consommé garnished with large truffled chicken quenelles.

Richelieu: Beef consommé garnished with strips of carrot and turnip, stuffed chicken quenelles and balls of stuffed lettuce.

Richepin: Chicken consommé garnished with chicken quenelles stuffed with chicken jelly, strips of carrot, turnip and stuffed lettuce leaves.

Risi-Bisi: Beef consommé garnished with rice and green peas; grated Parmesan cheese served separately.

Rivoli: Fish consommé garnished with fish quenelles and small pieces of spaghetti.

Robespierre: Rich beef consommé flavored with tomato juice, served in cups.

Rohan: Game consommé garnished with poached plovers eggs and shredded lettuce, game purée spread on small rounds of toast gratinated and served separately.

Rossini: Chicken consommé flavored with truffles, slightly thickened with tapioca; very small profiterolles stuffed with truffled goose liver purée served separately.

Rothschild: Game consommé with pheasant flavor and Sauterne wine, garnished with royal of equal parts of pheasant and chestnut purée, strips of truffles and ortolan breast.

Rotraud: Game consommé flavored with white wine, garnished with pheasant and chestnut royal and strips of pheasant meat and truffles.

Royal: Chicken consommé slightly thickened with tapioca, garnished with cubes of royal. Royal: An unsweetened custard of eggs with added egg yolks, broth or cream, variously flavored with chicken forcemeat, fish, almond milk, tomato purée etc. cut in cubes, round slices, diamonds etc.

Rubens: Chicken consommé flavored with tomato juice, garnished with hop shoots.

Russian Fish: de poisson à la russe: Fish consommé garnished with pearls of cucumbers and fish quenelles.

Rustic Style: à la paysanne: Beef consommé with braised vegetables cut in small thin slices, served with slices of fried French bread.

Rustical: à la villageoise: Beef consommé garnished with strips of leek and small square shaped noodles.

S

with Sago Pearls: aux perls de Nizam: Beef consommé garnished with sago pearls cooked in broth.

Salvator: Beef consommé flavored with tomato juice, garnished with diced tomatoes and chervil.

St. Charles: Beef consommé garnished with small poached eggs and shredded chervil.

St. George: Hare consommé flavored with claret, garnished with hare quenelles, strips of truffles and hare meat.

St. Germain: Beef consommé garnished with quenelles, peas, shredded lettuce and chervil.

Saint-Saëns: Chicken consommé garnished with pearl barley and potatoes balls.

San Remo: Chicken consommé garnished with rice and round slices of carrots; grated Parmesan cheese served separately.

Sans-gêne: Chicken consommé garnished with strips of truffles, cockscombs and cocks' kidneys.

Santa Maria: Chicken consommé flavored with tarragon, garnished with angels hair and quenelles; profiterolles stuffed with mushroom purée served separately.

Santos-Dumont: Chicken consommé thickened with tapioca, garnished with pearls of carrots and turnips and strips of French beans.

Sarah Bernhardt: Chicken consommé slightly thickened with tapioca, garnished with chicken quenelles with crayfish butter, sliced beef marrow, asparagus tips and strips of truffles.

Savarin: Beef consommé garnished with sweetbread quenelles stuffed with onion purée.

Saxon: Beef consommé garnished with strips of ham, ox tongue and sauerkraut cooked in broth and croûtons.

Ségurd: Chicken consommé garnished with strips of chicken meat and smoked ox tongue.

with Semolina: au semoule: Beef consommé with semolina cooked in the soup.

Semolina C. Beatrice: Beef consommé with semolina, round slices of broiled chicken forcemeat and cubes of tomato royal.

— C. Mireille: Chicken consommé with semolina, round slices of chicken forcemeat with tomato purée and cubes of plain royal.

— C. Tivoli: Chicken consommé with semolina garnished with small baked raviolis.

— C. Valencia: Beef consommé with semolina, garnished with shredded lettuce, sorrel and chervil.

Shepherds: à la bergère: Beef consommé thickened with tapioca, garnished with asparagus tips, diced mushrooms, tarragon and chervil.

Severin: Chicken consommé garnished with small slices of cooked chicken forcemeat.

Sévigné: Chicken consommé garnished with chicken quenelles, braised stuffed lettuce, very green peas and chervil.

Sevillian: à la sevillane: Beef consommé flavored with tomato juice, slightly thickened with tapioca, garnished with cubes of tomato royal.

Snail: à l'escargot: Chicken consommé flavored with snail broth, garnished with small snails, diced root vegetables and fine herbs; croûtons served separately.

Solange: Beef consommé garnished with pearl barley, diced chicken meat and shredded lettuce.
Solferino: Beef consommé garnished with pearls of carrots, turnips and potatoes.
Soubise: Beef consommé garnished with cubes of onion purée royal.
Soubrette: Chicken consommé flavored with tomato, slightly seasoned with Cayenne pepper, garnished with small round chicken quenelles decorated with a truffle ring and peeled shrimp-tails.
Sovereign: à la souveraine: Chicken consommé garnished with pearl sized chicken quenelles, peas and braised, diced root vegetables and chervil.
Spinners: à la filateur: Beef consommé garnished with noodles cut in very thin strips.
Spring: Printanier: Chicken consommé garnished with pearls or small round strips of braised carrots and turnips, peas, diced French beans, asparagus tips, shredded lettuce and chervil.
— **with poached eggs:** Printanier Colbert: Same as above but with very small poached eggs.
— **Royal:** Printanier royal: Chicken consommé Printanier with cubes of plain royal.
Surprise: Chicken consommé flavored and colored with the juice of red beetroots, garnished with chicken quenelles stuffed with chicken aspic jelly.
with Stuffed Lettuce: à la baigneuse: Beef consommé garnished with small balls of stuffed lettuce.

T

Talleyrand: Chicken consommé flavored with Sherry wine, garnished with diced truffles cooked in Sherry.
Talma: Chicken consommé garnished with rice and almond milk royal.
with Tapioca: Beef consommé slightly thickened with tapioca.
with Tarragon: à l'estragon: Beef consommé flavored with essence of tarragon, garnished with tarragon leaves.
Tewki Pasha: Mutton consommé flavored with tomato and peppers, garnished with rice and strips of red and green peppers.
Theodor: Chicken consommé garnished with diced chicken meat, asparagus tips and flageolets.
Theodora: Chicken consommé garnished with strips of chicken and truffles, asparagus tips and cubes of plain royal.
Theresa: Thérèse: Cold chicken sonsommé garnished with shredded chervil and filbert-sized balls of chicken mousse.
Tosca: Chicken consommé thickened with tapioca, garnished with chicken, goose liver and truffle quenelles and strips of carrots; profiterolles stuffed with chicken purée served separately.
Trévise: Chicken consommé thickened with tapioca, garnished with thin strips of chicken meat, truffles and ox tongue.
Trianon: Chicken consommé thickened with tapioca, garnished with slices of chicken, spinach and carrot royal.
Tunisian: à la tunisienne: Mutton consommé flavored with saffron, garnished with chick peas, rice, diced tomatoes and green peppers.

Turbigo: Chicken consommé garnished with strips of chicken meat and carrots and vermicelli.

Turtle Real: Tortue clair: Made with beef, veal, calve's feet, turtle meat and pot herbs, flavored with turtle herbs and Sherry wine, garnished with the diced turtle meat.

— **Lady Curzon:** Clear turtle soup, filled in small cups, covered with curry flavoured whipped cream, glazed rapidely.

— **Sir James:** Clear turtle soup flavored with Cognac and Madeira, served in small cups.

— **with Sturgeon:** Tortue au sterlet: Clear turtle soup garnished with strips of sturgeon meat cooked in champagne, sturgeon quenelles and slices of eel-pout liver.

Tuscan: à la toscane: Beef consommé garnished with diced mushrooms and tomatoes, small pieces of macaroni and diced baked aubergines.

V

Valencian: à la valencienne: Chicken consommé garnished with chicken quenelles, shredded lettuce and chervil.

Valentino: Chicken consommé garnished with strips of chicken meat, truffles and small heart-shaped chicken quenelles.

Vatel: Fish consommé garnished with diced sole fillets and cubes of lobster royal.

Vaudoise: Beef consommé with diced beef and root vegetables cooked in the soup; crusts of dried French bread and grated Swiss cheese served separately.

with Vermicelli: au vermicelle: Beef consommé garnished with cooked vermicelli.

Venetian: à la vénitienne: Beef consommé flavored with tarragon, chervil and sweet basil, garnished with rice; very small browned potato dumplings served separately.

Verdi: Beef consommé garnished with small pieces of macaroni and spinach, tomato and cream-quenelles.

Véron: Beef consommé flavored with truffle juice and Port, garnished with strips of red peppers and cubes of purée of flageolet royal.

with Vesiga: au vésiga à la russe: Chicken consommé flavored with Madeira, garnished with strips of cooked vesiga and three sorts of quenelles.

Victor Emanuel: Beef consommé garnished with diced tomatoes and macaroni; grated Parmesan cheese served separately.

Victoria: Beef or chicken consommé garnished with strips of chicken meat and truffles, chicken quenelles, peas and chervil.

— **Regina:** Fish consommé flavored with lobster, garnished with asparagus tips and truffle pearls; tiny puff paste patties filled with lobster ragoût served separately.

Viennese: à la viennoise: Rich beef consommé not clarified, flavored with smoked beef, bacon and root vegetables, garnished with rice, pearl barley, very small haricot beans and peas.

Villeneuve: Chicken consommé garnished with pancakes stuffed with ham purée cut in triangles, lettuce stuffed with chicken and ox tongue purée cut in squares and cubes of plain royal.

Villeroi: Chicken consommé garnished with chicken forcemeat, chopped carrots, onions, and tomatoes added, poached and cut in slices.

Vivian: Viviane: Chicken consommé garnished with slices of chicken breast and truffles.

Voltaire: Chicken consommé garnished with diced chicken meat, tomatoes and chicken quenelles.

Viveur: Chicken consommé flavored and colored with red beetroot garnished with strips of knob celery and diablotins (q. v.).

W

Westmoreland: Veal and calf's head consommé slightly thickened with arrowroot, flavored with Madeira, garnished with small slices of gherkins, truffles, chicken quenelles and diced calf's head.

White Lady: Dame Blanche: Chicken consommé thickened with tapioca, garnished with cubes of almond milk royal and strips of white chicken meat.

Windsor: Rich beef consommé flavored with turtle herbs and Sherry, slightly thickened with arrowroot, garnished with strips of calf's foot.

X Y Z

Xavier: Beef consommé flavored with Madeira, thickened with arrowroot, garnished with thin strips of unsweetened pancake.

Yvette: Chicken consommé flavored with turtle herbs, garnished with chicken quenelles and purée of spinach.

Zola: Beef consommé garnished with small cheese dumplings mixed with chopped white truffles; grated cheese served separately.

Zorilla: Chicken consommé flavored with tomato juice, garnished with rice and chick peas.

Thick Soups

A

African Soup: P. à l'africaine: curried chicken velouté, blended with cream of rice, garnished with diced artichoke bottoms and egg plants.

Agnes Sorel: Cr. Agnès Sorel: cream of chicken, blended with purée of mushrooms, garnished with strips of chicken, mushrooms and ox tongue.

Albert: P.: same as Parmentier, garnished with strips of root vegetables.

Alexandra: Cr. Cream of chicken with tapioca, garnished with strips of chicken meat and shredded lettuce.

Algerian: (Cr.) à l'algérienne: Purée of sweet potatoes and velouté, flavored with filberts, blended with filbert butter, thickened with cream.

— **Artichoke:** Pr. d'artichauts à l'algérienne: Purée of artichokes and sweet potatoes, flavored with filberts (hazelnuts), garnished with diced artichoke bottoms and croûtons.

Alice: Cr.: potato soup, blended with purée of turnips, thickened with cream, garnished with croûtons.
Amazone: Cream of chicken and rice, garnished with croûtons.
Ambassadors: P. à l'ambassadeur: Green pea soup, garnished with rice and shredded lettuce.
Andalusian: Cr. à l'andalouse: Cream of tomatoes, onions and rice, garnished with diced tomatoes and strips of green peppers.
Antonin Carême: V. Chicken velouté, purée of artichoke bottoms and mushrooms, garnished with strips of truffles.
Ardennes: V. à l'ardennaise: Velvet soup of pheasant and red kidney beans, flavored with Port, garnished with strips of pheasant and croûtons.
Argenteuil: Cr.: purée of asparagus, blended with cream sauce, thickened with cream, garnished with green asparagus tips and chervil.
Arménonville: P. Purée of green peas, garnished with sago, diced, vegetables and chervil.
Asparagus Soup: Cr. d'asperges: purée of white asparagus and rice, blended with cream, garnished with asparagus tips.
Arras Style: V. à l'artésienne: Purée of white haricot beans diluted with velouté, garnished with tapioca.
Artichoke: Cr. d'artichauts: Purée of artichokes and rice, improved with cream, garnished with croûtons.
— **Morlaix:** Cr. à la morlaisienne: Artichoke cream with tapioca, garnished with fried croûtons.
Aurora: Cr. à l'aurore: Chicken and tomato cream, garnished with chicken quenelles.

B

Bagration 1: V. Velouté of veal, garnished with macaroni; grated cheese served separately.
Bagration 2: V. Fish velouté flavored with mushrooms, garnished with strips of sole fillets, fish quenelles with crayfish butter and crayfish tails.
Balmoral: V. Velouté of calf's foot flavored with turtle herbs, garnished with strips of calf's foot and veal quenelles.
Balvais: P. Green pea soup garnished with diced vegetables.
Balzac: Cr. Purée of knob celery and cream of barley, garnished with strips of leek and celery.
Bankers Style: Cr. à la financière: Cream of woodcock blended with purée of goose liver, garnished with croûtons.
Barcelona: P. à la barcelonnaise: Tomato and tapioca soup, garnished with diced ham.
Barley Soup, French: Cr. d'orge: Strained barley soup, diluted with velouté, improved with cream.
— — **Westfalian:** Barley soup flavored with ham, garnished with chopped ham, diced carrots, knob celery and potatoes, blended with cream and egg yolks.
Beaucaire: Cr. Cream of barley, garnished with strips of knob celery, leeks and chicken meat.
Beaufort: P.: hare soup, garnished with strips of hare and small sliced sausages, cream added at the last minute.
Beaulieu: Pr. Purée of vegetables blended with tapioca consommé, garnished with diced root vegetables.

Bean Soup, Hungarian: P. de haricots à la hongroise: Purée of white haricot beans cooked with bacon, seasoned with paprika, blended with sour cream.

— **Turkish:** P. de haricots à la turque: Purée of white haricot beans, fried onions and rice, flavored with garlic.

of Beans Victoria: Pr. de haricots blancs Victoria: Purée of white haricot beans cooked in chicken broth, bound with cream and egg yolks, garnished with strips of chicken meat and chicken quenelles.

Beauharnais: Cr. Cream of barley blended with crayfish butter, garnished with veal quenelles and crayfish tails.

Belgian: P. Purée of Brussels sprouts, thickened with egg yolks and cream, garnished with fried croûtons.

Belle Otéro: V.: purée of sweet potatoes blended with velouté, garnished with slices of beef marrow.

Berchoux: P.: purée of lentils, diluted with strong game stock, thickened with cream, garnished with croûtons.

Bercy: Cr. Cream of turnips and potatoes, garnished with fried croûtons.

Bismarck: V. Velouté of calf's head blended with shrimp purée.

Bisque of Crabs: B. de crabes: same as bisque of crayfish but crayfish replaced by crabs.

— **of Crayfish:** B. d'écrevisses: diced root vegetables sautéd in butter, crayfish added, seasoned, ignited with brandy, white wine added, cooked in consommé. Cook rice in consommé at the same time or with crayfish. Shell crayfish and reserve tails, pound rice with shells and vegetables, dilute purée with consommé, reheat, blend with cream and butter, garnish soup with diced crayfish tails.

— **of Crayfish Princess Style:** d'écrevisses à la princesse: bisque, garnished with asparagus tips and fish quenelles blended with crayfish butter.

— **of Crayfish with Truffles:** B. d'écrevisses à la périgourdine: bisque of crayfish, flavored with truffle essence, garnished with pearls of truffles, crayfish tails and quenelles.

— **of Shrimps:** B. de crevettes: same as bisque of crayfish, crayfish replaced by shrimps.

Bloum: Pr. Purée of turnips, celery knobs, potatoes and leeks, blended with cream, garnished with croûtons and chervil.

Boatmans Soup: Cr. à la batelière: shrimp purée, blended with fish velouté, improved with cream, garnished with shrimp tails, bearded mussels and croûtons.

Boïldieu: V. Chicken velouté garnished with three sorts of quenelles: chicken, goose liver and truffle.

Bolivian: P. à la bolivienne: Tomato soup garnished with diced lamb and tomatoes and strips of cooked ham.

Bonvalet: V. Purée of potatoes, turnips and leeks diluted with velouté, garnished with lozenges of green beans and cubes of carrot royal.

Borely: V. Purée of whitings diluted with fish velouté, garnished with very small bearded mussels and whiting quenelles.

Botzari: Pr.: purée of green peas, diluted with mutton stock, garnished with diced lean mutton, root vegetables and rice.

Bourdalou: V. Velouté of chicken and cream of rice, garnished with cubes of royal of four different colours; grated cheese served separately.
Brahms: V. Chicken velouté slightly flavored with caraway seeds, garnished with small balls of turnips, carrots and potatoes.
Bread Soup, French: P. de pain à la française: Chopped onions lightly fried in butter, mixed with diced bread, cooked in beef stock, strained, blended with egg yolks and cream, garnished with poached eggs.
Bressane: Pr. Purée of pumpkin, blended with butter and cream, garnished with Italian paste.
Bretonish: Cr. à la bretonne: Cream soup of white haricot beans, leeks and onions, blended with cream, garnished with strips of leeks and mushrooms.
Brides: Pr. Petite mariée: Purée of white haricot beans, garnished with diced vegetables.
Brie Style: P. à la briarde: Purée of carrots and potatoes, garnished with croûtons and chervil.
Brillat-Savarin: V. Purée of chicken and rabbit, diluted with velouté, flavored with Madeira, garnished with strips of mushrooms, truffles and carrots.
Bristol: Cr. Green pea soup blended with cream, garnished with small strips of root vegetables, tarragon and chervil.
Broad Bean Soup: Pr. de fèves: purée of broad beans, thickened with arrowroot, mellowed with milk, garnished with small broad beans.
Brussels: Cr. à la bruxelloise: Purée of Brussels sprouts, improved with cream, garnished with croûtons.

C

Calabrian: P. à la calabraise: purée of white haricot beans and sorrel, garnished with rice.
Cambacérès: P. Crayfish velouté blended with pigeon velouté, garnished with pigeon quenelles stuffed with purée of crayfish.
Cambell: Fish velouté seasoned with curry powder, garnished with strips of sole fillets.
Camelia: Cr.: purée of peas and tapioca, blended with cream of chicken, garnished with strips of chicken and leeks.
Canoness: V. à la chanoinesse: velouté of fish, blended with crayfish butter, garnished with sliced soft roe.
Capri: P. brown game soup, flavored with quail, garnished with strips of quail and cockscombs.
Capuchin Soup: V.: chicken velouté, blended with cream of mushrooms, garnished with profiteroles stuffed with chicken purée.
Cardinals Soup: Cr. cardinal: lobster purée, blended with fish velouté, garnished with diced lobster and lobster royal cut in shape of a cross.
Carmelite: Cr. Purée of whiting blended with Béchamel and fish velouté, improved with cream, garnished with strips of sole fillets and whiting quenelles.
Carmen: V. Velouté of chicken, cream of rice and tomatoes, garnished with rice, diced tomatoes and shredded sweet peppers.
Caroline: V.: velouté of chicken, blended with cream of rice, garnished with rice and almond cream royal.

Carrot Soup: Pr. Crécy: Purée of carrots thickened with rice, mellowed with butter.

— — **Old fashioned:** Crécy à l'ancienne: Thickened with potatoes instead of rice, garnished with fried croûtons.

Castellan: P. à la castellane: brown game soup, flavored with woodcock, garnished with strips of woodcock and lentil and woodcock royal mixed with chopped hard-boiled egg yolks.

Catherine: V.: rich fish velouté, garnished with shrimp tails and green peas.

Cauliflower Soup: Pr. à la Dubarry: Purée of cauliflower and potatoes, mellowed with milk and butter, garnished with small cauliflower sprigs and chervil. May also be prepared as velouté or cream soup.

Cavalier: Cr. à la chevalière: cream of chicken, garnished with strips of truffle and ox tongue.

Celery Soup: A. — Pr. de céleri: purée of celery, blended with purée of potatoes, mellowed with milk and butter. **B.** V. de céleri: purée of celery, blended with veal velouté, thickened with cream and egg yolks.

Celestian: Cr. à la céléstine: Chicken cream soup blended with purée of artichokes, garnished with croûtons.

Cérès: Cr. Cream of green wheat blended with cream, garnished with chervil.

Chabrillan: P. Cream of tomatoes, garnished with vermicelli and chicken quenelles with tarragon.

Champagne: P. à la champenoise: Potato purée blended with celery purée, garnished with diced carrots and celery.

Chantilly: P. Lentil soup blended with whipped cream, garnished with quenelles.

Charlotte: Pr. Purée of leeks, potatoes and watercress, cohered with butter, garnished with chervil.

Charterhouse Soup: Cr. chartreuse: cream of chicken with tapioca, garnished with ravioli stuffed with goose liver and spinach.

Chasseur: P.: game soup, garnished with croûtons.

Châtelaine: Cr. Cream of chicken blended with purée of fresh green peas, garnished with quenelles and chervil.

Chatillon: P. Tomato soup, garnished with shredded sorrel and vermicelli.

Chayotte: Cr. Cream of chicken blended with purée of choyottes, garnished with croûtons.

Cheese Soup, Dutch: P. au fromage à la hollandaise: grated Gouda cheese cooked in beef consommé, strained, cohered with cream, mellowed with butter.

Chervil Soup: P.: velouté of veal, strongly flavored with chervil, garnished with croûtons.

— **Root Soup:** Cr. de cerfeuil: purée of root chervil and veal velouté, blended with cream, garnished with croûtons and shredded chervil.

Cherville: V.: velouté of rabbit, garnished with slices of rabbit, morrels and truffles, flavored shortly before serving with Madeira.

Chesterfield: Cr.: cream of veal, garnished with pieces of calf's tail.

Chestnut Soup: Pr. de marrons: purée of chestnuts blended with game velouté, garnished with croûtons.

Chevreuse: Cr. cream of chicken, blended with semolina cooked in consommé, garnished with julienne of chicken meat and truffles.

Chicago: P. Bisque of lobster blended with tomato soup, garnished with diced tomatoes, Nizam pearls and diced lobster.

Chicken, Cream of: Cr. de volaille: purée of chicken mixed with light Béchamel, creamed and seasoned, garnished with strips of white chicken meat.

— **Medici, Cream of:** Cr. de volaille à la Médicis: cream of chicken, blended with purée of lobster, garnished with chicken quenelles and stachy.

— **liver Soup:** V. de foies de volaille: purée of chicken liver, blended with velouté of veal, garnished with sliced fried chicken liver.

— **Soup, Supreme Style:** Cr. de volaille suprême: rich chicken soup, bound with double cream, garnished with diced chicken.

— **Soup Viennese:** P. de volaille à la viennoise: Purée of chicken blended with veal velouté, garnished with small slices of chicken meat and diced vegetables.

Choiseul: Cr. Purée of lentils and game, blended with cream, garnished with rice and shredded sorrel.

Choisy: Cr. Purée of lettuce mixed with Béchamel and cream, garnished with croûtons and chervil.

Claire fontaine: V.: same as watercress soup but garnished with diced potatoes and shredded watercress.

Clamart: Pr. Purée of green peas, garnished with green peas and croûtons.

Claremont: V. Chicken velouté flavored with champagne, garnished with asparagus tips, strips of chicken meat and chicken quenelles.

Clermont: Pr. Purée of chestnuts, celery and onions, mellowed with milk, garnished with crisp fried onion rings and Italian paste.

Colombine: Cr.: cream of chicken and pigeon, flavored with aniseed (anice), garnished with diced pigeon meat and pigeon quenelles.

Compiègne: Pr. Purée of white haricot beans mellowed with milk, garnished with shredded sorrel and chervil.

Conaught: P.: lentil soup, garnished with diced chicken and croûtons.

Condé: Pr. Purée of red haricot beans flavored with red wine, garnished with fried croûtons.

Condorcet: Pr. Purée of game, garnished with strips of game and game quenelles.

Conti: Pr. Purée of lentils, blended with butter, garnished with fried croûtons and chervil.

Coquelin: Pr. Green pea soup, garnished with strips of chicken meat and leeks.

Cormeilles: Pr. Purée of green beans and potatoes melowed with milk, garnished with green beans cut in lozenge shape.

Corneille: Cr.: cream of lettuce, garnished with sago.

Countess: Cr. à la comtesse: cream of asparagus and chicken velouté, garnished with asparagus tips, shredded lettuce and sorrel.

Count's: P. du comte: Purée of vegetables blended with lentil soup, garnished with strips of root vegetables.

Courland Soup: P. à la courlandaise: purée of carrots, knob celery, cabbage, turnips, onions and potatoes, cooked in duck stock; slices of duck breast served separately.

Crayfish Soup Joinville: V. d'écrevisses J.: Purée of crayfish blended with fish velouté, garnished with crayfish tails, diced mushrooms and truffles.

— — **Lucullus:** V. d'écrevisses L.: same as Joinville but garnished with crayfish tails and crayfish heads stuffed with fish forcemeat with chopped truffles.

— — **Oriental:** V. d'écrevisses à l'orientale: velouté of fish, blended with purée of crayfish, garnished with diced crayfish tails and rice.

Creole: P. à la créole: Purée of okra diluted with velouté, garnished with diced tomatoes and strips of sweet red peppers.

Cressonière: Purée of watercress and potatoes mellowed with milk, garnished with shredded watercress.

Cretan: P. à la crétoise: purée of vegetable marrow, blended with tomato soup, garnished with croûtons.

Croatian Soup: Cr. à la croate: cream of sweet corn, garnished with sweet corn.

Cussy: P.: game soup, garnished with chestnut royal and fine strips of partridge and truffle.

D

Danish Duck: Pr. de canard à la danoise: Purée of duck and artichokes, flavored with Marsala wine, garnished with duck quenelles.

— **Game:** Pr. de gibier à la danoise: Purée of lentils and game, garnished with strips of game and truffles, flavored with Madeira wine.

Darblay: Pr.: purée of potatoes, garnished with strips of root vegetables.

Dartois: V. d'Artois: Purée of white haricot beans diluted with velouté, garnished with strips of vegetables and sprigs of chervil.

Delicate Soup: Cr. délice: purée of chicken, diluted with chicken consommé, mixed when almost finished with unsweetened whipped cream, served in cups.

Délice: Cr. Cream of chicken, flavored with almond milk, garnished with pearl sized chicken quenelles; tiny puff pastry patties filled with chicken purée served separately.

Delicious Soup: Cr. délicieuse: cream of chicken blended with goose liver purée, served in cups, topped with unsweetened whipped cream with paprika; tiny puff pastry patties stuffed with chicken purée served separately.

Derby: V.: velouté and rice cream, flavored with curry and onions, garnished with chicken quenelles stuffed with goose liver, rice and pearls of truffles.

d'Estaing: V.: purée of crabs blended with fish velouté, garnished with strips of white fish and crab quenelles.

Diana: V. Diane: purée of partridge, blended with game velouté, garnished with strips of partridge and truffle.

Diplomate: V. Chicken and rice velouté, garnished with tapioca, truffle rings and chicken quenelles.

Divette: Cr.: velouté of smelts blended with cream of crayfish, garnished with diced crayfish tails, fish quenelles and truffle pearls.

Dolguruki: V. Chicken and onion velouté, flavored with ham, garnished with strips of chicken meat.
Doyen: P. Purée of green peas and chicken velouté, garnished with chicken quenelles and green peas.
Dubarry: Pr. Purée of cauliflower and potatoes, garnished with cauliflower buds or croûtons. May also be made as cream or velouté.
Dubelley: Cr.: cream of lettuce, blended with cream, thickened with tapioca.
Duchess: Cr. duchesse: cream of chicken, garnished with asparagus tips and strips of truffles.
— **Louise:** Cr. Duchesse Louise: Cream of chicken and mushrooms, garnished with shredded lettuce and strips of chicken and mushrooms.
Duck Soup, Rouenese: P. à la rouennaise: brown duck soup, flavored with red wine, purée of duck liver added when almost finished, garnished with strips of duck and croûtons.
Dunkirk: V. à la Dunkerque: Purée of cauliflower, potatoes and leeks, diluted with velouté, garnished with croûtons.
Durham: Cr. Chicken cream soup, garnished with chicken, lobster and spinach quenelles.

E

Egg-plant: Cr. d'aubergines: Cream of chicken blended with purée of aubergines, garnished with diced aubergines.
Egyptian Pr.: à l'égyptienne: Purée of rice, leeks and onions.
Elisabeth: V. Chicken and rice velouté, garnished with croûtons.
Eliza: V. Elise: Chicken velouté, garnished with shredded sorrel and chervil.
Endive: Pr. aux endives: Purée of endives and potatoes, mellowed with milk.
Erica: Cr.: cream of chicken, blended with purée of sweet red peppers, served in cup, topped at the last minute with unsweetened whipped cream.
Esau: Pr. Esaü: Purée of grey lentils garnished with rice.
Esmeralda: Cr. Purée of celery and morels, blended with cream of chicken; profiterolles stuffed with purée of goose liver served separately.
Estérel: P. Purée of white haricot beans and pumpkin, garnished with vermicelli.
Eveline: Cr. Chicken cream soup, garnished with a ring of thick tomato sauce while serving.
Excelsior: V. Cream of barley blended with asparagus velouté, garnished with pearl barley.

F

Fanchette: V. Velouté of chicken, garnished with asparagus tips, green peas and squares of stuffed cabbage.
Farmers Soup: P. paysanne: purée of vegetables, garnished with croûtons and chervil.
Faubonne: Pr. Purée of white haricot beans, garnished with strips of root vegetables and chervil.
Fieldfare Soup: P. de grives: game soup flavored with fieldfare and brandy, garnished with croûtons.

Flemish Soup: Cr. à la flamande: cream of Brussels sprouts, blended with potato soup, garnished with small Brussels sprouts.
Florence: Cr. à la florentine: Purée of spinach, improved with cream, flavored with nutmeg, garnished with croûtons.
Fleury: V. Velouté of barley, garnished with diced root vegetables and cauliflower buds.
Fontanges: Cr. Cream of green peas, garnished with shredded sorrel and chervil.
Francis Joseph: Cr. François Joseph: Cream of celery blended with purée of chestnuts and tomatoes, garnished with vermicelli.
Freneuse: Pr. Purée of turnips and potatoes, mellowed with milk.
Frog's Legs: Cr. de grenouilles: Purée of frogs legs, blended with velouté of veal, mellowed with cream; sautéd frogs' legs on toast served separately.
— — **Sicilian Style:** V. de grenouilles à la sicilienne: Purée of frogs' legs, blended with fish velouté, garnished with frogs' legs, strips of white fish and chopped pistachios.

G

Game Soup: P. de gibier: braise game bones and trimmings with pot herbs, spices, herbs, onions, pepper grains and bacon rind until brown, dust with flour, sweat the flour brown. Moisten with beef or veal stock, boil slowly for several hours, skim carefully. Strain, add red wine. Or prepare stock without flour, thicken with lentils and strain.
Gascon: V. gasconne: purée of tomatoes and onion, blended with velouté, garnished with diced preserved goose meat.
Gastronomers: Cr. à la gastronome: Cream of chicken and chestnuts, garnished with morels, cockscombs and strips of truffles.
Gaulish: Cr. à la gauloise: Cream of knob celery, chestnuts and tomatoes, garnished with croûtons.
Génin: Pr. Purée of carrots, leeks, tomatoes, mushrooms and rice, garnished with shredded sorrel and chervil.
George Sand: V. Rich fish velouté, garnished with crayfish tails and shredded lettuce.
Georgina: Pr. Georgette: Purée of artichokes, mellowed with milk, blended with artichoke butter, garnished with Nizam pearls.
Germinal: V. Chicken velouté flavored with tarragon, garnished with asparagus tips and chervil.
Germiny: P. Rich consommé thickened with egg yolks and cream, garnished with shredded sorrel.
Gervaise: Cr. Cream of chicken and barley, garnished with diced lamb meat and cocks' kidneys.
Goatherds Style: Pr. à la chevrière: Purée of potatoes, leeks, lettuce, sorrel and herbs, blended with fine herb butter, garnished with diced, sauted potatoes.
Gosford: P. Asparagus soup thickened with tapioca.
Gounod: Pr. Purée of green peas, garnished with diced chicken meat, croûtons and chervil.
Gourmets Game Soup: Cr. des gourmets: purée of pheasant, blended with brown game soup, purée of goose liver added, blended with cream, flavored with Portwine, garnished with strips of pheasant and pheasant quenelles.

Granada: P. Cream of chicken, garnished with diced tomatoes and strips of chicken meat.

Grand-duke: Cr. Grand-duc: Purée of partridge, mellowed with cream, garnished with chicken quenelles and diced mushrooms.

Grandmothers: P. Grand'mère: Potato soup, garnished with strips of leek and cabbage, shredded lettuce and macaroni.

Grand-veneur: Cr. Cream of pheasant, seasoned with Cayenne pepper, flavored with Sherry, garnished with diced pheasant meat and truffles.

Greek: V. à la grecque: Purée of tomatoes blended with purée of pumpkin, diluted with velouté, garnished with croûtons.

Green Kern or Green Wheat Soup: Cr. de blé-vert: veal stock, flavored with ham, thickened with meal of green wheat, mellowed with milk and blended with cream.

— **Meadow:** Cr. vert-pré: purée of spinach and potatoes, blended with cream, garnished with croûtons and chervil.

— **Soup:** P. aux herbes: shredded lettuce, spinach, sorrel, leeks and purslane sweated in butter, blended with potato soup, strained through a fine sieve, garnished with croûtons and chervil.

H

Helianti: V. de hélianthe: purée of helianti mixed with velouté of veal, seasoned with lemon juice and Cayenne pepper, garnished with croûtons.

Herbs Soup: P. aux herbes: spinach, sorrel, chervil, parsley, dandelion, nettle shoots etc. sweated in butter, blended with potato soup or velouté, strained, mellowed with cream, garnished with croûtons.

Holstein Soup: P. Tomato soup, garnished with asparagus tips, lobster quenelles and cauliflower buds.

Hortensia: Cr. Hortense: Cream of chicken, garnished with asparagus tips, pearls of carrots and chicken quenelles.

Hotel-keeper Style: Cr. à la hôtelière: Purée of green beans, lentils and potatoes, cohered with cream, garnished with croûtons and chervil.

Housewife Soup: P. à la bonne-femme: Purée of potatoes, leeks, lettuce and cucumber, mellowed with milk, garnished with croûtons.

I

Ilona: Cr.: purée of fresh green peas, blended with cream of chicken, served in cups, topped just before serving with unsweetened whipped cream, sprinkled with paprika.

Imperial: V. à l'impériale: rice cream blended with velouté, bound with cream and egg yolks, garnished with cubes of almond milk royal.

Imperial: P. à l'impériale: rich chicken consommé, thickened with tapioca, bound with cream and egg yolks.

Imperator: Cr. Cream of pheasant flavored with morels, garnished with goose liver and pheasant quenelles, strips of truffles and cubes of royal.

Indian Soup: V. à l'indienne: velouté of chicken, flavored with curry, blended with coconut milk and cream, garnished with rice.

Irma: V.: chicken velouté, garnished with curried chicken quenelles and asparagus tips.

J

Jackson: Pr. Purée of potatoes and flageolets, thickened with tapioca, garnished with strips of leeks.

Jacobine: P.: brown game soup, garnished with game quenelles and royal with Madeira wine.

Janin: Pr. Purée of white haricot beans, carrots and leeks, garnished with croûtons.

Japanese Soup: P. à la japonaise: purée of stachy (crosnes, japanese artichokes), blended with velouté, garnished with croûtons.

Jacqueline: V. Fish velouté, garnished with asparagus tips, pearls of carrots, peas and rice.

Jean Bart: V.: rich fish velouté, garnished with diced tomatoes, quenelles of brill, strips of leek and macaroni.

Jeanette: V.: purée of salsify, blended with veal velouté, garnished with diced chicken and rice.

Jenny Lind: Cr.: cream of chicken, garnished with sago.

Josephine: P. Purée of green peas blended with sago consommé, garnished with strips of vegetables.

Juanita: V.: cream of rice, blended with velouté, garnished with diced tomatoes and quenelles mixed with sieved hard-boiled egg yolks.

Jubilee: P. jubilé: same as Balvais, q. v.

Julius Cesar: V. Jules César: light game soup, blended with purée of hazel-hen, garnished with strips of hazel-hen, mushrooms and truffles.

Jussieu: V.: velouté of chicken, garnished with strips of chicken and chicken quenelles.

K

Kempinski: P. Purée of green peas blended with purée of carrots, garnished with rice.

Knickerbocker: P.: purée of white haricot beans, blended with velouté, garnished with tapioca and croûtons.

L

Lady Morgan: V.: velouté of chicken and cream of rice, garnished with diced chicken and cockscombs.

Lady Simone: Cr. Dame Simone: Very rich lettuce cream soup, garnished with shredded sorrel and Nizam pearls; small gratinated poached eggs served separately.

Lamballe: Pr. Purée of green peas, garnished with tapioca.

Languedoc Style: P. à la languedocienne: Green pea soup, garnished with small slices of vegetables and chervil.

Lavallière: V.: chicken velouté blended with purée of celery, garnished with cubes of celery royal; profiterolles stuffed with purée of chicken served separately.

Ledoyen: V.: purée of flageolets, blended with velouté, garnished with croûtons.

Leek Soup: Cr. de poireaux: purée of leeks blended with cream sauce, mellowed with cream, garnished with croûtons.

Lejeune: Cr.: cream of chicken, garnished with sago.
Lenclos: Cr.: cream of chicken, blended with purée of crayfish, garnished with pearl barley.
Lentil Soup: Cr. de lentilles: purée of lentils, blended with cream sauce, mellowed with cream, garnished with lentils.
— — **Bavarian:** P. de lentilles à la bavaroise: Purée of lentilles cooked with bacon, garnished with slices of smoked sausage.
— — **German:** P. de lentilles à l'allemande: lentil soup, mellowed with cream, garnished with diced bacon and slices of Frankfurters.
— — **Russian:** P. de lentilles à la russe: lentil soup, blended with purée of knob celery, onions and leeks, garnished with diced root vegetables and small slices of poached sturgeon.
— — **with Vegetables:** P. Conti à la brunoise: lentil soup, blended with butter, garnished with braised diced vegetables.
— — **with Vermicelli:** P. Conti Clermont: lentil soup, garnished with vermicelli and fried rings of onions.
Lettuce, Cream of: Cr. de laitue: purée of lettuce, blended with cream of chicken, garnished with shredded lettuce.
Liége Game Soup: V. à la liégoise: purée of fieldfare and rice, thickened with brown bread, garnished with strips of fieldfare.
Lisette: Cr.: cream of celery, garnished with strips of truffles.
Lison: Cr.: cream of celery and rice, garnished with Japan pearls or sago.
Lithuanian: P. à la lithuanienne: potato soup, garnished with diced knob celery, shredded sorrel, sliced sausage, and hard-boiled eggs dipped in bread crumbs and fried; sour cream served separately.
Little Duke: Cr. Petit-duc: purée of woodcock, blended with purée of goose liver, blended with cream, flavored with cognac, garnished with strips of woodcock and woodcock royal.
Lobster, Bretonish: P. de homard à la bretonne: Purée of lobster mixed with rich fish velouté, garnished with diced lobster and lobster quenelles.
Londonderry: V.: velouté of veal and rice, flavored with mushrooms and white wine, bound with cream and egg yolks, garnished with diced turtle meat.
Longchamps: P. Purée of green peas, garnished with shredded sorrel, vermicelli and chervil.
Longueville: Pr.: purée of green peas, garnished with shredded sorrel and spaghetti.
Louisette: Cr.: cream of celery, garnished with green peas, strips of chicken and truffle.
Lucullus: V.: velouté of chicken, bound with cream and egg yolks, garnished with chicken and truffle quenelles, cockscombs and cocks' kidneys.
Lyonese Soup: V. à la lyonnaise: velouté of chicken, garnished with cubes of chestnut royal.

M

Macdonald: V.: velouté of chicken, blended with purée of calf's brains, flavored with Sherry, garnished with diced cucumber.

Mac-Mahon: V.: velouté of veal and purée of calf's brain, garnished with diced cucumbers and calf's brain.

Magdalena: Cr. Madeleine: purée of white haricot beans and onion, blended with velouté of artichokes, garnished with sago.

Magellan: P.: purée of partridge, flavored with Madeira, garnished with croûtons.

Maintenon: Cr.: cream of chicken, garnished with braised, diced root vegetables.

Majordomo: Cr. majordome: pureé of lentils, blended with cream, garnished with chicken quenelles and chervil.

Malakoff: Pr.: purée of potatoes, blended with tomato soup, garnished with shredded spinach.

Malmsbury: V.: rich velouté of fish, garnished with pieces of pike, diced lobster and bearded mussels.

Mancelle: P.: purée of chestnuts and celery, blended with purée of game, garnished with strips of partridge.

Marchals: Cr. à la maréchale: cream of chicken, garnished with asparagus tips, diced chicken and truffles.

Marcilly: V.: purée of peas and chicken velouté, garnished with chicken quenelles and Nizam pearls.

Margaret: V. Marguérite: Velouté of barley, garnished with chicken quenelles and croûtons.

Maria: Cr. Purée of white haricot beans, blended with cream, garnished with diced carrots and turnips and chervil.

Marianne: Pr.: purée of potatoes and pumpkin, blended with cream, garnished with shredded lettuce and sorrel and croûtons browned with cheese.

Marie Antoinette: V.: purée of asparagus, blended with velouté, garnished with cubes of asparagus royal.

Marie Louise: V.: velouté of chicken and pearl barley, garnished with pearl barley and macaroni.

Maria Stuart: V.: velouté of chicken and barley, garnished with pearl barley and small balls of root vegetables

Market-gardeners Style: P. à la maraichère: Purée of green peas and onions, garnished with noodles and button onions.

Marquise: V.: velouté of chicken and rice, garnished with shredded lettuce and peas.

Masséna: P. Purée of pheasant, mellowed with cream, garnished with diced chestnut royal.

Martha: V.: velouté of chicken and purée of onion, garnished with chicken quenelles stuffed with braised diced vegetables.

Mathilda: V. Mathilde: velouté of cucumber, blended with cream of rice, garnished with small balls of cucumber.

Mathurine: V.: rich velouté of fish, garnished with salmon quenelles.

Medicis: Pr.: purée of green peas, blended with purée of carrots, garnished with shredded sorrel and chervil.

Médicis: P.: brown game soup, blended with tomato purée, garnished with game quenelles and macaroni; grated Parmesan cheese served separately.

Meissonier: Pr.: purée of onions, diluted with mutton velouté, garnished with diced lean mutton and croûtons.

Memphis: Cr.: cream of artichokes, garnished with diced artichoke bottoms and cubes of artichoke royal.

Mercédès: V.: velouté of chicken, blended with purée of artichokes, garnished with diced artichoke bottoms and chicken.

Metternich: P. Purée of pheasant, garnished with strips of pheasant meat and cubes of artichoke royal.

Mignon: Cr.: purée of shrimps, blended with fish velouté, cohered with cream, garnished with shrimp tails, fish quenelles and pearls of truffle.

Mikado: V.: purée of crosnes (stachy), blended with velouté, mellowed with milk, garnished with Japan pearls.

Milanese: Cr. à la milanaise: cream of chicken, blended with purée of tomatoes, garnished with strips of ham, truffle and mushrooms and diced macaroni; grated Parmesan cheese served separately.

Millers Soup: V. à la meunière: velouté of fish, bound with cream and egg yolks, garnished with strips of white fish and croûtons.

Miramont: P.: velouté of chicken, blended with purée of potatoes, bound with cream and egg yolks, garnished with croûtons.

Mistinguette: P.: purée of green peas, blended with chicken consommé, thickened with tapioca.

Modena: V. Modène: purée of spinach, blended with velouté, garnished with croûtons.

Mogador: V.: velouté of chicken, blended with purée of goose liver, garnished with fine strips of chicken, ox tongue and truffles.

Molière: Cr.: purée of green peas, blended with light cream sauce and cream, garnished with diced calf's sweetbread, asparagus tips and cockscombs.

Mongolian Soup: P. mongole: purée of yellow split peas, blended with tomato soup, garnished with strips of root vegetables.

Monte Christo: Cr. Cream of chicken and young nettle shoots, garnished with strips of mushrooms and truffles.

Montespan: V.: purée of asparagus, blended with velouté, garnished with tapioca and green peas.

Montesquieu: Cr.: cream of cucumber, blended with mushroom velouté, garnished with diced cucumber.

Montglas: Cr.: cream of chicken, garnished with diced boletus and truffles.

Montmorency: Cr.: cream of chicken mixed with grated Parmesan cheese, garnished with shredded lettuce, vermicelli and stuffed chicken wings.

Montorgeuil: V.: velouté of chicken, garnished with diced root vegetables, shredded sorrel and chervil.

Montpensier: Pr.: purée of cauliflower, blended with cream of rice, garnished with croûtons.

Montreuil: V.: velouté of chicken, garnished with chicken quenelles with spinach adorned at the last minute with a ring of tomato sauce.

Morrel Soup: V. de morilles: velouté of morrels, garnished with sliced morels and croûtons.

Mozart: Pr. Purée of white haricot beans and tomatoes, garnished with croûtons.

Mulligatawny Soup: curried cream of chicken, garnished with rice and diced chicken.

Musart: Cr. Purée of flageolets, blended with cream, garnished with flageolets.

Mussel Soup Rigo: P. de moules R.: velouté of fish and mussels, seasoned with paprika, garnished with bearded mussels.

N

Nanette: P.: chicken soup mixed with cream of tomatoes, garnished with peas, green beans cut in lozenge shape and strips of truffles.

Navarin: Cr.: purée of green peas, garnished with crayfish tails, green peas and blanched chopped parsley.

Navarra: Cr. à la navarraise: cream of tomato, garnished with vermicelli, grated cheese served separately.

Nelson: Cr.: cream of smelts, blended with lobster butter, garnished with rice and lobster quenelles.

Nelusko: V.: velouté of chicken, blended with filbert butter, garnished with chicken quenelles mixed with ground filberts.

Nemours: P.: purée of potatoes and mushrooms, mellowed with milk, garnished with tapioca and strips of mushrooms.

Nesselrode: P.: purée of woodcock and chestnuts, garnished with woodcock quenelles and croûtons.

Nice Soup: P. à la nissarde: vegetable marrow soup, garnished with tapioca.

Nimese Soup: V. à la nîmoise: velouté of fish, blended with purée of tomatoes, garnished with croûtons.

Nimrod: P.: light game soup, flavored with Sherry, garnished with profiterolles stuffed with purée of game.

Nivernaise Soup: P.: purée of carrots, blended with purée of turnips, garnished with diced root vegetables.

Noblemans Style: P. Gentilhomme: Purée of lentils and partridge, flavored with Madeira, garnished with partridge quenelles and truffle balls.

Norman Soup: P. à la normande: purée of potatoes, white haricot beans, leeks and turnips, mellowed with milk and cream, garnished with chervil.

Norvegian: P. à la norvegienne: purée of cabbage turnips, blended with velouté, garnished with strips of red beetroot.

O

Oatmeal Soup: oatmeal cooked in beef stock, blended with cream and egg yolks.

Okra Soup: purée of okra (gombos) and tomatoes, garnished with croûtons.

Onion Soup: V. Soubise: purée of onions, blended with veal velouté, bound with cream and egg yolks, garnished with croûtons.

Orléans: Cr.: cream of chicken, garnished with chicken quenelles, blended with purée of crayfish, and chicken quenelles with fine herbs.

Orloff: Cr.: cream of cucumber and onions, garnished with strips of truffle and diablotins.

Oxalis, Cream of: Cr. d'oxalis: purée of oxalis, blended with light cream sauce, finished off with cream.

Ox-tail Soup: P. de queues de boeuf: brown ox-tail soup, flavored with Madeira, garnished with diced ox-tail and root vegetables.

Oyster: V. aux huîtres: fish velouté with oyster liquor and white wine, garnished with poached, bearded oysters.

— **Cancal Style:** V. à la cancalaise: rich fish velouté flavored with oyster liquor, garnished with poached bearded oysters and fish quenelles.

P

Palestinian: Pr. palestine: purée of Jerusalem artichokes, mellowed with milk, garnished with croûtons.

Paquita: P.: purée of green peas, garnished with sago and diced tomatoes.

Parisian: Cr. à la parisienne: purée of potatoes and leeks, blended with veloutée of veal, bound with cream, garnished with croûtons.

Parmentier: Pr.: purée of potatoes and leeks, garnished with croûtons and chervil.

Patti: V.: purée of artichokes, blended with velouté, garnished with diced artichoke bottoms.

Pavillon: V.: purée of watercress and crosnes, blended with chicken velouté, garnished with diced celery and carrots.

Pea Soup with Crusts: Pr. aux croûtons: Purée of yellow split peas cooked with root vegetables, onions and ham bones, garnished with fried croûtons.

— — **German:** Löffelerbsen: Soup of yellow split peas cooked with pig's ears, not strained, garnished with diced pig's ear, diced fried bacon and croûtons.

— — **Greek:** P. de pois à la grecque: purée of green peas, diluted with mutton stock, garnished with diced root vegetables and lean mutton.

— — **with Mint:** Pr. de pois à la menthe: Purée of green peas cooked with mint, garnished with chopped mint.

— — **Polish:** P. de pois à la polonaise: Green pea soup, garnished with strips of red beetroot, knob celery, leeks and onions.

Peruvian Soup: Cr. à la péruvienne: purée of oxalis, blended with light cream sauce and cream, garnished with croûtons.

A. **Peter the Great:** P. Pierre-le-Grand: purée of hazel-hen blended with mushroom velouté, garnished with strips of carrots and knob celery.

B. **Peter the Great:** V. Pierre—le—Grand: purée of knob celery (celeriac), blended with velouté, bound with egg yolks and cream, garnished with diced knob celery.

Pheasant Soup Lucullus: Cr. de faisan L.: cream of pheasant blended with purée of goose liver, flavored with Port, garnished with pheasant quenelles and pearls of truffle; tiny puff pastry patties stuffed with purée of pheasant served separately.

Pimontese Soup: P. à la piémontaise: chicken velouté, blended with purée of tomatoes, garnished with diced chicken and macaroni.

Pomeranian: P. à la poméranienne: Purée of white haricot beans diluted with velouté of goose, flavored with marjoram, parsley and chervil, garnished with diced goose meat.

Pompadour: P. tomato soup, blended with cream, garnished with sago and shredded lettuce.

Potato Soup, Saxon: P. de pommes de terre à la saxonne: purée of potatoes, garnished with vermicelli.

Portuguese Soup: P. portugaise: purée of tomatoes, garnished with rice.

Princess Soup: Cr. à la princesse: cream of chicken, blended with cream of asparagus, garnished with asparagus tips and diced chicken.

Pumpkin Soup: P. de potiron: purée of pumpkin, mellowed with milk, garnished with croûtons.

Purslane Soup: Cr. de pourpier: purée of potatoes and purslane blended with cream, garnished with shredded purslane leaves.

Q

Quebec: same as Maria (q. v.).

Queens Soup: Cr. à la reine: cream of chicken and rice, garnished with diced chicken.

Queen Hortense: Cr. Reine Hortense: cream of chicken, blended with purée of asparagus, garnished with tapioca and asparagus tips.

— **Margot:** Cr. Reine Margot: cream of chicken, flavored with almond milk, garnished with chicken quenelles with pistachios.

Quirinal: P. Purée of pheasant, flavored with Sherry, garnished with strips of pheasant and truffles.

R

Rachel: Pr. Purée of peas and sorrel, blended with rice velouté, garnished with rice and croûtons.

Récamier: Cr.: cream of pigeon, garnished with asparagus tips.

Regency: V. à la régence: Barley and chicken velouté, blended with crayfish butter, garnished with crayfish quenelles, cockscombs and barley.

Rice Cream Soup: Cr. de riz: velouté, blended with rice cream, mixed with cream, garnished with rice.

— **Soup, Spanish:** V. de riz à l'espagnole: velouté of rice, garnished with diced chicken, small glazed onions and diced tomatoes.

Rich Soup: Cr. à la riche: cream of chicken, flavored with truffle essence, garnished with pearls of truffle and strips of chicken.

Rigoletto: Pr. Purée of green peas, garnished with shredded spinach and diablotins.

Rohan: P.: purée of plover, garnished with soft boiled or poached plovers' egg and game croûtons.

Romeo: Cr.: cream of potatoes, blended with purée of onion, garnished with diced ham, boiled egg white and chervil.

Rossini: V.: velouté of chicken, blended with truffled goose liver patty butter garnished with chicken quenelles with goose liver.

Rouenais: Cr. à la rouennaise: Purée of lentils diluted with duck velouté, garnished with croûtons.

Roumanille: Cr.: cream of onion, garnished with vermicelli; grated cheese served separately.

Royan: Pr. Purée of cauliflower, garnished with tapioca.

Rubens: Cr.: cream of rice, blended with white onion purée, garnished with diced mushrooms; grated Parmesan cheese served separately.

Rumford: P.: purée of yellow split peas, garnished with pearl barley, diced potatoes and diced fried bacon.

Rustic Soup: P. à la campagnarde: vegetable soup, blended with purée of haricot beans and leeks, garnished with diced carrots, green beans and peas.

S

Saint-Cloud: P.: purée of fresh green peas and lettuce, garnished with shredded lettuce, croûtons and chervil.

St. Cyr: P. Purée of potatoes, turnips and cauliflower, garnished with buds of cauliflower and green beans cut in lozenge shape.

St. Georges: V.: purée of hare, blended with velouté of mushrooms, flavored with red wine, garnished with strips of hare, mushrooms and truffles.

Saint-Germain: Pr. Purée of fresh green peas, garnished with green peas and chervil.

St. Hubert: Pr.: brown game soup with venison, chestnuts and lentils, blended with cream, a little gooseberry jelly added, garnished with strips of truffles.

St. John: Cr. St. Jean: Rich cream of fish, garnished with fried fish quenelles.

St. Louis: Cr.: cream of tomatoes, garnished with tapioca and chicken quenelles.

Saint-Malo: V. Velouté of fish, garnished with shrimps and fish quenelles.

St. Marceau: Pr. Purée of green peas and leeks, garnished with strips of leeks and shredded lettuce.

St. Martin: Pr.: purée of lentils and potatoes, garnished with croûtons.

St. Sebastian: Pr.: purée of tomatoes, garnished with strips of green peppers and truffle.

Salsify, Cream of: Cr. de salsifis: purée of salsify, blended with light cream sauce, mixed with cream, garnished with croûtons.

Savoyard: Pr. à la savoyarde: purée of oxalis, blended with potato soup, garnished with slices of French bread, sprinkled with cheese and gratinated.

Schönbrunn: V.: purée of pheasant, blended with velouté, bound with cream and egg yolks, flavored with Sherry and lemon juice, seasoned with Cayenne pepper.

Sevigné: Cr.: purée of lettuce, blended with cream of chicken, garnished with shredded lettuce and chicken quenelles.

Shepherds Soup: P. à la bergère: purée of white haricot beans, potatoes, onions and leeks, garnished with shredded tarragon and croûtons.

Shepherdess Soup: Pr. à la pastourelle: Purée of potatoes, leeks, onions and field mushrooms, mellowed with milk, garnished with sliced field mushrooms and small diced sauted potatoes.

Shrimp Soup: V. de crevettes: fish velouté blended with purée of shrimps, garnished with shrimps, quenelles of fish, green peas and truffle pearls.

— — **Norman:** V. de crevettes à la normande: fish velouté, blended with purée of shrimps, garnished with shrimps and oysters.

Sicilian: P. à la sicilienne: purée of tomatoes, thickened with tapioca, garnished with croûtons.

Sicilian: Cr. sicilienne: purée of froglegs, blended with light cream sauce, mixed with cream, flavored with white wine and lemon juice.

Sigurd: P.: purée of potatoes and tomatoes, garnished with chicken quenelles and diced green peppers.

Silver Soup: P. argenté: same as Parmentier, garnished with tapioca.

Simone: Cr. Purée of white haricot beans blended with cream, garnished with diced vegetables.

Snail Soup: V. d'escargots: fish velouté, blended with snails cooked in white wine, flavored with horseradish, strained, garnished with diced snails, fish quenelles and chopped fine herbs.

Soisson Style: Cr. à la soissonaise: Cream of white haricot beans, garnished with chervil.

Solferino: P.: purée of potatoes, carrots, leeks and tomatoes, cohered with butter, garnished with small balls of potato, green beans cut in lozenge shapes and chervil.

Sorrel Soup: P. d'oseille: purée of sorrel, blended with velouté, mixed with cream, garnished with croûtons.

Spanish Soup: Cr. espagnole: purée of tomatoes, blended with cream of rice and onions, garnished with rice.

Sport Soup: P.: potato soup, mellowed with butter, garnished with shredded sorrel, vermicelli and chervil.

Stamboul: Cr.: cream of rice, blended with purée of tomatoes, garnished with fried croûtons shaped like half moons.

Steward: P.: purée of lentils and partridge, flavored with ham and herbs, garnished with partridge quenelles.

Sultana: Cr. sultane: cream of chicken and almond milk, blended with pistachio butter, garnished with half moon shaped chicken quenelles decorated with truffle stars.

Surette: Cr.: cream of chicken, garnished with shredded sorrel; tiny puff pastry patties stuffed with asparagus tips served separately.

Susanne: Cr. Suzanne: cream of cucumber, blended with purée of fresh green peas, garnished with chopped hard-boiled egg yolks.

Susie: Cr. Suzon: cream of green peas topped at the last minute with unsweetened whipped cream, garnished with a small poached egg.

Suzette: V.: velouté of mushrooms, blended with purée of watercress, garnished with green beans cut like lozenges.

Sweet Potato Soup: P. de patates: purée of sweet potatoes, blended with purée of fresh tomatoes, diluted with veal stock, garnished with sago.

T

Tegetthoff: Pr. Purée of green peas, garnished with white asparagus tips.

Theresa: V. Thérèse: Purée of white haricot beans diluted with velouté, garnished with tapioca, strips of chicken and leek.

Tomato, American Cream of: Cr. de tomates à l'américaine: cream of tomatoes, blended with crayfish bisque, garnished with tapioca.

— **Soup, Chicago:** P. Tomato soup, garnished with sago, tarragon and croûtons.

— — **with Noodles:** fresh tomatoes sweated with mirepoix, thickened with roux or cornstarch, moistened with white stock, cooked, seasoned with salt and a little sugar, strained and garnished with noodles cooked separately.

Toulousian: V. à la toulousaine: velouté of chicken, blended with essence of mushrooms, garnished with chicken quenelles, diced goose liver, cockscombs, cocks' kidneys and diced truffles.

Tours Style: V. à la tourangelle: Purée of green beans and flageolets, diluted with velouté, garnished with lozenge shaped green beans and small flageolets.

Trouville Style: V. à la trouvillaise: velouté of fish blended with shrimp butter, garnished with shrimps.

Tsar: P. du tsar: hazel-hen soup, blended with purée of goose liver, flavored with essence of truffle, garnished with strips of truffles cooked in Madeira.

Tsarina: V. à la czarine: purée of hazel-hen, blended with velouté of celery, garnished with strips of knob celery.

Turenne: P.: same as Parmentier with diced cooked bacon.

Tyrolese: P. à la tyrolienne: purée of green peas, lettuce, sorrel and cucumber, garnished with croûtons of brown bread.

V

Valois: Pr. Purée of pheasant, garnished with green peas and pheasant quenelles.

Van Duzer: P.: purée of tomatoes, garnished with pearl barley.

Véfour: Cr.: cream of chicken, blended with tomato purée, garnished with tapioca and chicken quenelles.

Vegetable Marrow Soup: Cr. de courgettes: purée of vegetable marrow, blended with thin Béchamel and cream, garnished with croûtons.

— **Soup, Scotch:** purée of knob celery, potatoes, carrots, turnips, leeks and yellow split peas cooked in mutton broth, garnished with diced mutton and pearl barley.

Velvet Soup: P. velours: purée of carrots, blended with consommé thickened with tapioca.

Venetian: Cr. à la vénitienne: cream of chicken, garnished with raviolis, stuffed with spinach.

Verneuil: P. Purée of green peas blended with cream of barley, garnished with royal, diced carrots and mushrooms.

Victoria: V.: velouté of fish, blended with cream of rice, purée of lobster and tomatoes, garnished with croûtons.

Village Soup: P. Purée of potatoes and leeks, mellowed with milk, garnished with strips of spaghetti.

Villars: P.: purée of artichokes, blended with purée of flageolets and onions, garnished with croûtons.

Vintager: Cr. vigneronne: purée of pumpkin, white haricot beans and leeks, flavored with red wine, garnished with fried croûtons of brown bread.

Vintimille: bisque of crayfish, garnished with tapioca and crayfish tails.

Vivian: Cr. Viviane: cream of chicken, garnished with diced artichoke bottoms, truffles and carrots.

Voisin: Cr.: cream of chicken, garnished with diced spring vegetables, green beans and peas.

Vuillemot: P. Purée of white haricot beans and light Béchamel, garnished with rice and shredded sorrel.

W

Waldèze: P.: purée of fresh tomatoes, blended with consommé, thickened with tapioca, garnished with diced tomatoes; grated Parmesan mixed with Swiss cheese served separately.

Washington: Cr.: cream of sweet corn, garnished with grains of sweet corn, flavored with whisky and Port when serving.

Watercress Soup: V. à la cressonière: purée of watercress and potatoes blended with velouté, garnished with chervil.

Wellington: P.: purée of knob celery, blended with chicken velouté, garnished with rice.

White Lady: V. Dame Blanche: Velouté of chicken, flavored with almond milk, garnished with diced chicken meat and chicken quenelles.

White Friars Soup: V. à la carmelite: rich fish velouté, garnished with whiting quenelles and strips of sole fillets.

Wilhelmina: Cr. Wilhelmine: cream of chicken and rice, garnished with asparagus tips and strips of carrots and truffles.

Windham: P.: Purée of sweet corn, thickened with tapioca, garnished with rice.

Windsor: P.: cream of rice, blended with velouté of veal, flavored with turtle herbs, garnished with strips of calf's feet and chicken quenelles blended with hard-boiled egg yolks.

Wholesome Soup: P. de santé: Purée of potatoes and sorrel, blended with cream, garnished with shredded sorrel and chervil.

Woronzow: Cr.: cream of chicken with purée of goose liver, flavored with Madeira, garnished with strips of celery and carrots and raviolis stuffed with purée of goose liver.

X Y

Xavier: V.: cream of rice, blended with chicken velouté, garnished with diced chicken and royal.

Yvette: Cr. lobster purée blended with fish velouté, garnished with fish quenelles, diced lobster and truffles.

Cold Clear and Thick Soups

Cold soups are greatly appreciated on hot summer days and for supper partys. The stock or broth for these soups must be made of first class material, well skimmed and degreased. It is not admissible to add gelatine to consommés; good chicken or other broth containing sufficient gelatinous matter to jellify the consommé when chilled. Jellied to much consommés are not pleasing to the palate. Thick soups must always be well seasoned otherwise they will taste insipid when chilled; they ought to have the consistency of rich but not to thick cream.

Cold Clear Soups: Consommés froids et en gelée.

— **with Celery Flavor:** à l'essence de celery: rich beef broth with celery added to clarification.

Cold Clear Soup

— **with Gold Leaves:** aux pailletes d'or: rich chilled and lightly jellied chicken consommé with shredded gold leaf added; served in cups.

— **Love Apple Jelly:** Gelée aux pommes d'amour: cold Portuguese consommé flavored with Marsala.

— **Madrilene, Jellied:** Madrilène en gelée: rich chicken broth with plenty of raw tomatoes and a few red peppers added to clarification; served well chilled and lightly jellied.

— **with Morel Essence:** à l'essence de morilles: rich beef broth with soaked dried or fresh morels added to clarification.

— **with Mushroom Essence:** à l'essence de champignons: rich beef broth with plenty of mushroom waste added to clarification.

— **with Partridge Essence:** à l'essence de perdreau: rich game broth strongly flavored with roasted partridge bones and carcasses added to clarification. Cold pheasant and quail soups are prepared the same way.

— **Portuguese, Jellied:** Portugaise en gelée: purée of raw tomatoes added to rich chicken consomme, boiled slowly with lid on and strained with light pressure through an etamine cloth.

— **with Red Peppers:** aux piements doux: rich beef broth with purée of raw or preserved red peppers added to clarification.

— **with Tarragon Flavor:** à l'essence d'estragon: rich beef broth with a few tarragon leaves drawn out in the hot but not boiling soup.

— **with Truffle Essence:** à l'essence de truffes: rich beef or chicken broth with truffle peels added to clarification.

— **with Wine:** au vin: rich chicken consommé flavored with wine, the wine added when soup is perfectly chilled. Suitable wines are: with Madeira: au vin de madère; with Port: au porto; with Sherry: au Xérès; with Marsala: au vin de Marsala; with Malvasier: au vin de Malvoisie.

Cold Thick Soups: Potages liés froids.

— **Chicken, Cream of:** Crème de volaille: white roux moistened with strong chicken broth, seasoned, bunch of herbs added, cooked slowly, degreased, strained, cooled slowly stirring occasionally, strained again, finished off with thick cream and served well chilled.

— **Chicken Cream with Port:** Crème de volaille au porto: same soup flavored with white Port.

— **Chicken Cream Sultan:** Crème de volaille à la sultane: thick chicken cream with hazelnut milk and pistachio purée added, strained, chilled and finished off with heavy cream.

— **Crayfish, Cream of:** Crème d'écrevisses: crayfish prepared the American way, pounded in mortar, rubbed through a sieve, mixed with cream of chicken, strained, seasoned sharply with paprika, chilled, flavored with brandy, finished off with heavy cream.

— **Duck, Cream of:** Crème de caneton: prepared like cream of chicken with strong broth made of the bones and carcass of roast duck sweated in butter with mirepoix but not browned; flavored with Sherry, finished off with heavy cream.

Cold Thick Soup

— **Duquinha,** Cream: Crème Duquinha: cream of chicken with 20 % purée of fresh tomatoes and 20 % purée of red peppers added, chilled and finished off with heavy cream.

— **Margot,** Cream: Crème Margot: thick cream of chicken with almond milk added while still hot, chilled, finished off with heavy cream.

— **Mushroom, Cream of:** Crème de champignons: white roux moistened with strong veal stock, mushroom waste and essence added, seasoned, cooked slowly, strained, cooled, strained again and finished off with heavy cream.

— **Pigeon, Cream of:** Crème de pigeon: prepared like cream of chicken with rich pigeon broth.

— **Portuguese Chicken Cream:** Crème de vollaile à la portugaise: prepared like cream of chicken, when done a third of the amount purée of raw tomatoes added, strained, cooled, finished off with heavy cream.

— **Tomato, Cream of:** Crème de tomates: purée of raw fresh tomatoes boiled up with rich veal stock, thickened with arrow-root diluted with cream, boiled for a few minutes, seasoned, strained, chilled, mixed with cold tomato juice and finished off with heavy cream.

— **Vichysoise:** diced leeks and chopped onions simmered in butter until soft but not browned, diced potatoes added, seasoned with salt, cooked until potatoes are soft, strained through a sieve, brought to a boil with half cream and half milk, cooled stirring occasionally, strained again, finished off with heavy cream; served well chilled with chopped chives sprinkled on top.

National, Regional and Miscellaneous Soups

A

Abji l'Amid: Cold Potato Soup: a cold purée of potato soup, flavored with lemon juice. (Turkish)

Aïgo bouido: Garlic Soup: crushed garlic, and sage cooked in water with a little olive oil, seasoned with salt and pepper, strained, poured over slices of French bread dried in the oven. (French)

Aigo ménagère: Provençal Household Soup: sliced onions and leeks lightly fried in olive oil, diced tomatoes, crushed garlic, thick slices of potatoes, fennel and mixed herbs added, moistened with water, flavored with saffron and dried orange peel and boiled. Soup strained and poured over slices of French bread, the potatoes with poached eggs on top, sprinkled with chopped parsley served separately. (French)

Aïgo saou: Fish and Garlic Soup: pieces of fish, boiled in water with sliced onions, potatoes and tomatoes, seasoned with parsley, celery, bay leaves, salt and pepper, strongly flavored with garlic, the soup eaten with thin slices of French bread, moistened with olive oil, the fish is eaten separately, sometimes with aioli, garlic sauce (q. v.). (French)

Ajo blanco: Cold Garlic Soup: garlic and almonds pounded in a mortar with olive oil to a thick paste, moistened with water, seasoned with salt and pepper, small slices of bread added, served chilled. (Spanish)

Ajiaco Cubano: Cuban Soup: boiled salt pork, pickled pork and pork cooked with chick-peas, garlic, sliced egg-plant, sweet corn, diced pumpkin and potatoes, seasoned with saffron, salt and pepper. (Cuban)

Albigensian Soup: Soupe à l'albigeoise: calf's foot, ham, preserved goose, smoked sausage, diced carrots, turnips and leeks, shredded cabbage and lettuce and broad beans cooked in water in a special pot, served with thin slices of French bread. (French)

Al cuarto de hora: Mussel Soup: chopped onions, parsley, diced ham and rice sweated in butter, moistened with water and mussel liquor, seasoned, cooked, garnished with mussels, sprinkled with chopped hard-boiled eggs at serving. (Spanish)

American Soup: Potage à l'américaine: Half lobster and half tomato bisque garnished with diced lobster and tapioca.

Andalusian Chick-Pea Soup: Garbanzos à la Andaluza: chick-peas soaked over night, cooked with potherbs, seasoned with salt, saffron and Cayenne pepper, strained, sprinkled with crushed caraway seeds at serving. (Spanish)

Ardennes Soup: Soupe à l'ardennaise: sliced endives, leeks and potatoes, fried in butter, cooked slowly in milk, seasoned, thickened with butter, served with thin slices of French bread. (French)

Auvergne Pot Soup: Potée or Soupe à l'auvergnate: slices of carrots, turnips, leeks, potatoes and cabbage cooked in pig's head broth with a few lentils, garnished with diced pig's head and served with thin slices of rye bread. (French)

B

Balnamoon Skink: Chicken Soup: rich chicken broth, bound with egg yolks and milk, garnished with diced knob celery, green peas and shredded lettuce. (Irish)

Barcelonessa: Barcelona Mutton Soup: mutton broth, mixed with a little tomato purée, thickened with white bread crumbs fried in butter, garnished with small dumplings of mutton forcemeat, seasoned with salt, pepper and chopped parsley, mixed with eggs, turned in flour and baked in oil; sprinkle soup with chopped parsley and chervil. (Spanish)

Barszcz zimny czyli zupa: Cold Beetroot Soup: juice of pickled red beetroot and pickled cucumbers, boiled, thickened with semolina, bound with egg yolks and sour cream, seasoned, stirred on ice, served chilled with thick slices of hard-boiled eggs. (Polish)

Bier-Suppe: Beer Soup: light beer, boiled, thickened with brown roux, flavored with cinnamon, cardamom, lemon-peel, salt and sugar, strained and poured over small pieces of fried bread. (German)

Biskuitschöberl-Suppe: Biscuit Soup: mix butter with egg yolks, flour and milk, season with salt and nutmeg, fold in stiffly beaten whites of egg, fill batter in flat well greased pan and bake. Cut biscuit in lozenge shapes and serve as garnish for strong beef broth. (Austrian)

Boronia: Spanish Vegetable Soup: diced egg-plants, pumpkin and tomatoes, sweated in oil, moistened with water, strongly flavored with garlic, seasoned with salt, allspice and carraway seeds, cooked, rubbed through a sieve, thickened with breadcrumbs, colored with saffron. (Spanish)

Borschtsch polski: Polish Soup: roast duck cooked in rich beef broth, the broth strained, garnished with thin strips of red beetroot and shredded cabbage; slices of the roast duck's breast, beef, pellmenes, juice of red beetroot and sour cream served separately.

— **sjeloni:** Green Borschtsch: same as Borschtschock, shredded cabbage replaced by shredded spinach, sorrel and lettuce and not colored or served with beetroot juice. (Russian)

— **Skobeleff:** same as Russian National Soup with addition of diced potatoes, diced salt pork, small fried sausages and meat balls (bitkis); small slices of fried bread served separately. (Russian)

Borschtschock: Russian National Soup: the foundation of this soup are shredded cabbage and strips of root vegetables and red beetroots. It may be cooked with or without beef, ham bones, hazel-hen, duck etc. and is allways colored with the raw juice of red beetroots and served with sour cream. (Russian)

— **flotski:** Navy Soup: same as Borschtschock but made with diced vegetables. (Russian)

Boston Clam Chowder: see New England Clam Chowder.

— **Fish Chowder:** sweat chopped onions, diced green peppers and knob celery in butter, moisten with fish stock, season with Cayenne pepper and herbs, add diced potatoes and finally milk; garnish with flaked cod- or other fish and chopped parsley, serve crackers separately.

Botwinja (Batwinja): Cold Herb Soup: purée of sorrel and young beetroot tops, mixed with kwass, seasoned with salt, pepper and sugar, garnished with strips of fresh cucumber, chopped tarragon, dill and fennel, a piece of ice on each plate; small pieces of cold cooked salmon or sturgeon and grated horseradish served separately. If no kwass is available, it may be replaced by acid white wine. (Russian)

Bouillabaisse: Marseille Fish Soup: John Dory, dragons' head, devil-fish, baudreuil, chapon and other firm fish cut in pieces, moistened with water and cooked with chopped onions, leeks, parsley, tomatoes, fennel green, saffron, bay leaves and olive oil, ten minutes later soft fish such as whiting and red mullet added, seasoned, cooked quickly and served with slices of French bread. (French)

Bourride: Mediterranean Fish Soup: small sea fish, cut in pieces, sautéd in butter with chopped onions, knob celery and crushed garlic, moistened with water and white wine, seasoned with salt, pepper and herbs, boiled and strongly flavored with garlic; soup garnished with diced boiled potatoes, fish served separately on pieces of fried bread. (French)

Bramborová polevká: Czech Potato Soup: sweat carrots, knob celery and shredded green cabbage in butter, moisten with stock and cook. Mix brown roux with beef stock, season with garlic, marjoram, salt and pepper, cook and strain. Garnish with the diced vegetables, plenty of diced boiled potatoes, diced mushrooms and diced fried salt pork. (Czech)

Brandkrapferlsuppe: Beef broth with fried Profiterolles: cream puff paste the size of a large pea, baked in hot fat, served as garnish for strong beef broth. (Austrian)

Busecca: Tripe Soup: chopped onions, strips of leeks, carrots, cabbage and celery, sweated in olive oil, soaked kidney beans added, moistened with white stock and boiled slowly; a few minutes before serving add thin strips of cooked tripe and at the last minute chopped bacon, sage garlic, parsley and diced tomatoes. (Italian)

Butternockerlsuppe: Dumpling Soup: small dumplings made of creamed butter, egg yolks, flour, sour cream, salt, pepper and the stiffly beaten whites, poached in water and served in rich beef broth. (Austrian)

C

Caldo española: Spanish Soup: pork, smoked meat, potatoes, turnips, carrots and cabbage boiled in water, seasoned, later on a piece of smoked Spanish sausage added. (Spanish)

Cancha Mexicana: Mexican Chicken Broth; sweat chopped onions and diced tomatoes in butter, add rice, moisten with chicken broth boil, season and garnish with diced chicken and chopped mint. (Mexican)

Cebolla española: Onion Soup: chopped onions, slightly fried in olive oil, moistened with white stock, seasoned, mixed with diced bread, cooked slowly. (Spanish)

Chanfaina: Spanish Liver Soup: boil calf's and hog's liver in slightly salted water until tender, sweat chopped onions, mint and parsley in olive oil, moisten with the liver stock, season with salt, paprika, caraway seeds, cinnamon and saffron, cook, add the livers cut in dices and sprinkle with breadcrumbs at serving. (Spanish)

Chicken Broth: the clear broth of fat hens boiled with celery, onions, leeks, carrots and spices, garnished with rice, diced vegetables and pieces of fowl. (English)

Chinese birds' nest soup: Salangane soup: nests of South Asian swallows cleaned, soaked and cooked in rich beef stock. Rich beef consommé flavoured with turtle herbs and Sherry, garnished with the shredded nests. (Chinese)

Chotodriece: Polish Cold Soup: heat juice of pickled cucumbers with leaven, blend with sour milk, strain and garnish with chopped red beet roots, slices of hard-boiled eggs, crayfish tails, chopped chives and dill, served cold with a piece of ice on each plate. (Polish)

Chicken and Clam Broth Bellevue: half clam and half chicken broth served with unsweetened whipped cream.

— **Gumbo Creole:** dice peppers, onions, ham, okra and tomatoes, sweat in butter and simmer till they are done, each batch separately if desired. Boil rice separately and dice the cooked chicken and garnish strong chicken broth with these ingredients.

Clam Broth: clams scrubbed, placed in saucepan with enough water to cover the shells, cooked with chopped onions, celery, parsley and salt until clams are done. Discard shells, separate hard meat and dice soft parts. Strain broth through a cloth, combine diced meat with broth and enhance with strong chicken broth or meat extract for flavor and color.

— **Chowder:** sweat chopped onions, salt pork, diced green peppers, smother with flour to thicken, add clam stock, season with salt, pepper and herbs, add diced potatoes, finally milk and diced tomatoes and garnish with diced clams.

Cocido Andaluz: Andalusian Pot Soup: soak chick-peas, put them in a large earthen pot with a piece of lean beef, a small piece of bacon, beef bones, a ham bone, moisten with water, boil for an hour, add green beans cut in halves, diced potatoes and pumpkins, chorizos (a spicy garlic sausage), a morcilla (sort of black sausage) and cook till done; shortly before serving mix with pounded garlic and green peppers and saffron; the soup is eaten first and the meat and vegetables afterwards. (Spanish)

Cock-a-Leeky: rich chicken and veal broth, garnished with strips of chicken and leeks and, often, with stewed prunes. (Scotch)

Crab Gumbo Creole: diced onions, green peppers, ham, celery and leeks sweated in butter, simmered until done, strong fish or white stock added, seasoned, garnished with shredded crabmeat or shrimps, boiled rice and diced tomatoes.

Cream of Corn and Onions: chopped onions and sweet corn sweated in butter, smothered with flour, white stock added, cooked blended with milk, strained, well seasoned and bound with cream and butter.

— of Corn Washington: diced onions, leeks and celery sweated in butter, sprinkled with flour, well blended; stewed corn, chicken or white stock added, simmered for an hour, strained, fresh whole kernels, finely diced red piementos, egg yolks and light cream added before serving.

Cucumber Soup: slices of peeled cucumbers, stewed in butter, moistened with white stock, seasoned, cooked, thickened with arrowroot, strained, thickened with egg yolks and milk, garnished with shredded sorrel.

D

Duyne tchorbassi: Beef Soup: beef broth, thickened with flour, mixed with water, garnished with diced beef, sprinkled with melted butter, mixed with paprika, at serving. (Turkish)

E

Ekshili tchorba: Mutton Soup: mutton broth, garnished with diced rather fat mutton, thickened with a mixture of flour, eggs, lemon juice and cold water. (Turkish)

F

Finnlandskaia: Finnish Soup: strong beef broth; slices of pancakes made with sour cream, mixed with grated parsley root, placed on small pieces of toast, sprinkled with grated cheese and gratinated served separately.

Fishmongers Soup: chopped onions, diced salt pork, green peppers and celery, sautéd in butter, moistened with strong fish stock, diced tomatoes and chopped herbs added, seasoned with Cayenne pepper, garnished with small pieces of boiled codfish; crushed crackers served separately.

Fleckerlsuppe: rich beef broth, garnished with small squares of noodles. (Austrian)

Frankfurter Bohnensuppe: Frankfurt Bean Soup: kidney beans soaked in water, boiled with diced potherbs, seasoned, when done mellowed with butter and garnished with sliced Frankfurters; not strained. (German)

Friar's Chicken: squab chickens, cut in four pieces, cooked in veal stock until they are tender, stock seasoned, bound with egg yolks, garnished with the chicken and plenty of chopped parsley. (English)

Fridattensuppe: rich beef broth, garnished with shreds of very thin unsweetened pancakes, sprinkled with chopped chives. (Austrian)

G

Ganslsuppe: Goose Soup: necks, wings, feet and gizzards of goose cooked in white stock, strained and thickened with white roux, seasoned and garnished with cauliflower buds, marrow dumplings and the giblets cut in small pieces. (Austrian)

Garbanzos à la Andaluza: Andalusian Chick-Pea Soup: chick-peas soaked over night, cooked with potherbs, seasoned with salt, saffron and Cayenne pepper, strained, sprinkled with crushed carraway seeds. (Spanish)

— **Madrilena:** Chick-pea Soup: purée of chick-peas, diluted with beef stock seasoned, garnished with croûtons. (Spanish)

Garbure à la béarnaise: Bearnese House-hold Soup: salt pork, preserved goose, carrots, turnips, potatoes, cabbage, fresh kidney beans and green beans cooked slowly in water with herbs and seasoning until done. Arrange sliced salt pork, goose and vegetables alternately in a baking dish, moisten with a little fast stock, sprinkle with grated cheese and gratinated. Pour strained soup in a soup tureen and serve vegetables at the same time. (French)

— **à la Paysanne:** Farmers Soup: sliced carrots, turnips, leeks, onions and potatoes, simmered in white stock, mashed, reduced, seasoned, spread on triangles of farmers bread, sprinkled with grated cheese, a little stock fat poured over and gratinated; served separately with rich beef broth. (French)

Gesinka: Vegetable and Barley Soup: strips of knob celery, carrots, onions and mushrooms, cooked in very little water with butter, rubbed through a sieve, mixed with beef broth, bound with sour cream and yolks of eggs, seasoned with salt and lemon juice, garnished with pearl barley. (Polish)

Giblet Soup: necks, wings and gizzards of chicken, sautéd in butter, smothered with flour, browned, moistened with white stock, cooked with celery and a bouquet of herbs, seasoned with salt and pepper, strained, garnished with rice, strips of celery and the giblets. (English)

Green Turtle Soup: very strong clear consommé flavored with basil, marjoram, rosemary, fennel, sage and allspice, Madeira or Sherry, garnished with the diced turtle meat.

H

Hamburger Aalsuppe: Hamburg Eel Soup: eel cut in convenient pieces and cooked in well seasoned stock; small pears peeled and quartered, simmered in white wine with lemon-peel and a pinch of sugar. Reserve eel and pear stock, strain and mix with strongbeef broth, slightly thickened with brown roux, garnished with finely diced carrots, leeks, parsley root and green peas; this soup should have a slightly sweet-sour taste. Put eel, pears and small flour dumplings in a soup tureen and pour over the soup. (German)

— **Krebssuppe:** Hamburg Crayfish Soup: crayfish sauted in butter with mirepoix, ignited with brandy, cooked in white stock with a little white wine. Tails broken out, shells pounded, sweated in butter, sprinkled with flour, moistened with the crayfish stock, boiled, seasoned, strained and garnished with green peas, small dumplings and crayfish tails. (German)

Hare Soup: trimmings and legs of hare sauted in butter, smothered with arrowroot, moistened with stock, seasoned and cooked; add the sliced liver 10 minutes before the soup is done. Strain and mix with purée made of trimmings and liver, flavor with an infusion of turtle herbs and Port shortly before serving and garnish with the diced meat of the legs. (English)

Hirnschöberlsuppe: Brain Soup: boiled cold calf's brain, strained, mixed with butter, egg yolks, bread crumbs and stiffly beaten whites, seasoned with salt, pepper and nutmeg, filled in a well greased pan, baked and cut in lozenges shape as garnish for rich beef broth. (Austrian)

Hochepot Flamande: Flemish Hotpot: pigs' feet, pigs' ears, salt pork, a piece of beef brisket and shoulder of mutton, cooked with coarsely sliced carrots, potatoes, leeks, onions and a quarter of cabbage, seasoned with salt and pepper. Pour soup and a part of the vegetables in a soup tureen and serve meat, the remaining vegetables and small poached pork sausages separately. (Belgian)

Hollandse Palingsoep: Dutch Eel Soup: sweat skinned eels, cut in convenient pieces and parboiled, in butter with chopped onions, leeks and the heads and trimmings of sea fish, fill up with water and white wine, season with salt, peppercorns and cloves and boil till fish is done. Take out the eel and reserve, strain fish stock, season with Cayenne pepper and thicken with egg yolks and a little butter. Put small thin slices of toast, strips of leeks, celery and parsley root and the eel in a soup tureen and pour over the hot soup. (Dutch)

Hrachová polevká: Czech Pea Soup: thicken beef stock with white roux, boil with onions, garlic and marjoram, season with pepper and blend with purée of yellow split peas, strain and garnish with diced pigs' ears, croûtons and chopped parsley. (Czecho-Slovakian)

Huevos a la Casera: Household Soup: boiling water, seasoned with salt, a little olive oil added, thickened with fresh white breadcrumbs, garnished with eggs poached in the soup. (Spanish)

Hungarian Fish Soup: salt pieces of fresh water-fish and put aside. Slightly brown chopped onions in butter, add diced tomatoes, moisten with water, boil and poach fish in the stock, thicken with rice flour, season and serve.

K

Kale Brose: beef broth cooked with beef jowl and kale, thickened with oatmeal, garnished with sippets. (Scotch)

Kalia: Polish Chicken Broth: chicken broth, flavored with the juice of pickled cucumbers, garnished with diced chicken, knob celery, carrots and parsley root. (Polish)

Kapustniak: Polish Saurkraut Soup: saurkraut cooked in water with marrow bones, a piece of pork and bacon, carrots, knob celery, parsley root, onions and pork sausages; thickened with roux, vegetables taken out, garnished with the diced meat, bacon and the sausages. (Polish)

Kidney Soup: sauté calf's kidneys in butter, moisten with brown stock, season, boil and thicken with brown roux. Pound kidneys, rub through a sieve, mix with the strained soup, season with Cayenne pepper, flavor with Madeira and garnish with slices of calves' kidneys sauted in butter just before soup is served. (English)

Kissela Tschorva: Serbian Fish Soup: cut hucho (huck) in small pieces, salt and let them stand for a while. Slice onions and green peppers, sweat in oil or lard, moisten with water, season and boil; poach fish in this stock, take out carefully, strain stock, bind with egg yolks and cream, garnish with rice and the pieces of hucho. (Jugoslavian)

Kolodnik: Polish Herb Soup: chopped boiled red beetroots and double as many blanched young beetroot tops, mixed with chopped chives and dill, blended with the juice of pickled cucumbers and sour cream or milk, seasoned, garnished with diced fresh cucumbers, hard-boiled eggs cut in quarters, crayfish tails, sliced lemons and, sometimes, small pieces of parboiled cold sturgeon, served with a piece of ice in each plate. (Polish)

Krapiwa: Nettle Soup: chopped onions sweated with young nettle shoots, moistened with beef broth, cooked with a piece of brisket; dice of brisket and pearl barley as garnish. (Russian)

L

Lebersuppe: Liver Soup: sliced onions, carrots, shallots, diced salt pork, thyme and bay leaves sweated in butter, mixed with sliced calf's liver, deglazed with white wine, moistened with brown sauce, cooked gently; liver pounded, rubbed through a sieve, diluted with the strained soup and beef stock, seasoned and garnished with croûtons. (Austrian)

Ledvinková polevká: Kidney Soup: sliced onions and potatoes sweated in lard, sprinkled with flour, moistened with white stock, seasoned with salt, pepper, paprika, caraway seeds and garlic, cooked slowly, rubbed through a sieve, garnished with sliced sauted calf's kidneys. (Czecho-Slovakian)

Litowski Soup: Lithuanian Soup: purée of potato soup, blended with sour cream, garnished with shredded sorrel, strips of knob celery and smoked goose breast, small fried pork sausages and half an egg, hard-boiled, dipped in egg and breadcrumbs and fried in lard. (Russian)

Lobster Chowder: gently simmer chopped onions, celery, salt pork, leeks and green peppers in butter, sprinkle heavily with flour to thicken, moisten with fish or white meat stock, add seasoning, bay leaves or sage and thyme and later diced potatoes and tomatoes, cook and garnish with diced lobster.

— **Gumbo:** sweat chopped onions, diced peppers and strips of ham in lobster butter, add white wine and fish or white stock, later okra and diced tomatoes; season, cook and garnish with diced lobster.

Louisiana Soup: Consommé à la lousiannaise: clear chicken broth garnished with cut okra, crabmeat, rice, diced shrimps or lobster and sweet peppers, colored with saffron.

M

Magyar gulyás leves: Goulash Soup: fry chopped onions in lard until pale brown, add diced beef the size of a nut, season with paprika, marjoram, crushed caraway seeds and salt, and simmer for a while. Moisten with water, add strips of red peppers and later on diced tomatoes and potatoes and cook; ten minutes before soup ist ready, add coarse strips of noodle dough. (Hungarian)

— **halleves:** Hungarian Fish Soup: chopped onions sweated in lard, sprinkled with flour, moistened with fish stock, seasoned with paprika, blended with sour cream, garnished with small pieces of fish and carps' roes and just before done, with pieces of torn-up noodle dough. (Hungarian)

Mallorquina: Fish Soup: chopped onions, sweated in olive oil, chopped tomatoes, garlic and parsley added, moistened with rich fish stock and white wine, seasoned, cooked and garnished with croûtons fried in oil. (Spanish)

Manhattan Clam Chowder: same as New England clam chowder, Worcestershire sauce left out, diced reddish tomatoes added, crushed crackers served separately.

Markknödlsuppe: Marrow Dumpling Soup: chopped beef marrow, slightly warmed, rubbed through a sieve, mixed with bread soaked in milk, eggs and flour, seasoned, shaped into small dumplings and boiled in salted water; garnish for rich beef broth.

Mille-Fanti: Bread Soup: mix fresh white bread crumbs with grated Parmesan cheese, eggs, salt, pepper and nutmeg, pour mixture in boiling beef broth, stir thoroughly with an egg whisk, cover and let boil very slowly for 8 minutes and stir again before serving. (Italian)

Minestra al pomodoro: Italian Tomato Soup sweat chopped onions and sliced garlic in oil, add tomatoes cut in pieces, mint, sweet basil, marjoram, salt and pepper, fill up with water and boil slowly, strain; garnish with rice and serve grated Parmesan cheese separately. (Italian)

Minestra Turinese: Turinese Soup: diced knob celery, leeks, green cabbage, ham and tomatoes sweated in oil, moistened with water or white stock, flavored with garlic and saffron, garnished with rice; grated Parmesan cheese served separately. (Italian)

— **Veneziana:** Venetian Soup: chopped salt pork, onions and cabbage, boiled in water with blanched calf's foot, calf's ears, liver and tomatoes, seasoned with salt, pepper, bay leaves, marjoram and allspice, strained, garnished with rice. (Italian)

Minestrone: Vegetable Soup: sweat sliced carrots, turnips, leeks, shredded cabbage, diced salt pork and tomatoes in oil, add crushed garlic, green peas and green beans, moisten with stock or water, season, boil, later on add rice or Italian paste and serve grated Parmesan cheese separately. (Italian)

Mulligatawny Soup: chopped onions and ham sautéd in butter, generously sprinkled with rice flour seasoned with curry powder, moistened with chicken broth, boiled slowly, strained, mellowed with cream, garnished with rice, diced chicken and vegetables; sometimes a chopped apple is added while cooking. (Anglo-Indian)

N

New England Clam Chowder: diced onions, leeks, green peppers, salt pork and potatoes, sautéd in butter, moistened with fish stock, seasoned with salt, pepper, curry powder, sage and thyme, diced clams, parsley; a little Worcestershire sauce added shortly before serving; crushed crackers served separately.

Nga Yenn Wo. Birds' nest soup: rice cooked for hours in water with dried onion and dried orange peel. Soaked and cleaned birds' nests, diced white chicken meat, Chinese sauce, salt and pepper added and cooked. Garnished with green onion sprouts and dried onion sprouts, served in Bowls. (Chinese)

O

Okroschka: Sour Soup: half fill a soup tureen with: sour cream blended with sour milk, diluted with kwass (semi-sparkling Russian beverage, obtained by fermenting malt, rye flour and sugar with water), seasoned with mustard, salt and pepper; add chopped roast veal, breast of hazelhen, ox tongue and ham, crayfish tails and a piece of ice, and sprinkle with chopped dill. (Russian)

— **is riba:** Cold Fish Soup: fry small pieces of firm fish, sturgeon, sterlet etc. in oil; when cold place in soup tureen, add diced lobster and crayfish tails, fill up with kwass, season with salt and pepper, serve chilled sprinkled with chopped chervil and tarragon. (Russian)

Olla Podrida: Spanish Pot Soup: calves' and pigs' feet, sheep trotters, pork, game and chick-peas boiled in water, seasoned with salt and pepper, garlic sausage (chorizo) added later on, all served in a special pot or the soup eaten first and the meat and vegetables later on. (Spanish)

Oyster Chowder: chopped onions, diced green peppers and okra sweated in butter, moistened with white stock, seasoned with salt and pepper, diced tomatoes added, thickened with arrowroot, garnished with bearded oysters.

P

Philadelphia Pepperpot: chopped onions, diced ham, knob celery, green peppers and leeks, sweated in butter, moistened with white stock, simmered slowly, bouquet of herbs and later on diced potatoes added, garnished with strips of cooked tripe, chopped parsley and small spätzle, seasoned with crushed white pepper.

Pigeon Soup: rich chicken broth cooked with pigeons and ham bones, garnished with diced vegetables and strips of pigeon.

Polewka: Polish Rye Soup: water, thickened with rye flour, seasoned, blended with cream. (Polish)

Polpetti: Italian Cheese Soup: mix beef broth with grated Parmesan cheese and garnish with Italian paste. (Italian)

Potato Chowder: chopped onions, diced salt pork, leeks and celery, sweated in butter, cooked in white stock, diced potatoes added later, blended with cream, seasoned with salt and Cayenne pepper, served sprinkled with chopped parsley.

Potée Auvergnate: Auvergne Soup Pot: slices of carrots, turnips, leeks, potatoes and shredded cabbage, cooked in pig's head broth with a few lentils, garnished with the diced pig's head, served in an earthen pot, thin slices of French bread separately. (French)

— **Bourguignonne:** Burgundy Pot Soup: salted pork and knuckle, cooked with cabbage, carrots, turnips, leeks and potatoes, served in special earthen soup pot with dried slices of French bread. (French)

Potroka: Goose Giblet Soup: beef broth, flavored with the juice of pickled cucumbers, garnished with goose giblets, diced pot herbs, sliced pickled cucumbers, chopped parsley, fennel and dill, bound with sour cream and egg yolks. (Russian)

Preßkohlsuppe: Beef Broth with Stuffed Cabbage: leaves of white cabbage, stuffed with pork sausage meat, mixed with soaked bread, eggs and chopped chives, seasoned, shaped into small balls, braised and served as garnish for beef broth. (Austrian)

Puchero: Spanish National Soup: lean beef, raw ham and chick-peas, cooked in water, seasoned, a piece of choriza (garlic sausage) added later; soup garnished with small dumplings, made of ham, bacon, eggs, breadcrumbs and garlic, fried in oil. (Spanish)

— **mexicana:** Mexican Pot Soup: boil a piece of beef, veal and pickled pork and goose giblets in plenty of water slowly, season, add carrots, turnips, onions, parsley root and chick peas and serve in special earthen pot. (Mexican)

R

Real Turtle Soup: P. à la tortue clair: clear soup made of turtle, beef, chicken, calf's foot, aromatic and turtle herbs, seasoned with Cayenne pepper, flavored with Sherry or Madeira, sometimes slightly thickened with arrowroot and served with milk punch.

Rindersuppe mit Milzschnitten: Beef broth with Milt: mince milt, season with salt pepper and marjoram and spread on small pieces of white bread toasted on one side, cover with another slice of bread, toasted on one side only, bake in oven and serve with rich beef broth. (Austrian)

Rosol: Buckwheat Soup: beef and chicken broth, thickened with buckwheat groats, garnished with diced chicken and bacon, chopped parsley and fennel. (Polish)

Rossolnik: Russian Chicken Soup: strips of parsley root and knob celery cooked in white stock, strips of ogourzis (small pickled Russian cucumbers) added, moistened with chicken broth, flavored with juice of pickled cucumbers, bound with egg yolks and sour cream, garnished with strips of chicken. (Russian)

Rybi polevká: Czech Fish Soup: carrots, knob celery, onions, cabbage, parsley and cauliflower cooked in fish stock, seasoned with salt and nutmeg, rubbed through a sieve, mellowed with milk, bound with milk and egg yolks, garnished with hard carps' roes cooked in fish stock. (Czecho-Slowakian)

S

Schtschi: Russian Cabbage Soup: diced onions, carrots, knob celery, parsley root and leeks sweated in stock fat, shredded blanched cabbage added, moistened with beef and pork stock, seasoned with salt, peppercorns and bay leaves, boiled with a piece of brisket; sour cream and the sliced brisket served separately. (Russian)

— **Nikolaijewski:** Cabbage Soup: same as schtschi, but made with stock of pork bones roasted in fat, vegetables grated and not diced, and tomato purée added. (Russian)

— **i russki:** Russian Cabbage Soup: chopped white cabbage, sweated in lard with sliced onions, moistened with stock of pork bones, cooked with chopped vegetables, a piece of bacon and brisket, seasoned with salt, peppercorns and bay leaves; buckwheat groats (kacha) served separately. (Russian)

— **soldatski:** Soldiers Soup: same as schtschi, the cabbage replaced by saurkraut. (Russian)

Scotch Mutton Broth: rich mutton broth, garnished with diced vegetables, mutton and pearl barley. (Scotch)

Sharks' Fin Soup: Sharks' fins soaked over night. All loose particles cleaned out, fins covered with water, boiled, Chinese sauce, chicken stock, salt and cornstarch added. Garnished with shredded chicken meat and parsley. (Chinese)

Sjeloni: Green Soup: same as schtchi, shredded sorrel, spinach and slices of hard-boiled eggs added. (Russian)

Soljanka is riba: Fish Soup: sliced onions, sweated in oil, moistened with fish stock and juice of pickled cucumbers, garnished with small pieces of sterlet or sturgeon, poached in the stock; strips of pickled cucumbers and marinated mushrooms and capers, peeled sliced lemons, sprinkled with chopped dill, black olives and rastigai served separately. (Russian)

Sopa Victoria Ena: Bread Soup: fried dices of white bread, cooked in milk, rubbed through a sieve, moistened with beef broth, bound with egg yolks and butter, garnished with chopped hard-boiled eggs and chervil. (Spanish)

Soupe à l'ail: Garlic Soup: water, boiled with sliced garlic, sage, bay leaves, salt and pepper for 15 minutes. Sprinkle slices of French bread with grated cheese, brown in oven, place in earthen soup pot, put a few drops of oil on top, pour over the hot strained soup and wait 2 minutes before serving. (French)

— **à l'albigeoise:** Albigensian Soup: calf's foot, ham, preserved goose, smoked sausage, diced carrots, turnips and leeks, shredded cabbage and lettuce and broad beans cooked in water with seasoning in a special earthen pot, served with thin slices of French bread. (French)

— **à l'ardennaise:** Ardennes Soup: sliced endives, leeks and potatoes, sweated in butter, cooked slowly in milk, seasoned, mellowed with a little butter, served with thin slices of French bread. (French)

— **au fromage:** Cheese Soup: chopped onions, fried in butter, sprinkled with flour, moistened with stock, seasoned with salt, pepper and a bay leaf. Sliced French bread placed in an earthen soup pot, freely sprinkled with grated cheese, soup poured over, gratinated in the oven. (French)

— **à l'oignon:** chopped onions fried in butter, lightly browned, sprinkled with flour, moistened with water or white stock, seasoned, cooked and poured over layers of French bread, cut in slices, sprinkled with grated Parmesan cheese and placed in a special earthen soup pot. (French)

— **à l'oignon gratinée:** Gratinated Onion Soup: chopped onions, fried in butter, moistened with white stock, seasoned, cooked and poured in a special earthen soup pot; slices of French bread sprinkled with grated Parmesan cheese put on top, gratinated in hot oven. (French)

Southern Bisque: diced onions, celery, carrots and leeks sweated in butter, sprinkled with flour; bay leaf, peppercorns, cloves and chopped garlic added; well blended; tomato paste, stewed corn and ham bone added, moistened with white stock, simmered for two hours; strained, seasoned to taste and garnished with whole corn and diced green peppers.

Squash Soup: chopped onions, diced leeks and celery fried in butter, moistened with white stock, diced green squash added, seasoned with salt and pepper, blended with cream and garnished with boiled rice.

Sup Malorussiski: Hare Soup: purée of hare and barley, diluted with beetroot juice and sour cream, garnished with strips of hare. (Russian)

— **Meschanski:** Citizens Soup: beef broth, garnished with strips of carrots, leeks and celery; cabbage leaves, stuffed with veal forcemeat, shaped into small balls, braised, sprinkled with Parmesan cheese and gratinated, served separately. (Russian)

— **Moscowskaia:** Moscovite Soup: rich beef broth; small dumplings made of cottage cheese, mixed with butter, flour, egg yolks, sour milk, salt, sugar, grated lemon peel and stiffly beaten egg whites, poached, sprinkled with

Sup
grated Parmesan cheese and browned on top, served separately. (Russian)

— **Rakowa:** Crayfish Soup: strong fish stock, garnished with sliced carrots, parsley root, leeks and fried chopped onions, crayfish tails and fish quenelles, each portion served with a few drops of crayfish butter on top; peeled lemon slices, sprinkled with chopped dill and rastegai served separately. (Russian)

T

Tiroler Knödlsuppe: Tyrolese Dumpling Soup: rich beef broth, garnished with large dumpling made of diced bread, soaked in milk, mixed with flour, eggs, chopped onions and diced salt pork, boiled in water. (Austrian)

Tonnillo: Egg Soup: water, seasoned with salt and thyme, a little olive oil added, thickened with white breadcrumbs, bound with raw eggs, served hot. (Spanish)

U

Ucha is sterlett: fish stock made of ruffe, gudgeon, sliced onions, celery, peppercorns and bayleaves, clarified with press caviar, pounded with ice and egg whites, garnished with small pieces of sterlet, boiled in fish stock, lemon juice and Madeira, and slices of peeled lemon. (Russian)

Ulmer Gerstlsuppe: Barley Soup: rich beef broth, garnished with pearl barley, thickened with egg yolks and milk. (Austrian)

V

Velös leves: Brain Soup: sliced mushrooms and chopped parsley, calf's brain sweated in butter, smothered with flour, slightly browned, moistened with beef stock, seasoned with salt, pepper and mace, boiled, strained, mixed with purée of calf's brain, garnished with croûtons. (Hungarian)

W

Westfälische Bohnensuppe: Westphalian Bean Soup: purée of kidney beans, diluted with white stock, garnished with diced knob celery, carrots, leeks, potatoes and slices of Bologna sausage. (German)

Wiener Knödelsuppe: Dumpling Soup: soak half plain bread and half toast in milk, mix with flour, eggs and milk, season with salt and nutmeg, shape into small dumplings and boil in salt water; garnish rich beef broth with these dumplings. (Austrian)

Wilfredo Soup: chopped onions and green peppers sweated in olive oil, crushed garlic and tomato purée added, moistened with white stock, seasoned with salt and cinnamon, bound with eggs, garnished with croûtons and slices of black pudding. (Spanish)

Z

Zelná polevká: Cabbage Soup: white roux, mixed with chopped, blanched cabbage, moistened with beef stock, seasoned with salt, pepper and nutmeg, thickened with egg yolks blended with milk. (Czecho-Slovakian)

Zuppa Genovese: Genoese Soup: chopped fish, onions and parsley, simmered in butter, seasoned with salt, pepper and nutmeg, moistened with fish stock, cooked, rubbed through a sieve, thickened with egg yolks, garnished with fish dumplings fried in oil. (Italian)

— **Palermitana:** Palermo Soup: diced veal, beef, ham, calf's liver, onions, carrots, knob celery and leeks, sweated in butter with diced salt pork, moistened with water, seasoned with peppercorns, marjoram, bay leaves and salt, cooked, rubbed through a sieve, flavored with white wine, garnished with veal quenelles; grated Parmesan served separately. (Italian)

— **Pavese:** Italian Egg Soup: place slices of toasted French bread in earthen soup pot with a raw egg on top, sprinkle generously with grated Parmesan cheese, pour over beef broth and brown in a very hot oven. (Italian)

— **dei pescatore:** Fisherman's Soup: a variety of small seafish cut in pieces, moistened with water, seasoned with salt, pepper, allspice, thyme and bay leaves, cooked with onions, carrots, knob celery and leeks, taken out when done. Slices of bread, fried in oil, placed in a soup tureen, the fish put on top, the strained hot soup poured over; grated Parmesan cheese served separately. (Italian)

Hot and Cold Fruit and Wine Soups

These soups are mainly of German origin
and very refreshing in summer time

Ananas-Kaltschale: Cold Pineapple Soup: crushed pineapple mixed with sugar, boiled up, macerated for a while, strained, mixed with white wine, chilled and garnished with small pieces of pineapple, macerated in sugar and lemon juice.

Apfel-Kaltschale: Cold Apple Soup: apples peeled, sliced, cooked with water and sugar, rubbed through a sieve, when cold blended with white wine, garnished with diced apples and sultanas simmered in sugar syrup.

Aprikosen-Kaltschale: Cold Apricot Soup: ripe apricots, cut in thin slices and sprinkled with powder sugar, kernels scalded, peeled, pounded, mixed with sugar syrup, apricot slices macerated with this syrup, rubbed through a sieve, mixed with white wine, chilled, garnished with thin slices of skinned apricots.

Beer Soup: pale beer or ale, slightly sweetened, mixed with grated rye bread, currants and peeled slices of lemon, covered, chilled for two hours and served on soup plates or in glasses.

Cherry Soup: cherries, stoned, cooked with water, lemon peel and cinnamon, rubbed through a sieve, red wine and sugar added, thickened with cornflour, garnished with chopped stewed cherries, crushed rusks scattered on top.

Erdbeer-Kaltschale: Cold Strawberry Soup: wild strawberries, rubbed through a sieve, mixed with sugar and white wine, chilled, garnished with sugared wild strawberries.

Flieder-Kaltschale: hot milk, flavored with elder-blossoms, vanilla and cinnamon, sweetened, strained, thickened with egg yolks, chilled, served with crushed finger biscuits scattered on top.

Hagebutten-Suppe: Hips Soup: dried hips, soaked in water, scalded, cooked with rusks, seasoned with cinnamon, lemon peel, sugar and a pinch of salt, rubbed through a sieve, white wine added, thickened with egg yolks and butter, garnished with croûtons.

Hamburger Apfelsuppe: Hamburg Apple Soup: peeled and sliced apples, cooked in water with lemon peel, cinnamon, sugar, ground almonds and crushed rusks, rubbed through a sieve, mixed with apple wine, cooked for a few minutes, mellowed with a piece of butter, garnished with croûtons.

Himbeer-Kaltschale: Cold Raspberry Soup: raspberries, macerated in sugar syrup for an hour, rubbed through a sieve, mixed with white wine, flavored with lemon juice, garnished with sugared raspberries.

Johannisbeer-Kaltschale: Cold Red Currant Soup: red currants, cooked in sugar syrup, rubbed through a sieve, chilled, mixed with white wine, garnished with red currants, crushed finger biscuits scattered on top of soup.

Kirschen-Kaltschale: Cold Cherry Soup: Morellos pounded with their kernels, boiled in sugar syrup, rubbed through a sieve, diluted with white wine, chilled, garnished with stoned cherries.

Mandel-Kaltschale: Cold Almond Soup: sweet almonds and a few bitter almonds scalded, skinned and ground, infused in hot milk, pressed through a cloth, bound with egg yolks, sweetened, chilled and garnished with crushed macaroons.

Melonen-Kaltschale: Cold Melon Soup: diced melon, macerated with sugar and lemon juice, blended with white wine, served chilled.

Orangen-Kaltschale: Cold Orange Soup: julienne of orange peel cooked in sugar-syrup, flavored with orange juice, blended with white wine, garnished with segments of orange.

Pfirsich-Kaltschale: Cold Peach Soup: ripe peaches skinned, cut in slices, diluted with sugar syrup, mixed with a few peach kernels, ground and macerated in sugar syrup, rubbed through a sieve, blended with white wine, chilled, garnished with sliced, peeled peaches.

Reis-Kaltschale: Cold Rice Soup: prepared the same way as cold cherry soup, garnished with rice instead of cherries, served chilled.

Sago-Kaltschale: Cold Sago Soup: sago, cooked in half water and half white wine, flavored with lemon peel and cinnamon, sweetened, strained, blended with white wine, flavored with lemon juice, chilled.

Wine Soup: white wine and water, boiled with lemon peel and cinnamon for a few minutes, strained, sweetened with sugar, thickened with egg yolks and almond milk; for diabetics use saccharine instead of sugar.

Egg Dishes

French: Plats d'oeufs
German: Eierspeisen
Italian: Piatti d'uova
Spanish: Platas de Huevos

Plain egg dishes are usually served for breakfast and eggs with a more lavish garnish for lunch or supper, but not for dinner. Eggs should be prepared at the last minute and served at once. Always use special baking dishes of china or fire-proof glass for cooking eggs as silver turns black if it comes into direct connection with the eggs.

General Classification

1. **Scrambled eggs:** oeufs brouillés: first melt butter in a shallow pan (plat à sauter), add well beaten eggs, seasoned with salt and pepper, mixed with a spoonful of cream or milk, and cook slowly stirring the eggs with a wooden spoon until they are congealed. Keep the eggs soft.
2. **Eggs shirred in cocottes:** oeufs en cocottes: grease small individual fire-proof china or glass pots (cocottes) with butter, break an egg into each, salt the egg whites only, and poach in a water bath on top of the stove or in the oven for 4—5 minutes.
3. **Soft boiled eggs, Eggs in the shell:** oeufs à la coque: cook in boiling water $2^1/_2$—$3^1/_2$ minutes according to size.
4. **Medium boiled eggs:** oeufs mollets: cook eggs 5—6 minutes in boiling water according to size, hold under cold water and remove shell carefully. Before serving heat briefly in salt water.
5. **Hard-boiled eggs:** oeufs durs: cook eggs 8—10 minutes in boiling water according to size, hold under cold water and remove shell carefully.
6. **Stuffed eggs:** oeufs farcis: cut hard-boiled eggs lengthwise or crosswise as needed, remove yolk, mash and mix it with a purée, vegetables, salad etc., and garnish as desired.
7. **Cold eggs:** oeufs froids: poached, medium boiled or hard boiled eggs, coated with chaudfroid sauce or mayonnaise etc., glazed with aspic jelly, dressed on pastry cases, croûtons, tartlets etc. and garnished as desired.
8. **French fried or Baked eggs:** oeufs frits: heat oil in small frying pan, break only one egg at the time into the pan, shape with two small wooden spoons and fry; center should remain soft. Drain on cloth, sprinkle with a little salt and serve with sauce and garnish as desired.
9. **Fried eggs:** oeufs au plat, oeufs miroir: slightly brown butter in special frying dish and avoid spoiling the yolk.

Salt egg whites only, cook a few minutes on top of the stove and finish cooking in the oven until yolks have become covered with a sort of cloudy veil; the yolk and a part of the white should remain soft. Eggs may also be fried in a hot buttered frying pan on top of the stove until the whites are congealed; ragged edges are then trimmed with a round cutter.

10. **Poached eggs:** oeufs pochés: fill shallow pan with water and add a little vinegar. Bring water to a boil and slide the eggs — not to many at the same time — into the boiling water and poach for 4—5 minutes; the yolk must remain soft. Remove eggs from the water with a small skimmer and allow them to cool in cold water. Trim and heat them briefly in hot salt water before serving.
11. **Moulded eggs:** oeufs moulés: grease special moulds, similar to baba moulds, with butter or use cocottes. Break an egg into each mould, salt the whites slightly, and poach in a tray of hot water the same way as eggs in cocottes. Turn eggs out and serve on pastry cases, croûtons or other base and garnish as desired.
12. **Omelette:** beat eggs thoroughly adding a spoonful of milk or cream and season with salt and pepper. Heat a spoonful of butter in the omelette pan, pour in the mixture, and shake the pan continually until the eggs beginn to set. Gather the bulk with a palette toward the far end of the pan and tild pan in that direction to accumulate the eggs into an eliptical heap at one end; the center of the omelette must remain soft and the outside ought to be white, not brown. Turn omelette upside down on the platter and finish its eliptical shape. After the omelette has been stuffed an incision is often made on top and filled with a part of the stuffing.

Scrambled Eggs

Oeufs brouilles

Admirals Style: Oeufs brouillés à l'amiral: garnished with diced lobster, surrounded with lobster sauce.

with Anchovies: aux anchois: mixed with chopped anchovies, garnished with strips of anchovy fillets.

Antoine: mixed with diced fried bacon, herbs and capers, covered with brown butter.

Archduchess: à l'archiduchesse: mixed with diced ham and mushrooms, seasoned with paprika, filled in round potato croquettes with a cavity in the centre, asparagus tips on top, paprika sauce.

Arlesian Style: à l'arlésienne: mixed with diced eggplant and tomatoes tossed in butter.

with Asparagus: à l'Argenteuil: garnished with asparagus tips.

with Asparagus Tips: aux pointes d'asperges: mixed with cut green asparagus tips, small bunch of asparagus tips in centre.

d'Aumale: mixed with diced tomatoes, diced broiled veal kidneys in Madeira sauce in the centre.

Balzac: mixed with diced ox tongue and truffle, garnished with round croûtons coated with onion purée, surrounded with demi-glace tomatée.

Belly: mixed with diced salt pork and chopped chives, surrounded with demi-glace.

Benclan: garnished with diced green and red peppers, sprinkled with chopped truffles.

Boatsmans Style: à la batelière: mixed with chopped chives, filled in tartlets lined with purée of soles.

Bordeaux Style: à la bordelaise: mixed with diced mushrooms, garnished with triangles of fried bread, surrounded with bordelaise sauce.

Brasilian Style: à la brésilienne: mixed with strips of red peppers, filled in flat puff pastry patty, surrounded with tomato sauce, mixed with chopped ham.

Bresse Style: garnished with sauted chicken livers and slices of truffle, surrounded with demi-glace.

Burgundy Style: à la bourguignonne: mixed with chopped snails, diced bacon, garlic, chopped nuts and parsley, surrounded with Madeira sauce.

Cambridge Style: mixed with diced lobster, mushrooms and sweet peppers, surrounded with cream sauce.

Carême: mixed with diced gooseliver, chicken meat and truffles, filled in flat puff pastry shell, garnished with sliced truffle, surrounded with demi-glace.

Carnot: mixed with cockscombs and mushrooms, garnished with cocks' kidneys, surrounded with demi-glace.

Chalons Style: à la châlonaise: garnished with cockscombs and kidneys, cream sauce.

Chambord: on slices of fried eggplant, surrounded with demi-glace.

Châtillon Style: centre garnished with sliced, sauted mushrooms, sprinkled with chopped chives, centre surmounted with fried parsley, surrounded with fleurons.

with Chicken Livers: aux foies de volaille: garnished with sauted chicken livers, tossed in Madeira sauce.

Countess: à la comtesse: mixed with shrimps, garnished with asparagus tips, surrounded with demi-glace.

Crispi: garnished with diced, sauted tomatoes and croûtons fried in butter.

Dairy-maids Style: à la laitière: mixed with grated Emmenthal cheese, chopped parsley, chives and chervil.

Divette: mixed with diced crayfish and asparagus tips, crayfish tails in centre surrounded with crayfish sauce.

Don Juan: mixed with chopped green peppers, garnished with strips of anchovy fillets, surrounded with Madeira sauce.

Eierrösti: diced bread, soaked in warm milk, stirred, mixed with hot butter and beaten eggs, prepared the same way as scrambled eggs. (Swiss)

Elliot: dressed in border of rice, surrounded with Madeira sauce.

Elvira: mixed with diced truffles, filled in flat puff pastry shell, garnished with fried gooseliver coated with paprika sauce, green asparagus tips dressed in centre.

Epicurean: à l'épicurienne: mixed with diced gooseliver patty, truffles and mushrooms, surrounded with demi-glace.

Esau: Mixed with diced fried bacon, dressed on bed of lentils, surrounded with demi-glace.

Figaro: garnished with sliced sausage, surrounded with Montebello sauce.

with Fried Bread: aux croûtons: mixed with small croûtons fried in butter.

Georgette: mixed with diced crayfish, filled in hollow baked potatoes, surrounded with crayfish sauce.

Gordon: mixed with truffles, filled in flat puff pastry shell, garnished with a slice of poached beef marrow, surrounded with Chateaubriand sauce.

Grandmothers Style: à la grand'mère: mixed with chopped parsley and croûtons fried in butter.

Graziella: large brioche, hollowed out, filled with plain scrambled eggs, sauted slices of mushrooms in centre, surrounded with fried slices of veal kidneys.

Green Meadow: Vert-pré: tartlets half filled with purée of spinach or lettuce, topped with scrambled eggs, sprinkled with chopped herbs, surrounded with velouté.

with Ham: au jambon: mixed with diced or chopped ham.

Hamburg Style: à la hamburgeoise: garnished with strips of boned and skinned smoked herrings.

Hangtown fry: mixed with diced fried bacon and fried oysters.

Héloise: mixed with strips of ox tongue, chicken and mushrooms, surrounded with tomato sauce.

with Herbs: aux fines herbes: mixed with chopped parsley, tarragon, chervil and chives.

Housewife's Style: à la bonne femme: mixed with croûtons fried in butter, surrounded with demi-glace.

Huysmans: mixed with diced mushrooms and artichoke bottoms, filled in flat puff pastry shell, garnished slices of veal kidneys, masked with Madeira sauce.

Italian Style: à l'italienne: filled in border of risotto with diced tomatoes, surrounded with tomato sauce.

Jérôme: flat puff pastry shell half filled with hashed game, topped with scrambled eggs.

Joinville: mixed with diced shrimps, mushrooms and truffles, served in puff pastry patty, garnished with shrimps, slice of truffle and a mushroom.

Lesseps: garnished with slices of fried calf's brain, poured over with brown butter.

Leuchtenberg: mixed with chopped chives, caviar in the centre.

with Lobster: à l'homard: garnished with diced lobster in lobster sauce.

Lucullus: mixed with diced truffles, garnished with slices of truffles, surrounded with demi-glace.

Madrid Style: à la madrilène: mixed with cream and diced sauted tomatoes.

Magda: mixed with chopped herbs, mustard and grated Parmesan, garnished with fried triangular shaped croûtons.

Manon: mixed with chopped mushrooms and truffles, dressed on tartlet of chicken forcemeat croquette, surrounded with truffled velouté sauce.

Marie: mixed with grated Parmesan, filled in puff pastry patty, sprinkled with chopped truffles.

Marivaux: mixed with chopped truffles, large mushroom cap in centre, surrounded with sliced mushrooms and a thread of meat glaze.

Mary: mixed with chopped truffles and sweet red peppers, dressed in puff pastry patty.

Mercédès: mixed with chopped chives, dressed in flat hollow brioche or roll filled with diced tomatoes tossed in oil, surrounded with tomato sauce.

Mexican Style: à la mexicaine: mixed with diced green peppers, surrounded with tomato sauce.

Mezerai: garnished with grilled halved lamb kidneys and truffle slices, surrounded with truffle sauce.

Monaco: à la monégasque: garnished with slices of lobster, masked with lobster sauce.

Montbarry: mixed with diced mushrooms, truffles and asparagus tips, served on rice mixed with grated Parmesan and Swiss cheese.

Moorish Style: à la mauresque: mixed with chopped fried sausage and ham.

with Mushrooms: aux champignons: mixed with diced or sliced mushrooms, surrounded with Spanish sauce.

Nantese Style: à la nantaise: on fried bread croûtons, garnished with sardines.

Nantua: mixed with diced crayfish tails and truffles, garnished with sliced truffles, surrounded with crayfish sauce.

Norman Style: à la normande: garnished with poached oysters, surrounded with Norman sauce.

Norvegian Style: à la norvégienne: on anchovy toast, garnished with strips of anchovy fillets.

Opera: mixed with diced sauted chicken livers, garnished with asparagus tips, surrounded with buttered veal gravy.

Oriental Style: à l'orientale: mixed with diced tomatoes, sauted with onions, and diced green peppers, garnished with croûtons coated with onion purée, surrounded with a thread of meat glaze.

Ostend Style: à l'ostendaise: mixed with poached oysters, surrounded with oyster sauce.

Pantheon: mixed with diced chicken livers and mushrooms, garnished with fleurons, surrounded with truffle sauce.

Parmentier: diced pan fried potatoes, tossed in meat glaze with chopped parsley filled in center.

with Parmesan: mixed with grated Parmesan, sprinkled with chopped parsley.

Paulus: garnished with diced sauted tomatoes and sweet green peppers.

Pisto Manchego Española: mixed with diced bacon, tomatoes, chopped onions and parsley sauted in oil. (Spanish)

Portuguese Style: à la portugaise: mixed with diced tomatoes, surrounded with tomato sauce, sauted tomatoes in centre.

Princess: mixed with asparagus tips, garnished with asparagus tips and truffle slices, surrounded with cream sauce.

Princess Marie: mixed with grated Parmesan and diced truffles, served in pastry shells or cocotte dishes.

Provencal Style: à la provençale: mixed with diced tomatoes, garlic and chopped parsley.

Queen Hortense: à la reine Hortense: mixed with diced lobster and mushrooms, garnished with pilaw rice, mixed with diced red peppers and peas, pressed into small dariole moulds and turned out, surrounded with lobster sauce.

Rachel: mixed with diced truffles and asparagus tips, garnished with sliced truffles, surrounded with demi-glace.

Ranhofer: served in artichoke bottoms, garnished with ox marrow coated with Burgundy sauce.

Raspail: mixed with diced knob celery, tomatoes and cream.

Roman Style: à la romaine: mixed with chopped anchovy fillets, shredded spinach and a little garlic, surrounded with demi-glace mixed with tomato purée.

Rôtisserie Périgourdine: mixed with diced truffles, filled in flat puff pastry patty, garnished with slices of truffles cooked in Burgundy wine, coated with buttered Burgundy sauce.

Rotraud: mixed with a little crayfish sauce, bouquet of asparagus tips in center, garnished with sliced truffles and crayfish tails, surrounded with crayfish sauce.

St. Denis: filled in very large grilled mushroom caps, surrounded with red wine sauce.

Salamanca: Salamanque: mixed with diced truffles, served on artichoke bottoms covered with cheese sauce and glazed.

Sans-gêne: served on artichoke bottoms, garnished with slice of blanched ox marrow, masked with Burgundy sauce, sprinkled with chopped parsley.

Sappho Bernhardt: garnished with slices of truffles, cockscombs and cocks' knidneys, surrounded with cream sauce.

Saragossa: mixed with diced fried ham, garnished with thick fried slices of bananas and corn fritters, surrounded with tomato sauce

Schinkel: mixed with strips of ham, artichoke bottoms and mushrooms, filled in border of puff pastry, surrounded with buttered meatglaze mixed with chopped tarragon, crayfish butter dropped on top.

Scrambled Plovers Eggs, Spring Style: Oeufs de vanneau à la printanière: filled in flat puff pastry patty, topped with purée of morels, mixed with diced truffles, sprinkled with chopped herbs.

with Shrimps: aux crevettes: mixed with shrimps, surrounded with shrimp sauce.

Spanish Style: à l'espagnole: served on tomatoes fried in oil, garnished with fried rings of large onions.

Sultan's Style: à la sultane: finished with pistachio butter, served in baked border of duchess potatoes.

Swiss Style: à la suisse: mixed with diced Swiss cheese, filled in tartlets, sprinkled with grated cheese and gratinated.

Sylvette: served in puff pastry tartlet filled with crayfish purée, garnished with truffle, surrounded with Madeira sauce.

with Tarragon: à l'estragon: mixed with chopped tarragon, surrounded with demi-glace with tarragon essence.

Tartuffe: mixed with fried diced bacon, served in puff pastry patty, surrounded with truffle sauce.

with Tomatoes: aux tomates: mixed with diced sauted tomatoes.

Toronto: served in hollowed out tomatoes, covered with Bordeaux sauce, sprinkled with grated cheese and glazed rapidly.

with Truffles: aux truffes: mixed with diced truffles, garnished with truffle slices, surrounded with demi-glace.

Turkish Style: à la turque: half eggplant fried, stuffed with the chopped fruit meat, tomatoes and onions, seasoned with salt, pepper and saffron, the scrambled eggs on top.

Urbain Dubois: mixed with diced lobster, served in hollowed lobster claws, coated with lobster sauce.

Vaucourt: mixed with diced truffles and asparagus tips, served in border of baked duchess potatoes, garnished with truffle slices, surrounded with demi-glace.

Villemain: served in puff pastry tartlets or patties on chicken forcemeat, eggs mixed with diced mushrooms.

Waldorf: large grilled mushroom caps stuffed with scrambled eggs, small round slice of truffled gooseliver patty on top, surrounded with truffle sauce.

Walewska: garnished with dices of truffles and lobster, bound with cream sauce blended with lobster butter, surrounded with the same sauce.

Westphalian Style: à la westphalienne: mixed with fried diced Westphalian ham.

with Whipped Cream: Chantilly: mixed with whipped unsweetened cream, sprinkled with chopped chives.

Yvette: mixed with crayfish tails, garnished with asparagus tips, surrounded with crayfish sauce.

Eggs Shirred in Cocottes

Oeufs en cocottes

Bonaparte: poached in buttered cocotte lined with chopped snails, slice of truffle on top, surrounded with Sherry sauce.

Bordeaux Style: à la bordelaise: bottom of dish lined with slices of blanched ox marrow, egg when set surrounded with Bordeaux sauce.

Café Anglais: cocotte lined with chicken forcemeat, egg, when set, covered with lobster sauce.

Canoness' Style: à la chanoinesse: base of creamed shrimps and truffles; surrounded with cream sauce.

Carnegie: dish lined with purée of mushrooms mixed with chopped sweet peppers, when set adorned with tomato sauce.

with Chambertin: a little Chambertin sauce poured into the cocottes, eggs broken in and steamed until set.

Cherbourg Style: à la cherbourgeoise: base of light fish forcemeat, shrimp sauce poured around the edge.

with Chicken Purée: à la purée de volaille: cocottes lined with purée of chicken blended with velouté, eggs sprinkled with grated Parmesan and glazed.

Colbert: cocotte lined with chicken forcemeat with chopped herbs, surrounded with Colbert sauce.

Commanders Style: à la commodore: poached in buttered cocottes, covered with Béarnaise sauce.

with Cream: à la crème: spoonful of cream poured in each cocotte, eggs steamed until set, surrounded with cream.

Cuban Style: à la cubaine: base of minced creamed crabmeat; sprinkled with chopped parsley.

Diana: cocotte lined with game forcemeat, truffle slice on top, surrounded with game sauce.

Diplomats Style: à la diplomate: base of gooseliver slices, when done surrounded with tomato sauce.

Edison: cocotte lined with chicken forcemeat, surrounded with truffle sauce.

Florence Style: à la florentine: cocottes lined with spinach, mixed with a few chopped anchovy fillets, eggs coated with cream, sprinkled with grated cheese and glazed.

Foresters Style: à la forestière: cocottes lined with minced morels, slice of lean fried bacon at the bottom; game gravy poured around, sprinkled with chopped herbs.

Gipsies Style: à la Zingara: cocottes lined with purée of ham, when done garnished with large slice of mushroom, small truffle slice on top; surrounded with demi-glace blended with tomato purée.

Gouffé: cocottes lined with minced calf's brains, mixed with chopped ham and chives; tomato sauce around the edge.

Italian Style: à l'italienne: eggs covered with Italian sauce, sprinkled with Parmesan, poached and glazed.

Johanna: cocottes lined with purée of chicken blended with gooseliver; eggs surrounded with chicken velouté.

Josephine: cocottes lined with mushroom purée, eggs covered with cheese sauce colored with tomato purée.

Karola: base of chicken forcemeat, mushrooms and truffles; surrounded with demi-glace.

Leontine: base of creamed crayfish and truffles; surrounded with tomato sauce.

Lucullus: base of gooseliver purée, eggs covered with sliced truffles, surrounded with Madeira sauce.

Magdalena: à la Madeleine: base of chicken purée, slightly curried, surrounded with demi-glace.

Marigny: base of fried ham and poached oysters, covered cream sauce, sprinkled with Parmesan and glazed.

Marly: base of minced veal and mushrooms; surounded with demi-glace.

Nancy Style: à la nancéenne: cocottes lined with gooseliver purée, garnished with sliced truffles, coated with demi-glace.

Parisian Style: à la parisienne: base of minced chicken, ham, tongue, mushrooms and truffles; surrounded with demi-glace.

Pavillon: base of minced morels and truffles in cream sauce, eggs topped with sliced truffles and morels, covered with Chateaubriand sauce.

Porto Rico: base of diced tomatoes, chopped ham and asparagus tips; surrounded with cream sauce.

Portuguese Style: à la portugaise: base of tomato purée; surrounded with tomato sauce.

Princess Style: à la princesse: base of creamed asparagus tips; surrounded with cream sauce.

Queens Style: à la reine: base of minced chicken; surrounded with cream sauce.

Ribeaucourt: base of chopped ham, mushrooms and truffles in thick Spanish sauce; surrounded with demi-glace.

Rossini: base of gooseliver purée; surrounded with truffle sauce.

Rouenese Style: à la rouennaise: cocottes lined with duck liver forcemeat; surrounded with rouenese sauce.

St. George: base of onion purée, coated with cream sauce, sprinkled with Parmesan and glazed.

St. Hubert: cocottes lined with purée of game; eggs garnished with slice of truffle, covered with poivrade sauce.

Sagan: base: sliced calf's brain in velouté sauce; surrounded with demi-glace.

Scotch Style: à l'écossaise: base of chopped ox tongue, mushrooms and truffles; surrounded with tomato sauce.

Shepherdess Style: à la bergère: base of minced lamb; surrounded with demi-glace.

Tosca: base of sour cream, eggs covered with milk, sprinkled with Parmesan.

Valentine: base of tomato purée mixed with chopped mushrooms; surrounded with velouté sauce.

Voltaire: base of creamed chicken hash, covered with cream sauce, sprinkled with Parmesan and glazed.

Medium Boiled Eggs

Oeufs mollets

Auber: medium boiled eggs on tartlets filled with beef and mushrooms hash, coated with Madeira sauce.

Aurora: à l'aurore: dressed on puff pastry shell, coated with Aurora sauce.

Berlioz: dressed on hash of venison and mushrooms, surrounded with game gravy.

Bombay Style: dressed on rice, coated with curry sauce.

Bordeaux Style: à la bordelaise: dressed on oval fried croûtons, slightly hollowed out, garnished with blanched ox marrow, coated with Bordelaise sauce.

Brussels Style: à la bruxelloise: dressed on puff pastry tartlets filled with purée of endives, coated with cream sauce.

Cavour: dressed on bed of buttered macaroni, coated with Mornay sauce, sprinkled with grated Parmesan and glazed.

Cecelia: Cécilie: dressed on oval, hollowed out croûtons filled with asparagus purée, coated with Mornay sauce, sprinkled with cheese and glazed.

Clélia: dressed on bed of spinach, coated with Mornay sauce, sprinkled with grated cheese and glazed.

Clementine: dressed on asparagus tips and wax beans tossed glace.
in butter, coated alternately with cream sauce and demi-

Dauphiné Style: à la dauphinoise: dipped in egg and breadcrumbs, deep fried, dressed on fried parsley, tomato sauce served separately.

Devils Style: à la diable: dressed on oval croûtons, coated with sauce diable.

Divorced Eggs: Divorçons: dressed on pastry shells, one egg covered with cream sauce and sprinkled with chopped truffles, the other egg covered with tomato sauce and sprinkled with sieved hard egg whites.

Dubois: scallop shells, filled with diced lobster and truffles in cream sauce seasoned with curry, medium boiled eggs on top, coated with lobster sauce, sprinkled with grated Parmesan and glazed.

Flaubert: dipped in egg and bread crumbs, deep fried, dressed on croustade filled with ragout of diced mushrooms, lobster and bearded mussels; Dutch sauce blended with lobster butter served separately.

Gastronomers Style: dressed on oval croûton, scooped out, filled with asparagus tips in cream sauce, coated with cream sauce blended with asparagus purée.

with Horseradish Sauce: à la sauce raifort dressed on oval croûtons, coated with horseradish sauce.

Manon: dressed on pastry cases filled with diced chicken and mushrooms in cream sauce, coated with cream sauce, sprinkled with chopped truffles.

Milanese Style: à la milanaise: dressed on bed of macaroni Milanaise, coated with Mornay sauce, sprinkled with grated Parmesan and glazed.

Molay: dressed on bed of sorrel, coated with Spanish sauce.

Molière: dressed on grilled half-tomatoes filled with chicken purée, coated with Regency sauce.

Monseigneur: dressed on pastry cases filled with purée of sorrel, coated with Colbert sauce.

Nancy Style: à la nancéenne: point cut off of medium boiled eggs, carefully hollowed out, stuffed with purée of goose-liver, coated with Soubise sauce, dipped in bread crumbs, deep fried, dressed on fried parsley; truffle sauce served separately.

Nicolas: dressed on pastry cases filled with salmon purée, coated with Dutch sauce blended with caviar, garnished with cèpes in cream sauce.

Royal: à la royale: dressed on pastry cases filled with chicken purée, coated with cream sauce mixed with mushroom purée, sprinkled with chopped truffles.

Sovereigns Style: à la souveraine: dressed on pastry cases filled with purée of chicken or asparagus, coated with Madeira sauce, garnished with slice of truffle.

Taillevent: dressed on pastry cases filled with pheasant purée, coated with peppersauce blended with red currant jelly, seasoned with powdered ginger, garnished with slice of truffle.

Ursuline Style: à l'ursuline: dressed on cases of salmon forcemeat, slightly hollowed out and filled with white purée of mushrooms, truffles slices on top, coated with Mornay sauce, sprinkled with grated Parmesan and glazed.

Viéville: dressed on risotto, coated with Spanish sauce, garnished with grilled lamb kidneys and fleurons.

in White Sauce: à la poulette: dressed on oval croûtons, coated with Poulette sauce.

Hard-Boiled and Stuffed Eggs

Oeufs durs et farcis

with Anchovies: aux anchois: hard boiled, stuffed with the yolks creamed with anchovy butter, mixed with chopped mushrooms, dipped in egg and bread crumbs and fried; anchovy sauce served separately.

Antibes Style: à l'antiboise: hard-boiled eggs, halved lengthwise, stuffed with the creamed yolks mixed with diced lobster, tomatoes and stiffly beaten whites, sprinkled with grated cheese and baked.

Aurora: à l'aurore: slices of hard-boiled eggs, covered with Béchamel mixed with tomato purée, sprinkled with grated cheese, gratinated, chopped hard yolks sprinkled on top.

Avignon Style: à l'avignonnaise: hard boiled, halved lengthwise; stuffed with the yolks creamed with cream sauce, breadcrumbs and chopped anchovy fillets; sprinkled with Parmesan and glazed.

Bagration: hard-boiled, halved lengthwise, dressed on base of risotto, covered with cream sauce mixed with chopped ox tongue, ham, truffles and mushrooms.

Belloy: hard boiled, halved lengthwise, stuffed with the yolks creamed with cheese sauce, mixed with diced lobster, mushrooms and truffles, coated with cheese sauce, sprinkled with Parmesan and glazed.

Bennet: hard boiled, halved lengthwise, stuffed with the creamed yolks, mixed with onion purée and chopped mushrooms, coated with cream sauce, sprinkled with grated cheese and chopped hard-boiled eggs and baked.

Breton Style: à la bretonne: sliced leeks, onions and mushrooms stewed in butter, thickened with Béchamel; half of this sauce placed on the serving dish, hard-boiled eggs halved lengthwise on top, covered with the remaining sauce.

Calabrian Style: à la calabraise: hard-boiled, stuffed with the yolks blended with anchovy paste and purée of green peppers, dipped in egg and bread crumbs and fried; Bordeaux sauce served separately.

Carême: sliced hard-boiled eggs, artichoke bottoms and truffles, bound with Nantua sauce, dressed in timbales or cocottes, covered with Nantua sauce, garnished with sliced truffles.

Cecilia: hard-boiled, cut in half, stuffed with the yolks, mixed with cream sauce and diced mushrooms, dressed on large grilled mushrooms, covered with cheese sauce, sprinkled with Parmesan and glazed.

Coquelin: hard-boiled, halved lengthwise, stuffed with the yolks blended with purée of mushrooms, covered with cream sauce and fillets of anchovies, sprinkled with cheese and browned in the oven.

De Ruyter: layers of hard-boiled sliced eggs, sliced potatoes, small pieces of desalted herrings and poached soft carp roes dressed in baking dish, covered with cream, sprinkled with grated cheese and browned in the oven.

Fishmongers Style: hard-boiled, halved lengthwise, stuffed with the yolks blended with purée of salmon, coated with crayfish sauce, sprinkled with Parmesan and glazed.

Genuese Style: à la génoise: hard-boiled, halved lengthwise, stuffed with the creamed yolks, mixed with chopped anchovy fillets, herbs and breadcrumbs, coated with cheese sauce, browned in the oven.

Gourmets Style: hard-boiled, halved lengthwise, stuffed with the creamed yolks, mixed with diced lobster, crayfish and truffles, thickened with cheese sauce, sprinkled with grated cheese, browned in the oven.

Hortense: hard-boiled, halved lengthwise, stuffed with the yolks blended with purée of gooseliver and rice, covered with cheese sauce, sprinkled with grated Parmesan, melted butter dropped on top, browned in oven.

Hungarian Style: à la hongroise: sliced hard-boiled eggs, served in timbales, covered with paprika sauce, mixed with chopped onions and diced tomatoes.

Hunters Style: à la chasseur: hard-boiled stuffed with purée of game mixed with chopped mushrooms, parsley and the yolks, dipped in egg and bread crumbs and fried; poivrade sauce served separately.

Indian Style: à l'indienne: hard-boiled, halved lengthwise, stuffed with the yolks blended with cream sauce and purée of chicken, seasoned with curry powder, both halves put together, dipped in egg and bread crumbs and fried; curry sauce served separately.

Italian Style: à l'italienne: hard-boiled halved lengthwise, stuffed with purée of tomatoes, chopped mushrooms, parsley and the yolks, coated with cream sauce mixed with tomato purée, sprinkled with grated Parmesan and browned in oven.

Lenox: sliced hard-boiled eggs, thickened with cream sauce, dressed in fire proof dish, coated with tomato purée, sprinkled with Parmesan, melted butter on top, browned in oven.

Lucullus: hard-boiled, stuffed with the yolks blended with gooseliver purée, both halves put together again, dipped in egg and bread crumbs and fried; Madeira sauce served separately.

Maintenon: hard-boiled, dressed in oval tartlets filled with white onion purée, coated with cheese sauce, sprinkled with grated Swiss cheese, browned, thread of buttered meat glaze around.

Meissonier: hard-boiled, halved lengthwise, stuffed with mixture of the yolks, diced sweetbread and chicken, mushrooms and truffles in cream sauce, coated with cheese sauce, sprinkled with Parmesan cheese, browned in the oven.

Montglas: hard-boiled, stuffed with chopped chicken, ox tongue, mushrooms and truffles, blended with cream sauce, dipped in egg and bread crumbs and fried; demi-glace tomaté served separately.

Mortimer: hard-boiled, top cut off, yolk removed, stuffed with caviar, dipped in egg and bread crumbs and fried rapidly.

Piedmontese Style: à la piémontaise: hard-boiled, halved lengthwise, stuffed with the yolks, purée of white truffles and cream sauce, coated with cream sauce mixed with chopped white truffles, sprinkled with Parmesan, browned in the oven.

Princess Alice: hard-boiled, stuffed with the yolks mixed with asparagus purée, chopped truffles and grated Parmesan, dipped in egg and bread crumbs and fried; truffle sauce served separately.

— **Chimay:** hard-boiled, halved lengthwise, stuffed with the yolks blended with purée of mushrooms, covered with cheese sauce, sprinkled with Parmesan and browned in the oven.

Ristori: hard-boiled, halved lengthwise, stuffed with the yolks blended with gooseliver purée, coated with cream sauce.

Saint-Germain: hard-boiled, halved lengthwise, stuffed with the hard yolks mixed with purée of green peas and raw yolks, coated with cheese sauce, sprinkled with grated cheese and browned in the oven; garnished with small balls of glazed carrots; Béarnaise sauce served separately.

Sarah Bernhardt: hard boiled, halved lengthwise, stuffed with mixture of the hard yolks, chopped chicken, white breadcrumbs and raw yolks, baked, covered with truffle sauce.

Strassburg Style: à la strassbourgeoise: hard-boiled, stuffed with the yolks mixed with gooseliver purée, dipped in egg and bread crumbs and fried; suprême sauce blended with gooseliver purée served separately.

Tripe: à la tripe: hard-boiled, cut in slices, dressed in timbales, coated with onion sauce, chopped parsley sprinkled on top.

White Friars Style: à la carmelite: hard-boiled, halved lengthwise, stuffed with the yolks mixed with chopped shallots, parsley and purée of sorrel, coated with cheese sauce, sprinkled with grated Parmesan, browned in the oven.

Cold Eggs

Oeufs froids

Alexandra: cold poached eggs served on tartlets filled with lobster froth, decorated with truffles, glazed with aspic jelly, caviar around the base.

Ambassadress Style: à l'ambassadrice: hard-boiled eggs, dressed on pastry shell, coated with mayonnaise sauce, decorated with tarragon leaves, garnished with aspic jelly.

with Asparagus: aux asperges: cold medium boiled eggs, coated with white chaudfroid sauce, decorated, glazed with aspic jelly, served on asparagus salad.

Balzac: cold poached eggs dressed on pastry case filled with purée of knob celery, coated with white chaudfroid sauce blended with celery purée, garnished with truffle slice, glazed and garnished with aspic jelly.

Baroda: cold hard-boiled eggs, halved lengthwise, stuffed with the yolks creamed with anchovy butter and a little curry powder, coated with mayonnaise sauce seasoned with curry powder, garnished with aspic jelly.

Berlin Style: à la berlinoise: cold poached eggs, coated with mayonnaise blended with purée of smoked salmon, served on pastry case, lined with purée of smoked salmon.

Beyram Ali: cold poached eggs coated with green mayonnaise, decorated with shrimps, dressed on vegetable macédoine, sprinkled with chopped dill, garnished with sliced tomatoes.

Blissful Style: des viveurs: cold medium boiled eggs, coated with lobster-chaudfroid sauce, glazed with aspic jelly; dressed on slices of spiny lobster coated with mayonnaise, thickened with aspic, set around a cupola of Parisian potato salad, garnished alternately with slices of marinated potatoes and beetroot.

Carême: tartlets filled with diced salmon in mayonnaise, topped with fried eggs, cut round with pastry cutter, yolks decorated with slice of truffle, whites surrounded with caviar, garnished with triangles of aspic jelly.

Charterhouse Style: à la chartreuse: filled in small moulds lined with aspic jelly, cold cut vegetables arranged symmetrically on sides and bottom, sealed with aspic jelly, turned out on vegetable macédoine; mayonnaise served separately.

Colinette: poached eggs filled in oval moulds lined with aspic jelly, chequered with truffles and hard whites of egg, turned out on Rachel salad, garnished with aspic jelly.

Christopher Columbus: Christoph Colomb: cold hard-boiled eggs, halved lengthwise, stuffed with chopped chicken, the yolks, anchovy fillets, capers and pickled cucumbers; dressed on shredded lettuce, garnished with sliced radishes; cold mustard sauce served separately.

Columbus: à la Colomb: cold medium cooked eggs, dressed on pastry cases filled with purée of gooseliver, coated with mayonnaise, garnished with chopped aspic jelly mixed with tomato purée.

Danish Style: à la danoise: cold hard boiled eggs, cut lengthwise, stuffed with the yolks mixed with purée of smoked salmon, covered with mayonnaise sauce.

Eggs in Nests: Oeufs au nid: cold medium boiled eggs placed in nest made of maître d'hotel butter, filled with chopped aspic jelly, surrounded with salad of watercress.

Esterhazy: cold poached eggs dressed on oval croûtons covered with an oval slice of ox tongue, coated with Ravigote sauce, garnished with diced aspic jelly.

Frou-Frou: cold poached eggs coated with chaudfroid sauce mixed with chopped yolks of hard-boiled eggs, decorated with a ring of truffle, dressed on salad of peas, French beans and asparagus tips in mayonnaise, garnished with chopped aspic jelly.

Gabrielle: cold medium boiled eggs (mollet) set in oval mould filled with aspic jelly mixed with chopped lobster coral, dressed on oval tartlets filled with purée of white fish.

Gentleman Style: à la gentilhomme: cold hard-boiled eggs halved lengthwise, stuffed with purée of pheasant blended with the yolks, coated with brown chaudfroid sauce, decorated with truffle slice, glazed with aspic jelly.

Germaine: cold poached eggs set in moulds filled with aspic jelly blended with tomato juice, dressed on oval pieces of fried bread, slightly hollowed out and stuffed with chopped lobster bound with mayonnaise.

Harlequin: à l'arlequin: cold medium boiled eggs (mollet) coated with various sorts of chaudfroid sauce, decorated differently, glazed with aspic jelly, dressed on tartlets filled with vegetable macédoine bound with mayonnaise.

Hungarian Style: à la hongroise: sliced hard-boiled eggs, dressed on vegetable salad, sprinkled with paprika, garnished with tomato and cucumber salad dressed on lettuce leaves.

Hussar Style: à la hussarde: dressed on crayfish froth (mousse), coated with mayonnaise sauce mixed with grated horseradish and cream, decorated with thin strips of green peppers.

Imperial Style: à l'impériale: cold poached eggs dressed on artichoke bottoms filled with vegetable macédoine mixed with diced ox tongue and tomatoes, coated with Remoulade sauce.

Johanna: cold poached eggs glazed with aspic jelly, dressed in pastry shells filled with ham froth.

Lafond: cold hard-boiled eggs, dressed in pastry shells filled with salad of thin strips of calf's foot and green peppers, coated with mayonnaise.

with Lobster tartlets: aux tartelettes de homard: cold poached eggs, coated with jellied mayonnaise, sprinkled with chopped lobster coral, dressed an artichoke bottoms; garnished with tartlets filled with diced lobster and tomatoes mixed with mayonnaise, garnished with a slice of lobster, decorated and glazed with aspic jelly.

Margot: cold medium boiled eggs, dressed on ovals of fried bread, hollowed out and stuffed with chopped anchovies, ox tongue and pickles, bound with mayonnaise, coated with mayonnaise.

Maupassant: cold poached eggs coated with brown matelote sauce with red wine blended with fish jelly, glazed with fish jelly, garnished with pink colored fish jelly.

Mirabeau: cold fried eggs cut round with a pastry cutter, dressed on rounds of toast spread with anchovy butter mixed with chopped hard yolks, decorated with anchovy fillets and pitted olives, glazed with aspic jelly.

Modern Style: à la moderne: cold hard-boiled plovers eggs, dressed on pastry shells filled with vegetable macédoine in mayonnaise sauce.

Monte Christo: cold poached egg set in mould lined with aspic jelly, sealed with aspic, turned out on vegetable macédoine bound with mayonnaise.

Mortimer: cold hard-boiled eggs, cut at ends so as to stand upright, yolk removed, replaced by caviar, decorated with anchovy fillets and truffle slices, glazed with aspic jelly, dressed on artichoke bottom, garnished with aspic jelly.

Mosaic: medium boiled eggs (mollet) decorated mosaic-fashion with ox tongue, truffles, green beans and hard-boiled egg white, served on base of Russian salad in aspic jelly decorated in the same way.

Nice Style: à la niçoise: poached cold eggs dressed in pastry shells filled with salad of diced potatoes, French beans and tomatoes, bound with mayonnaise blended with tomato purée, coated with the same sauce, glazed with aspic jelly.

Nordenskjöld: mould lined with aspic jelly, decorated with hard-boiled egg white, poached egg placed in centre, sealed with aspic, turned out on asparagus salad; mayonnaise with chopped herbs served separately.

Norwegian Style: à la norvégienne: poached eggs decorated and glazed with aspic jelly, dressed on shrimp salad mixed with chopped anchovy fillets.

Oléa: cold hard-boiled eggs, halved lengthwise, stuffed with the yolks creamed with butter, chopped olives added, seasoned with Cayenne pepper, garnished with aspic jelly.

Olga: cold hard-boiled eggs, halved lengthwise, stuffed with the yolks creamed with a little mayonnaise, mixed with chopped olives and knob celery, coated with mayonnaise sauce, garnished with caviar.

Paganini: puff pastry shells stuffed with diced tomatoes in mayonnaise, cold poached egg placed on top, coated with thick mayonnaise, decorated with a truffle lyra.

Pretender Style: à la prétendant: poached eggs coated with mayonnaise, glazed with aspic jelly, filled in puff pastry tartlets stuffed with salad of raw diced mushrooms: garnished with white asparagus tips covered with green mayonnaise.

Prince of Wales: Prince de Galles: large tomatoes cut in half, hollowed out, marinated with vinegar and oil, stuffed with salad of diced stalk celery, half of a hard-boiled cold egg placed on each tomato, coated with mayonnaise.

Queen Style: à la reine: small brioches baked in round moulds, hollowed out, filled with diced chicken in mayonnaise, medium boiled egg (mollet) on top, coated with mayonnaise, truffle slice on top, glazed with aspic jelly.

Quirinal: poached egg, decorated with slice of truffle, glazed with aspic jelly, dressed on round base of lobster froth.

Romanow: cold poached eggs decorated with pitted olives and green peppers, placed on cold marinated artichoke bottoms filled with caviar.

Rosita: poached eggs coated with chaudfroid sauce mixed with chopped lobster coral, chequered with small slices of truffle, glazed with aspic jelly, dressed on round base of aspic jelly, garnished with tiny peeled tomatoes stuffed with purée of tunny fish.

Rubens: cold poached eggs coated with white chaudfroid sauce blended with gooseliver purée, decorated with blanched tarragon leaves, glazed with aspic jelly, placed on tartlet of hop shoots, mixed with tomato purée, chopped parsley and chervil, blended with aspic jelly.

Russian Style: à la russe: puff pastry tartlet filled with Russian salad, poached egg on top, garnished with smoked salmon, caviar and gherkins.

Sevilla Style: à la sevillanne: oval shaped toast spread with anchovy butter, half an egg cut lengthwise placed on top, garnished with stuffed olives.

Skobeleff: cold poached eggs coated with mayonnaise blended with tomato purée, decorated with strips of smoked salmon, placed on tartlets filled with diced crayfish tails in mayonnaise seasoned with anchovy essence.

Spring Style: à la printanière: poached eggs decorated and glazed with aspic jelly, placed in puff pastry tartlet filled with fine vegetable macedoine mixed with mayonnaise.

with Tarragon: medium boiled eggs (mollet) dressed on lettuce, coated with mayonnaise sauce, decorated with blanched leaves or sprinkled with chopped tarragon.

Tartar Style: 1. à la tartare: cold poached egg dressed on small flat beefsteak Tartar, seasoned with paprika, coated with thick sour cream, sprinkled with chopped chives.
2. hard-boiled eggs halved lengthwise, stuffed with the yolks creamed with mayonnaise, mixed with chopped red beet roots, pickles and anchovy fillets, garnished with caviar, surrounded with tartar sauce.

Tsarina: à la czarine: cold medium boiled eggs, coated with pink chaudfroid sauce, dressed on puff pastry tartlets filled with Russian salad, garnished with strips of smoked salmon, anchovy fillets, caviar and aspic jelly.

Valence Style: à la valencienne: cold poached eggs dressed on artichoke bottoms, coated with mayonnaise mixed with mustard and crushed garlic, garnished with tomato salad.

Wladimir: cold medium boiled eggs, dressed on asparagus salad, coated with green mayonnaise.

French Fried or Baked Eggs

Oeufs frits

Abyssinian Style: à l'abyssine: dressed on flat sweet potato fritters, surrounded with truffle sauce.

American Style: à l'américaine: fried in oil, dressed on slice of fried bacon; tomato sauce served separately.

Andalusian Style: à l'andalouse: fried in oil, dressed on slices of fried eggplant; tomato sauce served separately.

Bayonese Style: à la bayonnaise: dressed on fried tomatoes cut in halves and grilled slices of ham; Madeira sauce served separately.

Benoiton: served on hashed salt cod cooked in red wine, mixed with anchovy fillets and fine herbs, sprinkled with cheese and glazed, surrounded with a border of cooked sliced potatoes..

Bordeaux Style: à la bordelaise: fried in oil, dressed on tomatoes cut in halves, fried and stuffed with chopped mushrooms à la bordelaise.

Colbert: Poached eggs, dipped in egg and breadcrumbs, fried in oil, dressed on artichoke bottoms, coated with Chateaubriand sauce, sprinkled with chopped parsley.

Cosmopolitan: à la cosmopolite: cold poached eggs, dipped in egg and breadcrumbs, fried, dressed on croûtons, surrounded with truffle sauce.

d'Orignan: fried in oil, dressed on fried slices of eggplant, covered with diced tomatoes sauted with chopped onions, garlic and herbs, garnished with anchovy fillets.

English Style: fried in oil, dressed on fried ham, garnished with triangular fried croûtons.

Infante: fried in oil, garnished with chicken livers sauted in butter and bound with Madeira sauce.

Louisiana: fried in oil, dressed on fritters of sweet potatoes, garnished with moulded risotto, sliced fried bananas and creamed corn.

Maxim Ferronet: fried in oil, dressed on slices of fried eggplant, slightly coated with béarnaise sauce, garnished with mushrooms à la bordelaise.

Mexican Style: à la mexicaine: fried in oil, dressed on rice mixed with diced sauted tomatoes and garlic.

Nivernese Style: à la nivernaise: dressed on croûtons, garnished with glazed carrot balls and small glazed onions, surrounded with demi-glace.

Palmerston: fried in oil, dressed on a slice of buttered toast covered with a slice of fried ham, surrounded with poivrade sauce.

Reapers Style: à la moissonneur: fried in oil, dressed on grilled bacon, garnished with peas à la paysanne.

Roman Style: à la romaine: fried in oil, dressed on round croûtons, hollowed out and filled with chopped spinach sauted in butter and mixed with chopped anchovy fillets.

St. Hubert: fried in oil, dressed on game purée mixed with purée of lentils, surrounded with game gravy.

Shepherds Style: à la pastourelle: fried in oil, dressed on slices of grilled bacon garnished with sliced mushrooms sauted with chopped shallots, half a grilled mutton kidney placed on each egg.

Spanish Style: à l'espagnole: fried in oil, dressed on tomatoes, cut in halves and fried, garnished with fried onion rings; tomato sauce served separately.

with Sorrel: fried in oil, dressed on purée of sorrel.

Verdi: hard-boiled eggs halved lengthwise, stuffed with the creamed yolks mixed with cream sauce, chopped ham and fine herbs, dipped in egg and breadcrumbs and fried, garnished with asparagus tips; truffle sauce served separately.

Villeroi: poached or medium boiled eggs, coated with Villeroi sauce, dipped in egg and breadcrumbs and fried, garnished with fried parsley; tomato sauce served separately.

Yorkshire Style: fried in oil, surrounded with grilled York ham; tomato sauce served separately.

Fried Eggs

Oeufs au plat — Oeufs mirroir

Acrobats: à la saltimbanque: dressed on bed of diced mushrooms and tomatoes simmered with chopped challots, garlic, parsley and chervil in Spanish sauce.

Admirals Style: à l'amiral: dressed on ragoût of truffles and crayfish tails; white wine sauce, poured round the eggs.

Algerian: à l'algérienne: dressed on bed of diced tomatoes, eggplants and green peppers in tomato sauce.

Alsatian Style: à l'alsacienne: dressed on saurkraut, garnished with sliced sausage.

American Style: à l'américaine: 1. dressed on slice of grilled ham, border of tomato sauce poured around the edge. 2. dressed on slices of lobster, surrounded with American sauce.

with Anchovies: aux anchois: baked in dish covered with diced anchovy fillets, garnished with anchovy fillets.

Antibes Style: à l'antiboise: eggs cooked on dish rubbed with garlic and lined with anchovy fillets; border of tomato sauce poured around the edge.

Antonine: dressed on grilled ham; sprinkled with chopped herbs and capers, browened butter is then poured over.

Antwerp Style: à l'anversoise: dressed on bed of hop shoots bound with cream sauce; surrounded with cream.

Bacon and Eggs: grilled or fried bacon on dish, eggs broken on top, seasoned and fried.

with Bananas: aux bananes: cooked on bed of sliced bananas, slightly sauted in butter.

Bercy: garnished with very small pork sausages, surrounded with tomato sauce.

Bibesco: garnished with strips of ox tongue, surrounded with truffle sauce.

Bradford: fried, cut round with cutter, dressed on pastry shell filled with chopped ham in curry sauce.

Braganza: dressed on pastry tartlet filled with strips of chicken, mushrooms and truffles in velouté sauce; tomato sauce around the edge.

Breton Style: à la bretonne: dressed on onion purée, sprinkled with cheese, glazed under the salamander.

with Brown Butter: au beurre noir: covered with brown butter seasoned with a few drops of vinegar.

Butcher Style: à la bouchère: dressed on thin fried tenderloin or flat Hamburger; surrounded with demi-glace.

Canadian Style: à la canadienne: large half-tomatoes scooped out, filled with small egg, seasoned, placed on buttered egg dishes, baked in oven.

Cardinals Style: à la cardinal: garnished with slices of lobster and truffle, surrounded with lobster sauce.

Castellans Style: à la châtelaine: dressed on tartlets filled with mashed chestnuts bound with meat glaze; masked with chicken velouté blended with purée of onions.

Carême: garnished with sliced mushrooms and truffles, masked with cream sauce, glazed under the salamander.

Chalons Style: à la châlonnaise: garnished with cockscomb and cock's kidney, surrounded with suprême sauce.

Chartrese Style: à la Chartres: cut out round, dressed on croûtons, demi-glace with chopped tarragon poured over.

Clamart: dressed on green peas cooked the French way.

Cluny: garnished with very small chicken fritters, surrounded with tomato sauce.

Condé: dressed on bed of purée of red kidney beans with diced fried bacon, border of red wine sauce poured around the edge.

Conti: dressed on bed of lentils and grilled bacon.

Devilled Eggs: cooked on both sides, brown butter with a drop of vinegar poured over.

Doria: garnished with olive-shaped parboiled cucumbers in cream sauce.

in Dressing Gown: en robe de chambre: large baked potato, scooped out, filled with a raw egg, seasoned, butter dropped on top, cooked in the oven.

Duchess Style: à la duchesse: cut out round, dressed on base of duchesse potato, covered with cream sauce, decorated with slice of truffle.

Egyptian: à l'égyptienne: dressed on bed of creamed purée of leeks and onions.

Florence Style: à la florentine: dressed on bed of plain spinach sauted in butter, coated with cheese sauce, sprinkled with grated cheese, glazed under the salamander.

Foresters Style: à la forestière: dressed on bed of sliced morels, sauted with chopped shallots and diced bacon, garnished with morels.

French Style: à la française: dressed on bed of plain spinach, sauted in butter; garnished with grilled bacon, surrounded with Colbert sauce.

Grandduke: Grand-duc: cut out round, dressed on croûton. slice of truffle on yolks, garnished with crayfish tails and asparagus tips.

Grandmothers Style: à la grand'mère: dressed on fried bread, sprinkled with chopped chives.

Granier: dressed on bed of sliced truffles and asparagus tips; slice of truffle on the yolks, asparagus tips on the side.

Greek Style: dressed on bed of diced pumpkin, peppers and tomatoes simmered in oil with chopped onions.

Gounod: garnished with sauted mushrooms, surrounded with tomato sauce.

Ham and Eggs: ham fried on one side, raw eggs broken overit, finished in the oven.

Hungarian Style: dressed on bed of sliced stewed onions flavored with paprika, coated with sour cream, sprinkled with chopped chives, glaced under the salamander.

Hunters Style: à la chasseur: garnished with sauted chicken livers and diced mushrooms, surrounded with Madeira sauce.

Imperial: à l'impériale: dressed on diced sauted gooseliver, surrounded with Madeira sauce.

Isoline: garnished with tomatoes sauted provençale style, stuffed with diced chicken livers bound with Madeira sauce.

Japanese: à la japonaise: cut out round, dressed on half-tomatoes, garnished with stachys.

Jessica: garnished with fried morels and asparagus tips, surrounded with thick gravy.

Jockey Club: cut out round, dressed on round croûton spread with gooseliver paste, garnished with diced veal kidneys and truffles, surrounded with Madeira sauce.

Karoly: dressed on slices of smoked ox tongue, sprinkled with cheese and glazed.

Khedivial: à la Khédive: dressed on purée of onions, cream poured over, sprinkled with grated cheese and glazed; tomato sauce poured around the dish.

Lille Style: à la lilloise: dressed on bed of slightly crushed Brussels sprouts, surrounded with cream sauce.

Little Duke: Petit-duc: garnished with fried mushroom caps stuffed with grated horseradish, surrounded with Chateaubriand sauce.

Lothringian Style: à la lorraine: dressed on slices of grilled bacon and thin slices of Swiss cheese, covered with cream.

Lyonese Style: à la lyonnaise: dressed on bed of browned onions, surrounded with Lyonese sauce.

Marguerite: cut out round, dressed on flat round fish croquette, tomato sauce poured around the edge of dish.

Mariners Style: à la marinière: dressed on bearded mussels in matelote sauce.

Marquise: dressed on scooped out Marquise potatoes stuffed with hashed ham and veal bound with tomato sauce.

Mascot: à la mascotte: garnished with diced artichoke bottoms, truffles and potatoes, surrounded with Madeira sauce.

Maximilian: Maximilienne: dressed on half tomato, stuffed with purée of parsley roots, sprinkled with breadcrumbs mixed with chopped parsley and grated cheese, topped with butter and glazed.

Metternich: dressed on sliced sauted mushrooms, dusted with grated cheese, glazed under the salamander.

Mexican Style: à la mexicaine: dressed on diced pumpkin, tomatoes, onions and sweet peppers simmered in oil with garlic.

Mezerai: garnished with halved grilled mutton kidneys, surrounded with truffle sauce.

Mikado: dressed on half fried tomato, garnished with anchovy fillets, sprinkled with capers, surrounded with demi-glace.

Mirabeau: fried with anchovy butter in the dish, garnished with anchovy fillets and stuffed olives, decorated with blanched tarragon leaves.

Modern Style: dressed on sliced mushrooms and truffles in cream sauce, sprinkled with grated Parmesan, butter dropped on top and glazed.

Monaco Style: à la monégasque: dressed on bed of tomatoes concassées mixed with chopped tarragon, garnished with anchovy fillets, surrounded with tomato sauce.

Monselet: dressed on artichoke bottom, garnished with slice of truffle, demi-glace poured around the edge.

Montargis: cut out round, dressed on tartlet filled with strips of fried chicken livers, mushrooms and ox tongue, bound with cream sauce and a little meat glaze, coated with cheese sauce and glazed.

Montebello: dressed on shredded ham, chicken and truffles in Madeira sauce with chopped tarragon, decorated with blanched tarragon leaves.

Monte Carlo: baked with cream, garnished with salpicon of lamb kidneys and truffles and green asparagus tips.

Montmorency: cooked on base of creamed asparagus tips, garnished with asparagus tips and diced fried artichoke bottoms.

Mornay: only slightly set, covered with cheese sauce, sprinkled with grated cheese and glazed under the salamander.

Naiad: Naïade: dressed on toast coated with chopped sweated green peppers, surrounded with Colbert sauce mixed with chopped tarragon and chervil.

Nancy Style: à la nancéenne: dressed on purée of onions and sweet peppers, garnished with sliced sausage, surrounded with demi-glace.

Nantua: cooked on salpicon of crayfish, yolks decorated with slice of truffle, garnished with crayfish tails, border of Nantua sauce poured around the edge.

Negus: cut out round, dressed on round flat game croquette,

Nero: Néron: cut out round, dressed on flat chicken croquette, surrounded with tomato sauce.

Nice Style: à la niçoise: dressed on tomatoes concassées with chopped tarragon, garnished with anchovy fillets, demi-glace poured around the dish.

Normandy Style: à la normande: cooked on raw oysters in light cream sauce, surrounded with Norman sauce.

Olivet: dressed on creamed purée of sorrel, surrounded with cream sauce.

Omar Pacha: cooked on base of sliced onions simmered in butter, sprinkled with grated cheese, glazed and surrounded with tomato sauce.

Opera: garnished with asparagus tips and sauted chicken livers, surrounded with Madeira sauce.

Orléans: dressed on puff pastry tartlets filled with diced chicken in tomato sauce, coated with suprême sauce blended with pistachio butter.

Parma Style: à la parmesane: coated with cream, sprinkled with grated Parmesan and glazed.

Patti: dressed on purée of truffles, surrounded with Sherry sauce.

Perigord Style: à la périgourdine: set on truffle essence, garnished diced truffles, border of truffle sauce.

Persian Style: à la persane: base of sliced onions fried in butter, seasoned with Cayenne pepper, sprinkled with chopped parsley, a little lemon juice poured over the eggs.

Piedmontese: à la piémontaise: garnished with sliced white Italian truffles, sprinkled with grated Parmesan and glazed.

Portuguese Style: à la portugaise: dressed on stewed tomatoes, garnished with tomatoes concassées sprinkled with chopped parsley.

Provençal Style: à la provençale: dressed on half-tomatoes, sprinkled with chopped parsley and garlic, fried in oil.

Queens Style: à la reine: dressed on piped tartlets of duchesse potatoes filled with hashed chicken; suprême sauce poured around the edge.

Rachel: cut out with round cutter, dressed on round croûton, yolk surmounted with slice of blanched ox marrow and a slice of truffle; demi-glace poured around the dish.

Richemont: garnished with diced morels and truffles, surrounded with Madeira sauce.

Roman Style: dressed on plain spinach sweated in butter and anchovy fillets, dusted with grated Parmesan and glazed.

Rossini: cut out round, dressed on slice of sauted gooseliver, garnished with truffle slice, surrounded with truffle sauce.

Rothomago: garnished with fried ham, small pork sausage (Chipolata) and surrounded with tomato sauce.

Royal Style: à la royale: dressed on round base of poached chicken forcemeat, garnished with purée of mushrooms, surrounded with suprême sauce mixed with chopped truffles.

St. Hubert: dressed on game hash, surrounded with pepper sauce.

Sagan: garnished with fried calf's brain, surrounded with suprême sauce.

Sailors Style: à la matelote: congealed in dish covered with Matelote sauce, surrounded with the same sauce.

Savoy Style: à la savoyarde: base of sliced fried raw potatoes sprinkled with grated Parmesan, coated with cream, cooked in oven.

with Shrimps: cut out round, dressed on puff pastry tartlets filled with salpicon of shrimps; garnished with shrimps, shrimp sauce poured around the dish.

Sicilian Style: à la sicilienne: garnished with half tomatoes stuffed with Italian sauce, surrounded with Italian sauce.

Soubise: dressed on purée of onions, surrounded with demi-glace.

Spanish Style: à l'espagnole: cut out round, dressed on grilled half-tomatoes, garnished with fried onion rings.

Swiss Style: à la suisse: base of sliced bread and Swiss cheese, baked in the oven.

with Tarragon: dressed on tarragon sauce, garnished with blanched tarragon leaves and the same sauce poured round the eggs.

Tessin Style: à la tessinoise: cooked in oil on dish rubbed with garlic.

Trouville Style: à la trouvillaise: dressed on salpicon of shrimps, mussels and mushrooms bound with white wine sauce, surrounded with shrimp sauce.

Turandot: garnished with fried tomatoes stuffed with sauted chicken livers in Madeira sauce.

Turkish Style: à la turque: garnished with sauted chicken livers and fried onion rings; surrounded with tomato sauce.

Vaucourt: scrambled eggs mixed with diced truffles and asparagus tips dressed inside a ring of piped Duchess potatoes, a fried egg cut with a round cutter placed on top decorated with a slice of truffle; demi-glace poured around the potatoes.

Vegetable Gardners Style: à la maraîchère: dressed on bed of braised chiffonade of lettuce and sorrel, garnished with slices of bacon and sausage.

Véfour: covered with sliced calf's brain topped with thin slices of Swiss cheese, glazed under the salamander.

Victoria: garnished with salpicon of diced lobster and truffles in lobster sauce; surrounded with lobster sauce.

Villars: dressed on bed of sliced artichoke bottoms, bound with onion sauce; garnished with slices of fried bacon, a border of purée of white kidney beans piped around the dish.

Walewska: dressed on tartlet filled with diced spiny lobster bound with cream sauce blended with spiny lobster butter; egg cut out round, topped with slice of spiny lobster and truffle, coated with cream sauce blended with butter of spiny lobster.

Welcome Eggs: Bienvenu: dressed on bed of purée of fresh tomatoes on dish piped with a crown of Duchesse potatoes which were baked beforehand.

Wladimir: garnished with asparagus tips and sliced truffles, coated with cream, sprinkled with grated cheese and glazed.

Poached Eggs

Oeufs pochés

Abyssinian Style: à l'abyssine: dressed on flat croquettes of sweet potatoes, hollowed out and stuffed with chestnut purée, coated with white butter sauce mixed with shredded white Italian truffles.

Admirals Style: à l'amiral: dressed on tartlet filled with salpicon of crayfish tails and truffles, coated with white wine sauce.

African Style: à l'africaine: dressed on oval toast, garnished with slices of grilled bacon, pilaw rice and diced stewed tomatoes.

Algerian Style: à l'algérienne: dressed on tartlet filled with diced pumpkin, tomatoes, eggplant and green peppers simmered in oil and bound with tomato sauce.

Almassy: dressed on tartlets filled with purée of mushrooms and sardines, coated with Nantua sauce.

Alsatian Style: à l'alsacienne: dressed on saurkraut with slices of carrots and sausage, coated with demi-glace.

Ambassadrice: dressed on pastry cases filled with creamed purée of lettuce, coated with cream sauce.

American Style: à l'américaine: dressed on halved tomatoes fried in butter, slice of lobster on top, coated with lobster sauce.

Andalusian Style: à l'andalouse: dressed on slices of fried eggplant, coated with tomato sauce mixed with strips of green peppers.

André: dressed on halved tomatoes, filled with sliced mushrooms, coated with Bordeaux sauce.

Antwerp Style: à l'anversoise: dressed on tartlet filled with hop shoots in cream sauce, coated with German sauce.

Archduchess Style: à l'archiduchesse: Dressed on flat potato croquettes with a cavity in the centre, filled with sliced stewed onions and mushrooms, seasoned with paprika; coated with horseradish sauce.

Archdukes Style: à l'archiduc: dressed on tartlets filled with sauted chicken livers and truffles, deglazed with Cognac; coated with paprika sauce.

Archibald: dressed on oval croûtons, scooped out slightly and filled with chopped stewed red peppers, bound with mushroom sauce; coated with Colbert sauce mixed with purée of tomatoes and finely diced artichoke bottoms.

Argentine Style: à l'argentine: dressed on tartlets filled with diced sauted eggplants, coated with tomato sauce, covered with fried onion rings.

Armenonville: dressed on tartlets filled with creamed asparagus tips, coated with suprême sauce.

Artagan: dressed on tartlets filled with gooseliver, mushroom cap on top, coated with Dutch sauce.

Artists Style: à la diva: dressed on ring of poached chicken forcemeat, the centre filled with diced gooseliver and tomatoes in Béarnaise sauce.

d'Artois: dressed on croûtons masked with diced stewed tomatoes, coated with tomato sauce.

with Asparagus tips: aux pointes d'asperges: dressed on asparagus tips, coated with Mousseline sauce.

in Baked Potatoes: à la Parmentier: dressed on baked potatoes, scooped out, filled with the pulp mixed with butter, coated with cheese sauce, sprinkled with grated cheese and glazed.

Bakers Style: à la boulangère: dressed on oval croûton, hollowed out slightly and filled with diced sauted mushrooms, coated with cheese sauce, sprinkled with grated cheese and glazed.

Baltic Style: à la baltique: dressed on oval croûton, slightly hollowed out and filled with a little caviar, coated with cheese sauce, sprinkled with grated cheese and rapidly glazed under the salamander.

Barcelona Style: à la barcelonnaise: dressed on halved tomatoes, garnished with stewed green peppers, coated with demi-glace.

Bar-le-Duc: dressed on artichoke bottoms, coated with cream sauce mixed with chopped tarragon.

Beauce Style: à la beauceronne: dressed on croûton filled with white onion purée, coated with velouté blended with white onion purée.

Beauharnais: dressed on artichoke bottoms, coated with Beauharnais sauce.

Beaujolais Style: à la beaujolaise: dressed on croûton, coated with Colbert sauce.

Béchamel: dressed on croûton, coated with cream sauce.

Bedford: dressed on tartlet filled with purée of gooseliver, coated with Madeira sauce, shredded truffles and ox tongue on top.

Belleclaire: dressed on croûton filled with purée of mushrooms, coated with cream sauce mixed with chopped truffles, sprinkled with grated cheese, glazed under the salamander.

Benedict: dressed on toast covered with an slice of fried ham, coated with Dutch sauce, decorated with truffle slices.

Benedictine: dressed on tartlets filled with purée of salt cod, mixed with chopped truffles, coated with cream sauce.

Berlioz: dressed on oval croûtons, stuffed with partridge and mushroom hash, coated with Hunter sauce.

Bernadotte: dressed on oval croûton covered with anchovy fillets, coated with cream sauce, mixed with chopped green olives.

Bignon: dressed on ring of poached chicken forcemeat, coated with velouté sauce, decorated with blanched tarragon leaves, trickle of demi-glace poured around the dish.

Blanchard: dressed on toast covered with sliced ox tongue, coated with Colbert sauce.

Boieldieu: dressed on tartlet filled with salpicon of chicken, truffles and gooseliver, coated with chicken velouté.

Bonnefoy: dressed on tartlet filled with purée of game, coated with thick game gravy.

Bonvalet: dressed on oval croûton, coated with suprême sauce, a border of Choron sauce and a slice of truffle on each egg.

Boston Style: dressed on tartlet filled with purée of haddock, coated with cream sauce.

Braganza: dressed on halved tomatoes fried in oil, coated with Béarnaise sauce, a border of thick gravy poured around.

Brasilian Style: à la brésilienne: dressed on base of rice, coated with tomatoe sauce, mixed with chopped sweet peppers and ham.

Brébant: dressed on tartlet filled with purée of quails and gooseliver, coated with truffle sauce.

Brebigny: small poached eggs, dipped in egg and bread crumbs, rapidly fried in deep fat, dressed on pastry cases filled with purée of mushrooms; lobster sauce served separately.

Breton Style: à la bretonne: dressed on tartlet filled with purée of haricot beans, coated with thick gravy.

Brussels Style: à la bruxelloise: dressed on bed of creamed purée of chicory, coated with cream sauce, bread crumbs fried in butter on top.

Buckingham Palace: dressed on toast covered with a slice of ham, coated with cream sauce, sprinkled with grated cheese and glazed.

Burgundy Style: à la bourguignonne: poached in claret, dressed on croûtons, coated with the reduced thickened claret blended with demi-glace.

Café Anglais: dressed on piped ring of poached crayfish forcemeat, coated with Nantua sauce.

Cambridge: dressed on base of scooped out pumpkin, filled with chicken purée, coated with Venitian sauce.

Camerani: dressed on tartlets filled with braised saurkraut, topped with a round slice of fried ham, coated with thick gravy, sprinkled with chopped ham.

Cardinals Style: à la cardinal: dressed on pastry cases, filled with diced lobster in Béchamel sauce, coated with Cardinal sauce, chopped lobster coral sprinkled on top.

Carnot: dressed on artichoke bottoms filled with diced stewed tomatoes, coated with Spanish sauce mixed with tomato purée.

with Carrots: Crécy: dressed on hollowed out brioche, filled with carrot purée, coated with cream sauce, a star of carrot on each egg.

Castelians Style: à la châtelaine: dressed on tartlets filled with crushed chestnuts, bound with buttered meat glaze, coated with suprême sauce blended with onion purée, a slice of truffle on each egg.

Castro: dressed on artichoke bottoms, coated with cream sauce blended with Dutch sauce, mixed with chopped mushrooms, seasoned with Cayenne pepper.

Catalan Style: à la catalane: dressed on halved fried tomatoes, filled with diced sweet pepper in thick tomato sauce, coated with tomato sauce.

Celestian Style: à la célestine: dressed on fried bread spread with lobster butter, topped with anchovy fillets; coated with cream sauce blended with crayfish butter.

Cevennes Style: à la cévenole: dressed on purée of chestnuts, coated with velouté sauce.

Chalons Style: à la chalonnaise: dressed on pastry cases filled with cockscombs and cocks' kidneys in cream sauce, coated with suprême sauce.

Chambéry: dressed on scooped out croûtons filled with purée of chestnuts, coated with Madeira sauce.

Chambord: dressed on croûtons, coated with Chambord sauce.

Chamonix: dressed on tartlets filled with purée of mushrooms, coated with Madeira sauce.

Chantilly: dressed on pastry cases filled with creamed purée of green peas, coated with Mousseline sauce.

Chartrese Style: à la Chartres: dressed on croûtons, coated with tarragon sauce, decorated with blanched tarragon leaves.

Chateaubriand: dressed on toast covered with a slice of fried gooseliver, coated with Chateaubriand sauce.

Chivry: dressed on tartlets filled with purée of sorrel, spinach and watercress, coated with Chivry sauce.

Cinderella: Cendrillon: egg served on a large baked potato which has been scooped out; slice of truffle on top, coated with cheese sauce, sprinkled with grated cheese and glazed.

Clamart: dressed on pastry case filled with purée of green peas or peas cooked in the French way; coated with suprême sauce or cream sauce.

Clermont: dressed on croûtons covered with sliced mushrooms in tomato sauce, coated with curry sauce.

Colbert: dressed on tartlets filled with very fine vegetable macedoine in cream sauce; Colbert butter served separately.

Colonels Style: à la colonel: dressed on thick slices of tomato, dipped in egg and breadcrumbs and fried, coated with mushroom sauce.

Colonial Style: à la coloniale: dressed on base of risotto, mixed with chopped red and green peppers, coated with cheese sauce, sprinkled with grated cheese, glazed and surrounded with tomato sauce.

Colombine: poached pigeon eggs, dresseed on bed of chicken purée, coated with cream sauce.

Continental Style: à la continentale: dressed on croûton covered with gooseliver purée, coated with Madeira sauce mixed with tomato purée.

Coquelicot: dressed on ring of poached chicken forcemeat filled with stewed diced peppers, coated with cream sauce, mixed with chopped peppers.

Countess Style: à la comtesse: dressed on artichoke bottom a slice of truffle on each egg and a small bunch of asparagus tips on one side.

with Crayfish and Asparagus: aux écrevisses et asperges: dressed on pastry cases filled with diced crayfish tails and asparagus tips in cream sauce, coated with Nantua sauce.

Creole Style: à la créole: dressed on flat rice croquettes, mixed with chopped mushrooms, coated with Creole sauce.

on Cress Bed: à la cressonière: dressed on tartlets, filled with purée of watercress bound with Béchamel sauce, coated with suprême sauce mixed with chopped watercress.

Crown-Prince Style: à la dauphin: dressed on green asparagus tips on toast, coated with Madeira sauce, mixed with chopped mushrooms.

Czecho-Slovakian Style: à la tchèque: dressed on croûtons, coated with cream sauce, sprinkled with chopped ham and glazed.

Danish Style: à la danoise: dressed on pastry case filled with purée of smoked salmon.

Daumont: dressed on large mushrooms filled with diced crayfish tails in Nantua sauce, coated with Nantua sauce, a slice of truffle on each egg.

Derby: dressed on slices of gooseliver patty, coated with truffle sauce.

Diana: dressed on tartlets filled with game purée mixed with mushroom purée, coated with game sauce flavored with Madeira; a slice of truffle on each egg.

Dieppe Style: à la dieppoise: dressed on pastry cases, filled with mussels and shrimps in white wine sauce, coated with wine sauce.

Dijon Style: à la dijonnaise: dressed on a ring of piped baked Duchesse potatoes, coated with Burgundy sauce; a small mushroom cap on each egg.

Divorced Eggs: Divorçons: dressed alternately on pastry cases filled with tomatoes concassées, coated with cream sauce, sprinkled with chopped truffles, and cases filled with hashed chicken, coated with tomato sauce and sprinkled with chopped hard-boiled egg yolks.

Don Carlos: dressed on tartlet filled with diced chicken and ox tongue in cream sauce, coated with Béarnaise sauce.

Doria: dressed on tartlets filled with diced stewed cucumbers, coated with velouté sauce; a slice of white Italian truffle on each egg.

Dreux Style: à la Dreux: dressed on tartlets filled with diced chicken, mushrooms, truffles and olives bound with demi-glace blended with essence of truffles; a slice of truffle on each egg.

Dubarry: dressed on pastry cases filled with purée of cauliflower, coated with cheese sauce, sprinkled with grated cheese and glazed.

Duchess Style: à la duchesse: dressed on border of Duchess potato, coated with velouté sauce, a border of thick gravy poured around.

Dufferin: dressed on large grilled mushrooms, coated with horseradish sauce.

Duse: dressed on round flat croquettes of macaroni, mixed with diced ox tongue and mushrooms and very thick tomato sauce; coated with cheese sauce blended with tomato purée, sprinkled with grated cheese, rapidly glazed under the salamander.

Dutch Style: à la hollandaise: dressed on croûton, scooped out and filled with purée of smoked salmon, coated with Dutch sauce.

Easter Eggs: à la pascale: dressed on moulds made of Marquise potato, filled with spinach purée, each egg coated with a different colored sauce (Nantua, truffle, green and cream sauce).

Edmond: dressed on scooped out croûtons masked with chopped snails and sauted tomatoes, coated with tomato sauce, a cockscomb on each egg.

English Style: à l'anglaise: dressed on toast masked with melted Cheddar cheese seasoned with Cayenne pepper, a little melted butter poured over the eggs.

Elisabeth: dressed on artichoke bottoms, coated with Soubise sauce, sprinkled with grated cheese and glazed.

Escoffier: dressed on round scooped out brioche, filled with purée of mushrooms mixed with diced artichoke bottoms; coated with suprême sauce, sprinkled with chopped lobster coral, a slice of truffle topped with a dot of caviar on each egg.

Esmeralda: dressed on tartlets, filled with purée of gooseliver, coated with Maximilian sauce, sprinkled with chopped truffles and hard-boiled egg whites.

Eugenie: dressed on large mushrooms stuffed with gooseliver purée, coated with Dutch sauce.

Fédora: dressed on tartlets filled with diced gooseliver and truffles in suprême sauce, coated with suprême sauce.

Finnish Style: à la finnoise: dressed on croûtons, coated with tomato sauce mixed with diced green peppers and chopped chervil.

Flemish Style: à la flamande: dressed on pastry cases, filled with purée of Brussels sprouts, coated with cream sauce.

Flora: dressed on pastry cases, half of the eggs coated with suprême sauce and besprinkled with chopped truffles, the other half with tomato sauce besprinkled with chopped parsley.

Floréal: dressed on tartlets, coated with suprême sauce mixed with chopped parsley, a border of purée of green peas piped around the base.

Florence Style: à la florentine: dressed on tartlets filled with plain spinach sauted in butter; coated with cheese sauce, sprinkled with grated cheese and glazed.

Fontainebleau: dressed on croûtons masked with diced fried tomatoes, coated with cream sauce mixed with chopped red peppers.

Foresters Style: à la forestière: dressed on piped baked Duchess potato moulds, filled with sliced morels, coated with thick gravy, sprinkled with chopped parsley.

French Style: à la française: dressed on round flat potato croquettes, the cavity filled with diced sauted tomatoes, coated with demi-glace.

Gabriel: dressed on bed of rice, mixed with diced gooseliver and sauted diced veal kidneys; coated with Madeira sauce.

Garcia: dressed on tartlets filled with chicken purée, mixed with chopped sweet peppers, coated with Madeira sauce.

Gascon Style: à la gasconne: dressed on halved tomatoes, filled with lamb hash, mixed with chopped herbs, garlic and tomato sauce; coated with thick tomato sauce, sprinkled with grated cheese and glazed.

Gastronomers Style: à la gastronome: dressed on tartlets filled with purée of mushrooms, coated with gastronomers sauce, sprinkled with chopped truffles.

Gaulish Style: à la galloise: dressed on chopped ham on toast covered with stewed, diced tomatoes, coated with tomato sauce, garnished with cockscomb and cocks' kidney.

Georgette: dressed on baked, scooped out potatoes, filled with salpicon of lobster or crayfish in Nantua sauce; coated with cheese sauce, sprinkled with grated cheese and glazed.

Germaine: dressed on large grilled mushrooms, coated with Colbert sauce mixed with chopped tarragon.

German Style: à l'allemande: dressed on pastry cases, filled with saurkraut, topped with small slice of boiled salt pork and sausage, coated with demi-glace.

Gipsy Style: à la Zingara: dressed on croûtons, coated with demi-glace tomatée, mixed with strips of ham, mushrooms, ox tongue and truffles.
Gladstone: dressed on pastry case, filled with chestnut purée, coated with cream sauce, blended with purée of gooseliver.
Gladys: dressed on tartlet filled with purée of white fish mixed with diced stewed tomatoes, coated with cream sauce.
Gounod: dressed on slice of fried calf's sweetbread, coated with truffle sauce.
Gourmand: dressed on croûtons masked with anchovy butter, coated with truffle sauce, a slice of truffle on each egg.
Grandduke: Grand-duc: arranged like a crown in a large flat pastry shell with a truffle slice and a crayfish tail between each egg, coated with Mornay sauce, sprinkled with grated cheese and rapidly glazed; asparagus tips dressed in the center before serving.
Greek Style: à la grecque: dressed on fried slices of eggplant, coated with Dutch sauce.
Grimod: dressed on pastry case filled with salpicon of crayfish tails in Nantua sauce, coated with cheese sauce, sprinkled with grated cheese and glazed.
Halévy: dressed on tartlet filled with diced stewed tomatoes; each egg coated on one half with suprême sauce and the other half with tomato sauce, a line of meat glaze between both halves.
Harlequin: à l'arlequin: dressed on croûtons, coated with cream sauce, sprinkled with chopped ham, truffles and parsley, surrounded with demi-glace.
d'Hauteville: baked potatoes, scooped out, filled with the pulp mixed with diced chicken and cream, eggs dressed on top, coated with suprême sauce blended with crayfish butter, a slice of truffle on each egg, sprinkled with cheese and glazed.
Héloise: dressed on croûton, coated with German sauce, mixed with chopped chicken, truffles and ox tongue; a border of meat glaze poured around the dish.
Henri IV.: dressed on artichoke bottom, coated with Béarnaise sauce.
Hoyos: dressed on pastry case, filled with purée of sorrel, coated with cream sauce, sprinkled with grated cheese and glazed.
Huevos escalfados Catalana: cold poached eggs, dressed on pastry cases filled with salad of white kidney beans, onions and red peppers. (Spanish)
Humberto: dressed on flat croquette of spaghetti, coated with velouté blended with tomato purée, garnished with sliced white sauted Italian truffles.
Hungarian Style: à l'hongroise: dressed on tartlets filled with slices of stewed onions, mixed with tomatoes concassées, seasoned with paprika, coated with cream sauce, blended with tomato butter and seasoned with paprika.
Hunter Style: à la chasseur: dressed on tartlets filled with sauted chicken livers and mushrooms in Hunter sauce, coated with Hunter sauce.
Hussar Style: à la hussarde: dressed on halved fried tomatoes, filled with hashed onions and ham, bound with demi-glace, coated with velouté sauce seasoned with Cayenne pepper.

Imperial: à l'impériale: dressed on croûtons, slightly scooped out and filled with diced gooseliver and truffles in Madeira sauce.

— **Spring:** Printanière impériale: dressed on slices of spiny lobster, coated with American sauce finished off with thick cream, garnished with creamed morels and tiny tartlets filled with tomatoes concassées and sprinkled with very fine strips of truffles.

Indian Style: dressed on bed of curry rice, coated with curry sauce.

Infante: à l'infante: dressed on Pastry case, filled with purée of mushrooms, coated with cheese sauce and glazed, a slice truffle on each egg.

Irma: dressed on flat croquettes of noodles with a cavity in the center, filled with purée of gooseliver, coated with truffle sauce.

Isabella: dressed on flat chicken croquette with a cavity in the center, cavity filled with salpicon of ox tongue, truffles and pistachios, bound with suprême sauce; suprême sauce poured around.

Italian Style: à l'italienne: dressed on bed of risotto, mixed with diced tomatoes, coated with tomato sauce, garnished with slices of Zampino (stuffed, boiled pigs' trotters).

Jean Bart: dressed on pastry cases, filled with salpicon of mussels, mushrooms and shrimps in Béchamel sauce, coated with Norman sauce, a small button mushroom on each egg.

Jessica: dressed on croûtons, slightly scooped out and filled with salpicon of morels and asparagus tips, coated with Chateaubriand sauce.

Joan: Jeannette: dressed on tartlets filled with gooseliver purée, a small round slice of chicken on each egg, coated with chicken velouté.

Khédive: dressed on tartlets filled with chicken purée mixed with spinach purée, coated with velouté sauce.

Lafayette: dressed on croûtons, coated with Béarnaise sauce, garnished with diced stewed tomatoes.

Lakmé: dressed on croûtons, scooped out slightly and filled with diced sweetbread in curry sauce, coated with Colbert sauce mixed with chopped tarragon.

Lapérouse: dressed on tartlets, filled with creamed purée of artichoke bottoms, coated with suprême sauce, a slice of truffle on each egg.

Laurent: dressed on sliced smoked salmon on toast, coated with cream sauce.

La Vallière: dressed on pastry case filled with creamed purée of sorrel, coated with suprême sauce, decorated with asparagus tips.

Lenard: dressed on toast spread with caviar, coated with Madeira sauce.

Lithuanian Style: à la lithuanienne: dressed in tartlets filled with mushroom purée, coated with truffle sauce.

Little Duke: Petit-Duc: dressed on large grilled mushrooms, coated with Chateaubriand sauce.

Loie Fuller: dressed on croûtons, alternately coated with lobster sauce and green herb sauce.

Lorette: dressed on case made of baked Dauphine potato, filled with asparagus tips, coated with Spanish sauce, a slice of truffle on each egg.

Louis XIV.: dressed on pastry cases filled with mushroom purée mixed with diced ox tongue, coated with suprême sauce, sprinkled with chopped truffles.

Louisa: Louisette: dressed on Dauphine potato bottom, coated with Dutch sauce, mixed with chopped ham, sprinkled with chopped truffles.

Louisville: dressed on corn fritters, coated with tomato sauce, garnished with fried slices of bacon and bananas.

Macdonald: dressed on mushrooms purée, coated with truffle sauce.

Madras Style: à la Madras: dressed on pastry cases filled with curry rice, coated with curry sauce.

Madrid Style: à la madrilène: dressed on croûtons, masked with anchovy butter, coated with cream sauce mixed with chopped olives.

Magdalen: Madeleine: dressed on croûtons, masked with chicken purée, coated with German sauce.

Maharadja: dressed on croûtons, masked with creamed chopped peppers, coated with curry sauce.

Maintenon: dressed on tartlets, filled with mushroom purée, coated with Soubise sauce, sprinkled with grated cheese and glazed.

Maire: dressed on croûtons, scooped out and filled with salpicon of ox tongue, ham and truffles in Madeira sauce.

Malakow: dressed on croûtons, masked with caviar, coated with cream sauce mixed with grated horseradish.

Malmaison: dressed on pastry cases, filled with creamed green peas, diced French beans and asparagus tips, coated with Béarnaise sauce, sprinkled with chopped chervil and tarragon.

Maltese Style: à la maltaise: dressed on tartlets, filled with mushrooms purée, coated with Maltese sauce.

Marie Louise: dressed on artichoke bottoms, filled with mushrooms purée, coated with suprême sauce.

Marlborough: dressed on croûton masked with anchovy butter, coated with truffle sauce, garnished with slices of fried bacon.

Martha: dressed on artichoke bottoms filled with chopped chicken, coated with egg sauce.

Martin: dressed on ring of poached chicken forcemeat, coated with Nantua sauce.

Masséna: dressed on artichoke bottoms filled with Béarnaise sauce, coated with tomato sauce, a slice of blanched ox marrow, sprinkled with chopped parsley, on each egg.

Massenet: dressed on base of Duchess potato, mixed with diced artichoke bottoms, coated with cream sauce blended with green bean butter.

Maximilian: dressed on halved tomatoes, stuffed with sweated herbs, fried in oil, coated with Maximilian sauce.

Mazarin: dressed on pastry cases filled with diced mushrooms sauted in oil, coated with tomato sauce.

Médicis: dressed on pastry cases filled with Vichy carrots and sorrel purée, coated with cream sauce mixed with green pea purée.

Menton Style: à la mentonnaise: dressed on creamed, stewed leeks, coated with cream sauce, sprinkled with grated cheese and glazed.

Metternich: dressed on artichoke bottoms filled with strips of ox tongue in velouté sauce, coated with cheese sauce, sprinkled with grated Parmesan and glazed.

Metz Style: à la messinoise: dressed on thick croûtons, hollowed out and filled with saurkraut, coated with demi-glace, garnished with sliced Frankfurters in demi-glace.

Mexican Style: à la mexicaine: dressed on bed of diced tomatoes, mushrooms and green peppers, simmered in oil and mixed with tomato sauce.

Mignon: dressed on artichoke bottom, filled with green peas and diced crayfish tails sauted in butter, coated with crayfish sauce.

Milanese: à la milanaise: dressed on pastry cases, filled with macaroni Milanese style, coated with cheese sauce, sprinkled with grated cheese and glazed.

Mirabeau: dressed on croûtons, masked with anchovy butter, coated with anchovy sauce, garnished with anchovy fillets, half a stuffed olive on each egg.

Mireille: dressed on saffron rice, coated with cream sauce mixed with saffron, garnished with croûtons fried in oil and masked with tomatoes concassées.

Mirepoix: au mirepoix: dressed on grilled ham on toast, coated with Madeira sauce, mixed with diced pot herbs sautéd in butter.

Modern Style: à la moderne: dressed on pastry cases filled with gooseliver purée, coated with velouté sauce.

Mogador: dressed on base of Duchesse potato, coated with cream sauce mixed with gooseliver purée, glazed and decorated with slices of ox tongue and truffles.

Molnar: dressed on pastry cases, filled with plain spinach in butter and topped with a small slice of fried gooseliver, coated with cheese sauce mixed with spinach purée, sprinkled with grated cheese and glazed.

Monaco Style: à la monégasque: dressed on half tomatoes fried in oil, coated with tomato sauce, mixed with chopped tarragon, garnished with anchovy fillets.

Monselet: dressed on pastry cases filled with strips of artichoke bottoms and truffles mixed with demi-glace, coated with Madeira sauce blended with tomato purée.

Montglas: dressed on pastry cases filled with salpicon of ox tongue, gooseliver, mushrooms and truffles in Madeira sauce, coated with Madeira sauce.

Montmorency: dressed on artichoke bottoms filled with creamed asparagus tips, coated with suprême sauce blended with tomato purée.

Montpensier: dressed on tartlets filled with scrambled eggs, mixed with shrimps, coated with shrimp sauce.

Mornay: dressed on croûtons, coated with cheese sauce, sprinkled with grated cheese and glazed.

Mozart: dressed on croûtons masked with liver purée, coated with cream sauce, each egg decorated with a lyra of truffle.

Murger: dressed on artichoke bottoms filled with chopped ox tongue in cream sauce, coated with cream sauce, a slice of truffle on each egg.

Naples Style: à la napolitaine: dressed on risotto, coated with demi-glace, mixed with tomato sauce, sprinkled with grated cheese and glazed.

Navarre Style: à la navarraise: dressed on flat croquettes of spaghetti, red and green peppers, coated with Béarnaise sauce.

New York Style: à la New-Yorkaise: dressed on creamed corn or corn meal mush, coated with cream sauce.

Niniche: dressed on artichoke bottoms filled with creamed chicken purée, coated with cream sauce.

Ninon: dressed on croûtons or pastry cases filled with creamed asparagus tips, coated with suprême sauce, a slice of truffle on each egg.

Normandy Style: à la normande: dressed on pastry cases filled with poached bearded oysters in Normandy sauce, coated with Normandy sauce.

Olympus: à l'olympic: dressed on tartlets filled with mushroom purée, coated with cream sauce, blended with spiny lobster butter, a slice of spiny lobster and truffle on each egg.

Oran Style: à l'oranaise: dressed on pastry cases filled with chopped ham, mushrooms, red peppers and onions, coated with Colbert sauce.

Oriental Style: à l'orientale: dressed on slices of fried tomatoes and cucumbers, coated with Dutch sauce.

d'Orléans: dressed on pastry cases filled with salpicon of chicken in tomato sauce, coated with suprême sauce blended with pistachio butter.

Orsay: dressed on croûtons, coated with Chateaubriand sauce.

Otéro: dressed in baked potatoes, scooped out and filled with salpicon of shrimps, mushrooms and truffles in Nantua sauce, coated with Nantua sauce.

with Ox Tongue: dressed on croûtons masked with ox tongue purée, coated with tomato sauce.

Pacha: dressed on flat croquettes of saffron rice, mixed with chopped onions and diced tomatoes, coated with cream sauce, sprinkled with grated cheese and glazed.

Parmentier: dressed on base of Duchess potatoes, coated with Béchamel sauce, sprinkled with grated Parmesan and glazed.

Patti: dressed on tartlets filled with artichoke purée, coated with Madeira sauce, a slice of truffle on each egg, garnished with asparagus tips.

Paulus: dressed on croûtons, coated with cream sauce mixed with chopped truffles, and glazed.

Pavillon: dressed on tartlets filled with morel purée, covered with cream sauce, a slice of truffle on each egg and a border of Chateaubriand sauce around the edge.

Perigord Style: à la périgourdine: dressed on large slice of truffle, coated with demi-glace mixed with truffle essence.

Perrier: dressed on chicken croquettes filled with diced sweet peppers, coated with Parisian sauce.

Persian Style: à la persane: dressed on croûtons, coated with tomato sauce, sprinkled with chopped ham and chives.

Pfordte: dressed on artichoke bottoms filled with mushroom purée, coated with truffle sauce.

Phoenician Style: à la phocéenne: dressed on pastry cases filled with creamed purée of cod, coated with cream sauce mixed with chopped truffles.

Piedmontese Style: à la piémontaise: dressed on risotto Piedmontese style, coated with cream sauce, garnished with slices of white Italian truffles.

Plovers Eggs Royal Style: Oeufs de pluvier à la royale: poached plovers eggs, dressed on flat croquettes of chicken and mushrooms, coated with demi-glace, sprinkled with chopped truffles.

Poincaré: dressed on artichoke bottoms, coated with mousseline sauce, sprinkled with chopped chives.

Polish Style: dressed on hashed mutton mixed with chopped mushrooms, coated with pepper sauce.

Portuguese Style: à la portugaise dressed on halved tomatoes fried in oil, coated with Portuguese sauce.

President Style: à la président: dressed on artichoke bottoms filled with creamed hashed chicken, coated with truffle sauce, a slice of truffle on each egg.

Prince Nicolai: dressed on fried slices of eggplant, coated with cream sauce with a pinch of saffron, garnished with risotto, mixed with diced red peppers.

Princess Style: à la princesse: dressed on pastry shells filled with asparagus tips, coated with cream sauce, a slice of truffle on each egg.

Puerto Rico: dressed on tomatoes concassées, mixed with diced ham and asparagus tips, coated with tomato sauce.

Queen Style: à la reine: dressed on pastry cases filled with chicken purée, coated with suprême sauce.

Queen Hortensia: à la reine Hortense: dressed on border of pilaw rice, mixed with diced red peppers, green peas and saffron, coated with American sauce, a slice of truffle on each egg; center filled with diced lobster and mushrooms in American sauce.

Rachel: dressed on artichoke bottoms, coated with Bordeaux sauce, a slice of ox marrow on each egg sprinkled with chopped parsley.

Raphael: dressed on croûtons, coated with cream sauce mixed with anchovy paste, garnished with crayfish tails.

Richelieu: dressed on cases of Duchess potato, garnished with grilled mushrooms and braised lettuce, coated with demi-glace.

Richemont: dressed on pastry cases filled with fried morels, coated with Madeira sauce, sprinkled with strips of truffles.

Rienzi: dressed on croûtons masked with gooseliver purée, coated with Italian sauce, garnished with slices of fried bacon.

Ritz: dressed on pastry cases filled with salpicon of shrimps, coated with shrimp sauce, garnished with diced stewed green peppers.

Roland: dressed on croûtons masked with chopped chicken in cream sauce, coated with cream sauce mixed with chopped chicken and truffles and glazed.

Roman Style: à la romaine: dressed on pastry shells filled with spinach leaves tossed in butter and mixed with chopped anchovy fillets and just a little garlic, coated with demi-glace with tomato.

Romeo: dressed on pastry cases lined with anchovy paste, coated with cheese sauce mixed with chopped ham, sprinkled with grated cheese and glazed.

Rossini: dressed on toast masked with a slice of fried gooseliver, coated with truffle sauce, a slice of truffle on each egg.

Rotraud: dressed on croûtons masked with truffle purée, coated with truffle sauce.

Rouen Style: à la rouennaise: dressed on toast masked with duck liver purée, coated with Rouenese sauce.

Rougemont: dressed on flat macaroni croquettes, coated with cheese sauce, sprinkled with grated cheese and glazed; border of tomato sauce.

Sailor's Style: à la matelote: dressed on croûtons masked with anchovy butter, coated with sailor sauce.

Saint-Hubert: dressed on tartlets filled with hare purée, coated with pepper sauce, a slice of truffle on each egg.

Saint-Lawrence: St. Laurent: cold poached eggs, dipped in egg and breadcrumbs, fried, dressed on tartlets filled with creamed chopped ham.

Saint-Peter: St. Pierre: dressed on croûtons masked with anchovy butter, coated with anchovy sauce.

Sans-Gêne: dressed on artichoke bottoms, a slice of blanched ox marrow on each egg, coated with Bordeaux sauce, sprinkled with chopped parsley.

Sarah Bernhardt: dressed on croûtons masked with creamed chicken purée, coated with truffle sauce.

Sardinian Style: à la sarde: dressed on halved fried tomatoes, coated with cheese sauce, sprinkled with grated cheese and glazed.

Sardou: dressed on croûtons masked with artichoke purée, coated with cream sauce blended with artichoke butter, garnished with asparagus tips, a slice of truffle on each egg.

Savoy Style: à la savoyarde: dressed on Savoyard potatoes, coated with cheese sauce, sprinkled with grated cheese and glazed.

Scotch Style: à l'écossaise: dressed on pastry cases, filled with salmon purée, coated with creamed fish velouté, blended with crayfish butter.

Schinkel: dressed on pastry cases filled with shredded ham, mushrooms and artichoke bottoms in Colbert sauce, coated with suprême sauce, a little crayfish butter dropped on each egg.

Schouvalow: dressed on artichoke bottoms filled with goose-liver purée, mixed with chopped truffles and ox tongue, coated with demi-glace, garnished with tiny balls of braised cabbage.

Scribe: dressed on pastry cases filled with chicken liver purée, coated with demi-glace.

Sergius: dressed on pastry cases filled with chicken purée, coated with suprême sauce, blended with artichoke butter.

Sevigné: dressed on croûtons masked with creamed lettuce, coated with velouté sauce, a ring of truffle on each egg.

Sevilla Style: à la sévillane: dressed on croûtons masked with anchovy butter, coated with velouté sauce mixed with a little tomato purée, half a stuffed olive on each egg; garnished with tomatoes concassées mixed with chopped parsley and a little garlic.

Shepherds Style: à la bergère: dressed on hashed lamb, coated with demi-glace.

with Shrimps: aux crevettes: dressed on tartlets, filled with salpicon of shrimps, coated with shrimp sauce, garnished with shrimps.

Songstress Style: à la divette: dressed on croûtons, scooped out and filled with creamed corn, coated with suprême sauce, sprinkled with chopped truffles.

with Sorrel: à l'oseille: dressed on sorrel purée, coated with demi-glace.

Soubeyran: dressed on tartlets filled with creamed onion purée mixed with chopped truffles, coated with suprême sauce.

Soubise: dressed on pastry cases filled with white onion purée, coated with thick veal gravy.

with Spinach: aux épinards: dressed on creamed purée of spinach, coated with demi-glace.

Splendid View: Beau regard: dressed on tartlets filled with eggplant purée, coated with demi-glace mixed with tomato purée, a slice of truffle on each egg.

Stanley: dressed on rice pilaff, mixed with onion purée, coated suprême sauce flavored with curry.

Sully: dressed on tartlets filled with hashed creamed chicken, coated with Béarnaise sauce.

Sultans Style: à la sultane: dressed on tartlets filled with scrambled eggs, mixed with chopped truffles; a half moon shaped slice of truffle on each egg, a little Madeira sauce poured around the edge.

Susan: Suzette: dressed on baked potatoes, slightly scooped out and lined with cheese sauce, coated with cheese sauce, glazed, a slice of truffle on each egg.

Swiss Style: à la suisse: dressed on toast covered with a very thin slice of Swiss cheese, coated with cheese sauce, sprinkled with grated Swiss cheese and glazed.

Talleyrand: dressed on slice of gooseliver patty on toast, coated with truffle sauce.

with Tarragon: dressed on croûton, coated with tarragon sauce, decorated with blanched tarragon leaves.

Tewfik Pacha: dressed on croûtons, coated with mushroom sauce mixed with chopped red peppers.

Theodor: dressed on pastry cases filled with creamed calf's brain, coated with cream sauce.

on Toast: sur toast: dressed on buttered toast, coated with melted butter.

Toulouse Style: à la toulousaine: dressed on pastry cases filled with salpicon of sweetbreads, mushrooms and chicken, coated with German sauce, a slice of truffle and a small cockscomb on each egg.

Toupinel: dressed on baked potatoes, scooped out, filled with potato purée mixed with chopped ham, coated with cheese sauce, sprinkled with grated cheese and glazed.

Tours Style: à la tourangelle: dressed on tartlets filled with flageolet purée, coated with cream sauce, blended with green bean butter.

Toussenel: dressed on flat game croquettes, coated with salmi sauce mixed with chestnut purée, sprinkled with chopped truffles.

Troubadour: dressed on croûtons masked with gooseliver purée, coated with truffle sauce.

Troubetzkoy: dressed on tartlets filled with game purée, mixed with chopped truffles, coated with Madeira sauce.

Trouville Style: à la trouvillaise: dressed on salpicon of mussels and shrimps, coated with shrimp sauce, a small mushroom cap on each egg.

Tschilbir: dressed on a china dish, coated with Yoghourt mixed with a pinch of salt and crushed garlic, melted butter seasoned with paprika poured over the Yoghourt. (Bulgarian)

Turin Style: à la turinoise: dressed on flat spaghetti croquettes with a cavity in the centre, the cavity filled with diced fried chicken livers, coated with demi-glace mixed with tomato purée.

Turkish Style: à la turque: dressed on saffron rice, coated with tomato sauce, sprinkled with chopped pistachios.

Tyrolese Style: à la tyrolienne: dressed on croûtons, scooped out and filled with tomatoes concassées, coated with Tyrolese sauce, garnished with fried onion rings.

Vanderbilt: dressed on tartlets filled with diced lobster in American sauce mixed with white onion purée.

Vatel: dressed on tartlets filled with diced sweetbread, truffles and tomatoes in cream sauce, coated with cheese sauce and glazed.

Vediloff: dressed on pastry cases filled with creamed asparagus tips, coated with shrimp sauce, decorated with asparagus tips and sliced truffles.

Venetian Style: à la venitienne: dressed on slices of poached calf's brains, coated with Venetian sauce, a mushroom cap on each egg.

Verdi: dressed on pastry cases filled with chopped ham, mixed with chopped fine herbs and cream sauce, coated with demi-glace and truffle essence, a slice of truffle on each egg.

Victoria: dressed on tartlets filled with diced lobster and truffles in lobster sauce, coated with Victoria sauce.

Villeroi: cold poached eggs, dipped in beaten eggs and bread crumbs and fried, dressed on fried parsley.

Viroflay: dressed on brioche cases filled with creamed spinach, coated with cream or suprême sauce.

Voisin: dressed on tartlets filled with chicken purée, alternately coated with cream and tomato sauce.

Volnay: dressed on croûtons, decorated mushroom cap, coated with buttered Volnay sauce.

Walewska: dressed on pastry cases filled with diced spiny lobster in cream sauce, decorated with a slice of truffle, coated with cheese sauce, finished with spiny lobster butter, and glazed.

Washington: dressed in baking dish on creamed corn, coated with cheese sauce, sprinkled with grated cheese and glazed.

Waterloo: dressed on slice of gooseliver patty on toast, coated with Béarnaise sauce.

Westphalian Style: à la westphalienne: dressed on croûtons, coated with suprême sauce, sprinkled with chopped fried Westphalian ham.

Xavier: dressed on pastry cases filled with salpicon of crayfish tails, mushrooms and truffles mixed with shrimp sauce.

Yvette: dressed on corn fritters, coated with archduke sauce.

Zurio: dressed on flat potato croquettes, coated with cream sauce.

Moulded Eggs

Oeufs moulés

Antwerp Style: à l'anversoise: bottom of mould decorated with truffle slices, lined with hop shoots; served on round croûton, coated with German sauce.

Archdukes Style: à l'archiduc: mould sprinkled with fine herbs; served on duchesse potatoes or croûton, coated with paprika sauce.

Belmont: mould lined with Villeroi sauce with chopped herbs; coated with tomato sauce mixed with chopped truffles.

Bernadotte: mould lined with chopped parsley and truffles; coated with anchovy sauce.

Blériot: mould lined with chopped hard-boiled eggs and lobster coral; served cold on tartlets filled with French salad.

Boieldieu: fancy moulds decorated with star of truffle, lined with gooseliver purée; dressed on tartlets filled with diced chicken, gooseliver and truffles, coated with thick gravy.

Bresse Style: à la bressanne: mould lined with sliced truffles and cockscombs; dressed on artichoke bottoms filled with diced mushrooms, cockscombs and cock's kidneys bound with velouté sauce.

Carignan: Madeleine moulds lined with chicken forcemeat; dressed on toast, coated with Chateaubriand sauce.

Carini: Dariole mould decorated with dots of truffle and ox tongue; dressed on a slice of fried sweetbread, garnished with morels in cream sauce flavored with Madeira; Béarnaise sauce served separately.

Chartrese Style: à la Chartres: moulds decorated with blanched tarragon leaves; coated with tarragon sauce.

Cherville: eggs beaten as for omelette, mixed with purée of spinach, poached in moulds; coated with Mornay sauce, sprinkled with grated cheese and glazed.

Daumont: mould lined with sliced truffles and crayfish tails; served on large mushrooms, coated with Nantua sauce.

Dreux Style: à la Dreux: mould lined with aspic jelly, decorated with asparagus tips and sliced truffles, filled with hard-boiled egg, sealed with aspic jelly; turned out on croûton, garnished with diced aspic jelly.

Duchess Style: à la duchesse: mould lined with chopped truffles or decorated with sliced truffle; served on flat duchesse potato bottom, coated with velouté sauce.

Fancy Eggs: moulds lined with aspic jelly, decorated with truffle, hard-boiled egg white, ox tongue and French beans, filled with cold poached egg, sealed with aspic jelly; served on salad of diced knob celery, pickled cucumbers, potatoes and red beetroots.

Foresters Style: à la forestière: mould lined with chopped parsley; served on tartlets filled with sliced fried morels, coated with thick gravy.

Juliette: fancy mould lined with chopped truffles and pistachios; served on croûton, coated with thick gravy.

Kasimir: mould decorated with thin strips of red and green peppers, lined with chicken forcemeat; served on croûton, coated with Spanish sauce.

Lilly: mould lined with chopped lobster coral, filled with half scrambled eggs and half raw beaten eggs mixed with diced truffles and shrimps; coated with shrimp sauce.

Modern Style: à la moderne: fancy mould lined with aspic jelly, decorated with fancy cut truffles and root vegetables, filled with poached cold egg, sealed with aspic jelly; served on vegetable macedoine bound with mayonnaise.

Mortemar: mould filled with half scrambled eggs mixed with half raw eggs; served on tartlets filled with purée of mushrooms; Colbert sauce served separately.

Mortimer: small high moulds lined with aspic jelly, decorated with truffle, red beetroots and knob celery, filled with poached egg, sealed with aspic jelly, turned out on puff pastry shell filled with caviar.

Neapolitan Style: à la napolitaine: moulds filled with scrambled eggs mixed with grated Parmesan and raw beaten eggs; coated with thick demi-glace blended with tomato purée, sprinkled with grated cheese and gratinated.

Palermo Style: à la palermitaine: mould decorated with ox tongue and truffles; served on pastry shell filled with macaroni, coated with cream sauce.

Perigord Style: à la périgourdine: mould decorated with truffle; served on tartlets filled with purée of truffle, coated with Madeira sauce.

Princess: à la princesse: mould decorated with truffle, lined with chicken forcemeat, filled with scrambled eggs mixed with diced truffles and asparagus tips, mould sealed with chicken forcemeat; dressed on croûton, suprême sauce served separately.

Prüger: moulds lined with aspic jelly, decorated with thin strips of red and green peppers and hard-boiled egg white filled with cold poached egg, sealed with aspic jelly; served on tartlets filled with diced tomatoes in mayonnaise sauce.

Queen Style: à la reine: mould lined with slices of chicken and truffle; dressed on ring of poached chicken forcemeat, coated with suprême sauce.

My Queen Style: à la petit-reine: fancy mould chequered with truffles and hard-boiled egg white, lined with aspic jelly, filled with cold poached egg, sealed with aspic jelly; served on asparagus salad bound with mayonnaise, garnished with half-moons of aspic jelly.

with Risotto: au risotto: mould lined with chopped ox tongue; dressed on risotto mixed with diced red peppers and eggplants, surrounded with tomato sauce.

Spring Style: à la printanière: moulds lined with sliced spring vegetables; dressed on croûton, coated with German sauce blended with vegetable butter.

Tours Style: à la tourangelle: lined with purée of shelled green Lima beans (flageolets); dressed on croûton, coated with cream sauce blended with green bean butter.

Verdi: mould decorated with slice of truffle, filled with scrambled eggs mixed with raw eggs, grated Parmesan and diced truffles; coated with demi-glace prepared with truffle essence.

Omelettes

African Style: à l'africaine: stuffed with tomatoes concassées, mixed with onions sweated in oil, rice and chopped ham.

Agnes Sorel: stuffed with chicken purée, mixed with sliced mushrooms, garnished with round slices of pickled ox tongue, a border of thick gravy poured around.

Algerian Style: à l'algérienne: stuffed with chopped stewed onion, sweet peppers and tomatoes.

American Style: à l'américaine: diced fried bacon in the mixture, stuffed with tomatoes concassées.

with Anchovies: aux anchois: eggs mixed with chopped desalted anchovy fillets, surrounded with anchovy sauce or demi-glace.

Andalusian Style: à l'andalouse: stuffed with diced tomatoes, red peppers and mushrooms, garnished with fried onion rings.

Archduke: à l'archiduc: stuffed with fried chicken livers in Madeira sauce, garnished with truffle slices, archduke sauce poured around.

Argentine: à l'argentine: stuffed with diced eggplant, a border of tomato sauce poured around.

with Artichoke Bottoms: aux fonds d'artichauts: omelette mixture mixed with diced or thinly sliced artichoke bottoms, a trickle of demi-glace poured around the dish.

with Asparagus tips: egg mixture with asparagus tips or stuffed with creamed asparagus tips.

d'Aumale: stuffed with diced fried veal kidney in Madeira sauce, garnished with tomatoes concassées.

with Bacon: au lard: egg mixture poured over diced fried bacon, omelette finished off as usual.

Belle Arlesian: à la belle Arlésienne: stuffed with codfish purée seasoned with garlic and mixed with olive oil, coated with tomato sauce mixed with diced fried eggplants.

Belloy: stuffed with diced fried eelpout livers, anchovy sauce poured around.

Benedictine: stuffed with creamed purée of salted cod, mixed with chopped truffles, a border of Normandy sauce poured around.

Béranger: stuffed with tomatoes concassées, mixed with diced fried bacon and chopped herbs, tomato sauce poured around the edge.

Bertin: omelette mixture mixed with diced fried eggplants and tomatoes, a trickle of Colbert sauce poured around.

Bertrand: stuffed with creamed chicken purée, mixed with chopped truffles, garnished with thin round slices of chicken and truffles, coated with Dutch sauce blended with mushroom essence.

Boulogne Style: à la boulonaise: stuffed with diced fried mackerel, a little melted parsley butter poured over the omelette.

Breton Style: à la bretonne: egg mixture mixed with chopped leeks, onions and mushrooms.

Brillat Savarin: stuffed with diced woodcock meat and truffles in salmi sauce, garnished with sliced truffles, surrounded with salmi sauce.

Brussels Style: à la bruxelloise: stuffed with creamed shredded endives, cream sauce poured around.

Burgundy Style: à la bourguignonne: stuffed with chopped stewed snails, chopped parsley in the omelette mixture.

Butcher Style: à la charcutière: egg mixture, mixed with diced fried bacon and diced sausage, surrounded with mustard sauce.

with Calf's Brains: au cervelle de veau: stuffed with diced calf's brain in Madeira sauce.

Canino: egg mixture mixed with chopped onions, diced morels and garlic sausage fried in oil and mixed with chopped parsley.

Cardinal P.: omelette of plovers eggs stuffed with salpicon of lobster and truffles in creamed thick veal gravy, coated with cheese sauce, blended with lobster butter, sprinkled with grated cheese and glazed rapidly under the salamander.

with Soft Carp Roes: aux laitances de carpe: stuffed with diced soft roes stewed in claret.

Castelan Style: à la châtelaine: stuffed with crushed chestnuts bound with meat glaze, surrounded with creamed white onion sauce.

Catalonian: à la catalane: stuffed with diced tomatoes concassées, green peppers and diced fried potatoes and eggplants, all mixed together.

Chalons Style: à la châlonnaise: stuffed with cockscombs and cocks' kidneys in cream sauce, surrounded with suprême sauce.

Chambery: egg mixture mixed with diced leeks, bacon, potatoes and cheese.

Chambord: stuffed with soft roe purée, surrounded with Chambord sauce.

Chartrese Style: à la Chartres: egg mixture mixed with chopped tarragon, demi-glace mixed with chopped tarragon poured around.

Cherburg Style: à la cherbourgoise: stuffed with shrimps, garnished with shrimps, shrimp sauce poured around.

Chevreuse: omelette mixture mixed with chopped chervil and diced stewed chervil bulbs, border of demi-glace poured around.

Choisy: stuffed with creamed shredded lettuce, cream sauce poured around the border.

Clamart: stuffed with peas cooked the French way, incision on top filled with peas.

Cluny: stuffed with game purée, a border of tomato sauce poured around the dish.

Continental Style: à la continentale: chopped chives in the egg mixture, stuffed with diced fried poatoes and boletus, surrounded with demi-glace.

Cracovian: à la cracovienne: stuffed with diced fried sweet potatoes mixed with fried bread crumbs.

with Crayfish: aux écrevisses: stuffed with salpicon of crayfish tails, border of Nantua sauce, poured around.

Creole Style: plain omelette, surrounded with Creole sauce.

Czech Style: à la tchèque: stuffed with short strips of ham and truffle in cream sauce, the same sauce poured around the omelette.

Danitscheff: see Tanitscheff.

Dejardins: stuffed with tomatoes concassées mixed with diced anchovy fillets and mushrooms, a border of Colbert sauce poured around the dish.

Demidoff: stuffed with diced artichoke bottoms or purée, garnished with slices of blanched marrow, covered with demi-glace.

Dieppe Style: à la dieppoise: stuffed with salpicon of mussels and shrimps, surrounded with white wine sauce.

Diocletian: Dioclétien: stuffed with creamed lettuce purée, surrounded with velouté sauce.

Diplomat Style: à la diplomate: stuffed with diced artichoke bottoms and truffles in truffle sauce.

Doria: stuffed with diced cucumber in velouté sauce, surrounded with velouté sauce mixed with grated white Italian truffles.

Dretschena, Russian O.: eggs beaten with milk, a little flour, cream, salt and pepper, cooked on both sides, arranged flat on a round dish, covered with brown butter (Russian).

Durand: egg mixture mixed with thinly sliced mushrooms and artichoke bottoms sautéd in butter, stuffed with asparagus tips and truffles in suprême sauce, a border of demi-glace tomatée poured around the edge.

Duse: garnished with calf's brain and crayfish tails in Madeira sauce.

Dutch: Hollandaise: egg mixture mixed with strips of smoked salmon sautéd in butter, a border of Dutch sauce poured around.

with Eel-pout Liver: aux foies de lottes: stuffed with eel-pout livers, surrounded with demi-glace.

Egyptian Style: à l'égyptienne: eggs mixed with tomato purée, stuffed with saffron rice, tomato sauce poured around.

Eierhaber (Swiss Omelette): sort of unsweetened pancake made of eggs, milk, a litte flour, salt and pepper, cooked and cut in small pieces. (Swiss)

Favorite Style: à la favorite: stuffed with creamed asparagus tips and chopped ham, garnished with truffle slices, a border of cream sauce poured around.

Farmers Style: à la paysanne: eggs mixed with shredded sorrel, diced fried bacon and potatoes, served flat like a pancake.

with Field Fungi: aux mousserons: stuffed with sautéd small field fungi, surrounded with Madeira sauce.

— — **Mushrooms:** aux chanterelles: stuffed with chopped, fried field mushrooms, surrounded with cream sauce.

with Fine Herbs: aux fines herbes: omelette mixture mixed with chopped herbs (parsley, tarragon, chervil, chives etc.).

Fishmonger Style: à la poissonnière: stuffed with salpicon of white fish, white wine sauce poured around.

Foresters Style: à la forestière: stuffed with sliced morels and boletus, mixed with buttered meat glaze, border of thick veal gravy.

Foulard: egg whites beaten to snow, mixed with the double amount of egg yolks and chopped fine herbs, seasoned with salt and pepper and baked.

Francis Joseph: François-Joseph: stuffed with diced chicken and mushrooms in paprika sauce, coated with cheese sauce, sprinkled with grated Parmesan cheese and glazed under the salamander.

French Style: à la française: egg mixture mixed with whipped cream and chopped stewed shallots.

Frothy Omelette: O. mousseline: stiffly beaten eggwhites, mixed with egg yolks and a little whipped cream, seasoned with salt and pepper, baked in the oven, served open, not folded together.

Gardners Style: à la jardinière: stuffed with mixed diced vegetables in cream sauce, a trickle of demi-glace around the edge.

Genoese: Farinada genovese: thin flat omelettes made of eggs, chick pea flour, water and salt, baked in hot oven (Italian).

Gipsy: à la Zingara: stuffed with tomatoes concassées, mixed with strips of ham, mushrooms and truffles, a border of demi-glace tomatée.

with Goby: aux nonats: stuffed with the fried young of a small Mediterranean Goby fried like whitebait

Gordon: egg mixture mixed with diced parboiled ox marrow and truffles, garnished with slices of truffles and blanched ox marrow, border of Chateaubriand sauce.

Gounod: filled with diced fried sweetbread in truffle sauce. surrounded with truffle sauce.

Grandmothers Style: Grand'mère: omelette mixture mixed with croûtons fried in butter and chopped parsley.

with Gravy: aux jus: plain omelette with a little thick veal gravy poured around.

Grenoble Style: à la grenobloise: egg mixture mixed with shredded sorrel and sliced fried onions.

Grimaldi: purée of crayfish mixed with the omelette mixture, stuffed with salpicon of crayfish.

Guildford: stuffed with stewed chopped morels and red peppers in white wine sauce.

with Ham: au jambon: egg mixture, mixed with chopped boiled ham.

Harlequin: arlequin: four small omelettes, one plain, one mixed with spinach, one with tomato purée and one with chopped truffles, not folded, placed one on top of the other, surrounded with a cordon of demi-glace.

Havana: à la havanaise: stuffed with fried chicken livers, diced green peppers and tomatoes, a border of tomato sauce.

with Hop shoots: aux jets de houblon: stuffed with creamed hop shoots, cut an incision in the center of the omelette, fill with hop shoots, cream sauce poured around.

Housewifes Style: Bonne femme: egg mixture mixed with diced fried bacon, fried slices of onions and mushrooms.

Hungarian: à la hongroise: stuffed with chopped onions stewed in butter, mixed with diced ham, surrounded with cream sauce flavored with paprika.

Hunter Style: à la chasseur: stuffed with sauted chicken livers and sliced mushrooms in demi-glace, the incision filled with the same mixture, Hunter sauce poured around.

Imperial: à l'impériale: stuffed with diced gooseliver and truffles in Madeira sauce.

Indian: à l'indienne: stuffed with curry rice mixed with stewed chopped onions, surrounded with curry sauce.

Italien: à l'italienne: stuffed with risotto mixed with diced tomatoes, surrounded with tomato sauce.

Ivanhoe: stuffed with creamed purée of smoked haddock, cream sauce poured around.

Jessica: stuffed with sliced morels and asparagus tips in cream sauce, garnished with bouquets of morels and asparagus tips, a trickle of Chateaubriand sauce poured around.

Joinville: stuffed with salpicon of shrimps, truffles and mushrooms in shrimp sauce, shrimp sauce poured around.

Jura Style: à la jurassienne: egg mixture mixed with diced fried bacon and chopped chervil, stuffed with sorrel purée, surrounded with cream sauce.

with Kidneys: aux rognons: stuffed with diced sautéd kidneys in Madeira sauce, an incision made on the top and filled with kidneys, surrounded with Madeira sauce.

Lafontaine: mixture with grated cheese, stuffed with diced truffles and tomatoes in Madeira sauce.

Limoge Style: à la limousine: egg mixture mixed with diced fried potatoes and ham.

Little Duke: Petit-duc: stuffed with boletus or mushrooms, surrounded with Chateaubriand sauce.

with Lobster: à l'homard: stuffed with diced cooked lobster in lobster sauce.

Loti: stuffed with truffle purée, surrounded with Madeira sauce.

Louis XIV.: stuffed with chopped chicken and truffles in cream sauce, the same sauce poured around.

Lucerne: à la lucernoise: mixed with diced fried rye bread, cooked on both sides and served flat (Swiss).

Lyonese: à la lyonnaise: egg mixture mixed with sliced fried onions and chopped parsley.

Mancelle: stuffed with chestnut purée mixed with strips of partridge, game sauce poured around.

Maria: egg mixture mixed with chopped braised onions and fine herbs, the same mixture filled in the incision, white onion sauce poured around.

Marseille Style: à la marseillaise: stuffed with purée of salted cod mixed with tomatoes concassées, surrounded with Nantua sauce.

Mascotte: egg mixture mixed with diced fried potatoes, artichoke bottoms and truffles, border of Madeira sauce.

Masséna: stuffed with diced artichoke bottom in tomato sauce, garnished with blanched slices of ox marrow slightly coated with buttered meat glace, border of Béarnaise sauce.

Maxim: plain omelette garnished with slices of truffle and crayfish tails on top, surrounded with sautéd frog legs.

Mazarin: stuffed with sliced fried chipolatas and mushrooms in Madeira sauce.

Médicis: stuffed with diced roast fieldfare, truffles and morels bound with demi-glace, hunter sauce poured around the omelette.

Meissonier: stuffed with diced carrots and turnips in cream sauce, surrounded with the same sauce.

Metz Style: à la messinoise: strips of Frankfurters in the egg mixture, stuffed with saurkraut, surrounded with demi-glace.

Mexican: à la mexicaine: strips of sweet peppers and diced mushrooms in the egg mixture, stuffed with tomatoes concassées, surrounded with demi-glace tomatée.

Milanese: à la milanaise: stuffed with macaroni cut in small pieces and mixed with grated Parmesan cheese, truffle strips and tomato sauce, surrounded with the same sauce.

Mireille: stuffed with tomatoes concassées flavored with garlic, cream sauce colored with saffron poured around.

Mistral: fry diced eggplants in oil, pour egg mixture, mixed with diced sautéd tomatoes, a little crushed garlic and chopped parsley, over the eggplants, cook on both sides and serve flat.

Monaco: à la monégasque: tomato purée and chopped tarragon in the egg mixture, garnished with anchovy fillets, a trickle of anchovy sauce poured around.

Mona Lisa: stuffed with strips of fieldfare, surrounded with Hunter sauce.

with Morels: aux morilles: stuffed with sliced fried morels, demi-glace poured round around the omelette.

with Mushrooms: aux champignons: egg mixture, mixed with sliced sautéd mushrooms, thick gravy poured around.

with Mussels: aux moules: stuffed with bearded mussels in sailor sauce, surrounded with the same sauce.

Nana: strips of mushrooms and shredded lettuce in the omelette mixture, stuffed with diced sweetbreads in cream sauce, cream sauce blended with essence of truffles poured around.

Nantese Style: à la nantaise: stuffed with sardine purée, surrounded with white wine sauce.

Nantua: stuffed with salpicon of crayfish tails, garnished with crayfish tails, surrounded with Nantua sauce.

Newburg: stuffed with diced lobster in Newburg sauce, surrounded with the same sauce.

Nice Style: à la niçoise: stuffed with tomatoes concassées and diced green beans surrounded with demi-glace or thick veal gravy.

Nimese Style: à la nimoise: cooked in oil, stuffed with purée of salted codfish, garnished with truffle slices.

Ninon: stuffed with asparagus purée, garnished with sliced truffles, coated with light cream sauce.

Nivernese Style: à la nivernaise: stuffed with small glazed button onions, coated with demi-glace, garnished with glazed young carrots.

Noailles: stuffed with fried chicken livers and kidneys, cream sauce poured around.

Normandy Style: stuffed with ragoût of shrimps and mushrooms bound with Normandy sauce, garnished with sliced truffles and bearded oysters, a border of Normandy sauce poured around the omelette.

Olympia: stuffed with diced crabmeat and sweet peppers in cream sauce.

Omelette, Plain: Omelette nature: served without garnish of any kind.

Opera: stuffed with chicken livers and asparagus tips, surrounded with Madeira sauce.

Ostende Style: à l'ostendaise: stuffed with poached oysters in white wine sauce, garnished with sliced truffles, border of white wine sauce.

with Ox Marrow: à la moelle: stuffed with diced, blanched ox marrow in Madeira or Burgundy sauce, garnished with slices of blanched ox marrow, sprinkled with chopped parsley, surrounded with Madeira or Burgundy sauce.

with Oysters: aux huîtres: stuffed with poached bearded oysters in cream sauce.

Pantagruel: diced truffles in the egg mixture, stuffed with diced quail breasts in Madeira sauce, the same sauce poured round the omelette.

Parisian: à la parisienne:
1. egg mixture with strips of truffles, ox tongue and mushrooms, stuffed with chicken purée.
2. chopped stewed onions and chopped mushrooms in egg mixture, garnished with small fried pork sausages, thick veal gravy poured around.

Parmentier: egg mixture, mixed with fried diced potatoes and chopped parsley.

with Parmesan: aux parmesan: egg mixture, mixed with grated Parmesan cheese.

Patti: beaten eggs mixed with diced artichoke bottoms, truffles and asparagus tips, omelette garnished with sliced artichoke bottoms and truffles, surrounded with demi-glace.

with Peas: aux petits pois: stuffed with creamed green peas, surrounded with cream sauce.

Perigord Style: à la périgourdine: omelette mixture, mixed with finely diced truffles, truffle sauce poured round the omelette.

Poacher Style: à la braconnière: omelette mixture, mixed with fried diced bacon and sliced morels, stuffed with hashed hare.

Portuguese Style: à la portugaise: omelette stuffed with tomatoes concassées, surrounded with tomato sauce.

with Potatoes: aux pommes de terre: made with diced fried potatoes in the egg mixture.

Prelate: du prélat: egg mixture, mixed with shredded lettuce, stuffed with ragoût of lobster, crayfish tails and truffles in lobster sauce, border of Normandy sauce.

Prince Style: à la princière: made of guinea fowls eggs, mixed with strips of truffles, stuffed with asparagus tips in suprême sauce, coated with Dutch sauce blended with chicken essence.

Princess: à la princesse: finely diced truffles in the egg mixture, stuffed with creamed asparagus tips, garnished with asparagus tips, a little suprême sauce poured around.

Provençal Style: à la provençale: stuffed with large cubes of tomatoes, simmered in oil, mixed with a little crushed garlic and chopped parsley.

Queen Style: stuffed with creamed chicken purée, surrounded with suprême sauce.

Raspail: stuffed with chopped boiled beef, ham and fine herbs in demi-glace, surrounded with demi-glace.

Reform: à la réforme: stuffed with strips of ox tongue, hard-boiled egg whites, pickled cucumbers and truffles, mixed with peppersauce finished off with red currant jelly.

Regency: à la régence: stuffed with ragoût of cockscombs and cocks' kidneys, mushrooms, truffles, ham and ox tongue in Regency sauce.

Richemonde: stuffed with creamed, sliced mushrooms, flavored with Port, coated with cheese sauce, glazed under the salamander.

Rigoletto: stuffed with diced truffles and ox marrow in buttered meat glaze, border of tomato sauce.

Robert: egg mixture, mixed with diced fried bacon and chopped onions, surrounded with Robert sauce.

Roman: à la romaine: stuffed with braised shredded spinach, mixed with chopped anchovies and a little garlic, surrounded with demi-glace tomatée.

Rose Caron: stuffed with diced fried bacon and eggplants.

Rossini: diced truffles and gooseliver mixed with the beaten eggs, garnished with small slices of fried gooseliver and truffles, covered with Madeira sauce.

Rouenese: à la rouennaise: stuffed with duck liver purée, Rouenese sauce poured around.

Royal: à la royale: stuffed with creamed chicken purée mixed with chopped truffles, garnished with sliced truffles, cream sauce poured around.

Russian: à la russe: egg mixture seasoned with paprika, stuffed with cold caviar, surrounded with shallot sauce.

Sagan: stuffed with diced calf's brain surrounded with suprême sauce.

Saint-Hubert: stuffed with game purée, garnished with mushroom caps, demi-glace or salmi sauce poured around.

Salvator: stuffed with strips of ham and truffles in Madeira sauce.

Sarah Bernhardt: stuffed with diced truffles, cockscombs and cocks' kidneys in cream sauce, a border of cream sauce.

Saratoga: stuffed with diced crabmeat and green peppers in Creole sauce.

Savoy Style: à la savoyarde: egg mixture, mixed with very small cubes of Swiss cheese, poured over thin slices of sautéd potatoes, omelette arranged flat on round dish.

Schinkel: egg mixture, mixed with strips of artichoke bottom, mushrooms and ham, covered with a little crayfish butter, border of buttered meat glaze, mixed with chopped tarragon.

Sevilla: à la sevillane: stuffed with tomatoes concassées, mixed with diced green olives, flavored with garlic, surrounded with white velouté sauce mixed with a little tomato purée and blended with anchovy butter.

Shepherd Style: à la bergère: stuffed with hashed lamb, mixed with sliced mushrooms, surrounded with demi-glace.

with Shrimps: aux crevettes: stuffed with shrimps in shrimp sauce, surrounded with shrimp sauce.

Sigurd: omelette mixture made with sliced morels and truffles.

with Sorrel: à l'oseille: cooked with shredded sorrel in the egg mixture or stuffed with creamed shredded sorrel, border of demi-glace poured around the omelette.

Soubise: stuffed with white onion purée, surrounded with thick veal gravy.

Spanish I: à l'espagnole: stuffed with tomatoes concassées, garnished with deep fried onion rings.

Spanish II (La Frita): eggs mixed with chopped stewed onions and grated cheese, served flat and browned on both sides. (Spanish)

with Spinach: aux épinards: stuffed with creamed spinach purée, cream sauce poured around.

Sportsman: stuffed with game purée, surrounded with chief ranger sauce.

Stuffed Omelette: O. fourrée: a small omelette stuffed with any kind of purée and folded in a larger one of different taste; also term for any stuffed omelette.

Swiss: à la suisse: mixed with grated Swiss cheese, served flat on a round dish, sprinkled generously with grated Swiss cheese.

Tanitscheff: stuffed with ragoût of cockscombs and cocks' kidneys, mushrooms and truffles in German sauce, a little German sauce poured around.

Tenants Style: à la fermière: beaten eggs mixed with small thin slices of carrots, onions and celery and chopped parsley, poured over diced ham fried in butter, omelette arranged flat on round dish.

with Tomatoes: aux tomates: stuffed with tomatoes concassées, incision made on top of omelette, filled with tomatoes and sprinkled with chopped parsley.

Tortilla Espanola: Sliced onions and raw potatoes fried in oil, omelette mixture poured over, cooked on both sides and arranged flat on a round dish. (Spanish)

Trafalgar: stuffed with deep fried whitebait.

Trouville: à la trouvillaise: stuffed with ragoût of mussels, mushrooms and shrimps in white wine sauce, surrounded with shrimp sauce.

Tsarina: à la czarine: stuffed with diced ogourzi (q. v.) and mushrooms, border of cream sauce.

with Tunny-fish: au thon: stuffed with marinated tunny-fish.

Turinese: à la turinoise: stuffed with chicken liver and mushrooms, border of Madeira sauce.

Turkish: à la turque: stuffed with poultry liver, surrounded with demi-glace tomatée.

Valencia: stuffed with risotto, coated with cream sauce mixed with chopped red peppers.

Vichy: stuffed with Vichy carrots, border of cream sauce.

Victoria: stuffed with ragoût of lobster and truffles in lobster sauce, border of lobster sauce.

Village Style: à la villageoise: stuffed with diced sautéd mushrooms mixed with chopped herbs.

Vosges Style: à la vosgienne: stuffed with diced fried bacon, potatoes and small whitebread croûtons.

Walewska: stuffed with ragoût of spiny lobster and truffles in cream sauce, surrounded with cream sauce blended with spiny lobster butter.

Wedic: stuffed with saffron rice mixed with diced mangoes and tomatoes, surrounded with suprême sauce blended with pistachio butter.

Yarmouth Style: stuffed with flaked bloaters, surrounded with white wine sauce.

with Yellow Boletus: aux cèpes: mixed or stuffed with sliced boletus sautéd with chopped shallots, a border of thick gravy poured around the omelette.

Fish · Crustaceans (Shell-fish) · Molluscs

Poissons	French	Crustacés
Fische	German	Krustentiere
Pesci	Italian	Crostaci
Pescados	Spanish	Crustáceos

Fish is easily digested but not so appeasing as meat. It is healthy food rich in Albumen, Magnesium, Phosphorous and Vitamins. Saltwater fish is also high in Sulfur and Iodine.

Tasty fish dishes can only be prepared with absolutely fresh fish. Fast transportation, fast freezing and progressive service methods have advanced the fish supply greatly. Fish, in the first instance saltwater fish, is now marketed cleaned, trimmed and filleted ready for use. The quality of fish, however, varies greatly according to where it is caught.

Knowledge of how to prepare fish is essential as the majority of guests appreciate well-prepared fish dishes. Fish should, therefore, never be cooked long beforehand, especially if it is to be boiled, because it loses a lot of flavor if left in the water or stock for any length of time.

Large fish which are to be served whole, salmon, salmon-trout, turbot, giant pike-perch etc., are started in cold water or stock and brought to the boil, smaller fish or fish cut in portions are always placed in hot but not boiling liquid. In both cases the fish must only be allowed to simmer (poach) without actually boiling.

Fillets, steaks, cutlets and smaller fish are more tasty if poached in their own juices. They are placed in a pan greased with butter and covered with chopped shallots, seasoned, a little white or red wine etc. and fish stock poured over until the fish is covered by the liquor about one third. It is then covered with a greased paper, brought quickly to the boiling point and allowed to simmer without actually boiling. The stock is often used to make the sauce.

Only larger fish are braised. They are often larded and always placed in a fish kettle on a base of sliced vegetables, mushroom peels and herbs, covered to a third with wine and stock and braised in the oven. The fish ought to be basted from time to time. The liquor is used in making the sauce.

Only newly killed fish with an uninjured skin can be cooked "blue" — au bleu —. Brook trout trench, carp, pike etc. is **placed in well seasoned hot**, but not boiling water and only allowed to simmer. It is absolutely unnecessary to pour vinegar over the fish or to add vinegar to the water, vinegar spoils the taste of such fine fish as trout, tench or carp. If the scales and fins are left on and mucous adherring to the fish is not touched to much it will always cook "blue"

Fish Stock I: Court-Bouillon: water, salt, pepper-corns, sliced onions and carrots, bunch of herbs, very little vinegar, boiled and strained; pepper-corns added ten minutes before straining. This stock is used for whole salmon, carp, giant pike-perch, pike, salmon-trout etc. It can also be used for crustaceans.

Fish Stock II: water seasoned with salt, a little milk and a few peeled lemon slices added. Stock for turbot, brill and giant pike-perch. The water is poured cold over the fish. Bass is usually cooked in salted water, without any other ingredients.

Fish Stock III: Fonds de poisson: fish bones and parings, sliced onions, mushroom peels, parsley sprigs, pepper corns (added 10 minutes before straining), very little salt, 8 parts water to 1 part wine (white or red wine according to use) boiled 30 minutes.

Fish Stock IV: Essence de poisson: fish bones and parings of soles, whitings, turbot etc., mushroom peels and parsley sprigs sweated in butter, moistened with 4 parts fish stock III and 1 part white wine and a little lemon juice, boiled 15 minutes and strained.

Fish, Fried I: seasoned, dipped in beaten egg and breadcrumbs, deep fried in hot fat or oil.

Fish, Fried II: small pieces or fillets, dipped in frying batter, deep fried in hot fat or oil.

Fish, French Fried III: coated with flour, fried in deep fat or oil. Deep fried fish is always garnished with fried parsley and lemon wedges.

Fish, Shallow Fried: smaller fish or fillets and cutlets — whole fish mostly scored to allow the heat to penetrate quicker — coated with flour, fried in skillet in hot butter or oil to a golden brown. The technical term for shallow fried fish covered with lemon slices or lemon juice with chopped parsley scattered on top and bubbling brown butter poured over is "Millers's Style" — à la meunière.

Fish, Grilled (Broiled): smaller fish scored, coated with flour brushed with oil, grilled and seasoned when they are cooked. Fillets are often dipped in melted butter and white breadcrumbs before being grilled.

A

Abalone: Pacific shellfish resembling scallops but larger. Prepared like scallops.

— **Steak California:** cut in thick slices, soaked in milk for a few minutes, seasoned, coated with flour, dipped in beaten egg, deep fried, dressed on tomatoes concassées, covered with lemon juice and browned butter, garnished with black olives.

Able de mer: see kingfish.

Ablette: see bleak.

Aigrefin, aiglefin: see haddock.

Alose: see shad.

Anchois: see anchovies:

Anchovies: F. Anchois; G. Sardellen, Anchoven. Small deep-sea fish of the herring family found in the Atlantic, Black Sea and abundant in the Mediterranean. Chiefly imported, cleaned and packed in salt or filleted and canned.

Anchovies
- **Basque Style:** à la basque: dipped in eggs and breadcrumbs, deep fried, dressed on tomatoes Provencal style; Béarnaise sauce mixed with small capers served separately.
- **Beaulieu:** coated with flour, fried in a pan in butter, dressed in tomatoes concassées, covered with green herb sauce.
- **Fried:** frites: I. dipped in eggs and breadcrumbs, deep fried, Tartar sauce served separately.
  II. dipped in frying batter, deep fried, tomato sauce served separately.
- **Grilled:** grillées: coated with flour, brushed with oil, grilled, remoulade sauce served separately.
- **Nice Style:** à la niçoise: boned, stuffed with fish forcemeat mixed with chopped herbs, wrapped in marrow blossoms poached in white wine and fish stock; stock thickened with flour and butter and blended with anchovy paste poured over the fish.
- **Pisa Style:** boned, stuffed with fish forcemeat, poached in white wine with sliced mushrooms, dressed on coarsely chopped spinach mixed with diced sautéd tomatoes and anchovy butter, covered with cream sauce, sprinkled with breadcrumbs, dotted with butter, browned in oven.
- **Saint-Honorat:** dipped in egg and breadcrumbs, deep fried, dressed on tomatoes concassées; Béarnaise sauce made with mint served separately.

Atlantic Cod: French: Tancaud; German: Dorsch. Name for baby cod and the cod caught in the Baltic. Prepared like cod.
- **Indian Style:** cut in fillets, coated with flour and fried, served with curry sauce and boiled rice.

Anguille: see eel.
- **de mer:** see conger eel.

Angler: F. Baudroie; G. Seeteufel. Saltwater fish found off the European and American Coasts of the Atlantic and the Mediterranean. Chiefly used for making Bouillabaisse.

B

Baby Halibut: prepared like halibut, turbot and sole.
- **Pike:** Brocheton: see pike.
- **Turbot:** F. Turbotin. Prepared like turbot and sole.

Bar: see bass.
- **noir:** see black bass and black sea bass.
- **rayé:** see striped bass.

Barbeau: see barbel.

Barbel: F. Barbeau, Barbillon; G. Barbe; I. Barbio. Freshwater fish found all over Europe. The spawn is poisonous.
- **Burgundy Style:** à la bourguignonne: steamed in red wine with mushroom peel and bouquet garni, stock strained and thickened with butter paste.
- **Dijon Style:** à la dijonnaise: cooked in fish stock with butter and chopped shallots, stock thickened with white roux, finished with cream, French mustard and chopped parsley.
- **with Dutch Sauce:** à la sauce hollandaise: cooked in court-bouillon, Dutch sauce served separately.

Barbel

— **Fried:** frit: cut in pieces, dipped in eggs and breadcrumbs, deep fried, Tartar sauce served separately.

— **Gordon Bennet:** fillets cut into small round pieces, poached in white wine, fishstock and mirepoix; when cold glazed with aspic jelly, dressed on tartlets filled with fine vegetable salad.

— **Gratinated:** au gratin: fillets coated with Italian sauce, sprinkled with grated Parmesan, melted butter dropped on top, cooked and browned on top at the same time in the oven.

— **Grilled:** grillé: scored on both sides, grilled, served with herb butter.

— **with Horseradish Sauce:** scored on both sides, dipped in eggs and breadcrumbs, fried, served with horseradish sauce.

— **Nice Style:** à la niçoise: baked in the oven in oil, dressed on tomatoes concassées, mixed with garlic and chopped tarragon, garnished with anchovy fillets, black olives and lemon slices, sprinkled with capers, browned butter poured over the fish.

— **Provencal Style:** à la provençale: poached in fish stock, oil and a little garlic, coated with Provencal sauce, garnished with stuffed tomatoes.

— **Maître d'hôtel:** cut in pieces, grilled, served with herb butter.

— **Massena:** braised in fish stock and white wine, stock reduced, mixed with demi-glace, finished off with anchovy butter, diced lobster, mushrooms and mussels, and poured over the fish.

— **Menton Style:** à la mentonnaise: fillets stuffed with pike forcemeat, folded, fried in butter, coated with white wine sauce.

— **Miller Style:** à la meunière: coated with flour, fried in butter, sprinkled with chopped parsley, lemon juice and browned butter poured over the fish.

— **Mirabeau:** larded with anchovy fillets, baked in the oven with oil, anchovy butter served separately.

— **Montebello:** fillets stuffed with pike forcemeat, folded, poached in white wine, fish stock and butter, coated with Choron sauce, garnished with fleurons.

— **with Ravigote Sauce:** à la ravigote: cut in pieces, dipped in eggs and breadcrumbs, deep fried, Ravigote sauce served separately.

— **Russian Style:** à la russe: poached in white wine, butter and fish stock with sliced knob celery, coated with white wine sauce mixed with chopped chervil.

— **Saint-Charles:** poached in white wine and butter, coated with white wine sauce mixed with sliced truffles and diced lobster, sprinkled with chopped lobster coral.

— **Toulon Style:** à la toulonaise: stuffed with fish forcemeat, steamed in fish stock and mussel liquor, coated with mussel sauce.

— **in White Wine Sauce:** au vin blanc: fillets or small fish poached in white wine and fish stock, coated with white wine sauce.

Barbillon: see barbel.

Barbue: see brill.

Bass, Sea Bass: F. Bar, Loup de mer; G. See-Barsch, Wolfsbarsch. Saltwater fish found from the Mediterranean up to the British Isles, seldom in the Baltic. Prepared like salmon.

— **Blackfish:** cut in pieces, poached in fish stock, demi-glace, a little honey, chopped dates, currants and chopped almonds added; garnished with dumplings.

Black Bass: F. Bar noir; G. schwarzer Barsch. Freshwater fish of the Eastern States of the U.S.A. Best fried in butter, boiled with butter sauce or prepared à la Mornay.

— **Planked Bass:** baked on plank bordered with duchess potato mixture, garnished with parsley, lemon and herb butter.

— **Sea Bass:** F. Bar noir; G. Schwarzer Barsch. Saltwater fish caught along the eastern coasts of the United States. Prepared like salmon or salmon trout.

Blanchaille: see whitebait.

Bleak: F. Ablette; G. Ukelei, Lauben. Small freshwater fish found in European lakes and in some rivers north of the Alps. Usually fried.

Bloater: F. Hareng fumé; G. geräucherter Hering. Mildly cured and smoked herring served as breakfast dish.

— **Broiled:** grillé: seasoned with pepper, brushed with butter and broiled.

— **Fried:** frit: skinned and filleted, soaked in milk, coated with flour, fried in butter, served on toast.

— **with Fried Eggs:** aux oeufs: skinned, filleted and fried, served with fried eggs.

— **Livonian Style:** à la livonienne (cold): fillets, alternated with sliced boiled potatoes, sliced apples, chopped tarragon and fennel; French dressing poured on top.

— **Russian Style:** à la russe (cold): fillets alternated with sliced red beetroots, sliced hard-boiled eggs, capers and chopped parsley.

Bluefish: Atlantic saltwater fish akin to mackerel. Prepared like mackerel.

Bondelle: see whitefish.

Bonite: see bonito.

Bonito: F. Bonite; G. Bonito. Saltwater fish of the mackerel family found in the Atlantic and Pacific. Prepared like tunny-fish.

Bouillabaisse: dish made of several kind of fish, crustaceans and shell fish with onions, leeks, garlic, tomatoes, fennel, bay leaves, oil and seasoning.

— **Marseille Style:** à la marseillaise: fish used: dragon's head, John Dory, whiting, conger eel, red mullet, frogfish, rainbow fish and langoustines or crawfish; large fish cut in pieces, small fish left whole, langoustine split lengthwise, crawfish cut in pieces. Sweat sliced onions and leeks in oil, add crushed garlic, bay leaf, a pinch of saffron, fennel, thyme, diced tomatoes and the firmer fish and langoustines or crawfish; fill up with water, season, boil 7 to 8 minutes, add the other fish and boil rapidly until done. Dress fish on platter surrounded with the langoustines or crawfish and pour the soup in a soup tureen over thin slices of French bread lightly fried in oil.

Bouillabaisse
— **Parisian Style:** à la parisienne: prepared like Marseille style with conger eel, gurnards, mackerels, whitings, soles, dragon-fish, langoustines and mussels.
Bourride: see Provencal fish stew.
Bouquets: see prawns.
Bream: F. Brème; G. Brachsen, Bleie; I. Orada. Freshwater fish common in all European waters.
— **in Beer:** à la bière: cooked in pale beer with onions, spice, bayleaves and lemon slices, stock thickened with butterpaste.
— **Estonian Style:** à l'ésthonienne: stuffed with fish forcemeat blended with crayfish butter, baked in the oven, coated with brown mushrooms sauce finished off with sour cream.
— **Fisher Style:** mode du pêcheur: sprinkle mixture of chopped mushrooms, breadcrumbs and shallots on bottom of baking dish, place fish on top, cover with the same mixture, moisten with white wine, pour melted butter over the fish and bake slowly in the oven.
— **German Style:** à l'allemande: cooked in fish stock with mirepoix and sage leaves, stock thickened with butterpaste and finished with a little cream.
— **with Peas:** aux petits pois: fillets dipped in eggs and breadcrumbs, fried in butter, garnished with creamed green peas.
— **Pilgrim's Style:** à la pélerin: baked in the oven, deglaced with sour cream, reduced, mixed with strips of pickled cucumbers, sauce poured over the fish; green pea purée and boiled potatoes served separately.
— **with Root Vegetables:** aux racines: cooked in slightly acidulated fish stock with strips of knob celery, carrots, leeks and onions, stock thickened with white roux, mixed with the vegetables and poured over the fish.
Brème: see bream.
Brill: F. Barbue; G. Butt, Rautenscholle; I. Barbuta. Flat saltwater fish resembling turbot found off the European Atlantic coast and in the Baltic.
— **Admiral Style:** à l'amiral: cooked in court-bouillon with Sauternes, glazed with lobster butter, garnished with oysters and mussels Villeroy, mushroom caps and truffles arranged in bunches and small puff pastry patties filled with crayfish tails; Normandy sauce finished off with crayfish butter and fish potatoes served separately.
— **Balmoral:** cutlets poached in champagne with chopped shallots, arranged inside of a piped border of Duchess potato mixture on spinach leaves tossed in butter, garnished with crayfish tails, coated with Mornay sauce, crayfish butter dropped on top, glazed.
— **Bercy:** fillets steamed with chopped shallots in white wine and fish stock, coated with the concentrated stock finished off with butter and lemon juice.
— **Bonnefoy:** cut in pieces, coated with flour, fried in butter and served with wine sauce.
— **Boulogne Style:** à la boulonnaise: cut in pieces, steamed in fish stock, coated with butter sauce, garnished with bearded mussels.
— **with Browned Butter:** au beurre noir: cut in pieces, boiled in court-bouillon, browned butter to which a little

Brill

vinegar has been added poured over, sprinkled with capers and chopped parsley.

— **Cancal Style:** à la cancalaise: fillets poached in white wine and fish stock, covered with Normandy sauce, garnished with poached bearded oysters and shrimps.

— **Chauchat:** poached fillets surrounded with slices of boiled potatoes, covered with cheese sauce and glazed.

— **Dieppe Style:** à la dieppoise: fillets poached in white wine and fish stock, covered with white wine sauce finished off with mussel stock, garnished with bearded mussels and shrimps.

— **Dieudonné:** fillets poached in white wine and fish stock with sliced mushrooms and diced tomatoes, stock boiled down and finished off with butter, cream, fine herbs and lemon juice.

— **Donier:** fillets poached in white wine and fish stock, dressed on risotto, coated with Mornay sauce, grated cheese sprinkled on top, dotted with butter, glazed, border of crayfish sauce.

— **Dugléré:** filleted or cut in pieces, poached with chopped shallots, diced tomatoes, chopped parsley and seasoning, stock boiled down, mixed with fish velouté, butter and lemon juice added, poured over the fish, garnished with fleurons.

— **Edward VII.:** Edouard VII.: poached in white wine and fish stock, dressed on border of piped Duchess mixture, garnished with poached oysters, covered with mousseline sauce.

— **Fedorowna:** fillets coated with fish forcemeat, folded, turned in flour, fried in butter, garnished with sliced truffles, mushrooms and shrimps, covered with crayfish sauce and diced crayfish, surrounded with bearded mussels, dipped in egg and breadcrumbs and deep fried.

— **French Style:** à la française: cut in pieces, cooked in fish stock, covered with Choron sauce.

— **Fried:** frite: cut in pieces, dipped in egg and breadcrumbs, fried in butter.

— **Grandduke:** grand-duc: fillets poached in white wine and mushroom fond, garnished with sliced truffles, crayfish tails and asparagus tips, covered with Mornay sauce, sprinkled with grated cheese and gratinated.

— **Gratinated:** au gratin: fillets covered with Italian sauce, sprinkled with breadcrumbs, dotted with butter, cooked in the oven and gratinated at the same time.

— **Grilled:** grillée: cut in pieces, seasoned, turned in flour, greased with oil, grilled and served with fried parsley and lemon.

— **Housewife's Style:** à la bonne-femme: fillets poached in butter with sliced mushrooms, chopped shallots and parsley, white wine and velouté, stock boiled down, beaten with butter, poured over the fish and glazed.

— **Hyére Style:** à la hyéroise: small whole fish stuffed with fish forcemeat, poached in white wine with butter, sliced leeks and button onions, stock boiled down, thickened with egg yolks and cream, seasoned with Cayenne pepper and poured over the fish.

— **with Lobster Sauce:** au sauce homard: Boiled and served with lobster sauce.

Brill

— **Laguipière:** fillets poached in white wine and fish fumet, covered with white wine sauce, brunoise of truffles sprinkled on top.

— **Leopold I.:** fillets poached in white wine and fish stock, covered with Geneva sauce, garnished with small pastry shells filled with ragoût of shrimps, mushrooms and fish dumplings in shrimp sauce.

— **Magdalena:** Madeleine: fillets coated with fish forcemeat, poached in white wine and fish stock, when cold dipped in egg and breadcrumbs, deep fried; Dutch sauce mixed with tomato purée served separately.

— **Mantua:** fillets coated with fish forcemeat, folded, poached with sliced mushrooms and white wine, dressed in a border of piped and baked Duchess mixture covered with Italian sauce.

— **Mariner's Style:** à la marinière: fillets poached in white wine and fish stock, garnished with bearded mussels and shrimps, covered with sauce Marinière.

— **Montreuil:** fillets poached in white wine and fish fumet, covered with white wine sauce, garnished with large boiled potato balls covered with shrimp sauce.

— **Mornay:** fillets poached in fish fumet and white wine, covered with Mornay sauce, sprinkled with grated Swiss and Parmesan cheese and glazed.

— **Normandy Style:** à la normande: fillets poached in white wine and fish stock, covered with Normandy sauce, garnished with oysters, mussels, mushroom caps, sliced truffles, shrimps, very small smelts or strips of sole fillets dipped in egg and breadcrumbs and deep fried, whole crayfish.

— **Portuguese:** à la portugaise: fillets poached in white wine and fish stock, covered with tomatoes concassées, chopped parsley and sliced mushrooms, covered with white wine sauce and glazed, chopped parsley scattered on top.

— **Provencal:** à la provençale: fillets poached in white wine and oil with garlic and diced tomatoes, covered with sauce Provençale, chopped parsley scattered on top.

— **Regency Style:** à la régence: whole fish braised in white wine and fish fumet, garnished with poached oysters, white mushroom caps, olive shaped truffles, poached carps roes' and small whiting dumplings finished off with crayfish butter, covered with Normandy sauce mixed with mushroom and truffle essence.

— **Rich Style:** à la riche: fillets poached in white wine and fish stock, garnished with crayfish tails and truffle slices, covered with Nantua sauce.

— **Rosine:** fillets poached in white wine and fish stock, covered with white wine sauce mixed with tomato purée, garnished with small tomatoes stuffed with fish forcemeat.

— **Russian Style:** à la russe: strips of carrots and onions and shredded parsley steamed in white wine and fish stock, fillets poached in this stock, boiled down, butter and lemon juice added and poured over the fillets; sauce should be a little thin.

— **Saint-Germain:** fillets dipped in melted butter and white breadcrumbs, grilled with butter, garnished with potato balls fried in butter, Béarnaise sauce served separately.

Brill

— **Saint-Malo:** fillets grilled and served with sauce St.-Malo.

— **Sappho Bernhardt:** fillets poached, covered with green herb sauce mixed with strips of knob celery, carrots and truffles.

— **Turenne:** fillets coated with fish forcemeat, poached in white wine and fish stock, surrounded with diced tomatoes, mushrooms and cucumbers, covered with white wine sauce and glazed.

— **Tyrolese Style:** à la tyrolienne: fillets poached, garnished with button onions, diced tomatoes and chopped parsley, covered with white wine sauce.

— **Vatel:** 1. fillets poached in white wine and fish fumet, covered with Chambord sauce, garnished with stuffed pieces of cucumber and deep fried strips of sole fillets. 2. poached, garnished diced crayfish tails, truffle slices and poached soft roes, covered with crayfish sauce.

— **Venetian Style:** à la vénitienne: poached, covered with Venetian sauce, garnished with boiled potato balls.

— **Wellington:** fillets poached, dressed on onion purée, covered with Soubise sauce, sprinkled with grated cheese, glazed; border of Normandy sauce.

Brocheton: see baby pike.

Brodetto di pesce: see fish-stew, Italian.

C

Cabillaud: see cod.

Cadgéri, Kedgeree: alternate layers of boiled flaked cod or turbot, boiled rice, hard-boiled sliced eggs and chopped stewed onions with curried cream sauce, cover with the same sauce and pour slightly browned butter on top. Can also be made with salmon. (Anglo-Indian)

Calmar: see squid.

Cappon magro: see fish-ragoût, Italian II.

Caracoles Catalana: see snails Catalonian style.

— **Madrilena:** see snails Madrid style.

Caramote: F.: Scampi; G.: Scampi; I.: Scampo. Name of the giant prawns of the Adriatic, related to the Dublin Bay Prawns. Prepared like crayfish.

— **with Absinth:** à l'absinthe: tails sautéd in oil and butter with chopped shallots, carrots, a little garlic and diced tomatoes, flambéd with cognac, deglaced with white wine, fish stock, a bunch of herbs, salt, Cayenne pepper and a little tomato purée added and simmered until done. Tails shelled, cut in large pieces, mixed with the reduced stock, strained, beaten up with butter and finished of with a few drops of absinth, filled in baking dish, glazed and served with Creole rice.

— **Aspic:** en gelée: Charlotte mould lined first with aspic jelly and then with scampi tails, center filled with Russian salad, sealed with aspic jelly, when set turned out, garnished with aspic jelly; mayonnaise served separately.

— **Barcelona:** raw frozen scampi shelled, sautéd in oil, seasoned, flambéd with cognac, moistened with white wine and cooked until done, then mixed with tomatoes concassées with chopped onions and parsley, served in timbale dish.

Caramote
— **Bordeaux Style:** à la bordelaise: prepared like lobster.
— **Fried:** frites: tails prepared like crayfish.
— **Istrian Style:** à l'istrienne: parboiled tails tossed in oil and butter, flambéd with cognac, deglaced with white wine, seasoned, diced tomatoes added, simmered and served in the boiled down stock.
— **Italian Style:** à l'italienne: parboiled, sautéd in oil, mixed with tomatoes concassées with crushed garlic and chopped parsley added.
— **Lacroix:** parboiled, shelled, sautéd in butter with chopped shallots, sliced mushrooms and diced red peppers added, flambéd with cognac, cooked in cream, seasoned sharply with curry, thickened with egg yolks; pilaf rice served separately.
— **Norwegian Style:** à la norvégienne: parboiled tails, shelled, sautéd in browned butter, chopped dill and paprika added, seasoned, moistened with heavy cream, boiled down, flavored with Sherry, served in timbale dish garnished with sliced truffles; plain boiled rice served separately.
— **Quarnero:** parboiled tails sautéd in butter with chopped shallots and diced tomatoes, seasoned with lemon juice and mixed with chopped parsley.
— **with Rice:** al riso: parboiled, shelled, tossed in oil with chopped shallots, parsley, basilic and garlic, seasoned, rice added, moistened with fish stock and a little tomato purée, cooked, sprinkled with grated Parmesan. (Italian)
— **in Scallop Shells:** prepared like shrimps.
— **Trieste Style:** à la triestaine: boiled, shelled, filled in mould lined with aspic jelly alternately with scampi froth (mousse), sealed with aspic jelly, when set turned out, garnished with triangles of aspic jelly.

Carassin: see crucian.

Carp, Mirror Carp, Leather Carp: F. Carpe; G. Karpfen; I. Carpione. Fresh water fish found in ponds and sluggish waters all over Europe. The soft roe is considered a great delicacy.
— **Alsatian Style:** à l'alsacienne: stuffed with pike forcemeat, poached in white wine and fish stock, dressed on saurkraut; the boiled down stock thickened with butter-paste, fish potatoes served separately.
— **in Beer:** à la bière: sliced, browned in butter; chopped onions, diced knob celery and gingerbread added, filled up with pale beer, simmered until done, sauce thickened with butter paste, strained and poured over the fish.
— **Blue:** au bleu: cooked in salt water with a little vinegar added, served with melted butter, grated horseradish or horseradish cream and fish potatoes.
— **Boatman Style:** à la canotière: small carp stuffed, braised in white wine with chopped shallots and fluted mushrooms, sprinkled with breadcrumbs, dotted with butter and browned, garnished with fried gudgeons, whole crayfish and fleurons.
— **Breteuil:** broiled, covered with browned butter, garnished with very small puff pastry patties filled with poached diced soft roes in white wine sauce.
— **Burgundy Style:** à la bourguignonne: cooked in red wine and fish stock, garnished with mushroom caps and

Carp

small glazed onions, covered with red wine sauce blended with the reduced stock.

— **Chambord:** skinned, larded with truffles, stuffed with fish forcemeat mixed with the soft roes and chopped mushrooms, braised in oven with red wine and fish fumet on bed of herbs and root vegetables and well glazed, garnished with fish dumplings decorated with truffles, soft roes and thin strips of sole fillets dipped in egg and bread crumbs and deep fried, fluted mushrooms and whole crayfish, coated with Geneva sauce made with the reduced stock.

— **Frederick the Great:** Fréderic-le-Grand: stuffed with pike forcemeat mixed with chopped truffles, poached in red wine and fish stock, covered with sauce made of the reduced stock thickened with butterpaste, garnished with olive shaped truffles, gudgeons dipped in egg and breadcrumbs and deep fried and fillets of eels, cut in strips and fried.

— **Genoa Style:** à la génoise: poached in red wine and fish stock, covered with Genoa sauce made of the stock, garnished with soft roes, mushrooms and crayfish tails.

— **Jellied:** en gelée: cut in pieces, boiled in slightly acidulated water and white wine with strips of carrots, knob celery, leeks and parsley roots, when done stock jellied and clarified and poured over the fish together with the vegetable strips.

— **Jutland Style:** à la jutlandaise: cut in pieces, marinated in vinegar, pepper and powdered cloves, cooked in pale beer, a little marinade and grated lemon peel, stock thickened with gingerbread, raisins and a little butter added and poured over the fish.

— **Larded:** piqué: skinned, larded with strips of fat bacon and anchovy fillets, melted butter poured over, roasted in oven, served with browned butter.

— **Marinated:** marinée: boiled in fish stock with julienne of root vegetables and sliced onions, when done covered with the vegetables, slices of lemon and capers, stock thickened with gelatine, poured over the fish and sprinkled with chopped parsley. (Austrian)

— **Matelote:** en matelote: cut in pieces, cooked in red wine, flambéd with cognac, thickened with butter and flour, garnished with mushrooms and button onions, surrounded with fried heart shaped croûtons.

— **with Mayonnaise:** à la mayonnaise: fillets skinned and boned, dipped in egg and breadcrumbs, deep fried, mayonnaise and buttered fish potatoes served separately.

— **Moldavian Style:** à la moldavienne: braised in white wine with mirepoix, stock strained, thickened with arrowroot and mixed with grated horseradish, fish dressed on saurkraut, coated with the sauce and garnished with small roast potatoes.

— **with Onions:** aux oignons: cut in pieces, poached in white wine, fish stock, butter and plenty of chopped onions, stock thickened with breadcrumbs.

— **Oriental Style:** à l'orientale: cut in pieces, poached in oil, white wine, fish stock, chopped shallots and seasoning, stock boiled down, mixed with chopped almonds and a little saffron and poured over the fish.

Carp
— **with Paprika:** au paprika: cut in pieces, poached in white wine, fish stock, butter and mushroom essence, stock reduced, mixed with paprika sauce.
— **Polish:** à la polonaise: cut in pieces, poached in pale beer and a little red wine, sliced onions, thyme, bay leaves, pepper corns, cloves and parsley, stock thickened with grated rye bread or gingerbread, seasoned with salt, a pinch of sugar and a few drops of vinegar, finished off with chopped almonds and sultanas.
— **Pompadour:** poached in red wine and fish stock on bed of root vegetables, when cold coated with aspic jelly made of the stock, garnished with artichoke bottom filled with Russian salad.
— **Roumanian Style:** à la roumaine: large carp placed on sliced, fried onions, seasoned, covered with sliced lemons and tomatoes, crushed garlic, white wine, a generous amount of sunflower oil and light tomato sauce, braised in oven until the stock is nearly boiled down, served very cold with fresh slices of lemon and tomatoes on top.
— **Royal Style:** à la royale: fillets cut in escalopes, poached in white wine, fish fumet and herbs, garnished with fluted mushrooms, truffle slices and soft roes, covered with Normandy sauce with the reduced stock.
— **Saint-Menehould:** fillets stiffened in white wine and fish stock, when cold dipped in egg and bread crumbs mixed with chopped mushrooms, broiled or fried, garnished with sliced pickled cucumbers or gherkins, hachée sauce mixed with chopped anchovies and gherkins served separately.
— **with Saurkraut:** au choucroute: cut in pieces, poached, dressed on pickled cabbage, covered with white wine sauce.
— **in Sour Cream:** à la crème aigre: fillets placed in baking dish greased with butter, seasoned with salt, pepper and lemon juice, covered with sour cream and baked in oven.
— **Stuffed:** farcie: I. stuffed with mousseline forcemeat of pike, braised in white wine, fish stock and chopped shallots, covered with the reduced stock thickened with butter paste, garnished with mushrooms.
— **Stuffed:** farcie: II. stuffed with pork forcemeat, mixed with bread soaked in milk, chopped sweated onions, parsley and eggs, placed in baking dish, melted butter poured over, baked, sprinkled with bread crumbs, dotted with butter and browned in oven.
— **Volnay:** small carp poached in Volnay wine, mushroom essence and chopped shallots, stock thickened with flour and butter, poured over fish and glazed, surrounded with fleurons.

Carpe: see carp.

Carrelet: see sand dab.

Char: F. Omble chevalier; G. Saibling. Freshwater fish found mainly in the subalpine Swiss, Scandinavian, Scotch and English lakes. Some species live in rivers and streams. Prepared like trout.
— **Cubat:** fillets, dressed in baking dish on mushroom purée, covered with Mornay sauce, glazed, garnished with truffle slices coated with meat glaze.
— **Gourmet's Style:** du gourmet: stuffed with truffled fish forcemeat, poached in butter and Rhine wine, stock

Char
reduced, mixed with fish velouté, thickened with egg yolks and cream, finished off with crayfish butter, poured over the fish, garnished with small tartlets filled with salpicon of mushrooms and crayfish, bound with white wine sauce, a slice of truffle on top.
— **Maître d'hôtel:** seasoned, shallow fried in butter, served with herb butter.
— **Nelson:** fillets poached in white wine and butter, covered with white wine sauce, glazed, garnished with Parisian potatoes and poached fish roe.
— **Reynière:** fillets poached in white wine and fish stock, covered with shrimps and cream sauce blended with the boiled down stock, sprinkled with grated cheese, dotted with butter and glazed.
— **Saint-Cloud:** poached in white wine and fish stock, covered with Béarnaise sauce, garnished with Parisian potatoes.
— **Traviata:** poached in white wine and butter, one side covered with white wine sauce, the other side with Nantua sauce, the white side garnished with crayfish tails, the other side with bearded mussels.
Chevaine: see chub.
Chevanne: see chub.
Chub: F. Chevanne, chevainne; G. Alant, Nerfling. Freshwater fish found in all European rivers and streams. Prepared like carp.
Clam: F. Praire, Lucine; G. Venusmuschel, Sandmuschel. Name for a variety of bivalve shell-fish found on the North Atlantic coast. Clams are eaten both raw and cooked. Prepared like mussels.
— **Fried:** frites: parboiled, dipped in egg and breadcrumbs or frying batter, deep fried, served with parsley, lemon and Tartar sauce.
— **Fritters:** beignets: see clams fried.
— **on Half Shell:** opened, served on deep plate with cracked ice, garnished with lemon and parsley; cocktail sauce optional.
— **Risotto:** parboiled with onions, celery, thyme, bay leaf and seasoning, risotto prepared with the clam broth, mixed with the chopped clams, butter and grated Parmesan, pressed in mould, turned out on round silver dish, surrounded with cream sauce.
— **Roast:** roasted on hot stove surface, tossed in butter with chopped herbs, onions and parsley, served on toast.
— **Steamed:** à la vapeur: boiled in fish stock or water with onions, celery, thyme, bay leaf and seasoning, served in broth in shell.
— **Stewed:** étuvée: stewed in seasoned water with butter until soft, combined with hot milk or cream, sprinkled with fresh butter and paprika, served with crackers.
Cod, Codfish: F. Cabillaud, Morue fraîche; G. Kabeljau; S. Bacalao. Important saltwater fish found in the Atlantic Ocean from Newfoundland to the North of Great Britain, Ireland, Norway, Canada, the North and Baltic seas.
— **with Anchovy Butter:** au beurre d'anchois: slices coated with flour, fried in butter, covered with browned butter mixed with anchovy paste.
— **Andalusian Style:** à l'andalouse: fillets or steaks poached in white wine and fish stock, stock boiled down, mixed

Cod

with fish velouté, tomato purée and julienne of red peppers, poured over the fish, garnished with halved tomatoes filled with risotto and fried slices of egg plants.

— **Baked:** au four: fried diced salt pork and chopped onions, mixed with large flakes of boiled, skinned and boned cod, filled in baking dish alternately with sliced boiled potatoes, diced tomatoes and, chopped parsley, milk poured over, sprinkled with cracker meal and baked in oven.

— **Baker Style:** à la boulangère: whole fish scored on both sides, placed in baking dish greased with butter, surrounded with sliced raw potatoes and small onions, chopped parsley mixed with crushed garlic and bread-crumbs scattered on top, melted butter poured over, baked slowly in oven.

— **Bandong:** filleted, cut in thick slices, marinated in lemon juice with salt, curry powder, chopped shallots and parsley, coated with flour, fried in clarified butter, served with plain boiled rice, mango-chutney and mushroom ketchup.

— **Basle Style:** à la baloise: cut in thick slices, poached or fried, covered with sliced fried onion and chopped parsley, melted butter poured over.

— **Boiled:** bouilli: boiled in salt water, served with caper, shrimp, anchovy, lobster, Dutch sauce or melted butter and fish potatoes.

— **Boston Scrod:** tail piece split lengthwise, brushed with clarified butter, seasoned and broiled.

— **Braganza:** boiled, skinned and boned, flaked, mixed with chopped truffles and mushrooms, bound with paprika sauce, filled in baking dish, sprinkled with bread crumbs, dotted with butter and baked in oven.

— **with Butter:** au beurre: cut in steaks, boiled in salt water, served with melted butter poured on top.

— **with Crayfish Tails:** aux écrevisses: fillets poached in white wine and fish stock, covered with Nantua sauce, garnished with crayfish tails.

— **Curried:** filleted, cut in thick slices, seasoned with curry powder, coated with flour, fried with sliced apples and onions, simmered in cream, served with plain boiled rice.

— **Diaz:** boiled and flaked, mixed with sliced parboiled mushrooms and diced green peppers, bound with paprika sauce, filled in baking dish, sprinkled with bread crumbs, dotted with butter and baked in oven.

— **Dieppe Style:** à la dieppoise: fillets prepared like sole.

— **Dimitri:** boiled steaks covered with white wine sauce, finished off with anchovy butter and a few chopped anchovy fillets.

— **Diplomate:** fillets poached in white wine and fish stock, garnished with sliced truffles coated with meat glaze.

— **Don Carlos:** fillets poached in fish stock, half of them garnished with mushrooms and covered with tomato sauce, the other half garnished with sliced truffles and covered with white wine sauce.

— **Dumplings: Quenelles de cabillaud: boiled, skinned, boned,** flaked and mashed, mixed with bread soaked in milk, chopped onions sweated in butter, eggs, chopped anchovies and parsley, breadcrumbs and seasoning, shaped into

Cod

balls, flattened, fried in butter, covered with anchovy or tomato sauce.

— **Dutch Style:** boiled, served with melted butter and salt potatoes.

— **English Style:** à l'anglaise: prepared like sole fillets.

— **Flemish Style:** à la flamande: cut in thick slices, poached in white wine with chopped shallots and herbs, stock thickened with white bread crumbs; fish served with a peeled slice of lemon on top, covered with the sauce.

— **Florence Style:** à la florentine: fillets, dressed in baking dish on plain spinach sweated in butter, dish surrounded with piped Duchess mixture, coated with Mornay sauce, sprinkled with grated cheese and glazed.

— **Fried:** frit: cut in slices, dipped in egg and breadcrumbs, deep fried; Tartar or tomato sauce served separately.

— **Genoa Style:** à la génoise: fillets poached in red wine and chopped shallots, garnished with mushrooms, crayfish tails and poached soft roes, covered with the stock thickened with butterpaste.

— **Gratinated:** I. Crème au gratin: flaked cod dressed on cheese sauce in baking dish surrounded with piped border of Duchess potato mass, coated with cheese sauce, sprinkled with grated cheese and browned on top.

— **Gratinated:** II. fillets placed in baking dish on Italian sauce, garnished with sliced raw mushrooms, very little white wine poured around, covered with Italian sauce, sprinkled with bread crumbs, dotted with butter and baked in oven.

— **Halévy:** fillets poached, covered with white wine sauce blended with shrimp sauce, mixed with chopped truffles and lobster coral, garnished with Parisian potatoes.

— **Héloise:** fillets dressed on chopped mushrooms and shallots, poached in white wine and fish fumet, stock reduced, mixed with fish velouté and a little meat glaze, poured over the fish and glazed.

— **with Herb Sauce:** aux fines herbes: boiled, covered with cream sauce mixed with chopped fine herbs.

— **Indian Style:** à l'indienne: cut in slices, boiled, covered with Indian sauce, plain boiled rice served separately.

— **Larded:** piqué: whole fish skinned on one side, larded with strips of fat bacon, placed in buttered baking dish on bed of sliced onions, seasoned, covered with melted butter and baked in oven.

— **Maltese Style:** à la maltaise: fillets poached in white wine, fish stock and chopped shallots, covered with the reduced stock mixed with fish velouté, finished off with anchovy butter, capers and chopped herbs.

— **Mexican Style:** à la mexicaine: boiled, served with Mexican sauce and Creole rice.

— **Mornay:** fillets prepared like halibut.

— **with Mushrooms:** aux champignons: fillets covered with sliced mushrooms, poached in butter and lemon juice, stock mixed with fish velouté and poured over the fish.

— **Newburgh:** fillets poached in white wine and fish stock, garnished with slices of lobster, covered with Newburgh sauce.

— **with Noodles:** aux nouilles: boiled, flaked, placed in baking dish alternately with noodles, covered with cream

Cod

sauce, sprinkled with grated cheese and breadcrumbs, dotted with butter, baked in oven.

— **Northern Style:** à la nordique: boiled in salt water, flaked, filled in baking dish alternately with sliced boiled potatoes, covered with fish velouté finished off with milk and lemon juice, sprinkled with grated cheese and breadcrumbs, dotted with butter, baked in oven; sliced pickled cucumbers and red beets served separately.

— **Parisian Style:** à la parisienne: I. fillets poached in white wine and mushroom fond, covered with white wine sauce mixed with the reduced stock, garnished with mushroom caps, truffle slices and whole crayfish.
II. fillets garnished with mushrooms caps, one side covered with white wine, the other with shrimp sauce, border of meat glaze.

— **Portuguese Style:** à la portugaise: cut in slices, poached with chopped onions, garlic, diced tomatoes, chopped parsley and white wine, stock reduced and poured over the fish.

— **Provencal Style:** à la provençale: prepared like pike.

— **Queen Style:** à la reine: fillets poached, garnished with small dumplings of fish forcemeat, fish covered with cream sauce.

— **in Scallop Shells:** en coquilles: boiled flaked cod dresses in scallop shells bordered with piped Duchess mixture, coated with Mornay sauce, sprinkled with grated cheese and glazed.

— **in Scallop Shells Nantua:** en coquilles à la Nantua: prepared like scallop shells but coated with Nantua sauce, a round slice of truffle placed on each shell at serving.

— **Spanish Style:** à l'espagnole: fillets fried in oil, dressed on tomatoes concassées, garnished with fried onions and fried julienne of red peppers.

— **Spring Style:** à la printanière: steaks shallow fried in butter, but not browned too much, covered with cream sauce blended with green bean butter, garnished with buttered green peas and new potatoes.

Colin: see hake.

Conger Eel: F. Congre, anguille de mer; G. Meer-Aal, See-Aal. Saltwater fish found in all oceans, the North Sea, the Baltic and the Mediterranean. Prepared like eel.

— **Spanish Style:** à l'espagnole: cut in pieces, stewed in oil, red wine and a few drops of vinegar with chopped onions, red peppers, garlic, thyme, bay leaf and chopped fine herbs, stock slightly reduced.

— **on the Spit:** à la broche: seasoned, coated with flour, brushed with oil and grilled on the spit; Colbert or Tartar sauce served separately.

Congre: see conger eel.

Coulibiac: see Russian salmon pie.

Coquilles St. Jacques: see scallops.

Crab: F. Crabe; G. Krabbe. Generic name given to all crustaceans of the order decapoda; common crab, giant crab, spider crab etc. Crabs are found off the European and American Atlantic coasts and the Pacific coast.

Crab, Giant Crab: F. Tourteau, Poupart; G. Taschenkrebs; I. Granchio.

— **Baltimore:** boiled, flaked meat tossed in butter with chopped shallots, seasoned with Worcestershire sauce,

Crab

Cayenne pepper and mustard powder, filled in the shell, coated with Mornay sauce, sprinkled with grated Parmesan, dotted with butter and baked brown.

— **Bordeaux Style:** à la bordelaise: flaked meat, mixed with sliced sautéd mushrooms and Bordeaux sauce, served on toast or in croustades.

— **Croquettes:** I. flaked meat mixed with diced parboiled mushrooms, mixed with thick Béchamel sauce, thickened with egg yolks, when cold shaped into croquettes, dipped in egg and bread crumbs, deep fried, served with fried parsley and lemon.
II. crabmeat mixed with mayonnaise, stiffened with aspic jelly, croquette shaped, rolled in hard-boiled, chopped egg yolks, served cold on lettuce leaves or parsley.

— **Devilled: à la diable: meat flaked, tossed in** butter with chopped fried onions, mixed with cream sauce, seasoned with Cayenne pepper, mustard powder, Worcestershire and Chili sauce, refilled in shell, sprinkled with bread crumbs, dotted with butter and browned in oven.

— **Dewey:** prepared like Newburgh, bearded oysters and mushrooms added.

— **Dressed:** garnie: cold shredded crabmeat, seasoned with salt, Cayenne pepper, mustard powder, vinegar and oil or bound with mayonnaise, refilled in shell, decorated with hard-boiled egg yolks and whites, chopped parsley, capers, red beetroot and sliced lemon, served cold.

— **Greek Style:** à la grecque: chopped onions and leeks sweated in butter, diced tomatoes, garlic, flaked crabmeat, bearded mussels and a bunch of herbs added, seasoned with salt and a little saffron, simmered with very little water, served or mixed with plain rice.

— **Indian Style:** à l'indienne: flaked, mixed with curry sauce, served with plain rice.

— **Italian Style:** à l'italienne: flaked, mixed with chopped sweated onions, chopped parsley, garlic and a little tomato sauce, simmered for a few minutes, filled in the shell, sprinkled with grated Parmesan and bread crumbs, dotted with butter, browned in oven.

— **à la King:** diced sweet green and red peppers, sliced mushrooms and chopped shallots simmered in butter until done, seasoned with pepper and lemon juice, flaked crabmeat added, flavored with Sherry, liaison of egg yolks and cream, salt and a few drops of Worcestershire sauce added at the last minute; plain boiled rice served separately.

— **Maryland:** flaked, tossed in butter, simmered in cream, seasoned with Cayenne pepper, flavored with cognac, served in chafing dish with toast.

— **Mexican Style:** à la mexicaine: flaked, mixed with chopped fried onions, diced green peppers, garlic, mustard powder, Worcestershire sauce, refilled in shell, coated with cheese sauce and glazed.

— **Nelson:** flaked, mixed with cream sauce, filled in shells alternately with poached bearded oysters, covered with creamed crabmeat, sprinkled with grated Parmesan and glazed.

— **Newburgh:** flaked, heated in butter, seasoned sharply, boiled up in heavy cream, thickened with egg yolks and

Crab
cream, flavored with Sherry, served in chafing dish with toast.
— **Portuguese Style:** à la portugaise: flaked meat mixed with chopped fried onions, sliced mushrooms, diced tomatoes and chopped parsley, boiled up with a little tomato sauce, placed in baking dish, sprinkled with bread crumbs mixed with chopped parsley, dotted with butter and browned in oven.
— **Salad:** salade de crabes: flaked meat and diced celery, mixed with mayonnaise, dressed on lettuce leaves, garnished with capers, hard-boiled eggs and pickles.
— **Stuffed:** farcié: prepared like devilled crab.
— **Valencia:** flaked meat tossed in butter with chopped onions, sliced mushrooms, diced red and green peppers and garlic, seasoned with mustard powder, Cayenne pepper and Worcestershire sauce, refilled in shell, coated with Mornay sauce, sprinkled with grated Parmesan, dotted with butter, baked brown in oven.

Crab, Soft Shells: F. Crabes mous; G. weichschalige Krabben. Little crabs that shed their shells during the molting season to gain room for the body's growth.
— **Broiled; Grilled:** grillée: broiled, served on toast with herb butter.
— **Creole:** à la créole: fried in butter, plain rice and Creole sauce served separately.
— **Fried:** frites: coated with eggs and bread crumbs, fried in deep fat, garnished with fried parsley and lemon; Tartar or other cold sauce served separately.
— **Miller Style:** à la meunière: dipped in milk and flour, tossed in butter, garnished with lemon, browned butter poured over.

Crabe huître: see oyster crab.

Crawfish, Spiny Lobster: F. Langouste; G. Heuschreckenkrebs, Panzerkrebs, Languste. Large crustacean found in the Mediterranean, Adriatic and the southern coasts of England and Ireland. Related to the lobster but without claws, only the first pair of feet are formed into small pincers. Characteristic the very long feelers and the strong carapace with strong spines. Prepared like lobster.

Crayfish: F. Ecrevisse; G. Krebs; I. Gambero; S. Cangrejo. Freshwater crustacean found in European and American rivers and lakes.
— **American Style:** à l'américaine: prepared like lobster.
— **Boiled:** à la nage: cooked in prepared court-bouillon made of finely diced carrots, celery, onions, parsley sprigs, thyme, bay leaf, chopped shallots, white wine, fish stock and butter, served with the bouillon in soup tureen sprinkled with chopped dill or
boiled in court bouillon with butter, caraway seeds and served sprinkled with chopped parsley.
— **Bordeaux Style:** à la bordelaise: prepared like lobster.
— **Cardinal:** scallop shells piped with a border of Duchess mixture around the edge, baked light brown, bottom of shell covered with a little cardinal sauce, filled with crayfish tails, masked with cardinal sauce, a round slice of truffle placed on top.
— **Croquettes:** diced crayfish tails with half the amount diced mushrooms added, bound with thick Béchamel sauce, seasoned sharply, thickened with egg yolks, when

Crayfish

cold shaped into croquettes, dipped in eggs and bread crumbs, fried in deep fat; Nantua sauce served separately.

— **in Dill Sauce:** à l'aneth: crayfish tails bound with fish velouté finished with cream and chopped dill; pilaf rice served separately or tails served in border of rice.

— **Fried:** frites: tails marinated in lemon juice, oil, chopped shallots and parsley, dipped in eggs and bread crumbs or in frying batter, fried in deep fat, served with fried parsley and lemon.

— **Georgette:** baked potatoes scooped out, filled with crayfish tails, coated with Nantua sauce, sprinkled with grated cheese and glazed.

— **Lafayette:** tails tossed in butter, seasoned sharply, cooked in cream, thickened with egg yolks, flavored with cognac and Sherry, served in chafing dish.

— **Magenta:** living crayfish sautéd in oil with finely diced onions, carrots and celery; seasoned, flambéd with cognac, deglaced with white wine; diced tomatoes and fish velouté added, cooked, sauce boiled down, finished off with meat glaze, butter and a pinch of basil.

— **Mariner Style:** à la marinière: whole crayfish cooked in white wine with thyme and a bay leaf, stock strained, boiled down, mixed with fish velouté, beaten with butter, poured over the crayfish, chopped parsley sprinkled on top.

— **Mousselines:** raw forcemeat of pike or whiting mixed with purée of crayfish, rubbed through a sieve, thoroughly chilled on ice, seasoned, mixed with egg whites, heavy cream added gradually, filled in small dariole mould, poached in waterbath, turned out and covered with Nantua sauce.

— **Mousselines Alexandra:** same as above but moulds decorated with a truffle slice and cooked crayfish tails.

— **Patty:** Pâté d'écrevisses: veal forcemeat mixed with purée of crayfish and crayfish butter, chopped mushrooms and egg yolks, highly seasoned, filled alternately with crayfish tails in mould lined with pie dough, covered with pie dough, decorated and baked in oven.

— **Pilaf:** Pilaw d'écrevisses: crayfish tails in American sauce, dressed in centre of pilaf rice, sprinkled with chopped tarragon.

— **Pyramid:** en buisson: cooked in courtbouillon, when cold dressed like a pyramid with parsley.

— **with Rice:** Méridon d'écrevisses: plain boiled rice, mixed with diced crayfish tails and a little Nantua sauce, filled in individual moulds, turned out, garnished with crayfish tails, covered with Nantua sauce.

— **Salad:** en salade: crayfish tails marinated in lemon juice and oil, mixed with capers and diced pickles, bound with mayonnaise, garnished with asparagus tips, dressed on shredded lettuce.

— **Soufflé:** cheese soufflé mixture mixed with crayfish purée (coulis), placed in soufflé dish alternately with crayfish tails, baked in hot oven.

— **Soufflé Florence Style:** Soufflé d'écrevisses à la florentine: same as soufflé with sliced truffles added.

— **Soufflé Piedmont Style:** à la piémontaise; same as soufflé but crayfish tails and sliced white Italian truffles added.

Crayfish

— **Soufflé Rothschild:** same as soufflé Florence with asparagus tips added.

— **Supreme with Champagne:** Suprême au champagne: crayfish cooked Bordeaux style with champagne, tails broken off, coulis made of the bodies, when cold sharply seasoned, mixed with aspic jelly and unsweetened whipped cream, filled in glass dish, when set decorated with the tails, truffles slices and chervil, dish filled with champagne aspic jelly; served on ice block.

— **Timbale Nantua:** flat vol-au-vent filled with crayfish tails, very small whiting dumplings, mushrooms and truffle slices bound with cream sauce finished off with crayfish purée and butter, decorated with a crown of truffle slices.

— **Vinaigrette:** crayfish tails served cold in Vinaigrette sauce.

— **Voltaire:** thick mushroom slices tossed in butter, mixed with crayfish tails, cooked in cream, sharply seasoned, flavored with Sherry and cognac, thickened with egg yolks, served in timbal dish.

— **Zephyrs of Crayfish:** Zéphyrs d'écrevisses: prepared American style, meat pounded in mortar with the reduced sauce, rubbed through a sieve, whipped unsweetened cream and aspic jelly added, seasoned sharply, filled in dariole moulds decorated with truffle slice and lined with aspic jelly, sealed with aspic, turned out when set, garnished with aspic jelly.

Crevettes grises: see shrimps.

Crevettes roses: see prawns.

Crucian, Crucian Carp: F. Carassin, corassin; G. Karausche. Freshwater fish of the carp family found in streams and rivers in Central and North Europe. Prepared like carp, but mainly used for making soup.

— **with Browned Butter:** au beurre noisette: boiled in court-bouillon, covered with bread crumbs fried in butter and a little lemon juice.

— **with Dill Sauce:** à la sauce aneth: boiled in court-bouillon, served with dill sauce and salt potatoes.

— **with Herb Butter:** au beurre maître d'hôtel: fried, served with herb butter.

— **Russian Style:** à la russe: cut in pieces, simmered in cream, butter and water, stock thickened with butter-paste, mixed with chopped chives, parsley, capers and lemon peel, flavored with lemon juice and poured over the fish.

Cuisses de grenouilles: see frog legs.

Cuttlefish: French: Sépiole; German: Tintenfisch. Marine mollusc found especially in the Mediterranean. Prepared like squid, main ingredient of the frutti di mare.

D

Dab: F. Limande; G. Kliesche. Small saltwater flatfish of the flounder family found in the Atlantic and Pacific. Prepared like plaice.

Daurade: vraie dorade: see Gilt-poll.

Dentex: F. Denté; G. Zahnbrasse. Saltwater fish found in the Atlantic and Mediterannean. Prepared like mackerel.

Dorade commune: see sea-bream.

Dorée: see John Dory.
Dory: see John Dory.
Dragon-fish: F. grande vive; G. Petermännchen; I. Dragoni. Saltwater fish found off the European coast and in the Mediterranean. Prepared like whiting and used for Bouillabaisse.
— **with Caper Sauce:** au sauce capres: scored, grilled, caper sauce served separately.
— **Posillipo:** marinated in lemon juice, oil and chopped tarragon, shallow fried, when cold dressed on Italian salad, garnished with stuffed hard-boiled eggs and aspic jelly, julienne of carrots, knob celery, pickled cucumbers and capers scattered on top.
— **Sicilian Style:** à la sicilienne: larded, poached in Marsala wine and oil with sliced onions and carrots, fond thickened with butterpaste, strained and flavored with lemon juice.
— **Trieste Style:** à la triestaine: marinated in oil and lemon juice, shallow fried, dressed on shredded lettuce, chopped hard-boiled eggs scattered on top covered with melted herb butter.
Dwarf Dragonfish: F. Petite vive; G. Zwergpetermännchen. Saltwater fish found off the European coast and in the Mediterranean. Chiefly used for Bouillabaisse.

E

Ecrevisse: see crayfish.
Eel: F. Anguille; G. Aal; I. Anguilla S. Anguila. Migratory fish found in streams and rivers.
— **Arlesian:** à l' arlésienne: fillets cut in pieces, stuffed with fish forcemeat, wrapped in paper envelope together with chopped onions, shallots and a little garlic, baked, taken out of the envelope and served with the natural juice mixed with anchovy butter.
— **Beaucaire:** boned, stuffed with fish forcemeat mixed with chopped mushrooms, cooked in white wine with mushrooms, chopped shallots, button onions and brandy.
— **Benoiton:** boned, twisted in a spiral, coated with flour and deep fried, garnished with parsley. Red wine sauce with chopped shallots and parsley, finished off with butter served separately.
— **Berlin Style:** à la berlinoise: skinned, cut in pieces, stewed in pale beer with pepper corns and bayleaves, thickened with grated rye bread.
— **Blue:** au bleu: cooked in vinegar and water, served with melted butter, horseradish or caper sauce.
— **Bordeaux Style:** à la bordelaise: cut in pieces, seasoned with salt and pepper, cooked in white wine with chopped onions, stock reduced, mixed with Bordeaux sauce finished off with anchovy butter.
— **Braised:** braisée: cut in pieces, sautéd in butter, braised with chopped sage, parsley, onions and white stock, seasoned with salt, pepper and nutmeg, sauce strained, thickened with butter mixed with flour, flavored with Port and lemon juice.
— **Burgundy Style:** à la bourguignonne: cut in pieces, cooked in red wine, sauce thickened with flour and butter, garnished with glazed button onions and mushrooms.

Eel

— **Catalonian Style:** à la catalane: cut in thick slices, fried in oil, dressed on diced green peppers and tomatoes simmered in oil, seasoned with Cayenne pepper and garlic and mixed with chopped parsley.

— **Citizens Style:** à la bourgeoise: fried in butter with chopped sage, served with lemon and mustard.

— **Condé:** small eels twisted in a spiral, cooked in fish stock and white wine, stock reduced, buttered and poured over the fish, center filled with oyster ragoût.

— **Coulibiac of Eel:** see Appetizers: Fishpie, Russian.

— **in Cream Sauce:** à la crème: poached in white wine, served in cream sauce with button onions and mushrooms.

— **Deviled:** à la diable: cut in pieces, parboiled, dipped in egg and breadcrumbs, grilled or fried; Devil sauce served separately.

— **Durand:** skinned and boned, cut in pieces, stuffed with fish forcemeat, stewed in white wine with diced potherbs, glazed, stock reduced, buttered and served separately.

— **Dutch Style:** à la hollandaise: skinned, cut in pieces, boiled, garnished with parsley; melted butter and boiled potatoes served separately.

— **English Style:** à l'anglaise: skinned and boned, cut in pieces, dipped in melted butter and white breadcrumbs, fried in butter and served with Maître d'hôtel butter.

— **Flemish Style:** à la flamande: sautéd in butter, cooked in pale beer, coarsely chopped sorrel, parsley, sage, tarragon, chervil, burnet and young nettles added, stock thickened with potato-starch.

— **Florimonde:** marinated in lemon juice, rolled up in a ring, wrapped in greased paper and baked in the oven, served with herb butter and potato crisps.

— **French Style:** à la française: cut in pieces, sweated in butter, button mushrooms added, sprinkled with flour, moistened with white wine and fish stock, chopped onions, seasoning and fine herbs added, stock reduced, thickened with egg yolks, flavored with lemon juice.

— **Fricassee of Eel:** en fricassée: cut in thick slices, sweated in butter with mirepoix, dusted with flour, moistened with white wine and fish stock, stock strained, egg yolks and cream added, flavored with lemon juice and poured over the fish mixed with button mushrooms.

— **Fried:** Friture d'anguilles: cut in small pieces, dipped in egg and breadcrumbs, deep fried and served with Tartare or similar sauce.

— **Fried with Tomato Sauce:** Anguille frite à la sauce tomate: small eels left whole, rolled up in a spiral, tied, dipped in beaten egg and breadcrumbs and fried; tomato sauce served separately.

— **German Style:** à l'allemande: cut in pieces, cooked in acidulated water with pot herbs, sage and fine herbs, coated with German sauce.

— **Gourmet:** cut in pieces, cooked in white wine and fish stock, garnished with crayfish tails, coated with cream sauce finished off with crayfish butter.

— **Grilled:** Grillée: cut in pieces, parboiled, turned in flour, basted in oil, grilled slowly and served with herb or anchovy butter.

Eel

— **in Green Sauce:** au vert: cut in pieces, sweated in butter with chopped parsley, burnet, sorrel, chervil, tarragon, sage, green thyme and young nettles, moistened with white wine, simmered until done, stock reduced and thickened with egg yolks, acidulated with lemon juice; eaten hot or cold.

— **Hamburg Style:** à la hambourgeoise: skinned, cut in pieces, cooked in white wine and fish stock with button onions, stock reduced and thickened with butter and flour, sprinkled with chopped parsley, garnished with small flour dumplings.

— **House-keeper Style:** à la ménagère: cut in pieces, grilled, herb butter mixed with a little mustard spread on top, garnished with sliced gherkins.

— **Larded:** Piquée: skinned left whole, larded with anchovy fillets, gherkins and truffles, rolled up in a spiral, tied, and poached in fish stock with vinegar, bayleaves, pepper corns and onions; coated with tomato sauce.

— **Maconese Style:** à la mâconnaise: cut in pieces, cooked in red wine with button onions and mushrooms, stock thickened with flour and butter, mixed with crayfish tails, garnished with small heart shaped croûtons fried in butter.

— **Maître d'hôtel:** skinned, cut in pieces, boiled, coated with herb butter, garnished with boiled potatoes.

— **Malakoff:** cut in thick slices, simmered in white wine with diced tomatoes and chopped onions, dressed on plain spinach sautéd in butter, liquor reduced, not strained, and poured over the fish.

— **Mariner Style:** à la marinière: cooked in white wine and fish stock with chopped shallots, stock reduced and mixed with fish velouté, dressed with button onions, mushrooms and crayfish tails, coated with the sauce; garnished with heart shaped croûtons.

— **Marshal Style:** à la maréchale: fillets cut in pieces, dipped in melted butter and white breadcrumbs, mixed with chopped truffles, fried in butter, a slice of truffle coated with meat glaze on each piece, garnished with asparagus tips or green peas.

— **Melun Style:** à la melunoise: eel left whole, marinated, rolled up to a spiral and baked in oven, garnished with sliced gherkins; Robert sauce served separately.

— **Miller Style:** à la meunière: cut in pieces, coated with flour, fried, sprinkled with chopped parsley, lemon juice and browned butter poured over the fish.

— **Montespan:** cut in pieces, simmered in white wine with mushrooms and chopped herbs.

— **Normandy Style:** à la normande: cut in pieces, cooked in cider with button onions and mushrooms, stock thickened with flour and butter, mixed with poached bearded oysters, garnished with small heart shaped croûtons.

— **Orly:** fillets cut in thin strips, dipped in frying batter, deep fried; tomato sauce served separately.

— **in Paper Case:** en papillote: skinned, cut in pieces, coated with chopped mushrooms, anchovies, capers, parsley, shallots and lemon-peel, wrapped in greased paper, baked in the oven or grilled, served in the paper case.

Eel

— **Parisian Style:** à la parisienne: skinned and boned, cut in pieces, stuffed with fish forcemeat mixed with chopped truffles, cooked in white wine, dressed with mushrooms and crayfish tails, coated with Sailor sauce, garnished with fleurons.

— **Pie, English:** Pâté d'anguilles à l'anglaise: fillets cut in pieces, seasoned with salt, pepper and nutmeg, filled in pie dish alternately with slices of hard-boiled eggs, covered with white wine, sealed with short or puff paste and baked. When done a little demi-glace with fish essence is poured into the pie.

— **Pompadour:** whole eel rolled up in a spiral, tied, parboiled, coated with Villeroy sauce mixed with onion purée, egged and breadcrumbed, fried, dressed with Dauphine potatoes; Choron sauce served separately.

— **Provencal Style:** à la provençale: small eels left whole, stewed in a little white wine with diced tomatoes, chopped onions, herbs and garlic.

— **Riojana:** cut in pieces, stewed in oil and red wine with chopped onions, garlic, thyme, bayleaves, salt, pepper corns, a dash of vinegar, plenty of diced red peppers and fine herbs. (Spanish)

— **Roman Style:** à la romaine: cut in thick slices, sweated in butter, green peas and shredded lettuce added, moistened with white wine and cooked, thickened with butter paste.

— **Rouenese Style:** à la rouennaise: small eels rolled up in a spiral, tied, poached in red wine with mirepoix, glazed, dressed on round dish, center garnished with ragoût of mushrooms, oysters and soft roes, coated with the reduced red wine mixed with demi-glace, fried smelts dressed around the eel.

— **with Sage:** à la sauge: marinated in lemon juice, seasoned, coated with flour, fixed on skewers alternately with sage leaves, grilled and served with green peas.

— **Sailor's Style:** en matelote: cut in pieces, cooked in red wine, wine reduced and mixed with demi-glace, dressed with glazed button onions and mushrooms, coated with the sauce, garnished with fleurons.

— **Saint-Menehould:** cut in pieces, poached in white wine, when cold dipped in melted butter and breadcrumbs mixed with chopped mushrooms, grilled, garnished with sliced gherkins; Hachée sauce, mixed with chopped anchovies served separately.

— **Spanish Style:** à l'espagnole: cut in pieces, fried in oil, stewed in white wine with garlic, saffron and pepper, sprinkled with grilled shredded almonds.

— **Stew:** Ragoût d'anguilles: skinned eel cut in pieces, seasoned, dusted with flour, browned in butter and stewed with chopped anchovies, mushrooms, Sherry and a little vinegar.

— **Suffren:** larded with anchovy fillets, steamed in white wine and glazed, stock thickened with tomato purée, butter and anchovy paste, seasoned with Cayenne pepper.

— **Ticinese Style:** Anguilla alla ticinese: skinned and cut in pieces, browned with diced onions, carrots and sage, cooked in white wine and fish or meat stock with diced tomatoes, garlic and spices, stock reduced and served with polenta. (Italian)

Eel

— **Toulouse Style:** à la toulousaine: small eel rolled up in a spiral, tied, poached in fish stock and white wine, dressed on round dish, coated with fish velouté mixed with the reduced stock, center filled with mushrooms and button onions in velouté sauce.

— **Venetian Style:** à la vénetienne: cut in pieces, poached in white wine and glazed, coated with Venetian sauce, garnished with mushrooms and diced soft roes.

— **Villeroi:** cut in pieces, cooked in courtbouillon, when cold coated with Villeroi sauce, dipped in Eggs and breadcrumbs, deep fried; tomato sauce served separately.

— **Waldorf:** cut in pieces, marinated, dipped in milk, coated with flour and grilled; fish potatoes and mayonnaise sauce served separately.

— **in White Sauce:** à la poulette: cut in pieces, sweated in butter with chopped onions, sprinkled with flour, cooked in water, dressed with button mushrooms, coated with the strained sauce thickened with egg yolks, chopped parsley sprinkled on top.

Eel-pout, Burbot: F. Lotte; G. Aalraupe, Quappe; I. Lotta. Only member of the cod family living in fresh water. Found throughout Europe, in New England and the Great Lakes. The liver is very fat and highly esteemed.

— **Blue:** au bleu: cut in pieces, sprinkled with salt, marinated with hot vinegar, boiled, served with caper sauce.

— **in Cream Sauce:** à la crème: cut in pieces, parboiled, cooked in cream with butter and seasoning.

— **Housewife Style:** à la bonne-femme: cut in pieces, stewed with sliced mushrooms and chopped shallots in white wine and thin velouté sauce, coated with the sauce finished off with a little butter and glazed.

— **Villeroy:** cut in pieces, parboiled, when cold coated with Villeroy sauce, dipped in egg and breadcrumbs, deep fried and served with tomato sauce.

— **in White Wine:** au vin blanc: cut in pieces, parboiled, finish cooking with white wine and butter, reduce stock, mix with fish velouté and pour over the fish.

Empereur: see swordfish.

Eperlan: see smelt.

Espadon: see swordfish.

F

Fanshell: F. Pétoncle, Vanneau; G. Kamm-Muschel. Shellfish resembling the scallop found on the European and American Atlantic coasts and in the Mediterranean where its name ist pèlerine Prepared like scallop.

Féra: see whitefish.

Fish Balls: boiled flaked fish, seasoned, mixed with mashed potatoes and egg-yolks, when cold shaped into small balls, dipped in egg and breadcrumbs, deep fried; tomato sauce served separately.

Fish-Cake, Norwegian: Fiskkaggen: forcemeat of boiled white fish, mixed with butter, egg yolks, breadcrumbs and stiffly beaten egg whites, seasoned with salt, pepper and nutmeg, filled in soufflé-dish, baked, turned out and eaten cold. (Norwegian)

Fish Cakes: mashed boiled fish, mixed with the double amount of Duchess potato, egg yolks and a little cream, seasoned, shaped like small Hamburg steaks, dipped in egg and breadcrumbs, deep fried, tomato sauce, served separately.

Fiskkaggen: see Fish-Cake, Norwegian.

Fish-stew Belgian: Waterzooi: eel, pike, carp and tench, cut in pieces, boiled in seasoned water with butter, chopped herbs and strips of root vegetables, thickened with breadcrumbs, served with slices of buttered toast (Belgian).

— **Italian:** I. Brodetto di pesce: several sorts of saltwater fish cut in pieces, fried in oil with chopped onions, tomato purée and fine herbs added, moistened with fish stock, stewed, garnished with heart shaped croûtons fried in oil; served with polenta (Italian).

— **Italian:** II. Cappon magro: dress marinated slices of boiled celery, carrots, potatoes, cauliflower and green beans alternately with small slices of fried bread rubbed with garlic, top with cold fillets of fish and medaillons of crayfish, cover with green sauce made of mayonnaise mixed with chopped gherkins, capers and herbs and garnish with quarters of hard-boiled eggs, anchovy fillets, olives, tomatoes and shrimps (Italian).

Fish-rissoles: Rissoles de poisson, mixture of cold chopped boiled fish, shallots and seasoning bound with thick cream sauce and egg yolks, wrapped in puff paste, half moon-shaped, deep fried, garnished with fried parsley.

Fish Rolls: Roulades de poisson: chopped boiled fish, mixed with chopped onions and parsley sweated in butter, a little cream sauce and egg yolks added, spread on small pancakes baked on one side only, rolled together, dipped in eggs and breadcrumbs, fried and served with Brussels sprouts or cauliflower.

Flétan: see halibut.

Flounder: F. Flet; G. Flunder. Common saltwater flatfish found off the sandy coast of the Atlantic. Marketed fresh and in large quantities smoked. Prepared like plaice.

Fogas: Name for the giant pike-perch of the lake Balaton in Hungary. Prepared like pike-perch.

— **with Butter:** au beurre: cut in pieces, boiled in court bouillon; fish potatoes and melted butter served separately.

— **Croatian Style:** à la croate: whole fish, skinned and larded, simmered in sour cream.

— **Fried:** frite: filleted, dipped in eggs and breadcrumbs, deep fried, dressed with fried parsley and lemon; Tartar sauce served separately.

— **Grilled:** grillée: fillets, coated with flour, grilled; Tartar or Remoulade sauce served separately.

— **Miller Style:** à la meunière: filleted and prepared like sole fillets.

— **with Paprika:** au paprika: boiled; cream sauce flavored with paprika and fish potatoes served separately.

— **with Root Vegetables:** aux racines: fillets poached in white wine and fish stock, covered with white wine sauce mixed with julienne of carrots, knob celery and leeks, glaced.

— **Zichy:** boiled, coated with paprika sauce, sprinkled with grated cheese, glazed, garnished with asparagus tips.

Fried Fish: Friture: pieces or fillets of fish or seafood, usually dipped in eggs and breadcrumbs and deep fried.
— **of Eel:** Friture d'anguilles: parboiled, skinned and boned, cut in pieces, dipped in eggs and breadcrumbs, deep fried, Tartar or remoulade sauce served separately.
— **Marne Fry:** Friture de la Marne: the small "fry" of fresh water fish, coated with flour, deep fried, seasoned with salt and Cayenne pepper, served with lemon and fried parsley.
— **Monaco Style:** à la monégasque: fillets of small fish: soles, red mullets or mackerels — dipped in egg and breadcrumbs, deep fried, served with fried parsley and lemon.
— **Parisian Style:** à la parisienne: fillets of several kinds of small fish, coated with fish forcemeat, folded, dipped in egg and breadcrumbs, deep fried and served with fried parsley and lemon wedges.

Fritto misto di pesce: small smelts, gudgeons, fish fillets, frog legs, prawns, mussels, small fish croquettes, pieces of artichoke bottoms, broccoli and tomatoes etc, dipped in egg and breadcrumbs, sometimes dipped in frying batter, fried in oil, dressed with parsley and lemon; tomato sauce served separately (Italian).

Friture: see fried fish.

Frogs' legs: F. Cuisses de grenouilles; G. Froschkeulen. The hindlegs of the common march frog and large bull frog, usually "farmed" in France and the USA. Marketed fresh and frozen.
— **Aurora:** à l'aurore: poached in white wine and butter, when cold coated with white chaud-froid sauce, mixed with tomato purée, filled in mould lined with Champagne jelly, sealed with aspic jelly, turned out and decorated with jelly.
— **Ball Nymphs:** Nymphes ballerines: poached in white wine, when cold coated with paprika chaud-froid sauce and glazed with aspic jelly, dressed on wine leaves; mayonnaise with fine herbs or green sauce served separately.
— **in Butter:** au beurre: seasoned, coated with flour, fried in butter, lemon juice dropped on top, covered with browned butter.
— **Canadian Style:** à la canadienne: poached in white wine and butter, dressed in large pastry case on Newburgh sauce, covered with Newburgh sauce, sealed with light fish forcemeat, cooking of forcemeat finished in oven, glazed with butter.
— **Farmer Style:** : à la paysanne: poached in lemon juice and butter, covered with cream sauce mixed with chopped chervil.
— **with Fine Herbs:** aux fines herbes: I. seasoned, sautéd in butter, chopped parsley, lemon juice and browned butter on top.
II. poached in white stock, stock thickened with butter paste, egg yolks and cream, served in timbale with chopped parsley scattered on top.
— **Fricassee:** en fricassée: I. poached in white wine and butter, covered with sliced onions, diced tomatoes and red and green peppers simmered in butter.
— **Fricassee:** en fricassée: II. poached in white wine and butter, stock boiled down, mixed with velouté, cream and sliced, parboiled mushrooms and poured over the legs.

Frogs' legs

— **Fried:** frite: marinated in oil, lemon juice, chopped onions and parsley, coated with flour, dipped in egg and breadcrumbs, deep fried, served with fried parsley and lemon wedges.

— **Froth:** Mousselines de grenouilles: raw forcemeat of frog legs and pike or other fish, seasoned, mixed with raw egg whites and unsweetened whipped cream, filled in small moulds greased with butter and decorated with truffle slices, steamed in hot water bath, turned out, garnished with frog legs poached; in white wine, covered with Mousseline sauce.

— **in Frying Batter:** à l'Orly: dipped in frying batter, deep fried, dressed with fried parsley and lemon wedges, tomato sauce served separately.

— **Gratinated:** gratinées: prepared like fricassee, dressed in border of piped Duchess potato mixture, covered with the sauce, grated cheese and breadcrumbs sprinkled on top, gratinated in oven.

— **Italian Style:** à l'italienne: poached in butter and lemon juice, covered with Italian sauce, chopped parsley sprinkled on top.

— **Lyonese Style:** à la lyonnaise: parboiled, sautéd in butter with sliced shallow fried onions, lemon juice, chopped parsley and browned butter on top.

— **Mariner Style:** à la marinière: sautéd in butter and poached in white wine, covered with mariner's sauce.

— **Miller Style:** à la meunière: prepared like soft roes.

— **Nimese Style:** à la nîmoise: fried in butter, covered with diced tomatoes sautéd with chopped onions and garlic, diced green peppers and eggplants, chopped parsley scattered on top.

— **Princess Style:** à la princesse: poached in lemon juice and butter, covered with cream sauce, garnished with a bunch of asparagus tips.

— **Provencal Style:** à la provençale: sautéd in oil with diced tomatoes, chopped shallots, garlic and chopped herbs.

— **with Ragoût of Crayfish:** au ragoût d'écrevisses: small legs parboiled, coated with Villeroi sauce, dipped in egg and breadcrumbs, deep fried and dressed on large fried mushrooms stuffed with fine ragoût of crayfish tails.

— **with Risotto:** au risotto: legs poached in white wine and butter, mixed with crayfish tails and perch fillets fried in butter, bound with Nantua sauce, dressed in border of risotto; grated cheese served separately.

— **Spanish Style:** frite à l'espagnole: seasoned with salt and pepper, dipped in egg and breadcrumbs, shallow fried in oil; Creole sauce served separately.

— **Steuben:** marinated in lemon juice, salt and pepper, sautéd in butter, covered with sweet cream, cream slightly boiled down, thickened with egg yolks mixed with Sherry, finely chopped chives scattered on top.

— **Theodor:** fried in butter, filled in large puff pastry patty, covered with diced tomatoes sautéd with chopped onions, red peppers, garlic and parsley.

— **in White Sauce:** à la poulette: poached in white wine and butter with thyme, bay leaves, sliced onions and parsley stalks, covered with poulette sauce.

Frost-Fish, also called Tom cod. Salt water fish, prepared like cod.

Fruits de mer: see seafood.
Frutti di mare: seafood: smelts, fish fillets, pieces of cuttlefish, oysters, mussels and other marine delicacies marinated in lemon juice and oil, dipped in eggs and breadcrumbs, fried in oil, garnished with parsley and lemon; tomato sauce served separately. (Italian)

G

Gardon: see roach.
Gilt-poll: F. Daurade, vraie dorade; G. Goldbrasse. Saltwater fish of perch-like appearance found in the Mediterranean, off the African and occasionaly off the coast of the British Isles.
— **with Butter:** boiled in court bouillon; melted butter and fish potatoes served separately.
— **Calcutta Style:** fillets coated with fish forcemeat, folded, poached in fish stock, covered with curry sauce mixed with sliced mushrooms; pilaff rice served separately.
— **Grilled:** grillée: smaller fish coated with flour, grilled and served with herb butter, Tartar sauce or mustard mayonnaise.
— **Icarian Style:** à l'icarienne: poached in white wine with shallots and mushroom peel, stock strained, boiled down, thickened with butter paste, poured over the fish, garnished with heart shaped croûtons.
— **Miller's Style:** à la meunière: prepared like barbel.
— **with Parsley Butter:** à la persillade: grilled and served with parsley butter.
— **Roman Style:** à la romaine: cut in pieces, sweated in butter, shredded lettuce, green peas and white wine added, cooked slowly, thickened with butter paste, served in timbale dish.
— **Venetian Style:** à la vénetienne: steamed with butter, lemon juice and fish stock, surrounded with Venetian sauce.
— **in White Wine Sauce:** au vin blanc: small fish or fillets poached in white wine and fish stock, covered with white wine sauce; fish potatoes served separately.
Gilthead: F. Pagel; G. Roter Meerbrassen. Saltwater fish of the sea-bream family, found in the Mediterranean, the warmer waters off the American coasts and occasionally in the Atlantic. Prepared like gilt-poll.
Goujon: see gudgeon.
Grande vive: see dragon-fish.
Grayling: F. Ombre-écailles, ombre-commun, G. Äsche. Freshwater fish. Prepared like trout.
— **Blue:** au bleu: prepared like trout au bleu.
— **Geneva Style:** à la genévoise: poached in red wine with mirepoix, garnished with fried mushrooms, coated with the reduced stock thickened with butter paste.
— **Lausanne Style:** à la lausannoise: poached in white wine with shallots and sliced mushrooms, stock reduced, mixed with demi-glace, finished off with butter and lemon juice.
— **Maître d'hôtel:** boiled in vinegar water, melted herb butter poured over.
— **Provencal:** à la provençale: scored on both sides, fried in oil with diced tomatoes and garlic.
Grélin: see rock salmon.

Grey Mullet: F. Mulet gris, mulet porc; G. Graubarbe. Saltwater fish found in the Mediterranean, the Atlantic, Pacific and in the North Sea. Prepared like giltpoll.

Grondin: see gurnard.

Gudgeon: F. Goujon; G. Gründling; I. Chiozzo. Small freshwater fish found in nearly all European lakes. Served fried or as a garnish.

— **Deviled:** à la diable: coated with flour, deep fried, seasoned with salt mixed with Cayenne pepper, served with fried parsley and lemon.

— **English Style:** à l'anglaise: dipped in eggs and breadcrumbs, fried in butter, covered with half melted herb butter.

— **Francillon:** coated with flour, grilled, dressed on toast coated with anchovy butter, garnished with straw potatoes and fried parsley; tomato sauce and anchovy butter served separately.

— **Fried:** frit: I. dipped in frying batter and deep fried; II. dipped in egg and breadcrumbs, deep fried very crisp, served with fried parsley and lemon wedges.

Gurnard, Gurnet: F. Grondin; G. Knurrhahn; I. Triglia. Saltwater fish found in the Mediterranean and in the warmer waters of the Atlantic coasts. Prepared like red mullet.

— **Egyptian Style:** à l'égypienne: cut in pieces, simmered in oil, white wine, strips of leeks, diced tomatoes and chopped parsley, stock reduced and beaten with garlic butter.

— **with Herb Butter:** à la maître d'hôtel: broiled and served with herb butter.

— **with Shrimp Sauce:** au sauce crevette: stuffed with fish forcemeat mixed with chopped shrimps, braised, covered with shrimp sauce.

H

Haddock: F. Aiglefin; G. Schellfisch; I. Baccalà fresco. Saltwater fish caught off the American and North European Atlantic coasts. Prepared like cod.

— **with Anchovies:** aux anchois: fillets fried in butter, covered with browned butter mixed with chopped anchovies.

— **Ancient Style:** à l'ancienne: boiled, covered with caper sauce mixed with sliced gherkins.

— **Boatman's Style:** à la batelière: fillets poached in fish stock, dressed on pastry boats filled with ragoût of mussels and shrimps, covered with white wine sauce, garnished with strips of soles egged, breadcrumbed and deep fried.

— **with Browned Butter:** au beurre noir: cut in pieces, shallow fried, covered with browned butter with a few drops of vinegar added, chopped parsley sprinkled on top; boiled potatoes served separately.

— **Buena Vista:** fillets, poached in white wine and fish stock, covered with Sailor sauce mixed with diced lobster, tomatoes and mushrooms.

— **with Butter:** au beurre: boiled; melted butter and fish potatoes served separately.

— **Étretat:** cutlets or fillets poached in butter and white wine, garnished with poached oysters and shrimps, covered with Normandy sauce.

Haddock

— **with Fine Herbs:** I. cutlets, poached, covered with white wine sauce with chopped herbs;
II. fillets arranged on chopped shallots, mushrooms and parsley in greased baking dish, covered with chopped mushrooms, chopped onions and parsley, moistened with white wine, sprinkled with breadcrumbs, dotted with butter and baked in oven.

— **Flemish Style:** à la flamande: fillets poached in white wine, garnished with button onions, mushrooms and chopped herbs, stock boiled down, mixed with white wine sauce and poured over the fish.

— **Lyon Style:** à la lyonnaise: fillets fried in butter, covered with slices of fried onions and chopped herbs, browned butter with a few drops of vinegar on top.

— **Maître d'hôtel:** cutlets fried in butter, herb butter on top; fish potatoes served separately.

— **Portuguese Style:** à la portugaise: cut in large pieces, arranged in baking dish largely greased with oil and butter with chopped sweated onions, garlic, diced tomatoes, chopped parsley and rice, moistened with white wine, seasoned, cooked in oven.

— **Saint-Nazaire:** cutlets, poached in courtbouillon, garnished with poached bearded oysters and lobster slices, covered with white wine sauce, fleurons around.

— **with various Sauces:** boiled and served with anchovy, caper, parsley, herb, lobster, crayfish, Dutch sauce or melted butter and boiled potatoes.

— **Scotch Style:** à l'écossaise: boiled, covered with Dutch sauce mixed with finely diced root vegetables simmered in butter.

Haddock, Smoked: Finnan Haddie, Finon Haddie; F. Aigrefin fumé; G. geräucherter Shellfish. Split, cured and smoked haddock is a favorite breakfast dish.

— **Broiled:** grillé: soaked in milk, cut in pieces, brushed with butter, broiled, served with plain or herb butter.

— **with Butter:** au beurre: cut in pieces, cooked in milk or milk and water, drained, melted butter poured on top.

— **in Cream Sauce:** à la crème: cut in pieces, poached in milk and water, covered with cream sauce.

— **Delmonico:** boiled, boned, flaked, covered with cream sauce, garnished with truffle slices, shrimps and quarters of hard-boiled eggs.

— **Park Hotel:** boiled, boned, flaked, filled in baking dish masked with cream sauce, Duchess mixture piped around the edges, covered with cream sauce blended with Dutch sauce and glazed.

Hake: F. Colin; G. Seehecht; I. Luccio marino: Saltwater fish found in the Atlantic and Pacific.

— **Ancient Style:** à l'ancienne: boiled, covered with caper sauce with chopped gherkins added.

— **Basle Style:** à la baloise: cutlets prepared like cod.

— **Boistelle:** prepared like sole fillets.

— **Fried:** fillets prepared like sole.

— **Gambetta:** fillets, poached, one fillet covered with Nantua and the other with green herb sauce, a slice of truffle on each fillet.

— **Leopold:** escalopes poached in white wine and fish stock, one escalope covered with lobster sauce, chopped truffles scattered on top, the other escalope covered with Geneva

Hake
sauce with chopped coral on top, garnished with shrimps in white wine sauce.
— **Miller Style:** à la meunière: prepared like sole fillets.
— **Polish Style:** à la polonaise: fillets fried in butter, chopped parsley and hard-boiled eggs scattered on top, breadcrumbs browned in plenty of butter poured over.
— **in Red Wine:** au vin rouge: poached in red wine with chopped shallots, covered with Genoese sauce, garnished with fleurons.
— **with Sorrel:** à l'oseille: braised in white wine and butter, arranged on sorrel purée, garnished with glazed button onions and diced fried bacon, covered with the stock thickened with butterpaste.
— **Toulouse Style:** à la toulousaine: poached in court-bouillon, covered with white wine sauce, garnished with mushrooms, button onions, pitted olives and small fish dumplings.

Halászlé: see Hungarian fish stew.

Halibut: F. Flétan; G. Heilbutt. The largest species of the flatfish family found off the western shores of North America, in the Northern Atlantic, the North Sea and the western Baltic. Prepared like turbot.
— **Boiled:** bouilli: cut in pieces, boiled and served with caper, egg, Dutch, mousseline sauce or melted butter and boiled potatoes.
— **Boistelle:** fillets poached in white wine and fish fumet with chopped parsley, shallots and sliced raw mushrooms, covered with the stock, reduced, beaten up with butter and glazed.
— **Bristol:** cut in pieces, boiled in salt water with a little milk, dressed with poached bearded oysters on top, covered with cream sauce, sprinkled with grated cheese and glazed.
— **with Browned Butter:** au beurre noir: cut in pieces, coated with flour fried in butter, covered with well browned butter mixed with chopped parsley and a few drops of vinegar.
— **Cette Style:** à la cettoise: fillets poached, dressed on tomatoes concassées, covered with lobster sauce, sprinkled with chopped herbs.
— **Creamed:** crème au gratin: boiled, skinned and boned, flaked, arranged in baking dish on a little Mornay sauce in a border of piped duchess potato mixture, covered with Mornay sauce, sprinkled with grated cheese and glazed.
— **Cuban Style:** à la cubaine: fillets coated with flour, fried in butter, Creole sauce and plain rice served separately.
— **Duchess:** à la duchesse: fillets, arranged on dish in prebaked border of piped duchess potato mass, covered with cream sauce.
— **Gratinated:** poached fillets, dressed in baking dish greased with butter, covered with Italian sauce, sprinkled with breadcrumbs, dotted with butter and gratinated in oven.
— **Housewife Style:** à la bonne femme: fillets prepared like sole.
— **Lille Style:** à la lilloise: fillets poached in white wine and fish stock, covered with white wine sauce mixed with tomato purée, chopped tarragon and small thin strips of fried bacon.

Halibut
— **Maître d'hôtel:** fillets coated with flour, fried in butter and served with herb butter.
— **Mathilde:** cut in pieces, boiled, covered with Mexican sauce mixed with diced tomatoes tossed in butter.
— **Miller Style:** à la meunière: cut in pieces or fillets, prepared like barbel.
— **Mornay:** fillets poached, dressed in baking dish, surrounded with piped Duchess potato mixture, covered with Mornay sauce, sprinkled with grated cheese and glazed.
— **Murat:** prepared like sole.
— **with Mussels:** au moules: cut in pieces, boiled, garnished with bearded mussels, covered with mussel sauce.
— **Venetian Style:** fillets poached in white wine and fish stock, covered with Venetian sauce, garnished with fleurons.

Hareng: see herring.
— **fumeé:** see bloater and kipper.

Herring: F. Hareng; G. Hering; I. Aringa; S. Arenque. Important saltwater fish caught in the Atlantic both on the European and American coasts and in the Pacific. Small herrings up to 8 inch. are called streamlings, young female herrings Matjes. Processed herrings, salted, marinated, pickled or smoked, are an important commercial article.
— **Bismarck:** fat salt Matjes soaked, cleaned, filleted, boiled in pickle of white wine, vinegar and spices, served with raw onion rings and lemon slices on top.
— **Boiled:** bouilli: boiled in salt water with a few drops of vinegar, served with melted butter and fish potatoes.
— **Boulogne Style:** à la boulonnaise: poached in white wine and fish stock, garnished with bearded mussels, mussel sauce poured over the fish.
— **Bratheringe:** fried pickled herrings: fresh herrings, seasoned, coated with flour, fried in pan in fat until well browned, when cold covered with boiled pickle of water, vinegar, sliced onions, a little sugar, bayleaves and spices and left in pickle for a few days before serving. (German)
— **Cakes Esthonian Style:** Crêpes de hareng à l'estonienne: fillets of salt herrings, soaked, chopped finely, mixed with butter, breadcrumbs and cream, baked in skillet like small thin pancakes; sour cream served separately.
— **Calais Style:** à la calaisienne: opened from the back, bones removed, stuffed with the soft roes mixed with chopped mushrooms, shallots and herb butter, wrapped in greased paper and baked in oven.
— **Courland Style:** po kurlandski: coated with flour, fried in butter, placed in baking dish on fried onion rings and strips of fried bacon, covered with sour cream mixed with tomato purée and flavored with Kabul sauce, sprinkled with breadcrumbs, butter dotted on top, baked in oven. (Russian)
— **Devilled:** à la diable: scored on both sides, brushed with mustard, coated with breadcrumbs, grilled in oil; ravigote sauce served separately.
— **Dieppe Style:** à la dieppoise: poached in white wine, mussel and mushroom stock, garnished with bearded mussels and shrimps, covered with white wine sauce mixed with the reduced stock.

Herring

— **Door-keeper Style:** à la portière: scored, brushed with mustard, coated with breadcrumbs and chopped parsley, fried in butter, covered with browned butter mixed with a few drops of vinegar.

— **in Dressing Gown:** en robe de chambre: salt herrings, soaked, skinned, filleted, dipped in frying batter, deep fried; potato salad served separately.

— **Egyptian Style:** à l'égyptienne: fried in oil, covered with fried diced tomatoes and fried onion rings.

— **English Style:** à l'anglaise: opened from the back, boned, flattened, dipped in eggs and breadcrumbs, fried in butter, half melted herb butter poured over the fish.

— **Farmer Style:** à la paysanne: fillets poached in white wine and stock with small thin slices of carrots, onions, leeks and knob celery simmered in butter beforehand, stock boiled down, beaten up with butter and poured over the fillets, chopped parsley sprinkled on top.

— **Flemish Style:** à la flamande: poached in white wine with chopped shallots, butter and lemon segments without peel or pips, stock thickened with cracker meal and poured over the fish.

— **Fried:** frit: I. seasoned with salt, pepper and lemon juice, coated with eggs and breadcrumbs, deep fried, mustard butter served separately.
II. scored on both sides, coated with flour, fried in butter, served with herb butter.
III. scored on both sides, coated thinly with mustard, dipped in breadcrumbs, fried in oil; Tartar or remoulade sauce served separately.

— **Kippered:** split, salted and smoked, grilled or fried in butter, served with or without scrambled eggs as breakfast dish.

— **Nantese Style:** à la nantaise: scored on both sides, coated with eggs and breadcrumbs, fried in butter; sauce made of purée of soft roes, stirred on the fire with mustard, seasoning and butter, served separately.

— **Paramé:** scored on both sides, sautéd in butter, wrapped in greased paper with Duxelles, baked in oven.

— **Sill-lada:** salt herrings skinned, washed, soaked in milk, filled in baking dish alternately with slices of boiled potatoes and onions, sprinkled with grated cheese and breadcrumbs, baked in oven, melted butter poured over top. (Swedish)

— **Strömmings-lada:** young herrings opened from the back, bones removed, salted, filled in greased baking dish, sprinkled with grated Parmesan and breadcrumbs, dotted with butter, baked in oven. (Swedish)

— **Stroganoff:** coated with flour, arranged in baking dish greased with butter on slices of boiled potatoes, sour cream mixed with chopped sweated shallots and Kabul sauce poured over, sprinkled with grated Parmesan, dotted with butter, baked in oven. (Russian)

— **Stuffed:** farci: opened from back, boned, stuffed with fish forcemeat mixed with chopped herbs, wrapped in greased paper, baked in oven.

Homard: see lobster.

Huch: see huck.

Huck, Hucho: F. Huch; G. Huchen. Freshwater fish of the salmon family found in the Danube and in rivers north of the Alps. Prepared like salmon.

— Cutlet, Escalope: filleted, sliced, sautéd in butter and served with Nantua sauce.

Hungarian Fish Stew: Halászlé: sliced onions fried in butter, dusted with paprika, tench, carp, fogas, pike and eel, cut in pieces, added, mixed with tomatoe purée, moistened with water and sour cream, cooked, stock strained, thickened with egg yolks, seasoned with lemon juice and poured over the fish. (Hungarian)

John Dory, Dory: F. Dorée, Saint-Pierre, Poule de mer; G. Petersfisch, Heringskönig. Saltwater fish found in all European seas. Used chiefly in making bouillabaisse.

K

Kingfish: F. Able de mer; G. Weissbarsch. Saltwater fish found in the Atlantic and Pacific.

— with Devil's Sauce: à la sauce diable: scored, coated with flour, brushed with oil, grilled; devil's sauce served separately.

— Dutch Style: à la hollandaise: boiled, served with Dutch sauce and fresh, boiled potatoes.

— Miranda: scored, coated with flour, pan fried in butter, capers and chopped parsley scattered on top, a little tomato catsup and lemon juice poured over, covered with browned butter.

Kippers: F. harengs fumés; G. geräucherte Heringe: split herrings mildly cured and smoked. Popular breakfast dish usually broiled or fried.

Klippfish: F. Morue séchée; G. Klippfisch. Name for cod, first cut up, salted and then dried in the air. Prepared like salt cod.

Kulibijaka: see Russian salmon pie.

L

Laberdan: cod salted and packed in barrels at port of landing. Prepared like salt cod.

Laitance d'alose: see shad roe.

Laitances: see soft roes.

Lake Trout: F. Truite du lac; G. Seeforelle. Large variety of the river trout found chiefly in Swiss lakes. Prepared like salmon and salmon trout.

Lamprey: F. Lamproie; G. Lamprete, Neunauge. Eel-like fish living both in rivers and seas of the north and south temperate regions. Prepared like eel.

Lamproie: see lamprey.

Langouste: see crawfish.

Langoustine: F. Langoustine; G. Langustine. Crustacean resembling lobster but much smaller found in the Mediterranean, related to Dublin Bay prawns and the Norwegian lobster. Prepared like crayfish.

Lavaret: see whitefish.

Lemon Sole, Dab-sole: F. Vraie limande, limande-sole; G. Rotzunge, echte Rotzunge. Saltwater flatfish found off the European and American Atlantic coasts. Prepared like sole and dab.

Lemon Sole, Dab-sole

— **Antwerp Style:** à l'anversoise: poached in butter, lemon juice and water, covered with Dutch sauce, seasoned with a little mustard, garnished with potato croquettes.

— **Carnot:** poached in white wine and fish stock, covered with white wine sauce, garnished with tiny puff pastry patties stuffed with salpicon of shrimps.

— **David:** coated with flour, pan fried in butter, sprinkled with chopped parsley, seasoned with lemon juice, breadcrumbs browned in plenty of butter on top.

— **Flemish Style:** à la flamande: fillets, poached in butter and lemon juice, covered with white wine sauce seasoned with mustard, garnished with fish potatoes.

— **Gaillard:** poached in white wine and fish stock, placed in baking dish greased with butter, garnished with poached bearded oysters, covered with cream sauce, chopped hard-boiled eggs and breadcrumbs scattered on top, dotted with butter, glazed rapidly under the salamander.

— **Grenoble Style:** à la grenobloise: fillets prepared like sole.

Lieu jaune: see pollack.

Lieu noir: see rock salmon.

Limande: see dab.

Limande-sole: see lemon sole.

Ling: F. Lingue; G. Lengfisch. Saltwater fish caught chiefly in the North Sea and in the Channel. Marketed fresh, dried and smoked. Prepared like cod.

Lingue: see ling.

Lobster: F. Homard; G. Hummer; I. Arragosta. Very popular crustacean resembling crayfish but much larger. Lobsters are caught along almost all the European coasts, the Atlantic coasts of America and Canada and especially around Newfoundland.

— **Alexandra:** boiled, in court-bouillon, when cold split lengthwise, flesh taken out of body and claws, both halves filled with shredded lettuce mixed with the diced meat of the claws and bound with Alexandra sauce, garnished with the sliced meat of the body, slices of hard-boiled eggs and truffles, coated with Alexandra sauce, dressed on shredded lettuce and served with lemon wedges.

— **American Style:** à l'américaine: cut body of living lobster in pieces, crack the claws open, season with salt and Cayenne pepper, reserve the creamy parts of the entrails. Sauté pieces in oil and butter with chopped onions, add chopped shallots just before done, flambé with brandy, moisten with white wine, add diced tomatoes or tomato purée and simmer for 20 minutes. Dress lobster pieces in timbale dish, reduce the stock, strain through a wire sieve, reheat, thicken with the reserved entrails and coral rubbed through a sieve, without allowing to boil, beat with butter, finish off with chopped herbs and pour over the lobster pieces; serve with rice. The lobster pieces may be shelled before pouring the sauce over.

— **Bagration:** cold lobster slices dressed on rounds of toast or pastry cases filled with Russian salad, coated with mayonnaise, chopped chervil and fennel green sprinkled on top.

— **Bahiana:** raw lobster split lengthwise, the claws cracked lightly, sautéd in oil with chopped onions, diced green peppers, tomatoes, oil and seasoning added, simmered in

Lobster

fish stock; stock boiled down and poured over the lobster. (Brasilian)

— **Belle View:** en belle-vue: boiled cold lobster halved lengthwise, meat taken out of shell, shell filled with vegetable, Russian or other salad, meat replaced in shell with round red side upwards, glazed with aspic jelly, dressed on round silver dish with the lobster heads upright in the center, garnished with aspic jelly, parsley or watercress and lemon; mayonnaise served separately. Any sumptuous lobster dish may be called Belle View.

— **Bordeaux Style:** à la bordelaise: prepared like américaine, but lobsters split open lengthwise, fine mirepoix added to sauce, finished off with meat glaze and lemon juice.

— **Brillat-Savarin:** boiled in court-bouillon, flesh of body cut in thick slices; arrange like a turban alternately with fried slices of small vegetable marrow, covered with American sauce, center filled with ragoût of mushrooms, truffles and the diced flesh of the claws bound with American sauce.

— **Broiled:** grillé: living lobster tapped on head to stun it, split in half by inserting strong pointed knife in center of back, knife pressed down first towards nose and then turned round to split tail end, seasoned with salt and Cayenne pepper, brushed with butter or oil, broiled, garnished with lemon and parsley, melted butter served separately.

— **Cardinal Style:** à la cardinal: cooked in court-bouillon, flesh of tail sliced, flesh of claws diced. Half shells filled with ragoût of sliced mushrooms and truffles bound with a little lobster sauce, lobster slices arranged alternately with truffle slices on top, covered with sauce cardinal and glaced, the stuffed claws placed on both sides.

— **Carnot:** cold medaillons of lobster, decorated with truffle slices, glazed with aspic jelly, dressed on lobster froth filled in border mould and turned out on round silver dish, decorated with aspic jelly; Russian sauce served separately.

— **Chantecler:** live lobster split in half lengthwise, seasoned with curry powder, sautéd in butter, flesh taken out of shells, shells filled with curry rice, sliced lobster dressed on top, covered with curry sauce mixed with Nantua sauce, glazed, garnished with a mushroom in the center and a cockscomb on each side.

— **Chevreuse:** boiled in court-bouillon, when cold taken out of the shell, cut in medaillons, dressed alternately with sliced truffles on asparagus tips in the shells, glazed with jelly; mayonnaise sauce served separately.

— **Churchill:** raw lobster split lengthwise, coated with a mixture of butter, mustard powder, salt and Cayenne pepper, baked in oven.

— **Curried:** sliced boiled lobster sautéd in butter, simmered for a while in curry sauce, dressed in timbale dish, plain rice served separately.

— **Cutlets:** Côtelettes de homard: diced lobster, mushrooms and truffles bound with fish velouté with lobster butter and egg yolks, when cold shaped into cutlets, coated with egg and breadcrumbs, deep fried, dressed with fried parsley; lobster or other convenient sauce served separately.

Lobster

— **Clarence:** boiled in court-bouillon. Split open lengthwise, flesh taken out and cut in slices, entrails passed through a sieve, mixed with Béchamel sauce and seasoned with curry powder. Shells filled with curry rice, lobster slices alternated with truffle slices arranged on top, covered with a part of the prepared sauce and the rest served separately.

— **Delmonico:** prepared like Newburgh but with Madeira instead of Sherry wine.

— **Devilled:** à la diable: raw lobster split lengthwise in two halves, the claws cracked slightly, seasoned with salt and Cayenne pepper, brushed with oil and grilled; Devil sauce served separately.

— **Dumas:** sliced lobster sautéd in butter, deglaced with white wine, simmered in demi-glace with tomato purée, garnished with fleurons.

— **Edison:** sliced lobster sautéd in butter, simmered in fresh cream, seasoned with paprika, served on toast.

— **French Style:** à la française: pieces of raw lobster sautéd in clarified butter, cognac, white wine and vegetable julienne added, seasoned lightly, cooked, stock mixed with fish velouté, boiled down, beaten with butter and poured over lobster.

— **Fritters:** Croquettes de h.: salpicon prepared as for cutlets, shaped into longish croquettes, dipped in eggs and breadcrumbs, deep fried, dressed with fried parsley; lobster sauce served separately.

— **Froth:** mousse de homard: mousseline forcemeat prepared from raw lobster and well seasoned, filled in charlotte or other round mould greased with butter, steamed in water bath in oven, turned out on round dish and covered with lobster sauce.

— **Froth Cold:** mousse de h.: flesh of cooked lobster pounded in mortar with a little cream sauce, rubbed through fine wire sieve, highly seasoned, mixed with liquid aspic jelly and whipped, unsweetened cream, filled in mould lined with aspic jelly, when set turned out and garnished with triangles of aspic jelly.

— **Froth Infante Style:** à l'infante: boiled cold lobster halved lengthwise, flesh removed and cut in slices, shells filled half full with mousseline forcemeat of lobster, lobster slices arranged alternately with truffle slices and poached bearded oysters on top, covered with forcemeat, greased paper put on top, baked in oven with a little water in baking pan.

— **Grammont:** boiled, when cold halved lengthwise, shells filled with cold lobster froth, lobster slices arranged on top, garnished alternately with cold poached and bearded oysters and truffle slices, coated with aspic jelly, dressed with lettuce hearts and parsley.

— **Grilled:** grillé: see broiled.

— **Hamburg Style:** à la hamburgeoise: slices of boiled lobster, placed in shallow saucepan with Madeira and meat glaze, boiled up and thickened with breadcrumbs mixed with butter, sauce finished off with a little thick cream, chopped parsley, salt, Cayenne pepper and lemon juice, lobster dressed in timbale dish with sauce poured over the top.

Lobster

— **Hungarian Style:** à la hongroise: prepared like Newburgh, but with raw lobster, adding chopped onions and paprika sweated in butter and leaving out the Sherry.

— **Lord Randolph:** raw lobster halved lengthwise, grilled, flesh taken out of shells, diced, mixed with butter, anchovy paste and chopped parsley, filled in the shells, coated with Mornay sauce, sprinkled with grated Parmesan and glazed.

— **Majestic:** prepared like Bordeaux style, flesh taken out of the shells, filled in timbale dish with truffle slices, covered with Nantua sauce.

— **Merville:** Blanquette de homard Merville: raw lobster cut in pieces, sautéd in butter, ignited with cognac, deglaced with Rhine wine, simmered in cream with fine mirepoix, flesh taken out of shells and dressed in timbale dish with mushrooms and poached bearded oysters, covered with the sauce thickened with egg yolks, highly seasoned and finished off with the entrails and butter; plain rice served separately.

— **Monaco Style:** à la monégasque: raw lobster halved lengthwise, prepared like American style, flesh sliced and filled in the shells, covered with the reduced and strained sauce mixed with diced tomatoes and chopped tarragon, sprinkled with grated Parmesan and glazed.

— **Mornay:** half shells filled with ragout of mushrooms and the flesh of the claws in lobster sauce, slices of boiled lobster and truffles arranged on top, covered with Mornay sauce, sprinkled with grated cheese and glazed.

— **Mousselines:** mousseline forcemeat of raw lobster filled in small oval or round moulds, decorated with a slice of truffle, steamed, turned out, dressed in shape of a turban, covered with lobster, Nantua or other appropriate sauce, center garnished with asparagus tips, mushrooms or other garnish.

— **Newburgh:** slice cooked lobster, sautéd in butter on both sides, cook in thick cream and Sherry, thicken with mixture of egg yolks and cream, season lightly, serve in chafing dish with toast.

— **Palestine:** raw lobster cut in small pieces, sautéd in butter with fine mirepoix, ignited with cognac, moistened with white wine and fish stock, simmered until done, flesh taken out of shells and kept warm. Shells pounded in mortar, sautéd in oil with mirepoix, moistened with the lobster stock, fish velouté, the entrails and coral mixed with butter added and seasoned with a pinch of curry powder. Sauce strained, mixed with thick cream and butter and poured over the lobster dressed in border of curry rice.

— **Parisian Style:** à la parisienne: sliced lobster decorated and glazed with aspic jelly, dressed on trimmed shell filled with shredded lettuce and placed on sloping bread or rice base, garnished with artichoke bottom and hard-boiled eggs stuffed with Russian salad, glazed with aspic jelly and crowned with a truffle slice; mayonnaise served separately.

— **Phonician Style:** à la phocéenne: prepared like American style with a little saffron and garlic, sauce finished off with julienne of red peppers, served without the shells in border of pilaf rice with saffron.

Lobster

— **Pilaf:** Pilaw: pilaf rice with saffron mixed with diced lobster, diced sautéd eggplants, tomatoes and green peppers, lobster sauce served separately; or lobster prepared American style, taken out of the shells and dressed in the center of pilaf rice pressed into a round border mould, turned out on a round silver dish.

— **Pompadour:** prepared like American style but moistened with fish stock and cream, flesh taken out of the shells and dressed in timbale dish, stock reduced, bound with entrails, finished off with butter and poured over the lobster.

— **in Port:** au porto: small lobster split lengthwise, claws cracked open, sautéd in butter, seasoned with salt and paprika, cooked, covered with dry Port. Flesh taken out of the shells, stock reduced, thickened with a blend of egg yolks and cream, finished off with a few drops of Port and poured of the sliced lobster dressed in timbale or chafing dish.

— **in Scallop Shells:** en coquille: boiled diced lobster, mixed with diced mushrooms, bound with cheese sauce, filled in scallop shells, coated with cheese sauce, sprinkled with grated cheese and glazed.

— **Soufflé 1:** raw or boiled flesh of lobster, pounded im mortar with thick Béchamel sauce, rubbed through a fine sieve, seasoned highly, mixed with cream, egg yolks and stiffly beaten egg whites, filled in soufflé dish greased with butter, baked in water bath in oven; lobster sauce served separately.

— **Soufflé 2:** mousseline forcemeat prepared from raw lobster, seasoning and cream, filled in the half shells, decorated with truffle slices, covered with greased paper, baked in the oven with a few drops of fish stock in baking dish, dressed with parsley and lemon; lobster or mousseline sauce blended with lobster butter served separately.

— **Stuffed:** boiled in court-bouillon, split lengthwise, flesh taken out of tails and claws, diced, mixed with diced mushrooms, seasoned with Cayenne pepper, bound with cream sauce, filled in the half shells, sprinkled with grated cheese and glazed under the salamander.

— **Thermidor:** boiled lobster halved lengthwise, flesh sliced, refilled in shells, covered with Bercy sauce mixed with mustard and Mornay sauce, sprinkled with grated cheese and glazed.

— **Tourville:** ragoût of boiled lobster, cut in slices, mixed with sautéd mushroom slices, bearded oysters, mussels and truffle slices in Normandy sauce, filled in border of risotto, coated with cheese sauce, sprinkled with grated cheese and glazed.

— **Turkish Style:** à la turque: prepared like American style, dressed without shells in border of pilaf rice with saffron.

— **Vanderbilt:** raw lobster halved lengthwise and prepared American style, shells filled with ragoût of crayfish tails, mushrooms and truffles in American sauce, the sliced lobster arranged alternately with truffle slices on top, coated with creamed American sauce, sprinkled with grated Parmesan and glazed.

Lobster

— **Victoria:** half shells filled with salpicon of lobster, truffles and mushrooms in Victoria sauce, lobster slices dressed on top, covered with Victoria sauce, sprinkled with grated cheese and glazed.

— **Winterthur:** prepared like Victoria but lobster in salpicon replaced by shrimps, and shrimp sauce used instead of Victoria sauce.

— **Wladimir:** flesh of raw lobster pounded in mortar with a little cream sauce, rubbed through a wire sieve, mixed with cold cream sauce, truffle purée, paprika, salt, lobster butter, egg yolks and stiffly beaten egg whites, filled in split lobster shells and baked in oven.

— **Xavier:** ragoût of boiled lobster and mushrooms in Nantua sauce filled in split shells, sprinkled with grated cheese and glazed.

Lotte: see eel-pout.

Loup marin: see wolf-fish.

M

Mackerel: F. Maquereau; G. Makrele. Saltwater fish found off all the coasts of the Atlantic, the Pacific coast of North America, in the Mediterranean, the North Sea and the Baltic.

— **with Anchovy Cream:** au crème d'anchois: poached, covered with cream sauce blended with anchovy butter.

— **Bonnefoy:** fillets coated with flour, shallow fried, covered with bordeaux sauce; fish potatoes served separately.

— **Boulogne Style:** à la boulonnaise: poached in white wine and fish stock, garnished with bearded mussels, covered with bastard sauce.

— **Calais Style:** à la calaisienne: opened at the back, boned, stuffed with mixture of herb butter, chopped soft roes, mushrooms and shallots, wrapped in greased paper, baked in oven.

— **Citizen Style:** à la bourgeoise: stuffed with fish forcemeat mixed with chopped herbs, coated with flour, shallow fried, covered with cream sauce mixed with chopped mushrooms.

— **Dieppe Style:** fillets prepared like brill.

— **Francillon:** fillets grilled, arranged on croûtons masked with anchovy butter, garnished with straw potatoes; tomato sauce served separately.

— **Fried:** frit: fillets marinated in oil, lemon juice, chopped shallots and parsley, coated with flour, deep fried, tomato sauce served separately.

— **Grilled, Broiled:** grillé: split lengthwise, seasoned, coated with flour, brushed with oil, grilled; Tartar or Ravigotte sauce or herb butter served separately.

— **Old English Style:** à l'ancienne mode anglaise: cut in pieces, boiled in fish stock with plenty of fennel; purée of green gooseberries served separately.

— **with Peas:** aux petits pois: poached, covered with cream sauce blended with green pea butter, garnished with buttered green peas.

Mackerel

— **Rosalie:** fillets shallow fried in nut oil, covered with chopped onions, shallots, mushrooms and a little garlic sautéd in nut oil, a few drops of vinegar and chopped parsley added.

— **Spring Style:** à la printanière: fillets poached, covered with bastard sauce beaten up with vegetable butter, garnished with buttered green peas and new potatoes.

— **Stuffed:** farci: stuffed with fish forcemeat mixed with chopped herbs and anchovy paste, wrapped in oiled paper, baked in oven, taken out of the paper, sprinkled with chopped parsley; anchovy sauce served separately.

— **in White Wine:** au vin blanc: fillets poached in white wine and fish stock, covered with wine sauce.

Maquereau: see mackerel.

Marena: F. Marène; G. Maräne. Freshwater fish of the salmon family related to the lavaret, found mainly in North German lakes. Prepared like trout.

Marène: see marena.

Matelote, Sailor's Dish, Fish Stew: F: Matelote; G: Matrosengericht: fish stew made mainly of freshwater fish cut in pieces, cooked with wine, onions, parsley sprigs, bay leaf, thyme and pepper corns, stock boiled down and thickened with flour and butter or mixed with fish velouté, garnished in many different ways. Meurette, Pochouse and Waterzoi are typical matelotes.

— **Boatman Style:** à la canotière: carp and eel cut in pieces, flambéd with cognac, cooked in withe wine, stock thickened with flour and butter, garnished with mushrooms, button onions, whole crayfish and small gudgeon, egged, breadcrumbed and fried crisp in deep fat.

— **of Eel:** d'anguille: cut in pieces, sautéd in butter, flambéd with cognac, cooked in red wine, thickened with butter and flour, garnished with button onions, mushrooms, crayfish tails and heart shaped croûtons.

— **Fisher Style:** des pêcheurs: carp, eel, pike, perch and trout, cut in pieces, cooked in red wine, thickened with flour and butter, garnished with button onions and mushrooms.

— **Italian Style:** à l'italienne: tench and pike cut in pieces, cooked in red wine with chopped onions and herbs, thickened with flour and butter, garnished with mushrooms and button onions.

— **Meurette:** pike, carp, eel and chub cut in pieces, flambéd with Marc (spirit distilled from the husk of grapes) cooked in red wine, thickened with flour and butter, garnished withs slices of French bread, spread with butter, dried in the oven and rubbed with garlic.

— **Miller Style:** à la meunière: freshwater fish cooked in red wine, flambéd with cognac, stock thickened with flour and butter, garnished with crayfish and heart shaped croûtons.

— **Normandy Style:** à la normande: soles, gurnards and small conger eels cut in pieces, flambéd with Calvados (Apple Jack), cooked in cider, stock boiled down, mixed with fish velouté and cream, garnished with bearded poached oysters, mushrooms, bearded mussels, crayfish tails and heart shaped croûtons.

Matelote
— **Parisian Style:** à la parisienne: carp, eel, pike, perch and trout cut in pieces, cooked in red wine, thickened with flour and butter, garnished with crayfish tails, button onions, small fish dumplings, mushrooms and truffles.
— **Reims Style:** à la rémoise: pike cut in pieces, poached in fish stock and dry champagne, stock boiled down and mixed with fish velouté, garnished with poached fish roes, mushrooms, truffle slices and heart-shaped croûtons.
— **Sailor Style:** à la marinière: carp, pike, eel and tench cut in pieces, flambéd with cognac, cooked in white wine, stock reduced and mixed with fish velouté, garnished with white button onions, mushrooms, whole crayfish and heart shaped croûtons.
— **Spanish Style:** à l'espagnole: freshwater fish cut in pieces, flambéd with brandy, cooked in cider, stock boiled down and mixed with fish velouté, garnished with crayfish tails, bearded poached oyster and fleurons.
— **Verdun Style:** Pochouse de Verdun-sur-le-Doubs: carp, pike, eel and tench cut in pieces, flambéd with cognac, cooked in red wine with a bunch of herbs, stock thickened with flour and butter, garnished with diced fried bacon, glazed onions, mushrooms and croûtons rubbed with garlic.
Merlan: see whiting.
Morue fraîche: see cod.
— **salée:** see salt cod.
— **séchée:** see stockfish.
Muge: see surmullet.
Mulet: see mullet.
— **gris:** see grey mullet.
— **porc:** see grey mullet.
Mullet: F. Mulet; G. Meerbarbe, Atlantic and Pacific saltwater fish of which there are various species. Some live in the North Sea and the Baltic, the best of all the red mullet in the Mediterranean. Prepared like shad.
Murena, Muraena, Murry: F. Murène; G. Muräne. Saltwater fish of the eel species caught in the Mediterranean and off the Atlantic coast. Prepared like eel.
Murène: see murena.
Muskellunge, Maskalonge: F: Muscalonge; G: Muskallonga: freshwater fish related to pike found in North American lakes. Prepared like pike.
Mussel: F. Moule; G. Muschel, Miesmuschel. Small oval-shaped bivalve sea shellfish. To open mussels steam or boil with a little white wine, herbs, spices and sliced onions, discard all mussels that are reddish or black after cooking.
— **Alexandra:** parboiled, warmed up in Newburgh sauce with diced knob celery cooked in butter.
— **American Style:** à l'américaine: parboiled, bearded, covered with American sauce, sprinkled with chopped chervil and tarragon.
— **Baked:** au four: bearded, filled in half shells, covered with herb sauce, sprinkled with breadcrumbs, dotted with butter and baked in oven.
— **Burgundy Style:** à la bourgignonne: parboiled, bearded, covered with Burgundy sauce.
— **Californian Style:** à la californienne: bearded mussels, filled in small china caisses (cocottes) greased with butter, covered with chopped mushrooms, knob celery, chervil,

Mussel
parsley and a little mussel stock, dotted with butter and baked in oven.
— **Catalonian Style:** à la catalane: parboiled, removed from the shells, stock mixed with chopped onions sweated in butter and sprinkled with flour, boiled, bound with egg-yolk, seasoned with lemon juice, poured over mussels filled in shells and glazed.
— **Commander Style:** à la commodore: parboiled, filled in shells, covered with herb butter mixed with finely diced bacon, baked in oven.
— **Creole Style:** à la créole: parboiled, bearded, bound with Creole sauce; Creole rice served separately.
— **Deviled:** à la diable: parboiled, bearded, dipped in egg and breadcrumbs, fixed on skewers alternately with square slices of bacon, brushed with oil, broiled and seasoned with Cayenne pepper.
— **Fried:** frites: parboiled, bearded, marinated in lemon juice, oil and chopped parsley, dipped in frying batter, deep fried, served with fried parsley and lemon.
— **Fried:** frites: parboiled, taken out of shells, bearded, dipped in egg and breadcrumbs, deep fried, served with fried parsley and lemon.
— **Giardinetto:** mussels in half shells covered alternately with Bèarnaise, Poulette, American and herb sauce, fried and prepared à la Villeroi, all dressed on one dish.
— **Greek Style:** à la grecque: cooked in preboiled stock of white wine, oil, water, shallots, onions, bay leaf, fennel and parsley sprigs, bearded and served cold in part of the stock.
— **Housewife Style:** à la bonne-femme: prepared like marinière with julienne of mushrooms and raw celery added.
— **Hunter Style:** à la chasseur: parboiled, bearded, placed in half shell covered with chopped shallots, mushrooms, bacon and parsley, sprinkled with breadcrumbs and paprika and gratinated.
— **Mariner Style:** à la marinière: steamed with chopped shallots, parsley sprigs, bay leaf, thyme and white wine until open, removed from shells, bearded, each mussel placed in one shell. Part of decanted stock boiled down with white wine sauce, seasoned with lemon juice, poured over the mussels, chopped parsley sprinkled on top.
— **Mexican Style:** à la mexicaine: bearded, filled in baking dish, covered with diced tomatoes, chopped shallots and green peppers sautéd in oil, sprinkled with breadcrumbs, dotted with butter and gratinated in oven.
— **Newburgh:** bearded, tossed in butter, cooked in cream, bound with egg yolks mixed with Sherry, seasoned with Cayenne pepper.
— **Pompadour:** parboiled, bearded, tossed in cream sauce blended with lobster butter.
— **President Grant:** parboiled, bearded, chopped, mixed with chopped cooked green peppers, bound with Béchamel sauce, thickened with egg yolks, when cold shaped into croquettes, dipped in egg and breadcrumbs and fried in deep fat; Creole sauce served separately.
— **Rochelle Style:** à la rochelaise: parboiled, opened, one shell removed, stuffed with butter mixed with chopped

Mussel
shallots, fine herbs and thyme, seasoned with lemon juice, baked in oven.
— **Sicilian Style:** à la sicilienne: parboiled, bearded, mixed with macaroni ut in small pieces, bound with cream sauce blended with a little of the decanted stock, butter and grated Parmesan cheese.
— **Toulon Style:** à la toulonnaise: bearded mussels mixed with white wine sauce and a little of the decanted, boiled down stock, dressed in border of risotto.
— **Villeroi:** bearded, coated with Villeroi sauce, dipped in eggs and breadcrumbs and fried in deep fat.
— **in White Sauce:** à la poulette: parboiled, removed from shells, bearded, each mussel placed in one shell, dressed in timbale dish, covered with poulette sauce, chopped parsley sprinkled on top.

O

Omble: see grayling.
Ombre-écailles: see grayling.
Ombre commun: see grayling.
Oursin: see sea-urchin.
Oysters: huîtres: see appetizers.
Oyster Crab: Crab huître; G. Austernkrabbe. Little crab living with the oyster in the same shell, found mainly on the American Atlantic coast.
— **Fried:** frite: dipped in milk, turned in flour, fried in deep fat, served with fried parsley and lemon.

P

Pagel: see giltpoll.
Pagre: F. Pagre; G. Rötlicher Brassen. Saltwater fish akin to gilthead. Prepared like giltpoll.
Palée: see whitefish.
Pélerine: see fanshell.
Perch: F. Perche; G. Barsch; I. Pesce persico. Freshwater fish found in European rivers and larger lakes. American perch of different species.
— **with Anchovy Sauce:** à la sauce anchois: marinated with oil, lemon juice, chopped parsley, salt and pepper, dipped in egg and breadcrumbs, coated with oil, grilled and served with anchovy sauce.
— **with Asparagus:** aux asperges: cooked in white wine, coated with Dutch sauce, garnished with asparagus tips.
— **Blue:** au bleu: boiled in salt water with vinegar added, served with fresh or melted butter.
— **with Crayfish Sauce:** à la sauce aux écrevisses: cut in pieces, dipped in egg and breadcrumbs, fried, crayfish sauce served separately.
— **Dutch Style:** boiled in court-bouillon, dressed on serviette with parsley and lemon segments; melted butter and fresh boiled potatoes served separately.
— **with Eggs and Butter:** boiled in court-bouillon, sprinkled with chopped hard-boiled eggs and parsley, browned butter poured over.
— **with Herb Sauce:** aux fines herbes: cooked in white wine and lemon juice, coated with herb sauce.

Perch

— **Joinville:** fillets stuffed with fish forcemeat, folded, poached in white wine, garnished with truffle slices, mushrooms and shrimps, coated with Joinville sauce.

— **Marshal Style:** à la maréchale: fillets dipped in melted butter and white breadcrumbs, fried in butter, garnished with truffle slices dipped in meat glaze, served with asparagus tips or green peas.

— **with Oysters:** steamed in court-bouillon, served with oyster sauce.

— **Swedish Style:** à la suédoise: filled in baking dish greased with butter, sprinkled with white breadcrumbs mixed with chopped lemon-peel and parsley, a little fish stock poured on both sides, melted butter dropped on top, baked in the oven.

— **Villeroi:** prepared like eel.

Perche dorée: see ruffe.

— **noir:** see black bass.

Petite vive: see dwarf dragon fish.

Pétoncle: see fanshell.

Pike: F. Brochet; G. Hecht; I. Luccio. Freshwater fish found in lakes, ponds and rivers in Central and Northern Europe and America.

— **Alsatian Style:** à l'alsacienne: skinned, larded, baked in the oven with butter and white wine, slightly browned, covered with the reduced stock mixed with fish velouté, garnished with tartlets filled with braised saurkraut, garnished with a round slice of ham.

— **Ancient Style:** à l'ancienne: fillets poached covered with white wine sauce mixed with truffle slices, capers and very small balls of cucumbers.

— **Baden Style:** Badischer Hecht: baked in pan in the oven covered with sour cream and surrounded with button onions; when half done sprinkled with grated cheese and breadcrumbs and gratinated. (German)

— **in Beer:** à la bière: boiled in pale beer with sliced onions and lemons, pepper corns, cloves and a little salt, stock strained, thickened with rye bread, finished off with butter and lemon juice and poured over the fish.

— **Benoiton:** fillets, dipped in eggs and breadcrumbs, deep fried, served with red wine sauce.

— **Bordeaux Style:** à la bordelaise: cut in pieces, poached with red wine, chopped shallots and herbs, stock thickened with butterpaste and poured over the fish.

— **Burgundy Style:** à la bourguignonne: cut in pieces, poached in red wine with chopped shallots, button mushrooms and small glazed onions, stock thickened with butter paste, poured over the fish and glazed.

— **Castiglione:** fillets poached in white wine, covered with white wine sauce mixed with sliced mushrooms and lobster, glazed and garnished with boiled potato balls.

— **Chambord:** prepared like salmon trout.

— **Clermont:** cut in pieces, grilled, garnished with gratinated oysters and deep fried carp roes; maître d'hôtel sauce served separately.

— **Dutch Style:** à la hollandaise: cut in pieces, boiled in court-bouillon, covered with sauce made of the stock thickened with roux and egg yolks, finished off with butter and chopped parsley and mixed with small strips of poached sole fillets.

Pike

— **English Style:** à l'anglaise: I. fillets dipped in egg and breadcrumbs, fried in butter, half melted herb butter poured over;
II. boiled, dressed with parsley and lemon; caper sauce and salt potatoes served separately.

— **Fried:** frit: cut in pieces or filleted, dipped in egg and breadcrumbs, deep fried and served with Tartar sauce.

— **Gayarre:** cut in pieces and boiled, covered with fish velouté colored with saffron, flavored with Sherry and mixed with thin strips of pimiento, garnished with boiled potato balls. (Spanish)

— **German Style:** à l'allemande: steamed in white wine and fish stock with sliced onions and lemons, parsley stalks and bayleaves; stock boiled down, thickened with butter paste, blended with anchovy butter, mixed with capers and poured over the skinned fish.

— **Green:** au vert: cut in pieces, boiled in salt water with sliced onions, carrots, knob celery, bayleaves, pepper corns and parsley stalks, stock strained, thickened with white roux, mixed with butter and chopped parsley, chervil and dill.

— **Grenadins:** oval medaillons cut from the fillets, larded with truffles, poached in white wine and fish stock, stock reduced, poured over the grenadins and glazed, dressed in shape of a turban, garnish and sauce to taste.

— **with Sorrel:** à l'oseille: grenadins larded with thin strips of carrots and gherkins, sweated in butter, simmered in fish fumet, fumet reduced with a little velouté and glaced; sorrel purée served separately.

— **Grilled:** grillé: cut in thick slices, seasoned, coated with flour, grilled; Tartar sauce served separately.

— **Harlequin Style:** à l'arlequin: whole fish skinned, larded with strips of carrots, truffles, gherkins and anchovies, simmered in fish stock, dressed on oval dish, one half covered with lobster, the other half with herb sauce; garnished with plain fish dumplings, dumplings mixed with spinach purée and dumplings mixed with lobster butter.

— **with Horseradish:** à la raifort: cut in pieces, boiled in court-bouillon, covered with grated horseradish, sprinkled with breadcrumbs, browned butter poured on top.

— **Hungarian Style:** à la hongroise: whole fish, seasoned with paprika, covered with chopped onions sweated in butter, chopped anchovies and sour cream added; sprinkled with breadcrumbs, dotted with butter and baked in the oven.

— **Italian Style:** à l'italienne: fillets slightly fried in oil, arranged in baking dish, covered with Italian sauce, breadcrumbs sprinkled on top, dotted with oil and browned in oven.

— **with Knob Celery:** au celeri: cut in pieces, boiled, covered with velouté mixed with diced knob celery simmered in butter.

— **Mariner Style:** à la marinière: fillets or thick slices poached in white wine and fish fumet, stock reduced and mixed with fish velouté; garnished with mushrooms, glazed onions, crayfish and heart-shaped croûtons, covered with the sauce.

— **Martinière:** baby pike marinated in white wine, oil and fine herbs, grilled; mayonnaise sauce mixed with chopped hazelnuts served separately.

Pike

— **Montebello:** whole fish skinned on one side only, stuffed with fish forcemeat, the skinned side coated with forcemeat and covered with small fillets of sole larded with truffles, braised on bed of sliced onions, carrots and parsley stalks in white wine, arranged on oval dish, covered with white wine sauce blended with anchovy butter, garnished with shrimp croquettes, pastry boats filled with poached oysters, soft roes and crayfish.

— **with Mushrooms:** aux champignons: fillets poached in white wine and fish stock with sliced mushrooms, stock thickened with butter paste, egg yolks and cream, seasoned with Cayenne pepper and poured over the fillets.

— **Norman Style:** à la normande: cut in thick pieces or whole fish stuffed with fish forcemeat, barded with thin slices of fat bacon, braised in white wine, covered with Normandy sauce; garnished with bearded oysters and mussels, crayfish tails, mushrooms, truffle slices and strips of deep fried sole fillets or smelts.

— **Orly:** fillets cut in long strips, dipped in frying batter, deep fried; tomato sauce served separately.

— **with Oysters:** aux huîtres: coated with butter, baked in the oven, basted with white wine and a few drops of vinegar, covered with the reduced stock mixed with white wine sauce and poached, bearded oysters.

— **Parisian Style:** à la parisienne: whole fish braised in white wine and mushroom fond, back garnished with sliced truffles and mushrooms, covered with the reduced stock mixed with white wine sauce, surrounded with boiled crayfish.

— **with Parmesan:** au parmesan: fillets fried with sliced onions, covered with cream sauce, sprinkled with grated Parmesan, anchovy butter dropped on top and glazed.

— **with Parsley Butter:** persillé: fillets coated with flour, fried in butter, covered with browned butter mixed with chopped parsley and lemon juice.

— **with Parsley Sauce:** à la sauce au persil: whole fish boiled; parsley sauce and fish potatoes served separately.

— **with Pickled Cabbage:** Hecht mit Sauerkraut: boiled skinned, boned and flaked, mixed with saurkraut, filled in baking dish, covered with cream and baked in oven. (German)

— **Cake:** Pain de brochet: pike flesh boned and skinned, pounded in mortar with half the quantity of panade and butter, rubbed through a fine sieve, seasoned, mixed with eggs and egg yolks so that a homogeneous mixture is formed, filled in mould, poached in water bath, turned out, decorated with sliced truffles, covered with mousseline or bastard sauce, sometimes garnished with mushrooms.

— **Polish Style:** cut in pieces, boiled in water with slices of apple, onions, knob celery and parsley roots, pepper corns, bay leaves, cloves, white wine and a few drops of vinegar; stock strained, thickened with ginger bread and poured over the fish. (Polish).

— **Pompadour:** I. fillets dipped in egg and breadcrumbs, fried in butter, garnished with fried parsley and small potato croquettes; Tartar sauce served separately;
II. fillets dipped in egg and breadcrumbs fried in butter, a slice of truffle on each fillet, a border of Béarnaise sauce between the fillets, garnished with nut potatoes.

Pike

— **Prince Henry:** whole fish stuffed with salmon forcemeat, skinned, larded with truffles, braised in Rhenish wine, Madeira and fish stock, stock thickened with white roux, poured over the fish: garnished with bearded mussels, crayfish tails, mushrooms and small fish dumplings.

— **Provencal Style:** à la provençale: fillets poached in white wine and fish stock covered with diced tomatoes simmered in oil with chopped shallots, garlic, chopped mushrooms and parsley, the reduced stock added.

— **Prussian Style:** à la prusse: equal parts of pike and eel cut in thick slices and boiled in court- bouillon, covered with parsley sauce; cucumber salad served separately.

— **Ragoût:** cut in thick slices, poached in lemon juice and butter, garnished with crayfish tails and small pike dumplings, covered with Nantua sauce.

— **Regency Style:** à la régence: fillets poached in butter and white wine, garnished with poached bearded oysters, poached soft roes, mushrooms, truffle slices and small fish dumplings with crayfish purée, covered with Regency sauce.

— **Roger de Flor:** fillets poached in white wine and fish stock, one half covered with cream sauce blended with anchovy butter, the other half with tomato sauce; garnished with bearded mussels in half shell, covered with cheese sauce and gratinated.

— **Roland Köster:** skinned, larded with truffles, stuffed with truffled whiting forcemeat, simmered in white wine and mushroom essence, covered with cream sauce, mixed with the reduced stock and little Dutch sauce; garnished with poached bearded oysters, large mushrooms and lobster croquettes.

— **Russian Style:** à la russe: cut in pieces, parboiled, mixed with sliced onions fried in butter and grated horseradish, filled in baking dish, covered with sour cream and baked in oven.

— **Saint-Germain:** fillets dipped in melted butter and bread-crumbs, fried in butter or grilled, garnished with nut potatoes; Béarnaise sauce served separately.

— **Sevilla Style:** à la sevillane: fillets larded with strips of anchovies and gherkins, dipped in oil and breadcrumbs, grilled; tomato sauce mixed with strips of red peppers served separately.

— **Sluice-keeper Style:** à l'éclusière: place pike on bed of chopped shallots and sliced mushrooms, season and steam with butter and white wine in oven, when nearly done moisten generously with sweet cream, reduce stock and pour over the fish.

— **in Sour Cream:** à la crème aigre: baked in the oven with butter, basted with sour cream and simmered until done.

— **Stewed:** étuvé: fillets larded with bacon, seasoned and stewed with lemon juice and butter, covered with Colbert sauce.

— **Stuffed:** farci: whole fish stuffed with forcemeat mixed with chopped mushrooms, parsley and a little sage, skinned, barded with thin slices of fat bacon, simmered in butter and white wine with diced green peppers and tomatoes.

Pike

— **Suffren:** fillets larded with strips of anchovies, poached in butter, white wine and fish stock, stock thickened with butter paste, blended with anchovy butter and tomato purée, seasoned with Cayenne pepper and poured over.

— **Truffled:** truffé: skinned, stuffed with fish forcemeat mixed with diced truffles, bacon and ox tongue, barded, simmered in white wine and fish stock; stock reduced, mixed with fish velouté, blended with a little Dutch sauce and poured over the fish after the bards have been removed.

Pike Dumplings: Quenelles de brochet: pike flesh boned and skinned, pounded in mortar with the same amount of beef-suet, mixed with an equal amount of panade, egg whites and seasoning or raw flesh pounded in mortar with egg whites and seasoning, stirred to a smooth paste on ice, cooled for 2 hours and slowly mixed with sweet cream. Shaped into oval or round dumplings and poached in salt water or light fish stock.

— **Lyonese Style:** à la lyonnaise: dumplings made with suet-forcemeat, poached in salt water, arranged in baking dish greased with butter, covered with fish velouté and simmered in the oven.

— **Morland:** dumplings made of pike forcemeat with cream, stuffed with a poached carp roe, dipped in beaten eggs and chopped truffles, fried slowly in clarified butter, dressed in shape of a turban with mushroom purée in the center.

— **Nantua:** dumplings of creamed pike forcemeat, poached, garnished with crayfish tails and sliced truffles, covered with Nantua sauce.

— **Royal Style:** à la royale: prepared like dumplings Morland, poached in salt water covered with oyster sauce.

— **Turkish Style:** à la turque: flesh of cooked pike mixed with white bread soaked in milk, pounded in mortar, passed through a sieve, mixed with eggs, seasoned with salt, pepper and powdered cloves, shaped into oval dumplings and fried in oil.

Pike-perch, Giant Pike-perch: F. Sandre; G. Zander. Freshwater fish found mainly in North and Eastern Europe, in the Danube, Elbe and sometimes in the Rhine.

— **Ambassadress Style:** à l'ambassadrice: fillets, stuffed with crayfish forcemeat, folded, poached in butter and Madeira, covered with cream sauce beaten with crayfish butter mixed with diced crayfish tails and the reduced stock.

— **Baked:** au four: whole fillets poached in white wine and fish stock, placed in greased baking dish, covered with ragoût of mussels, mushrooms and small fish dumplings bound with fish velouté, masked with fish velouté, sprinkled with grated cheese, browned in oven.

— **Berlin Style:** à la berlinoise: greased baking dish filled alternately with layers of pike-perch forcemeat, sliced and seasoned fillets, covered with breadcrumbs and grated Parmesan, dotted largely with crayfish butter, poached slowly in waterbath in the oven.

— **with Butter:** au beurre: boiled, melted butter and fish potatoes served separately.

— **with Calvilles:** aux calvilles: fillets, coated with flour, fried in pan in butter, covered with calville slices fried in butter, lemon juice and browned butter on top.

Pike-perch

— **with Crayfish Tails:** aux queues d'écrevisses: fillets, poached, covered with crayfish sauce, garnished with crayfish tails and fleurons.

— **Embassy Style:** à l'ambassade: fillets prepared like sole.

— **Fried:** frite: cutlets dipped in egg and breadcrumbs, deep fried; tartar sauce served separately.

— **Gratinated:** au gratin: fillets prepared like sole.

— **Grilled:** grillée: slices, coated with flour, brushed with clarified butter, grilled; ravigote or tartar sauce served separately.

— **Hatzfeld:** fillets, poached in white wine and fish stock, covered with white wine sauce with chopped pickles.

— **Homely Style:** à la bourgeoise: poached in sour cream on bed of sliced carrots, knob celery, onions, peppercorns and bay leaf, stock thickened with butter-paste, seasoned with lemon juice and poured over the fish.

— **with Lobster Sauce:** au sauce homard: fillets, stuffed with lobster and fish forcemeat, folded, poached, covered with lobster sauce, lobster eggs scattered on top.

— **Milanese Style:** à la milanaise: fillets marinated in lemon juice, dipped in flour, egg and breadcrumbs, fried in butter, arranged on macaroni tossed in butter and grated Parmesan.

— **Minister Style:** à la ministre: fillets, poached in white wine and fish stock, garnished with bearded oysters, crayfish tails and sliced truffles, covered with oyster sauce.

— **Mousselines with Crayfish:** Mousselines aux écrevisses: mousseline forcemeat of pike-perch poached in small oval moulds, turned out, arranged like a crown, covered with crayfish sauce, a slice of truffle on each mousseline, center filled with crayfish tails in white wine sauce.

— **with Paprika Sauce:** au sauce paprika: boiled, served with paprika sauce and fish potatoes.

— **Polish Style:** à la polonaise: boiled, coovered with fish velouté finished off chopped fennel green and grated horseradish.

— **Portuguese Style:** à la portugaise: fillets prepared like sole.

— **Provencal Style:** à la provençale: fillets, prepared like sole.

— **Radzivill:** fillets, poached in white wine, covered with white wine sauce mixed with sliced mushrooms, truffles and gherkins, garnished with fish dumplings.

— **in Red Wine:** au vin rouge: fillets, poached in red wine with chopped shallots, stock thickened with butter-paste and poured over the fillets.

— **Roumanian Style:** à la roumaine: poached in white wine, oil and lemon juice with tomato purée, sliced fried onions and garlic, covered with raw sliced tomatoes and lemon slices, served cold in the stock.

— **Spring Style:** à la printanière: boiled, covered with cream sauce beaten with asparagus butter, garnished with shaped glazed carrots and turnips, asparagus tips and boiled potato balls.

— **Victoria:** fillets, prepared like sole.

— **Walewska:** fillets prepared like sole.

— **Warsawian Style:** à la varsovienne: I. poached in acidulated water, covered with white butter sauce mixed with chopped hard-boiled eggs.
II. fillets, coated, with flour, fried in butter, covered with

chopped hard-boiled eggs, parsley and breadcrumbs in plenty of browned butter.

Pilchard; Gipsy herring; F. Pilchard; G. Pilchard. Sort of fat sardine caught off the French and English coasts.

Plaice: F. Plie; G. Scholle; I. Passera di mare. Flatfish of the flounder family found off the coasts of the North Sea and the Baltic. Also marketed smoked and marinated,

— **Baked:** au four: small whole fish or fillets, arranged in baking dish greased with butter, covered with Hachée sauce, sprinkled with grated cheese and breadcrumbs, cooked and gratinated in oven.

— **with Browned Butter:** au beurre noisette: boiled or shallow fried, covered with browned butter.

— **with Dutch Sauce:** à la sauce hollandaise: boiled, covered with Dutch sauce, fish potatoes served separately.

— **in Frying Batter:** frite: fillets dipped in light frying batter, deep fried, served with fried parsley and lemon.

— **Gratinated:** au gratin: dressed in baking dish greased with butter, covered with Italian sauce, sprinkled with breadcrumbs, dotted with butter, baked and gratinated in oven.

— **Grilled:** grillée: scored on both sides, grilled with oil, served with herb butter.

— **Housewife Style:** Bonne femme: prepared like sole.

— **Miller Style:** à la meunière: scored on both sides and prepared like barbel.

— **Nice Style:** à la niçoise: fillets coated with flour, grilled or fried in oil, garnished with tomatoes concassées, decorated with anchovy fillets and pitted black olives; anchovy butter served separately.

Plie franche: see plaice.

Pollack, Pollock: F. Lieue jaune; G. Pollack. Saltwater fish resembling the rock salmon found from the Bicaya up to Greenland and off the Atlantic coast of North America. Prepared like cod.

Polyp: French: Poulpe; German: Polyp, Tintenschnecke. Marine mollusc found in the Mediterranean and South Atlantic.

— **Fried:** frit: tentacles cut in pieces, seasoned, coated with flour, dipped in beaten eggs, deep fried, served with lemon.

— **Provencal Style:** à la provençale: cut off tentacles, beat well to soften the fibres, parboil, dry and sweat in oil with chopped onions. Season, add peeled chopped onions, crushed garlic and a bunch of herbs, moisten with half white wine and half water stew until done, serve with chopped parsley on top.

— **Stuffed Marseille Style:** farci à la marseillaise: remove ink-sac and spines from pouch, cut off tentacles, wash pouch and tentacles well, stuff with chopped onions sweated in oil mixed with the finely chopped tentacles, tomatoes, bread soaked in milk, garlic, chopped parsley and egg yolks, season highly, sew pouch to enclose the stuffing and place squids in stewpan greased with oil. Sweat onions in oil, add a piece of bay leaf and crushed garlic, sprinkle with flour, moisten with white wine and water, season, bring to a boil, boil for 15 minutes, strain over the squids, sprinkle with breadcrumbs, pour a little oil on top and brown them very slowly in the oven.

Pompano: saltwater fish found in the South Atlantic, the Carribean Sea and the Gulf of Florida. Prepared like perch.
— **Grilled:** grillé: scored, brushed with oil, grilled and served with herb butter.
— **in Paper Bag:** en papillote: scored, wrapped in greased paper bag with chopped mushrooms, shallots and parsley, baked in oven, served in the bag.
— **rellena:** stuffed with chopped onions and diced tomatoes sweated in oil mixed with chopped hard-boiled eggs, parsley and spices, poached and covered with fish velouté. (Mexican)
Pope: see Ruffe.
Poulpe: see polyp.
Prawns: F. Crevettes roses, Bouquets; G. Granat, Garnat, Flohkrebs. Small saltwater crustacean of the lobster type improperly called shrimp. Prepared like shrimps, but served mainly cold as appetizer or as a garnish. Dublin Bay prawns are considered the best.
Provencal Fish Stew: Bourride: cut small firmer fish in pieces, add chopped onions, tomatoes, garlic, a bunch of herbs and a piece of bitter orange peel, moisten with water, season, add a pinch of saffron and a few spoons full of oil and boil rapidly until done. Strain stock, thicken with egg yolks, mix with aiolli sauce and pour over slices of French bread placed in a soup tureen; serve fish on a separate dish.

R

Red Mullet, Red Surmullet: F. Rouget; Rouget Barbet; G. Rot-Barbe. Saltwater fish found in the Mediterranean, off the French and Italien coasts and near Malta. Having no gall it is prepared without being gutted, only the fins are removed.
— **Armenian Style:** à l'arménienne: grilled, garnished with crabmeat and oysters in white wine sauce sprinkled with chopped chives.
— **Baron Brisse:** coated with flour, brushed with oil, broiled, garnished with Parisian potatoes, herb butter on top of the fish.
— **Bordeaux Style:** à la bordelaise: shallow fried in clarified butter, covered with Bordeaux sauce prepared with white wine.
— **with Butter:** au beurre: broiled, melted butter mixed with lemon juice on top.
— **Chesterfield:** fillets fried in butter, dressed on shrimp ragoût, covered with shrimp sauce.
— **Danicheff:** poached in fish fumet with julienne of truffles, chopped shallots and butter, stock boiled down, beaten with butter, poured over the fish and glazed.
— **Don Carlos:** poached in white wine and butter, garnished with sliced mushrooms, one half covered with white wine and the other with tomato sauce.
— **Duse:** poached, dressed on risotto with crayfish tails, covered with Mornay sauce mixed with chopped truffles and crayfish tails, sprinkled with Parmesan and glazed.
— **Epicurean Style:** à l'épicurienne: fried in butter, covered with diced sautéd tomatoes mixed with shallot butter and a little thick gravy.

Red Mullet, Red Surmullet

— **with Fennel:** au fenouil: marinated in oil, lemon juice and chopped fennel with coarsely chopped fat bacon and parsley, fish wrapped with the marinade in oiled paper, grilled slowly and served in paper bag.

— **with Fine Herbs:** aux fines herbes: poached in white wine with chopped shallots, mushrooms, herbs and garlic, stock boiled down, mixed with demi-glace and poured over the fish.

— **Francillon:** scored, broiled, dressed on toast of same size as fish, garnished with straw potatoes and fried parsley; tomato sauce and anchovy butter served separately.

— **Gratinated:** au gratin: placed in greased baking dish on chopped shallots, covered with sliced mushrooms and Italian sauce, sprinkled with chopped parsley and breadcrumbs, butter dotted on top, baked brown in oven.

— **Grenoble Style:** à la grenobloise: scored, fried, chopped parsley, capers and lemon slices on top, covered with browned butter.

— **Indian Style:** à l'indienne: grilled and served with curry sauce.

— **Italian Style:** à l'italienne: poached in white wine and fish stock, covered with Italian sauce.

— **Jean d'Arc:** fillets fried in a pan in oil, dressed on rice mixed with crayfish tails covered with Nantua sauce, garnished with crayfisch tails, bearded oysters, mushrooms and small fish dumplings.

— **Leghorn Style:** à la livournaise: poached in fish fumet with chopped shallots, diced tomatoes and julienne of truffles, stock boiled down, beaten with butter, poured over the fish and glazed.

— **Marocco Style:** à la marocaine: simmered in oil with chopped onions, pepper, saffron and very little water, beaten eggs poured over, baked in oven.

— **Marseille Style:** à la marseillaise: cooked in white wine and oil with chopped onions sweated in oil, garlic and saffron.

— **Marshal Style:** à la maréchale: fillets, dipped in melted butter, coated with breadcrumbs mixed with chopped truffles, fried in butter.

— **Messaline:** fillets poached in white wine and butter, dressed on purée of fresh tomatoes, covered with Mexican sauce.

— **Montesquieu:** fillets dipped in melted butter, rolled in finely chopped onions and parsley, fried in butter, seasoned with lemon juice.

— **Nantese Style:** à la nantaise: grilled, dressed on chopped shallots, sweated in butter, cooked in white wine, reduced and mixed with chopped soft roes and demi-glace, garnished with sliced lemon.

— **Nice Style:** à la niçoise: grilled, garnished with tomatoes concassées flavored with garlic, and black olives, anchovy fillets on top of the fish.

— **Oriental Style:** à l'orientale: poached in oil and white wine with chopped onions, diced tomatoes, garlic and saffron, served hot or cold in the stock.

— **in Paper Bag:** en papillote: prepared like trout.

— **Polish Style:** à la polonaise: fried, covered with fish fumet, boiled down, bound with egg yolks and cream, breadcrumbs fried in butter on top.

Red Mullet, Red Surmullet

— **Portuguese Style:** à la portugaise: poached, covered with Portuguese sauce.

— **Provencal Style:** à la provençale: grilled, covered with browned butter, garnished with tomatoes concassées flavored with garlic, anchovy fillets and green pitted olives places on top.

— **Richelieu:** grilled, dressed on half-melted herb butter, garnished with sliced truffles.

— **Spanish Style:** à l'espagnole: fillets shallow fried in oil and butter, dressed on halved tomatoes fried in oil, garnished with fried onion rings and strips of fish fillets, dipped in egg and breadcrumbs and fried in oil.

— **Theodora:** stuffed with fish forcemeat mixed with chopped mushrooms, poached in white wine and fish stock, covered with white wine sauce.

— **Trouville Style:** à la trouvillaise: boned, filled with fish forcemeat, poached in white wine, covered with Colbert sauce.

— **Venetian Style:** à la vénitienne: fillets shallow fried in oil, covered with Venetian sauce, garnished with mushroom caps and stuffed olives.

— **Villeroi:** fillets marinated in oil and lemon juice, coated with Villeroi sauce, dipped in egg and breadcrumbs, fried in deep fat, garnished with fried parsley and lemon.

Roach: F. Gardon; G. Plötze, Rotauge: Freshwater fish found in the lakes and rivers of Central and East Europe and in the Baltic. Chiefly filleted and fried.

Rock Salmon: F. Grélin, lieu noir; G. Köhler, Seelachs. Saltwater fish caught mainly off the Norwegian, Icelandic and Scottish coasts. Marketed fresh, dried and smoked. Prepared like cod.

Rouget: see red mullet.

Rouget-Barbet: see red mullet.

Royans: large sardines caught off the French coast. See sardines.

Ruffe, Pope: F. Perche dorée; G. Kaulbarsch. Freshwater species of perch found mainly in Scandinavia, Siberia and in the Midlands and South of England. Prepared like pike.

S

Saint-Pierre: see John Dory.

Salmon: F. Saumon; G. Lachs, Salm; I. Salmone; S. Sálmon. Migratory fish living in fresh water and the sea. The best river salmon are caught in the Rhine, the Loire and the Weser, sea salmon off the American Atlantic, the Canadian and Pacific coasts and in Europe off the Scotch, English, Norwegian, Swedish and Dutch coasts.

— **Admiral Style:** à l'amiral: prepared like brill.

— **Artois:** à la d'Artois: darne, skinned, coated with whiting forcemeat, decorated with truffle slices, poached in butter and white wine, covered with shrimp sauce, garnished with large dumplings of whiting mousseline forcemeat mixed with shrimp coulis and small pastry shells filled with shrimps, a fluted mushroom cap and a slice of truffle.

— **Balmoral:** poached in court-bouillon, covered with Chambord sauce mixed with shrimps, garnished with small fish dumplings, boiled potato balls and truffles.

Salmon

— **Baron Brisse:** cut in slices, grilled, covered with Madeira sauce, garnished with poached oysters and shrimp dumplings.

— **Béarnaise:** cut in slices, grilled, Béarnaise sauce served separately.

— **Bellevue:** (cold) whole fish poached in court-bouillon, when cold, skinned, decorated with truffle, hard-boiled egg whites, chervil, tarragon etc., glazed with aspic jelly and garnished to taste.

— **Brillat-Savarin:** braised with chopped onions and julienne of carrots, leeks and celery in white wine, fish and crayfish stock, stock reduced, beaten with butter, finished with cream and poured over the fish; garnished with small glazed truffles, fluted mushrooms and crayfish heads stuffed with salpicon of crayfish tails, mushrooms and chopped parsley bound with white wine sauce.

— **Cardinal:** cutlets poached in white wine and butter, a slice of lobster and truffle on each cutlet, covered with cardinal sauce, chopped lobster coral scattered on top.

— **Chambord:** prepared like carp.

— **Champerré:** cutlets poached in white wine and fish stock, dressed on pilaf rice, covered with Normandy sauce, garnished with glazed button onions and fried parsley.

— **Condorcet:** cut in steaks, poached in white wine and fish stock, each steak covered with diced tomatoes and olive shaped fresh cucumbers simmered in butter, coated with white wine sauce, chopped parsley sprinkled on top.

— **Courbet:** smaller fish skinned, coated with fish forcemeat, decorated with truffle slices to imitate the scales, braised carefully in fish stock and champagne; stock reduced, mixed with Normandy sauce, poured over the fish, garnished with fluted mushrooms, truffles, whole boiled crayfish and half moon shaped fish dumplings.

— **Crown Prince Style:** à la dauphin: slices poached in white wine and fish stock, garnished with lobster slices, fluted mushrooms and small fish dumplings, covered with lobster sauce.

— **with Cucumbers:** aux concombres: cut in slices, broiled, served with sliced cucumbers with French dressing poured over.

— **Cutlets:** Côtelettes de saumon: I. fillets, cut in thick slices and shaped like cutlets;
II. salpicon of boiled salmon, diced mushrooms and truffles, mixed with thick Béchamel sauce, thickened with egg yolks when cold shaped into cutlets, dipped in egg and breadcrumbs and deep fried;
III. mousseline forcemeat of salmon mixed with diced mushrooms, truffles or crayfish tails, filled in cutlet moulds poached and served with appropriate sauce and garnish; also dipped in egg and breadcrumbs and fried in deep fat.

— **Cutlets Alaska:** cutlets Nr. I poached in white wine and fish stock, when cold coated with pink chaufroid sauce, glazed with aspic jelly, dressed on pastry shells filled with Russian salad; cold caviar sauce, served separately.

— **Cutlets Edward VII:** Côtelettes de saumon Edouard VII.: Cutlets Nr. III poached, covered with creamed curry sauce, a slice of truffle on each cutlet.

Salmon

— **Cutlets Italian Style:** à l'italienne: Cutlets Nr. I coated with thick mushroom purée, dipped in egg and breadcrumbs mixed with grated Parmesan, deep fried; anchovy sauce served separately.

— **Cutlets Marshal Style:** à la maréchal: cutlets Nr. I dipped in melted butter and breadcrumbs mixed with chopped truffles, fried in butter, a slice of truffle coated with meat glaze on each cutlet, garnished with asparagus tips.

— **Cutlets Pojarski:** 3 parts of raw chopped salmon to 1 part white bread soaked in milk, mixed with a little butter, seasoned, shaped into cutlets, dipped in egg and breadcrumbs, fried in clarified butter, garnished to taste.

— **Cutlets Russian:** à la russe: (cold) cutlet moulds lined with aspic jelly and caviar, filled with salmon froth, sealed with aspic jelly, when set turned out on Russian salad.

— **Danish Style:** à la danoise: darne poached in court-bouillon, garnished with boiled potatoes, bastard sauce finished with anchovy butter served separately.

— **Darne:** middle section of large fish.

— **Daumont:** darne or slices poached in white wine and fish stock, garnished with pastry boats filled with crayfish tails in Nantua sauce, large fish dumplings decorated with a truffle slice, mushrooms and truffle slices; Nantua sauce served separately.

— **Dieppe Style:** à la dieppoise: prepared like brill.

— **Diplomat Style:** à la diplomate: steaks poached, covered with diplomat sauce, a large slice of truffle coated with meat glaze on each steak.

— **Duchess Alice:** large middle section braised with mirepoix, fish stock, Rhine wine and mushroom peels; stock strained, boiled down with cream, thickened with egg yolks, buttered, mixed with julienne of mushrooms and poured over the fish, garnished with tiny puff pastry patties filled with salpicon of crayfish, small peeled tomatoes stuffed with asparagus tips and fried bearded oysters.

— **Duchess Style:** à la duchesse: steamed in court-bouillon, covered with oyster sauce beaten with crayfish butter, garnished with stuffed morels, small lobster dumplings, boiled potato balls and breaded, deep fried oysters.

— **with Dutch Sauce:** à la sauce hollandaise: boiled, served with Dutch sauce and fish potatoes.

— **English Style:** à l'anglaise: I. fillets dipped in eggs and breadcrumbs, fried in butter, covered with half melted herb butter.
II. darne poached in court-bouillon; boiled potatoes, cucumber slices slightly salted and melted butter or Dutch sauce served separately.

— **Epicurean Style:** à l'épicurienne: darne poached in white wine, Madeira, fish stock and truffle essence, stock reduced, thickened with butter paste, finished with anchovy butter, lemon juice and chopped parsley.

— **Escalopes, Médaillons, Suprêmes:** fillets of salmon cut into diagonal slices, prepared like sole fillets.

— **Fedorowna:** darne poached in court-bouillon, covered with sliced mushrooms, truffles, shrimps and crayfish

Salmon

tails; shrimp sauce poured over the fish, garnished with bearded, breaded and deep fried mussels.

— **Gardner Style:** à la jardinière: (cold) steaks poached, when cold decorated to taste, glazed with aspic jelly, dressed on bed of vegetable salad bound with mayonnaise, garnished with aspic jelly.

— **with Geneva sauce:** à la génevoise: poached in court-bouillon, served with Geneva sauce and fish potatoes.

— **German Style:** à l'allemande: steaks seasoned, coated with melted butter mixed with egg yolks, breaded and fried in butter, garnished with creamed mushrooms.

— **Gismonda:** (cold) cutlets poached, when cold one side coated with plain jellied mayonnaise, the other side with jellied mayonnaise mixed with crayfish butter and chopped crayfish eggs, a line of caviar in the center, garnished with moulded Russian salad, watercress and aspic jelly.

— **Hungarian Style:** à la hongroise: escalopes poached with diced tomatoes, chopped onions sweated in butter, white wine, paprika and fish stock; stock boiled down, beaten with butter, poured over the fish and glazed.

— **Lafayette:** cut in slices, poached, garnished with crayfish tails, covered with white wine sauce blended with tomato purée, chopped truffles scattered on top.

— **with Lobster Sauce:** au sauce homard: boiled, served with lobster sauce with diced lobster and fish potatoes.

— **Lucullus:** whole fish or darne, skinned, larded with truffles, braised in champagne and fish stock, covered with the reduced stock thickened with egg yolks and cream and beaten up with crayfish butter; garnished with small puff pastry patties alternately filled with salpicon of crayfish, soft roes and bearded poached oysters.

— **Marcel Prévost:** cutlets poached, dressed on spinach leaves sweated in butter, covered with mariner sauce, garnished with poached bearded mussels.

— **Marguery:** escalopes prepared like sole fillets.

— **Médicis:** escalopes, dipped in egg and breadcrumbs, fried in butter, garnished with small fried tomatoes filled with Béarnaise sauce.

— **Metternich:** escalopes, poached in butter and white wine, covered with white wine sauce with paprika, a slice of truffle on each escalope,.

— **Mirabeau:** prepared like sole fillets.

— **Modern Style:** à la moderne: cutlets, broiled, Colbert sauce and cucumber salad served separately.

— **Moldavian Style:** à la moldavienne (cold): whole fish dressed on bed of sliced fried onions, tomato slices, slices of peeled lemons, chopped parsley and crushed garlic, covered with strips of red and green peppers and sliced eggplants, moistened with white wine, sunflower oil and tomato purée, braised in oven, served chilled.

— **Monte Carlo:** prepared like sole fillets.

— **Montmorency:** preparated like sole fillets.

— **Mousselines Alexandra:** mousselines of salmon forcemeat, shaped with a spoon, a thin slice of raw salmon placed on each mousseline, poached, topped with a truffle slice, coated with Mornay sauce, sprinkled with cheese, glazed and garnished with buttered asparagus tips or green peas.

— **Mousselines Tosca:** mousseline forcemeat mixed with crayfish purée, shaped with a spoon, poached, garnished

Salmon
with fried soft roes, crayfish tails and truffle slices, coated with Mornay sauce blended with crayfish butter, sprinkled with grated cheese and glazed.
— **Nantese Style:** à la nantaise: poached in white wine and mushroom essence, garnished with crawfish slices, poached bearded oysters and truffle slices, covered with Dutch sauce mixed with the boiled down stock.
— **Nesselrode:** whole fish, skinned and boned, stuffed with pike forcemeat mixed with lobster forcemeat, wrapped in sliced fat bacon and pie dough, baked in oven; lobster sauce with poached bearded oysters served separately.
— **Normandy Style:** à la normande: prepared like sole fillets.
— **with Oysters:** aux huîtres: cut in pieces, poached in white wine, fish stock and mirepoix, covered with the boiled down stock mixed with fish velouté and oyster liquor, garnished with bearded oysters.
— **Parisian Style:** à la parisienne: escalopes, poached in white wine, butter and mushroom essence, a slice of truffle and a fluted mushroom cap on each escalope, covered with white wine sauce mixed with the boiled down stock, garnished with whole crayfish.
— **Pie:** Pâté: (cold) rectangular mould lined with pie dough, sides and bottom coated with pike forcemeat mixed with chopped truffles, filled alternately with two layers of salmon fillets, sliced truffles and forcemeat, covered with pie dough, decorated with leaves of dough, eggwashed and baked. When cold filled with aspic jelly through a hole in the center of the crust.
— **Polignac:** escalopes, poached, covered with creamed white wine sauce with julienne of mushrooms and truffles added, garnished with fleurons.
— **Pompadour:** escalopes dipped in melted butter and breadcrumbs, fried in clarified butter, a slice of truffle on each escalope; bordered with Béarnaise sauce, garnished with Parisian potatoes.
— **Prince of Wales:** Prince de Galles: darne poached in butter and champagne, dressed on dish with prebaked border of piped Duchess mixture, covered with curry sauce mixed with the reduced stock, beaten with crayfish butter, garnished with bearded oysters and mussels.
— **Quirinal:** steaks, poached, garnished with crayfish tails and mushrooms, covered with red wine sauce.
— **Radzivill:** steak, poached, covered with ragoût of shrimps in shrimp sauce topped with sliced truffles, garnished with olive shaped cucumbers stewed in butter.
— **Regency Style:** à la régence: whole fish stuffed with whiting forcemeat and prepared like pike.
— **Réjane:** escalopes, poached, covered with white wine sauce beaten with watercress butter, garnished with piped Duchess potatoes.
— **Richelieu:** medaillons, fried in clarified butter, covered with half melted herb butter, a slice of truffle on each medaillon.
— **Riga:** (cold): whole fish poached in court-bouillon, when cold coated with jellied mayonnaise, decorated and glazed with aspic jelly, garnished with pieces of marinated cucumbers stuffed with vegetable salad, tartlets filled with the same salad, a crayfish head filled with cray-

Salmon
fish froth placed on top, and halves hard-boiled eggs filled with caviar.
— **Royal Style:** à la royale: whole fish or large middle section braised in white wine, garnished with small tartlets stuffed with salpicon of crayfish in Nantua sauce, fluted mushroom caps, olive shaped truffles and boiled potato balls, fish covered with Normandy sauce.
— **Royal Style** (cold): cutlets poached, when cold coated with salmon froth, covered with jellied mayonnaise, decorated with truffle slices, hard-boiled egg whites, egg yolks, tarragon or chervil leaves etc., glazed with aspic jelly, dressed in glass dish and filled with half set aspic jelly. Served surrounded with crushed ice.
— **Russian Salmon Pie; Kulibijaka:** Coulibiac: thin sheet of yeast dough made with eggs and butter, covered with layers of semolina, sliced hard-boiled eggs, salmon fillets, chopped onions and herbs, chopped vesiga, etc.; the edges of the dough wrapped over to close the pie, egg washed and baked in oven, served with melted butter.
— **Saint-Germain:** prepared like sole fillets.
— **in Scallop Shell Mornay:** en coquilles: flakes of boiled salmon, filled in shells masked with Mornay sauce, Duchess mixture piped around the edges, coated with Mornay sauce, sprinkled with grated cheese, browned in top.
— **Scallops Victoria:** same as Mornay with lobster slices added, coated with Nantua sauce, a slice of truffle on top.
— **Scotch Style:** à l'écossaise: poached in white wine and fish stock, covered with Dutch sauce mixed with the reduced stock and vegetable brunoise simmered in butter.
— **Susie:** Suzette: poached escalopes, covered with Joinville sauce, garnished with ragoût of mushrooms and truffles bound with lobster sauce.
— **Turenne:** prepared like brill.
— **Vanderbilt:** darne, poached in court-bouillon, covered with shrimp sauce mixed with sliced truffles, garnished with mushroom caps, bearded poached oysters and shrimps.
— **Venetian Style:** à la vénetienne: darne, poached, Venetian sauce served separately.

Salmon Trout: F. Truite saumonnée; G. Lachsforelle: Migratory fish of the salmon family living in European rivers and fresh water lakes and in the sea. Sea trout is found in the North Sea and in the Baltic, the name is also given to the Alaska trout and the Australian King Salmon. Prepared like trout and salmon.
— **American Style:** à l'américaine: fillets, poached in white wine, covered with lobster slices and American sauce.
— **Banker Style:** à la banquière: poached in court-bouillon, covered with fish velouté mixed with diced lobster, garnished with sautéd quarters of artichoke bottoms, fluted mushrooms, truffle slices and oval shaped cucumbers simmered in butter.
— **Cambacérès:** skinned on one side, larded with strips of truffles and red carrots, bones removed, leaving head intact, stuffed with fish forcemeat, wrapped in fat bacon, braised in white wine; bacon removed, fish dressed on long platter, covered with the boiled-down stock mixed

Salmon Trout
with white wine sauce and beaten with butter; garnished with pitted olives, fried soft roes, sautéd morels and truffle slices.

— **Caruso:** escalopes coated with lobster forcemeat, covered with truffle slices and a crayfish tail, poached in white wine, butter and fish stock, stock reduced and thickened with butter and flour, garnished with tiny puff pastry patties filled with caviar.

— **Clarence:** fillets stuffed with truffled forcemeat of pike-perch, folded, poached in white wine, fish stock and chopped shallots, fish placed in buttered baking dish on pilaf rice, covered with the boiled-down stock, mixed with Béchamel sauce, flavored with curry, finished with cream and butter and glazed.

— **George Sand:** fillets, poached, decorated with truffle slices, garnished with small fish dumplings and shrimps, covered with shrimp sauce.

— **Imperial Style:** à l'impériale: skinned on one side, larded with truffles, braised in champagne and fish stock, garnished with shrimps and poached soft roes; stock reduced, beaten with butter, poured over the fish, julienne of truffles scattered on top.

— **Ivanhoe:** fillets shallow fried in fireproof dish, sliced fried apples and artichoke and peeled lemon segments on top, covered with white wine sauce beaten with crayfish purée.

— **Mermaids:** Ondines (cold): froth (mousse) filled in oval moulds about the size of an egg, stuffed with salpicon of shrimps. When set turned out, a shrimp tail stuck into each, dressed in deep glass dish, covered with half set aspic jelly mixed with chervil leaves.

— **Monseigneur:** whole fish poached in red wine with vegetables and herbs, garnished with fluted mushroom caps, covered with red wine sauce; surrounded with tartlets filled with a poached egg coated with red wine sauce, and pastry boats filled with poached soft roes coated with white wine sauce and decorated with truffle slices.

— **Montgolfier:** boned, stuffed with truffled fish forcemeat, poached in court-bouillon, skinned, decorated with truffle slices, covered with white wine sauce, garnished with lobster slices and mushroom caps.

— **Montrouge:** prepared like sole fillets.

— **Vatel:** prepared like sole fillets.

Salt Cod: F. Morue salée; G. Laberdan, gesalzener Kabeljau. Before boiling in water or milk taken out of salt and soaked in water overnight.

— **Bamboche:** cut in long strips, dipped in milk and flour, deep fried, dressed on macedoine of vegetables.

— **Bénédictine:** poached, flaked, mashed together with boiled potatoes, mixed with oil and milk like thick mayonnaise, filled in baking dish and glazed.

— **Benoiton:** sliced onions slightly browned in butter and oil, sprinkled with flour moistened with fish fumet and red wine; garlic, sliced raw potatoes and flaked salt cod added, cooked, filled in baking dish, sprinkled with breadcrumbs and baked in oven.

— **Biscaya Style:** à la biscaienne: diced parboiled salt cod sautéd in oil with diced tomatoes, chopped parsley and

Salt Cod
garlic added, dressed alternately with strips of peppers in baking dish, simmered in oven, garnished with heart shaped croûtons.

— **Brandade:** prepared like Bénédictine with less potatoes, a little garlic added and sharply seasoned.

— **Brandade, Creamed:** à la crème: same as brandade but prepared with cream.

— **Brandade, Truffled:** truffée: prepared like brandade with chopped truffles added and garnished with sliced truffles.

— **in Cream Sauce:** à la crème: poached, flaked and covered with cream sauce.

— **Creole Style:** à la crèole: baking dish filled alternately with sliced fried onions, tomatoes Provencal style and boiled, flaked salt cod, covered with browned butter and served very hot.

— **English Style:** à l'anglaise: boiled, dressed with boiled potatoes and parsnips; English egg sauce served separately.

— **Italian Style:** à l'italienne: soaked raw salt cod, cut in large dice, coated with flour, fried in deep fat; tomato sauce served separately.

— **Lyonese:** à la lyonnaise: boiled and flaked, mixed with sliced onions and potatoes sautéd in butter, deglaced with a few drops of vinegar, dressed in timbale dish with chopped parsley scattered on top.

— **Mornay:** poached and flaked, filled in baking dish masked with Mornay sauce, covered with Mornay sauce, sprinkled with grated cheese and gratinated.

— **Provencal:** à la provençale: chopped onions and diced tomatoes sautéd in oil, capers, black olives, a little garlic, chopped parsley and boiled flaked salt cod added, simmered for a few minutes and dressed in timbale dish.

— **Spanish Style:** à l'espagnole: same as Biscaya, alternated with sliced boiled potatoes, each layer covered with tomato sauce diluted with a little of the fish stock.

— **with Spinach:** aux epinards: coarsely chopped spinach, seasoned with pepper, salt, nutmeg and garlic, mixed with boiled flaked salt cod, chopped parsley, anchovy fillets, bound with Béchamel sauce, filled in baking dish, sprinkled with breadcrumbs, dotted with butter and browned in oven.

— **Valencia:** boiled flaked salt cod dressed alternately in timbale dish with pilaf rice, tomato purée and fried onion rings, rice as last layer; garnished with quarters of hard-boiled eggs, browned butter mixed with breadcrumbs poured on top, finished in oven and served very hot.

Sand Dab: F. Carrelet; G. gemeine Scholle. Saltwater fish found off the American and European Atlantic coasts but not in the Mediterranean. Prepared like plaice.

Sardine: F. Sardine: G. Sardine. Small saltwater fish resembling herring caught off the Atlantic coasts and in the Mediterranean, mainly processed and packed in oil.

— **Antibes Style:** à l'antiboise: boned, dipped in egg and breadcrumbs, deep fried, in oil, dressed around tomatoes concassées prepared with garlic.

— **Basque Style:** prepared like anchovies.

Sardine

— **Canteen-woman's Style:** à la vivandière: stuffed, placed in pieces of scooped out cucumbers, filled in buttered plat à sauter poached in oven in mushroom essence, drained, covered with tomato sauce, sprinkled with chopped herbs.

— **Courtier Style:** à la courtisane: boned, stuffed with fish forcemeat mixed with chopped mushrooms, poached in white wine, dressed on croûtons of same size, masked with white wine sauce mixed with spinach purée, glazed, garnished with potato croquettes the size of a large marble.

— **Devilled:** à la diable: dipped in egg and breadcrumbs, deep fried, seasoned with Cayenne pepper; devil's sauce served separately.

— **Havre Style:** à la havraise: prepared like courtiers style, the stuffing without mushrooms, coated with white wine sauce with a cordon of meat glaze, garnished with fried mussels.

— **Housewife Style:** bonne-femme: small sliced onions slightly fried in oil, moistened with white wine, boiled down, diced tomatoes added, filled in baking dish, sardines placed on top, sprinkled with mixture of breadcrumbs and powdered fennel seeds, a little oil dropped on top, baked in oven.

— **Hyère Style:** à la hyèroise: poached in white wine and mushroom essence mixed with chopped sautéd leeks, dressed on fried croûtons; stock boiled down, thickened with egg yolks, beaten with butter, seasoned with Cayenne pepper, chopped parsley added and poured over the fish.

— **Nice Style:** prepared like anchovies.

— **Orly:** dipped in frying batter, deep fried; tomato sauce served separately.

— **Provencal Style:** à la provençale: shallow fried in oil together with crushed garlic, bay leaf and thyme; browned butter with a few drops of vinegar and chopped herbs poured over.

— **Saint-Honorat:** prepared like anchovies.

— **Sicilian Style:** à la sicilienne: opened from the back, boned, dipped in egg and breadcrumbs, fried in butter, dressed on peeled lemon slices, chopped hard-boiled eggs and capers scattered on top, garnished with anchovy fillets, browned butter poured over.

— **Toulon Style:** à la toulonaise: boned, stuffed, poached, garnished with bearded mussels, covered with white wine sauce.

— **Trieste Style:** à la triestaine: boned, stuffed with fish forcemeat with chopped herbs, poached, covered with fish velouté blended with herb butter, garnished with very small rice croquettes.

Saumon: see salmon.

Scallops: F. Coquilles St. Jacques; G. Jakobsmuscheln. Bivalve mollusc characterized by the radially ribbed shell found on both sides of the Atlantic. American scallops are smaller then the European variety.

— **in Cream Sauce:** à la crème: parboiled, sliced, deglaced with white wine, moistened with cream, cooked, thickened with egg yolks, seasoned with Cayenne pepper and lemon juice.

Scallops
— **Creole:** à la créole: sliced, sautéd in butter, simmered in Creole sauce, served with Creole rice.
— **Curried:** au curry: sliced, sautéd in butter with chopped onions and diced tomatoes, simmered in fish velouté flavored with curry powder, dressed in timbale dish, plain boiled rice and Mango Chutney served separately.
— **Fried:** frite: poached, dipped in egg and breadcrumbs, deep fried; Tartar sauce served separately.
— **Gratinated:** au gratin: parboiled, sliced, braised in white wine and mushroom essence, replaced in shells masked with gratin sauce, coated with gratin sauce, sprinkled with breadcrumbs, gratinated in oven.
— **Mornay:** parboiled, sliced, braised, replaced in shells masked with Mornay sauce, coated with Mornay sauce, sprinkled with grated cheese and glazed.
— **Nantes Style:** à la nantaise: sliced, poached in white wine and mushroom essence, dressed in shells with poached bearded oysters and mussels, coated with white wine sauce and glazed.
— **Newburgh:** sliced, sweated in butter, cooked in cream, seasoned with Cayenne pepper; thickened with egg yolks, flavored with Sherry; rice served separately.
— **Ostende Style:** à l'ostendaise: prepared like Nantese style with bearded oysters, shrimps and mushrooms, coated with Nantua sauce and decorated with a truffle slice.
— **Parisian Style:** à la parisienne: parboiled, sliced, stewed in white wine and mushroom essence, dressed in shells surrounded with piped Duchess mixture alternated with sliced mushrooms, coated with white wine sauce mixed with chopped truffles and glazed.
— **on Skewers:** en brochette: parboiled, sliced, dipped in egg and breadcrumbs, impaled on skewers alternately with thin slices of bacon, broiled and served with Colbert sauce.

Scampi: see caramote.

Seafood: F. fruits de mer; G. Meeresfrüchte; I. Frutti di mare. All kinds of fish, particularly shellfish, bivalves, molluscs and other marine delicacies, usually combined and in various forms of preparation.
— **Alabama:** steamed scallops, shrimps and lobster slices tossed in butter, moistened with Sherry, boiled down, bound with cream sauce, seasoned with Cayenne pepper and lemon juice, filled in individual casseroles, sprinkled with grated cheese and glazed.
— **Florida** (cold): chopped onions slightly fried in butter, equal parts bearded mussels, shrimps and oysters added, boiled up in white wine sauce, seasoned with Cayenne pepper and lemon juice, chilled, served cold sprinkled with chopped tarragon and parsley, garnished with sliced avocados and lemon.

Sea-bream: F. Dorade commune; G. Meerbrasse. Saltwater fish found in the Atlantic and chiefly off the Norwegian coast.
— **Commander Style:** à la commodore: poached in court-bouillon, garnished with oysters Villeroy, whole crayfish, small lobster croquettes, small fish dumplings and large boiled potato balls; Normandy sauce finished off with anchovy butter served separately.

Sea-bream
— **Grilled:** grillé: scored, seasoned, coated with flour, brushed with oil and grilled; herb butter or tartar sauce served separately.
— **Grimaldi:** poached folded fillets dressed on creamed spaghetti, decorated with a slice of lobster and truffle, covered with Nantua sauce.
— **Murillo:** seasoned with lemon juice and paprika, fried in butter, garnished with stuffed cucumbers and large mushrooms stuffed with gooseliver purée, covered with Dutch sauce.

Sea-Robin: saltwater fish similar to the European gurnards. Prepared like red mullet.

Sea-Urchin, Sea-Hedgehog: F. Oursin; G. See-Igel. Marine animal shaped like a round spiny ball, found off the coast of Europe, America and Asia. Cut open and eaten raw as an appetizer, also boiled and used for sauces.

Sépiole: see cuttlefish.

Shad: F. Alose; G. Alse, Maifisch. Saltwater fish of the herring species found off the coasts of Western Europe, North America, the North Sea and the Mediterranean. Shad roe is considered a great delicacy.
— **American Style:** à l'américane: fillets, poached in butter and white wine, garnished with lobster slices, covered with American sauce.
— **Andalousian Style:** fillets prepared like sole.
— **Baker Style:** à la boulangère: poached in white wine with shredded sorrel, sliced onions, bacon and butter.
— **Bercy:** scored on both sides, seasoned, baked in oil in the oven, covered with Bercy sauce.
— **Broiled, Grilled:** grillée: scored, marinated in oil, lemon juice, chopped shallots and parsley, broiled, covered with herb butter, garnished with parsley and lemon.
— **Brussels Style:** à la bruxelloise: fillets coated with lobster forcemeat, folded, dipped in egg and breadcrumbs, fried in deep fat; Dutch sauce served separately.
— **in Cases:** en caisses: small china cases (cocottes) filled with a tablespon of fresh tomato purée, seasoned and mixed with chopped herbs, small pieces of poached shad fillets placed on top, covered with tomato sauce, sprinkled with grated cheese and glazed.
— **Dutch Style:** à la hollandaise: poached in court-bouillon, served with fish potatoes, Dutch sauce or melted butter.
— **Flemish Style** à la flamande: prepared like cod.
— **Fried:** frite: fillets dipped in egg and breadcrumbs, deep fried; Tartare or Remoulade sauce served separately.
— **with Horseradish Sauce:** à la sauce raifort: scored, shallow fried, covered with horseradish sauce.
— **Irish Style:** à l'irlandaise: fillets stuffed with whiting forcemeat mixed with crayfish purée, folded, coated with flour, grilled with oil; crayfish sauce served separately.
— **Italian Style:** à l'italienne: baking dish masked with chopped mushrooms sweated in butter with chopped shallots, the seasoned fish placed on top, covered with Italian sauce, sprinkled with breadcrumbs, dotted with butter, baked and browned in oven.
— **Maître d'hôtel:** scored, marinated, grilled; herb butter served separately.
— **Milanese Style:** à la milanaise: fillets marinated in oil, lemon juice, chopped herbs and a pinch of salt, dipped

Shad
in egg and breadcrumbs mixed with grated Parmesan, fried in oil; spaghetti Milanese style served separately.
— **Nantese Style:** à la nantaise: fillets prepared like salmon.
— **in Paper Bag:** en papillote: scored, wrapped in greased paper bag with chopped shallots and mushrooms, baked in oven, served in the bag; tomato sauce served separately.
— **Planked:** baked on plank with border of Duchess potatoes, garnished with parsley, lemon and herb butter.
— **Provencal Style:** à la provençale: fillets prepared like cod.
— **Saint-Malo:** fillets, broiled; St. Malo sauce served separately.
— **with Sorrel:** à l'oseille: fillets, dipped in egg and breadcrumbs, grilled with oil, covered with browned butter and a little lemon juice; sorrel purée served separately.
— **Soubise:** scored, coated with flour, broiled, dressed on white onion purée.
— **Stuffed:** farcie: stuffed with pike forcemeat mixed with chopped fine herbs, poached in red wine fish stock, stock boiled down and thickened with butter and flour, mixed with sliced sautéd mushrooms, poured over the fish, chopped parsley scattered on top.
— **Village Style:** à la villageoise: scored, coated with flour, fried in oil and butter, covered with butter mixed with chopped parsley, just a little chopped sage, a few drops of vinegar and a little juice of green tomatoes.

Shad-roe Bordeaux Style: oeufs d'alose à la bordelaise: seasoned, fried in oil, topped with slices of blanched ox marrow, covered with Bordeaux sauce.
— **Newburgh:** cut in pieces, cooked in cream, seasoned with Cayenne pepper, thickened with egg yolks mixed with Sherry, served on toast.
— **and Spinach:** Laitance d'alose aux épinards: fried, dressed on plain spinach tossed in butter, covered with cream sauce.

Shrimp: F. Crevette, crevette gris; G. Krevette, Garnele; I. Gamberetti. Varieties of small shellfish related to lobster found on the Atlantic coast of Europe and America. Marketed fresh, canned and frozen in various sizes. The most common are the grey shrimps which only turn faintly pinkish when boiled. Used for soups, garnishes and cold as an appetizer.
— **Creole Style:** tails tossed in butter, bound with Creole sauce, plain rice served separately.
— **Curried:** au curry: tails bound with curry sauce, plain boiled rice served separately.
— **Danish Style:** large shrimps mixed with asparagus tips, bound with shrimp sauce, served in timbale dish garnished with fried heart shaped croûtons.
— **Devilled:** à la diable: prepared like fried shrimps, Cayenne pepper and mustard powder added to breadcrumbs.
— **Fried:** frites: large tails, dipped in egg and breadcrumbs or in frying batter, fried in deep fat; Tartar sauce served separately.
— **Gustave:** large tails arranged in baking dish on layer of asparagus tips tossed in butter, covered with cheese sauce, sprinkled with grated cheese and browned on top.
— **Pudding:** Pouding de crevettes: pounded to paste with a litte cream sauce, pitted olives and chutney; rubbed

Shrimp
through a sieve, mixed with whole eggs, seasoned with Cayenne pepper, filled in greased moulds lined with breadcrumbs, poached lightly in water bath, turned out, served hot with shrimp sauce.
— **Pudding, Danish:** Pouding à la danoise: chopped tails mixed with white bread soaked in milk and egg yolks, seasoned with salt, pepper and nutmeg, finished off with stiffly beaten egg whites, filled in pudding mould, steamed in water bath turned out and covered with shrimp sauce.
— **in Scallop Shells:** en coquilles: filled in shells masked with Mornay sauce and a border of Duchess mixture piped around the edges, covered with Mornay sauce, sprinkled with grated cheese and browned in oven. Sliced sautéd mushrooms, asparagus tips or truffle slices may be added to shrimps.

Silure, Common Silure: F. Silure; G. Wels, Waller. One of the largest European freshwater fish, found mainly in the Danube, Elbe, Vistula and Oder.
— **Boiled:** Bouilli: served with fish potatoes and Dutch, caper, shrimp, butter or Robert sauce.
— **Escalopes:** dipped in eggs and breadcrumbs, fried in butter, lemon juice and browned butter on top.
— **Fried:** frit: cut in slices, dipped in frying batter, deep fried; tomato sauce served separately.
— **Grilled:** grillé: steaks, coated with flour, brushed with oil, grilled, served with herb or anchovy butter.

Skate: F. Raie; G. Rochen. North Atlantic flatfish of the ray family of which the skate and the thornback ray are the most important.
— **with Browned Butter:** au beurre noir: cut in pieces, boiled in salt water, browned butter to which a little vinegar has been added poured over at the last minute, chopped parsley and capers scattered on top.
— **with Caper Sauce:** au sauce câpres: boiled, covered with caper sauce, fish potatoes served separately.
— **Fried:** frite: small skate cut in half, each half in small strips, marinated in lemon juice, oil, sliced onions and fine herbs, dipped in frying batter, deep fried, served with fried parsley and lemon.
— **Italian Style:** cut in pieces, boiled in prepared stock of milk, water, sliced onions, garlic, pepper corns, thyme, bay leaf and salt, stock strained, thickened with flour and butter, poured over fish arranged in baking dish, sprinkled with grated Parmesan, dotted with butter and glazed.
— **Provencal:** à la provençale: cut in pieces, parboiled, covered with Provencal sauce, sprinkled with chopped parsley.

Smelt: F. Eperlan; G. Stint; I. Pesce argentino; S. Esperinque. Small silvery fish thriving in both salt and fresh water. Smelts are found off the Atlantic and Pacific coasts.
— **Bercy:** prepared like sole.
— **Colbert:** prepared like sole.
— **English Style:** à l'anglaise: opened from the back, back bone removed, dipped in melted butter and breadcrumbs, fried in clarified butter, herb butter in the opening at serving.

Smelt

— **Fried:** frites: dipped in egg and breadcrumbs, fried in deep fat, served with fried parsley and lemon.

— **Gratinated:** au gratin: arranged in fireproof dish on Italian sauce, covered with sliced mushrooms, Italian sauce poured over, sprinkled with breadcrumbs, dotted with butter, baked in the oven.

— **Greek Style:** à la grecque: poached in prepared stock of white wine, oil, vinegar, onion slices, fennel, pepper corns, parsley sprigs, bay leaf and garlic, served cold in a part of the strained stock.

— **Grilled:** grillés: opened from the back, backbone removed, coated with flour, dipped in melted butter, grilled, served with herb butter or tartar sauce.

— **with Horseradish:** mit Essigkren: poached, covered with sauce prepared with cream mixed with grated horse-radish, apple purée, vinegar, sugar and salt (Austrian).

— **Mousselines Alexandra:** prepared like salmon.

— **Mousselines Pacelli:** mousseline forcemeat of smelts mixed with chopped dill, filled in small oval moulds, poached, turned out on oval pastry shells filled with diced mush-rooms in cream sauce, arranged like a crown on a round dish, covered with Nantua sauce, center filled with oval-shaped cucumber pieces in cream sauce.

— **Orly:** dipped in frying batter, deep fried, tomato sauce served separately.

— **Planked:** prepared like bass.

— **Polignac:** prepared like sole.

— **Polish Style:** à la polonaise: stuffed with fish forcemeat, poached in butter and white wine, chopped hard-boiled eggs scattered on top, covered with breadcrumbs fried in plenty of butter mixed with chopped parsley.

— **Stanley:** poached in fish stock and white wine, dressed on risotto mixed with diced mushrooms and truffles, covered with white wine sauce blended with white onion purée, seasoned with curry powder.

Snails: F. escargots; G. Schnecken; I. lummacha. Only edible mollusc living on dry land. To prepare wash shells, remove lid, blanch in water and vinegar, take snails out of shells, remove black alimentary truck and braise snails in rich stock with white wine and pot herbs. Allow to Cool off in their liquor, refill in shells or serve as specified. Snails are marketed fresh in shells or canned.

— **Burgundy Style:** à la bourguignonne: shells filled with a little Burgundy butter (shallot butter mixed with garlic, parsley, snail stock, salt and pepper) snails put in, closed with Burgundy butter, heated in special snail pan.

— **Catalonian Style:** Caracoles Catalana: parboiled, sautéd in oil with chopped onions, garlic, chopped parsley and a little thyme (Spanish).

— **Chablis Style:** à la chablisienne: same as Burgundy style but with butter with chopped shallots boiled down in white wine, garlic, chopped parsley, meat glaze and seasoning.

— **Dijon Style:** à la dijonnaise: prepared like Burgundy style but with butter mixed with strained ox marrow, chopped truffles, very little garlic, seasoning and chopped shallots boiled down in white wine.

Snails

— **Fried:** frits: parboiled, dipped in egg and breadcrumbs, deep fried, served with fried parsley and lemon.

— **Fritters:** Beignets: parboiled, marinated in lemon juice, oil, chopped shallots and parsley, dipped in frying batter, deep fried, served with lemon and fried parsley.

— **Genoble Style:** à la grenobloise: prepared like Burgundy style, mashed hazelnuts added to the butter.

— **with Horseradish:** mit Essigkren: parboiled and simmered in white wine and chopped herbs; grated horseradish mixed with a little vinegar served separately (Austrian).

— **Madrid Style:** Caracoles Madrilena: parboiled, taken out of shells, sautéd in oil, simmered in sauce made of chopped onions fried in butter with chopped ham and garlic, moistened with white wine, diced tomatoes, strips of green peppers and chopped parsley added, seasoned with salt, Cayenne pepper and nutmeg, served in this sauce (Spanish).

— **Marinated:** marinés (cold): parboiled, simmered in white wine with a little vinegar, oil, seasoning and sliced mushrooms, served cold in the stock.

— **Monastry Style:** mode de l'abbaye: parboiled taken out of shells, sautéd in butter with chopped onions, sprinkled with flour, seasoned, moistened with thin cream, simmered until done, thickened with egg yolks.

— **Red Devils:** Diables rouges: parboiled, sautéd in oil with chopped onions and garlic, chopped red peppers and tomatoes added, seasoned highly with Cayenne pepper and a few drops of Tabasco sauce, served in timbale dish sprinkled with chopped parsley.

— **Salad:** parboiled, marinated in oil, vinegar, salt, pepper, chopped shallots and parsley, mixed with chopped anchovy fillets, garnished with slices of hard-boiled eggs.

— **on Skewers:** Brochettes d'escargots: parboiled, taken out of the shells, fixed on skewers alternately with small slices of bacon, dipped in egg and breadcrumbs, deep fried, served with herb butter.

— **Villebernier:** taken out of shells and simmered a few minutes in sauce made of chopped shallots cooked in red wine, seasoned with a few drops of vinegar and Cayenne pepper, boiled down and beaten with butter.

— **Wine-grower Style:** à la vigneronne: parboiled, taken out of the shells, sautéd in butter with chopped shallots and garlic, dipped in frying batter mixed with chopped chives, fried in oil, dressed with fried parsley.

Soft Roe: F. Laitance; G. Fischmilcher. Usually the milt of carp, herring, mackerel and cod.

— **in Aspic Jelly:** en gelée: poached in white wine, lemon juice and seasonning; when cold filled in mould lined with aspic jelly mixed with chopped tarragon, sealed with aspic jelly, turned out when set.

— **Creole Style:** à la créole: poached in lemon juice and butter, covered with Creole sauce.

— **Florence Style:** à la florentine: poached served on tartlets filled with plain spinach tossed in butter, covered with cheese sauce, sprinkled with grated cheese and glazed.

— **Fried:** frite: cooked in slightly acidulated water, when cold dipped in egg and breadcrumbs or frying batter, deep fried, served with fried parsley and lemon segments.

Soft Roe

— **Fritters:** Beignets de laitances: poached, when cold dipped in frying batter, deep fried, served with fried parsley and lemon segments.

— **Hungarian Style:** à la hongroise: seasoned with paprika, dressed in pastry boats, covered with paprika sauce.

— **with Lobster Sauce:** à la cardinal: poached, dressed in pastry shells, coated with lobster sauce, a slice of truffle on top.

— **Marshal Style:** à la maréchale: parboiled, dipped in melted butter and white breadcrumbs, mixed with chopped trufles, fried in butter; truffle sauce served separately.

— **Miller Style:** à la meunière: parboiled, coated with flour, fried in butter, chopped parsley scattered on top, lemon juice and browned butter poured over.

— **Ostende Style:** à l'ostendaise: poached in white wine and butter, dressed in pastry boats, covered with herb sauce mixed with diced shrimps and oysters.

— **Parisian Style:** à la parisienne: poached in butter and white wine, dressed in scallop shells, covered with velouté sauce mixed with sliced mushrooms, sprinkled with grated cheese and glazed.

— **in Scallop Shells:** en coquille: poached in white wine and butter, filled in scallop shells, coated with lobster sauce, sprinkled with grated Parmesan and glazed.

— **Scotch Style:** à l'écossaise: poached, dressed in flat pastry shell filled with scrambled eggs, covered with cheese sauce, sprinkled with grated cheese and rapidly glazed under the salamander.

— **Soufflé of Roes:** Soufflé de laitances: parboiled, mashed, mixed with thick cream sauce, salt, pepper, egg yolks and stiffly beaten egg whites, filled in small china soufflé moulds, baked in the oven.

— **on Toast:** sur toast: fried in butter, seasoned with Cayenne pepper, dressed on buttered toast.

— **Tsarina** à la czarine: poached in white wine, dressed on pastry boats or shells, covered with white wine sauce, garnished with caviar.

— **Villeroi:** parboiled, coated with Villeroi sauce, dipped in egg and breadcrumbs and deep fried.

Sole: F. Sole; G. Seezunge; I. Sogliola; S. Lenguado. Saltwater flat fish found off all Westeuropean coasts,and in the Baltic, Channel soles are considered the best.

— **Adlon:** poached in white wine, garnished with scampi tails, truffle slices and mushrooms, covered with Dutch sauce blended with tomato purée.

— **Admiral Style:** à l'amiral: large sole poached in white wine and fish stock with chopped shallots and butter, covered with the boiled down stock mixed with white wine sauce and blended with crayfish butter, garnished with crayfish tails, fluted mushroom caps, sliced truffles, mussels and oysters à la Villeroi.

— **Adrienne:** fillets, poached, garnished with poached soft roes, covered with white wine sauce mixed with sliced mushrooms and finished off with unsweetened whipped cream; a tiny puff pastry patty filled with salpicon of crayfish tails for each portion.

— **Aiglon:** sole poached in white wine, dressed on mushroom purée, covered with white wine sauce mixed with white

Sole

onion purée, meat glaze dotted on top, garnished with fleurons.

— **Alexandra:** fillets, poached, garnished with lobster and truffle slice, covered with Nantua sauce, glazed, surrounded with fleurons.

— **Alexandrine:** fillets poached in fish fumet and white wine, dressed on tomatoes concassées mixed with sliced mushrooms, garnished with lobster slices, covered with Bercy sauce and glazed.

— **Alice:** fillets poached in fish fumet and white wine with chopped onions and thyme, served at table with 4 raw oysters, 1 oz butter and cracker meal for each portion. Waiter thickens stock with cracker meal, poaches oysters in sauce, the sauce finished of with butter poured over the fillets.

— **with Almonds:** Amandine: coated with flour, shallow fried in butter, slivered almonds fried in butter scattered on top, covered with lemon juice and browned butter.

— **Alphonse XIII.:** fillets, shallow fried in butter, dressed on slices of fried eggplants, covered with tomato sauce mixed with julienne of green peppers

— **Alsatian Style:** à l'alsacienne: fillets, poached, served on saurkraut, covered with Mornay sauce, sprinkled with grated cheese, glazed.

— **Altona Style:** auf Altona Art: shallow fried in butter, covered with diced mushrooms, shrimps and mussels sautéd in butter, chopped parsley and lemon juice on top, covered with browned butter; poached oysters in Dutch sauce and boiled potato balls tossed in butter served separately (German).

— **Ambassador Style:** à l'ambassadeur: fillets poached, dressed on mushroom purée, covered with white wine sauce, glazed, sliced truffles on top, surrounded with fleurons.

— **Ambassadrice Style:** fillets folded and poached, covered with Normandy sauce, garnished with stuffed crayfish heads.

— **Amelia:** Amélie: poached, bordered with sliced truffles and boiled potatoes, covered with Nantua sauce.

— **American Style:** à l'américane: fillets folded poached in white wine and fish stock, a slice of lobster on each fillet, covered with American sauce.

— **Amphytrion:** fillets, coated with pike forcemeat mixed with diced oysters and anchovy paste, seasoned with Cayenne pepper, folded, dipped in egg and breadcrumbs, fried in deep fat, served with fried parsley and lemon.

— **Amundsen** (cold): fillets, folded, poached, when cold dressed on halved tomatoes scooped out, marinated with oil, vinegar, salt and pepper, stuffed with diced marinated carps roes, fillets decorated with crayfish tails and glazed with aspic jelly.

— **Ancient Style:** poached in white wine, garnished with button onions and mushroom caps, covered with white wine sauce.

— **Andalusian Style:** à l'andalouse: fillets coated with fish forcemeat with chopped sweet peppers, rolled into paupiettes, poached, filled in halved cooked tomatoes stuffed with risotto mixed with diced peppers, each

Sole

tomato placed on slice of fried eggplant, browned butter poured on top.

— **Archduke Style:** à l'archiduc: poached in fish stock, Whisky and Port; stock reduced, creamed, beaten with butter, mixed with vegetable brunoise and finely diced truffles and poured over the sole.

— **Arlesian Style:** à l'arlésienne: poached in fish stock with chopped onions, diced tomatoes and a little garlic, stock reduced, beaten with butter, mixed with olive-shaped pieces of baby marrows simmered in butter, poured over the sole, garnished with fried onion rings.

— **Armenonville:** fillets folded with a crayfish claw inside, dipped in egg and breadcrumbs, fried, garnished with olive-shaped cucumbers in cream sauce, surrounded with Nantua sauce.

— **with Asparagus:** à l'Argenteuil: poached in white wine, covered with white wine sauce garnished with white asparagus.

— **with Baby Marrows:** aux courgettes: fillets, dressed in baking dish greased with butter, slices of peeled baby marrows, diced tomatoes, seasoning and a pinch of sweet basil on top, seasoned with lemon juice, sprinkled with breadcrumbs, melted butter dotted on top, baked and gratinated slowly in oven.

— **Bagration:** I. poached, covered with Mornay sauce mixed with truffle julienne, sprinkled with grated cheese and glazed.

II. cold poached fillets glazed with aspic jelly, dressed on lobster slices around a cupola of Russian salad.

— **Baron Brisse:** I. fillets stuffed with pike forcemeat mixed with purée of crayfish, folded, poached in white wine and mushroom essence, covered with sliced truffles, mushrooms and crayfish tails, coated with cream sauce flavored with Sherry, glazed.

II. stuffed paupiettes, poached, dressed on border of poached fish forcemeat, a slice of truffle on each paupiette, covered with white wine sauce; centre filled with crayfish tails in American sauce.

— **Beatrice:** poached rolls dressed on large poached mushrooms surrounded with poached soft roes, covered with white wine sauce mixed with shrimp purée and shrimps, a slice of truffle and a fluted mushroom cap on each paupiette.

— **Beaufort:** poached, covered with lobster sauce mixed with diced lobster, mushrooms and poached bearded oysters.

— **Beaumanoir:** fillets, poached, covered alternately with white wine sauce, a slice of truffle on top, and lobster sauce with a fried oyster.

— **Bedford:** grilled sole dressed on herb butter, garnished alternately with small round croûtons, scooped out, stuffed with mushroom purée with chopped truffles, and with spinach purée coated with Mornay sauce, sprinkled with grated cheese and glazed.

— **Belle de Nuit:** fillets coated with crayfish forcemeat, folded, poached in white wine and mushroom essence, covered with Normandy sauce mixed with diced tomatoes, garnished with mushrooms and boiled potato balls.

Sole

— **Benedictine:** fillets, folded, poached, dressed around a cupola of truffled brandade (which see), fillets covered with white wine sauce.

— **Benevenuto:** shallow fried in butter, dressed on tomatoes concassées with garlic, garnished with sliced truffles and fried slices of yellow boletus, covered with browned butter, chopped tarragon sprinkled on top.

— **Benjamin:** folded, dipped in egg and breadcrumbs, fried, dressed on baked potatoes, scooped out and filled with diced mushrooms in cream sauce; American sauce served separately.

— **Bercy:** fillets poached with chopped shallots and parsley in white wine and fish fumet, stock boiled down, beaten with butter, poured over the fillets and glazed.

— **Birkouff:** poached in white wine, covered with white wine sauce mixed with brunoise, chopped fennel and savory, chopped parsley on top.

— **Biron:** poached, covered with Geneva sauce mixed with chopped truffles, garnished with fleurons.

— **Bismarck:** fillets coated with fish forcemeat mixed with chopped truffles, dressed on artichoke bottoms with a mushroom cap and a poached bearded oyster on each, covered with white wine sauce mixed with the reduced oyster liquor and Dutch sauce, glazed rapidly under the salamander, garnished with ragoût of mussels, shrimps and mushrooms in Dutch sauce.

— **Boatman Style:** à la batelière: prepared like haddock.

— **Boïeldieu:** fillets coated with fish forcemeat mixed with salpicon of truffles, shrimps and crayfish, folded, poached, dressed on flat croquettes of spiny lobster, covered with Nantua sauce, a slice of truffle on each fillet.

— **Boistelle:** prepared like Bercy, raw sliced mushrooms added.

— **Bolivar:** boned, stuffed with fish forcemeat mixed with onion purée and diced tomatoes, poached in white wine and fish stock, covered with white wine sauce mixed with white onion purée.

— **Bordeaux Style:** à la bordelaise: poached in red wine with chopped shallots, stock boiled down, mixed with Bordeaux sauce and poured over the fish.

— **Breteuil:** sole poached in court-bouillon, garnished with pastry boats filled with poached soft roes; fish potatoes and melted butter served separately.

— **Breton Style:** à la bretonne: poached, garnished with mushroom caps, covered with Breton sauce, glazed, fleurons around.

— **Bristol:** paupiettes poached in white wine, dressed on artichoke bottoms with a slice of truffle on top, covered with white wine sauce, garnished with Parisian potatoes.

— **Brouns:** fillets stuffed with fish forcemeat mixed with lobster purée, filled in soufflé dish greased with butter, lobster soufflé mass on top, baked; white wine sauce with mushroom slices and chopped fine herbs served separately.

— **Buckingham:** stuffed fillets, folded, poached, dressed on slices of stuffed cabbage, covered with Newburgh sauce and glazed.

— **Burgundy Style:** à la bourguignonne: poached in red wine, garnished with button onions and mushrooms,

Sole

covered with Burgundy sauce mixed with the reduced stock.

— **Byron:** poached in red wine, fish stock and mushroom essence with mirepoix, stock reduced, beaten with butter, poured over the fish, chopped truffles scattered on top.

— **Café de Paris:** poached with truffle julienne, decorated with fluted mushrooms, asparagus tips, poached bearded oysters and large shrimps; border of Victoria sauce.

— **Café Riche:** fillets, folded, poached in fish stock, dressed so as to resemble a turban, center filled with ragoût of spiny lobster and truffles, fillets and ragoût covered with Victoria sauce.

— **Cancal Style:** à la cancalaise: fillet, folded, poached in butter and oyster liquor, garnished with bearded oysters and shrimps, covered with Normandy sauce mixed with the boiled down stock.

— **Cape Martin:** Cap Martin: boned, stuffed with crayfish tails and oysters, poached in white wine and fish fumet, stock reduced, mixed with white wine sauce, poured over the sole, meat glaze dropped on top.

— **Capricious Style:** à la caprice: fillets dipped in melted butter and breadcrumbs, grilled, dressed on fried half bananas, covered with buttered sauce Robert Escoffier.

— **Cardinal Style:** fillets coated with fish forcemeat with lobster, folded, poached, arranged in a circle with a slice of lobster between each fillet and a slice of truffle on top, covered with cardinal sauce, chopped lobster coral scattered on top.

— **Carême:** fillets or whole fish poached, garnished with poached soft roes, fluted mushrooms and poached bearded oysters, covered with white wine sauce blended with celery purée, fleurons around.

— **Carmen:** shallow fried in butter, decorated with strips of red peppers and blanched tarragon leaves, red pepper butter served separately.

— **Carmencita:** poached in white wine, dressed on tomatoes concassées with garlic and chopped parsley, covered with fish velouté beaten with butter and mixed with julienne of green peppers, garnished with small pastry shells stuffed with creamed brandade of salt cod.

— **with Carrots:** Crécy: fillets coated with pike forcemeat mixed with carrot purée, folded, poached in white wine, fish stock and carrot purée, stock reduced, beaten with butter, poured over the fillets, garnished with artichoke bottoms filled with tiny carrot balls tossed in butter.

— **Casanova:** poached, decorated with truffle slices, covered with white wine sauce, garnished with poached bearded oysters and mussels, surrounded with fleurons.

— **Casino:** fillets, cut in squares, poached, mixed with shrimps, bearded oysters and mussels, bound with cream sauce, filled in china or earthenware cases, sprinkled with grated cheese and glazed.

— **Castellan Style:** à la castellane: fillets, poached, garnished with lobster slices, mushrooms and boiled potato balls, covered with white wine sauce and glazed.

— **Castiglione:** fillets poached, a mushroom cap and a slice of lobster on each fillet, bordered with slices of boiled potatoes, covered with white wine sauce mixed with cream sauce and glazed.

Sole

— **Catalonian Style:** à la catalane: fillets, folded, poached in white wine, dressed on halved tomatoes sautéd in oil and stuffed with sliced onions cooked in oil, covered with white wine sauce and glazed.

— **Cavalier Style:** à la chevalière: paupiettes stuffed with crayfish forcemeat, poached in white wine, dressed like a crown, center filled with ragoût of mushrooms, truffles and spiny lobster bound with lobster sauce, paupiettes covered with white wine sauce.

— **Caylus:** fillets poached in white wine with vegetable brunoise, stock boiled down, beaten with butter and poured over the fillets, garnished with fried mushroom caps and snail croquettes.

— **Cazenave:** paupiettes poached in lemon juice and mushroom essence, placed in small Calville apples, peeled, scooped out and poached, covered with the reduced stock mixed with Dutch sauce, julienne of red peppers scattered on top.

— **Cecil Rhodes:** fillets, folded, poached in oyster stock, garnished with asparagus tips, olive-shaped truffles and bearded oysters, covered with the boiled down stock beaten with butter and glazed.

— **Cecilia:** fillets, shallow fried in butter, garnished with asparagus tips, covered with browned butter.

— **Celina:** fillets, poached, dressed on spaghetti mixed with butter, grated Parmesan, shrimps and oysters, covered with white wine sauce blended with Dutch sauce and glazed.

— **Ceylon Style:** à la cingalaise: fillets, poached, dressed on pilaf rice mixed with diced green and red peppers, covered with white wine sauce seasoned with curry.

— **in Chambertin:** au Chambertin: poached in Chambertin wine, stock thickened with butterpaste and beaten with butter, garnished with sole strips, dipped in egg and breadcrumbs, deep fried.

— **Charlemagne:** fillets coated with truffled salmon forcemeat, dipped in egg and breadcrumbs, deep fried, dressed on pastry boats filled with mushroom purée; lobster sauce mixed with truffle julienne served separately.

— **Charlotte** (cold): fillets, folded, poached, chilled, dressed on artichoke bottoms stuffed with froth of soft roes seasoned with grated horseradish, decorated with chervil leaves and lobster coral, glazed with aspic jelly.

— **Chauchat:** sole poached in white wine and fish stock, bordered with sliced boiled potatoes, covered with white wine sauce, glazed, garnished with fleurons.

— **Cherbourg:** rolled fillets, poached, garnished with ragoût of shrimps, poached bearded oysters and mussels, covered with shrimp sauce and glazed.

— **Chevigné:** fillets coated with salmon forcemeat, folded, dipped in egg and breadcrumbs, fried in butter, garnished with creamed mushrooms flavored with Port; Béarnaise sauce served separately.

— **Chevreuse:** fillets coated with fish forcemeat and chopped herbs, folded, poached in white wine, covered with Béarnaise sauce mixed with tomato purée and the boiled down stock.

— **Chilian Style:** à la chilienne: fillets, poached, garnished with poached bearded oysters, covered with Creole sauce,

Sole

sprinkled with grated cheese, butter dropped on top and gratinated.

— **Chivry:** fillets, folded, poached, covered with Chivry sauce, garnished with fleurons.

— **Choiseul:** poached, covered with white wine sauce with julienne of white Italian truffles added.

— **Choisy:** fillets, poached, dressed on braised lettuce, covered with Mornay sauce mixed with mushroom julienne and glazed.

— **Circassian Style:** à la circassienne: fillets, arranged in a baking dish greased with butter, covered with cucumber slices, seasoned, moistened with white wine, melted butter dropped on top, baked in the oven.

— **Clara Ward:** fillets cut in strips, sautéd in butter with diced knob celery and artichoke bottoms, sprinkled with chopped herbs, browned butter poured over.

— **Claremont:** poached, covered with white wine sauce with diced tomatoes and chopped fine herbs added, garnished with halfmoon-shaped fried croûtons.

— **Clarence:** I. fillets, poached, garnished with soft roes and shrimps, covered with white wine sauce blended with anchovy butter.

II. fillets, poached, dressed on flat baked Duchess potatoes, covered with American sauce mixed with diced lobster, seasoned with curry; a slice of truffle on each fillet.

— **Claudine:** fillets, folded, poached in white wine with fine mirepoix, diced tomatoes and chopped herbs, stock boiled down and mixed with lobster purée; china cases filled with shrimps bound with this sauce, fillets dressed on top and covered with fish velouté blended with crayfish butter.

— **Cleopatra:** Cléopatre: boned, stuffed with creamed whiting forcemeat mixed with chopped truffles, covered with white wine sauce with julienne of truffles.

— **Colbert:** filleted on the upper side but fillets left attached to the fish at both ends. Fillets turned back from bone, coated with flour dipped in egg and breadcrumbs and shallow fried in butter, backbone removed through the opening with scissors, center filled with herb butter.

— **Colinette:** fillets coated with pike forcemeat with chopped herbs, folded, dipped in egg and breadcrumbs, deep fried, tomato sauce served separately.

— **Condé:** sole poached, covered with white wine sauce, a border of fresh tomato purée and a cross of purée in the centre, glazed.

— **Cornelin:** poached, covered with white wine sauce, chopped lobster coral and truffles scattered on top.

— **Countess Style:** à la comtesse: fillets, stuffed with fish forcemeat, folded, dipped in egg and breadcrumbs, deep fried, dressed on halved cooked tomatoes filled with salpicon of shrimps.

— **Crownprince Style:** à la dauphine: fillets, stuffed, folded, poached, chilled, coated with Villeroy sauce, dipped in egg and breadcrumbs, deep fried; tartar sauce mixed with diced tomatoes served separately.

— **Cubat:** sole, poached, dressed on mushroom purée, covered with Mornay sauce, glazed, truffle slices on top.

— **Dartois:** rectangular sheet of puff paste coated with fish forcemeat, folded fillet placed on top, covered with a

Sole

second sheet of puff paste, brushed with egg yolk and baked.

— **Daumier:** fillets, folded, poached, dressed on poached base of fish forcemeat mixed with rice, covered with Mornay sauce, glazed, border of Nantua sauce.

— **Daumont:** rolls, stuffed with fish forcemeat mixed with crayfish purée, poached in fish fumet, dressed on large mushroom stuffed with salpicon of crayfish, covered with Normandy sauce, garnished with stuffed crayfish heads and fried soft roes.

— **Deauville Style:** à la deauvillaise: poached with chopped onions and fish fumet stock boiled down with thick cream, beaten with butter, poured over the sole, garnished with fleurons.

— **Déjazet:** fillets dipped in egg and breadcrumbs, fried in butter, decorated with blanched tarragon leaves, covered with tarragon butter.

— **Desmoulin:** poached in white wine and fish stock with diced tomatoes, sliced mushrooms and chopped herbs, stock boiled down, beaten with butter and poured over the sole.

— **Devilled:** à la diable: grilled, devil sauce served separately.

— **Dieppe Style:** à la dieppoise: fillets poached in white wine, fish and mussel stock, garnished with bearded mussels and shrimps, covered with white wine sauce with reduced mussel stock.

— **Dieudonné:** poached in white wine with fish fumet, diced tomatoes, sliced mushrooms, chopped chervil and parsley, stock boiled down with cream, thickened with flour and butter and poured over the fish.

— **Dimitri:** fillets poached in white wine, covered with white wine sauce, garnished with anchovy strips and fish potatoes.

— **Diplomate:** poached in white wine and fish stock, covered with diplomat sauce, truffle slices on top.

— **Don Carlos:** fillets, folded, poached, alternately covered with white wine sauce with chopped truffles on top, and with tomato sauce with chopped mushrooms.

— **Doria:** coated with flour, fried in butter, garnished with olive-shaped pieces of cucumber simmered in butter, browned butter poured over the sole.

— **Dubarry:** fillets, poached, garnished with truffle slices and poached soft roes, covered with Mornay sauce, glazed, border of demi-glace beaten with lobster butter.

— **Dubois:** fillets, cut in strips, coated with flour, fried in butter, covered with Colbert sauce.

— **Duchess Alice:** large flat open puff pastry patty filled with ragoût of crayfish tails, mushrooms and diced sweetbreads in Nantua sauce, folded fillets poached in mushroom essence and white wine arranged on top with the points towards the center, covered with Dutch sauce mixed with the reduced stock, center filled with creamed morels.

— **Dugléré:** sole or fillets poached in white wine and butter with chopped shallots, diced tomatoes, parsley and seasoning, stock boiled down, mixed with fish velouté, beaten with butter, seasoned with lemon juice and poured over the fish.

Sole

— **Duke Style:** à la ducale: poached in dry champagne with fresh sliced truffles, stock boiled down with cream, mixed with Dutch sauce, poured over the fish, garnished with poached bearded oysters and pea-sized boiled potato balls tossed in butter.

— **Dumas:** poached, covered with white wine sauce, chopped herbs and diced tomatoes added.

— **Duperré:** poached in butter and lemon juice, covered with fish velouté mixed with the reduced stock, garnished with mushrooms, poached oysters and shrimps.

— **D'Urville:** fillets coated with fish forcemeat, folded, larded with truffles, poached in lemon juice and butter, placed on baked, boat-shaped Duchess potatoes, scooped out and stuffed with salpicon of shrimps in shrimp sauce.

— **Duse:** fillets, stuffed with fish forcemeat, folded, poached, filled in Savarin mould greased with butter, sealed with pilaf rice, turned out, covered with Mornay sauce, sprinkled with cheese, browned in oven, center filled with ragoût of shrimps in white wine sauce, chopped truffles scattered on top.

— **with Dutch Sauce:** à la sauce hollandaise: sole boiled in court-bouillon, covered with Dutch sauce, fish potatoes served separately.

— **Dutch Style:** à la hollandaise: sole poached in court-bouillon, served on serviette with parsley, melted butter and fish potatoes separately.

— **Edward:** Edouard: fillets marinated in Cognac, coated with flour, fried in butter, covered with white wine boiled down with chopped shallots, meat glace added, beaten with butter and anchovy paste, seasoned with lemon juice.

— **Egyptian Style:** à l'égyptienne: fillets cut in strips, poached in lemon juice and butter, filled in small china cases (cocottes) with sliced truffles, mushroom caps and tiny fish dumplings, covered with red wine sauce finished off with lobster butter.

— **Elisabeth:** fillets coated with fish forcemeat, folded, poached, dressed on artichoke bottoms, a slice of truffle and a mushroom cap on top, covered with Mornay sauce, sprinkled with Parmesan, dotted with butter and gratinated.

— **Embassy Style:** à l'ambassade: fillets poached in white wine and fish stock, garnished with lobster and truffle slices covered with white wine sauce, glazed, surrounded with a border of American sauce and fleurons.

— **Empress Style:** à l'impératrice: fillets stuffed and folded, poached, dressed on croûtons, covered with white wine sauce with truffle julienne, a poached bearded oyster on each fillet.

— **English Style:** à l'anglaise: fillets dipped in egg and breadcrumbs, fried in butter, herb butter on top.

— **Epicurian Style:** à l'épicurienne: poached in white wine, truffle stock and Madeira, stock boiled down, beaten with butter, mixed with chopped parsley, seasoned with anchovy paste and lemon juice.

— **Escoffier** (cold): fillets, one part coated with fish forcemeat and lobster purée, the other part with forcemeat and truffle purée, rolled into paupiettes and poached. When cold each paupiette cut in four slices, filled along the

Sole

sides of a mould lined with aspic jelly, alternating colors of paupiettes; mould filled with crayfish froth, sealed with aspic jelly, chilled, turned out, garnished with aspic jelly.

— **Etretat:** poached, covered with Nantua sauce, garnished with poached oysters, mushrooms, shrimps and sliced truffles.

— **Excelsior:** Paupiettes, poached covered with Normandy sauce with julienne of mushrooms, a slice of truffle on top, garnished with lobster ragoût Newburgh.

— **Farmer Style:** à la paysanne: poached in white wine and fish stock with chopped shallots and thin slices of root vegetables, stock poured of, boiled down, beaten with butter and poured over the fish, chopped parsley on top.

— **Fécamp Style:** à la fécampoise: fillets, poached in white wine and fish stock, garnished with bearded mussels and shrimps, covered with shrimp sauce, meat glaze dropped on top, surrounded with fleurons.

— **Fedorowna:** fillets stuffed with pike forcemeat, folded, poached, covered with Nantua sauce mixed with diced truffles, mushrooms and shrimps, garnished with shrimps and fried mussels.

— **with Fine Herbs:** aux fines herbes: poached in court bouillon, covered with herb sauce.

— **in Fish Stock:** sole poached in courtbouillon and white wine with thin strips of root vegetables, served in the stock with chopped parsley on top; Dutch sauce and melted butter served separately.

— **Floréal:** paupiettes stuffed with fish forcemeat, poached, dressed in small china cases on creamed asparagus tips, covered with white wine sauce beaten with green asparagus butter, a round slice of carrot and chervil leaf on top.

— **Florence Style:** à la florentine: fillets poached, dressed in baking dish greased with butter on spinach leaves tossed in butter, covered with Mornay sauce, sprinkled with grated cheese and glazed.

— **Fontainbleau:** fillets, poached, covered with shrimp sauce, garnished with asparagus tips and shrimps.

— **Foyot:** prepared like Bercy, meat glace added to sauce.

— **Francis Joseph:** François Joseph: fillets, coated with crayfish forcemeat, folded, poached, dressed on fried slices of eggplants, covered with Béarnaise sauce blended with tomato purée.

— **French Style:** à la française: poached in court-bouillon, covered with Béarnaise sauce mixed with tomato purée.

— **Fried:** frite: I. dipped in milk, coated with flour, deep fried, served with fried parsley and lemon.
II. sole or fillets dipped in egg and breadcrumbs, deep fried, served with fried parsley and lemon.

— **Fried:** dorée: III. sole coated with flour, fried in butter, garnished with sliced lemon, covered with browned butter.

— **Fried:** à l'Orly: fillets dipped in frying batter, fried in deep fat; tomato sauce served separately.

— **Friquet:** fillets, poached, dressed in baking dish on shredded lettuce simmered in butter, garnished with bearded oysters, covered with Mornay sauce with spinach julienne, chopped hard-boiled eggs scattered on top.

Sole
- **Gastronomer Style:** à la gastronome: fillets coated with truffle slices, mushrooms and shrimps, covered with white covered with Riche sauce, garnished with shrimps.
- **Geisha:** fillets, folded, poached, dressed on flat potato croquettes, covered with curry sauce, diced tomatoes and chopped parsley.
- **George Sand:** fillets, poached, garnished with small fish dumplings and crayfish tails, covered with Normandy sauce blended with crayfish purée.
- **Gismonda:** fillets, poached in fish stock and Port, stock reduced, thickened with cream and egg yolks, seasoned with Cayenne pepper, poured over the fish, garnished with fish potatoes.
- **Glazed:** sur le plat: poached in white wine and fishstock with chopped shallots in baking dish greased with butter, stock boiled down, beaten with butter, poured over fish and glazed rapidly.
- **Godard:** poached in white wine, dressed on dish edged with Duchess potato mixture and baked, garnished with truffle slices, mushrooms and shrimps, covered with white wine sauce beaten with lobster butter.
- **Gondolier:** à la gondolière: fillets, folded, poached, dressed on baked boats of Duchess potato mixture filled with salpicon of shrimps in shrimp sauce, covered with green herb sauce.
- **Gounod:** fillets coated with fish forcemeat, poached, garnished with bearded oysters and lobster slices, coverred with lobster sauce.
- **Gourmet:** I. poached in fish fumet, mushroom essence and Port, stock reduced, beaten with butter and poured over the fish.
  II. fillets cut in thick strips, fried in butter with thick mushroom and artichoke bottom strips, dressed in timbale dish with fried, olive-shaped potatoes, chopped parsley, lemon juice and browned butter on top.
  III. fillets poached in white wine and fish stock, stock boiled down, mixed with cream sauce and diced crayfish tails.
- **Grammont:** fillets, folded, poached in white wine, dressed on mushroom purée with chopped shallots, a slice of truffle and a bearded oyster on each fillet, covered with mushroom purée sprinkled with grated cheese, dotted with butter and gratinated; Dutch sauce served separately.
- **Grand-duchess:** Grand duchesse: fillets, folded, poached, garnished with sliced truffles and asparagus tips, coveed with Mornay sauce, glazed.
- **Grand-duke:** Grand-duc: fillets, folded, poached in mushroom essence and white wine, garnished with asparagus tips and crayfish tails, covered with Mornay sauce, sprinkled with grated cheese and glazed.
- **Grand Hotel:** fried, garnished with diced sautéd potatoes and artichoke bottoms, chopped parsley and a little meat glaze on top, covered with browned butter.
- **Gratinated:** au gratin: placed on baking dish greased with butter, masked with chopped shallots and gratin sauce, surrounded with sliced mushrooms and mushroom caps on top, covered with gratin sauce, sprinkled with breadcrumbs, dotted with butter, baked in oven.

Sole

— **Greek Style:** à la greque: fillets coated with flour, fried in oil, dressed on pilaf rice, tomato sauce mixed with diced red peppers poured around.
— **Grenoble Style:** prepared like red mullet.
— **Grilled:** grillée: sole coated with flour, brushed with oil, grilled, garnished with parsley and lemon.
— **Grimaldi:** fillets folded or paupiettes, poached in white wine, dressed on spaghetti in cream sauce, a slice of lobster and truffle on each paupiette, covered with Nantua sauce.
— **Grimod de la Reynière:** sole poached in white wine, garnished with shrimps, covered with Mornay sauce, blended with tomato purée, sprinkled with cheese and glazed.
— **Halévy:** fillets, poached in white wine, dressed in the center of a piped border of Duchess potatoes, covered alternately with white wine sauce with chopped truffles and Nantua sauce with chopped hard-boiled egg whites scattered on top.
— **Half-mourning:** demi-deuil: poached in white wine, covered with white wine sauce, a line of truffle slices placed on top.
— **Hamburg Style:** à la hambourgeoise: poached in white wine and fish stock, covered with white wine sauce with strips of knob celery, turnips and chopped parsley.
— **Havre Style:** à la havraise: fillets poached in white wine, covered with Bercy sauce, garnished with breaded fried mussels.
— **Hélèna:** Hélène: poached, dressed on bed of creamed noodles, covered with Mornay sauce, sprinkled with grated cheese, glazed.
— **Héloise:** prepared like Bercy with chopped mushrooms instead of shallots.
— **Horcher:** sole poached in Rhine wine, dressed on spaghetti mixed with butter, grated Parmesan and mushroom julienne, covered with white wine sauce mixed with cooked shredded lettuce, glazed.
— **Hotelkeeper Style:** à l'hôtelière: fried in butter, dressed on herb butter mixed with duxelles, dish bordered with lemon slices.
— **Housekeeper Style:** à la ménagère: poached in red wine with chopped shallots and herbs, stock thickened with flour and butter.
— **Housewife Style:** bonne-femme: placed on sliced or chopped mushrooms, chopped shallots and parsley, poached in white wine and fish stock; stock boiled down, beaten up with butter, poured over the fish, glazed.
— **Hungarian Style:** à la hongroise: poached in white wine and butter with chopped onions and diced tomatoes, covered with paprika sauce.
— **Imperial Style:** à l'impériale: sole poached, garnished with poached soft roes and crayfish tails, covered with white wine sauce with julienne of truffles, surrounded with fleurons.
— **Indian Style:** à l'indienne: stuffed with fish forcemeat seasoned with curry, poached, covered with creamed curry sauce; rice separate.
— **Infante Style:** à l'infante: poached, dressed on mushroom purée, covered with Mornay sauce, sprinkled with grated cheese, glazed.

Sole

— **Ismailia:** fillets, folded, poached in butter and fish stock, dressed on pilaf rice mixed with diced red peppers and green peas, covered with the boiled down stock beaten with butter.

— **Jackson:** sole poached in court-bouillon, garnished with small onions, covered with cream sauce, sprinkled with chopped parsley, surrounded with fleurons.

— **Jean Bart:** fillets, folded, poached, arranged like a crown and covered with Normandy sauce, center filled with ragoût of mussels, mushrooms and shrimps in cream sauce, surrounded with mussels in half shell, coated with Mornay sauce, sprinkled with grated cheese and glazed.

— **Joan:** Jeannette: fillets coated with fish forcemeat finished off with gooseliver purée, folded, poached, covered with white wine sauce, a slice of truffle on each fillet. Served hot or cold.

— **Joinville:** fillets, folded, poached, arranged like a crown with a slice of truffle on each fillet, covered with Joinville sauce, center filled with ragoût of truffles, mushrooms, shrimps and small dumplings in the same sauce.

— **Joseph:** fillets arranged in baking dish greased with butter on chopped onions, sliced tomatoes, crushed garlic and chopped parsley on top, seasoned, moistened with white wine, sprinkled with breadcrumbs, melted butter poured over, baked in oven.

— **Josette:** fillets, poached, placed on shredded lettuce and sliced carrots simmered in butter and mixed with cream sauce, covered with cream sauce and glazed.

— **Jouffroy:** poached in white wine with sliced mushrooms, covered with white wine sauce, glazed, garnished with tiny puff pastry patties filled with asparagus tips, a slice of truffle on each patty.

— **Judic:** fillets, folded, poached in lemon juice and butter, dressed on braised halved lettuces, garnished with small fish dumplings, covered with Mornay sauce, glazed, border of meat glaze.

— **Juggler Style:** à la jongleur: fillets, coated with salmon forcemeat, poached, dressed on oval pastry shells filled with diced artichoke bottoms and mushrooms in fish velouté, fillets covered with the same sauce.

— **Jules Janin:** poached in Rhine wine with mirepoix bordelaise, dressed on duxelles mixed with chopped truffles, garnished with poached bearded mussels and crayfish tails, covered with turtle sauce finished off with crayfish purée, sliced truffles on top.

— **Kotchoubey:** fillets, folded, dipped in egg and breadcrumbs, fried in butter, dressed on pilaf rice; Dutch sauce mixed with white wine sauce, seasoned with Worcestershire sauce and Cayenne pepper served separately.

— **Lacharme:** prepared like Bercy without parsley, garnished with truffle slices.

— **Lady with Camellias:** Dame aux camélias: fillets cut in strips, poached, bound with paprika sauce seasoned with mango chutney, dressed on artichoke bottoms, a truffle slice and a shrimp on top, surrounded with white wine sauce.

— **Lady Egmont:** fillets, poached in white wine with sliced mushrooms, garnished with green asparagus tips, stock

Sole

reduced with cream, beaten with butter, poured over the fillets and glazed.

— **Lady Hamilton:** poached, covered with Venetian sauce mixed with chopped olives, garnished with anchovy strips.

— **Laguipierre:** fillets, poached, covered with white wine sauce, tiny truffle cubes scattered on top.

— **Lavallière:** fillets coated with truffled fish forcemeat, folded, poached, dressed on border of poached fish forcemeat, covered with Normandy sauce, a slice of truffle on each fillet, center of border filled with ragoût of crayfish tails, mushrooms, bearded oysters and soft roes in Normandy sauce.

— **Leghorn Style:** à la livournaise: dressed in baking dish on tomatoes concassées with chopped onions and garlic, moistened with a little white wine, sprinkled with breadcrumbs, a litte oil poured over, baked in oven, lemon juice and chopped parsley on top at serving.

— **Leopold:** fillets, folded, poached, half of them covered with lobster, the other with Geneva sauce, chopped truffles on the shrimp and chopped lobster coral on the Geneva sauce, garnished with shrimps bound with white wine sauce.

— **Little-duke:** petit duc: poached in white wine and fish stock with sliced mushrooms, a slice of truffle on each fillet, covered with the reduced stock mixed with white wine sauce, glazed, garnished with bunches of asparagus tips.

— **Livonian Style:** à la livonienne: fillets coated with fish forcemeat mixed with chopped mushrooms and truffles, folded, poached in white wine and fish stock with julienne of fennel and parsley root, stock reduced, beaten with butter, poured over the fish and glazed.

— **Loie Fuller:** fillets, poached in white wine, covered alternately with white wine, shrimp and green herb sauce.

— **Londonderry:** fillets, coated with crayfish forcemeat, folded, poached, covered with fish velouté beaten with anchovy butter, garnished with bearded mussels and mushrooms.

— **Louis XV.** poached, covered with white wine sauce, chopped coral scattered on top, garnished with halfmoon-shaped truffle slices.

— **Louisette:** poached in court-bouillon, covered with cream sauce, garnished with diced boiled potatoes bound with Nantua sauce.

— **Louisiana:** fillets fried in butter, covered with diced fried bananas, red peppers and diced tomatoes, browned butter poured over the fillets.

— **Lutèce:** fried in butter, dressed on buttered spinach leaves, covered with sliced fried artichoke bottom and fried onion rings, bordered with slices of boiled potatoes, browned butter and a little lemon juice on top.

— **Lydia:** fillets, poached, garnished with shrimps and asparagus tips, covered with white wine sauce, glazed, garnished with fleurons.

— **Macon Style:** à la mâconnaise: fillets, poached in red wine, garnished with small onions and mushrooms, covered with red wine sauce, garnished with heart-shaped croûtons.

Sole

— **Manchester Style:** boiled sole covered with shallot sauce.

— **Manon:** paupiettes, dressed in center of piped ring of prebaked Duchess potato mixture, paupiettes covered with white wine sauce with chopped herbs, center filled with asparagus tips mixed with julienne of mushrooms and truffles tossed in butter.

— **Marcadet:** fillets, poached in white wine, and mussel stock, covered with white wine sauce mixed with the reduced stock, garnished with fried bearded mussels, mushrooms filled with purée of sea-urchins and small fried gudgeons.

— **Marcanton:** fillets, coated with truffled fish forcemeat, folded, poached in butter and a little maraschino, stock boiled down and mixed with Dutch sauce, poured over fillets, garnished with fried seafood.

— **Marcel Prévost:** sole, poached in white wine, dressed on mushroom purée, covered with Mornay sauce, sprinkled with grated Parmesan and glazed.

— **Marcelle:** fillets coated with truffled fish forcemeat, a slice of truffle on each folded fillet, poached in butter and lemon juice, dressed on pastry boats filled with soft roe purée.

— **Margaret:** Marguerite: poached in white wine, covered with white wine sauce, a line of truffle slices on top.

— **Margarete Devillier:** poached dressed on tomatoes concassées, covered with Mornay sauce, chopped truffles added, sprinkled with grated cheese, glazed.

— **Marguery:** poached in fish fumet and white wine, garnished with bearded mussels and shrimps, covered with white wine sauce, glazed, surrounded with fleurons.

— **Marie Louise:** I. fillets, poached in white wine and mushrooms essence, covered with mousseline sauce colored with spinach purée, dressed in border of piped duchess potatoes, sprinkled with chopped truffles, glazed. II. whole sole, stuffed with fish forcemeat mixed with chopped truffles and mushrooms, poached, one half covered lengthwise with white wine and the other with Italian sauce, garnished with fried gudgeons.

— **Marie Stuart:** fillets, folded, poached, covered with Newburgh sauce garnished with round flat fish dumplings decorated with truffle slices.

— **Marigny:** sole coated with flour, fried in butter, dressed on tomatoes concassées, garnished with small puff pastry tartlets filled with diced blanched ox marrow in Bercy sauce.

— **Mariner Style:** à la marinière: prepared like Marguery, chopped herbs, mushrooms and oysters added, not glazed.

— **Marinette:** fillets, coated with thick Béchamel sauce mixed with grated Parmesan and seasoned with Cayenne pepper, poached, when cold coated with Villeroy sauce, dipped in egg and breadcrumbs, deep fried, served with fried parsley and lemon.

— **Marlaise, Blanquette of Sole:** fillets, cut in thick strips, poached in mushroom essence and white Burgundy, mixed with sliced truffles, crayfish tails and mushrooms, bound with the reduced stock thickened with eggs and cream, seasoned with Cayenne pepper, finished off with meat glaze and butter; Creole rice served separately.

Sole

— **Marquise:** fillets, folded, poached, arranged like a turban on dish bordered with piped duchess potatoes mixed with tomato purée and prebaked, center filled with shrimps, truffles and fish dumplings, ragoût and fillets covered with shrimp sauce.

— **Marseille Style:** à la marseillaise: cooked in oven in baking dish with chopped onions, garlic, saffron, diced tomatoes, oil and a little white wine; chopped parsley on top at serving.

— **Marshal Style:** à la maréchale: fillets, dipped in melted butter and white breadcrumbs mixed with chopped truffles, fried in butter, a slice of truffle on each fillet, garnished with asparagus tips.

— **Mascotte:** fillets, folded, fried in butter, garnished with fried olive potatoes, diced artichoke bottoms and truffle olives, Colbert sauce on top.

— **Mathilda:** Mathilde: poached in white wine, covered with white wine sauce blended with white onion purée, garnished with olive-shaped cucumber pieces simmered in butter.

— **Maurice:** fillets, garnished with bearded mussels and shrimps, covered with shrimp sauce, glazed, border of fish glaze.

— **Meissonier:** poached, covered with white wine sauce with chopped herbs, sprinkled with chopped parsley.

— **Messaline:** fillets poached in champagne and fish stock, stock boiled down, mixed with tomato purée, beaten with butter, poured over, garnished with quartered artichoke bottoms, dipped in frying batter and deep fried.

— **Metternich:** fillets, poached in white wine and fish stock, covered with paprika sauce mixed with the reduced stock, garnished with sliced truffles.

— **Mexican Style:** à la mexicaine: fillets, folded, poached, dressed on large mushrooms filled with tomatoes concassées, covered with cream sauce blended with tomato purée mixed with diced red peppers.

— **Mignon:** poached in court-bouillon, covered with Portuguese sauce.

— **Mignonette:** fillets cut lengthwise in halves, sautéd in butter, dressed in timbale dish with pea-sized potato balls fried in butter, slices of fresh truffles on top, covered with meat glaze beaten with butter and seasoned with lemon juice.

— **Miller Style:** à la meunière: sole coated with flour, fried in butter, chopped parsley and lemon juice on top, covered with browned butter.

— **Minerva:** poached in fish stock with diced tomatoes, chopped onions and shallots, covered with anchovy strips and sliced boiled potatoes, the reduced stock beaten with butter poured over.

— **Mirabeau:** I. poached in butter and white wine, one half covered with white wine sauce, decorated with anchovy fillets, the other half covered with Geneva sauce decorated with tarragon leaves.
II. fillets fried in anchovy butter, garnished with anchovy strips and blanched tarragon leaves.

— **Miramar:** fillets cut in thick strips, sautéd in butter, dressed alternately on rice with slices of shallow fried egg plant, covered with browned butter.

Sole
- **Mireille:** prepared like Colbert, opening filled with Béarnaise sauce made with olive oil, sole surrounded with tomatoes concassées in oil with garlic and chopped herbs.
- **Miromesnil:** poached in white wine and fish stock with shredded lettuce, julienne of truffles and diced tomatoes, stock boiled down and beaten with butter.
- **Miroton:** fillets poached in white wine and chopped shallots, dressed on mushroom purée, stock boiled down with cream, beaten with butter, poured over the fillets, sprinkled with breadcrumbs, dotted with butter, baked in oven.
- **Mogador:** fillets coated with fish forcemeat, folded, decorated with truffle slices, poached, dressed in border of poached fish forcemeat filled with Nantua garnish, surrounded with stuffed crayfish bodies; Nantua sauce served separately.
- **Moïna:** I. fillets folded, fried in butter, arranged like a crown, center filled with morels and pieces of artichoke bottoms in cream sauce. Pan deglaced with Port, meat glaze added, beaten with butter, poured over the fillets. II. sole poached, covered with Chambord sauce mixed with diced morels and artichoke bottoms.
- **Monaco:** fillets, poached, covered with white wine sauce blended with tomato sauce with chopped herbs, garnished with poached bearded oysters and croûtons.
- **Moncey:** poached, covered with mussel sauce, tomatoes concassées in the center of sauce.
- **Montalban:** fillets, coated with flour, shallow fried, dressed on purée of artichoke bottoms, covered with browned butter.
- **Monte Carlo:** fillets, coated with flour, fried in butter, capers, anchovy essence and browned butter on top.
- **Montespan:** fillets, poached in white wine and fish stock with sliced mushrooms and chopped herbs, stock reduced beaten with butter, poured over fillets.
- **Montgolfier:** poached, covered with white wine sauce, julienne of mushrooms, carrots and truffles added, garnished with fleurons.
- **Montreuil:** poached, garnished with small round boiled potatoes. Sole covered with white wine sauce, potatoes with shrimp sauce.
- **Montreux:** fillets, poached, garnished with sliced boiled potatoes and truffles, covered with Mornay sauce and glazed.
- **Montrouge:** fillets, folded, poached, arranged like a turban, center filled with sliced mushrooms in cream sauce, fillets covered with cream sauce mixed with mushroom purée.
- **Mornay:** poached in white wine and fish stock, placed in baking dish on Mornay sauce, covered with Mornay sauce, sprinkled with grated Parmesan, dotted with butter and glazed.
- **Murat:** fillets cut in strips, sautéd in butter, dressed with sautéd diced potatoes and artichoke bottoms, sprinkled with chopped parsley, lemon juice and meat glaze on top, covered with browned butter.
- **with Mushrooms:** aux champignons: poached in white wine and mushroom essence with sliced mushrooms,

Sole

covered with white wine sauce mixed with the reduced stock.

— **with Mussels:** aux moules: poached in court-bouillon, garnished with bearded mussels, covered with mussel sauce.

— **My Dream:** mon rêve: fillets, coated with fish forcemeat, folded, poached in mushroom essence and white wine, dressed on pilaf rice mixed with diced green peppers and tomatoes, half a scampi on each fillet, covered with mousseline sauce finished off with the reduced stock and scampi butter.

— **Nantua:** poached in fish stock and mushroom essence, garnished with crayfish tails, covered with Nantua sauce, sliced truffles on top.

— **Naples Style:** à la napolitaine: fillets, poached, dressed on macaroni mixed with butter and grated cheese, covered with Mornay sauce, sprinkled with grated Parmesan and glazed.

— **Narragansett:** fillets, poached, covered with shrimp sauce, garnished with clams.

— **National:** fillets, poached, covered alternately with white wine, white wine with pistachio purée and Nantua sauce.

— **Nelson:** fillets poached in white wine, covered with Mornay sauce and glazed, garnished with poached soft roes and tiny potato dumplings.

— **Nemours:** fillets, stuffed, folded, poached, arranged like a crown with a slice of truffle on each fillet, covered with shrimp sauce, center of crown filled with mushrooms, soft roes and fish dumplings bound with Normandy sauce, the crown surounded with tiny shrimp croquettes.

— **Newburgh:** poached, garnished with lobster and truffle slices, covered with Newburgh sauce.

— **Nice Style:** à la niçoise: grilled, lemon slices and capers on top, garnished with tomatoes concassées in oil with a little garlic, anchovy butter poured around.

— **Normandy Style:** à la normande: prepared like salmon.

— **Offémont:** poached in fish stock with chopped shallots, stock boiled down and blended with white wine sauce and cream, garnished with creamed morels and olive shaped pieces of truffles.

— **Opera:** poached in court-bouillon, covered with white wine sauce, garnished with asparagus tips and truffles.

— **Oriental Style:** à l'orientale: I. poached, covered with Newburgh sauce flavored with curry; pilaf rice served separately.

II. small soles or fillets poached in white wine and oil with diced tomatoes, saffron, bay leaf, fennel, garlic, coriander and pepper corns, served cold in stock garnished with lemon slices.

— **Orléans Style:** fillets, coated with fish forcemeat, folded, poached, dressed in china cases on salpicon of crayfish tails, mushrooms and truffles, covered with shrimp sauce, decorated with a slice of truffle and a small shrimp.

— **Ostende Style:** à l'ostendaise: fillets stuffed, folded and poached in oyster liquor and butter, decorated with truffle slices, covered with Normandy sauce, garnished with bearded oysters and small sole croquettes.

— **Otéro:** fillets, folded, poached, dressed on baked potatoes, scooped out and filled with shrimp salpicon, covered

Sole

with Mornay sauce, sprinkled with cheese and glazed.

— **with Oysters:** aux huîtres: poached in white wine and oyster liquor, covered with white wine sauce with poached bearded oysters mixed with the reduced stock.

— **Paillard:** prepared like Bercy, sauce mixed with meat glaze, garnished with morels sautéd in butter, whole crayfish and heart-shaped croûtons.

— **Palace Hotel:** raw tomato and mushroom slices placed on sole, poached in white wine with chopped shallots and tarragon, stock reduced, flambéd with cognac, beaten with butter, poured over sole and glazed.

— **Palestine:** fillets wrapped round a stuffed crayfish body, poached, covered with white wine sauce mixed with diced crayfish tails, garnished with croûtons.

— **Palestrina:** poached in white wine, dressed on spaghetti mixed with truffle and mushroom julienne bound with Mornay sauce, covered with white wine sauce, shredded lettuce added, sprinkled with grated Parmesan, dotted with butter, glazed, surrounded with fleurons.

— **Parisian Style:** à la parisienne: I. poached, sliced truffles and mushroom caps on top, covered with white wine sauce, garnished with whole crayfish.
II. poached in court-bouillon, garnished with mushroom caps, one half of the fish covered with white wine and the other half with shrimp sauce, border of meat glaze.

— **Parmentier:** fillets, folded, poached, dressed on scooped out, baked potatoes, covered with Mornay sauce and glazed.

— **Patty:** Pâté de soles: mould lined with hot-water paste, coated with fish forcemeat, filled alternately with forcemeat, sole fillets, raw oysters, truffles, mushrooms and shrimps, forcemeat as the last layer; a little melted butter poured on top, sealed with paste, decorated, egg washed and baked. Served hot, white wine sauce separately.

— **Paul Bert:** poached in white wine and fish stock, covered with white wine sauce blended with Béarnaise sauce and tomato purée.

— **Perroquet:** fillets, folded, poached, covered with Mornay sauce, glazed, garnished with round croûtons, scooped out, filled alternately with poached bearded oysters, mussels, shrimps, and tiny fish dumplings covered with white wine sauce.

— **Peter the Great:** Pierre-le-Grand: poached, covered with white wine sauce, one half dusted with chopped ham, the other with chopped truffles, glazed.

— **Picardy Style:** à la picarde: prepared like Marguery, truffle slices and bearded oysters added, but not glazed.

— **Piccadilly:** poached in white wine with chopped tarragon and shallots, stock reduced, finished off with brandy and Worcester sauce, beaten with butter.

— **Polignac:** poached, covered with creamed white wine sauce, julienne of truffles and mushrooms added.

— **Pompadour:** fillets, dipped in melted butter and breadcrumbs, grilled, a slice of truffle on each fillet, a thread of Béarnaise sauce with a little meat glaze between the fillets, garnished with Parisian potatoes.

Sole

— **Portuguese Style:** à la portugaise poached, covered with white wine sauce, tomatoes concassées mixed with sliced mushrooms and chopped parsley around.

— **Pratt:** fillets, poached in fish stock and very dry French vermouth, stock reduced and mixed with white wine sauce, garnished with mushroom caps, sauce poured over the fillets.

— **Pretty Helena:** Belle Hélène: poached in red wine, covered with red wine sauce, truffle slices on top, garnished with small pastry shells filled with poached soft roes in paprika sauce.

— **Prince Style:** à la princière: fillets, poached, covered with Nantua sauce with diced truffles added, glazed, truffle slices on top.

— **Princess Style:** à la princesse: poached, covered with white wine sauce blended with asparagus butter, garnished with duchess potatoes in nest-shape filled with asparagus tips, a slice of truffle on top.

— **Provencal Style:** à la provençale: poached in white wine and fish stock, covered with Provencal sauce, sprinkled with chopped parsley, garnished with tomatoes Provencal.

— **Queen Style:** à la reine: poached, covered with creamed fish velouté, garnished with truffle slices and small fish dumplings.

— **Rabelais:** poached, covered with Normandy sauce, chopped lobster eggs scattered on top.

— **Rachel:** fillets, stuffed with truffled fish forcemeat, folded, poached in butter and mushroom essence, covered with white wine sauce with diced truffles and asparagus tips added.

— **Rangoon Style:** fillets marinated in lemon juice, mustard oil, chopped shallots, cinnamon and powdered coriander, sautéd in mustard oil, dressed in timbale dish with sliced fried bananas, chopped parsley sprinkled on top; mango chutney, melted butter and plain boiled rice served separately.

— **with Ravigote Sauce:** fillets, dipped in egg and breadcrumbs, fried in deep fat, dressed with fried parsley and lemon; ravigote sauce served separately.

— **in Red Wine:** au vin rouge: poached in red wine and fish stock, covered with the stock thickened with butter-paste and beaten with butter.

— **Regency Style:** à la régence: prepared like salmon.

— **Réjane:** fillets, poached in white wine, covered with white wine sauce beaten with crayfish butter, garnished with baked rosettes of duchess potatoes.

— **Remy Martin:** poached in butter, fish stock, mirepoix bordelaise and cognac Remy Martin, garnished with mushroom caps, covered with the reduced stock beaten with butter, tomatoes concassées around.

— **Renaissance:** poached, covered with white wine sauce, garnished with carrots, green peas, turnips, cauliflower, asparagus tips and round boiled potatoes.

— **Renoir:** paupiettes, poached in champagne, dressed on halved Calville apples, poached, scooped out and filled with mushroom purée, covered with Dutch sauce mixed with the reduced stock, chopped truffles scattered on top.

— **Rhodesia:** paupiettes, poached, dressed on lobster slices, covered with creamed American sauce.

Sole

— **Rich Style:** à la riche: poached, garnished with diced truffles and crayfish tails, covered with Nantua sauce, slices of truffles on top.

— **Richelieu:** prepared like Colbert, shallow fried in butter, opening filled with herb butter with sliced truffles on top.

— **Richemberg:** poached in court-bouillon, bearded oysters on top, covered with cream sauce seasoned with powdered thyme, bayleaf and mixed with chopped parsley.

— **Riviera:** fillets cut in strips, sautéd in butter, mixed with thick julienne of mushrooms and artichoke bottoms sautéd in butter, dressed in timbale dish with tomatoes concassées on top, covered with lemon juice and browned butter.

— **Robert:** poached, garnished with bearded mussels, covered with Robert sauce.

— **Rochele Style:** à la rochelaise: poached in red wine, garnished with bearded mussels, oysters and soft roes, covered with the reduced stock mixed with demi-glace beaten with butter.

— **Roman Style:** à la romaine: fillets poached in white Italian wine and fish stock, served on baking dish filled with macaroni mixed with shredded spinach, butter, grated Parmesan and chopped anchovy fillets; covered with cream sauce mixed with the reduced stock, sprinkled with cheese and gratinated.

— **Romulus:** poached in fish stock, red wine and mushroom essence, stock thickened with butterpaste, blended with anchovy butter, capers added, garnished with small pastry tartlets alternately filled with artichoke purée, tomatoes concassées and pea-sized sautéd potatoes.

— **Rosalie:** fillets shallow fried in nut oil with chopped shallots, onions, sliced mushrooms and a little garlic, sprinkled with chopped parsley.

— **Rose Caron:** fillets poached in white wine, half of them covered with shrimp sauce, chopped truffles added, the other half with white wine sauce finished off with pistachio butter.

— **Rosine:** fillets, poached in white wine, covered with white wine sauce blended with tomato purée, garnished with small tomatoes stuffed with fish forcemeat.

— **Rossini:** fillets, stuffed with fish forcemeat mixed with gooseliver purée, rolled to paupiettes, poached in white wine, covered with white wine sauce, chopped truffles scattered on top; garnished with tiny tartlet filled with the same forcemeat as above, poached and garnished with a truffle slice.

— **Royal Style:** à la royale: poached in fish fumet and butter, garnished with sliced truffles, crayfish tails, mushrooms and small fish dumplings, covered with Normandy sauce, surrounded with small boiled potato balls.

— **Russian Style:** à la russe: poached in white wine and fish stock with zig-zag sliced carrots, turnips, sliced onions and parsley leaves, stock reduced, beaten with butter and seasoned with lemon juice.

— **Saint-Cloud:** poached, covered with white wine sauce, a diagonal line of tomato sauce on top, garnished with fried mussels.

— **Saint-George:** fillets, stuffed with lobster forcemeat, folded, poached, dressed on scooped out baked potatoes

Sole

filled with lobster ragoût, covered with Bercy sauce, glazed.

— **Saint-Germain:** fillets, dipped in melted butter and breadcrumbs, fried in butter, Béarnaise sauce between the fillets, garnished with Parisian potatoes.

— **Saint-Michel:** fillets, stuffed with fish forcemeat, gooseliver purée added, folded, poached, dressed on buttered green peas, covered with Nantua sauce mixed with diced crayfish tails.

— **Salisbury:** fillets, folded, poached, dressed on pilaf rice, covered with white wine sauce with diced lobster and truffles.

— **Sappho Bernardt:** poached, covered with green herb sauce, julienne of carrots and truffles added.

— **Savoy:** poached in white wine, mushroom and truffle essence and fish stock, a line of mushroom caps on top, garnished alternately with bunches of asparagus tips and tomatoes concassées, stock boiled down, beaten with butter, poured over and glazed.

— **Scotch Style:** à l'écossaise: poached in white wine with fine brunoise of vegetables, covered with Dutch sauce mixed with the boiled down stock and brunoise.

— **with Shrimps:** aux crevettes: poached, garnished with shrimps, covered with shrimp sauce.

— **Sicilian Style:** à la sicilienne: fillets, stuffed with fish forcemeat mixed with anchovy paste and chopped hard-boiled eggs, folded, dipped in egg and breadcrumbs, deep fried, garnished with tomatoes concassées and diced sautéd potatoes, covered with melted butter.

— **Spanish Style:** à l'espagnole: fillets, fried in butter, dressed on tomatoes concassées, garnished with fried onion rings and fried julienne of green peppers.

— **Spring Style:** à la printanière: fillets, folded, poached in fish stock and butter, covered with cream sauce beaten with green herb butter, garnished with shaped spring vegetables and asparagus tips tossed in butter.

— **Sullivan:** fillets, stuffed, folded, poached, garnished with asparagus tips, covered with Mornay sauce, glazed, a truffle slice on each fillet.

— **Sully:** fillets, dipped in egg and breadcrumbs, deep fried, served with lemon and fried parsley; Béarnaise sauce and anchovy butter served separately.

— **Sultan Style:** à la sultane: fillets, poached, covered with white wine sauce beaten with pistachio butter, a half moon-shaped truffle slice on each fillet, garnished with puff pastry patties filled with shrimps in shrimp sauce.

— **Stettin Style:** à la stettinoise: poached, covered with Dutch sauce blended with salmon butter, garnished with tiny puff pastry patties filled with creamed purée of smoked salmon.

— **Sylvette:** fillets, folded, poached in fish fumet and Sherry with diced mushrooms, truffles and vegetable brunoise, stock boiled down, creamed, beaten with butter and poured over the fillets, garnished with small tomatoes stuffed with sole purée, sprinkled with cheese and glazed.

— **Taillevent:** poached in white wine, dressed on hashed creamed morels, covered with Mornay sauce, glazed, garnished with tartlets filled with purée of salted cod flavored with garlic.

Sole

— **Talleyrand:** fillets, folded, poached, dressed on spaghetti in cream sauce mixed with truffle julienne, coated with white wine sauce, glazed, a slice of truffle on each fillet.

— **Talma:** fillets, coated with flour, fried in butter, covered with sautéd diced potatoes, mushrooms, artichoke bottoms, capers and chopped parsley, browned butter and a little meat glaze poured on top.

— **Tanagra:** fillets coated with truffled salmon forcemeat, poached, dressed in a large flat pastry shell on ragoût of morels, asparagus tips and crayfish tails bound with Dutch sauce, fillets covered with Normandy sauce, a little crayfish butter dropped on top.

— **Tenant Style:** à la fermière: I. poached in white wine and fish stock with thin slices of root vegetables, stock boiled down with cream, beaten with butter and poured over the fish.
II. poached in red wine and chopped shallots, stock thickened with butter paste, poured over the fish, garnished with sliced sautéd mushrooms.

— **Theodora:** fillets, poached, covered alternately with white wine sauce, white wine sauce with chopped truffles scattered on top, Venitian and Nantua sauce.

— **Thermidor:** poached, covered with Bercy sauce seasoned with mustard, bordered with meat glaze.

— **Tolstoi:** fillets, cut in thick strips coated with flour, deep fried, white wine sauce served separately.

— **Tosca:** fillets, poached in white wine, a poached soft roe on each fillet, covered with white wine sauce blended with crayfish purée, garnished with flat salmon dumplings, half a crayfish tail and a slice of truffle on top, covered with Mornay sauce beaten with crayfish butter, glazed.

— **Tout-Paris:** fillets, poached in white wine, alternately covered with white wine and shrimp sauce.

— **Traviata:** coated with flour, fried in butter, garnished with fried tomatoes filled with salpicon of crayfish tails.

— **Trois-Frères:** poached, one half covered with white wine sauce with chopped truffles and parsley, the other half with white wine sauce, border of tomato sauce over both sauces.

— **Troubetzkoi:** paupiettes, poached in champagne, dressed on pastry shells filled with purée of soft roes, covered with luke warm Dutch sauce blended with the reduced stock and a little caviar.

— **Trouville Style:** à la trouvillaise: prepared like Fécamp style.

— **Urbain Dubois:** poached, covered with very little Mornay-sauce mixed with diced truffles and crayfish tails, topped with crayfish soufflé mass, baked in oven.

— **d'Urville:** fillets, stuffed, folded, larded with truffles, poached, covered with American sauce, garnished with pastry boats filled with crayfish tails in crayfish sauce.

— **Valentine:** fillets, poached, dressed on sliced sautéd mushrooms, covered with browned butter.

— **Valentino:** fillets, folded, poached, covered with Mornay sauce, glazed, served on flat potatoe croquettes stuffed with risotto mixed with diced white Italian truffles.

— **Valois:** I. poached, covered with white wine with Béarnaise reduction.

Sole Valois
II. poached in fish stock and white wine, garnished with poached soft roes, boiled olive-shaped potatoes and whole crayfish, covered with Valois sauce.
— **Van den Berg:** poached, covered with white wine sauce mixed with diced mushrooms, tomatoes and chopped herbs.
— **Vanderbilt:** fillets, folded, prepared like salmon.
— **Vatel:** I. fillets, poached, covered with Chambord sauce, garnished with pieces of cucumber, scooped out and stuffed with fish forcemeat, and fried sole strips.
II. poached, garnished with truffle slices and soft roes, covered with crayfish sauce with diced crayfish tails.
— **Vaucluse Style:** à la vauclusienne: coated with flour, shallow fried in olive oil, chopped parsley and lemon juice on top, covered with the oil in which the fish was fried.
— **with Vegetable Salad:** à la jardinière (cold): fillets, folded, poached, pared, when cold dressed in border mould lined with aspic jelly and decorated with truffles and red peppers, sealed with aspic jelly, chilled, turned out on round silver dish, center filled with vegetable salad.
— **Venetian Style:** I. à la venetienne: poached, covered with Venetian sauce.
II. Belle Venice: fillets, folded, poached, when cold coated with Villeroi sauce mixed with grated Parmesan, dipped in frying batter, deep fried; Venetian sauce served separately.
— **Verdi:** fillets, poached, dressed on creamed macaroni mixed with diced lobster and truffles, covered with Mornay sauce, glazed.
— **Vernet:** poached, covered with Vernet sauce.
— **Véron:** fillets, dipped in melted butter and breadcrumbs, fried in butter, dressed on Véron sauce.
— **Veronika:** Veronique: poached in fish stock and a little Curaçao, garnished with peeled pitted grapes, covered with the reduced stock beaten with butter, glazed.
— **Victor Hugo:** poached, covered with white wine sauce blended with tomato purée, mixed with diced truffles, mushrooms and chopped tarragon.
— **Victoria:** fillets or whole sole, poached, garnished with diced truffles and spiny lobster, covered with Victoria sauce, glazed.
— **Viennese Style:** à la viennoise: fillets, marinated in lemon juice, oil, chopped herbs and onions, dipped in egg and breadcrumbs, shallow fried, garnished with fried parsley and lemon.
— **Villeroi:** fillets, stuffed, poached, coated with Villeroi sauce, dipped in egg and breadcrumbs, deep fried; tomato sauce served separately.
— **Virgin Style:** à la vierge: poached, covered with virgin sauce, sprinkled with chopped tarragon and chervil.
— **Virginia:** fillets, folded, poached, served on baked, scooped out potatoes filled with salpicon of crayfish tails, covered with Mornay sauce, glazed.
— **Walewska:** fillets, poached in fish fumet, half a langoustine or scampi tail, cut lengthwise, and two truffle slices on each fillet, covered with Mornay sauce, glazed.
— **Walkyrie:** fillets, poached, garnished with lobster and truffle slices, covered with white wine sauce; American sauce served separately.

Sole

— **Washington:** fillets, shallow fried in butter, dressed with lobster slices on top, covered with American sauce, julienne of truffles scattered on top.

— **in White Wine:** poached in white wine, covered with white wine sauce, the reduced stock added.

— **White Friars Style:** à la carmélite: boned, stuffed with fish forcemeat mixed with crayfish purée, poached in white wine, decorated with truffle slices, covered with fish velouté blended with crayfish butter, garnished with small puff pastry patties filled with salpicon of crayfish tails.

— **Wilhelmine:** fillets, folded, poached, dressed on baked, scooped out potatoes filled with creamed diced cucumbers, a bearded oysters on each fillet, covered with Mornay sauce, glazed.

— **Windsor:** poached in fish stock, lemon juice and mirepoix, covered with oyster sauce finished off with purée of soft roes.

— **Wine-merchant Style:** marchand de vin: poached in red wine, butter and chopped shallots, stock reduced, beaten with butter and meat glaze.

— **Xenia:** fillets, stuffed with thick duxelles, folded, coated with Mornay sauce, wrapped in puff pastry, eggwashed, baked in oven; oyster sauce served separately.

— **Yvette:** poached in white wine, covered with green herb sauce, garnished with small tomatoes stuffed with fish purée cooked in the oven.

Spiny Lobster: see crawfish.

Squid: F. Calmar; G. Kalmar. Saltwater mollusc found off the Atlantic coast and in the Mediterranean. Before preparation the upper side must be carefully opened for the removal of the ink-sack.

— **Braised:** braisé: tentacles shallow fried in butter with onion slices, braised with white wine, chopped anchovies, garlic and parsley, stock reduced and mixed with tomato sauce.

— **Housekeeper Style:** à la ménagère: tentacles blanched and skinned, shallow fried in oil, stewed with chopped onions, fennel, diced tomatoes, saffron and summer savory, when done mixed with boiled rice.

— **Sailor Style:** en matelote: tentacles cut in pieces, shallow fried in oil with chopped onions, garlic, diced tomatoes and bunch of herbs added, moistened with white wine, cooked, stock reduced, mixed with white wine sauce, garnished with mushrooms and buttor onions, sprinkled with chopped parsley.

Sterlet: F. Sterlet, petit esturgeon; G. Sterlet; I. storioncello; S. esturion, R. sterlett. Migratory fish found in American lakes, the Pacific coast, the Caspian and Black Seas. The sterlet is the smallest member of the sturgeon family.

— **in Champagne:** au champagne: poached in champagne, fish stock and mushroom essence, covered with Dutch sauce blended with the reduced stock, garnished with crayfish tails, mushrooms and truffles.

— **Demidoff:** bay sterlet poached in white wine and the pickle of pickled cucumbers with chopped fennel and knob celery, stock mixed with meat gravy, thickened with butter-paste, garnished with crayfish tails, mushrooms, truffles and olives.

— **Grilled:** grillé: fillets, dipped in melted butter and bread-crumbs, grilled, garnished with fried parsley and lemon; tartar sauce served separately.

Sterlet

— **Latvian Style:** à la lithuanienne: fillets, poached in white wine, covered with anchovy sauce, garnished with rice croquettes seasoned with Cayenne pepper.

— **Mabillon:** poached in white wine, fish stock and mushroom essence, covered with Dutch sauce blended with the reduced stock and crayfish butter, garnished with dumplings of truffled fish forcemeat.

— **Mariner Style:** à la marinière: poached in fish and mussel stock, garnished with bearded oysters, mussels and shrimps, covered with mariner's sauce.

— **Moldavian Style:** à la moldavienne: cooked in white wine and sunflower oil with fried sliced onions, diced tomatoes, garlic, sliced lemons, lemon juice and chopped parsley; served cold.

— **Monastry Style:** po monastrirski: fillets, lightly fried in butter, arranged in fireproof dish covered with sliced mushrooms and surrounded with slices of boiled potatoes, covered with sour cream, sprinkled with breadcrumbs and grated Parmesan, dotted with butter and baked in the oven. (Russian)

— **Orloff:** poached in white wine, fish stock, mushroom essence and cucumber pickle, garnished with cucumbers shaped like little barrels, stuffed with fish forcemeat and simmered in butter, stuffed olives, stuffed crayfish heads, mushrooms and vesiga. (Russian)

— **Petrograd Style:** fillets, poached in white wine, covered with American sauce, garnished with sautéd yellow boletus, small carrots, olive-shaped cucumbers, crayfish tails and fleurons.

— **Polish Style:** à la polonaise: poached in white wine and fish stock with julienne of root vegetables, fennel and sliced onions, stock thickened with butter-paste, garnished with button onions and small boiled potato balls.

— **porowi:** poached in fish stock, white wine and mushroom essence, stock thickened with butter-paste, seasoned with lemon juice and Cayenne pepper, garnished with crayfish tails and mushrooms; grated horseradish served separately. (Russian)

— **po russki:** poached in white wine, fish stock and mushroom essence, stock boiled down with tomato purée and gravy, thickened with butter-paste and poured over the fish; garnished with fancy sliced carrots, parsley roots and knob celery, thick strips of mushrooms and pickled cucumbers, peeled lemon slices, olives and grated horseradish. (Russian)

— **rassol:** poached in white wine, fish stock and cucumber pickle, stock thickened with butter-paste, garnished with stuffed cucumbers, mushrooms, stuffed crayfish heads and vesiga. (Russian)

— **Russian Style:** à la russe: I. baby sterlet placed in fireproof dish greased with butter, surrounded with sliced boiled potatoes, moistened with fish stock, sprinkled with breadcrumbs and grated Parmesan, dotted with butter, baked in the oven; sliced slightly salted cucumbers served separately.

II. poached in white wine, cucumber pickle and butter with chopped parsley and chopped knob celery, stock thickened with butter-paste, chilled, mixed with chopped

Sterlet
hard-boiled egg yolks and caviar, poured over the cold fish, garnished with aspic jelly and grated horseradish.
— **Tsarina:** à la czarine: medaillons, poached, dressed on tartlets filled with chopped truffles and chopped hard-boiled eggs in paprika sauce, covered with caviar sauce.
— **Turtle Style:** en tortue: larded with anchovy strips, braised in white wine with aromatic herbs and pot herbs, covered with turtle sauce, garnished with mushrooms, olives, fish dumplings, gherkins and fleurons.

Stockfish: F. Morue séchée; G. Stockfish; I. Baccalà; S. Bacalao seco. Cod boned and dried in the air. Must be soaked in water for 24 hours before it is used.
— **Bénedictine:** prepared like salt cod.
— **Brandade,** creamed brandade, truffled brandade: prepared like salt cod.
— **Brasilian Style:** Bacalhao bahiana: boiled, covered with sauce made of chopped onions fried in oil, diced tomatoes, red peppers and fish stock added, garnished with manioc meal cooked in fish-stock with oil, tomatoes, salt and pepper, when cold cut in pieces and fried. (Brasilian)
— **with Butter:** au beurre fondu: poached in milk, melted butter and fish potatoes served separately.
— **with Caper Sauce:** à la sauce câpres: boiled, served with caper sauce.
— **Cartusian Style:** à la chartreuse: oval or round mould lined with slices of boiled carrots and turnips, filled with boiled flaked stockfish bound with cream sauce and egg yolks, poached in water-bath, turned out, chopped mushrooms scattered on top, surrounded with cream sauce.
— **Citizen Style:** à la bourgeoise: poached in milk, boned, simmered in butter with chopped onions, covered with breadcrumbs fried in plenty of butter, served with saurkraut.
— **Dutch Style:** à la hollandaise: boiled, served with boiled potatoes and melted butter.
— **English Style:** prepared like salt cod.
— **with Garlic:** à l'ail: boiled, flaked, simmered in oil with crushed garlic and chopped parsley.
— **in Garlic Sauce:** à la Mithridate: boiled, flaked, bound with cream sauce flavored with garlic, sprinkled with grated cheese, gratinated.
— **with Honey:** Bacalao con miel: cooked, flaked, mashed, made into a stiff dough with flour, honey, saffron, salt and pepper, cut into squares, turned in flour, shallow fried in oil. (Spanish)
— **Indian Style:** à l'indienne: boiled, flaked, covered with curry sauce, plain rice served separately.
— **Madrid Style:** Bacalao Madrilena: boiled, flaked, simmered in oil and lemon juice with diced tomatoes, pine-kernels, chopped parsley and spices. (Spanish)
— **Marseille Style:** Brandade à la marseillaise: poached, flaked, mashed with fresh boiled potatoes, mixed with chopped stewed onions, crushed garlic and nutmeg, beaten with oil and milk like mayonnaise.
— **with Onions:** aux oignons: boiled, flaked, covered with onions fried in butter, fish potatoes served separately.
— **with Peas:** aux petits pois: boiled, flaked, mixed with green peas, tossed in butter and thick cream, sprinkled with chopped parsley.

Stockfish

— **with Peas Spanish Style:** Bacalao con guisantes: boiled, flaked, bound with sauce made of fried garlic and chopped parsley, sprinkled with flour, moistened with water, seasoned with pepper and bay leaf; mixed with cooked peas. (Spanish)

— **Provencal Style:** à la provençale: boiled and flaked, mixed with chopped onions sweated in oil, capers, diced tomatoes, black olives, crushed garlic and chopped parsley, simmered in oil.

— **Roman Style:** à la romaine: boiled, flaked, simmered in oil with chopped onions, parsley, garlic and diced tomatoes.

— **with Sorrel:** à l'oseille: boiled, flaked, bound with cream sauce, dressed on sorrel leaves simmered in butter, sprinkled with grated cheese, glazed.

— **Soufflé with Truffles:** Soufflé aux truffles: boiled, flaked, mashed, seasoned, bound with thick Béchamel sauce and egg yolks, mixed with stiffly beaten egg whites, filled in greased soufflé dish alternately with sliced truffles, baked in the oven.

— **Spanish Style:** Bacalao español: boiled, garnished with quarters of hard-boiled eggs, green beans and potatoes, olive oil poured on top. (Spanish)

— **Swedish Style:** à la suédoise: fireproof baking dish greased with butter, lined with thin slices of bread, filled alternately with layers of flaked boiled stockfish mixed with fried onions and herring fillets, covered with cream, sprinkled with grated cheese, bake in the oven.

— **Viennese Style:** à la viennoise: cut in pieces, boiled, skinned and boned, covered with fried onions and breadcrumbs fried in butter, browned butter poured over.

— **Viscaina:** boiled, flaked, dressed in baking dish on tomatoes concassées mixed with chopped onions, garlic and chopped parsley, sprinkled with grated Parmesan, moistened with oil, baked.

Striped Bass: F. Bar rayé; G. gestreifter Barsch. A native of the Atlantic coasts of the United States, also found in the Pacific. Small fish best fried in butter, larger fish prepared like halibut.

Sturgeon, Common Sturgeon: F. Esturgeon; G. Stör; I. Sturione; S. Esturion; R. Ossetrina. Salt and fresh-water fish found in almost all seas, on the Pacific coast, the Caspian and Black Seas, the rivers Rhine, Vistula, Weser, Elbe, Oder and Garrone. Sturgeon roe yields very good caviar.

— **Citizen Style:** à la bourgeoise: thick slices poached in fish stock with butter and sliced root vegetables, bunch of herbs and sliced onions, covered with sauce made of the reduced stock thickened with butter-paste, served with German fried potatoes.

— **Finnish Style:** Ossetrina Findlandskaïa: slices simmered in butter, dressed on buckwheat gruel mixed with chopped mushrooms sautéd in butter, covered with Smitane sauce, sprinkled with grated Parmesan, dotted with butter, glazed, decorated with anchovy strips. (Russian)

— **Greek Style:** à la grecque: escalopes cooked in parboiled and strained stock of white wine, oil, vinegar, lemon

Sturgeon
slices, parsley sprigs, fennel and pepper corns, served cold in part of the stock sprinkled with chopped herbs.
— **Italian Style:** à l'italienne: steaks prepared like sole.
— **Normandy Style:** large piece, poached in white wine and fish stock, prepared like sole.
— **Perronet:** steaks, sprinkled with flour, brushed with oil, grilled, dressed on sautéd mushroom slices; Beauharnais sauce served separately.
— **Provencal Style:** à la provençale: steaks larded with anchovy strips, marinated in oil and lemon juice, sautéd in oil with diced tomatoes, chopped onions and a little garlic, moistened with white wine and white stock, braised, stock reduced, mixed with capers and chopped parsley and poured over the fish.
— **Tsarina:** à la czarine: steaks poached in white wine and fish stock, garnished with mushrooms, sliced yellow boletus, slices of bulb fennel and pickled cucumbers, covered with Mornay sauce, sprinkled with grated Parmesan, glazed.

Sturgeon, Great: F. Grand esturgeon; G. Hausen; R. Beluga. The largest member of the sturgeon family, salt and fresh-water fish found in the Caspian and Black Seas, Volga, Ural and Danube. Its roe yields the „Beluga malossol" caviar, the marrow is known as „Vesiga" and largely used for culibijaka. Cut into cutlets and prepared like common sturgeon.

Sudak: Russian pike-perch found in nearly all Russian rivers. Prepared like pike-perch, also marketed smoked.
— **po russki:** scored, poached in white wine, fish stock and mushroom essence, arranged in baking dish with pickled cucumbers cut in thick strips, sliced mushrooms, crayfish tails and oysters, moistened with a little stock, covered with browned breadcrumbs, dotted with butter, baked in the oven; remaining stock boiled down, beaten with butter and served separately. (Russian)
— **po ruski na skoworodke:** in pans: fillets, arranged in baking dish, covered with thin slices of boiled potatoes and pickled cucumbers, dusted with flour, moistened with fish stock, sprinkled with grated cheese and breadcrumbs, dotted with butter, baked in the oven. (Russian)

Surmullet, Common Surmullet: F. Muge, mulet cabot; G. Meerbarbe. Saltwater fish found mainly in the Mediterranean and off the French Atlantic coast. Prepared like sea bass.

Swordfish: F. Espadon, Empereur; G. Schwertfish. Saltwater fish found in the Atlantic, Pacific and Mediterranean. Weight up to 400 1b, marketed fresh and salted.
— **Boatman Style:** à la batelière: escalopes prepared like haddock.
— **with Browned Butter:** au beurre noisette: steaks poached in court bouillon, browned butter poured on top.
— **in Cream Sauce:** à la sauce crème: fillets poached in butter and lemon juice, covered with cream sauce, garnished with fish potatoes.
— **Delphi:** fillets coated with flour, shallow fried, garnished with cucumber pieces stuffed with duxelles and small broiled tomatoes, capers and chopped parsley scattered over the fish, browned butter and lemon juice on top.
— **Dieppe Style:** à la dieppoise: prepared like sole fillets.

Swordfish

— **English Style:** à l'anglaise: escalopes prepared like cod.

— **Florence Style:** à la florentine: fillets poached in fish stock and white wine, arranged in buttered baking dishes on leaf spinach sautéd in butter, covered with Mornay sauce, sprinkled with grated cheese, dotted with butter and browned in oven.

— **Genoa Style:** à la génoise: escalopes poached in red wine, garnished with mushrooms, crayfish tails and poached soft roes, covered with Genoese sauce.

— **Turkish Style:** à la turque: small square pieces fixed on skewers alternately with bay leaves, brushed with oil, broiled and served on Creole rice; hot sauce made of tomato purée flavored with onion juice and garlic, beaten up with oil served separately.

T

Tancaud: see Atlantic cod.

Tench: F. Tanche; G. Schleie; I. Tinca. Freshwater fish. Used for matelotes, can also be prepared like trout.

— **in Beer:** à la bière: browned in butter, simmered in pale beer with chopped sweated onions, parsley and knob celery, stock thickened with gingerbread, seasoned and finished with butter.

— **Blue:** au bleu: prepared like all fish au bleu, served with melted butter, grated horseradish and fish potatoes.

— **Broiled:** grillée: scored, coated with flour, brushed with oil, broiled; ravigote sauce served separately.

— **in Cream Sauce:** à la crème: placed in baking dish greased with butter masked with chopped shallots and very little garlic, moistened with white wine, simmered in oven, when half done fresh cream poured over to finish cooking; served in baking dish.

— **in Dillsauce:** au sauce aneth: cooked au bleu, covered with fish velouté blended with a little Dutch sauce and mixed with chopped dill.

— **Fried:** frite: cut in pieces, dipped in egg and breadcrumbs fried in deep fat; lettuce salad and ravigotte sauce served separately.

— **Green:** au vert: chopped shallots, parsley, sorrel, spinach, dill, chervil and tarragon sweated in butter, fish placed on top, moistened with fish stock and a little white wine, cooked, stock thickened with egg yolks and cream, seasoned with lemon juice and poured over the fish.

— **Housewife Style:** à la bonne-femme: poached in white wine with chopped shallots, sliced mushrooms, chopped parsley and a pinch of sweet basil, stock thickened with flour and butter.

— **Italian Style:** à l'italienne: poached in fish stock and white wine, covered with Italian sauce.

— **in Paper Bag:** en papillote: prepared like trout.

— **in Parsley Sauce:** persilée: poached in butter and lemon juice with chopped shallots and parsley sprigs, stock reduced, mixed with fish velouté and chopped parsley and poured over the fish; fish potatoes served separately.

— **with Peas:** aux petits pois: dipped in egg and breadcrumbs, shallow fried in butter, served with green peas tossed in butter, with breadcrumbs browned in butter poured on top.

Tench
— **with Sage:** à la sauge: placed in baking dish greased with butter and a few fresh sage leaves on the bottom, seasoned, moistened with cream, simmered in oven and basted with the cream.
— **Silesian Style:** à la silésienne: poached in white wine and fish stock with julienne of root vegetables, stock thickened with egg yolks and cream, seasoned with lemon juice, chopped parsley added.
— **Stuffed:** farcie: stuffed with pike forcemeat, poached in white wine, butter and lemon juice with chopped shallots, mushrooms and parsley, stock boiled down and blended with German sauce.
— **Tyrolese Style:** à la tyrolienne: fried in butter, dressed on tomatoes concassées, covered with Tyrolese sauce, garnished with fried onion rings.

Terrapène: see terrapin.

Terrapin: F Terrapène; G. Terrapine. Small sea turtle found on the Atlantic coast of the Southern States of the U.S.A.
— **Baltimore:** cooked in salt water with spices, cut in pieces, meat simmered in browned butter, stock added, thickened with potato starch, seasoned with Cayenne pepper, flavored with Sherry and lemon juice.
— **in Chafing Dish:** parboiled, cut in pieces, tossed in nut butter, seasoned with freshly ground pepper, Cayenne pepper and salt, cream added, reduced, thickened with blended egg yolks, cream and Sherry.
— **Fricassee:** en fricassée: parboiled, cut in pieces, simmered in white stock with onions, bouquet garni, lemon peel, bayleaves and spice, stock thickened with white roux, boiled down with white wine, strained, thickened with egg yolks and flavored with lemon juice. Meat arranged in small china or silver dish with button mushrooms, morels and crayfish tails covered with the sauce, garnished with fleurons.
— **Jockey Club:** prepared like Maryland, brandy and sliced truffles added.
— **in Madeira:** au madère: parboiled, cut in pieces, seasoned with freshly ground pepper, Cayenne pepper and salt, moistened with demi-glace, stewed and flavored with Madeira.
— **Maryland:** cooked in salt water with spice, meat cut in pieces, stewed in Sherry and butter, seasoned with Cayenne pepper, thickened with egg yolks and cream.

Trout: F. Truite; G. Forelle; I. Trota; S. Trucha. One of the finest species of the salmon family found in many countries. Varieties are: lake trout, river trout, rainbow trout, brook trout. Fish hatcheries maintain a constant supply of live brook trout.
— **Astronomer Style:** à l'astronome: boiled in court-bouillon, covered with Italian sauce, garnished with pieces of eggplants stuffed with Duxelles, sprinkled with grated cheese and gratinated.
— **Blue:** au bleu: poached in salt water with vinegar added when fish is freshly killed; served with melted butter or Dutch sauce and fish potatoes separately.
— **Bordeaux Style:** poached in white wine with chopped shallots, covered with Bordeaux sauce.

Trout

— **Burgundy Style:** à la bourguignonne: poached in red wine, dressed with glazed button onions and mushrooms, covered with the red wine thickened with butterpaste.

— **Café de Paris:** arranged in fire proof dish on chopped shallots and parsley, seasoned, covered with a little white wine and fish stock, butter dotted on top, cooked in the oven.

— **Cambacérès:** fillets of large trout larded with strips of truffles and carrots, coated with forcemeat of pike and crayfish, re-shaped, wrapped in thin slices of fat bacon, braised in white wine with slices of onions and carrots, bacon taken off, stock reduced, mixed with white wine sauce and finished off with crayfish butter. Fish dressed on platter, garnished with fried morels, soft roes, sliced truffles and pitted olives, covered with the sauce.

— **in Champagne:** au champagne: poached in champagne, stock reduced, mixed with fish velouté, buttered, poured over the skinned fish and glazed.

— **in China Cases:** en caisses: fillets cut in thick strips, fried in butter, dressed in china cases on tomatoes concassées mixed with sliced mushrooms, covered with Italian sauce, sprinkled with grated cheese and breadcrumbs, dotted with butter and gratinated in the oven.

— **Cleopatra:** à la Cléopatre: prepared like Miller's style, garnished with shrimps, fried soft roes and capers.

— **Courtier Style:** à la courtisane: stuffed with herb forcemeat, poached in white wine, covered with fish velouté, garnished with potato croquettes.

— **Doria:** prepared like Miller style, garnished with oval shaped pieces of cucumber cooked in butter.

— **Fried:** frite: small trout dipped in egg and breadcrumbs, deep fried; mayonnaise or Tartar sauce served separately.

— **Froth:** Mousse de truites: forcemeat of boiled trout, seasoned, mixed with unsweetened whipped cream and aspic jelly, filled in mould lined with aspic jelly and decorated, sealed with aspic jelly, turned out when set and garnished with aspic jelly.

— **Gautier:** small fish dipped in egg and breadcrumbs, fried in butter, a little white wine sauce poured on both sides.

— **Gavarni:** wrapped in paper bag with herb butter, baked in the oven, served in the paper bag with fish potatoes separately.

— **Grandduke:** grand-duc: prepared like brill fillets.

— **Hotel-keeper Style:** à l'hôtelière: opened from the back, bones removed, dipped in melted butter and white breadcrumbs, fried in butter, filled with herb-butter mixed with Duxelles, garnished with slices of lemons.

— **Hussar Style:** à la hussarde: boned, stuffed with fish forcemeat mixed with chopped stewed onions, poached in white wine, covered with white wine sauce mixed with onion purée and glazed.

— **Jeanne d'Arc:** fillets, coated with flour fried in butter, dressed on flat rice croquettes, garnished with ragoût of oysters, mussels, crayfish tails and mushrooms in crayfish sauce, covered with crayfish sauce.

— **Maître d'hôtel:** fish scored, coated with flour, fried in butter, covered with herb butter.

— **Milanese Style:** à la milanaise: marinated in oil, lemon juice, salt and pepper, coated with flour, dipped in beaten

Trout
egg and breadcrumbs mixed with grated Parmesan cheese, fried in oil; Italian sauce served separately.
— **with Caper Sauce:** au gras: slices, simmered in white wine and butter with sliced onions, herbs and carrots, stock strained, thickened with butter-paste and mixed with capers and chopped gherkins.
— **Miller Style:** à la meunière: coated with flour, fried in clarified butter, chopped parsley and lemon juice on top, covered at the last minute with browned butter.
— **Mirabeau:** poached in white wine and fish stock, half of the fish covered with Geneva sauce, sprinkled with chopped tarragon, the other half covered with white wine sauce and sprinkled with chopped truffles.
— **in Paper Envelope:** en papillote: seasoned with salt, pepper and lemon juice, wrapped in paper envelope, greased with butter, chopped shallots added, baked in oven and served in the envelope.
— **Rachel:** fillets folded and poached in white wine, covered with white wine sauce mixed with diced truffles and asparagus tips.
— **in Red Wine:** au vin rouge: poached in red wine and fish stock, stock boiled down, thickened with roux, poured over the skinned fish and glazed.
— **Romanow:** cooked in court-bouillon, covered with Mousseline sauce with chopped anchovy fillets, garnished with lemon slices.
— **Russian Style:** à la russe: cooked in court-bouillon, covered with cream or Dutch sauce mixed with caviar.
— **Saint-Florentin:** stuffed with fish forcemeat mixed with chopped herbs, poached in white wine with chopped shallots, a bunch of herbs and spice, stock thickened with butterpaste and poured over the fish.
— **Swedish Style:** à la suédoise: boiled in court-bouillon, when cold glazed with aspic jelly, garnished with cucumbers and smoked salmon, cold horseradish sauce served separately.
— **Swimming:** à la nage: freshly killed trout cooked in court-bouillon in a table fish-kettle; melted butter and fish potatoes served separately.
— **Stuffed:** farcie: boned, stuffed with finely truffled fish forcemeat, wrapped in greased paper and grilled or baked in oven, garnished with sliced lemons; marinière sauce served separately.
— **Tyrolese Style:** à la tyrolienne: coated with flour, dipped in egg and breadcrumbs, deep fried, served with Tyrolese sauce.
— **Vaucluse Style:** à la vauclusienne: prepared like Miller style but with oil instead of butter.
— **Wallisian Style:** à la valaisienne: seasoned, poached in Dôle (a Swiss red wine) with chopped shallots and a bunch of herbs, skinned fish arranged on dish with button mushrooms on top, covered with the stock thickened with roux, chopped parsley sprinkled on top.

Truite: see trout.
— **arc-en-ciel:** Rainbow trout: see trout.
— **du lac:** see lake trout.
— **de rivière:** see trout.
— **saumonée:** see salmon trout.

Tunny-fish, Tunny, Tuna: F. Thon; G. Thunfish; I. Tonno; S. Atun. Giant salt water mackerel found chiefly in southern seas, specially in the Mediterranean. Sold only in pieces when fresh, mainly marketed canned in oil.
— **with Caper Sauce:** au gras: slices, simmered in white wine and butter with sliced onions, herbs and carrots, stock strained, thickened with butter-paste and mixed with capers and chopped gherkins.
— **Chioggiola:** cutlets simmered in oil with sliced onions, diced tomatoes, garlic and green peas. (Italian)
— **Fried:** frit: sliced, dipped in egg and breadcrumbs, deep fried, tartar sauce served separately.
— **Indiana:** steaks, larded with anchovy strips, marinated in white wine, chopped shallots and herbs, poached in the marinade with butter, fine mirepoix, saffron and curry powder, stock boiled down, blended with fish velouté; plain rice served separately.
— **Leghorn Style:** à la livournaise: steaks larded with anchovy strips, poached in white wine, Marsala wine, oil, chopped onions, diced blanched bacon, chopped ham and butter, served with the stock, garnished with crayfish dumplings covered with aurora sauce.
— **with Macedoine:** à la macédoine: slices, dipped in egg and breadcrumbs, fried in butter; vegetable macedoine and tartar sauce served separately.
— **Orly:** cut in small thin slices, marinated with lemon juice, oil, salt and pepper, dipped in frying batter, deep fried; tomato sauce served separately.

Turbot: F. Turbot; G. Steinbutt; I. rombo; S. rodaballo. Large saltwater flat fish resembling halibut but fuller, rounder and more delicate in flavor. Main fishing areas: France, England, Belgium, Holland and the Baltic.
— **Admiral Style:** à l'amiral: braised and prepared like sole.
— **Aida:** fillets prepared like sole Florence Style.
— **American Style:** à l'américaine: fillets or baby turbot prepared like sole.
— **Andalusian Style:** baby turbot placed on earthenware dish greased with butter, onions rings, slightly fried in butter, diced tomatoes, mushroom slices and strips of red peppers on top, sprinkled with breadcrumbs, dotted with butter, moistened with white wine and fish stock, braised in the oven.
— **Antoinette:** baby turbot boiled in court-bouillon, covered with cream sauce beaten with anchovy butter mixed with capers and shrimps.
— **Arlesian Style:** à l'arlésienne: baby turbot braised in white wine and fish stock, covered with Bercy sauce, glazed, garnished with halved fried tomatoes filled with fried onions.
— **Bayard:** fillets, poached in white wine and fish stock, garnished with lobster slices, mushroom caps and truffle slices, covered with lobster sauce.
— **Beauharnais:** cut in slices, boiled; Beauharnais sauce and fish potatoes served separately.
— **Boiled:** bouilli: large fish cut in slices of the desired size, baby turbot boiled whole. Appropriate sauces: Dutch, caper, lobster, shrimp, crayfish, mousseline, caviar, Venitian and melted butter. Fish potatoes are always served with boiled turbot.

Turbot

— **Boistelle:** fillets, prepared like sole.

— **with Browned Butter:** au beurre noir: thick slices, boiled, covered with browned butter with a few drops of vinegar; fish potatoes served separately.

— **Cambacérès:** braised in white wine, fish stock, truffle essence and mirepoix, covered with fish velouté mixed with the reduced stock, garnished with fried mussels, crayfish croquettes and fried mushrooms.

— **Chauchat:** fillets prepared like sole.

— **Daumont:** prepared like sole fillets.

— **Drunkard Style:** à la pocharde: boiled, one half covered with white wine sauce, the other half with red wine sauce.

— **Duchess Style:** à la duchesse: baby turbot, poached, dressed on platter surrounded with piped prebaked duchess potato mixture, covered with cream sauce.

— **Dugléré:** cut in slices, prepared like sole.

— **Dutch Style:** prepared like sole.

— **Embassy Style:** à l'ambassade: fillets prepared like sole.

— **Feuillantine:** stuffed with lobster mousseline forcemeat, poached in fish stock and white wine, dressed with the white side upwards, covered with Nantua sauce with truffle slices and bearded oysters on top; cream sauce blended with the boiled down stock and seasoned with Cayenne pepper served separately.

— **Florence Style:** à la florentine: fillets prepared like sole.

— **Francis I.:** François I.: fillets prepared like sole Dugléré sliced mushrooms added.

— **French Style:** à la française: baby turbot, braised, covered lengthwise on one side with white wine sauce and on the other with white wine sauce finished off with tarragon butter, garnished with puff pastry patties filled with mussels in poulette sauce, a slice of truffle on top, and whole crayfish.

— **Grilled:** grillé: baby turbot, slices or fillets, brushed with clarified butter, grilled, served with herb butter.

— **Halévy:** fillets prepared like sole.

— **Heligoland Style:** à la héligolandaise: slices, boiled, covered alternately with lobster, white butter and green herb sauce.

— **Hungarian Style:** à la hongroise: poached, covered with white wine sauce seasoned sharply with paprika; fish potatoes served separately.

— **Joan:** Jeanette: stuffed with leaf spinach tossed in butter, braised in fish stock and white wine, covered with Mornay sauce finished off with crayfish butter, glazed, garnished with puff pastry patties filled with crayfish salpicon.

— **Laguipierre:** poached, covered with Normandy sauce with diced truffles scattered on top, garnished with small potato croquettes and oyster shells filled with salpicon of shrimps and glazed.

— **Mirabeau:** poached, covered alternately with Geneva sauce, decorated with blanched tarragon leaves, and white wine sauce, decorated with truffle slices, anchovy fillets between the two sauces.

— **Montrouge:** fillets prepared like sole.

— **Olga:** paupiettes, poached in lemon juice and butter, dressed in baked potatoes, scooped out and filled with

Turbot
shrimp ragoût in white wine sauce, covered with Mornay sauce, glazed.
— **Ostende Style:** à l'ostendaise: prepared like sole.
— **with Oyster Sauce:** aux huîtres: boiled served with oyster sauce.
— **Polignac:** fillets, prepared like sole.
— **Prince of Wales:** Prince de Galles: I. braised, covered with white wine sauce seasoned with curry and finished off with crayfish purée; garnished with mussels and oysters Villeroi and rice croquettes.
II. braised, covered with Chambord sauce beaten with crayfish butter, garnished with poached bearded mussels, oysters and rice croquettes.
— **Queen Style:** à la reine: fillets prepared like sole.
— **Rachel:** fillets, prepared like sole.
— **Regency Style:** à la régence: prepared like salmon.
— **Reynière:** boned, stuffed with whiting forcemeat, poached in white wine and fish stock, center of fish garnished with mushrooms caps, on both sides poached soft roes interlaced with anchovy fillets; white wine sauce blended with white onion purée served separately.
— **Rostand:** poached in fish fumet and truffle essence with sliced yellow boletus and truffle julienne, stock reduced, beaten with butter, poured over the fish and glazed; garnished with puff pastry patties filled with salpicon of lobster in American sauce, tartlets filled with asparagus tips and fried whitebait.
— **Saint-Malo:** baby turbot, scored, brushed with oil, grilled, garnished with Parisian potatoes; Saint-Malo sauce served separately.
— **Sappho Salvatore:** poached, covered with green herb sauce mixed with julienne of truffle, knob celery and carrots.
— **Stuffed:** farci: fillets opened from dark side, backbones removed, stuffed with fish forcemeat, poached or braised in butter, white wine and fish stock, served with fish potatoes and sauce to taste.
— **Vatel:** fillets, poached, covered with Geneva sauce, garnished with deep fried sole strips dipped in breadcrumbs and pieces of stuffed stewed cucumbers.
— **Wine-merchant Style:** marchand de vin: slices, prepared like sole.
— **Wladimir:** baby turbot, poached, covered with creamed white wine sauce with vegetable strips, diced tomatoes and clams added.

Turbotin: see baby turbot.

Turtle: F. Tortue; G. Schildkröte; I. Tartaruga. Marine reptile. The best green turtles come from the West Indies, Florida and Cuba. Mainly used for making soup.
— **Braised:** braisée: parboiled in rich stock, braised in Madeira with sliced root vegetables, stock boiled down and mixed with demi-glace.
— **Financier Style:** à la financière: boiled in rich stock until half done, then braised in Madeira, garnished with cockscombs and cocks' kidneys, pitted olives, chicken dumplings, fluted mushrooms and truffle slices, covered with the stock boiled down and mixed with demi-glace.
— **Fried:** frite: parboiled in rich stock, cut in convenient pieces, dipped in frying batter, deep fried, served with

fried parsley and lemon; mayonnaise sauce served separately.

Turtle-flippers: F. nageoires de tortue; G. Schildkrötenflossen; I. Alette di tartaruga.

— **American Style:** à l'américaine: cooked in rich stock till nearly done, then braised in Madeira, covered with American sauce.

— **in Madeira Sauce:** à la sauce madère: parboiled in rich stock, braised in Madeira, stock thickened with arrow-root and poured over the flippers.

— **Maryland:** parboiled in rich stock, drained, shallow fried in butter, moistened with stock, boiled up, thickened with arrow-root, favored with Sherry.

V

Vive: see dragon fish.

Vraie limande: see lemon sole.

W

Waterzooi: see Fish-stew, Belgian.

Whitebait: F. Blanchaille; G. Weissfischchen. Very small white fish, probably a separate variety of the herring family, found in large numbers off the North Sea coast, in the Thames and along the American Atlantic coasts.

— **Devilled:** à la diable: coated with flour, crisp-fried in deep fat, seasoned with salt mixed with Cayenne pepper, served with lemon.

— **Fried:** frites: coated with flour, crisp-fried in deep fat, seasoned with salt and pepper, garnished with lemon.

— **Indian Style:** à l'indienne: deep fried, seasoned with salt and curry powder.

Whitefish: freshwater fish with numerous varieties found in the Great Lakes of America. Prepared like salmon trout and trout.

Whitefish: Fish of the species salmonidae found chiefly in the subalpine Swiss, upper Bavarian and Austrian lakes.
I. F. Féra; G. Felchen, Renke, Sandfelchen.
II. F. Bondelle; G. Silberfelchen.
III. F. Palée; G. Balchen.
Prepared like trout.

Whitefish: F. Lavaret; G. Renke, Felchen. One of the whitefish species found in French lakes. Prepared like trout.

— **American Style:** à l'américaine: stuffed with fish forcemeat, poached in butter and fish stock, covered with American sauce.

— **Basle Style:** à la bâloise: shallow fried in butter, covered with anchovy butter, fried onions rings and chopped parsley, browned butter poured on top.

— **Bavarian Style:** à la bavaroise: scored, shallow fried in butter, covered with diced tomatoes simmered with chopped sautéd onions, chopped parsley and herbs, lemon juice and browned butter on top.

— **Blue:** au bleu: boiled au bleu, fresh butter and fish potatoes served separately.

Whitefish

— **Brussels Style:** à la bruxelloise: fillets placed in baking dish well greased with butter, covered with sautéd mushroom slices, a few drops of white wine poured over, breadcrumbs and a little grated cheese sprinkled on top, baked in oven; chopped parsley on top at serving.

— **Doria:** fried in butter, peeled lemon slices on top, garnished with oval-shaped pieces of cucumber simmered in butter, browned butter poured over the fish.

— **English Style:** prepared like trout.

— **Grenoble Style:** à la grenobloise: shallow fried, garnished with sliced lemon, capers and chopped parsley scattered on top, browned butter poured over the fish.

— **Grilled:** grillé: scored, coated with flour, brushed with oil, grilled, garnished with parsley and lemon; Béarnaise sauce or herb butter served separately.

— **Hotelkeeper Style:** à l'hôtelière: opened from the back, bones removed, dipped in eggs and breadcrumbs, shallow fried in butter, dressed on herb butter mixed with dry duxelles, browned butter, chopped parsley and lemon slices on top.

— **Lucerne Style:** à la lucernoise: shallow fried in butter, covered with anchovy butter, chopped lightly fried onions, chopped tomatoes, capers and chopped herbs, browned butter on top.

— **Mascotte:** fillets poached in white wine and fish stock, filled in oval pastry shell, garnished with small fish dumplings and sliced truffles, covered with wine sauce.

— **Neuchâtel:** neuchâteloise: fillets poached in white wine and fish stock, stock boiled down with cream and poured over the fillets, garnished with branch spinach mixed with chopped anchovy fillets and small peeled tomatoes cooked in butter.

— **Piedmont Style:** à la piémontaise: fillets, coated with fish forcemeat mixed with chopped white Italian truffles, folded, poached in white wine and fish stock, stock reduced, beaten with butter and poured over the fish.

— **Polish Style:** à la polonaise: scored, shallow fried in butter, chopped parsley and chopped hard-boiled eggs scattered on top, breadcrumbs fried brown in plently of butter poured over the fish.

— **in Red Wine:** au vin rouge: simmered in red wine with a little meat glaze, seasoning and a bunch of herbs, stock boiled down, thickened with flour and butter, completed with anchovy butter and poured over the fish.

White Sea Bass: Pacific saltwater fish. Prepared like halibut.

Whiting, Silver Hake, Jack Salmon: F. Merlan; G. Weissling, Wittling. Saltwater fish found chiefly in the North Atlantic.

— **in Baking Dish:** au plat: poached in white wine and fish stock, chopped shallots added, stock reduced, beaten with butter, poured over the fish and glazed.

— **Bercy:** opened from the back, backbone removed, prepared like sole.

— **Binoculars:** en lorgnette: split from tail to head without detaching the fillets from head, backbone removed, each fillet rolled outward to form the shape of binoculars, dipped in milk, eggs and breadcrumbs, deep fried, served with fried parsley and lemon.

Whiting

— **Boulogne Style:** à la boulonnaise: cut in pieces, poached in fish stock and white wine, garnished with bearded mussels, covered with butter sauce blended with the reduced stock.

— **Cécilia:** fillets, fried in butter, garnished with asparagus tips, sprinkled with grated Parmesan, glazed.

— **Dieppe Style:** prepared like sole.

— **Dumplings with Onion Sauce:** Quenelles à la Soubise: mousseline forcemeat of whiting shaped with a table spoon, poached, covered with Soubise sauce, garnish to taste.

— **Dumplings in Puff Pastry Shell Cardinal:** Vol-au-vent de quenelles de merlan Cardinal: large open puff pastry patty filled with whiting mousseline dumplings, slices of spiny lobster and fluted mushrooms bound with Béchamel sauce finished off with lobster butter, decorated with truffle slices, a fluted mushroom cap in the center.

— **English Style:** à l'anglaise: prepared like smelt.

— **Enraged:** en colère: tail inserted in the mouth, dipped in egg and breadcrumbs, fried in deep fat; tomato sauce served separately.

— **Fisher Style:** des pêcheurs: poached in white wine and fish stock with chopped shallots, garnished with mussels, mushrooms and button onions, covered with the boiled down stock thickened with butter-paste, sprinkled with grated cheese, glazed.

— **Flemish Style:** à la flamande: poached in white wine and butter with chopped shallots and peeled lemon slices, stock thickened with cracker meal.

— **French Style:** à la française: fillets, coated with flour, deep fried, garnished with fried parsley and lemon; sauce to taste.

— **Gaditana:** tail inserted into the mouth, dipped in flour and beaten egg, fried in oil, garnished with fried parsley and lemon.

— **Gratinated:** au gratin: prepared like sole.

— **Grenoble Style:** prepared like red mullet.

— **with Herbs:** aux fines herbes: poached in white wine and fish stock, covered with herb sauce.

— **Jackson:** poached in white wine, fish stock and chopped shallots, stock reduced, mixed with white onion purée and chopped herbs, beaten with butter and poured over the fish, garnished with button onions, glazed, surrounded with fleurons.

— **Jeannine:** stuffed with fish forcemeat mixed with chopped herbs, poached in white wine, Madeira and fish stock, garnished with crayfish tails, sliced truffles, covered with the reduced stock beaten with butter, diced tomatoes added.

— **Jutland Style:** à la jutlandaise: fillets, marinated in oil, vinegar and chopped parsley, folded, dipped in frying batter, deep fried; Joinville sauce served separately.

— **Jutta:** fillets, fried in oil, tartar sauce served separately.

— **Medicis:** opened from the back, backbone removed, dipped in melted butter and breadcrumbs, fried flat in butter, garnished with small tomatoes, scooped out, grilled and stuffed with Béarnaise sauce.

— **Montreuil:** prepared like sole.

— **Nice Style:** à la niçoise: prepared like red mullet.

Whiting

— **Nilsson:** poached in white wine with chopped shallots, garnished with button mushrooms and stewed button onions, covered with white sauce mixed with chopped tarragon, glazed.

— **Riviera:** Côte d'azur: scored, poached in white wine, fish stock, meat glaze and lemon juice with diced tomatoes, chopped shallots, garlic, chopped herbs, sliced mushrooms, shredded lettuce and knob celery, served in the boiled down stock.

— **Tabellion:** paupiettes stuffed with fish forcemeat, poached in white wine, covered with Normandy sauce, chopped truffles scattered on top, garnished with fish dumplings.

— **Tyrolese Style:** à la tyrolienne: I. shallow fried in butter, covered with Tyrolese sauce, garnished with fried onion rings and tomatoes concassées. II. prepared like „enraged" withing; Tyrolese sauce served separately.

— **in White Wine:** au vin blanc: prepared like sole.

Wolf-fish: F. Loup marin; G. Seewolf. Saltwater fish found off the Atlantic coasts of Europe and North America.

— **Bellavista:** medaillons coated with flour, shallow fried in butter, arranged en couronne with a fried tomato slice on each medaillon, sprinkled with chopped parsley, covered with browned butter, oval-shaped pieces of cucumber simmered in butter in the center of the crown.

— **Bercy:** fillets prepared like sole fillets.

— **Berlin Style:** à la berlinoise: fillets poached in butter and lemon juice, garnished with white asparagus tips, morels and crayfish tails, covered with white wine sauce, meat glaze and crayfish butter dropped on top, surrounded with fleurons.

— **Borghese:** Fillet, stuffed with duxelles mixed with chopped parsley and grated Parmesan, folded, coated with flour, shallow fried in oil, seasoned with lemon juice, the frying oil mixed with browned butter poured over the fish.

— **Doria:** prepared like sole fillets.

— **Geneva Style:** à la génevoise: escalopes poached in red wine and chopped shallots, covered with Geneva sauce.

— **Houswifes Style:** fillets prepared like sole fillets.

— **Modern Style:** à la moderne: cutlets, poached, covered with Nantua sauce mixed with diced truffles and crayfish tails.

— **Valentino:** médaillons, poached in white wine and fish stock, dressed on baked tartlets of Duchess potato, scooped out, filled with risotto mixed with chopped Italian truffles, fish coated with Mornay sauce, sprinkled with grated cheese and glazed.

Garnishes

French: Garnitures
German: Garnituren
Italian: Guarnizioni
Spanish: Guarniciones

Garnishes are ingredients used to complete or to decorate a dish or to add eye-appeal. In classical cookery nearly all dishes are named after their garnishes. Many groups of garnishes are identified by special names, referring to countries, cities, trades, events or to persons more or less famous. The names of the various methods of preparation are decisive for the expert. To use classical names for dishes that do not conform to the generally known standard is not honorable. Unfortunately far-fetched or bombastic names are frequently given to mediocre dishes; the result is a disappointment for the guest. It is far better to name a simple garnish according to its ingredients than to use a classical name if the dish is not up to the generally accepted methods of preparation. This does, of course, not mean that only dishes with classical names should be served; new dishes with new names are invented nearly daily by creative chefs.
Complicated garnishes for large pieces of meat or poultry are better dressed separately to facilitate quick service. It is almost impossible to serve a dish hot if it is garnished with a great number of vegetables or other ingredients.
Where the name of the sauce is not mentioned in the text it is customary to serve the pan juice or the juice formed in roasting, the stock resulting from braising, thick veal gravy or browned butter according to the dish. For dishes garnished with vegetables tossed in butter or bound with cream sauce it is safer to serve meat glaze whipped with butter or thick veal gravy than demi-glace or other thick brown sauces.

A

Admiral: amiral: (for fish): bearded oysters and mussels Villeroy, large fluted mushrooms caps, truffle slices, Normandy sauce whipped with crayfish butter.

African: africaine (for fish): fried, garnished with sliced fried bananas, devil sauce.
(for butchers' meat) olive-shaped cucumbers und eggplants, yellow boletus, tomatoes cut in quarters, pips removed, all sautéd in oil, castle potatoes.

Agnès Sorel: (for poultry): small tartlets of chicken mousseline-forcemeat stuffed with sliced mushrooms, round slices of red ox tongue, German sauce.

Albertine: (for fish): poached, covered with white wine sauce with chopped mushrooms, truffles and parsley, garnished tomatoes concassées and asparagus tips.

Albuféra: (for poultry): stuffed with risotto mixed with diced truffles and goose-liver, garnished pastry tartlets filled with tiny chicken dumplings, small mushroom caps, cockscombs and truffle pearls bound with Albuféra sauce separately.

Alexandra (for fish): poached, truffle slices, Mornay sauce, glazed, garnished green asparagus tips.
(for poultry): truffle slices, Mornay sauce with truffle essence, glazed, garnished green asparagus tips.

Algerian: algerienne (for butchers' meat): small tomatoes simmered in oil, croquettes of sweet potatoes, light tomato sauce with julienne of sweet peppers.

Alhambra: (for butchers' meat): sautéd quarters of artichoke bottoms, sautéd tomatoes and very small green peppers.

Allemande: see German.

Alliance (for butchers' meat): small glazed onions and carrots, artichoke bottoms, demi-glace.

Alphonso: Alphonse (for butchers' meat): mushroom caps, artichoke bottoms, Madeira sauce.

Alsatian Style: à l'alsacienne (for butchers' meat): I. tartlets filled with saurkraut, a round slice of ham on top, demi-glace.
II. noodles tossed in butter, mixed with diced truffles and goose-liver.

Amazonian: amazone (for butchers' meat): tartlet-shaped lentil fritters scooped out, stuffed with morel and chestnut purée, hunter sauce.

Ambassador: ambassadeur (for butchers' meat): duchess potatoes, artichoke bottoms stuffed with mushroom puree, grated horseradish.

Ambassadress: ambassadrice (for tournedos and noisettes): chicken livers and mushrooms sautées, cockscombs and kidneys, braised lettuce, Parisian potatoes, deglaced with veal gravy and Madeira.
(for poultry): braised white, breasts cut out, caracass filled with buttered asparagus tips, carved breast arranged on top, covered with suprême sauce, garnished buttered green asparagus tips and lamb sweetbreads larded with truffles.

Amelia: Amélie (for fish): white wine sauce colored with tomato purée, garnished sliced truffles, mushrooms and small potato croquettes.

American: américaine (for fish): sliced lobster, American sauce.
(for poultry and butchers' meat): mais fritters, sliced fried sweet potatoes.

Ancient Style: à l'ancienne (for fish): poached, covered with white wine sauce with sliced mushrooms and white button onions, sprinkled with chopped parsley, garnished with heart-shaped croûtons.
(for poultry): white braised button onions and mushroom caps.

Andalusian: andalouse (for butchers' meat): half sweet peppers stuffed with rice Greek style, thick egg-plant slices, scooped out, fried, filled with tomatoes concassées sautéd in oil, small pork sausages (chipolatas), thick veal gravy.

Antoinette (for fish): poached, herb sauce whipped with anchovy butter, mixed with capers and diced shrimps.

Antwerp: anversoise (for butchers' meat): pastry shells filled with creamed hop shoots, boiled potatoes, tomato sauce.

Argenteuil (for fish): white wine sauce, asparagus tips.
(for butchers' meat): asparagus tips covered with Dutch sauce.

Arlesian: arlesienne (for tournedos and noisettes): sliced eggplants fried in oil, tomatoes concassées in oil, fried onion rings, demi-glace with tomato purée.

Armand (for butchers' meat): soufflé potatoes, red wine sauce garnished with truffle strips and diced sautéd goose liver.

Armenonville (for butchers' meat): I. Anna potatoes and creamed morels.
II. tomatoes concassées, French beans, olive potatoes, quarters of artichoke bottoms.

Artois (for tournedos and noisettes): tartlet-shaped potato croquettes filled with green peas, Madeira sauce.
(for poultry): glazed carrots and button onions, artichoke quarters sautéd in butter, the natural juice of the roast deglaced with Madeira, mixed with liquid meat glaze, whipped with butter.

Athenian: athénienne (for tournedos and noisettes): thick fried slices of eggplant stuffed with duxelles, Madeira sauce.

Auber (for poultry, tournedos and noisettes): artichoke bottoms stuffed with chicken purée, Madeira sauce.

Augusta (for fish): fillets poached in white wine with chopped shallots and sliced yellow boletus, covered with Mornay sauce, glazed.

B

Badish: badoise (for butchers' meat): braised red cabbage, potato purée and sliced bacon.

Bagration (for fish): fillets coated with fish forcemeat mixed with crayfish butter, poached, covered with fish velouté mixed with mushroom purée, glazed.

Bahama (fish): white wine sauce, shrimps, red pepper strips, turtle meat.

Baker Style: boulangère (for butchers' meat): sliced onions and potatoes sweated in butter, mixed, and baked together with the meat.
for poultry): olive-shaped shallow fried potatoes and glazed small onions.

Balzac (for fish): larded with truffles, crayfish sauce.
(for tournedos and noisettes): large chicken dumplings, olives stuffed with game purée, hunter sauce.

Banker Style: à la banquière (for tournedos and noisettes): boned stuffed larks, chicken dumplings, truffle slices, demi-glace with truffle essence.

Bardoux (for butchers meat): green peas tossed in butter, mixed with chopped ham.

Barigoule (for game): stuffed artichokes Barigoule, pepper sauce.

Baron Brisse (for butchers' meat): artichoke bottoms filled with truffle pearls, tomatoes concassées and soufflé potatoes, demi-glace with truffle essence.

Basque (for fish): egged and breadcrumbed, shallow fried, dressed on tomatoes concassées Provencal style; Béarnaise sauce with small capers served separately.

Bayard (for entrées): round croûtons scooped out stuffed with goose-liver purée, sliced mushroom, truffles, artichoke bottoms and ox tongue bound with Madeira sauce; Madeira sauce.

Bayol (for butchers' meat): salsify simmered in butter, flavored with garlic, diced shallow fried potatoes.

Bayonne Style: à la byonnaise (for butchers' meat): macaroni in cream sauce mixed with julienne of Bayonne ham or macaroni croquettes with chopped Bayonne ham, Madeira sauce with tomato purée.

Beatrice: Béatrix (for butchers' meat): morels sautéd in butter, artichoke bottoms cut in quarters, well formed fresh carrots, new potatoes fondantes, Sherry sauce.

Beaucaire (for tournedos and noisettes): braised lettuce, potato croquettes.

Beaufort (for fish): mushrooms, bearded poached oysters, diced lobster, lobster sauce.

Beaugency (for tournedos and noisettes): artichoke bottoms stuffed with tomatoes concassées, a poached slice of beef marrow on top, Béarnaise sauce.

Beauharnais (for tournedos and noisettes): stuffed mushrooms, quartered artichoke bottoms, castle potatoes, Beauharnais sauce.

Belle-Alliance (for tournedos and noisettes): sautéd slices of goose-liver and truffle slices, Madeira sauce with tomato purée.

Belle Vue: whole fish such as salmon or salmon trout and crustaceans, lobster or crawfish etc. cold in jelly, pompously displayed and garnished, usually as a center piece.

Belmont (for butchers' meat): stuffed tomatoes and small stuffed sweet peppers.

Benedictine (for fish): dressed on flat pastry shell filled with truffled purée of salt cod, cream sauce.

Benjamin (for butchers' meat): round croquettes of truffled dauphine-potatoes, large stuffed mushrooms, Madeira sauce.

Bercy (for grilled meat): Bercy butter, French fried potatoes.

Bern Style: bernoise (for fish): fried, sautéd diced artichoke bottoms, mushrooms and potatoes.
(for butchers' meat): noodles tossed in butter, French fried potatoes.

Bernard (for butchers' meat): sliced sautéd yellow boletus, tomatoes concassées and potato croquettes, tomato sauce.

Berny (for game): Berny potatoes, tartlets filled with lentil purée, a slice of truffle on top, pepper sauce.

Berry Style: à la berrichonne (for butchers' meat): braised cabbage balls, small glazed onions, glazed chestnuts, bacon slices, demi-glace.

Bignon (for butchers' meat): baked potatoes, scooped out and filled with pork forcemeat.

Bijou (for entrées): puff pastry patties filled with diced lamb sweetbreads bound with tomato sauce.

Bizontine (for tournedos and noisettes): tartlets made of duchess potato-mass stuffed with cauliflower purée, stuffed braised lettuce and buttered veal gravy.

Boatman Style: à la batelière (for fish): 1. mushrooms, glazed button onions, French fried eggs, whole crayfish, white wine sauce.
2. fillets dressed on pastry boats filled with small mussels and shrimps in white wine sauce, covered with green herb sauce, small fried gudgeons around.

Bohemian Style: à la bohémienne (for tournedos, noisettes and entrées): 1. tartlets filled with diced goose liver and truffles bound with buttered meat glaze.
2. rice pilaff, tomatoes concassées, fried onion rings, thick veal gravy. (for poultry and game): stuffed with whole goose liver studded with truffles and roasted en casserole.

Boitelle (for fish): sliced raw mushrooms cooked with the fish.

Bombay (for fish): poached, covered with curry sauce, plain rice and Indian condiments served separately.

Bontoux (for butchers' meat): macaroni croquettes, Madeira sauce.

Bordeaux Style (for fish): Bonnefoy sauce. (for grilled meat): sliced poached ox marrow and Bordeaux sauce.

Bourgeoise: see citizen style.

Bouquetière: see florist style.

Brabant Style: à la brabançonne (for butchers' meat): tartlets filled with Brussels sprouts covered with Mornay sauce and glazed, flat potato croquettes.

Bragance (for tournedos and noisettes): stuffed tomatoes, croquette potatoes, Béarnaise sauce.
(for entrées): scooped out croûtons stuffed with goose-liver purée, a slice of truffle on top, puff pastry tartlets filled with asparagus tips, truffle sauce.

Branicka (for tournedos, noisettes and fillets mignons): pastry shells filled with mushroom purée, asparagus croquettes, Madeira sauce.

Brantôme (for fish): white wine sauce with julienne of truffles and root vegetables, moulded risotto.

Bréhan (for butchers' meat): artichoke bottom stuffed with flageolet purée, a slice of truffle on top, parslied potatoes, cauliflower buds covered with Dutch sauce, thick gravy.

Bréteuil (for fish): shallow fried, garnished with fried oysters, browned butter poured over.

Breton Style: à la bretonne (for butchers' meat): white kidney beans in breton sauce, chopped parsley.

Bride Style: petite-mariée (for poultry): poached in veal stock, button onions braised white, fresh carrots, green peas, new potatoes, suprême sauce with the boiled down stock.

Brie Style: à la briarde (for butchers' meat): stuffed lettuce, fresh or shaped carrots in cream sauce.

Brighton (for fish): poached bearded oysters, button onions, white wine sauce seasoned with English mustard.

Brillat-Savarin (for feathered game): tartlets filled with woodcock soufflé, baked in the oven, truffle slices, demi-glace boiled down with game essence.

Bristol (for butchers' meat): apricot-shaped rice croquettes, flageolets in cream sauce, Parisian potatoes tossed in meat glaze, thick veal gravy.

Brussels Style: à la bruxelloise (for butchers' meat): braised endives, Brussels sprouts, castle potatoes, Madeira sauce.

Burgundy Style: à la bourguignonne (for fish): cooked in red wine with mushroom waste, stock thickened with butter-paste, strained.
(for butchers' meat): braised or deglaced with red wine, glazed onions, diced fried bacon, mushrooms cut in quarters and sautéd in butter.

C

Café Anglais (for tournedos and noisettes): artichoke bottoms stuffed alternately with mushroom and truffle purée, Madeira sauce with truffle essence.

Camargo (for entrées): tartlets filled with creamed noodles, a round shallow fried slice of goose-liver and a truffle slice on top, truffle sauce separately.

Cambacérès (for fish): crayfish tails, mushroom slices, white wine sauce with crayfish coulis, chopped truffles scattered on top.
(for entrées): truffle slices, mushrooms, pitted olives, Madeira sauce.

Camerani (for poultry and sweetbread): small tartlets stuffed with goose-liver purée, truffle slices, slices of red ox tongue shaped like cockscombs, macaroni Italian style, suprême sauce.

Cancal Style: à la cancalaise (for fish): poached bearded oysters and shrimps bound with Normandy sauce.

Canon Style: à la chanoine (for fish): fillets stuffed with shrimp forcemeat, anchovy sauce.

Canova (for tournedos and noisettes): artichoke bottoms filled with diced truffles, cockscombs and kidneys bound with thick Madeira sauce, sliced shallow fried goose-liver.

Canteen-woman Style: à la vivandière (for fish): fillets stuffed with duxelles, coated with tomato sauce with chopped chervil and tarragon, sprinkled with grated cheese, glazed.

Capuchin Style: à la capucine (for butchers' meat): stuffed cabbage balls, large stuffed mushrooms, Madeira sauce.

Cardinal Style (for fish): slices of lobster and truffle, cardinal sauce.

Carême (for fish): decorated fish dumplings, truffle slices, fleurons, cream sauce.
(for tournedos and noisettes): potato croquettes, large pitted olives stuffed with ham forcemeat, Madeira sauce.

Carignan (for cutlets): dipped in eggs and breadcrumbs mixed with grated Parmesan, shallow fried, garnished with cockscombs and kidneys, dipped in frying batter and deep fried, sharp tomato sauce served separately.

Carmencita (for butchers' meat): tomatoes concassées, sweet peppers simmered in butter.

Carnegie (for tournedos and noisettes): artichoke bottoms filled with asparagus tips, truffle slices.

Carnot (for butchers' meat): braised stuffed pieces of cucumber, red wine sauce mixed with chopped tarragon.

Casanova (for fish): bearded oysters and mussels, truffle slices, white wine sauce.

Castellan: châtelaine (for butchers' meat): I. artichoke bottoms stuffed with white onions purée, glazed chestnuts, Parisian potatoes, Madeira sauce.
II. braised celery, artichoke bottoms cut in quarters, halved tomatoes, castle potatoes.

Castilian: à la castillane (for tournedos and noisettes): small nest-shaped potato croquettes filled with tomatoes concassées in oil, fried onion rings, tomato sauce.

Catalonian: à la catalane (for tournedos and noisettes): artichoke bottoms, grilled tomatoes, demi-glace with tomato purée.

Catalonian
(for butchers' meat): I. diced egg-plants sautéd in oil, pilaf rice, tomato sauce.
II. stuffed tomatoes, glazed onions, glazed chestnuts, mushrooms, small fried pork sausages, demi-glace with tomato purée.

Cavour (for entrées): round flat polenta cakes mixed with grated Parmesan, large mushrooms stuffed with chicken liver purée, thick veal gravy with tomato purée flavored with Marsala.

Centenary: centenaire (for tournedos and noisettes): stuffed braised lettuce, potato croquettes, thick veal gravy.

Cevennes Style: à la cévenole (for butchers' meat): larded, glazed chestnuts, mushrooms, demi-glace with the boiled down meat gravy.

Chambord (for large braised fish): large fish dumplings decorated with truffles, olive-shaped truffles, fluted mushrooms, soft roes sautéd in butter, heart-shaped croûtons, whole crayfish, Chambord sauce.

Champagne Style: à la champenoise (for butchers' meat): stuffed braised onions, stuffed braised cabbage balls, Anna potatoes, demi-glace or thick meat gravy.

Chancelor Style: à la chancelier (for butchers' meat): glazed onions, Parisian potatoes, demi-glace.

Chancy (for butchers' meat): green peas and small round carrots tossed in butter, mushrooms, Madeira sauce.

Chanoine: see canon style.

Charles V. (for entrées): mushrooms, cocks' combs, truffle slices, game dumplings, Madeira sauce.

Charolles Style: à la charollaise (for butcher's meat): cauliflower buds Villeroy, glazed carrots, pastry shells filled with turnip purée.

Chartres Style (for tournedos and noisettes): blanched tarragon leaves, small fondant potatoes, thick veal gravy flavored with tarragon.

Chatelaine (for tournedos, butcher's meat and poultry): artichoke bottoms stuffed with white onion purée, braised chestnuts, nut potatoes, Madeira sauce.

Chatham (for butchers' meat, especially veal): noodles tossed in butter and garnished with slices of ox tongue, light white onion sauce mixed with sliced mushrooms.

Chauchat (for fish): dressed in border of sliced boiled potatoes, covered with Mornay sauce, glazed.

Chavette (for fish): dressed on sliced artichoke bottoms tossed in butter, covered with Mornay sauce mixed with truffle strips, glazed.

Cherbourgh (for fish): bearded oysters and mussels, shrimps, shrimp sauce, glazed.

Cheron (for tournedos and noisettes): artichoke bottoms filled with vegetable macedoine, Parisian potatoes.

Chevreuse (for tournedos and noisettes): I. truffle slices, semolina croquettes stuffed with chopped mushrooms, Bonnefoy sauce.
II. artichoke bottoms stuffed with mushroom purée, a slice of truffle on top, Parisian potatoes.

Chinon Style: à la chinonaise (for butchers' meat): braised balls of green cabbage stuffed with pork forcemeat, parsley potatoes, demi-glace.

Chipolata (for butchers' meat and poultry): braised chestnuts, glazed button onions, small pork sausages (chipolatas), diced fried bacon, glazed carrots, demi-glace with the reduced meat or poultry stock.

Choiseul (for tournedos and noisettes): artichoke bottoms stuffed with goose-liver purée, mushroom sauce.

Choisy (for tournedos and noisettes): braised lettuce, castle potatoes, buttered meat glaze.

Choron (for tournedos and noisettes): artichoke bottoms filled with green peas, Parisian potatoes, Choron sauce.

Cinderella: Cendrillon (for butchers' meat): artichoke bottoms stuffed with white creamed onion purée mixed with chopped truffles.

Citizen Style: à la bourgeoise (for butchers' meat): glazed button onions, glazed carrots, diced blanched and fried bacon, large olive potatoes.

Clamart (for butchers' meat): tartlets filled with green peas cooked in the French way with shredded lettuce added, round flat Macaire potatoes, thick veal gravy.

Claremont (for butchers' meat): stuffed braised onions, stuffed cucumbers, tomatoes concassées.

Clermont (for butchers' meat): stuffed braised cabbage balls, rectangles of salt pork cooked with the cabbage, boiled potatoes, demi-glace.
(for tournedos and noisettes): braised chestnuts crushed with a fork, mixed with butter, egg yolks and onion purée, filled in small moulds, poached and turned out, fried onion rings, light Soubise sauce.

Colbert (for fish): deep fried, Colbert sauce.
(for butchers' meat, tournedos, noisettes and sweetbread): small chicken croquettes, very small French fried eggs, truffle slices, Colbert sauce.

Colinette (for fish): fillets stuffed with truffled fish forcemeat, egged and breadcrumbed, deep fried. tomato sauce.

Commodore (for large fish): oval crayfish croquettes, mussels Villeroi, dumplings made of whiting forcemeat mixed with crayfish butter, Normandy sauce whipped with crayfish butter.

Compote (for spring chickens and pigeons) glazed button onions, raw mushrooms halved sautéd in butter, diced fried bacon.

Concordia (for butchers' meat): French beans, fresh carrots, potato purée, demi-glace or thick veal gravy.

Condé (for butchers' meat): purée of red haricot beans cooked with bacon, the bacon cut in triangles, red wine sauce whipped with butter.

Connaught (for feathered game): stuffed with chestnuts, thick game gravy, watercress salad.

Conti (for butchers' meat): lentil purée cooked with bacon, the bacon cut in triangles.

Continental (for tournedos and noisettes): quartered artichoke bottoms and split lamb kidneys sautéd in butter, Madeira sauce.

Countess: à la comtesse (for butchers' meat): larded with truffles, braised lettuce, veal dumplings, thick veal gravy.

Count of Brabant: comte de Brabant (for feathered game): small Brussels sprouts tossed in butter with diced fried bacon, salmi sauce.

Courbet (for fish): bearded oysters, fluted mushrooms, white wine sauce seasoned with curry powder.

Creole (for eggs, small poultry and entrées): risotto, stuffed green peppers, Creole sauce.

Cuban: à la cubaine (for butchers' meat, tournedos and noisettes): tartlets filled with tomatoes concassées in oil mixed with diced red peppers flavored with garlic.

Cussy (for poultry, tournedos and noisettes): large mushrooms stuffed with chestnut purée, very small truffles cooked in Madeira, cocks' combs, Madeira sauce.

Cyrano (for tournedos and noisettes) artichoke bottoms stuffed with mushroom purée, thick veal gravy.

D

Danicheff (for fish): covered with diced tomatoes simmered in butter and chopped braised onions, sprinkled with grated cheese, melted butter on top, glazed.

Daumont (for fish): mushrooms filled with halved crayfish tails bound with Nantua sauce, round dumplings made of creamed fish forcemeat, decorated with truffles, soft roes dipped in eggs and breadcrumbs and deep fried, Nantua sauce.

Dauphine (for butchers' meat): dauphine potatoes, demi-glace with Madeira.

Déjazet (for fish): fillets dipped in eggs and breadcrumbs, shallow fried, dressed on half-melted tarragon butter, decorated with blanched tarragon leaves.

Delagrange (for butchers' meat): green peas, glazed carrots and turnips, pieces of celery dipped in frying batter and deep fried, demi-glace.

Delicious: délicieuse (for fish): boiled potato balls, Dutch sauce mixed with tomatoes concassées.

Delphine (for butchers' meat): macaroni mixed with truffle strips and game purée, thick veal gravy.

Demidoff (for fish): crayfish tails, pitted olives, fish dumplings, mushrooms, financier sauce.

Denise (for butchers' meat): small mushroom croquettes, unsweetened soufflé fritters; white haricot beans bound with Dutch sauce and thick meat gravy separately.

Descartes (for poultry and feathered game): pastry cases with a small quail stuffed with truffled forcemeat in each.

Dieppe Style: à la dieppoise (for fish) shrimps, bearded mussels, white wine sauce with the reduced fond of the fish.

Dijon Style: à la dijonnaise (for butchers' meat): quartered potatoes shallow fried in butter, veal dumplings mixed with chopped ox tongue, Madeira sauce.

Diplomate (for entrées): slices of calf's sweetbread, cockscombs, cocks kidneys and small mushrooms bound with Madeira sauce.

Don Carlos (for butchers' meat): braised red peppers, mushrooms, Madeira sauce.

Doria (for fish): shallow fried in butter, peeled pitted lemon slices on top, olive-shaped pieces of cucumber simmered in butter, browned butter, lemon juice and chopped parsley.

D'Orsay (for tournedos and noisettes): mushrooms, stuffed olives, castle potatoes, Madeira sauce.

Dreux (for butchers' meat): larded with ox tongue, truffles and fat bacon; veal or chicken dumplings, cockscombs and kidneys, mushrooms, truffle slices, blanched pitted olives and financier sauce.

Dragomirow (for fish): garnished with bearded mussels, covered with Mornay sauce, glazed.

Dubarry (for butchers' meat, tournedos and noisettes): cauliflower buds ball-shaped, covered with Mornay sauce, sprinkled with grated cheese and glazed, castle potatoes, thick meat gravy.

Dubley (for butchers' meat): nest-shaped duchess potatoes stuffed with mushroom purée, grilled mushrooms.

Duchess (for butchers' meat, tournedos and noisettes): duchess potatoes, Madeira sauce.

Dufferin (for fish): bearded oysters and mussels, genoise sauce whipped with anchovy butter.

Dumas (for butchers' meat): glazed carrots, braised cabbage balls, diced fried bacon, demi-glace.

Durance (for fish): diced lobster and shrimps, Dutch sauce whipped with lobster butter.

Durand (for butchers' meat): braised lettuce, blanched pitted olives, veal dumplings, truffle slices, demi-glace.

Duroc (for sautéd poultry, tournedos and noisettes): small new potatoes browned in butter, Madeira sauce with sliced mushrooms.

Duse (for butchers' meat): French beans, peeled tomatoes simmered in butter, raw diced potatoes shallow fried in butter, Madeira sauce.

E

Edward VII.: Edouard VII. (for poultry): risotto stuffing mixed with diced truffles and goose-liver; olive-shaped cucumbers in cream sauce, suprême sauce seasoned with curry powder mixed with diced red peppers.

Egyptian: égyptienne (for fish) 1. fried in oil, tomatoes concassées, fried onions, curry sauce.
2. poached, dressed on pilaf rice, covered with Portuguese sauce mixed with strips of red peppers.

Elyssée-Palace (for entrées): sliced sweetbreads egged, breadcrumbed and shallow fried, mushrooms, Béarnaise sauce.

Emperor Style: à l'empereur (for butchers' meat): halved fried tomatoes with a large blanched ox marrow slice on top, asparagus tips, Parmentier potatoes, truffle sauce.

Empress Style: à l'impératrice (for poached poultry): lamb sweetbreads, large dices of calf's brains, button onions simmered in velouté, suprême sauce blended with chicken purée.

English Style: à l'anglaise (for boiled butchers' meat): I. boiled bacon, parsley sauce.
II. mashed parsnips or turnips, boiled potatoes, caper sauce.
(for boiled poultry): olive-shaped carrots and turnips, celery, green peas and slices of ox tongue, all boiled, cream sauce.
(for fish) fillets dipped in eggs and white breadcrumbs, shallow fried, half-melted herb butter.

Excelsior (for tournedos and noisettes): braised lettuce, fondantes potatoes, thick veal gravy.

Exquisite (for fish): small mushroom croquettes, lobster sauce mixed with chopped truffles.

F

Falstaff (for fish): shallow fried, sautéd yellow boletus, tomatoes concassées.

Favart (for poultry and sweetbread): chicken dumplings with chopped tarragon, pastry shells filled with sliced yellow boletus in cream sauce, chicken velouté whipped with crayfish butter.
(for butchers' meat): noodles mixed with truffle strips, tossed in butter, thick veal gravy.

Favorite (for tournedos and noisettes): goose-liver slices sautéd in butter, truffle slices, asparagus tips, thick veal gravy.

Fédora (for fish): stuffed with duxelles, Geneva sauce, fish potatoes.
(for butchers' meat): tartlets filled with olive-shaped carrots, turnips and asparagus tips, glazed chestnuts and orange fillets.

Ferval (for entrées): brioche-shaped duchesse potatoes or potato croquettes with chopped ham, quartered artichoke bottoms sautéd with chopped herbs, thick meat gravy.

Financier Style: à la financière (for poultry and sweetbreads): chicken mousseline dumplings, cockscombs and kidneys, pitted blanched olives, truffle slices, fluted mushrooms, financier sauce.

Finnish Style: à la finnoise (for fish): small stuffed tomatoes, white wine sauce with chopped red peppers.

Flemish Style: à la flamande (for fish): poached in fish stock and pale beer, stock thickened with butter-paste and mixed with chopped herbs.
(for butchers' meat): braised cabbage balls, olive-shaped carrots and turnips, sliced boiled bacon, slices of garlic sausage, boiled potatoes.

Fleury (for tournedos and noisettes): nest-shaped potato croquettes filled with diced sautéd veal kidneys, demi-glace with tomato purée.

Florentine, Florence Style (for fish): leaf spinach, Mornay sauce, glazed.
(for butcher's meat): semolina croquettes with grated Parmesan and egg-yolks, tiny spinach pancakes, demi-glace highly flavored with tomato purée.

Florian (for butchers' meat): braised lettuce, glazed button onions, olive-shaped carrots, foantantes potatoes, veal gravy.

Florist Style: à la bouquetière (for butchers' meat): artichoke bottoms filled alternately with glazed pearls of turnips and carrots, diced green beans and peas, small bunches of cauliflower covered with Dutch sauce and small castle potatoes, thick veal gravy.

Fontainebleau (for tournedos and noisettes): nest-shaped duchess potatoes filled with diced spring vegetables in cream sauce.

Forester Style: à la forestière (for butchers' meat, tournedos and noisettes): sautéd morels, diced fried bacon, diced raw potatoes sautéd in butter. thick veal gravy or demi-glace.

Française: see French style.

Franklin (for butchers' meat): stuffed braised onions, potatoes cut in quarters sautéd in butter, demi-glace.

Frascati (for poultry and butchers' meat): asparagus tips, small truffles, sautéd slices of goose-liver, fluted mushrooms, half-moon-shaped duchess potatoes, thick veal gravy.

French Style: à la française (for butchers' meat): tartlets filled with vegetable macédoine, asparagus tips, braised lettuce, cauliflower buds covered with Dutch sauce, demi-glace or thick veal gravy.

G

Gabrielle (for fish): covered with white wine sauce mixed with tomato purée, whipped with butter, glazed.
(for tournedos and noisettes): flat potato croquettes with chopped chicken and truffles, braised lettuce, slices of truffles and blanched ox marrow, Madeira sauce whipped with butter.

Gambetta (for tournedos and noisettes): stuffed egg-plants, small tomatoes simmered in butter, Madeira sauce.

Gardner Style: à la jardinière: green peas, flageolets, carrots, turnips and cauliflower buds covered with Dutch sauce arranged in bunches around the meat, thick veal gravy.

Gastronomer Style: à la gastronome (for poultry and sweetbreads): glazed chestnuts, very small whole truffles, sautéd morels, cockscombs rolled in liquid meat glaze, demi-glace with truffle essence.
(for feathered game): sautéd morels, glazed chestnuts, braised lamb sweetbreads, cockscombs and kidneys rolled in liquid meat glaze.

Gaulish Style: à la gauloise (for tournedos, noisettes and small poultry): tartlets filled with cocks' kidneys, cocks' combs Villeroi, mushrooms, truffle slices, the natural juices deglaced with white wine.

Gautier (for fish): mushrooms, fish dumplings, bearded oysters, fish velouté whipped with butter.

Georgian Style: à la georgienne (for butchers' meat): small rice dumplings dipped in eggs and breadcrumbs and deep fried, tomato sauce.

German Style: à l'allemande (for butchers' meat): sliced calf's kidneys sautéd in butter, glazed button onions, small red peppers simmered in butter, German fried potatoes, Madeira sauce.

Gipsy Style: à la zingara (for veal and poultry): julienne of ham, ox tongue, mushrooms and truffles sweated in butter, demi-glace with tomato and tarragon flavor.

Girardi (for fish): bearded oysters, shrimps, mushrooms, herb sauce.

Godard (for butchers' meat and poultry): veal dumplings mixed with chopped mushrooms and truffles, shaped with a spoon, large chicken dumplings decorated with truffles and ox tongue, fluted mushrooms, olive-shaped truffles, cockscombs, slices of glazed lamb sweetbreads, Godard sauce.

Gorenflot (for braised butchers' meat): red cabbage, slices of Bologna sausage, cooked with the meat, boiled potatoes, the stock thickened with butter-paste.

Gouffé (for butchers' meat): olive-shaped truffles, shaped risotto, veal dumplings, mushrooms, demi-glace.

Gourmet (for butchers' meat): artichocke bottoms, mushrooms, truffles, Madeira sauce.

Grand-duke: grand-duc (for fish): asparagus tips tossed in butter, crayfish tails, truffle slices, Mornay sauce, glazed.

Grand Hotel (for tournedos and noisettes): artichoke bottoms filled with Béarnaise sauce, braised celery hearts, soufflé potatoes, the meat juice deglaced with white wine and boiled down with demi-glace.

Grandmother Style: à la grand'mère (for fish): shallow fried, browned button onions, sautéd olive potatoes, lemon juice, chopped parsley, browned butter.

Greek Style: à la greque (mainly for saddles of lamb and veal): rice prepared in the Greek way.

H

Harvester Style: à la moissoneuse (for butchers' meat): green peas prepared in the French way, shredded lettuce, sliced potatoes and diced blanched bacon added, thickened with butter-paste; thick veal gravy.

Hauser (for grilled meat): fried onion rings, Parisian potatoes, Colbert sauce.

Havanna Style: à la havanaise (for fish): tomatoes concassées, diced red or green peppers, glazed button onions, mushrooms, herb sauce.

Helder (for tournedos and noisettes): I. Béarnaise sauce on top of the meat with tomatoes concassées in the center, Parisian potatoes, thick veal gravy.
II. artichoke bottoms filled alternately with shallow fried potato balls and green asparagus tips, tomatoes concassées, Béarnaise sauce.

Helvetia (for butchers meat, tournedos and noisettes): tomatoes stuffed alternately with spinach and white onion purée, Madeira sauce.

Henri IV. (for tournedos and noisettes) artichoke bottoms filled with Parisian potatoes rolled in liquid meat glaze, Béarnaise sauce.

Hotel Plaza (for tournedos and noisettes): purée of green peas, small braised cabbage balls, truffle slices, Madeira sauce.

Housekeeper Style: à la ménagère (for small poultry and sweetbreads): sliced carrots, green peas, French beans and button onions simmered in butter.

Hungarian Style: à la hongroise (for fish): poached in white wine and fish stock with chopped onions sweated in butter, paprika and diced tomatoes, stock boiled down with thick cream.
(for tournedos, noisettes and butchers' meat): cauliflower sprigs coated with Mornay sauce mixed with paprika and chopped onions sweated in butter and glazed, fondantes potatoes, the pan juice of the meat boiled down with cream and paprika.

Hussar Style: à la hussarde (for butchers' meat, tournedos and noisettes): I. duchess potatoes, stuffed with white onion purée, hussar sauce.
II. potatoes stuffed with onion purée, stuffed egg-plants, grated horseradish.

I

Imperial: à l'impériale (for poultry): mushrooms, sliced braised sweetbreads, truffle slices, cocks' combs, escalopes of goose-liver, Madeira sauce.

Independant Style: à l'indépendance (for tournedos and entrées): artichoke bottoms stuffed with chicken purée, green peas, tomatoes concassées.

Indian Style: à l'indienne (for fish, meat and poultry): boiled rice, Indian sauce.

Infant: à l'infante (for tournedos and noisettes): stuffed tomatoes, grilled mushrooms, straw potatoes, Madeira sauce, macaroni mixed with truffle strips and tossed in butter separately.

Ismaîl Bayaldi (for tournedos, noisettes and poultry): fried sliced eggplants, tomatoes concassées with garlic, pilaf rice, Portuguese sauce.

Italian Style: à l'italienne (for meat and poultry): macaroni croquettes with Parmesan, quartered artichoke bottoms prepared in the Italian way, Italian sauce.

J

Jacques (for feathered game): stuffed with forcemeat of chicken or other livers, mushrooms, shallots, soaked white bread and seasoning, prepared en casserolle.

Japanese Style: à la japonaise (for butchers' meat): tartlets filled with stachys bound with velouté, potato croquettes, demi-glace or veal gravy.

Jessica (for eggs, suprême of chicken, noisettes and medaillons): small artichoke bottoms stuffed with salpicon of blanched ox marrow and shallots, bound with thick demi-glace, sautéd morels, Anna potatoes baked in tartlet moulds, German sauce with truffle essence.

Jockey Club (for tournedos, noisettes and sweetbreads): crayfish dumplings mixed with chopped mushrooms, stuffed tomatoes, truffle slices, potato croquettes, demi-glace flavored with Marsala.

Joinville (for fish): salpicon of shrimps, truffles and mushrooms bound with Normandy sauce, Normandy sauce whipped with crayfish butter.

Judic (for entrées): braised lettuce, cocks' combs, truffle slices, very fine demi-glace.

Jules Verne (for butchers' meat): stuffed braised turnips, stuffed potatoes, large quartered mushrooms sautéd in butter.

Jussière (for butchers' meat): stuffed onions, stuffed braised lettuce, castle potatoes, thick meat gravy.

K

Khedive (for entrées): asparagus tips, tomatoes concassées, diced mushrooms and goose-liver in Madeira sauce.

Kléber (for tournedos and noisettes): artichoke bottoms stuffed with goose-liver purée, truffle sauce.

Kotschoubey (for feathered game): cooked en casserole with raw truffle slices, garnished with Brussels sprouts cooked in butter with diced bacon, chopped coarseley, meat glaze added.

L

Lady Morgan (for entreées): cockscombs, creamed corn, okra, Madeira sauce.

Lakmé (for tournedos and noisettes): tartlets filled with purée of broad beans, grilled mushrooms, tomato sauce.

Languedoc Style: à la languedocienne (for butchers' meat, poultry, tournedos and noisettes): sliced egg-plants fried in oil, sliced yellow boletus sautéd in oil, tomatoes concassées in oil with garlic and chopped parsley, thick veal gravy.

Lavallière (for tournedos and noisettes): artichoke bottoms filled with green asparagus tips, castle potatoes, Bordeaux sauce.

Leo XIII. (for poultry): I. poached, small chicken dumplings, crayfish tails, macaroni tossed in butter, suprême sauce. II. stuffed with saffron rice mixed with diced mushrooms and white truffles, panned, truffle sauce.

Leopold (for tournedos, noisettes and small poultry): tartlets filled with sliced mushrooms and chopped shallots in cream sauce, Madeira sauce blended with goose-liver purée.

Ligurian: à la ligurienne (for butchers' meat): stuffed tomatoes, risotto with saffron, duchess or croquette potatoes, veal gravy.

Lilly (for tournedos and noisettes): Anna potatoes baked in tartlet moulds, artichoke bottoms with a slice of sautéd goose-liver and a truffle slice on top, truffle sauce.

Lison (for butchers' meat): chopped braised lettuce mixed with cream and egg-yolks poached in tartlet moulds, flat croquettes of duchess mass mixed with chopped ox tongue, thick meat gravy.

Lithuanian Style: à la lithuanienne (for butchers' meat and entrées): small mushrooms simmered in sour cream, Madeira sauce.

Little-Duke: petit-duc (for entrées): tartlets stuffed with chicken purée, truffle slices, green asparagus tips, Madeira sauce.

Lombarde (for butchers' meat, tournedos and noisettes): tomatoes stuffed with risotto mixed with Parmesan and chopped Italian truffles, Madeira sauce.

Lorette (for tournedos and noisettes): small chicken croquettes, buttered asparagus tips or green peas, truffle slices, thick veal gravy.

Lothringian Style: à la lorraine (for butchers' meat and large poultry): braised red cabbage balls, braised saurkraut, potato dumplings, thick meat gravy.

Louis XIV. (for tournedos and noisettes): artichoke bottoms stuffed with mushroom purée, truffle slices, round flat cakes of Anna potatoes, devil sauce.

Louis XV. (for entrées and sweetbreads): diced truffles, mushrooms and artichoke bottoms, truffle sauce.

Louisiana (for tournedos, noisettes and poultry): creamed corn, moulded risotto, deep fried slices of sweet potatoes and bananas, thick poultry or veal gravy.

Lucullus (for poultry and entrées): truffles cooked in Madeira, filled with cocks' kidneys rolled in liquid meat glaze, dumplings made of chicken forcemeat and purée of the scooped out truffles, shaped with a tea spoon, cockscombs; demi-glace with truffle essence.

Lyonese Style: à la lyonnaise (for butchers' meat): middle sized braised onions, fondantes potatoes, Lyonese sauce.

M

Macedonian Style: à la macédoine (for butchers' meat and entrées): diced or pearl-shaped carrots, turnips and knob celery simmered in butter, diced green beans, green peas, flageolets and cauliflower sprigs bound with light cream sauce, veal gravy.

Mac-Mahon (for butchers' meat): potatoes cut in quarters and pan fried, truffles, flageolets, Madeira sauce.

Macon Style: à la mâconnaise (for fish): poached in red wine with mushrooms, red wine sauce.

Magdalena: Madeleine (for fish): cream sauce whipped with crayfish butter, diced knob celery and crayfish tails. (2. for tournedos and noisettes): tartlets stuffed with purée of white haricot beans, artichoke bottoms stuffed with white onion purée, demi-glace.

Maillot (for butchers' meat, especially for braised ham): olive-shaped carrots and turnips cooked in broth, glazed button onions, braised lettuce, green peas and French beans tossed in butter, thick veal gravy.

Maintenon (for veal cutlets and steaks): stuffed with mushroom slices bound with thick cream sauce mixed with white onions purée, sautéd, garnished with truffle slices, truffle sauce.

Majestic (for fish): poached in champagne, artichoke bottoms stuffed alternately with mushroom purée and spinach purée, salmon mousseline dumplings and sole mousseline dumplings; fish stock boiled down, bound with cream and egg-yolks, whipped with butter and mixed with truffle julienne.
(for tournedos and noisettes): potatoe croquettes mixed with chopped mushrooms, fried tomatoes, okra, sliced fried veal kidneys, Béarnaise sauce.

Mancelle (for game): mushroom and celery purée, tartlets stuffed with game purée, demi-glace with game essence.

Mantua (for fish): fillets coated with Italian sauce, sprinkled with grated Parmesan and breadcrumbs, gratinated.

Marianne (for fish): poached in white wine, dressed on spinach leaves tossed in butter, garnished with bearded mussels, covered with white wine sauce.

Maria Stuart (for entrées): tartlets stuffed with white onion purée and covered with a slice of poached ox marrow, demi-glace.

Maria Theresia: Maria Thérèse (for butchers' meat): croquettes of truffled risotto, demi-glace with tomato purée.

Marie Louise (for tournedos, noisettes and poultry): artichoke bottoms stuffed with mushroom purée mixed with white onion purée, thick veal gravy.

Marietta (for butchers' meat and poultry): open noodle patties filled with cockscombs and tomato purée, Madeira sauce.

Marigny (for butchers' meat): tartlets filled alternately with buttered green peas and French beans, fondantes potatoes, thick veal gravy.

Mariner Style: à la marinière (for fish): bearded mussels cooked in white wine, shrimp tails, mariner's sauce.

Marinetta (for butchers' meat and poultry): tartlets stuffed with spinach purée bound with cream sauce, fleurons, tomato sauce.

Marion Delorme (for tournedos, noisettes and poultry): same as Marie Louise.

Marquise (for tournedos, noisettes and poultry): tartlets filled with poached calf's marrow cut in pieces, truffles strips and asparagus tips all bound with German sauce whipped up with crayfish butter, marquise potatoes.

Marseille Style: à la marseillaise (for butchers' meat): halved tomatoes fried in oil with a little garlic, a large olive encircled with an anchovy fillet on top, large potato chips, Provencal sauce.

Marshal Style: à la maréchale (1. for sweetbreads, butchers' meat and poultry): dumplings made of chicken forcemeat with chopped truffles shaped with a spoon, truffle slices bound with Italian sauce, cockscombs, demi-glace flavored with Madeira.
(2. for lamb cutlets, chicken breasts and escalopes of sweetbread): dipped in melted butter and white breadcrumbs mixed with chopped truffles, pan fried, a slice of truffle on top, asparagus tips or green peas tossed in butter.

Marsini (for fish): fillets or small fish dressed on bed of fish forcemeat mixed with chopped truffles and green peppers, garnished bearded oysters, fish dumplings and truffle slices, coated with white wine sauce.

Mary Jane: Marie Jeanne (for tournedos and noisettes): 1. tartlets stuffed with mushroom purée, a slice of truffle on top, Parisian potatoes, demi-glace.
2. artichoke bottoms stuffed with white onion purée mixed with mushroom purée, Parisian potatoes, Madeira sauce.

Mascagni (for butchers' meat): tartlets stuffed with chestnut purée a slice of fried calf's brains on top, straw potatoes, tomato sauce.

Mascot: Mascotte (for tournedos, noisettes and poultry): artichoke bottoms cut in quarters and sautéd in butter, olive potatoes, truffle balls, the meat juice dissolved with white wine and boiled up with veal gravy. All preparation Mascot are cooked "en cocotte".

Masséna (for noisettes and tournedos): poached slices of ox marrow, small artichoke bottoms stuffed with thick Béarnaise sauce, tomato sauce.

Massenet (for tournedos and noisettes): artichoke bottoms with a slice of poached ox marrow on top, French beans tossed in butter, round flat Anna potatoes, Madeira sauce.

Mazarin (for fish): tartlets filled alternately with truffle cubes and shrimps in shrimp sauce, crayfish sauce.
(for entrées): artichoke bottoms filled with vegetable macédoine, rice croquettes, mushrooms, decorated veal dumplings, Madeira sauce.

Médicis (for butchers meat, tournedos and noisettes): tartlets filled with Vichy carrots and green peas, round potato croquettes fried, scooped out and filled with sorrel purée, thick veal gravy.

Melba (for butchers' meat): stuffed tomatoes, braised lettuce, fluted mushroom caps, truffle slices, demi-glace flavored with Portwine.

Melun Style: à la melunoise (for fish): boiled, covered with Robert sauce.

Menton Style: à la mentonnaise (for butchers' meat): pieces of chard stuffed with duxelles, artichoke bottoms filled with tiny potato balls sautéd in butter, meat gravy.

Mephisto (for fish): fillets or small fish pan fried or grilled, devil sauce served separately.

Mercédès (for butchers' meat, tournedos, noisettes and cutlets): braised lettuce, large mushroom caps, fried tomatoes, potato croquettes, Madeira sauce.

Metro (for butchers' meat) artichoke bottoms filled alternately with small carrot and potato balls, green beans and peas, demi-glace.

Metternich (for saddles of veal or lamb): braised, carved, each slice coated with Béchamel sauce seasoned with paprika and a truffle slice between the meat slices, placed back into position, coated with Béchamel sauce with paprika, sprinkled with grated cheese, glazed in the oven; pilaff of rice and veal gravy served separately.

Mexican Style: à la mexicaine (for butcher's meat and poultry): large grilled mushroom caps stuffed with tomatoes concassées, grilled sweet peppers, sharply seasoned meat gravy with tomato juice.

Mignon (for entrées): artichoke bottoms filled with buttered peas, small chicken dumplings decorated with truffle, the pan juice dissolved in white wine and whipped with butter.

Mikado (for tournedos and noisettes): fried halved tomatoes, stachys sautéd in butter, Provencal sauce.

Milanese Style: à la milanaise (for butcher's meat): macaroni tossed in butter, mixed with grated Parmesan and julienne of ox tongue, mushrooms and truffles; tomato sauce.

Milton (for poultry): cock's combs and kidneys, green asparagus tips, truffle slices, suprême sauce.

Mirabeau (for grilled meat): garnished criss-cross with anchovy fillets, pitted olives and blanched tarragon leaves; anchovy butter served separately.

Mireille (for butcher's meat): Mireille potatoes, tomato sauce.

Mirette (for tournedos, noisettes and cutlets): small timbals of Mirette potatoes, the meat juice and a little meat glaze whipped with butter.

Modern: à la moderne (for butchers' meat): cabbage braised in dariole moulds with a slice of truffle, braised lettuce, veal forcemeat dumplings decorated with red ox tongue, thick veal gravy.

Moïna (for tournedos and noisettes): artichoke bottoms cut in quarters and sautéd in butter, pan fried mushrooms, Madeira sauce.

Monaco (for entrées): slices of fried calf's brains, fried ham slices, large mushroom caps, demi-glace with julienne of mushrooms and truffles.

Monseigneur (for fish): fillets or small fish stuffed with fish forcemeat poached in white wine and fish stock, small puffpastry patties filled with shrimps in white wine sauce, green herb sauce.

Monselet (for tournedos and noisettes): stuffed egg plants, Parisian potatoes, Foyot sauce.

Montagné (for tournedos and noisettes): stuffed tomatoes, artichoke bottoms filled with sliced sautéd mushrooms, Madeira sauce.

Montansier (for fish): poached in fish stock, one half covered with white wine the other half with red wine sauce, garnished with fleurons.

Montbazon (for poultry): lamb sweetbreads larded with truffles, oval chicken forcemeat dumplings decorated with truffles, large fluted mushroom caps, truffle slices, suprême sauce.

Montebello (for fish): coated with fish forcemeat, larded with truffles, braised in white wine, garnished with shrimp croquettes, pastry boats filled with soft roes and whole crayfish; fish velouté whipped with anchovy paste and garnished with bearded oysters.
(for tournedos and noisettes): tartlets filled with diced ox tongue and truffles bound with Choron sauce.

Monte Carlo (for tournedos, noisettes and butchers' meat): stuffed cucumbers, potato croquettes, tartlets filled alternately with diced green beans and green peas tossed in butter, thick veal gravy.

Montglas (for small and large puff pastry patties): diced goose liver, ox tongue, truffle and pearl-sized chicken forcemeat dumplings bound with Madeira sauce.

Montgomery (for butchers' meat): thin pancakes stuffed with spinach purée cut in pieces, tartlets stuffed with white onion purée, truffles slices, meat gravy.

Montmorency (for butchers' meat and poultry): artichoke bottoms filled with vegetable macedoine, bunches of green asparagus tips, Madeira sauce.

Montpensier (for tournedos, noisettes and poultry): bunches of green asparagus tips, truffle slices on top of the meat, the pan juices deglaced with white wine and whipped with butter.

Montreuil (for fish): covered with white wine sauce, garnished with large boiled potato balls covered with shrimp sauce.

Monvoisin (for fish): covered with white wine sauce with chopped shallots and shrimps, sprinkled with chopped parsley, garnished with tomatoes concassées.

Morlaix Style: à la morlaisienne (for fish): bearded mussels and shrimps, covered with green herb sauce, sprinkled with grated cheese, glazed.

Mozart (for tournedos and noisettes): artichoke bottoms stuffed with purée of knob celery, soufflé potatoes, pepper sauce.

N

Nantes Style: à la nantaise (for butcher's meat: glazed turnips, green peas, potato purée, thick meat gravy.

Nantua (for fish): crayfish tails bound with Nantua sauce, truffle slices, Nantua sauce.

Naples Style: à la napolitaine (for fish): dressed on spaghetti tossed in butter and mixed with grated Parmesan, covered with Mornay sauce, sprinkled with grated Parmesan, glazed, border of tomato sauce poured around.

Naples Style
(for veal collops and cutlets): meat dipped in eggs, half breadcrumbs and half grated Parmesan, shallow fried, garnished spaghetti tossed in butter and mixed with grated Parmesan and tomato sauce.

Nelson (for fish): fillets poached, covered with white wine sauce, garnished with soft roes and Parisian potatoes.
(for lamb or veal cutlets and steaks): coated with veal forcemeat mixed with white onion purée, breadcrumbs sprinkled on top, gratinated in the oven.
(for saddles of veal or lamb) braised, carved, each slice covered with white onion purée, placed back into position with small ham slice between the meat slices, covered with cheese soufflé mass mixed with truffle purée, baked rapidly in the oven; thick veal gravy separately.

Nemours Style: (for entrées): buttered green peas, olive-shaped carrots, duchess potatoes, meat gravy.

Nemrod (for feathered game): rissoles stuffed with diced ox marrow, croquette potatoes, small puff pastry patties filled with cranberries, large mushrooms caps stuffed with chestnut purée, French beans, game gravy.

Nesle (for fish): fillets stuffed with fish forcemeat, folded, shallow fried, mushrooms, crayfish tails, white wine sauce.

Nesselrode (for fish): fillets stuffed with pike forcemeat, diced lobster added, wrapped in puff pastry, baked in oven, lobster sauce with bearded oysters separately.
(for butcher' meat): glazed chestnuts, mushrooms, truffles, Madeira sauce.

Nevers Style: à la nivernaise (for butcher's meat): I. glazed olive-shaped carrots, glazed button onions, meat gravy. II. glazed olive-shaped carrots and turnips, glazed onions, braised lettuce, boiled potatoes, meat gravy.

Nice Style: à la niçoise (for fish): pan fried, diced tomatoes sautéd in oil with garlic, chopped tarragon added, black olives, anchovy fillets, capers, lemon slices, anchovy butter.
(for meat and poultry): diced tomatoes as above, French beans tossed in butter, very small castle potatoes, thick veal gravy.

Nicolas (for entrée): fried gooseliver, truffle slices, Madeira sauce.

Ninon (for tournedos, noisettes and poultry): Mireille potatoes baked in dariol moulds, small puff pastry patties filled with green asparagus tips mixed with truffle strips, Madeira sauce whipped with butter.

Normandy Style: à la normande (for fish): bearded oysters and mussels, shrimps, truffle slices, gudgeons or very small smelts egged, breadcrumbed and deep fried, fleurons, Normandy sauce, whole crayfish.

Norwegian Style: à la norvégienne (for cold fish): whole fish, poached, when cold skinned, decorated to taste, glazed with aspic jelly, garnished with prawns, scooped out pieces of cucumber stuffed with purée of smoked salmon, red beet boats filled with shrimp salad, halved hard-boiled eggs, very small skinned and marinated tomatoes; Russian mayonnaise sauce separately.

Norwegian Style with noodles (for meat and poultry): noodles tossed in butter, Madeira sauce.

O

Odalisc Style: à l'odalisque (for lamb): sliced fried eggplants, buttered peas, Italian sauce.

Opera: à l'Opéra (for fish): asparagus tips, white wine sauce. (for tournedos and noisettes): tartlets filled with sautéd chicken liver slices, small patties of duchess potato mass, egged, breadcrumbed, deep fried and hollowed out, filled with buttered asparagus tips; the natural juices of the meat whipped with butter.

Ophelia (for fish): cream sauce finished off with tomato purée and tomato catsup, small pieces of deep fried salsify, potato croquettes.

Oriental Style: à l'orientale (for fish): I. fillets or small fish poached in white wine and oil with diced tomatoes, seasoned with salt, peppercorn, fennel, bay leaf, garlic, parsley roots and saffron, served cold in the stock with lemon slices.
II. fillets, lobster slices prepared à la Newburgh, Newburgh sauce seasoned with curry powder; plain rice separately.
(for butcher's meat): halved tomatoes stuffed with rice Greek style, croquettes of sweet potatoes, tomato sauce.

Orleans Style: à l'orléanaise (for butcher's meat): braised curly endives bound with eggs and buttered, maître d'hôtel potatoes separately, meat gravy.

Orloff (1. for saddles of veal and lamb): braised, carved, each slice coated with white onion purée, placed back into position with a truffle slice between the meat, masked with Béchamel sauce mixed with onion purée, glazed; asparagus tips, creamed cucumber olives or braised celery and veal gravy separately.
(2. for other butcher's meat): braised celery, braised stuffed lettuce, castle potatoes, Navarra tomatoes, thick meat gravy.

Ostende Style: à l'ostendaise (for fish): fillets stuffed with fish forcemeat, poached in oyster liquor, poached bearded oysters and truffle slices on top, Normandy sauce, very small deep fried sole croquettes.

Othello (for tournedos, noisettes and grilled meat): buttered green peas, straw potatoes, truffle sauce.

Oyster-merchant Style: à l'écaillière (for feathered game): stuffed with forcemeat mixed with chicken livers, diced bacon and oysters, garnished with glazed button onions, thick game gravy.

P

Palermo Style: à la palermitaine (for butcher's meat): stuffed egg plants, macaroni croquettes, grilled tomatoes, tomato sauce.

Palestinian Style: à la palestine (for butcher's meat and poultry): small fried semolina dumplings, glazed button onions, quartered artichoke bottoms sautéd in butter, Madeira sauce.

Paquita (for fish): white wine sauce whipped with anchovy butter, small puff pastry patties stuffed with diced mushrooms and lobster in crayfish sauce.

Parisian Style (for fish): poached, garnished with sliced mushrooms and truffles, covered with white wine sauce, surrounded with whole crayfish.
(for butcher's meat and poultry): Parisian potatoes, artichoke bottoms stuffed with salpicon of ox tongue. mushrooms and truffles bound with velouté sauce and glazed, Madeira sauce.

Parmentier (for butcher's meat and poultry): diced or oval-shaped potatoes pan-fried in butter, chopped parsley scattered on top, veal gravy.

Pergamon (for tournedos and noisettes): truffle slice on the meat, croquette potatoes, Madeira sauce.

Perigord Style: à la périgourdine (for fillets of beef, tenderloins): small whole truffles cooked in Madeira with fine mirepoix, truffle sauce.
(for poultry): truffle slices placed under the skin of the breast, poached, suprême sauce with truffle essence.

Persian Style: à la persane (for butcher's meat and poultry): small green peppers stuffed with rice, fried banana slices, halved grilled tomatoes; Chateaubriand sauce.

Peruvian Style: à la péruvienne (for tournedos and entrées): scopped out oxalis stuffed with chopped raw ham and chicken, the pulp of the oxalis added, and treated like stuffed tomatoes; light tomato sauce.

Piedmontese Style: à la piémontaise (for butcher's meat and poultry): small timbals of risotto mixed with grated white truffles, tomato sauce.

Pisane Style: (for fish): paupiettes dressed on buttered spinach leaves mixed with anchovy fillets and garlic, covered with cream sauce, diced tomatoes added, surrounded with quarters of hard-boiled eggs, sprinkled with breadcrumbs and grated Parmesan, moistened with oil, gratinated in the oven.

Polignac (for poultry): stuffed with chicken mousseline forcemeat mixed with sliced truffles and mushrooms, poached, covered with suprême sauce finished off with mushroom purée, mushroom and truffle julienne added.

Polish Style: à la polonaise (for poultry): tartlets filled with braised saurkraut, small grilled smoked sausages, small veal dumplings, Madeira sauce.

Pompadour (for fish): fillets dipped in melted butter and white breadcrumbs, pan fried, truffle slices dipped in melted meat glaze on top, Parisian potatoes, Choron sauce separately.
(for tournedos and entrées) artichoke bottoms filled with lentil purée, a slice of truffle on top, marble-sized potato croquettes, light truffle sauce.

Pontigny (for fish): crayfish tails, mushrooms, fish forcemeat dumplings stuffed with white onion purée, sailors sauce mixed with diced shrimp tails.

Portuguese Style: à la portugaise (for butcher's meat and poultry): stuffed tomatoes, castle potatoes, Portuguese sauce.

Pretty Helena: Belle-Hélène (for tournedos and noisettes): small round croquettes of green asparagus tips, truffle slices, thick veal gravy.

Prince of Wales: Prince de Galles (for fish): bearded mussels and oysters, small rice croquettes, Chambord sauce whipped with crayfish butter, seasoned with curry powder.

Princess Style: à la princesse (for tournedos, noisettes and sweetbreads): truffle slices, creamed asparagus tips, German sauce finished off with mushroom essence.

Printanière: see Spring Style.

Provencal Style: à la provençale (for entrées): small grilled tomatoes, stuffed mushroom caps with a little garlic, Provencal sauce.

Providence (for butchers' meat and poultry): pitted olives, mushrooms, truffles, veal or chicken dumplings, goose liver, the natural juice of the meat or poultry.

Q

Queen Margot: reine Margot (for poultry): stuffed with chicken mousseline-forcemeat blended with almond purée, chicken mousseline dumplings blended alternately with pistachio purée and crayfish butter; suprême sauce blended with almond milk.

Queen Style: à la reine (for poached poultry): chicken purée blended with eggs, moulded and poached, truffle slices on top of each mould, suprême sauce.

Quirinal (for fish): mushrooms, crayfish tails, red wine sauce. (for tournedos and noisettes): mushroom caps stuffed with ox marrow, straw potatoes, watercress, Italian sauce with chopped tarragon.

R

Rachel (for fish): fillets stuffed with fish forcemeat and a slice of truffle, folded, poached in white wine, green asparagus tips, truffle strips, white wine sauce.
(for tournedos and noisettes): artichoke bottoms with a large blanched slice of ox marrow on top, chopped parsley, red wine sauce.

Radzivill (for fish): mushrooms, truffle slices, soft carps roes, eel-pout liver, crayfish dumplings, Geneva sauce.

Rakoczy (for butchers' meat): sliced eggplants simmered in butter, bound with paprika sauce.

Raphael (for tournedos and noisettes): artichoke bottoms filled alternately with sliced creamed carrots and Béarnaise sauce, straw potatoes.

Reform: à la réforme (for lamb cutlets): dipped in melted butter and white breadcrumbs mixed with chopped ham, pan fried, Reform sauce.

Regency Style: à la régence (for fish): bearded oysters, small whiting dumplings finished off with crayfish butter, fluted mushroom caps, sliced soft roes, olive-shaped truffles, Normandy sauce with truffle essence.
(for sweetbreads and poultry): truffled chicken dumplings, large veal dumplings decorated with truffle, small round goose liver collops, fluted mushroom caps, olive-shaped truffles, cockscombs, German sauce finished off with truffle essence.

(for feathered game): same garnish as for poultry, no veal dumplings and game instead of chicken dumplings, salmi sauce with truffle essence.

Regina (for butcher's meat): tomatoes stuffed with risotto with Parmesan, mushrooms, grilled sweet peppers, Madeira sauce mixed with chopped pickles.

Réjane (for fish): rosette-shaped duchess potatoes, white wine sauce whipped with meat glaze and crayfish butter. (for entrées): tartlets stuffed alternately with goose liver purée and asparagus tips, Madeira sauce.

Renaissance (for butchers' meat): young carrots, turnips, French beans, green peas, asparagus tips and sprigs of cauliflower covered with Dutch sauce all dressed around the meat in question, new pan fried potatoes, meat gravy. This garnish is usually served separately nowadays.

Reynière (for poultry): small fried pork sausages, glazed chestnuts, Madeira sauce mixed with diced sautéd calf's kidneys.

Richelieu (for fish): dipped in melted butter and white breadcrumbs, pan fried, covered with herb butter, truffle slices on top.
(for tournedos, noisettes and butcher's meat): stuffed tomatoes, stuffed mushroom caps, braised lettuce, small egg-shaped potatoes cooked in butter, thick veal gravy.

Rich Style: à la riche (for fish): fillets, a slice of spiny lobster and truffle on each, covered with Victoria sauce. (for tournedos, noisettes and poultry) goose liver medaillons, truffle slices, artichoke bottoms filled with asparagus tips, Madeira sauce.

Robinson (for entrées): tartlets or artichoke bottoms filled with diced sautéd chicken livers in Madeira sauce.

Rochambeau (for butchers' meat): tartlet-shaped duchess potatoes filled with Vichy carrots, stuffed lettuce, cauliflower sprigs Polish style, Anna potatoes, demi-glace.

Rohan (for poultry): poached, artichoke bottoms covered with meat glaze, a round slice of goose liver and a truffle slice on top, tartlets filled with cocks' kidneys bound with German sauce, cocks' combs, German sauce finished off with mushroom essence.

Romanoff (for butchers' meat): stuffed cucumbers, tartlet-shaped duchess potatoes filled with diced mushrooms and knob celery bound with horseradish sauce, thick meat gravy.

Roman Style (for butchers' meat): tartlets filled with tiny Italian dumplings sprinkled with cheese and glazed, spinach subrics mixed with chopped anchovies, Roman sauce with tomato purée.

Roosevelt (for game): tartlets stuffed alternately with lentil purée, diced sautéd morels and truffles, chiefranger sauce.

Roseberry (for butchers' meat): semolina croquettes scooped out and stuffed with diced, sautéd morels, stuffed tomatoes, French beans, olive-shaped cucumbers, meat gravy.

Rossini (for tournedos, medaillons and chicken breasts): small goose liver collops fried in butter, thick truffle slices, demi-glace with truffle essence.

Rostand (tournedos, noisettes and butchers' meat): quartered artichoke bottoms sautéd in butter, creamed mushrooms, Colbert sauce.

Rouenese Style: à la rouennaise (for fish): poached in red wine with chopped shallots, covered with the boiled down stock whipped up with butter, bearded oysters and mussels, shrimps, mushrooms and small deep fried smelts.

Roumanille (for tournedos, noisettes and veal medaillons): sautéd in butter, coated with Mornay sauce mixed with tomato purée, glazed, garnished anchovy fillets, pitted olives and slices of egg plants fried in oil.

Royal Style: à la royale: same as Regency.

S

Sagan (for veal collops, sweetbreads and suprêmes of poultry): dressed on risotto, mushroom caps stuffed with purée of calf's brains mixed with chopped truffles, the natural juices boiled down, mixed with thick veal gravy and flavored with Madeira.

Sailor Style: à la matelote (for fish and certain ragoûts): glazed button onions, button mushrooms cooked in butter, small heart-shaped croûtons fried in butter, sometimes crayfish tails or whole crayfish cooked in court-bouillon.

Saint-André (for fish): pan fried, dressed on sorrel purée, chopped hard-boiled eggs scattered on top, chopped parsley, browned butter.

Saint-Cloud (for butchers' meat): peas prepared in the French way, braised lettuce, Madeira sauce.

Saint-Florentin (for butchers' meat): Saint-Florentin potatoes, morels prepared in the Bordeaux way, Bonnefoy sauce.

Saint-Germain (for fish): dipped in eggs and breadcrumbs, pan fried, nut potatoes, Béarnaise sauce.
(for sweetbreads): purée of green peas dressed in artichoke bottoms, Béarnaise sauce.
(for butchers' meat): purée of green peas bound with egg yolks and poached in dariol moulds, olive-shaped glazed carrots, fondantes potatoes, Béarnaise sauce.

Saint-Henri (for fish)· pan fried, chopped parsley, lemon juice and browned butter on top, sea urchin purée separately.

Saint-Lambert (for butchers' meat): glazed button onions, glazed carrots, French beans, green peas, cauliflower sprigs, thick meat gravy.

Saint-Mandé (for butcher's meat): Macaire potatoes, green peas and French beans tossed in butter, thick veal gravy.

Saint-Marc (for game): chestnut croquettes, demi-glace with game and juniper berry essence.

Saint-Nazaire (for fish): bearded oysters and diced lobster in white wine sauce and fleurons.

Saint-Saëns (for suprêmes of poultry): small goose liver truffle croquettes, cockscombs, asparagus tips, suprême sauce with truffle essence.

Salvator (for fish): Portuguese sauce with chopped thyme, fish potatoes.

Samaritaine (for butcher's meat): rice timbales, braised lettuce, Dauphine potatoes, demi-glace.

Sarlat Style: à la sarladaise (for lamb and mutton): raw sliced potatoes and truffles pan fried in the oven, thick meat gravy.

Sardinian Style: à la sarde (for butchers' meat): ball-shaped risotto croquettes with saffron, stuffed tomatoes, stuffed braised cucumbers, light tomato sauce.

Savary (for tournedos and noisettes): tartlet-shaped duchess potatoes stuffed with chopped braised celery bound with demi-glace.

Savoyard Style: à la savoyarde (for butchers' meat): braised, Savoyard potatoes, thick meat gravy with tomato purée.

Saxon Style: à la saxe (for poultry): poached, crayfish tails, cauliflower sprigs, crayfish sauce.

Scotch Style: à l'écossaise (for fish): Normandy sauce mixed with diced pot herbs.
(for butchers' meat): buttered green beans, fondantes potatoes, Scotch sauce.

Schubert (for tournedos, noisettes and poultry): tartlets filled with asparagus tips, round pieces of potato scooped out, pan fried and filled with green peas, round pieces of knob celery scooped out, simmered in butter and stuffed with potato purée, Madeira sauce.

Scribe (for tournedos and noisettes): rice tartlets stuffed with goose liver purée.

Sens Style: à la sénonaise (for fish): covered with sailor sauce whipped with anchovy butter and glazed.

Serge (for sweetbreads and veal collops): dipped in eggs and white breadcrumbs mixed with chopped mushrooms and truffles, pan fried in butter, artichoke quarters cooked in butter, large ham julienne warmed up in Madeira, demi-glace with truffle essence.

Sevigné (for tournedos and noisettes): stuffed lettuce, fried mushrooms, castle potatoes, Madeira sauce.

Sevilla Style: à la sévillane (for tournedos, noisettes and poultry): tartlets stuffed with tomatoes concassées and sweet red peppers, Parmentier potatoes, Valois sauce.

Sicilian Style: à la sicilienne: (for fish): dipped in eggs and breadcrumbs, pan fried, covered with lemon slices, hard-boiled chopped eggs, chopped parsley, capers and anchovy fillets, browned butter poured over.
(for entrées): ribbon macaroni bound with butter, grated Parmesan, velouté and chicken liver purée.
(for meat in general): stuffed tomatoes, timbals of Piedmont rice, croquette potatoes, light tomato sauce.

Sigurd (for butchers' meat): stuffed tomatoes, small ham croquettes, truffle sauce.

Soissons Style: à la soissonnaise (for mutton): white haricot beans bound with tomato sauce and a little garlic or purée of haricot beans finished off with cream and butter, light tomato sauce.

Southern Style: à la méridionale (for fish): fillets or small fish simmered in fish stock and oil with diced tomatoes and saffron.
(for meat in general): stuffed tomatoes, green peas, tartlets stuffed with sorrel purée, sliced sautéd yellow boletus, light tomato or Madeira sauce.

Spanish Style: à l'espagnole (for fish): pan fried in oil, tomatoes concassées, strips of fried green peppers, fried onion rings.
(for butchers' meat): rice pilaff mixed with diced red peppers, green peas and diced garlic sausage, fried tomatoes, meat gravy.

Spring Style: à la printanière: (for butchers' meat): olive-shaped glazed carrots and turnips, asparagus tips, green peas, French beans.

Staël (for tournedos, noisettes and small pieces of poultry): round flat chicken croquettes, large mushroom caps stuffed with chicken purée and green peas, Madeira sauce.

Steward Style: maître d'hôtel (for grilled meat): herb butter, French fried or soufflé potatoes, watercress.

Strassburg Style: à la strasbourgeoise (for butchers' meat): braised saurkraut, triangles of bacon cooked with the sauerkraut, sautéd collops of goose liver, meat gravy.

Suchet (for fish): white wine sauce with strips of carrots, leeks, celery and truffles simmered in butter.

Sully (for tournedos, noisettes and poultry): same as Judic, Parisian potatoes added.

Sultan Style: à la sultane (for chicken breasts): dipped in eggs and white breadcrumbs mixed with chopped truffles, cutlet-shaped poached chicken forcemeat as support for the breasts, tartlets stuffed with truffle purée decorated with pistachios, cockscombs, suprême sauce seasoned with curry powder.

Susan: Suzanne (for tournedos and noisettes): stuffed braised lettuce, artichoke bottoms, demi-glace with tarragon essence and chopped tarragon leaves.

Suzeraine (for butchers' meat): stuffed tomatoes, stuffed pieces of cucumber, Madeira sauce.

T

Talleyrand (for butchers' meat and poultry): macaroni cut in small pieces, bound with butter and grated Parmesan and mixed with truffle julienne and diced goose liver, Perigord sauce with truffle julienne.

Tenant Style: à la fermière (for poultry and butchers' meat): carrots, turnips, celery and onions in small thin slices simmered in butter, diced fried bacon, olive-shaped pan fried potatoes, the natural juice of the meat or poultry.

Tivoli (for entrées): green asparagus tips, large grilled mushrooms stuffed with sliced cockscombs and kidneys in suprême sauce, thick veal gravy.

Tosca (for fish): fillets stuffed with fish forcemeat mixed with crayfish butter, crayfish tails, truffle slices and sliced fried soft roes, covered with Mornay sauce whipped with crayfish butter, glazed.
(for poultry): stuffed with rice, poached, braised fennel bulbs, the boiled down stock whipped up with butter.

Toulon Style: à la toulonaise (for fish): stuffed with whiting forcemeat, poached in fish stock, bearded mussels, buttered fish velouté.

Toulouse Style: à la toulousaine (for poultry, sweetbreads and large puff pastry patties): chicken forcemeat dumplings, braised sweetbread collops, very white mushroom caps, cockscombs, truffle slices, German sauce with mushroom essence.

Tours Style: à la tourangelle (for butchers' meat): French beans and flageolets mixed together and bound with light Béchamel sauce, thick meat gravy.

Tourville Style: à la tourvillaise (for fish): truffle und mushroom slices, bearded mussels and oysters, covered with Mornay sauce, glazed.

Trevise Style (for tournedos and noisettes): scooped out fried croûtons stuffed with mushroom purée, quartered artichoke bottoms dipped in frying batter and deep fried, noisette potatoes, Choron sauce.

Trianon (for fish): covered alternately with Nantua, green herb and white wine sauce mixed with chopped truffles. (for tenderloins — fillet of beef — and tournedos): tartlets filled alternately with green peas, carrot purée and chestnut or mushroom purée, Madeira sauce.

Trieste Style: à la triestoise (for fish): dressed on shredded lettuce simmered in butter, surrounded with quarters of hard-boiled eggs and noisette potatoes, browned butter poured over.

Trouville Style: à la trouvillaise (for fish): shrimps tails, small mushroom caps, bearded mussels, shrimp sauce.

Tsar Style: du tsar (for fish): olive-shaped agoursis cooked in butter, fluted mushrooms or gribuis, covered with Mornay sauce, glazed.

Tsarina: à la tsarine (for fish): garnished with olive-shaped cucumbers cooked in butter, covered with Mornay sauce with paprika, glazed.
(for chicken breasts): poached in butter, olive-shaped cucumbers in cream sauce, suprême sauce with julienne of fennel bulbs.

Turbigo (for tournedos and noisettes): small fried pork sausages (Chipolatas), grilled or fried mushrooms, the pan juices deglaced with white wine and boiled down with demi-glace and tomato purée.

Turkish Style: à la turque (for fish): pan fried in butter, dressed on rice pilaff with saffron, garnished with slices of eggplants fried in oil, browned butter on top.

Turtle Style: en tortue (for calf's head): small veal dumplings, mushroom caps, stuffed blanched olives, olive-shaped gherkins, sliced calf's tongues, sliced calf's brains, truffle slices, very small French fried eggs, heart-shaped croûtons fried in butter, turtle sauce.

Tuscan Style: à la toscanne (for veal collops, sweetbreads and chicken breasts): macaroni cut in pieces, bound with goose liver purée and mixed with diced truffles, thick veal gravy. All preparations Tuscan style are dipped in eggs and breadcrumbs mixed with grated Parmesan and pan fried in butter.

Tyrolian Style: à la tyrolienne (for fish): pan fried, dressed on tomatoes concassées,, garnished with fried onion rings. (for dark grilled meat): fried onion rings, tomatoes concassées, Tyrolian sauce.

U

Upsala Style (for fish): poached, covered with white wine sauce with coarse julienne of fennel bulbs simmered in butter.

Urbain-Dubois (for fish): 1. fillets, poached covered with aurora sauce mixed with diced crayfish tails and truffles, topped with crayfish soufflé, baked in oven.

Urbain-Dubois
2. poached, covered with lobster soufflé, baked in oven, garnished with sliced truffles and small whiting dumplings covered with Normandy sauce.

V

Valaisan Style: à la valaisienne (for fish): boiled, Geneva sauce mixed with chopped pickles and capers served separately.

Valenciennes Style (for tournedos, noisettes and poultry): rice pilaff mixed with diced ham und sweet red peppers. For meat thick veal gravy with tomato purée, for poultry suprême sauce slightly colored with tomato purée.

Valkyrie Style (for game): potato croquettes, stuffed mushroom caps, the pan juice deglaced with cream and flavored with juniper berries.

Valois (for fish): boiled potato balls, soft roes simmered in butter, whole crayfish, Valois sauce.
(for small pieces of butchers' meat and poultry): sliced raw potatoes and artichoke bottoms sautéd in butter, the pan juices deglaced with white wine, boiled down with veal gravy and whipped with butter. Served en cocotte.

Van Swieten (for fish): covered with shrimps and truffles in crayfish sauce, topped with very small dices of white bread fried in butter.

Vaucluse Style: à la vauclusienne (for small fish or fillets): pan fried in olive oil, lemon juice and chopped parsley on top, covered with the frying oil mixed with browned butter.

Vegetable Gardner Style: à la maraichère (for butchers' meat): salsify cut in pieces, bound with cream sauce, Brussels sprouts, large castle potatoes, demi-glace or thick veal gravy.

Venetian Style: à la vénetienne (for fish): fillets poached in white wine, covered with Venetian sauce, garnished with heart-shaped croûtons fried in butter.
(for poultry): poached, covered with suprême sauce finished off with green herb butter, cockscombs, sliced poached calf's brains and fluted mushrooms.

Verdi (for fish): fillets, poached, dressed on macaroni cut in small pieces and mixed with diced lobster, truffles, butter and grated Parmesan, covered with Mornay sauce, glazed.

Verneuil (for small pieces of veal, lamb and chicken breasts): dipped in melted butter and white breadcrumbs, pan fried, artichoke purée and Colbert sauce served separately.

Vert-pré (for grilled meat and poultry) straw potatoes, watercress, herb butter.
(for white meat): French beans, green peas and green asparagus tips tossed in butter.

Vichy Style (for butchers' meat): carrots prepared in the Vichy way, castle potatoes, brown gravy.

Victoria (for fish): sliced or diced spiny lobster and truffles, covered with Victoria sauce, glazed.
(for tournedos, noisettes and chicken breasts): small tomatoes stuffed with mushroom purée and gratinated, arti-

choke quarters cooked in butter, the pan juice deglaced with Portwine and boiled down with veal gravy.

Viennese Style: à la viennoise (for fish fillets, veal cutlets and collops and chicken breasts): dipped in eggs and breadcrumbs, pan fried, garnished with lemon slices, capres, chopped parsley, hard-boiled egg yolks and whites each part chopped separately, and pitted olives, browned butter on top.

This is the French style, in Vienna these preparations are only served crisp pan fried with a slice of lemon on top, nothing else.

Viroflay (for butchers' meat): spinach cakes Viroflay, artichoke quarters sautéd in butter, castle potatoes, thick veal gravy.

W

Walewska (for fish): sliced langoustine or spiny lobster tails and truffles, covered with Mornay sauce whipped with langoustine butter, glazed.

Washington (for poultry): stuffed with corn prepared Greek style, poached, suprême sauce.

White Lady: dame blanche (for fish): cream sauce with chopped truffles, fleurons,

Windsor (for fish): soft roes, bearded oysters, oyster sauce. (for veal cutlets and steaks): cut open, stuffed with veal forcemeat with chopped mushrooms, braised, garnished with sliced ox tongue, meat gravy; any vegetable purée served separately.

Wladimir (for tournedos and noisettes): olive-shaped cucumber pieces stewed in butter, diced vegetable marrow sautéd in butter, the pan juice deglaced with sour cream and seasoned with paprika, grated horseradish scattered on top.

Y

Yvette (for fish): covered with herb sauce, glazed, small tomatoes stuffed with sole purée.

Main Dishes

Meat, Poultry Game etc.
Hot Appetizers, Entrées, Relevés, Roasts

French: Plats de viande, volaille et gibier
German: Fleisch-, Geflügel- und Wildgerichte
Italian: Piatti di carne, pollame, selvaggina
Spanish: Comivas de carne, volatil, salvaje

General Rules for Cooking Meat, Poultry and Game

Roasting: Rôtis: roasting in oven should be done in an uncovered pan. Under no circumstances is water to be added. The meat is seasoned, placed in a pan on hot fat, roasted in the oven and basted frequently. Heat must be regulated according to size and sort of meat. If roasted on the spit, large pieces must be seared first and the heat regulated to allow the meat to get done in the interior; frequent basting is essential. Large roasts will continue to cook after leaving the oven. Temperature of place where the finished roast is kept warm must therefore be watched.

Braising: Braisés ordinaires: meat must first be well seared to keep the juices in. It is then placed in a special braising pan with a tight fitting cover on sliced onions and carrots browned beforehand, moistened with wine, stock or a light sauce or a concoction of all three and braised slowly in the oven with the cover on.

White Braising: Braisés à blanc: this method is applied principally to poultry or white meat, veal and lamb. The meat is stiffened in butter only but not allowed to get browned. It is placed in a braising pan on sliced pot herbs lightly fried in butter, moistened with white wine or white stock or both and braised at a moderate temperature with the cover on.

Pan-Roasting: Poêlés: it is impossible to translate the culinary term poêler literally. To poêler meat or poultry it is placed in a good fitting pan or fireproof casserole on sliced pot herbs, seasoned, melted butter poured on top and roasted in oven with the cover on. Shortly before meat is done, cover is taken of to allow the top side to get brown. Moderate temperature is essential for pan-roasting. As soon as the meat is browned it is taken out of the pan, the fat is poured off and the residue deglaced with wine, stock, gravy or sauce and used for making the sauce.

Poaching: Pochés: term applied to cooking poultry or meat in stock just a little before the boiling point. The meat is placed in a casserole, boiling stock is poured over and simmered below boiling point until the meat is tender. This applies to large pieces of meat, ham or poultry only. Small pieces, fillets, breasts etc are placed in a pan greased with butter, seasoned, a little lemon juice, wine or stock poured over, covered with a greased papper and poached in oven at moderate temperature for a few minutes.

Deep Fat Frying: Traitement à la friture: frying of small pieces of meat, poultry etc in hot fat. There must be enough fat in pan to allow them to swimm and hot enough, to sear meat etc. Before frying food is often dipped in egg and breadcrumbs or in frying batter. Don't **boil** fod in deep fat as the absortion of fat will make the food indigestible. Guard against overheating the fat. Fried food is deposited on a clean towl to absorb the surplus fat and sprinkled with salt while still hot. Fried food is never served with a cover on dish.

Pan or Shallow Frying: to roast or fry in a skillet with little butter or fat.

Sautéing: Sautés: roasting or frying in a heavy flat sort of casserole called plat à sauter or sautoir on a quick fire tossing i. e. shaking the pan to and fro so that the contents become mixed and change their places. This method is especially suited for disjointed chicken (poulet sauté) and very small pieces of meat etc. Essential for all sautés is the deglacing of the residues in the pan with wine, stock or sauce after the fat has been poured off. Shallow frying of steaks, tournedos etc. is also called sautéing.

Grilling: Grillés: the action of cooking food by dry heat close to an open fire on a grill (broiler), a hot griddle or on a spit.

A

Abatis de volaille: see giblets.

Agnello al forno: roast baron of lamb: larded with onions and garlic, sprinkled with salt and rosemary, roasted in hot lard surrounded with raw potatoes cut in quarters. (Italian)

Agnelotti: kind of ravioli stuffed with lamb hash mixed with chopped onions sautéd in butter, boiled rice, brain, cheese and seasoning; boiled, drained, sprinkled with grated Parmesan, melted butter dropped on top, gratinated or served in tomato sauce or demi-glace with grated Parmesan separately. (Italian)

Aiguillettes: see breast strips.

Ailerons: see wing tips.

Albóndigas: Spanish meat balls: tenderloin and half as much fat bacon chopped finely, seasoned with salt and red pepper, chopped garlic and whole eggs added, shaped into small flat dumplings, fried in the pan on both sides, covered with white wine, light tomato sauce and brown gravy, braised. (Spanish)

— **con guisantes:** Spanish meat dumplings: round flat dumplings made of raw chopped beef and chopped onions sautéd in butter, browned on both sides, simmered in demi-glace with tomato purée and garlic; sauce mixed with green peas poured over the dumplings. (Spanish)

Albóndiguillas: Spanish dumplings: minced roast or boiled meat, poultry or game mixed with breadcrumbs, eggs, a little white wine, chopped parsley and herbs, seasoned with salt and pepper, shaped into nut-sized flat dumplings, dipped in eggs and breadcrumbs, fried in the pan in oil, served with tomato sauce.

— **a Criolla:** Creole Style: same as above but the sauce mixed with chopped sweet peppers simmered in butter, rice pilaff with saffron served separately. (Spanish)

Alligator Steak: cut from the tail, sautéd in butter, served with Madeira sauce.

Allumettes: see puff pastry sticks.

Alouette: see lark.

Aloyau de boeuf: see sirloin of beef.

Amourettes: the marrow of ox or more often veal bones. See ox marrow.

Andouilles: particular kind of pork sausage served as hors d'oeuvre. See pork sausages.

Arrostino annegato alla milanaise: calf's liver cut lengthwise, rolled in a boned veal loin, cut into thick slices held together with wooden skewers, sprinkled with chopped sage and rosemary, salted, coated with flour, fried on both sides in oil, stewed in white wine, lemon juice and brown stock, glazed in oven; risotto and the thickened gravy served separately. (Italian)

Arroz Valenciana: Rice Valencian Style: chicken meat stewed together with rice, thick strips of ham, shredded red and green peppers, green peas and boletus, served with demi-glace with tomato. (Spanish)

Asado: meat or poultry roasted over an open fire with garlic, ham, saffron and red peppers. (Spanish)

Aspic: Aspic Jelly: boiled or roasted meat, fish, poultry, game or vegetables filled in mould lined with aspic jelly and decorated, sealed with jelly, turned out, garnished, served with an appropriate sauce.

— **Banker Style:** à la banquière: mould decorated with hard-boiled egg whites and truffle slices, filled with diced goose liver, mushrooms, cockscombs and cocks' kidneys, sealed with aspic jelly.

— **Carnot:** mould lined with aspic jelly, filled with slices of lobster and truffles, sealed with aspic jelly, chilled, garnished with tartlets filled with lobster salad mixed with diced green peppers; remoulade sauce mixed with grated horseradish served separately.

— **Gaulish Style:** à la gauloise: slices of chicken breast, cockscomb and cocks' kidney, coated with white chaud-froid sauce set alternately with truffle slices in mould lined and sealed with aspic jelly.

— **of Goose Liver:** de foie gras: goose liver studded with truffles, wrapped in fat bacon, poached in Madeira or Port, when cold placed in mould lined with Madeira or Portwine jelly and decorated with truffle, sealed with jelly, chilled.

— **of Hare:** de lièvre: mould lined with aspic jelly, filled alternately with small slices of roast hare, mushrooms, truffles and gooseliver, sealed with jelly, chilled.

Aspic
- **Italian Style:** à l'italienne: mould lined with aspic jelly, decorated with truffle, filled with small slices of chicken breast, ox tongue and truffles, sealed with aspic jelly, chilled, Italian salad served separately.
- **of Lobster:** de homard: slices of lobster and truffles set in mould in very clear aspic jelly, chilled; mayonnaise or Gloucester sauce served separately.
- **Medicis:** fieldfare breasts and gooseliver froth filled alternately in mould lined with Madeira aspic jelly.
- **Modern Style:** à la moderne: chicken, ham and spinach froth set alternately in mould lined with aspic jelly.
- **of Salmon:** de saumon: small poached salmon slices decorated with tarragon leaves, hard-boiled egg whites-truffle or tomato slices, set in aspic jelly, chilled, garnished with darioles of vegetable macedoine bound with jellied mayonnaise; Chantilly, Tartar oder mayonnaise sauce served separately.
- **of Sterlet:** de sterlet: mould lined with fish jelly, decorated with hard-boiled egg whites, truffle and gherkin slices and crayfish tails, filled with small slices of poached sterlet, sealed with aspic, chilled, turned out, garnished with halved hard-boiled eggs stuffed with vegetable salad; mayonnaise sauce served separately.
- **of Woodcock:** de bécasse: breast of roast woodcock and woodcock froth filled alternately in mould lined with game jelly, chilled, turned out on shredded lettuce.

Attereaux: see skewers.

B

Backhendl: fried chicken: young cockerels, fryers, cut in four, dipped in eggs and breadcrumbs together with liver and gizzard, fried in deep fat, garnished with fried parsley, lettuce salad served separately. (Austrian)

Ballotine: culinary term of a sort of galantine of white meat, pork or chicken, stuffed with forcemeat, braised white or brown. served hot with an appropriate sauce and garnish or cold in aspic jelly.

Ballotines de volaille: see chicken legs, stuffed.

Bárány paprikás: see Goulash.

Bárány pörkölt: Hungarian Lamb Goulash: diced lamb, fried with chopped onions, diced bacon and paprika in lard, seasoned with salt, stewed with brown stock and tomato purée; Tarhonya served separately. (Hungarian)

Baron: name for the two legs and back in one piece, especially for lamb and mutton.

Baron of Beef: Baron de boeuf: joint of beef consisting of the two sirloins joined together at the backbone. Can only be roasted in front of an open fire being to large for any oven.

Barquettes: see pastry boats.

Bartavelle; F. Bartavelle; G. Steinhuhn: Greek or red-legged partridge, prepared like partridge.

Bavarian Liver Dumplings: see bayrische Leberknödel.

Bayerische Leberknödel: Bavarian Liver Dumplings: raw chopped calf's liver rubbed through a sieve, mixed with eggs, chopped fat bacon and onions, a little flour, small croûtons fried in butter and seasoning, shaped into balls the size of a tangerine, poached in salt water, drained, covered with browned butter and served with saurkraut. (German)

Bear; F. Ours; G. Bär: the European brown bear, the American black bear and the polar white bear are edible, the meat is considered very tasty, especially the paws, ham and steaks.

Bear's Ham in Burgundy: Jambon d'ours au vin de Bourgogne: marinated in Burgundy wine, sliced pot herbs and onions, braised in a part of the marinade, red wine sauce made with the stock and saurkraut served separately.

— **Cumberland:** braised with a part of the marinade, the stock boiled down with demi-glace, strained, mixed with apple purée and a little red currant jelly.

— **Francis Joseph:** Francois Joseph: braised in champagne, served with the boiled down stock mixed with chief ranger's sauce.

— **Northern Style:** à la nordique: smoked, watered over night, wrapped in dough made of water and rye flour, baked in the oven, whipped unsweetened cream mixed with grated horseradish and caviar served separately.

— **Russian Style:** à la russe:
1. larded, braised in the marinade, garnished with saurkraut, mixed with diced apples, and glazed button onions.
2. braised in the marinade, served with sauce prepared with the boiled down marinade and sour cream.

— **Tsarina:** à la czarine: same as Northern Style.

Bear's Paws: Pattes d'ours: kept for a few days in a boiled marinade, stewed in white wine with pot herbs and a part of the marinade.

— **Grilled:** grillées: boiled in marinade until tender, when cold cut in pieces, marinated in lemon juice and oil, dipped in eggs and breadcrumbs, moistened with oil or butter, grilled; devil sauce served separately.

— **Russian Style:** à la russe: boiled until tender, when cold bones removed, cut in slices, dipped in eggs and breadcrumbs, deep fried; caper sauce served separately.

— **Stuffed:** farcies: boiled until tender, when cold bones removed, stuffed with pork forcemeat with chopped fine herbs, wrapped in greased paper bag, baked in oven; Portwine sauce served separately.

Bear, Saddle of: Selle d'ours: marinated in a boiled marinade of red wine, pot herbs, onions, thyme, sage and a bayleaf, braised with crushed juniper berries and a part of the marinade, garnish to taste.

— **Russian Style:** à la russe: larded, braised in a part of the marinade, served with sour cream sauce.

— **Trapper Style:** à la trappeur: larded, marinated in red wine and whisky with pot herbs and onions, braised in the marinade, the stock thickened with arrow root, strained and mixed with rose hip purée, garnished with topinambours simmered in butter; creamed corn and plain boiled rice served separately.

Beaver: Castor: seldom eaten nowadays, prepared like furred game.

Beaver

— **Ragout:** Ragoût de bièvre: meat cut in large cubes, pan-fried with chopped onions, sprinkled with flour, moistened with white wine, brown stock and a dash of vinegar, seasoned, chopped lemon peel and anchovy fillets added, braised in oven.

— **Tail:** Queue de bièvre: marinated in red wine with pot herbs, sliced onions, fine herbs, water and a little vinegar, stewed in brown stock and a part of the marinade, stock reduced, strained, thickened with arrow root.

— **Tail, grilled:** Queue de bievre grillée: cooked in the marinade, dipped in eggs and breadcrumbs, moistened with oil, grilled, served with devil sauce.

Bécasse: see woodcock.

Bécassine: see snipe.

Bec-figue: see Fig-Pecker.

Beef; F. Boeuf; G. Ochsenfleisch, Rindfleisch: beef is the meat of an ox which is one year old or more, fattened for food before it is slaughtered. The quality of prime beef depends upon the breed, age, mode of fattening and the manner in which it was slaughtered.

Beef, Boiled: Boeuf bouilli: brisket or short ribs etc. simmered in boiling water with onion, pot herbs and cabbage until quite tender. Served with the vegetables taken from pot when done, boiled potatoes and horseradish or other appropriate sauce.

— **Russian Style:** à la russe: boiled, covered with sour cream sauce mixed with grated horseradish, flavored with vinegar, sprinkled with breadcrumbs, dotted with butter and browned in oven.

Beef, Braised: Boeuf braisé: see rump of beef.

Beef, Brisket of: Poitrine de boeuf: the brisket contains the rib ends and breast bones and is used fresh or corned. Corned brisket is usually boned before pickling. Fresh boiled brisket is served with the pot herbs used for flavoring the broth and horseradish, mustard, paprika, piquant or Robert sauce.

— **Berlin Style:** à la berlinoise: fresh boned breast, boiled, garnished with the pot herbs; horseradish sauce, bouillon potatoes, pickled cucumber, pickled red beetroots and cranberries served separately.

Beef: Chateaubriand: a double tenderloin steak cut out of the center of the tenderloin, at least 16 ozs. net for two people, grilled or sautéd. All garnishes for tournedos may be served with chateaubriand.

— **Béarnaise:** grilled, garnished with castle or soufflé potatoes, Béarnaise sauce with a little liquid meat glaze dropped on top served separately.

— **Chateaumeillant:** fried in butter, taken out, chopped shallots lightly sautéd in the butter, deglazed with red wine, boiled down with demi-glace, whipped up with butter, poured over the meat, garnished with straw potatoes and large mushrooms stuffed with duxelles.

— **Marquise:** fried in butter, dressed with Marquise garnish and Marquise potatoes.

— **with Ox Marrow:** à la moëlle: fried in butter, a few slices of blanched ox marrow on top, covered with Madeira sauce, sprinkled with chopped parsley.

Beef: Chateaubriand
— **Savarin:** fried in butter, a slice of goose liver on top, covered with truffle sauce, garnished with artichoke bottoms, filled with green asparagus tips, and sautéd mushrooms.
Beef, Corned: pickled brisket of beef boiled very lightly until done. Corned beef is also marketed in cans.
— **Baked:** boiled, when done studded with cloves, covered with maple syrup, baked, basted several times.
— **and Cabbage:** served with cabbage, which should not be boiled with the beef in the same kettle, and boiled potatoes.
— **Hash:** diced corned beef trimmings mixed with diced cold potatoes, boiled or steamed in jacket, and chopped onions fried together lightly. served omelette shaped.
Beef Cutlet, Rib Steak: Côte de boeuf: a cut from the ribs including the bone; bone trimmed at the end for cutlet, not trimmed for steak. Grilled or fried, served with the same garnishes as for Chateaubriand.
Beef, Fillet Mignon of: Filet mignon de boeuf: fillets mignons are usually cut from the end of the tenderloin too thin to be utilized for tournedos or fillet steaks, cut in triangular shape, lightly flattened, seasoned, dipped in melted butter and breadcrumbs, grilled slowly and served with a suitable garnish.
— **American style:** à l'américaine. Served with fried slices of bacon and fried tomatoes.
— **Bayard:** placed on croûton spread with gooseliver purée, garnished with small chicken croquettes and buttered green peas; truffle sauce served separately.
— **with Béarnaise sauce:** à la sauce Béarnaise: grilled, Béarnaise sauce and Parisian potatoes served separately.
— **Beaufrémont:** grilled, macaroni tossed in butter, mixed with grated Parmesan and truffle strips, and tomato sauce served separately.
— **Green Meadow:** à la vert-pré: served with watercress and straw potatoes.
— **Labori:** served with truffle sauce mixed with chopped mushrooms.
— **Reform:** à la réforme: placed on a small slice of fried ham; Reform sauce served separately.
— **Tyrolian Style:** à la tyrolienne: garnished with fried tomatoes and deep fried onion rings; Tyrolian sauce served separately.
Beef Heart, Braised: Coeur de boeuf braisé: soaked in water, trimmed, larded, marinated in wine vinegar, browned in butter, braised in light demi-glace with mirepoix.
Beef Kidney: Rognon de boeuf: fat removed, skinned, used for frying, braising and stewing, in pies, also prepared like calf's kidney.
— **Bercy:** sliced, sautéd in butter, served in Bercy sauce.
— **in Madeira Sauce:** à la sauce madère: sliced, sautéd, bound with Madeira sauce.
— **Sour:** à l'aigre: sliced, browned in lard with chopped onions, fat poured off, deglaced with vinegar, seasoned, moistened with demi-glace, braised; chopped parsley scattered on top.

Beef

— **in White Wine:** au vin blanc: sliced, browned with chopped shallots, deglaced with white wine, braised in light demi-glace.

Beef, Liver: Foie de boeuf: not so tender and not as esteemed as calf's liver. Skinned, all strings removed, best boiled or braised; sliced very thin and prepared like calf's liver.

Beef, Loin of: Contrefilet, faux filet: the loin is the part of the back from the last rib to the rump. If it is roasted whole, it must be boned, the side nerve removed, trimmed and tied. Prepared like sirloin and tenderloin.

Beef, Medaillons of: Medaillons de boeuf: same as tournedos.

Beef Marrow: Amourettes: soaked in water to rid marrow of blood, poached in lightly acidulated stock made of water and pot herbs and cooled off in the stock before further use.

— **in Caper Sauce:** à la sauce câpres: served in hot caper sauce.

— **Croquettes:** Croquettes d'amourettes: diced, mixed with diced mushrooms and truffles, bound with thick German sauce; when cold shaped into croquettes, dipped in egg and breadcrumbs and deep fried; truffle sauce served separately.

— **French Style:** à la française: diced, mixed with diced mushrooms and truffles, bound with thick German sauce, allowed to cool, shaped into small round cakes, dipped in frying batter, deep fried; ravigote sauce served separately.

— **Fried:** Frites: coated with Villeroy sauce, dipped in egg and breadcrumbs, fried in deep fat; tomato sauce.

— **Genoese Style:** à la génoise: diced, mixed with chopped ham and plain boiled rice, bound with beaten eggs; dropped with a soup spoon in hot oil and fried; tomato sauce served separately.

— **Polish Style:** à la polonaise: diced, mixed with chopped truffle and yellow boletus, bound with thick demi-glace; a soupspoonful wrapped in a very small thin unsweetened pancake, dipped in frying batter, deep fried; herb sauce served separately.

— **in Poulette Sauce:** à la poulette: simmered for a few minutes in poulette sauce, chopped parsley scattered on top.

— **Russian Style:** à la russe: diced, mixed with diced boletus, bound with demi-glace, wrapped in pig's caul, dipped in frying batter and deep fried; herb sauce served separately.

— **Sailor Style:** en matelote: cut in thick slices, mixed with crayfish tails, poached soft roes, mushrooms and button onions, bound with red wine sauce.

— **Scotch Style:** à l'écossaise: charlotte mould greased with butter, lined with thin slices of ox tongue, coated with veal forcemeat, filled with diced marrow and ox tongue bound with thick German sauce, sealed with forcemeat, cooked in oven in a waterbath; when done turned out and covered with Scotch sauce.

Beef, Miroton of: Miroton de boeuf: sliced onions lightly browned in lard, dredged with flour, browned, moistened with beef stock and seasoned; sliced boiled beef placed in the sauce, simmered for a while and served with a dash of vinegar or white wine.

Beef and Onions: Zwiebelfleisch: small slices of raw beef browned in fat with plenty of sliced onions, seasoned, moistened with beef stock and stewed; served with small flour dumplings or rice. (Austrian)

Beef: Ox Tail: Queue de boeuf: the heaviest kind are the best for stewing. The tail is divided into convenient pieces, the thin end used for soup.

— **Alsatian Style:** à l'alsacienne: prepared like old fashioned style, served with saurkraut.

— **Auvergne Style:** à l'auvergnate: browned in fat, sprinkled with flour, moistened with white wine and brown stock, stewed; when nearly done glazed button onions, chestnuts and diced fried bacon added.

— **Cavour:** cut in pieces, browned, stewed in white wine and brown stock; stock strained, bound with arrow-root, poured over the tail, mushrooms sautéd beforehand added, boiled up; chestnut purée served separately.

— **Charollais Style:** à la charollaise: browned, stewed in white wine and light demi-glace with a little garlic; shortly before serving olive-shaped carrots, turnips and small pork forcemeat dumplings added; served in border ob prebaked duchess potatoes, triangles of boiled bacon around the edge.

— **Chipolata:** prepared like with Madeira; garnished with glazed button onions, carrots, chestnuts and fried chipolatas.

— **in Cream Sauce:** à la crème: cut in pieces, boiled in white stock with root vegetables, when done drained and simmered for a short while in light cream sauce.

— **with Dumplings:** Ochsenschweif mit Knödeln: browned in butter, stewed in brown stock with grated root vegetables, when nearly done cooking finished with sour cream; served with bread dumplings. (Austrian)

— **Fried:** frite: cut in pieces, boiled, dipped in egg and breadcrumbs, deep fried; tartar sauce served separately.

— **Genoese Style:** à la génoise: browned in oil, simmered in brown stock with garlic, diced raw ham and tomato purée; when done green asparagus tips and parboiled ravioli added.

— **Hotpot of:** Hochepot de queues de boeuf: cut in pieces, boiled together with blanched pig's feet boned and cut in strips, pig's ears cut in strips and seasoning; when more then half done olive-shaped carrots, turnips and the heart of a white cabbage added; filled in timbale dish with fried chipolatas on top; boiled potatoes served separately.

— **in Madeira sauce:** à la sauce madère: browned with mirepoix and bacon waste, sprinkled with flour, moistened with brown stock and red wine, tomato purée added; when done taken out, sauce flavored with Madeira strained over the tail.

— **Old Fashioned Style:** à l'ancienne: cut in pieces, stewed, when cold dipped in egg and breadcrumbs, deep fried; served with saurkraut, purée of green peas or potato purée.

— **with Vegetables:** aux légumes: browned, mirepoix added, sprinkled with flour, moistened with brown stock and stewed; when nearly done pieces taken out and put in clean casserole, olive-shaped carrots, turnips, knob celery

Beef: Ox Tail
and diced bacon sautéd beforehand added, sauce strained over and cooked until done; flavored with Madeira before serving.

— **Vinaigrette:** cut in pieces, boiled; vinaigrette sauce served separately.

Beef Palate: Palais de boeuf: scalded until the skin can be removed, cooked thoroughly until white and well done, cut in squares.

— **in Anchovy Sauce:** à la sauce anchois: parboiled, simmered in red wine sauce blended with anchovy butter before serving.

— **in Cream Sauce:** à la sauce crème: parboiled, simmered in light Béchamel sauce, finished off with sweet cream.

— **with Curry Sauce:** à la sauce au curry: parboiled, simmered in curry sauce; plain boiled rice served separately.

— **Danish Style:** à la danoise: parboiled, dipped in egg and breadcrumbs, grilled; remoulade sauce served separately.

— **Farmer Style:** à la paysanne: parboiled, simmered in light demi-glace with small slices of carrots, turnips, celery and onions; green peas added shortly before serving.

— **Fricassee of:** en fricassée: parboiled. simmered in velouté, bound with egg yolks and cream, flavored with lemon juice, served with parboiled button onions and button mushrooms, bordered with fleurons.

— **Fried:** frit: parboiled, dipped in egg and breadcrumbs, deep fried; tomato sauce served separately.

— **Gratinated:** au gratin: parboiled, cut in broad strips, simmered in herb sauce, filled in buttered baking dish, sprinkled with grated Parmesan, dotted with butter and gratinated in oven.

— **Italian Style:** à l'italienne: parboiled, coated with flour, fried in oil, covered with Italian sauce.

— **Lyonese Style:** à la lyonnaise: parboiled, simmered in butter with sliced onions lightly browned beforehand and a little light demi-glace; finished off with chopped parsley and a few drops of vinegar.

— **with Madeira Sauce:** à la sauce madère: parboiled, simmered in light Madeira sauce.

— **in Poulette Sauce:** à la poulette: parboiled, served in poulette sauce.

— **Villeroi:** cold parboiled squares coated with Villeroi sauce, dipped in egg and breadcrumbs, deep fried, garnished with fried parsley; tomato sauce served separately.

Beef, Point of Rump: Pointe de culotte: best for braising, see rump of beef.

Porterhouse Steak: a steak cut through the thicker part of the loin including sirloin, bone and tenderloin. Prepared like Chateaubriand.

— **London Style:** à la londonienne: grilled, garnished with watercress, halved grilled lamb kidneys, fried sliced bacon, fried tomatoes, grilled mushrooms and straw potatoes; herb butter.

Beef, Pressed: smoked pickled brisket pressed in special mould, when cold cut in slices.

Beef, Ribs of, Prime Ribs of: Roastbeef: consists of seven ribs, the 6th to the 12th. If roasted entirely it is trimmed, the short ribs cut off from the end of the ribs, the vertebra bones sawed of. Ribs of beef are roasted and served rare, medium or well done with the pan gravy and Yorkshire pudding.

Beef, Rump, Aitchbone, Silverside, Flank: Culotte de boeuf, Pointe de boeuf, Pièce de boeuf; entirely boned these are excellent for braising. They are usually transversed with thick strips of fat bacon spiced or marinated beforehand, browned on all sides thoroughly to prevent the juices from escaping, placed on mirepoix browned beforehand, moistened with stock, wine or a light brown sauce or a combination of all three and braised in oven with the lid on in a braising pan.

— **Bordeaux Style:** à la bordelaise: braised in light Bordeaux sauce; boletus prepared in the Bordeaux way served separately.

— **braised in Champagne:** braisé au champagne: braised in veal stock and champagne with mirepoix and glazed; the reduced stock lightly thickened with arrow-root served separately.

— **Brillat Savarin:** larded with truffle, braised in red wine and light demi-glace; garnished with small stuffed onions and lamb sweetbreads; the strained sauce served separately.

— **Bülow:** larded, marinated in brandy and Madeira, browned, braised in white wine, brown stock, the marinade and mirepoix; when done stock strained and thickened with corn starch; garnished with potato croustades filled alternately with turnip and spinach purée.

— **Burgundy Style:** à la bourguignonne: transversed with thick strips of fat bacon marinated in brandy, braised in red wine and light demi-glace with mushroom waste and a bunch of herbs. When two thirds done, placed in a clean casserole with diced fried bacon, glaced button onions and lightly sautéd mushrooms, sauce strained over the beef, finished in oven.

— **Dauphiné Style:** boeuf braisé au gratin dauphinoise: braised in white wine and light demi-glace; served with the strained sauce and potatoes gratinated in the Dauphiné way.

— **Etterbeek Style:** à l'instar d'Etterbeek: marinated in pale beer with thyme, bayleaf, cloves, peppercorns, mirepoix and a little oil; larded, braised with the mirepoix, the strained marinade and brown stock, carved, garnished with glazed button onions and sautéd mushrooms; a part of the strained and reduced stock, to which seeded and peeled grapes have been added, poured over the beef and the rest served separately.

— **Flemish Style:** à la flamande: braised and glazed, served with the degreased and reduced braising stock and Flemish garnish.

— **German Style:** Sauerbraten: marinated for 48 hours in cold preboiled marinade of wine vinegar, sliced onions, root vegetables, allspice, bayleaves, peppercorns and a little water; browned, placed on top of the browned onions and vegetables, braised in the marinade; sauce boiled up with sour cream, thickened with rye bread, strained or only thickened with corn starch; served with potato purée or potatoe dumplings and the sauce.

Beef, Rump

— **Greek Style:** à la grecque: braised in veal stock with tomato purée; the thickened braising stock and rice prepared the Greek way served separately.

— **Italian Style:** à italienne: larded with fat bacon and anchovy fillets, seasoned with salt, pepper and powdered cloves; braised in red wine, brown stock and tomato purée; the reduced and lightly thickened and strained stock and macaroni tossed in butter and grated Parmesan served separately.

— **Japanese Style:** à la japonaise: braised in light demi-glace; sauce and creamed stachy served separately.

— **Limoux Style:** Fondant Limousin: larded, marinated in Madeira, braised until very soft with mirepoix in rich brown stock and the Madeira, tomatoes and mushroom waste added; glazed and served covered with the degreased, strongly reduced and strained stock.

— **Lothringian Style:** à la lorraine: braised in white wine and demi-glace, glazed; garnished with stuffed braised cabbage balls, fancy-shaped glazed turnips and triangles of the bacon braised with the cabbage; the strained sauce served separately.

— **Lyonese Style:** à la lyonnaise: marinated in white wine, vinegar and sliced onions; garnished with sliced onions fried in butter and bound with meat glaze; the reduced, strained stock served separately.

— **Malesherbes:** braised in light Madeira sauce, garnished with fancy-shaped root vegetables.

— **à la mode:** boeuf à la mode: transversed with thick strips of lard marinated beforehand with salt, allspice, parsley and brandy, rubbed with salt and marinated for a few hours in red wine and the brandy; braised as usual with three boned, blanched calf's feet tied together. When two thirds done, placed in clean casserole with the calf's feet cut in triangles, button onions lightly browned in butter and half cooked olive-shaped carrots, covered with the degreased strained stock braised until done. Served with the garnish and the stock boiled down with demi-glace.

— **à la mode** (cold): prepared like beef à la mode. When done, stock boiled down with aspic jelly, beef placed in a turreen or cocotte with the garnish around, the strained degreased stock poured over the meat, allowed to set and served cold.

— **Nevers Style:** à la nivernaise: braised in red wine and demi-glace; garnished with olive-shaped glazed carrots and glazed button onions.

— **Parisian Style:** à la parisienne: larded with truffle and ox tongue, braised in white wine and demi-glace; garnished with artichoke bottoms filled with diced mushrooms, ox tongue and truffle bound with velouté and Parisian potatoes; the strained sauce served separately.

— **Provencal Style:** à la provençale: braised in white wine and brown stock with tomatoes and garlic; garnished with mushroom caps stuffed with duxelles flavored with garlic and small fried tomatoes; Provencal sauce blended with the strained reduced braising stock served separately.

— **Providence:** braised in white wine and demi-glace; garnished with shaped cauliflower covered with Dutch

Beef, Rump
sauce, glazed olive-shaped carrots and buttered wax beans; the strained sauce served separately.
— **Soubise** marinated in white wine; braised in the white wine and veal gravy with root vegetables and glazed; white onion purée and the degreased, reduced and strained stock served separately.
— **with Spring Vegetables:** aux primeurs: braised, served with spring vegetables.
— **Tohubohu:** braised in light demi-glace with tomato; garnished with glazed button onions, braised cabbage balls, small pieces of braised leek, macaroni tossed in butter and grated Parmesan and cream puff paste fritters with Parmesan.
— **Waldmeisterbraten:** Braised Beef with Woodruff: point of rump marinated in light vinegar pickle with a bunch of woodruff, browned in butter with sliced carrots and onions and braised in a part of the pickle; stock thickened with flour diluted with red wine and finished off with sour cream; macaroni or German fried potatoes served separately. (Austrian)

Beef: Rumpsteak: Rumpsteak, Tranche de tête d'aloyau: cut from high quality beef and properly stored the rump is excellent for steaks and as juicy as a sirloin steak. The steaks are cut rather thick, triangular shape, and grilled or fried. Prepared like sirloin steak.
— **English Style:** à l'anglaise: fried in butter, covered with deep fried onion rings.
— **Grilled:** grillé: grilled, served with grated horseradish.
— **Grandmother Style:** à la grand'mère: fried in butter, deglaced with lemon juice and meat gravy; garnished with diced fried bacon, roasted olive-shaped potatoes and glazed button onions.
— **Meyerbeer:** fried in butter, a lamb kidney split lengthwise and sautéd on top, covered with truffle sauce.
— **Mirabeau:** prepared like sirloin steak.

Beef, Sirloin of: Aloyau de boeuf: the sirloin is the part between the rump and the ribs and consists of loin, tenderloin (fillet) and part of the rump. There ought not to be more then five ribs attached to the sirloin. It is usually roasted, seldom braised.
— **Alsatian Style:** à l'alsacienne: prepared like tenderloin.
— **Antwerp Style:** à l'anversoise: prepared like tenderloin.
— **Breton Style:** à la bretonne: roasted, white Lima beans prepared the Breton way and the clear meat gravy served separately.
— **Bristol:** roasted, garnished with Parisian potatoes, ball-shaped rice croquettes and flageolets bound with velouté; thick meat gravy.
— **with Celery:** aux céleris: roasted, braised celery covered with light demi-glace and clear meat gravy served separately.
— **Citizen Style:** à la bourgeoise: roasted, garnished with glazed button onions, glazed olive-shaped carrots and diced fried bacon; thick meat gravy.
— **English Style:** à l'anglaise: roasted, served with Yorkshire pudding and the clear meat gravy.
— **Favorite Style:** à la favorite: prepared like tenderloin.

Beef, Sirloin of
— **Florence Style:** à la florentine: roasted, garnished with spinach cakes, and semolina croquettes; demi-glace with tomato.
— **French Style:** à la française: roasted, garnished with tartlets filled with spinach purée and Anna potatoes baked in small beaker moulds; thick meat gravy.
— **Godard:** prepared like tenderloin.
— **Hungarian Style:** à la hongroise: same garnish as for tournedos; thick meat gravy.
— **Infante Style:** à l'Infante: prepared like tenderloin.
— **Italian Style:** à l'italienne: roasted, served with Italian garnish and sauce.
— **Languedoc Style:** à la languedocienne: prepared like tenderloin.
— **Lothringian Style:** à la lorraine: roasted, garnished with balls of red cabbage, braised in red wine with juniper berries, and fondantes potatoes; horseradish sauce served separately.
— **Menton Style:** à la mentonaise: prepared like tenderloin.
— **Milanese Style:** à la milanaise: roasted, served with macaroni prepared the Milanese way and light tomato sauce.
— **Nevers Style:** à la nivernaise: braised, garnished with olive-shaped carrots and glazed button onions; thick meat gravy.
— **Nice Style:** à la niçoise: prepared like tenderloin.
— **Portuguese Style:** à la portugaise: prepared like tenderloin.
— **Quimperlé Style:** à la mode de Quimperle: braised in cider, sauce prepared with the stock boiled down with demi-glace; Lima beans prepared the Breton way served separately.
— **Renaissance:** roasted, garnished with fancy-shaped vegetables of all kinds or the vegetables served separately; thick meat gravy.
— **Richelieu:** prepared like tenderloin.
— **Roman Style:** à la romaine: prepared like tenderloin.
— **Romanoff:** roasted, garnished with potato croustades, filled alternately with diced knob celery and mushrooms bound with demi-glace, and fancy-shaped cucumber simmered in butter; thick meat gravy.
— **Saint-Florentin:** prepared like tenderloin.
— **Sardinian Style:** à la sarde: garnished with rice croquettes with saffron, stuffed tomatoes and cucumber; light tomato sauce.
— **with Spring Vegetables:** aux primeurs: roasted, spring vegetables of all kinds and clear meat gravy served separately.
— **Westmoreland:** roasted, garnished with stuffed tomatoes, fancy-shaped cucumber pieces, green peas; thick meat gravy and German fried potatoes served separately.

Beef: Sirloin Steak: Entrecôte: cut from the trimmed short loin into individual pieces more or less thick. Served as single, double or larger portions and grilled or sautéd. Cut double thick the steak is called entrecôte double.
— **Antibes Style:** à l'antiboise: sautéd, covered with tomatoes concassées Provencal Style.
— **Béarnaise:** grilled, brushed with liquid meat glaze, garnished with castle potatoes; Béarnaise sauce served separately.

Beef, Sirloin Steak

— **Bercy:** grilled, coated lightly with meat glaze; Bercy sauce served separately.

— **Bordeaux Style:** à la bordelaise: sautéd, blanched slices of ox marrow on top; Bordeaux sauce served separately.

— **Braised:** braisé: browned, braised in white wine and demi-glace; garnished with fancy-shaped glazed carrots, turnips, knob celery and button onions and quartered potatoes fried in butter.

— **Burgundy Style:** à la bourguignonne: sautéd, deglaced with red wine, boiled up with meat glaze, buttered, seasoned with lemon juice and poured over the steak; garnished with fried diced bacon, glazed button mushrooms and button onions.

— **Cavour:** sautéd, blanched ox marrow slices on top, covered with light demi-glace; garnished with moulded Anna potatoes, glazed button onions and fried tomatoes.

— **Cecilia:** same garnish as tournedos.

— **Chatelaine:** sautéd; garnished with artichoke bottom filled with white onion purée, glazed chestnuts and nut potatoes; Madeira sauce.

— **Choron:** same sauce and garnish as tournedos.

— **Clamart:** sautéd, same garnish as tournedos.

— **Danitcheff:** grilled, covered with a broad strip of Béarnaise sauce with a line of caviar lengthwise; garnished with potato croquettes and green peas.

— **English Style:** à l'anglaise: grilled, garnished with slices of fried bacon and boiled potatoes; herb butter.

— **Forester Style:** à la forestière: sautéd, deglaced with white wine and veal gravy; garnished with sautéd morels and diced fried potatoes, both sprinkled with chopped parsley, and triangles of blanched and fried bacon; jus served separately.

— **Georgian Style:** à la georgienne: sautéd blood rare, when cold coated with anchovy butter, wrapped in puff pastry, brushed with egg yolk, baked in oven.

— **Grandmother Style:** à la grand'mère: fried in cocotte, deglaced with a little veal gravy; garnished with glazed button onions, diced fried bacon and olive-potatoes; served in the cocotte with the lid on.

— **Green Meadow:** au vert-pré: grilled, covered with herb butter; garnished with watercress and straw potatoes.

— **Hotelkeeper Style:** à la hôtelière: sautéd, covered with herb butter mixed with chopped mushrooms and shallots; deglaced with white wine, reduced, meat glaze added and poured over the steak.

— **Hungarian Style:** à la hongroise: 1. sautéd in butter, taken out of pan, diced lard and chopped onions browned in the butter, dusted with paprika, deglaced with white wine. boiled up with velouté and poured over steak; garnished with boiled potato balls.
2. browned in lard with chopped onions, dusted with paprika, braised in stock and sour cream; garnished with stuffed red peppers and potato balls

— **Judic:** sautéd, deglazed with white wine, truffle essence and veal gravy; truffle slices and cock's kidneys coated with liquid meat glace placed on top, garnished with braised lettuce; jus served separately.

Beef: Sirloin Steak

— **Jussieu:** sautéd, covered with Madeira sauce; garnished with braised lettuce and glazed button onions.

— **Lorette:** sautéd, covered with Madeira sauce; garnished with artichoke bottoms filled with asparagus tips, and Lorette potatoes.

— **Lyonese Style:** à la lyonnaise: same garnish as tenderloin.

— **Marquise:** sautéd, same garnish as tournedos.

— **with Marrow:** à la moelle: grilled or sautéd, covered with marrow sauce.

— **Marseille Style:** à la marseillaise: grilled, covered with herb butter mixed with a little tomato purée and crushed garlic; garnished with copeaux potatoes and halves of fried tomatoes flavored with garlic and herbs.

— **Mexican Style:** à la mexicaine: grilled, garnished with grilled mushrooms and red peppers; tomato gravy served separately.

— **Meyerbeer:** sautéd, two half grilled lamb kidneys on top, covered with truffle sauce.

— **Minute:** à la minute: cut thin, beaten flat, grilled, fresh butter on top; garnished with Pont-neuf potatoes and watercress.

— **Mirabeau:** grilled, a few anchovy fillets and stoned olives bordered with blanched tarragon leaves arranged on top; anchovy butter served separately.

— **Monaco Style:** à la monegasque: same garnish as tournedos.

— **Montagné:** grilled, garnished with artichoke bottoms filled alternately with tomatoes concassées and chopped mushrooms bound with thick Madeira sauce.

— **Monastery Style:** du couvent: browned, braised in white wine and demi-glace mixed with truffle, ox tongue, mushroom strips and green peas when done; placed on base of Anna potatoes, covered with the sauce.

— **Mountaineer Style:** à la montagnarde: sautéd rare, covered with blanched ox marrow slices coated with white onion purée, glazed.

— **with Mushrooms:** aux champignons: sautéd, deglaced with white wine and mushroom stock, boiled up with demi-glace; garnished with cooked mushrooms warmed up in the sauce, covered with the sauce.

— **Nicolas II.:** sautéd in cocotte; garnished with sliced fried gooseliver and small whole truffles cooked in Madeira; bordered with demi-glace boiled up with the truffle stock.

— **Parisian Style:** à la parisienne: sautéd; same garnish as tenderloin.

— **Pergamon:** grilled, covered with Béarnaise sauce with truffle slices on top; garnished with potato croquettes, bordered with tomato sauce.

— **Planked:** grilled or sautéd, served on appropriate plank bordered with duchess potatoes and an assortiment of fresh vegetables; mushrooms on top, herb butter.

— **Portuguese Style:** à la portugaise: sautéd; garnished with stuffed tomatoes and castle potatoes; Portuguese sauce.

— **Quirinal:** same garnish as tournedos.

— **Regina:** sautéd; garnished with tomatoes stuffed with risotto; Madeira sauce with chopped red peppers, mushrooms and pickles.

Beef: Sirloin Steak
— **Soldatski Gowjadina:** browned in butter, braised in beef stock with shredded cabbage and parsley root, balls of carrots and turnips and a bunch of herbs. (Russian)
— **Spanish Style:** à l'espagnole: sautéd in oil; garnished with fried tomatoes, deep fried onion rings and sliced egg plants.
— **Steeple-chase:** grilled, same garnish as tenderloin steak.
— **Steward Style:** à la maître d'hôtel: grilled, served with herb butter.
— **Tyrolian Style:** à la tyrolienne: grilled, covered with sliced onions fried in butter and bound with a little pepper sauce, bordered with tomatoes concassées.
— **with Watercress:** au cresson: grilled, garnished with watercress.
— **Winemerchant Style:** à la marchand de vin: grilled, covered with red wine butter.

Beefsteak: see tenderloin steak.

Beef Steak Pudding: pudding bowl lined with suet dough, filled with small slices of beef, chopped onions and thick slices of potato (optional), seasoned, closed with dough, tied in a napkin and boiled.
— **Steak and Kidney Pudding:** same as above but with sliced beef kidney instead of potatoes.
— **Steak and Oyster Pudding:** beef steak pudding with oysters added.

Beef Stew: flank or chuck, boned, cut in cubes, stewed in water with onions, carrots, potatoes, seasoning and a bay leaf.
— **French:** Estouffade de boeuf: diced bacon fried, taken out of the fat, beef cut in cubes browned in the fat with chopped onions, sprinkled with flour, moistened with red wine, garlic added, stewed in oven with the lid on; when nearly done meat taken out and put in a clean casserole, the fried bacon and quartered sautéd mushrooms added, sauce strained over, cooking finished in oven.

Beef Tea: Jus de viande de boeuf: pure undiluted juice of ground lean beef extracted by boiling the meat in a double boiler tightly covered. Article of diet.

Beef: T-bone Steak: same as Porterhouse steak but cut thinner. Prepared like Chateaubriand.

Beef, Tenderloin or Fillet of Beef: Filet de boeuf: the undercut of the loin, the tenderest of all cuts of beef. It is carefully trimmed, larded and served whole roasted or pan-roasted hot and cold.
— **Agnès Sorel:** larded with truffle and ox tongue, pan-roasted, garnished with tartlets filled with mushroom purée with a round slice of ox tongue and a truffle slice on top; the deglaced pan gravy with veal stock served separately.
— **Alsatian Style:** à l'alsacienne: roasted, garnished with tartlets filled with saurkraut and a round slice of fried ham on top; demi-glace.
— **Andalusian Style: à** l'andalouse: roasted, garnished with red or green peppers prepared the Greek way, tiny pork sausages and small halved eggplants filled with tomatoes concassées; thick veal gravy flavored with Sherry served separately.

Beef, Tenderloin

— **Antwerp Style:** à l'anversoise: roasted, garnished with tartlets, filled with creamed hop shoots, and boiled potatoes; tomato sauce.

— **Arlesian Style:** à l'arlésienne: roasted, garnished with sautéd eggplant, tomatoes concassées and fried onion rings; demi-glace with tomato served separately.

— **Beatrice:** roasted, Beatrice garnish.

— **Berry Style:** à la berrichonne: larded, roasted, garnished with braised cabbage balls, large glazed chestnuts, glaced button onions; thick veal gravy served separately.

— **Bisontine:** roasted, garnished with baked duchess potato-croustade filled with cauliflower purée, stuffed lettuce; thick veal gravy.

— **Brabant Style:** à la brabançonne: roasted, garnished with round potato croquettes and tartlets filled with small Brussels sprouts covered with Mornay sauce and glazed; thick veal gravy.

— **Bréhan:** roasted, garnished with parsley potatoes and artichoke bottoms filled with cauliflower sprigs covered with Dutch sauce; the deglaced pan gravy mixed with thick veal gravy served separately.

— **Bristol:** roasted, garnished with rice croquettes, flageolets in cream sauce and castle or croquette potatoes; Madeira sauce or thick veal gravy.

— **Camargo:** opened on one side, hollowed out slightly, meat chopped and mixed with raw chopped gooseliver and truffles, stuffed in tenderloin, studded with truffle, wrapped in bacon, roasted, unwrapped and glazed; garnished with tartlets filled with buttered noodles, a slice of fried goose liver and a truffle slice on each tartlet, truffle sauce served separately.

— **Caprivi:** pan-roasted, garnished with stuffed cucumber, stuffed onions, veal dumplings, diced calf's sweetbread and macaroni croquettes; Madeira sauce.

— **Capuchin Style:** à la capucine: pan-roasted, garnished with stuffed cabbage balls and stuffed mushrooms; Madeira sauce.

— **Chatelaine:** roasted, garnished with glazed chestnuts, artichoke bottoms filled with white onion purée and nut potatoes; Madeira sauce.

— **Chief Ranger Style:** à la grand-veneur: marinated in white wine, braised, garnished with tartlet-shaped lentil croquettes filled with morel purée; chief ranger sauce mixed with the reduced stock served separately.

— **Chipolata:** roasted, garnished with glazed chestnuts, button onions and olive-shaped carrots, diced fried bacon and tiny pork sausages; thick veal gravy.

— **Clamart:** roasted, garnished with round Macaire potatoes and tartlets filled with peas prepared in the French way; thick veal gravy.

— **Coquelin** (cold): roasted, when cold carved and placed in oval cocotte covered with the deglaced, degreased and lighty jellied pan gravy mixed with julienne of carrots, celery and truffles; cocotte filled with light Madeira jelly, chilled and served in the cocotte.

— **Crown Prince Style:** à la dauphine: roasted, garnished with dauphine potatoes; Madeira sauce.

Beef, Tenderloin

— **Diplomat Style:** à la diplomate: larded with bacon, truffle and ox tongue, marinated in white wine, pan roasted, deglaced with the white wine and demi-glace; garnished with diced calf's sweetbread, mushrooms, cockscombs and cocks' kidneys bound with diplomat sauce.

— **Doria:** roasted, garnished with olive-shaped cucumbers simmered in butter; deglaced with demi-glace.

— **Dubarry:** roasted, garnished with cauliflower balls coated with Mornay sauce and glazed; thick veal gravy.

— **Duchess Style:** à la duchesse: roasted, garnished with duchess potatoes; Madeira sauce.

— **Egyptian Style:** à l'égyptienne: roasted, garnished with croquettes of saffron rice and stuffed red peppers; sharp veal gravy with tomato.

— **Favorite Style:** à la favorite: roasted, garnished with fried slices of gooseliver with a truffle slice on top and green asparagus tips; thick meat gravy served separately.

— **Fervaal:** pan-roasted, garnished with potato croquettes, mixed with chopped ham, and sautéd artichoke bottoms; the pan gravy deglaced with thick veal gravy served separately.

— **Financier Style:** à la financière: roasted, financier garnish and sauce.

— **Flemish Style:** à la flamande: roasted, garnished with braised cabbage balls, glazed fancy shaped carrots and turnips, strips of fried bacon and boiled potatoes; demi-glace.

— **Florist Style:** à la bouquetière: roasted, garnished with vegetables in season arranged in bunches around the tenderloin; clear veal gravy served separately.

— **Forester Style:** à la forestière: roasted, garnished with sautéd morels, diced sautéd potatoes and fried diced bacon; Italian sauce.

— **Frascati:** larded, pan-roasted, garnished with crescent-shapped truffled duchess potatoes, sautéd triangles of gooseliver, fluted mushrooms, olive-shaped truffles and asparagus tips; thick pan gravy.

— **Gardner Style:** à la jardinière: roasted, garnished with fancy shaped vegetables, green beans, peas and cauliflower sprigs coated with Dutch sauce; clear veal gravy.

— **Gastronomer Style:** à la gastronome: studded with truffle, marinated in Madeira, wrapped in bacon, tied, braised in Madeira, unwrapped and glazed; garnished with large glazed chestnuts, morels, thick raw truffle slices cooked in champagne and cockcombs rolled in liquid meat glaze; demi-glace boiled down with the braising stock and the truffle stock served separately.

— **Godard:** pan-roasted, served with Godard garnish and sauce.

— **Gouffé:** roasted, placed on base of risotto, garnished with mushrooms, truffles and small veal dumplings; Madeira sauce.

— **Harlequin:** à l'arlequine: roasted, garnished with tartlets filled alternately with spinach purée, tiny carrot and turnip balls, tiny nut potatoes, tomatoes concassées and cauliflower sprigs coated with Dutch sauce; thick veal gravy served separately.

Beef, Tenderloin

— **Hungarian Style:** à la hongroise: larded, roasted, garnished with shaped cauliflower coated with Mornay sauce, mixed with chopped ham and paprika and glazed, and small stewed and glazed onions; light Soubise sauce condimented with paprika served separately.

— **Hussar Style:** à la hussarde: roasted, garnished with rosette-shaped duchess potatoes and large mushroom caps filled with thick white onion purée; hussar sauce served separately.

— **Infante Style:** à l'infante: roasted, garnished with straw potatoes, stuffed tomatoes, mushroom caps and macaroni mixed with butter, grated Parmesan and truffle strips; Madeira sauce.

— **Italian Style:** à l'italienne: larded, pan-roasted, garnished with quartered artichoke bottoms prepared in the Italian way and macaroni croquettes; Italian sauce served separately.

— **Japanese Style:** à la japonaise: roasted, garnished with tartlets filled with creamed stachy and potato croquettes; thick veal gravy.

— **Jockey Club:** larded, marinated in white wine and Madeira, roasted, garnished with stuffed tomatoes, potato croquettes, chicken dumplings, crayfish tails and olive-shaped truffles; demi-glace with the reduced marinade served separately.

— **Lacroix:** raw tenderloin opened from one side, stuffed with thick strips of truffled gooseliver parfait, wrapped in thin slices of fat bacon, tied, roasted; unwrapped, browned, garnished with cocotte potatoes; Madeira sauce.

— **Languedoc Style:** à la languedocienne: roasted, garnished with slices deep fried eggplants, yellow boletus sautéd in oil and tomatoes concassées with garlic and chopped parsley; thick meat gravy.

— **Laxenburg Style:** à la laxenbourgeoise: browned on both sides, brushed with melted butter mixed with egg yolk, coated with breadcrumbs mixed with grated Parmesan and finished off in the oven; garnished with artichoke bottoms filled alternately with green peas and diced green beans; Madeira sauce served separately.

— **Little Duke:** à la petit duc: roasted, garnished with puff pastry shells filled with creamed asparagus tips and artichoke bottoms filled with diced truffles bound with Madeira sauce; Madeira sauce served separately.

— **London House:** opened on one side, stuffed with small slices of raw gooseliver alternated with truffle slices, studded with truffles, tied, pan roasted and glazed; garnished with small truffles cooked in Madeira and mushroom caps; demi-glace mixed with the deglaced pan gravy and the Madeira served separately.

— **Lorette:** larded, pan-roasted and glazed, garnished with Lorette potatoes and buttered asparagus tips; light demi-glace with tomato served separately.

— **Lothringian Style:** à la lorraine: roasted, braised red cabbage and horseradish sauce served separately.

— **Lyonese Style:** à la lyonnaise: roasted, garnished with sliced fried onions bound with demi-glace and sprinkled with chopped parsley; demi-glace boiled up with the pan

Beef, Tenderloin

gravy deglaced with vinegar and white wine served separately.

— **Madeleine:** roasted, garnished with artichoke bottoms filled with white onion purée, and purée of white Lima beans, bound with egg yolk, filled in beaker moulds, poached and turned out; light demi-glace.

— **Mariposa:** roasted, garnished with grilled red peppers, tartlets filled with creamed sweet corn, and fried bananas; demi-glace flavored with Sherry served separately.

— **Masséna:** same garnish as for tournedos.

— **Massenet:** same garnish as for tournedos.

— **Mazarin:** roasted, garnished with tartlets filled with diced truffles and sweetbread bound with Madeira sauce and artichoke bottoms filled alternately with diced buttered green beans and tiny veal dumplings in Madeira sauce; Madeira sauce.

— **Medicis:** roasted, Medicis garnish.

— **Melba:** roasted, garnished with stuffed braised lettuce, stewed tomatoes and tartlets filled with chestnut purée; Madeira sauce.

— **Menton Style:** à la mentonnaise: roasted, garnished with stuffed pieces of chard and artichoke bottoms filled with small Parisian potatoes; thick veal gravy.

— **Mexican Style:** à la mexicaine: roasted, garnished with grilled mushrooms and red peppers; highly spiced tomato sauce served separately.

— **Milhaud** (cold): larded with truffle, roasted, when cold carved, reshaped with equal-sized slices of gooseliver parfait between the tenderloin slices, glazed with aspic jelly; garnished with small tangerines, scooped out, edge indented, filled with gooseliver froth, decorated with two tangerine pieces and glazed with aspic jelly flavored with tangerine juice, and triangles of aspic jelly.

— **Mireille:** 1. shaped Mireille potatoes; tomato sauce.
2. mushrooms, sautéd artichoke quarters, spinach cakes; Madeira sauce.

— **Modern Style:** à la moderne: roasted, garnished with vegetable chartreuse, braised lettuce and decorated veal dumplings; thick veal gravy served separately.

— **Montmorency:** roasted, garnished with artichoke bottoms, filled with vegetable macedoine, and bunches of asparagus tips; Madeira sauce served separately.

— **Nevers Style:** à la nivernaise: larded, pan-roasted and glazed, garnished with glazed carrots and button onions; the degreased pan gravy served separately.

— **Nice Style:** à la niçoise: roasted, garnished with tomatoes concassées with garlic and chopped parsley, French beans and castle potatoes; thick veal gravy served separately.

— **Old Fashioned Style:** à l'ancienne: roasted, garnished with mushrooms and glazed button onions; thick veal gravy.

— **Oriental Style:** à l'orientale: roasted, garnished with halved tomatoes fried in oil with shaped rice prepared the Greek way on top, alternated with croquettes of sweet potatoes; highly spiced tomato sauce served separately.

— **Palestine Style:** à la palestine: roasted, served with Palestine garnish.

— **Parisian Style:** à la parisienne: roasted, served with Parisian garnish and Madeira sauce.

Beef, Tenderloin

— **Park Hotel** (cold): larded, pan-roasted, when cold coated with the deglaced, degreased jellied pan gravy, decorated on top with small round slices of tomato and hard-boiled egg white, glazed with Madeira jelly; garnished alternately with tartlets filled with Waldorf salad, truffles en surprise and small peeled tomatoes filled with salad of diced French beans.

— **President Style:** à la présidente (cold): cold larded tenderloin glazed with Madeira aspic jelly, garnished with tartlets filled alternately with salad of diced tomatoes, diced knob celery and cauliflower sprigs bound with jellied mayonnaise and glazed with aspic jelly.

— **Portuguese Style:** à la portugaise: roasted, garnished with stuffed tomatoes and castle potatoes; light tomato sauce served separately.

— **Provencal Style:** à la provençale: roasted, garnished with stuffed tomatoes and stuffed mushrooms; Provencal sauce served separately.

— **Regency Style:** à la régence: marinated in white wine, coated with Matignon, wrapped in thin slices of bacon, tied, braised in white wine and glaced; served with regency garnish and demi-glace with the reduced stock.

— **Renaissance:** roasted, served with renaissance garnish and clear veal gravy.

— **Rich Style:** à la riche (cold): roasted, when cold carved, arranged on oval silver platter with round slices of gooseliver parfait between the tenderloin, coated with Madeira jelly; garnished with artichoke bottoms filled with asparagus tips in jellied mayonnaise and small skinned tomatoes filled with chicken froth, decorated with a truffle star and coated with Madeira jelly, and diced aspic jelly.

— **Richelieu:** roasted, garnished with stuffed tomatoes, stuffed mushrooms caps, braised lettuce and castle potatoes; thick veal gravy.

— **Roman Style:** à la romaine: garnished with tartlets filled with Roman dumplings, sprinkled with grated Parmesan and gratinated, and spinach subrics with anchovy butter; Roman sauce.

— **Romanoff:** roasted, garnished with olive-shaped cucumbers simmered in butter and crustades of duchess potato filled with diced creamed mushrooms and knob celery; light demi-glace served separately.

— **Russian Style:** à la russe: cold roasted tenderloin glazed with aspic jelly, garnished with tiny tartlets filled alternately with grated horseradish, mixed with whipped cream seasoned with paprika, and short julienne of pickled cucumber.

— **Saint-Florentin:** roasted, garnished with sautéd yellow boletus and Saint-Florentin potatoes; Bonnefoy sauce served separately.

— **Saint-Germain:** roasted, garnished with glaced carrots, beakers of green pea purée bound with egg yolks, poached and turned out, and fondantes potatoes; Bèarnaise sauce served separately.

— **Saint-Mandé:** roasted, garnished with Macaire potatoes, asparagus tips and buttered green peas; thick veal gravy.

Beef, Tenderloin

— **Sardinian Style:** à la sarde: roasted, garnished with rice croquettes, stuffed tomatoes and stuffed cucumber; light tomato sauce served separately.

— **Saxon Style:** à la saxe: roasted, garnished with stuffed cucumber and fried tomatoes; demi-glace with tomato.

— **Talleyrand:** studded with truffles, marinated in Madeira, larded, braised and glazed; served with Talleyrand garnish and demi-glace mixed with the braising stock and chopped truffles.

— **Tivoli:** roasted, garnished with stuffed mushrooms and bunches of asparagus tips; thick buttered veal gravy served separately.

— **Trianon:** roasted, garnished with tartlets filled alternately with carrot purée, green pea purée and chestnut purée (when out of season, mushroom purée); Madeira sauce served separately.

— **Tuscan Style:** à la toscanne: roasted, garnished with tomatoes concassées and tartlets filled with Brussels sprouts; thick veal gravy with tomato served separately.

— **Tyrolian Style:** à la tyrolienne: roasted, garnished with deep fried onion rings and tomatoes concassées; Tyrolian sauce served separately.

— **Vegetable Gardner Style:** à la maraîchère: roasted, garnished with Brussels sprouts, short pieces of salsify in cream sauce and castle potatoes; clear veal gravy.

— **Viroflay:** roasted, garnished with sautéd quartered artichoke bottoms, spinach Viroflay and castle potatoes; thick veal gravy.

— **Wellington:** browned on both sides, allowed to cool lightly, coated on all sides with duxelles mixed with fine mirepoix, wrapped in puff pastry, decorated with strips of dough, baked; Madeira sauce with chopped truffles served separately.

Beef: Tenderloin Steak, Beefsteak, Fillet Steak: Beefsteak, Bifteck: tenderloin or fillet steaks may be cut from any part of the tenderloin except the Point, especially from the middle piece towards tenderloin head. Usually grilled or sautéd, seldom braised.

— **Alsatian Style:** à l'alsacienne: same garnish as tournedos.

— **American Style:** à l'américaine: garnished with sliced fried sweet potatoes and corn fritters.

— **Baron Brisse:** prepared like tournedos.

— **Béarnaise:** grilled, French fried or soufflée potatoes; Béarnaise sauce served separately.

— **Berlin Style:** à la berlinoise: sautéd, covered with blanched slices of ox marrow, covered with red wine sauce; garnished with sautéd chanterelles, glazed olive-shaped carrots, soufflée potatoes and tartlet filled with gooseliver purée.

— **Bordeaux Style:** à la bordelaise: fried, blanched ox marrow placed on top, covered with Bordeaux sauce.

— **Cecil:** same garnish as tournedos.

— **Cecilia:** same garnish as tournedos.

— **Choron:** sautéd, garnished with artichoke bottoms filled alternately with buttered green peas and nut potatoes; Choron sauce served separately.

— **Dutch Style:** à la hollandaise: larded with anchovy fillets, braised in gravy with chopped onions, sauce finished off with cream.

Beef: Tenderloin Steak

— **Duval:** sautéd rare, coated with thick mushroom purée, slices of truffle on top, wrapped in pig's caul, placed in oven for a short time; Madeira sauce with chopped truffle served separately.
— **Egyptian Style:** à l'egyptienne: broiled, same garnish as for tenderloin.
— **Forester Style:** à la forestière: prepared like tournedos.
— **Franco-Russe:** sautéd, covered with demi-glace mixed with diced tomatoes and sliced mushrooms; garnished with Parmentier potatoes and grated horseradish.
— **with Fried Eggs:** à cheval: sautéd, two fried eggs cut round with a cutter placed on top.
— **Gourmet Style:** du gourmet: sautéd blood rare, placed between two small slices of sautéd gooseliver, wrapped in puff paste, baked in hot oven; truffle sauce.
— **Greek Style:** à la grecque: chopped, mixed with cold boiled rice and chopped onions lightly fried in butter, seasoned, reformed, fried and covered with tomato sauce.
— **Hamburg Style:** à la hambourgeoise: chopped, mixed with chopped onions lightly fried in butter, seasoned, reformed, fried in butter, covered with fried onions.
— **Heligoland Style:** à la heligolandaise: sautéd, placed on croûton, covered alternately with strips of thick tomato, green herb and Dutch sauce; served with French fried potatoes.
— **Hunter Style:** sautéd, deglaced with white wine and hunter sauce.
— **Kempinski:** fried, covered with two halved fried tomatoes filled with Béarnaise sauce; garnished with straw potatoes and watercress.
— **Lord Seymour:** same garnish as tournedos.
— **Lyonese Style:** à la lyonnaise: same garnish as tenderloin.
— **Madrid Style:** à la madrilène: fried, garnished with a large stuffed, braised onion covered with Mornay sauce and gratinated.
— **Marschall Style:** à la maréchale: fried, truffle slices on top, garnished with tartlet filled with asparagus tips.
— **Meier:** fried in butter, covered with deep fried onion rings, garnished with German fried potatoes.
— **Metropole:** prepared like tournedos.
— **Murillo:** fried blood rare, coated with mushroom purée bound with cream and egg yolk, baked in oven.
— **Nelson:** lightly flattened, seasoned, fried blood rare, placed in small round cocotte with chopped onions sautéd in butter, deglaced with Madeira and boiled up with a spoon full of demi-glace, glazed button onions and fancy shaped carrots, sautéd button mushrooms and boiled potato balls; cocotte closed, simmered for a few minutes and served with chopped pickles scattered on top.
— **Nilson:** marinated in red wine pickle with pot herbs; larded, browned, braised in half demi-glace and half pickle; garnished with pieces of carrots, parsnips and cabbage simmered in butter and white stock.
— **Nimese Style:** à la nimoise: chopped, mixed with bread soaked in milk, egg, seasoning and chopped sautéd onions: reformed, dipped in egg and breadcrumbs, fried, served covered with tomato sauce flavored with garlic.

Beef: Tenderloin Steak
— **in Paper Bag:** en papillote: coated with anchovy butter, wrapped in greased paper bag, grilled; truffle sauce served separately.
— **Polish:** à la polonaise: fried, covered with chopped fried onions and breadcrumbs browned in butter; garnished with German fried potatoes tossed in anchovy butter, and grated horseradish.
— **Potted:** en casserole: dredged with flour, seasoned, browned in butter, placed in fireproof earthenware or China casserole fancy-shaped carrots, turnips and potatoes added, moistened with a little beef gravy, stewed with lid on.
— **Republican Style:** à la républicaine: browned in oil, simmered with chopped onions and ham in demi-glace; when done green peas and sautéd fairy ring mushrooms added; served with half a red pepper stewed and filled with a small poached egg.
— **Reynière:** same garnish as tournedos.
— **Russian:** à la russe: 1. prepared like Hamburg steak with two fried eggs cut out round on top instead of the onions; bordered with clear gravy.
2. larded with fat bacon and ham, browned, stewed in white wine and sour cream mixed with chopped fennel; garnished with boletus.
— **Salisbury:** 1. scraped or chopped with suet, seasoned, mixed with eggs, breadcrumbs and capers, reformed, broiled. 2. chopped bacon mixed with the ground meat, chopped onions, green peppers, parsley and seasoning, shaped, broiled. 3. scraped or chopped, mixed with chopped onions and seasoning, shaped square, wrapped in pig's caul, broiled, fried onions on top, bordered with cream sauce.
— **Salisbury Steak Creole:** same as 1 served with Creole sauce.
— **with Smothered Onions:** aux onions: fried, covered with onion slices browned in butter and stewed in light demi-glace; chopped parsley sprinkled on top.
— **Spanish:** à l'espagnole: chopped, mixed with chopped fat bacon, soaked bread, garlic, parsley and seasoning, shaped round, dipped in egg and breadcrumbs, fried; tomato sauce.
— **Steeple Chase:** fried, a fried egg placed on top; garnished with a sardine, a cornet of smoked salmon filled with grated horseradish and potato, cucumber and lettuce salad arranged in bunches.
— **Stock Exchange Style:** Hôtel des monnaies: boiled potatoes and mushrooms cut in thin slices sautéd pale brown in butter, beaten eggs poured over and fried like thin pancake. Steak sautéd rare, wrapped in the pancake, covered with browned butter; served with lettuce salad.
— **Swedish:** à la suédoise: browned in butter, stewed with chopped onions and sliced raw potatoes.
— **Tartar:** à la tartare: chopped or scraped, shaped round with an egg yolk in cavity in center; garnished with capers, anchovy fillets, chopped onions and pickles arranged in bunches.

Beef Tongue, Ox Tongue: Langue de boeuf: pickled or pickled and smoked tongue is cooked slowly in plenty of water, simmering until done, cooled off in running water, skinned and served hot or cold. Fresh, unpickled tongue may

Beef Tongue
be braised or boiled with a larded onion and pot herbs. They must be soaked in water and trimmed before being boiled or braised.
— **Alsatian Style:** à l'alsacienne: lightly pickled tongue braised; saurkraut with small slices of ham on top, mashed potatoes and the sauce served separately.
— **Bigarade:** lightly pickled tongue, braised and served with bigarade sauce.
— **with Broad Beans:** aux fèves: braised in white wine and demi-glace; sauce and broad beans tossed in butter served separately.
— **Christiania:** pickled tongue boiled, garnished with artichoke bottoms filled with diced mushrooms and diced blanched ox marrow bound with demi-glace; pepper sauce mixed with chopped sour cherries.
— **Citizen Style:** à la bourgeoise: fresh tongue braised in red wine and brown stock; shortly before tongue is done placed in clean casserolle with browned button onions, diced lightly fried bacon and parboiled olive-shaped carrots, the lightly thickened and strained sauce poured over the tongue, braised until done.
— **Conti:** fresh tongue braised in white wine and demi-glace; lentil purée garnished with triangles of bacon cooked with the lentils and the sauce served separately.
— **with Cucumbers:** aux concombres: fresh tongue braised in demi-glace and Madeira; fancy-shaped pieces of cucumber in cream sauce served separately.
— **Czech Style:** à la tcheque: braised in white wine and brown stock with mirepoix; sauce thickened with light roux and grated gingerbread, strained, mixed with sultanas and slivered almonds, lightly sweetened.
— **Flemish Style:** à la flamande: lightly pickled tongue braised, covered with a little sauce; Flemish garnish and the remaining sauce served separately.
— **German Style:** à l'allemande: fresh tongue parboiled, braised in light demi-glace; served with spinach purée, mashed potatoes and the sauce flavored with Madeira.
— **Italian Style:** à l'italienne: pickled tongue parboiled, braised in light Italian sauce; garnished with artichoke bottoms prepared the Italian way, and macaroni croquettes; the sauce served separately.
— **Julien:** pickled tongue, boiled, served with piquant sauce with tomato purée and mashed potatoes.
— **Leopold:** fresh tongue, braised in white wine and demi-glace; sauce and braised French endives served separately.
— **Mandragora** (cold): pickled tongue, boiled, cooled off, skinned, glazed with Madeira aspic jelly and placed in center of long or rectangular silver dish; garnished with small skinned tomatoes scooped out and filled with a salad of rice, diced bananas and mangoes bound with mayonnaise flavored with curry powder, grilled slivered almonds on top, and tartlets filled with egg yolk creamed with butter, mixed with chopped chives and decorated with a truffle star.
— **Mentschikoff:** fresh tongue braised in white wine and demi-glace; covered with the sauce mixed with glazed button onions, olive-shaped cucumber pieces simmered in

Beef Tongue
butter, quartered mushrooms simmered in butter and peeled seeded grapes.
— **Milanese Style:** à la milanaise: fresh tongue braised in brown stock and tomato purée; macaroni prepared the Milanese way and the thickened sauce served separately.
— **Naples Style:** à la napolitaine: pickled tongue boiled or fresh tongue braised; covered with tomato sauce; spaghetti prepared the Naples way served separately.
— **Nelson:** pickled tongue, boiled, cooled off, skinned cut in slices; two slices always spread with cold white onion purée and put together like a sandwich, dipped in egg and breadcrumbs, deep fried and garnished with buttered green peas and nut potatoes.
— **Nignon:** pickled tongue boiled until three quarters done, then braised in veal gravy and Muscat wine and glazed; garnished with sliced fried eggplant, fried tomatoes and sautéd yellow boletus; the stock thickened with arrowroot served separately.
— **Orlow:** fresh tongue, parboiled, braised in white wine and white stock; when done carved, put together again with thick onion purée and a slice of truffle between the slices, coated entirely with onion purée, covered with Mornay sauce and glazed.
— **Palermo Style:** à la palermitaine: fresh tongue braised in light tomato sauce and white stock; garnished with fried halved tomatoes and macaroni croquettes.
— **with Parmesan:** au parmesan: greased baking dish sprinkled with grated Parmesan, filled with layers of cold sliced pickled beef tongue, demi-glace and grated Parmesan; covered with demi-glace, sprinkled with grated Parmesan, dotted with butter and browned in oven.
— **Perigord Style:** à la périgourdine: fresh tongue braised in demi-glace and Madeira with truffle peels; served with truffle sauce prepared with the strained braising sauce.
— **Saint-Flour:** boiled, served with buttered noodles mixed with grated Parmesan, chestnut croquettes and Madeira sauce.
— **Sardinian Style:** à la sarde: boiled or braised in light tomato sauce; garnished with stuffed pieces of cucumber, stuffed tomatoes and rice croquettes with saffron; tomato sauce.
— **with Sorrel:** à l'oseille: braised or boiled, served with sorrel purée and Madeira sauce.
— **Soubeyran:** fresh tongue braised in demi-glace and Madeira; garnished with tartlets filled with white truffled onion purée.
— **with Spinach:** aux epinards: parboiled, braised in white wine, Madeira and demi-glace; served with spinach purée.

Beef: Tournedos: a small fairly thick slice of the tenderloin weighing about 4 oz., trimmed and shaped round, tied, sautéd or grilled, untied and usually served on round fried croûton. After the fat has been poured off, the residue in the pan is always deglaced with wine, stock or other fluid and added to the sauce.
— **Adelaide:** grilled, garnished with tartlets filled with creamed corn and thick slices of banana dipped in egg and breadcrumbs and deep fried; thick tomato sauce

Beef: Tournedos
seasoned with catsup and blended with butter served separately.
— **Aida:** sautéd rare, coated with shrimps bound with thick Béchamel sauce, sprinkled with grated Parmesan, dotted with butter and glazed rapidly; Madeira sauce.
— **Aiglon:** placed on round flat potato croquette mixed with chopped truffle, a round slice of fried gooseliver or a small dumpling of gooseliver forcemeat placed on top; Madeira sauce.
— **Alexandra:** 1. a truffle slice on top of the tournedos covered with buttered meat glaze; garnished with tartlets filled with green asparagus tips.
2. a truffle slice on top, garnished with sautéd quarters of artichoke bottoms; Madeira sauce.
— **Algerian Style:** à l'algérienne: placed on flat sweet potato croquette, garnished with fried tomatoes; light demi-glace with tomato.
— **Alsatian Style:** à l'alsacienne: placed on croûton, garnished with saurkraut and fried bacon; demi-glace.
— **Ambassadress Style:** à l'ambassadrice: garnished with truffled lamb sweetbread and green asparagus tips; Madeira sauce with truffle essence.
— **American Style:** à l'américaine: placed on croquette of sweet potatoes, garnished with corn fritters; light tomato sauce.
— **Andalusian Style:** à l'andalouse: garnished with stuffed peppers and tiny pork sausages, a fried slice of egg plant on top of the tournedos; thick veal gravy with tomato.
— **Antwerp Style:** à l'anversoise: garnished as for tenderloin.
— **d'Arenberg:** a slice of truffle on the tournedos, covered with the deglacage with Madeira and demi-glace; garnished with tartlets filled alternately with buttered leaf spinach and creamed carrots; Béarnaise sauce served separately.
— **Arlesian Style:** à l'arlésienne: same garnish as for tenderloin.
— **Armand:** garnished with tartlets filled with gooseliver purée, a slice or small ball of truffle on top; red wine sauce.
— **Armenonville:** placed on base of Anna potatoes, garnished with creamed morels; deglaced with Madeira and veal gravy.
— **Baltimore:** placed on tartlet filled with creamed corn, a fried tomato slice and a smaller slice of green pepper on each tournedos; Chateaubriand sauce.
— **Balzac:** covered with hunter sauce, garnished with small chicken dumplings and blanched stuffed olives.
— **Banker Style:** à la banquière: deglaced with Madeira and demi-glace; banker garnish.
— **Baroda:** placed on shaped risotto; garnished with artichoke bottoms and small veal dumplings decorated with truffle; regency sauce.
— **Baron Brisse:** tomatoes concassées on top of the tournedos; garnished with souffle potatoes and artichoke bottoms filled with small truffle balls; demi-glace with truffle essence.
— **Basque Style:** à la basque: sautéd, garnished with stuffed tomatoes, Anna potatoes and creamed knob celery.

Beef: Tournedos

— **Bayard:** placed on croûton spread with gooseliver purée. garnished with strips of mushrooms, truffles, ox tongue and artichoke bottoms bound with Madeira sauce; Madeira sauce served separately.

— **Bayonne Style:** à la bayonnaise: garnished with macaroni croquettes mixed with chopped ham; tomato sauce.

— **Beatrice:** garnished with sautéd morels, fancy-shaped carrots, artichoke quarters and new potatoes; covered with demi-glace.

— **Beaugency:** deglaced with Madeira and demi-glace; tournedos bordered with Choron sauce, center filled with tomatoes concassées with a blanched slice of ox marrow and chopped parsley on top; deglacage poured around the tournedos.

— **Beauharnais:** 1. garnished with artichoke bottoms, filled with Beauharnais sauce, blanched tarragon leaves placed crisscross on top, and French fried potatoes.
2. garnished with stuffed mushrooms and sautéd artichoke quarters; truffle sauce.

— **Belleclaire:** placed on halved fried tomatoes; garnished with mushroom caps, filled with diced red peppers simmered in butter, and tartlets filled with tiny potato balls sautéd with chopped shallots.

— **Belle-Hélène:** placed on round flat asparagus croquette, a slice of truffle on top of tournedos.

— **Belmont:** a truffle slice on top, covered with Madeira sauce; garnished with mushrooms and cucumber balls simmered in butter.

— **Benjamin:** a stuffed mushroom on each tournedos, garnished with truffled dauphine potatoes; deglaced with Madeira and demi-glace.

— **Bercy:** grilled, brushed with liquid meat glaze; Bercy sauce served separately.

— **Bernardi:** garnished with game croquettes and puff pastry patties filled with vegetable macedoine; Madeira sauce.

— **Berny:** marinated beforehand, dried, sautéd in oil, a large truffle slice on the tournedos, garnished with Berny potatoes; pepper sauce.

— **Berthier:** garnished with stuffed tomatoes and olives stuffed with anchovy paste; tomato sauce mixed with grated horseradish.

— **Bizontine:** tournedos placed on croustade made of duchess potato filled with creamed cauliflower purée; garnished with braised lettuce; thick veal gravy.

— **Blanchette:** large truffle slice on top of tournedos, covered with Bordeaux sauce mixed with julienne of mushrooms, ham and truffle.

— **Bonaparte:** garnished with artichoke bottom filled with salpicon of chicken bound with suprême sauce; covered with truffle sauce.

— **Bonnefoy:** sautéd and covered with Bonnefoy sauce.

— **Bordeaux Style:** à la bordelaise: grilled, a large blanched slice of ox marrow sprinkled with chopped parsley on top; Bordeaux sauce served separately.

— **Brabant Style:** same garnish as for tenderloin.

— **Bragance:** placed on croûton spread with gooseliver purée, a slice of truffle on top of tournedos; garnished with puff pastry patty filled with green asparagus tips; truffle sauce.

Beef: Tournedos

— **Brébant:** covered with Béarnaise sauce, garnished with straw potatoes and watercress.

— **Bréhan:** sautéd, placed on tartlet filled with purée of broad beans, garnished with cauliflower sprigs and parsley potatoes.

— **Breton Style:** à la bretonne: garnished with white Lima beans prepared in the Breton way; thick veal gravy.

— **Bristol:** placed on round flat rice croquette, garnished with buttered flageolets and nicely shaped boiled potatoes rolled in liquid meat glace and chopped parsley.

— **Brussels Style:** à la bruxelloise: deglaced with Madeira and demi-glace; garnished with Brussels sprouts, braised French endives and castle potatoes.

— **Calypso:** grilled, placed on artichoke bottom, covered with red wine sauce, a blanched slice of marrow on top of the tournedos, sprinkled with chopped chervil.

— **Canova:** a round slice of fried gooseliver on top of tournedos; garnished with artichoke bottom filled with truffles, cockscombs and cocks' kidneys bound with Madeira sauce.

— **Carême:** potato croquettes, olives stuffed with ham purée; Madeira sauce.

— **Carignan:** deglaced with Port and veal gravy with tomato; placed on base of Anna potato, garnished with artichoke bottoms filled with asparagus tips and baked duchess potato nests filled with gooseliver purée.

— **Carnot:** stuffed cucumber; red wine sauce with chopped chervil.

— **Catalonian Style:** à la catalane: same garnish as for tenderloin.

— **Catherine:** deglaced with white wine and Bonnefoy sauce; placed on base of Macaire potato, a blanched slice of ox marrow on top of tournedos.

— **Cavaignac:** garnished with half-moon shaped potato croquettes, stuffed olives, and sauted chicken livers, cockscombs, cocks' kidneys and truffle slices bound with thick tomato sauce.

— **Cecil:** garnished with soufflé potatoes, asparagus tips and sautéd mushrooms; Madeira sauce.

— **Cecilia:** grilled, garnished with large mushroom caps filled with creamed green asparagus tips and soufflé potatoes; thick veal gravy.

— **Chancy:** garnished with creamed carrot balls, sautéd mushrooms and buttered green peas; Madeira sauce.

— **Chantecler:** sautéd, half a sautéd lamb kidney and a cockscomb on top of the tournedos, covered with Port sauce mixed with truffle julienne; garnished with potato nests filled alternately with chicken purée and asparagus tips.

— **Chartres Style:** à la Chartres: deglaced with thick veal gravy with tarragon flavor; blanched tarragon leaves on top of the tournedos; garnished with castle potatoes.

— **Chatelaine:** sautéd, placed on artichoke bottom filled with onion purée; garnished with glazed chestnuts and nut potatoes; Madeira sauce.

— **Chéron:** 1. artichoke bottoms filled with vegetable macedoine and Parisian potatoes; thick veal gravy.
2. stuffed tomatocs, artichoke bottoms filled with buttered

Beef: Tournedos
green peas, stuffed mushrooms; one half of tournedos covered with Béarnaise and the other half with Choron sauce.
— **Chevreuse:** placed on round flat semolina croquette with chopped mushrooms; a large truffle slice on top of tournedos, covered with Bonnefoy sauce.
— **Chiefranger Style:** à la grand-veneur: marinated, dried, sautéd, served with chiefranger sauce.
— **Choisy:** placed on croûton coated with meat glaze; garnished with braised lettuce and castle potatoes.
— **Choron:** grilled, placed on artichoke bottom filled with green peas or green asparagus tips; garnished with nut potatoes; Choron sauce.
— **Cinderella:** Cendrillon: placed on artichoke bottom filled with truffled onion purée and glazed.
— **Clamart:** placed on base of Macaire potatoes; garnished with tartlets filled with peas prepared in the French way shredded lettuce added.
— **Claude:** garnished with braised lettuce and nest-shaped potato croquettes filled with tiny creamed carrot balls; thick veal gravy.
— **Colbert:** deglaced with Madeira and meat glaze; dressed on round flat chicken croquette, a french fried egg surmounted with a truffle slice on top of tournedos; Colbert sauce.
— **Continental Style:** à la continentale: grilled, garnished with grilled tomatoes, grilled mushroom caps, soufflé potatoes and watercress; herb butter served separately.
— **Countess Style:** à la comtesse: garnished with artichoke bottom filled with asparagus tips and potato croquettes; truffle sauce.
— **Countess Maritza:** grilled, garnished with small pieces of braised celery wrapped in puff pastry, brushed with egg yolk and baked, almond potatoes and slices of baby marrow dipped in frying batter and deep fried; herb butter.
— **Crecy:** sautéd, garnished with small carrot balls simmered in butter; Madeira sauce.
— **Crispi:** placed on tartlet filled with risotto, covered with tomato sauce; tartlet filled with cauliflower covered with Mornay sauce and glazed as a garnish.
— **Crownprince Style:** à la dauphine: garnished with dauphine potatoes; Madeira sauce.
— **Cussy:** placed on artichoke bottom filled with chestnut purée (when out of season, mushroom purée) and gratinated; a truffle slice, a cockscomb and a cocks' kidney rolled in Italian sauce on top of tournedos; Madeira sauce.
— **Czech Style:** à la tchèque: placed on base of risotto; garnished with tomatoes concassées and deep fried onion rings.
— **Delagrange:** garnished with gratinated asparagus tips, fancy shaped carrots, turnips and green peas; Madeira sauce.
— **Deslignac:** grilled, covered with Choron sauce, garnished with castle potatoes.
— **Dubarry:** garnished with cauliflower balls coated with Mornay sauce and glazed; buttered veal gravy.
— **Duquina:** sautéd, covered with cream sauce mixed with red pepper purée; garnished with tartlets filled with short

Beef: Tournedos

coarse julienne of pickled cucumber bound with sour cream sauce and sprinkled with chopped dill.

— **Duroc:** covered with hunter sauce, garnished with nut potatoes and tomatoes concassées.

— **Elysée-Palace:** sautéd, a slice of fried calf's sweetbread and a fluted mushroom cap on top; Béarnaise sauce.

— **Embassy Style:** à l'ambassade: covered with Choron sauce, garnished with artichoke bottom filled with cucumber balls simmered in butter.

— **Eugen:** sautéd, covered with pepper sauce mixed with chopped mustard fruit; garnished with small stuffed green peppers and almond potatoes.

— **Favorite Style:** à la favorite: sautéd, a sautéd slice of gooseliver and truffle slice placed on top; garnished with asparagus tips and Parisian potatoes.

— **Florence Style:** à la florentine: sautéd, placed on spinach subric or leaf spinach tossed in butter, garnished with semolina croquettes; Chateaubriand sauce.

— **Forester Style:** à la forestière: sautéd, garnished with sautéd morels, Parmentier potatoes and fried bacon triangles; buttered veal gravy.

— **Foyot:** grilled, garnished with straw potatoes and watercress; Foyot sauce.

— **Frascati:** same garnish as for tenderloin.

— **Gabrielle:** sautéd, placed on round flat truffled chicken croquette, a blanched slice of ox marrow and truffle on top of tournedos, covered with buttered Madeira sauce; garnished with braised lettuce.

— **Gambetta:** sautéd, a fried egg cut out round and a strip of truffle on top; garnished with Parmentier potatoes and green peas; thick veal gravy.

— **Gastronomers Style:** à la gastronome: sautéd, garnished with glazed chestnuts, small truffles cooked in champagne and cocks' kidneys rolled in liquid meat glaze; demi-glace with truffle essence.

— **Gouffé:** sautéd, placed on shaped risotto, garnished with mushrooms, olive-shaped truffles and small veal dumplings; demi-glace.

— **Gourmet Style:** du gourmet: 1. sautéd rare, a small slice of fried gooseliver placed on top, cooled, wrapped in puff pastry dough, brushed with egg yolk, baked in oven; truffle sauce served separately.
2. cut open on one side, stuffed with a piece of gooseliver, dipped in egg and breadcrumbs, fried in butter; garnished with mushroom caps and castle potatoes; truffle sauce.

— **Grandduke Style:** à la grandduc: sautéd, a blanched ox marrow and a truffle slice placed on top, covered with truffle sauce flavored with Madeira; garnished with asparagus tips.

— **Green Meadow:** à la vert-pré: grilled, garnished with straw potatoes and watercress; herb butter on top.

— **Hauser:** grilled, garnished with deep fried onion rings and straw potatoes; Colbert sauce.

— **Helder:** sautéd, a border of Béarnaise sauce, the center filled with tomatoes concassées on top tournedos: garnished with Parisian potatoes.

Beef: Tournedos

— **Henry IV.:** Henri IV.: grilled, garnished with artichoke bottom filled with small Parisian potatoes; Béarnaise sauce served separately.

— **Hotelier Style:** à l'hotelière: sautéd, deglazed with white wine and demi-glace; garnished with artichoke bottom filled with Béarnaise sauce, braised celery hearts and soufflé potatoes.

— **Hungarian Style:** à la hongroise: sautéd, garnished with cauliflower balls coated with Mornay sauce mixed with chopped ham and paprika, sprinkled with grated Parmesan and glazed.

— **Hussar Style:** à la hussarde: same garnish as for tenderloin.

— **Iman Bayaldi:** placed on thick slice of deep fried eggplant, a fried tomato on the tournedos; garnished with shaped pilaf rice; thick veal gravy with tomato.

— **Italian Style:** à l'italienne: garnished as for tenderloin.

— **Japanese Style:** à la japonaise: sautéd, garnished with tartlet filled with creamed stachy; thick veal gravy.

— **Jetée-Promenade:** grilled, a fried half tomato filled with Béarnaise sauce on top; garnished with soufflé potatoes and watercress.

— **Judic:** sautéd, a large slice of truffle and a cocks' kidney on top of each tournedos; garnished with braised lettuce.

— **Jussieu:** sautéd, garnished with braised lettuce and glazed onions; Madeira sauce.

— **Kléber:** sautéd, covered with truffle sauce; garnished with artichoke bottom filled with truffled gooseliver purée.

— **Laguipierre:** sautéd, a round slice of ox tongue and a slice of fried gooseliver placed on top, covered with truffle sauce.

— **Lakmé:** sautéd, placed on tartlet stuffed with broad bean purée, a fluted mushroom on top of tournedos; bordered with tomato sauce.

— **Langtry:** sautéd, placed on artichoke bottom, a peeled stewed tomato surmounted with a stoned olive and decorated with blanched tarragon leaves on top of tournedos; bordered with truffle sauce.

— **Lavallière:** sautéd, placed on artichoke bottom filled with green asparagus tips, covered with Bordeaux sauce; garnished with castle potatoes.

— **Leopold:** sautéd, placed on tartlet filled with finely sliced yellow boletus sautéd with chopped shallots and bound with cream sauce; covered with Madeira sauce blended with gooseliver purée.

— **Lesdiguières:** grilled, placed on large Spanish onion stuffed with spinach, covered with Mornay sauce and glazed.

— **Lesseps:** sautéd, placed on rice croquette mixed with saffron and diced red peppers; garnished with tomatoes stuffed with brain purée; Madeira sauce.

— **Levasseur:** sautéd in oil, covered with Provencal sauce mixed with sautéd slices of yellow boletus; garnished with straw potatoes.

— **Lili:** sautéd, placed on base of Anna potatoes; garnished with artichoke bottom filled with a round slice of sautéd gooseliver and a truffle slice.

Beef: Tournedos

— **Little Duke:** à la petit duc: sautéd, placed on tartlet filled with chicken purée, a slice of truffle on top of tournedos; garnished with asparagus tips.

— **Lola Montez:** sautéd, placed on tartlet filled with tomatoes concassées garnished with large mushroom caps filled with diced red peppers simmered in butter; Madeira sauce with tomato.

— **Lord Seymour:** sautéd, garnished with artichoke bottom filled with Béarnaise sauce mixed with chopped truffles; Madeira sauce mixed with chopped olives.

— **Lorette:** sautéd, placed on croûton, garnished with chicken croquettes, tartlet filled with asparagus tips and a slice of truffle on top.

— **Louis XV.:** placed on base of Anna potatoes, garnished with tartlet filled with minced mushrooms simmered in butter and a truffle slice on top; tournedos covered with devil sauce.

— **Louise:** fried tomatoes, stuffed mushrooms and nut potatoes; Parisian sauce.

— **Lucullus:** sautéd, placed on croûton coated with liquid meat glaze; garnished with small chicken dumplings, olive-shaped truffles and cockscombs covered with demiglace with truffle essence.

— **Lyonese Style:** à la lyonnaise: same garnish as for tenderloin.

— **Mac-Mahon:** sautéd, deglaced with white wine and meat glaze beaten with butter; arranged in cocotte on base of sliced raw potatoes sautéd in butter with chopped onions; covered with the deglacage.

— **Magenta:** placed on croûton scooped out and filled with diced blanched ox marrow bound with buttered meat glace; Madeira sauce.

— **Maire:** sautéd, covered with Madeira sauce; maire potatoes served separately.

— **Marc Aurel:** sautéd, garnished with chicken dumplings and lamb's sweetbread covered with Madeira sauce.

— **Marianne:** sautéd, garnished with artichoke bottom filled with creamed purée of green peas; thick veal gravy.

— **Marigny:** sautéd, garnished with tartlets filled alternately with green peas and diced green beans, and fondantes potatoes; veal gravy.

— **Marion-Delorme:** same as Mary Jane.

— **Marly:** garnished with artichoke bottom filled with small carrot balls; Madeira sauce.

— **Marquise:** sautéd, garnished with tartlet filled with marquise garnish, and marquise potatoes.

— **with Ox Marrow:** à la moelle: grilled, a large slice of blanched ox marrow on top: covered with marrow sauce.

— **Marseille Style:** à la marseillaise: sautéd in oil, covered with Provencal sauce with a stoned olive and an anchovy ring on top; garnished with tomatoes prepared the Provencal way and ribbon potatoes.

— **Marshall Style:** à la maréchale: sautéd, a large truffle slice coated with liquid meat glaze on top; garnished with green asparagus tips.

— **Mary Jane:** Marie-Jeanne: sautéd, garnished with artichoke bottom filled with mushroom purée blended with onion purée covered with Madeira sauce with tomato.

Beef: Tournedos

— **Mary-Louise:** Marie-Louise: prepared like Mary Jane.

— **Mary-Theresia:** Marie-Thérèse: sautéd, a slice of truffle on top, covered with demi-glace with tomato; garnished with shaped risotto.

— **Mascagni:** placed on tartlet filled with chestnut purée, a slice of fried calf's brain on top of tournedos covered with tomato sauce; garnished with straw potatoes.

— **Mascott:** à la mascotte: sautéd in a cocotte, garnished with sautéd artichoke quarters, olive-shaped truffles and potatoes; deglaced with white wine and thick veal gravy.

— **Masséna:** sautéd, a slice of blanched ox marrow on top; garnished with artichoke bottom filled with Béarnaise sauce; truffle sauce served separately.

— **Massenet:** placed on base of Anna potatoes, a slice of blanched ox marrow sprinkled with chopped parsley on top of tournedos; garnished with artichoke bottom filled with diced green beans; Madeira sauce.

— **Maxim's:** placed on round asparagus croquette, a fried slice of tomato covered with Béarnaise sauce surmounted with a truffle slice on top of tournedos; garnished with potato nests filled alternately with buttered green peas and French fried potatoes.

— **Medicis:** same garnish as for tenderloin.

— **Melba:** sautéd, deglaced with Port and demi-glace; garnished with tomatoes, stuffed with salpicon of chicken, mushrooms and truffles bound with velouté and glazed, and braised lettuce.

— **Mercedes:** Mércédès: sautéd, garnished with braised lettuce, fried tomatoes, large mushroom caps and potato croquettes; Madeira sauce.

— **Metropole:** sautéd, a slice of fried calf's sweetbread and a mushroom cap on top, covered with truffle sauce; Madeira sauce served separately.

— **Metropolis:** deglaced with Sherry, cream and demi-glace; garnished with tartlets, filled with okra mixed with tomatoes concassées, and shoestring potatoes.

— **Mexican Style:** à la mexicaine: garnished as for tenderloin.

— **Mignon:** sautéd, a small chicken dumpling and a truffle slice placed on top; garnished with artichoke bottoms filled with green peas.

— **Mikado:** sautéd, placed on a grilled half tomato; garnished with stachy tossed in butter; bordered with Provencal sauce.

— **Mirabeau:** grilled, decorated with blanched tarragon leaves and a rolled anchovy filled with a stoned olive; anchovy butter served separately.

— **Mireille:** sautéd, coated with liquid meat glaze; Mireille garnish; light tomato sauce.

— **Mirette:** sautéd, deglaced with white wine and meat glace, beaten with butter; tournedos placed on base of Mirette potatoes and covered with the sauce.

— **Modern Style:** same garnish as for tenderloin.

— **Monaco:** sautéd, same garnish as for tenderloin.

— **Monte Carlo:** sautéd, garnished with stuffed cucumber, tartlets, filled alternately with green beans and green peas, and croquette potatoes; buttered veal glaze.

Beef: Tournedos

— **Montespan:** sautéd, placed on artichoke bottom, a fluted mushroom cap on top; Madeira sauce mixed with chopped mushrooms.

— **Monthabor:** placed on base of shaped rice pilaf mixed with diced red peppers, covered with tomato sauce.

— **Montmorency:** sautéd, placed on artichoke bottom filled with vegetable macodoine; garnished with asparagus tips.

— **Montmort:** sautéd, placed on croûton made of a slice of fried brioche, scooped out and filled with gooseliver purée mixed with diced truffle; a slice of truffle dipped in liquid meat glace on top of tournedos, a border of Madeira sauce blended with gooseliver purée poured around.

— **Montpensier:** sautéd, garnished with tartlet filled with asparagus tips and a slice of truffle on top.

— **with Morels:** aux morilles sautéd, covered with demi-glace, garnished with morels sautéd in butter with chopped shallots.

— **Mozart:** sautéd, garnished with artichoke bottoms filled with celery purée and potato nests with soufflée potatoes; pepper sauce.

— **with Mushrooms:** aux champignons: sautéd, covered with Madeira sauce with sliced mushrooms, or garnished with sautéd mushrooms, covered with Madeira sauce.

— **Nancy Style:** à la nancéenne: sautéd, a slice of sautéd goose liver on top, covered with truffle sauce.

— **Naples Style:** à la napolitaine: sautéd in oil, bordered with tomato sauce; macaroni prepared the Naples way served separately.

— **Nesselrode:** sautéd, garnished with olive-shaped truffles and glazed chestnuts; Madeira sauce.

— **Nice Style:** à la nicoise: same garnish as for tenderloin.

— **Nichette:** sautéd, garnished with mushroom caps filled with grated horseradish, and cockscombs and cocks' kidneys coated with marrow sauce.

— **Ninon:** sautéd, deglazed with Madeira and veal gravy, reduced and beaten with butter; tournedos placed on base of Mirette potatoes, garnished with small puff pastry patty filled with asparagus tips mixed with truffle strips.

— **Noailles:** placed on base of chicken forcemeat poached in tartlet mould; a slice of gooseliver on top, garnished with cockcombs and cocks' kidneys; Madeira sauce.

— **Opera:** à l'opéra: sautéd, placed on tartlet filled with sautéd chicken livers bound with Madeira sauce; garnished with croustade filled with asparagus tips.

— **Oriental Style:** à l'orientale: sautéd in oil, placed on flat croquette of sweet potatoes; garnished with halved stewed tomatoes and shaped rice prepared the Greek way.

— **Orleans Style:** à l'orléanaise: sautéd, garnished with creamed chicory mixed with egg yolks; maître d'hôtel potatoes and thick veal gravy served separately.

— **Oscar:** sautéd, garnished with potato croustades filled alternately with creamed carrot balls and a small ball of braised cabbage; thick veal gravy.

— **Othello:** sautéd, a small poached egg placed on tournedos, covered with truffle sauce; garnished with straw potatoes and green peas.

Beef: Tournedos

— **Palace Hotel:** sautéd, garnished with potato nests filled alternately with green peas and diced green beans, and tomatoes stuffed with gooseliver purée; demi-glace.

— **Palatine:** sautéd, garnished with glazed button onions, diced fried bacon and apple wedges sautéd in butter.

— **Palermo Style:** à la palermitaine: sautéd, garnished with macaroni croquettes, stuffed eggplant and fried tomatoes; tomato sauce.

— **Parisian Style:** à la parisienne: same garnish as for tenderloin.

— **Parmentier:** sautéd, deglaced with Madeira and demi-glace; garnished with Parmentier potatoes sprinkled with chopped parsley.

— **Pau Style:** à la paloise: sautéd, garnished with nut potatoes; Pau sauce served separately.

— **Péra Palace Hotel:** sautéd, a slice of truffle on top; garnished with potato nest filled with green peas, and tomatoes stuffed with gooseliver purée; Tyrolian sauce.

— **Perrier:** placed on potato croustade filled with salpicon of lamb sweetbread, mushrooms and truffle bound with Madeira sauce; a fluted mushroom cap on top of tournedos.

— **Peruvian Style:** à la peruvienne: sautéd, garnished with occa filled with hashed chicken and ox tongue bound with demi-glace; tomato sauce.

— **Piedmont Style:** à la piémontaise: sautéd, deglaced Madeira and demi-glace; garnished with shaped risotto prepared in the Piedmont way.

— **Pompadour:** 1. sautéd, a slice of truffle on top, garnished with tiny ball-shaped potato croquettes and artichoke bottom filled with lentil purée; truffle sauce.
2. coated with Choron sauce, garnished with artichoke bottom filled with nut potatoes; truffle sauce served separately.

— **Portuguese Style:** à la portugaise: same garnish as for tenderloin.

— **Prince Impériale:** grilled, coated with Béarnaise sauce; garnished with straw potatoes and green peas.

— **Princess Style:** same garnish as for tenderloin.

— **Provencal Style:** same garnish as for tenderloin.

— **Quirinal:** sautéd, garnished with mushroom caps filled with blanched diced ox marrow, straw potatoes and watercress; bordered with Italian sauce mixed with chopped tarragon.

— **Rachel:** covered with Bordeaux sauce; garnished with artichoke bottom with a large blanched slice of ox marrow on top.

— **Raphael:** sautéd, garnished with artichoke bottoms, filled alternately with Béarnaise sauce and small creamed carrot balls, and straw potatoes.

— **Regina:** garnished with tomatoes filled with risotto; Madeira sauce mixed with chopped pickles and green peppers.

— **Rich Style:** à la riche: sautéd, deglaced with Madeira and demi-glace; a slice of gooseliver and a truffle slice on top of tournedos; garnished with artichoke bottom filled with asparagus tips.

— **Richelieu:** same garnished as for tenderloin.

Beef: Tournedos

— **Richemont:** sautéd, deglaced with Madeira and thick veal gravy with sliced sautéd morels and truffles added.

— **Ristori:** sautéd, covered with Madeira sauce with chopped truffles; garnished with small puff pastry patties filled alternately with truffled quail puréé and diced pot herbs simmered in butter and bound with thick Madeira sauce.

— **Rivoli:** placed on base of Anna potatoes, covered with truffle sauce.

— **Rohan:** sautéd, deglaced with Sherry and demi-glace; garnished with artichoke bottom, filled with round slice of gooseliver and a truffle slice, and a tartlet filled with cockscombs and cocks' kidneys bound with German sauce.

— **Roman Style:** à la romaine: same garnish as for tenderloin.

— **Rossini:** sautéd, a round sautéd slice of gooseliver and a truffle slice on top of tournedos, covered with Madeira sauce with truffle essence.

— **Rostand:** sautéd, garnished with sautéd quartered artichoke bottoms and creamed mushrooms; Colbert sauce.

— **Roumanille:** sautéd, placed on a half grilled tomato, covered with Mornay sauce blended with tomato purée, sprinkled with grated cheese and glazed rapidly, a rolled anchovy fillet with a stoned olive on top of tournedos; garnished with sliced deep fried eggplant.

— **Roxy:** grilled, placed on thick slice of fried apple, covered with pepper sauce mixed with shredded green peppers; garnished with fried halved bananas and tartlets filled with okra mixed with tomatoes concassées.

— **Saint-Didier:** sautéd, garnished with tomatoes concassées sprinkled with chopped chives; Madeira sauce.

— **Saint-Germain:** sautéd, covered with Béarnaise sauce; garnished with tartlets filled with purée of green peas, glazed carrots and castle potatoes.

— **Saint-Laurent:** sautéd, garnished with tomato filled with Béarnaise sauce and soufflée potatoes; demi-glace.

— **Saint-Mande:** placed on base of Anna potatoes, garnished with green peas and asparagus tips.

— **Sarah Bernhardt:** sautéd, garnished with small peeled and stewed tomatoes and braised lettuce; a blanched slice of ox marrow on top of tournedos, covered with demi-glace flavored with Port.

— **Sardinian Style:** à la sarde: sautéd, garnished with rice croquettes with saffron and stuffed cucumber; tomato sauce.

— **Sévigné:** stuffed lettuce, mushrooms and castle potatoes; Madeira sauce.

— **Sevilla Style:** à la sevillane: sautéd, garnished with tartlets filled alternately with tomatoes concassées and diced red peppers simmered in butter, and fondantes potatoes; Valois sauce.

— **Shepherd Style:** à la bergère: garnished with glazed button onions, fried diced bacon and straw potatoes.

— **Sicilian Style:** à la sicilienne: sautéd, served with noodles tossed in butter and bound with purée of sautéd chicken livers mixed with velouté, covered with grated Parmesan; veal gravy with tomato.

— **Sigurd:** stuffed tomatoes, potato croquettes with chopped ham; truffle sauce.

Beef: Tournedos

— **Spanish Style:** à l'espagnole: sautéd, garnished with small glazed Spanish onion, tomato filled with rice pilaf with chopped ham, and nut potatoes; demi-glace with Sherry.
— **Staël:** sautéd, placed on round chicken croquette, a mushroom cap filled with chicken purée on top of tournedos; garnished with buttered green peas; thick veal gravy.
— **Stephanie:** sautéd, a slice of truffle on top covered with Madeira sauce; garnished with potato nests filled alternately with green peas and Parmentier potatoes.
— **Steward Style:** à la maître d'hôtel: grilled, covered with herb butter.
— **Sully:** garnished with braised lettuce and Parisian potatoes; covered with Madeira sauce cockscombs and cocks' kidneys added.
— **Sultana:** à la sultane: sautéd, placed on base of rice pilaf, a small poached egg on top of tournedos covered with truffle sauce; garnished with Parmentier potatoes with chopped parsley and gratinated slices of eggplant.
— **Sylvestre:** sautéd, garnished with tartlets filled with gooseliver purée blended with truffle purée; red wine sauce.
— **Talleyrand:** same garnish as for tenderloin.
— **with Tarragon:** à l'estragon: sautéd, blanched tarragon leaves crisscross on top; tarragon sauce.
— **Tivoli:** grilled, placed on croûton brushed with liquid meat glaze; garnished with large mushroom caps filled with small cockscombs and cocks' kidneys bound with German sauce, and bunches of asparagus tips.
— **Tosca:** placed on base of risotto; garnished with pieces of braised fennel bulbs; deglaced with veal gravy.
— **Toulouse Style:** à la toulousaine: Toulouse garnish and truffle sauce.
— **Touraine Style:** à la tourangelle: sautéd, garnished with diced green beans and flageolets in light cream sauce.
— **Trianon:** sautéd, garnished with tartlets filled alternately with carrot, chestnut and green peas purée.
— **Turbigo:** sautéd, deglaced with white wine and demi-glace; a large fluted mushroom cap on top, garnished with tiny fried pork sausages.
— **Tyrolian Style:** same garnish as for tenderloin.
— **Valencay:** sautéd, placed on flat croquette of noodles mixed with chopped ham; financier garnish.
— **Valois:** placed on base of Anna potatoes; Valois sauce.
— **Vatel:** sautéd, deglaced white wine and demi-glace; placed on base of Anna potatoes, a border of piped green peas purée filled with tomatoes concassées on top; garnished with sautéd yellow boletus and braised endives.
— **Vendôme:** sautéd, a small fried tomato filled with Béarnaise sauce on top; garnished with soufflée potatoes and deep fried onion rings.
— **Ventadour:** sautéd, placed on tartlet filled with artichoke purée; blanched slice of ox marow and truffle slice on top of tournedos covered with Chateaubriand sauce; garnished with nut potatoes.
— **Verdi:** sautéd, deglaced Madeira and demi-glace; placed on round slice of gooseliver, covered with white onion sauce and glazed; garnished with potato croustade filled with buttered carrot balls, and braised lettuce.

Beef: Tournedos
— **Victor Hugo:** sautéd, covered with tomatoes concassées with a slice of truffle on top; border of Béarnaise sauce mixed with grated blanched horseradish poured around the edge.
— **Victoria:** sautéd, placed on round flat chicken croquette; half a fried tomato placed on top of tournedos.
— **Villaret:** grilled, placed on tartlet filled with flageolet purée; a mushroom cap on top of tournedos covered with Chateaubriand sauce.
— **Villemer:** grilled, placed on croûton scooped out and filled with truffled onion purée; a slice of truffle coated with liquid meat glace on top of tournedos; Madeira sauce.
— **Visconti:** sautéd, placed on tartlet filled with purée of flageolets; a mushroom cap filled with Chateaubriand sauce on top of tournedos.
— **Voisin:** placed on base of Anna potatoes, a fried half tomato decorated with blanched tarragon leaves on top of tournedos; garnished with artichoke bottoms filled alternately with green peas and spinach purée, tarragon gravy.
— **Wellington:** sautéd blood rare, cooled off, coated with duxelles, wrapped in puff paste, brushed with egg yolk, baked in oven; truffle sauce served separately.
— **Winterthur:** sautéd, garnished with artichoke bottoms filled with a slice of blanched ox marrow covered with truffle slices; Colbert sauce.
— **Wladimir:** sautéd, placed on base of chicken forcemeat poached in tartlet mould; a slice of gooseliver on top of tournedos, covered with Colbert sauce mixed with chopped fennel greens.
— **Xavier:** sautéd, deglaced with Port and thick veal gravy; placed on base of spinach mixed with chicken forcemeat poached in tartlet mould, covered with the sauce; garnished with tartlet filled with chicken purée and asparagus tips placed on top, artichoke bottoms filled alternately with carrot balls and stewed red beetroot balls, and nut potatoes.
— **Zola:** sautéd blood rare, covered with anchovy fillets, wrapped in unsweetened brioche dough, baked; truffle sauce served separately.

Bengalines de bécasse: see woodcock.

Berner Platte: Berne dish: smoked pork ribs, boiled beef, tongue or smoked sausage, lean bacon, salt tongue and a marrow bone arranged on saurkraut or beans. (Swiss)

Biche: Hind, Female Deer: prepared like roe deer.

Bifteck: see beef, tenderloin steak.

Bitki: plural for bitok.

Bitok: sort of small round flattened Russian dumplings made of raw or cooked meat, mainly fried and served with a suitable sauce and garnish.
— **Carnot:** veal forcemeat mixed with bread soaked in water, butter and eggs, shaped into flat round cakes indented in the center, center filled with a litle gooseliver purée, sealed with forcemeat, shaped into flat balls, poached, allowed to cool, coated with thick Mornay sauce, dipped in egg and breadcrumbs and deep fried; garnished with straw potatoes and buttered green peas; tomato sauce served separately.

Bitok
— **po Kassatzki:** prepared like Carnot stuffed with scrambled eggs mixed with chopped truffle, poached lightly, cooled, dipped in egg and breadcrumbs, fried, placed on oval croûton, covered with tomato sauce; garnished with shaped tomato rice with a slice of truffle on top. (Russian)
— **Nowgorodski:** made of raw chopped beef like po russki, fried in butter, covered with deep fried onion rings, bordered with Madeira sauce; German fried potatoes served separately. (Russian)
— **po russki:** raw chopped beef mixed with soaked white bread, chopped fried onions, salt and pepper, shaped into small round flat dumplings rolled in breadcrumbs, fried in butter, placed in a greased baking dish, bordered with sliced boiled potatoes, covered with thick sour cream sauce, sprinkled with breadcrumbs and grated Parmesan, browned in oven. Can also be prepared with veal. (Russian)
— **Skobeleff:** prepared like po Kassatzki stuffed with salpicon of ham, ox tongue, mushrooms and truffle, fried, covered with truffle sauce; garnished with potato nest filled with buttered peas mixed with braised shredded lettuce.
— **tatarski:** chopped raw beef, seasoned, mixed with an egg-yolk and a little butter, shaped into very small flat dumplings, browned quickly on both sides in butter, the inside kept blood rare, served in the small skillet in which they where fried; boiled potatoes and lettuce salad separately. (Russian)

Black Pudding: see blood sausage.

Blanquette: white stew: veal or lamb cut large dices, cooked in white stock or water with a larded onion, carrot and bunch of herbs, when done strained, stock thickened with white roux, seasoned, strained over the meat, garnished with small mushroom caps and button onions, sauce blended with egg yolks and cream, seasoned with lemon juice.
— **Ancient Style:** à l'ancienne: garnished with mushrooms and button onions.
— **Housekeeper Style:** à la ménagère: garnished with small new potatoes simmered in butter, small young carrots and button onions.

Blood Sausage, Black Pudding: Boudin noir: pigs' blood mixed with chopped onions fried in diced fried bacon, filled in narrow hog casings, blanched, fried or broiled.
— **Flemish Style:** à la flamande: fried in butter, garnished with diced fried apples flavored with a dash of vinegar.
— **Lyonese Style:** à la lyonnaise: cut in thick slices, fried, covered with sliced onions browned in butter and chopped parsley, a few drops of lemon juice on top.

Boeuf bouilli: see beef, boiled.

Boeuf braisé: see beef, braised.

Bolitas espanolas: Spanish Dumplings: minced meat mixed with breadcrumbs, eggs, white wine, chopped parsley and seasoning, shaped into walnut-sized dumplings, fried in oil, covered with Madeira sauce and tomato purée and simmered until done. (Spanish)

Border: Bordure: ragoût, salpicon, minces etc. served in border of poached forcemeat, duchess potatoes, puff pastry etc. Forcemeat is filled in a special border mould, poached in waterbath in oven, turned out on round platter, center filled with the respective food.

Border
— **Countess Style:** à la comtesse: border of chicken forcemeat, center filled with slices of chicken breast, diced artichoke bottoms and asparagus tips bound with suprême sauce blended with truffle essence.
— **Hunter Style:** à la chasseur: border of partridge forcemeat, center filled with game dumplings, mushrooms and truffle slices bound with hunter sauce.
— **Parisian Style:** buttered rice pressed in border mould and turned out; center filled with diced sautéd chicken livers, cockscombs, cocks' kidneys and mushrooms bound with demi-glace.
— **Princess Style:** à la princesse: border of duchess potato, baked, center filled with small chicken dumplings and green asparagus tips bound with German sauce blended with asparagus butter; truffle slices on top.
— **Queen Style:** à la reine: greased border mould lined with truffle slices, filled with chicken purée mixed with boiled rice, bound with egg yolks and poached; center filled with diced chicken bound with cream sauce.

Bordure: see border.

Borju pörkölt: Hungarian Veal Stew: chopped onions lightly fried in lard, diced veal, paprika and crushed garlic added, fried quickly for a few minutes, tomato purée or quartered tomatoes, water and seasoning added, simmered until done. (Hungarian)

Boudin: see forcemeat sausage.

Bouchées: small puff pastry patties of various shapes filled with purées, ragoûts, fine minces or salpicons, served as an appetizer or light luncheon dish. After having been filled a slice of truffle, a mushroom etc. is placed on top instead of the pastry lid.
— **Ambassadress Style:** à l'ambassadrice: filled with diced lamb sweetbreads, truffles and asparagus tips bound with suprême sauce.
— **American Style:** à l'américaine: stuffed with diced lobster in American sauce, a slice of lobster on top.
— **Bohemian:** à la bohémienne: small brioches baked in fluted moulds, scooped out, filled with salpicon of truffles and goose liver bound with Madeira sauce.
— **Bresse Style:** à la bressanne: oval patty filled diced sautéd chicken livers and mushrooms bound with Duxelles sauce.
— **Crown-prince:** à la dauphine: cockscombs, cocks' kidneys and truffles bound with Dutch sauce.
— **Diana:** à la Diane: diced feathered game and truffle bound with salmi sauce, a slice of truffle on top.
— **Don Juan:** diced chicken meat, mushrooms and truffles bound with demi-glace.
— **Duchess Style:** à la duchesse: filled with chicken purée and asparagus tips bound with suprême sauce, a slice of truffle on top.
— **Dutch Style:** à la hollandaise: oval patty filled with diced smoked salmon bound with Dutch sauce, an oyster on top.
— **Elysée:** filled with diced chicken meat and mushrooms in Nantua sauce.

Bouchées
— **Financier Style:** à la financière: Cockscombs, cocks' kidneys, pitted olives, truffles and mushrooms in financier sauce, a stuffed olive on top.
— **Flower Girl Style:** à la bouquetière: filled with finely diced vegetables bound with suprême sauce, a round slice of carrot on top.
— **Grandduke:** à la grand-duc: filled with coarse julienne of truffles and asparagus tips bound with suprême sauce.
— **Hungarian:** à la hongroise: filled with ham purée bound with paprika sauce.
— **Hunter Style:** à la chasseur: filled with diced game and mushrooms bound with hunter sauce.
— **Imperial Style:** à l'impériale: diced shrimps and oysters bound with shrimp sauce, a slice of truffle on top.
— **Indian Style:** à l'indienne: rice mixed with diced fish or chicken meat and hard boiled eggs bound with fish or chicken velouté flavored with curry powder.
— **Infante Style:** cockscombs, cocks' kidneys, diced knob celery, truffles, ox tongue and carrots bound with velouté sauce.
— **Isabella:** Isabella: filled with diced ox tongue and truffles bound with light chicken purée, a slice of truffle on top.
— **Joinville:** oval patty filled with diced shrimps, mushrooms and truffles bound with Joinville sauce, an oval slice of truffle on top.
— **with Lobster:** à l'homard: filled with diced lobster and mushrooms bound with lobster sauce.
— **Lucullus:** square patty filled with cockscombs and truffles bound with demi-glace and truffle essence, a square slice of truffle on top.
— **Mary-Rose:** Marie-Rose: lozenge-shaped patty filled with tiny shrimps, pearl-sized smelt dumplings and short truffle julienne, bound with shrimp sauce, a lozenge-shaped slice of smelt forcemeat with tomato on top.
— **Mascot:** à la mascotte: diced chicken breast, artichoke bottoms and truffles, bound with thick veal gravy boiled down with white wine.
— **Metternich:** chicken meat and truffles in cream sauce, a slice of truffle on top.
— **Milanese:** à la milanaise: macaroni cut in small pieces mixed with diced ox tongue, mushrooms and truffles, bound with tomato sauce and filled in oval patties.
— **Mirabeau:** filled with sole salpicon bound with cream sauce whipped up with anchovy butter, a stuffed olive on top.
— **Mogador:** filled with salpicon of tongue and chicken breast bound with Béchamel sauce blended with gooseliver purée.
— **Monseigneur:** oval patty filled with truffled purée of soft roes, covered with shrimp sauce, an oval slice of truffle on top.
— **Montglas:** square patty filled with diced gooseliver, ox tongue, mushrooms and truffles in excellent Madeira sauce, a square truffle slice on top.
— **Montpensier:** filled with small truffled chicken dumplings bound with shrimp sauce, a slice of truffle on top.
— **Montrose:** filled with chicken purée mixed with finely diced ham, a truffle slice on top.
— **Nantua:** filled with diced crayfish tails and truffles bound with Nantua sauce, a crayfish tail on top.

Bouchées
— **Neptun:** flaked fresh haddock, diced mushrooms and truffles bound with German sauce, filled in oval patty.
— **Nesles:** à la Nesles: filled with hashed lamb, diced truffles and mushrooms bound with German sauce.
— **with Oysters:** aux huîtres: filled with poached diced oysters in Normandy sauce.
— **Perigord Style:** à la périgourdine: square patty filled with truffle purée bound with thick Madeira sauce.
— **Princess:** à la princesse: filled with diced chicken meat, truffles and green asparagus tips bound with German sauce with mushroom essence.
— **Queen Style:** 1. à la reine: filled with diced chicken breast, mushrooms and truffles bound with suprême sauce. 2. stuffed with very white chicken purée.
— **Regency Style:** à la régence: filled with salpicon of mushrooms, chicken, gooseliver, tiny veal dumplings, cockscombs and truffles bound with German sauce with truffle essence.
— **Richelieu:** filled with salpicon of truffles, ox tongue and chicken bound with truffle sauce, a round slice of ox tongue on top.
— **Royal Style:** à la royale: stuffed with truffle purée bound with truffle sauce.
— **Russian:** à la russe: filled with chopped vesiga and hard boiled eggs bound with sour cream sauce.
— **Saint-Hubert:** stuffed with game purée, a fluted mushroom cap on top.
— **with Shrimps:** aux crevettes: filled with diced shrimps in shrimp sauce, a slice of truffle on top.
— **with Soft Roes:** aux laitances: filled with sliced poached soft roes in shrimp sauce.
— **Souvaroff:** filled with salpicon of veal sweetbread, chicken, artichoke bottoms and cucumber bound with German sauce.
— **Spring Style:** à la printanière: filled with finely diced spring vegetables and green peas bound with velouté sauce.
— **Stuart:** filled 3/4 full with minced chicken and mushrooms bound with suprême sauce, the last quarter with suprême sauce mixed with crayfish purée.
— **Toulouse Style:** à la toulousaine: same filling as for vol-au-vent.
— **Turbigo:** diced sautéd ducks' liver, artichoke bottoms and truffles bound with German sauce with tomato, filled in oval patty.
— **Vatel:** square patty filled with chicken and gooseliver purée in suprême sauce.
— **Victoria:** filled with diced lobster and truffles bound with Victoria sauce, a truffle slice on top.
— **Virgin Style:** à la vierge: diced lamb sweetbreads and brain bound with cream sauce.

Boudin noir: see blood sausage.

Boulettes: see meat balls.

Brasciole Milanese: Stuffed Veal Rolls: small veal slices stuffed with minced raw veal and ham bound with egg yolk and rolled up, fixed on skewer alternated with slices of raw ham, coated with flour, fried in butter. (Italian)

Breast Strips: Aiguillettes: long thin strips of roasted poultry served with an appropriate sauce and garnish.

Breast Strips
— **of Rouen Duck with Cherries:** de rouennais aux cerises: strips of blood rare roasted Rouen duck, covered with gravy prepared with the bones, thickened with arrow-root and mixed with stoned cooked morellos.
— **of Rouen Duck in Orange Sauce:** de rouennais à l'orange: prepared as above, covered with thick gravy prepared with the bones flavored with orange juice and mixed with blanched julienne of orange peel.
— **of Poularde Saint-Albin:** de poularde Saint-Albin (Cold): strips of roasted poularde breast coated with brown chaud-froid sauce, decorated with hard-boiled egg whites and ox tongue, placed upright in charlotte mould lined with aspic jelly, center filled with chicken froth prepared with the poularde legs, sealed with aspic jelly, chilled, turned out on round dish, a small cooked truffle glazed with aspic jelly placed on top.
Brebis: ewe.
Brochettes: see skewers.
Bruant: see yellow hammer.
Bubble and Squeak: popular British dish of heated up "left-overs", beef, mutton or veal, with cabbage and potatoes.
Bünder Wurst: Bündner Sausage: lean pork chopped finely, mixed with diced bacon, salt pepper, powdered cloves and a little water, filled in calf's bladder, smoked, boiled served hot or cold. (Swiss)
Bustard: F. Outarde; G. Trappe: name of various comestible birds, in particular: the Great Bustard; F. Grande Outarde, the largest of European land birds found from Spain eastwards to China;
the Little Bustard; F. Bastardau, the best of both, found in nearly all countries bordering the Mediterranean. Prepared like wild duck.
— **Tsarina:** à la tsarine: browned in butter, deglazed with brandy and Madeira, braised in beef stock, stock thickened with arrow-root and strained; garnished with tartlets filled alternately with small cucumber balls simmered in butter, bound with sour cream sauce mixed with chopped dill, and sautéd boletus, Berny potatoes and shaped truffled rice.

C

Cabbage, Stuffed: chou farci: prepared in different ways and filled with forcemeat of various kinds.
— **Armenian Style:** à l'armenienne: stuffed with raw chopped mutton mixed with boiled rice, diced tomatoes and garlic; braised in light tomato sauce, sauce flavored with lemon juice before serving.
— **Balls Hungarian Style:** à la hongroise: blanched cabbage leaves stuffed with pork sausage meat, shaped into balls, fried lightly in lard, covered with paprika sauce and sour cream and braised in oven.
— **Bomb:** Bombe au choux: greased bomb mould lined thickly with half cooked cabbage leaves, filled alternately with veal forcemeat, cabbage leaves and slices of cooking partridges braised in red wine in the center, sealed with forcemeat; cooked in waterbath in oven, turned out and covered with demi-glace blended with the reduced partridge stock.

Cabbage

— **Golduny po litowski:** Stuffed cabbage Lithuanian Style: stuffed with chopped raw mutton, boiled rice, chopped onions fried in butter and chopped dill, placed on sliced carrots and bacon, covered with sour cream mixed with a little tomato purée and braised in oven; served on the bacon slices with a carrot slice on top, covered with the strained sauce and sprinkled with chopped dill. (Russian)

— **Little-Russian Style:** à la petite-russienne: stuffed with minced pork and mutton mixed with boiled rice, diced tomatoes, chopped dill and majoram; braised, covered with sour cream sauce mixed with tomato purée and seasoned with Kabul sauce.

— **Pirog domaschnuy:** roast pork and braised cabbage or saurkraut, chopped coarsely, mixed with lightly fried chopped onions, seasoning and a little sour cream; plain yeast dough rolled and cut out with a round cutter the edges moistened with water, a spoonful of the cabbage mixture placed in the center, covered with a second base of dough and pressed down; cooked in boiling water, drained and covered with chopped onions fried in butter. (Russian)

— **Rolls, Stuffed:** Chou farci: cabbage leaves blanched, allowed to cool, stuffed with pork sausage meat, rolled together and sealed on both sides, braised on bed of sliced carrots, onions and bacon waste in brown stock; stock strained, thickened and poured over the rolls.

— **Stuffed, Provencal Style:** Sou-Fassum Provençal: large cabbage leaves blanched, coated with a mixture of pork sausage meat, the chopped interior leaves, blanched chopped red beetroot leaves, diced fried bacon, chopped onions lightly fried in butter, plain boiled rice, chopped tomatoes. garlic, seasoning and fresh cooked green peas if in season; cabbage head reformed, tied and boiled until tender in mutton or beef stock.

Caille: see quail.

Caisse: small container round or square in silver, glass, earthenware or fireproof china. See also appetizers.

— **Aiglon:** lined with gooseliver forcemeat, filled with ragout of gooseliver and truffles bound with demi-glace, sealed with gooseliver soufflé, poached in waterbath in oven.

— **Alice:** filled with sliced chicken in suprême sauce, covered with duchess-potato mixture, brushed with egg yolk, browned in oven.

— **Carême:** sliced poached soft roes and very small fish dumplings bound with shrimp sauce finished off with anchovy butter, a slice of truffle on top.

— **Cupidon:** filled with financier garnish in financier sauce.

— **Gourmet Style:** du gourmet: ragoût of lamb sweetbreads, truffles and morels, bound with demi-glace, a slice of truffle on top.

— **Mirabeau:** lined with fish purée mixed with chopped tarragon, filled with diced sole fillets bound with cream sauce blended with anchovy butter, decorated with anchovy fillets and a stoned olive.

— **Montglas:** lined with gooseliver forcemeat, filled with ragoût of gooseliver, mushrooms and ox tongue bound with Madeira sauce, sealed with gooseliver forcemeat,

Caisse
poached in water-bath in oven, a slice of truffle coated with liquid meat glaze on top.
— **Rôtisserie Périgourdine:** filled with small slices of chicken breast and truffles bound with suprême sauce flavored with Port, covered with puff paste, baked in oven.
— **Susie:** Suzanne: filled with asparagus tips in cream sauce, a nice slice of chicken breast and a truffle slice on top, covered lightly with cream sauce.

Calderata de Cordero: Phillipine Lamb Ragoût: chopped onions and garlic sautéd in oil, mixed with chopped lambs' liver, moistened with stock, seasoned with salt and pepper, boiled, rubbed through a sieve; diced lamb without bones simmered in this sauce, garnished with stewed button onions.

Calf; F. Veau; G. Kalb: the young of various mammals, especially that of the cow up to one year of age. The meat of the calf is called veal (q. v.). Calf has been retained in connection with brains, chitterlings, ears, feet, lungs, pluck, tongue and sweetbread.

Calf's Brain: Cervelle de veau: steeped in water, thin skin taken off, washed till blood is extracted, cooked in aromatic water acidulated with vinegar or lemon juice, kept in water for future use.
— **Archduke Style:** à l'archiduc: sliced, covered with velouté sauce mixed with white onion purée, finished off with cream, brandy and Madeira, truffle slices on top.
— **with Artichoke Bottoms:** aux fonds d'artichauts: cut in thick slices, each slice placed on an artichoke bottom, covered with Dutch sauce, a little chopped tarragon scattered on top.
— **with Asparagus:** aux asperges: parboiled, cut in slices, dipped in egg and breadcrumbs, fried in butter, garnished with creamed asparagus tips.
— **Beaumont:** cut in thick slices, coated with gooseliver forcemeat, a second slice covered with forcemeat placed on top, sprinkled with chopped truffle, wrapped in puff paste, baked in oven; truffle sauce served separately.
— **with Browned Butter:** au beurre noir: boiled, covered with well browned butter seasoned with a few drops of vinegar, capers and chopped parsley scattered on top.
— **Burgundy Style:** à la bourguignonne: boiled, covered with Burgundy sauce with mushroom caps and browned button onions added, bordered with heart-shaped croûtons fried in butter.
— **Carola:** parboiled, cut in thick slices, coated with very thick German sauce mixed with chopped mushrooms, dipped in egg and breadcrumbs, fried in deep fat, garnished with fried parsley and lemon.
— **in Cream Sauce:** à la crème: boiled, covered with Béchamel sauce finished off with cream.
— **Cromesquis of:** Cromesquis de cervelle: parboiled, chopped coarsely, mixed with diced mushrooms and truffle, bound with thick German sauce and egg-yolk, chilled, cut into triangles, dipped in frying batter, fried in deep fat; truffle or tomato sauce served separately.
— **Croquettes:** Croquettes de cervelle: boiled, when cold diced, mixed with diced mushrooms, bound with thick velouté and egg-yolk, allowed to cool, shaped, dipped in

Calf's Brain
egg and breadcrumbs, fried in deep fat, garnished with fried parsley; tomato sauce served separately.

— **with Fine Herbs:** aux fines herbes boiled, covered with herb sauce.

— **Florence Style:** à la florentine: slices heated up in butter, placed on spinach leaves tossed in butter, covered with Mornay sauce, sprinkled with grated Parmesan, glazed.

— **Fried:** frite: cut in slices, dipped in egg and breadcrumbs, fried in deep fat, served with buttered green peas.

— **Fries:** greased scallop shells filled with spinach leaves, a small piece of butter on top, covered with a slice of brain with more spinach leaves on top, sprinkled generously with breadcrumbs and grated Parmesan, butter dropped on top, browned in hot oven.

— **Fritters:** Beignets de cervelle: boiled, cut in slices, dipped in light frying batter, fried in deep fat; tomato sauce served separately.

— **Gipsy Style:** à la zingara: cut in thick slices raw, coated with flour, fried in butter, placed on a small slice of fried ham, covered with Gipsy sauce.

— **Hirn mit Zwiebeln:** with Onions: boiled, chopped coarsely, sautéd in butter, mixed with chopped fried onions. (Austrian)

— **Hirnpalatschinken:** Brain Pancakes: boiled chopped brains sautéd in butter, well seasoned, filled in very thin unsweetened pancakes, rolled together, cut in small pieces, dipped in egg and breadcrumbs, fried in deep fat. (Austrian)

— **Italian Style:** à l'italienne: cut raw in slices, coated with flour, fried in half butter and half oil, covered with Italian sauce.

— **in Large Puff Pastry Shell:** Vol-au-vent de cervelle: parboiled sliced brain, mushrooms and small veal forcemeat dumplings bound with German sauce, filled in large puff pastry shell, garnished with truffle slices.

— **Marianne:** parboiled, sliced, fried in butter, dressed on chopped spinach leaves mixed with sorrel and purslane and tossed in butter, covered with Madeira sauce.

— **Marshall Style:** à la maréchale: parboiled, sliced, dipped in egg and breadcrumbs, fried in butter, a slice of truffle coated with liquid meat glaze on top, garnished with asparagus tips.

— **Mazagran:** en mazagran: ragoût of brain, mushrooms and truffle slices bound with German or suprême sauce, filled in nest made of duchess potato-mixture, covered with the same mixture, brushed with egg-yolk, browned in oven, covered lightly with tomato sauce.

— **Miller Style:** à la meunière: raw slices seasoned, coated with flour, fried in butter, chopped parsley, lemon juice and browned butter on top.

— **Montrouge:** parboiled, sliced, filled in flat tart of unsweetened short pastry, covered with sliced mushrooms, coated with Mornay sauce, sprinkled with grated Parmesan and glazed rapidly.

— **with Mustard Sauce:** à la sauce moutarde: parboiled, covered with cream sauce flavored with mustard and mixed with finely diced parsley root simmered in butter.

Calf's Brain

— **Parisian Style:** à la parisienne: parboiled, diced, mixed with sliced mushrooms and truffle, bound with German sauce, filled in scallop shells bordered with duchess potato-mixture, sprinkled with grated Parmesan, glazed.

— **Patty:** Vol-au-vent de cervelle: boiled, cut in large cubes, mixed with white button onions, diced blanched and fried bacon and slices of pickled cucumber, bound with red wine sauce finished off with anchovy butter, filled in large open puff pastry patty.

— **Poulette:** boiled, covered with poulette sauce, chopped parsley scattered on top.

— **Rambouillet:** parboiled, arranged in timbale dish with mushroom caps and white button onions, covered with German sauce, chopped parsley sprinkled on top.

— **Ravigote:** parboiled, sliced, filled in baking dish bordered with duchess potato-mixture and browned beforehand, covered with ravigote sauce.

— **Rosita:** parboiled, diced, mixed with sliced mushrooms, truffles and macaroni cut in small pieces, bound with Mornay sauce, filled in flat pastry shell, sprinkled with grated cheese and glazed rapidly.

— **Sailor Style:** en matelote: poached in parboiled stock with sliced onions, carrots and red wine, sliced, garnished with glazed onions and mushrooms, covered with the strained, reduced stock thickened with butter-paste, bordered with heart-shaped croûtons fried in butter.

— **in Scallop Shell:** en coquille: parboiled, diced, filled in scallop shell, covered with Italian sauce, sprinkled with grated Parmesan and breadcrumbs, dotted with butter, gratinated.

— **Spanish Style:** Sesos Españolas: parboiled, diced, fried in butter, chopped parsley and lemon juice, filled in scallop shells, covered with cream sauce with a streak of tomato sauce in the center, sprinkled with grated Parmesan, glazed. (Spanish)

— **Tosca:** parboiled, cut in large dice, mixed with macaroni cut in small pieces, crayfish tails and grated Parmesan, bound with crayfish sauce, filled in pastry shell.

— **Villeroi:** parboiled, when cold cut in thick slices, coated with Villeroi sauce, dipped in egg and breadcrumbs, fried; truffle sauce served separately.

Calf's Ears: Oreilles de veau: scalded and prepared like calf's head.

— **Dressel:** scalded, braised, cut in strips, coated with flour, fried to a pale brown in oil and butter, chopped parsley, sweet basil, marjoran and a pinch of sage added at the last minute, dressed in timbale dish, lemon juice and browned butter poured over, capers scattered on top.

— **Fried:** frites: parboiled, braised in Madeira, cut in strips, dipped in frying batter, fried in deep fat, garnished with fried parsley; tomato sauce served separately.

— **Grilled:** grillées: scalded, braised, cut lengthwise, brushed with mustard, dipped in melted butter and breadcrumbs, grilled; devil sauce served separately.

— **Italian Style:** à l'italienne: scalded, braised, covered with Italian sauce.

Calf's Ears
— **Poulette:** parboiled, cut in pieces, braised in white stock, served with poulette sauce.
— **Toulouse Style:** à la toulousaine: scalded, braised, served with Toulouse garnish and sauce.
— **Turtle Style:** en tortue: scalded, braised, served with turtle garnish and sauce.

Calf's Foot: Pied de veau: blanched, cooked in a blanc (water mixed thoroughly with a little flour and a pinch of salt)
— **Catalonian Style:** à la catalane: blanched, boned, fried lightly in oil, braised in white wine with demi-glace and diced tomatoes, browned button onions, sautéd mushrooms cut in quarters and very small fried pork sausages added later on.
— **Citizen Style:** à la bourgeoise: boned, simmered, in Madeira sauce, garnished with glazed button onions, carrots and small boiled or roasted potatoes.
— **Croquettes of:** Croquettes de pied de veau: blanched, boned, braised, cut into small cubes, mixed with chopped mushrooms and parsley, bound with very thick German sauce, allowed to cool, shaped into croquettes, dipped in egg and breadcrumbs, fried in deep fat, garnished with fried parsley; white mustard sauce served separately.
— **Custine:** blanched, braised in white wine and brown stock, cut into small cubes, mixed with sliced mushrooms, bound with very thick duxelles sauce, allowed to cool, divided into rectangular pieces, wrapped in pig's caul, brushed with melted butter, browned in hot oven, served with demi-glace.
— **English Style:** à l'anglaise: cooked, boned, dipped in egg and breadcrumbs, fried in butter, covered with half-melted herb butter.
— **Fried:** frit: cooked, boned, both halves dipped in egg and breadcrumbs, deep fried; tomato sauce served separately.
— **Grilled:** grillé: 1. blanched, cooked, boned, brushed thinly with mustard, dipped in butter, grilled; devil sauce served separately.
2. blanched, cooked, boned, brushed with mustard, dipped in egg and breadcrumbs, moistened with oil or butter, grilled; tartar sauce served separately.
— **Poulette:** blanched, cooked, boned, dressed in timbale dish, covered with poulette sauce, sprinkled with chopped parsley.
— **Provencal Style:** à la provençale: blanched, cooked, boned, simmered in Provencal sauce.
— **Tartar Style:** à la tartare: blanched, cooked, boned, dipped in egg and breadcrumbs, fried in deep fat, garnished with fried parsley; tartar sauce served separately.
— **Tyrolian Style:** à la tyrolienne: blanched, cooked, boned, simmered in sauce prepared with chopped onions lightly fried in oil, diced tomatoes, crushed garlic, chopped parsley and light pepper sauce.
— **Vinaigrette:** blanched, cooked, boned, served with vinaigrette sauce.

Calf's Head: Tête de veau: boned, soaked, scalded, rubbed with lemon, cooked in lightly salted water mixed thoroughly with a little flour to prevent darkening; the tongue is usually cooked and served with the head.

Calf's Head

— **American Style:** à l'américaine: parboiled, cut in square pieces, simmered in butter with diced tomatoes, chopped onions, fennel and chopped herbs.

— **Boiled:** bouillie: parboiled, cut in square pieces, served hot with chopped chives scattered on top; vinaigrette sauce separately.

— **English Style:** à l'anglaise: whole head cooked without being boned, a piece of boiled salt pork and parsley sauce served at the same time.

Financier Style: à la financière: parboiled, cut in square pieces, served with financier garnish and sauce.

— **French Style:** à la francaise: parboiled, cut in square pieces, served hot garnished with raw chopped onions, parsley and capers; vinaigrette sauce served separately.

— **Fried:** frite: parboiled, cut in rectangles, marinated in lemon juice and oil, dipped in frying batter or egg and breadcrumbs, deep fried; tomato or tartar sauce served separately.

— **Godard:** parboiled, cut in squares or rectangles, served with Godard sauce and garnish.

— **with Gribiche Sauce:** parboiled, cut in squares, served in timbale dish covered with a little hot white stock; gribiche sauce served separately.

— **Indian Style:** à l'indienne: parboiled, cut in strips, bound with Indian sauce; plain boiled rice served separately.

— **Livonian Style:** à la livonienne (cold): whole head carefully boned, stuffed with veal forcemeat mixed with diced fat bacon, ox tongue, pistachios and diced truffles, reformed, wrapped in greased cloth, tied, boiled in white stock with white wine, Madeira and mirepoix, allowed to cool in the stock, carved, covered with aspic jelly prepared with the stock.

— **with Madeira Sauce:** à la sauce madère: parboiled, cut in squares, covered with Madeira sauce.

— **Medicis:** parboiled, cut in squares, filled in timbale dish with mushroom caps, truffle slices, veal dumplings and cockscombs, covered with velouté sauce.

— **with Parsley Sauce:** à la sauce persil: parboiled, cut in squares, covered with parsley sauce; boiled potatoes served separately.

— **Polish Style:** à la polonaise: 1. parboiled, cut in squares, dressed in timbale dish, chopped hard-boiled egg and parsley scattered on top, breadcrumbs browned in plenty of butter poured over.

2. cut in squares, dipped in egg and breadcrumbs, fried in butter, covered with chopped parsley and browned butter; red currants cooked with a pinch of sugar and a little white stock, rubbed through a sieve and reduced served separately.

— **Poor Man Style: pauvre homme: parboiled, cut in** squares, covered with demi-glace mixed with chopped shallots simmered in butter, chopped parsley, chives and fried breadcrumbs.

— **Poulette:** parboiled, cut in squares, covered with poulette sauce, sprinkled with chopped parsley.

— **Ravigote:** parboiled, cut in squares, covered with hot ravigote sauce.

Calf's Head

— **Steward Style:** à la maître d'hôtel: parboiled, cut in squares, dipped in egg and breadcrumbs, fried, covered with half-melted herb butter.

— **Tertillière:** parboiled, cut in square pieces, coarse julienne of ox tongue, mushrooms and truffles and Madeira sauce added, simmered for a while, shortly before serving a little blanched julienne of lemon peel added, arranged in timbale dish and garnished with halved hard-boiled eggs.

— **Titus:** parboiled, cut in squares, covered with poulette sauce seasoned with mustard, bordered with heart-shaped croûtons fried in butter.

— **Toulouse Style:** parboiled, cut in squares, arranged in timbale dish with Toulouse garnish and sauce.

— **Turtle Style:** en tortue: parboiled, cut in squares, served with turtle garnish and sauce.

— **Vinaigrette:** parboiled, cut in squares, served hot with vinaigrette sauce.

— **mit Wurzeln:** with Root Vegetables: blanched, cut in squares, cooked in water acidulated with vinegar and coarse julienne of root vegetables, served in timbale dish with the strained vegetables, covered with white horseradish sauce. (Austrian)

Calf's Heart: Coeur de veau: steeped in water for a short time, boiled, braised or sautéd.

— **Bavarian Style:** à la bavaroise: boiled in white stock with sliced onions and shredded root vegetables, served in the boiled down stock with the vegetables, acidulated with a little vinegar.

— **Braised:** braisé: browned in stock fat with sliced onions and carrots, deglaced with white wine, water or stock added, seasoned, braised. braising stock strained and thickened with light roux.

— **Burgundy Style:** à la bourguignonne: braised in red wine and light demi-glace, garnished with sautéd mushroom caps, diced fried bacon and glaced button onions.

— **Citizen Style:** à la bourgeoise: browned in butter, braised, when half done browned button onions, diced fried bacon and shaped carrots browned beforehand added; braising stock thickened with brown roux or arrow-root.

— **Gratinated:** au gratin: boiled, cut in small thin slices, mixed with sliced mushrooms, bound with German sauce, filled in scallop shells, sprinkled with breadcrumbs, butter dotted on top, gratinated in oven.

— **Sainte-Menehould:** boiled, allowed to cool, cut in slices, coated with Villeroi sauce and chopped raw mushrooms, wrapped in pig's caul, dipped in melted butter and breadcrumbs, broiled.

— **Sautéd:** sauté: cut lengthwise in thin slices, sautéd rapidly in butter, placed in demi-glace, piquant, tomato or pepper sauce for a minute or two but not allowed to boil, boiling would toughen the meat.

— **Stuffed:** farci: opened, stuffed with well seasoned veal forcemeat, wrapped in thin slices of fat bacon, tied, braised.

Calf's Kidney: Rognon de veau: if the kidney is to be prepared whole, a little more then half an inch of fat is left on; if sliced, fat, skin and gristle must be removed. Kidney is always cooked a little underdone.

Calf's Kidney

— **Bercy Style:** sliced, sautéd, filled in timbale dish covered with Bercy sauce.

— **Berry Style:** à la berichonne: sliced, sautéd, drained, mixed with sliced sautéd mushrooms, residue delaced with red wine and the drained off juice, boiled up with Bordeaux sauce without ox marrow, diced fried bacon added to mushrooms and kidney, bound with the sauce, chopped parsley sprinkled on top.

— **Bordeaux Style:** à la bordelaise: sliced, sautéd, mixed with sautéd sliced boletus and chopped parsley, bound with Bordeaux sauce with diced blanched ox marrow added.

— **in Casserole:** an casserole: whole kidney, seasoned, placed in fireproof casserole with a little butter, fried slowly in oven turning the kidney frequently, served in the casserole with a little rich veal gravy poured over at serving.

— **Cecil Hotel:** whole kidney fried in butter, garnished with soufflé potatoes asparagus tips and grilled mushroom caps; Madeira sauce served separately.

— **in Champagne:** au champagne: sliced, sautéd with chopped shallots, taken out of pan and drained, deglaced with dry champagne, the drained-off juice and demi-glace added, boiled down, kidneys tossed in this sauce.

— **Chef Style:** à la mode du chef: whole kidney prepared in casserole, taken out, residue in casserole deglaced with Sherry and boiled up with cream and demi-glace, kidney replaced in casserole, garnished with sautéd mushrooms, pineapple strips sautéd in butter scattered on top.

— **Demidoff:** whole kidney prepared in casserole with Demidoff garnish.

— **Devilled Kidney and Bacon:** kidney split open lengthwise without separating one end, slightly flattened, seasoned with salt, brushed with a mixture of mustard powder, Worcestershire sauce, tomato catsup and Tabasco sauce, coated with breadcrumbs, moistened with melted butter, broiled, dressed on slices of fried bacon.

— **Empire:** sliced, sautéd, mixed with sautéd chicken livers, shredded ham and mushrooms, bound with sour cream sauce mixed with tomato purée and seasoned with Kabul sauce, sprinkled with grated cheese, glazed rapidly, bordered with halved fried tomatoes (Russian).

— **Housewife Style:** à la bonne-femme: whole kidney fried in casserole, garnished with diced fried bacon and diced potatoes, a little rich veal gravy poured over at serving.

— **Hunter Style:** à la chasseur: sliced, sautéd, taken out and drained, chopped shallot lightly fried in the frying butter, deglaced with brandy and white wine and boiled up with hunter sauce; kidney tossed in the sauce, served in timbale dish sprinkled with chopped parsley, chervil and tarragon.

— **Indian Style:** à l'indienne: chopped onions sautéd in butter, a little curry powder and velouté sauce added, cooked and strained, sliced sautéd kidney bound with this sauce, dressed in timbale dish; plain boiled rice served separately.

— **Liege Style:** à la liègoise: whole kidney prepared in casserole, a minute before serving ignited with a little

Calf's Kidney

Genever, two crushed juniper berries and a tablespoonful of rich veal gravy added and served in the casserole.

— **Montpensier:** cut in thick slices and sautéd, taken out of pan, residue deglaced with Madeira, a little lemon juice, liquid meat glaze and chopped parsley added and blended with butter; kidney slices arranged like a crown on dish, covered with the sauce, center filled with buttered asparagus and a few truffle slices placed on top.

— **Mother Catherine Style:** à la mère Catherine: whole kidney fried in casserole, when done taken out, deglaced with Port and boiled up with sweet cream and veal glace, kidney replaced in casserole with garnish of sautéd mushrooms and truffle slices, closed and served in casserole.

— **Nierndl mit Hirn:** Kidney and Brains: brains, boiled, chopped coarsely, fried in butter with chopped fried onions added, mixed with sliced sautéd kidneys, chopped parsley scattered on top. (Austrian)

— **Parma Style:** à la parme: thick slices sautéd, truffle slice on each, garnished with straw potatoes and artichoke bottoms, filled with asparagus tips, covered with Mornay sauce and glazed; bordered with demi-glace.

— **Portuguese Style:** à la portugaise: cut in thick slices, sautéd, arranged like a crown, half a stuffed tomato placed on each slice, center filled with tomatoes concassées, sauce prepared as for Montpensier poured around.

— **Robert:** fried whole in casserole and kept rare. Sent to the dining room where waiter takes kidney out of casserole and keeps it warm between two plates. In the meantime the residue in casserole is ignited with brandy and boiled half down, a little mustard, butter, lemon juice, and chopped parsley added, well mixed, kidney slices, and warmed up in this sauce without allowing it to boil and served on hot plates.

— **Russian Style:** à la russe: 1. sliced, sautéd rare, mixed with olive-shaped carrots, turnips, knob celery, stoned olives, olive-shaped fried potatoes, sliced sautéd mushrooms and slices of pickled cucumber, bound with tomato sauce.
2. slices sautéd with chopped shallots, sliced sautéd mushrooms and glazed olive-shaped cucumbers added, bound with demi-glace finished off with sour cream and lemon juice.

— **Saint-Germain:** whole kidney fried in butter, garnished as for sweetbread.

— **Sour:** à l'aigre: sliced, sautéd with chopped onions, besprinkled with flour, moistened with brown stock, seasoned, a little vinegar added, stewed.

— **Tyrolian Style:** à la tyrolienne: whole kidney fried, garnished with fried tomatoes or tomatoes concassées and deep fried onion rings.

— **with various Wines:** aux vins divers: prepared as with champagne, but deglaced with Madeira, Marsala, Sherry, Port, Rhine wine or Burgundy etc.

Calf's Liver: Foie de veau: the tastiest of all butcher's livers, mainly sliced thin, coated with flour, fried in butter and kept rare.

Calf's Liver

— **American Style:** à l'américaine: sliced, fried in butter, served with sliced fried bacon and fried tomatoes.

— **with Bananas:** aux bananes: sliced, fried in butter, each slice covered with half a banana divided lengthwise, coated with flour and fried in butter, lemon juice and browned butter on top.

— **Bercy:** sliced, coated with flour, dipped in melted butter and broiled, covered with Bercy butter.

— **Berlin Style:** à la berlinoise: sliced, coated with flour, fried in butter, garnished with fried apple and onion rings; browned butter poured on top.

— **Bordeaux Style:** à la bordelaise: whole liver, skinned, lightly fried in butter on all sides, wrapped in pig's caul with chopped shallots, onions and boletus sautéd in butter, stewed in white wine and demi-glace with tomato; garnished with sliced boletus sautéd in butter.

— **Citizen Style:** à la bourgeoise: whole liver, skinned, larded, braised in demi-glace, garnished with glazed button onions and small carrots sautéd in butter.

— **Dumplings, Viennese:** Quenelles de foie de veau à la viennoise: raw liver, chopped, rubbed through a sieve, white breadcrumbs, flour, chopped onions lightly fried in butter, chopped parsley, whole eggs and egg-yolk and seasoning added, dumplings shaped with a table spoon, poached in white stock, dressed in timbale dish, lemon juice and browned butter poured on top.

— **English Style:** à l'anglaise: sliced, fried in butter, dressed alternately with sliced fried bacon, sprinkled with chopped parsley. Browned butter poured on top.

— **with Fine Herbs:** aux fines herbes: sliced, fried in butter; brown herb sauce served separately.

— **Fried:** frite: seasoned, rolled in flour, dipped in egg and breadcrumbs, fried in butter, served with vegetables to taste.

— **Harvester Style:** à la moissoneusse: fried slices placed on green peas prepared in the French way and mixed with slices of boiled potatoes and diced fried bacon.

— **Hashed:** Hachée de foie de veau. Liver skinned, cooked in white stock, minced, mixed with chopped onions stimmered in butter and chopped parsley, bound with sauce prepared with the boiled down stock thickened with butter paste, seasoned, served with poached egg on top.

— **Italian Style:** fried slices bordered with Italian sauce.

— **Jutland Style:** à la jutlandaise: whole liver, skinned, larded, browned in goose fat, simmered in pale beer with sliced root vegetables, peppercorns and a bay leaf; covered with the strained stock thickened with butter-paste.

— **Lyonese Style:** à la lyonnaise: sliced, fried in butter and oil, garnished with sliced fried onions bound with a little liquid meat glaze, a few drops of vinegar heated up in the frying pan poured over the meat.

— **Milanese Style:** à la milanaise: sliced, fried in oil, dressed on macaroni prepared in the Milanese way; tomato sauce served separately.

— **Oriental Style:** à l'orientale: sliced, fried in oil, residue in frying pan deglaced with a little vinegar and a pinch of sugar, boiled up with demi-glace with soaked dried Malaga grapes and raisins added.

— **in Paper Bag:** en papillote: sliced liver marinated in oil, lemon juice, chopped shallots, pepper and salt; placed on

Calf's Liver

a small slice of ham and covered with a slice of bacon, wrapped in paper bag, roasted in oven.

— **Patty:** Pain de foie de veau: raw liver pounded in mortar with green lard, bread soaked in cream, chopped onions sweated in butter and whole eggs, rubbed through a sieve, seasoned, egg whites and a little cream added, mixed well, filled in greased charlotte mould, poached in water-bath in oven, turned out and covered with an appropriate brown sauce.

— **in Pig's Caul:** en crépine: whole liver, skinned, larded, wrapped in pig's caul, braised in white wine, white stock and sour cream with chopped onions; sauce prepared with the braising stock.

— **Provencal Style:** à la provençale: sliced, fried, covered with Provencal sauce.

— **with Red Wine Sauce:** à la sauce au vin rouge: sliced, fried, covered with Bordeaux sauce mixed with fried diced bacon.

— **with Risotto:** raw liver, skinned diced, sautéd rapidly in butter, filled in the center of a border of risotto placed on a flat baking dish, covered with Mornay sauce, sprinkled with grated cheese, grated rapidly.

— **Schweizer Leberspiessli:** Liver Skewers: square pieces of sliced liver and bacon fixed on a skewer, brushed with melted butter, seasoned, sprinkled with chopped sage, wrapped in pig's caul, dipped in melted butter, broiled. (Swiss)

— **Soufflé of:** Soufflé de foie de veau: skinned, cooked in stock, pounded together with a little cold Béchamel sauce and butter, rubbed through a sieve, seasoned, mixed with a little cream, egg yolks and stiffly beaten egg-whites, filled in greased soufflé dish, baked in oven; Madeira or other brown sauce optional.

— **in Sour Sauce:** à la sauce aigre: sliced, fried, residue in frying pan deglaced with vinegar, boiled up with demi-glace and poured over the meat.

— **Spanish Style:** à l'espagnole: sliced, fried in oil, half a fried tomato placed on each slice, garnished with onion rings fried in oil and fried parsley.

— **Turinese Style:** à la turinoise: sliced, fried, served on risotto, covered with browned butter.

Calf's Lungs: Mou de veau: blanched strongly in water, then cooked in white stock with pot and aromatic herbs and kept for future use in the stock.

— **Fried:** frit: parboiled, cut in strips, simmered in butter with chopped onions and parsley, bound with thick sauce prepared with the stock and egg yolk, when cold shaped in triangles, dipped in egg and breadcrumbs, deep fried; tomato sauce served separately.

— **Hashed:** Hachée de mou de veau: parboiled, minced, mixed with chopped onions sautéd in butter, chopped parsley, lemon peel and a little stock, thickened with white roux, cooked, served with a poached egg on top.

— **Jugged:** en civet: cut raw in thick strips, fried lightly in butter, dredged with flour, moistened with red wine and a little white stock, crushed garlic and a bunch of herbs added, cooked gently until nearly tender, taken out and put in a clean casserole, blanched fried and diced bacon,

Calf's Lungs
browned button onions and raw quartered mushrooms added, the sauce strained over, cooked until done.
— **Poulette:** parboiled, cut in strips, bound with poulette sauce, chopped parsley scattered on top.
— **Tripe-Merchand Style:** à la tripière: cut raw in thick strips, sautéd in butter, moistened with white stock, seasoned, raw potatoes cut in quarters, a bunch of herbs and crushed garlic added, cooked until tender.
— **Wiener Lungenbeuschel:** parboiled, cut in strips, simmered in sauce prepared with white roux and white stock, chopped anchovies, capers, lemon peel, parsley and rosemary added; served with white bread or semolina dumplings. (Austrian)

Calf's Marrow: Amourettes de veau: prepared like beef marrow.

Calf's Sweetbreads: Ris de veau: glands of which the one is longer and the other larger, rounder and more tasty. Sweetbreads must be trimmed first, tubes and gristle cut off, then soaked until they are white, blanched for a few minutes, skin and nerves removed and pressed between two boards with a small weight on top to shape them nicely. They are then braised with stock, white wine and vegetables, served whole, often glazed, or sliced and prepared in the manner desired.
— **Alexandra:** braised white, garnished as for suprême of chicken.
— **Arlesian Style:** à l'arlesienne: sliced, fried in butter, garnished as for suprême of chicken.
— **with Asparagus Tips:** aux pointes d'asperges: parboiled, sliced, dipped in egg and breadcrumbs, fried in butter, garnished with buttered green asparagus tips.
— **Baden-Baden:** sliced, fried in butter, placed on Anna potatoes, covered with Madeira sauce, garnished with mushroom caps and asparagus tips.
— **Bonne-Maman:** braised in cocotte, placed on coarse vegetable julienne, moistened with veal stock, served in the cocotte covered with the boiled down stock.
— **Bravoura:** sliced, fried in butter, placed on spinach leaves tossed in butter, covered with cream sauce, grated cheese sprinkled on top, glazed.
— **Brighton Style:** (cold): larded with bacon and truffles, braised, when cold glazed with aspic jelly, garnished with artichoke bottoms filled with vegetable macedoine bound with mayonnaise and aspic jelly.
— **Bristol:** sliced, fried, a poached egg on each slice, garnished with straw potatoes and tomatoes concassées; Béarnaise sauce served separately.
— **in Caisse:** en caisse: braised, cut in small slices, filled in china or silver container, garnished with sliced mushrooms and truffles, covered with suprême sauce.
— **Calabrian Style:** à la calabraise: sliced, fried, served with macaroni prepared in the Naples way.
— **Camargo:** braised, covered with Madeira sauce, garnished with small flat brioches scooped out and filled with green peas prepared in the French way mixed with Vichy carrots.
— **Carême:** braised white, cut open lengthwise, stuffed with strips of cockscombs, mushrooms and truffles bound with

Calf's Sweetbreads

mushroom purée, coated with thick German sauce, breadcrumbs and grated Parmesan sprinkled on top, glazed.

— **Century's End:** Fin de siècle: braised in cocotte, garnished with sautéd gooseliver slices, mushrooms and sliced truffles, thick veal gravy poured over.

— **Cevennes Style:** à la cévenole: braised, covered with the strained reduced stock, garnished with glazed chestnuts, button onions and crescent-shapes croûtons fried in butter.

— **Chancelor Style:** à la chancelière: parboiled, sliced, coated with chicken forcemeat, dipped in egg and breadcrumbs, fried in butter, placed on artichoke bottom, covered with suprême sauce mixed with chopped truffles.

— **with Chestnut Purée:** à la purée de marrons: braised, covered with Madeira sauce, chestnut purée served separately.

— **Chivry:** braised white, covered with Chivry sauce, spring vegetables served separately.

— **Choiseul:** sliced, two slices joined together with very fine mirepoix with chopped truffles in between, dipped in egg and breadcrumbs, fried in butter; truffle sauce served separately.

— **Cinq Clous:** studded with five truffle points, braised, garnished with cockscombs, cocks' kidneys, mushroom caps, truffle slices and small veal dumplings, covered generously with German sauce.

— **Clamart:** braised brown, glazed, served with Clamart garnish and thick veal gravy.

— **Collops or Escalopes of:** Escalopes de ris de veau: steeped in water, blanched, skinned, nerves removed, pressed lightly, cut in thick slices, trimmed round, fried in clarified butter and served with veal collops garnish or as desired.

— **Columbus:** Colomb: braised, sliced, placed on slice of sautéd gooseliver, covered with Colbert sauce with cockscombs and cocks' kidneys, garnished with small chicken dumpling in two colors, mixed with bright red tomato purée and with green herb purée.

— **Coquelin:** larded, braised brown, glazed, dressed on oval pastry shell filled with green peas, diced red peppers and sliced mushrooms bound with Melba sauce.

— **Cordon bleu:** larded with truffles, braised, glazed, covered with the reduced stock, garnished with straw potatoes and artichoke bottoms filled with diced sautéd calf's kidney bound with Madeira sauce.

— **Countess Style:** à la comtesse: larded with truffles, braised brown, glazed, covered with the reduced thickened gravy, garnished with braised lettuce and small decorated chicken dumplings.

— **with Crayfish Tails:** aux queues d'écrevisses: braised white, garnished with crayfish tails bound with cream sauce and crayfish noses stuffed with chicken forcemeat blended with crayfish butter and poached.

— **Demidoff:** larded with bacon and truffles, braised when half done crescent-shaped carrots, turnips and truffles as well as sliced small onions, simmered in butter beforehand, added, finished braising, covered with the vegetables and the degreased reduced gravy.

Calf's Sweetbreads

— **Diana:** braised brown and glazed, garnished with small game dumplings; chestnut purée and Diana sauce served separately.

— **Don Carlos:** braised, covered with Madeira sauce mixed with sliced mushrooms and strips of red peppers.

— **Dom Pedro:** braised in cocotte, when half done strips of red peppers, simmered in butter, parboiled fennel bulbs cut in quarters and a few drops of white Port added, braising finished in oven in closed cocotte.

— **Doria:** braised white, garnished with olive-shaped cucumbers, covered with velouté sauce blended with the reduced stock.

— **Dreux:** larded with truffles and ox tongue, braised, served with garnish and sauce financier.

— **Dumas:** braised white, covered with suprême sauce mixed with diced artichoke bottoms.

— **Egyptian Style:** à l'egyptienne: braised, dressed on flat rice croquette, covered with marrow sauce, garnished with braised stuffed peppers.

— **Empress Style:** à l'impératrice: braised white, covered with suprême sauce blended with chicken purée, garnished with asparagus tips, button onions kept white and diced calf's brains bound with velouté sauce.

— **Erima:** blanched, placed in fireproof china cocotte together with diced green peppers and tomatoes simmered in butter with chopped shallots and deglaced with white wine, sliced raw mushrooms added.

— **Excelsior:** larded with truffles, braised white, covered with white onion sauce mixed with julienne of truffle, ox tongue and mushrooms, garnished with three sorts of small chicken dumpling, white, mixed with tomato purée and with green herb purée.

— **Favorite Style:** à la favorite: parboiled, sliced, fried in butter, arranged alternately with sautéd gooseliver slices, decorated with truffle slices, garnished with buttered asparagus tips: Madeira sauce with truffle essence served separately.

— **Figdor:** sliced, fried in butter, placed on Anna potatoes, garnished with fried tomatoes and large grilled mushroom caps, bordered with tomato sauce.

— **Financier Style:** à la financière: braised, served with financier garnish and sauce.

— **Florence Style:** à la florentine: braised white, dressed on spinach leaves tossed in butter, covered with Mornay sauce, sprinkled with grated Parmesan and glazed.

— **Fréville:** larded, braised in Port and veal stock with sliced raw truffles and mushroom caps, stock boiled down with cream and veal glace and poured over the sweetbreads; asparagus tips served separately.

— **Fried:** frit: sliced, dipped in egg and breadcrumbs, fried in butter, served with vegetable macedoine.

— **Gardner Style:** à la jardinière: braised, covered with Madeira sauce, garnished gardeners style.

— **Gastronomer Style:** à la gastronome: braised brown, glazed, garnished with glazed chestnuts, small whole truffles cooked in champagne, cockscombs coated with liquid meat glaze and large sautéd halfed morels; demi-glace finished off with truffle essence served separately.

Calf's Sweetbreads

— **German Style:** à l'allemande: larded, braised white, garnished with mushroom caps and olive-shaped cucumbers, covered with German sauce.

— **Gismonda:** sliced, grilled, arranged on shell of short pastry filled with quartered artichoke bottoms and small mushroom caps simmered in butter, covered with Chateaubriand sauce.

— **Godard:** braised brown, served with Godard garnish and sauce.

— **Grand Mother Style:** à la grand'mère: fried in closed cocotte with sautéd olive potatoes, browned half cooked button onions and diced bacon.

— **Gratined:** gratiné: braised white, sliced, arranged on baking dish bordered with duchess potato-mixture and masked with duxelles, covered with sliced cooked mushroom, coated with duxelles sauce, sprinkled with breadcrumbs, dotted with butter, gratined in oven.

— **with Green Peas:** aux petits pois: sliced, dipped in egg and breadcrumbs, fried in butter, garnished with buttered green peas or braised brown, covered with the strained boiled down stock blended with Madeira sauce; buttered green peas served separately.

— **Grilled:** grillé: parboiled, cut in thick slices, coated with flour, dipped in melted butter, grilled, served with Colbert sauce or buttered meat glace.

— **Guizot:** braised, covered with Madeira sauce finished off with an infusion of mint, garnished with stuffed tomatoes and potato croquettes.

— **Henri IV.:** sliced, fried in butter, coated with liquid meat glace, placed on artichoke bottom, garnished with nut potatoes; Béarnaise sauce served separately.

— **Isabella:** roasted, garnished with artichoke bottoms, mushrooms and braised green peppers; thick veal gravy served separately.

— **Joceline:** sliced, grilled, placed on thick slices of potatoes, shaped like artichoke bottoms, fried in butter and filled with onion purée seasoned with curry powder, half a grilled tomato and green pepper on top of the sweetbread.

— **Judic:** braised, dressed on croûton, garnished with braised lettuce and truffle slices, covered with Madeira sauce mixed with cockscombs and cocks' kidneys.

— **à la King:** parboiled, cut in thick slices, sautéd in butter on both sides, moistened with cream, seasoned with Cayenne pepper, diced green peppers simmered in butter and sliced mushrooms added, thickened with egg-yolks blended with Sherry, bordered with heart-shaped croûtons fried in butter.

— **Lausanne Style:** à la lausannoise: larded, braised, sliced, each slice placed on a slice of ox tongue, covered with Madeira sauce; mushroom purée served separately.

— **Lavallière:** larded, braised, covered with suprême sauce blended with white onion purée and mixed with chopped ham, garnished with buttered green peas and glazed button onions.

— **with Lettuce:** au laitue: braised, glazed, covered with Madeira sauce, garnished with braised lettuce and castle potatoes.

Calf's Sweetbreads

— **with Lobster:** à l'homard: braised white, cut in oblique slices, arranged with lobster slices in between, covered with cream sauce blended with the strained reduced stock and lobster butter.

— **Lucullus:** larded with truffle, braised brown, glazed, Lucullus garnish and demi-glace with truffle essence.

— **Madame Sans-gêne:** braised brown, glazed, covered with Colbert sauce, garnished with stuffed mushroom caps.

— **Margaret:** Marguerite: braised white, covered with Dutch sauce mixed with chopped truffles.

— **Marigny:** braised brown, glazed, garnished alternately with tartlets filled with buttered green peas and with buttered diced French beans; thick veal gravy served separately.

— **Marion Delorme:** parboiled, sliced, fried in butter, garnished with artichoke bottoms filled with chestnut purée; thick veal gravy served separately.

— **Marshall Style:** à la maréchale: sliced, prepared like suprême of chicken.

— **Mary Stuart:** Marie-Stuart: larded with truffle and ox tongue, braised, covered with the reduced and thickened stock; garnished with small puff pastry patties filled with purée of knob celery.

— **Maubeuge Style:** braised in cocotte, when half done cockscombs, cocks' kidneys, sautéd mushroom caps und sliced truffles added, moistened with a little light Madeira sauce, cocotte closed, cooking finished in oven.

— **Melba:** fried slices placed on ring of puff pastry filled with mushroom purée, covered with Madeira sauce mixed with short truffle strips.

— **Milanese Style:** à la milanaise: blanched, sliced, dipped in egg and breadcrumbs mixed with grated Parmesan, fried in oil and butter, arranged like a crown with macaroni prepared in the Milanese way in the center; light tomato sauce served separately.

— **Montauban:** braised brown, glazed, garnished with slices of chicken forcemeat-sausage, small rice croquettes, mixed with chopped ox tongue, and mushrooms; velouté with mushroom essence served separately.

— **Montebello:** braised, covered with light Béarnaise sauce, garnished with artichoke bottom filled with mushroom purée.

— **Montglas:** braised brown, glazed, deglaced with Madeira, reduced and mixed with demi-glace, garnished with sliced, sautéd gooseliver and truffle slices.

— **Montpensier:** braised, same garnish as for tournedos.

— **with Mushrooms:** aux champignons: 1. braised white, covered with German sauce blended with the reduced stock and mixed with sliced mushrooms.
2. braised brown, covered with brown mushroom sauce, garnished with sautéd mushrooms.

— **Naples Style:** à la napolitaine: braised, served with macaroni prepared in the Naples way.

— **Nesselrode:** braised brown, covered with the reduced and thickened braising stock, served with chestnut purée.

— **Noailles:** sliced, fried in butter, placed on sautéd gooseliver slice, covered with suprême sauce with cockscombs and cocks' kidneys added.

Calf's Sweetbreads

— **Nobleman Style:** à la gentilhomme: braised white, when cold sliced, coated with Villeroy sauce mixed with chopped truffles, dipped in egg and breadcrumbs, fried; truffle sauce served separately.

— **Old Fashioned Style:** à l'ancienne: braised white, garnished with button onions and mushroom caps prepared white, covered with velouté blended with the reduced stock.

— **Orloff:** 1. braised, placed in cocotte, garnished with braised celery, covered with truffle julienne and the strained and reduced stock, served in closed cocotte.
2. parboiled, sliced, two slices stuffed with thick white onion purée and a slice of truffle in between, covered with Mornay sauce, sprinkled with grated cheese and glazed.

— **with Oysters:** aux huîtres: braised white, covered with suprême sauce mixed with poached oysters and the oyster liquor.

— **in Paper Bag:** en papillote: braised, sliced, each slice filled in greased paper bag together with a small fried slice of ham and fine mirepoix, finished off in oven.

— **with Paprika Sauce:** à la sauce paprika: braised, covered with paprika sauce.

— **Parisian Style:** à la parisienne: larded with truffles, braised, glaced, served with Parisian garnish and the reduced and strained gravy.

— **Perigord Style:** à la périgourdine: studded with truffle, braised, covered with truffle sauce.

— **Piedmont Style:** à la piémontaise: braised, dressed on risotto mixed with sliced white truffles; light tomato sauce served separately.

— **Pompadour:** braised brown, served with Pompadour garnish and truffle sauce.

— **Portuguese Style:** à la portugaise: sliced, fried, prepared like sautéd chicken.

— **Prince of Wales:** Prince de Galles: braised, garnished with sautéd chicken livers, mushrooms, truffle slices and small halved grilled peppers, covered with Madeira sauce.

— **Princess Style:** à la princesse: braised, glazed, placed on flat pastry shell filled with buttered green asparagus tips, decorated with truffle slices coated with meat glaze; German sauce with mushroom essence served separately.

— **Princess Mary:** Princesse Marie: sliced, fried in butter, placed on artichoke bottom, garnished with sautéd chicken livers and cauliflower sprigs covered with Dutch sauce.

— **Provencal Style:** à la provençale: sliced, fried, garnished with grilled mushroom caps and stuffed tomatoes, covered with Provencal sauce.

— **Queen Style:** à la reine: braised white, covered with suprême sauce, garnished with chicken purée bound with egg yolks, filled in beaker mould, poached and turned out.

— **Rachel:** braised, glazed, garnished with artichoke bottoms with a large slice of blanched ox marrow covered with Bordeaux sauce and sprinkled with chopped parsley on top; the thickened braising stock served separately.

Calf's Sweetbreads

— **Richelieu** (cold): braised in rich veal stock with fine julienne of carrots, turnips, celery and truffles, when done placed in cocotte with the julienne on top and the strained, degreased and reduced stock poured over, served cold.

— **Roman Style:** à la romaine: braised brown, garnished with spinach croquettes and tartlets filled with Roman gnocchi, covered with Roman sauce.

— **Rossini:** braised, sliced, each slice placed on a sautéd gooseliver slice, a large truffle slice on the sweetbread, covered with Madeira sauce.

— **Rostand:** braised, garnished with tartlets filled alternately with knob celery purée and buttered green peas; the thickened stock served separately.

— **Royal Style:** à la royale: braised white, covered with suprême sauce, regency garnish.

— **Russian Style:** à la russe (cold): braised white, when cold covered with white chaudfroid sauce and glazed with aspic jelly, garnished with tartlets filled with Russian salad; Russian mayonnaise served separately.

— **Saint-Alban:** braised, sliced, each slice placed on a flat chicken croquette with a fluted mushrom cap on top; tomato sauce served separately.

— **Saint-Cloud:** 1. larded with truffle and ox tongue, braised, garnished with braised lettuce and tartlets filled with purée of green peas; Madeira sauce served separately. 2. larded and braised as above, served with Regency garnish and the thickened braising stock.

— **Saint-Germain:** parboiled, sliced, grilled, garnished with Parisian potatoes and olive-shaped carrots; Béarnaise sauce and purée of fresh green peas separately.

— **Saint-Mandé:** sliced, fried, each slice placed on base of Anna potatoes, garnished with buttered green peas and French beans; thick veal gravy served separately.

— **Saint-Saëns:** larded with truffle, braised, covered with the thickened braising stock, garnished with artichoke bottoms filled with mushroom purée mixed with chopped truffles.

— **Sarah Bernhardt:** braised, covered with Madeira sauce, garnished with very small braised red peppers stuffed with risotto mixed with mushroom purée.

— **with Sorrel:** à l'oseille: braised white or brown, covered with German or Madeira sauce; sorrel purée served separately.

— **Soubise:** braised white, covered with Soubise sauce; white onion purée served separately.

— **Spanish Style:** à l'espagnole: larded with truffle, braised, served on risotto mixed with diced red peppers, mushrooms and stoned olives; tomato sauce served separately.

— **with Spinach:** aux epinards: braised, covered with Madeira sauce, spinach purée served separately.

— **Surcouf:** braised, covered with the thickened stock, garnished with spring carrots and turnips, quartered artichoke bottoms and asparagus tips, all tossed in butter.

— **Swedish Style:** à la suédoise (cold): braised white, when cold cut in slices, each slice coated with horseradish butter, decorated with a round slice of ox tongue and glazed with aspic jelly. Slices arranged on round flat pastry

Calf's Sweetbreads
shell filled with vegetable salad bound with mayonnaise; Russian mayonnaise served separately.
— **Talleyrand:** braised, sliced, served with Talleyrand garnish.
— **Tegetthoff:** braised, covered with Madeira sauce, garnished with asparagus tips and tartlets filled with purée of fresh green peas.
— **Timbale of, Condé:** Timbale de ris de veau Condé: timbale mould lined with pie dough, baked to a pale color, filled with sliced sweetbreads, truffles and mushrooms bound with thick Madeira sauce, covered with chicken forcemeat mixed with chopped mushrooms and truffles, finished off in the oven; Madeira sauce served separately.
— **Toulouse Style:** à la toulousaine: braised white, covered with suprême sauce, Toulouse garnish.
— **Truffled:** truffé: studded with fresh truffles, placed in small cocotte with a little butter, white wine and meat glace, hermetically sealed with dough, braised in oven, cocotte first opened at serving.
— **Tsarina:** à la tsarine: braised white, covered with creamed velouté, garnished with olive-shaped cucumber pieces in cream sauce.
— **Verdi:** braised in brown stock and Marsala, garnished with sautéd slices of gooseliver and Roman gnocchi; the reduced stock mixed with demi-glace served separately.
— **Viard:** parboiled, sliced, dipped in egg and breadcrumbs, fried in butter, each slice placed on tartlet filled with mushroom purée mixed with chopped truffles.
— **Viennese Style:** à la viennoise: collops dipped in egg and breadcrumbs, fried in butter, garnished with lemon and parsley.
— **Villeroi:** parboiled, sliced, each slice coated with Villeroi sauce, dipped in egg and breadcrumbs, deep fried, garnished with buttered green peas or other suitable vegetable; tomato or truffle sauce served separately.
— **Virginia:** parboiled, sliced, simmered in cream and demi-glace, each slice placed on round croûton fried in butter with a small slice of fried ham on top, covered with the sauce seasoned with paprika.
— **Volnay:** braised brown, glazed, covered with the reduced thickened stock, garnished on one side with white onion and on the other with mushroom purée.
— **Waldorf:** parboiled, sliced, fried in butter, garnished with artichoke bottoms filled with tiny veal or chicken dumplings bound with Madeira sauce.

Calf's Tail: Queue de veau: cut in convenient pieces, blanched and usually braised.
— **Italian Style:** à l'italienne: parboiled, simmered in Italian sauce.
— **Marengo:** prepared like veal ragoût Marengo.

Calf's Tongue: Langue de veau: usually served with calf's head. For separate dish boiled with pot herbs, skinned and cut lengthwise or in thick slices. If tongue is to be braised it must be parboiled and skinned beforehand.
— **with Cucumber Sauce:** à la sauce aux concombres: boiled, covered with pepper sauce mixed with chopped gherkins.

Calf's Tongue
— **with Devil Sauce:** à la diable: boiled and served with devil sauce.
— **Fried:** frite: cut in thick slices, dipped in egg and breadcrumbs, deep fried; anchovy or caper or tomato sauce served separately.
— **Housekeeper Style:** à la ménagère: two slices of boiled tongue filled with mirepoix simmered in butter and bound with thick demi-glace, dipped in flour, egg and breadcrumbs, deep fried; Italian sauce and spinach or potato purée served separately.
— **Italian Style:** à l'italienne: parboiled, braised, covered with Italian sauce mixed with the strained reduced stock; spaghetti prepared in the Italian way served separately.
— **with Malaga Sauce:** à la sauce au Malaga: boiled, sliced, covered with demi-glace flavored with Malaga.
— **Munich Style:** à la munichoise: boiled in white stock, white wine and a little vinegar with peppercorns, bay leaf and allspice, covered with strips of carrot, turnip, knob celery and sliced onions boiled in a part of the stock, a little stock poured over, garnished with sliced pickled cucumbers and rasped horseradish.
— **with Mustard Sauce:** à la sauce moutarde boiled, when cold cut lengthwise, dipped in egg and breadcrumps, moistened with melted butter, grilled; mustard sauce served separately.
— **in Paper Bag:** en papillote: boiled, cut in two lengthwise, wrapped in a greased paper bag placed on a slice of ham and covered with duxelles; baked in oven and served in the bag.
— **Polish Style:** à la polonaise: parboiled, braised in light demi-glace with chopped almonds, dates and figs, currants and a little honey.
— **Portuguese Style:** à la portugaise: braised, covered with Portuguese sauce, garnished with stuffed tomatoes and castle potatoes.
— **with Purée:** au purée: braised, served with the reduced and thickened stock and potato, knob celery, green pea, turnip, Lima bean or chestnut purée.
— **Westmoreland:** boiled, covered with Madeira sauce mixed with chopped pickles.

Calf's Udder: Tétine de veau: steeped in water, blanched, skinned, cooked in white stock or milk.
— **Fried:** frite: 1. boiled until tender, cut in squares, dipped in egg and breadcrumbs, deep fried; tomato or ravigote or tartar sauce served separately.
2. cut in squares, seasoned, fried in butter, covered with browned butter; saurkraut, lentils or green peas served separately.

Canard: see duck.
Canard sauvage: see wild duck.
Caneton: duckling, see duck.
Caneton Rouennais: See Rouenese duck.
Cannelons: see pastry cones.
Canvasback Duck: the largest North American bay or sea duck, so named because its white and gray back feathers resemble a canvas mottling.
— **American Style:** à l'américaine: roasted rare, breast removed, the carcass and lower legs chopped roughly,

Canvasback Duck
placed in a special duck press to extract blood and juices, mixed with purée of the sautéd liver previously strained, breast heated in chafing dish with this sauce, but not over-heated, as it is liable to curdle; garnished with corn fritters.
— **broiled:** cut open from the back, lightly flattened, broiled, served with herb butter and red currant jelly.
— **Roast:** rôti: roasted rare, breast removed and kept warm in chafing dish, pressed as for American style, juices mixed with demi-glace, Madeira and Cognac, strained over the breast, heated slowly, wild rice served separately.

Capercailzie, Mountain Cock; F. Coq de bruyère; G. Auerhahn: the largest of all feathered game, found in the Alps, the Jura, Carpathians and in some parts of Scotland.
— **Braised:** en daube: larded, marinated in red wine with sliced pot herbs, braised in light demi-glace.
— **with Pineapple:** à l'ananas: roast breast, sliced, dressed alternately with small thin slices of pineapple cooked in white wine, covered with demi-glace with game essence.
— **Stuffed:** farci: stuffed with pork forcemeat mixed with chopped shallots, diced truffles and mushrooms, seasoned with thyme, sweet basil and chopped parsley, wrapped in thin slices of salt pork, roasted, served with the pan juice boiled down with game stock.
— **Westphalian Style:** à la westphalienne: wrapped in thin slices of salt pork, roasted with juniper berries and herbs, served with the pan juice boiled up with game gravy, thickened with arrowroot, strained and mixed with fried strips of ham and sautéd diced apples.

Capitolade de volaille: see chicken ragoût, French.

Capon: Chapon: prepared like poularde.

Carnatz: Roumanian Croquettes: minced boiled or roast beef mixed with finely minced lean pork trimmings, seasoned with salt, paprika, pepper and marjoram, shaped into croquettes, dipped in egg and breadcrumbs, deep fried, tomato sauce served separately. (Roumanian)

Carré de veau: see rack of veal.

Cassoulet: see French mutton stew.

Castor: see beaver.

Cerdo asado ala Riojano: Roast pork: pork larded with garlic, roasted by an open fire, garnished with whole pimientos fried in oil. (Spanish)

Cerf: see stag.

Cervelle de veau: see calf's brain.

Chamois: see goat, alpine.

Chanfaina: Stewed pig's liver: diced pig's liver pre-fried in oil with chopped onions, moistened with stock, stewed with chopped parsley, mint, cinnamon, paprika, saffron, pepper corns and cloves; breadcrumbs scattered on top at serving. (Spanish)

Chapon: see capon.

Charterhouse Dish: Chartreuse: greased charlotte mould lined with fancy shaped vegetables, mushrooms or cabbage etc. coated inside with forcemeat, lined with thin slices of fat bacon, filled with ragoût of some kind, sealed with forcemeat, covered with fat bacon, steamed in oven in water-bath, allowed to rest for a while, turned out and covered with a suitable sauce.

Charterhouse Dish

— **of Calf's Sweetbread:** de ris de veau: greased mould lined with fancy shaped vegetable slices, coated with veal forcemeat, filled with cooked sliced sweetbread, mushrooms and truffle slices bound with thick German sauce, sealed with forcemeat and steamed; turned out, a large fluted mushroom cap placed on top, garnished with braised lettuce, German sauce served separately.

— **of Partridge:** de perdreau: prepared as of pheasant but with old partridges.

— **of Pheasant:** Chartreuse de faisan: old pheasant braised with cabbage; bottom and sides of mould lined thickly with cabbage, filled alternately with the carved pheasant, slices of garlic sausage and small slices of blanched bacon, sealed with cabbage, steamed, turned out and covered with demi-glace with pheasant essence.

— **of Pigeon:** de pigeon: same preparation but with young pigeons.

— **of Quails:** de cailles: prepared as with calf's sweetbread but with quails breast stiffened in butter.

Chartreuse: see charterhouse dish:

Chicken: F. Poulet; G. Huhn; I. Pollo; S. Gallina: is the best of all domesticated birds known as poultry. Chickens are graded for the table according to age, weight and quality, viz:

Squab Chicken: Baby Chicken; F. Poussin; G. Küken.
Spring Chicken: Broiler; F. Poulet de grain; G. Junghahn.
Roasting Chicken: F. Poulet reine; G. Brathuhn.
Capon: F. Chapon; G. Kapaun: castrated cock.
Poularde: F. Poularde; G. Masthuhn, Poularde: fat speyed hen.
Boiling Fowl: F. Poule; G. Suppenhuhn: best used for broth, salad, mayonnaise, forcemeat etc.

Chicken Breast: see suprême of chicken.

Chicken, Chaudfroid of: Chaudfroid de volaille; poached or roasted chicken or poularde breast, allowed to cool, left whole or cut in slices according to size, trimmed, coated with chaudfroid sauce, decorated to taste and glazed with aspic jelly.

— **Gounod:** Chaudfroid de volaille Gounod: slices of cold poached poularde, trimmed, coated with chicken froth; when set covered with white chaudfroid sauce, decorated with a lyra made of truffle, glazed and garnished with aspic jelly.

— **Rossini:** coated with white chaudfroid sauce, decorated with truffle and glazed with Madeira aspic jelly; placed on a slice of gooseliver patty or parfait of the same size, decorated with aspic jelly.

— **Scotch Style:** de volaille à l'écossaise: coated with white chaudfroid sauce mixed with finely diced truffle, ox tongue, hard-boiled egg white and gherkins, glazed with aspic jelly; served on base of salad of diced green beans bound with jellied mayonnaise and a small slice of ox tongue on top.

— **Spring Style:** Chaudfroid de poulet à la printanière: small skinned breast of poached cold spring chicken coated with green herb chaudfroid sauce, decorated and glazed with aspic jelly; garnished with artichoke bottoms filled with vegetable salad bound with jellied

Chicken Chaudfroid
mayonnaise, decorated with a truffle star and glazed with aspic jelly.

— **Vincent:** slices, trimmed, coated with green herb chaudfroid sauce and glazed; placed on tartlet filled with salad of celery and hard-boiled egg; cucumber salad served separately.

Chicken Chop Suey: Chinese chicken ragoût: sliced onions, mushrooms, celery, green peppers and bean sprouts stewed together with sliced fried chicken meat in brown stock flavored with Soja sauce, served with plain rice. (Chinese)

Chicken, Creamed: minced cooked chicken meat boiled in light cream to a thick consistency, seasoned with salt, paprika and a little Sherry, served in chafing dish or on toast.

— —, **Baked:** creamed chicken filled in baking dish surrounded with a border of piped Duchess potato mixture, sprinkled with breadcrumbs, melted butter dropped on top, browned in oven.

Chicken Cutlet: Côtelette de volaille: may be prepared in three different ways:

1. breast of spring chickens with the wing tip, skinned and treated like suprême.

2. roasted or boiled chicken meat diced and mixed with finely diced mushrooms, truffles etc., mixed with thick Béchamel sauce, thickened with egg yolks, when cold shaped in the form of a small lamb chop, dipped in egg and breadcrumbs, fried in deep fat or in butter and served with an appropriate garnish.

3. chicken mousseline forcemeat filled in greased cutlet mould, poached, sometimes dipped in egg and breadcrumbs and fried, also served with sauce and garnish.

— **Albuféra:** prepared like suprême of chicken.

— **American Style:** à l'américaine: prepared with diced meat and mushrooms, dipped in egg and breadcrumbs, fried in butter, garnished with tiny turtle croquettes; Newburgh sauce served separately.

— **Amphytrion:** fried in butter, dressed on mushroom purée, covered with Madeira sauce with chopped truffles.

— **Barberina:** raw breast coated with chicken forcemeat mixed with raw gooseliver and chopped truffles, dipped in egg and breadcrumbs, fried, garnished with artichoke bottoms filled with chopped mushrooms bound with cream sauce.

— **Béarnaise:** raw breast cut open lengthwise, stuffed with veal forcemeat mixed with chopped herbs, sautéd in butter, bordered with thick veal gravy; Béarnaise sauce served separately.

— **Berchoux:** raw breast stuffed with truffled forcemeat, sautéd, dressed on tartlet filled with creamed mushroom purée, covered with truffle sauce.

— **Bérenger:** breast poached, dressed on tartlet filled with mushroom purée, covered with suprême sauce, garnished with decorated veal or chicken dumplings.

— **Carpathian Style:** à la carpathique: prepared like Pojarsky, placed on small broiled red pepper, garnished with slices of egg plant coated with flour and deep fried; tomato sauce acidulated with lemon juice served separately.

— **Chartres Style:** à la Chartres: raw breast stuffed with

Chicken Cutlet
chicken forcemeat with chopped tarragon, fried in butter, covered with tarragon sauce with chopped tarragon.
— **with Chestnut Purée:** à la purée de marrons: fried in butter, covered with Madeira sauce, garnished with chestnut purée.
— **Colbert:** raw breast dipped in egg and breadcrumbs, fried in butter, placed on artichoke purée; Colbert sauce served separately.
— **Dubarry:** cutlets of chicken mousseline forcemeat, poached, chilled, dipped in egg and breadcrumbs, fried, garnished with shaped cauliflower covered with Mornay sauce and glazed; thick chicken gravy served separately.
— **Duchess Style:** à la duchesse: fried, dressed on base of baked duchess potato, financier garnish and sauce.
— **English Style:** à l'anglaise: raw breast dipped in egg and breadcrumbs, fried in butter, garnished with any kind of green vegetable tossed in butter, bordered with thick veal gravy beaten with butter.
— **Epicurean Style:** à l'épicurienne: fried, dressed on flat oval chicken dumpling, covered with cream sauce mixed with sliced mushrooms.
— **d'Estrées:** cutlet mould filled with chicken mousseline forcemeat, poached, turned out, truffle slice placed on top, covered with suprême sauce, garnished with creamed mushrooms.
— **Favorite Style:** à la favorite: fried in butter, dressed on fried slice of gooseliver, truffle slice placed on top, covered with buttered meat glaze, garnished with green asparagus tips.
— **Gatchina:** raw breast meat, chopped finely, mixed with butter and cream, shaped, rolled in cracker meal, fried in butter, garnished with macedoine of root vegetables tossed in butter.
— **Gaulish Style:** à la gauloise: fried, placed on small slice of fried ham, covered with Madeira sauce with cockscombs and cocks' kidneys added.
— **Georgette:** fried in butter, placed on Georgette potato, a truffle slice laid on top, covered with buttered meat glaze.
— **Gudrun:** cutlet mould lined with chicken mousseline forcemeat, filled with diced crayfish tails bound with cream sauce, sealed with forcemeat, poached, turned out, covered with cream sauce blended with crayfish butter, garnished with creamed morels.
— **Helder:** raw breast poached in butter and lemon juice, covered with chicken velouté boiled down with a little tomato juice and blended with butter, garnished with salpicon of artichoke bottoms, mushrooms, truffles and the red parts of carrot simmered in butter.
— **Henri IV.:** fried in butter, placed on artichoke bottom with a slice of truffle dipped in liquid meat glaze on top, garnished nut potatoes; Béarnaise sauce served separately.
— **Londonderry:** fried, served on salpicon of chicken, ox tongue and mushrooms bound with truffle sauce.
— **Lucullus:** raw breast stuffed with chicken mousseline farce with chopped truffles, poached in lemon juice and butter, covered with demi-glace with truffle essence,

Chicken Cutlet
garnished with cockscombs and a small truffle cooked in champagne.
— **Lyonese Style:** fried in butter, covered with thick veal gravy mixed with plenty of sliced fried onions, sprinkled with chopped parsley.
— **Marie Louise:** dipped in egg and breadcrumbs, fried, dressed on artichoke bottom filled with white onion purée, browned butter poured over.
— **Marquise Style:** à la marquise: poached, deglaced with Port and cream, boiled up with a little cream sauce, truffle purée added and poured over the chicken; garnished with small puff pastry patty filled with salpicon of cockscombs, cocks' kidney and truffles bound with cream sauce.
— **Mirabeau:** grilled, decorated with anchovy fillets and blanched tarragon leaves, garnished with blanched pitted olives in thick demi-glace; anchovy butter served separately.
— **Miramar:** prepared in the second way with mushrooms, fried, dressed on risotto mixed with diced fried egg plant, covered with browned butter; light tomato sauce with chopped tarragon served separately.
— **with Mushrooms:** aux champignons: poached in butter and lemon juice, covered with suprême sauce mixed with sliced mushrooms.
— **My Fancy:** Mon désir: prepared with chicken mousseline forcemeat mixed with chopped mushrooms, filled in cutlet mould, poached, turned out, covered with Portuguese sauce, garnished with olive-shaped cucumbers simmered in butter.
— **Oriental Style:** à l'orientale: fried in oil, dressed on rice pilaf colored with saffron, covered with suprême sauce mixed with tomato purée and saffron.
— **Pojarsky:** raw breast chopped finely with cream and butter added, seasoned, shaped with a small piece of chilled butter placed in the center, dipped in egg and breadcrumbs and fried in butter; garnished with vegetable macedoine or to taste. May also be prepared with the chopped meat mixed with cream and soaked white bread only.
— **Queen of Hearts:** reine de coeur: cutlets prepared in the second way with chicken meat and braised celery, dipped in egg and breadcrumbs, fried in butter, garnished with tartlet filled with diced green peppers and tomatoes simmered in butter with chopped shallots and parsley; thick boiled down chicken gravy beaten with butter served separately.
— **Rohan:** fried in butter, a slice of blanched ox marrow coated with liquid meat glaze placed on top; garnished with sautéd mushrooms mixed with chopped parsley and a few drops of lemon juice.
— **Saint-Germain:** raw breast fried in butter, garnished with purée of green peas bound with egg yolks and cream, poached in small moulds and turned out, and castle potatoes; Béarnaise sauce served separately.
— **Ségurd:** raw breast chopped, mixed with cream, egg yolk and butter, seasoned, shaped, dipped in egg and breadcrumbs, fried in butter, truffle slice dipped in liquid

Chicken Cutlet
meat glaze placed on top, Madeira sauce with truffle slices served separately.
— **Turkish Style:** à la turque: poached, covered with German sauce blended with pistachio butter and mixed with truffle slices cut in crescent shape; rice pilaf with saffron served separtely.
— **Waselewitch:** prepared like Pojarsky, garnished with gribuis (Russian mushrooms) bound with sour cream sauce; sour cream sauce mixed with strips of pickled cucumber served separately.
— **Wladimir:** fried in butter, dressed on shaped risotto, a slice of calf's sweetbread, a truffle slice and a cockscomb placed on top, covered with Wladimir sauce.

Chicken, Fricassée of: Fricassé de poulet: cut in pieces, stiffened in butter, smothered with flour, moistened with white stock, a larded onion and a bunch of herbs added, stewed until done, pieces taken out and placed in a clean casserole, covered with velouté sauce made of the stock thickened with egg yolks and cream, seasoned with lemon juice, garnished.
— **Ancient Style:** à l'ancienne: garnished with small mushroom caps and stewed button onions, sauce finished off with chopped chives and parsley, surrounded with puff pastry fleurons.
— **Archduke Style:** à l'archi-duc: covered with the sauce mixed with button mushrooms and truffle slices.
— **Aurora:** à l'aurore: mixed with veal dumplings finished off with tomato purée covered with the sauce blended with tomato purée.
— **Berlin Style:** à la berlinoise: boiled fowl, cut in pieces, skinned, garnished with morels, mushroom caps, small slices of sweetbread and veal dumplings, covered with velouté sauce made with the stock and a little white wine, thickened with egg yolks and cream, seasoned with lemon juice; capers and crayfish butter dropped on top, bordered with crayfish noses stuffed with semolina boiled in chicken stock with butter, thickened with egg yolks.
— **Breton Style:** à la bretonne: served with the sauce mixed with coarse julienne of mushrooms, leeks and knob celery.
— **Bride Style:** à la petite mariée: covered with the sauce mixed with very small boiled potato and carrot balls, button onions and green peas.
— **Chevalière:** sauce mixed with mushroom caps, sliced truffles, cockscombs, cocks' kidneys and small chicken dumplings.
— **Chimay:** garnished with morels and green asparagus tips.
— **with Crayfish Tails:** aux écrevisses: sauce blended with the boiled down crayfish stock, whipped up with crayfish butter and mixed with crayfish tails, bordered with fleurons.
— **Demidoff:** sauce mixed with halfmoon-shaped slices of carrots, turnips, knob celery and sliced onions simmered in butter, half-moon-shaped truffle slices scattered on top.
— **Duchess Style:** à la duchesse: covered with suprême sauce, garnished with white asparagus tips.
— **French Style:** à la française: sauce mixed with green peas and very small boiled potato and carrot balls.

Chicken Fricassée

— **Ivory Style:** à l'ivoire: covered with the creamed sauce finished off with meat glaze and mixed with button mushrooms and sliced artichoke bottoms.

— **Leo X.:** mixed with mushroom caps and small veal dumplings, macaroni served separately.

— **Modern Style:** à la moderne: garnished with button onions, mushroom caps and olive-shaped truffles, sauce finished off with Port and truffle extract, garnished with fleurons and crayfish tails, truffle julienne scattered on top.

— **Princess Style:** à la princesse: mixed with green asparagus tips and sliced truffles.

— **Queen Margot:** à la reine Margot: mixed with chicken dumplings finished off with crayfish butter and chicken dumplings mixed with pistachio purée, covered with the sauce blended with almond milk.

— **Rakoczy:** covered with the sauce finished off with paprika and cream, garnished with slices of eggplant sautéd in butter.

— **Richemonde:** sauce mixed with julienne of carrots and truffles.

— **Spring Style:** à la printanière: sauce mixed with small olive-shaped carrots and turnips, button onions and lozenges of green beans, green peas scattered on top.

— **Sultan Style:** à la sultane: dressed in border of rice, covered with the sauce finished off with pistachio butter, diced cooked red peppers scattered on top.

— **Trianon:** mixed with truffled chicken dumplings, veal dumplings with purée of fine herbs and chicken dumplings mixed with minced red tongue; sauce finished off with gooseliver purée.

— **Victor Hugo:** covered with velouté sauce with paprika and cream, mixed with quartered artichoke bottoms.

— **Westphalian Style:** à la westphalienne: covered with German sauce; buttered noodles mixed with chopped Westphalian ham served separately.

Chicken, Fried: Poulet frit: disjointed, each leg and breast cut in two, mostly dipped in egg and breadcrumbs, fried in deep fat and garnished with fried parsley.

— **Croissy:** fried in deep fat, Béarnaise sauce served separately.

— **English Style:** à l'anglaise: bones removed, dipped in egg and breadcrumbs, deep fried, garnished with lemon and watercress; herb butter served separately.

— **Maryland:** deep fried, garnished with sliced fried bacon, fried pieces of banana, corn fritters; horseradish cream served separately.

— **Provencal Style:** à la provençale: deep fried; Provencal sauce served separately.

— **Savoy Hotel:** deep fried, served with asparagus tips in cream sauce and tomato sauce.

— **Viennese Style:** à la viennoise: disjointed, legs and breasts left whole, dipped in egg and breadcrumbs including the liver, deep fried, garnished with fried parsley; lettuce salad served separately.

— **Villeroi:** chicken parboiled, when cold boned, coated with Villeroi sauce, dipped in egg and breadcrumbs, deep fried; truffle sauce served separately.

Chicken, Fritot: Fritot de poulet: thin slices of chicken breast marinated in oil, lemon juice and chopped herbs, dipped in frying batter, deep fried, dressed with fried parsley; tomato sauce served separately.

Chicken, Grilled: Poulet grillé: broiler, either half or whole, split in the back, back bone chopped off, opened, flattened, legs stuck in the abdominal walls, seasoned, brushed with butter and grilled.

— **American Style:** à l'américaine: grilled, garnished with fried bacon slices and fried tomatoes.

— **with Devil Sauce:** à la diable: brushed with mustard powder mixed with Cayenne pepper and a little water, dipped in breadcrumbs, grilled; devil sauce served separately.

Chicken à la King: diced white cooked chicken breast tossed in butter, seasoned lightly, simmered in sweet cream. Meanwhile toss in butter diced green and red peppers and fresh mushrooms until done and combine with the chicken, thicken with egg yolks blend with cream, take from fire to prevent curdling, season with Sherry and a dash of Cognac; served in chafing dish with toast.

Chicken Legs, Stuffed: Ballotines de volaille: prepared with the raw legs of chicken of which the wings and breasts have been used otherwise, boned, stuffed with forcemeat, braised white or brown, served with an appropriate sauce and garnish, often-shaped like a small ham and then called jambonneau de volaille.

— **with Fine Herbs:** aux fines herbs: chicken legs stuffed with chicken forcemeat mixed with chopped fine herbs, braised in white wine and demi-glace, sauce finished off with chopped tarragon, parsley and chervil.

— **Florence Style:** Cuisses de poulet à la florentine: poached, dressed on leaf spinach tossed in butter, covered with Mornay sauce finished off with chicken essence, sprinkled with grated cheese, glazed.

— **Garibaldi:** turkey's legs stuffed with chicken and veal forcemeat mixed with chopped ox tongue and truffles, braised brown, served with tomato sauce.

— **Grilled:** Cuisses de poulet grillées: left over roast chicken legs brushed with mustard, dipped in melted butter and breadcrumbs, grilled; devil sauce served separately.

— **Italian Style:** à l'italienne: chicken legs stuffed with chicken forcemeat mixed with chopped mushrooms, braised in light Italian sauce, covered with the sauce, garnished with quartered artichoke bottoms prepared in the Italian way.

— **Nice Style:** à la nicoise: chicken legs stuffed with chicken forcemeat, braised in white wine, chopped onions, garlic, diced tomatoes and demi-glace, covered with the sauce, garnished with French beans and diced sautéd potatoes.

— **Princess Style:** à la princesse: chicken legs stuffed with chicken forcemeat with chopped truffles added, braised white, dressed on flat potato croquettes, covered with German sauce mixed with the boiled down stock, a truffle slice on each leg, garnished with green asparagus tips.

Chicken Livers, Poultry Livers: Foies de volaille: the livers of large chicken, poulardes or turkeys are the best. The gall must be removed carefully and the livers sautéd

Chicken Livers
rare. They may be served on toast as a breakfast dish or with rice as an entrée.

— **Bordeaux Style:** à la bordelaise: sautéd with chopped shallots and herbs, deglaced with red wine, boiled down with demi-glace.

— **English Style:** à l'anglaise: sautéd, arranged on slice of fried bacon, sprinkled with chopped parsley, covered with browned butter.

— **Farmer Style:** à la paysanne: sautéd with chopped shallots and chopped raw mushrooms, seasoned with lemon juice, chopped parsley sprinkled on top.

— **with Fine Herbs:** aux fines herbes: sautéd in butter with chopped shallots, mushrooms, parsley, chervil and tarragon, bound with the deglacage mixed with demi-glace and tomato purée.

— **Forester Style:** à la forestière: sautéd, mixed with sautéd morels, bound with Madeira sauce.

— **Hunter Style:** à la chasseur: sautéd with chopped shallots, bound with hunter sauce.

— **Italian Style:** à l'italienne: turned in flour, sautéd, bound with Italian sauce, served in border of risotto.

— **with Madeira:** au madère: sautéd with chopped shallots, bound with Madeira sauce.

— **Oriental Style:** à l'orientale: sautéd in oil with finely chopped onions and a little garlic, mixed with soaked chopped currants, a pinch of sugar, deglaced with lemon juice and light tomato sauce.

— **Pilaf of:** en pilaw: sautéd, bound with tomato sauce, served in border of rice pilaf.

— **Pilaf of, Merville:** Pilaw de foies de vollaille Merville: poularde livers cut in large dice, sautéd, mixed with diced sautéd mushrooms, deglaced with Port and boiled down with cream; livers bound with this sauce and dressed in a border of rice pilaf mixed with diced tomatoes and green peppers.

— **on Skewers:** en brochette: large livers fixed on skewers alternately with small squares of bacon and thick mushroom slices, dipped in egg and breadcrumbs, turned in melted butter and broiled.

— **on Tomato-Rice:** sautéd, placed on buttered rice mixed with tomato sauce, covered with tomato sauce, chopped truffles scattered on top.

Chicken Mousse: Mousse de volaille: raw chicken meat pounded in mortar with egg white, rubbed through a hair sieve, seasoned, chilled on ice, mixed with thick cream, filled in greased mould decorated with truffle etc., poached in water bath, turned out, served with sauce and garnish as for chicken mousselines.

Chicken Mousselines: Mousselines de volaille: same preparation as for mousse, filled in small beaker or dariole moulds or shaped with a table spoon, poached and served with an appropriate sauce and garnish.

— **Agnès Sorel:** served with sauce and garnish as for suprême of chicken.

— **Ambassadress Style:** served with the same sauce and garnish as for suprême of chicken.

Chicken Mousselines

— **Countess Style:** à la comtesse: mould decorated with truffle and pistachio, filled with mousseline forcemeat mixed with chopped mushrooms, poached, turned out, covered with suprême sauce.

— **Lovely Irma:** Belle Irma: oval mousseline shaped with a spoon, placed on flat potato croquette mixed with chopped truffle, garnished with asparagus tips, covered with suprême sauce.

— **Mosaic:** à la mosaique: moulds tesselated with hard-boiled egg white, truffle, ox tongue and pickled cucumber, filled in layers with chicken mousseline forcemeat, chopped truffles and gooseliver forcemeat, poached, turned out, bordered with Colbert sauce.

— **Nancy Style:** Ursulines de Nancy: round mousseline, dressed on tartlet filled with gooseliver purée bound with demi-glace flavored with Port, truffle slice placed on top, covered with buttered chicken glaze, garnished with asparagus tips.

— **Principessa:** oval mousseline, dressed on oval tartlet filled with tomatoes concassées, covered with suprême sauce finished off with purée of red peppers, chopped tarragon sprinkled on top, garnished with sliced egg plant fried in deep fat.

— **Sicilian Style:** à la sicilienne: oval mousseline dressed on oval tartlet filled with macaroni cut in small pieces and prepared Naples way, covered with suprême sauce finished off with purée of chicken liver, sprinkled with grated Parmesan, glazed rapidly.

Chicken Pie: chicken prepared as for fricassée, filled in pie dish together with diced bacon, small potato balls, vegetables and the sauce, **covered with puff pastry** or pie dough, baked in oven until brown, served hot.

— **English:** chicken cut as for chicken sauté, filled in pie dish with quartered eggs, quartered mushrooms, olives, small fried potato balls, seasoned, thick veal gravy added, covered with puff paste, brushed with egg yolk, baked in oven until done and nicely browned; served hot or cold.

Chicken Purée: Purée de volaille: boiled or roasted chicken without skin or bones pounded in mortar with a little cream sauce, rubbed through a sieve, mixed with German or suprême sauce, filled in puff pastry patty or served in timbale dish surrounded with fleurons.

— **Queen Style:** à la reine: purée of chicken filled in center of flat border of poached chicken mousseline forcemeat, small slices of ox tongue and poached eggs arranged on top, covered with suprême sauce.

Chicken Ragoût, French: Capitolade de volaille: slices of roasted or boiled chicken meat without bones with sliced mushrooms added, warmed up in Italian sauce without allowing the sauce to boil, served with chopped parsley sprinkled on top.

Chicken, Sautéd: Poulet sauté: disjoint spring chicken or broiler detaching the legs first and severing them at the joint. Then the two halves of the breast are cut off with a piece of the wing-bone and carefully pulled away from the breast-bone; if the chicken is very large the upper part of the wing with a piece of the breast is cut off first

Chicken, Sautéd

and the two breast halves pulled away from the breast-bone. The back-bone is trimmed and cut into two or three pieces according to size. Chicken may be sautéd brown or white. If it is to be sautéd brown, season the pieces and fry them to a rich brown in butter or oil, cover sautoir and finish off in the oven. The breastpieces which are more quickly done are taken out first and as soon as the legs are done too arrange chicken in timbale dish or cocotte. Deglace the residue with wine or other liquid and brown gravy or sauce as the case may warrant. If the chicken is to be prepared white it is sautéd in butter without being allowed to discolor and always deglaced with white wine or a white stock etc. and finished off with cream or a white sauce or with both. In both cases the chicken is sautéd first, then covered and cooked in the oven until done and taken out before the sauce is prepared. With rare exceptions it is never simmered in the sauce.

— **Alexandra:** sautéd white, deglaced with white onion sauce and cream, garnished with asparagus tips and truffle slices.

— **Algerian Style:** à l'algérienne: browned, deglaced with wine, diced tomatoes and a little garlic added, garnished with olive-shaped sweet potatoes simmered in butter.

— **Annette:** browned, deglaced with white wine, boiled up with demi-glace, arranged on Anna potatoes mixed with diced artichoke bottoms, covered with the sauce mixed with chopped herbs.

— **Anvers Style:** à l'anversoise: prepared white, deglaced with cream, suprême sauce, hop shoots and julienne of red ox tongue added and poured over chicken.

— **Archduke Style:** à l'archiduc: prepared white with chopped onions, chicken taken out and arranged in timbale dish, pan juice deglaced with brandy, cream and velouté, boiled up, strained, flavored with Madeira and lemon juice and blended with butter, poured over the chicken and garnished with lemon slices.

— **Arlesian Style:** à l'arlésienne: sautéd in oil, deglaced with white wine, demi-glace with tomato, a little crushed garlic added and boiled down, poured over the chicken, garnished with tomatoes concassées, deep fried onion rings and slices of egg plant.

— **Armagnac:** prepared white, deglaced with Armagnac brandy, boiled up with cream and finished off with crayfish butter and lemon juice.

— **Armenonville:** sautéd, deglaced with brandy, boiled up with demi-glace, served with Armenonville garnish.

— **d'Artois:** sautéd, deglaced with Madeira and liquid meat glace, beaten with butter; garnished with glazed button onions, olive-shaped carrots and artichoke bottoms.

— **Bayonne Style:** à la bayonnaise: sautéd, deglaced with Sherry, boiled up with demi-glace and tomato purée, chopped ham added; served with buttered rice.

— **Beaulieu:** sautéd, deglaced with white wine, a little lemon juice and veal gravy, arranged in cocotte with tomatoes concassées, quartered artichoke bottom and potato balls sautéd in butter and black olives, covered with the gravy.

Chicken, Sautéd

— **Belle-Otéro:** prepared white, deglaced with cognac brandy, Port, cream and veal stock, boiled down, cockscombs and cock's kidneys and truffle slices added, poured over the bird, garnished with French fried eggs and tiny chicken croquettes.

— **Bercy:** sautéd in butter and taken out when done, chopped shallots slightly fried in the butter, deglaced with white wine, boiled down, liquid meat glace and lemon juice added, beaten with butter, mixed with sliced pork sausage and mushrooms sautéd in butter, poured over the chicken, chopped parsley scattered on top.

— **Berlin Style:** à la berlinoise: sautéd, deglaced with brandy and white wine, boiled up with demi-glace, garnished with mushrooms, tomatoes concassées and chicken dumplings.

— **Biarritz:** sautéd in oil, deglaced with white wine, boiled up with demi-glace, garnished with glaced button onions, sautéd potato balls, boletus and diced fried egg plants.

— **Boivin:** sautéd with parboiled button onions, quarters of blanched artichoke bottoms and strongly blanched potato balls, covered and finished in oven, arranged in timbale dish, deglaced with chicken broth, boiled down, liquid meat glace added, blended with butter, seasoned with lemon juice and poured over the chicken.

— **with Boletus:** aux cèpes: sautéd, when half done sliced sautéd boletus added, deglaced with Madeira and demi-glace.

— **Bordeaux Style:** sautéd, chopped shallots lightly fried in the butter, deglaced with white wine, boiled up with demi-glace, garnished with slices of raw potatoes sautéd in butter, sliced sautéd boletus and artichoke quarters sautéd in butter and deep fried onions rings.

— **Burgundy Style:** à la bourguignonne: sautéd, deglaced with red wine, boiled up with demi-glace, garnished with glazed button onions, sautéd mushrooms and diced fried bacon, covered with the sauce.

— **Catalonian Style:** à la catalane: sautéd in oil, deglaced with chopped shallots and white wine, diced tomatoes and peppers, crushed garlic, sliced mushrooms and tomato sauce added, poured over the chicken and garnished with glazed button onions, chestnuts and slices of garlic sausage.

— **Cecil Hotel:** sautéd, deglaced with red wine and demi-glace, garnished with sautéd boletus, quartered artichoke bottoms and stuffed tomatoes.

— **with Champagne:** au champagne: sautéd, deglaced with dry champagne and thick veal gravy, raw truffle slices added, cooked and poured over the chicken.

— **Champeaux:** sautéd, deglaced with white wine, veal stock and meat glace, beaten with butter, poured over the chicken, garnished with glazed button onions and olive potatoes.

— **Chantecler:** sautéd, deglaced with champagne and demi-glace, garnished with cockscombs and olive-shaped oast potatoes.

— **Citizen Style:** à la bourgeoise: sautéd, deglaced with white wine and demi-glace, garnished with glaced onions, olive-shaped carrots and fried diced lean bacon.

Chicken, Sautéd

— **Côte d'Azur:** sautéd, deglaced with Madeira and demi-glace, garnished with diced green beans, green peas, diced artichoke bottoms, green asparagus tips and olive potatoes.

— **Delmonico:** prepared white, deglaced with veal velouté seasoned with paprika, garnished with diced boletus, red peppers, artichoke bottoms and sliced truffles.

— **Demidoff:** sautéd, same garnish as for poularde added, finished with truffle crescents and a little veal gravy shortly before serving.

— **Dora:** sautéd, deglaced with brandy and white wine, boiled up with demi-glace, garnished with asparagus tips.

— **Doria:** browned with olive-shaped cucumbers, covered and finished in oven; chicken and cucumbers arranged in timbale dish, pan juice deglaced with lemon juice and veal gravy, poured over the chicken and in the last instance a little browned butter.

— **Durand** (modern way): chicken coated with flour, sautéd in oil and arranged in timbale dish on small slices of fried ham, bordered with tomatoes concassées with chopped shallots and parsley, chicken covered with fried onion rings.

— **Duroc:** same as hunter style with olive potatoes and tomatoes concassées.

— **Duse:** sautéd in oil, deglaced with tomato sauce, garnished with diced artichoke bottoms, dressed in rice border sprinkled with chopped truffles.

— **Egyptian Style:** à l'egyptienne: sautéd in oil with chopped onions, diced ham and mushroom slices, dressed in timbale dish with fried tomato slices on top, deglaced with veal gravy.

— **Embassy Style:** à l'ambassade: prepared white, deglaced with cream and suprême sauce, garnished with diced sautéd gooseliver, truffle slices and buttons mushrooms.

— **Farmer Style:** à la paysanne: sautéd, deglaced with white wine and demi-glace, garnished with green peas, diced green beans and small slices of carrots, turnips and onions simmered in butter.

— **with Fairy Ring Mushrooms:** aux mousserons: sautéd together with the mushrooms and chopped shallots, deglaced with white wine and demi-glace, chopped parsley scattered on top.

— **Fédora:** prepared white with raw truffle slices, deglaced with cream and a little Béchamel sauce, boiled down, blended with crayfish butter and seasoned with Cayenne pepper and lemon juice, garnished with green asparagus tips.

— **with Fine Herbs:** aux fines herbes: sautéd, deglaced with chopped shallots, white wine, veal stock and demi-glace, boiled down, blended with butter, mixed with chopped parsley, chervil and tarragon and poured over the chicken.

— **Forester Style:** à la forestière: browned with chopped shallots, morels cut in pieces or mushrooms, covered and finished in oven, arranged in timbale dish, deglaced with white wine and veal gravy, boiled down and poured over the chicken, garnished with fried triangles of bacon and large diced sautéd potatoes.

— **Frou-Frou:** sautéd, deglaced with Madeira and demi-glace, arranged in cocotte, garnished with truffle slices, quartered artichoke bottoms, olive potatoes and spinach croquettes.

Chicken, Sautéd

— **Gabrielle:** prepared white, deglaced with mushroom stock, a little Béchamel sauce added, boiled down, beaten with butter and poured over the chicken, coarse julienne of truffle scattered on top, surrounded with fleurons.

— **George Sand:** prepared white, deglaced with cream, chicken glaze and crayfish purée, garnished with crayfish tails and truffle slices.

— **Georgina:** prepared white with button onions and a bunch of herbs containing fennel, deglaced with Rhine wine and mushroom stock, sauce reduced with cream, garnished with mushroom caps, chopped tarragon and chervil scattered on top.

— **Gounod:** sautéd, deglaced with brandy and light tomato sauce, sliced mushrooms, artichoke bottoms, truffle and carrots added and poured over the chicken.

— **Grand Hotel:** sautéd, deglaced with brandy, white wine and thick veal gravy, garnished with truffle slices and sautéd potato balls.

— **Hotel Four Seasons:** prepared white with chopped shallots and sliced mushrooms added, deglaced with brandy, cream and chicken stock, reduced, beaten with crayfish butter, seasoned with paprika, crayfish tails and truffle slices added and poured over the chicken.

— **Hotel Knickerbocker:** sautéd, deglaced with white wine and Madeira, reduced, demi-glace added, garnished with diced fried bacon, mushroom caps and cocotte potatoes.

— **Housewife Style:** à la bonne-femme: sautéd, deglaced white wine and thick veal gravy, garnished glazed button onions, cocotte potatoes and diced fried bacon.

— **Hungarian Style:** à la hongroise: sautéd in lard with choppped onions, deglaced with sour cream and veal gravy condimented with paprika, diced tomatos added, cooked and poured over the fowl.

— **Hunter Style:** à la chasseur: chicken sautéd, taken out, sliced mushrooms sautéd in the butter with chopped shallots added, moistened with brandy and white wine, boiled down with demi-glace with tomato, finished off with chopped tarragon and chervil and poured over the chicken.

— **Indian Style:** à l'indienne: sautéd in oil with chopped onions added, sprinkled with curry powder, deglaced with coconut milk and velouté, reduced and poured over the chicken; plain boiled rice served separately.

— **Italian Style:** à l'italienne: sautéd, deglaced with Italian sauce, garnished with quartered artichoke bottoms prepared in the Italian way.

— **Japanese Style:** à la japonaise: sautéd, deglaced with white wine and demi-glace, garnished with stachy sautéd in butter.

— **Josephine:** sautéd, when half done mirepoix bordelaise, chopped lean ham and mushrooms chopped coarsely added, deglaced with cognac and mushroom stock, reduced, thick veal gravy added and beaten with butter, chicken bordered with small boletus sautéd in oil.

— **Judic:** sautéd, deglaced white wine and demi-glace, garnished with truffle slices and braised lettuce.

Chicken, Sautéd

— **Jura Style:** à la jurassienne: sautéd, when nearly done diced blanched and fried bacon added, deglaced with demi-glace, chopped chives added and poured over the chicken.

— **Lathuile:** sautéd together with diced potatoes and artichoke bottoms, garnished with fried onion rings and fried parsley, little liquid meat glace and after that browned butter poured on top.

— **Leopold:** prepared white, deglaced with white wine, chopped shallots and cream, garnished with braised French endives.

— **Lothringian Style:** à la lorraine: sautéd, deglaced with white wine, demi-glace and cream, chopped chives and chervil scattered on top.

— **with Madeira:** au madère: sautéd, deglaced with chopped shallots and Madeira, boiled down with demi-glace.

— **Madeleine:** prepared white, deglaced with cream, suprême sauce and finely diced root vegetables simmered in butter added.

— **Marengo:** sautéd, deglaced with brandy and white wine, reduced, diced tomatoes, garlic, demi-glace, tomato purée, mushroom caps and truffle slices added, boiled up, poured over the chicken, garnished with whole crayfish, French fried eggs and heart-shaped croûtons, chopped parsley scattered on top.

— **Marigny:** browned in butter, diced French beans and green peas added, sautoir covered and chicken and vegetables finished in oven, chicken taken out, pan juice deglaced with veal gravy and poured over chicken when the vegetables are done, bordered with small fondantes potatoes.

— **Marseille Style:** à la marseillaise: sautéd, when half done crushed garlic, shredded green peppers and peeled quartered tomatoes fried in oil beforehand added, deglaced with white wine and a little lemon juice, reduced and poured over the chicken, chopped parsley scattered on top.

— **Mascotte:** sautéd, deglaced white wine demi-glace, Mascott garnished.

— **Masséna:** sautéd, deglaced white wine and truffle sauce. garnished with diced artichoke bottoms and sliced blanched ox marrow.

— **Mathilde:** sautéd with chopped onions, cucumbers shaped like large olives added, when done arranged in timbale dish, deglaced with cognac brandy and suprême sauce and poured over the chicken.

— **Mazarin:** sautéd, deglaced with Madeira and demi-glace, garnished with olive-shaped carrots, knob celery, glazed button onions and truffle slices.

— **Mexican Style:** à la mexicaine: sautéd in oil, deglaced with white wine and thick veal gravy with tomato purée, garnished with grilled red or green peppers and large grilled mushroom caps filled with tomatoes concassées.

— **Mireille:** sautéd, dressed on Mireille potatoes, deglaced with very little veal gravy, poured over the chicken and after that a little browned butter.

— **Monselet:** sautéd, deglaced with Sherry and demi-glace with sliced artichoke bottoms and truffles added.

Chicken, Sautéd

— **Montmorency:** sautéd, deglaced with Madeira and demi-glace, garnished with quartered artichoke bottoms sautéd in butter and green asparagus tips.

— **with Morels:** aux morilles: sautéd, when nearly done morels simmered in butter beforehand added, deglaced with brandy, morel stock and meat glaze, reduced, beaten with butter and poured over the fowl.

— **Mother-in-law Style:** belle-mère: sautéd, deglaced with Madeira and demi-glace, garnished with diced fried salt pork, green peas, sautéd potato balls, glaced button onions and diced artichoke bottoms.

— **with Mushrooms:** aux champignons: sautéd, when nearly done chopped shallots and sliced raw mushrooms or small mushrooms caps added, deglaced with Madeira and demi-glace, chopped parsley scattered on top.

— **Nice Style:** à la nicoise: sautéd in oil, deglaced with white wine and demi-glace with tomato; Nice garnish.

— **Nimrod:** sautéd, deglaced with white wine and demi-glace with chopped shallots and diced tomatoes, garnished with sautéd mushrooms.

— **Old Fashioned Style:** à l'ancienne: sautéd white, deglaced with chicken velouté, garnished with button onions and mushrooms.

— **Orléans Style:** à la orléanaise: sautéd, deglaced with red wine and veal stock, boiled down, blended with butter, garnished with glazed button onions and fluted mushrooms.

— **with Oysters:** aux huîtres: prepared white, deglaced with white wine and oyster liquor, boiled up with veal velouté, garnished with poached oysters.

— **Palestrina:** prepared white, deglaced with Sherry and cream, boiled down and mixed with sliced mushrooms and shredded lettuce simmered in butter; risotto mixed with truffle and mushroom julienne served separately.

— **Parmentier:** sautéd with olive-shaped potatoes slightly browned in butter added, deglaced with white wine and veal gravy, reduced and poured over the chicken, chopped parsley scattered in top.

— **Portuguese Style:** à la portugaise: sautéd in oil, chopped onions lightly browned in the oil, diced tomatoes, sliced mushrooms a little white wine and chopped parsley added, cooked and poured over the fowl.

— **Provencal Style:** à la provençale: sautéd in oil, deglaced with white wine and Provencal sauce, garnished with blanched black olives.

— **Ritz:** sautéd, deglaced with white wine and demi-glace, garnished with olive potatoes, boletus, mushrooms and artichoke bottom filled with tomatoes concassées, chopped parsley scattered on top.

— **Rivoli:** sautéd, deglaced with Sherry, demi-glace and tomato purée, dressed on Anna potatoes mixed with chopped truffles.

— **Rostand:** sautéd, deglaced with brandy and thick veal gravy with tomato purée, half moon-shaped slices of carrots, turnips and celery, truffle slices and morels added.

— **Roumanian Style:** à la roumaine: sautéd with chopped onions and diced egg plant, deglaced with plum gin and white wine, diced tomatoes, garlic, strips of green peppers

Chicken, Sautéd
and tomato sauce added, cooked and poured over the chicken.
— **with Samos:** au Samos: sautéd with diced tomatoes, deglaced with Samos wine and thick veal gravy, seeded and peeled grapes added.
— **Spanish Style:** browned in oil, rice pilaf, mixed with diced red peppers, parboiled green peas and sliced garlic sausage, added, finished in oven and served in cocotte.
— **with Spring Vegetables:** aux primeurs: sautéd, deglaced with white wine and demi-glace, garnished with spring vegetables.
— **Stanley:** prepared white with chopped onions, deglaced with chicken stock, cream and curry powder, strained, mixed with truffle slices, poured over the chicken, garnished with mushroom caps.
— **with Tarragon:** à l'estragon: sautéd, deglaced with white wine, boiled up with brown tarragon sauce, poured over the chicken, sprinkled with chopped tarragon.
— **Tenants Style:** à la fermière: sautéd, Tenants garnish added, deglaced with thick veal gravy, served in cocotte.
— **with Truffles:** aux truffes: sautéd, when half done sliced raw truffles added, cooked covered and dressed in timbale dish, deglaced with Madeira and a little demi-glace, boiled down, buttered and poured over the chicken.
— **Turbigo:** sautéd, deglaced with white wine, demi-glace and tomato purée garnished with tiny fried pork sausages and sautéd mushrooms.
— **Turenne:** sautéd, deglaced with Madeira and demi-glace, garnished with truffle slices and diced sautéd potatoes.
— **Van Dyck:** prepared white, deglaced with cream, suprême sauce and blanched hop shoots added.
— **Vendé Style:** à la vendéenne: prepared white with button onions, deglaced with white wine, reduced, velouté added, buttered, mixed with chopped parsley and poured over the chicken.
— **Verdi:** sautéd, deglaced with Asti wine and demi-glace, arranged on rice prepared in the Piedmont way, garnished with truffles slice and sliced sautéd gooseliver.
— **Wissmann:** sautéd, deglaced with white wine, curry powder and velouté, mixed with finely diced root vegetables simmered in butter, garnished with mushrooms, button onions and pitted olives, sauce poured over; plain boiled rice served separately.

Chicken, Spring, Young Chicken: Poulet de grain: young chickens, also called broilers, from 1,½ to 2,½ lbs, chiefly prepared en casserole or cocotte, grilled or roasted.
— **Belle-Meunière:** stuffed with sliced chicken livers and coarsely chopped mushrooms sautéd in butter, a few slices of truffle placed between the skin and the flesh, browned in butter, placed in a cocotte with butter, blanched triangles of lean bacon and quartered mushrooms sautéd in butter, roasted with lid on, when done a few drops of veal gravy poured over the chicken.
— **in Casserole:** Poulet en casserole: roasted in earthen or china fireproof casserole basting frequently, a little veal gravy poured over at serving; no garnish
— **in Cocotte:** Poulet en cocotte: roasted in fireproof cocotte, when half done olive-shaped, half fried potatoes, diced

Chicken, Spring
fried bacon and glazed onions added, a little veal gravy poured over at serving.
— **in Cocotte Bazar:** simmered in cocotte with diced artichoke bottoms, fried diced bacon, sliced boletus, small sautéd potato balls and diced tomatoes.
— **in Cocotte Housewife Style:** en cocotte bonne-femme: roasted in cocotte, placed on sliced potatoes sautéd in the roasting butter, surrounded with blanched and fried triangles of bacon, a little veal gravy poured over the chicken.
— **Compote of:** en compote: browned in cocotte, taken out, deglaced with white wine and mushroom stock, boiled down, demi-glace added, chicken replaced in cocotte with blanched diced bacon, button onions and mushroom caps sautéd in butter and simmered in oven until done.
— **Hotelier Style:** à l'hôtelière: boned, stuffed with pork sausage meat, roasted in cocotte with sliced mushrooms added, a little veal gravy poured over at the last minute.
— **Judic:** roasted, placed in cocotte, garnished with braised lettuce, cocks' kidneys and truffle slices, Madeira sauce poured over.
— **Katoff:** prepared like grilled chicken, placed on round baked cake of duchess potato-mixture, bordered with veal gravy; buttered meat glaze served separately.
— **Limoux Style:** à la limousine: stuffed with pork sausage meat mixed with chopped mushrooms, roasted in fireproof china cocotte, finished off with triangles of lean bacon and glazed chestnuts, a little veal gravy added at the last minute.
— **Mascotte:** browned in fireproof china casserole, artichoke bottoms cut in large dice and olive-shaped potatoes, both sautéd in butter beforehand, added, cooked in oven, finished off with truffle slices and a little veal gravy.
— **Mireille:** split at the back, backbone chopped off, opened, flattened, fried in butter, when half done, placed on Anna potatoes mixed with sliced raw artichoke bottoms baked in an earthenware dish of suitable size and nearly done, melted butter poured over and finished off in oven.
— **with Morels:** aux morilles: prepared in casserole, when half done morels lightly sautéd in butter and a few drops of veal gravy added, lid put on casserole and finished off in oven.
— **Rouzier:** disjointed, backbone chopped off, slightly sautéd in butter, when cold placed in fireproof cocotte with raw truffle slices, a little Burgundy, veal gravy and seasoning added, **covered with puff pastry,** decorated with dough with a funnel in the center, brushed with egg yolk and baked in oven.
— **Toad Style:** à la crapaudine: prepared like grilled chicken, but brushed with melted butter and dipped in breadcrumbs beforehand; sharp sauce such as devil sauce served separately.

Chicken, Squab, Baby Chicken: Poussin: tender young chicklets weighing about $^3/_4$ lb.
— **Barigoule:** boned, stuffed with chicken forcemeat mixed with diced truffles and ox tongue, braised, placed in

Chicken, Squab
round earthenware cocotte on artichoke bottoms stuffed with duxelles and braised in white wine; clear veal gravy poured around.

— **Cinderella:** Cendrillon: split open, flattened, seasoned, only heated in butter on both sides, wrapped in pig caul between two layers of truffled veal forcemeat, dipped in melted butter and breadcrumbs, grilled; truffle sauce served separately.

— **Gourmet:** prepared like grilled chicken, arranged on Anna potatoes, garnished with sliced pickled cucumbers; Chateaubriand sauce mixed with sliced mushrooms served separately.

— **Grandmother Style:** à la grand'mère: prepared like chicken in cocotte.

— **Hamburg Style:** à la hambourgeoise: boned, stuffed with veal forcemeat, roasted in fireproof china casserole, garnished with diced artichoke bottoms, diced roasted potatoes and sliced truffle, a little veal gravy poured over.

— **Jacques:** stuffed with forcemeat of duck livers, chopped shallots, mushrooms, soaked bread, chopped parsley and seasoning, browned on all sides, placed in cocotte with a little veal gravy and Madeira, closed hermetically and cooked in oven.

— **Piedmont Style:** à la piémontaise: stuffed with white Italian truffles pounded together with fresh fat bacon, trussed, roasted, served on risotto mixed with sliced Italian truffles and grated Parmesan, browned butter poured over the squab.

— **Polish Style:** à la polonaise: stuffed with gratin forcemeat mixed with soaked bread, butter and chopped parsley, roasted, served in cocotte with a few drops of lemon juice and breadcrumbs fried in plenty of butter poured over.

— **Richelieu:** split in the back, opened, flattened, dipped in egg and breadcrumbs, fried in butter, covered with half-melted herb butter and a line of truffle slices on top.

— **Tartar Style:** à la tartare: split in half, flattened, brushed with mustard, dipped in breadcrumbs, grilled; tartar sauce served separately.

— **Usuroff:** browned on all sides in butter, placed in cocotte with shredded celery, truffle strips, melted butter, a little meat glaze and veal gravy, cocotte closed hermetically, finished off in oven.

— **Villani:** stuffed with a small piece of gooseliver dusted with paprika, roasted, deglaced with Tokay, veal gravy and thick cream, boiled down, seasoned with paprika and poured over the squab.

Chicken, Supreme of: Suprême de volaille: for suprêmes or fillets of chicken only the raw breast of spring chicken or capons with the upper joint of the wing left on are used. They may be prepared brown or white. In the first case they must be seasoned, coated with flour, placed in a sautoir with hot clarified butter and quickly browned on both sides and served at once otherwise they will be dry and tasteless.
If they are to be prepared white (poached), they are placed in a sautoir with melted but not hot butter, turned in the butter, seasoned, a little lemon juice is dropped on

Chicken, Supreme of

top, the lid put on and placed in a hot oven; a few minutes are sufficient to cook them.

Suprêmes may also be dipped in egg and breadcrumbs and fried in clarified butter.

— **Agnes Sorel:** poached in lemon juice and butter, placed on tartlet of chicken mousseline forcemeat stuffed with sliced sautéd mushrooms, covered with suprême sauce, decorated with a ring of ox tongue, a round truffle slice in the center.

— **Albuféra:** cut in shape of a heart, stuffed with chicken mousseline forcemeat, poached, placed on tartlet filled with Albuféra garnish, covered with Albuféra sauce.

— **Alexandra:** poached lightly, a few truffle slices placed on top, covered with Mornay sauce with chicken essence, glazed, garnished with asparagus tips.

— **Ambassadress Style:** à l'ambassadrice: poached, garnish and sauce as for poularde.

— **Andalusian Style:** à l'andalouse stuffed with chicken mousseline forcemeat, poached, covered with suprême sauce mixed with diced red peppers simmered in butter.

— **Archduke Style:** à l'archiduc: poached, dressed on croûton, truffle slices placed on top, covered with archduke sauce.

— **Arlesian Style:** à l'arlesienne: fried, garnished with sliced egg plant fried in oil, fried onion rings and tomatoes concassées prepared in oil; demi-glace with tomato served separately.

— **Belleclaire:** poached, covered with suprême sauce seasoned with curry powder and mixed with julienne of mushrooms and shredded red peppers simmered in butter.

— **Belle-Hélène:** sautéd in butter. dressed on flat asparagus croquette, a slice of truffle placed on top, covered with browned butter; thick veal gravy served separately.

— **Bellevue** (cold): poached, when cold coated with chicken chaudfroid sauce, decorated to taste, glazed with aspic jelly, garnished with aspic jelly.

— **Berlin Style:** à la berlinoise: poached, garnished with crayfish tails, small veal dumplings, mushrooms, morels and slices of calf's sweetbread, covered with suprême sauce, capers scattered and crayfish butter dropped on top.

— **Carmen:** poached, dressed on croûton on a slice of ox tongue, covered with cream sauce blended with tomato purée, garnished with tartlets filled with green asparagus tips and grilled red peppers.

— **Clementine:** poached, placed on chicken mousseline forcemeat poached in a tartlet mould, covered with suprême sauce, garnished with creamed salsify.

— **Countess Style:** à la comtesse: poached, covered with suprême sauce mixed with chopped truffles, garnished with small puff pastry patties filled with asparagus tips.

— **in Cream Sauce:** à la crème: fried in butter, deglaced with brandy and cream, boiled down, cream sauce added and poured over the suprême.

— **Cumberland:** dipped in light frying batter, fried in deep fat; Cumberland sauce served separately.

— **Cussy:** sautéd in butter, dressed on artichoke bottom, a slice of truffle and a cockscomb on top; thick chicken gravy served separately.

Chicken, Supreme of

— **Doria:** dipped in egg and breadcrumbs, fried in butter, garnished with olive-shaped cucumbers simmered in butter, lemon juice and browned butter poured on top.

— **Dreux Style:** larded with truffle and ox tongue, poached, garnished with cockscombs and cocks' kidneys and sliced truffles, covered with German or suprême sauce.

— **Financier Style:** à la financière: poached, placed on croûton, served with financier garnish and sauce.

— **Florence Style:** à la florentine: poached lightly, placed on spinach leaves tossed in butter, covered with Mornay sauce and glazed rapidly.

— **Grandduke Style:** à la grandduc: poached, a large truffle slice placed on top, covered with Mornay sauce blended with crayfish butter, glazed, garnished with green asparagus tips and crayfish tails.

— **Imperial Style:** à l'impériale: stuffed with chicken forcemeat, poached, dressed on border of risotto filled with financier garnish, covered with suprême sauce, garnished with tartlets filled with asparagus tips.

— **Indian Style:** à l'indienne: poached lightly, placed for a few minutes in Indian sauce without allowing the sauce to boil, arranged in timbale dish covered with the sauce; plain boiled rice served separately.

— **Irma:** fried in butter, placed on flat potato croquette, garnished with asparagus tips mixed with truffle strips tossed in butter; thick veal gravy served separately.

— **Italian Style:** à l'italienne: fried in clarified butter, covered with Italian sauce; artichokes prepared in the Italian way served separately.

— **Japanese Style:** à la japonaise: sautéd in butter, dressed on shaped rice, garnished with tartlets filled with creamed stachy; thick veal gravy served separately.

— **Jeanette** (cold): poached, when cold coated with chicken chaudfroid sauce, decorated with blanched tarragon leaves, dressed on oval slices of gooseliver parfait in oval silver dish or plat russe, covered entirely with half-set chicken aspic jelly, served well chilled.

— **Judic:** sautéd, placed on halved braised lettuce, a truffle slice and a cockscomb on each suprême, covered with thick veal gravy.

— **Jules Verne:** stuffed with gooseliver forcemeat, poached in butter and lemon juice, placed on ring of puff pastry filled with financier garnish, covered with Wladimir sauce and a slice of truffle on top.

— **Kiew Style:** à la kiewoise: cut open lengthwise, stuffed with a piece of chilled butter, dipped in egg and breadcrumbs, fried in butter, placed on a croûton, garnished with vegetable macedoine tossed in butter and straw potatoes.

— **Maria Theresia:** Marie Thérèse: poached, arranged on rice pilaf, covered with suprême sauce mixed with diced ox tongue.

— **Marie Louise:** dipped in egg and breadcrumbs, fried in butter, placed on artichoke bottom filled with mushroom purée blended with white onion purée, covered with browned butter.

— **Marquise Style:** poached, placed on tartlet filled with ragoût of green asparagus tips, truffle slices and diced blanched calf's marrow bound with German sauce blended

Chicken, Supreme of
with crayfish butter, covered with suprême sauce, garnished with marquise potatoes.
— **Marshall Style:** à la maréchale: dipped in egg and white breadcrumbs mixed with chopped truffles, fried in butter, a slice of truffle coated with liquid meat glace on each suprême, garnished with green asparagus tips tossed in butter.
— **Moïna:** fried in butter, placed on artichoke bottom filled with chopped morels simmered in butter, covered with demi-glace flavored with Port.
— **Montpensier:** dipped in egg and bread crumbs, fried in butter, a slice of truffle on top, covered with browned butter, garnished with asparagus tips tossed in butter.
— **My Dream:** mon rêve: fried in butter, placed on half a peeled and scooped out apple, poached carefully and filled with banana purée, covered with pepper sauce.
— **Orly:** marinated in oil and lemon juice chopped shallots and parsley, dipped in frying batter, fried in deep fat; garnished with fried parsley; tomato sauce served separately.
— **with Paprika:** au paprika: fried in butter, covered with cream sauce seasoned with paprika; noodles or rice served separately.
— **Parisian Style:** à la parisienne: poached, covered with German sauce, decorated with crescents of truffle and ox tongue coated with liquid glace, garnished with chicken forcemeat dumplings mixed with chopped truffle and ox tongue.
— **Patti:** stuffed with chicken and gooseliver forcemeat, poached, covered suprême sauce with paprika, garnished with artichoke bottoms filled with glazed truffle balls.
— **Polignac:** poached, covered with suprême sauce mixed with julienne of mushrooms and truffle.
— **with Port:** au porto: fried in butter covered with thick veal gravy flavored with Port.
— **Princess Style:** poached, garnished as for poularde.
— **Princess Chimay:** fried in butter, garnished with sautéd morels and asparagus tips, bordered with thick veal gravy.
— **Provencal Style:** à la provençale: prepared like sautéd chicken.
— **Providence:** larded with truffle, coated with chicken forcemeat, poached, covered with suprême sauce, garnished with cockscombs, mushroom caps, truffle olives and small chicken dumplings.
— **Regency Style:** à la régence: poached, served with regency garnish and sauce.
— **Richelieu:** dipped in egg and breadcrumbs, fried in butter, truffle slices coated with liquid meat glaze placed on top; herb butter served separately.
— **Rimini:** larded with truffle, poached, dressed on pastry boat filled with mushroom purée; German sauce served separately.
— **Rixensart:** fried in butter, garnished with tartlets filled with creamed hop shoots and potatoes, shaped like large artichoke bottoms, fried in butter and filled with coarsely chopped morels simmered in butter; Colbert sauce served separately.

Chicken, Supreme of

— **Rossini:** fried in butter, placed on gooseliver slice sautéd in butter, covered with Madeira sauce mixed with sliced truffles.

— **Saint-Germain:** fried in butter, Béarnaise sauce and purée of green peas served separately.

— **Scarlet:** à l'écarlate: larded with red ox tongue, poached, placed on flat chicken forcemeat dumpling, covered with suprême sauce, chopped red ox tongue scattered on top.

— **Tsarina:** à la tsarine: poached, covered with supême sauce mixed with coarse julienne of fennel, garnished with olive-shaped cucumber simmered in sour cream.

— **Valois:** dipped in egg and breadcrumbs, fried in butter, garnished with stuffed olives; Valois sauce served separately.

— **Verneuil:** marinated as for Orly, dipped in egg and breadcrumbs, fried in butter, covered with Colbert sauce; artichoke purée served separately.

— **Villeroi:** poached lightly, when cold coated with Villeroi sauce, dipped in egg and breadcrumbs, fried rapidly in deep fat; truffle sauce served separately.

Chicken Wings: Ailerons de volaille: wing tips of large poultry such as poulardes or capons, usually boned and stuffed.

— **Butcher Style:** à la charcutière: tender wings stuffed with pork sausage meat, wrapped in pig's caul, dipped in egg and breadcrumbs and grilled slowly.

— **Chipolata:** braised in light demi-glace served with Chipolata garnish.

— **Risotto of:** Risotto d'ailerons: boned, stuffed with truffled pork forcemeat, simmered in white wine and veal stock, cut in thick slices and bound with the boiled down stock blended with cream and thickened with arrow-root, arranged in the center of a border of risotto.

— **d'Uzès:** boned, stuffed with truffled pork forcemeat, simmered in light Madeira sauce, garnished with truffle slices and cocks' kidneys.

Poularde: the flesh of these fattened chickens must be white, firm and tender. They are excellent for roasting, braising and poaching especially the poulardes of Le Mans, Bresse and Houdans in France, of Brussels and Styria.

— **Albuféra:** stuffed with rice pilaf mixed with diced gooseliver and truffles, poached, covered with Albuféra sauce, garnished with tartlets filled with mushrooms, cockscombs and truffle pearls bound with Albuféra sauce, a slice of ox tongue cut like a cockscomb between each pair of tartlets.

— **Alexandra:** studded with ox tongue and truffle, poached, breast with backbone cut out, carcass stuffed dome-shape with chicken mousseline forcemeat and steamed, the carved breast replaced on top, covered with Mornay sauce, glazed, garnished with tartlets filled with buttered asparagus tips, a small breast slice on top, bordered with liquid meat glaze.

— **Ambassadress Style:** à l'ambassadrice: studded with truffles, breast covered with thin slices of vegetables simmered in butter, bird wrapped in a cloth, braised white, unwrapped, breast cut out with breastbone, carcass filled with buttered asparagus tips, breast carved and

Poularde

replaced on top, covered with thick suprême sauce, garnished with lamb sweetbreads studded with truffles and green asparagus tips.

— **American Style:** à l'américaine: stuffed with breadcrumb stuffing mixed with chopped steamed onions, chopped sage and parsley, roasted, garnished with fried slices of lean bacon; pan gravy.

— **Amphytrion:** stuffed with mixture of soaked bread, pork sausage meat, crushed braised chestnuts and chopped truffles, braised, garnished with stuffed mushrooms and stuffed tomatoes; Madeira sauce.

— **Andalusian Style:** à l'andalouse: poached, covered with supreme sauce finished off with pimiento butter, garnished with red peppers stuffed with rice, sliced sautéd eggplants and slices of Spanish garlic sausage (chorizos).

— **Argenteuil:** poached, covered with suprême sauce finished off with green asparagus butter, garnished with asparagus tips.

— **d'Aumale:** studded with truffles, stuffed with chicken mousseline forcemeat, braised, garnished with tartlets filled with creamed cucumber pearls and small onions stuffed with hashed ox tongue and gooseliver bound with thick demi-glace; the boiled down gravy blended with butter served separately.

— **Aurora:** à l'aurore: stuffed with veal forcemeat mixed with thick fresh tomato purée, poached, covered with aurora sauce.

— **Banker Style:** à la banquière: stuffed with chicken mousseline forcemeat mixed with diced gooseliver, pan-roasted (poêler), deglaced with truffle essence blended with chicken glaze and improved with butter, garnished with tartlets filled with salpicon of gooseliver and truffles, a stuffed lark and two tiny chicken dumplings on top.

— **Bresse Style:** à la bressanne: stuffed with risotto mixed with diced sautéd chicken livers, roasted, Madeira sauce.

— **Bride Style:** à la petite-mariée: poached in rich white stock, placed in fireproof casserole, garnished with young carrots, button onions and small new potatoes cooked in butter and freshly cooked green peas, covered with the boiled down stock blended with a little suprême sauce.

— **Californian Style:** à la californienne: stuffed with bread, soaked in milk, mixed with chopped onions, chicken livers and diced lean bacon sautéd in butter, chopped parsley and seasoning, roasted, served with the pan gravy.

— **Cardinal Style:** à la cardinale: stuffed with chicken forcemeat blended with lobster butter, mixed with diced lobster and truffles, poached, garnished with lobster and truffle slices, covered with suprême sauce blended with lobster butter.

— **Cavour:** larded with fat bacon and truffles, braised white, covered with suprême sauce; buttered noodles mixed with grated Parmesan served separately.

— **Chancelor Style:** à la chancelière: larded with fat bacon and truffles, poached covered with suprême sauce, breast decorated with truffle slices, garnished with truffled chicken mousseline dumplings.

Poularde

— **Chantilly:** stuffed with pilaf rice mixed with diced gooseliver and truffles, poached, covered with Chantilly sauce blended with a little chicken glace, garnished with chicken forcemeat dumplings.

— **Chatelaine:** pan-roasted, deglaced with white wine and veal gravy, served with Chatelaine garnish.

— **Chevalière:** breast cut out, larded with ox tongue and truffles, legs boned and stuffed with veal forcemeat, both poached, legs arranged on oval dish with ragoût of button mushrooms, cockscombs and cocks' kidneys, bound with suprême sauce, between them, breast placed on top and covered with suprême sauce.

— **Chimay:** stuffed with noodles sautéd in butter and mixed with diced gooseliver patty, pan-roasted, covered with a little pan gravy thickened with arrowroot, raw noodles browned in clarified butter scattered on top; thickened pan gravy served separately.

— **Chipolata:** pan-roasted and served with Chipolata garnish.

— **Chivry:** poached, covered with Chivry sauce, garnished with creamed or buttered vegetable macedoine.

— **Claridge Hotel:** filled with bread stuffing mixed with diced sautéd boletus and truffles, roasted, deglaced with white wine and thick veal gravy.

— **with Coarse Salt:** au gros sel: poached in rich white stock with fancy shaped carrots and button onions, garnished with carrots and onions; a sauceboat with stock and coarse salt served separately.

— **Crown Prince Style:** à la dauphine: larded, roasted, garnished with chicken croquettes and olive-shaped truffles; pan gravy.

— **Demidoff:** roast poularde in casserole until three quarters done, add carrots and turnips cut in small crescents, small sliced onions and diced celery, simmered in butter beforehand, put lid on casserole and finish cooking in oven with crescent-shaped truffle slices and boiled down chicken stock added at the last minute; serve in the fireproof casserole.

— **Derby:** stuffed with rice pilaf with diced gooseliver and truffles added, roasted in closed fireproof china casserole, garnished with truffles cooked in champagne and gooseliver collops sautéd in butter; the pan gravy deglaced with truffle stock and veal gravy, thickened with arrowroot served separately.

— **Diva:** stuffed with rice, diced gooseliver and truffles added, poached, covered with suprême sauce with paprika, garnished with sliced creamed boletus.

— **Doria:** poached, covered with suprême sauce finished off with cucumber purée, garnished with cucumber balls simmered in butter.

— **Dreux Style:** à la Dreux: larded with truffles and ox tongue, poached, covered with German sauce, breast decorated with truffle slices, garnished with chicken dumplings and bouquets of cockscombs and cocks' kidneys.

— **Edward VII.:** Edouard VII.: stuffed as for Diva, poached, covered with suprême sauce seasoned with curry powder, diced red peppers added; creamed cucumber balls served separately.

Poularde

— **Elysée Palace:** studded with truffles, stuffed with mousseline chicken forcemeat mixed with gooseliver purée, poached, garnished with regency garnish, served with supreme sauce.

— **Emile Bernard:** stuffed with morels, braised with diced fried bacon, diced root vegetables and mushrooms added, deglaced with brandy, boiled down with Sauternes wine, tomato sauce and demi-glace, finished off with chopped truffles.

— **Empress Style:** à l'imperatrice: poached, covered with supreme sauce blended with chicken purée, garnished with braised lamb sweetbreads, sliced poached calf's brains and button onions cooked in chicken stock.

— **End of Century:** Fin de siecle: roasted, garnished with olive-shaped cucumbers, celery knobs and potatoes, all simmered in butter, small stuffed onions, sliced sautéd boletus, fried tomatoes and fried eggplant slices; Madeira sauce.

— **English Style:** à l'anglaise: poached, covered with supreme sauce, surrounded with sliced ox tongue, garnished with olive-shaped carrots and turnips, green peas and braised celery.

— **Escoffier:** poached, covered with suprême sauce, garnished with morels, mushrooms, truffles and chicken dumplings.

— **Escurial:** stuffed with rice pilaff mixed with diced ham and mushrooms, roasted in casserole with lid on, deglaced with demi-glace and white wine, garnished with stuffed Spanish olives and French fried eggs.

— **Eugen Lacroix** (cold): roasted, when cold breast and breastbone cut out, breast carved in oblique slices, each slice placed on small pastry boat filled with ham froth and glazed with Madeira jelly; cavity of bird filled like a cupola with gooseliver patty froth mixed with grilled powdered hazelnuts, decorated entirely with thin apple slices of equal size poached in white wine, glazed with Madeira jelly, garnished alternately with the pastry boats and truffles en surprise.

— **Favorite Style:** à la favorite: stuffed with chicken forcemeat mixed with truffled gooseliver, poached, covered with suprême sauce, garnished with cockscombs, cocks' kidneys and truffle slices.

— **Fédora:** poached, covered with suprême sauce finished off with crayfish butter, garnished with asparagus tips.

— **Flemish Style:** à la flamande: prepared as described for goose.

— **Florida:** roasted, garnished with fried tomatoes, fried sliced bananas and peaches, covered with the pan gravy boiled up with thick veal gravy.

— **Florist Style:** à la bouquetière: poached, covered with suprême sauce blended with reduced mushroom stock, florist garnish.

— **Gastronomer Style:** à la gastronome: stuffed with lightly sautéd morels, roasted with lid on, deglaced with champagne, garnished with small truffles and glazed chestnuts, a cocks' kidney placed between the two; demi-glace finished off with the deglacage served separately.

— **Godard:** braised, served with Godard garnish and Godard sauce.

Poularde

— **Greek Style:** à la grecque: stuffed with Greek rice, braised, covered with tomato sauce with the boiled down braising stock.

— **Half-Mourning:** à la demi-deuil: sliced truffles placed between the skin and the flesh, stuffed with chicken mousseline forcemeat with truffle purée added, poached, covered with suprême sauce mixed with sliced truffles.

— **Hungarian Style:** à la hongroise: roasted in closed casserole, covered with Hungarian sauce, garnished with shaped rice pilaff mixed with diced tomatoes.

— **Italian Style:** à l'italienne: stuffed with risotto mixed with sautéd chicken livers, garnished with artichoke bottoms prepared in the Italian way, covered with Italian sauce.

— **in Ivory Sauce:** à la sauce ivoire: poached, covered with ivory sauce, garnished to taste.

— **Jellied:** en gelée (cold): poached, cooled off in the stock, coated with white chicken chaufroid sauce, decorated with hard-boiled egg white and truffle, glazed with chicken aspic jelly, garnished with small moulds of tomato froth in jelly.

— **Lady Curzon:** stuffed as for Diva, poached, covered with suprême sauce flavored with curry powder; creamed cucumbers or boletus served separately.

— **Lambertye** (cold): poached, when cold breasts and breastbone cut out, carcass stuffed with chicken froth mixed with gooseliver purée, breasts carved in oblique slices, coated with white chaudfroid sauce, garnished with truffle and replaced into position, glazed with aspic jelly, garnished with aspic jelly.

— **Languedoc Style:** à la languedocienne: roasted in closed casserole, served with Languedoc garnish.

— **Leghorn Style:** à la livournaise: braised, garnished with fried diced bacon, sliced sautéd boletus, button mushrooms and glazed button onions, covered with the thickened stock.

— **Leo XIII.:** Leon XIII.: stuffed with risotto mixed with sliced mushrooms, sliced white Italian truffles and Parmesan, colored with saffron, braised, served with the thickened braising stock mixed with slices of Italian truffles.

— **Lothringian Style:** à la lorraine: stuffed with veal forcemeat with chopped herbs, poached, covered with cream sauce mixed with chopped fine herbs.

— **Louise of Orleans:** Louise d'Orléans: stuffed with a small whole gooseliver studded with truffles and poached for 20 minutes,, browned quickly in oven, breast covered with truffle slices, first wrapped in thin slices of fat bacon and then entirely in pie dough, a small funnel left open in center, baked in oven, served hot or cold.

— **Louisiana Style:** à la Louisiane: stuffed with creamed corn mixed with diced red peppers, roasted, garnished with shaped rice, fried bananas and tartlets filled with creamed corn; pan gravy.

— **Lucas:** stuffed with veal forcemeat mixed with chopped herbs, roasted, garnished with stuffed braised lettuce, stuffed onions, pitted olives, potato croquettes and diced sautéd knob celery; pan gravy.

Poularde

— **Lucullus:** stuffed with chicken mousseline forcemeat mixed with raw gooseliver purée, braised, garnished with truffles cooked in champagne and cockscombs; demi-glace with truffle essence and the reduced braising stock served separately.

— **Lucy:** stuffed with risotto mixed with diced red peppers and green peas, braised in chicken stock and Tokay wine, stock boiled down, seasoned with paprika, finished off with thick cream and poured over the poularde, garnished with artichoke bottoms filled with braised hashed celery bound with demi-glace and grilled sweet peppers.

— **Maintenon:** larded with ox tongue and truffles, braised white, covered with suprême sauce, garnished with fluted mushroom caps, chicken dumplings and artichoke bottoms filled with a large truffle slice, coated with Mornay sauce and glazed.

— **May Rose:** Rose de mai (cold): poached, when cold skinned, breast and breastbone cut out, breast carved, coated with white chaudfroid sauce, decorated with truffle, glazed and placed on pastry boats filled with tomato froth; carcass with legs coated with white chaud-froid sauce, cavity filled with tomato froth, decorated with hard-boiled egg white and truffle, glazed with aspic jelly, garnished with the pastry boats.

— **Metropole:** poached, covered with suprême sauce, garnished with quartered artichoke bottom sautéd in butter, mushrooms and button onions cooked in chicken stock, bordered with heart-shaped croûtons fried in butter.

— **Milton:** stuffed with veal forcemeat mixed with diced gooseliver, poached, garnished with cockscombs, cocks' kidneys and button mushroom caps bound with suprême sauce; suprême sauce served separately.

— **Moïna:** prepared in casserole with morels and quartered artichoke bottoms, deglaced with champagne and thick veal gravy.

— **Monte Carlo:** poached, covered lengthwise on one side with suprême and the other side wit aurora sauce; the white side garnished with chicken dumplings with tomato purée, the pink side with ordinary chicken dumplings.

— **Montmorency:** larded with truffles, braised in demi-glace and Madeira, covered with the sauce, Montmorency garnish.

— **Nantua:** poached, covered with suprême sauce, finished off with crayfish coulis, truffle slices placed on the breast, garnished with crayfish tails and chicken dumplings blended with crayfish butter.

— **Neva Style:** à la Néva (cold): poached, when cold breast and breastbone cut out, skinned, carcass filled with gooseliver froth, breast carved and replaced into position, coated with white chicken chaudfroid sauce, decorated with truffle, glazed with aspic jelly, garnished with Russian salad bound with jellied mayonnaise, filled in small moulds lined with aspic jelly and tourned out.

— **Nice Style:** à la nicoise: braised, covered with the thickened stock, Nice garnish with pitted black olives instead of potatoes.

— **with Olives:** aux olives (cold): roasted, when cold, breast and breastbone cut out, carcass stuffed with chicken froth

Poularde

mixed with chopped Spanish olives, breast carved in thin slices, replaced in position, decorated with olive slices, glazed with aspic jelly, garnished with quarters of peeled and scooped out tomatoes filled with the same stuffing as for the poularde, a slice of roast poularde decorated with an olive slice on top and glazed with aspic jelly, and large stuffed Spanish olives.

— **Oriental Style:** à l'orientale: stuffed with saffron rice, poached, covered with suprême sauce flavored with curry powder, garnished with fancy-shaped Bryonis simmered in butter.

— **Orlow:** poached, covered with suprême sauce blended with white onion purée, truffle slices placed on breast, garnished with braised lettuce.

— **with Oysters:** aux huitred: poached, covered with suprême sauce mixed with the oyster liquor, poached oysters in the sauce.

— **Paramé:** barded, roasted in closed casserole, garnished with fancy-shaped carrots, turnips and braised lettuce; thick veal gravy served separately.

— **Parisian Style:** à la parisienne: poached, covered with German sauce, breast decorated with half-moons of truffle and ox tongue, garnished with truffled chicken dumplings and dumplings mixed with chopped ox tongue.

— **Parsival:** boned, stuffed with truffled chicken mousseline forcemeat, poached, garnished with artichoke bottoms filled with green pea purée mixed with fine herbs and moulded risotto mixed with diced tomatoes and mushrooms; suprême sauce blended with purée poularde livers.

— **Patti:** stuffed as for Diva, poached, covered with suprême sauce seasoned with paprika, garnished with artichoke bottoms with a small whole truffle coated with liquid meat glaze in each.

— **Piedmont Style:** à la piemontaise: stuffed with risotto mixed with sliced white truffles, roasted in closed casserole, deglaced with Madeira and demi-glace.

— **Polignac:** poached, breast and breastbone cut out, cavity stuffed with chicken mousseline forcemeat with julienne of chicken and truffles, forcemeat cooked at the open oven door, breast carved, replaced into position alternated with truffle slices, covered with suprême sauce blended with mushroom purée and mixed with julienne of mushrooms and truffles.

— **Portuguese Style:** à la portugaise: stuffed with risotto mixed with tomatoes concassées, roasted, covered with Portuguese sauce finished off with the deglacage, garnished with stuffed tomatoes.

— **Préval:** boned entirely, stuffed with chicken forcemeat mixed with raw gooseliver and truffle purée, flavored with cognac and Madeira, rolled in a cloth as for galantine, poached in chicken stock; rice pilaf mixed with slivered almonds and suprême sauce served separately.

— **Prince of Wales:** Prince de Galles: stuffed with gooseliver and woodcock forcemeat mixed with diced truffles, pan-roasted, garnished with sautéd wood-cock breast, truffles and mushrooms.

— **Princess Style:** poached, covered with suprême sauce blended with asparagus purée, garnished with artichoke

Poularde
bottoms or croustades of duchess potato mixture filled with asparagus tips.
— **Queen Blanche:** Reine Blanche: stuffed with chicken mousseline forcemeat with diced ox tongue and truffles added, poached, garnished with cockscombs, button mushrooms and truffle slices bound with German sauce.
— **Queen Frederica:** roasted, garnished with thick banana, peach and pineapple slices dipped in light frying batter and deep fried; pan gravy deglaced with Port and thick veal gravy served separately.
— **Queen Margot:** à la reine Margot: stuffed with chicken mousseline forcemeat with almond purée, poached, covered with suprême sauce finished off with almond milk, garnished with chicken forcemeat dumplings blended with pistachio purée and chicken forcemeat dumplings finished off with crayfish butter.
— **Queen Olga:** Reine Olga: larded with ham, filled with bread stuffing, roasted, covered with Madeira sauce with diced fried bacon and blanched julienne of lemon peel added.
— **in Red Wine:** au vin rouge: disjointed, legs and breast cut in two pieces, browned in butter, seasoned, mushroom waste, sliced onions, thyme, a bay leaf and garlic added, moistened with red wine, braised, when half done taken out and put in a clean stewpan, the stock thickened with butter paste strained over, diced fried bacon, sautéd button mushrooms and glazed button onions added, braised until done.
— **Regency Style:** à la régence: stuffed with chicken mousseline forcemeat blended with crayfish purée, covered with suprême sauce, Regency garnish.
— **Renaissance:** poached, covered with German sauce finished off with truffle stock, Renaissance garnish.
— **Revue:** poached, covered with suprême sauce, garnished with round intented rice croquettes filled with chicken purée.
— **Rose Marie** (cold): prepared like May Rose using ham froth instead of tomato froth.
— **Russian Style:** à la russe: poached covered with suprême sauce blended with beetroot juice, garnished with braised fennel.
— **Sainte-Anne:** stuffed with risotto mixed with diced tomatoes, braised in demiglace and Madeira, garnished with stuffed tomatoes and grilled mushroom caps.
— **Saint-Cyr** (cold): poached, when cold skinned, breast and breastbone cut out, breast carved, each slice coated with white chaudfroid sauce, half a stuffed cold lark coated with brown chaudfroid sauce placed on top and glazed with aspic jelly; carcass coated with brown chaufroid sauce, cavity filled with gooseliver froth, decorated to taste and glazed with jelly, garnished with the sliced breast.
— **Saint-James:** stuffed with veal forcemeat mixed with chopped herbs, prepared en casserole, deglaced with brandy, Madeira and thick veal gravy, garnished with spring vegetables sautéd in butter.
— **Saxon Style:** à la saxonne: poached, covered with crayfish sauce, garnished with shaped gratinated cauliflower and crayfish tails.

Poularde

— **Scotch Style:** à l'écossaise: stuffed with veal forcemeat mixed with diced root vegetables simmered in butter, poached, covered with Scotch sauce; creamed French beans served separately.

— **Simone:** stuffed with grilled truffled pig's feet chopped coarsely and crushed braised chestnuts, wrapped in slices of fat bacon, browned in casserole, bacon removed, surrounded with small raw truffles and button onions browned in butter, braised in champagne and veal gravy with lid on; creamed morels served separately.

— **Souwaroff:** stuffed with gooseliver and truffles cut in large dice, roasted until three quarters done, placed in fireproof casserole with middle sized truffles cooked for a few minutes beforehand in Madeira, a little rich chicken stock added, casserole sealed hermetically with dough, placed in oven for half an hour, served in the casserole.

— **Spring Style:** à la printanière: stuffed with a little herb butter, roasted, when half done placed in fireproof casserole with Spring garnish and a little veal gravy, lid put on and finished off in oven.

— **Sylvia:** marinated in olive oil, truffle stock, chopped truffles, mushrooms, shallots, parsley and sweet basil, wrapped in greased paper with all these ingredients, roasted in oven, unwrapped; thick chicken gravy served separately.

— **Talleyrand:** roasted, breast and breastbone cut out, breast cut in large dice, mixed with Talleyrand garnish and filled in cavity of bird, coated thinly with chicken forcemeat, decorated with truffle slices, covered with greased paper and finished off in oven; paper removed, covered lightly with demi-glace with truffle extract and a little sauce served separately.

— **with Tarragon:** à l'estragon (cold): poached with tarragon leaves, when cold breast garnished with blanched tarragon, coated with aspic jelly flavored with tarragon, garnished with aspic jelly.

— **Tivoli:** roasted, deglaced white wine, lemon juice and veal gravy, boiled down and blended with butter, garnished with large grilled mushroom caps filled with cockscombs and cocks' kidneys, bound with German sauce, and asparagus tips.

— **Tosca:** stuffed with rice pilaf mixed with diced gooseliver, roasted in closed casserole, garnished with braised fennel, covered with the deglaced pan gravy beaten with butter.

— **Toulouse Style:** à la toulousaine: poached, covered with German sauce, Toulouse garnish.

— **Truffled:** truffée: raw truffle sliced between the skin and the flesh, stuffed with forcemeat of gooseliver and leaf lard, seasoned, flavored with Madeira and mixed with diced truffles, barded, roasted; the pan gravy boiled up with veal gravy and truffle stock served separately.

— **Tuscan Style:** à la toscane: stuffed with noodles mixed with diced gooseliver, truffles, butter and grated Parmesan cheese, roasted in closed casserole, deglaced with white wine and demi-glace; noodles mixed with chopped ham, truffles, ox tongue and Parmesan, tossed in butter, served separately.

Poularde

— **Valenciennes Style:** roasted, garnished with risotto mixed with diced ham, small grilled ham slices on top; suprême sauce finished off with tomato purée served separately.

— **Van Dyck:** poached, covered with surpême sauce mixed with hop shoots.

— **Victoria:** stuffed as for Souwaroff, roasted in closed casserole, when more then half done potatoes cut in large dice, sautéd in butter, added and finished off in oven.

— **Villars:** poached, garnished with lamb sweetbreads, mushrooms and cocks' kidneys, a crescent-shaped slice of ox tongue between them, bird covered with suprême sauce.

— **Virgin Style:** à la vierge: poached, covered with suprême sauce, garnished with sliced calf's sweetbread, brain and cockscombs.

— **Washington:** stuffed with corn prepared in the Greek way, braised, glazed; creamed corn and the boiled down degreased braising stock served separately.

— **White Lady:** Dame Blanche: poached, covered with suprême sauce, garnished with mushroom caps and truffles.

— **Windsor:** larded, roasted in casserole, garnished with mushrooms, diced truffles, cockscombs and cocks' kidneys, deglaced with Madeira and veal gravy.

— **Wladimir:** poached, covered with suprême sauce blended with Béarnaise sauce mixed with julienne of celery, carrots and truffles, decorated with blanched tarragon leaves.

Chili con carne: Mexican beef stew: diced lean beef browned in beef suet, chopped onions, garlic and Chili peppers added, stewed, served smothered with frijole bean (Mexican).

Chipolatas: kind of very small pork sausage, fried and mainly used as a garnish.

Chitterlings, Pluck: F. Fraise, Fressure; G. Gekröse; lamb or calf's pluck, cleaned, blanched, simmered or fried.

— **Fricassee:** blanched and prepared like fricassee of veal.

— **Fried:** frite: blanched, cut in pieces, dipped in egg and breadcrumbs, deep fried, dressed with fried parsley, devil sauce served separately.

— **Housekeeper Style:** à la ménagère: blanched, cut in pieces, simmered in velouté, slices of carrotts, button onions and small new potatoes added.

— **Lyonese Style:** à la lyonnaise: blanched, cut in thick strips, seasoned, sauted in hot oil, mixed with sliced onions fried in butter, arranged in timbale dish with chopped parsley on top, a few drops of vinegar heated in the frying pan poured over.

— **in Poulette Sauce:** de veau à la poulette: blanched, cut in pieces, simmered in white stock, drained, served in poulette sauce.

— **with Ravigote Sauce:** à la ravigote: blanched, cut in pieces, cooked in white stock, arranged in a timbale dish with a few drops of the stock; light ravigote sauce served separately.

— **with Vinaigrette:** blanched, cut in pieces, cooked in white stock, arranged in timbale dish with a few drops of the stock; vinaigrette served separately.

Civet de lièvre: see jugged hare.

Chop Suey: prepared like chicken chop suey but with diced pork instead of chicken.
Chou farci: see stuffed cabbage.
Chuck: Paleron: mainly braised like rump of beef.
Cimier: saddle of venison.
Civet de chevreuil: see ragoût of roebuck.
Cochon de lait: see suckling pig.
Cockscombs: Crêtes de coq: the crest of male fowls, cut off steeped in cold water and heated sufficiently to strip the thin skin off the meat, kept in cold water until all the blood is drained out, cooked in chicken broth with lemon juice and used as garnish, hot appetizer or light entrée. Being a delicacy cockscombs should not be discarded. They are also commercially packed in glasses.
— **Demidoff:** parboiled, simmered in butter together with small oval slices of carrots, turnips, celery and onions, bound with suprême sauce, a few oval truffle slices added at the last minute.
— **Fried:** frites: parboiled, dipped in frying batter, deep fried, served with fried parsley and lemon.
— **Greek Style:** à la grecque: parboiled cockscombs and cocks' kidneys mixed with rice pilaf and diced red peppers, garnished with fried slices of eggplants.
— **on Skewers:** en brochette: boiled in chicken broth, drained, 6 combs fixed on each skewer, dipped in melted butter and white breadcrumbs, grilled; Béarnaise sauce served separately.
— **Villeroi:** Parboiled, coated with Villeroi sauce, dipped in egg and breadcrumbs, deep fried; truffle sauce served separately.
Cocks' Kidneys: Rognons de coq: steeped in cold water, blanched in water mixed with flour, used as garnish in fine ragouts and as hot hors d'oeuvre.
— **Greek Style:** à la grecque: sautéd in butter, mixed with rice pilaf colored with saffron and mixed with diced green peppers, garnished with sliced egg plant fried in oil.
— **Patty of:** à la Montrouge: simmered in white stock, bound with cream sauce flavored with Madeira, filled in flat open puff pastry patty, sprinkled with breadcrumbs and chopped truffles, dotted with butter, gratinated rapidly.
— **Royal Style:** à la royale: cooked white, bound with cream sauce flavored with Madeira and mixed with a little truffle purée, filled in small china container, sprinkled with breadcrumbs, dotted with butter and gratinated.
Coeur de veau: see calfs' heart.
Contrefilet: see loin of beef.
Coq de bois: see heathcock.
Coq de bruyère: see capercailzie.
Coquille: see ragoût in scallop shell.
Coquilles: medium-sized scallop shells in which ragoût in scallop shells is served.
Coratello d'agnello: lamb's heart, liver and lungs, parboiled, cut in strips, stewed in white wine, oil and lemon juice with chopped onions, butter, chopped parsley and seasoning. (Italian)
Côte. Côtelette: see cutlets and chops.
— **de boeuf:** see rib of beef.
Côtes d'agneau: see lamb cutlets or chops.
— **de chevreuil:** see roebuck.

Côtes de marcassin: see young wild boar.
— **de mouton:** see mutton cutlets and chops.
— **de pigeon:** see pigeon breast.
— **de porc:** see pork, spare ribs.
— **de veau:** rib or cutlet of veal.
— **de volaille:** see chicken cutlets and breast.

Cotochinjos: Brasilian chicken legs: chicken legs, parboiled, coated with thick mush of tapioca boiled in broth, deep fried, served with vegetables and tomato sauce. (Brasilian)

Couscous: diced chicken or mutton cooked in an earthen steamer, in the lower part, and semolina in the upper part. To the meat is usually added, vegetables, chilies and a sort of sausage meat ball. (Arabian)

Crème de volaille: see chicken froth.

Crépinette: sort of flat round sausage made of poultry, game or other forcemeat or salpicon coated with forcemeat, wrapped in pig's caul, dipped or brushed with melted butter, rolled entirely in fresh white breadcrumbs, grilled and served with a suitable sauce. Weight: 3,½ to 4 oz.
— **of Brain:** de cervelle: prepared with pork sausage meat mixed with raw minced calf's brains.
— **of Chicken:** de volaille: raw chicken, gooseliver, lean pork and truffle, minced, seasoned, a little brandy added, shaped into round flat cakes, a truffle slice placed on top, wrapped in pig's caul, grilled and served with Madeira sauce.
— **Cinderella:** à la cendrillon: pork sausage meat mixed with chopped truffle and chopped cooked pig's feet, wrapped in pig's caul.
— **Hunter Style:** à la chasseur: filled with pork forcemeat mixed with chopped feathered game, mushrooms and game glaze; served with hunter sauce.
— **Italian Style:** à l'italienne: salpicon of calf's sweetbread and mushrooms bound with thick Italian sauce; pig's caul coated with pork sausage meat, filled with salpicon, covered with sausage meat, caul folded over on top.
— **of Lamb:** d'agneau: salpicon of lamb and mushrooms bound with thick German sauce or demi-glace, wrapped in pig's caul.
— **Liege Style:** à la liègeoise: made of diced cooked lamb, soaked bread, chopped sautéd onions, eggs, seasoning and a pinch of powdered juniper berries, wrapped in pig's caul; potato purée served separately.
— **Perigord Style:** à la périgourdine: fine pork forcemeat mixed with diced truffles, wrapped in pig's caul; served with potato purée and truffle sauce.
— **Queen Style:** à la reine: prepared like chicken crépinette without truffle; suprême sauce served separately.
— **Saint-Hubert:** pork sausage meat mixed with raw chopped furred game; served with chestnut purée and game sauce.
— **Sainte-Menehould:** prepared with parboiled diced pig's feet and diced truffles bound with very thick demi-glace, enclosed in sausage meat and wrapped in pig's caul.
— **of Sweetbread:** de ris de veau: diced parboiled calf's sweetbread mixed with diced truffles and hard-boiled eggs, bound with thick German sauce; tomato sauce served separately.
— **Turkish Style:** à la turque: made of pork forcemeat mixed with minced cooked mutton, seasoned with allspice and

Crépinette
wrapped in pig's caul; garnished with sliced deep fried eggplant, tomato sauce served separately.
— **of Veal:** de veau: prepared like lamb crépinette.
— **Vivarais Style:** à la vivaraise: raw chopped pork, pig's liver, lungs and onions fried lightly in butter, mixed with parboiled chopped spinach and mangold leaves, seasoned with salt, pepper and garlic, bound with beaten eggs; when cold wrapped in pig's caul, rolled in Breadcrumbs and grilled.

Crêtes de coq: see cockscombs.

Cromesqui: sort of croquette which is not dipped in egg and breadcrumbs but prepared with the same mixtures as for croquettes, i. e. meat, fish, crustaceans, poultry or game diced finely, mixed with finely diced mushrooms, truffle etc., bound with very thick sauce, sometimes thickened with egg yolk, spread on a plafond, allowed to cool and either cylindrical, cone or ball-shaped etc. Prepared in the French way they are only dipped in frying batter; prepared in the Polish way wrapped in a very thin pancake and dipped in frying batter; in the Russian way wrapped in pig's caul and dipped in frying batter; all cromesquis are fried in deep fat and served with fried parsley; for some kinds of cromesquis a sauce is served separately.
— **Bohemian Style:** à la bohémienne: salpicon of gooseliver, tongue, truffles and mushrooms bound with thick demi-glace.
— **Cardinal Style:** à la cardinale: same salpicon as for croquettes.
— **Duchess Style:** à la duchesse: salpicon of chicken meat, mushrooms and truffles bound with thick cream sauce; dipped in frying batter, deep fried.
— **Egg Cromesquis:** aux oeufs: hard-boiled diced eggs, diced truffle and mushrooms, bound with thick demi-glace; dipped in frying batter, deep fried.
— **French Style:** à la française: salpicon of blanched ox marrow, mushrooms and truffle; dipped in frying batter, deep fried.
— **Genoese Style:** à la genoise: diced blanched ox marrow, ham and boiled rice, bound with very thick tomato sauce; dipped in frying batter, fried in oil; tomato sauce served separately.
— **of Gooseliver:** de foie gras: diced poached gooseliver and truffles bound with very thick Madeira sauce; wrapped in pancake, dipped in frying batter, deep fried.
— **Gourmet Style:** du gourmet: diced game and truffle, bound with thick velouté; deep fried, not to thick chestnut purée served separately.
— **Hunter Style:** à la chasseur: salpicon of feathered game, mushrooms and truffles, bound with demi-glace with game essence; dipped in frying batter, deep fried; demi-glace with game essence served separately.
— **Nantese Style:** à la nantaise: prepared like croquettes.
— **Nowgorod:** salpicon of boiled beef, mushrooms, pickled cucumber and red beetroot bound with thick sour cream sauce; wrapped in pig's caul, dipped in frying batter, deep fried.

Cromesqui

— **Polish:** à la polonaise: salpicon of boiled beef, yellow boletus and truffle, bound with thick demi-glace; wrapped in a square of thin pancake, dipped in frying batter, deep fried.

— **Rossini:** 1. salpicon of chicken meat and truffle bound with truffle sauce; 2. salpicon of gooseliver and truffle bound with thick Madeira sauce; both dipped in frying batter and deep fried.

— **Russian:** à la russe: salpicon of blanched ox marrow, yellow boletus or gribuis and feathered game bound with thick sour cream sauce; wrapped in pig's caul, dipped in frying batter, deep fried.

— **Shepherd Style: à la bergère:** same salpicon as for croquettes.

— **of Sweetbread:** de ris de veau: salpicon of calf's sweetbread, ox tongue and mushrooms bound with thick Madeira sauce; dipped in frying batter, deep fried.

— **Victoria:** salpicon of lobster and truffle bound with thick lobster sauce.

Croquettes are unvariably prepared with a mixture of finely diced fish, meat, crusteaceans, poultry or game and mushrooms, truffles etc etc. cooked beforehand, bound with a very thick sauce, often thickened with egg yolks and allowed to cool. The croquette mass is then cylindrical, ball, pear, cube or triangle shaped, dipped in egg and breadcrumbs, deep fried, served with fried parsley and, not always, with some kind of sauce separately.

— **Bohemian:** à la bohémienne: salpicon of gooseliver and truffles bound with German sauce, pear shaped.

— **of Brain:** de cervelle: salpicon of calf's brain, mushroom and ham bound with thick German or Madeira sauce; pear shaped; tomato sauce served separately.

— **Cardinal Style:** à la cardinal: diced lobster and truffles bound with thick cardinal sauce; triangular shaped; cardinal sauce served separately.

— **of Chicken:** de volaille: salpicon of chicken, mushrooms and truffles bound with chicken velouté with mushroom essence and egg yolks; triangular shape; light demi-glace or truffle sauce and if desired buttered green peas, asparagus tips or vegetable macedoine served separately.

— **of Chicken Liver:** de foies de volaille salpicon of chicken livers sautéd blood rare, mushrooms and truffles bound with thick Madeira sauce; round shaped; Madeira sauce served separately.

— **Club Style:** du club: salpicon of chicken, mushrooms and green peppers bound with Béchamel mixed with grated Parmesan and Swiss cheese; apricot shaped; buttered green peas served separately.

— **of Cod American Style:** de morue à l'américaine: flaked boiled cod mixed with duchess potato mass and a little Béchamel; ball shaped; tomato sauce served separately.

— **Diana:** à la diane: salpicon of feathered game and truffle bound with salmi sauce; cylindrical shape.

— **Dominican:** à la dominicaine: poached diced oysters and mushrooms bound with Béchamel and white onion purée finished off with lobster butter and Cayenne pepper, oval shaped; white wine sauce with the oyster liquor served separately.

Croquettes

— **Duchess Style:** à la duchesse: same salpicon as for cromesqui; cylindrical shaped.

— **Easter:** à la pasquale: lamb sweetbread, lamb tongue, ham and truffle bound with thick velouté and white onion purée; round shaped.

— **of Egg:** aux oeufs: diced hard-boiled eggs, mushrooms and truffles bound with thick velouté; egg shaped; curry sauce served separately.

— **Empress Style:** à l'impératrice: salpicon of chicken, calf's brain and lamb sweetbread bound with thick velouté and onion purée; pear shaped; chicken velouté finished off with chicken purée served separately.

— **Erimar:** salpicon of furred game, bananas, mushrooms and green peppers bound with peppers sauce with red currant jelly; square shape; pepper sauce finished off with red currant jelly and a little mustard served separately.

— **of Fish:** de poisson: flaked boiled fish and mushroom bound with thick fish velouté; cylindrical shaped.

— **of Game:** de gibier: salpicon of game, mushrooms and truffles bound with thick salmi sauce; shaped as desired; hunter sauce served separately.

— **Gastronomer Style:** à la gastronome: salpicon of feathered game and truffles bound with thick suprême sauce with a little truffle purée added; cylindrical shaped; light chestnut purée served separately.

— **Gipsy Style:** à la zingara: julienne of ham, ox tongue, mushrooms and truffle bound with thick demi-glace; oval shaped; gipsy sauce served separately.

— **of Gooseliver:** de foie gras: diced gooseliver and truffles bound with thick demi-glace; ball shaped; Madeira sauce served separately.

— **Gourmet:** prepared as for cromesqui.

— **of Ham:** de jambon: diced ham bound with thick German sauce; cylindrical shaped; light tomato sauce served separately.

— **Hungarian:** à la hongroise: salpicon of calf's foot, ham and mushrooms bound with thick paprika sauce; triangular shaped; demi-glace seasoned highly with paprika served separately.

— **Hunter Style:** à la chasseur: salpicon of feathered game, mushrooms and truffle peels bound with thick demi-glace with game essence; triangular shape; demi-glace with truffle essence served separately.

— **Indian:** à l'indienne: hard-boiled diced eggs, chicken and boiled rice bound with thick curry sauce with coconut milk; cylindrical shaped; curry sauce served separately.

— **Italian:** à l'italienne: salpicon of ox tongue, calf's sweetbread and mushrooms bound with Italian sauce; cylindrical shaped; tomato sauce served separately.

— **Jean Bart:** poached oysters and lobster bound with thick Béchamel finished off with lobster butter; ball shaped; cream sauce finished off with lobster butter served separately.

— **Joinville:** salpicon of shrimps, mushrooms and truffles bound with thick shrimp sauce; cylindrical shaped; shrimp sauce without garnish served separately.

Croquettes
— **of Lobster:** de homard: lobster, mushrooms and truffles bound with Béchamel finished off with lobster butter and seasoned with Cayenne pepper; oval shaped; lobster sauce served separately.
— **Marquise:** chicken, ox tongue, mushrooms and truffles bound with thick aurora sauce; oval shaped; tomato sauce served separately.
— **Milanese:** à la milanaise: macaroni, julienne of truffle, ox tongue and chicken bound with Béchamel mixed with tomato purée and grated Parmesan; square shaped; light buttered tomato sauce served separately.
— **Nantese Style:** à la nantaise: flaked fish and mushrooms bound with thick white wine sauce; cylindrical shaped; tomato sauce served separately.
— **of Oysters:** aux huîtres: poached diced oysters and mushrooms bound with thick velouté blended with the oyster liquor.
— **Savigny:** ham, artichoke bottoms and morels bound with with thick Béchamel and egg yolks; round flat shape; light creamed white onion sauce served separately.
— **Shepherd:** à la bergère: salpicon of lamb, ham and fairy ring mushrooms bound with Béchamel; apricot shaped; brown herb sauce served separately.
— **Soubise:** chicken, mushrooms and truffles bound with suprême sauce mixed with white onion purée; apricot shaped; light white onion sauce served separately.
— **of Sweetbread:** de ris de veau: diced sweetbread, ox tongue, mushrooms and truffle bound with thick Madeira sauce; cylindrical shaped.

Croustade: a small container made of unsweetened short pastry baked dry beforehand; or rice cooked very soft, mixed with egg yolks and grated Parmesan, when cold cut out with a round cutter, scooped out, dipped twice in egg and breadcrumbs and deep fried; or made of duchess potato-mixture filled in greased dariol moulds, turned out, dipped in egg and breadcrumbs, deep fried and scooped out. Different shaped croustades are also made commercially. Croustades may be filled with the same salpicons as for bouchées.
— **Agnes Sorel** made of short pastry, lined with chicken forcemeat, filled with salpicon of chicken and mushrooms bound with German sauce; a small slice of chicken breast decorated with a round slice of ox tongue and a fluted mushroom covered with buttered meat glaze on top.
— **Andalusian:** à l'andalouse: made of rice, filled with salpicon of red peppers, chicken and egg plant bound with suprême sauce finished off with red pepper butter; a round slice of red pepper on top as lid.
— **Condé:** filled with salpicon of calf's sweetbread, mushrooms bound with truffle sauce.
— **Copacabana:** oval croustade of duchess potato filled with diced turkey, bananas and sweet potatoes bound with pepper sauce; slivered grilled almonds scattered on top.
— **Duchess Style:** à la duchesse: croustade of duchess potato filled with salpicon of chicken, truffle and mushrooms bound with creamed velouté.
— **Financier Style:** à la financière: filled with financier garnish and financier sauce.

Croustade

— **Joinville:** made of rice, same filling as for bouchée.

— **Lucullus:** 1. puff pastry croustade filled with salpicon of truffles, cooked in champagne, tiny chicken dumplings, cockscombs and cocks' kidneys bound with demi-glace with the reduced truffle stock added. 2. oval duchess potato croustade filled with sliced quails breast, tiny quail dumplings and truffle slices covered with demi-glace with quail essence.

— **Nantese Style:** à la nantaise: diced white fish and mushrooms bound with tomato sauce in croustade of short pastry.

— **Nantua:** short pastry croustade filled with diced crayfish tails and truffles bound with Nantua sauce, a stuffed crayfish head placed on top.

— **Piedmont Style:** à la piémontaise: rice croustade filled with diced chicken, truffles and tiny veal dumplings bound with Italian sauce.

— **Royal:** à la royale: short pastry croustade filled with salpicon of cockscombs, cocks' kidney, calf's sweetbread, mushrooms and truffles bound with suprême sauce.

Cuisseau de veau: see leg of veal.

Cuisses de volaille: see chicken legs.

Cuissot: leg of venison or wild boar.

Culotte de boeuf: see rump of beef.

Curry, Curry and Rice: fish, crustaceans, eggs, meat, poultry, game or vegetables prepared with curry sauce and served with plain boiled rice as well as clarified butter, Bombay ducks, chutney, mango, catsup or other relishes according to circumstances.

— **of Beef Madras Style:** de boeuf à la Madras: beef cut into large dice, marinated in mustard oil, chopped onions, lemon peel, parsley and garlic, simmered in own juice with a piece of cinnamon until done, boiled up with curry sauce and grated coconut; rice, clarified butter, Bombay ducks and mango chutney served separately.

— **of Chicken and Rice:** Curry de volaille au riz: disjointed, browned in mustard oil with chopped onions added, sprinkled with curry powder, smothered with flour, flour lightly browned, moistened with coconut milk, brown stock and tomato purée crushed garlic added, stewed, served with rice.

— — — **Malayan Style:** de volaille à la malaisienne: disjointed, browned in butter, smothered with flour and sprinkled with curry powder, moistened with coconut milk and stock, chopped lemon peel and grated coconut added, stewed, when done slivered roasted almonds scattered on top: rice served separately.

— **of Lamb:** d'agneau: prepared like chicken curry with diced lamb.

— **of Mutton:** Curry de mouton: prepared like chicken curry with diced mutton.

— **of Rabbit:** de lapereau: prepared likė chicken curry.

— **of Turbot:** de turbot: turbot skinned and boned, cut into large dice, marinated in mustard oil, chopped parsley, lemon peel and garlic, browned, cooked in curry sauce, served with rice.

D

Daube: ancient term for a meat stew with wine and spices, braised in a hermetically closed earthenware casserole.

— **Nice Style:** beef cut in small thick slices, browned rapidly in butter with diced bacon, carrots and raw ham, filled in earthen pot with a piece of dried lemon and orange peel, a bayleaf, a sprig of celery and a little thyme, seasoned lightly, a little beef stock poured in the pot, closed hermetically and braised in oven.

— **Provencal Style:** à la provençale: small slices of beef marinated in oil, white wine, brandy, herbs and chopped onions; browned in oil, diced bacon, diced tomatoes, stoned olives, mushrooms and garlic added, marinade poured over the meat, closed hermetically and braised in oven.

Dahorp: Jougo-Slavian mutton stew: diced mutton cooked in water seasoned with salt, onions and pot herbs added, rice cooked in the strained stock with diced green peppers, mixed with the meat, lightly flavored with vinegar. (Jougo-Slavian)

Daim: see fallow deer.

Darioles: different kinds of food cooked in small beaker moulds.

— **Saint-Germain:** moulds greased with butter, lined with purée of green peas bound with egg-yolks, filled with diced mushrooms, truffles and lamb sweetbreads in thick suprême sauce, sealed with purée of green peas, poached in bain-marie, turned out, covered with suprême sauce.

D'Artois: see puff pastry strips.

Deutsches Beefsteak: German Meat Dumpling: raw chopped beef mixed with bread soaked in milk, minced beef suet and chopped onions sweated in butter, seasoned, shaped into flattish dumplings, fried in butter, covered with fried onions rings; mashed potatoes served separately. (German)

Dinde: turkey hen, see turkey.

Dindon: turkey cock, see turkey.

Dindonneau: baby turkey, see turkey.

Dolmas: stuffed vine leaves: blanched vine leaves stuffed with chopped chicken meat mixed with mutton fat, boiled rice, chopped parsley, fennel and onions, seasoned, shaped into balls, wrapped in thin slices of fat bacon, stewed in broth or water, covered with the stock thickened with egg yolks and flavored with lemon juice. (Turkish)

Doppskov: left over boiled or roast veal, beef and ham diced finely, tossed in butter with chopped onions, simmered in cream sauce, mixed with diced boiled potatoes, a fried egg on top. (Swedish)

Double: term applied to the two legs of lamb or mutton.

Duck; F. Canard; G. Ente: domestic, semiwild and wild, webfooted and short-legged diving bird of various sizes. There are three distinct sorts: 1. domestic ducks such as Nantais, Aylesbury and Hamburg ducks;
2. Rouennais, a large duck which is smothered so as to loose no blood;
3. wild ducks of various species which are usually shot.
Wild duck and Rouennais are described under their respective names.

Duck

— **Alsatian Style:** à l'alsacienne: braised, cut in pieces, dressed on saurkraut cooked in white wine, garnished with small boiled potatoes, the thick gravy served separately.

— **Ancient Style:** à l'ancienne: braised, dressed on saurkraut, garnished with sliced bacon, cooked with the saurkraut, sliced sausage and glazed carrots; the thickened gravy served separately.

— **Badish Style:** à la badoise: braised with mirepoix, ham and mushroom waste in Rhine wine, dressed on saurkraut, stock boiled down with demi-glace with truffle julienne added, bordered with sliced bacon cooked with the saurkraut.

— **Béarnaise Style:** à la Béarnaise: simmered in white stock with bacon, carrots, turnips, cabbage, fresh white beans and green beans, dressed in fireproof dish garnished with the vegetables and small slices of French bread sprinkled with grated Parmesan, browned and a little of the duck fat poured over; the boiled down stock served separately.

— **Beaulieu:** roasted, dressed in fireproof casserole, garnished with stoned olives, quartered artichoke bottoms and new potatoes, pan juice deglazed with Madeira and boiled down with demi-glace.

— **Bigarade:** rosted rare, deglaced with bigarade sauce, breast of duck cut into thin long slices and covered with the sauce.

— **Boiled,** bouilli: 1. boiled in water with pot herbs and a larded onion, served with horseradish or onion sauce.
2. stuffed with bread soaked in milk, mixed with the chopped liver, parsley, herbs and seasoning, wrapped in a clean cloth, boiled.

— **Bordeaux Style:** à la bordelaise: stuffed with bread soaked in milk mixed with the chopped liver, chopped parsley and green olives, sliced sautéd yellow boletus, eggs, garlic, salt and pepper, roasted, pan juice served separately.

— **Burgundy Style:** à la bourguignonne: braised in red wine and light demi-glace, garnished with glazed button onions, fried button mushrooms and diced fried bacon; the degreased sauce served separately.

— **with Cabbage:** au chou: cut in pieces, browned in butter, braised with cabbage, blanched and cut in quarters, and diced bacon in a fireproof china dish with the lid on.

— **Carmen** (cold): roasted; when cold breast and breast bone cut off, cavity filled with gooseliver froth, the sliced breast placed back into position, decorated with tangerine slices and red cherries, glazed with aspic jelly, garnished with tangerines stuffed with almond jelly, bordered with aspic jelly.

— **with Cherries:** aux cerises: prepared like Bigarade, deglazed with Madeira and thick veal gravy, stoned cherries added, boiled up and poured over the slices.

— **Chipolata:** braised, garnished with small pork sausages (chipolatas) and braised chestnuts; the thickened gravy served separately.

— **with Cucumbers:** aux concombres: braised, garnished with cucumber balls simmered in butter and heart-shaped croûtons fried in butter; the thickened gravy served separately.

Duck

— **Duclair:** stuffed with bread soaked in milk, mixed with the chopped liver, heart and parsley, seasoned, roasted, deglazed with red wine and orange juice, boiled up with demi-glace.

— **English Style:** à l'anglaise: stuffed with sage and onion stuffing, braised or roasted, gravy made with the pan juice.

— **Flemish Style:** à la flamande: braised, garnished with braised cabbage balls, triangles of bacon cooked with the cabbage, glazed carrots and turnips and slices of garlic sausage; the degreased and thickened gravy served separately.

— **German Style:** à l'allemande: stuffed with white bread soaked in milk, mixed with the chopped liver and lungs, chopped parsley, salt and pepper, roasted, the pan juice deglazed with brown stock and cucumber salad served separately.

— **with Grapes:** aux raisins: braised in red wine and thick veal gravy with thin orange peel, stock strained, boiled up with peeled and seeded grapes and poured over the duck; rice pilaf with sautéd diced yellow boletus served separately.

— **with Green Peas:** aux petits pois: roasted, when more then half done green peas, shredded lettuce, diced bacon, button onions and light demi-glace added and braised.

— **Italian Style:** à l'italienne: browned in butter, braised with blanched calf's feet, onions, raw ham waste and bacon, seasoned with bay leaf, salt and pepper; sauce made of chopped mushrooms, parsley and chives sautéd in oil, boiled up with the strained stock and thickened, served with the duck.

— **Japanese Style:** à la japonaise (cold): braised, when cold breast and backbone cut out, the cavity filled with duck froth, the sliced breast placed back again in position, coated with brown chaudfroid sauce made with the braising stock, glazed with aspic jelly, garnished with small tangerines filled with duck froth mixed with gooseliver patty, glazed with aspic jelly.

— **Lyonese Style:** à la lyonnaise: braised, garnished with glazed button onions and chestnuts.

— **with Malaga:** au Malaga (cold): braised with sliced onions and carrots in red wine, brown stock and Malaga, when cold, breast sliced and put back into position, covered with brown chaudfroid sauce made with the stock, glazed and garnished with aspic jelly flavored with Malaga.

— **Maltese Style:** à la maltaise: braised in white wine, light demi-glace and the juice of blood oranges with mirepoix, the strained sauce mixed with blanched julienne of blood oranges, flavored with the juice of blood oranges.

— **Marshall Robert** (cold): roasted, when cold, breast cut out and cut into thin slices, each slice spread with purée of gooseliver patty, placed back into position, coated with brown chaudfroid sauce finished off with the deglazed pan juice, glazed with aspic jelly, garnished with orange quarters without skin or pips, coated with aspic jelly.

— **with Mint:** à la menthe: roasted en casserole, deglazed with thick veal gravy with chopped mint added.

Duck

— **Modern Style:** à la moderne: cut into pieces, seasoned, browned in butter, braised in Port and light demi-glace with chopped shallots and anchovies added, sauce strained and poured over the pieces.

— **Molière:** boned, stuffed with half gratin forcemeat with gooseliver and half fine pork sausage meat mixed with chopped truffles, wrapped in a cloth like galantine, poached in duck stock, glazed, Madeira sauce with duck essence and sliced truffles served separately.

— **Mousse of:** Mousse de caneton: boned, meat pounded in mortar with egg whites, chilled, seasoned with salt and pepper, rubbed through a sieve, mixed on ice with unsweetened whipped cream until light and fluffy, filled in mould greased with butter and decorated with truffle slices, poached in a water bath, served with sauce made with the bones or an other appropriate sauce and served hot. Mousse is often mixed with gooseliver, diced truffles or mushrooms etc.

— **Nevers Style:** à la nivernaise: braised, dressed with Nevers garnish, the thickened stock served separately.

— **Normandy Style:** à la normande: browned, flambéd with apple jack, braised in brown stock and cider, stock boiled down with sweet cream, garnished with apple quarters sautéd in butter.

— **Northern Style:** à la nordique (cold): stuffed with gooseliver forcemeat, braised, when cold coated with brown chaudfroid sauce, decorated, glazed with aspic jelly, served with Russian salad.

— **with Olives:** aux olives: braised in white wine and light demi-glace, pitted olives added when nearly done, sauce flavored with Madeira, served en cocotte.

— **with Orange:** à l'orange: braised in light demi-glace, sauce finished off with orange and lemon juice, fine blanched julienne of orange peel added, bordered with orange wedges.

— **with Pineapple:** à l'ananas: roast duck garnished with small pineapple slices slightly sautéd in butter, pan juice deglaced with pineapple juice and brandy, boiled up with thick veal gravy.

— **with Port Wine:** au Porto: roasted underdone, breast cut in long thin slices and kept warm in chafing dish, deglazed with Port and thick veal gravy, mixed with the juice crushed out of the carcass in a special duck press, warmed up but not boiled and poured over the aiguillettes (breast).

— **Potted:** en terrine: stuffed with duck forcemeat mixed with gooseliver and chopped shallots lightly fried in butter, cooked in hermetically closed china or earthenware cocotte with very little gravy, served hot or cold.

— **à la Presse:** the roast duck, blood rare, is sent into the dining room together with a purée of the slightly sautéd liver. Legs and breasts removed from bones, breasts cut into thin slices and placed on a warm chafing dish, legs sent back to kitchen to be grilled. The juice and blood of the carcass extracted in a special duck press, warmed up with the mashed liver in a chafing dish, seasoned with orange juice, brandy, Madeira or Port, salt and a pinch of Cayenne pepper, but not allowed to boil as overheating is likely to curdle the sauce, poured over the breasts and

Duck
warmed up until they are sufficiently done and served immediately.

— **Provencal Style:** à la provençale: cut into pieces, browned in oil, simmered in white wine with diced tomatoes and garlic, shortly before duck is done chopped anchovies, blanched black olives and a pinch of sweet basil added.

— **Russian Style:** à la russe: braised, when nearly done sliced pickled cucumbers added, stock boiled down with sour cream.

— **Savoy Style:** à la savoyarde:
1. braised with sliced onions, dressed on Savoy style potatoes, covered with the thickened stock.
2. browned with diced bacon and button onions, braised in brown stock, tomatoes concassées and sliced yellow boletus added, served in cocotte with the garnish and the sauce seasoned with lemon juice.

— **Sevilla Style:** à la sévillanne (cold): boned, stuffed with half gratin and half mousseline forcemeat mixed with thick tomato purée and diced gooseliver, wrapped in a cloth poached in white stock, when cold unwrapped, breast cut into thin slices and put back into position, coated with brown chaudfroid sauce flavored with Sherry, decorated, glazed with aspic jelly garnished with large olives stuffed with gooseliver patty.

— **Simone:** boned, stuffed with pork forcemeat mixed with diced truffles and braised lightly crushed chestnuts, browned, braised in champagne and veal gravy, when nearly done glazed button onions and small raw truffles added, dressed with the garnish and the boiled down, strained stock; morels in cream sauce served separately.

— **Stuffed German Style:** farci à l'allemande: stuffed with apples, roasted, braised red cabbage, boiled potatoes and the thickened gravy served separately.

— **Suprême of:** suprême de canard: ducks breast sautéd in butter and prepared like duck.

— **Tenant Style:** à la fermière: braised in white wine with light demi-glace, small slices of carrots, turnips, knob celery and onions, lozenges of green beans and green peas added.

— **with Turnips:** aux navets: braised in demi-glace, garnished with olive-shaped turnips sautéd in butter and cooked with the duck.

Dumplings; F. Quenelles; G. Klösse: are made of various sorts of forcemeat, filled in oval-shaped greased moulds or shaped with two soup spoons, poached in boiling fluid and served with a suitable sauce and garnish.

— **Alsatian:** à l'alsacienne: diced chicken and veal livers sautéd blood rare in butter with chopped onions, rubbed through a sieve, mixed with egg yolks and soaked bread, seasoned, poached, covered with herb butter.

— **Breton:** Quenelles à la bretonne: made of chicken forcemeat mixed with brown onion purée, shaped, poached and covered with bastard sauce mixed with chopped mushrooms.

— **Crayfish, Cardinal Style:** d'écrevisses à la cardinale: crayfish mousseline forcemeat filled in oval greased moulds, turned out, arranged like a crown on a round platter with a truffle slice on each dumpling, covered with cream

Dumplings
sauce finished off with crayfish butter and truffle essence; crayfish tails bound with the same sauce in the center.

— **Ham, Viennese Style:** de jambon à la viennoise: minced boiled ham mixed with bread soaked in milk, a little flour, eggs, chopped onions sweated in butter and tiny fried croûtons, seasoned, shaped with two spoons, poached in lightly salted water, drained and served covered with browned butter.

— **Hermann Senn:** duck forcemeat mixed with finely diced and blanched fat bacon, shaped with two spoons, poached, arranged in a border of poached chicken forcemeat, covered with financier garnish and sauce.

— **Montglas:** chicken forcemeat moulded with two spoons, poached in chicken stock, arranged like a crown on small slices of ox tongue, a slice of truffle on each dumpling, covered with Madeira sauce, ragoût of diced gooseliver, truffle slices and mushrooms in the center.

— **Morland:** de volaille Morland: chicken forcemeat with panade moulded in shape of an egg, rolled in chopped truffle, fried in clarified butter, served with mushroom purée.

— **Richelieu:** de volaille Richelieu: oval greased mould lined with chicken forcemeat with panade, filled with salpicon of chicken, mushrooms and truffles bound with German sauce, sealed with forcemeat, poached, allowed to cool, dipped in egg and breadcrumbs, fried in butter, garnished with fried parsley; truffle sauce served separately.

— **Rothschild:** made of pheasant forcemeat, garnished with salpicon of cockscombs, gooseliver and truffles bound with Madeira sauce; Madeira sauce with truffle and pheasant essence served separately.

— **Soubise:** moulded chicken dumplings, poached, allowed to cool, dipped in egg and breadcrumbs, deep fried and served with white onion purée.

— **Talleyrand:** chicken forcemeat dumpling filled with salpicon of mushrooms and truffles bound with Madeira sauce, poached, covered with German sauce mixed with sliced mushrooms and cockscombs.

— **d'Uzès:** oval dumpling of chicken forcemeat mixed with chopped chicken, poached, covered with aurora sauce mixed with truffle julienne.

— **Veal:** de godiveau: veal pounded in mortar with veal suet, eggs and ice, rubbed trough a sieve, seasoned, shaped with two soup spoons, poached and served with German or other suitable sauce.

— **Swedish:** Quenelles à la suédoise: ground beef mixed with breadcrumbs, eggs, salt and pepper; round dumplings formed, fried in diced salt pork, when done finished off with demi-glace.

Dutch Kraut: sauerkraut braised in white wine and white stock with a piece of boned pork, sliced apples, onions and seasoning, bound with butterpaste, the kraut garnished with the sliced meat and boiled potatoes.

Duyune eti: Mutton stew: Mutton cut into large cubes, fried in mutton fat together with onions cut in quarters, stewed in water with tomato purée, seasoned with lemon juice. (Turkish)

E

Echine de porc: see spare rib.
Eisbein: see pickled pork shank.
Ekshili keuftés: meat balls: chopped raw beef mixed with bread soaked in water, eggs and chopped parsley, seasoned with salt and pepper, cooked in a rather thin sauce made of chopped onions lightly fried in butter, tomato purée and water, mixed before serving with crushed garlic, cinnamon and a little vinegar. (Turkish)
Emincé: meat, poultry or game cut into small thin slices (not minced), heated in special sauce and served hot, often in a border of risotto or rice pilaf. See mince.
Entrecôte: see beef, sirloin steak.
Entrecôte double: see beef, sirloin steak.
Epaule d'agneau: see shoulder of lamb.
Epaule de mouton: see shoulder of mutton.
Epaule de porc: see shoulder of pork.
Epaule de veau: see shoulder of veal.
Epigram: Epigramme: dainty entrée particularly of lamb or mutton.

Epigram of Lamb: Epigramme d'agneau: braised breast of lamb, bones removed, put under pressure, when cold cut like cutlets, dipped in egg and breadcrumbs, fried in butter, dressed like a turban alternated with lamb cutlets, dipped in egg and breadcrumbs and also fried in butter, center filled with fresh vegetables, sauce poured around or served separately.
— **with Asparagus Tips:** aux pointes d'asperges: served with green asparagus tips tossed in butter.
— **Parma Style:** à la Parme: breast and cutlet dipped in egg and breadcrumbs mixed with grated Parmesan, fried in butter, garnished with creamed mushrooms or sliced white Italian truffles.

Epigram of Mutton: Epigramme de mouton: prepared like epigram of lamb.

Escalope de veau: see veal collop.

Esterhazy rostélyos: Esterhazy sirloin steak: thin sirloin steak seasoned with salt and pepper, browned in lard and placed in a casserole, sliced onions, carrots and parsley root sautéd in the lard, besprinkled with flour and slightly browned, moistened with water or stock, paprika, a bay leaf, marjoran, a few lemon slices and chopped capers added, poured over the steak and steak stewed until done. Meantime coarse julienne of carrots and parsley root is fried lightly in butter, moistened with stock and simmered until done, the steak placed on top, the sauce strained over, sour cream added and simmered for another few minutes; Rice, small flour dumplings or noodles served separately. (Hungarian)

Estofado Rosalia: Spanish beef stew: thick beef slices browned in lard with sliced onions, mixed with sliced raw ham, seasoned with garlic, thyme, sweet basil, cloves, bay leaf and pepper corns, stewed in beef stock, served with chopped parsley scattered on top.

Estouffade de boeuf: see beef stew, French.

F

Favorites: beaker moulds lined with unsweetened short pastry, baked light brown, filled with ragôut of gooseliver and truffle bound with thick Madeira sauce, covered with gooseliver soufflé mass and a slice of truffle on top, baked in slow oven; truffle sauce served separately.

Faisan: see pheasant:

Falscher Hase: false hare: chopped beef, veal and pork mixed with eggs, butter, capers, chopped onions sweated in butter, lemon juice, salt and pepper, shaped like a tenderloin, rolled in breadcrumbs, roasted in butter, the pan juice boiled up with sweet cream and poured over the meat. (German)

Får i kål: Swedish Lamb stew: lamb shoulder cut in large dice, browned in butter, stewed with white cabbage and potatoes. (Swedish)

Fauxfilet: see loin of beef.

Fawn: F. Faon; G. Hirschkalb: young deer prepared like roe deer.

Fejoada: redbrown Frijole beans cooked together with brisket of beef, salt pork, smoked beef, ham, pigs ears, ox tongue, spicy garlic sausage (chorizos) and red and green peppers. (Brasilian)

Fieldfare: F. Grieve; G. Krammetsvogel: kind of European thrush much esteemed as small game.

— **with Genever:** au genièvre: roasted in cocotte, when nearly done a few crushed juniper berries scattered on top, deglaced with old genever and a little game stock, lid put on cocotte and served hot.

— **with Gooseliver:** au foie gras: boned, stuffed with a small piece of gooseliver, roasted, deglaced with Madeira and demi-glace.

— **with Grapes:** aux raisins: roasted, placed in cocotte with peeled and seeded grapes; covered with the pan juice deglaced with a trickle of brandy and a little grape juice and put in the oven a few minutes before serving.

— **Housewife Style:** à la bonne-femme: roasted together with diced blanched bacon; placed in cocotte covered with tiny croûtons fried in butter, the pan residue deglaced with a trickle of brandy poured on top.

— **Hunter Style:** à la chasseur: roasted, covered with hunter sauce.

— **Imperial Style:** à l'impériale: boned, stuffed with truffled gooseliver forcemeat, barded, roasted, placed on oval fried croûton coated with truffle purée; the pan juice deglaced with a trickle of brandy poured over the birds.

— **Italian Style:** à l'italienne: barded with two fresh sage leaves and a thin slice of fat bacon, tied and roasted.

— **Liege Style:** à la liégeoise: fried open in a cocotte on the stove, when nearly done crushed juniper berries and tiny croûtons fried in butter scattered on top, lid put on, served very hot.

— **with Madeira:** au madère: roasted, deglaced with Madeira and a little demi-glace.

— **Modern Style:** à la moderne (cold): roasted, breast detached, when cold covered with brown chaudfroid

Fieldfare
sauce prepared with the bones, decorated with truffle and hard-boiled egg white, placed in tartlet mould lined with aspic jelly and sealed with aspic jelly; when set turned out and arranged around fieldfare froth filled in a bomb mould lined with aspic jelly and turned out on a round silver platter.

— **Old Fashioned Style:** à l'ancienne: fried in cocotte, garnished with glazed button onions and button mushrooms; a little veal gravy added at serving.

— **in Paper Bag:** en papillote: boned, stuffed with liver forcemeat and a juniper berry, larded, two or three birds wrapped in a greased paper bag and roasted in oven.

— **Piedmont Style:** à la piemontaise: roasted, deglaced with brandy, truffle essence and demi-glace; arranged on top of risotto mixed with diced Italian truffles, the sauce poured over the birds.

— **Polish Style:** à la polonaise: stuffed with liver forcemeat, roasted in cocotte, a trickle of lemon juice and veal gravy poured around the birds, covered with breadcrumbs browned in butter.

— **Rabelais:** boned, stuffed with a small piece of gooseliver, poached in champagne with fine mirepoix; placed in a truffle cooked in champagne and scooped out to hold the bird; covered with the reduced stock of the birds and the truffle pulp chopped and mixed with German sauce.

— **with Risotto:** au risotto: boned, stuffed with liver forcemeat, roasted, arranged on risotto, covered with the pan juice deglaced with brandy and game stock.

— **with Saurkraut:** à la choucroûte: roasted, served on saurkraut braised in white wine with apples and a few juniper berries.

— **Stuffed:** farcies: boned, stuffed with liver forcemeat, roasted, placed on croûton coated with liver forcemeat; the pan juice deglaced with brandy poured over the birds.

Fig-Pecker: F. Bec-figue; G. Feigendrossel: prepared like ortolan.

Filet de boeuf: fillet of beef, see tenderloin.

— **de chevreuil:** see roebuck.

— **de lapereau:** see fillet of rabbit.

— **de lièvre:** see fillet of hare.

— **mignon de boeuf:** see beef, fillet mignon of.

— **mignon de chevreuil:** see roe-deer.

— **de mouton:** see mutton tenderloin.

— **de porc:** see pork tenderloin.

— **de renne:** see fillet of reindeer.

— **de volaille:** see chicken breast and suprême.

Filets mignons: smal tenderloins of lamb, mutton or beef.

Findik keuftessi: Mutton dumplings: chopped mutton mixed with chopped onions fried in butter, flour, eggs, butter and seasoning, shaped into walnut-sized dumplings, fried in butter, moistened with water or mutton stock and simmered with chopped fresh mint leaves. (Turkish)

Finnisk far-stuvning: Lamb Stew: breast of lamb cut into convenient pieces, fried in butter, moistened with stock, stewed with carrots, turnips and potatoes. (Finnish)

Fläsk korv-stuvning: Pork Sausage with potatoes: thick slices of special pork sausage cooked in pork stock with sliced onions and potatoes cut in large dice. (Swedish)

Foie de boeuf: see beef liver.
— **gras:** Foie d'oie: see gooseliver.
— **de veau:** see calf's liver.
Foies de volaille: see chicken livers.
Fondant: a very thick purée bound with strongly reduced sauce, sometimes mixed with a second purée, allowed to cool, shaped like a tiny pear, dipped in flour, egg and breadcrumbs, fried rapidly in very hot deep fat and served with fried parsley.
— **Bohemian Style:** à la bohemienne: made of ham purée bound with thick cream sauce mixed with diced gooseliver.
— **Countess Style:** à la comtesse: made of chicken purée mixed with purée of ox tongue.
— **Dreux Style:** à la Dreux: purée of chicken livers sautéd rare, bound with thick demi-glace, mixed with thick mushroom purée.
— **Duchess Style:** à la duchesse: made of chicken and ox tongue purée mixed with finely chopped pistachios.
— **Georgette:** game purée mixed with gooseliver purée.
— **Louisette:** two parts chicken and one part each gooseliver and ox tongue purée mixed with very thick German sauce.
— **Marion:** made of chicken and game purée.
— **Marly:** made of three parts pheasant and one part chicken purée bound with salmi sauce.
— **Metternich:** made of gooseliver purée mixed with diced gooseliver.
— **Monselet:** gooseliver and truffle purée mixed with thick Madeira sauce.
— **Queen Style:** à la reine: chicken purée mixed with very thick suprême sauce.
Forcemeat sausage: Boudin: forcemeat shaped like a small sausage or piped in shape of an oval dumpling, sometimes stuffed with salpicon, poached, dipped in egg and breadcrumbs, fried in butter, served hot as a light entrée.
Forcemeat, Chicken: de volaille: chicken forcemeat spread on paper greased with butter, center, stuffed with salpicon of chicken in thick cream, rolled together, poached cut in pieces, covered with suprême sauce.
— — **Carignan:** stuffed with chopped mushrooms simmered in butter and bound with thick German sauce, poached, cut into thick slices, dipped in egg and breadcrumbs, fried in butter, garnished with cockscombs dipped in frying batter and deep fried; tomato sauce served separately.
— — **Marshall Style:** de volaille large chicken forcemeat sausage, poached, cut into thick slices, dipped in egg and breadcrumbs, fried in butter, a slice of truffle on each slice, garnished with green asparagus tips.
— — **Morland:** chicken forcemeat shaped into very small sausages, rolled in chopped truffles, fried, served on mushroom purée.
— — **Richelieu:** chicken forcemeat mixed with chopped truffles and mushrooms, shaped into small sausages, fried in butter; truffle sauce served separately.
— — **Uzès:** oval dumplings of chicken forcemeat, poached but not breaded, covered with Aurora sauce mixed with truffle julienne.

Forcemeat
— **of Game with Chestnut Purée:** de gibier à la purée de marrons: made of furred game mixed with chopped mushrooms, poached, dipped in egg and breadcrumbs, fried garnished with chestnut purée; pepper sauce served separately.
— **with Onion Purée:** à la Soubise: oval dumplings of veal forcemeat stuffed with thick white onion purée, poached, covered with Soubise sauce.
— **of Partridge:** de perdreau: prepared with partridge forcemeat, poached, dipped in egg and breadcrumbs, fried; salmi sauce served separately.
— **of Pheasant Prince Charles:** Boudin de faisan Prince Charles: forcemeat of pheasant mixed with chopped truffles, shaped into very small sausages, poached, dipped in egg and breadcrumbs, fried; pepper sauce prepared with game stock served separately.
Fraise: see chitterlings.
French Lamb Chop: see lamb cutlet.
— **Mutton Chop:** see mutton cutlet.
— **Mutton Stew:** see navarin (mutton ragoût).
Fressure: see chitterlings.
Fricadelle: lean pork trimmings and other meat, raw or cooked, chopped moderately fine, mixed with eggs, soaked bread, chopped chives and parsley, seasoned, shaped into flat round or oval cakes, dipped in egg and breadcrumbs, fried in butter.
Fricandeau de veau: see veal, fricandeau of.
Fricassée d'agneau: see lamb fricassée.
— **de poulet:** see fricassée of chicken.
— **de veau:** see fricassée of veal.
Fritots: slices or pieces of precooked brains, calf's head, sheep's or calf's trotters, chicken etc. marinated in oil, lemon juice and fine herbs, dipped in frying batter, deep fried, dressed with fried parsley; tomato sauce served separately.
Fritto Misto: Mixed Fry: sliced cooked lamb brains, sweetbreads, small slices of calf's liver, small pieces of zucchini and artichokes, lamb cutlets and chicken croquettes, dipped in egg and breadcrumbs, deep fried in oil, served with lemon. (Italian)
— — **alla siciliana:** Sicilian Mixed Fry: slices of calf's brains, liver and lungs, small thin slices of precooked veal and calf's head, quartered artichoke bottoms and sardines, dipped in frying batter, deep fried, served with lemon and tomato sauce. (Italian)
— **Scelto alla Romana:** Roman Mixed Fry: sliced calf's brains, sweetbreads, calf's liver, calf's marrow, small potatoes, artichoke bottoms and small pieces of bread, dipped in egg and breadcrumbs, deep fried and served with lemon. (Italian)

G

Galantine d'agneau: see lamb.
— **Duck:** Galantine de canard: boned, prepared like chicken galantine; may be served hot with a sauce prepared with

Galantine
the chopped bones browned with mirepoix and cooked with light demi-glace, flavored with Madeira.

— **de volaille:** see chicken galantine.

Geflügelreis: Chicken Rice: risotto mixed with butter, diced boiled chicken and grated Parmesan, pressed into a greased mould, turned out, sprinkled generously with grated Parmesan, tomato sauce poured around. (Austrian)

Gelinotte: see hazel-hen.

Giblets: Abatis de volaille: hearts, neck, gizzard, liver, ends of wings etc. of poultry, braised or stewed, served in sauce with an appropriate garnish or plain boiled rice.

— **Chicken Burgundy Style:** à la bourguignonne: browned with chopped onions and diced lean bacon, besprinkled with flour, moistened with red wine and brown stock, when done giblets taken out, mixed with glazed button onions and diced fried bacon, the sauce strained over, boiled up, served with chopped parsley on top.

— **Chipolata:** browned, braised in light demi-glace, garnished with glazed button onions, glazed chestnuts and diced fried bacon, surrounded with small fried pork sausages.

— **Goose, German Style:** à l'allemande: cooked in water with pot herbs, onions, bay leaf, peppercorns and allspice, when done stock strained, thickened with white roux, finished off with a little sweet cream, poured over the giblets, mixed with plenty of chopped parsley; plain boiled rice served separately.

— **Housekeeper Style:** à la ménagère: braised brown, mixed with sliced fried onions, slices of boiled new potatoes and carrots.

— **Housewife Style:** à la bonne-femme: braised in brown stock and white wine with garlic and chopped herbs, thickened with brown roux, boiled up with diced fried bacon and parboiled button onions.

— **Marseille Style:** Abatis d'oie à la marseillaise: browned in oil, braised in white wine with diced tomatoes, shredded green peppers, onions and garlic, seasoned with lemon juice, chopped parsley sprinkled on top.

— **Mecklenburg Style:** à la mecklenbourgeoise: boiled with pot herbs, a larded onion, peppercorns and allspice, sauce prepared with the stock and white roux bound with goose blood, seasoned with salt, a pinch of sugar and a dash of vinegar, strained, poured over the giblets mixed with quartered peeled, cored and cooked pears; flour dumplings served separately.

— **Pomeranien Style:** à la poméranienne: blanched, fried in butter with chopped onions, dredged with flour, moistened with white stock, seasoned, cooked, when done bound with goose blood.

— **Russian Style:** à la russe: cooked in water with pot herbs, a larded onion, ginger, peppercorns, allspice and salt, stock strained, thickened with white roux, mixed with cooked prunes, raisins, dried pears and apples, poured over the giblets, boiled up and served.

— **Turkey, Farmer Style:** de dinde à la paysanne: browned, braised with small slices of onions, carrots and turnips, lozenges of green beans and green peas added at the last minute.

Giblets
— **with Turnips:** aux navets: stewed in white stock, thickened with white roux, mixed with oval-shaped turnips simmered in butter.
— **with Vegetables:** Abatis de poulet aux légumes: browned in butter with chopped onions, dredged with flour moistened with stock, seasoned, stewed, mixed with parboiled oval-shaped carrots and turnips, lozenges of green beans and green peas.
— **with Root Vegetables:** aux racines: braised in light demi-glace with sliced onions, small pieces of salsify, carrot, turnip and potato balls added.

Gigot d'agneau: see leg of lamb.
— **de mouton:** see leg of mutton.
— **de pré-salé:** see leg of lamb.

Gigue de chevreuil: see haunch of vension.
— **de renne:** see haunch of reindeer.

Gjuwetch: Bulgarian Mutton Stew: diced mutton simmered in oil with chopped onions, diced green peppers, eggplants diced green beans, squash and potatoes, okra and garlic, covered with sliced tomatoes, seasoned, oil dropped on top, stewed in the oven. (Bulgarian)

Goat, Alpine: F. Chamois; G. Gemse: goat belonging to the antilope family found in Europe in the Alps and the Pyrenees, and in Asian and American mountains. Prepared like deer but usually marinated beforehand
— **Haunch, Citizen Style:** Gigue à la bourgeoise: marinated in vinegar, water, and sliced carrots, onions, peppercorns and bay leaf, browned, braised in brown stock and a part of the marinade, stock boiled down with sour cream; rice or noodles tossed in butter served separately.
— **Haunch, Swiss Style:** Gigue à la suisse: marinated, larded, browned in butter, braised in red wine and brown stock with sliced onions, peppercorns, bay leaf and toasted bread as thickening, stock, boiled up and strained over the meat.
— **Saddle, Chief Ranger Style:** Selle à la grand-veneur: larded, if more than six months old marinated in red wine with pot herbs, peppercorns, sliced onions and bay leaf, if young roasted medium, if old braised; served with chief ranger sauce prepared with the stock, buttered noodles and sautéd mushrooms, morels or boletus.
— **Saddle, German Style:** Selle à l'allemande: marinated in red wine, sliced onions and pot herbs, browned in butter, braised with the marinade, gravy boiled down with sour cream and demi-glace, seasoned with lemon juice and strained: red cabbage and potato purée served separately.
— **Saddle, Snagow Style:** Selle à la Snagow: young saddle, larded, roasted medium, deglaced with white wine, brandy and demi-glace, sauce boiled up, mixed with peeled and seeded grapes and poured over the saddle; noodles tossed in butter and mixed with strips of red peppers served separately.

Golden Plover: F. Pluvier; G. Regenpfeiffer: the most esteemed member of the plover family, found in Europe, America and still abundant in many parts of the British Isles. Plover's eggs are considered a delicacy and protected by law in some countries to prevent the extinction of the bird.

Golden Plover

— **Dumanoir:** roasted, deglaced with brandy and truffle sauce.

— **with Armagnac:** à l'Armagnac: roasted, at serving ignited with a little Armagnac, deglaced with game stock.

— **Catalonian Style:** à la catalane: prepared like partridge.

— **Douglas:** stuffed with truffled forcemeat, roasted, deglaced with brandy and game stock.

— **Lady Morgan:** roasted, deglaced and ignited with Armagnac, meat glaze and a little sweet cream added, boiled up and poured over the bird; garnished with skinned and seeded grapes heated up with a trickle of brandy.

— **Stuffed:** farci: boned, stuffed with game forcemeat mixed with chopped shallots, chopped fat bacon, parsley and seasoning; roasted, served with Italian sauce.

Golubzy po litowski: Lithuanian Cabbage Rolls: blanched white cabbage leaves stuffed with mutton forcemeat mixed with boiled rice, chopped onions sweated in butter, chopped dill and seasoning, rolled together, arranged on sliced carrots and slices of lean bacon, moistened with stock and tomato purée, braised in oven, served with the bacon placed on top, covered with the strained stock boiled up with sour cream and chopped dill sprinkled on top. (Russian)

Goose: F. Oie; G. Gans: domesticated aquatic fowl belonging to the duck family, best under two years of age. Geese are found in all parts of the world and important because of their flesh and feathers. The fat liver, abnormaly enlarged, is considered as a delicacy. Goose is roasted, boiled, salted and smoked, particulary the breast.

— **Alsatian Style:** à l'alsacienne: stuffed with pork sausage forcemeat, roasted, garnished with saurkraut braised with goose fat and triangles of lean bacon cooked with the saurkraut.

— **in Aspic Jelly** (cold): browned, braised, when cold breast removed, carved, put back into position, whole bird coated with the degreased cold thickened gravy mixed with aspic jelly, when set glazed with aspic jelly, garnished with jelly triangles.

— **Bismarck:** roasted, dressed on shredded white cabbage braised with goose fat and white wine, garnished with halved cooked apples stuffed with chestnut purée.

— **Boiled:** Bouillie: boiled in white stock with pot herbs, a larded onion and a bunch of herbs; fat rice or, noodles tossed in butter and almond horseradish cream served separately.

— **Bordeaux Style:** à la bordelaise: stuffed with a mixture of sliced sautéd boletus, soaked white bread, the chopped liver, anchovy butter, pitted green olives, eggs, garlic and seasoning, roasted and served with the natural gravy.

— **with Chestnuts:** aux marrons: stuffed with pork sausage meat mixed chestnuts cooked in stock until more then half done, roasted, served with the natural gravy.

— **Chipolata:** braised, carved, garnished with glazed button onions, glazed olive-shaped carrots, glazed chestnuts, diced fried lean bacon and chipolata sausages, covered with the boiled down thickened stock.

— **Danish Style:** à la danoise: stuffed with apples and raisins, roasted, garnished with baked apples.

Goose

— **English Style:** à l'anglaise: stuffed with sage and onion stuffing, roasted; warm apple sauce served separately.

— **Farmer Style:** à la paysanne: braised, garnished with small slices of carrots, turnips, knob celery and onions, green peas and lozenges of green beans simmered in butter and mixed with the degreased thickened gravy.

— **Flemish Style:** à la flamande: braised, garnished with braised cabbage balls, carrots, turnips, slices of lean boiled bacon and boiled potatoes, covered with the boiled down thickened gravy.

— **French Style:** à la française: cut in pieces, braised with shredded lettuce and green peas.

— **Hamburg Style:** à la hambourgeoise: stuffed with peeled apple wedges simmered in butter and stoned prunes, roasted, served with the natural gravy.

— **Little-Russian Style:** à la petite-russienne: stuffed with thick gruel of buckwheat, braised with sliced onions, sauce finished off with sour cream.

— **Mecklenburg Style:** à la mecklenbourgeoise: filled with white bread stuffing mixed with goose fat, raisins, diced sautéd apples and gooseliver, braised in brown stock and white wine, garnished with braised red cabbage.

— **with Morellos:** aux griottes: browned, braised with mirepoix, red wine and demi-glace, carved, covered with the sauce mixed with stoned cooked morellos.

— **Northern Style:** à la nordique: seasoned with salt and crushed caraway seeds, stuffed with sliced apples and onions seasoned with marjoram, roasted, served with the natural gravy.

— **Pickled:** salé: cut in pieces, rubbed with a mixture of salt, pepper and a little sugar, placed in an earthenware pot and pickled for a few days, cleaned, cooked in white stock with pot herbs and a larded onion, served with saurkraut.

— **Provencal Style:** à la provençale: prepared like duck.

— **Russian Style:** à la russe: cut in pieces, poached in white stock with pot herbs and mushroom waste, covered with white sauce prepared with the stock and sour cream and mixed with sliced boletus.

— **Steamed:** en daube: boned, stuffed with pork sausage meat mixed with diced ox tongue, salt pork, truffles and brandy, tied, placed in an earthenware casserole just large enough to hold the goose, half filled with stock prepared with the bones, calf's feet and white wine, closed hermetically, steamed in oven, served cold in the jellied stock.

— **Strassburg Style:** à la strassbourgeoise: stuffed with apples, roasted, served with braised saurkraut mixed with chestnuts.

— **Stuffed:** farcie: stuffed with apples and chestnuts, braised; the thickened gravy served separately.

— **Visé Style:** à la mode de Visé: boiled in white stock with the giblets and garlic, cut in pieces and kept warm with the degreased stock fat; covered with velouté prepared with the stock, thickened with egg yolks and finished off with sweet cream and purée of garlic cooked in milk.

Goose Giblet Pie: Pâté d'abatis d'oie: wings, gizzard, heart, neck and liver browned in butter, sprinkled with flour, moistened with white stock, seasoned and cooked, when cold placed in pie dish, covered with pie or puff paste and baked.

Gooseliver: F. Foie gras; G Gänseleber: the abnormally enlarged liver of geese fattened especially for this purpose. Prepared as patty, parfait and for other hot and cold dishes and as a garnish.

— **with Apples:** sautée aux pommes fruit: cut in thick slices, seasoned, fried in butter, covered with apple slices fried in butter, fried onion rings and the browned butter.

— **in Aspic Jelly:** see aspic.

— **Braised:** braisée: studded with truffles, wrapped in a thin slice of fat bacon, placed in a service casserole with a little Madeira and rich stock, seasoned, hermetically closed and cooked in oven.

— **Brioche:** Brioche de foie gras: studded with truffles, wrapped in a thin slice of fat bacon, poached 20 minutes, when nearly cold placed in the center of a mould lined with brioche dough, covered with brioche dough, brushed with egg yolk, allowed to raise, baked in the oven; served hot or cold.

— **Celestines** (cold): cold poached gooseliver cut into oval medaillons, covered with chopped truffles, coated with brown chaudfroid sauce, glazed with aspic jelly, dressed on oval slice of gooseliver froth.

— **en Cocotte:** studded with truffles, wrapped in thin slice of fat bacon, seasoned, lightly sautéd in butter, deglaced white wine and veal gravy, placed in a fireproof earthen or china casserole, the stock strained over, closed hermetically with plain dough of flour and water, cooked in oven; Madeira sauce served separately.

— **Cutlets:** côtlettes de foie gras: 1. poached cold gooseliver cut in cubes mixed with half as much diced truffles and mushrooms, bound with thick cream sauce finished with egg yolks, when cold-shaped into cutlets, dipped in egg and breadcrumbs, fried in butter; Madeira or truffle sauce and asparagus tips served separately. 2. (cold) poached cold gooseliver or gooseliver patty rubbed through a sieve, mixed with jelly and whipped cream, seasoned filled in cutlet moulds, chilled, turned out, coated with brown chaudfroid sauce, decorated with a truffle slice, glazed with aspic jelly.

— **Financier Style:** à la financière: studded with truffles, wrapped in a slice of fat bacon, poached in Madeira and rich stock, unwrapped, served with financier garnish.

— **Fried:** frite: cut in thick slices, seasoned, dipped in egg and breadcrumbs, fried in butter.

— **Froth:** Mousse de foie gras (cold): cold poached liver, rubbed through a sieve, seasoned, mixed with aspic jelly and whipped cream, filled in mould lined with aspic jelly and decorated with truffle slices, sealed with aspic jelly, chilled, turned out and garnished with triangles of aspic jelly.

— **Froth Modern Style:** Mousse de foie gras à la moderne: (cold) froth prepared as above but kept very light, filled in a glass or crystal dish, decorated with truffle, bordered

Gooseliver

with triangles of cold poached gooseliver, filled with very light aspic jelly flavored with Sherry, Port or Madeira, chilled.

— **Godard:** studded with truffles, wrapped in thin slice of fat bacon, braised in white wine, mushroom extract and white stock, unwrapped, dressed with Godard garnish and sauce.

— **Hungarian Style:** à la hongroise: dusted with paprika and a little salt, lightly fried in butter, wrapped in a thin slice of fat bacon, placed in cocotte, half filled with Tokay and rich stock, closed hermetically and cooked in oven.

— **Hunter Style:** à la chasseur: cut in slices, seàsoned, coated with flour, fried in butter, dressed on game purée, hunter sauce poured over.

— **Ilona:** braised in Port and rich stock, boiled up with sweet cream, thickened with egg yolk, seasoned with paprika and poured over the liver; buttered noodles served separately.

— **Marshall Style:** à la maréchale: cut in slices, seasoned, dipped in egg and breadcrumbs, fried in butter, a slice of truffle dipped in liquid meat glaze placed on each gooseliver slice, garnished with green asparagus tips; thick veal gravy flavored with Madeira served separately.

— **Nectarines:** Nectarines de foie gras (cold): cupola mould lined first with aspic jelly and then with white chaudfroid sauce, filled with small slices of truffled gooseliver patty, sealed with Madeira aspic jelly, chilled, turned out, garnished with aspic jelly.

— **in Paper Bag:** en papillote: seasoned, fried in butter until half done, wrapped in greased paper with truffle slices and a thin slice of raw ham sautéd in butter, finished off in oven: Madeira sauce served separately.

— **with Paprika:** au paprika: cut in slices, dusted with paprika, sautéd in butter, covered with paprika sauce finished off with cream.

— **Parfait:** the best of all gooseliver confections made exclusively of the finest livers and the blackest truffles in an open terrine and set in fine Madeira jelly.

— **Patty:** Pâté de foie gras: rich confection of fat gooseliver and truffles in round, oval or rectangular pie crust usually marketed as no kitchen can compete nowadays with the patties made by noted firms. Patties are also prepared in terrines. Fresh patties will keep well for 8 to 10 days if stored cold.

— **Perigord Style:** à la Périgord: studded with truffles, marinated in brandy with a bay leaf, seasoning and whole peeled truffles, barded with fat bacon, braised, when ³/₄ done placed in cocotte with the truffles, the marinade and a little veal gravy, closed hermetically and finished in oven; time 20 minutes. Served in the cocotte.

— **in Port:** au porto: seasoned, wrapped in thin slice of fat bacon, lightly fried in butter, braised in Port and veal gravy, unwrapped and served with sauce made with the stock boiled down with thick cream.

— **in Port Jelly:** au gelée de porto (cold) studded with truffles, wrapped in fat bacon, poached in Port and veal

Gooseliver

gravy, when cold unwrapped, placed in glass dish or cocotte, covered with light aspic jelly prepared with the stock and well chilled.

— **in Puff Pastry:** en chausson: studded with truffles wrapped in a thin slice of fat bacon and then in puff pastry decorated, baked in oven; Madeira sauce served separately.

— **Saint-Alliance:** seasoned, placed in fireproof cocotte surrounded with large peeled truffles, moistened with dry champagne, closed hermetically, poached in oven and served in the cocotte.

— **Soufflé:** see soufflé.

— **Strassburg Style:** à la strassbourgoise: sliced, sautéd in butter, arranged on slices of apple fried in butter, a truffle slice on each gooseliver slice, the frying butter poured on top.

— **Talleyrand:** cut in slices, seasoned, coated with flour, fried in butter, dressed in flat croustade filled with macaroni tossed in butter mixed with grated Parmesan, diced truffles and gooseliver; chicken glaze blended with butter and truffle extract served separately.

— **Tartlet in Jelly:** tartlet de foie gras en gelée: tartlet filled with a little gooseliver froth, a round slice of gooseliver parfait placed on top, decorated with truffle and ox tongue, glazed with Madeira aspic jelly.

— **Timbale Montesquieu:** buttered charlotte mould garnished with round slices of truffled chicken forcemeat poached beforehand, lined with chicken mousseline forcemeat mixed with gooseliver, filled with lightly sautéd small slices of gooseliver and truffle slices bound with thick Madeira sauce, sealed with forcemeat, poached in water bath, turned out, garnished with triangles of fried gooseliver covered with Madeira sauce; Madeira sauce severed separately.

— **Tosca (cold):** poached with whole truffles in Madeira and veal stock and kept pink, when cold cut in round medaillons, a slice of truffle on top, glazed with aspic jelly prepared with the clarified stock, placed in halved peeled and cored cold calville apples, poached in white wine, bordered with chopped grilled hazel nuts.

— **Villeroi:** slices of cold poached liver coated with Villeroi sauce, dipped in egg and breadcrumbs, deep fried; Madeira sauce served separately.

Goulash; F. Goulash; G. Gulasch; H. Gulyas: a brown beef stew of Hungarian origin, prepared with beef, veal, lamb or pork or a mixture of all with plenty of sliced onions, paprika and other ingredients.

— **Bárány paprikás:** Lamb Goulash: diced lean bacon and chopped onions lightly fried in lard, diced lamb added, dusted with paprika, allowed to draw for a few minutes, tomato purée, shredded green peppers and a little water added, seasoned with salt and stewed until done, sour cream added at the last minute, boiled up and served with rice, flour dumplings or tarhonya. (Hungarian)

— **of Beef:** goulash de boeuf: diced shin of beef browned in lard with plenty of sliced onions, dusted with paprika, sprinkled with flour, moistened with water, seasoned and stewed; boiled rice, noodles or macaroni served separately.

Goulash

— **Debreszin Style:** beef goulash mixed with plenty of sliced pickled cucumbers.

— **of Deer:** de cerf: prepared like beef goulash, finished off with sour cream.

— **Esterházy:** beef goulash seasoned with paprika, thyme, bay leaf, allspice, garlic, pepper and vinegar, when done finished off with sour cream and mixed with coarse julienne of parsley roots, carrots and knob celery.

— **Gipsy Style:** à la tsigane: prepared like Hungarian goulash but with equal parts of beef, veal, pork and mutton.

— **Hamburg Style:** à la hambourgeoise: beef goulash moistened with half white wine and half stock, seasoned with paprika, garlic and chopped lemon peel, mixed with capers.

— **Hungarian:** à la hongroise: sliced onions and crushed garlic lightly fried in lard, three times as much diced beef shin, paprika, marjoran and crushed caraway seeds added, seasoned with salt and simmered for a while, moistened with water, when half done diced green peppers, chopped tomatoes and potatoes cut in quarters or large cubes added and stewed until done; it should swim in a sort of clear red gravy.

— **Hunyady:** prepared like veal goulash but with pork, large potato dices added.

— **Karlsbad Style:** beef goulash finished off with sour cream and served with very small flour dumplings.

— **Karolyi:** beef goulash with plenty of tomatoes and large diced potatoes in the sauce.

— **Old Vienna Style:** same as beef goulash with large potato dices added shortly before meat is done, sauce seasoned with a little vinegar.

— **Stroganoff:** see Govia Dina Stroganoff.

— **Székely Style:** sliced onions lightly fried in lard, dusted with paprika, allowed to draw for a minute and moistened with water, not to lean pork cut into large dices, crushed garlic, salt and crushed caraway seeds added, simmered for a few minutes, moistened with water, seasoned with salt and as much saurkraut as meat added, stewed, a little sour cream added when nearly done.

— **of Veal:** de veau: chopped onions fried in lard until yellow, shoulder or breast of veal cut into large dice added, dusted with paprika, allowed to draw for a minute, moistened with very little water, seasoned with salt and simmered for a while in a closed casserole, flour mixed with sour cream and a little tomato purée added and stewed until done.

— **Viennese:** à la viennoise: half as much sliced onions as beef sautéd in lard, dusted with paprika, a few drops of water and the diced beef added, simmered for a while in a closed stewpan, seasoned with crushed garlic, majoran and crushed caraway seeds, after a while dusted with flour, moistened with rich stock, potatoes cut in quarters added and stewed.

— **Zelný gulyas:** Cabbage Goulash: beef goulash seasoned with paprika and caraway seeds, moistened with white wine and a little vinegar, mixed with shredded white cabbage. (Tchecho Slovakian)

Goulash

— **Znaim Style:** prepared with half pork and half veal, seasoned with paprika, majoran, garlic and caraway seeds, stewed in own gravy, not thickened with flour, mixed with plenty of small sliced pickled cucumbers.

Gosling: F. Oison; G. Junggans: young goose when five or six months old is called gosling or green goose and principally roasted.

Govia Dina Stroganoff: Sauté of beef Stroganoff: tenderloin of beef cut in cubes and sautéd rapidly in butter blood rare; plenty of chopped onions browned separately in butter, boiled up in demi-glace and seasoned with mustard, a little lemon juice and vinegar and finished off with thick sour cream. Beef tossed in the sauce but not boiled and served immediately. (Russian)

Gras double: see tripes.

Green Goose: see gosling.

— **Plover:** see lapwing.

Grenadin de lapereau: see rabbit.

— **de veau:** see veal.

— **de volaille:** see chicken.

Grive: see fieldfare.

Grouse; F. Grouse; G. Schottisches Waldhuhn: very fine game bird found in Great Britain, especially in Scotland. American varieties are ruffled, blue and spruce grouse and sage cock. Prepared like partridge but best roasted and served with the pan gravy.

— **English Style:** à l'anglaise: roasted, placed on croûton, garnished with watercress and lemon; bread sauce and fried breadcrumbs served separately.

— **with Orange Sauce:** à l'orange: barded, roasted, served on croûton; orange jelly diluted with a little white wine, seasoned with lemon juice and mixed with blanched orange julienne served separately.

— **Rob Roy:** barded with lard marinated beforehand with whisky, roasted, ignited with whisky, boiled up with veal gravy.

Guinea Fowl; F. Pintade; G. Perlhuhn: a native of West Africa now domesticated in Europe and America. Young birds are barded and must be roasted rare and basted frequently as their flesh is rather dry by nature. Older birds are best braised or stewed.

— **Alsatian Style:** à l'alsacienne: stewed in veal stock with cabbage, carrots and a piece of lean bacon; served carved on top of cabbage, garnished with the sliced carrots, bacon, fried pork sausages and boiled potatoes.

— **American Style:** à l'américaine: cut open at the back, flattened; seasoned, brushed with butter, grilled; garnished with fried tomatoes and fried sliced bacon.

— **Borsdorp Style:** barded, roasted, deglaced with white wine and pepper sauce; garnished with peeled apples, scooped out, poached in butter and lemon juice and filled with cooked cranberries spiced with cinnamon and a little sugar and thickened with corn starch.

— **in Casserole:** en casserole: roasted in fireproof China or glass casserole; served in the closed casserole with a spoonful of rich gravy.

Guinea Fowl

— **with Celery:** aux céleris: old bird braised in light demi-glace, garnished with braised celery with blanched slices of ox marrow on top.

— **Charterhouse Style:** à la chartreuse: prepared like pheasant.

— **in Cream Sauce:** à la crème: roasted, shortly before bird is done sour cream added.

— **Creole Style:** à la créole: disjointed, browned in butter, braised in light demi-glace with chopped onions, diced tomatoes. Green peppers, mushrooms and chopped ham.

— **Czech Style:** à la tcheque: stuffed with a gooseliver lightly poached and dusted with paprika; roasted, deglaced with Madeira sauce.

— **Forester Style:** à la forestière: barded, roasted, shortly before bird is done bacon removed to allow breast to brown; placed in cocotte garnished with sautéd morels, diced fried potatoes and bacon; covered with the deglacage boiled up with duxelles sauce.

— **German Style:** à l'allemande: larded, braised, served on saurkraut mixed with poached oysters; Madeira sauce.

— **Knickerbocker:** boned breasts dipped in melted butter and breadcrumbs, brushed with oil, grilled; garnished with French fried potatoes; Colbert sauce served separately.

— **Mirabeau:** disjointed, browned in butter, braised in light demi-glace with diced fried bacon, mushrooms, fancy shaped turnips and chopped tarragon.

— **Nesselrode:** disjointed, coated with flour, fried; demi-glace with tomato and chestnut purée served separately.

— **with Oranges:** à l'orange: barded, roasted, deglaced with brandy, orange juice and thick veal gravy; garnished with orange fillets.

— **Polish Style:** à la polonaise: filled with bread stuffing; served in cocotte covered with chopped hard-boiled eggs, chopped parsley and breadcrumbs browned in plenty of butter.

— **Singapore:** Singapoure: disjointed, marinated with curry powder, chopped shallots and lemon juice; coated with flour and sautéd; deglaced with pineapple juice, cream and veal gravy, boiled down, diced pineapple added and poured over the bird.

— **Stuffed:** farcie: stuffed with soaked bread mixed with eggs, chopped onions simmered in butter, chopped fat bacon, parsley, sage, pepper and salt; roasted, served with the pan gravy and red current jelly.

— **Suprême of:** Suprême de pintade: prepared like suprême of pheasant.

H

Hachis: see hash.

Ham: F. Jambon; G. Schinken: hind leg of hog pickled in brine and smoked. Ham differs greatly in size, taste, colour and quality according to breed and the method of curing. Regions famous for hams are Virginia in America, Prague in Tschechoslowakia, Bayonne in France, Westphalia in Germany and York in England. Ham which is

Ham
to be baked or braised is parboiled, taken out of the stock half an hour before it is done and skinned and trimmed.

— **Alsatian Style:** à l'alsacienne: parboiled, braised in Riesling with saurkraut and a piece of lean bacon; carved, dressed on the saurkraut with the sliced bacon and Stassburg sausages; Madeira sauce and boiled potatoes served separately.

— **Ambassador Style:** à l'ambassadeur (cold): boiled, when cold skinned with exception of a small piece near end of shank bone which is left on and cut zig-zag; with a slanting cut, top side of ham cut off up to about an inch from end of skin, halved lengthwise, carved in thin slices and put aside, the cavity formed by the piece cut off filled with gooseliver froth mixed with diced truffles and allowed to set. The sliced ham arranged with a truffle slice looking out between the ham slices right and left on top of the froth with a line of small fluted mushrooms lengthwise between them, glazed with Madeira aspic jelly, placed on a long silver platter and garnished with aspic jelly.

— **Baked:** au four: Prague ham parboiled, wrapped in pie dough, decorated, brushed with egg yolk, a hole left in the center to permit the steam to escape; when done a little Sherry or Port poured through the hole; meat glaze flavored with Port and buttered lightly served separately.

— **Bayonne Style:** à la bayonnaise: parboiled, braised in Madeira, glazed; risotto mixed with diced tomatoes, small mushroom caps, tiny chipolatas, and Madeira sauce served separately.

— **Bellevue:** en belle vue (cold): boiled, when cold top side cut off and carved, replaced into position, decorated to taste with truffle, hard-boiled egg white, blanched tarragon leaves etc., glazed with aspic jelly and garnished with triangles of aspic jelly.

— **in Bread Crust:** en croûte: parboiled, allowed to cool, wrapped in dough of rye flour, baked; warm potato salad served separately.

— **Burgundy Style:** à la bourguignonne: parboiled, braised in white Burgundy with mirepoix bordelaise and mushroom waste; Madeira sauce mixed with sliced sautéd mushrooms or fairy ring mushrooms and the reduced and strained stock served separately.

— **with Chestnut Purée:** au purée de marrons parboiled, braised in white wine, glazed; served with pepper sauce and chestnut purée.

— **Clamart:** parboiled, braised in Madeira; Macaire potatoes, green peas prepared in the French way with shredded lettuce and Madeira sauce served separately.

— **Countess Style:** à la comtesse: parboiled, studded with truffle, braised in Madeira, glazed; garnished with braised lettuce and chicken mousseline dumplings; Madeira sauce.

— **Courland Style:** à la courlandaise: thick slice of mild cured ham fried and covered with deep fried onion rings; sauce made of onions simmered in butter and white wine, strained, boiled up with sour cream and seasoned with Kabul sauce served separately.

Ham

— **English Style:** à l'anglaise: parboiled, wrapped in bread dough, baked; served with fancy shaped boiled root vegetables and Madeira sauce.

— **Financier Style:** à la financière: braised in Madeira; financier garnish and sauce.

— **Fitz-James:** parboiled, braised in Madeira, glazed; garnished with shaped tomato rice and stuffed mushrooms, Madeira sauce mixed with the reduced braising stock and small cockscombs and cock's kidneys served separately.

— **Flemish Style:** à la flamande: boiled, garnished with cabbage balls, slices of garlic sausage and lean boiled bacon, shaped carrots, turnips and boiled potatoes; Madeira sauce.

— **with French Endives:** aux endives: boiled, served with Madeira sauce and braised French endives.

— **Godard:** parboiled, braised in Madeira; Godard garnish and sauce.

— **Lacroix** (cold): thin slices of Prague ham with a thin slice of truffled gooseliver parfait between two slices, placed in glass dish and covered with very light Madeira aspic jelly.

— **in Madeira**: au madère: parboiled, braised in Madeira, served with Madeira sauce and a vegetable to taste.

— **Mecklenburg Style:** à la mecklenbourgeoise: boiled, coated thickly with grated rye bread mixed with sugar, powdered cloves and cinnamon, melted butter dropped on top, gratinated in oven.

— **Metternich:** parboiled, baked in pie dough with slices of sautéd gooseliver with a large truffle slice on top, buttered asparagus tips and demi-glace with truffle essence served separately.

— **Milanese Style:** à la milanaise: parboiled, braised in white wine, glazed; macaroni prepared the Milanese way and demi-glace with tomato served separately.

— **Muskau:** parboiled, braised in Sherry, glazed; served with spinach croquettes with chopped ham and financier sauce with the reduced Sherry and sliced truffles.

— **with Noodles:** aux nouilles: braised, served with buttered noodles and Madeira sauce.

— **Norfolk Style:** à la Norfolk: parboiled, baked in pie dough; slices of braised calf's sweetbread, green peas prepared farmer's way and the braising stock of the sweetbread served separately.

— **with Pommard:** au Pommard: parboiled, braised in Pommard and glazed; garnished with button mushrooms, glazed button onion and sautéd cock's kidneys; demi-glace with the boiled down braising stock served separately.

— **with Saurkraut:** au choucroute: boiled, served with braised saurkraut, boiled potatoes and demi-glace flavored with Rhine wine.

— **Souabian Style:** à la souabe: braised in pale beer with sliced onions and brown stock; stock strained and thickened with arrow-root.

— **with Spinach:** aux epinards: braised, served with Madeira sauce and spinach purée.

Ham

— **Valencienne Style:** à la valencienne: parboiled, braised in white wine; served with risotto mixed with diced tomatoes and green peas, and demi-glace mixed with the reduced braising stock.

— **Virginia Style:** parboiled, studded with cloves, dusted with powder sugar, baked and glazed; crushed peppercorns covered with wine vinegar, reduced, boiled up with rich veal gravy, strained, mixed with caramel sugar and soaked seedless sultanas, boiled up, flavored before serving with Sherry and served separately.

— **Wagram:** parboiled, braised in Marsala and glazed; garnished with glazed chestnuts, saurkraut, very small black puddings and chicken sausages; Marsala sauce.

Ham Mousse: Mousse de jambon: mild cured raw ham, ground, pounded in mortar with raw egg white, rubbed through a fine sieve and chilled, blended carefully with heavy cream and seasoned; filled in Charlotte mould greased with butter, poached covered in water bath and allowed to rest for a few minutes before mousse is turned out.

— **Alexandra:** mould decorated with truffle slices and rhombic shaped pieces of raw ham before mousse is filled in; poached, turned out, covered with German sauce mixed with grated Parmesan and glazed; served with buttered green asparagus tip.

— **Chartrese Style:** à la Chartres: filled in cylindrical mould, poached; turned out, covered with thick veal gravy flavored with Port and blended with butter, center filled with small pieces of green asparagus tips; mushroom purée mixed with chicken purée served separately.

— **Clamart:** poached, covered with Madeira sauce; garnished with shaped Macaire potatoes and tartlets filled with green peas prepared in the French way mixed with shredded lettuce.

— **Florence Style:** à la florentine: poached, covered with German sauce colored with spinach purée; spinach leaves tossed in butter served separately.

— **Hungarian Style:** à la hongroise: covered with paprika sauce and glazed; garnished with small gratinated cauliflower balls.

Ham Mousselines: Mousselines de jambon: same forcemeat as mousse filled in small oval individual moulds greased with butter, shaped with two soup spoons or with a piping bag, poached and served with the same sauces and garnishes as mousse.

Hamburger Rauchfleisch: smoked brisket of beef cut in very thin slices and served with grated horseradish (German).

Hare; F. Liêvre; G. Hase: esteemed game quadruped which inhabits the plains and woods of Central Europe from France up to the Caucasus and North Russia and North Sweden, North Italy, South of France, Scotland, parts of England and the Americas. Young hares, whole or in part, are larded and roasted rare, old ones and trimmings used for soup, patties, forcemeat or fumet.

— **Cutlets:** Cotelettes de lîèvre: prepared in three different ways: 1. with leftovers, mushrooms and truffles, chopped finely, bound with Béchamel sauce, shaped like cutlets,

Hare
dipped in egg and breadcrumbs and fried.
2. chopped raw hare flesh mixed with soaked bread, butter and seasoning, cutlet-shaped, coated with flour and fried in clarified butter.
3. hare forcemeat mixed with panade and seasoning, filled in greased cutlet moulds and poached.
— **Berlin Style:** à la berlinoise: prepared in the 3rd. way, covered with pepper sauce finished off with sour cream, garnished with very small apples, peeled, center cored out, poached in white wine and water and filled with braised red cabbage.
— **Diana:** Diane: prepared in the 2nd. way, fried in butter, served with chestnut purée and Diana sauce.
— **Mirza:** prepared in the 2nd. way, fried in butter, placed on half an apple, peeled, center bored out, fried and filled with red currant jelly; pepper sauce served separately.
— **Morland:** prepared in the 2nd. way, dipped in melted butter and chopped truffles, fried in clarified butter, dressed on mushroom purée, bordered with pepper sauce or the sauce served separately.
— **with Mushrooms:** aux champignons: prepared in the 1st. way, fried in butter, garnished with sautéd mushrooms; mushroom sauce served separately.
— **Pojarski:** prepared in the 2nd. way, fried in clarified butter, sauce and garnish to taste.
— **Saint-Marc:** prepared in the 3rd. way but shaped by hand, coated with flour, fried in butter and garnished with chestnut croquettes; pepper sauce and cranberries served separately.
— **English Style:** rôti à l'anglaise: belly stuffed with mixture of chopped suet, soaked bread, the chopped liver, chopped ham, lemon peel, eggs and chopped herbs seasoned with salt, pepper and nutmeg, sewed together, roasted and basted with butter, served with the pan gravy and red currant jelly.
— **German Style:** à l'allemande: larded, roasted, pan gravy boiled up with sour cream, served with red cabbage and potato purée.
— **Potted:** Hase im Topf: boned, cut in pieces, seasoned and sprinkled with grated rye bread, filled in fireproof pot alternately with diced pork belly, covered with red wine mixed stock and a little vinegar, sealed hermetically with dough and stewed in oven; potato dumplings served separately (German).

Hare, Fillets of: Filets de lièvre: the two fillets removed from loin (saddle), skinned, larded with fat bacon or truffles and always roasted, sautéd or grilled rare.
— **Charles V.:** sautéd in butter on one side only, this side coated with goose liver forcemeat, covered with greased paper and finished off in oven, garnished with ragoût of button mushrooms, truffle slices, hare kidneys and tiny game dumplings bound with Madeira sauce.
— **Diana:** prepared like saddle of hare.
— **Mirza:** prepared like hare cutlet.
— **Norman Style:** à la normande: pan fried, deglaced with cider, boiled up with cream and hare stock, seasoned, strained and poured over the fillets, garnished with apple slices sautéd in butter.

Hare, Fillets of

— **Roman Style:** à la romaine: roasted, served with chestnut, celery or lentil purée and Roman sauce.

— **Sully:** larded, shaped and tied like a crescent, cooked in butter and brandy, untied, center of one fillet filled with lentil purée, center of the other with celery purée, a slice of truffle on top, covered with pepper sauce.

— **Vendôme:** shaped as for Sully, roasted, dressed on base of poached hare forcemeat, center filled with ragoût of mushroom and truffle slices sauced with the pan gravy deglaced with brandy; chestnut purée and pepper sauce served separately.

Hare, Jugged: Civet de lièvre: cut in pieces, marinated with brandy, oil, salt, pepper and sliced onions. Fry diced blanched lean bacon and quartered onions light brown in butter, sprinkle with flour, brown lightly, add the hare pieces wiped dry and sauté them in the butter stirring continously, moisten with red wine, add garlic and a bunch of herbs, cover stewpan and cook slowly. Shortly before the hare is done add the reserved blood and the liver cut in small slices. Pick out hare and liver in a clean stewpan, add glazed button onions and sautéd button mushrooms, strain sauce over the meat and serve surrounded with heart-shaped croûtons.

— **Brussels Style:** à la bruxelloise: with diced fried bacon, glazed button onions and peeled seeded grapes.

— **Flemish Style:** à la flamande: cooked in red wine with a little vinegar, plenty of sliced onions and a little brown sugar, garnished with croûtons coated with red currant jelly.

— **German Style:** à l'allemande: marinated in wine vinegar, water, pot herbs and sliced onions, prepared as above but moistened with bouillon and a part of the marinade, bound with the hare blood, garnished with button onions, mushrooms and fried diced bacon.

— **Lyonese Style:** à la lyonnaise: prepared as usual but with glazed chestnuts and without button onions or mushrooms.

Hare, Legs of: Cuisses de lièvres: skinned, larded, roastet, served with chestnut purée, braised red cabbage or lentil purée and pepper or sour cream sauce.

Hare, Mumbled: jugged, mixed when done with raw beaten eggs.

Hare, Parfait of: Parfait de lièvre (cold): roast cold hare pounded in mortar with a little cold Béchamel sauce and a quarter as much poached gooseliver, rubbed through a sieve, seasoned with salt, pepper and Madeira, mixed with cold aspic jelly and when beginning to set with whipped cream, filled in parfait mould lined with aspic jelly, chilled, turned out and garnished with aspic triangles.

Hare Pie: Pâté chaude de lièvre: charlotte mould lined with pie dough, sides and bottom coated with hare forcemeat mixed with panade, filled with very small slices of hare fillets very lightly sautéd in butter, covered with a few spoons of salmi sauce with red wine, prepared with the hare bones, sealed with forcemeat, closed with pie dough, baked in oven and turned out on round platter; salmi sauce served separately.

Hare, Saddle of: Râble de lièvre: back of hare from the haunch up to the first ribs, skinned, larded and roasted rare.

— **Chief Ranger Style:** à la grand-veneur: marinated, larded, roasted, served with chief ranger sauce and chestnut purée.

— **Diana:** larded, roasted, served with chestnut purée and Diana sauce.

— **Forester Style:** à la forestière: larded, roasted, garnished with sautéd morels, diced fried bacon and pan fried diced potatoes; duxelles sauce blended with the pan gravy served separately.

— **German Style:** à l'allemande: marinated, larded, roasted, deglaced with sour cream and brown gravy.

— **with Grapefruit:** larded, roasted, deglaced with white wine, boiled up with demi-glace, seasoned with grapefruit juice and mixed with julienne of blanched grapefruit peel, garnished with sections of fresh grapefruit warmed up in butter, covered with the sauce.

— **Morand:** larded, roasted, served with pepper sauce with strips of blanched lemon zest and truffle julienne.

— **Rôtisserie Périgourdine:** flanks left long, stuffed with the minced liver, heart, lungs, chicken livers, green bacon and soaked bread mixed with eggs, grated fresh truffles, chopped shallots and garlic, well seasoned, wrapped entirely in thin slices of fat bacon, tied together, braised in Madeira with brown stock and truffle extract, when cold bacon removed, top side covered with truffle slices, wrapped in puff paste, decorated, brushed with egg yolk, baked, served with the boiled down thickened gravy mixed with julienne of truffles and chestnut purée.

— **Russian Style:** à la russe: marinated in vinegar and water with sliced onions, carrots and seasoning, browned in butter, braised in sour cream, sauce prepared with the cream boiled down with chopped onions, demi-glace and a little of the strained pickle, finished off with cooked chopped beetroots.

— **Saint-Hubert:** larded, roasted with a few crushed juniper berries added, deglaced with game sauce and strained, garnished with sautéd mousserons and hare forcemeat poached in tartlet mould, covered with the sauce.

— **Swiss Style:** à la suisse: larded, browned with diced lean bacon in butter, braised with brown stock and sour cream, seasoned with vinegar and chopped lemon peel, gravy thickened with breadcrumbs and strained.

— **Viennese Style:** à la viennoise: marinated, roasted, deglaced with sour cream and boiled down with brown gravy, strained, mixed with capers and poured over the saddle; small flour dumplings served separately.

Hare, Suprême of: Suprême de lièvre: prepared with loin fillets cut into thick oblique slices, trimmed, seasoned and fried rare.

— **with Cranberries:** aux airelles: 1. fried in butter, placed on tartlet filled with warm cranberries, covered with pepper sauce boiled up with hare stock.

Hare, Suprême of

2. (cold) trimmed round, fried, pressed lightly, when cold covered with brown chaudfroid sauce prepared with hare stock, decorated with truffle and hard-boiled egg white, glazed with aspic jelly, placed on tartlet filled with jellied cranberries.

— **Montmorency:** fried in butter, placed on artichoke bottom filled with creamed vegetable macedoine, covered with demi-glace flavored with Madeira and reduced hare stock; garnished with greeen asparagus tips.

— **with Orange:** à l'orange: fried rare, dressed like a turban with an orange fillet on each suprême, covered with pepper sauce flavored with orange juice and a little curaçao; center filled with braised glazed chestnuts.

— **Rabelais:** fried, placed on pastry boat filled with chestnut purée, a small fried slice of gooseliver on top, covered with Madeira sauce mixed with truffle julienne.

Hash: Hachis: combination of finely diced meat and vegetables thickened with a suitable sauce. Dark meats are bound with a brown, tomato sauce or thick gravy, white meats with velouté, cream, German or Béchamel sauce and served hot.

— **Beef and Brain:** de boeuf au cervelle de veau: roast beef mixed with diced green peppers and diced boiled potatoes, bound with thick tomato sauce, a slice of fried calf's brain on top.

— **Chicken:** de volaille: minced chicken and mushrooms, bound with thick cream sauce, served on toast.

— **Chicken, Italian Style:** de volaille à l'italienne: roasted or boiled chicken hashed, mixed with Italian sauce, filled in fireproof dish, sprinkled with grated Parmesan, a little oil dropped on top and gratinated; macaroni tossed in butter and mixed with grated Parmesan served separately.

— **Corned Beef:** corned diced beef, lightly fried chopped onions and diced potatoes bound with demi-glace.

— **Gipsy Style:** à la zingara: hashed corned beef mixed with hashed potatoes, and green diced peppers, bound with tomato sauce, a French fried egg on top.

— **Grandmother Style:** à la grand'mère: three parts of beef hash mixed with one part potato purée, filled in soufflé dish, covered with potato purée, sprinkled with a mixture of breadcrumbs and grated cheese, butter dropped on top, browned in oven.

— **Gratinated:** au gratin: scallop shell bordered with piped duchess potato-mixture, filled with lamb, beef or chicken hash bound with a suitable sauce, sprinkled with grated Parmesan, melted butter dropped on top, gratinated.

— **Hare:** de lièvre: chopped onions, lightly fried in butter, mixed with finely diced roast hare and chopped parsley, bound with game sauce or demi-glace served with very small croûtons browned in butter scattered on top.

— **Housewife Style:** à la bonne-femme: finely diced chicken and mushrooms in cream sauce, surrounded with German fried potatoes.

— **Lamb, American:** d'agneau à l'américaine: roast diced lamb mixed with chopped onions, green peppers, diced tomatoes and potatoes, bound with demi-glace.

Hash

— **Lamb, with fried Bananas:** d'agneau aux bananes frites: minced lamb and potatoes bound with cream sauce, garnished with halved bananas coated with flour and fried in butter.

— **Mexican:** d'agneau à la mexicaine: roast diced lamb mixed with chopped fried onions, chopped chili peppers, diced red and green peppers, bound with thick tomato sauce.

— **Mutton:** de mouton: finely diced boiled mutton, mixed with brown onion sauce, a fried egg on top.

— **and Poached eggs:** Hachis de boeuf aux oeufs pochés: corned beef hash served with poached eggs.

— **Polish Style:** de volaille à la polonaise: finely diced chicken mixed with diced boletus or mushrooms sautéd in oil, bound with pepper sauce, chopped parsley and hard boiled egg scattered on top, a litte browned butter poured over the hash.

— **Portuguese Style:** à la portugaise: diced roast beef and lightly fried chopped onions mixed with tomatoes concassées, sprinkled with grated white bread and cheese, browned in oven, garnished with halved stuffed tomatoes.

— **Saint-Hubert:** game hash bound with game sauce, a poached egg on top.

— **and Spinach:** Hachis Marianne: diced chicken bound with cream sauce, dressed on leaf spinach tossed in butter, bordered with potato purée.

Haunch of Roe-Deer: see roe-deer, leg of.

Hazel-Hen; F. Gelinotte; G. Haselhuhn: game bird which inhabits the pine forests in Europe from the Alps to Russia, Siberia and Japan. The flesh is white, tender and tasty but a little dry. It must, therefore, be barded and frequently basted with butter. Young birds are roasted or broiled, the old ones braised. Most recipes for partridge may be used.

— **Chaudfroid Savoy Style:** Chaudfroid de gelinotte à la savoyarde: roasted breast coated with brown chaudfroid sauce mixed with truffle purée, glazed with aspic jelly; placed on slice of gooseliver parfait, served with truffle salad.

— **Courland Style:** à la courlandaise: cut in pieces, browned in butter with chopped shallots, simmered in sour cream with diced tomatoes, chopped anchovy fillets, mushrooms and seasoning.

— **German Style:** à l'allemande: prepared like pheasant.

— **Grandmother Style:** à la grand'mère: roasted en cocotte, deglazed with brandy and game fumet, garnished with sautéd mushroom, diced whitebread fried in butter scattered on top.

— **Monseigneur:** stuffed with pork sausage meat mixed with grated truffles and diced gooseliver, barded, roasted en casserole, deglaced with Madeira, garnished with sautéd mushroom caps, glazed button onions and fried diced bacon.

— **Polish Style:** à la polonaise: roasted, covered with finely chopped egg-yolks and breadcrumbs browned in plenty of butter.

— **Savoy:** cooked en casserole of which the sides have been rubbed with garlic.

Hazel-Hen
— **Smitane:** roasted, deglaced with white wine, boiled down with sour cream sauce and poured over the bird.
— **Souwaroff:** prepared like pheasant.
— **Timbale Nesselrode:** charlotte mould lined with pie dough, coated thickly with hazel-hen and gooseliver forcemeat, filled with hazel-hen breasts and olive-shaped truffles, sealed with forcemeat, covered with pie dough, baked in oven, turned out on round platter, bordered with demi-glace boiled up with the hazel-hen bones and trimmings, a little sauce served separately.
— **Tsarina Style:** à la tsarine: roasted, garnished with olive-shaped pickled cucumbers and Russian mushrooms (gribuis), covered with the pan juice deglaced with white wine and sour cream.
— **Victoria:** filled with diced gooseliver and truffles, braised, garnished with diced roast potatoes sprinkled with chopped parsley.

Hazel-Hen Breasts: Suprêmes de gelinotte: sautéd, braised or grilled and served with a suitable sauce.
— **Lautrec:** seasoned, dipped in butter, grilled, brushed with liquid meat glaze seasoned with lemon juice, garnished with fried mushroom caps stuffed with herb butter.
— **Lithuanian Style:** à la lithuanienne: sautéd, breadcrumbs fried in plenty of butter poured on top, garnished with sliced fried boletus; Madeira sauce served separately.
— **Little-Russian Style:** à la petite-russienne: sautéd in butter, placed on flat cake of kacha, covered with pepper sauce flavored with cinnamon and Malaga, mixed with chopped morellos.
— **Livonian Style:** à la livonienne: sautéd in butter, covered with pepper sauce finished off with sour cream, garnished with sliced boletus sautéd in butter and sprinkled with chopped parsley.
— **Nicolas:** sautéd, placed on pastry boat filled with chopped boletus, sautéd in butter and bound with thick Madeira sauce, covered with sour cream sauce with strips of pickled cucumbers added.

Heath Cock: F. Coq de bois; G. Birkhahn: prepared like hazel-hen.
— **Roast:** rôti: barded, roasted in hot oven, dressed on croûton garnished with watercress, the pan juice boiled down with game stock served separately.
— **Stuffed:** farci: breastbones removed, stuffed with forcemeat prepared with fat bacon, gooseliver, chopped shallots, diced truffles and seasoning, barded and roasted in oven.

Heron: F. Héron; G. Fischreiher: long-legged voracious bird which lives in many of the European lakes and rivers. It is edible and was formerly bred for food but now protected by law in many countries. Served as a lenten dish.
— **poached:** poché: poached in broth with pot herbs, a larded onion and a little vinegar, served with the boiled down stock seasoned with lemon juice.
— **roasted:** rôti: young bird barded with salt pork, roasted, served with the natural juice boiled up with sour cream.

Hunyadi töltöt: sirloin steak beaten flat, covered with mixture of creamed butter, egg yolk, chopped ham, macaroni cut in slices and egg white whipped stiffly, rolled together, tied with a piece of twine, seasoned, browned in lard, moistened with brown stock with fried onion slices, sliced tomatoes, shredded green peppers and plenty of paprika, stewed, when half done sour cream added (Hungarian).

Husarenfilet: tenderloin steak larded with ham and strips of pickled cucumber, browned, stewed in thin cream sauce, served with boiled potatoes. (Austrian)

Husarenfleisch: small thin slices of tenderloin, veal and pork seasoned with salt and paprika, browned, fried onion slices added, dredged with flour, flour browned lightly, moistened with brown stock, a little vinegar added, when half done moistened with sour cream, served with boiled potatoes (Austrian).

Hure de sanglier: see appetizers, wild boar's head.

I J

Innocents: French name sometimes used for squab pigeons.

Irish Stew: mutton, boned or not, cut into covenient pieces, seasoned with salt and pepper, a good deal of sliced onions added, moistened with water, boiled slowly, when half done sliced potatoes added, chopped parsley sprinkled on top at serving.

Isard: the alpine goat of the Pyrenees, prepared like venison.

Izmir keuftessi: Chopped Mutton Roll: raw mutton; chopped, mixed with soaked white bread, eggs, onion juice, salt, pepper and nutmeg, shaped into longish rolls, fried, covered with tomato purée boiled up with a little water. (Turkish)

Jambon: see ham.

— **d'ours:** see bear's ham.

Jambonneaux: see stuffed chicken legs.

Jarret de veau: see knuckle of veal.

Jungfernbraten: Braised pork Tenderloin: pork tenderloin larded, browned, placed on sliced browned onions and carrots, moistened with sour cream and a little stock, braised, sauce strained and finished off with a few drops of vinegar. (Austrian)

Jungschweinskarree: Loin of Pork: loin blanched, scored, salt and crushed caraway seeds rubbed in, roasted and served with the pan gravy. (Austrian)

K

Kadine-bouton: Beef Dumplings: raw chopped beef mixed with boiled rice, chopped parsley and salt, shaped into oval flat dumplings, boiled, when cold dipped in beaten egg and fried. (Turkish)

Kaiserfleisch: rack of smoked pickled pork, boiled, served with saurkraut and white bread dumplings or with purée of green split peas. (Austrian)

Kangaroo: F. Kangourou; G. Känguruh: the largest of the herbivorous leaping animals native of Australia, com-

Kangaroo
parable to venison. Its heavy tail yields a good soup and is also appreciated for stews.
— **Oriental Style:** à l'orientale: steeped in water, cut into convenient pieces, browned, stewed, garnished with stuffed tomatoes, sliced fried egg plant, fried bananas and sautéd artichoke bottoms; sauce prepared with the braising stock.
— **Saddle of:** Selle de kangourou: marinated in boiled pickle of red wine, sliced onions and carrots, herbs and spices, larded, roasted or braised according to age, garnished as for venison.
— **Stuffed:** farci: stuffed with veal forcemeat mixed with diced bacon and eggs, well seasoned, wrapped in a cloth, cooked in light demi-glace with red wine, onions carrots and mushroom waste, served, with sauce prepared with the gravy flavored with Marsala.
— **Tail, Fried:** Queue de kangourou frit: steeped in water, boned, stuffed with veal and pork forcemeat mixed with eggs, brandy and spices, boiled in stock, chilled, cut in pieces, dipped in egg and breadcrumbs, deep fried, served with mangold, spinach or salsify and tomato sauce.

Kapama: Ragoût of lamb: boned lamb cut into large dice, coated with flour, sautéd in oil with sliced onions, seasoned with paprika and salt, stewed with just a little water until nearly done, plenty of green onions added and stewed until done; covered with spinach leaves and the meat juice, sour cream served separately. (Bulgarian)

Kasseler Rippespeer: see smoked spare ribs of pork.

Kebab, Kabab: Turkish Skewers: slices or cubes of mutton or chicken, seasoned, fixed alternately on skewers with onion slices, dipped in melted butter, oil or mutton fat, grilled and served on saffron rice etc. (Turkish)
— **Chachi-Kebassi:** leg of mutton cut in cubes, marinated with onion and lemon juice, seasoned with salt and pepper, fixed on skewers and grilled; at serving slivered roasted almonds scattered on top and sour cream poured over the kebassi. (Turkish)
— **Osmanie Kébabi:** fat diced mutton marinated in vinegar with chopped onions, salt and pepper; fixed on skewers without the onions and grilled or only stewed with a little water. (Turkish)

Keuftés: Turkish Meat Rolls: chopped raw mutton mixed with bread soaked in water, eggs, pounded garlic, cinnamon and salt, shaped into thumb-sized rolls and fried in mutton suet. (Turkish)

Kid; F. Chevreau; G. Kitz: young goat is very palatable and can be prepared like lamb but it must be highly seasoned.
— **Stuffed:** farci: boned, stuffed with forcemeat prepared with the finely chopped lungs, heart, liver and kidneys mixed with soaked bread, eggs, salt, pepper, nutmeg, majoram and chopped onions sweated in butter, sewed together, roasted and served with the pan gravy or the gravy boiled up with sour cream and condimented highly.

Kisela Dahorp: diced mutton boiled in water with pot herbs, drained, mixed with half-cooked rice, chopped lightly fried onions and a little of the strained stock, seasoned with paprika and vinegar, cooking finished in oven. (Jugo-slavian)

Koenigsberger Klops: raw minced beef and pork mixed with chopped onions, bread soaked in water, chopped anchovies, eggs and seasoning, shaped into round dumplings, boiled in water with sliced onions, a bay leaf, peppercorns and allspice; sauce prepared with the strained stock and white roux mixed with chopped anchovy fillets and capers seasoned with vinegar; dumplings simmered in the sauce for a few minutes before serving. (German)

Köttbullar: Swedish Meat Balls: raw minced beef mixed with chopped beef suet, bread soaked in milk and eggs, seasoned, shaped into flattened balls, browned in butter and simmered in demi-glace; macaroni or creamed green beans served separately. (Swedish)

Kurinuy Koteletki Pojarski: half a raw chicken breast chopped finely with sweet cream, a small piece of white bread soaked in cream, an egg-yolk and a little bit of butter added, seasoned, shaped into two cutlets, turned in bread-crumbs, fried in butter; garnished with a spring vegetable and German fried potatoes, bordered with demi-glace a little browned butter poured over the cutlets. (Russian)

Kurnik: Polish Chicken Pie: pasty mould lined with puff pastry, filled alternately with very thin unsweetened pancakes, boiled rice mixed with hard-boiled eggs, chopped onions and a little cream sauce, pancake, cold sliced sautéd yellow boletus bound with sour cream sauce, pancake, diced chicken in suprême sauce, a pancake on top, closed with puff pastry, decorated, a funnel in the center, brushed with egg yolk and baked; served hot with suprême sauce separately. (Polish)

L

Labskaus: Sailor's Beef: pickled brisket of beef boiled in water with a larded onion, pot herbs and peppercorns; ground, mixed with chopped onions fried in butter, a chopped desalted herring and mashed freshly boiled potatoes; served hot with pickled cucumbers and red beetroots. (German)

Laemmernes Gebackenes: see lamb shoulder fried Austrian style.

Lamb; F. Agneau; G. Lamm: the flesh of young sheep: from the age of nine months to about one year lamb becomes yearling. In lamb the color of the flesh is light to dark pink, the fat soft and creamy white.

Lamb, Breast of: Poitrine d'agneau: cut derived from the breast roasted or braised, if stewed cut into convenient squares.

— **Baker Style:** à la boulangère: browned in butter, surrounded with sliced potatoes mixed with sliced onions sautéd in butter lightly beforehand, butter or fat poured on top, roasted in oven.

— **with Crayfish:** aux écrevisses: boned, opened on one side, stuffed with white bread soaked in milk, mixed with chopped onions sautéd in butter, chopped herbs, diced crayfish, eggs and seasoning finished off with crayfish butter; roasted served with the pan gravy blended with thick veal gravy.

Lamb Breast
— **Deviled:** à la diable: grilled squares; devil sauce served separately.
— **Fried:** frite: boiled, boned, allowed to cool under light pressure, cut in squares, dipped in egg and breadcrumbs, deep fried, served with fried parsley; light tomato sauce separately.
— **à la Gratar:** grilled: boiled, boned, allowed to cool under light pressure, cut in squares, finely chopped onions and garlic rubbed into the squares, coated with flour, dipped in sunflower oil, grilled on charcoal fire; garnished with sliced red beetroots, pickled green tomatoes, pickled scallions and chilis. (Rumanian)
— **Green Meadow:** à la vert-pré: grilled, garnished with watercress and straw potatoes; half-melted herb butter served separately.
— **Grilled:** grillée: boiled, boned, cooled under light pressure, cut in squares, dipped in egg and breadcrumbs, dipped in clarified butter, grilled; garnished with lemon, potato, lentil or celery purée served separately.
— **Hamburg Style:** à la hambourgeoise: boiled, boned, brushed with butter, breadcrumbs and grated Parmesan sprinkled on top, gratinated in oven; tomato sauce served separately.
— **Shepherd Style:** à la bergère: boiled or braised, boned, allowed to cool under light pressure, cut in squares, dipped in egg and breadcrumbs mixed with chopped mushrooms, coated with melted butter, grilled; garnished with straw potatoes; sauce duxelles served separately.
— **Stuffed:** farcie: boned, opened from on side, stuffed with veal forcemeat; roasted, served with the pan gravy blended with veal gravy and a green vegetable.

Lamb Cutlet, French Lamb Chop: Côtelette d'agneau: cut from the rack, backbone and tip of ribs removed and trimmed, fried and kept a little underdone.
— **Alsatian Style:** prepared like mutton cutlet.
— **Ambassadress Style:** prepared like mutton cutlet.
— **Argenteuil:** dipped in egg and breadcrumbs, fried in butter; creamed asparagus tips served separately.
— **Arlesian Style:** à l'arlésienne: fried, garnished with deep fried onion rings, sliced eggplant and tomatoes concassées
— **Armenonville:** prepared like mutton cutlet.
— **with Artichoke Purée:** à la purée d'artichaut: dipped in egg and breadcrumbs, fried in butter, arranged on artichoke purée, bordered with Madeira sauce.
— **Beaucaire:** fried, garnished with artichoke bottoms filled with tomatoes concassées sprinkled with chopped herbs.
— **Beaugency:** prepared like mutton cutlet.
— **Belle-Alliance:** fried, a slice of sautéd gooseliver and a truffle slice on top, covered with Madeira sauce blended with tomato purée.
— **Bellevue** (cold): fried, allowed to cool under light pressure, decorated to taste, glazed with aspic jelly, arranged like a crown with diced aspic jelly in the center; vegetable or other suitable salad served separately.
— **Bignon:** fried, garnished with tomatoes stuffed with risotto, covered with Madeira sauce mixed with chopped truffles.

Lamb Cutlet

— **Bresse Style:** à la bressanne: fried, garnished with sautéd chicken livers bound with truffled demi-glace and sautéd mushrooms.

— **Breton Style:** à la bretonne: fried, served with purée of navy beans or navy beans prepared in the Breton way and veal gravy.

— **Buloz:** prepared like mutton cutlet.

— **Cambon:** fried, garnished with stuffed eggplant and tartlets filled with diced red peppers simmered in butter; veal gravy.

— **Carême:** cut open on one side, stuffed with thick mushroom purée mixed with salpicon of truffle, cockcombs and cocks' kidneys, fried lightly on both sides, allowed to cool, coated with **Villeroi sauce,** dipped in egg and breadcrumbs, deep fried; tomato sauce served separately.

— **Carignan:** prepared like mutton cutlet.

— **Catalonian Style:** à la catalane: browned on both sides, braised in white wine and demi-glace with sautéd sliced mushrooms and diced tomatoes; shortly before cutlet is done glazed button onions and fried halved chipolatas added.

— **Champvallon:** prepared like mutton cutlet.

— **Charleroi:** prepared like mutton cutlet.

— **Chartres Style:** à la Chartres: grilled, covered with demi-glace with tarragon flavor and chopped tarragon; vegetable as desired served separately.

— **Chatelaine:** grilled or fried, garnished with artichoke bottoms filled with white onion purée, glazed chestnuts and nut potatoes; Madeira sauce.

— **Chatillon:** fried on one side only, this side coated thickly with sliced cooked mushrooms bound with thick Béchamel, grated Parmesan sprinkled on top, glazed and finished off in oven; garnished with green bean purée, bordered with buttered meat glaze.

— **Choiseul:** prepared like mutton cutlet.

— **Constance:** fried on one side, this side coated with veal forcemeat mixed with chopped fine herbs, covered with greased paper and finished off in oven; cream sauce mixed with cockscombs served separately.

— **Conti:** browned on both sides, braised in white wine, a small slice of ox tongue placed on top, covered with pepper sauce; garnished with tartlet filled with lentil purée.

— **Cova:** prepared like mutton cutlet.

— **Crownprince Style:** à la dauphine: grilled garnished with dauphine potatoes; Madeira sauce served separately.

— **Cussy:** prepared like mutton cutlet.

— **Cyrano:** prepared like mutton cutlet.

— **Dénise:** grilled, garnished with small mushroom croquettes and unsweetened soufflé fritters; white navy beans bound with light Dutch sauce and buttered meat glaze served separately.

— **in Dressing Gown:** en robe de chambre: fried blood rare, allowed to cool, **wrapped in puff pastry, baked**; mushroom sauce served separately.

— **Dubelly:** grilled, garnished with potato croquettes mixed with mushroom purée; thick veal gravy served separately.

Lamb Cutlet

— **Durand:** prepared like mutton cutlet.
— **Forester Style:** à la forestière: fried, garnished with sauted morels, diced fried bacon and Parmentier potatoes; Italian sauce served separately.
— **Francillon:** grilled, placed on oval croûton spread with anchovy butter, garnished with straw potatoes; tomato sauce finished off with anchovy butter served separately.
— **Frascati:** fried, garnished with halfmoon shaped potato croquettes, mushroom caps, asparagus tips, small slice of gooseliver and olive-shaped truffles; thick veal gravy served separately.
— **Gardner Style:** à la jardinière: fried garnished with fancy shaped carrots, turnips, green beans, green peas and cauliflower sprigs coated with Dutch sauce; thick veal gravy served separately.
— **Gordon Bennet:** fried, garnished with artichoke bottom with a sautéd round slice of gooseliver on top covered with Mornay sauce and glazed.
— **Greek Style:** à la grecque: fried on one side only, this side coated thickly with rice prepared in the Greek way, sprinkled with grated Parmesan, gratinated in oven; thick veal gravy with tomato served separately.
— **Henriot:** prepared like mutton cutlet.
— **Henry IV:** Henri IV.: grilled, garnished with artichoke bottoms filled with small Parisian potatoes: Béarnaise sauce served separately.
— **Housewife Style:** prepared like mutton cutlet.
— **Imperial Style:** à l'impériale: fried on one side, this side coated with salpicon of lamb's sweetbread bound with cream sauce, sprinkled with grated cheese, glazed in oven; served on truffled rice; Madeira sauce.
— **Italian Style:** prepared like mutton cutlet.
— **Joan of Arc:** Jeanne d'Arc: flattened, dipped in frying batter, deep fried, garnished with nut potatoes; Madeira sauce.
— **Lavallière:** prepared like mutton cutlet.
— **Limoux Style:** Prepared like mutton cutlet.
— **Maintenon:** prepared like mutton cutlet.
— **Maison Dorée:** fried, a slice of sautéd gooseliver and a truffle slice on top, covered with truffle sauce.
— **Malmaison:** prepared like mutton cutlet.
— **Marie Louise:** prepared like mutton cutlet.
— **Marly:** garnished with artichoke bottoms filled with tiny carrot balls tossed in butter; thick veal gravy
— **Marshall Style:** prepared like sweetbread.
— **Mirecourt:** fried on one side, this side coated cupola-shaped with chicken forcemeat, covered with greased paper and finished in oven; garnished with tartlet filled with artichoke purée; a border of velouté finished off with mushroom essence.
— **Modern Style:** prepared like mutton cutlet.
— **Monaco:** prepared like veal steak.
— **Montglas:** fried, covered with Madeira sauce with truffle essence mixed with julienne of mushrooms and ox tongue; garnished with small veal dumplings.
— **Morland:** prepared like mutton cutlet.

Lamb Cutlet

— **Morly:** fried lightly, coated with gooseliver forcemeat, dipped in egg and breadcrumbs, fried in butter; chestnut purée served separately.

— **Muscovite Style:** à la moscovite: browned, braised in sour cream and light stock, when nearly done coarse julienne of pickled cucumber added; covered with the reduced stock and the julienne, garnished with mushrooms, julienne of red beets scattered on top.

— **Navarra Style:** à la navarraise: fried on one side, this side coated with salpicon of red peppers, mushroom and ham bound with thick Béchamel reduced with mushroom stock, sprinkled with grated Parmesan, finished off and glazed in oven; garnished with tomatoes prepared the Navarrese way.

— **Nelson:** prepared like mutton cutlet.

— **Ninon:** fried on one side, this side coated with gooseliver forcemeat; finished in oven, garnished with asparagus tips; Colbert sauce.

— **d'Orsay:** fried, garnished with coarse julienne of mushrooms, truffles and ox tongue bound with velouté.

— **Parisian Style:** grilled, served with Parisian garnish.

— **Perigord Style:** prepared like mutton cutlet.

— **Pompadour:** fried, served with Pompadour garnish.

— **Portuguese Style:** à la portugaise: fried, garnished with stuffed tomatoes and castle potatoes; Portuguese sauce.

— **Queen Style:** prepared like mutton cutlet.

— **Rachel:** prepared like mutton cutlet.

— **Reform:** prepared like mutton cutlet.

— **Roman Style:** à la romaine: fried, garnished with tartlets filled with tiny Roman dumplings sprinkled with cheese and gratinated and spinach purée mixed with chopped anchovies, bound with egg yolks, filled in greased beaker moulds and turned out; Roman sauce with tomato purée served separately.

— **Royal Style:** à la royale: fried, placed on croûton scooped out and filled with gooseliver purée; garnished with soufflé potatoes; Madeira sauce.

— **Saint-Hilier:** opened from one side, stuffed with chicken forcemeat, dipped in egg, chopped truffles and ox tongue, fried in clarified butter; Madeira sauce mixed with tomatoes concassées and strips of red pepper served separately.

— **Saint-James:** fried, garnished with shaped tomato risotto and stuffed mushrooms; Madeira sauce with truffle julienne served separately.

— **Saint-Lô:** fried, garnished with sautéd artichoke bottoms cut in quarters and tomatoes concassées; Colbert sauce with chopped tarragon.

— **Saint-Ouen:** fried, garnished with artichoke bottoms filled alternately with green peas, tomatoes concassées and tiny fried potato balls; demi-glace with chopped tarragon.

— **Sandringham:** dipped in egg and breadcrumbs, fried in butter, garnished with French beans, asparagus tips and fondantes potatoes; demi-glace.

— **Savary:** fried, garnished with tartlets of duchess potato filled with chopped braised celery bound with demi-glace, sprinkled with breadcrumbs, butter dropped on top and gratinated.

Lamb Cutlet

— **Shepherd Style:** à la bergère: 1. dipped in egg and breadcrumbs, fried, garnished with a slice of fried ham, sautéd fairy ring mushrooms, straw potatoes and glazed button onions;
2. fried, served in cocotte with fried triangles of bacon, glazed button onions, sautéd morels and straw potatoes.

— **Sicilian Style:** à la sicilienne: fried; broad noodles tossed in butter, mixed with grated Parmesan and purée of sautéd chicken livers blended with a little velouté served separately

— **Susie:** Suzanne: fried, placed on artichoke bottom, decorated with blanched tarragon leaves; garnished with stuffed lettuce; demi-glace with chopped tarragon.

— **Swedish Style:** à la suédoise: marinated, dipped in egg and breadcrumbs, moistened with butter, grilled; Swedish sauce served separately.

— **Talma:** fried on one side, this side coated cupola-shaped with chicken forcemeat mixed with gooseliver purée, sprinkled with chopped truffles, dotted with butter, finished off in oven; cream sauce mixed with chopped mushrooms and truffle served separately.

— **Unequaled Style:** à la nonpareille: fried on one side, this side coated with chicken forcemeat mixed with chopped green peppers, finished off in oven; border of cream sauce.

— **Villeroi:** prepared like mutton cutlet.

— **Westend Hotel:** fried, garnished with green peas, small stuffed onion, carrots and Parmentier potatoes; Madeira sauce.

Lamb's Ears: Oreilles d'agneau: blanched, parboiled in white stock.

— **Condé:** parboiled, allowed to cool, stuffed with chicken croquette concoction, dipped in egg and breadcrumbs, deep fried; garnished with fried parsley and lemon.

— **Stuffed:** farcies: parboiled, stuffed with chicken forcemeat with chopped herbs, allowed to cool, dipped in egg and breadcrumbs, deep fried; served with fried parsley and lemon.

Lamb Fricassee: Fricassée d'agneau: prepared like chicken fricassee.

Lamb, Galantine of: Galantine d'agneau: lamb shoulder boned, spread out, flattened, coated with lamb forcemeat mixed with eggs, chopped parsley, chopped onions sweated in butter, the diced sautéd liver, diced ox tongue and pickled cucumber, tied in a cloth, poached, allowed to cool under light pressure, cloth removed, glazed with aspic jelly; served carved with a cold sauce as desired.

Lamb Kidneys: Rognons d'agneau: prepared like mutton kidneys.

Lamb, Leg of: Gigot d'agneau: shank bone removed, trimmed and roasted; a clove of garlic inserted in the leg bone will add to flavor.

— **Brabant Style:** à la brabanconne: served with Brabant garnish and the deglaced pan gravy blended with thick veal gravy.

— **Chivry:** salted, coated with flour, wrapped in a napkin, boiled; Chivry sauce served separately.

Lamb, Leg of

— **English Style:** à l'anglaise: boiled with carrots, turnips and onions, garnished with the vegetables; caper sauce served separately.

— **Liege Style:** à la liègeoise: pan-roasted in oval cocotte, a few minutes before serving finely crushed and chopped juniper berries added and ignited with a little Genever.

— **with Mint sauce:** à la menthe: roasted, served hot or cold with mint sauce.

— **Sarlat Style:** à la sarladaise: browned, placed in oval cocotte on sliced raw potatoes mixed with sliced raw truffles, sautéd lightly in butter beforehand; butter dropped on top and finished off in oven.

— **with Tarragon:** à l'estragon: braised with a little bunch of tarragon added and glazed; served with the reduced thickened stock with chopped tarragon.

Lamb Noisette: Noisette d'agneau: a slice of the boned loin about an inch thick nicely trimmed and fried or grilled. Two noisettes are usually served for a portion. Prepared like lamb cutlet.

— **Belle-Hélène:** fried, placed on flat asparagus croquette, a truffle slice on top; thick veal gravy.

— **Dénise:** prepared like lamb cutlet.

— **Dreux:** larded with strips of truffle, ox tongue and ham, fried, financier garnish.

— **English Style:** à l'anglaise: fried, a small slice of fried bacon and a fried lamb kidney placed on top; garnished with watercress.

— **Favorite Style:** à la favorite: fried, a slice of fried gooseliver and a truffle slice placed on top; garnished with green asparagus tips; thick veal gravy.

— **Florence Style:** à la florentine: fried, placed on small semolina croûton with grated Parmesan, garnished with spinach subric; demi-glace with tomato served separately.

— **Frascati:** prepared like lamb cutlet.

— **Greek Style:** fried, placed on croûton, garnished with shaped rice prepared the Greek way; tomato sauce served separately.

— **Henry IV.:** prepared like lamb cutlet.

— **Judic:** fried, dressed on croûton, a slice of truffle and a cocks' kidney on top; garnished with braised lettuce; demi-glace.

— **Maintenon:** prepared like veal cutlet.

— **Marigny:** fried, garnished with tartlets, filled alternately with green peas and diced green beans, and castle potatoes; thick veal gravy.

— **Marshall Style:** prepared like sweetbread.

— **Masséna:** fried, placed on artichoke bottom filled with thick Béarnaise sauce, a slice of blanched ox marrow on top, covered with tomato sauce.

— **Montpensier:** fried, deglaced Madeira and demi-glace mixed with truffle strips and poured over noisette; garnished artichoke bottom filled with asparagus tips.

— **Provencal Style:** à la provençale: fried, garnish and sauce Provencal.

— **Soubise:** fried, placed on croûton, garnished with artichoke bottoms filled with white onion purée; Madeira sauce.

Lamb Noisette

— **with Tarragon:** à l'estragon: fried, a slice of blanched ox marrow and two blanched tarragon leaves placed on top; garnished with Parisian potatoes; tarragon sauce served separately.

Lamb Ragoût, Egyptian Style: Ragout d'agneau à l'égyptienne: diced lamb browned in oil with chopped onions and garlic, sprinkled with flour, moistened with stock and stewed with diced tomatoes added; when done filled in timbale dish with whole green beans, parboiled and sautéd in oil until colored light brown, and chopped parsley on top.

Lamb, Saddle of: Selle d'agneau: prepared like saddle of mutton.

Lamb, Shoulder of: Épaule d'agneau: cut from the forequarters, mainly boned, rolled, tied and roasted or braised.

— **Baker Style:** prepared like lamb breast.

— **Breton Style:** à la bretonne: roasted, served with purée of navy beans prepared the Breton way; veal gravy mixed with the deglaced pan gravy served separately.

— **Chevet:** boned, rolled, roasted, garnished with quartered roast potatoes; demi-glace with chopped parsley and shallots cooked in white wine served separately.

— **English Style:** à l'anglaise: boned, rolled, boiled with carrots and turnips; garnished with the vegetables and boiled potatoes; caper sauce served separately.

— **Florian:** roasted, when nearly done brushed with butter, sprinkled with breadcrumbs and gratinated; garnished with braised lettuce, glazed olive-shaped carrots, glazed onions and nut potatoes; clear veal gravy served separately.

— **Fried Austrian Style:** Laemmernes Gebackenes: boned, cut in squares, dipped in egg and breadcrumbs, fried in lard; lettuce salad served separately. (Austrian)

— **Housewife Style:** à la bonne-femme: browned, roasted together with sliced raw potatoes sautéd beforehand and browned button onions.

— **Milanese Style:** à la milanaise: stuffed, roasted; macaroni prepared in the Milanese way and demi-glace with tomato served separately.

— **with Minth Sauce:** à la sauce menthe: roasted, served with mint sauce.

— **Scotch Style:** à l'écossaise: boned, rolled, boiled in water with a larded onion and carrots; garnished with small onions, stuffed with forcemeat with chopped herbs, and parsley potatoes; covered with velouté prepared with the stock.

— **Stuffed:** farcie: boned, stuffed with pork sausage meat, rolled, braised, served with the thickened stock.

— **Warsawian Style:** à la varsovienne: boned, stuffed with sausage meat mixed with soaked bread, eggs, diced hard-boiled eggs and pickled cucumber; braised, the stock boiled down with sour cream; red beet root salad served separately.

— **Windsor:** boned, stuffed with veal forcemeat with panade, chopped parsley and duxelles, rolled, braised, carved, arranged with slices of ox tongue between the lamb slices; the clear gravy and a green vegetable served separately.

Lamb Sweetbreads: Ris d'agneau: prepared like calf's sweetbread.

Lamb Tongue: Langue d'agneau: parboiled, prepared like mutton tongue.

— **Fried:** frite: parboiled, skinned, dipped in egg and breadcrumbs, deep fried; tomato or tartar sauce served separately.

— **Grilled:** grillée: parboiled, allowed to cool, split lengthwise, dipped in melted butter and breadcrumbs, grilled; tomato sauce served separately.

— **in Pig's Caul:** en crépinette: parboiled, skinned, studded with truffle, coated with veal forcemeat, wrapped in pig's caul, dipped in egg and breadcrumbs, moistened with butter, grilled.

Lamb Trotters: Pieds d'agneau: prepared like sheep's trotters.

Landrail, Corncrake: F. Roi de cailles; G. Wachtelkönig: very fine little game bird found in Europe and Africa. Prepared like quail.

Langue de boeuf: see beef tongue.

— **de porc:** see pork tongue.

— **de veau:** see calf's tongue.

Lapereau: young rabbit, prepared like rabbit.

Lapskojs: leftover boiled or roast veal, beef and ham diced, mixed with diced raw potatoes and chopped onions, moistened with stock or broth, seasoned, a bunch of herbs added, cooked, when done bound with cream sauce. (Swedish)

Lapwing, Green Plover; F. Vanneau; G. Kiebitz: game bird found in Europe and America. Prepared like quail. Lapwing eggs are considered a great delicacy and are protected by law in many countries to prevent the extinction of the bird.

Lark; F. Alouette, Mauviette; G. Lerche: small meadow bird widely distributed in Europe and Asia; protected by law in some countries. Larks are chiefly roasted and greatly esteemed baked in pies.

— **Ballotine of:** Ballotine de mauviettes (cold): boned, stuffed with chopped gooseliver mixed with chopped ox tongue and truffle, each lark shaped round and tied in a greased cloth; poached in stock prepared with the bones, cooled in the stock, dried, coated with brown chaudfroid sauce, decorated to taste and glazed with Madeira aspic jelly.

— **English Style:** à l'anglaise: seasoned, brushed with beaten egg, breadcrumbs mixed with chopped parsley sprinkled on top, covered with melted butter and roasted in oven.

— **Farmer Style:** à la paysanne: browned in butter with diced bacon, sprinkled with flour, moistened with warm water, seasoned, a small bayleaf, button onions and olive-shaped potatoes browned in butter added and stewed until done; larks arranged in cocotte together with the garnish, sauce reduced and strained over the birds.

— **Father Philipp Style:** du père Philippe: browned in butter, placed together with diced fried bacon in a round potato with a lid cut off, scooped out and baked until half done beforehand; lid put on top again, potato wrapped in oiled paper and baked until done in oven.

— **Housewife Style:** à la bonne-femme: roasted with diced fried bacon, when done covered with the butter in which

Lark

tiny croûtons have been fried; deglaced with a trickle of brandy and poured around the birds.

— **Mother Marian Style:** à la mère Marianne: larks stiffened in browned butter, placed in a cocotte on sliced apples sautéd in butter and when only a little more then half done, sprinkled with breadcrumbs, melted butter poured on top and finished off in oven.

— **Normandy Style:** à la normande: lid cut off of a middle-sized apple, scooped out, filled with two larks, seasoned, stuffed with a small piece of butter and stiffened rapidly in hot butter beforehand, a few drops of applejack poured on top, lid replaced into position, apple wrapped in unsweetened short paste, brushed with egg yolk and baked in oven.

— **with Olives:** aux olives: browned in butter, deglaced with Madeira and light demi-glace, stoned blanched olives added, simmered slowly until done.

— **in Paper Cases:** en caisses: boned, stuffed with forcemeat prepared with chopped chicken livers and truffle, each lark placed in greased paper case on top of a little forcemeat, a few drops of brandy poured on top, covered with a thin slice of fat bacon, baked in oven and served in the cases.

— **Pie:** Pâté d'alouettes (cold): oval pastry mould lined first with pie dough and then on sides and bottom with thin slices of fat bacon, filled alternately with veal forcemeat and larks, boned and stuffed with highly seasoned veal and liver forcemeat, covered with veal forcemeat, a thin slice of fat bacon and a bayleaf on top. Mould sealed with dough, a paper funnel placed in center to allow steam to escape, brushed with egg yolk, decorated with leaves made of dough, brushed with egg yolk once more and baked. When cold a little aspic jelly poured into the pie through the funnel and allowed to set before serving.

— **Provencal Style:** à la provençale: roasted, when half done quartered sautéd mushrooms, blanched pitted olives, tomatoes concassées with garlic added, a few drops of white wine poured on top, and finished in oven.

— **Ragoût of:** Ragoût de mauviettes: split lengthwise, browned in butter, simmered in a little white stock with chopped ham, a little thyme and finely diced pot herbs; when done dressed in timbale dish covered with the strained lightly thickened and well seasoned sauce.

— **Southern Style:** à la méridionale: boned, stuffed with veal forcemeat with chopped herbs, roasted, served with truffle sauce.

— **Turkish Style:** à la turque: chopped onions sweated in butter with rice, diced sautéd eggplant, saffron, salt, pepper and the larks browned in butter beforehand added, moistened with white stock and prepared like rice pilaf; when done pressed in greased mould, turned out and covered with thick game gravy.

Levraut: young hare, prepared like hare.

Lièvre: see hare.

Liver Cheese: Fromage d'Italie: pork liver and fat unsalted bacon ground finely, mixed with eggs, seasoned with powdered thyme, sage, bay leaf, nutmeg, garlic, salt and

Liver
pepper, filled in rectangular mould lined with fat bacon, baked slowly in oven, when cold coated with aspic jelly, carved.

— **Sausage:** diced pork and calf's liver sautéd rare with chopped onions and fat bacon, seasoned, made into a paste, filled in casings, poached (not boiled) and cooled in cold water.

Lonchas de Ternera: Veal Steak Spanish Style: veal steak dipped in egg and breadcrumbs mixed with grated Parmesan, placed in baking dish greased with butter, covered with melted butter, fried in oven; light tomato sauce poured around the steak. (Spanish)

Longe de veau: see loin of veal.

Lothringian Tart: Quiche Lorraine: tart tin lined with unsweetened short paste, bottom masked with sliced bacon blanched and fried lightly, filled with unsweetened custard seasoned with salt and paprika, butter dotted generously on top, baked in moderate oven.

Love in disguise: calf's heart, soaked in water, larded, boiled until tender, dried, coated with veal forcemeat, rolled in crushed raw noodles, roasted in butter in oven and basted frequently.

M

Majoranfleisch: point of rump or tail piece cut in thick slices, browned in lard with sliced onions, moistened with brown stock, marjoram and seasoning added and braised (Austrian).

Malácz Kovesonya: Hungarian Headcheese: pork and pork swards boiled with just enough water to cover them, garlic, carrots, onions, parsley roots, salt and spice added, when done meat and swards diced, filled in suitable dish, the degreased and boiled down stock poured over the meat and chilled; when set sliced and sprinkled with paprika (Hungarian).

Mandarines de cailles: see quails breast jellied.

Marcassin: see wild boar, young.

Marha Gulyás: chopped onions and garlic lightly fried in lard, diced beef, beef heart, liver and udder added, seasoned with paprika, crushed caraway seeds, majoram and salt, moistened with water, a little tomato purée and stewed; when half done diced potatoes and shortly before serving csipetke (q. v.) added (Hungarian).

Marinebraten: Marine Stew: pan greased with butter, covered with sliced onions, carrots and celery knobs, tenderloin placed on top, browned in oven, moistened with white wine and stock, braised and basted frequently; stock strained, boiled down with sweet cream, mixed with strips of carrots, onions, knob celery and parsley root simmered in butter and poured over the tenderloin; spätzle or rice served separately. (Austrian)

Marrow Bone: Os de moelle: ox marrow bone, split, poached, served hot in napkin as an appetizer.

— **Fritters:** Beignets de moelle: ox marrow poached, allowed to cool off, cut in thick slices, dipped in friying batter, deep fried and served with fried parsley and lemon.

Mauviette: see lark.

Meat Balls: Boulettes: flattish dumplings made of chopped raw veal and pork, bread soaked in milk, chopped onions sweated in butter, eggs and seasoning, fried in butter, the frying butter poured over the dumplings.

Medaillon de boeuf: see tournedos.

Mehemalou: Lamb or Mutton Ragoût: lamb or mutton cut in fairly large dice and marinated in lemon juice with chopped onions, bayleaf, crushed garlic, peppercorns and cloves; browned sharply in mutton fat, dusted with flour, moistened with stock, salt, sugar and saffron added and stewed: when half done soaked stoned prunes and dried muscadel raisins added; sauce finished off with grape sirup, served with slivered roasted almonds on top. (Persian)

Mince: Emincé: small thin slices of boiled, braised or roast meat heated up (not boiled) in sauce, mixed with sliced mushrooms or other ingredients.

— **of Chicken and Rice:** de volaille au riz: small slices bound with suprême sauce, filled in center of a border of risotto.

— **with Cucumbers:** aux concombres: sliced mutton bound with demi-glace mixed with chopped gherkins, garnished, with slices of raw cucumber simmered in butter.

— **Geisha:** sliced chicken bound with curry sauce mixed with tomato purée, flavored with chutney and red currant jelly; plain boiled rice served separately.

— **Housewife Style:** à la bonne-femme: sliced chicken bound with velouté, surrounded with sliced boiled potatoes and mushroom caps.

— **Italian Style:** à l'italienne: sliced chicken bound with Italian sauce.

— **Marianne:** sliced beef bound with pepper sauce, garnished with baked potatoes scooped out and filled with the mash mixed with butter and chopped parsley.

— **with Ox Tongue:** de langue de boeuf: sliced beef bound with demi-glace, slices of pickled ox tongue on top.

— **of Roe-Deer:** de chevreuil: sliced, mixed with truffle slices and sliced sautéd morels, bound with Madeira sauce; garnished with tiny game croquettes.

Miroton de boeuf: see beef, miroton of.

Mixed Grill: a combination of grilled food chiefly served as a luncheon dish, such as lamb chops, lamb kidneys, farm sausages, tournedos, slices of ham, rashers of bacon, veal noisettes, chicken breast etc. with a garnish of tomatoes, mushrooms. sliced potatoes etc.

— **London:** a grilled lamb chop, tournedos, lamb kidney. two rashers of bacon and a small farm sausage garnished with two large mushrooms. two half-tomatoes and watercress; served with herb butter.

— **Master Thuillier's:** du maître Thuillier: for each person: a small veal noisette, a lamb tenderloin, a roe noisette, a breast of spring chicken, a small slice of calf's liver, a rasher of bacon, a large mushroom and two large crayfish tails or a jumbo shrimp. all grilled and garnished with watercress and straw potatoes; herb butter and salad of lettuce hearts served separately.

Mountain Cock: see capercailzie.
Mousse de jambon: see mousse of ham.
— **de volaille:** see chicken mousse.
Mousselines de jambon: see mousselines of ham.
— **de volaille:** see chicken mousselines.
Mudjemeri: Mutton fritters: chopped raw mutton with chopped onions, cold boiled rice passed through a mincer, and eggs, seasoned with salt and chopped herbs, shaped with a soup spoon and fried in mutton fat; tomato sauce optional. (Turkish)
Mussaka, Moussaka: dish of Oriental origin consisting of diced or chopped mutton, onions, garlic, eggplant, tomatoes and other ingredients.
— **Egyptian:** à l'égytienne: raw mutton chopped coarsely, mixed with chopped onions and garlic, seasoned and simmered in mutton fat. Sliced tomatoes and eggplants as well as shredded green peppers each part simmered separately, in butter and seasoned with salt, pepper, paprika and chopped herbs filled alternately with the meat in a baking dish, sprinkled with grated cheese and browned in oven; served covered with browned butter and tomato sauce poured round the edge.
— **Roumanian:** à la roumaine: mixed with diced eggplants and diced tomatoes; border of tomato sauce.
— **Servian:** à la serbe: mixed with diced tomatoes and turnips, browned in oven, border of tomato sauce.
— **Turkish:** à la turque: filled in baking dish alternately with sliced lightly sautéd tomatoes and chopped leeks simmered in butter; browned in oven, bordered with tomato sauce.
Mutton; F. Mouton; G Hammel, Schaf: the flesh of sheep from one to five years old. Well-bred and well-fed sheep three or four years old are the best.
For brains, kidneys, trotters (feet) etc. see sheep.
Mutton Chop: Chop de mouton:
Double chop: same as loin chop but without splitting the loin.
English chop: a 2 inch thick chop from the split loin, backbone removed, rolled the full length with the kidney in the center and fastened by means of a skewer.
French chop: see cutlet.
Loin chop: a cut from the loin split lengthwise including the tenderloin and containing the T-bone.
— **Collops:** Escalopes de mouton: thin slices cut from a tender leg of mutton, trimmed, seasoned, dipped in egg and breadcrumbs, fried in butter, garnished with straw potatoes.
Mutton Cutlet: Côtelette de mouton: chops cut from the loin split lengthwise, trimmed and the topside of the bone well pared, sautéd or grilled.
— **Alberta:** sautéd, arranged on mushroom purée, covered with Colbert sauce, garnished with pan fried potato balls.
— **Alsatian Style:** à l'alsacienne: grilled, garnished with tartlets filled with braised saurkraut, a round slice of fried ham on top, meat covered with thick veal gravy.
— **Ambassadress Style:** à l'ambassadrice: 1. sautéd, deglaced with Madeira and thick veal gravy, garnished with chicken livers and mushrooms sautéd in butter, cockscombs and kidneys, braised lettuce and Parisian potatoes.

Mutton Cutlet

2. sautéd, a slice of braised lamb sweetbread larded with truffle on top, garnished with green asparagus tips.

— **Armenonville:** sautéd, dressed on flat cake of Anna potatoes, covered with Madeira gravy, garnished with creamed morels and cockscombs.

— **Bardoux:** dipped in egg and breadcrumbs fried in butter, garnished with green peas tossed in butter and mixed with chopped ham.

— **Baron Brisse:** 1. browned and stewed en casserole with diced knob celery, garnished with artichoke bottom filled with mushroom purée and Parisian potatoes.
2. sautéd, covered with tomatoes concassées, garnished with soufflé potatoes and artichoke bottoms filled with truffles; truffle sauce served separately.

— **Beaugency:** sautéd, placed on crouton garnished with artichoke bottom filled with tomatoes concassées and bordered with Béarnaise sauce, a blanched slice of ox marrow in the center.

— **Beauharnais:** sautéd, placed on croûton, garnished with watercress and French fried, straw or soufflé potatoes; Beauharnais sauce served separately.

— **Bennet:** sautéd, garnished with artichoke bottoms filled with gooseliver purée, covered with Mornay sauce, sprinkled with grated cheese and glazed.

— **Biarritz:** fried in butter on one side only, this side coated dome-shaped with finely truffled ham forcemeat, placed in a greased pan and finished in oven, bordered with truffle sauce.

— **Billancourt:** sautéd, covered with Madeira sauce, garnished with buttered shelled green Lima beans and chestnut purée.

— **with Boletus:** aux cêpes: sautéd, garnished with stuffed boletus.

— **Breton Style:** à la bretonne: sauted, garnished with cooked navy beans bound with Breton sauce.

— **Buloz:** grilled on one side only, this side coated thickly with thick Béchamel sauce mixed with grated Parmesan, covered with half breadcrumbs and half grated Cheese, melted butter dropped on top, browned; risotto mixed with chopped truffles served separately. The cutlet can also be dipped in egg and breadcrumbs mixed with grated cheese and fried in clarified butter.

— **Burgundy Style:** à la bourguignonne: browned, stewed in casserole with browned button onion, mushrooms and fried diced bacon, the stock boiled up with Burgundy sauce.

— **Cabaret:** browned en cocotte with chopped shallots, deglaced with white wine, demi-glace added, stewed, served in the dish with chopped herbs sprinkled on top.

— **Carignan:** dipped in egg and breadcrumbs mixed with grated Parmesan, fried in oil, garnished with cockcombs and cocks' kidneys dipped in frying batter and deep fried; tomato sauce served separately.

— **Castilian Style:** à la castillane: sautéd, garnished with tartlets made of duchess potato-mixture, filled with tomatoes concassées with a little garlic, and deep fried onion rings, bordered with the pan gravy boiled up with tomato sauce.

Mutton Cutlet

— **Cette Style:** à la cettoise: dipped in egg and breadcrumbs, fried in oil, garnished with fried tomatoes; Madeira sauce flavored with garlic and tomato purée served separately.

— **Champvallon:** rib lamb chops browned in butter, placed in baking dish with sliced onions, seasoned, moistened with white stock, garlic and a bunch of herbs added, stewed 20 minutes in oven, sliced potatoes added replaced in oven and basted frequently until done; served in the baking dish.

— **Charleroi Style:** sautéd on one side only, this side coated thickly with thick white onion purée, sprinkled with grated cheese and finished in oven.

— **Chatelaine:** prepared like noisette.

— **Châtillon:** sautéd, dressed on base of Anna potatoes, coated with chopped mushrooms bound with Béchamel sauce, sprinkled with grated cheese and glazed.

— **Clamart:** dressed on base of Anna potatoes, garnished with tartlets or artichoke bottoms filled with peas prepared in the French way, border of thick veal gravy.

— **Clementine:** sautéd, placed on a slice of ox tongue, a slice of fried sweetbread on top, covered with German sauce mixed with sliced mushrooms, garnished with straw potatoes.

— **Cussy:** sautéd, placed on artichoke bottom filled with chestnut purée — out of season with mushroom purée —, a slice of truffle on each cutlet, covered with Madeira sauce, garnished with large cocks' kidneys rolled in thick Italian sauce.

— **Cyrano:** sautéd, garnished with artichoke bottoms filled with mushroom purée.

— **D'Orsay:** sautéd, garnished with stuffed olives, sautéd mushrooms and castle potatoes, covered with Madeira sauce.

— **Dubarry:** sautéd or grilled, garnished with shaped cauliflower sprigs coated with Mornay sauce, sprinkled with grated cheese and glazed.

— **Durand:** prepared like noisettes.

— **Elysée Palace:** sautéd, a slice of fried calf's sweetbread and a mushroom cap on top; Béarnaise sauce served separately.

— **Farmer Style:** à la paysanne: sautéd, dressed on thin slices of carrots, turnips, celery and onions simmered in butter, garnished with olive-shaped pan fried potatoes and diced fried bacon.

— **Favorite Style:** sautéd, a fried slice of gooseliver and a truffle slice on top, covered with thick veal gravy, garnished with green asparagus tips.

— **Financier Style:** à la financière: sautéd, garnished with financier garnish, financier sauce.

— **with Fine Herbs:** aux fines herbes: browned in butter, taken out of pan, chopped shallots and fine herbs lightly fried in the butter, deglaced with white wine, cutlet replaced in pan, moistened with light demi-glace and simmered until done.

— **Gavarni:** sautéd, covered with Colbert sauce with chopped tarragon leaves, garnished with braised lettuce and glazed button onions.

Mutton Cutlet

— **Hashed:** hashée: kernel cut out but fat left on bone, kernel minced finely, mixed with a third of the weight in butter, seasoned, cutlet reformed with the hash, sautéd carefully in butter, garnished to taste or, after having been reformed, dipped in egg and breadcrumbs, fried in butter and garnished.

— **Henriot:** sautéd rare, when cold coated with Villeroy sauce, dipped in egg and breadcrumbs, deep fried, garnished with creamed morels.

— **Housewife Style: à la bonne-femme:** rapidly browned on both sides, placed in baking dish with parboiled navy beans, sliced carrots and onions, crushed garlic and seasoning, melted butter poured over, finished off in oven.

— **Hungarian Style:** à la hongroise: browned on both sides in lard with chopped onions, sprinkled with paprika, diced fried bacon added, simmered in stock until done, stock boiled down with sour cream and poured over the meat.

— **Hunter Style:** à la chasseur: sautéd, deglaced with white wine, boiled up with hunter sauce and poured over the cutlet.

— **Italian Style:** dipped in egg and breadcrumbs mixed with grated Parmesan, fried in half oil and half butter, garnished with quartered artichoke bottoms prepared in the Italian way.

— **Laura:** fried rare, wrapped in pig caul containing creamed spaghetti cut in small pieces and mixed with tomatoes concassées, dipped in melted butter and breadcrumbs, grilled, bordered with demi-glace with tomato.

— **Lavallière:** prepared like noisette.

— **Limoux Style:** à la limousine: browned on both sides, placed en cocotte with glazed onions and braised chestnuts, finished in oven, a little thick veal gravy poured over.

— **Louisiana:** sautéd, garnished with fried slices of sweet potatoes and bananas, rice fritters and creamed corn.

— **Maintenon:** fried on one side, this side coated thickly with thick Béchamel sauce mixed with white onion purée and sliced cooked mushrooms bound with egg-yolk, arranged on a greased pan, glazed; truffle sauce served separately.

— **Malmaison:** dipped in egg and breadcrumbs, fried, dressed on flat cake of duchess potato-mixture, garnished with fried tomatoes and tartlets filled with purée of lentils and purée of green peas.

— **Mancelle:** sautéd, covered with pepper sauce, garnished with tartlets filled with purée of chestnuts cooked in game stock with celery.

— **Marie-Louise:** dipped in egg and breadcrumbs, fried, garnished with artichoke bottoms filled with mushroom purée blended with white onion purée, bordered with thick veal gravy.

— **Marquise:** sautéd, garnished with tartlets filled with veal marrow, asparagus tips and truffle strips, bound with German sauce blended with crayfish butter, and small piped duchess potatoes mixed with tomato purée.

— **Marshall Style:** à la maréchale: dipped in egg and breadcrumbs, fried, a slice of truffle dipped in liquid meat glaze on top, garnished with green asparagus tips.

Mutton Cutlet

— **Milan Style:** à la milanaise: dipped in egg and breadcrumbs mixed with grated Parmesan, fried in butter, garnished with macaroni prepared in the Milan style; light tomato sauce served separately.

— **Mirecourt:** sautéd on one side only, this side coated cupola-shaped with creamed veal forcemeat with mushroom purée, finished off in oven, garnished with artichoke purée; suprême sauce with mushroom extract served separately.

— **Modern Style:** à la moderne: sautéd, place on tartlet filled with chestnut purée; Madeira sauce mixed with julienne of mushrooms, truffles and artichoke bottoms served separately.

— **Montglas:** sautéd on one side only, this side coated with salpicon of ox tongue, mushrooms and truffles bound with thick Madeira sauce, sprinkled with breadcrumbs, dotted with butter and glazed, bordered with demi-glace.

— **Morland:** dipped in egg and chopped truffles, fried in clarified butter, garnished with mushroom purée, bordered with buttered meat glaze.

— **Murillo:** sautéd on one side only, this side coated with thick Mornay sauce with chopped mushrooms added, sprinkled with cheese, glazed, garnished with grilled red peppers, bordered with tomato sauce.

— **Musketeer Style:** à la mousquetaire: marinated in oil, lemon juice, salt and pepper, sautéd on one side, this side coated with veal forcemeat, dry duxelles and chopped herbs added, sprinkled with grated cheese, browned in oven, garnished with ragoût of sliced mushrooms and artichoke bottoms bound with duxelles sauce.

— **Navarese Style:** à la navarraise: sautéd on one side, this side coated with salpicon of ham, green peppers and mushrooms bound with thick Béchamel sauce, sprinkled with grated Parmesan, glazed in oven, garnished with tomatoes Navarese style.

— **Nelson:** prepared as above but coated with white onion purée blended with chicken forcemeat, sprinkled with breadcrumbs, browned in oven, garnished with croquette potatoes, bordered with Madeira sauce.

— **Nonpareille:** sautéd on one side, this side coated with chicken forcemeat mixed with chopped green and red peppers, finished off in oven; Béarnaise sauce served separately.

— **Parisian Style:** à la parisienne: grilled, served with Parisian garnish.

— **Plaza Hotel:** sautéd on one side, this side coated thickly with purée of baked eggplants mixed with egg yolk, covered with breadcrumbs, dotted with butter, finished off in oven; brown horseradish sauce served separately.

— **Pompadour:** sautéd, garnished with artichoke bottom, filled with lentil purée and a slice of truffle on top, and ball-shaped croquette potatoes; truffle sauce served separately.

— **Provencal Style:** 1. à la provençale: one side sautéd in oil, this side coated with thick Béchamel mixed with garlic purée and egg yolk, sprinkled with breadcrumbs and finished in oven, a grilled mushroom cap filled with a stuffed olive on each cutlet, bordered with Provencal

Mutton Cutlet

sauce. 2. sautéd in oil, garnished with tomatoes fried in oil, sautéd mushrooms and blanched pitted olives; thick veal gravy with tomato and garlic flavor served separately.

— **Queen Style:** à la reine: fried in butter on one side only, this side coated with chicken forcemeat mixed with chopped truffles, finished off in oven, garnished with creamed asparagus tips.

— **Rachel:** grilled, garnished with artichoke bottom with a large blanched slice of ox marrow on top, cutlet covered with Bordeaux sauce.

— **Reform:** à la reforme: dipped in melted butter and egg-crumbs mixed with chopped ham, fried in butter, served with Reform sauce.

— **Richmond:** sautéd on one side, this side coated with thick mushroom purée bound with thick Béchamel sauce and egg yolks, sprinkled with breadcrumbs, melted butter on top, baked in oven, bordered with Madeira sauce.

— **Robinson:** sautéd, garnished with sautéd chicken livers and mushrooms, covered with Madeira sauce.

— **Saint-Cloud:** sautéd, garnished with tartlets filled with peas prepared in the French way, braised lettuce and castle potatoes, covered with demi-glace.

— **Saint-Germain:** sautéd, with Saint-Germain garnish and Béarnaise sauce.

— **Saint-Ouen:** sautéd, garnished with artichoke bottoms filled with peas, fried tomatoes, Parisian potatoes, bordered with tomato sauce mixed with chopped tarragon.

— **Sardinian Style:** à la sarde: sautéd, with Sardinian garnish and tomato sauce.

— **Sevigné:** sautéd on one side, this side coated with salpicon of mushrooms and artichoke bottoms bound with thick Béchamel sauce, dipped in egg and breadcrumbs, fried in butter, bordered with buttered meat glaze.

— **Shepherd Style:** à la bergère: sautéd, a small slice of fried ham placed on top, garnished with glazed onions, sautéd morels, boletus or mushrooms and straw potatoes.

— **Sicilian Style:** à la sicilienne: dipped in egg and breadcrumbs mixed with Parmesan cheese, fried, garnished with broad noodles tossed in butter, mixed with Parmesan, cream sauce and purée of chicken livers.

— **Soubise:** sautéd, dressed on white onion purée, bordered with demi-glace.

— **Sully:** sautéd, garnished with braised lettuce, cockscombs, cocks' kidneys and Parisian potatoes, bordered with Madeira sauce.

— **Swedish Style:** à la suédoise: grilled, Swedish sauce served separately.

— **Tyrolian Style:** à la tyrolienne: sautéd, garnished with fried tomatoes and fried onion rings, Tyrolian sauce.

— **Valois:** prepared like Montglas, garnished with stuffed olives; Valois sauce served separately.

— **Verdi:** prepared as specified for noisette.

— **Victor Hugo:** sautéd on one side, this side coated with thick Béchamel mixed with grated, boiled up horseradish and egg yolk, finished off in oven, thick veal gravy poured around.

Mutton Cutlet
— **Village Style:** à la villageoise: sautéd, coated with brown onion purée, sprinkled with breadcrumbs, butter dropped on top and gratinated.
— **Villeroi:** fried rare, when cold coated with Villeroi sauce, dipped in egg and breadcrumbs, fried.
— **Westmoreland:** dipped in egg and chopped truffles, fried in clarified butter, served on mushroom purée, bordered with Madeira sauce.

Mutton Kidneys: Rognons de mouton see sheep's kidneys.

Mutton, Leg of: Gigot de mouton; gigot de pré-salé.
— **Australian Style:** à l'australienne: boned carefully, opening stuffed with forcemeat of mutton, salt pork, chopped onions, pickled cucumbers and parsley, barded, bound, braised in brown stock with sliced carrots, onions and a bunch of herbs; sauce prepared with the thickened stock.
— **Baker Style:** à la boulangère: roasted slowly in lard surrounded with thick slices of potatoes and onions, the carved slices of meat served on a layer of potatoes.
— **Bayonne Style:** à la bayonnaise: boned, larded with strips of mushrooms, pickled cucumbers and anchovy fillets, marinated in oil, vinegar, sliced lemon, thyme and bay leaf, wrapped in greased paper, roasted in oven; red wine sauce served separately.
— **Boiled:** bouilli: boiled with pot herbs and a larded onion, garnished with boiled carrots and onions; sauce prepared with the stock and white roux served separately.
— **Bordeaux Style:** à la bordelaise: main bone removed, larded with strips of ham, braised, when a little more then half done, blanched diced bacon, carrots and turnips cut in quarters and a little garlic added, braised until done and arranged on a dish with the garnish; tomato sauce blended with the boiled down and strained stock served separately.
— **Breton Style:** à la bretonne: roasted; navy beans prepared Breton style or purée of Lima beans and the natural gravy served separately.
— **with Caper Sauce:** au sauce câpres: boiled, served with caper sauce and boiled potatoes.
— **Dubouzet:** skinned, larded with fat bacon and ox tongue, braised, garnished with small potato dumpling the center stuffed with a little pork forcemeat; tomato sauce boiled up with the gravy served separately.
— **English Style:** à l'anglaise: boiled in water with carrots, turnips, celery, a little salt and a few peppercorns, garnished with the vegetables and boiled potatoes; caper sauce served separately.
— **Housewife Style:** à la bonne-femme: boned, stuffed with pork sausage meat, rolled, bound and braised, when half done sliced carrots, parboiled navy beans, sliced sautéd onions and a little garlic added and braised until done.
— **Liége Style:** à la liégeoise: roasted, the pan gravy deglaced with Genever, boiled down with crushed juniper berries and brown stock, thickened and strained.
— **with Mint Sauce:** à la sauce menthe: roasted, served with cold mint sauce.
— **Ninon:** skinned, larded, marinated in oil, a little vinegar and white wine with sliced shallots, thyme, sweet basil parsley, garlic, a bay leaf and allspice, browned, braised

Mutton, Leg of
with the marinade and white wine, stock thickened, strained and mixed with chopped herbs.
— **Polish Style:** à la polonaise: braised, sauce finished off with sour cream, garnished with stuffed pieces of cucumber.
— **Spanish Style:** à l'espagnole: braised in brown stock with tomato purée and garlic added, garnished with fried onion rings, grilled peppers and fried tomatoes; the strained thickened sauce served separately.
— **Stuffed:** farci: boned, stuffed with veal forcemeat mixed with chopped herbs, bound together, browned, braised, garnished with tartlets filled with green pea purée; the thickened gravy served separately.
— **Tenant Style:** à la fermière: braised, when a little more then half done sliced carrots, turnips, celery and onions added and when done a few small parboiled potatoes.
— **with Turnips:** aux navets: braised, when a little more then half done olive-shaped turnips and button onions, browned in butter, added.

Mutton, Noisette of: Noisette de mouton, noisette de pré-salé: meat from the loin fillet cut in thick slices of the desired size, trimmed and usually sautéd or grilled.
— **with Asparagus Purée:** au purée d'asperges: sautéd, garnished with tartlets filled with asparagus purée, covered with thick veal gravy.
— **Brabant Style:** à la brabançonne: sautéd, garnished with tartlets filled with small Brussels sprouts, covered with Mornay sauce and glazed, and croquette potatoes; bordered with thick veal gravy or Madeira sauce.
— **Braganza:** sautéd, arranged on flat cake of Macaire potatoes, covered with tomatoes concassées, bordered with truffle sauce.
— **Bréhan:** sautéd, garnished with tartlet filled with purée of broad beans and cauliflower sprigs coated with Dutch sauce, bordered with thick veal gravy.
— **Breton Style:** à la bretonne: sautéd garnished with navy beans bound with Breton sauce.
— **Chatelaine:** sautéd, dressed on tartlet filled with white onion purée, garnished with braised chestnuts and Parisian potatoes, bordered with Madeira sauce.
— **Chevreuse:** sautéd, dressed on flat round semolina croquette mixed with chopped mushrooms, a large truffle slice on each noisette, bordered with Bordeaux sauce prepared with white wine.
— **Cinderella:** Cendrillon: 1. browned on both sides, when cold spread with veal forcemeat mixed with chopped truffles on both sides, wrapped in hog caul, dipped in melted butter and breadcrumbs, grilled; truffle sauce served separately.
2. sautéd, dressed on artichoke bottom stuffed with white onion purée, bordered with thick veal gravy with tomato.
— **Cyrano:** sautéd, garnished with artichoke bottoms filled with mushroom purée, bordered with Madeira sauce.
— **Dickson:** prepared like mutton tenderloin.
— **Durand:** sautéd, dressed on croûton, garnished with artichoke bottom, filled with half a braised lettuce and a slice of blanched ox marrow on top, and a small

Mutton, Noisette of
truffled veal dumpling; Madeira sauce with chopped olives served separately.

— **Lavallière:** sautéd, garnished with artichoke bottoms filled with asparagus purée and castle potatoes, covered with Bordeaux sauce.

— **Suzanne:** sautéd, dressed on artichoke bottom, garnished with Parisian potatoes, covered with demi-glace blended with tarragon extract.

— **Verdi:** sautéd, dressed on slice of fried gooseliver, coated with white onion purée, sprinkled with grated cheese and rapidly glazed, garnished with pre-baked croustades of duchess potato-mixture filled with very small carrot balls, and braised lettuce.

— **Voisin:** 1. sautéd, deglaced with tarragon gravy, dressed on flat cake of Anna potatoes, covered with the gravy, garnished with small moulds of spinach purée mixed with chicken forcemeat.
2. sautéd, dressed on Anna potatoes, garnished with halved fried tomatoes, with chopped tarragon sprinkled on top, and artichoke bottoms filled alternately with spinach purée and green peas; tarragon sauce poured over the noisettes.

Mutton Ragout: Ragoût de mouton: brown mutton stew usually prepared with shoulder, neck or the upper part of the rack. Meat cut in pieces, browned together with diced carrots and onions, sprinkled with flour, browned, moistened with stock, seasoned, tomato purée or fresh tomatoes, garlic and bunch of herbs added, cooked for about 90 minutes, meat picked out and put in a clean casserole, small browned onions and small nicely-shaped potatoes browned in butter added, sauce strained over the meat and cooked until potatoes are done; served in timbale dish sprinkled with chopped parsley.

— **Catalonian Style:** à la catalane: diced: browned in lard with onions and garlic, moistened with red wine and demi-glace, seasoned and stewed; when done fried diced potatoes, small slices of fried bacon and diced headcheese added.

— **Citizen Style:** à la bourgeoise: prepared like ragoût with small carrot and turnip balls lightly browned in butter added.

— **with Green Beans:** aux haricots verts: prepared like ragoût with cubes of boned meat, diced potatoes and diced green beans added.

— **Indian Style:** à l'indienne: meat browned with plenty of chopped onions, curry powder and flour sprinkled on top, braised with brown stock, sauce improved with cream; plain boiled rice served separately.

— **Navarin:** Navarin de mouton: French mutton stew with glazed onions, small shaped potatoes and carrot balls added.

— **Navarin Spring Style:** Navarin à la printanière: same as navarin with olive-shaped turnips, carrots, potatoes and glazed onions added, dressed in timbale dish with green peas and green beans cut in lozenges scattered on top.

— **and Navy Beans:** Haricot de mouton: mutton diced, browned in lard, sprinkled with flour, allowed to brown, moistened with water or stock, seasoned and stewed with

Mutton Ragout
garlic, tomato purée and a bunch of herbs; when nearly done picked out and put in clean saucepan, fried diced bacon, glazed button onions and parboiled navy beans added, sauce strained over, cooked until done and served with chopped parsley on top.

— **Persian:** à la perse: see Mehemehalou.

— **Rhenish Style:** à la rhénane: diced mutton browned in lard with chopped onions and diced bacon, dredged with flour, moistened with stock and stewed; when done seasoned generously with pepper and vinegar; mixed with parboiled navy beans.

— **with Rice:** Ragoût de mouton au riz: prepared like ragout but without onions or potatoes, rice added at the second phase of cooking.

— **and Vegetables:** Schoepsengulasch: diced mutton browned in lard, sprinkled with flour, moistened with white wine, brown stock and tomato purée, seasoned and stewed; when done parboiled potato balls, green peas, diced green beans and fancy-shaped carrots and turnips added. (Austrian)

Mutton Cassoulet: a special mutton stew always prepared with boned meat, navy beans and other ingredients and baked in oven.

— **Carcasson Style:** à la Carcasonne: prepared like Castelnaudary with half mutton and half pork, the garlic sausage replaced by a pickled leg of goose previously browned in lard.

— **Castelnaudary Style:** Navy beans cooked in water with a carrot, a larded onion, a piece of blanched lean bacon, a garlic sausage, a few strongly blanched rinds of bacon tied together, a little tomato purée and seasoning. Boned mutton cut in medium dice, browned in lard with plenty of chopped onions and a little crushed garlic, moistened with the bean water and stewed until done. Beans mixed with the diced rinds, arranged in layers in baking dishes alternately with the meat, the bacon cut in small slices and the sliced sausage; beans on top; sprinkled with breadcrumbs, baked in oven to a rich brown while basted with the stock several times.

— **Toulouse Style:** à la toulousaine: prepared like Castelnaudary but principally with goose meat.

Mutton, Saddle of: Selle de mouton: consists of the entire loin with backbone, tenderloins, kidneys and flank, which is folded in to protect the roast from below; the loin is tied with fine string to hold its shape.

— **Belle Alliance:** roasted, garnished with stuffed tomatoes, braised lettuce and croquette potatoes; the pan gravy boiled up with thick veal gravy.

— **Breton Style:** à la bretonne: roasted and garnished as for leg of mutton.

— **Brillat-Savarin:** roasted, garnished with artichoke bottoms filled with truffle purée and baked nests of duchess potato-mixture filled with tomatoes concassées; the pan juice deglaced with Madeira and boiled up with demiglace served separately.

— **Duchess Style:** à la duchesse: roasted, garnished with duchess potatoes, served with Madeira sauce.

Mutton, Saddle of

— **Farmer Style:** à la paysanne: prepared with the same garnish as for cutlet.

— **Lafayette:** roasted, garnished with artichoke bottoms filled with tiny carrot balls, tartlets filled with diced green beans, stuffed tomatoes and chestnut croquettes; Madeira sauce.

— **Lison:** roasted, garnished with croquette potatoes mixed with chopped smoked tongue and lettuce purée mixed with egg-yolks and cream, filled in small moulds and poached in waterbath.

— **Merville:** prepared like Metternich with a slice of goose-liver between the meat slices, coated with Mornay sauce, sprinkled with grated Parmesan, browned, garnished with stuffed tomatoes and a salpicon of sliced fresh truffles and mushrooms sautéd in butter, mixed with blanched slices of ox marrow, bound with thick demi-glace; the thickened meat gravy separately.

— **Metternich:** roasted rare, carved, each slice coated with Béchamel with paprika, replaced in original shape on back bone with a slice of truffle between the slices, coated entirely with Béchamel with paprika, browned rapidly and served with rice pilaf.

— **Nice Style:** à la nicoise: roasted, garnished with French beans, castle potatoes and tomatoes concassées with garlic and chopped tarragon; thick meat gravy separately.

— **Prince Orloff:** prepared like Metternich, slices coated with mushroom and white onion purée, the entire saddle coated with Mornay sauce, sprinkled with grated Parmesan and gratinated.

— **Sarah Bernhardt:** roasted, garnished with croustades prepared with duchess potato-mixture filled with cauliflower, covered with Mornay sauce and gratinated, tomatoes stuffed with pearl potatoes fried in butter; the thickened gravy served separately.

— **Sicilian Style:** à la sicilienne: roasted, garnished with broad noodles tossed in butter, mixed grated Parmesan, cream sauce and purée of sautéd chicken livers; thick veal gravy.

— **Tenant Style:** à la fermière: prepared as specified for leg of mutton.

Mutton Shoulder: prepared like lamb shoulder.

Mutton Tail: Queue de mouton: mostly used for soup but also stewed or grilled.

— **Fried:** frite: parboiled, cut in suitable pieces, dipped in egg and breadcrumbs, fried in deep fat; tomato sauce separately.

— **Grilled:** grillée: parboiled, when cold cut in pieces, dipped in melted butter and breadcrumbs, grilled served with anchovy butter.

— **in Madeira:** au madère: cut in pieces, braised in light demi-glace and flavored with Madeira at serving.

Mutton Tenderloins, Mutton Fillets: Filets mignons: culinary term for the two small fillets underneath the mutton saddle.

— **Arlesian Style:** à l'arlésienne: fried in oil, garnished with fried tomatoes and deep fried slices of eggplant, fried onion rings on top of the tenderloin.

Mutton Tenderloins

— **Byron:** coated with onion purée, rolled in breadcrumbs mixed with chopped parsley, fried in butter, garnished with halved fried sheep's kidneys and Byron potatoes.

— **Dickson:** braised in demi-glace with a little truffle stock, covered with the sauce mixed with truffle julienne and pitted olives.

— **Durand:** prepared like mutton noisettes.

— **Gascon Style:** à la gasconne: larded with anchovy fillets, simmered in gascon sauce.

— **Goethe:** fried in butter, covered with light scrambled eggs mixed with chopped mushrooms, garnished with chipped potatoes.

— **Nevers Style:** à la nivernaise: braised, garnished with glazed olive-shaped carrots, turnips and button onions and the gravy boiled down with demi-glace and tomato purée.

— **Persian Style:** à la perse: fried in butter, dressed on halved grilled tomatoes, garnished with green peppers stuffed with rice and halved fried bananas; Chateaubriand sauce finished off with the boiled down stock of the peppers served separately.

— **Provencal Style:** à la provençale: fried in oil, garnished with stuffed tomatoes and stuffed mushroom caps, covered with Provencal sauce.

Mutton Tongue: Langue de mounton: soaked, boiled, trimmed and skinned, or blanched and braised. Prepared like calf's tongue.

— **Fried:** frite: parboiled, skinned, cut in thick slices, dipped in egg and breadcrumbs, deep fried; tomato sauce.

— **Gratinated:** au gratin: boiled, skinned, split lengthwise, placed in greased fireproof dish on sliced mushrooms, coated with Italian sauce, dotted with butter gratinated in oven.

— **Grilled:** grillée: parboiled, skinned, split lengthwise, marinated in oil with chopped shallots and herbs; grilled, piquant sauce served separately.

— **Liege Style:** à la liègeoise: parboiled, braised, crushed juniper berries added, stock thickened with arrowroot and flavored with Genever.

— **in Paper Bag:** en papillote: boiled, skinned, cut lengthwise in three, a slice of ham on each side, coated with duxelles wrapped in greased paper bag, closed and baked in oven.

— **in Pig's Caul:** en crépinette: boiled, skinned, split lengthwise, studded with truffle, coated with pork forcemeat; wrapped in pig's caul, dipped in egg and breadcrumbs, baked in oven.

— **Provencal Style:** à la provençale: parboiled, braised, covered with Provencal sauce: garnished with large mushroom caps filled with duxelles flavored with garlic.

— **Ragoût of:** Ragoût de langues de mouton: boiled, simmered in light velouté prepared with the stock, sliced onions, pepper-corns, a bay leaf, allspice and a dash of tarragon vinegar, cut in slices, mixed with sliced pickled cucumbers and mushrooms, the sauce strained over.

— **Ramadura:** parboiled, cut in slices and stewed in white stock with diced tomatoes, chopped lightly fried onions and apples, garlic and cream mixed with curry powder;

boiled down with coconut milk and cream when done; rice pilaf mixed with saffron, diced green peppers and tomatoes served separately.

N

Navarin: see mutton ragoût.
New England Boiled Dinner: smoked boneless shoulder of pork and corned beef cooked together with carrots, turnips, cabbage and potatoes; pickled red beetroots served separately.
— — **Stew:** diced salt pork, sliced turnips and button onions fried lightly, seasoned, covered with water, boiled, diced potatoes added later on; served covered with the thickened stock.
Noisettes de veau: see veal noisettes.
Noix de veau: see veal nut.

O

Oie: see goose.
Oie sauvage: see wild goose.
Oison: see gosling.
Olivette glacate: Stewed Veal Roulade: veal slice, flattened, stuffed with veal forcemeat mixed with chopped ham, parsley and grated Parmesan, rolled, tied and stewed in white wine, demi-glace or brown stock and tomato purée. (Italian)
Oreilles d'agneau: see lamb's ears.
Ortolan: F. Ortolan; G. Fettammer: also called reed bird, a small bird of the finch family, about 6 inches long, the plumage a mixture of brown, black and white, greatly esteemed by gastronomers as small game.
— **Apicius:** boned, stuffed with chicken and gooseliver forcemeat, wrapped in a cloth and poached in game stock, unwrapped, filled in a scooped out raw truffle, first wrapped in thin slices of bacon and then in a greased paper and baked in the oven.
— **Baked:** en feuilleté: fried gently in butter, when cold wrapped in puff pastry, brushed with egg-yolk and baked in oven.
— **in Baked Potato:** en surprise: boned, stuffed with gooseliver forcemeat, poached in game stock, placed in a large baked and scooped out potato, covered with truffle sauce.
— **in Case:** en caisse: roasted, placed in a small china container on diced truffles and gooseliver bound with Madeira sauce.
— **in Champagne:** au champagne: stuffed with a small piece of raw truffle, placed in a small china fireproof container with a little champagne and seasoning, covered with puff paste, baked in oven.
— **with Cherries:** aux cerises: stuffed with bread stuffing mixed with chopped sautéd chicken livers, poached in game stock and Port, covered with stoned cherries bound with demi-glace boiled down with the stock.

Ortolan

— **Housewife Style:** à la bonne-femme: cooked in butter en cocotte with diced fried bacon and glazed button onions, flambéd with brandy, deglaced with a little game stock.

— **with Juniper Berries:** au genièvre: cooked in butter en cocotte with a few crushed juniper berries, deglazed with brandy and game stock.

— **Lothringian Style:** à la lorraine: large ripe stoned plums slightly fried in butter, a slightly moistened ortolan placed on half a plum, wrapped in wine leaf, cooked in the oven, unwrapped and served with unripe grape juice poured over the bird.

— **Lucullus:** cooked en casserole, dressed in a large truffle cooked in Madeira and scooped out, deglacéd with game stock, poured over the ortolan, the lid of the truffle placed on top.

— **Marianne:** cooked en cocotte and dressed on leaf spinach tossed in butter.

— **with Pineapple Juice:** au suc d'ananas: roasted, deglaced and flambéd with brandy, boiled up with a dash of lemon juice and a few spoonsfull of fresh pineapple juice and poured over the birds.

— **Rothschild** (cold): large truffle cooked in champagne, scooped out, filled with a roast cold ortolan, covered with champagne aspic jelly mixed with gold leaf.

— **on Skewer:** en brochette: stuck on a skewer alternated with small slices of lean bacon, roasted on the spit.

— **in Tangerine:** à la pomme d'or (cold): poached in game stock, when cold breasts removed and glazed with Port jelly, dressed on scooped out tangerine filled with purée of goose-liver patty blended with aspic jelly and whipped cream.

— **Toulouse-Lautrec:** cooked en cocotte, flambéd with Armagnac, deglaced with grape juice, garnished with peeled and seeded Chasselas grapes.

— **with Truffles:** aux truffes: roasted, covered with Madeira sauce with sliced truffles.

Osso Buco: veal shank divided into thick pieces, seasoned, coated with flour, browned in butter, braised in white wine and very little white stock with diced tomatoes, chopped onions and garlic until stock is nearly entirely reduced, a little lemon juice and chopped parsley on top. (Italian)

— — **alla Gremolada:** large veal shank divided in 4 pieces, seasoned, coated with flour, browned in butter, moistened with white wine and veal stock, finely diced knob celery, carrots and chopped onions sweated in the poured off butter, a little tomato purée, chopped lemon peel, parsley, garlic, sage and rosemary added to the veal shank, braised and served with risotto. (Italian)

Oxbringa: boiled brisket of beef served with creamed potatoes. (Swedish)

P

Paella: (Spanisch Ragoût): diced beef, veal, mutton and pork sautéd in oil with chopped onions, stewed in broth, sliced Chorizzo (Spanish sausage), rice, cauliflower sprigs, green

Paella
peas, pieces of green beans, prawns and mussels added, seasoned with salt, pepper and saffron. (Spanish)

Palais de boeuf: see beef palate:

Paleron: see chuck.

Palten: Black Pudding: creamed butter mixed with hog's blood, cream, flour, egg yolks and stiffly beaten egg whites, seasoned with salt, nutmeg and marjoram, filled in greased mould, poached in water bath in oven; turned out and covered with browned butter. (Russian)

Papaz yahnissi: Mutton collops: thick slices of mutton, stewed in mutton fat with sliced onions, garlic, salt, pepper, cinnamon and a little vinegar. (Turkish)

Paprikás borjut szelet: Veal Collops with paprika: veal collops seasoned with salt and paprika, turned in flour, fried in lard with chopped onions, moistened with white stock, shredded green peppers added and stewed; when done sauce boiled down with sour cream and served with boiled rice, noodles or Tarhonya. (Hungarian)

— **csirke:** Paprika Chicken: chopped onions and crushed garlic lightly fried in lard, sprinkled with flour and paprika, chicken disjointed as for poulet sauté, the parboiled gizzard, green chopped peppers, a few tomatoes cut in pieces added, moistened with water and stewed; when nearly done the chicken liver and sour cream added; served with flour dumplings or noodles. (Hungarian)

Partridge; F. Perdreau; G. Rebhuhn, Feldhuhn: the common or grey partridge is found all over Europe, Persia and parts of Asia. There are several varieties of American partridges entirely different to the European or Asian kind. Young birds have a tender beak, sharp toes and a fine skin over the legs. Only young birds are fit for roasting and should be trussed and barded; old birds are stewed, braised or used for soup.

— **Agnes Sorel:** breasts larded with ox tongue and truffle, sauted, placed on partridge forcemeat poached in tartlet moulds and filled with sliced mushrooms; salmi sauce prepared with the bones.

— **Alsatian Style:** à l'alsacienne: pan roasted, deglaced with white wine and demi-glace; saurkraut cooked in white wine with a piece of lean bacon served separately with the sliced bacon on top.

— **with Anchovy Butter:** au beurre d'anchois: roasted, garnished with watercress; anchovy butter poured over the bird.

— **Andrassy:** roasted, when nearly done shredded green peppers, simmered in butter beforehand and sour cream added.

— **Bacchus:** roasted, deglaced with white wine and game sauce; Malaga raisins boiled up in the sauce and poured over partridge.

— **Béarnaise:** browned in oil, braised in white wine, brown stock and tomato purée with garlic.

— **Brabant Style:** à la brabançonne: pan-roasted, garnished with Brussels sprouts, chipolatas and croquette potatoes; the pan juice boiled up with light demi-glace served separately.

— **Burgundy Style:** à la bourguignonne: pan roasted, placed in cocotte with glazed button onions and mushroom caps;

Partridge

deglaced with red wine, boiled up with demi-glace and poured over bird.

— **Carême:** pan-roasted, deglaced with suprême sauce, cream and a little celery purée; garnished with braised celery.

— **in Casserole:** en casserole: roasted in casserole; when done a few drops of brandy and game gravy poured in casserole and served with the cover on.

— **Catalonian Style:** à la catalane: cut in pieces, browned in oil with garlic, sliced mushrooms and diced tomatoes, braised in game sauce flavored with Sherry; garnished with chipolatas and glazed button onions.

— **Charterhouse Style:** à la chartreuse: prepared like pheasant.

— **Châtelaine:** pan roasted, garnished with glazed chestnuts and artichoke bottoms filled with white onion purée; the thickened pan gravy served separately.

— **Chaudfroid Old Fashioned Style** (cold): chaudfroid à l'ancienne: roasted, breast sliced when cold; flesh of legs pounded in mortar with truffles, mushrooms and chopped shallots, boiled up with a bay leaf, rubbed through a sieve, a little aspic jelly added; breast coated with this sauce, garnished with truffle slice and glazed with aspic jelly.

— **Conti:** pan-roasted, deglazed with Madeira and demi-glace; garnished with tartlets filled with lentil purée and a round slice of the bacon cooked with the lentils on top.

— **D'Artois:** roasted, garnished with artichoke bottoms filled alternately with asparagus tips and lentil purée with a mushroom cap on top; pan gravy.

— **Diana:** Diane: roasted, served with chestnut purée and Diana sauce.

— **Diplomat Style:** à la diplomate: stuffed with truffled game forcemeat and larded; roasted, deglaced with Madeira sauce and truffle essence, finished off with gooseliver purée; placed in cocotte with mushrooms, stoned olives and gooseliver dumplings, sauce poured over, served with cover on.

— **English Style:** à l'anglaise: roasted, placed on croûton, garnished with watercress and lemon; pan gravy, bread sauce and browned breadcrumbs served separately.

— **Epigrammes of:** Epigrammes de perdreau: breasts taken off with the wing bone, seasoned and fried lightly in butter; forcemeat prepared with the remaining flesh poached in cutlet moulds, dipped in egg and chopped truffles and also fried in butter; breasts and cutlets arranged like a crown on round platter; demi-glace prepared with the bones, and chestnut purée served separately.

— **Forester Style: à la forestière: roasted,** garnished with morels; deglaced with white wine and demi-glace, finished off with liver purée and chopped parsley.

— **Fried:** frit: cut in four pieces, dipped in egg and breadcrumbs, deep fried; garnished with fried parsley and lemon.

— **German Style:** à l'allemande: roasted; deglaced with sour cream; served with saurkraut.

— **Grenoble Style:** à la grenobloise: browned, cut in pieces, simmered in Madeira sauce with garlic and diced fried bacon.

Partridge

— **Grévy:** browned in oil, braised in light Madeira sauce with tomato purée garnished with glazed button onions, stoned olives and boletus sautéd with garlic.

— **Grilled:** à la crapaudine: split at the back, flattened, dipped in melted butter, grilled; devil sauce served separately.

— **Housewife Style:** à la bonne-femme: prepared like pheasant.

— **Hungarian Style:** à la hongroise: cut in pieces, browned in lard with chopped onions and very fine mirepoix, sprinkled with paprika, shredded green peppers added, braised in sour cream and a little white stock.

— **Kléber:** prepared like pheasant.

— **Lady Clifford:** roasted in service casserole; when two thirds done raw truffle slices, a jigger of flambéd brandy and a spoonful of meat glaze added; light Soubise sauce served separately.

— **Lautrec:** young partridge split at the back, fixed on a skewer, brushed with butter and grilled; lemon juice dropped on the bird, garnished with grilled mushroom caps filled with herb butter; bordered with liquid meat glaze.

— **marinated:** see perdiz en ecabeche.

— **Marly:** browned in butter, placed in service casserole surrounded with fairy ring mushrooms sautéd in butter; casserole closed hermetically, finished roasting in oven and served with cover on.

— **Mignonettes of:** Mignonettes de perdreau: breast cut off, opened a little from the thick side and stuffed with a small slice of raw gooseliver and a truffle slice, dipped in egg and breadcrumbs and fried in butter; garnished with asparagus tips; game sauce with truffle and mushroom slices served separately.

— **Mirbach:** stuffed with partridge forcemeat. browned, braised in light truffle sauce; garnished with tartlets filled with lentil purée.

— **Norman Style:** à la normande: roasted, deglaced with apple jack, cider and cream; garnished with fancy-shaped apple pieces sautéd in butter.

— **with Olives:** aux olives: browned in butter, simmered in Madeira sauce with stoned green olives.

— **Patti:** roasted in oil; garnished with glazed button onions, stoned olives and sautéd boletus; tomato sauce flavored with garlic.

— **Piedmont Style:** à la piemontaise: boned, stuffed with risotto with grated Italian truffles, pan-roasted; deglaced with tomato sauce mixed with strips of Italian truffles.

— **Polish Style:** à la polonaise: filled with herb stuffing. roasted; breadcrumbs browned in plenty of butter poured over the partridge.

— **Prince Victor:** boned, stuffed with partridge forcemeat, trussed, poached in game stock; dressed on croûton; stock reduced, ignited with brandy, bound with arrow-root and poured over the bird.

— **Provencal Style:** à la provençale: cut in pieces, browned in oil, simmered with diced tomatoes, crushed garlic, diced artichoke bottoms and eggplants, sautéd beforehand, and blanched black olives.

Partridge

— **with Red Cabbage:** au chou rouge: barded, roasted, carved; served on red cabbage braised in red wine and the pan gravy deglaced with sour cream.

— **Salmi:** roasted blood rare, cut in pieces, heated up in salmi sauce with truffle slices and mushroom caps, bordered with heart-shaped croûtons masked with liver purée.

— — **Hunter Style:** à la chasseur: roasted blood rare, deglaced with brandy, white wine and salmi sauce mixed with sliced mushrooms sautéd with finely chopped shallots; bird cut in pieces, heated up in the sauce, chopped tarragon and chervil scattered on top.

— — **Seaman Style:** à la marinière: same as salmi with truffle slices and mushrooms; crayfish tails, a French fried egg and heart-shaped croûtons on top.

— **with Saurkraut:** au choucroute: old bird barded and browned, braised together with saurkraut in white wine and fat beef stock with sliced apples.

— **Sierra Leone:** roasted in oil with strips of raw ham; served covered with the ham and breadcrumbs browned in oil.

— **Soubise:** roasted in casserole; when two thirds done raw truffle slices added; served in casserole with cover on; Soubise sauce served separately.

— **Souwaroff:** prepared like pheasant.

— **Spanish Style:** espagnol: cut in pieces raw, dipped in flour, egg and breadcrumbs mixed with chopped garlic and parsley, fixed on a skewer and grilled; cold sauce made of garlic, pickled cucumbers, olives, mint and parsley, pounded in mortar, seasoned with vinegar and beaten with oil like mayonnaise served separately. (Spanish)

— **Stewed:** à l'estouffade: browned, placed in service casserole greased with butter on thin slices of carrots and onions lightly browned beforehand and crushed juniper berries; residue in pan deglaced with brandy and a little game stock, poured over the bird, closed hermetically, stewed in oven and served in the casserole.

— **Stuffed:** en demi-deuil: boned, stuffed with truffled game forcemeat, truffle slices placed between skin and breastflesh, wrapped in a cloth and poached in game stock prepared with the bones; unwrapped, stock reduced, mixed with ignited brandy and served separately.

— **Tenant Style:** à la fermière: prepared like spring chicken.

— **Victoria:** filled with diced truffles and gooseliver, roasted; served with diced sautéd potatoes and a few drops of game gravy in service casserole.

— **Viennese Style:** 1. Rebhuhn Wiener Art: barded, wrapped in blanched cabbage leaves, trussed, simmered in butter with chopped onions and very little stock; taken out, gravy boiled up with sour cream and thickened with flour. (Austrian)

— **Viennese Style:** 2. Wiener Art: larded, roasted and basted frequently with sour cream; lentils mixed with diced fried bacon served separately. (Austrian)

Partridge Breast: Suprême de perdreau: breasts separated from breastbone with a small piece of the wing bone, mainly sautéd rare in butter; prepared like suprême of pheasant.

Partridge Breast

— **with Grapes and Gooseliver:** aux foie gras et raisins: sautéd, deglaced with brandy and stock prepared with the bones; placed in service cocotte with diced sautéd gooseliver and skinned, seeded grapes; gravy poured over, heated up for a minute, served with cover on.

— **Magenta:** breasts flattened lightly, sautéd for a minute on one side only, allowed to cool lightly pressed; browned side coated with partridge soufflé mass with a slice of truffle on top, placed in oven for a few minutes to cook soufflé; served with Madeira sauce with truffle essence.

— **Véron:** legs boned; flesh and partridge liver poached, mixed with the same amount of truffles, pounded in mortar, rubbed through a sieve, bound with a little velouté, mixed with the same amount of chestnut purée, buttered lightly; breast sautéd, arranged like a turban alternately with heart-shaped croûtons; purée filled in the center, breasts bordered with demi-glace with game essence.

Pastry Boats, Boats: Barquettes: small boat-shaped moulds lined with pie dough, puff or short pastry, a concoction of rice or semolina, filled with salpicon or purée, sometimes browned in oven. Barquettes Chevreuse are always made with cooked semolina, seasoned, bound with egg and mixed with butter. The moulds are lined with this mixture, filled, covered with the mixture, turned out, dipped in egg and breadcrumbs and deep fried. These boats are always called: Barquettes Chevreuse with Lobster, Chicken etc. Pastry boats are served as a hot appetizer or light entrée.

— **Chevreuse with Chicken:** Barquettes de volaille à la Chevreuse: lined with semolina mass, filled with diced chicken bound with thick German sauce, sealed with semolina mass, dipped in egg and breadcrumbs, deep fried.

— — **with Game:** de gibier à la Chevreuse: filled with game purée mixed with diced game.

— — **with Ham:** de jambon à la Chevreuse: filled with diced ham bound with curry sauce.

— — **Mirabeau:** lined with semolina mass, filled with sole purée mixed with anchovy butter and chopped olives, sealed with semolina mass, dipped in egg and breadcrumbs, deep fried, served with fried parsley.

— **Choisy:** lined with short pastry, baked; filled with salpicon of sole and mushrooms bound with cream sauce, half a braised lettuce placed on top, covered with Mornay sauce, glazed.

— **Creole Style:** à la créole: short pastry; filled with rice mixed with diced tomatoes and okra, seasoned with allspice.

— **Devil Style:** à la diable: lined with puff pastry; filled with salpicon of calf's head and crayfish tails bound with red wine sauce seasoned with Cayenne pepper.

— **Diana:** lined with short pastry, baked, coated inside with game forcemeat, filled with salpicon of truffle and mushrooms bound with Diana sauce, sealed with game forcemeat and placed in oven for a few minutes to allow the forcemeat to get done; brushed with butter at serving.

— **Florence Style:** à la florentine: lined with puff pastry, baked a pale yellow; filled with spinach leaves sautéd in

Pastry Boats

butter, covered with cheese soufflé mixed with anchovy paste, baked in oven.

— **Gaulish Style:** à la gauloise: salpicon of cockscombs and cock's kidneys bound with demi-glace, covered with chicken forcemeat mixed with diced ham, finished off in oven.

— **Ivanhoe:** lined with puff pastry; filled with creamed purée of smoked haddock, a mushroom cap on top.

— **Joinville:** puff pastry; filled with salpicon of shrimps bound with velouté blended with shrimp butter; covered with shrimp sauce, a shrimp placed on top.

— **Nantua:** lined with puff pastry trimmings baked; filled with salpicon of crayfish tails bound with fish velouté finished off with crayfish butter, covered with Nantua sauce; two small crayfish tails placed in the center and a small stuffed crayfish head on both ends.

— **Ostend Style:** à l'ostendaise: lined with puff pastry trimmings; filled with poached bearded oysters bound with light Béchamel sauce finished off with fish essence; diced truffles scattered on top.

— **with Oysters:** à la normande: lined with puff pastry trimmings, baked; filled with salpicon of mushrooms and crayfish tails bound with Norman sauce, covered with poached oysters, masked with Norman sauce.

— **Regina:** lined with short pastry, lightly baked; bottom masked with mushroom purée, filled with Chester soufflé, baked.

— **Russian Style:** à la russe: puff pastry; filled with salpicon of vesiga, leeks, knob celery and carrots bound with velouté.

— **with Soft Roes:** aux laitances: lined with short pastry, baked; filled with soft roes poached in butter and lemon juice, covered with mustard or paprika sauce.

— **Tosca:** lined with puff pastry trimmings; filled with diced crayfish tails bound with American sauce, covered with cheese soufflé, finished in oven.

Pasty: Pâté: pasties are made of forcemeat of various kind, mixed with dices or strips of the main ingredient, gooseliver, bacon, truffles, pistachios etc., filled in pasty mould lined with slices of fat bacon, coated with forcemeat, covered with pie dough and baked. To allow the steam to escape one or more holes are made on top of dough and filled with small funnel of greased paper. When the pasty is cold, aspic jelly is poured through the funnel in the pasty and the paper taken out.

— **d'Abbeville:** commercial article made of woodcock.

— **d'Amiens:** duck pasty marketed in oval crust.

— **de Beaugency:** golden plover pasty, factory made and sold fresh.

— **de Chartres:** factory made lark and gooseliver pasty.

— **Chicken:** de volaille: made like pheasant pasty in oval mould.

— **of Duck:** de canard: duck boned and stuffed with duck and liver forcemeat as for galantine, placed in oval mould lined with fat bacon, coated with veal forcemeat, sealed with forcemeat, covered with sliced fat bacon,

Pasty

finished off with pie dough, decorated and baked; when cold aspic jelly filled in pasty through small hole in center of crust.

— **Fieldfare:** de grives: fieldfare boned and stuffed with liver forcemeat seasoned with powdered juniper berries; filled in oval mould lined with pie dough alternately with game and liver forcemeat and diced truffles; sealed with forcemeat, covered with pie dough, decorated and baked; when cold aspic jelly with fieldfare essence, made of the bones, filled in pasty.

— **Ham:** de jambon: prepared like veal and ham pasty with pork forcemeat mixed with diced lean ham; when cold Madeira aspic jelly is filled in the pasty.

— **Hare:** de lièvre: hare boned, skinned, saddle cut into long strips and marinated in brandy with spices together with long strips of ham and fat bacon. Baked in rectangular mould filled with forcemeat prepared with the rest of the hare, veal and green bacon; when cold aspic jelly made with the hare bones poured into the patty.

— **de Lyon:** factory made turkey pasty marketed fresh.

— **de Marseille:** factory made truffled tunny pasty sold fresh.

— **Parisian:** Parisien: oval mould lined with pie dough, coated with veal and beef forcemeat, filled with layers of sliced raw tenderloin, marinated beforehand with chopped shallots, white wine, brandy and spices, and sliced lightly sautéd mushrooms, sealed with forcemeat, a little melted butter poured on top, covered with pie dough and baked; when done a little demi-glace poured in the patty through a hole in center of crust; served hot.

— **de Périqueux:** factory made pasty of gooseliver and truffles sold fresh.

— **Pheasant:** de faisan: oval mould lined with sliced fat bacon, coated with pheasant and liver forcemeat, filled alternately with layers of forcemeat, pheasant breasts cut in strips, truffles cut in quarters, strips of gooseliver and beef tongue, sealed with forcemeat, fat slices of bacon on top, covered with pie dough, decorated and baked; when cold aspic jelly poured in pasty.

— — **American:** de faisan à l'américaine: pheasant boned entirely, breast cut in strips and marinated with chopped shallots, spices and Sherry; bones chopped, browned with mirepoix, moistened with very little water, cooked, strained and concentrated. Forcemeat made of pheasant legs, veal and fat pork seasoned with salt, pepper and allspice. Pasty mould lined with pie dough, filled alternately with layers of forcemeat, salt pork, pistachios and the pheasant breasts, sealed with forcemeat, sliced fat bacon on top, covered with pie dough, decorated and baked. When cold aspic jelly prepared with the concentrated stock filled in pasty through small hole in center.

— **Pigeon:** de pigeon: prepared like chicken pasty; filled with aspic jelly made of the pigeon bones.

— — **Schwarzenberg:** de pigeons Schwarzenberg: oval mould lined with pie dough and forcemeat made of pigeon legs, veal, pork and green bacon, filled alternately with skinned

Pasty
pigeon breasts, sautéd beforehand in butter and allowed to cool off, diced gooseliver, truffles and forcemeat, closed with dough, decorated and baked; when cold filled with aspic jelly.
— **de Pithiviers:** factory made lark pasty sold fresh.
— **Rabbit:** de lapereau: prepared like hare pasty.
— **de Reims:** factory made pork pasty sold fresh.
— **de Saumur:** factory made veal pasty sold fresh.
— **Veal and Ham:** de veau et jambon: oval mould lined with pie dough and thin slices of fat bacon, filled with forcemeat of lean pork and green bacon mixed with diced veal, ham and salt pork marinated beforehand in brandy, sliced fat bacon on top; covered with pie dough, decorated and baked; when cold filled with aspic jelly through small hole in center of crust.

Pâté: see pasty.

Pâté anglais: see pie.

Patties, Small: Petits Pâtés: minced meat, poultry, game or salpicon bound with sauce stuffed between two small round sheets of puff pastry, brushed with egg yolk and baked. Filling prepared as for bouchées.
— **Manon:** stuffed with diced veal and ox tongue bound with thick Madeira sauce.
— **Nérac:** stuffed with salpicon of game and truffle bound with thick Madeira sauce.
— **Oriental Style:** à l'orientale: stuffed with salpicon of mutton and red peppers bound with thick tomato sauce.
— **Parisian Style:** de deux sous: stuffed with veal forcemeat mixed with a little thick Madeira sauce.
— **Tours Style:** à la tourangelle: stuffed with salpicon of larks and truffles bound with thick game sauce.

Paupiette: Polpetti: thin slice of meat used as wrapper for various fillings, tied with thin string, braised in an appropriate sauce, gravy, stock or wine covered with buttered paper, garnished to taste.

Peacock: F. Paon; G. Pfau: fowl allied to the pheasant and reared for ornamental purposes. Formerly popular at banquets, now seldom eaten except the young chicks.
— **Contadino:** larded, braised in light demi-glace mixed with tomato purée; carved, arranged on risotto mixed with pistachios and black currents, lightly sauced.
— **English Style:** à l'anglaise: larded, stuffed with veal forcemeat, roasted, served with pan gravy and bread sauce.
— **Swabian Style:** à la souabe: larded, savory herbs stuffed in belly, roasted, served with oyster sauce.

Pellmènes: Russian Raviolis: squares of noodle dough rolled out thinly, center filled with beef or veal hash seasoned with salt, pepper and marjoram, sides brushed with egg yolk and folded over on top, boiled in salt water; when done drained, covered with melted butter and sprinkled with grated Parmesan.
— **Siberian Style:** à la sibirienne: shaped round, filled with finely diced ham and hazelhen, seasoned and bound with thick demi-glace; poached, drained, arranged in timbale dish covered with melted butter, a few drops of lemon juice and a little liquid meat glace, sprinkled with chopped parsley.

Perdiz en Escabeche: marinated partridge: young partridge browned in oil, moistened with white stock, garlic, button onions and julienne of carrots and knob celery added, seasoned with thyme, bay leaf, peppercorns, cloves and salt and stewed until tender; placed in an earthenware dish with the stock and garnish, finely diced ham, white wine and a little mild vinegar added and marinated in the stock for two days. Served cold in the stock with sliced lemon and chopped parsley on top. (Spanish)

Perdreau: see partridge.

Perisoare cu Verdaturi: Green Meatballs: forcemeat made of one part ground beef and three parts of ground fat pork with plenty of onions fried lightly in butter, seasoned, shaped into small balls, rolled in chopped herbs, parsley, chervil, dill, spinach and tarragon; fried slowly with very little butter, finished off with demi-glace. (Roumanian)

Peru Paulistano: Stuffed Turkey: turkey stuffed with bread stuffing mixed with tapioca and chopped ham; braised and served with the thickened gravy. (Brasilian)

Pfeffer Potthast: Pepper Pot: boned beef chuck cut in large cubes, plenty of sliced onions, a bay leaf and pot herbs added, covered with hot water, seasoned with salt and pepper and cooked until done; pot herbs and bayleaf removed, stock thickened with breadcrumbs and seasoned sharply with pepper. (German)

Pheasant: F. Faisan; G. Fasan: fine game bird native of Europa and Asia, now also to be found in America. The tastiest pheasants come from Bohemia and Hungary. Young pheasants are identified by their grey legs and pliable breasts. Before being roasted they must be barded with thin slices of fat bacon or salt pork to protect the breast and to prevent them drying out.

— **Alsatian Style:** à l'alsacienne: stuffed with pork sausage meat, browned, braised with saurkraut and a piece of lean bacon, arranged on the saurkraut and garnished with the sliced bacon.

— **Angoulême Style:** à l'angoumoise: stuffed with chestnuts and truffles cut in quarters and wrapped in unsalted fat bacon and roasted; truffle sauce served separately.

— **Bohemian Style:** à la bohémienne: stuffed with truffled gooseliver seasoned with salt and paprika, trussed, roasted en cocotte, deglaced and flambéd with brandy, gravy boiled up with game stock.

— **Brillat-Savarin:** roasted in butter, garnished with tartlets filled with souffle of woodcock with a truffle slice on top: demi-glace boiled down with game stock.

— **with Brussels Sprouts:** à la comte de Brabant: roasted, when nearly done fried diced lean bacon and parboiled Brussels sprouts added, the cooking finished in a closed cocotte.

— **Burgundy Style:** à la bourguignonne: roasted, served en cocotte with glazed button onions, button mushrooms and diced fried lean bacon, deglaced with red wine and boiled up with demi-glace.

— **with Cabbage:** au chou: old pheasant braised together with blanched white cabbage, a piece of lean bacon, carrots and a larded onion; pheasant carved, arranged on the cabbage, garnished with the sliced bacon, carrots and

Pheasant

small fried pork sausages (chipolatas); young pheasants are roasted and the cabbage braised separately.

— **Carthusian Style:** Chartreuse de faisan: timbale mould greased with butter, decorated with sliced carrots and turnips, lined with braised, well-drained cabbage, roast and carved pheasant placed in the middle, filled up with cabbage, steamed in water bath, turned out, served with demi-glace boiled up with the pheasant bones.

— **en Casserole:** roasted in butter, dressed in earthenware or china fireproof casserole with small roast potatoes, diced fried lean bacon and quartered mushrooms placed around the bird: the natural gravy poured over.

— **with Celery:** au céleri: braised with celery waste, stock boiled up with cream, strained and poured over the bird, garnished with braised celery.

— **Chaudfroid Beaulieu:** Charlotte mould lined with aspic jelly, coated inside with white chaudfroid sauce, filled with pheasant mousse mixed with gooseliver purée, sealed with aspic jelly; when set turned out on a round base of Russian salad bound with jellied mayonnaise and decorated with truffle slices and hard-boiled egg white.

— — **Châtelaine:** cold roast pheasant breast cut in slices, trimmed round, one half coated cupola-shaped with partridge froth covered with white chaudfroid sauce, the other half with chicken froth coated with brown chaudfroid sauce, decorated alternately with hard-boiled egg white and truffle; placed alternately in color in deep square dish and covered completely with light Madeira aspic jelly.

— — **Gastronomer Style:** Chaudfroid de faisan à la gastronome: breast sliced, coated with brown chaudfroid sauce, decorated and glazed; froth made with the legs filled in parfait mould lined with aspic jelly and sealed with aspic jelly; when set parfait turned out on round silver dish, bordered with the breast slices and garnished with small cold truffles poached beforehand in Madeira and glazed with aspic jelly.

— — **of Pheasant Hilda:** Chaudfroid de faisan Hilda (cold): pheasant roasted rare, when cold, breasts removed and cut diagonally in thin slices, masked with froth prepared with the legs and a little gooseliver, coated with brown chaudfroid sauce, decorated with a small thin slice of pineapple and glazed with aspic jelly; dressed in a deep round or square glass or crystal dish on Waldorf salad bound with a little jelly, covered with light game jelly flavored with Sherry.

— **Connaught:** stuffed with stuffing made of soaked bread, eggs, seasoning and braised chestnuts crushed coarsely, roasted, served with the pan juice deglaced with brandy and game stock and watercress salad.

— **with Cranberries:** aux airelles: roasted, pan juice deglaced with white wine, boiled up with demi-glace and flavored with orange juice, garnished with tartlets filled with cranberries cooked with sugar, flavored with cinnamon and slightly thickened with cornstarch.

— **in Cream Sauce:** à la crème: roasted in casserole with sliced onions, deglaced with sweet cream and meat glaze.

— **Demidoff:** prepared like poularde.

Pheasant

— **Flemish Style:** à la flamande: browned in butter, braised with carrots, turnips and a heart of cabbage cut in quarters.

— **Froth:** Mousse de faisan (cold): purée of roast pheasant mixed with a little poached gooseliver, pounded fine and rubbed through a sieve, seasoned, mixed with velouté sauce, aspic jelly, pheasant essence and whipped cream, filled in a mould lined with aspic jelly and decorated to taste, sealed with jelly, when set turned out on a round dish and garnished with aspic jelly, or
the froth kept very light and fluffy and filled in a deep round crystal dish, chilled, bordered with pheasant breasts decorated with truffle slices, covered with very light aspic jelly prepared with the pheasant bones.

— **Galantine of:** Galantine de faisan (cold): bird boned carefully, spread out, filled with pheasant forcemeat seasoned with brandy and seasoning salt, mixed with diced truffles, gooseliver, ox tongue, salt pork and pistachios, rolled with strips of pheasant breast in the middle, tied in a napkin and boiled slowly in pheasant stock. Allowed to cool in the broth, put under light pressure, chilled, removed from cloth covered with brown game chaudfroid sauce, decorated with hard-boiled egg white, tarragon leaves etc., glazed with aspic jelly prepared with the clarified stock and flavored with Sherry or Madeira. When served as buffet dish, only a part of the galantine is carved and dressed with the uncarved part on a long dish garnished with aspic jelly.

— **Georgian Style:** à la géorgienne: poached with Malvasier, orange and grape juice, extract of green tea, butter and skinned new hazelnuts; stock boiled down with demi-glace and poured over the bird.

— **German Style:** à l'allemande: roasted, served with the pan gravy, boiled up with sour cream, and braised red cabbage.

— **Gipsy Style:** à la zingara: braised in demi-glace with tomato purée flavored with tarragon; sauce strained, mixed with coarse julienne of ham, tongue, mushrooms and truffles sautéd in butter, poured over the bird.

— **Gourmet Style:** stuffed with woodcock forcemeat mixed with diced lean bacon and truffles, wrapped in pork caul, roasted on spit, garnished with croûtons spread with purée of sautéd woodcock livers and entrails.

— **Grandmother Style:** à la grand'mère roasted, arranged with diced fried lean bacon, diced bread croûtons and diced fried potatoes en cocotte.

— **Grilled:** grillé: prepared like grilled chicken, devil sauce served separately.

— **Gunsbourg:** stuffed with truffled woodcock forcemeat, roasted. deglaced with brandy and woodcock essence.

— **Housewife Style:** à la bonne-femme: braised en casserole with diced ham, button onions, small mushrooms and red wine.

— **Jacques:** stuffed with forcemeat made of bread soaked in milk, pheasant livers, chopped shallots sweated in butter and chopped mushrooms; roasted en casserole.

— **Kempinski:** stuffed with forcemeat of lean pork, unsalted fat bacon and chopped truffles between breast and skin,

Pheasant

barded, roasted, deglaced with sour cream, garnished with fried mushrooms and braised chestnuts.

— **Lacroix:** (cold) roasted rare, when cold breast and breastbone cut out, breasts cut in long thin slices, coated with brown chaudfroid sauce with pheasant essence, decorated with truffle and glazed with aspic jelly; rest of the bird coated with brown chaudfroid sauce and glazed with aspic jelly, carcass filled with pheasant and gooseliver froth mixed with diced red peppers and truffles, the breast slices replaced in position; pheasant dressed on long silver dish on a set sheet of aspic jelly, garnished with small tangerines, scooped out and filled with purée of gooseliver parfait, mixed with the juice of the tangerines and powdered grilled hazelnuts, decorated with halved red cherries and glazed with aspic jelly flavored with tangerine juice.

— **Leghorn Style:** à la livournaise: browned, braised, garnished with mushrooms and sliced fried yellow boletus, the thickened gravy poured over.

— **Lucullus:** stuffed with pheasant mousseline forcemeat mixed with truffle purée, browned, braised, garnished with small whole truffles cooked in champagne and cockscombs; the boiled down stock blended with demiglace and truffle essence served separately.

— **Mousse of:** Mousse de faisan: see pheasant froth.

— **Mousselines of:** Mousselines de faisan (cold): prepared like froth but filled in small round or oval moulds lined with jelly and decorated with truffle, sealed with aspic jelly, chilled, turned out and garnished with aspic jelly.

— **Napoleon:** stuffed with rice mixed with diced truffles and chestnuts, breast studded with truffles, barded, braised; truffle sauce finished off with gooseliver purée served separately.

— **Normandy Style:** à la normande: browned, flambéd with apple jack, moistened with cider and cooked in casserole; when done, stock boiled down with sweet cream, garnished with quartered apples sautéd in butter.

— **with Oysters:** aux huîtres: stuffed with forcemeat of fat unsalted bacon, gooseliver waste, pheasant livers and chopped raw oysters, seasoned with salt, pepper, nutmeg, sweet basil and thyme, barded and roasted on the spit.

— **Parisian Style:** à la parisienne: roasted, garnished with artichoke bottoms alternately filled with truffle pearls, gooseliver purée and very small dumplings made of pheasant forcemeat.

— **with Pineapple:** à l'ananas: roasted, garnished with small slices of pineapple fried in butter, the natural gravy poured over the bird.

— **Prince Nicolai:** fried blood rare, when cold, coated with duxelles mixed with a purée of the sautéd livers and chopped fine herbs, wrapped in puff pastry, decorated with puff paste, brushed with egg yolk, baked, Madeira sauce served separately.

— **Regency Style:** à la régence: roasted, garnished with mushroom caps, cocks' combs and pheasant dumplings; salmi sauce with truffle essence.

Pheasant

— **Richemonde:** stuffed with bread stuffing mixed with diced lean bacon and truffles, braised, served with the thickened stock flavored with Madeira.

— **Sainte-Alliance:** stuffed with woodcock forcemeat mixed with ox marrow and chopped truffles, roasted, dressed on fried croûton masked with a purée of the sautéd livers and intestines of woodcock mixed with finely chopped salt pork, anchovy paste and truffles, garnished with quarters of bitter oranges.

— **Salmi of:** roasted blood rare, cut in pieces, heated up in salmi sauce with the juice of the pressed out carcass, truffle slices and quartered sautéd mushrooms added, surrounded with heart-shaped croûtons fried in butter.

— **Souvaroff:** stuffed with diced gooseliver slightly sautéd in butter, roasted en cocotte, when a little more then half done small truffles parboiled in Madeira with their stock added, cocotte hermetically closed and placed in the oven for 15 minutes.

— **Strassburg Style:** à la strassbourgeoise: roasted, dressed on saurkraut, garnished with small fried pork sausages and triangles of lean bacon cooked with the saurkraut.

— **Thackeray:** roasted blood rare, cut in pieces, spread with duxelles, dipped in egg and breadcrumbs, deep fried, garnished with game dumplings; demi-glace with game essence served separately.

— **Titania:** roasted rare, placed in an earthenware or fireproof china casserole surrounded with black peeled and seeded grapes, orange fillets without skin or pips, the pan juice deglaced with pomegranate juice and game stock poured over the pheasant, just boiled up once and served immediately.

— **Victoria:** boned, stuffed with gooseliver and truffles, roasted, served en cocotte surrounded with diced potatoes fried in butter.

— **Viennese Style:** à la viennoise: boned entirely excepting the forelegs, stuffed with pork forcemeat mixed with unsalted fat bacon, diced truffles and gooseliver marinated in Madeira, seasoned with patty seasoning, trussed, barded and kept cool for 24 hours; roasted, carved and served with demi-glace boiled up with the bones of the bird.

Pheasant, Suprême of: Suprême de faisan: pheasant breast gently fried in butter but kept rare or just allowed to draw in butter without allowing the breasts to discolor; they are often served on croûtons of the same shape fried in butter.

— **Alexandrine:** drawn in butter and kept white, a large truffle slice on each suprême, covered with suprême sauce, garnished with tartlets filled with creamed asparagus tips.

— **Ambassadress Style:** à l'ambassadrice: kept white, covered with suprême sauce, garnished with lamb sweetbreads larded with truffles and asparagus tips.

— **Gaulish Style:** à la gauloise: fried in butter, dressed on croûton, covered with cockscombs and cocks' kidneys in truffle sauce.

— **German Style:** à l'allemande: fried in butter, dressed on Savoy cabbage. garnished with sliced lean bacon which

Pheasant, Suprême of
has been cooked with the cabbage, the natural juice boiled up with sour cream poured over the suprême.

— **Imperial Style:** à l'impériale: larded with truffles and ham, fried in butter, covered with Madeira sauce to which julienne of truffles and mushrooms has been added.

— **with Lentils:** à la gentilhomme: dressed on tartlets filled with lentil purée, covered with truffle sauce.

— **with Mushrooms:** aux champignons: fried in butter, deglaced with mushroom essence and white wine, boiled down with demi-glace, sliced sautéd mushrooms added and poured over the suprême.

— **with Orange Juice:** au suc d'orange: prepared like with pineapple juice, using orange juice instead of the pineapple.

— **with Oysters:** aux huîtres: fried in butter, dressed on braised saurkraut, garnished with poached oysters, covered with demi-glace boiled up with the pheasant bones.

— **with Pineapple Juice:** au suc d'ananas: seasoned, fried in butter, deglaced with brandy, flambéd, a dash of lemon and 2 or 3 spoonfuls of fresh pineapple juice added, and poured over the suprême.

— **Royal Style:** à la royale: fried in butter, dressed on oval shaped flat pheasant dumplings, a truffle slice on each suprême, covered with truffle sauce.

— **with Tangerine Juice:** au suc de mandarines: same as with pineapple but with tangerine juice.

Philadelphia Pepperpot: diced beef shoulder or shanks, tripe cut in shreds, sliced onions, shredded green peppers and crushed peppercorns cooked in beef stock until nearly tender, diced potatoes and spaetzle added, when done thickened with grated rusks, chopped dill pickles added for additional flavor.

— — **Scrapple:** pork neck bones cooked in lightly salted water until meat can be removed from bones; remove meat and shred finely, add to strained stock, bind with corn meal mixed with water and cook until thickened. Season, pour thoroughly thickened scrapple in cake pans dipped in water, chill, slice and fry like corn meal mush. Serve hot with butter and syrup.

Piche-Pache: Turkey Ragôut: turkey giblets browned in butter with chopped onions and garlic, moistened with stock, cooked with cabbage cut in quarters, turnips, carrots, potatoes and ox marrow; served with tomato sauce. (Spanish)

Pichelsteiner or Püchelsteiner Fleisch: fireproof serving pot filled alternately with sliced ox marrow, slices of beef, pork, veal and mutton, all mixed together, and sliced onions, carrots, knob celery, potatoes and Savoy cabbage, seasoned with salt and pepper, moistened with water, cooked and served in the pot (German)

Pie: Pâté anglais: food baked in deep dishes, covered with a crust, or surrounded entirely by a dough crust or with the crust open. English style pies are baked in firepoof China or glass dishes and always covered with a crust. In America they are called deep-dish pies and those baked in a tin open pies. Meat pies are invariably baked in

Pie

deep dishes and covered either with short pastry or puff pastry. All pies decribed here are made with puff paste if not otherwise stated.

— **Chicken:** de poulet: chicken disjointed as for fricassee, quartered eggs, quartered mushrooms, olives and small fried potatoes filled in pie dish, seasoned with salt, pepper and chopped shallots, moistened with lightly thickened gravy, closed with puff paste and baked.

— **Chicken and Ham Pot:** pie dish lined with ham, filled with pieces of boiled chicken, mushrooms and parboiled potato balls, covered with light chicken velouté and ham slices on top; sealed with pie dough, brushed with egg yolk and baked.

— **Mutton:** de mouton: mutton cut in large dice, mixed with thick slices of mutton kidneys, mushrooms and blanched calf's sweetbreads, seasoned with salt, pepper and chopped shallots, filled in pie dish, moistened with white stock, covered with puff pastry, decorated, brushed with egg yolk, baked and served hot.

— **Rabbit, English:** de lapin à l'anglaise: large boned pieces of rabbit sautéd lightly, diced lean ham, mushrooms, quartered hard-boiled eggs and chopped onions, seasoned with salt, pepper and thyme, filled in pie dish, moistened with white stock made of the bones, covered with puff pastry, decorated, brushed with egg yolk, baked and served hot.

— **Steak:** de filet de boeuf: sliced rump of beef or tenderloin, very small potatoes, quartered eggs, mushrooms and olives, chopped onions and parsley, seasoned with salt, pepper and nutmeg, arranged in pie dish, moistened with gravy, closed with short pastry, brushed with egg and baked.

— **Steak and Kidney:** de steak et rognons de boeuf: same as steak pie, but instead of potatoes add beef or calf's kidneys cut in strips.

— **Steak and Kidney, American:** de steak et rognons à l'américaine: coarsely chopped onions, cubed beef chuck and quartered lamb kidneys browned in suet, seasoned, stewed in gravy until tender and cooled. Filled in pie dish moistened with a little more gravy lightly thickened, closed with flaky short crust, baked until crust is browned.

— **Sweetbread:** de ris de veau: diced blanched calf's sweetbreads, button mushrooms, small veal dumplings, quartered hard-boiled eggs and asparagus tips seasoned with salt, pepper and a dash of Worcestershire sauce, filled in pie dish, moistened with white stock, baked and served hot.

— **Veal and Ham:** de veau et jambon: boned and sliced loin of veal filled in pie dish, covered with sliced ham and chopped shallots, seasoned, moistened with gravy, closed with pie dough and baked.

— **Veal Pot:** large cubes of veal prepared as blanquette, filled in pie dish with mushrooms and covered with the sauce; sealed with pie dough, brushed with egg yolk and baked.

Pièce de boeuf: see rump of beef.
Pied de veau: see calf's foot.
Pieds de mouton: see sheep's trotters.
Pieds de porc: see pig's feet.

Pig: F. Porc; G. Schwein: a young swine of either sex before it attains sexual maturity. The meat of the pig is known as pork with the exception of the innards. For main preparations of pig see pork.

Pig's Ears: Oreilles de porc: cleaned and boiled in white stock with pot herbs.

— **Fried:** frits: parboiled, dipped in egg and breadcrumbs, deep fried; devil sauce served separately.

— **Grilled:** grillé parboiled; dipped in butter and breadcrumbs, grilled; devil sauce served separately.

— **Italian Style:** à l'italienne: parboiled, simmered in Italian sauce.

— **Lyonese Style:** à la lyonnaise: parboiled, cut in strips, browned in butter, mixed with sliced fried onions mixed with liquid meat glaze, seasoned with vinegar.

— **with Mustard Sauce:** à la sauce moutarde: boiled, served with mustard sauce.

— **Rouenese Style:** à la rouennaise: parboiled, when cold stuffed with pork forcemeat, wrapped in pig's caul, dipped in melted butter and breadcrumbs, grilled; Madeira sauce.

— **Sainte-Menehould:** parboiled, brushed with mustard, dipped in egg and breadcrumbs, deep fried; mashed potatoes.

— **with Saurkraut:** au choucroute: parboiled, served with saurkraut.

— **Stuffed:** farcis: stuffed with pork forcemeat, wrapped in a cloth, boiled in stock; served with Madeira sauce.

— **Swiss Style:** à la suisse: parboiled, dipped in melted butter and breadcrumbs mixed with chopped parsley, tarragon, thyme and marjoram, fried in butter; caper sauce served separately.

Pig's Feet: Pieds de porc: marketed cleaned; boiled in white stock with a larded onion, carrot and a bunch of herbs and allowed to cool under light pressure before further use.

— **Cinderella:** Cendrillon: parboiled, boned, diced finely, mixed with chopped mushrooms and truffle, bound with thick demi-glace and wrapped in pig's caul; grilled, truffle sauce served separately.

— **Fried:** frits: parboiled, boned, dipped in egg and breadcrumbs, deep fried; tomato sauce served separately.

— **Rouenese Style:** à la rouennaise: parboiled, boned, two halves stuffed with pork forcemeat mixed with chopped herbs, rejoined, dipped in egg and breadcrumbs, moistened with melted butter, grilled; Madeira sauce served separately.

— **Sainte-Menehould:** parboiled, boned, dipped in egg and breadcrumbs, grilled; pepper sauce optional.

— **Truffled:** truffé: parboiled, boned, when cold diced and mixed with chopped truffle and pork forcemeat; wrapped in pig's caul with truffle slices, brushed with butter, grilled; truffle sauce served separately.

— **Villeroi:** parboiled, boned, cut in pieces, coated with Villeroi sauce, dipped in egg and breadcrumbs, deep fried; tomato sauce served separately (optional).

Pig's Head: Tête de porc: usually split in two halves and boiled in lightly salted water with pot herbs, spice and a little vinegar.

Pig's Head
— **with Horseradish:** au raifort: boiled, boned, cut in squares; grated horseradish seasoned with salt and vinegar served separately.
— **Stuffed** (cold): farcie: prepared like wild boar's head.
— **Vinaigrette:** boned, cut in squares and served hot with vinaigrette sauce.

Pig's Liver: Foie de porc: mainly used for forcemeat otherwise prepared like calf's liver.
— **Citizen Style:** à la bourgeoise: skinned, braised in light demi-glace, garnished with glazed button onions and pan fried potatoes cut in quarters.
— **Italian Style:** à l'italienne; fried, served with Italian sauce.
— **in Red Wine:** au vin rouge: cut in cubes, browned in butter, dredged with flour, seasoned, stewed in red wine and brown stock; when done covered with deep fried onion rings.

Pig's Trotters: see pig's feet.

Pigeon; F. Pigeon; G. Taube: a large number of different kinds of pigeon are found in the world. Young birds fattened for the table are highly esteemed, older bird mainly used for boiling or for soup.
— **Berlin Style:** à la berlinoise (cold): large squab pigeon, boned, stuffed with chicken forcemeat mixed with diced truffle, red peppers and pistachios, wrapped in a cloth and poached in chicken stock; when cold coated with white chaudfroid sauce prepared with the stock, glazed with aspic jelly; served with a slice cut off to show the stuffing, garnished with small skinned tomatoes stuffed with Waldorf salad and diced aspic jelly.
— **Bordeaux Style:** à la bordelaise: split at the back, flattened and fried in butter; garnished with quartered artichoke bottoms and sliced raw potatoes sautéd in butter and deep fried onion rings
— **Bresse Style:** à la bressanne: boned, stuffed with risotto mixed with sautéd chicken livers, roasted, served with the pan gravy.
— **Breton Style:** à la bretonne: split lengthwise, browned in butter, simmered in butter and white stock with sliced onions, mushroom slices and shredded leeks sweated in butter beforehand; when half done heavy cream and velouté added.
— **Broiled:** grillé: split at the back but not separated, lightly flattened, seasoned with salt, pepper and Cayenne pepper, fixed on a skewer, dipped in melted butter and breadcrumbs, broiled; melted butter served separately.
— **Casanova:** split at the back, flattened but not separated; brushed with mustard, dipped in egg and breadcrumbs mixed with chopped parsley, ham and garlic, grilled; served with Anna potatoes and Chateaubriand sauce.
— **Catalonian Style:** à la catalane: disjointed, sautéd in oil, deglaced with white wine and demi-glace, quartered mushrooms, button onions browned beforehand and diced tomatoes added and all simmered together until pigeon is done.
— **Charterhouse Style:** à la chartreuse: prepared with old pigeons like partridge.

Pigeon

— **Chipolata:** browned in butter, deglaced with white wine, half demi-glace and half brown stock added and braised until done; served with Chipolata garnish.

— **Citizen Style:** à la bourgeoise: roasted in casserole with glazed button onions, mushrooms and diced fried bacon added when nearly done; deglaced with Madeira and meat gravy.

— **Compote of:** en compote: prepared like spring chicken.

— **Crispi:** stuffed, roasted, served covered with diced mushrooms, truffles and ham sautéd in the frying butter; hot ravigote sauce separately.

— **with Cucumbers:** au concombres: browned in butter, simmered in white stock; when done stock boiled down with cream and blended lightly with butter; served with olive-shaped cucumber pieces in cream sauce.

— **Diplomat Style:** à la diplomate: disjointed, boned, sautéd in butter, allowed to cool, coated with Villeroy sauce, dipped in egg and breadcrumbs and deep fried; demi-glace with pigeon essence mixed with sliced truffles and mushrooms served separately.

— **English Style:** à l'anglaise: split at the back, flattened, not separated, fixed on a skewer, grilled; garnished with fried slices of bacon, straw potatoes and watercress; devil sauce served separately.

— **Farmer Style:** à la paysanne: roasted in cocotte, when nearly done diced fried bacon and sautéd potato cubes added; a few spoonfuls of veal gravy poured over the bird at serving.

— **Fried:** frit: disjointed, poached, when cold dipped in frying batter, deep fried; served with asparagus tips or green peas.

— **Gautier:** split lengthwise, poached in plenty of butter with lemon juice; when done drained, dried and served covered with German sauce blended with crayfish butter.

— **Grandmother Style:** à la grand'mère: prepared like chicken in cocotte.

— **with Green Peas:** aux petits pois: diced bacon and button onions fried in butter and taken out of the pan; pigeon browned in the butter, placed in service casserole together with the bacon, onions and green peas, the pan gravy and demi-glace added and simmered slowly until done.

— **Gumbo:** browned in butter with chopped onions, diced ham and tomatoes and okra added, seasoned, moistened with stock and simmered until done; rice served separately.

— **Holstein Style:** à la Holstein: disjointed, seasoned, poached in butter and white stock with diced bacon; sauce thickened with butterpaste, mixed with capers.

— **Housewife Style:** à la bonne-femme: prepared like spring chicken.

— **Laurette** (cold): boned, stuffed with forcemeat, roasted; when cold cut in thick slices, coated with brown chaud-froid sauce, decorated with hard-boiled egg white and pistachios, glazed with aspic jelly.

— **Lavallière:** roasted in cocotte, garnished with green peas, diced ham and glazed button onions, covered with Madeira sauce.

Pigeon

— **with Malaga:** au Malaga: browned in butter, deglaced with Malaga and braised in demi-glace; soaked Malaga raisins added shortly before bird is done.
— **with Morels:** aux morilles: roasted, garnished with sautéd morels, Madeira sauce.
— **Nana:** prepared in casserole with diced truffles, stoned olives, small nut potatoes and glazed button onions; deglaced with white wine and veal gravy.
— **Naples Style:** à la napolitaine: roasted, served on macaroni prepared the Naples way.
— **with Oysters:** aux huîtres: stuffed with oysters, roasted, served on croûton; served with the pan gravy flavored with sage.
— **Polish Style:** à la polonaise: prepared like squab chicken.
— **in Puff Pastry:** en feuilletage: barded and roasted blood rare; allowed to cool, wrapped in puff pastry, baked, gravy served separately.
— **Saint-Charles:** larded with ox tongue, roasted, deglaced with veal gravy; garnished with stuffed mushrooms.
— **with Sauternes:** au Sauternes: roasted, deglaced with Sauternes wine and thick veal gravy.
— **Sevigné:** split in half, stiffened in butter and cooled under light pressure; inside filled with salpicon of chicken, mushrooms and truffle bound with thick German sauce, dipped in egg and breadcrumbs and fried slowly in clarified butter; served with light Madeira sauce and asparagus tips.
— **Sierra Morena:** disjointed, browned in oil, moistened with brown stock and simmered with truffle slices, mushrooms, garlic and chopped chives; sauce flavored with Malaga.
— **Spanish Style:** à l'espagnole: split in half, roasted in oil; served on saffron rice garnished with fried tomatoes green peas and grilled red peppers.
— **Stuffed: farci:** stuffed with bread stuffing mixed with chopped mushrooms, roasted in service casserole; pan gravy.
— **Stuffed, Austrian Style:** farci à l'autrichienne: boned, stuffed with bread stuffing mixed with eggs, butter and chopped chives; roasted, served with the pan gravy.
— **Sylvain:** disjointed, browned in butter in service casserole with sliced mushrooms, boletus or fairy ring mushrooms, wild thyme and sage added, moistened with veal gravy and simmered in oven with the cover on; served in the casserole.
— **Tenant Style:** à la fermière: browned in butter, placed in cocotte with small slices of celery, carrots, turnips and onions, a little veal stock added and simmered in oven with the cover on until done.
— **Thiers:** disjointed, poached; when cold dipped in frying batter, deep fried; piquant sauce and gratinated cauliflower served separately.
— **Toad Style:** à la crapaudine: prepared like spring chicken.
— **Valenciennes Style:** à la valenciennes: boned, stuffed with veal forcemeat with diced gooseliver and mushrooms, braised in light demi-glace, white wine and tomato purée; served on Valenciennes rice.

Pigeon
— **Verdi:** pigeon breasts fried in butter, arranged on rice prepared the Piedmont way alternately with slices of sautéd gooseliver and truffle; deglaced with Asti wine and veal gravy, reduced, blended with butter and poured over the breasts.
— **Vivian:** Stuffed, roasted, garnished with Parisian potatoes; Colbert sauce served separately.

Pigeon Cutlet: Côtelette de pigeon: split in half, breast boned, stiffened in butter; when cold dipped in egg and breadcrumbs and fried.
— **Crownprince Style:** à la dauphine: coated with Villeroy sauce, dipped in egg and breadcrumbs, deep fried; buttered green peas served separately.
— **Pompadour:** dipped in egg and breadcrumbs fried in butter; garnished with artichoke bottoms filled with lentil purée, a truffle slice on top, and tiny round potato croquettes; truffle sauce served separately.
— **Valois:** dipped in egg and breadcrumbs, fried in butter; asparagus tips and Valois sauce served separately.

Pigeonneau: see squab.

Pilaw, Pilaf or Pilau: oriental dish of rice similar to risotto. As a main dish it is served with fish, meat or fowl with spices and other ingredients.
— **Arabian:** à l'arabe: well blanched and drained rice simmered in mutton fat and mixed with small cubes of fat mutton seasoned and simmered in its own fat.
— **of Chicken Livers:** de foies de volaille: large dices of chicken livers sautéd rare, mixed with diced mushrooms, bound with Madeira sauce, filled in border of rice pilaf.
— **Egyptian:** à l'egyptienne: diced mutton simmered in fat, diced tomatoes, eggplants and rice added, seasoned, moistened with mutton stock and cooked.
— **Greek:** à la grecque: 1. diced lamb simmered in its own fat with chopped onions, diced tomatoes, rice and gumbos added, moistened with lamb stock, cooked.
2. chicken disjointed and cut in small pieces, lightly fried in mutton fat with chopped onions, well blanched rice, diced sweet peppers, tomatoes, raisins and currants added moistened with stock and simmered until done.
— **Indian:** à l'indienne: chicken disjointed, browned in butter with chopped onions, sprinkled with curry powder, moistened with stock, garlic and raisins added and simmered until done; arranged on top of rice pilaf seasoned with curry powder and Cayenne pepper colored with saffron.
— **Mutton:** de mouton: diced mutton and chopped onions fried lightly in mutton fat, well blanched rice and tomato purée added, seasoned and cooked moistened with mutton stock.
— **Oriental:** à l'orientale: pieces of chicken slightly browned in butter with chopped onions, seasoned with ginger powder, moistened with a little stock; Malaga raisins, diced red peppers and currants added, stewed and served with plain boiled very dry rice.
— **Parisian:** à la parisienne: pilaf rice mixed with small thin slices of boiled chicken and diced tomatoes, pressed in an oval mould; turned out, sprinkled with grated Parmesan, bordered with tomato sauce.

Pilaw
— **Persian:** à la perse: diced fat mutton simmered in mutton fat with chopped onions, when two thirds done rice and saffron added, cooked until done.
— **Turkish:** à la turque: same as oriental with saffron added.
Pintade: see Guinea fowl.
Pintadeau: young Guinea fowl: see Guinea fowl.
Piroschki: Pirogues: sort of small Russian patty prepared mainly with yeast dough, filled with fish, meat, hard-boiled chopped eggs, cabbage, semolina etc. and baked.
— **with Bacon:** au lard: filled with chopped bacon and onions lightly fried.
— **pó finnski: squares of puff pastry, center filled with small** cold poached slice of pike-perch fillet, chopped onions sweated in butter and a small piece of pickled herring on top; ends folded over, patty closed, brushed with egg white and baked; when done glazed with crayfish butter. (Russian)
— **s' kapusstoi:** with Cabbage: squares of yeast dough rolled out thin, center filled with chopped white cabbage simmered with chopped onions, chopped bacon and cream, seasoned, mixed with butter and hard-boiled egg white; ends folded over, patty closed, brushed with egg white and baked; when done brushed generously with butter. (Russian)
— **rewelski:** Rewal Style: made of yeast dough, filled with a small slice of poached fillet of pike-perch covered with chopped onions simmered in butter; when baked brushed with butter. (Russian)
— **Russian:** à la russe: made of yeast dough, filled with chopped vesiga, chopped hard-boiled eggs, chopped onions simmered in butter and chopped herbs bound with thick demi-glace; when baked brushed generously with butter.
— **with Salmon:** au saumon: made of yeast dough, filled with a small piece of boiled salmon covered with chopped onions simmered in butter, chopped hard-boiled eggs and herbs; when baked a little light Dutch sauce poured into the patty through a hole in the center.
Pluvier: see Golden Plover.
Poerkoelt: Pörkölt: beef, veal or pork cut in large cubes, browned in lard with coarsely chopped onions, seasoned, paprika, garlic and tomato purée added, moistened with very little stock, stewed; rice or small flour dumplings served separately. (Hungarian)
Pointe de boeuf: see rump of beef.
Poitrine d'agneau: see lamb breast.
Polo al riso: Chicken and Rice: chicken disjointed, simmered in oil with chopped onions, strips of ham, mushrooms and parsley; when half done rice and diced tomatoes added, seasoned, moistened with a little stock and simmered until done; served with grated Parmesan and lettuce salad. (Italian)
— **español:** Chicken Spanish: disjointed, browned, simmered in demi-glace with tomato purée, diced fried bacon, chick peas, diced red peppers and Chorizos. (Spanish)
Polpettino Casalungo: ground beef, veal and pork, seasoned, mixed with eggs, shaped into small rolls, browned in oil and simmered with diced tomatoes, garlic and chopped parsley; grated Parmesan served separately. (Italian)

Pope's Eye: see nut of veal.

Pork; F. Porc; G. Schweinefleisch: the name of the meat of young pigs. Pork must always be cooked slowly and thoroughly done, rather overcooked than undercooked. For innards of pork see pig.

Pork, Bacon: Lard, Lard de poitrine: sides and belly of pig, cured and smoked. Gammon: term for a flitch of bacon with the ham on it. Rasher of bacon: a thin slice of bacon. Good bacon is evenly streaked with red lean meat, white and tender, the skin should be thin.

— **with Cabbage:** au chou: piece of bacon boiled with blanched quarters of cabbage with a larded onion added; when done bacon sliced, arranged on top of the cabbage and served with boiled potatoes.

— **Fried:** frit: rashers fried and served with fried pork sausage or tomatoes as a breakfast dish.

Pork Chop, French Chop, Cutlet: Côte de porc: cut from the loin with rib bone, fried or grilled, plain, coated with flour or dipped in egg and breadcrumbs.

— **with Apples:** au pommes fruits: seasoned, coated with flour, fried in butter; garnished with peeled apple wedges poached in butter, white wine, lemon juice and a little sugar.

— **Berlin Style:** à la berlinoise: dipped in egg and breadcrumbs, fried; mashed potatoes and braised red cabbage with sliced apples served separately.

— **Butcher Style:** à la charcutière: not trimmed, lightly flattened, dipped in melted butter and breadcrumbs, grilled; mashed potatoes and butcher sauce served separately.

— **Courland Style:** à la courlandaise: dipped in melted butter and breadcrumbs, grilled; served with red cabbage, glaced chestnuts and Madeira sauce.

— **Debreczin Style:** browned on both sides, wrapped in blanched cabbage leaf, tied, braised in light paprika sauce; boiled potatoes served separately.

— **Eszterházy:** browned, seasoned with paprika, simmered in sour cream with strips of root vegetables.

— **Farmer Style:** à la paysanne: fried, served with fried sliced onions and pan fried potatoes cut in quarters.

— **with Fine Herbs:** aux fines herbes: browned, braised in very little brown stock with chopped shallots, mushrooms and parsley.

— **Flemish Style:** à la flamande: browned in butter, placed in baking dish garnished with peeled and coarsely sliced apples, cooking finished in oven.

— **Grandmother Style:** à la grand'mère: chopped, mixed with chopped onions simmered in butter, eggs and butter, seasoned, reformed with the rib bone, wrapped in pig's caul, brushed with butter, grilled; mashed potatoes served separately.

— **Hungarian Style:** à la hongroise: browned in lard, braised in light paprika sauce; served with noodles or Tarhonya.

— **in Jelly:** en gelée: loin boiled in lightly salted water with pot herbs; when cold chops cut without bones, aspic jelly prepared with the stock and lightly acidulated with vinegar; cutlet mould lined with jelly, decorated with sliced carrots and pickled cucumber, chop placed in

Pork Chop
mould, sealed with jelly; when set turned out and served with German fried potatoes.
— **Mexican Style:** à la mexicaine: browned in butter, braised in light demi-glace with tomato and strips of red peppers.
— **Milanese Style:** à la milanaise: dipped in egg and bread-crumbs mixed with grated Parmesan, fried in oil; macaroni prepared the Milanese way served separately.
— **Moldavian Style:** à la moldavienne: chopped, seasoned, mixed with egg, reformed with the rib bone, fried in butter; covered with fried sliced onions, garnished with grated horseradish; mustard sauce served separately.
— **with Piquant or Robert Sauce:** sauce piquante ou sauce Robert; seasoned, coated with flour, fried in butter and served either with Piquant or Robert sauce and mashed potatoes.
— **with Root Vegetables:** aux racines: browned in butter, placed in baking dish alternately with sliced carrots, onions, turnips and potatoes, seasoned, a little stock added, braised in oven.
— **with Saurkraut:** au choucroute: browned in lard, placed in baking dish with prebraised saurkraut, covered with raw apple slices, moistened with white wine and a little beef stock, braised in oven.
— **Soissons Style:** à la soissonaise: fried in butter, served with navy beans prepared the Soissons way.
— **in Sour Cream Sauce;** au crème aigre: seasoned, coated with flour, fried in butter; deglaced with sour cream and a little meat glaze, seasoned with lemon and poured over cutlet; boiled potatoes served separately.
— **Westmoreland:** fried in butter, covered with demi-glace with chopped pickles added.

Pork, Head Cheese; Hungarian Brawn: Fromage de Hongrie: head, feet and swards cooked in water with root vegetables, onions, bayleaf, marjoram, thyme, salt and allspice; when done head and feet boned and diced, and aspic jelly made of the clarified stock. Rectangular mould lined with aspic, decorated with the sliced root vegetables, gherkins and hard-boiled eggs, filled with the diced meat and covered entirely with aspic jelly; when set turned out, garnished with aspic jelly and served with vinaigrette sauce.

Pork, Leg of: Gigot de porc, Jambon frais: skin scored diamond fashion, roasted whole or boned and rolled. Served sliced with its own gravy and mashed or roast potatoes, saurkraut, braised red cabbage, spinach purée or sautéd fruits. In Great Britain apple sauce is always served with roast pork.

Pork, Loin of: Carré de porc: vertebrae removed, trimmed and roasted, served with the degreased pan gravy. All garnished for pork chops are applicable to roast loin.
— **Austrian Style:** Jungschweinsbraten: loin of young hog, blanched, scored diamond fashion, crushed caraway seeds and salt rubbed into the flesh, roasted; pan gravy thickened, degreased and strained, served separately with boiled potatoes. (Austrian)
— **with Brussels Sprouts:** aux choux de Bruxelles: roasted in a fireproof serving dish; 20 minutes before pork is done parboiled well drained Brussels sprouts added.

Pork, Loin of

— **Farmer Style:** à la paysanne: roasted; when half done potatoes cut in quarters and sliced onions added, cooking finished in oven.

— **with Purées:** aux purées diverses: roasted, served with the degreased pan gravy and purée of lentils, celery, onions, green peas or potatoes.

— **with Red Cabbage:** au chou rouge: roasted, served with the degreased pan gravy and braised red cabbage.

— **with Saurkraut:** au choucroute: roasted, served with braised saurkraut, boiled potatoes and the degreased pan gravy.

— **Smoked:** fumé: the cured and smoked loin is boiled or roasted and served with saurkraut, red cabbage or spinach and boiled or mashed potatoes.

— **Soissons Style:** à la soissonnaise: roasted, served with navy beans parboiled and cooked with the meat.

Pork, Loin and Spare Ribs, Smoked: Kasseler Rippenspeer: the cured and smoked ribs are chiefly roasted, less often boiled, and served with the pan gravy, saurkraut, braised red cabbage or spinach, and mashed or boiled potatoes. (German)

Pork Sausage: Saucisse de porc: fresh finely minced lean pork and green bacon with salt and spices, or half lean and half fat pork minced finely and seasoned with salt, spices, nutmeg, herbs etc. and filled in sheep casing. Pork sausages filled in very thin casings and only about 2 inch. long are called Chipolatas.

— **Burgundy Style:** à la bourguignonne: poached, cut in pieces and fried in Burgundy butter (snail butter).

— **Fried:** frite: blanched, fried and served with mashed potatoes.

— **Grilled:** grillée: blanched, coated with flour, brushed with melted butter, grilled; served with mashed potatoes.

— **in Night Dress:** en robe de chambre blanched, when cold wrapped in puff paste, baked in oven.

— **with Risotto:** au risotto: Chipolatas cooked in butter and white wine, stock boiled down with demi-glace; filled in center of risotto border covered with the sauce.

— **in White Wine:** au vin blanc: stiffened in butter and cooked in white wine; stock boiled down with demi-glace and poured over sausage.

Pork, Scrambled: boiled smoked spare ribs diced or sliced and mixed with scrambled eggs.

Pork, Pickled Shank: Eisbein: boiled, served with saurkraut, pease-pudding and boiled potatoes. (German)

— **au four:** boiled, when half done placed in fireproof china casserole, surrounded with raw potatoes cut in quarters, sprinkled with chopped parsley mixed with a little garlic, white wine and a little meat gravy added, lid sealed hermetically with dough, baked in the oven.

Pork, Pickled Spare Ribs of: boiled, served with saurkraut, pease pudding or mashed potatoes.

— **Gratinated:** boiled, sliced, arranged in baking dish on a layer of saurkraut alternately with layers of mashed potatoes, saurkraut and the meat; mashed potatoes on top, sprinkled with breadcrumbs, dotted generously with butter and browned in oven.

Pork, Tenderloin of: Filet mignon de porc: removed from inside of loin, sinew trimmed, split lengthwise, opened and flattened or sliced across in small steaks.

— **with Apples:** aux pommes fruits: seasoned, coated with flour, fried in butter and served with thick pared and cored apple slices poached in butter and white wine and glazed with sugar.

— **Austrian Style:** à l'autrichienne: simmered in stock and sour cream with root vegetables and onions; sauce strained and poured over meat, served with boiled potatoes.

— **French Style:** à la française: wrapped first in thin slice of salt pork and then in a blanched cabbage leaf; tied, stewed in white wine and demi-glace.

— **Gastronomer Style:** à la gastronome: whole tenderloin larded with anchovy fillets and salt pork, browned, braised in brown stock, strained and finished off with sour cream; garnished with sautéd boletus and stoned olives.

— **German Style:** à l'allemande: fried in butter, deglaced with sour cream, served with mashed potatoes.

— **Hungarian Style:** à la hongroise: browned in butter, braised in light paprika sauce; served with noodles or boiled potatoes.

— **Lyonese Style:** à la lyonnaise: fried, covered with sliced fried onions mixed with a little liquid meat glaze and seasoned with vinegar.

— **with Pineapple:** à l'ananas: cut in small steaks, fried in butter, deglaced with pineapple juice, boiled up with demi-glace; garnished with small slices of glazed pineapple.

— **Russian Style:** à la russe: split lengthwise, opened, browned in butter, coated with duxelles, wrapped first in a blanched cabbage leaf and then in pig's caul, fried in oven; served with brown herb sauce.

— **Wellington:** fried blood rare and allowed to cool; coated with duxelles mixed with chopped parsley, lemon peel and tomato purée, wrapped in puff paste and baked.

— **Westmoreland:** fried, served with demi-glace mixed with chopped pickles and mushrooms.

Pork Tongue: Langue de porc: prepared like calf's tongue.

Port Arthur Dish: half a roast squab chicken, a tournedos placed on a croûton with an artichoke bottom filled with blanched ox marrow on top, a fried veal collop with a mushroom on top and German fried potatoes arranged on a suitable platter; sauce made of chopped shallots sweated in butter, deglaced with white wine, boiled up with demi-glace and tomato purée, seasoned with Cayenne pepper and lemon juice served separately.

Potpourri: a fried mutton cutlet, pork chop, veal collop and tournedos arranged on a platter, covered alternately with demi-glace and tomato sauce; garnished with sautéd mushrooms, green peas, potato croquettes and French beans.

Pot Roast: Estouffade: diced meat browned in fat with sliced or chopped onions added, dredged with flour, moistened with stock, wine or water, seasoned, bunch of herbs added, stewed in oven in china or earthenware casserole hermetically closed with dough.

Pot Roast
— **Alsatian Style:** à l'alsacienne: diced pork stewed in demi-glace with morels.
— **Burgundy Style:** à la bourguignonne: diced beef stewed in red wine with diced bacon, button onions, button mushrooms and light demi-glace.
— **Provence Style:** à la provençale: diced beef stewed in white wine and demiglace with diced tomatoes, pitted olives and garlic.

Potwarak: Duck Yougoslavian Style: sliced onions fried a pale yellow, mixed with chopped saurkraut and pepper corns, a duck browned on all sides placed on top, seasoned, moistened with a little saurkraut pickle and braised; when done carved and arranged on the saurkraut (Yougoslavian).

Poularde: see chicken.

Poulet frit: see chicken, fried.

Poulet de grain: see spring chicken.

Poulet reine: see roasting chicken.

Poulet sauté: see chicken, sautéd.

Poussin: see squab chicken.

Ptarmigan; F. Perdrix blanche; G. Schneehuhn: game bird of the northern Regions of Europe and Siberia allied to the grouse. In the U. S. A. it is represented by an identical species known as White-Tailed Ptarmigan. Ptarmigan is mainly marketed in a frozen state and prepared like partridge or pheasant.

Puchero Argentina: cubes of brisket of beef, lamb and pig's head, pieces of disjointed chicken and chick peas boiled slowly in water, later on diced bacon, Chorizos, cabbage cut in quarters, potato balls, rice and diced tomatoes added and seasoned sharply (Argentine).
— **Madrileña:** chick peas soaked, boiled with cubes of brisket of beef, disjointed chicken, bacon, Chorizos, diced tomatoes and green peppers; shortly before Puchero is done potato balls added and stock boiled down (Spanish).

Puff Pastry Patties, Small: see bouchées.
— — **Shells, Large:** see vol-au-vent.
— — **Sticks:** Allumettes: sheet of puff pastry spread with forcemeat or some kind of purée, covered with another sheet of puff pastry, egg washed, cut into thin strips and baked.
— — — **Saint Hubert:** spread with game forcemeat mixed with chopped morels.
— — **Strips:** D'Artois: sheet of puff pastry spread with forcemeat or fine ragoût in thick sauce, covered with another sheet of puff pastry, egg washed, bake, cut into strips, served hot.

Pumpkin Egyptian Style: Courge à l'egyptienne: lid cut off of a baby pumpkin or squash, seeds removed, blanched, stuffed with risotto prepared with chopped onions and garlic sweated in oil and tomato purée, allowed to cool and mixed with raw minced mutton, chopped fresh mint, parsley, garlic, fennel and peeled tomatoes, covered with sliced onions, carrots and tomatoes, lid put on, wrapped in greased paper, braised in brown stock and tomato purée, served covered with browned butter.
— **Mexican Style:** à la mexicaine: stuffed with beef, chopped olives, red peppers and currants, braised in brown stock.

Pumpkin
— **Stuffed:** farcie: prepared like Egyptian style filled with minced raw mutton mixed with boiled rice and diced tomatoes, braised in light tomato sauce.
Pytt i panna: left overs of roast beef, veal and ham mixed with diced boiled potatoes and chopped fried onions, sautéd in butter and served with a fried egg on top (Swedish).

Q

Quail; F. Caille; G. Wachtel: migratory little game bird wintering in Africa and India and breeding throughout the greater part of Europe. The European bird is smaller than the American, of which there are several species such as Virginia, California and Mountain quail etc.
— **Alexandra:** poached in white stock, arranged in baking dish with a slice of truffle on top, covered with Mornay sauce with truffle essence, sprinkled with grated cheese, glazed; green asparagus tips served separately.
— **Alexis:** roasted in cocotte, deglaced with Curaçao and sweet cream, veal glaze and Malaga raisins added.
— **Baked:** sous la cendre: boned, stuffed with truffled game forcemeat, wrapped in bacon and pie dough, baked. Formerly these quails where wrapped in a piece of greased paper and baked directly in hot cinders.
— **Beaconsfield:** simmered in butter with a little white stock; served on green pea purée, garnished with sautéd mushrooms, covered with the stock boiled down with demi-glace.
— **Berlin Style:** à la berlinoise: boned, stuffed with gooseliver forcemeat; shaped like a ball, wrapped in a cloth and poached in veal stock; unwrapped, placed on an artichoke bottom, covered with German sauce prepared with the stock chopped truffle scattered on top.
— **Bohemian Style:** à la bohémienne: boned, filled with a piece of gooseliver and truffle; roasted, deglaced with veal gravy.
— **Café de Paris:** roasted, served on baked potatoes, piece cut of off the top, scooped out and filled with gooseliver purée.
— **Canadian Style:** à la canadienne: roasted, garnished with fried apple wedges, salmi sauce.
— **Carmen** (cold): poached in rich veal stock flavored with white Port; when cold glazed with aspic jelly prepared with the stock; served with pomegranate granité.
— **in Casserole:** en casserole: roasted in service casserole, deglaced with brandy and game stock.
— **Cecilia** (cold): roasted, when cold breasts removed, placed on small slice of gooseliver, coated with brown chaud-froid sauce; when set filled in border mould lined with aspic jelly and decorated with truffle slices, sealed with aspic jelly; chilled and turned out on round silver dish.
— **Charente Style:** à la charentaise: wrapped in vine leaf and bacon, roasted, deglaced with Cognac.
— **with Cherries:** aux cerises: roasted in casserole, deglaced with brandy and lemon juice, garnished with stoned stewed sour cherries.

Quail

— **with Cherries** (cold): à la cerisette: poached in rich veal stock with champagne; when cold glazed with aspic jelly prepared with the stock, garnished with poached stoned sour cherries, drained and bound with the same aspic jelly; served with cherry granité.

— **Clermont:** boned, stuffed with cooked coarsely chopped chestnuts mixed with butter and chopped onions simmered in butter; poached, covered with light white onion sauce.

— **in Cream Sauce:** à la créme: roasted, deglaced with brandy, boiled up with sweet cream and a little meat glaze, seasoned with lemon juice.

— **Crownprince Style:** à la dauphine: roasted, placed in baked potato scooped out lightly, covered with truffle sauce.

— **Diana:** Diane: roasted, served with chestnut purée and Diana sauce.

— **Demidoff:** braised in cocotte with small half-moon shaped slices of carrots, turnips, celery and onions; when done half-moon shaped truffle slices added; served in the cocotte with the cover on.

Egyptian Style: à l'egyptienne: roasted, placed on rice pilaf mixed with diced tomatoes; tomato sauce.

— **Farmer Style:** à la paysanne: prepared like partridge.

— **Father Philippe Style:** roasted, served on baked potato scooped out lightly.

— **Félix:** poached in white stock, served with archduke sauce.

— **Figaro:** stuffed with a piece of truffle, filled in sausage skin with a small piece of veal glaze, poached in veal stock, served in the skin.

— **Financier Style:** à la financière: poached, served with financier garnish and sauce.

— **Frères Provençaux:** stuffed, browned in butter, when cold coated with duxelles, wrapped in puff paste, decorated, brushed with egg yolk, baked in oven.

— **with Grapes:** aux raisins (cold): poached in rich veal stock; when cold placed in glass dish with peeled seeded aromatic grapes, covered entirely with aspic jelly prepared with the stock flavored with Rhine wine.

— **Greek Style:** à la grecque: cooked in butter in casserole, deglaced with game stock served on rice prepared the Greek way, covered with the gravy.

— **with Green Peas:** aux petits pois: roasted, served with green peas cooked in butter with chopped ham and seasoning in closed casserole without water or any other liquid.

— **George Sand:** stuffed with gooseliver forcemeat, browned in butter, allowed to cool; wrapped in puff paste, brushed with egg yolk, baked in oven.

— **Housewife Style:** à la bonne-femme: prepared like partridge.

— **Italian Style:** à l'italienne: roasted, deglaced with white wine, boiled down with Italian sauce; garnished with artichoke quarters prepared the Italian way.

— **Judic:** roasted, served on braised lettuce, garnished with cock's kidneys and truffle slices; demi-glace with quail essence.

— **Julia:** Julie: split at the back, flattened, dipped in butter and chopped truffle, wrapped in pig's caul, grilled.

Quail

— **Kléber:** roasted, served on pastry shell filled with salpicon of mushrooms and gooseliver, covered with Madeira sauce with mushroom essence.

— **with Lettuce:** aux laitues: roasted in casserole, garnished with braised lettuce.

— **Liege Style:** à la Liègeoise: roasted in cocotte with crushed juniper berries, deglaced with Genever.

— **Little Duke:** à la petit duc: split at the back, flattened, seasoned, dipped in egg and breadcrumbs, moistened with butter, grilled; garnished with mushroom caps stuffed with grated horseradish; Madeira sauce.

— **Lucullus:** large round truffle cut in half, scooped out and cooked in Madeira; quails boned, stuffed with game forcemeat mixed with the chopped truffle pulp, egg yolks and brandy, shaped round, tied in a cloth and poached in veal stock. Unwrapped, placed on the truffle, covered with rich demi-glace, glazed and served with demi-glace with quail essence poured around.

— **Maintenon:** boned, stuffed with truffled game forcemeat, poached; garnished with cockscombs, truffle slices and mushrooms, covered with white truffle sauce.

— **with Malaga Sauce:** au Malaga: roasted, deglaced with Malaga and thick veal gravy, garnished with Malaga raisins.

— **Mandarinette:** Mandarines de cailles: tangerine scooped out, filled with quail froth mixed with diced gooseliver, a quails breast coated with brown chaudfroid sauce and two tangerine fillets placed on top, glazed with aspic jelly, served very cold.

— **Marianne:** roasted in service casserole with small slices of apple, sprinkled with breadcrumbs, dotted with butter and browned in oven.

— **Medicis:** poached, garnished with diced gooseliver and truffles, covered with salmi sauce; Macaroni served separately.

— **Milanese Style:** à la milanaise: split at the back, flattened, dipped in egg and breadcrumbs mixed with half grated Parmesan; fried in butter, devil sauce served separately.

— **Norman Style:** à la normande: apple cut in half, scooped out, a quail browned in butter placed in each half with a few drops of applejack poured on top, wrapped in short paste, brushed with egg yolk and baked in hot oven.

— **Oriental Style:** à l'orientale: roasted, deglaced with tomato juice and veal gravy, served on rice pilaf with saffron.

— **in Paper Bag:** en papillote: boned, lightly browned in butter; when cold coated with duxelles mixed with chopped truffle and parsley, wrapped in greased paper and baked in oven.

— **Parmentier:** boned, stuffed with gooseliver forcemeat, placed in a large potato, scooped out and filled with a piece of butter, wrapped in greased paper and baked in oven.

— **Perigord Style:** à la périgourdine: roasted in casserole, deglaced with Madeira and veal gravy, garnished with olive-shaped or cubed truffles.

— **Piedmont Style:** à la piemontaise: cooked in butter, served on risotto mixed with diced sautéd chicken livers and white Italian truffles.

Quail

— **with Pineapple:** à l'ananas: roasted in cocotte, deglaced with pineapple juice and thick veal gravy; diced pineapple boiled up in the gravy and poured over the bird.

— **with Pommard:** glacée au Pommard (cold): poached in rich veal stock with Pommard; when cold glazed with aspic jelly prepared with the stock; served with granité made with the juice of sour grapes.

— **Pompadour:** boned, stuffed with thick mushroom purée bound with egg yolks and mixed with diced truffle; roasted, served with truffle sauce.

— **Princess Style:** à la princesse: boned, stuffed with gooseliver forcemeat, poached in veal stock; placed on nest made of duchess mixture, baked and filled with green asparagus tips tossed in butter, covered with German sauce finished off with green asparagus butter.

— **Queen Amelia:** Reine Amélie (cold): prepared like Carmen but served with tomato granité.

— **with Quinces:** aux coings: marinated 48 hours with brandy and quince peels; cooked in butter with the brandy, but without the peels in a fireproof cocotte closed hermetically; served in the cocotte with quince jelly separately.

— **with Red Cabbage:** au chou rouge: roasted, served on braised red cabbage mixed with apple and chestnut purée.

— **Richelieu:** boned, filled with a small piece of raw truffle, poached in rich veal stock with julienne of carrots, celery and onion, when nearly done julienne of truffle added; served in the stock with the julienne on top. May also be served cold.

— **Rossini:** boned, stuffed with truffled gooseliver forcemeat; roasted, placed on a fried slice of gooseliver, a truffle slice on top, covered with Madeira sauce.

— **Rôtisserie Périgourdine:** boned, stuffed with a piece of gooseliver, placed in a fireproof China cocotte on slices of raw truffle, moistened with a little Madeira and veal gravy; cocotte covered with puff pastry with a funnel in the center to allow the steam to escape. Decorated, brushed with egg yolk, baked.

— **Royal Style:** à la royale: boned, stuffed with gooseliver and truffle, poached in veal stock; placed in China case on salpicon on cockscombs, cock's kidneys, mushroom, truffles and tiny chicken dumplings bound with German sauce.

— **with Saurkraut:** au choucroute: wrapped in bacon, browned in butter, placed on half-cooked saurkraut and braised in oven with the saurkraut.

— **Spanish Style:** à l'espagnole: roasted in oil, served on risotto mixed with diced green peppers, green peas and garlic sausage, garnished with fried tomatoes.

— **Suwaroff:** prepared like woodcock.

— **in Tangerine:** en mandarine (cold): boned, stuffed with game forcemeat, poached in rich veal stock; slice cut of the top of a tangerine, scooped out, juice pressed out and filtered, aspic prepared with the stock and flavored highly with the tangerine juice. Quail placed in tangerine, covered entirely with this aspic jelly.

Quail

— **Turkish Style:** à la turque: browned in butter, cooked in rice pilaf mixed with cooked chopped eggplants; served on top of the rice with a border of game gravy.

— **Urban Dubois:** boned, stuffed, cooked in light Madeira sauce with finely diced carrots, mushrooms and button onions.

— **Valenciennes:** roasted, served on risotto mixed with diced tomatoes, artichoke bottoms, green peas and chopped ham.

— **Victoria:** stuffed with gooseliver and truffle, roasted in casserole with diced blanched potatoes, deglaced with brandy and very little veal gravy.

— **Vintager Style:** à la vigneronne: wrapped in vine leaf and bacon, roasted, deglaced with Madeira and veal gravy, garnished with peeled seeded grapes.

Quenelles: see dumplings.

Quiche Lorraine: see Lothringian tarte.

R

Rabbit; F. Lapin; G. Kaninchen: tame or hutch rabbit; F. lapin de chou or lapin de clapier; G. zahmes Kaninchen: wild rabbit; F.lapin de garenne; G. Wildkaninchen: young rabbit; F. lapereau; G. junges Kaninchen. Young rabbits are best für roasting, frying, baking or fricassée, older rabbits are stewed or used for making pies and soups.

— **Baked:** au four: cut in pieces, fried when half done brushed with mustard, sprinkled with breadcrumbs mixed with a little chopped thyme, dotted with melted butter and finished in oven.

— **Burgundy Style:** à la bourguignonne: prepared like citizen style but with red wine, button mushrooms and glazed button onions, bordered with heart-shaped croûtons fried in butter.

— **Citizen Style:** à la bourgeoise: carved, browned in lard, dredged with flour, moistened with white wine and brown stock, when nearly done browned button onions, olive-shaped carrots and diced fried bacon added.

— **English Style:** à la l'anglaise: stuffed with sage and onion stuffing, tied, boiled with pot herbs, served with caper sauce.

— **French, Ragoût:** Gibelotte de lapin: prepared like jugged hare with half red wine and half brown stock.

— **Fried:** frit: back and legs cut in convenient pieces, marinated in oil, lemon juice, chopped shallots, salt and pepper, wiped dry, dipped in egg and breadcrumbs, fried; tomato sauce served separately.

— **Hungarian Style:** à la hongroise: cut in pieces, browned with chopped onions added, dusted with paprika, simmered in sour cream and white stock.

— **Hunter Style:** à la chasseur: cut in pieces, browned, dredged with flour, braised in white wine and brown stock, when nearly done button onions and mushrooms added and at serving chopped chervil and tarragon.

— **Marengo:** cut in pieces and prepared like veal ragoût.

— **with Mushrooms:** aux champignons: cut in pieces, browned in butter, simmered in light demi-glace and white wine, button mushrooms added shortly before rabbit is done.

Rabbit

— **Old Fashioned Style:** à l'ancienne: cut in convenient pieces, sweated in butter but not browned, dredged with flour moistened with white stock and white wine, when nearly done parboiled button onions and mushroom caps added; bound with egg yolks and cream, chopped chives sprinkled on top, bordered with fleurons.

— **Pie Farmer Style:** Tourte de lapereau à la paysanne: tart ring lined with plain pie dough, coated inside and at the bottom with pork sausage meat mixed with soaked bread, chopped onions and parsley, thick cold slices of rabbit fillet, stiffened in butter beforehand placed on top, covered with sliced mushrooms, closed with pie dough brushed with egg yolk and baked; when done a little demiglace poured in the pie through a hole in the center.

— **Poulette:** cut in pieces and simmered in poulette sauce.

— **Provencal Style:** à la provençale: cut in pieces, fried in oil, simmered in Provencal sauce.

— **with Prunes:** aux pruneaux: cut in pieces, marinated in vinegar pickle, dried, browned lightly in butter, moistened with half water and half marinade, stoned prunes soaked in water beforehand added, simmered until done, stock thickened at the last minute with a little red currant jelly. (Belgian)

— **Spanish Style:** à la l'espagnole: cut in pieces, browned in oil with chopped onions and diced bacon, seasoned with salt and paprika, chopped peeled tomatoes, strips of red and green peppers and a little stock added, simmered until done and bordered with heart-shaped croûtons fried in butter.

— **Sweet-Sour:** à la l'aigre-doux: cut in pieces and marinated 24 hours in white wine, vinegar, sliced onions and herbs; browned in butter, moistened with demi-glace, stock and a little marinade, stewed until done, picked out in a clean stewpan with pickled cherries added; the boiled down sauce to which a little melted chocolate has been added strained over the rabbit. (Belgian)

Rabbit, Fillet of: Filet de lapereau: cut from the loin of young rabbits, skinned, larded and mainly fried in butter.

— **Conti:** larded with fat bacon and ox tongue, fried, arranged on a slice of bacon cooked with the lentils, covered with game sauce prepared with the rabbit bones; lentil purée served separately.

— **Dampierre:** larded with truffle and ox tongue, poached in butter and a little brandy, arranged on rabbit mousse, garnished with glazed button onions, chestnuts and mushrooms; pepper sauce served separately.

— **with Fine Herbs:** au fines herbes: larded, simmered in butter, white wine, chopped bacon, mushrooms, shallots and parsley; stock boiled down with a little demi-glace and poured over the fillet.

— **Milanese Style:** à la milanaise: flattened, dipped in egg and breadcrumbs mixed with grated Parmesan, fried in butter; macaroni prepared in the Milanese way and tomato sauce served separately.

— **with Oranges:** à l'orange: larded, fried in butter, taken out of skillet, deglaced with orange juice and a little brandy, boiled up with pepper sauce finished off with

Rabbit, Fillet of
red currant jelly; garnished with orange fillets tossed in butter.
— **with Pepper Sauce:** à la sauce poivrade: larded, fried, covered with pepper sauce, bordered with heart-shaped croûtons fried in butter.
— **Provencal Style:** à la provençale: larded, fried, in oil, taken out of skillet, deglaced with white wine, chopped peeled tomatoes, garlic, chopped anchovies, sweet basil and stoned olives added, cooked for a while and poured over the fillet.

Râble de lièvre: see saddle of hare.

Ragoût: a white or brown spicy stew or a compound of meat, fowl or game with vegetables or other ingredients with a rich sauce. Usually a dish by itself but also used as a garnish or filler for vol-au-vent etc. Fricassées and blanquettes are white ragoûts. For ragoût see also meat, poultry and game.
— **Alsatian Pork:** de porc à l'alsacienne: diced lean pork browned in lard, chopped onions added, stewed in light demi-glace; garnished with glazed button onions, served with chopped chives scattered on top.
— **of Chicken, Brown:** de poulet à brun: chicken disjointed, browned in butter, sprinkled with flour, moistened with stock, seasoned and braised with cover on; when done mixed with diced sweetbread, capers, button mushrooms, small veal dumplings and sliced truffles; served in border of puff pastry or in large puff pastry patty.
— **of Chicken, White:** de poulet à blanc: disjointed, sweated in butter with mirepoix, moistened with white stock and simmered until done; skinned, mixed with button mushrooms, morels, small slices of sweetbread and truffle slices; the stock thickened with white roux, boiled up with white wine, seasoned with salt, Cayenne pepper and lemon juice strained over; bordered with fleurons.
— **Cream Stew:** Rahmfleisch: diced veal browned in butter with chopped onions and paprika, dredged with flour, moistened with white stock and stewed; finished off with sour cream and served with small dumplings. (Austrian)
— **of Duck:** de canard: duck roasted, when half done carved and stewed in duck stock with a larded onion, lemon slices and pepper corns; stock thickened with roux, strained, flavored with Port and poured over the duck; bordered with heart-shaped croûtons.
— **Financier Style:** à la financière: diced sweetbreads, small chicken dumplings, button mushrooms, cockscombs, cock's kidneys and stoned olives bound with demi-glace with truffle essence, dressed in border of puff pastry or large puff pastry shell, truffle slices on top.
— **German Style:** à la l'allemande: small slices of beef and beef kidneys browned in butter with chopped onions, stewed in light demi-glace with tomato purée and diced green peppers added; sauce flavored with Sherry, served with raw sliced fried potatoes and chopped parsley on top.
— **Gourmet Style:** du gourmet: poached soft roes, pike liver and oysters, crayfish tails, soaked anchovy fillets, diced ox tongue, mushrooms and sliced truffles bound with German sauce with chicken essence, filled in baked border of puff pastry.

Ragoût

— **Hunter Style:** à la chasseur: cubes of stag, wild boar or roe browned in butter, dredged with flour, moistened with white wine, brown stock and tomato purée, garlic and a bunch of herbs added, stewed; when nearly done picked out in clean saucepan, sliced sautéd mushrooms added, the sauce strained over and cooked until done.

— **Italian Style:** l'italienne: macaroni cut in small pieces, diced artichoke bottoms, ham, cockscombs and sliced partridge breast bound with tomato sauce; grated Parmesan served separately.

— **of Kangoroo:** de kangorou: cubes marinated in red wine, browned in oil with mirepoix, stewed in demi-glace with the marinade, seasoned with salt, pepper, allspice and a bayleaf.

— **Mexican Style:** à la mexicaine: diced lean pork browned in butter, seasoned, moistened with brown stock and stewed; when half done diced tomatoes, green peppers and rice added, cooking finished with cover on.

— **of Mutton and Green Beans:** Hammelfleisch mit grünen Bohnen: large cubes of mutton cooked in water with broken green beans, seasoned with salt, pepper and summer savory, diced potatoes added later on. (German)

— **Stragonoff:** see Govia Dina Stragonoff.

— **Strassburg Style:** à la strassbourgeoise: diced beef, veal and pork browned in lard with chopped onions, moistened with red wine and stock, seasoned with paprika, marjoram, sage, bay leaf, ginger, salt and pepper, stewed; served with small flour dumplings.

— **Tolstoi:** Sauté de boeuf Tolstoï: head of tenderloin of beef cut in large cubes, browned rapidly in butter, diced tomatoes, chopped onions, a little white stock, tomato purée and diced pickled cucumbers added, stewed; served in timbale dish with boiled potato balls separately.

— **Toulouse Style:** à la toulousaine: small slices of calf's sweetbread, cockscombs, cock's kidneys and sliced truffles bound with German sauce finished off with mushroom and truffle essence; filled in timbale dish with chicken dumplings on top, bordered with fleurons.

— **Trieste Style:** à la triestaine: diced beef browned in lard, seasoned and moistened with stock, mixed with shredded white cabbage, diced fried bacon and sautéd potato cubes.

Ragoût in scallop shells: Coquilles: border of duchess potato piped round the edge of shell, bottom masked with sauce, sliced meat, poultry etc placed on top, covered with sauce, sprinkled with grated cheese, butter dropped on top and gratinated in oven.

— **Aurora:** à l'aurore: sliced chicken, ham and mushrooms covered with Aurora sauce, gratinated.

— **Cardinal Style:** à la cardinale: filled with diced lobster and truffle bound with cardinal sauce, gratinated, a lobster and a truffle slice placed on top.

— **of Chicken:** Coquille de volaille: bottom of shell masked with cream or suprême sauce, sliced boiled chicken arranged on top, covered with sauce and gratinated.

— **Lucullus:** bottom masked with demi-glace with game essence, quail breasts, quail dumplings and truffle slices arranged on top, covered with thick demi-glace with game essence, gratinated.

Ragoût in scallop shells

— **Mother Catherine Style:** Coquille à la mère Catherine: bottom coated with demi-glace, filled with hashed duck mixed with diced mushrooms and bound with demi-glace with duck essence; sprinkled with breadcrumbs, melted butter dropped on top and gratinated.

— **Parisian Style:** à la parisienne: sliced poached calf's brain, sliced mushrooms and truffles, covered with German sauce and gratinated.

— **Richelieu:** slices of chicken, ox tongue and truffle covered with German sauce and gratinated.

— **Toulouse Style:** à la toulousaine: same filling as for bouchées, covered with German sauce with mushroom essence and gratinated.

Rakott káposza: Hungarian Saurkraut: saurkraut braised with a piece of smoked bacon; chopped lean pork browned in lard with chopped onions, garlic and paprika; baking dish filled alternately with layers of saurkraut and sliced bacon, covered with the pork and slices of Debreszin sausage topped with saurkraut; salt and paprika sprinkled on top, sour cream poured over, cooking finished in oven. (Hungarian)

Red Peppers, Stuffed: Gefüllter Paprika: red peppers stuffed with pork sausage meat mixed with boiled rice and chopped onions; stewed in light tomato sauce. (Austrian)

Regensburger Braten: ground beef and pork mixed with chopped suet, soaked bread, chopped onions sweated in butter, chopped parsley and eggs, seasoned with salt, pepper, garlic and marjoram; longish sort of loaf formed, placed in greased roasting pan, melted butter poured over, roasted; deglaced with beef stock and sour cream; potato dumplings served separately. (German)

Reindeer: F. Renne; G. Renntier: member of the deer family native to Northern Europe, America and Asia. In America it is often marketed frozen. The smoked tongue is considered a great delicacy.

Reindeer, Haunch of, Russian Style: Cuissot de renne à la russe: skinned, marinated in light wine pickle, larded, roasted; garnished with round croûtons scooped out and filled with caviar; boletus in sour cream sauce and Madeira sauce served separately.

Reindeer, Saddle of: Selle de renne: skinned, larded and roasted or braised.

— **Finnish Style:** à la finlandaise: roasted, deglaced with light demi-glace boiled up with sour cream and seasoned with lemon juice; buttered noodles, cranberry jelly and pickled cucumbers served separately.

— **Livonian Style:** à la livonienne: braised, stock boiled down with sour cream; garnished with mushroom caps filled with grated horseradish and tiny shells filled with iced caviar; sauce and pickled cucumbers served separately.

— **Norwegian Style:** à la norvégienne: roasted, served with chief ranger sauce, chestnut purée and salsifis in cream sauce.

— **Russian Style:** à la russe: roasted, served with Madeira sauce and boletus in sour cream sauce.

Reindeer Steak: Filet de renne: steak cut from a tender loin, sautéd in butter.
— **Gourmet Style:** du gourmet: fried on one side only, this side coated with gooseliver forcemeat with chopped truffle; brushed with melted butter, finished in oven; Madeira sauce.
— **Norwegian Style:** à la norvégienne: sautéd, garnished with tartlets filled alternately with chestnut purée and salsify in cream sauce; chief ranger sauce served separately.
— **Siberian Style:** à la sibirienne: sautéd deglaced with brown stock and sour cream, boiled down with coarse julienne of pickled cucumbers added and poured over the meat.
Reindlbiftek: Potted Tenderloin Steak: tenderloin steak browned in butter, lightly braised in demi-glace; served garnished with German fried potatoes and sliced gherkins, a fried egg on top. (Austrian)
Renne: see reindeer.
Ris d'agneau: see lamb sweetbreads.
Ris de veau: see calf's sweetbreads.
Rissoles: mincemeat fritters: minced fish, meat, poultry or game, mixed with mushrooms, truffles or other ingredients, bound with thick cold sauce, wrapped in puff or unsweetened short pastry, sometimes in fine yeast dough, shaped into half moons, patties, turnovers etc., fried in deep fat, dressed with fried parsley and lemon and always served without sauce. Rissoles are served as hot appetizer or light entrée.
— **of Beef:** de boeuf: minced boiled beef, chopped anchovy fillets, hard-boiled eggyolks and parsley, bound with thick demi-glace, wrapped in puff pastry and shaped like a turnover.
— **with Eggs:** aux oeufs: half moon-shaped puff pastry rissoles filled with chopped hard boiled egg, mushrooms and truffles bound with thick cream sauce.
— **of Ham:** de jambon: filled with purée of ham, bound with thick Madeira sauce.
— **of Lamb:** à la bergère: hash of lamb and morels bound with thick Béchamel mixed with white onion purée, made of puff pastry shaped like small fluted patties.
— **of Lobster:** de homard: salpicon of lobster, mushrooms and truffles, bound with thick lobster sauce, encased in puff pastry and shaped like fluted turnovers.
— **Montglas:** salpicon of chicken, mushrooms, sweetbreads and truffles, bound with thick suprême sauce, crescent-shaped.
— **Nantua:** diced crayfish tails and truffles, bound with Béchamel sauce blended with crayfish butter, wrapped in puff pastry, oval-shaped.
— **with Oysters:** aux huîtres: diced poached oysters bound with thick cream sauce blended with the oysters liquor, wrapped in puff pastry, half moon-shaped, fried in deep fat and served with fried parsley.
— **Pheasant:** de faisan: pheasant purée encased in puff pastry, fried in deep fat, garnished with fried parsley.
— **Pompadour:** made of puff pastry filled with salpicon of gooseliver, ox tongue, mushrooms and truffles bound with thick truffle sauce with a small slice of blanched beef marrow in the center, shaped like small round patties.

Rissoles

— **Queen Style:** à la reine: filled with minced chicken bound with thick cream sauce.

— **of Shrimps:** de crevettes: made of unsweetened short pastry filled with diced shrimps and mushrooms in thick shrimp sauce.

Rate pe Varza: Duck and Saurkraut: duck well browned on all sides, placed on saurkraut mixed with a large amount of sliced onions fried pale brown in lard; moistened with a little saurkraut pickle and braised in oven. When done the superfluous fat drained off, duck carved and served on the saurkraut. (Roumanian)

Roastbeef: see ribs of beef.

Roe-Deer, Roe-Buck, Roe: F. Chevreuil; G. Reh: roe is the finest of all furred game and the most used in hotel and restaurant kitchens. It is found all over Europe from Scotland and Sweden down to the Mediterranean and parts of Asia. The best parts are the back, saddle, and the haunch. Roe deer is always well larded with fat bacon before roasting.

Roe-Deer, Chaudfroid of: Chaudfroid de chevreuil: oblique slices of a cold roast saddle, trimmed, coated with brown game-chaudfroid sauce, decorated to taste and glazed with aspic jelly, placed on oval tartlet filled with roe-deer purée highly spiced; Cumberland sauce served separately.

Roe-Deer Collops: Escalopes: Escalopes de chevreuil: thin slices cut from a very tender loin, sautéd and prepared like cutlet.

— **Condé:** thin slice beaten flat, coated with game forcemeat with chopped herbs; browned, braised in game stock, stock thickened with arrow-root and poured over collop; chestnut purée served separately.

— **with Olives:** aux olives: thin slice, flattened, coated with game forcemeat, rolled together, wrapped in thin slice of salt pork, tied, braised in light Madeira sauce with stoned green olives.

— **Rolled:** en paupiette: thin slice beaten flat, coated with veal forcemeat mixed with chopped herbs; rolled, dipped in egg and breadcrumbs, fried slowly in butter.

Roe Cutlet: Côtelette de chevreuil: chops cut from the loin split lengthwise, trimmed and topside of bone pared. Roe cutlets being very small, it is best to cut the chops double thick, i. e. with two bones and to remove one. The chop is then lightly flattened, trimmed and fried medium done.

— **Caucasian Style:** à la caucasienne: sautéd taken out of sautoir and dressed on shaped kascha; chopped shallots lightly fried in the butter, crushed coriander and garlic added, deglaced with a trickle of white wine and pepper sauce, boiled up, strained, finished off with anchovy butter and chopped fennel and poured over the cutlets.

— **with Cherries:** aux cerises: sautéd, covered with pepper sauce with stoned sour cherries added.

— **Conti:** sautéd, deglaced with white wine and pepper sauce; served interlaced with heart-shaped slices of ox tongue and covered with the sauce; lentil purée served separately.

— **Diana:** Diane: sautéd, served on croûton masked with liver purée; Diana sauce and chestnut purée served separately.

Roe Cutlet

— **D'Orsay** (cold): sautéd, allowed to cool under light pressure, covered with brown game chaudfroid sauce mixed with chopped truffles and glazed with aspic jelly; arranged on border of game froth in jelly with paper frills on the cutlet bones.

— **Hunter Style:** à la chasseur: sautéd, deglaced with white wine and hunter sauce.

— **with Juniper Berries:** au genièvre: sautéd and arranged alternately with heart-shaped croûtons; deglaced with Genever, a crushed juniper berry and a little sweet cream added and reduced, finished off with a few spoonfuls of pepper sauce and a trickle of lemon juice, strained and poured over cutlets; hot apple sauce served separately.

— **Lacroix** (cold): sautéd rare, allowed to cool under light pressure, glazed with aspic jelly, a border of gooseliver cream piped on top, garnished with orange fillets and a cherry quarter in between; arranged on long dish garnished with half-oranges filled with Waldorf salad decorated with a walnut and small pieces of red cherries.

— **Little-Russian Style:** à la petite-russienne: sautéd and placed on baked tartlet of kasha flavored with cinnamon; covered with pepper sauce with chopped sour cherries and whole Malaga raisins.

— **Minute:** à la minute: sautéd in oil with finely chopped onions, deglaced with brandy, pepper sauce added, blended with butter and poured over cutlets; garnished with slices sautéd mushrooms.

— **Montmorency:** larded with truffle, sautéd, deglaced with Madeira and boiled up with game sauce; garnished with artichoke bottoms filled with asparagus tips.

— **Morand:** sautéd, deglaced with white wine and sour cream, boiled up with a little pepper sauce, seasoned with mustard and finished off with chopped orange peel; cutlets dressed on shaped Anna potatoes, sauce poured on top.

— **Nesselrode:** fried on one side only, this side coated cupola-shaped with game forcemeat with a truffle slice on top and finished off in oven; demi-glace boiled up with game stock and chestnut purée served separately.

— **with Olives:** aux olives: sautéd, served with pepper sauce and stuffed olives.

— **with Orange:** à l'orange: sautéd, deglaced with orange juice, boiled up with game sauce mixed with parboiled julienne of orange peel; garnished with orange fillets warmed in butter, covered with the sauce.

— **in Paper Bag:** en papillote: sautéd blood rare and allowed to cool; coated with duxelles, covered with a small slice of ham, wrapped in greased paper bag, cooking finished in oven; served in the paper bag.

with Pears: aux poires: marinated in oil, lemon juice and a little allspice, sautéd in butter, deglaced with brandy and pepper sauce; hot compote of pears spiced with cinnamon and lemon, and red currant jelly served separately.

— **with Pepper Sauce:** à la sauce poivrade: sautéd, covered with pepper sauce.

Roe Cutlet
— **Romanoff:** sautéd; garnished with stuffed pieces of cucumber and sautéd, creamed boletus; pepper sauce served separately.
— **Scotch Style**: à l'écossaise: sautéd, covered with pepper sauce mixed with julienne of ox tongue; garnished with French beans and nut potatoes.
— **Steward Style:** à la maître d'Hôtel: grilled, garnished with straw potatoes and watercress; herb butter.
— **with Truffles:** aux truffes: sautéd, deglaced with truffle stock and truffle sauce with sliced truffles added.
— **Valencia Style:** sautéd, served with bigarade sauce and orange fillets.
— **Valkyra:** Walkyrie: sautéd, placed on a flat Berny potato, a mushroom cap filled with thick white onion purée on top of cutlet; cream sauce flavored with juniper berries served separately.
— **Villeneuve:** stiffened in butter and cooled under light pressure; coated on one side cupola-shaped with cold salpicon of game, wrapped in pig's caul and fried in oven for a few minutes; game sauce with truffle julienne served separately.
— **Tsarina:** à la tsarine: sautéd, garnished with olive-shaped cucumbers simmered in butter and half a hard-boiled plover's egg filled with caviar; truffle sauce.

Roe-Deer, Haunch of: Cuissot de chevreuil: the haunch is skinned, aitchbone removed, end of shank bone trimmed, larded, roasted medium to rare and garnished like saddle of roe. The haunch is sometimes marinated in a light red wine pickle.

Roe-Deer, Jugged: Civet de chevreuil: prepared like jugged hare.

Roe-Deer Liver: Foie de chevreuil: sliced, coated with flour, fried in butter and garnished as cutlet.

Roe-Deer, Noisettes of: Noisettes de chevreuil: cut like lamb noisettes from the boned loin. Sautéd and prepared like cutlets.

Roe, Saddle of: Selle de chevreuil: the best part of the back is the saddle piece. Before roasting it must be skinned and larded. It is only tasty if roasted rare and frequently basted. A cold saddle of roe is an excellent show piece for cold buffets.
— **Baden-Baden:** marinated, pan-roasted, deglaced with game stock, degreased and thickened with arrow-root; garnished with pears cooked as compote with cinnamon and lemon, but without sugar; sauce and red currant jelly served separately.
— **Beaujeu:** larded, roasted, garnished with artichoke bottoms filled with lentil purée and glazed chestnuts; game sauce.
— **Berny**: roasted, garnished with tartlets filled with lentil purée, a truffle slice on top, and Berny potatoes; pepper sauce.
— **with Cherry Sauce:** à la sauce aux cerises: roasted served with pepper sauce blended with red currant jelly, mixed with stoned cooked cherries.
— **with Cream Sauce:** à la crème: roasted, deglaced with cream and a little meat glaze, seasoned with lemon juice.
— **Creole Style:** à la créole: larded, marinated in red wine; roasted, garnished with fried bananas; deglaced with the

Roe, Saddle of,
red wine, boiled down with pepper sauce and blended with butter.

— **Cumberland:** larded, roasted; chestnut purée and Cumberland sauce served separately.

— **Diana:** Diane: roasted, served with chestnut purée and Diana sauce.

— **German Style:** à l'allemande: roasted, deglaced with sour cream and meat glaze, seasoned with lemon juice; braised red cabbage, mashed potatoes and sauce served separately.

— **Lucullus** (cold): larded, roasted, allowed to cool; carved, each slice coated with gooseliver paste, replaced in position on back, decorated with a line or truffle slices along the back, glazed with Madeira aspic jelly; garnished with surprise truffles (paste of gooseliver patty shaped into round balls, rolled in chopped truffles and glazed with aspic jelly).

— **Montague** (cold): larded, roasted, allowed to cool, carved, middle bone chopped off, carcass and cavity filled with Waldorf salad bound with jellied mayonnaise; carved meat replaced into position, center garnished with a line of thin banana slices with half a red cherry on top, saddle glazed entirely with aspic jelly; garnished small medaillons of jellied gooseliver parfait and aspic jelly.

— **Park Hotel** (cold): roasted rare, allowed to cool, fillets lifted out and carved, back bone chopped off, cavity filled with gooseliver purée, the carved slices placed back in position with a line of small poached slices of apple along the center and half a cherry on each slice, glazed with aspic jelly; placed on rectangular dish, garnished on both sides with round poached apple slices with pineapple on top, and at both ends with tartlets filled with Waldorf salad, surprise truffles and fluted mushroom caps, all glazed with aspic jelly.

— **with Pepper Sauce:** à la sauce poivrade: roasted, served with pepper sauce.

— **with Pineapple:** à l'ananas: roasted, deglaced with fresh pineapple juice, boiled down with pepper sauce, thick strips of pineapple sautéd in butter beforehand added.

Roe-Deer, Tenderloin of: Filet mignon de chevreuil: the tenderloin is very small and tender, two or three should be served for one portion. Larded and prepared like roe cutlet.

— **in Cream Sauce:** à la crème: sautéd, deglaced with cream, meat glaze added, seasoned with lemon juice.

— **Douglas:** sautéd, placed on slice of fried gooseliver; deglaced with brandy and a little meat glaze, blended with butter and poured over tenderloin.

— **Dubarry:** sautéd, garnished with balls of gratinated cauliflower; Madeira sauce.

— **Josephine:** dipped in egg and chopped truffle, fried in butter; garnished with tartlets filled with game purée, a mushroom cap on top; truffle sauce.

Rognon de boeuf: see beef kidney.

Rognons d'agneau: see lamb kidneys.

— **de mouton:** see sheep's kidneys.

— **de veau:** see calf's kidneys.

Roi de cailles: see landrail.

Rostbraten: sirloin steak cut from the fat end about 3/4 inch thick, beaten flat, pan fried or stewed. (Austrian)
— **with Anchovies:** Rostbraten mit Sardellen: fried in butter, covered with chopped anchovy fillets sautéd in butter.
— **Dämpfrostbraten:** chopped onions lightly fried in lard, a seasoned rostbraten placed on top, covered with raw vegetables such as asparagus tips, green peas, mushrooms, diced potatoes, carrots and knob celery etc., dotted with butter, a little stock poured on top, stewed slowly in oven wih the cover on.
— **with Garlic:** Knoblauch Rostbraten: fried, covered with crushed garlic sweated in butter.
— **Gipsy Style:** Zigeuner Rostbraten: beaten flat, browned in butter with diced bacon and chopped onions, stewed in brown gravy with shredded cabbage, sliced potatoes, seasoned with marjoram.
— **Girardi:** seasoned, coated with flour, browned in butter with chopped onions, moistened with a little stock, chopped mushrooms, herbs and capers added, braised; gravy thickened with flour and seasoned with mustard and lemon juice; garnished with potato croquettes.
— **Italian Style:** Italienischer Rostbraten: browned in butter, braised in very little stock with chopped anchovies and parsley; gratinated macaroni served separately.
— **Machine:** Maschinrostbraten: fried in butter, stewed with paprika, sliced onions and potatoes; served in service casserole with the potatoes and sliced pickled cucumbers on top and the cover on.
— **Meran Style:** Meraner Rostbraten: browned in lard, braised with sliced bacon and cabbage.
— **with Must:** mit Most: browned in butter, covered with must, stewed with sliced onions and strips of root vegetables; stock thickened with grated gingerbread.
— **with Onions:** Zwiebelrostbraten: fried in butter, covered generously with fried onions.
— **Paprika:** browned, stewed in white stock and sour cream with paprika; noodles, flour dumplings or rice served separately.
— **Pressburg Style:** Pressburger Rostbraten: stewed in cream sauce, covered with sliced hard-boiled eggs and green peas.
— **Reindl:** seasoned, coated with flour, browned in lard with chopped onions, dusted with paprika and mustard, placed in small service casserole with white stock and cream, stewed with chopped pickles and capers; boiled potatoes served separately.
— **Russian Style:** Russischer Rostbraten: fried in butter, brushed with mustard and coated with grated horseradish.
— **Styrian Style:** Steirischer Rostbraten: beaten very flat, coated with chopped onions, anchovy fillets and chopped parsley sweated in butter and covered with a thin slice of bacon: rolled, tied, placed in service casserole on sliced root vegetables sweated in butter, covered with white stock and sour cream, stewed and served with cover on.
— **Swedish Style:** Schwedischer Rostbraten: fried in diced melted ox marrow, stewed with chopped onions, anchovy fillets and parsley in sour cream.
— **Swiss Style:** Schweizer Rostbraten: beaten flat, coated with potato croquette mass mixed with finely diced Swiss

Rostbraten
cheese and grated Parmesan; rolled, tied, browned in butter and braised in sour cream.
— **Tegetthoff:** browned, braised in demi-glace with strips of root vegetables; served with stoned olives and scampi tails on top.
— **Trobloff:** beaten very thin, a medium boiled egg, seasoned and wrapped in a thin slice of raw ham placed in center, rolled, tied and braised in beef stock; served on mashed potatoes.
— **Westmoreland:** braised in light cream sauce, served covered with sliced pickles.

Rouenese Duck: Canard Rouennais: a large special breed of duck weighing from 5 to 6 lb., which has been smothered so that it has lost none of its blood before cooking. Rouenese duck is seldom braised and always roasted rare.
— **Breast Strips Bigarade:** Aiguillettes à la bigarade: roasted blood rare, deglaced with a little veal gravy, reduced, strained and mixed with bigarade sauce; breast cut in long thin strips, placed on luke warm platter and covered with the sauce.
— **Breast Strips with Cherries:** Aiguillettes de Rouennais aux cerises: pan-roasted blood rare, deglaced with Madaira and veal gravy, degreased, thickened with arrow-root and strained; stoned sour cherries boiled up for a minute with the sauce and poured over the breast cut in long thin strips and arranged on luke warm platter.
— **in Champagne:** au champagne: pan-roasted, deglaced with dry champagne, reduced and mixed with thick veal gravy.
— **Edward VII.:** Edouard VII. (cold): roasted, stuffed with duck and duckliver froth, the carved breast replaced in position, coated with brown chaudfroid sauce, decorated, glazed with aspic jelly; garnished with tartlets filled with fine vegetable salad, decorated and glazed with jelly.
— **Japanese Style:** à la japonaise (cold): pan-roasted, when cold glazed with aspic jelly; garnished with small tangerines, lid cut off, scooped out and filled with gooseliver and duckliver froth, decorated and glazed with aspic jelly, and small beaker moulds filled with aspic jelly made of duck gravy flavored with tangerine juice and turned out.
— **Montmorency** (cold): roasted rare, when cold breast and breastbone cut of in such a way that the carcass forms a sort of case; breast carved in thin slices, each slice coated with brown chaudfroid sauce, carcass filled with duck and gooseliver froth, shaped like the ducks back and allowed to set. The breast-slices replaced into position, duck placed in a deep square dish, surrounded with stoned morellos poached in red wine and well drained, covered entirely with light aspic jelly prepared with duck stock.
— **Mousseline of:** Mousseline de Rouennais: prepared like chicken mousseline and always served either with Rouenese or Bigarade sauce. The only permissible garnishes are oranges, pineapple, cherries or tangerines and fine vegetable purées.
— **with Port:** au porto: prepared like duck.
— **à la Presse:** prepared like duck.
— **Stuffed Rouenese Style:** farci à la rouennaise: stuffed with forcemeat of duck livers, green bacon, chopped

Rouenese Duck
shallots, spices etc., roasted rare, served with Rouenese sauce.
— **with Truffles:** aux truffes: pan-roasted blood rare, deglaced with Chambertin, reduced and mixed with Rouenese sauce; breast cut in long thin strips, placed on luke warm dish, covered with slices of truffle cooked in Chambertin, the hot sauce poured on top.

S

Sarcelle: see teal.
Sarma: prepared like Sarmale. (Jugo-Slavian)
Sarmale: Saurkraut Rolls: ground beef and pork mixed with boiled rice, seasoned with garlic, salt, pepper and finely chopped onions, wrapped in leaves of cabbage pickled in whole heads and rolled together. Bottom of braising pan covered with plenty of sliced fried onions, the cabbage rolls placed on top between two layers of plain saurkraut, a little saurkraut pickle and tomato sauce poured over, braised in oven; sour cream served separately. (Roumanian)
— **in foi de spanac:** in Spinach Leaves: large blanched spinach leaves filled with same forcemeat as sarmale, placed on base of sliced fried onions, braised in oven with light tomato sauce; thick sour cream served separately. (Roumanian)
— **in foi de vin:** in Wine Leaves: same as above, blanched vine leaves instead of spinach leaves. (Roumanian)
Saucisse de porc: see pork sausage.
Saucisson: see sausage.
Sauerbraten: see beef, rump of, German style.
Saure Hachsen: knuckle of veal parboiled in stock with potherbs and spices, generously seasoned with vinegar; drained, placed in clean saucepan with plenty of shredded root vegetables, covered with stock and cooked until done; served covered with the reduced stock and the vegetables, chopped parsley scattered on top. (German)
Saurkraut, Garnished: 1. Choucroute garnie: saurkraut braised in white wine and fat stock with lard, onions, juniper berries, a piece of ham or bacon and fresh or pickled goose; when done meat carved and placed on top, garnished with Francfort sausages and boiled potatoes.
2. braised with ham, pickled pork and whole carrots; when done meat carved, placed on top, garnished with the sliced carrots, Francfort sausages and boiled potatoes.
—, **Polish Style:** Choucroute à la polonaise: saurkraut braised with sliced apples, lean bacon, garlic sausage and smoked beef: when done meat placed on top of kraut, garnished with pickled cucumbers.
Sausage: F. Saucisse; G. Wurst: the name sausage covers a large variety of chopped meat preparations, filled in casings of various sizes, boiled, smoked and dried. For pork sausage see pork.
— **Frankfurter or Vienna:** Saucisses de Francfort ou de Vienne: poached, served either with saurkraut and mashed potatoes or with hot potato salad, with grated horseradish, goulash sauce or only with mustard.

Sausage

— **Frankfurter, Baked:** poached lightly, skinned, wrapped in puff pastry, brushed with egg yolk, baked.

— **Frankfurter, Fried:** frit: poached, skinned, dipped in frying batter and deep fried.

— **Game:** Saucisson de gibier: forcemeat of game, green bacon, game livers, truffle, chopped herbs, seasoning and brandy, filled in casing, blanched and fried; served with game sauce.

— **in Pig's Caul:** see crépinette.

Sauté: sort of brown stew for which the meat is sliced or cubed, browned in butter, deglaced with wine, brandy etc. and stewed in a sauce prepared beforehand.

— **of Beef Arlesian Style:** de boeuf à l'arlesienne: diced beef browned with mirepoix, deglaced with white wine, stewed in demi-glace with tomato purée; when nearly done placed in clean casserole with diced tomatoes and diced eggplants sautéd in oil; served covered with fried onion rings.

— **of Beef Citizen Style:** de boeuf à la bourgeoise: diced, browned, stewed in demi-glace, garnished with fancy-shaped carrots, glazed button onions and diced fried bacon.

— **of Lamb Farmer Style:** d'agneau à la paysanne: diced, browned in butter, deglaced with white wine, stewed in demi-glace; when nearly done small slices of carrots, tunips, celery and onions, sautéd beforehand, and diced parboiled green beans and green peas added.

— **of Lamb Flemish Style:** d'agneau à la flamande: cut in large cubes, browned, stewed in light demi-glace; when done mixed with diced fried bacon, olive-shaped carrots, potatoes, turnips and slices of garlic sausage, garnished with small balls of braised cabbage.

— **of Lamb Forester Style:** d'agneau à la forestière: stewed in white wine and demi-glace, mixed with sautéd quartered morels, diced fried bacon and diced sautéd potatoes.

— **of Lamb Hunter Style:** d'agneau à la chasseur: browned in oil and butter, chopped shallots added, deglaced with white wine, stewed in tomato sauce; sautéd mushrooms added at serving.

— **of Lamb Spanish Style:** d'agneau à l'espagnole: sliced, browned in oil with chopped onions and garlic, stewed in tomato sauce.

— **of Mutton Armenian Style:** de mouton à l'armenienne: diced, sautéd in oil with chopped onions and garlic, stewed in tomato sauce with a piece of cinnamon and diced green peppers; served with saffron rice.

— **of Veal Devil Style:** de veau à la diable: sliced, browned in butter, stewed in devil sauce.

— **of Veal Gardner Style:** de veau à la jardinière: diced, browned, deglaced with white wine, stewed in demi-glace and tomato purée, mixed with fancy-shaped carrots, turnips, flageolets and sprigs of cauliflower; at serving diced green beans and green peas scattered on top.

— **of Veal Hungarian Style:** de veau à la hongroise: browned in lard with chopped onions, stewed in light paprika sauce; sour cream added at serving.

Sauté

— **of Veal Marengo:** de veau Marengo: diced, browned in oil with chopped onions and garlic, deglaced with white wine, stewed in brown stock with diced tomatoes; when nearly done button onions and button mushrooms browned in butter added; garnished with heart-shaped croûtons.

Schafsragoût Emmenthaler Art: a blanquette of mutton colored with saffron and mixed with diced or shredded root vegetables. (Suisse)

Schaschlik: Turkish Skewers: sliced mutton marinated in oil with chopped parsley, mint, salt and pepper, fixed on skewer alternately with sliced bacon, grilled; served on rice cooked in fat mutton stock with chopped onions. (Turkish)

Schwäbische Kalbsvögel: Swabian Veal Birds: slice of topside of veal flattened, covered with veal forcemeat and strips of fat bacon rolled, tied, browned, braised on bed of sautéd root vegetables, sliced onions and herbs in brown stock and white wine; stock strained, boiled down, thickened, mixed with capers and chopped anchovy fillets and poured over the birds. (German)

Selle d'agneau: see saddle of lamb.

— **de chevreuil:** see roe-deer, saddle of.

— **de renne:** see reindeer.

— **de veau:** see saddle of veal.

Serbisches Reisfleisch: cubes of veal, chopped onions and finely diced bacon browned in butter, seasoned with salt and paprika, rice added, moistened with white stock and prepared like risotto; when done pressed into a mould, turned out and sprinkled with grated Parmesan. (Austrian)

Serpenyös rostélios: Braised Sirloin Steak: sirloin steak flattened, seasoned, coated with flour, browned in lard with chopped onions and garlic; dusted generously with paprika, sprinkled with flour, moistened with water and braised with crushed caraway seeds, marjoram, tomato purée and chopped green peppers; shortly before steak is done thick slices of parboiled potatoes added. (Hungarian)

Sheep Brains: Cervelle de mouton: soaked in cold water, skin removed, cooked in water with a little vinegar, or lemon juice and seasoning, cooled off in the stock for future use.

— **Gipsy Style:** à la zingara: parboiled cut in slices, coated with flour, fried in butter, dressed on slice of fried ham, covered with gipsy sauce.

— **Parisian Style:** à la parisienne: parboiled, sliced, covered with German sauce mixed with sliced mushrooms and truffles, sprinkled with grated cheese, gratinated.

— **Poulette Style:** cooked, cut in slices, covered with poulette sauce, sprinkled with chopped parsley.

Sheep's Kidneys: Rognons de mouton: fat removed, skinned, usually halved and broiled, sautéd, seldom stewed.

— **American Style:** à l'américaine: halved, dressed on halved fried tomatoes, filled with herb butter, garnished with fried slices of lean bacon and watercress.

— **Bercy:** cut in thick slices, sautéd in butter, arranged in timbale dish, covered with Bercy sauce.

— **Berry Style:** à la berrichonne: cut in half, sautéd, mixed with diced fried lean bacon and fried mushroom slices,

Sheep's Kidneys

pan gravy deglaced with red wine, boiled up with demi-glace, poured over the kidney, chopped parsley scattered on top.

— **Bonvalet:** cut in slices, sautéd in butter, pan gravy boiled up with demi-glace, flavored with Madeira, poured over the kidney, garnished with sliced truffles and morels.

— **Bordeaux Style:** à la bordelaise: cut in thick slices, sautéd, deglaced with red wine, boiled down, Bordeaux sauce added; kidneys mixed with sliced sautéd boletus, diced blanched ox marrow and the sauce arranged in timbale dish, chopped parsley scattered on top.

— **Butcher Style:** à la bouchère: cut in half, broiled, dressed on tartlet filled with beef hash, garnished with tiny fried pork sausages.

— **Carvalho:** cut in half, sautéd, dressed on croûton with a mushroom cap placed on top, deglaced with Madeira, boiled up with Madeira sauce, sliced truffles added, poured over the kidney.

— **with Champagne:** au champagne: cut in thick slices, deglaced with champagne, boiled down, mixed with liquid meat glace and lemon juice, buttered and poured over the kidneys.

— **Chateaubriand:** opened on one side, fixed on a skewer, grilled, garnished with straw potatoes and watercress; Chateaubriand sauce served separately.

— **Chipolata:** grilled, garnished with tiny fried pork sausages, glazed button onions, chestnuts and small slices of fried bacon, covered with demi-glace.

— **Curried:** cut in slices, sautéd, covered with curry sauce, plain boiled rice served separately.

— **English Style:** à la l'anglaise: cut in half, grilled, a grilled slice of bacon placed on top; boiled potatoes tossed with butter and chopped parsley served separately.

— **French Style:** à la française: sautéd dressed on croûton, covered with truffle sauce, garnished with asparagus tips.

— **Fried:** frit: cut in thick slices, cooked in red wine and butter, when cold drained, dipped in egg and breadcrumbs, fried in deep fat; tomato or truffle sauce served separately.

— **Green Meadow:** Vert-pré: opened, grilled, herb butter in the opening, garnished with straw potatoes and watercress.

— **Henry IV.:** Henri IV.: 1. opened on one side but not cut through, grilled, opening filled with Béarnaise sauce, garnished with French fried potatoes and watercress. 2. same as above but garnished with artichoke bottoms filled with very small fried potato balls.

— **Hunter Style:** à la chasseur: cut in slices, sautéd with sliced mushrooms and chopped shallots, tossed in hunter sauce, chopped parsley scattered on top.

— **Japanese Style:** à la japonaise: 1. cut in half, sautéd, dressed on flat potato croquette, covered with thick veal gravy, garnished with stachy tossed in butter.
2. cut in half, sautéd, one half filled with tomatoes concassés, the other half filled with a tiny French fried egg, garnished with straw potatoes and watercress.

— **with Juniper Berries:** à la liégeoise: cut in half, sautéd in butter, deglaced with Genever, crushed juniper berries

Sheep's Kidneys
and demi-glace added, boiled up, strained and poured over the kidneys.

— **Louis XIV.:** cut open on one side, fixed on a skewer, grilled, dressed on small slice of fried ham, covered with thick veal gravy, garnished with watercress.

— **Mexican Style:** à la mexicaine: cut in half, grilled, dressed on large mushroom caps filled with tomatoes concassees, garnished with halved grilled red peppers, covered with thick veal gravy with tomato.

— **Michel:** flat open tart baked of pie dough, filled with braised saurkraut mixed with diced sautéd gooseliver, kidneys cut in half and sautéd in butter arranged like a crown on top and covered with buttered meat glace.

— **Montpensier:** cut in half, sautéd, dressed with a slice of truffle on top, covered with Madeira sauce, garnished with asparagus tips and pan fried potato balls.

— **with Mushrooms:** aux champignons: cut in slices, sautéd in butter with chopped shallots and sliced mushrooms, deglaced with white wine, demi-glace added and mixed with the kidneys.

— **Oriental Style:** à l'orientale: thick slices sautéd in butter, mixed with rice pilaf, diced tomatoes and green peppers, pressed into a mould, turned out and covered with tomato sauce.

— **with Paprika Sauce:** à la sauce paprika: cut in slices, sautéd in butter with chopped onions, simmered in light paprika sauce; plain boiled rice served separately.

— **Piedmont Style:** à la piemontaise: cut in half, dressed in a border of risotto Piedmont style, covered with sliced white truffles, surrounded with demi-glace with tomato and extract of white truffles.

— **Portuguese Style:** à la portugaise: cut in half, grilled, arranged on half fried tomatoes, covered with Portuguese sauce.

— **Saint-Lazare:** cut in half, sautéd, dressed on croûton, covered with marrow sauce with blanched sliced ox marrow.

— **on Skewer:** on brochette: opened, fixed on skewer with small pieces of bacon, grilled, covered with herb butter, garnished with watercress.

— **Spanish Style:** à l'espagnole: pan fried, garnished with half fried tomatoes and fried onion rings.

— **Turbigo:** cut in two lengthwise, sautéd, dressed on croûtons, deglaced with white wine, boiled up with demi-glace and tomato purée, garnished with tiny fried pork sausages and sautéd mushroom caps.

— **Viéville:** fried in butter, dressed on croûton, garnished with tiny fried pork sausages, fried mushroom caps and glazed button onions, covered with Madeira sauce.

— **in White Wine:** au vin blanc: cut in thick slices, pan fried in butter with chopped shallots, deglaced with white wine, boiled down, chopped parsley and a few drops of lemon juice added, buttered and poured over the kidneys.

— **Wine Merchant Style:** à la marchand de vin: cut in thick slices, sautéd in butter with chopped shallots, pan deglaced with red wine, boiled down, mixed with liquid meat glace and chopped parsley, blended with butter and poured over the kidneys.

Sheep's Trotters: Pieds de mouton: steeped in cold water, blanched, cooked in slightly salted water mixed with flour to keep them white, mostly boned beforehand.

— **Catalonian Style:** à la catalane: blanched, boned, parboiled, cut into large pieces, arranged in a baking dish, covered with tomato sauce mixed with crushed garlic, chopped parsley and a little white wine, sprinkled with breadcrumbs, melted butter dropped on top, gratinated.

— **Fried:** frits: 1. boned, cooked, allowed to cool under light pressure, cut in large pieces, dipped in frying batter, deep fried, served with fried parsley and lemon. 2. cut in pieces, marinated with lemon juice and oil, dipped in egg and breadcrumbs, deep fried; tomato sauce served separately.

— **Italian Style:** à l'italienne: blanched, boned, parboiled, simmered in Italian sauce.

— **Poulette Style:** à la poulette: boned, cooked, garnished with button onions and mushroom caps, covered with poulette sauce, chopped parsley sprinkled on top.

— **Sainte-Menehould:** blanched, boned, parboiled, pressed, dipped in egg and breadcrumbs, grilled.

— **Stuffed:** farcis: parboiled, boned, stuffed with forcemeat, dipped in egg and breadcrumbs, deep fried; tomato sauce served separately.

— **Tyrolian Style:** à la tyrolienne: blanched, boned, parboiled, cut in pieces, simmered in sauce prepared with chopped sweated onions, tomatoes concassées, chopped parsley and a little pepper sauce.

— **Villeroi:** cut in pieces, coated with Villeroi sauce, dipped in egg and breadcrumbs, deep fried; tomato sauce served separately.

Shoveller, Spoonbill; F. Rouge de rivière; G. Löffelente: one of the wild ducks common in the Northern Hemisphere. Its meat is tender and tasty. Prepared like wild duck.

Silverside of Veal: see fricandeau.

Skewers: Brochettes: equal-sized pieces of parboiled or fried meat, poultry, game etc. fixed alternately on skewers with another ingredient such as mushrooms, bacon, lean ham etc., coated with thick duxelles and dipped in breadcrumbs, grilled and garnished with watercress; herb butter or an appropriate sauce served separately.

— **Bohemian:** à la bohémienne: Gooseliver, ham and truffle slices; paprika sauce.

— **with Chicken Livers:** au foies de volaille: chicken livers, mushrooms and bacon; herb butter.

— **Financier Style:** à la financière: Cockscombs, Cock's kidneys, truffle slices, mushroom caps and ham; financier sauce.

— **Florida:** turkey, ham, pineapple and large olives, dipped in egg and breadcrumbs, no duxelles; orange butter.

— **Geneva Style:** à la génevoise: chicken liver, lamb sweetbread, truffle slices, artichoke bottoms, thick slices of blanched ox marrow; Italian sauce.

— **Kidneys, Spanish Style:** de rognons à l'espagnole: mutton kidneys, bacon and mushroom caps seasoned with Cayenne pepper.

— **Lamb Kidney:** de rognons: lamb kidneys split lengthwise and bacon; garnished with watercress; herb butter.

Skewers

— **Leda:** calf's liver, calf's sweetbread, mushrooms and artichoke bottoms dipped in melted butter, beaten egg and breadcrumbs mixed with chopped summer savory.

— **Pahlen:** slices of boiled lobster, raw oysters and mushroom caps; served on risotto.

— **Piedmont Style:** à la piemontaise: polenta mixed with grated Italian truffles and grated Parmesan, cut in cubes, and chicken livers; tomato sauce.

— **Stucchi:** Italian Skewers: chicken liver, lamb sweetbread, artichoke bottom, ham and Italian truffle cut in equal size, coated with veal forcemeat, dipped in egg and breadcrumbs, fried; tomato sauce served separately.

Snipe; F. Bécassine; G. Sumpfschnepfe, Moosschnepfe: esteemed game bird of the woodcock type found in Europe, America, parts of Africa and Asia. There are many kinds of snipe of which the Great Snipe is the largest and the Jack Snipe the smallest. The American Snipe is called „Wilson's" Snipe in the U. S. A. Snipe is prepared like woodcock.

Soufflé: cooked, preparation of raw or cooked meat, fish, shellfish, poultry or game pounded in the mortar to paste, mixed with thick Béchamel sauce, rubbed through a sieve, seasoned, eggyolks and stiffly beaten whites added, filled in china soufflé cases, silver casseroles or ramekins greased with butter and baked in the oven; an appropriate sauce served separately.

— **of Calf's Liver:** de foie de veau: prepared with paste made of diced calf's liver slightly sautéd in butter.

— **of Chicken:** à la reine: prepared with paste made of white chicken meat; suprême sauce served separately.

— **of Goose Liver:** de foie gras: gooseliver paste mixed with chopped truffles; served with truffle sauce.

— **of Hazelhen:** de gelinotte: prepared with hazelhen paste mixed with diced truffles and mushrooms; salmi sauce served separately.

— **of Partridge:** de perdreau: prepared with paste of the meat of underdone partridges mixed with chopped truffles.

— **of Pheasant:** de faisan: prepared with faisan paste, mashed gooseliver added; demi-glace with essence of game served separately.

— **of Woodcock:** de bécasse: prepared with a paste made of the meat of underdone woodcock mixed with gooseliver paste; demi-glace with essence of woodcock served separately.

Soufflé of Ham: de jambon: paste of mild cured raw ham mixed with thick Béchamel sauce, cream and raw egg whites, seasoned, stiffly beaten whites added, baked in bainmarie in the oven.

— **Alexandra:** dressed alternately in soufflé case with green asparagus tips and truffle slices.

— **Carmen:** dressed alternately in soufflé case with tomatoes concassées and diced green peppers.

— **with morels:** aux morilles: ham soufflé mass mixed with chopped sautéd morels, chopped truffles scattered on top.

— **Perigord Style:** à la périgourdine: dressed alternately in soufflé case with thick truffle slices, chopped truffles scattered on top; Perigord sauce served separately.

Soufflé of Ham
— **Spanish Style:** à l'espagnole: prepared with ham paste mixed with thick tomato purée and chopped red peppers.
— **with Spinach:** aux épinards: prepared with ham mass filled in the soufflé case alternately with blanched spinach leaves sautéd in butter.
Soufflés, Small: petits soufflés: prepared the same way as large soufflés but filled in small soufflés cases, glass containers, paper cases or very small silver casseroles.
Squab, Squab Pigeon: Pigonneau: young pigeon about four weeks old raised specially for the table. Prepared like pigeon.
Squab Chicken: see chicken.
Stag, Red Deer; F. Cerf; G. Hirsch: ruminant with solid antlers found, in Europe, North Amerika, Asia and North Africa. Young stag and all deer in general is prepared like roe deer, older stags are usually braised or used for ragoût etc.
— **Berny:** marinated, larded, roasted, garnished with tartlets filled with lentil purée and Berny potatoes; game sauce served separately.
— **Breast of, Stuffed:** Poitrine de cerf farcie: boned, spread with game forcemeat, rolled, tied, boiled until half done in water with pot herbs, a larded onion and a little vinegar, wrapped in greased paper, roasted, pan juice deglaced with game stock, thickened and finished off with anchovy paste.
— **Collop:** Escalope de cerf: slices cut from the haunch of a young stag, prepared like fillets of hare.
— **German Style:** à l'allemande: marinated, larded, roasted, covered with grated rye bread mixed with red wine and a pinch of cinnamon and brown sugar, melted butter dropped on top, browned in oven; Chief ranger sauce served separately.
— **Polish Style:** à la polonaise: marinated, browned in butter, braised in white stock, sour cream and fennel, garnished with saurkraut and sautéd boletus; the boiled down, strained sauce served separately.
— **Saddle of:** Cimier de cerf: skinned, larded, roasted and prepared like saddle of roe deer.
— **Shoulder of, German Style:** Epaule de cerf à l'allemande: skinned, larded, roasted in butter, pan gravy deglaced with sour cream; buttered noodles served separately.
Stag Liver: Foie de cerf: cut in large dice, browned in butter with chopped onions, seasoned, sprinkled with flour, browned lightly, moistened with brown stock, stewed, sauce finished off with mustard and vinegar.
Steak de veau: see veal steak.
Steirisches Schoepsernes: Stewed Mutton: breast of mutton cut in cubes boiled in water with shredded root vegetables, sliced onions and potatoes. (Austrian)
Stekt fläsk: bacon cooked with brown frijole beans and served sliced. (Swedish)
Suckling Pig; F. Cochon de lait; G. Spanferkel, Milchschwein: the baby pig is considered a great delicacy. It must be soaked thoroughly to rid it from blood and to whiten the meat. It is stuffed and roasted whole, served hot or cold, also boned and stuffed with forcemeat and poached in a cloth like galantine.

Suckling Pig

— **Alsatian Style:** à l'alsacienne: stuffed with pork sausage meat mixed with braised saurkraut and the diced sautéd pork liver, roasted.

— **American Style:** à l'américaine: stuffed with sausage meat mixed with chopped herbs, sage, onion, soaked bread, eggs and seasoning, roasted.

— **Bavarian Style:** à la bavaroise: brushed with oil, covered with an oiled paper and roasted; deglazed with thick veal gravy and served with the gravy, potato dumplings and cole slaw made with diced bacon.

— **English Style:** à l'anglaise: filled with sage and onion stuffing, roasted; apple sauce mixed with blanched currants served separately.

— **German Style:** à l'allemande: stuffed with apple slices and currants, roasted; thick pan gravy.

— **Italian Style:** à l'italienne: boned, stuffed with risotto mixed with grated Parmesan and diced salami, roasted.

— **with Liver Stuffing:** à la farce de foie de porc: stuffed with mixture of creamed butter, eggs, soaked bread and the boiled chopped liver seasoned with salt, pepper and nutmeg, roasted.

— **Piedmont Style:** à la piémontaise: stuffed with risotto mixed with grated white truffles, roasted; light tomato sauce served separately.

— **Polish Style:** à la polonaise: stuffed with braised shredded cabbage mixed with diced ham, roasted.

— **with Prunes:** aux pruneaux: stuffed with stoned half cooked prunes and mixed with a little majoram, roasted.

— **Russian Style:** à la russe: roasted (not salted or seasoned otherwise) and basted frequently with sour cream; carved and served on kascha (q. v.) mixed with the cooked diced liver and diced hard-boiled eggs.

Suckling Pig's Feet: Pieds de cochon de lait: soaked, cleaned and parboiled.

— **Czech Style:** à la tchèque: blanched, cooked in pale beer with caraway seeds, a larded onion and seasoning; stock strained and thickened with grated rye bread.

Suprême de Bécasse: see woodcock.

— **de Faisan:** see pheasant.

— **de gelinotte:** see hazel-hen breasts.

— **de Perdreau:** see partridge.

— **de volaille:** see chicken, suprême of.

Svenks panna: small veal and pork collops and thick slices of calf's kidney, seasoned, lightly sautéd in butter, placed in service casserole with sliced blanched onions and sliced raw potatoes, moistened with stock, a small linnen bag containing peppercorns, allspice and a bayleaf on top, stewed in oven with the cover on. (Swedish)

Szirke gulyás, szegedi módra: Gulyas Chicken: diced knob celery, onions, carrots and parsley root lightly fried in lard, seasoned with salt and paprika, moistened with white stock, a disjointed chicken, shredded green peppers, diced tomatoes and diced potatoes added and stewed; noodle dough torn by hand in small pieces, boiled and tossed in butter served separately. (Hungarian)

T

Tartelette: see tartlet.

Tartlet: Tartelette: tartlet shells are baked in small corrugated tin moulds lined with puff pastry, pie dough or short pastry. The inside is covered with a paper disk and is filled with peas or beans, to weight down the dough, and the shells baked a light brown; if they are to be lined with forcemeat to a pale yellow. After baking the paper is removed and the shells filled as desired. Tartlets are served as an appetizer, light entrée or garnish.

— **Brillat-Savarin:** filled with game salpicon bound with thick truffle sauce, coated with game forcemeat and placed in an oven with moderate temperatur for a few minutes to poach the forcemeat.

— **Cavalier Style:** à la chevalière: filled with cockscombs and cock's kidneys bound with Madeira sauce, coated with gooseliver mousseline forcemeat.

— **Cavour:** filled with diced truffles bound with Madeira sauce, coated with chicken mousseline forcemeat.

— **Châtillon:** filled with sautéd mushroom slices bound with cream sauce, coated with chicken mousseline forcemeat.

— **with Chicken Livers:** aux foies de volaille: lined with chicken forcemeat mixed with purée of chicken livers, filled with diced sautéd chicken livers bound with Madeira sauce, coated with forcemeat; poached, a truffle slice glazed with meat glaze on top.

— **Condé:** filled with salpicon of lamb sweetbread, truffle and champignons bound with Madeira sauce, coated with chicken forcemeat.

— **Diana:** Diane: lined with game forcemeat, filled with small partridge and truffle slices, covered with game sauce, coated with game forcemeat.

— **Diplomat Style:** à la diplomate: filled with diced truffles and gooseliver bound with truffle sauce, coated with pheasant mousseline forcemeat.

— **Favorite Style:** à la favorite: lined with gooseliver forcemeat, filled with diced truffles and green asparagus tips bound with Madeira sauce, coated with gooseliver. forcemeat and poached.

— **Gaulish Style:** à la gauloise: lined with chicken forcemeat and poached; filled with salpicon of cockscombs and cock's kidneys bound with buttered meat glaze, coated with chicken and ham forcemeat, poached.

— **Gooseliver:** de foie gras: filled with gooseliver forcemeat, poached, a truffle slice dipped in liquid meat glaze on top.

— **Gourmet's:** du gourmet: truffle and gooseliver diced, bound with gastronomer's sauce coated with chicken forcemeat mixed with chopped ox tongue.

— **Hungarian:** à la hongroise: filled with diced chicken bound with paprika sauce, coated with cheese soufflé with paprika.

— **Hunter Style:** à la chasseur: filled with diced sautéd chicken livers and sliced sautéd mushrooms bound with hunter sauce.

— **Irving:** diced feathered game bound with champagne sauce, coated with game forcemeat.

— **Italian:** à l'italienne: filled with macaroni cut in small pieces tossed in butter and grated Parmesan, coated with cheese soufflé, baked.

Tartlet

— **Marly:** lined with game forcemeat, filled with sliced pheasant breast and truffles covered with salmi sauce, coated with game forcemeat.

— **with Mushrooms:** aux champignons: coated with chicken forcemeat, poached, filled with mushrooms purée, a fluted mushrooms cap on top.

— **Nonette:** filled with gooseliver purée, coated with chicken forcemeat.

— **Palmerston:** filled with diced chicken bound with cream sauce, covered with mushroom purée.

— **Piedmont Style:** à la piemontaise: filled with light semolina soufflé with grated Parmesan and grated Italian truffles.

— **Queen Style:** à la reine: coated with chicken mousseline forcemeat, poached, filled with sliced chicken, mushrooms and truffle bound with supreme sauce, coated with chicken forcemeat.

— **Rouenese:** à la rouennaise: diced duck bound with Rouenese sauce, coated with duck forcemeat.

— **Saint-Hubert:** filled with game purée mixed with chopped sautéd morels, coated with game forcemeat.

Teal, Teal Duck: F. Sarcelle; G. Knäkente: one of the smaller wild ducks allowed to be eaten on abstinence days, native of the British Isles and Central Europe up to Scandinavia. In the U.S.A. the teal is represented by various species of which the Green-Winged Teal is the most widely distributed. Teal like all wild ducks is roasted blood rare, seldom braised.

— **with Anchovies:** aux anchois: stuffed with veal forcemeat braised; served with sauce prepared with the braising stock boiled down with sour cream, seasoned with mustard and lemon juice and finished off with chopped chives.

— **with Cranberry Sauce:** à la sauce aux airelles: roasted, garnished with watercress and lemon; hot cranberry sauce served separately.

— **English Style:** à la l'anglaise: roasted, garnished with watercress and lemon; apple sauce served separately.

— **Japanese Style:** à la japonaise: roasted, deglaced with tangerine juice and brandy, boiled up with veal stock, thickened with arrow-root and mixed with blanched shredded tangerine peel; surrounded with tangerine fillets lightly warmed, covered with the sauce.

— **with Oranges:** à l'orange: roasted, deglaced with orange and lemon juice boiled up and mixed with blanched shredded orange peel; garnished with warmed up orange fillets, covered with a part of the sauce, the rest served separately.

— **with Port:** à la sauce au porto: roasted, garnished with watercress and lemon; veal gravy lightly thickened with arrowroot and flavored with Port served separately.

— **à la Presse:** roasted blood rare, prepared like domestic duck.

— **Strips with Cherries:** Aiguillettes de sarcelle aux cerises: roasted blood rare, breasts detached, carved in long strips and placed on a luke-warm dish; deglaced with Madeira and veal gravy, thickened with arrow-root, sour cherries added, boiled up and poured over the strips.

Teal

— **Walter Scott:** stuffed with a piece of butter, wrapped in noodle dough, baked in oven; unwrapped, served covered with breadcrumbs fried in plenty of butter.

Tcherkez tâouk: Chicken Turkish Style: poached in water with sliced onions fried in oil; when cold disjointed and boned, covered with sauce made of soaked bread crust mashed with haselnut kernels blended with chicken stock, seasoned with paprika; served cold with hot oil mixed with paprika dropped on top. (Turkish)

Tendjéré kébabi: fat mutton cut in cubes, browned in oil with chopped onions, simmered in water, mixed with chopped parsley. (Turkish)

Tendron de veau: see veal gristle.

Terbiyéli keuftés: Turkish Dumplings: flat dumplings made of ground beef mixed with soaked bread, eggs, chopped onions, parsley, salt and pepper, browned in butter and simmered in stock; covered with sauce made of flour mixed with water, beaten with boiling water, egg yolks and lemon juice, seasoned with salt and paprika. (Turkish)

Terrine: oval or round earthenware or China pot lined with thin slices of fat bacon, coated with forcemeat, filled alternately with forcemeat, strips or layers of meat, poultry or game etc., sealed with forcemeat and a slice of fat bacon on top; poached in waterbath in oven, served cold.

— **Chicken:** de volaille: prepared like terrine of duck with chicken forcemeat.

— **Duck:** Terrine de canard: duck boned and stuffed as for galantine, placed in terrine lined with bacon and coated with veal forcemeat, covered with forcemeat and fat bacon and poached; when cold taken out of terrine, trimmed, replaced in terrine, covered with duck aspic jelly and chilled.

— **of Hare:** de lièvre: lined with bacon, coated with hare forcemeat, filled alternately with forcemeat, strips of fat bacon, ham, saddle of hare, pistachios and truffles, covered with hare forcemeat and bacon, poached and finished off like terrine of duck.

— **of Partridge:** de perdreau: boned, stuffed as for galatine with diced truffles and gooseliver; terrine lined with bacon, coated with veal forcemeat mixed with chopped shallots and thyme, sealed with forcemeat, poached.

Tête de porc: see pig's head.

Timbale: pastry shell baked in a round or half-conical mould of tin filled with an appropriate garnish or round meat loaf, fine forcemeat or mousse poached in waterbath with various garnishes and sauces; some very fine ragoûts dressed in a timbale dish are also often called timbale.

— **Agnes Sorel:** mould lined thickly with chicken forcemeat, filled with small chicken breasts drawn in butter, sliced mushrooms, truffles and ox tongue bound with thick German sauce, sealed with forcemeat, poached, turned out, topped with truffle slices, covered with German sauce finished off with chicken essence.

— **Alexandra:** pastry shell made of fine short pastry, filled with poached chicken or pigeon breasts, green asparagus tips and truffle slices, covered with Mornay sauce finished

Timbale Alexandra
off with chicken essence, sprinkled with grated Parmesan, glazed rapidly.

— **Ambassadress Style:** à l'ambassadrice; buttered mould decorated with rings of ox tongue with a round truffle slice in the center, lined with chicken forcemeat, filled alternately with noodles tossed in butter and sliced mushrooms, truffles, chicken livers and lamb sweetbreads sautéd in butter, bound with Madeira sauce with tomato, sealed with forcemeat, poached, turned out; Madeira sauce served separately.

— **Badish Style:** à la badoise: timbale made with noodle dough, baked, filled with sliced sweetbreads and ham in financier's sauce.

— **Beaumarchais:** mould greased with butter, decorated with truffle slices, lined with game forcemeat, filled with diced gooseliver and mushrooms in thick Madeira sauce, sealed with game forcemeat, poached, turned out, covered with Madeira sauce.

— **Bontoux:** mould lined with pie dough, baked, filled alternately with macaroni cut in small pieces, bound with butter, grated Parmesan and thick tomato purée, and thick slices of truffled chicken forcemeat poached in sausage shape, truffle slices, cockscombs and cocks' kidneys bound with demi-glace with tomato.

— **Calais Style:** à la calaisienne: ragoût of lobster, mussels, shrimps and button mushrooms, bound with Normandy sauce, filled in round flat timbale baked of pie dough.

— **Cavour:** shell of pie dough filled with sliced lamb sweetbreads, mushrooms, pitted olives and sliced truffles bound with Madeira sauce, garnished with slices of sautéd gooseliver on top.

— **Duchess Style:** à la duchesse: round shell of pie dough, baked, filled with white chicken meat, button mushrooms and truffle slices bound with cream sauce.

— **Milanese Style:** à la milanaise: shell of noodle dough baked white, bottom and sides lined with macaroni cut in small pieces, tossed in butter, tomato purée and grated Parmesan, center filled with a financier garnish in financier sauce, covered with macaroni, closed with a decorated lid of noodle paste.

— **Princess Style:** à la princesse: croustade of duchess potato-mixture baked to a rich brown, filled with small poached chicken breasts, chicken mousseline dumplings and asparagus tips, covered with German sauce finished off with asparagus butter.

— **Rachel:** shell of unsweetened short pastry, baked, filled with sliced sweetbreads, sliced artichoke bottoms and blanched slices of ox marrow bound with Bordeaux sauce.

— **Rothschild:** mould lined thickly with pheasant forcemeat, filled with diced gooseliver bound with thick Madeira sauce, sealed with pheasant forcemeat, poached, turned out, slices of truffle on top, covered with Madeira sauce.

— **Royal Style:** à la royale: mould greased with butter, decorated with round slices of ox tongue and truffles, lined thickly with chicken forcemeat, filled with sliced truffles, mushrooms and diced gooseliver bound with thick Madeira sauce, sealed with chicken forcemeat,

Timbale
poached in water bath, turned out, covered with Madeira sauce.
— **Talleyrand:** mould lined thickly with chicken forcemeat, filled with macaroni cut in small pieces, bound with butter, cream sauce and grated Parmesan, mixed with diced chicken, gooseliver and truffles, sealed with forcemeat, poached turned out, covered with demi-glace with truffle essence and truffle strips.

Tocana cu Mamaliga: Pork and Corn Mush: boned shoulder of pork cut in cubes, seasoned, browned in lard mixed with the same quantity of sliced browned onions, moistened with white wine and a little meat stock, powdered thyme added and braised slowly; served with thick corn mush. (Roumanian)

Töltölt Káposzta: Stuffed Cabbage: blanched cabbage leaves coated with pork sausage meat mixed with chopped onions, boiled rice, eggs, garlic, marjoram, paprika and salt, rolled together, arranged in a braising pan greased with lard between two layers of saurkraut, sprinkled with flour and paprika, moistened with water and stewed with the cover on; when half done sour cream added. (Hungarian)

Tourte: culinary name of a puff pastry crust, round and low, filled with any kind of prepared fish, meat, poultry etc.

Tripe: Tripe: is a part of the stomach; the part used for food are the paunch, which yields plain tripe and the smaller reticulum yielding the so-called honeycomb tripe. Cooked tripe as bought from the butcher's is not ready for eating and must be given additional cooking, braising, boilling or frying.
— **Andaluza:** chopped onions and ham lightly fried in butter, chopped tomatoes added, dredged with flour, moistened with white stock, parboiled tripe cut in strips and parboiled chick peas added, seasoned with salt, pepper, cinnamon, garlic and chopped mint, braised, thickened with oil and breadcrumbs. (Spanish)
— **Blanchard:** chopped onions fried lightly, smothered with flour, moistened with white stock, seasoned, cooked for a while, parboiled diced tripe, white wine, a bunch of herbs and diced potatoes added and cooked until done.
— **Caen Style:** à la mode de Caën: parboiled, cut in squares, placed in fireproof earthen dish with sliced onion, carrots and leeks, blanched ox feet, bunch of herbs, garlic and seasoning, moistened with brandy and white wine, closed hermetically and braised in bakers oven for 12 hours.
— **Citizen Style:** à la bourgeoise: sauce prepared with the tripe stock, brown roux, plenty of sliced onions, garlic, vinegar and a bunch of herbs, boiled, strained over the tripe cut in strips and cooked for a while.
— **Creole Style:** à la créole: sliced green peppers and onions lightly fried in butter, mixed with parboiled tripe cut in strips, diced peeled tomatoes and garlic, moistened with a little stock and simmered slowly; creole rice served separately.
— **with Fine Herbs:** aux fines herbs: parboiled, cut in strips, simmered in butter with chopped shallots, parsley and chervil, chopped herbs sprinkled on top at serving.

Tripe

— **Fried:** frite: cut in squares, dipped in egg and breadcrumbs, deep fried; tomato sauce served separately.

— **Gratinated:** au gratin: parboiled, cut in strips or squares, placed in fireproof baking dish greased with butter, covered with cream sauce mixed with grated Parmesan; grated Parmesan sprinkled on top and gratinated in oven.

— **Holland House:** parboiled, cut in squares, seasoned, coated with flour, fried, covered with chive sauce.

— **Housekeeper Style:** à la ménagère: parboiled, cut in squares, seasoned, mixed with parboiled diced ox foot, sliced onions, carrots, knob celery, marjoram, garlic, chopped tomatoes and a bunch of herbs, moistened with brandy, white wine and water and braised until done.

— **Housewife Style:** à la bonne-femme: chopped onions sweated in butter, smothered with flour, lightly browned, moistened with white wine and stock, seasoned, strips of parboiled tripe and a bunch ob herbs added, simmered in oven.

— **Hungarian Style:** à la hongroise: parboiled, cut in strips, simmered in paprika sauce with strips of red peppers.

— **Irish Style:** à l'irlandaise: parboiled, cut in squares, cooked in half milk and half water with sliced onions and seasoning; stock thickened with butterpaste and seasoned with mustard and lemon juice.

— **Königsberger Fleck:** Koenigsberg Style: boiled with pot herbs, sliced onions and seasoning, cut in strips and cooked until done in sauce prepared with the stock, white roux, marjoram, bay leaf, peppercorns and nutmeg. (German)

— **Lyonese Style:** à la lyonnaise: parboiled, cut in strips, fried in hot lard, mixed with sliced fried onions; a few drops of vinegar heated up in the pan poured over, chopped parsley scattered on top.

— **with Mustard:** à la moutarde: parboiled, cut in squares, brushed with mustard, dipped in egg and breadcrumbs, deep fried; tomato sauce served separtely.

— **Orly:** parboiled, cut in strips dipped in frying batter, deep fried; tomato sauce served separately.

— **Poulette:** parboiled, cut in strips and served in poulette sauce.

— **Provencal Style I:** à la provençale: sliced onions and chopped salt pork sweated in oil, dredged with flour, lightly browned, moistened with stock and boiled; tripe cut in strips, the sauce poured over and cooked until done; sauce bound with egg yolks and finished off with lemon juice, chopped parsley and sweet basil.

— **Provencal Style II:** à la provençale: parboiled, cut in strips, simmered in oil with chopped onions, garlic, diced tomatoes, sliced mushrooms and white wine.

— **Roumanian Style:** à la roumaine: parboiled, cut in strips, mixed with strips of parboiled pig's trotters, simmered in demi-glace seasoned with allspice and a little vinegar.

— **in Sour Sauce:** à la sauce aigre: prepared like citizen style strongly flavored with vinegar.

— **Spanish Style:** à la l'espagnole: parboiled in water and white wine with pot herbs, spices, calf's feet and a ham bone, cut in strips, cooked in sauce prepared with sliced onions lightly fried in oil with chopped tomatoes, dredged

Tripe
with flour, moistened with the strained stock, seasoned with pepper and caraway seeds, sliced garlic sausage added.

— **with Tartar Sauce:** à la sauce tartare: parboiled, cut in squares, coated with flour, dipped in oil, grilled; tartar sauce served separately.

— **Troyes Style:** à la mode de Troyes: parboiled, cut in squares, brushed with mustard, dipped in egg and breadcrumbs, deep fried; vinaigrette sauce served separately.

— **Venetian Style:** à la venetienne: parboiled, cut in strips, simmered in butter with sliced mushrooms and tomato sauce, sprinkled with grated Parmesan, butter dropped on top, browned in oven.

— **Vinaigrette:** parboiled cut in squares, dipped in egg and breadcrumbs, deep fried; vinaigretten sauce served separately.

Tscheburek: Caucasian Rissoles: squares of noodle dough rolled out thin, center filled with raw ground mutton mixed with boiled rice, chopped fat bacon, diced tomatoes, chopped dill, parsley and seasoning, sides folded over the filling and closed; fried in butter and served brushed with fresh butter. (Russian)

Turban: food arranged in shape of a turban or served in center of forcemeat poached in a round border or turban-shaped mould.

— **of Chicken:** de volaille: border mould lined with chicken forcemeat, filled with small slices of poached chicken, sealed with chicken forcemeat and poached; turned out, covered with suprême sauce, center filled with ragoût of cockscombs, cock's kidneys, truffle slices and button mushrooms bound with suprême sauce.

— **of Hare:** de lièvre: greased border mould lined with hare forcemeat, filled with small slices of roast hare, sealed with forcemeat and poached; turned out, covered with Madeira sauce, center filled with chestnut purée.

Turkey: F. Dinde, Dindon; G. Truthahn, Puter: large American game bird domesticated for nearly four hundert years and one of the most valuable domestic fowls. Turkeys with large breasts and small bones are the best as they yield the most white meat. Turkeys are roasted, poached or braised. When serving, slices of the carved breast are placed on top of a piece of leg. Before preparing the bird, the sinews must be drawn carefully out of the legs.

— **Algerian Style:** à l'algérienne: pan-roasted, deglaced with white wine, chopped shallots, diced tomatoes, crushed garlic added and boiled down with demi-glace; garnished with olive-shaped sweet potatoes and deep fried slices of egg plant.

— **with Almonds:** aux amandes: breastbone removed, stuffed with stuffing made of creamed butter mixed with egg yolk, bread crumbs, grated almonds and stiffly beaten egg white seasoned with nutmeg and salt; roasted, pan gravy.

— **American Style:** à l'amércaine: baby turkey split open at the back, both halves separated, coated with liver forcemeat, dipped in egg and breadcrumbs, moistened with melted butter, grilled very slowly.

— **Bismarck:** stuffed with sliced apples and raisins, wrapped in greased paper, roasted slowly; pan gravy.

Turkey

— **with Boletus:** aut cèpes: stuffed with forcemeat of veal, green bacon, soaked bread and finely chopped boletus stems; braised, when threequarters done diced blanched bacon sautéd in butter and small sautéd boletus added.

— **Brasilian Style:** à la brésilienne: boned, stuffed with pork sausage meat mixed with soaked bread, the chopped parboiled gizzard, the chopped liver, chopped hard-boiled eggs, ham, shallots and garlic, seasoned and barded; roasted on the spit.

— **Breast Chef Style:** Suprême de dindonneau à la mode du chef: breasts of baby turkey poached until very tender in white stock; carved, garnished with poached oysters and stuffed olives, covered with suprême sauce made with the stock, julienne of red peppers scattered on top.

— **Breast Michael:** Suprême de dindonneau Michael: turkey breasts roasted, deglaced with pineapple juice, white wine and brandy, reduced and boiled up with demi-glace; breasts sliced, arranged on risotto, garnished with halved-slices of pineapple dusted with curry powder, turned in flour and browned in butter, sweet potatoes and fried tomatoes; lightly sauced, rest of sauce served separately.

— **Broiled:** grillé: small baby turkey split open at the back, flattened, placed between racks covered with fat bacon, broiled slowly; served with hunter sauce, sweet potatoes and cranberries.

— **Caseros:** breastbone removed, stuffed with pork sausage meat mixed with eggs, diced fat bacon, pine nuts and stoned prunes, seasoned with salt, nutmeg and moistened with a little Port; browned in lard with chopped onions, a bunch of herbs and white wine added, moistened with demi-glace and braised; served with the strained sauce.

— **Catalonian Style:** à la catalane: disjointed and cut as for fricassée, sautéd in oil, deglaced with white wine, seasoned with garlic, salt and pepper, moistened with demi-glace and tomato purée and braised; served in the sauce with Catalonian garnish.

— **with Celery:** aux céleris braisés: pan-roasted with celery waste; deglaced with white wine and demi-glace, strained, garnished with braised celery.

— **with Chestnuts:** aux marrons: stuffed with half-cooked chestnuts mixed with pork sausage meat; roasted; pan gravy.

— **Chipolata:** prepared like poularde.

— **Citizen Style:** à la bourgeoise: braised, garnished with glazed button onions, olive-shaped glazed carrots and diced fried bacon; served with the braising stock boiled down with thick veal gravy.

— **Conti:** breastbone removed, stuffed with truffled veal forcemeat, roasted; garnished with veal dumplings, cockscombs and truffle slices; truffle sauce served separately.

— **with Cucumbers:** aux concombres: roasted, garnished with cucumber pieces shaped like large olives sautéd and bound with demi-glace.

— **English Style:** à la l'anglaise: prepared like poularde.

— **Gastronomer Style:** à la gastronome: stuffed with morels, pan-roasted; deglaced with champagne and truffle essence, boiled down with demi-glace and strained; garnished with small truffles cooked in champagne, glazed chestnuts and cockscombs.

Turkey

— **Godard:** pan-roasted, served with Godard garnish and sauce.

— **Gourmet Style:** du gourmet: stuffed with chestnuts, roasted; garnished with small fried sausages; pan gravy.

— **Grandmother Style:** à la grand'mère: roasted, carved and served with the same garnish as pigeon; pan gravy boiled down with thick veal gravy.

— **with Green Peas:** aux petits pois: disjointed, cut in pieces, seasoned, sautéd in butter with diced bacon, deglaced with white wine, reduced, moistened with demi-glace and simmered with the cover on; when nearly done parboiled green peas added.

— **Imperial Style:** à l'impériale: stuffed with truffled veal forcemeat; poached, covered with suprême sauce, garnished with cockscombs and mushrooms.

— **York Style:** à la yorkaise: filled with creamed butter mixed with egg-yolks, soaked bread, seasoning, diced York ham, cream, green peas and diced parboiled root vegetables; braised and served with the thickened pan gravy.

— **Mascot:** à la mascotte: disjointed, cut in pieces, sautéd in butter, deglaced with white wine and braised in light demi-glace; arranged in cocotte garnished with olive-shaped truffles and potatoes sautéd in butter and quartered artichoke bottoms, covered with the sauce.

— **Médicis:** roasted, garnished with tartlets filled with purée of fieldfare; deglaced with essence of fieldfare, Madeira and demi-glace.

— **with Mushrooms:** aux champignons: disjointed and cut in suitable pieces; seasoned, sautéd in butter, deglaced with white wine and mushroom stock, moistened with demi-glace; when nearly done quartered mushrooms lightly sautéd in butter added.

— **Nevers Style:** à la nivernaise: disjointed, cut as for fricassée, braised, garnished with olive-shaped carrots and glazed button onions.

— **with Oysters:** aux huîtres: stuffed with rice mixed with diced oysters, poached, covered with suprême sauce mixed with the oyster liquor and poached oysters.

— **Parisian Style:** à la parisienne: prepared like poularde.

— **Phantastic Style** (cold): baby turkey poached in white stock; when cold breast and breastbone cut out and the breast carved in thin oblique slices; carcass filled with gooseliver froth mixed with finely chopped grilled haselnuts, flavored with Madeira and shaped in form of the breast; when froth is set breast replaced into position and turkey glazed entirely with Madeira aspic jelly. Turkey placed on a large silver platter on which aspic jelly has been poured beforehand so as to form a mirror, when set garnished with very small tartlets filled with salad of diced apple, chopped celery, red peppers and ham bound with jellied mayonnaise with a round slice of pineapple glazed with aspic jelly on top, tiny nicely-shaped halved marinated red peppers filled with vegetable salad in jellied mayonnaise decorated with a truffle star, glaced with aspic jelly, and cubes of aspic jelly.

Turkey

— **Portuguese Style:** à la portugaise: stuffed with risotto mixed with diced tomatoes; pan-roasted, covered with Portuguese sauce mixed with the deglaced and strained pan gravy; garnished with stuffed tomatoes.

— **Provencal Style:** à la provençale: prepared like chicken sauté.

— **Queen Style:** à la reine: poached, served with suprême sauce and small beakers filled with chicken forcemeat mixed with boiled rice, poached, turned out, a truffle slice placed on top.

— **Regency Style:** à la régence: prepared like poularde.

— **Russian Style:** à la russe: filled with bread stuffing mixed with chopped onions sweated in butter and diced sautéd boletus; browned, braised in brown stock flavored with fennel and anice, when half done sour cream added; garnished with stuffed boletus, the strained sauce served separately.

— **Stuffed:** farci: breast boned, stuffed with bread stuffing mixed with chopped shallots sweated in butter, finely chopped ham, eggs and diced truffle, seasoned with salt and mixed spice; roasted; pan gravy.

— **Stuffed** (cold): farci: breast boned, stuffed with pork sausage meat mixed with diced truffles, bacon, and ox tongue, moistened with brandy; poached in white stock prepared with calf's feet, veal bones, white wine, pot herbs and spices; when cold placed in a suitable dish and covered entirely with well seasoned aspic jelly prepared with the stock.

— **Stuffed, English Style:** farci à l'anglaise: stuffed with sage and onion stuffing, served with fried rashers of bacon and the pan gravy.

— **with Tarragon:** à l'estragon: poached in white stock with a small bunch of tarragon; carved, served with a few leaves of blanched tarragon placed crisscross on top; the reduced stock thickened with cornstarch served separately.

— **Truffled:** Dindonneau truffé: filled with stuffing prepared with gooseliver and green bacon, seasoned with salt, pepper and nutmeg, mixed with small truffles cut in quarters; a few raw truffle slices slipped between the breast skin and flesh; kept in a cool place for 24 to 48 hours to allow the flavor of the truffle to penetrate the whole turkey; trussed, barded and roasted in oven or on the spit; served with the degreased pan gravy or truffle sauce.

— **with Turnips:** aux navets: braised in white wine and light demi-glace, garnished with olive-shaped turnips sautéd in butter and glazed button onions.

Turkey, Baby or Chicken: Dindonneau: a young turkey weighing up to 8—10 lb. Prepared like turkey.

Turlu: diced mutton sweated in butter with chopped onion, diced tomatoes, pumpkin and red peppers, sliced egg-plants and green beans broken in pieces added, seasoned, moistened with very little water, stewed. (Turkish)

V

Vanneau: see lapwing.

Veal; F. Veau; G. Kalbfleisch: the meat of the calf when killed from two to three months old; the meat from milk-fed calves is the best. Veal should be white, not pink and still less reddish. For veal see also calf.

Veal Birds, Swabian: Schwäbische Kalbsvögel: veal collop beaten flat, coated with veal forcemeat, rolled and tied; placed on sliced onions, carrots, lemon and a bayleaf, seasoned with salt and allspice, covered with half white wine and half white stock; stewed; when done covered with sauce prepared with pale brown roux and the stock, chopped anchovy fillets added, strained and mixed with chopped capers. (German)

Veal, Blanquette of: Blanquette de veau: boned veal cut into fairly large dice, moistened with white stock; seasoned, a bunch of herbs and a larded onion added, stewed slowly, when done meat picked out and placed in a clean casserole, stock thickened with white roux, boiled, thickened with egg-yolk and cream, seasoned with lemon juice, garnish added.

— **with Celery, French Endives or Salsify:** au celeri, chicorée ou salsifis: blanquette with the parboiled vegetables cut in small pieces added.

— **Old Fashioned Style:** à l'ancienne: garnished with mushroom caps cooked in butter and lemon juice and button onions kept white.

— **with Noodles:** aux nouilles: blanquette with buttered noodles served separately.

Veal, Breast of: Poitrine de veau: the breast is usually boned and stuffed with a well seasoned bread or sausage meat stuffing mixed with chopped mushrooms, herbs and egg, roasted or braised and glazed.

— **Alsatian Style:** à l'alsacienne: stuffed with well seasoned bread dressing, braised, served with saurkraut mixed with diced gooseliver and the thickened braising stock.

— **Courland Style:** à la courlandaise: stuffed with stoned prunes, browned, placed on slices of browned onions and carrots, moistened with stock, braised, stock boiled down with demi-glace; garnished with potato purée and stewed onions.

— **English Style:** à l'anglaise: filled with bread stuffing with chopped fine herbs, boiled, served with caper sauce.

— **Fried:** frite: boned but not stuffed, boiled in white stock, when cold cut in pieces, dipped in egg and breadcrumbs, fried, served with tomato sauce and a vegetable garnish.

— **German Style:** à l'allemande: stuffed, boiled slowly in white stock, served with horseradish sauce.

— **with Gooseberry Sauce:** à la sauce aux groseilles vertes: browned in butter, braised with gooseberries, white wine, lemon peel and a pinch of cinnamon and sugar, sauce rubbed through a sieve, thickened with egg-yolk and served separately.

— **Jutland Style:** à la jutlandaise: boiled in water with onions, lemon peel, allspice and a little salt, drained, brushed with goose fat, sprinkled generously with breadcrumbs, goose fat dropped on top, browned in oven.

Veal, Breast of
— **with Macaroni:** au macaroni: stuffed, braised, glazed, braising stock thickened and mixed with tomato purée; macaroni tossed in butter and mixed with grated Parmesan served separately.
— **with Onions Sauce:** à la sauce Soubise: filled with bread stuffing with chopped sweated onions, braised white, garnished with potato croquettes; white onion sauce served separately.
— **Rolled:** roulée: boned entirely, opened from the side, spread with veal forcemeat, rolled together, tied, braised, pressed a little before carving, served with the strained boiled down braising stock mixed with thick veal gravy; garnished with vegetables to taste.
— **Viennese Style:** à la viennoise: stuffed with bread stuffing mixed with chopped sweated onions and chopped herbs, salt and crushed caraway seeds rubbed into the meat, roasted; demi-glace flavored with caraway seeds served separately.

Veal Chop: see veal cutlet.

Veal Collop or Escalope: Escalope de veau: thin slice cut from the topside or nut, nicely trimmed and shaped round or oval.
— **Badish Style:** à la badoise: fried in butter; noodles or spätzle tossed in butter and creamed leaf spinach served separately.
— **Baked:** au four: fried on one side, this side covered with salpicon of mushrooms, ox tongue and truffle bound with tomato or cream sauce, sprinkled with grated Parmesan, melted butter dropped on top, gratinated in hot oven.
— **Bismarck:** fried, a hard-boiled plovers egg cut in half, mushroom caps and truffle slices placed on top, covered with tomato sauce.
— **Carmen:** fried, one half covered with truffle and the other half with light Béarnaise sauce, garnished with fried tomatoes and straw potatoes.
— **Cordon bleu:** two very small collops, flattened, seasoned, a small slice of ham or Swiss cheese or both placed in between, dipped in flour, egg and breadcrumbs and fried in plenty of clarified butter.
— **Creamed:** à la crème: fried in butter covered with light cream sauce.
— **English Style:** à l'anglaise: dipped in egg and breadcrumbs, fried, arranged with a slice of fried ham between the collops, browned butter poured on top.
— **Esterhazy:** browned on both sides, stewed with coarse julienne of root vegetables in veal stock and sour cream seasoned with paprika; tiny flour dumplings served separately.
— **Flemish Style:** à la flamande: fried served with Flemish garnish.
— **Fleury:** prepared like veal cutlet.
— **Holstein:** shallow-fried, a fried egg placed on top and sprinkled with capers; garnished with 3 sippets, one with a sardine, one with smoked salmon and one with anchovy fillets; beetroot salad, gherkins and German fried potatoes served separately.
— **Hungarian Style:** à la hongroise: seasoned with salt and paprika, coated with flour, browned in lard, braised in light sour cream sauce with paprika; small flour dumplings, tarhonya or noodles served separately.

Veal Collop

— **Hunter Style:** à la chasseur: fried, chopped shallots and sliced mushrooms sautéd in the butter, moistened with half tomato sauce and half demi-glace, boiled up, chopped chervil and tarragon added, poured over the collop.

— **Italian Style:** à l'italienne: prepared like veal cutlet.

— **Kaiser Schnitzel:** larded, fried in butter, braised in veal stock and sour cream, seasoned with lemon juice or vinegar, thickened slightly with flour, strained, capers added and poured over the schnitzel. (Austrian)

— **Leipziger Schnitzel:** fried, a poached egg covered with Béarnaise sauce placed on top, garnished with Leipziger Allerlei (q. v.). (German)

— **Marshall Style:** prepared like sweetbread.

— **Metropole:** dipped in egg and breadcrumbs, fried, a fried egg placed on top, garnished alternately with fresh vegetables tossed in butter and small containers with vegetable, red beetroot and other salads as well as various pickles. (Russian)

— **Milanese:** à la milanaise: dipped in egg and breadcrumbs mixed with grated parmesan, fried; macaroni prepared the Milanese way served separately.

— **Modern Style:** à la moderne: two small round collops fried on one side only; fixed together with truffled veal forcemeat with the fried sides inside, fried until done, covered with Madeira sauce; green peas tossed in butter served separately.

— **Moldavian Style:** à la moldavienne: fried, arranged on buttered rice, covered with light tomato sauce, garnished with stuffed tomatoes and tiny tartlets filled with caviar.

— **Montholon:** fried, an oval fried slice of ham, two truffle slices and two mushroom caps placed on top, bordered with suprême sauce.

— **with Mushrooms:** aux champignons: 1. dipped in egg and breadcrumbs, fried, garnished with button mushrooms sautéd in butter.
2. fried, covered with sliced sautéd mushrooms, coated with Madeira sauce.

— **Napoleon:** fried in butter, dressed on buttered rice mixed with fried diced gooseliver and truffles, covered with Mornay sauce and glazed rapidly; garnished with chanterelles bound with red wine sauce and diced sweetbread bound with cream and egg yolks, filled in beaker moulds, poached and turned out.

— **Nevers Style:** à la nivernaise: fried, garnished with glazed button onions and glazed olive-shaped carrots, covered with thick veal gravy.

— **Oscar:** prepared like veal cutlet.

— **with Paprika:** au paprika: seasoned with salt and paprika, coated with flour, fried in butter, covered with paprika sauce prepared with demi-glace and sour cream.

— **Paradeis Schnitzel:** browned on both sides, braised in light tomato sauce; buttered rice or noodles served separately. (Austrian)

— **Parisian Style:** à la parisienne: prepared like calf's sweetbread.

— **Plain:** naturel: fried, served with the frying butter but without any garnish.

Veal Collop

— **Prince Henry:** fried, covered with hunter sauce, chopped hard-boiled egg white and truffles scattered on top; garnished with fondantes potatoes, green peas and tartlets filled with diced creamed knob celery.

— **Rhenish Style:** à la rhenane: dipped in egg and breadcrumbs, fried, chequered with anchovy fillets, capers scattered on top; German fried potatoes and anchovy sauce served separately.

— **Rich Style:** à la riche: dipped in egg and breadcrumbs, fried, garnished with artichoke bottoms filled with purée of fresh green peas; Madeira sauce served separately.

— **Russian Style:** à la russe: fried in butter, covered with sour cream sauce mixed with thick strips of tomatoes, yellow boletus and pickled cucumbers, a slice of lemon with a little caviar placed on top.

— **Swabian Style:** à la souabe: fried in butter, a little lemon juice dropped on top, covered with cream sauce; spätzle generously covered with breadcrumbs fried in plenty of butter served separately.

— **Westphalian Style:** à la westphalienne: prepared like veal cutlet.

— **Wiener Schnitzel:** Viennese Collop: dipped in flour, egg and breadcrumbs, fried in lard, served quite dry with lemon wedges and parsley. (Austrian)

— **Yorkshire Style:** à la yorkaise: fried, frying butter boiled up with white wine, reduced, demi-glace added and poured over collop, a fried slice of ham and capers on top of the meat.

— **Zigeuner Schnitzel:** browned, simmered in light tomato sauce mixed with strips of smoked ox tongue, mushrooms and truffles. (Austrian)

Veal Cutlet: Côtelette or Côte de veau: the term "veal cutlet" is often used erroneously for "veal collop" in America, although there is a distinct difference between the two. Cutlets are cut from the rack or rib of veal, between the ribs, the backbone removed, the cutlet bone trimmed and the cutlet slightly flattened. Cutlets are fried in butter plain or dipped in egg and breadcrumbs and served with a suitable garnish and sauce.

— **with Anchovies:** aux anchois: larded with anchovy fillets, strips of ham and pickled cucumber, marinated in oil with lemon juice and chopped herbs, coated with flour, fried in butter; anchovy butter or sauce served separately.

— **Badish Style:** à la badoise: fried in butter, covered with scrambled eggs mixed with chopped herbs.

— **Barigoule:** browned in butter, braised in light Madeira sauce, garnished with artichoke Barigoule.

— **with Sweet Basil:** au basilic: sautéd in butter, deglaced with white wine, boiled down with meat glaze added, finished off with basil butter.

— **Beaulieu:** fried in butter, garnished with small stewed tomatoes, artichoke hearts, Parisian potatoes and stoned black olives; thick veal gravy.

— **Bellevue** (cold): larded with truffle and ox tongue, braised, chilled under light pressure, glazed with aspic jelly, garnished with artichoke bottoms filled with vegetable salad or another suitable garnish.

Veal Cutlet

— **Berlin Style:** à la berlinoise: fried blood rare, coated with sausage meat mixed with gooseliver purée, wrapped in pig's caul, fried in oven, garnished with gratinated knob celery pieces; truffle sauce served separately.

— **Bonaparte:** dipped in melted butter and breadcrumbs mixed with chopped parsley and a little thyme, fried slowly in oil and butter; truffle essence boiled up with a little white wine served separately.

— **Bordeaux Style:** à la bordelaise: fried, a large slice of blanched ox marrow placed on top, covered with Bordeaux sauce without ox marrow.

— **Braised:** braisée: larded, braised in light Madeira sauce with tomato, garnish to taste.

— **Buloz:** prepared like mutton cutlet.

— **Byzantine Style:** à la byzantine: fried, garnished with potato croquettes and braised lettuce; thick veal gravy served separately.

— **with Chestnut Purée:** à la purée de marrons: dipped in egg and breadcrumbs, fried, chestnut purée and pepper sauce served separately.

— **Citizen Style:** à la bourgeoise: braised and prepared like loin of veal.

— **Clamart:** fried, served with Clamart garnish.

— **Colbert:** fried, covered with Colbert sauce, a French fried egg and a slice of truffle placed on top, garnished with a round flat chicken croquette.

— **Crownprince Style:** à la dauphine: fried, garnished with dauphine potatoes; Madeira sauce served separately.

— **Dampierre:** fried, served with hussar sauce and purée of green peas.

— **Dreux:** larded with truffle and ox tongue, fried, served with financier garnish.

— **Dubarry:** fried, served with Dubarry garnish.

— **Duke of Reichstadt:** Duc de Reichstadt: fried without coloring cutlet to much, covered with velouté sauce, garnished with tiny puff pastry patties filled with mushroom purée and a slice of truffle instead of the lid.

— **Düsseldorf Style:** à la duesseldorfoise chopped, mixed with chopped shallots, parsley, mushrooms and bacon, seasoned, cutlet reformed, dipped in egg and breadcrumbs, fried in butter; demi-glace served separately.

— **English Style:** à l'anglaise: dipped in egg and breadcrumbs, fried in butter, served with herb butter.

— **Farmer Style:** à la paysanne: browned in butter, placed in cocotte with sliced root vegetables and onions, lightly sautéd in butter beforehand, finished off in oven, a little clear veal gravy poured over at serving.

— **Financier Style:** à la financière: fried, deglaced with Madeira, served with financier garnish mixed with the deglacage.

— **with Fine Herbs:** aux fines herbes: fried in butter, taken out, deglaced with white wine and boiled up with brown herb sauce and poured over the cutlet.

— **Fleury:** grilled, garnished with flat round and indented potato croquettes filled with diced sautéd calf's kidney; thick veal gravy.

Veal Cutlet

— **Forester Style:** à la forestière: fried, garnished with sautéd morels, diced sautéd potatoes, diced fried bacon, covered with the pan gravy boiled down with veal gravy and beaten with butter.

— **au Four:** fried on one side, this side coated cupola-shaped with chicken forcemeat mixed with diced mushrooms and truffles, covered with greased paper, finished in oven, paper taken of, brushed with crayfish butter; suprême or German sauce served separately.

— **with French Endives:** aux endives: fried, covered with demi-glace; braised French endives served separately.

— **Fried:** frite: dipped in egg and breadcrumbs, fried in butter, served with lemon.

— **Gendarme:** seasoned with paprika, dipped in egg and breadcrumbs, fried in butter; tomato sauce served separately.

— **German Style:** à l'allemande: dipped in egg and breadcrumbs, fried in butter; potato purée served separately.

— **Gipsy Style:** à la zingara: fried, a fried ham slice placed on top, covered with gipsy sauce.

— **with Gravy:** au jus: fried in butter, deglaced with rich veal gravy and poured over cutlet.

— **Greek Style:** à la grecque: fried, served with rice prepared in the Greek way and tomato sauce.

— **Green Meadow:** Vert-pré: grilled, covered with half-melted herb butter, garnished with straw potatoes and watercress.

— **Holstein:** prepared like veal Collops.

— **Hungarian Style:** à l'hongroise: flattened, coated with flour, fried in lard, cutlet taken out of pan, chopped onions and bacon fried lightly in the lard, seasoned generously with paprika, sprinkled with flour, white stock and sour cream added, boiled, strained and poured over the cutlet.

— **Italian Style:** à l'italienne: fried, garnished with macaroni croquettes and artichoke bottoms prepared the Italian way; Italian sauce served separately.

— **Kinsky:** Grilled, a slice of fried calf's sweetbread on top, garnished with German fried potatoes; piquant sauce mixed with chopped ox tongue and ham served separately.

— **Larded:** lardée: larded, braised in white wine, veal stock or gravy with bacon waste and onions, gravy strained, boiled down, thickened and poured over cutlet, garnished to taste.

— **Lyonese Style:** à la lyonnaise: fried, deglaced with white wine and a little vinegar, reduced, boiled up with demi-glace and poured over cutlet, garnished with fried onion slices bound with a little meat glaze.

— **Maintenon:** cut open on one side, stuffed with a cold concoction of sliced mushrooms bound with very thick Béchamel sauce mixed with white onion purée prepared beforehand, browned in butter on both sides, braised lightly with very little stock, covered with truffle sauce with sliced truffles.

— **Marchand:** fried on one side only, this side coated thickly with thick artichoke purée, sprinkled with grated Parmesan, butter dropped on top, cooked and glazed in

Veal Cutlet

oven, garnished with small round croûtons, with a slice of blanched ox marrow on top, and nut potatoes.

— **Marigny:** fried, garnished as for calf's sweetbread.

— **Marshall Style:** prepared like calf's sweetbread.

— **Mascot:** à la mascotte: fried in fireproof cocotte, deglaced with white wine and thick veal gravy, garnished with quartered artichoke bottoms sautéd in butter, olive-shaped truffles and olive potatoes.

— **Mazarin:** fried, garnished with stuffed cucumber and potato croquettes; Madeira sauce with tomato served separately.

— **Milanese Style:** à la milanaise: dipped in egg and bread-crumbs mixed with grated Parmesan, fried; macaroni prepared the Milanese way and tomato sauce served separately.

— **Montholon:** fried, a slice of ox tongue, a truffle slice and a fluted mushroom cap on top, bordered with suprême sauce.

— **Montmort:** fried, deglaced with Madeira and veal gravy, reduced, bound with gooseliver purée and a little veal glace and beaten with butter, cutlet brushed with liquid meat glaze, a slice of truffle on top, garnished with small round croûtons, scooped out and filled with gooseliver purée mixed with diced truffles; sauce served separately.

— **Morland:** dipped in egg and breadcrumbs mixed with chopped truffle, fried in butter, garnished with tartlet filled with mushroom purée; buttered veal glace served separately.

— **Murillo:** fried on one side, this side coated thickly with sliced mushrooms bound with thick Béchamel sauce and egg yolk, sprinkled with grated Parmesan, melted butter dropped on top, cooked and glazed in oven, garnished with tomatoes concassées and grilled peppers.

— **with Mushrooms:** aux champignons: fried, covered with Madeira sauce with sliced mushrooms.

— **Naples Style:** à la napolitaine: sautéd lightly in butter, dried, both sides coated with thick Béchamel bound with egg yolks and mixed with grated Parmesan, dipped in egg and breadcrumbs, browned in clarified butter, garnished with spaghetti prepared the Naples way.

— **Nelson:** fried on one side, this side coated with veal forcemeat with thick white onion purée added, sprinkled with breadcrumbs, melted butter dropped on top, browned in oven, served bordered with Madeira sauce.

— **Noailles:** browned, braised in light Madeira sauce, a slice of fried ham placed on top; buttered noodles served separately.

— **Orleans Style:** à l'orléanaise: fried in butter, garnished with chicory purée bound with Béchamel and egg yolks, filled in small greased beaker moulds, poached and turned out, bordered with the deglacage; maître d'hôtel potatoes served separately.

— **Orloff:** sautéd rare, cut open lengthwise on one side, stuffed with 2 truffle-slices and thick white onion purée, top side coated thickly with onion purée, covered with Mornay sauce, sprinkled with grated Parmesan and glazed.

Veal Cutlet

— **Oscar:** fried in butter, covered with diced green asparagus tips and crayfish tails bound with cream sauce, masked with Choron sauce.

— **in Paper Bag:** en papillote: sautéd in butter, wrapped in oiled paper bag on slice of ham covered with duxelles and a slice of ham with duxelles on top, finished in oven, served in the paper bag.

— **Parisian Style:** à la parisienne: larded with truffle and ox tongue, braised and glazed with garnish as for calf's sweetbread.

— **Parma Style:** à la parme: dipped in egg and breadcrumbs mixed with grated Parmesan, fried in clarified butter; tomato sauce served separately.

— **Parmentier:** fried, garnished with Parmentier potatoes, bordered with demi-glace.

— **Pasteur:** dipped in egg and breadcrumbs mixed with chopped truffles, fried, garnished with tartlets filled with mushroom purée; Madeira sauce with truffle essence served separately.

— **Perigord Style:** à la périgourdine: sautéd, wiped dry, coated on one side with pork sausage meat mixed with chopped truffles and gooseliver purée, wrapped in pig's caul, melted butter poured over, grilled, bordered with truffle sauce.

— **Pojarski:** meat detached from bone chopped with butter and bread soaked in milk, seasoned, reformed on bone, fried carefully in clarified butter, garnished to taste.

— **Provencal Style:** à la provençale: fried on one side, this side coated with Béchamel mixed with egg yolks and pounded garlic, sprinkled with grated Parmesan, melted butter dropped on top, cooked and glazed in oven, Provencal sauce poured around.

— **Rubens** (cold): braised, pressed lightly, when cold glazed with aspic jelly, dressed on salad of hop shoots and diced tomatoes, garnished with aspic jelly.

— **Russian Style:** à la russe: browned in butter, braised in white stock, stock boiled down with sour cream and a little demi-glace, seasoned with lemon juice and poured over cutlet; garnished with sautéd sliced boletus.

— **Saint-Cloud:** larded with truffles, fried, Saint-Cloud garnish.

— **Seymour:** dipped in egg and breadcrumbs mixed with chopped truffles, fried, served on mushroom purée, garnished with small calf's sweet bread croquettes; Madeira sauce served separately.

— **Sicilian Style:** à la sicilienne: fried; noodles mixed with grated Parmesan and velouté blended with purée of lightly sautéd chicken livers served separately.

— **Spanish Style:** española: fried, garnished with glazed button onions, German fried potatoes and tomatoes stuffed with risotto mixed with chopped ham and a little saffron; Sherry sauce served separately.

— **Spring Style:** à la printanière: fried, garnished with glazed button onions, glazed fancy shaped carrots and turnips, asparagus tips, French beans and green peas.

Veal Cutlet

— **Stanley:** browned, braised with sliced onions in white stock, stock boiled down with cream, seasoned with curry powder, strained and poured over the cutlet; truffle slices and mushroom caps on top of the cutlet.

— **Talleyrand:** sautéd in butter and allowed to cool, both sides coated with chicken forcemeat, rolled in chopped truffles fried slowly in clarified butter; macaroni mixed with butter, grated Parmesan, diced gooseliver and truffle strips, and truffle sauce served separately.

— **Tenant Style:** à la fermière: browned in butter, small slices of carrots, turnips and knob celery added, braised, when done glazed onions and small roast potatoes added.

— **with Truffles:** aux truffes: fried, large truffle slices placed on top, pan gravy deglaced with truffle essence and veal glaze, boiled up and beaten with butter poured over the cutlet.

— **Turkish Style:** à la turque: fried, garnished with sliced deep fried egg-plant and shaped risotto mixed with diced sautéd chicken livers; Madeira sauce with tomato served separately.

— **Vegetable Gardener Style:** à la maraîchère: fried, garnishsed like veal nut.

— **Veronese Style:** à la véronaise: fried, placed on base of polenta, covered with tomatoes concassées, garnished with French beans; bordered with thick veal gravy with tomato.

— **Vichy Style:** à la Vichy: fried, garnished with Vichy carrots.

— **Viennese Style:** à la viennoise: dipped in egg and breadcrumbs, fried, a lemon slice with a rolled anchovy fillet and a pitted olive on top; garnished with chopped hard-boiled egg yolk and egg white, capers and chopped parsley.

— **Virgin Style:** à la vierge: coated with flour, fried, deglaced with cream, seasoned with lemon juice, cutlet covered with a slice of calf's brain a cockscomb and a truffle slice, the sauce poured on top.

— **Virieu:** browned on both sides, braised slowly with diced tomatoes, diced fried bacon and veal gravy, placed on sautéd sliced boletus, the reduced and strained gravy poured over the cutlet.

— **Westmoreland:** dipped in egg and chopped truffles, fried slowly in clarified butter, dressed on mushroom purée; Madeira sauce with truffle essence served separately.

— **Yard:** browned, braised, garnished with a silver skewer on which a slice of calf's sweetbread, a fluted mushroom cap, a thick truffle slice and a cockscomb have been fixed: the boiled down gravy mixed with veal glaze and a little Dutch sauce served separately.

Veal Escalope: see veal collop.

Veal, Fricassée of: Fricassée de veau: boned veal cut in fairly large dice, stiffened in butter without allowing the meat to discolor, dredged with flour, moistened with white stock, seasoned, a bunch of herbs and a larded onion added, stewed slowly, when done meat picked out and placed in a clean casserole with the garnish, sauce strained over, bound with egg yolks and cream, seasoned with lemon juice; garnished as for chicken fricassée.

Veal, Fricandeau of: Fricandeau de veau: the long kernel or silverside of the leg of veal larded and roasted or braised. Prepared like loin or saddle of veal.

Veal Grenadin: Grenadin de veau: small slice of veal cut from the kernel of the leg (pope's eye), larded, sautéd or braised and served with a garnish as for fricandeau (silverside).

Veal Gristle: Tendron de veau: individual pieces of breast cut lengthwise braised with very little liquid and usually glazed.

— **with Celery:** aux céleris: braised, garnished with pieces of braised celery.

— **with Cucumbers:** aux concombres: braised, covered with Madeira sauce, garnished with fancy-shaped pieces of cucumber simmered in butter.

— **Farmer Style:** à la paysanne: braised, sauce flavored with Madeira, mixed with olive-shaped carrots, turnips and knob celery, button onions and green peas.

— **Fried:** frit: stewed in white stock, when cold dipped in egg and breadcrumbs, deep fried, served with tomato, mushroom or tarragon sauce.

— **German Style:** à l'allemande: braised, covered with mushroom sauce, plain rice served separately.

— **Grilled:** grillé: stewed in white stock, when cold dipped in egg and breadcrumbs, grilled, Madeira sauce served separately.

— **Homely Style:** à la bourgeoise: braised in brown stock and white wine with mirepoix, tomatoes and herbs, stock thickened and strained, garnished with glazed button onions, carrots and knob celery, pieces of salsify and braised lettuce.

— **Marengo:** braised in oil, white wine and brown stock, garlic and diced tomatoes added, stock boiled down, garnished with button onions and mushrooms, sprinkled with chopped parsley, border of heart-shaped croûtons fried in oil.

— **with Tarragon:** à l'estragon: braised, stock flavored with tarragon, thickened with corn starch, strained, mixed with chopped tarragon.

— **Turkish Style:** à la turque: braised in white stock, dressed on halved fried eggplants, scooped out, filled with Greek rice with the chopped flesh of the eggplants added; gristle arranged on top of the eggplant, covered with Mornay sauce, sprinkled with grated cheese, glazed.

— **with Turnips:** à la nivernaise: braised, served with fancy-shaped glazed turnips and the boiled down stock.

— **Villeroi:** stewed in white stock, when cold coated with Villeroi, sauce, dipped in egg and breadcrumbs, deep fried tomato sauce served separately.

Veal, Knuckle of: Veal Shank: Jarret de veau: both the fore and hind shanks contain a large bone and tasty connective tissue.

— **Bavarian Style:** Abgebräunte Kalbshachse: boiled in water with pot herbs and onions, allowed to cool in the stock, drained, coated with flour. dipped in egg and breadcrumbs, browned in lard and then fried in butter, covered with browned butter, served with potato salad. (German)

— **Braised:** braisé: browned, braised with very little rich brown stock, glaced; lettuce salad served separately.

Veal, Knuckle of

— **Munich Style:** Münchener Kalbshachse: boiled in lightly acidulated water with strips of carrot, parsley root, knob celery, onions, a bay leaf, peppercorns, allspice and nutmeg, served with the vegetables and a little stock. (German)

— **Simmered in Butter:** etuvé au beurre: cooked in white stock, when half done taken out of the stock and simmered slowly in butter with strips of root vegetables and chopped herbs in a closed casserole; served with the vegetables and boiled potatoes.

— **Spring Style:** à la printanière: divided into thick pieces, braised, served in the thickened braising stock with green peas, diced green beans and shaped carrots and turnips added.

Veal, Leg of: Cuisseau de veau: skinned, larded and roasted or braised.

— **Hamburg Style:** browned, placed on bed of sliced onions, carrots and bacon waste browned beforehand, braised with veal stock boiled down with sour cream; garnished with sautéd morels or mushrooms.

— **Italian Style:** à l'italienne: roasted, garnished with small balls of gratinated cauliflower, rice croquettes and stuffed egg-plant, served with tomato sauce.

— **Old Fashioned Style:** marinated for a few days in pickle of water, vinegar, sliced carrots, onions and parsley root, bay leaf and spices, then larded, roasted and served with a garnish to taste.

— **Saint-Peterburgh Style:** browned, braised, braising stock boiled down with sour cream, strained and mixed with strips of pickled cucumber, garnished with sautéd gribuis (Russian mushrooms); sauce and German fried potatoes served separately.

Veal, Loin of: Longe de veau: saddle split lengthwise, vertebra removed also smaller bones and sinews, loin rolled with the kidneys inside, flank folded over and tied securely, either roasted, braised or panned.

— **Alsatian Style:** à l'alsacienne: roasted, deglaced with veal stock, boiled down and thickened, garnished with tartlets filled with braised saurkraut and a round fried slice of ham on top: gravy served separately.

— **Basle Style:** à la baloise: roasted without the kidney, garnished with French beans, sautéd morels and artichoke bottoms filled with the diced sautéd kidney bound with demi-glace.

— **Brie Style:** à la briarde: larded, braised, garnished with braised lettuce stuffed with veal forcemeat with fine herbs; creamed carrots and the boiled down, degreased and strained braising stock served separately.

— **Brussels Style:** à la bruxelloise: larded, roasted, garnished with braised French chicoree, Brussels sprouts and castle potatoes; the deglaced residue boiled up with Madeira and demi-glace served separately.

— **Casablanca:** roasted, garnished with small grilled green peppers and tomatoes stuffed with rice cooked in mutton broth; corn mixed with diced tomatoes and chopped onions simmered in butter and the pan gravy served separately.

— **Citizen Style:** braised, when a little more then half done olive-shaped carrots, diced fried bacon and browned button onions added, stock boiled down with demi-glace.

Veal, Loin of

— **Crown Prince Style:** à la dauphine: roasted, garnished with dauphine potatoes, Madeira sauce.

— **Duchess Style:** à la duchesse: roasted, garnished with duchess potatoes, Madeira sauce served separately.

— **English Style:** à l'anglaise: stuffed with forcemeat prepared with the chopped kidney, chopped veal suet, soaked bread, chopped sweated onions, fine herbs, eggs and seasoning, rolled, tied and braised, served with a piece of boiled bacon and the degreased and boiled down stock.

— **Flemish Style:** à la flamande: roasted, deglaced with thick veal gravy, garnished with braised cabbage balls, carrots, turnips, fried triangles of bacon and boiled potatoes.

— **Florence Style:** à la florentine: roasted, garnished with spinach cakes and semolina croquettes; demi-glace blended with tomato sauce served separately.

— **French Style:** à la française: roasted, garnished with creamed spinach purée and Anna potatoes; Madeira sauce served separately.

— **Gardener Style:** à la jardinère: roasted, served with gardener garnish and veal gravy.

— **Lausanne Style:** à la lausannoise: braised, garnished with Robert potatoes and tartlets filled with liver purée; the thickened braising stock served separately.

— **Lison:** braised, garnished with small brioches prepared with duchess potato-mixture with chopped ox tongue, brushed with egg and baked in oven and small cakes of chopped braised lettuce mixed with thick Béchamel sauce and egg-yolks filled in tartlet moulds and poached in oven; the reduced and degreased braising stock served separately.

— **Milanese Style:** à la milanaise: larded, braised; macaroni prepared in the Milanese way and the stock boiled down with tomato purée served separately.

— **Monarch Style:** roasted, garnished with fancy shaped carrots, turnips and knob celery; Madeira sauce.

— **Nemours Style:** à la Nemours: larded, roasted, glazed, garnished with Vichy carrots, asparagus tips and potato balls cooked in butter; veal gravy.

— **Nevers Style:** à la nivernaise: roasted, Nevers garnish and pan gravy.

— **Old Fashioned Style:** à l'ancienne: roasted, garnished with sautéd mushrooms and glazed button onions; pan residue deglaced with veal stock and boiled down served separately.

— **Parisian Style:** à la parisienne: larded with ox tongue and truffle, pan-roasted, served with Parisian garnish and the thickened gravy.

— **Peruvian Style:** à la péruvienne: roasted, garnished with oka (oxalis), scooped out, filled with the chopped flesh, chicken and ham, bound with thick demi-glace and braised in oil; light tomato sauce served separately.

— **Piedmont Style:** à la piémontaise: roasted, served with risotto mixed with sliced Italian truffles and the pan gravy.

— **Pompadour:** roasted, served with Pompadour garnish; truffle sauce separately.

Veal, Loin of

— **Portuguese Style:** à la portugaise: roasted, garnished with stuffed tomatoes and castle potatoes; Portuguese sauce served separately.

— **Princess Style:** à la princesse: roasted, garnished with tartlets filled with creamed green asparagus tips with a slice of truffle on top and potato croquettes; pan gravy boiled up with mushroom essence and demi-glace served separately.

— **Richelieu:** roasted, garnished with braised lettuce, stuffed tomatoes, stuffed mushroom caps and castle potatoes; the thickened pan gravy served separately.

— **Riga Style:** roasted, garnished with fancy shaped root vegetables, glazed button onions and German fried potatoes; sour cream sauce served separately.

— **Riviera Style:** à la côte d'azur: roasted, garnished with straw potatoes, tomatoes stuffed with spinach purée and a fluted mushroom cap on top and artichoke bottoms filled alternately with green asparagus tips and diced green beans; pan gravy.

— **Romanoff:** larded with fat bacon and anchovy fillets, roasted, garnished with braised quartered fennel bulbs; pan gravy.

— **Russian Style:** à la russe: roasted, garnished with sautéd boletus, glazed button onions, green peas and sweetbread croquettes; thick pan gravy.

— **Saint-Cloud:** roasted, garnished with braised lettuce and tartlets filled with green pea purée or peas prepared in the French way; Madeira sauce.

— **with Spring Vegetables:** aux primeurs: roasted, deglaced with veal stock, garnished with spring vegetables tossed in butter.

— **Suzerain Style:** à la suzeraine: roasted, garnished with stuffed tomatoes and stuffed cucumber; veal gravy.

— **with Tarragon:** à l'estragon: roasted, served with tarragon sauce.

— **Trianon:** roasted, garnished with tartlets filled alternately with green pea purée, tiny buttered balls of carrots and potatoes; thick veal gravy with tomato served separately.

— **with Vegetable Macedoine:** à la macédoine: roasted; buttered or creamed vegetable macedoine and veal gravy served separately.

— **Viroflay:** roasted, garnished with spinach cakes Viroflay, quartered artichoke bottoms simmered in butter with fine herbs and castle potatoes; thick veal gravy.

Veal, Noisettes of: Noisettes de veau: small steaks cut from the loin shaped like mutton noisettes but a little larger, sautéd in butter, served and garnished like veal cutlet. Veal noisettes may also be cut from the nut of veal but the loin is preferable.

— **in Cocotte:** en cocotte: sautéd in cocotte, garnished with sautéd mushrooms and diced sautéd potatoes, a little veal gravy poured over at serving.

— **English Style:** à l'anglaise: dipped in egg and breadcrumbs, fried in butter, half melted herb butter on top.

— **with Lettuce:** au laitue: fried in butter, garnished with braised lettuce, bordered with thick veal gravy.

Veal, Noisettes of
— **Marigny** fried in butter, covered with thick veal gravy, garnished with tartlets, filled alternately with buttered diced green beans and green peas, and fondantes potatoes.
— **Royal Palace:** palais royal: sautéd rare, covered with a small piece of braised sweetbread, coated with white onion purée mixed with a little Dutch sauce, glazed rapidly under the salamander, garnished with Berny potatoes and braised celery.
— **Ujest Style:** sautéd in butter, covered with sour cream sauce mixed with chopped anchovies and capers, sprinkled with chopped chives.

Veal Nut, Pope's Eye: Noix de veau: one of the three major muscles of the leg of veal. It is almost heart shaped, usually larded, roasted, pan-roasted or braised but may also be used for collops, steaks or roulades.
— **Alsatian Style:** à l'alsacienne: prepared like loin of veal.
— **Beatrice:** roasted, served with Beatrice garnish and thick veal gravy.
— **Bordeaux Style:** à la bordelaise: roasted, served with slices boletus sautéd in oil with chopped shallots and Bordeaux sauce.
— **Brabant Style:** à la brabançonne: roasted garnished with potato croquettes and tartlets, filled with very small Brussels sprouts covered with Mornay sauce and glazed; pan gravy.
— **Bréhan:** larded, roasted, garnished with artichoke bottoms, filled with purée of broad beans with a truffle slice on top, and cauliflower sprigs coated with Dutch sauce; parsley potatoes and pan gravy served separately.
— **Brie Style:** prepared like loin of veal.
— **Caucasian Style:** à la caucasienne (cold): braised, when cold cut first in slices and then in triangles in the size of a small sandwich, one triangle is spread with softened butter mixed with chopped anchovy fillets and chives a second placed on top. Triangles chilled, lightly pressed, trimmed and glazed with aspic jelly, Bomb mould filled with tomato froth, when set turned out and bordered with the triangles.
— **Chatam:** larded, braised and glazed; noodles bound with butter, filled in timbale dish and bordered with oval slices of ox tongue, and light Soubise sauce with sliced cooked mushrooms added served separately.
— **with Chicory:** au chicorée: braised, chicory purée and thick veal gravy served separately.
— **Choisy:** roasted, garnished with braised lettuce and castle potatoes; buttered meat glace served separately.
— **Choron:** served with Choron garnish and Choron sauce.
— **Clamart:** prepared like loin of veal.
— **Doris** (cold): braised, allowed to get cold, cut in regular slices, slices spread with purée of gooseliver patty mixed with chopped pistachios, truffles and red ox tongue, nut reshaped, covered with brown chaudfroid sauce, decorated to taste glazed with aspic jelly, garnished with marinated artichoke bottoms filled with tiny marinated cucumber balls, tartlets filled with tomato froth with a truffle star on top and triangles of aspic jelly.
— **Dreux Style:** larded with ox tongue and truffle, braised, served with financier garnish and sauce.

Veal Nut

— **Florence Style:** prepared like loin of veal.

— **Florist Style:** à la bouquetière: roasted, garnished with fancy-shaped glazed carrots and turnips, castle potatoes, buttered French beans, green peas and cauliflower sprigs coated with Dutch sauce; thick veal gravy served separately.

— **Gourmet Style:** du gourmet: larded with ox tongue and truffle, braised in light Madeira sauce with root vegetables, garnished with glazed button onions, fried tomatoes, fancy-shaped turnips and diced fried potatoes, the strained sauce served separately.

— **Italian Style:** à l'italienne: garnished with macaroni croquettes and quartered artichoke bottoms prepared in the Italian way; Italian sauce served separately.

— **Japanese Style:** à la japonaise: roasted, garnished with tartlets filled with creamed stachy and potato croquettes; pan gravy.

— **Lison:** prepared like loin of veal.

— **Milanese Style:** à la milanaise: prepared like loin of veal.

— **Nemours Style:** prepared like loin of veal.

— **Northern Style:** à la nordique: larded, roasted, garnished with stuffed mushroom caps, artichoke bottoms filled with mushroom purée and croquettes potatoes; pan gravy deglaced with sour cream served separately.

— **Orleans Style:** à l'orléanaise: roasted, garnished with braised chicory, chopped, bound with egg-yolks and butter, maître d'hôtel potatoes and clear veal gravy served separately.

— **Roman Style:** à la romaine: roasted, served with Roman garnish and Roman sauce.

— **Saint-Mandé:** roasted, garnished with buttered green beans, green peas and small cakes of Anna potatoes; thick veal gravy served separately.

— **Sardinian Style:** à la sarde: roasted, garnished with small round risotto croquettes with saffron, stuffed tomatoes and stuffed, gratinated pieces of cucumber; demi-glace with tomato served separately.

— **Slavonian Style:** à la slavonienne: roasted blood rare, when cold coated with thick onion purée, wrapped in puff paste and baked; Madeira sauce and vegetable macedoine served separately.

— **with Sorrel:** à l'oseille: braised, deglaced with thick veal gravy; sorrel purée and the gravy served separately.

— **a Surprise:** en surprise: braised, when done lid cut of, scooped out carefully, filled with vegetable macedoine tossed in butter, lid put on, glazed, bordered with the sliced meat of the interior; the boiled down buttered gravy served separately.

— **Trianon:** prepared like loin of veal.

— **Vegetable-Gardener Style:** à la maraîchère: roasted, garnished with small pieces of salsify, buttered Brussels sprouts and castle potatoes; thick pan gravy served separately.

— **Viroflay:** prepared like loin of veal.

Veal Paupiette: Paupiette de veau: thin slice of veal, usually cut from the nut, flattened, filled with forcemeat or thick purée, tied, braised and served with garnish and an appropriate sauce.

Veal Paupiette

— **Algerian Style:** à l'algérienne: stuffed with veal forcemeat mixed with chopped red peppers, braised, placed on small fried tomato, covered with tomato sauce mixed with shredded red peppers, garnished with croquettes of sweet potatoes.

— **Antwerp Style:** à l'anversoise: stuffed with veal forcemeat, braised, placed on tartlet filled with creamed hop shoots, covered with tomato sauce, served with boiled potatoes.

— **Beautiful Helena:** Belle-Hélène: stuffed with veal forcemeat, braised, a slice of truffle on top, garnished with small asparagus croquettes, bordered with thick veal gravy.

— **Brabant Style:** à la brabançonne: filled with creamed veal forcemeat, braised, placed on tartlet filled with small Brussels sprouts covered with Mornay sauce and glaced, garnished with very small potato croquettes, bordered with thick veal gravy.

— **Fontanges:** stuffed with veal forcemat, braised, placed on flat potato croquette, garnished with creamed purée of Lima beans, bordered with thick veal gravy.

— **Hussar Style:** à la hussarde: stuffed with veal forcemeat, braised, placed on baked rosette of duchess potato, garnished with small tomatoes stuffed hussar style.

— **Madeleine:** stuffed with creamed veal forcemeat, braised, placed on artichoke bottoms filled with white onion purée, garnished with purée of Lima beans bound with cream and egg yolk, filled in beaker moulds poached and turned out; demi-glace boiled up with the braising stock served separately.

— **Marie Louise:** spread thin with veal forcemeat, stuffed with mushroom purée blended with thick white onion purée, tied, braised, covered with the thickened strained gravy.

— **with Mushrooms:** aux champignons: stuffed with creamed veal forcemeat mixed with raw chopped mushrooms, braised, a fluted mushroom cap placed on top, covered with mushroom sauce.

— **Noailles:** stuffed with veal forcemeat mixed with chopped mushrooms and fine herbs, rolled, tied, braised, covered with truffle sauce with chopped truffles blended with the reduced gravy.

— **Portuguese Style:** à la portugaise: stuffed with veal forcemeat, braised, dressed on a fried half tomato, covered with Portuguese sauce, garnished with castle potatoes.

— **Ria:** stuffed with veal forcemeat mixed with chopped tarragon, placed on baked boat of duchess potato-mixture filled with mushroom purée, covered with demi-glace with chopped tarragon, garnished with small stewed tomatoes.

— **with Sorrel:** à l'oseille: stuffed with veal forcemeat, braised, placed on creamed sorrel purée, bordered with thick veal gravy.

Veal, Quasi of: Quasi de veau: a thick slice cut between end of leg and loin, prepared like pope's eye.

Veal, Rack of: Carré de veau: prepared like loin of veal.

Veal, Ragoût of: Sauté de veau: shoulder, breast or skrag cut in convenient pieces, browned in oil or butter, chopped onions, crushed garlic and seasoning added, moistened with white wine, veal stock or sauce, when nearly done picked out in clean stewpan, garnish added, stock or sauce poured over and finished as prescribed.

— **Catalonian Style:** à la catalane: browned in oil with chopped onions and crushed garlic, stewed in white wine and demi-glace, shortly before serving glazed button onions, sautéd mushroom quarters, peeled quartered tomatoes, sautéd in oil and stoned olives added.

— **with Eggplants:** aux aubergines: stewed in white wine and tomato sauce, garnished with sliced eggplants coated with flour, fried and added at serving.

— **Hunter Style:** à la chasseur: stewed in brown stock with tomato purée, stock boiled down with hunter sauce, served with chopped parsley scattered on top.

— **Marengo:** browned in oil with chopped onions, deglaced with white wine, reduced, moistened with brown stock and tomato sauce, garlic and bunch of herbs added, stewed, garnished with sautéd button onions and button mushrooms, reduced stock poured over, bordered with heart-shaped croûtons.

— **with Mushrooms:** aux champignons: stewed in brown stock with demi-glace and bunch of herbs, garnished with button mushrooms sautéd in butter, chopped parsley scattered on top.

— **with Noodles:** aux nouilles: prepared like ragoût with mushrooms replacing the mushrooms with noodles cooked half done and finished in the sauce.

— **Oran Style:** à l'oranaise: stewed as for Marengo, picked out and put in clean stewpan, garnished with olive-shaped briony sautéd in butter, tomatoes concassées added, the reduced stock poured over; when done dressed in timbale dish with deep fried onion rings on top.

— **Portuguese Style:** à la portugaise: prepared like Marengo, without mushrooms and onions, a generous amount of tomatoes concassées added, sauce strained over, chopped parsley scattered on top.

— **Spring Style:** à la printanière: garnished with fancy-shaped vegetables in season.

Veal, Saddle of: Selle de veau: this is an excellent piece for party purposes, and either roasted or braised. For whole saddle of veal the entire loin is trimmed, the sinews removed, the kidneys taken off leaving just a little fat on the tenderloins, the flank folded under the saddle, larded and tied.

— **Basle Style:** à la bâloise: roasted, garnished with stuffed morels and tartlets filled with diced buttered green beans with a fried slice of calf's sweetbread on top; veal gravy served separately.

— **Brie Style:** à la briarde: prepared like loin of veal.

— **Charterhouse Style:** à la chartreuse: braised and glazed, served on long dish with a vegetable chartreuse on both ends; the degreased and reduced clear braising stock served separately.

— **Chatham:** larded, braised and glazed; buttered noodles garnished with oval ham slices and white onion sauce mixed with mushroom slices served separately.

Veal, Saddle of

— **Duchess Style:** à la duchesse: roasted, garnished with duchess potatoes; Madeira sauce served separately.

— **Flemish Style:** à la flamande: roasted, garnished with braised cabbage balls, fancy-shaped carrots and turnips, boiled potatoes and sliced sausage; thick veal gravy served separately.

— **Francfort Style:** à la francfortoise (cold): braised, allowed to cool, carved, replaced into position with gooseliver cream between the slices; gooseliver cream piped lengthwise to replace the chopped out vertebrae, decorated left and right of this line with halved pitted grapes and glazed with Madeira aspic jelly; garnished on both sides with tangerines, scooped out and filled with salad of diced tangerines, red peppers and knob celery, bound with jellied mayonnaise seasoned witl tangerine juice and tomato catsup and glazed with aspic jelly flavored with tangerine juice.

— **Italian Style:** à l'italienne: prepared like nut of veal.

— **Matignon:** braised until half done, coated with Matignon, wrapped first in thin slices of bacon and then in pig's caul, braised slowly until done; the degreased and reduced braising stock served separately.

— **Metternich:** braised, carved, replaced in position with two truffle slices and a little thick Béchamel with paprika in between, whole saddle coated with Béchamel with paprika and glazed rapidly; rice pilaf and the degreased and reduced braising stock served separately.

— **Nelson:** prepared like Metternich but with a small ham slice and thick white onion sauce between the veal slices; coated thickly with cheese soufflé mass mixed with chopped truffles and finished in oven; the degreased and reduced braising stock served separately.

— **Nemours Style:** prepared like loin of veal.

— **Oriental Style:** à l'orientale: prepared like Metternich with thick Béchamel seasoned with curry powder between the slices, whole saddle coated with Béchamel mixed with tomato purée, glazed, garnished with celery braised in the stock; rice pilaf served separately.

— **Orloff:** prepared like Metternich with truffle slices and thick white onion purée between the veal slices; coated entirely with Mornay sauce blended with white onion purée, glazed; the degreased and reduced braising stock and asparagus tips in cream sauce served separately.

— **Parisian Style:** à la parisienne: prepared like loin of veal.

— **Piedmontese Style:** à la piémontaise: prepared like Metternich with Mornay sauce mixed with grated white truffles between the slices, coated with the same sauce and glazed; the clear stock and rice prepared in the Piedmont way served separately.

— **Portuguese Style:** à la portugaise: prepared like loin of veal.

— **Princess Style:** à la princesse: prepared like loin of veal.

— **Renaissance:** roasted, garnished with all sorts of vegetables in season; clear veal gravy.

— **Richelieu:** roasted, garnished with stuffed tomatoes, large stuffed mushroom caps, braised lettuce and castle potatoes; thick veal gravy.

Veal, Saddle of

— **Richemont** (cold): larded with truffles, roasted, when cold carved and glazed with aspic jelly, garnished with scallop shells filled with vegetable salad, decorated to taste, and aspic jelly.

— **Romanoff:** prepared like Metternich with Béchamel mixed with finely sliced sautéd boletus, coated with Béchamel finished off with crayfish butter and glazed; garnished with fennel braised in white wine; the degreased and reduced braising stock served separately.

— **Saint-Germain:** larded, roasted and glazed, garnished with purée of fresh green peas, bound with cream and egg yolks, filled in beaker moulds, poached and turned out, castle potatoes and fancy-shaped carrots; the degreased and reduced stock as well as Béarnaise sauce served separately.

— **Salazar:** prepared like Metternich with Béchamel mixed with thickly reduced tomatoes concassées between the slices; coated with cheese soufflé mass mixed with thickly reduced fresh tomato purée and glazed; the reduced, degreased and thickened braising stock and braised onions stuffed with duxelles served separately.

— **Spanish Style:** à l'espagnole: braised in white wine and light demi-glace, garnished with very small fried tomatoes, shaped rice mixed with green peas, diced red peppers and fried crushed pork sausage, and castle potatoes; the degreased and reduced stock served separately.

— **Talleyrand:** studded with truffles, barded and braised, lightly covered with the degreased, reduced and strained stock; Talleyrand garnish and the rest of the stock served separately.

— **Tosca:** prepared like Metternich, the cavity filled with macaroni cut in small pieces, mixed with truffle julienne and bound with cream, slices replaced in position with sliced truffles and thick Béchamel mixed with onion purée in between, coated with the same sauce and glaced; the degreased, reduced and strained stock served separately.

— **with Vegetables:** aux légumes: roasted, garnished with vegetables to taste and castle potatoes; clear veal gravy served separately.

— **Versailles:** larded, roasted and prepared like Metternich with Mornay sauce between the slices; coated with Mornay sauce, sprinkled with grated Parmesan, butter dropped on top and glazed, garnished with mushroom caps filled with purée of green peas and artichoke bottoms filled with potato purée; thick veal gravy.

— **Westphalian Style:** à la westphalienne: roasted, carved, put back into position with a slice of Westphalian ham of the same size, covered with thick veal gravy; garnished with oval puff pastry tartlets filled with a small piece of braised celery with a blanched slice of ox marrow on top, covered with a little liquid meat glaze; thick veal gravy served separately.

Veal Shank: see knuckle of veal.

Veal, Shoulder of: Epaule de veau: mainly boned and rolled, prepared like loin of veal.

— **Stuffed:** farcie: boned, filled with pork sausage meat mixed with soaked bread, eggs, chopped shallots, onions, mushrooms and parsley, rolled, tied and braised; braising stock boiled down, thickened and strained served separately.

Veal Steak: Steak de veau: thick slice cut from the loin or topside of leg, trimmed carefully and usually fried in butter.

— **Archduke Style:** à l'archiduc: fried, truffle slices placed on top; deglaced with brandy, cream, velouté and white onion purée, boiled up, strained, flavored with Madeira and lemon juice and poured over the steak.

— **Berlin Style:** à la berlinoise: fried, poached oysters and truffle slices placed on top, covered with cream sauce blended with the oyster liquor, bordered with fleurons.

— **in Cocotte:** en cocotte: fried in oval cocotte in butter, when half done sautéd button mushrooms, diced sautéd potatoes and diced fried bacon added, covered and finished in oven; served in the closed cocotte with a little veal gravy poured over at serving.

— **Hotel Adlon:** fried, covered with scrambled eggs and sliced sautéd veal kidney on top, garnished with straw potatoes; Madeira sauce served separately.

— **Horcher:** fried, covered with Béarnaise sauce, garnished with artichoke bottoms, filled alternately with gooseliver purée and mushroom purée, and straw potatoes.

— **Marquise:** fried, served with marquise garnish.

— **Maryland:** dipped in egg and breadcrumbs, fried, placed on slice of fried bacon, garnished with fried bananas and cornfritters; horseradish cream served separately.

— **Merry Widow:** Veuve joyeuse: fried, halved fried bananas placed on top, covered with hot Cumberland sauce beaten with butter; garnished with straw potatoes and green peppers, shredded coarsely, blanched and sautéd in butter.

— **Mirbach:** fried, placed on shaped buttered rice mixed with grated Parmesan and saffron, a small braised sweetbread larded with truffle, ham and ox tongue on top; bordered with tomato sauce beaten with butter.

— **Monaco:** fried, placed on croûton brushed with liquid meat glaze, covered with a slice of fried ham, a slice of fried calf's brain and a fluted mushroom cap; bordered with demi-glace with sliced mushrooms and truffles.

— **My Wish:** Mon désir: fried rare, placed in oval baking dish with a thin slice of Swiss cheese dusted with paprika on top and a trickle of white wine poured around, glazed rapidly in hot oven, surrounded with tomatoes concassées mixed with a little garlic and chopped parsley.

— **Rachel:** prepared like calf's sweetbread.

— **Rich Style:** à la riche: prepared like veal collop.

— **Saxon Style:** à la saxe: fried, covered with scrambled eggs mixed with chopped parsley and sliced sautéd boletus; German fried potatoes served separately.

— **with Tarragon:** à l'estragon: fried, covered with tarragon sauce with chopped tarragon.

Venison; F. Venaison; G. Wild: collective name for the meat of any wild animal hunted for food, more particular for deer, elk, reine deer and antilope.

Vol-au-vent: pasty of puff pastry — puff paste shell — suitable for at least four persons with different kinds of fillings.

— **Agnés Sorel:** mushrooms, tiny chicken dumplings and diced chicken meat bound with German sauce, garnished with ox tongue and truffle slices covered with liquid meat glace.

— **Ancient Style:** à l'ancienne: calf's sweetbreads, cockscombs and kidneys, calf's brains and mushrooms bound with Madeira sauce, garnished with slices of larded sweetbreads, truffles and crayfish tails.

— **Beaumarchais:** lined with truffled game purée, filled with diced gooseliver and asparagus tips in Madeira sauce.

— **Benedictine:** filled with mashed salt cod mixed with freshly boiled mashed potatoes, oil and hot milk, highly seasoned.

— **with Calf's Brains:** au cervelle de veau: cooked calf's brains cut in small slices, small mushroom caps and truffle slices bound with Madeira sauce.

— **Cardinal Style:** à la cardinal: diced lobster and truffles bound with cardinal sauce, garnished with a border of truffle and lobster slices covered with the same sauce.

— **Chevet:** lined with coarsely chopped noodles bound with grated Parmesan and Béchamel sauce, filled with diced chicken meat, ox tongue, ham and mushrooms in Portuguese sauce, covered with noodles, sprinkled with grated Parmesan, glazed.

— **of Chicken:** de volaille: sliced chicken breasts, small chicken dumplings bound with German sauce.

— **Condé:** filling: calf's sweetbreads, mushrooms and truffles bound with Madeira sauce:

— **Cussy:** filling: diced artichoke bottoms, mushrooms, truffles, chicken meat, cockscombs in Madeira sauce.

— **d'Orsay:** filling: diced chicken meat, artichoke bottoms, mushrooms and truffles bound with paprika sauce.

— **Duchess Style:** à la duchesse: filled with chicken meat, ox tongue, mushrooms and truffles in cream sauce.

— **Dumonteil:** filled with sliced lobster and truffles in Newburgh sauce.

— **Epicurian Style:** à l'épicurienne: minced game mixed with diced gooseliver, braised beef palate and truffles in Madeira sauce.

— **Favorite Style:** à la favorite: slices of gooseliver sautéd in butter, sliced chicken breasts and truffles and asparagus tips bound with thick veal gravy whipped up with butter.

— **Financier Style:** à la financière: filled with financier garnish bound with financier sauce.

— **Frascati:** filled with sliced chicken breast, truffle slices and asparagus tips bound with velouté, garnished with a bunch of asparagus tips in the center surrounded with a border of truffle slices.

— **Gaulish Style:** à la gauloise: mushrooms, truffles, cockscombs and kidney and diced ham bound with suprême sauce.

— **Isabella:** hashed chicken and ox tongue in cream sauce, decorated with truffle slices.

— **Laguipierre:** filled with sliced calf's sweetbreads, cockscombs, sautéd chicken livers, small mushroom caps, truffle slices and pitted green olives bound with Madeira sauce.

Vol-au-Vent

— **Mariner Style:** à la marinière: shrimps, bearded mussels and strips of sole fillets in mariner's sauce.

— **Mazarin:** filling: small veal dumplings, mushrooms and truffle slices bound with Madeira sauce.

— **Medicis:** filled with diced gooseliver, ox tongue and truffles, bound with German sauce, covered with tomatoes concassées.

— **Milanese Style:** à la milanaise: filled with macaroni cut in pieces, tossed in butter, mixed with grated Parmesan, tomato sauce and strips of truffles, ox tongue, mushrooms and ham.

— **Mirabeau:** filled with small fillets of sole alternated with truffle slices in Geneva sauce, garnished with anchovy fillets, pitted olives and blanched tarragon leaves covered lightly with white wine sauce.

— **Mogador:** filling: small whiting dumplings, pieces of sole fillets, crayfish tails and truffle slices bound with Nantua sauce.

— **Noah's Ark:** diced chicken and pigeon meat, gooseliver, calf's sweetbreads, mushrooms, cockscombs and kidneys, truffles and tiny veal dumplings bound with suprême sauce whipped up with meat glaze.

— **Normandy Style:** à la normande: filled with small folded fillets of sole, bearded oysters, mussels, crayfish tails, truffle slices and small mushroom caps bound with Normandy sauce, garnished with truffle slices, the pastry shell surrounded with whole crayfish.

— **Queen Style:** à la reine: filled with chicken purée or diced chicken in suprême sauce, garnished with truffle slices.

— **Queen Frederica:** Reine Frédérique: oval puff pastry shell filled with small pike forcemeat dumplings, crayfish tails, diced tomatoes and green peppers simmered in butter, and small mushroom caps bound with Dutch sauce, a little crayfish butter dropped over and capers and chopped dill scattered on top.

— **Regency Style:** à la régence: filled with small truffled chicken dumplings, small mushroom caps, cockscombs, olive-shaped truffles and gooseliver slices bound with German sauce with truffle essence.

— **Réjane:** filled with sautéd morels, asparagus tips and truffle slices bound with thick Madeira sauce.

— **of Sweetbread:** de ris de veau: sliced braised calf's sweetbreads, truffle and mushroom slices bound with Madeira sauce, filled in oval pastry shell.

— **Talleyrand:** filled with short pieces of macaroni tossed in butter, mixed with grated Parmesan, diced gooseliver and truffles bound with demi-glace with truffle essence.

— **Toulouse Style:** à la toulousaine: filled with slices of chicken breasts, calf's brains and sweetbreads, small chicken dumplings, cockscombs and cock's kidneys, small mushroom caps and truffle slices all bound with German sauce with truffle essence.

— **Victoria:** strips of sole fillets, diced spiny lobster and truffles bound with Victoria sauce.

W

Wiener Backhuhn: see fried chicken Viennese style.

Wild Boar, Young: F. Marcassin; G. Frischling: wild boar is really good only when young, not over six months old. Saddle, leg, cutlets and noisettes are prepared like roebuck.

— **Breast, Fried:** frite: cut into convenient pieces, cooked in red wine and veal stock, when cold bones removed, brushed with mustard powder mixed with lemon juice, Worcestershire sauce and a little water, dipped in frying batter and deep fried; creamed hop shoots, chard or stachy served separately.

— **Breast in Jelly** (cold): Poitrine de marcassin en gelée: boiled in white stock with pot herbs and a little vinegar, when cold the bones removed, cut into convenient pieces, arranged in a mould, covered with jelly made from the stock, chilled, turned out; Cumberland sauce served separately.

— **Cutlets Ardennes Style:** Côtelettes de marcassin à l'ardennaise: braised in pale beer and demi-glace seasoned with crushed juniper berries and mustard, served with a slice of fried ham on each cutlet and the strained sauce poured over.

— **Cutlets Chief Ranger Style:** à la grand-veneur: braised in red wine and game stock, brushed with a mixture of grated rye bread, red wine and cinnamon, melted butter dropped on top, gratinated; chief ranger sauce served separately.

— **Cutlets Cumberland:** sautéd, dressed on croûtons fried in butter; Cucumberland sauce served separately.

— **Cutlets Kaunitz:** braised in red wine and game stock with pot herbs, dipped in egg and rye breadcrumbs, fried in a skillet; unsweetened apple purée cooked in white wine served separately.

— **Cutlets Little-Russian Style:** à la petite russienne: larded, braised in stock with sour cream and chopped fennel, dipped in frying batter made of buckwheat flour flavored with cinnamon, fried; the strained sauce flavored with Malaga and cinnamon, mixed with cooked stoned cherries served separately.

— **Cutlets Moldavian Style:** à la moldavienne: braised in pepper sauce and the juice of unripe grapes with onions and fennel, arranged on croûtons fried in butter, covered with the strained sauce mixed with chopped mushrooms, garnished with potato croquettes.

— **Cutlets Roman Style:** à la romaine: cutlets sautéd in butter, covered with Roman sauce; chestnut, lentil or celery purée served separately.

— **Cutlets Saint-Hubert:** sautéd on one side only, lightly pressed, when cold the fried side coated with forcemeat prepared with fat wild boar meat, chopped mushrooms, powdered juniper berries and seasoning, wrapped in pig's caul, arranged on a flat baking dish, sprinkled with breadcrumbs, melted butter dropped on top, fried in oven and served with game sauce and warm unsweetened apple purée.

Wild Boar

— **Cutlets Saint-Marc:** larded with ox tongue, braised, dressed on flat chestnut croquettes, the thickened and strained gravy and cranberry purée served separately.

— **Cutlets Slavonian Style:** à la slavonienne: braised in stock and red wine, dipped in egg yolk mixed with melted butter and grated rye bread mixed with cinnamon, a little sugar and ginger powder, fried; stachy in paprika sauce served separately.

— **Ham in Breadcrust:** Jambon de marcassin en croûte: marinated, braised in stock and red wine, when cold wrapped in rye bread dough mixed with a little butter and red wine, baked in the oven; Cumberland sauce served separately.

— **Ham German Style:** Jambon à l'allemande: marinated, braised and glazed, stock boiled up with pepper sauce and cream, finished off with red currant jelly.

— **Ham Roman Style:** à la romaine: marinated, braised in brown stock, a part of the marinate, red wine and onions; glazed, Roman sauce served separately.

— **Ham Russian Style:** à la russe: marinated, braised in the marinate with red wine and pot herbs, brushed with a mixture of grated rye bread, a little sugar and cinnamon moistened with a part of the strained stock, browned in oven; sauce made from the thickened stock served separately.

— **Ragoût of:** Ragoût de marcassin: cut into convenient pieces, browned, braised in demi-glace with red wine, brown stock, chopped onions and a few crushed juniper berries.

— **Saddle of:** Selle de marcassin: marinated but more often only larded, roasted, served with the thickened gravy and a garnish to taste.

— **Saddle in Crust:** en croûte: roasted, carved, put together again, brushed with a mixture of grated rye bread, cinnamon and red wine, melted butter dropped on top, browned in oven; cherry sauce served separately.

— **Saddle Modern Style:** à la moderne: larded, roasted medium, carved, prepared like saddle in crust, garnished with small deep fried balls prepared with cream puff paste mixed with cranberries, tartlets filled with sautéd diced boletus and castle potatoes; pepper sauce finished off with sweet cream and red currant jelly served separately.

Wild Duck; F. Canard Sauvage; G. Wildente: wild duck in America and the British Isles is usually a Mallard (F. Malart). Other species for the table are: Shoveler (F. Souchet) and Black Scoter (F. Macreuse). Wild duck is prepared like Teal or Rouenese duck and roasted rare or braised.

— **American Style:** à l'américaine: stuffed with game forcemeat, braised, served with salmi sauce flavored with Port and finished off with a purée of ducks liver.

— **Bigarade:** prepared like duck.

— **Braised:** braisé: browned in butter, braised with ham waste, a larded onion, celery, parsley root, juniper berries and peppercorns; served with mushroom sauce.

Wild Duck

— **with Cranberry Sauce:** à la sauce aux airelles: roasted rare, garnished with watercress and lemon; cranberry sauce served separately.

— **English Style:** à l'anglaise: roasted rare, garnished with watercress and lemon; apple sauce served separately.

— **Hunter Style:** à la chasseur: roasted rare, served with hunter sauce.

— **Little-Russian:** à la petite russienne: barded, roasted blood rare and allowed to cool; wrapped in puff paste, baked, served with Madeira sauce.

— **Orangine:** roasted rare, deglaced with Curaçao, white wine and thick veal gravy, boiled down, flavored with orange juice and mixed with blanched julienne of orange peel; garnished with orange fillets sautéd lightly in butter and ignited with Curaçao and brandy.

— **Palestinian Style:** à la palestine: pan-roasted rare, deglaced with veal gravy; garnished with fancy-shaped fried sweet potatoes.

— **with Port:** au porto: prepared like Rouenese duck.

— **à la Presse:** prepared like duck.

— **Salmi of:** Salmi de canard sauvage: prepared like partridge.

— **Stuffed:** farci: stuffed with soaked bread mixed with chopped fat bacon, the parboiled heart and liver, eggs, parsley and seasoning, braised; served with sauce made of the strained and thickened braising stock.

— **Syrian Style:** à la syrienne: disjointed, sautéd in butter, simmered in red wine and game sauce; garnished with glazed button onions, pitted olives and heart-shaped croûtons masked with duck liver purée.

— **Westerland Style:** roasted rare with crushed juniper berries, deglaced with sour cream and veal gravy; served with heart-shaped croûtons coated with forcemeat made of the liver, parboiled chopped heart, fat bacon, herbs and seasoning.

Wild Goose, Barnacle Goose, Fen Goose; F. Oie Sauvage; G. Wildgans: the ancestress of our tame goose is found only in the northern part of Europe from Germany to Norway, Russia, North India, North West Africa and China. Prepared like wild duck and tame goose.

— **Alsatian Style:** à l'alsacienne: stuffed with pork sausage meat, braised in white wine and light demi-glace; garnished with glazed chestnuts and tartlets filled with saurkraut and a round slice of ham on top.

— **Farmer Style:** à la paysanne: braised, when nearly done thin slices of carrots, turnips, celery and onions, sautéd lightly in butter, and parboiled green peas and diced green beans added.

— **with Saurkraut:** à la choucroute: stuffed with soaked bread mixed with egg yolks, chopped onions sweated in butter, chopped herbs and seasoning, braised in red wine and light demi-glace; served with saurkraut and boiled potatoes.

— **Stewed:** à l'étuvée: barded with fat bacon, stewed with butter, water, ham and bacon waste, root vegetables, juniper berries, seasoning and a dash of vinegar.

Woodcock; F. Bécasse; G. Schnepfe: prized game bird widely distributed in Europe and the British Isles, parts of Asia and America. The woodcock found in the U. S. A. is a

Woodcock

somewhat smaller bird then the European. It is served roasted a little underdone or broiled; the entrails including the liver, but without gizzard; sautéd, puréed, spread on croûtons and served with the bird.

— **Bengalines of:** Bengalines de bécasse (cold): egg-shaped mould lined with woodcock froth, filled with a small slice of cold roasted woodcock breast and a truffle slice, sealed with woodcock froth; when set turned out, coated with brown chaudfroid sauce and decorated with truffle slice; placed in deep silver dish and covered entirely with very light aspic jelly made of woodcock stock; served on ice block.

— **Burgundy Style:** à la bourguignonne: roasted in cocotte, deglaced with brandy and a little red wine; garnished with glazed button onions, button mushrooms and diced fried bacon.

— **Carême:** cut in pieces, sautéd rare, deglaced with brandy and the juice pressed out of the carcass, seasoned with mustard and lemon juice and poured over bird.

— **in Casserole:** flambée en casserole: roasted in service casserole; when done ignited with brandy, the chopped liver and entrails seasoned with Cayenne pepper and a few drops of lemon juice added, casserole closed and served.

— **Catalonian Style:** à la catalane: cut in pieces, sautéd rapidly in butter with fine mirepoix, chopped shallots, bacon and garlic; taken out of sautoir, pan gravy boiled up with demi-glace, the chopped liver and entrails added, flavored with Sherry, strained and poured over the bird.

— **Cecilia** (cold): roasted rare, allowed to cool, breast coated with brown chaudfroid sauce prepared with the bones, placed on slices of gooseliver patty coated with purée of woodcock and gooseliver, served in deep glass or silver dish covered entirely with light Madeira aspic jelly.

— **with Champagne:** au champagne: roasted, breasts cut out and kept warm; carcass, liver and entrails browned in butter, pounded in mortar, boiled up with a glass of champagne, reduced and rubbed through a sieve; sauce heated up but not boiled, seasoned with lemon juice and Cayenne pepper and poured over the breasts.

— **Chaudfroid of:** Chaudfroid de bécasse: roasted, when cold breasts coated with brown chaudfroid sauce made of the carcass with red wine and mirepoix; decorated, glazed with Sherry or Madeira aspic jelly, each breast served on a slice of gooseliver parfait.

— **with Cognac:** au fine champagne: roasted, cut in six parts; deglaced with fine old brandy, a little game essence added, boiled down, the entrails chopped and mixed with the juice pressed out of the carcass added but not allowed to boil, seasoned with lemon juice and Cayenne pepper and poured over the bird which has been kept warm in the meantime.

— **Favart:** roasted blood rare; breasts cut out with breastbone and kept warm. Carcass filled with gooseliver mousseline forcemeat mixed with a purée of the entrails, the carved breast alternated with truffle slices arranged on top, cooking finished in moderate oven; when done covered with a little demi-glace boiled up with woodcock stock, sauce also served separately.

Woodcock

— **Galitzin:** stuffed with game forcemeat mixed with the chopped liver and entrails, roasted, served with truffle sauce.

— **Lucullus:** roasted, deglaced with truffle essence and demi-glace; garnished with truffle cooked in Madeira, scooped out and filled with cock's kidneys coated with liquid meat glaze and game dumpling mixed with the livers, entrails and the inner parts of the scooped out truffles.

— **Monaco Style:** à la monegasque: roasted, deglaced with truffle stock and gravy; breasts carved, placed on croûton masked with purée of the livers, entrails and chopped truffle.

— **Mousse of:** Mousse de becasse: mousseline forcemeat of woodcock prepared as usual, filled in greased mould, poached in water bath, turned out and covered with demi-glace cooked with red wine and the carcass.

— **Mousselines of:** Mousselines de bécasse: prepared like mousse but filled in small oval moulds or shaped with two soup spoons.

— **Oyster-Merchant Style:** à l'écaillière: stuffed with chopped chicken livers, oysters, bacon and the entrails seasoned with paprika; barded, roasted, deglazed with sour cream and meat glaze, seasoned with anchovy butter and lemon juice.

— **in Paper Bag:** en papillote: split lengthwise, sautéd blood rare; chopped onions, mushrooms, truffles and parsley sweated in the butter, boiled up with a little Madeira sauce to thick purée, the chopped liver and entrails added; both halves of bird coated with the mixture, placed in greased paper bag and placed in the oven for a few minutes.

— **Parker-Gilbert** (cold): roasted, when cold breast cut out and coated with brown chaudfroid sauce made of the bones and glazed; legs and entrails sautéd beforehand and sautéd gooseliver pounded in mortar, rubbed through a sieve, brandy and seasoning added blended with aspic jelly and whipped cream and filled in parfait mould lined with aspic jelly and decorated to taste. When set turned out on round platter, garnished with the breasts and aspic jelly.

— **Rich Style:** à la riche: roasted rare, breasts placed on croûton masked with purée of the liver and entrails: deglaced with brandy and a little game stock, reduced, thickened with gooseliver purée blended with butter and poured over the breasts.

— **Roasted:** rôtie: 1. barded, roasted rare, served on croûton coated with the chopped entrails and livers, garnished with watercress and lemon: the pan juice deglaced with brandy and a little game stock served separately.
2. au fumet: roasted rare, breasts placed on croûton scooped out and filled with diced fried bacon: deglaced with brandy and red wine mixed with the juice pressed out of the carcass and poured over the bird.

— **Salmis of:** en salmis: cut in pieces, sautéd in butter, arranged in timbale dish with mushrooms and sliced truffles, covered with salmi sauce prepared with the carcass.

— **Salmis Hunter Style:** en salmis à la chasseur: cut in pieces, placed in timbale dish with sautéd mushroom

Woodcock
quarters; deglazed with white wine, boiled up with salmi sauce prepared with the carcass, finished off with purée of the liver and entrails, poured over the bird, garnished with heart-shaped croûtons.
— **Souvaroff:** prepared like pheasant.
— **Timbale Metternich:** prepared like with champagne; breasts placed alternately with sautéd slices of gooseliver in a flat round decorated crust made of pie dough; covered with the sauce blended with butter and truffle slices on top.
— **with Truffles:** aux truffles: prepared like "with champagne" using truffle stock instead of the champagne and adding sliced truffles to sauce.
— **Victoria:** boned, filled with diced gooseliver and truffles, roasted in cocotte with diced raw potatoes sautéd in butter; when done deglaced with a trickle of brandy and served with the cover on.

Woodcock, Suprême of: prepared like partridge.
— **Naples Style:** à la napolitaine: suprêmes sautéd rare, arranged on spaghetti tossed in butter, mixed with grated Parmesan and a purée of the entrails and the liver; covered with demi-glace with tomato cooked with the chopped sautéd carcass.
— **Nignon:** breasts sautéd blood rare and kept warm with a trickle of brandy; legs and carcass chopped finely, sautéd with chopped shallots, deglaced with red wine, reduced, boiled up with demi-glace and strained through a sieve; sauce mixed with coarse sautéd strips of mushrooms and game forcemeat dumplings shaped like small almonds, poured over the suprêmes, truffle julienne scattered on top.

Y and Z

Yahni: thick cut from a leg of mutton with the bone, browned in mutton fat with sliced onions, seasoned, moistened with water, stewed in fireproof casserole with the cover on. (Turkish)
— **with Rice:** au riz: diced mutton fried in mutton fat with chopped onions, when half done rice and tomato purée added and stewed until done. (Turkish)

Yambalaya: diced raw ham sautéd in butter with chopped shallots, red and green peppers and simmered until done, mixed with roast chicken cut in cubes; served mixed with rice pilaf. (Indian)

Yellow Hammer; F. Bruant; G. Goldammer: small wading bird found in Europe, Asia and America, prepared like wild duck. Protected by law in most countries.

Zadéjávané drsky: Tripe Checho-Slovakian Style: parboiled tripe cut in thin strips, sautéd in butter with chopped onions and garlic, sprinkled with flour, moistened with stock, mixed with chopped ham and parsley and simmered until done. (Checho-Slovakian)

Zamponi di Modena: Stuffed Pig's Foot: pig's foot boned, stuffed with forcemeat made of pork, green bacon, truffles and seasoning, cured, smoked, boiled and served with lentils. (Italian)

Zéphir: very light mousseline forcemeat of fish, crustacean, white meat, poultry or game with stiffly beaten egg white added, filled in small China or silver containers, baked in oven and served as hot appetizer.

Zrázy: sirloin steak, beaten flat, coated with mixture of chopped sweated onions, bacon, breadcrumbs, eggs and seasoning, rolled together, tied, browned in butter, stewed in red wine with chopped onions, diced bacon and a bunch of herbs; stock thickened with butterpaste. (Polish)

— **Nelson:** two small tenderloin steaks beaten flat, fried in service casserole with chopped onions and diced bacon; deglaced with Madeira, served with nut potatoes and sautéd mushrooms. (Polish)

Vegetables and Farinaceous Dishes

French: Légumes et Pâtes alimentaires
German: Gemüse und Teigwaren
Italian: Legume e paste
Spanish: Verduras y pastas.

General Rules

All vegetables must be thoroughly washed as very often small insects are to be found on and between the leaves. Some vegetables are scalded to take away the pungent or acrid taste and cooled in running cold water before they are cooked, although this is not in conform to the ideas of modern nutritionists.
Green vegetables must be cooked rapidly in boiling salt water or they will lose their color.
No vegetable should be cooked longer than necessary, otherwise it will lose its taste, color and nutritive value. Whenever it is possible vegetables ought to be simmered in butter with very little water or stock to preserve their essential values, such as minerals and vitamins, which are easily destroyed by heat.
Don't spoil the taste of vegetables by binding them with too much sauce or by seasoning them too much.
Italian paste, such as macaroni, spaghetti, taglitatelli etc. should always be cooked **shortly before serving them "al dente", i. e. they must be** done but not too soft.
Vegetables may be served as a garnish, a separate course — as in France —, as an appetizer and sometimes as a light entrée.

A

Ail: see garlic.
Artichaut: see artichoke.
Artichoke: F. Artichaut; G. Artischoke: the flower of a thistle native of Europe and Africa and also cultivated in America. The edible part is the „bottom" and the base of the leaves. If served whole the top ist cut off and the ends of the leaves are trimmed. The artichoke is then tied and boiled in salt water. Very small species may be boiled and eaten whole as long as they are young. The smallest buds are preserved in olive oil. Artichoke bottoms are served fresh and are also imported canned.
— **American Style:** à l'américaine: tender young artichoke, the inner parts, the so-called hay, removed, braised in white stock, center filled with ragout of chicken, ox tongue and truffle bound with American sauce.

Artichoke

— **Baker Style:** à la boulangère: trimmed, parboiled, hay removed, filled with pork forcemeat, wrapped in pie dough, baked.

— **Barigoule:** small tender artichoke, parboiled, hay removed, filled with duxelles mixed with chopped salt pork, wrapped in bacon, braised in white wine; when done stock strained, boiled down with demi-glace and poured over artichoke.

— **Béarnaise Style:** blanched, hay removed, braised in white wine, lemon juice and white stock; Béarnaise sauce served separately.

— **Bresse Style:** à la bressanne: blanched, hay removed, filled with chicken forcemeat mixed with purée of sautéd chicken livers; wrapped in bacon, tied, braised in white wine, when done stock boiled down with demi-glace and poured over artichoke.

— **Clamart:** middle-sized tender artichoke trimmed, placed in buttered cocotte, with a new carrot cut in quarters, a handfull of fresh green peas and a bunch of herbs, seasoned, moistened with water and cooked with the cover on; when done, bunch of herbs taken out and stock thickened with butterpaste.

— **Dietrich:** quarters of tender young artichokes, blanched, cooked in light velouté with chopped onions sweated in butter; served in border of risotto.

— **Dutch Style:** à la hollandaise: boiled, served with Dutch sauce.

— **Farmer Style:** à la paysanne: trimmed, cut in quarters, hay removed, simmered in white stock with diced bacon, button onions and very small new potatoes.

— **Forestas:** middle-sized tender artichoke, trimmed, parboiled, hay removed, stuffed with hashed rabbit mixed with tomatoes concassées, wrapped in bacon, tied, placed on sliced carrots and onions, braised in white stock and Madeira; stock thickened with butterpaste strained and poured over the artichoke.

— **Greek Style:** à la grecque: see appetizers.

— **Housewife Style:** à la bonne-femme: boiled, hay removed, served with butter sauce.

— **Jewish Style:** à la juive: small tender artichokes, blanched, center removed, filled with stuffing of breadcrumbs, chopped mint, garlic and seasoning; pan fried in oil until quite crisp, a few drops of water added at the last minute.

— **Moldavian Style:** Anghinará Moldovenesti: tender young artichoke trimmed, cut in quarters, hay removed, placed on sliced onions fried in oil, braised in white wine and oil with diced tomatoes, garlic, chopped lemon peel and dill, seasoned, and served cold in the stock. (Roumanian)

— **Oriental Style:** à l'orientale: tender young artichoke cut in quarters, braised in white wine, oil and white stock with sliced onions, garlic and fennel.

— **with Pepper Sauce:** à la poivrade: cut in quarters, cooked in lightly acidulated salt water; vinaigrette sauce mixed with chopped shallots and freshly ground pepper served separately.

Artichoke

— **Provencal Style:** à la provençale: very small tender artichokes, trimmed, seasoned, cooked slowly in oil with the cover on; fresh green peas and shredded lettuce added, cooked very slowly without addition of water with cover on.

— **Stuffed:** farci: parboiled, stuffed with beef hash mixed with duxelles and breadcrumbs, sprinkled with breadcrumbs, dotted with oil and browned in oven. Madeira sauce.

— **with Vinaigrette sauce:** à la vinaigrette: boiled in salt water, served hot or cold with vinaigrette sauce separately.

Artichoke Bottoms: Fonds d'artichauts: middle-sized artichokes, leaves and hay removed, bottom trimmed, blanched in salt water, drained and simmered for a few minutes in butter.

— **Alice:** blanched, simmered in butter, filled with blanched ox marrow, covered with truffle sauce.

— **Artagnan:** filled with mushroom purée mixed with egg yolks, diced artichoke bottoms sautéd in butter and chopped parsley; sprinkled with grated Parmesan, browned in oven; border of tomato sauce.

— **with Asparagus:** aux asperges: filled with white asparagus tips covered with Dutch sauce.

— **Bayard:** stuffed with gooseliver purée, coated entirely with chicken forcemeat, decorated with a truffle slice, butter dotted on top, finished off in moderate oven; border of Madeira sauce.

— **Bordeaux Style:** à la bordelaise: blanched, cooked in red wine and demi-glace, filled with diced blanched ox marrow, covered with the boiled down sauce; chopped parsley sprinkled on top.

— **Brussels Style:** à la bruxelloise: large bottoms, blanched, simmered in white wine and white stock; filled with tiny Brussels sprouts mixed with chopped ham and bound with demi-glace.

— **with Butter:** au beurre: blanched, simmered in butter and lemon juice, covered with the butter mixed with chopped parsley.

— **Castiglione:** filled with diced knob celery, truffles, cucumbers and asparagus tips bound with cream sauce.

— **Cavour:** boiled, drained, dipped in butter and grated Parmesan, placed in baking dish, browned in oven; covered with bubbling hot butter mixed with chopped hard-boiled eggs and anchovy essence.

— **Colbert:** very small bottoms put together with liver forcemeat mixed with duxelles, fixed on a skewer, dipped in frying batter, deep fried; Colbert sauce.

— **Cream of:**Crème de fonds d'artichauts: blanched, simmered in butter, rubbed through a sieve, mixed with half as much potato purée, finished off with butter and sweet cream.

— **in Cream Sauce:** à la crème: boiled, covered with light cream sauce bound with egg yolk, seasoned with Cayenne pepper.

— **Croquettes:** boiled, diced finely, bound with thick Béchamel and egg yolks; when cold shaped into small croquettes, dipped in egg and breadcrumbs, fried in deep fat.

Artichoke Bottoms

— **Cussy:** small bottoms filled with truffled gooseliver purée, coated with Villeroy sauce, dipped in egg and breadcrumbs, fried in deep fat; Madeira sauce.

— **Descartes:** filled with salpicon of calf's sweetbread, truffle and gooseliver bound with Madeira sauce.

— **Dubarry:** filled with cauliflower, covered with Mornay sauce, sprinkled with grated cheese, gratinated.

— **Fairy Queen:** Reine de fées: blanched, cooked in white stock, filled with cheese souffle mixed with diced chicken and crayfish tails, baked in oven.

— **with Fine Herbs:** aux fines herbes: blanched, simmered in demi-glace with chopped herbs.

— **Flemish Style:** à la flamande: filled with tiny carrot balls bound with German sauce.

— **Florence Style:** à la florentine: filled with chopped spinach simmered in butter with chopped onions and garlic, mixed with chopped anchovies and velouté; covered with Mornay sauce, sprinkled with grated Parmesan, glazed.

— **Fritters:** Beignets de fonds d'artichauts: small parboiled bottoms filled with duxelles, two bottoms put together, dipped in frying batter, fried in deep fat.

— **Gardner Style:** à la jardinière: filled with vegetable macedoine bound with cream sauce, chopped parsley sprinkled on top.

— **Georgette:** blanched, simmered in white stock with diced bacon and chopped herbs; filled with lamb brains, covered with Dutch sauce, decorated with blanched tarragon leaves.

— **Gourmet Style:** du gourmet: blanched, simmered in butter and lemon juice, filled with tomatoes concassées, a fried oyster placed on top.

— **Grandduke:** Grand-Duc: large bottoms filled with green asparagus tips bound with cream sauce; covered with Mornay sauce, glazed, a truffle slice dipped in liquid meat glaze on top.

— **Hungarian Style:** à la hongroise: 1. simmered in white wine on base of sliced carrots, onions and bacon waste, filled with chopped onions, mushrooms and red peppers, simmered in butter, flavored with garlic, bound with the thickened stock.
2. blanched, simmered in light paprika sauce.

— **Imperial Style:** à l'impériale: filled with green asparagus tips, covered with suprême sauce.

— **Italian Style:** à l'italienne: blanched, simmered in white wine and brown stock: stock reduced, mixed with Italian sauce, poured over bottoms.

— **Lucullus:** covered with demi-glace with Madeira mixed with truffle purée.

— **Lyonese Style:** à la lyonnaise: blanched, cut in quarters, cooked in white wine and brown stock with plenty of sliced onions browned in butter beforehand; chopped parsley sprinkled on top.

— **Maltese Style:** à la maltaise: boiled, covered with Maltese sauce.

— **Milanese Style:** à la milanaise: arranged in cocotte greased with butter, sprinkled generously with grated Parmesan, melted butter dropped on top, browned in oven.

Artichoke Bottoms

— **Monico:** filled with mushroom purée bound with egg yolks and mixed with stiffly beaten egg white, sprinkled with cheese, baked in oven.

— **Montault:** blanched, simmered in Madeira and meat glaze, filled with chopped ham bound with Madeira sauce, decorated with sliced mushrooms; arranged like a crown on service dish with buttered asparagus tips in the center.

— **Mornay:** coated with Mornay sauce, sprinkled with grated Parmesan, butter dropped on top, gratinated.

— **Nice Style:** à la niçoise: blanched, simmered in oil and white wine with chopped shallots, diced tomatoes and chopped anchovy fillets; served in the stock with chopped tarragon sprinkled on top.

— **in Oil:** à l'huile: blanched, simmered in white wine and oil with chopped onions, seasoned with lemon juice, served cold in the stock.

— **Piedmont Style:** à la piemontaise: filled with risotto mixed with grated Italian truffles; border of tomato sauce.

— **Polish Style:** à la polonaise: filled with chopped hard-boiled eggs, covered with breadcrumbs browned in plenty of butter.

— **Poulette:** boiled, cut in quarters, served with poulette sauce.

— **Princess Style:** à la princesse: filled with green asparagus tips, a flat round chicken dumpling and a truffle slice on top, covered with suprême sauce.

— **Purée of:** Purée de fonds d'artichauts: blanched, simmered in butter and lemon juice, rubbed through a sieve, bound with very thick velouté.

— **Queen Style:** à la reine: filled with chicken purée, covered with suprême sauce, a truffle slice on top.

— **Rachel:** filled with a large blanched slice of ox marrow, covered with Bordeaux sauce.

— **Ristori:** small bottoms filled with risotto mixed with diced sautéd chicken livers, truffles and grated Parmesan, put together, dipped in egg and breadcrumbs, deep fried; tomato sauce served separately.

— **Sagan:** filled with purée of calf's brains mixed with egg yolk, chopped herbs and grated Parmesan; baked in oven.

— **Siberian Style:** à la sibirienne: cold bottoms covered with mayonnaise mixed with mustard, chopped hard-boiled eggs, tarragon, chervil, capers and pickled cucumbers.

— **Sicilian Style:** à la sicilienne: large bottoms filled with macaroni cut in small pieces, bound with supreme sauce mixed with purée of chicken livers, butter and grated Parmesan; sprinkled with grated Parmesan, browned in oven.

— **Spanish Style:** à l'espagnole: filled with chopped red peppers simmered in butter with chopped onion, bound with demi-glace.

— **Stanley:** simmered in white wine with butter, blanched sliced onions, raw ham and light Béchamel sauce, when done sauce reduced with heavy cream, strained, blended with butter and poured over the bottoms; chopped boiled ham scattered on top.

— **with Tarragon Sauce:** à l'estragon: boiled, covered with tarragon sauce mixed with chopped tarragon.

Artichoke Bottoms

— **Trieste Style:** à la triestaine: blanched, simmered in oil with water, sliced onions and parsley roots, seasoned with lemon juice.

— **Turkish Style:** à la turque: filled with hashed mutton mixed with chopped fried onions, bound with tomato sauce.

— **Vegetable-Gardner Style:** à la maraîchère: blanched, sweated in oil with chopped onions, white of leeks, diced tomatoes, garlic und new potatoes shaped like the bottoms, moistened with white wine, seasoned, covered with sweated in oil with chopped onions, white of leeks, diced cover on.

— **Venetian Style:** à la venitienne: blanched, simmered in butter, covered with Venetian sauce.

— **Villeroi:** boiled, when cold cut in quarters, coated with Villeroi sauce, dipped in egg and breadcrumbs, deep fried, served with fried parsley.

Asparagus; F. Asperge; G. Spargel: the young stalks sprouting from the roots of the asparagus plant, cultivated in many varieties. White asparagus is grown deep and cut before it reaches the surface, the green stalks are grown above the ground. The very thin green asparagus tips are used as a garnish, salad, filling for omelette and as a decoration. Asparagus is peeled carefully, all the stalks cut in equal length, bundled, tied and boiled in salt water. They are usually served on a napkin or a special asparagus holder.

Thin green asparagus tips: the tips are broken off about 2 inches long, tied in bundles, the ends as far as they are not tough cut in small pieces. They are then boiled in salt water, refreshed in cold water and tossed in butter.

— **Bern Style:** à la bernoise: boiled, drained, arranged in baking dish, tips covered with grated Gruyère, chopped fried onions and breadcrumbs, dotted with butter (stalks shielded with buttered paper), gratinated in oven.

— **Branches:** en branches: boiled in salt water, dressed on a napkin or special asparagus holder, served with melted butter, Dutch, mousseline, Chantilly or vinaigrette sauce.

— **with Butter:** au beurre: asparagus tips, boiled, drained, tossed lightly in melted butter.

— **with Carrots and Peas:** aux carottes et petits pois: white tips cut in small pieces, boiled, drained, mixed with freshly cooked green peas and cooked carrot balls, tossed in butter, seasoned, bound with German sauce.

— **Chilled:** glacées: boiled, drained, marinated in oil, vinegar, salt and pepper with chopped capers, pickles, chervil, tarragon and a few drops of Worcestershire sauce; served chilled.

— **Colbert:** green asparagus tips, boiled, drained, dressed on toast, covered with mousseline sauce, a small poached egg on top.

— **Creamed:** à la crème: cut in pieces, boiled, bound with cream sauce.

— **Don Carlos:** boiled, drained, allowed to cool off, covered with mayonnaise finished off with herb purée and a little aspic jelly, when set glazed with aspic jelly, served cold.

Asparagus

— **English Style:** à l'anglaise: end of stalk cut of, tips boiled, drained, placed on slice of buttered toast, covered with egg yolk mixed with melted butter.
— **with Fine Herbs:** aux fines herbes: white tips, scalded, cooked in white stock with diced bacon, seasoned, stock boiled down, served with chopped herbs scattered on top.
— **Flemish Style:** à la flamande: 1. served with mashed egg yolks beaten with melted butter.
2. served with melted butter and medium boiled eggs.
— **Friburg Style:** à la fribourgeoise: boiled, drained, grated Gruyere scattered over the tips, covered with melted butter.
— **Geneva Style:** à la génevoise: boiled, drained, arranged in layers with grated Gruyère cheese between the tip, grated cheese on top, covered with browned butter.
— **German Style:** à l'allemande: covered with breadcrumbs browned in a generous amount of butter.
— **Gratinated:** au gratin: same as Mornay.
— **with Gravy:** au jus: boiled, drained, tips covered with thick veal gravy.
— **Ideal Style:** à l'idéale: served with mousseline sauce mixed with a little tomato purée.
— **Isigny:** boiled, drained, tips covered with butter mixed with raw egg yolk.
— **Italian Style:** à l'italienne: boiled, drained, arranged in greased baking dish, tips covered with grated Parmesan (stalks shielded with greased paper), melted butter dropped on top, gratinated.
— **Maltese Style:** à la maltaise: served with Maltese sauce.
— **Melba:** white tips, boiled, drained, covered with Melba sauce.
— **Milanese Style:** à la milanaise: same as Italian style.
— **Monselet:** white asparagus tips covered with thick veal gravy.
— **with Morels:** aux morilles: cut in pieces, boiled, drained, mixed with stewed morels, bound with butter sauce.
— **Mornay:** boiled, drained, arranged in greased baking dish, covered with Mornay sauce, sprinkled with grated cheese, dotted with butter, gratinated in oven.
— **with Oil:** à l'huile: served cold or luke warm with vinaigrette sauce with plenty of oil.
— **Orly:** tips of white asparagus, boiled, drained, dipped in frying batter, deep fried.
— **Piedmont Style:** à la piémontaise: same as Friburg Style.
— **Pompadour:** served with sauce made of oil, vinegar, chopped hard-boiled egg yolks, salt and pepper.
— **Princess Style:** à la princesse: boiled, served cold with mayonnaise finished off with whipped cream.
— **Sevilla Style:** à la sevillane: bottom and sides of a charlotte mould lined thickly with asparagus purée bound with chicken forcemeat, filled with cut cooked asparagus bound with cream sauce, sealed with asparagus purée, poached in water bath in oven; when done allowed to rest for a few minutes, turned out, covered with cream sauce mixed with julienne of red peppers, sprinkled with cheese and glazed.
— **Siberian Style:** à la sibirienne: boiled, served cold with Gribiche sauce separately.

Asparagus

— **Spanish Style:** à l'espagnole: boiled, garnished with eggs poached in the asparagus water; vinaigrette sauce served separately.

— **Tips in Butter:** au beurre: green tips, boiled, seasoned with salt and a pinch of sugar, tossed quickly in hot melted butter.

— **Tips, Creamed:** à la créme: same preparation as with butter, served in timbale dish with a border of heavy cream poured around.

— **Tips Imperial Style:** à l'impériale: green tips, boiled, drained, placed on buttered toast, covered with light Dutch sauce, truffle julienne scattered on top.

— **Tips Royal Style:** à la royale: boiled, drained, mixed with half the amount of course truffle julienne, bound with German sauce.

— **Tips with smoked Salmon:** au saumon fumé: boiled, bound with cream sauce, served with thin slices of smoked salmon.

— **Tips with Virgin Sauce:** Pointes d'asperges à la sauce vierge: green tips, boiled, drained, covered with virgin sauce.

— **Villeroi:** white tips, boiled, coated with **Villeroi sauce**, dipped in egg and breadcrumbs, deep fried.

— **Westphalian Style:** à la westphalienne: boiled, thin slices of raw Westphalian ham and melted butter served separately.

Asparagus Bean; F. Haricot asperge; G. Spargelbohne: a slender green snap bean native of South America and grown extensively in the U. S. A. Prepared like green beans.

Asperge: see asparagus.

Aubergine: see eggplant.

B

Bamia: see gombo.

Barley, Pearled; F. Orge perlé; G. Perlgraupen: a small variety of barley with both the inner and outer husk removed and polished. Prepared like risotto.

— **with Vegetables:** aux légumes: parboiled, cooked in bouillon with diced knob celery, carrots and onions.

— **Italian Style:** à l'italienne: prepared like risotto, mixed with tomato sauce; grated Parmesan served separately.

— **with Pears:** aux poires: blanched, cooked in bouillon with cubes of rather hard pears, seasoned, served covered with diced fried lean bacon.

Batata: see sweet potato.

Bean, Broad, Large Bean, Large Lima bean; F. Fève de marais; G. Puffbohne, Saubohne: beans grown in a fuzzy pod. They should be eaten as long as they are quite small, when they get older the seeds or beans of the pod grow a parchment skin which grows thicker and tougher every day. In this case the skin must be removed after they have been blanched.

— **with Bacon:** au lard: chopped onions fried lightly in butter, blanched diced bacon added, dredged with flour,

Bean, Broad
lightly browned, moistened with stock, cooked beans added, simmered for a while.
— **Breton Style:** à la bretonne: prepared like navy beans.
— **with Butter:** au beurre: cooked, drained, seasoned, tossed in butter.
— **Creamed:** à la crème: blanched, simmered in butter, finished off with cream.
— **English Style:** à l'anglaise: boiled in salt water, drained, served with a pad of fresh butter on top.
— **German Style:** à l'allemande: cooked, mixed with diced cooked carrots, moistened with bouillon, seasoned, mixed with chopped parsley and summer savory, thickened with butterpaste.
— **Greek Style:** à la grecque: blanched, simmered in oil with chopped onions, moistened with a little water, cooked, seasoned with salt and a pinch of sugar; served cold flavored with lemon juice.
— **Janina:** blanched, simmered in mutton fat with chopped onions and diced tomatoes, mixed with hashed mutton.
— **Mashed:** en purée: cooked, mashed, finished off with cream and butter.
— **Westphalian Style:** à la westphalienne: cooked, mixed with fried diced bacon and chopped parsley, bound with velouté sauce, boiled up, seasoned with salt and pepper.

Beans, Butter: Haricots Mange-tout: a French bean of which the pods have no lining membrane so that they may be eaten whole with their fully grown seeds. Chiefly boiled and tossed in butter.

Beans, Frijole: Haricots Frijole: reddish brown beans from Mexico and the Southwest of the U. S. A. marketed fresh and dried. Prepared like navy beans.
— **Feyjar mechada:** Brasilian Style: boiled, drained, mixed with chopped fried onions and beef stock, thickened with tapioca; fried in skillet like a pancake. (Brasilian)

Beans, Green, French Beans, String Beans; F. Haricots verts; Grüne Bohnen: the green pods of an annual plant with many varieties. Boiled in salt water and well drained before further use or simmered in own juice with a little butter in casserole with the cover on.
— **Austrian Style:** Eingebrannte Fisolen: diced, boiled, drained; chopped onions sweated in butter, sprinkled with flour, moistened with white stock and sour cream, boiled, seasoned, mixed with chopped parsley and dill, a dash of vinegar added; beans boiled up in this sauce. (Austrian)
— **with Bacon:** au lard: boiled, tossed in butter mixed with fried diced bacon.
— **Belgian Style:** à la belge: diced bacon and chopped onions lightly browned in butter, blanched green beans added, seasoned, covered with brown stock, cooked, thickened with butter paste; chopped parsley on top.
— **Broken:** concassées: broken in pieces, boiled, tossed in butter with chopped parsley.
— **with Brown Butter:** au beurre noisette boiled, drained, covered with brown butter, sprinkled with chopped parsley.
— **with Butter:** au beurre: boiled, drained, tossed in butter.
— **with Carrots:** aux carottes: broken in pieces, mixed with small new carrots, tossed in butter or bound with light Béchamel sauce.

Beans, Green

— **in Cream Sauce:** à la sauce crème: boiled, drained, bound with light Béchamel sauce finished off with cream.
— **English Style:** à l'anglaise: boiled, well drained, served with a piece of fresh butter on top.
— **French Style:** à la française: parboiled, drained, simmered in butter and lemon juice with chopped parsley.
— **German Style:** à l'allemande: blanched; chopped onions sweated in butter, sprinkled with flour, moistened with white stock, seasoned; beans cooked in this sauce until done.
— **Hotelier Style:** à l'hôtelière: boiled, mixed with velouté flavored with garlic and a dash of vinegar, sprinkled with chopped parsley.
— **Hungarian Style:** à la hongroise: shredded, blanched, simmered in lard with chopped onions, cooked in paprika sauce.
— **Jewish Style:** à la juive: cut in strips, simmered in water and goose fat, seasoned with salt, pepper, cloves, grated lemon peel, vinegar, cinnamon, sugar and lemon juice, thickened with brown roux, flavored with red wine.
— **Judias verdes a la Campesina:** Spanish Style: parboiled, mixed with diced ham, chopped onions and a little crushed garlic, simmered in oil. (Spanish)
— **Lyonese Style:** à la lyonnaise: boiled, drained, bound with demi-glace mixed with fried sliced onions; chopped parsley scattered on top.
— **Mecklenburg Style:** à la mecklenbourgeoise: blanched, cooking finished in light Béchamel sauce mixed with chopped parsley and summer savory.
— **Mixed:** panachés: half small boiled green beans and half green haricot beans, drained, mixed, tossed in butter, sprinkled with chopped parsley.
— **North German Style:** Norddeutsche Art: parboiled simmered in light velouté mixed with chopped parsley. (German)
— **with Parmesan:** au parmesan: large whole beans, boiled, drained, sprinkled generously with grated Parmesan, covered with browned butter.
— **with Pears:** aux poires: diced, simmered in butter and white stock with diced raw pears and potatoes, seasoned with salt, a pinch of sugar and cinnamon; served in the stock thickened with butterpaste.
— **Polish Style:** à la polonaise: large boiled beans prepared like cauliflower.
— **with Poulette sauce:** à la poulette: boiled, drained, bound with poulette sauce.
— **Purée of:** Purée de haricots verts: boiled, drained, rubbed through a sieve, mixed with a little purée of green haricot beans, seasoned, finished off with butter and cream.
— **Shredded:** ciselés: shredded, boiled, drained, tossed in butter or bound with light cream sauce; chopped parsley sprinkled on top.
— **with Sorrel:** à l'oseille: boiled, drained, mixed with shredded sorrel cooked in butter.
— **Steward Style:** à la maître d'hôtel: boiled, drained, tossed in herb butter.
— **with Tomatoes:** aux tomates: largely diced tomatoes, seasoned, simmered in butter, mixed with boiled green beans tossed in butter, mixed with chopped parsley.

Beans, Green

— **Tours Style:** à la tourangelle: blanched, cooked in light cream sauce, mixed with chopped parsley and very little garlic.

Beans, Green Haricot: Haricots Flageolets: sort of small green Lima bean marketed fresh, dried and canned. Prepared like navy beans.

— **Purée Musard:** boiled, drained, rubbed through a sieve, finished off with butter and cream.

Beans, Lima: a native of South America, grown extensively in California and Florida. Prepared like navy beans.

— **Succotash:** Lima beans and sweet corn buttered or creamed.

Beans, Navy, Kidney or White Haricot; F. Haricots blancs; G. weiße Bohnen: haricot beans are the seeds of different strains of French beans. They are marketed fresh or dried. If dried they must be soaked for a few hours before boiling. They are usually boiled in light salt water with pot herbs, a larded onion and a ham bone or bacon waste.

— **American Style:** à l'américaine: cooked with a piece of bacon; mixed with the diced bacon, bound with tomato sauce.

— **Austrian Style:** Eingebrannte Fisolen: boiled, thickened with white roux with chopped onions, flavored with a little vinegar. (Austrian)

— **Boston Baked:** parboiled with salt pork, placed in earthenware pot with the scored pork, covered with water mixed with brown sugar, molasses and mustard, baked in slow oven, uncovered to brown beans during the last half hour.

— **Brasilian Style:** à la brésilienne: drained beans mixed with tomatoes concassées and small croûtons fried in butter, a few spoonfuls of the bean stock added, simmered for a few minutes.

— **Breton Style:** à la bretonne: drained, seasoned, bound with Breton sauce; chopped parsley on top.

— **with Butter:** au beurre: drained, seasoned, mixed with chopped parsley, a piece of fresh butter placed on top.

— **with Carrots:** au carottes: parboiled, drained, mixed with diced parboiled carrots, simmered in fat mutton stock.

— **with Chervil:** au cerfeuil: boiled, drained, seasoned, tossed in butter with chopped chervil.

— **in Cream Sauce:** à la crème: drained, bound with cream sauce.

— **with Dutch Sauce:** à la sauce hollandaise: drained, bound with light Dutch sauce; chopped parsley on top.

— **English Style:** à l'anglaise: boiled, drained, a piece of fresh butter on top.

— **with Garlic:** à l'ail: parboiled with garlic, drained, simmered with chopped parsley and goose greaves.

— **German Style:** à l'allemande: drained, bound with German sauce.

— **Gratinated:** au gratin: drained, bound with demi-glace, filled in greased baking dish, covered with breadcrumbs, melted butter dropped on top, gratinated in oven.

— **with Gravy:** au jus: drained, mixed with thick veal gravy.

— **Indian Style:** à l'indienne: tossed in butter, bound with curry sauce.

Beans, Navy

— **Italian Style:** à l'italienne: parboiled, simmered in demi-glace with fried diced bacon, chopped onions and leeks.

— **Lyonese Style:** à la lyonnaise: drained, seasoned, tossed in butter with sliced onions fried in butter beforehand.

— **Peruvian Style:** à la péruvienne: parboiled, drained, mixed with cream sauce; placed in greased baking dish alternately with sliced boiled potatoes and chopped sweated onions, last layer boiled potatoes, covered with cream sauce, baked in oven.

— **with Potatoes:** aux pommes de terre: parboiled, drained, mixed with potato cubes, simmered in demi-glace.

— **Provencal Style:** à la provençale: parboiled, simmered in oil with diced tomatoes, chopped anchovy fillets and a little garlic; capers scattered on top.

— **Purée of:** Purée de haricots blancs: boiled, strained, rubbed through a sieve, seasoned, finished off with butter and cream.

— **Purée Breton:** Purée bretonne: purée mixed with Breton sauce.

— **Robert:** boiled, drained, bound with brown onion sauce.

— **Steward Style:** à la maître d'hôtel: boiled, drained, tossed in butter with chopped parsley, seasoned with salt, pepper and lemon juice.

— **with Tomatoes:** aux tomates: parboiled, drained, mixed with chopped lightly fried onions, butter and diced tomatoes, simmered for a few minutes.

— **Viennese Style:** à la viennoise: drained, covered with breadcrumbs browned in a generous amount of butter.

— **Westphalian Style:** à la westphalienne: boiled, drained, mixed with apple wedges cooked in water with butter and a pinch of sugar; bound with brown roux with chopped onions, seasoned with nutmeg, filled in service dish, breadcrumbs browned in butter on top.

Beans, Red Kidney: Haricots rouges: marketed dried and canned. Dried beans soaked in water, boiled in half water and half red wine with a larded onion, carrot, bunch of herbs and salt. Prepared like Navy beans.

— **with Bacon:** au lard: drained, mixed with butter, diced fried bacon and glazed button onions.

— **Burgundy Style:** à la bourguignonne: parboiled, simmered in red wine with browned button onions, diced fried bacon, tiny parboiled carrots and chopped herbs, thickened lightly with butter paste.

— **Stewed:** étuvés: parboiled, stewed in red wine with butter, seasoning and button onions browned beforehand.

Beet, Red Beet, Beetroot; F. Betterave; G. Rote Rübe: name of a large variety of roots grown for their sugar (beet-sugar) and for cattle fodder; the small crimson-red kind is used as a vegetable or salad when cooked.

— **American Style:** à l'américaine: boiled, sliced, bound with butter sauce, flavored with vinegar.

— **Bordeaux Style:** à la bordelaise: boiled, sliced, sautéd in oil with finely chopped onions, bound with red wine saucc.

— **Buttered:** au beurre: chopped onions simmered in butter until done, boiled sliced beets added, seasoned with salt and pepper, tossed in the butter, flavored with a dash of vinegar.

Beet

— **Buttered, and Celery:** et céleri au beurre: same as buttered beets with an equal amount of chopped cooked celery added.

— **with Caraway:** au cumin: boiled, sliced, marinated in vinegar, bound with velouté flavored with white caraway seeds.

— **Creamed:** à la crème: boiled, olive-shaped, seasoned, bound with cream sauce.

— **Croquettes:** boiled, peeled, diced finely, heated up in butter, bound with thick Béchamel sauce and egg yolks, seasoned with salt, mustard powder and a dash of vinegar; allowed to cool off, shaped into croquettes of the desired shape, dipped in egg and breadcrumbs, deep fried.

— **Farmer Style:** à la paysanne: boiled, sliced, mixed with sliced fried onions, bound with cream sauce.

— **in Mustard Sauce:** à la sauce moutarde: boiled, cut in cubes, bound with mústard sauce flavored with vinegar.

— **Old Fashioned Style:** à l'ancienne: boiled, peeled, sliced, simmered in butter with chopped onions, bound with butter sauce, flavored with vinegar.

— **in Orange Sauce:** à la sauce orange: cooked, olive-shaped, simmered in butter, seasoned with salt, pepper and sugar, moistened with half water and half orange juice, grated orange peel added, thickened with cornstarch, cooked for a few minutes.

— **Polish Style:** à la polonaise: boiled, sliced, simmered in butter with salt, pepper, sugar, vinegar and cloves.

— **Russian Style:** à la russe: boiled, sliced, simmered in butter, chopped mint added shortly before serving.

— **Sautéd:** sautées: boiled, sliced, sautéd in butter.

— **Spiced:** épicées: chopped onions simmered in butter, boiled sliced beets added, moistened with water, seasoned with salt, pepper, sugar, vinegar, powdered cloves and cinnamon, cooked until moisture is nearly evaporated.

— **Stewed:** étuvées: parboiled, olive-shaped, simmered in butter.

Bette: see mangold.

Betterave: see red beet.

Blé vert: see green kern.

Blette: see chard.

Blini: Russian Pancake: a very small pancake made of half wheat and half buckwheat flour, yeast, butter, milk and stiffly beaten egg whites, served as an appetizer but also with meat, poultry and game. Blini are always served with smetana (sour cream).

— **Livonian Style:** à la livonienne: made of buckwheat flour, egg yolks, milk and stiffly beaten egg whites.

Boletus, Edible: F. Cèpe; G. Steinpilz: a large fungus with a thick, white stem and a head with a large rounded cap yellowish to warm brown in color, the tubes are white to green-grey. This very fine mushroom is a native of Central and Northern Europe and is marketed fresh, dried and canned.

— **Bordeaux Style:** à la bordelaise: sliced, sautéd in hot oil with chopped shallots, seasoned, mixed with chopped parsley, a little lemon juice added.

Boletus

— **Creamed:** à la crème: sliced, simmered in butter with chopped onion, cream added, seasoned, boiled down, served in timbale dish.

— **Cutlet:** Cotelette de cèpes: chopped, simmered in butter with chopped onions, seasoned, mixed with bread soaked in water, eggs and breadcrumbs; allowed to cool off, cutlet-shaped, dipped in egg and breadcrumbs, fried in butter.

— **Fried:** frites: caps, cooked, allowed to cool off, seasoned, dipped in frying batter, deep fried.

— **Gratinated:** au gratin: sliced, sautéd in oil with chopped onions and diced tomatoes, filled in greased baking dish, sprinkled with breadcrumbs, dotted with butter, gratinated in oven.

— **Grilled:** grillées: large caps marinated in oil with chopped onions and garlic, dried, dipped in clarified butter, grilled, served with herb butter.

— **Harlequin Style:** à l'arlequin: diced carrots and knob celery fried lightly in butter with chopped onions, moistened with white wine and cooked, mixed with sliced sautéd boletus, chopped chervil and seasoning, bound lightly with tomato sauce.

— **Italian Style:** à l'italienne: sliced, sautéd, bound with Italian sauce.

— **Moldavian Style:** à la moldavienne: sliced, sautéd in oil with chopped shallots, simmered in sour cream, chopped fennel greens and chives added.

— **Northern Style:** à la nordique: sliced, sautéd in oil, seasoned, dredged lightly with flour, moistened with white stock and sour cream, cooked.

— **Piedmont Style:** à la piémontaise: caps stuffed with duxelles prepared with the chopped stems, garlic and chopped parsley.

— **Provencal Style:** à la provençale: same as Bordeaux style with chopped garlic added.

— **Russian Style:** à la russe: sliced, simmered in butter with chopped onions, sour cream added, cooked, finished off with chopped fennel and parsley.

— **Sautéd:** sautées: sliced, sautéd in half butter and half oil with chopped shallots, chopped parsley added.

— **Stuffed:** farcies: caps, stuffed with the chopped stems sautéd in butter with chopped onions, seasoned, a little tomato sauce and chopped parsley added, thickened with breadcrumbs; caps placed on greased baking sheet sprinkled with breadcrumbs, oil dropped on top, browned in oven.

— **Toulouse Style:** à la toulousaine: sliced, sautéd in butter and oil with chopped onions, shallots and garlic, mixed with diced fried ham and tomatoes concassées.

Brionne: see chayotte.

Broccoli: F. Brocoli; G. Spargelkohl: a vegetable, native of Southern Europe, developed by cultivation from the cabbage plant, and similar to cauliflower but deep green. Grown extensively in the U. S. A., marketed all the year fresh and frozen. Prepared like cauliflower.

— **with Butter:** au beurre: boiled, drained, served covered with browned butter and a few drops of vinegar.

Broccoli
— **with Dutch Sauce:** à la sauce hollandaise. boiled, served covered with Dutch sauce.
— **Italian Style:** à l'italienne: sprigs, parboiled, simmered in meat gravy, gravy finished off with anchovy butter.
— **Lille Style:** à la lilloise: sprigs, scalded, simmered in butter with chopped onions, chopped parsley scattered on top.
— **Polish Style:** à la polonaise: prepared like cauliflower.
— **Roman Style:** à la romaine: sprigs, parboiled, drained, dipped in unsweetened pancake batter, deep fried, served with lemon wedges.

Brussels Sprouts: F. Choux de Bruxelles; G. Rosenkohl, Sprossenkohl: a variety of cabbage cultivated for its sprouts, which shoot from the axils of the leaves along the stems.
— **with Butter:** au beurre: boiled, drained, tossed in butter.
— **with Brown Butter:** au beurre noisette: cooked in salt water, drained, covered with browned butter, chopped parsley scattered on top.
— **with Chestnuts:** aux marrons: cooked, drained, tossed in butter, garnished with glazed chestnuts.
— **Creamed:** à la crème: cooked, drained, chopped coarsely, simmered in butter, seasoned, cooking finished in heavy cream.
— **English Style:** à l'anglaise: cooked in salt water, drained, served with fresh butter on top.
— **Grandmother Style:** à la grand'mère: cooked, drained, sautéd in butter with chopped fried onions and diced bacon; covered with very small croûtons fried in a generous amount of butter.
— **Gratinated:** au gratin: cooked, drained, filled in greased baking dish, covered with Mornay sauce, sprinkled with grated cheese, dotted with butter, gratinated.
— **Housewife Style:** à la bonne-femme: parboiled, drained, simmered in butter, seasoned, chopped parsley scattered on top.
— **Italian Style:** à l'italienne: cooked in salt water, drained, arranged in timbale dish, grated Parmesan sprinkled on top, covered with chopped anchovy fillets lightly fried in browned butter.
— **Limoux Style:** à la limousine: cooked, drained, mixed with cooked, coarsely chopped chestnuts and simmered in butter for a while.
— **Milanese Style:** à la milanaise: cooked, drained, filled in greased baking dish, covered with Italian sauce mixed with tomatoes concassées, sprinkled with grated Parmesan, oil dropped on top, gratinated in oven.
— **Polish Style:** à la polonaise: cooked, drained, covered with breadcrumbs browned in plenty of butter.
— **Purée of:** en purée: cooked, drained, strained, mixed with a small amount of mashed potatoes, finished off with butter and cream.

C

Cabbage, Red: F. Chou-rouge; G. Rotkohl: a purple variety of cabbage, native of China, but now grown all over the world. It is usually shredded raw and stewed with pork

Cabbage, Red

or goose fat, ham or bacon waste, without being blanched beforehand.

— **Alsatian Style:** à l'alsacienne: stewed in red wine with lard, seasoned with salt and sugar; garnished with braised chestnuts.

— **with Apples:** aux pommes fruits: stewed in fat stock with peeled and sliced apples, seasoned, thickened with butter-paste.

— **Berlin Style:** à la berlinoise: scalded, drained, stewed with sliced onions and apples, sweated in goose or pork fat beforehand, in bouillon, seasoned with salt, sugar, allspice, cinnamon and vinegar, thickened with cornstarch, a little red currant jelly added shortly before serving.

— **Brasilian Style:** à la brésilienne: shredded, stewed in stock with chopped onions, diced bacon and a piece of fat pork; the carved pork placed on top at serving.

— **Chef Style:** à la manière du chef: sliced onions fried lightly in goose fat, shredded scalded red cabbage added, simmered for a few minutes, dredged with flour, moistened with red wine and bouillon, seasoned with salt and pinch of cinnamon, a piece of lean bacon added, braised; when done mixed with a few spoonfuls of apple purée, served mixed with the diced bacon.

— **Dutch Style:** à la hollandaise: chopped onions sweated in butter, moistened with water, chopped red cabbage and diced apples added, seasoned with vinegar, salt, cloves, allspice and sugar, stewed.

— **Flemish Style:** à la flamande: braised in butter and bouillon with chopped onions, apple slices and sugar.

— **German Style:** à l'allemande: simmered in lard with sliced onions and bouillon, seasoned with allspice and juniper berries.

— **Greek Style:** à la grecque: shredded, simmered in mutton fat with chopped onions, shredded lettuce, diced red peppers, peas, a smoked sausage and very little mutton stock; served with the sliced sausage on top.

— **Housewife Style:** à la bonne-femme: stewed with diced lean bacon, tomato purée, fat stock and seasoning.

— **Limoux Style:** à la limousine: braised in bouillon with lard, garnished with braised chestnuts.

— **Pomeranian Style:** à la pommeranienne: scalded, braised in water with lard, apple slices and caraway seeds, seasoned with salt, sugar and vinegar.

— **with Prunes:** aux pruneaux: simmered in fat bouillon with prunes and seasoning, thickened with butterpaste.

— **Russian Style:** à la russe: shredded, mixed with sliced onions, shredded knob celery and parsley roots, moistened with fat stock, seasoned with vinegar, sugar, allspice and cloves, stewed, thickened with cornstarch.

— **Steeple-chase Style:** à la grande-chasse: shredded, simmered in lard, moistened with hot vinegar, dredged with flour, apple slices and red wine added, seasoned with salt, pepper, caraway seeds and sugar, braised until done.

— **Valenciennes Style:** à la valenciennes: braised in bouillon with lard, diced fried bacon, apple slices and salt; served with fried chipolatas.

Cabbage, Red

— **Westphalian Style:** à la westphalienne: shredded, braised in butter, bouillon and red wine with sliced fried onions and a ham bone; flavored with vinegar at serving.

Cabbage, Savoy; F. Chou-vert; G. Wirsingkohl: a curly leaved cabbage native of Western Europe and now grown all over the world. Prepared like white cabbage.

— **Braised:** braisé: cut in quarters, scalded, braised in fat stock with chopped onions and diced bacon, covered with demi-glace.

— **Bremen Style:** à la bremoise: scalded, chopped, simmered in goose fat with a little water and chopped onions, seasoned with cloves, salt and sugar, thickened with butterpaste.

— **English Style:** à l'anglaise: cut in quarters, the stalk cut out, boiled in salt water, drained, pressed between two plates, cut in pieces, covered with melted butter.

— **French Style:** à la française: cut in quarters, scalded, braised in fat stock with bacon, a larded onion and a carrot.

— **Magdebourg Style:** à la magdebourgeoise: cut in quarters, scalded, braised in fat stock, served covered with breadcrumbs browned in butter.

— **Sou-fassu:** Stuffed: whole head blanched, refreshed, the inner leaves removed, chopped, mixed with chopped blanched mangold, diced fried bacon, chopped lightly fried onions, pork sausage meat, tomatoes concassées, fresh green peas, blanched rice, garlic and seasoning; cabbage reformed, tied in a greased cloth, cooked in bouillon for 3 to 4 hours.

Cabbage Turnip: F. Chou-rave; G. Kohlrabi: a hybrid of the cabbage family with a tuber growing above the ground. Young quickly grown cabbage turnips are excellent, the older ones often woody and hollow. The leaves are cooked separately like spinach and added to the stewed or boiled cabbage-turnips.

— **Austrian Style:** à l'autrichienne: peeled, sliced, boiled, the boiled chopped leaves added, mixed with chopped onions, thickened with white roux, moistened with bouillon, seasoned, stewed.

— **Bavarian Style:** à la bavaroise: boiled, rubbed through a sieve, thickened with white roux, moistened with white stock, seasoned with salt and nutmeg, stewed in oven.

— **Creamed:** à la crème: peeled, sliced, parboiled, simmered in butter and cream.

— **Czech Style:** à la tchèque: peeled, sliced, cooked in pale beer with a pinch of sugar, thickened with pale roux.

— **Gratinated:** au gratin: sliced, boiled, drained, filled in baking dish greased with butter, covered with Mornay sauce, sprinkled with grated cheese, dotted with butter, gratinated.

— **Homely Style:** à la chez-soi: parboiled, sliced, simmered in butter, a pinch of sugar, salt and a little of the water in which the tubers have been boiled added, thickened with butterpaste, mixed with the boiled chopped leaves.

— **Hungarian Style:** à la hongroise: parboiled, simmered in paprika sauce.

— **Russian Style:** à la russe: peeled, sliced, parboiled, simmered in butter and sour cream, sprinkled with chopped parsley; served with slices of smoked sausage.

Cabbage Turnip

— **Stuffed:** farcis: small equal-sized cabbage turnips peeled, boiled, a lid cut off, hollowed out, the pulp chopped finely, mixed with the boiled chopped leaves, fried chopped onions, breadcrumbs, butter and seasoning, filled in the turnips, sprinkled with breadcrumbs, melted butter dropped on top, browned in oven.

— **Viennese Style:** à la viennoise: diced, parboiled, simmered in butter with a pinch of sugar, sprinkled with flour, moistened with bouillon and boiled up.

Cabbage, White; F. Chou-blanc; G. Weisskohl: a native of Asia and Western Europe grown for its leaves. Used raw as a salad, in soups and chiefly as a vegetable.

— **with Apples:** aux pommes fruits: shredded, mixed with shredded red cabbage, simmered in water and butter, mixed with sliced apples, cooked, seasoned with salt, sugar and vinegar.

— **Bayrisch Kraut:** Bavarian Style: diced lean bacon and chopped onions sweated in butter, shredded cabbage added, seasoned with salt, vinegar, sugar, pepper and caraway seeds, moistened with water, stewed and thickened with pale brown roux. (German)

— **with Cheese:** au fromage: leaves boiled in salt water, drained, chopped coarsely, seasoned, filled in greased baking dish, covered with small very thin slices of Gruyère cheese, dotted generously with butter, baked in oven.

— **with Chestnuts:** aux marrons: shredded, sweated in lard with chopped onions, dredged with flour, moistened with bouillon and white wine, seasoned and stewed; served garnished or mixed with braised chestnuts.

— **Cole Slaw:** tender leaves shredded finely, seasoned with chopped onions, salt, pepper, oil and vinegar.

— **Coulibijaka of:** Coulibiac de chou: leaves boiled in salt water, drained, chopped, mixed with chopped onions sweated in butter and chopped dill and parsley, seasoned with salt and pepper; yeast dough rolled out thin, cut out to a large oval or square, filled with the cold cabbage mixture, covered with sliced hard-boiled eggs, a little melted butter poured on top, closed over the cabbage, brushed with egg yolk, a little hole left in the center to allow the steam to escape; decorated with fancy cut pieces of dough, brushed once more with egg yolk, allowed to raise, baked in fairly hot oven.

— **Creamed:** à la crème: shredded, cooked in white stock, drained, mixed with light cream sauce.

— **Dumplings:** Quenelles de chou-blanc: leaves, boiled in salt water, drained, remaining water pressed out, chopped, seasoned with salt and pepper, mixed with thick Béchamel and egg yolks, a little flour added; shaped into round dumplings, poached in salt water, drained, covered with browned butter.

— **English Style:** à l'anglaise: leaves boiled in salt water, drained, placed between two plates to press out the remaining water, cut in squares, served covered with melted butter.

— **French Style:** à la française: braised in fat stock with diced bacon, ham and chopped onions.

Cabbage, White

— **Italian Style:** à l'italienne: shredded, simmered for a while in oil, cooked in thin Italian sauce; garnished with braised chestnuts and slices of Zampino.

— **Lithuanian Style:** à la lithuanienne: shredded, cooked in bouillon with diced fried bacon, sliced peeled apples and chopped lightly fried onions; served with small slices of boiled beef.

— **Mexican Slaw:** same as cole slaw with chopped red and green peppers added.

— **Swabian Style:** à la souabe: shredded, braised in stock with chopped onions, mixed with soaked bread, beaten eggs, diced fried bacon and seasoning; filled in greased baking dish, baked in oven.

— **Spanish Style:** à l'espagnole: shredded, scalded, mixed with carrot strips, simmered in butter, stewed in bouillon with Madeira, chopped onions, parsley, thyme, garlic and a bayleaf.

— **Stuffed:** farci: whole leaves, blanched, the thick ribs cut out, filled with sausage stuffing, rolled together, braised on bed of sliced onions, carrots and bacon waste with fat stock; served covered with demi-glace, tomato or Madeira sauce.

— **Süsses Kraut:** Sweet Cabbage: shredded, cooked in bouillon with chopped onions, diced bacon and caraway seeds, seasoned with salt, sugar and vinegar. (Austrian)

— **Swiss Style:** à la suisse: shredded, simmered in butter with very little water until the cabbage is done and the moisture evaporated; filled in greased baking dish, covered with cream mixed with egg yolks, grated Emmenthal cheese, salt and nutmeg, baked in oven.

— **in White Wine:** au vin blanc: shredded, scalded, cooked in white wine with butter, sliced peeled apples, salt and sugar.

Cannelloni: a sort of tubular form of ravioli filled with chopped braised beef, calf's brain and chopped spinach bound with thick demi-glace, placed in greased baking dish, covered with thick veal gravy, sprinkled with grated Parmesan, oil dropped on top, gratinated in oven.

Carotte: see carrot.

Carrot; F. Carotte; G. Mohrrübe, Karotte: a native of Europe but now cultivated in every part of the world. Carrots are grown for their roots and there are many different varieties, some of them long and tapering and others short and round; the freshest and smallest are the best. Young small carrots may be left whole, old carrots which are apt to have a woody core may be cut out with an oval or round vegetable cutter or shaped with a knife like large olives.

— **Argenteuil Style:** à l'Argenteuil: fresh small carrots blanched, simmered in butter, seasoned, mixed with pieces of cooked asparagus.

— **with Boletus:** aux cèpes: cut in strips, simmered in butter and a little white stock, sliced boletus added, thickened with butterpaste.

— **with Butter:** au beurre: boiled in salt water, drained, tossed in fresh butter.

Carrot

— **Candied:** young carrots, cooked, drained, seasoned, placed in flat greased baking dish, dusted generously with sugar, dotted with butter, glazed in oven.

— **Creamed:** à la crème: prepared like glazed; when nearly done cream added and boiled down to the desired consistency.

— **Croquettes:** Croquettes de carottes: cooked, drained, mashed, mixed with butter, thick Béchamel sauce, egg yolks and seasoning; allowed to cool off, shaped into croquettes, dipped in egg and breadcrumbs, deep fried.

— **English Style:** à l'anglaise: 1. young carrots cooked in salt water, drained, pieces of fresh butter placed on top. 2. cooked in bouillon, mixed with milk, thickened with butter paste.

— **Farmer Style:** à la paysanne: cooked, drained, simmered in butter with diced fried bacon and glazed button onions.

— **with Fine Herbs:** aux fines herbes: glazed and mixed with chopped herbs shortly before serving.

— **Flemish Style:** à la flamande: sliced, simmered in butter and water, seasoned with pepper and salt, bound with egg yolks mixed with cream, chopped parsley added.

— **Fried:** frites: longish carrots cut in halves or quarters, blanched, coated with flour, fried in lard.

— **Glazed:** glacées: cooked in water with butter, salt and sugar until they are done, the moisture completely evaporated and the carrots glazed.

— **with Green Peas:** aux petits pois: diced, cooked, mixed with the same amount of cooked green peas, seasoned with salt and sugar, tossed in butter or bound with cream sauce.

— **Homely Style:** à la bourgeoise: simmered in butter with water, salt and a pinch of sugar, bound with butterpaste.

— **Housekeeper Style:** à la ménagère: cut in slices, cooked in bouillon and white wine with a bunch of herbs, salt, pepper and nutmeg; when done bunch removed, thickened with butter paste.

— **Lille Style:** à la lilloise: sliced, cooked in butter and water with pepper and salt, thickened with egg yolks and cream, chopped parsley added.

— **Marianne:** cut in strips, blanched, simmered in butter, mixed with the same amount of sliced sautéd fairy ring mushrooms, tossed in butter with chopped herbs and meat glaze.

— **Mashed:** en purée: cooked, drained, mashed, mixed with cream and butter, seasoned with salt and nutmeg, served covered with browned butter.

— **with Navy Beans:** aux haricots blancs: cut in small cubes, cooked in water with butter, mixed with cooked navy beans, thickened with butter paste.

— **Nevers Style:** à la nivernaise: olive shaped, simmered in butter and bouillon, seasoned with salt and sugar, cooked until the moisture is completely evaporated.

— **with Onions:** aux oignons: sliced carrots and onions fried lightly in butter, sprinkled with flour, moistened with bouillon, seasoned, cooked; thickened with egg yolks beaten with milk, flavored with vinegar, chopped parsley scattered on top.

Carrot

— **with Parsnips:** au panais: sliced carrots and parsnips cooked in white stock, thickened with pale brown roux.
— **Poulette:** cut in slices, blanched, simmered in butter, bound with poulette sauce.
— **Prussian Style:** à la prusse: diced, cooked in bouillon with butter, salt and a pinch of sugar; thickened with butter paste, plain boiled rice added shortly before serving.
— **Rhenish Style:** à la rhenanne: strips cooked in water and butter with prefried sliced onions; when done mixed carefully with sliced fried apples.
— **with Salsify:** aux salsifis: cut in large cubes, cooked, mixed with small pieces of cooked salsify, bound with cream sauce.
— **Soufflé:** cooked, strained, rubbed through a sieve, mixed with butter, cream and egg yolks, seasoned, stiffly beaten egg whites folded in, filled in greased soufflé dish, baked in oven.
— **Steward Style:** à la maître d'hôtel: cooked, drained, bound with Béchamel sauce, mixed with chopped parsley.
— **Sweet-Sour:** à l'aigre-doux: sugar burnt to light caramel with butter, young parboiled carrots added, deglaced with vinegar, stock and seasoning added, cooked, thickened with corn starch.
— **Vichy:** sliced, cooked with butter, if possible, in Vichy water, salt and sugar until glazed, chopped parsley scattered on top.
— **Viennese Style:** à la viennoise: cut in strips, blanched, cooked in bouillon with fried sliced onions, salt and sugar, thickened with pale brown roux, chopped parsley scattered on top.

Cardon: see cardoon.

Cardoon; F. Cardon; G. Kardi, Karde: a plant of the thistle family cultivated for the stems and roots. The main root is usually boiled, sliced and served as a salad, the stalks or ribs of the inner leaves are cleaned, the filaments removed, cut in 4 inch pieces and boiled in acidulated water with kidney fat to keep them white.
— **Andalusian Style:** à l'andalouse: parboiled, simmered in demi-glace and Port; placed in greased baking dish, covered with the sauce, sprinkled with breadcrumbs, dotted with butter, gratinated.
— **with Butter Sauce:** au maigre: parboiled, drained, served covered with white butter sauce.
— **Citizen Style:** à la bourgeoise: parboiled, simmered in butter and white stock with chopped onions and ham; stock thickened with butter paste, seasoned with lemon juice and poured over the cardoons.
— **in Cream Sauce:** à la crème: parboiled, simmered in butter, covered with cream sauce.
— **Fried:** à l'Orly: parboiled, drained, dipped in frying batter, deep fried; tomato sauce served separately.
— **Gratinated:** au gratin: parboiled, drained, placed in greased baking dish, covered with Mornay sauce, sprinkled with grated cheese, dotted with butter, gratinated in oven.
— **with Gravy:** au jus: parboiled, simmered in butter, covered with thick rich veal gravy.
— **Italian Style:** à l'italienne: parboiled, placed in baking dish, covered with Italian sauce, sprinkled with grated

Cardoon
Parmesan and breadcrumbs, oil dropped on top, gratinated in oven.
— **Milanese Style:** à la milanaise: parboiled, drained, arranged in layers with grated Parmesan between the layers, grated Parmesan on top, covered with browned butter.
— **Nevers Style:** à la nivernaise: cut in small pieces, parboiled, simmered in butter; mixed with olive-shaped carrots and turnips, bound with poulette sauce.
— **with Ox Marrow:** à la moelle: parboiled, drained, arranged with blanched slices of ox marrow on top, covered with demi-glace, chopped parsley sprinkled on top.
— **with Ox Marrow, Gratinated:** à la moelle gratinée: same as with ox marrow, sprinkled with grated cheese, gratinated.
— **Polish Style:** à la polonaise: parboiled, prepared like cauliflower.
— **with Poulette Sauce:** à la poulette: parboiled, simmered in butter and cream; sauce thickened with butter paste and egg yolks, seasoned with lemon juice.
— **Purée of:** Purée de cardons: parboiled, simmered in butter, rubbed through a sieve, mixed with mashed potatoes, finished off with butter and cream.
— **in Red Wine Sauce:** au vin rouge: parboiled, simmered in beef stock and red wine; stock thickened with butter paste, seasoned with lemon juice and poured over the cardoons.
— **Spanish Style:** à l'espagnole: parboiled, simmered in demi-glace with diced tomatoes and glazed button onions; bordered with fleurons.
— **Stewed:** étuvée: parboiled, simmered in light demi-glace with Sherry, seasoned with Cayenne pepper.

Cauliflower; F. Choux-Fleurs; G. Blumenkohl: a variety of the common cabbage or kale cultivated for its undeveloped flowers, not for its leaves, similar to Brocolli, but with a larger and more compact head. After the leaves have been removed and the stem cut even it is boiled in salt water. Cauliflower may also be grated and eaten raw or used for salads.
— **Cardinal Style:** à la cardinale: boiled, covered with cardinal sauce, sprinkled with grated Parmesan, gratinated.
— **with Crayfish Tails:** aux queues d'écrevisses: sprigs, boiled, drained, mixed with crayfish tails, bound with crayfish sauce.
— **with Cream Sauce:** à la sauce crème: boiled, covered with Béchamel sauce finished off with cream.
— **Dubarry:** Purée Dubarry: boiled, drained, rubbed through a sieve, mixed with mashed potatoes, finished off with butter and cream.
— **with Dutch Sauce:** à la sauce hollandaise: boiled, covered with Dutch sauce or sauce served separately.
— **English Style:** à l'anglaise: the small green leaves left on, boiled; melted butter served separately.
— **Florence Style:** à la florentine: boiled, arranged in greased baking dish on spinach leaves tossed in butter; covered with Mornay sauce, sprinkled with breadcrumbs and grated cheese, dotted with butter, gratinated.
— **French Style:** à la française: boiled, bastard sauce flavored with nutmeg served separately.

Cauliflower

— **Fried:** frite: sprigs, boiled, when cold dipped in frying batter, fried in deep fat.

— **Gratinated:** au gratin: boiled, covered with Mornay sauce, sprinkled with grated cheese, gratinated in oven.

— **Ignatieff:** same as Polish Style.

— **Italian Style:** à l'italienne: boiled springs, placed in greased baking dish, covered with Italian sauce mixed with diced tomatoes, sprinkled with grated Parmesan and breadcrumbs, gratinated in oven.

— **Milanese Style:** à la milanaise: boiled, placed in greased baking dish, covered generously with grated Parmesan, melted butter dropped on top, gratinated in oven, covered with browned butter at serving.

— **Polish Style:** à la polonaise: boiled, chopped hard-boiled eggs and parsley scattered on top, covered with breadcrumbs browned in plenty of butter.

— **Rebecca:** sprigs, parboiled, dipped in frying batter, deep fried; tomato sauce served separately.

— **Snagow Style:** Snagow: small red peppers cut open on top, seeds and filaments removed, blanched; filled with cauliflower sprigs, boiled, drained, bound with Béchamel sauce finished off with tomato purée flavored with garlic; sprinkled with grated cheese, browned in slow oven.

— **Soufflé of:** Soufflé de choux-fleurs: boiled, well drained, rubbed through a sieve, mixed with thick Béchamel sauce and egg yolks, seasoned, stiffly beaten egg whites added; filled in greased soufflé dish, baked.

— **Swiss Style:** à la suisse: boiled in half milk and half white stock with butter added; covered with sauce prepared with the thickened stock.

— **Victorine:** boiled, placed in greased baking dish, covered with Béchamel sauce finished off with crayfish butter, grated cheese sprinkled on top, dotted with melted crayfish butter, gratinated in oven.

— **Villeroi:** sprigs, boiled, drained, when cold coated with Villeroi sauce, dipped in egg and breadcrumbs, deep fried.

Celeriac: see knob celery.

Céleri en branches: see celery stalks.

Céleri-rave: see knob celery.

Celery, Knob, Celeriac; F. Céleri-rave; G. Knollensellerie: celery cultivated for its round turnip-like stem-base. The foliage is used for flavoring soups and stocks. Knob celery is used for salads, appetizers, soups and as a vegetable.

— **Braised:** braisé: parboiled, when half done peeled and sliced, cooking finished in thin Madeira sauce.

— **Creamed:** à la crème: olive-shaped or cut in cubes, cooked in white stock, seasoned, stock boiled down with cream.

— **Dutch Style:** à la hollandaise: olive-shaped, cooked in water, lemon juice and salt, drained, bound with light Dutch sauce.

— **Fried:** frit: boiled, peeled, cut in slices, dipped in frying batter, deep fried.

— **Fried Italian Style:** frit à l'italienne: parboiled, peeled, cut in small slices, seasoned, dipped in egg and breadcrumbs, deep fried; tomato sauce served separately.

Celery, Knob

— **with Gravy:** au jus: olive-shaped, cooked until half done, cooking finished in rich veal gravy.

— **Greek Style:** à la grecque: prepared like artichoke bottoms.

— **Italian Style:** à l'italienne: parboiled, when half done cut in slices, simmered in Italian sauce, chopped parsley scattered on top.

— **Mashed:** en purée: boiled, passed through a sieve, seasoned, finished off with butter and cream.

— **Meran Style:** à la méranienne: baking dish lined with thin slices of bacon, filled with raw slices of knob celery, seasoned, moistened with white stock, dotted with butter, braised in moderate oven; when nearly done sour cream added.

— **with Ox Marrow:** à la moelle: peeled, cut raw in thick slices, shaped like artichoke bottoms, cooked in white stock; drained, filled with brown onion purée, blanched ox marrow slices placed on top, sprinkled with chopped parsley.

— **with Parmesan:** au parmesan: boiled, sliced, filled in greased baking dish, covered with demi-glace, sprinkled generously with grated Parmesan, dotted with butter, gratinated in oven.

— **Spanish Style:** à l'espagnole: olive-shaped, scalded, cooked in demi-glace with chopped onions and diced tomatoes.

— **Villeroi:** boiled, peeled, cut into small convenient slices, coated with Villeroi sauce, dipped in egg and bread-crumbs, deep fried.

— **Vinaigrette:** boiled, peeled, sliced, served luke-warm or cold with vinaigrette sauce.

Celery, Stalk: F. Céleri en branches; Staudensellerie: vegetable, native of Europe, cultivated for its leaf-stalks, which must be bleached to be tender enough to be eaten. Used raw with cheese or in salads, stewed and braised. The green leaves and filaments removed, washed carefully, blanched and braised in fat stock.

— **Braised:** braisé: blanched, split lengthwise, folded, placed on sliced onions, carrots and bacon waste, moistened with fat stock, braised; drained, covered with Madeira sauce or demi-glace.

— **with Dutch Sauce:** à la sauce hollandaise: braised in white stock, drained, covered with light Dutch sauce.

— **Farmer Style:** à la paysanne: blanched, split lengthwise, folded, braised in thin demi-glace with diced fried bacon.

— **Fried:** frit: parboiled, cut in pieces, dipped in frying batter, deep fried.

— **Geneva Style:** à la génevoise: braised, drained, arranged in greased baking dish, covered with cream sauce, bread-crumbs and grated Gruyère sprinkled on top, melted butter poured over, gratinated in oven.

— **with Gravy:** au jus: blanched, split lengthwise, folded, braised in fat stock with sliced onions, carrots and bacon waste, drained, covered with thick veal gravy.

— **Hungarian Style:** à la hongroise: blanched, split lengthwise, folded, braised in white stock with lard, chopped onions, paprika and aniseed; stock strained, boiled down, mixed with paprika sauce and poured over the celery.

— **Italian Style:** à l'italienne: 1. small stalks, cut in two, braised in white stock, drained, arranged in layers with

Celery, Stalk

grated Parmesan between the layers and on top, covered with browned butter.

2. braised, served covered with Italian sauce.

— **with Madeira Sauce:** au sauce madère: braised, covered with Madeira sauce.

— **with Malaga Sauce:** à la sauce au malaga: braised, served with Malaga sauce.

— **with Ox Marrow:** à la moelle: braised, blanched ox marrow slices placed on top, covered with demi-glace and sprinkled with chopped parsley.

— **Spanish Style:** à l'espagnole: braised in demi-glace with chopped shallots, garlic and diced tomatoes.

— **Steward Style:** à la maître d'hôtel: braised in white stock, covered with butter sauce, chopped parsley scattered on top.

— **Tessin Style:** à la tessinoise: braised in white stock, cut in pieces, dipped in frying batter, deep fried; placed on baking sheet, dusted with powder sugar, glazed rapidly.

— **Villeroi:** boiled in salt water, allowed to cool off, cut in pieces, coated with Villeroi sauce, dipped in egg and breadcrumbs, deep fried; tomato sauce served separately.

Cèpe: see boletus, edible.

Cerfeuil bulbeux: see chervil bulb.

Champignon: see mushroom.

Chantarelle: F. Chanterelle, Girolle; G. Pfifferling, Eierschwamm: egg-yellow colored edible fungi with pleasant taste and smell. It is sautéd in oil and butter or stewed in butter with chopped onions.

— **Bern Style:** à la berneoise: sautéd in lard with chopped onions, simmered in white stock, stock boiled down, mixed with chopped parsley; grated Swiss cheese scattered on top.

— **with Fine Herbs:** aux fines herbes: sautéd in butter, mixed with chopped herbs.

— **Housekeeper Style:** à la ménagère: sautéd in butter with chopped onions, simmered in white stock, thickened with butter paste, mixed with chopped fennel and chives.

Chard, Swiss Chard, Leaf Beet: F. Bette, Blette, Poirée à carde; G. Mangold: a variety of beet cultivated for its ribs which are tender when young and stringy when old. The ribs are cooked like seakale and the leaves like spinach. The chards (ribs) are peeled carefully, cut into pieces about 4 in. long and cooked in a blanc, water with butter, lemon juice and a pinch of salt, to keep them white.

— **with Butter:** au beurre: cooked in a "blanc", drained, simmered for a while with plenty of butter with the cover on and served covered with the butter.

— **in Cream Sauce:** à la crème: cooked in a "blanc", drained, placed in a stewpan with a little butter, simmered for a few minutes, moistened with heavy cream and cooked until the sauce is thickened sufficiently.

— **with Dutch Sauce:** à la sauce hollandaise: peeled, left fairly long, bundled, cooked in salt water like asparagus; drained, dressed on a napkin; Dutch sauce served separately. Melted butter, mousseline, cream or vinaigrette sauce may also be served with chard.

— **Gratinated:** au gratin: cooked in a "blanc"; drained, placed in a baking dish on Mornay sauce, covered with

Chard, Gratinated
Mornay sauce, sprinkled with grated Parmesan, butter dropped on top, gratinated in oven.
— **with Gravy:** au jus: cooked in a "blanc", drained, simmered for a few minutes in thick veal gravy, served covered with the gravy finished off with butter.
— **Italian Style:** à l'italienne: prepared like chard with gravy using Italian sauce instead of the gravy.
— **Milanese Style:** à la milanaise: prepared like asparagus.
— **with Ox Marrow:** à la moelle: cooked in a "blanc", drained, simmered in demi-glace; served with sliced blanched ox marrow on top, covered with the demi-glace, sprinkled with chopped parsley.
— **Polish Style:** à la polonaise: prepared like asparagus.

Chayotte: F. Chayotte, Brionne; G. Eierkürbis, Chayotte: the fruit of a Central-American food plant cultivated in California and Florida. The fruit is of various sizes and colors and used as a vegetable or for salads. Prepared like egg-plant or cucumber.
— **in Cream Sauce:** à la crème: peeled, cut lengthwise in quarters, seeds removed, sliced, stewed in white stock until tender; stock reduced, mixed with heavy cream, seasoned, mixed carefully with the sliced chayottes.
— **Parma Style:** à la Parme: peeled, cut first in quarters and then in not too thin slices, half as much sliced potatoes added, simmered in butter with chopped onions, seasoned with salt, pepper and paprika, finished off with heavy cream; filled in greased baking dish, sprinkled with grated Parmesan, dotted with butter, gratinated.
— **Stuffed:** farcie: parboiled in skin, cut in half lengthwise, seeds removed, scooped out lightly; contents chopped, mixed with chopped onions fried lightly in butter, chopped mushrooms, boiled rice and a little tomato purée, seasoned, sprinkled with breadcrumbs and grated cheese, oil dropped on top, baked in oven.

Cheese: F. Fromage; G. Käse: the curd of milk of various domestic animals — cows, goats, sheep, asses etc. — separated from the whey by the action of rennet, made into different compact forms and ripened suitably. Cheese is used extensively for dishes of various kinds, especially Parmesan, Swiss and Cheddar cheese.
— **Cheddar Soufflé with Paprika:** Soufflé de Cheddar au paprika: soufflé mixture of milk, butter, grated Cheddar cheese very little flour and egg yolks seasoned sharply with paprika, stiffly beaten egg whites added, filled in greased soufflé dish, baked in oven and served immediately.
— **Fondue:** diced Gruyère cheese placed in special fondue dish, covered with dry white wine, seasoned with Cayenne pepper, melted, thickened with potato flour, served with bread cut into coarse cubes.
— **Fondue Brillat-Savarin:** beaten eggs mixed with grated Emmenthal cheese, butter and white wine, seasoned with Cayenne pepper, placed in special fondue dish above a spirit flame which can be regulated, allowed to thicken; served with bread cut into coarse cubes.
— **Fondue Neuchâtel Style:** à la neuchâteloise: fondue dish rubbed with garlic, diced Gruyère placed in dish, covered with Neuchâtel white wine, seasoned, allowed to boil up

Cheese

slowly to smooth cream stirring constantly, thickened with potato flour mixed with water; coarsely cut bread cubes served separately.

— **Fonduta:** diced Fontina cheese placed in fondue dish, moistened with milk, butter, egg yolks and seasoning added, allowed to boil up slowly to a smooth cream stirring constantly; served immediatly mixed with sliced white Italian truffles. (Italian)

— **Soufflé with Crayfish Tails:** Soufflé de fromage aux queues d'écrevisses: same as Cheddar soufflé but made with half grated Swiss and half Parmesan cheese; filled in greased soufflé dish with layers of crayfish tails between the soufflé mixture.

— **Soufflé Geneva Style:** Soufflé de fromage à la génevoise: noodles, parboiled, drained, mixed with Emmenthal cheese soufflé mixture, filled in soufflé dish greased with butter, covered with soufflé mixture, baked in oven.

Chervil Bulb, Turnip Rooted Chervil; F. Cerfeuil bulbeux; G. Kerbelrübchen: a plant grown for its tasty roots which make a very agreeable vegetable and salad. Prepared like stachys.

Chestnut; F. Marron; G. Kastanie, Edelkastanie: the nut or seeds of various kinds of chestnut trees, but chiefly of the European variety known as Sweet or Spanish chestnut. They are marketed without the prickly husk encased in an brown skin. To cook them the skin is pierced and the chestnuts immersed for a short time in deep fat, boiling water or on a baking sheet with a few drops of water placed in the oven; the skin will then come off quite easily.

— **Braised:** braisés: braised with rich veal gravy, the gravy reduced to glace the chestnuts.

— **Deviled:** à la diable: peeled, simmered in butter, seasoned with salt and Cayenne pepper.

— **Glazed:** glacés: peeled, cooked in rich veal gravy with a little sugar and butter and glazed.

— **Purée of:** Purée de marrons: stewed in white stock, rubbed through a sieve, finished off with butter and cream.

— **Stewed:** étuvés: peeled, stewed in white stock with a small piece of celery.

Chick-Peas; F. Pois chiches; G. Kichererbsen: S. Garbanzos: a native of western Asia now cultivated in all countries bordering the Mediterranean, in Turkey and India. It is larger than the common pea and especially popular in Spain. Chick-peas must be soaked in cold water for several hours and are then cooked in lightly salted water.

— **with Butter:** au beurre: cooked, drained, bound with butter, chopped herbs scattered on top.

— **Catalonian Style:** à la catalane: cooked, drained, mixed with tomatoes concassée, crushed garlic and chopped fine herbs.

— **Creamed:** à la crème: boiled, drained, cooked up with cream and butter.

— **Purée of:** Purée de pois-chiches: cooked, drained, rubbed through a sieve, finished off with cream and butter.

Chick-Peas
— **Vinaigrette:** cooked, drained, served cold in vinaigrette sauce.
Chicorée de Bruxelles: see French Endive.
Chicorée frisée: see chicory.
Chicory; F. Chicorée frisée; G. Endivie: a salad plant with narrow curly leaves, the center leaves are usually bleached. Chicory may be prepared like spinach.
— **in Cream Sauce:** à la crème: blanched, cooked in white stock, drained, chopped, bound with cream sauce.
— **Farmer Style:** à la paysanne: blanched, chopped, simmered in butter with chopped onions and diced fried bacon.
— **Loaf:** Pain de chicorée: boiled, drained, rubbed through a sieve, seasoned, mixed with eggs, filled in a greased mould, poached in waterbath; turned out, covered with velouté sauce.
— **Purée of:** blanched, simmered in butter and white stock, drained, rubbed through a sieve, mixed with half as much potato purée, seasoned, finished off with butter and cream.
— **Russian Style:** à la russe, blanched, simmered in butter with chopped onions and fennel, finished off with sour cream and cream sauce.
— **Spanish Style:** à l'espagnole: blanched, chopped, simmered in butter, bound with demi-glace.
Chinese Artichoke: see stachy.
Chinese Cabbage: see Pe-Tsai.
Chou-blanc: see cabbage, white.
Chou-marin: see sea-kale.
Chou-palmiste: see palmiste.
Chou-rave: see cabbage turnip.
Chou-rouge: see cabbage, red.
Chou-vert: see cabbage, Savoy.
Chou-vert non pommé: see green cabbage.
Choucroute: see saurkraut.
Choux de Bruxelles: see Brussels sprouts.
Choux-Fleurs: see cauliflower.
Ciernikis: Russian Cheese Cakes: pressed cottage cheese mixed with flour, eggs and melted butter, seasoned with salt, pepper and nutmeg, shaped into round flat cakes, poached in boiling water, served in timbale dish covered with melted butter. (Russian)
Coeur de palmier: see palm shoots.
Concombre: see cucumber.
Corn, Indian, Maize, Sweet Corn; F. Maïs; G. Mais, Kukurutz: the tallest of all grain grasses, native of America. Corn is excellent as a fresh vegetable, picked in green husks and boiled before being fully ripe, i. e. as fresh as possible. Corn is also marketed frozen and canned.
— **and Celery:** au céleri: cut cooked corn, diced cooked celery, chopped green peppers and chopped olives arranged in alternate layers in greased baking dish, covered with hot cream mixed with salt, pepper and a little butter, sprinkled with breadcrumbs, dotted with butter, baked in moderate oven.
— **off the Cob:** cooked, kernels removed from cob with a fork, seasoned with salt and paprika, tossed in butter.
— **on the Cob:** husks and silk removed, cooked in boiling water, drained, served on the cob with butter and salt.

Corn, Indian

— **Creamed:** à la crème: raw kernels simmered in cream, seasoned with salt and pepper.

— **Croquettes of:** Croquettes de maïs: cooked drained kernels bound with thick Béchamel and egg yolks, seasoned with paprika, allowed to cool; shaped into small croquettes or little round cakes, dipped in egg and breadcrumbs, deep fried.

— **Fritters:** Beignets de maïs: corn meal cooked in milk with butter and seasoning, cooled off, cut in squares or little round cakes, dipped in egg and breadcrumbs, deep fried.

— **Fritters American Style:** à l'américaine: flour sifted with baking powder, salt and paprika, cooked cold corn and egg yolks added, stiffly beaten egg whites folded in, dropped in deep fat with a soup spoon and fried.

— **Gratinated:** au gratin: cooked kernels bound with cream sauce, filled in greased baking dish, sprinkled with grated cheese, dotted with butter, gratinated in oven.

— **Grilled:** grillé: husk and silks removed from raw cob, brushed with butter, grilled, served with fresh butter and salt.

— **Mamaliga:** Corn Mush: corn meal cooked slowly in salt water and butter, served with melted butter on top. (Roumanian)

— **Mamaliga cu Ochiuri Romanesti:** mamaliga with poached eggs covered with melted butter on top; sour cream served separately. (Roumanian)

— **Maryland:** diced tomatoes sautéd in butter, cooked corn added, seasoned with salt, pepper and a pinch of sugar and simmered together for a few minutes.

— **Mexican Style:** à la mexicaine: cooked corn mixed with chopped cooked green beans, green peppers, chopped fried onions, butter and tomato purée.

— **Mush:** meal cooked in salt water in double boiler, served as a breakfast dish with cream and sugar.

— **O'Brien:** shredded green peppers cooked in butter, cooked corn and chopped pimiento added, seasoned and simmered for a while.

— **Soufflé:** Soufflé de maïs: cooked corn drained, rubbed through a sieve, seasoned with paprika and salt, mixed with heavy cream, butter and egg yolks, stiffly beaten egg whites added, filled in greased soufflé dish, baked in oven.

— **Southern Style:** corn simmered in cream and butter, seasoned, chopped green and red peppers added.

— **Stewed:** étuvé: kernels parboiled, stewed in milk and butter.

— **and Tomatoes:** aux tomates: diced tomatoes simmered in butter with cooked corn, seasoned with salt and pepper.

— **Tomerl:** Corn Pancake: corn meal mixed with eggs, milk, chopped fried onions and salt to a medium thick batter, fried in skillet like pancake. (Austrian)

Courge: see squash and marrow, vegetable.

Courgette: see marrow, small.

Cresson, Cresson Alenois: see watercress.

Crosnes du Japon: see stachy.

Cucumber; F. Concombre; G. Gurke: creeping plant native of North-West India of which there are many varieties. Cucumbers are eaten raw, pickled or cooked.

Cucumber

— **Andalusian Style:** à l'andalouse: peeled, split lengthwise, seeds removed, cut in thick pieces, simmered in tomato sauce; when done placed in baking dish, covered with the sauce, sprinkled with grated Parmesan, oil dropped on top, gratinated in oven.

— **Clermont:** peeled, seeds removed, diced, simmered in butter, mixed with diced cooked artichoke bottoms and chopped parsley.

— **Creamed:** à la crème: olive-shaped, blanched, seasoned, cooked in cream.

— **Duchess Style:** à la duchesse: peeled, cut in round pieces, scooped out, blanched, stuffed with chicken forcemeat, arranged in baking dish greased with butter; a little sweet cream poured around the cucumbers, sprinkled with grated cheese, cooked and browned in oven.

— **with Fennel:** à la tsarine: olive-shaped, simmered in light cream sauce with chopped fennel greens and parsley.

— **Fried:** frits: 1. peeled, cut in thick slices, seasoned with salt and pepper, dipped in frying batter, fried in deep fat. 2. cut in thick slices, seasoned, dipped in egg and breadcrumbs, fried in butter.

— **German:** à l'allemande: peeled, cut in cubes, sautéd in butter with chopped onions and diced bacon, moistened with demi-glace, cooked, seasoned with a dash of vinegar.

— **Glazed:** glacés: olive-shaped, blanched, cooked in butter, a little water and a pinch of salt until the water is completely evaporated and the cucumbers glazed.

— **Italian Style:** à l'italienne: peeled, cut in round pieces, scooped out, stuffed with bread soaked in milk mixed with egg yolks, chopped hard-boiled egg yolks, grated Parmesan, salt and nutmeg; simmered in oil in slow oven.

— **Polish Style:** à la polonaise: peeled, split lengthwise, seeded, cut in fairly large pieces, cooked in salt water and drained; served covered with chopped hard-boiled eggs and parsley, breadcrumbs browned in a generous amount of butter poured on top.

— **Roman Style:** à la romaine: peeled, olive-shaped, cooked in butter, bound with Roman sauce.

— **Saxon Style:** à la saxonne: peeled, seeds removed, cut in large pieces, simmered in butter with finely chopped onions, dusted with flour, cooking finished in sour cream.

— **Spanish Style:** à l'espagnole: peeled, cut in round pieces, scooped out, blanched; stuffed with pork sausage meat mixed with duxelles and chopped herbs, simmered in light demiglace, served covered with the sauce.

— **Stephanie:** round pieces scooped out, filled with pork sausage meat mixed with chopped truffle and gooseliver purée, covered with a thin slice of salt pork, simmered in light cream sauce; when done covered with the sauce, crayfish butter dropped on top.

— **Stewed:** étuvés: peeled, seeded, cut in pieces the size of a small finger, fried lightly in butter, cooked in white stock; thickened with butter paste and egg yolks, seasoned with vinegar or lemon juice.

— **Stuffed:** 1. peeled, cut in round pieces of about 2 inch., scooped out and blanched; stuffed with chicken forcemeat, arranged in buttered baking dish, cooking finished in slow oven.

Cucumber

2. stuffed with duxelles, sprinkled with breadcrumbs, dotted with butter, cooked and gratinated in oven.

— **Tenant Style:** à la paysanne: peeled, split lengthwise, seeded, cut in finger long pieces, blanched, stuffed with pork sausage meat, arranged in baking dish greased with butter, sprinkled with breadcrumbs, melted butter poured on top, cooked and browned in slow oven.

— **Turkish Style:** à la turque: round pieces, scooped out and blanched; stuffed with rice pilaf mixed with chopped cooked mutton, simmered in slow oven in fat mutton stock.

— **in Velouté:** à la velouté: peeled, seeds removed, cut in large cubes, blanched, simmered in veal velouté.

Czipetke: noodle dough, dried, torn by hand, boiled in salt water. (Hungarian)

D

Dandelion; F. Dent de lion, Pissenlit; G. Löwenzahn: a wild-growing spring weed which grows in poorest soil and should be picked before flowering. It is cultivated for its leaves, which may be bleached and used as a salad.

— **Purée of:** Purée de dent de lion: blanched, chopped, braised in fat stock, thickened with white roux, seasoned and braised in oven; served with a border of hot cream.

Dent-de-lion: see dandelion.

Dumpling; F. Quenelle; G. Kloss, Knödel: small balls or fancy shaped preparations of fish, meat, poultry or game, yeast dough, potato or other starchy compositions thickened with eggs, poached in water or steamed.

— **Buckwheat:** de gruau de sarrasin: buckwheat grits, soaked, mixed with a little flour, butter and egg yolks, stiffly beaten egg whites added, shaped into small balls, poached in salt water.

— **Erdapfelknödl:** Potato Dumpling: potatoes baked in jacket, hollowed out, mashed, mixed with butter, egg yolks, flour, semolina, chopped chives and small croûtons fried in butter; shaped into small dumplings, poached in salt water. (Austrian)

— **Herb:** aux fines herbes: cold boiled potatoes, grated, mixed with bread soaked in milk, eggs, flour, salt and chopped chervil, tarragon, thyme, marjoran, basil and burnet; shaped into dumplings, poached, served covered with browned butter.

— **Klosski:** Russian Dumpling: creamed butter mixed with eggs, chopped lightly fried onions, flour, chopped ham and diced bread; shaped into dumplings, poached in salt water, sour cream served separately.

— **Pignatelli:** cream puff paste mixed with grated Parmesan and finely diced ham, shaped into walnut-sized dumplings, fried in deep fat. (Italian)

— **Potato, Holstein Style:** de pommes de terre à la holsteinoise: cold boiled potatoes, grated, mixed with eggs, milk, buckwheat meal and salt, diced fried bacon added, shaped into small dumplings, poached in salt water.

— **Potato, Thuringian Style:** de pommes de terre à la thuringienne: raw potatoes, grated, soaked in water, squeezed

Dumpling

out thoroughly, mixed with rice or semolina mush, beaten eggs, salt and small croûtons fried in butter; shaped into small dumplings, poached in salt water.

— **Semmelknödl:** Bread Dumpling: bread soaked in milk, pressed out, mixed with butter, eggs, flour and chopped chives; shaped into small dumplings, poached in salt water. (Austrian)

— **Semolina:** de semoule: milk boiled up with butter, semolina cooked in the milk, thickened with eggs, allowed to cool; mixture shaped into small dumplings, poached in salt water.

— **Speckknödl:** Bacon Dumpling: same as Semmelknödl, diced fried lean bacon added. (Austrian)

E

Egg Plant: F. Aubergine; G. Eierapfel, Eierpflanze, Eierfrucht: fruit vegetable native of Asia of which there are several varieties of different sizes, shapes and colors. The most popular kinds are the small purple-black.

— **Algerian Style:** à l'algériene: prepared like Egyptian style but coated with tomato sauce, sprinkled with breadcrumbs and baked in oven.

— **American Style:** à l'américaine: split lengthwise, fried, hollowed out, filled with the chopped flesh mixed with chopped cooked mutton, boiled rice, chopped tomatoes and garlic, sprinkled with breadcrumbs, butter dropped on top, baked in oven.

— **Andalusian Style:** à l'andalouse: cut in thick slices, fried, scooped out, filled with the chopped flesh mixed with tomatoes concassées, diced red peppers and ham simmered in butter; border of demi-glace with tomato.

— **Baked:** au four: sliced, fried lightly in oil with garlic, filled alternately in greased baking dish with layers of hashed mutton and sliced tomatoes, sprinkled with breadcrumbs mixed with chopped parsley, oil dropped on top, baked in oven.

— **Benjamin:** split lengthwise, scored inside, seasoned with salt mixed with finely crushed garlic, dotted with butter, baked in oven.

— **in Cream Sauce:** à la crème: sliced, salted and soaked for an hour, wiped dry, simmered in butter, bound with light cream sauce.

— **Egyptian Style:** à l'égyptienne: split lengthwise, fried in oven in oil, scooped out; flesh chopped, mixed with chopped onions lightly fried in oil, seasoned, replaced in skin, a trickle of oil poured on top, baked; served with sliced fried tomatoes sprinkled with chopped parsley on top.

— **Fried:** frites: sliced, seasoned, turned in flour, fried in oil.

— **Fried Turkish Style:** frites à la turque: peeled, cut in slices, salted, after an hour salt washed off, fried in oil; at serving, yogurt seasoned with salt and garlic, poured over the slices.

— **Fritters:** Beignets: sliced, salted, dipped in egg and breadcrumbs, deep fried; tomato sauce served separately.

Egg Plant

— **Gratinated:** au gratin: split lengthwise: fried, scooped out, filled with the chopped flesh mixed with duxelles, sprinkled with grated Parmesan, dotted with butter, gratinated in oven.

— **Greek Style:** à la grecque: cut in thick slices, simmered for a few minutes in oil, cooked in marinade of white wine, oil, vinegar, sliced onions, fennel, garlic and spices; served cold in the stock.

— **Grilled:** grillées: split in half, seasoned, brushed with oil, grilled.

— **Haydée:** cut in slices, marinated in brandy and white wine; drained, dipped in egg and breadcrumbs, fried in oil; tomato sauce served separately.

— **Iman Bayaldi:** baking dish filled alternately with slices of eggplant sautéd in oil and tomatoes concassées, sprinkled with breadcrumbs, oil dropped on top, baked in oven.

— **Karni Yarik:** an incision made on one side, flesh scooped out, chopped, mixed with chopped onions fried in butter and hashed mutton, refilled in the fruit, placed on greased baking dish, covered with melted butter and a few drops of water, stewed in oven. (Turkish)

— **Lyonese Style:** à la lyonnaise: split lengthwise, fried, scooped out, flesh chopped, mixed with chopped fried onions, refilled in skin, sprinkled with breadcrumbs, butter dotted on top, browned in oven.

— **Mexican Style:** à la mexicaine: peeled, chopped, seasoned, filled in greased baking dish alternately with layers of chopped onions, diced tomatoes and green peppers, flavored with a little garlic, browned butter poured on top, baked in oven.

— **Naples Style:** à la napolitaine: peeled, sliced, seasoned, coated with flour, placed in greased baking dish, covered lightly with tomato sauce, sprinkled with grated Parmesan and breadcrumbs, oil dropped on top, baked in oven.

— **Nice Style:** à la niçoise: split lengthwise, fried in oil, scooped out; filled with the chopped flesh mixed with diced tomatoes, chopped anchovy fillets and garlic, sprinkled with grated Parmesan, oil dropped on top, gratinated in oven.

— **sautéd Nice Style:** sauté à la niçoise peeled, cut in slices, coated with flour, sautéd in oil; sliced tomatoes and thick strips of green peppers sautéd separately in oil, mixed with the eggplants served sprinkled with chopped herbs.

— **Nimese Style:** à la nimoise: split lengthwise, fried, scooped out; filled with the chopped flesh mixed with chopped green peppers and tomatoes, seasoned with garlic, refilled in the skin, baked in oven.

— **Oriental Style:** à l'orientale: split lengthwise: fried in oil, scooped out; filled with chopped flesh mixed with chopped onions fried in oil, chopped red peppers, hashed mutton, boiled rice and garlic, sprinkled with grated Parmesan, oil dropped on top, baked in oven.

— **Parisian Style:** à la parisienne: halves filled with the chopped flesh mixed with chopped ham, lamb, blanched chopped ox marrow and onions fried in butter.

— **with Parmesan:** au parmesan: cut in slices, salted, allowed to stand for a while, drained, placed in greased baking

Egg Plant

dish, sprinkled generously with grated Parmesan, melted butter dropped on top, baked in slow oven.

— **Pera Palace Hotel:** peeled, cut lengthwise in slices, always two slices put together with forcemeat made of chopped fried eggplant flesh mixed with diced tomatoes, breadcrumbs, chopped sweated onions, egg yolks and seasoning; placed on baking dish, trickle of oil on top, baked in oven.

— **Provencal Style:** à la provençale: prepared like stuffed eggplant but with more tomatoes; border of tomato sauce at serving.

— **Roumanian Style:** à la roumaine: small eggplant simmered in oven with sliced onions in oil and tomato sauce; when done an incision made on one side, opened but not separated, and filled with crisp fried onion slices.

— **Salata de vinete:** Eggplant salad: baked, skinned, washed, chopped fine with a wooden knife, seasoned with salt and pepper, mixed with lemon juice and grated onion, blended with oil and prepared like mayonnaise; served very cold as an appetizer garnished with tomatoes cut in quarters. (Roumanian)

— **Sicilian Style:** à la sicilienne: split lengthwise, fried in oil, filled with the chopped flesh mixed with grated Parmesan and egg yolks; baked in oven, bordered with tomato sauce.

— **Sidney:** split in half, fried in oil, arranged in baking dish with sliced tomatoes on top, sprinkled with grated Parmesan, oil dropped on top, baked in oven.

— **Soufflé of:** Aubergines soufflées: split lengthwise, fried, scooped out; flesh chopped, mixed with thick Béchamel sauce and stiffly beaten egg whites, refilled in the skin, baked in oven.

— **Stuffed:** farcies: split in half, fried, scooped out; flesh chopped, mixed with chopped onions simmered in oil, chopped mushrooms, tomatoes, garlic and parsley, seasoned, refilled in the skin, sprinkled with breadcrumbs, a trickle of oil on top, baked in oven.

— **Stuffed Turkish Style:** farcies à la turque: prepared like stuffed eggplant, the flesh chopped, mixed with chopped onions, simmered in oil, chopped skinned tomatoes and boiled rice, seasoned with salt, pepper, cinnamon and chopped mint; placed in baking dish with a few drops of water, oil dropped on top baked in oven.

Endive, Belge: see French endive.

Endive, French; Witloof; F. Endive, Endive Belge, Chicorée de Bruxelles; G. Echte Endivie, Brüsseler Chicoree: the best variety of cultivated chicory, long shoots forced and bleached in cellars. To keep endives white they ought not to be blanched but simmered in butter with very little water, lemon juice and a pinch of salt with a greased paper on top and the cover on.

— **Ardennes Style:** à l'ardennaise: simmered in butter and water with diced blanched bacon and chopped lean ham, covered with the lightly thickened stock.

— **Beulemanns:** same as Ardennes but simmered only with sliced onions; covered with demi-glace mixed with chopped mushrooms.

— **Bradford:** blanched, simmered in butter and veal gravy; when done, stock thickened with arrow-root, strained,

Endive, French
mixed with mushroom slices sautéd in butter, poured over the endives, chopped parsley on top.
— **with Cream Sauce:** à la crème: cooked, finished off with heavy cream.
— **with Dutch Sauce:** à la sauce hollandaise: cooked, drained, covered with Dutch sauce.
— **with Gravy:** au jus: cooked, drained, covered with rich veal gravy.
— **Milanese Style:** à la milanaise: cooked, drained, arranged in baking dish in layers, each leayer covered with grated Parmesan; covered with browned butter.
— **Mornay:** cooked, drained, arranged in baking dish greased with butter, covered with Mornay sauce, sprinkled with grated Parmesan, gratinated.
— **Polish Style:** à la polonaise: cooked, drained, covered with chopped hard-boiled eggs and parsley, breadcrumbs browned in plenty of butter poured on top.

Epinards: see spinach.

F

Fairy Ring Mushroom: F. Mousseron; G. Moosschwamm, Blätterpilz: small fungus found among short grass and after rain in summer and autumn. The cap is a reddish buff, stem and gills pale-buff colored. Prepared like field mushrooms but chiefly dried and used for flavoring ragoûts and soups.
— **with Herbs:** aux fines herbes: sliced, sautéd in butter with chopped shallots, mixed with chopped herbs.
— **Provence Style:** à la provençale: sliced, sautéd with chopped shallots and garlic in oil, mixed with tomatoes concassées, chopped parsley scattered on top.
— **Sautéd:** sautés: sliced, sautéd in butter with chopped shallots, finished off with chopped parsley and lemon juice.

Fennel, Fennel Bulbs: F. Pieds de fenouil; G. Fenchelknollen; I. Finocchi: plant grown for it seeds, roots, shoots and stems. The rootstocks are bulbous, somewhat sweet, tender and fleshy and can be cooked like knob celery. They are served hot or cold. Shoots and stems may be eaten raw as or in a salad. The bulbs are washed, cut lengthwise in halves or quarters, according to size, blanched and simmered in white stock with sliced onions and carrots.
— **Fried:** frit: 1. cooked, wiped dry, dipped in frying batter, fried in deep fat; tomato sauce served separately.
2. cooked, dried, dipped in flour, egg and breadcrumbs, fried in deep fat; Béarnaise sauce served separately.
— **with Gravy:** au jus: blanched, cooked in rather fat stock, drained, covered with thick veal gravy.
— **Gratinated:** au gratin: blanched, braised in white wine and demi-glace with chopped mushrooms, skinned tomatoes, chopped herbs and seasoning; when done arranged in baking dish greased with butter, the reduced braising stock poured on top, sprinkled with grated cheese and breadcrumbs, dotted with butter and gratinated.

Fennel

— **Greek Style:** à la grecque: (cold) blanched, braised in white wine and oil with knob celery, thyme, orange peel, lemon juice, vinegar and seasoning, served cold in the stock.

— **Italian Style:** à l'italienne: 1. blanched, cut in slices, simmered in butter and a little white wine, seasoned with salt and pepper, the chopped fennel greens added. 2. (cold) blanched, braised in oil and white wine with diced tomatoes, button onions, sliced mushrooms, chopped parsley, thyme and seasoning.

— **with Mousseline Sauce:** à la sauce mousseline: blanched, simmered in white stock, drained, served covered with mousseline sauce.

Fève de marais: see broad bean.

Finocchi: see fennel.

Fond d'artichaut: see artichoke bottom.

G

Garbanzo: Spanish name for chick-peas.

Garlic: F. Ail; G. Knoblauch: the most pungent member of the onion family cultivated from the earliest times on account of its characteristic flavor. Must be used with care and discretion. The bulb is divided into sections called cloves.

— **Provencal Style:** à la provençale: cloves, scalded, simmered in butter with chopped mushrooms, seasoned with Cayenne pepper and lemon juice.

Ghiveci Calugarest: Macedoine Monastry Style: green peas, diced green beans, cauliflower sprigs, Brussels sprouts, potato cubes, carrots, asparagus tips, diced squash, sliced tomatoes and eggplants, seeded green peppers and gombo all mixed together, seasoned, simmered in oil in slow stove with plenty of sliced fried onions and a little garlic. (Roumanian)

Globe Artichoke: same as artichoke.

Girolle: see chantarelle:

Gnocchi: Italian Dumplings: small dumplings about walnut-size made of semolina, cream puff paste, potatoes etc. and invariably mixed or served with grated cheese.

— **Gratinated:** au gratin: cream puff paste made with milk, mixed with grated Parmesan, shaped into balls the size of a walnut, poached; drained, filled in greased baking dish masked with Mornay sauce, covered with Mornay sauce, sprinkled with grated Parmesan, melted butter dropped on top, gratinated in oven.

— **Italian:** à l'italienne: boiled strained potatoes mixed with flour, eggs, butter and grated Parmesan, shaped into small balls, poached in salt water, drained; placed in greased baking dish, sprinkled with grated Parmesan, melted butter dropped on top, browned in oven.

— **with Parmesan:** au Parmesan: creamed butter mixed with flour, eggs and egg yolks, seasoned with salt, pepper and nutmeg, very little stiffly beaten egg white folded in, shaped hazelnut-size and poached; drained, arranged in timbale dish, sprinkled with grated Parmesan, covered with browned butter.

Gnocchi

— **Piedmont Style:** à la piémontaise: prepared with potatoes like Italian style, shaped into balls of hazelnut-size with flour and rolled on fork to decorate them, poached in salt water and drained; covered with grated Parmesan and breadcrumbs, browned butter poured on top, bordered with tomato sauce.

— **Potato:** de pommes de terre: same as Italian gnocchi.

— **Roman:** à la romaine: semolina cooked slowly in milk, seasoned with salt, pepper and nutmeg, bound with egg yolks and allowed to cool on greased baking sheet; cut round or halfmoon-shaped with a cutter, arranged in a greased baking dish, sprinkled with grated Parmesan and Gruyère cheese, melted butter dropped on top, gratinated in hot oven.

Gombo, Okra: F. Gombos; G. Eibisch, Bamia: a native of South America cultivated for the sake of its seed vessels. The long and narrow ones are commonly known as Okra and the smaller and round kind is called Bamia. Gombo is marketed fresh and canned. Bamia also dried.

— **American Style:** à l'américaine: parboiled, simmered in oil with diced tomatoes, garlic, chopped herbs and seasoning; served cold flavored with lemon juice.

— **Bame Sultanine:** in Tomato Sauce: boiled carefully in salt water with a dash of vinegar, drained, simmered in hot oil with a generous amount of sliced fried onions and tomato purée, seasoned with salt and lemon juice; served cold with skinned tomatoes cut in quarters and simmered in oil on top. (Roumanian)

— **with Butter:** au beurre: parboiled, seasoned, covered with melted butter mixed with lemon juice.

— **in Cream Sauce:** à la crème: blanched, simmered in butter, seasoned finished off with heavy cream.

— **Garnish:** pour garniture: blanched, simmered in butter with tomatoes concassées.

— **Janina:** chopped onions sweated in mutton fat, diced tomatoes and diced raw mutton added, sautéd for 7 to 8 minutes, bamia (soaked over night if dried) added, moistened with very little water, seasoned sharply and stewed slowly until done.

— **Oriental Style:** à l'orientale: parboiled, simmered in butter with diced tomatoes, seasoned with salt, garlic and cloves; served in border of saffron rice.

— **Stewed:** étuvés: blanched, stewed in demi-glace with lightly fried sliced onions.

— **with Tomatoes:** aux tomatoes: parboiled, simmered in butter with skinned chopped tomatoes.

— **Turkish Style:** à la turque: same as Janina taking oil instead of mutton fat.

Green Cabbage, Kale: F. Chou vert non pommé; G. Grünkohl, Braunkohl: name of any cabbage with finely dented curled leaves which do not form a head. Kale is green to purple in color and used in the manner of spinach.

— **French Style:** à la francaise: blanched, chopped finely, simmered in butter with chopped onions and a little stock; when done finished off with heavy cream, garnished with glazed chestnuts.

Green Cabbage
— **Holstein Style:** blanched, chopped with leeks added, sweated in lard, seasoned, braised in beef stock, thickened with oatmeal.
— **with Pickled Goose:** à la oie confit: blanched, chopped coarsely, simmered in rich stock with a pickled goose leg; when done thickened with white roux and served with the carved meat.

Green Kern: F. Blé vert; G. Grünkern: the polished immature kernels of a species of wheat, dried and husked. The meal derived from the kernels is chiefly used for making a soup very popular in Europe: F. Crème de blé vert; G. Grünkern Suppe.

Gruau: see gruel.

Gruel: F. Gruau; G. Grütze: groats of hulled ground grain-wheat, barley, buck-wheat, oats etc. — boiled and served as a breakfast dish, garnish etc.
— **Kascha:** Russian Gruel: buckwheat groats lightly grilled, mixed with butter, hot water, seasoned with salt and cooked in slow oven with the cover on; served with melted butter, sweet or sour cream. (Russian)
— **Porridge:** the meal or groats of any kind of grain boiled in water or milk and salt in double boiler, served hot with sugar, cream and or milk as a breakfast dish.
— **Smolenska Kascha:** Gruel Smolensk Style: buckwheat groats mixed with raw eggs, dried in slow oven, moistened with hot milk, seasoned, a little butter added, cooked in slow oven; served with fresh butter. (Russian)

H

Haricot asperge: see Asparagus bean.

Haricots blancs: see navy beans.
— **Flageolets:** see green haricot beans.
— **Mange-tout:** see butter beans.
— **rouges:** see red beans.
— **Verts:** see green beans.

Hélianthe: see helianti.

Helianti: F. Hélianthe; G. Helianthus: a tuberous vegetable similar to Jerusalem artichoke tasting somewhat like potato. It is scraped, blanched 5 minutes in salt water, cooled in cold water, drained and fried, creamed, mashed or prepared otherwise. It must be seasoned sharply, the taste being rather insipid, and not cooked to soft.
— **Glazed:** glacé: shaped like small eggs, blanched, simmered in butter and rich beef stock until all moisture is evaporated and the helianti nicely glazed.
— **Gratinated:** au gratin: blanched, simmered in butter; arranged in baking dish greased with butter, covered with Mornay sauce, sprinkled with grated Parmesan, dotted with butter, gratinated.
— **Housewife Style:** à la bonne-femme: blanched, simmered in veal stock, a little milk and butter, seasoned with pepper, and drained when done; stock bound with butter paste, chopped parsley added and poured over the helianti.
— **Mashed:** Purée de hélianthe: peeled or scraped, blanched, cooked in white stock with lemon juice until the stock

Helianti

is completely evaporated; rubbed through a sieve, mixed with hot milk or cream, seasoned with salt and paprika, garnished with heart-shaped croûtons.

— **Nimrod:** cut in thick slices, blanched and simmered lightly in butter; half as much yellow boletus cut in slices, sautéd in butter with chopped shallots and mixed with chopped parsley and a little finely crushed caraway seeds. Helianti and boletus filled alternately in baking dish greased with butter, boletus as last layer on top, sprinkled with grated Parmesan and breadcrumbs, dotted with butter, gratinated in oven.

— **Sautéd:** sauté: shaped like large olives, blanched, sautéd in butter until nicely browned.

— **Steward Style:** à la maître d'hôtel: cooked in salt water, drained, tossed carefully in herb butter.

Helvella: F. Helvelle; G. Lorchel: a conical, very tasty fungus similar to the conical morel to which it is related. It must be boiled for at least 5 minutes before further preparation and the water, which may be poisonous, thrown away. It is then absolutely harmless and may be prepared like morels.

Himmel und Erde: Heaven and Earth: sliced apples and sliced potatoes cooked in bouillon with salt and a piece of bayleaf; strained to make purée, served with black pudding or pork. (German)

Hominy: the kernel of white flint corn, hulled and split, more or less coarsely ground and sifted. It is used for puddings, cookies and as a breakfast cereal. As breakfast food it is cooked in water or milk in a double boiler and eaten with sugar and cream.

— **Fried:** shortly before finishing boiling the grits a little wheat flour added to prevent splitting when frying. Grits poured in pan, cooled off, cut in convenient pieces, fried in butter; served with syrup.

Hop Shoots: F. Jets de houblon; G. Hopfensprossen: the shoots of a climbing plant belonging to the nettle family, cultivated in America, Asia and Europe. The young shoots are washed in several changes of water, cooked in salt water with lemon juice and well drained.

— **with Butter:** au beurre: scalded, drained, simmered in butter and lemon juice.

— **Citizen Style:** à la bourgeoise: cooked, bound with bastard sauce.

— **Colbert:** scalded, simmered in butter and lemon juice, bound with cream sauce; served on toast with a poached egg brushed with melted butter on top.

— **with Egg and Breadcrumbs:** à la polonaise: cooked, drained, arranged in timbal dish mixed with chopped hard-boiled eggs, covered with breadcrumbs browned in a generous amount of butter.

— **with Fine Herbs:** aux fines herbes: scalded, cooked in butter and lemon juice, bound with velouté, a generous amount of chopped herbs added.

— **Fried:** frits: scalded, cooled off, dipped in frying batter, fried in deep fat.

— **Gratinated:** au gratin: cooked, drained, mixed with Mornay sauce; filled in baking dish greased with butter,

Hop Shoots
sprinkled with grated cheese, butter dropped on top, gratinated in oven.
— **Miller Style:** à la meunière: cooked in salt water with lemon juice, drained, lemon juice dropped on top, covered with browned butter.
— **Nürnberg Style:** à la nuerenbergoise: scalded, simmered in butter and lemon juice with a pinch of sugar, salt and nutmeg; bound with German sauce chopped parsley added.
— **Royal Style:** à la royale: scalded, cooked in butter and chicken stock; stock reduced with cream, shoots bound with this sauce truffle strips added.
— **Vinaigrette:** cooked in salt water and lemon juice, drained, served with vinaigrette sauce.

Hopping John: rice prepared like risotto with diced fried salt pork and green peas added.

I - J

Italian Dumplings: see gnocchi.

Jahnie de Ciuperci: Ragoût of Mushrooms: chopped onions fried lightly in oil, sliced mushrooms added, fried until light brown, mixed with tomato purée, seasoned with salt, pepper and chopped dill. (Roumanian)
— **de Fasole:** Navy Beans in Oil: boiled, drained, whilst hot mixed with oil and a generous amount of sliced fried onions; seasoned with salt, pepper, lemon juice and chopped dill; served cold. (Roumanian)

Jarmuz: Stewed Cabbage: white cabbage, scalded, drained, chopped coarsely, cooked in stock, bound with brown roux, mixed with sour cream, garnished with braised chestnuts. (Polish)

Jerusalem Artichoke: F. Topinambour; G. Erdbirne, Topinambur: the tubers of a sunflower resembling potatoes with a sweetish but pleasant taste. Containing no starch they are useful for many diets.
— **Coligny:** shaped like small eggs, blanched, cooked in butter and lemon juice; when nearly done liquid meat glaze and chopped parsley added.
— **Cracovian Style:** à la cracovienne: cut in slices, blanched, fried in butter, served covered with breadcrumbs fried in butter.
— **in Cream Sauce:** à la crème: olive-shaped, blanched, cooked in light cream sauce, finished off with heavy cream.
— **Dutch Style:** à la hollandaise: boiled, sliced, bound with Dutch sauce.
— **Duxelles:** large chokes parboiled in skin, cut open lengthwise, scooped out slightly, the contents chopped, mixed with duxelles, chopped herbs and onions lightly fried in butter; refilled in the halves, sprinkled with breadcrumbs dotted with butter, baked in oven.
— **English Style:** à l'anglaise: peeled, boiled, served with fresh butter.
— **Fried:** frits: cut in slices, seasoned, coated with flour, fried in hot oil.

Jerusalem Artichoke

— **Georgian Style:** à la georgienne: sliced, mixed with raw sliced potatoes, simmered in butter, white stock and a little sugar until glazed.

— **Gratinated:** au gratin: sliced, cooked in salt water, drained, placed in baking dish greased with butter, covered with Mornay sauce, sprinkled with grated cheese and gratinated.

— **Mashed:** Purée de topinambour: boiled, rubbed through a sieve, mixed with a little potato purée, finished off with butter and cream.

— **Oriental Style:** à l'orientale: baked in skin in hot oven; fresh butter served separately.

— **Orly:** shaped like large olives, parboiled, dipped in frying batter, fried in deep fat; tomato sauce served separately.

— **Parisian Style:** à la parisienne: cut in slices, blanched, cooked in light cream sauce, flavored with mustard and lemon juice.

— **Polish Style:** à la polonaise. sliced, cooked, drained, served covered with chopped parsley and breadcrumbs browned in a generous amount of butter.

— **Sautéd:** sautés: sliced, sautéd in butter.

— **Steward Style:** à la maître d'hôtel: parboiled, sliced, mixed with light cream sauce with chopped herbs.

— **Tunesian Style:** à la tunesienne: parboiled, cut open on top, scooped out and filled with chestnut purée.

K

Kale: see green cabbage.

Katalou: broken green beans, cubes of eggplants and green peppers, tomatoes cut in quarters and okra simmered in oil with garlic and chopped parsley. (Turkish)

Kohlrabi: see cabbage turnip.

L

Laitue: see lettuce.

Lasagne: a long broad undulating ribbon-like sort of macaroni. Prepared like macaroni.

— **alla piemontese:** Piedmont Style: mixed with finely sliced white truffles, bound with rich meat gravy; grated Parmesan served separately. (Italian)

— **alla bolognese:** Bologna Style: lasagne for which the paste has been made with green herb purée; boiled, tossed in butter and served with grated Parmesan. (Italian)

Leaf Beet: see chard.

Leek: F. Poireau; G. Lauch, Poree: a delicate member of the allium family, less pungent than onions or garlic, esteemed for its white long stem. The green tops are used for the stock pot. They are cut off when leeks are used as a vegetable.

— **braiséd:** braisé: cut into pieces of equal size, braised in fat stock with sliced carrots, onions and bacon waste,

Leek
covered with the degreased and strained stock boiled up with demi-glace.
— **with Butter:** au beurre: blanched, simmered in stock, drained, served with fresh butter.
— **German Style:** à l'allemande: split lengthwise, blanched, simmered in fat stock with raisins, stock thickened with white roux, seasoned with salt, sugar and vinegar.
— **Gratinated:** au gratin: cooked in salt water, drained, placed in baking dish, covered with Mornay sauce, sprinkled with grated Parmesan, dotted with butter, gratinated in oven.
— **Milanese Style:** à la milanaise: cut in pieces of equal size, cooked in salt water, drained, arranged in layers with grated Parmesan sprinkled between the layers, covered with grated Parmesan, browned butter poured on top.
— **in Oil:** à l'huile: boiled, served cold with vinaigrette sauce.
— **Polish Style:** à la polonaise: cooked in salt water, drained, covered with breadcrumbs browned in plenty of butter.
— **Sardinian Style:** à la sarde: boiled in salt water, drained, chopped coarsely, mixed with diced sautéd eggplants, bound with hash sauce.
— **Turkish Style:** à la turque: cut in pieces of equal size, blanched, placed on chopped onions lightly fried in oil, seasoned, simmered in oil and water; when half done rice added, served cold or luke warm with a little sugar sprinkled on top.
— **Vaudois Style:** à la vaudoise: simmered in fat stock with a piece of lean bacon and a sausage; served with the carved bacon and the sausage on top of the leeks, garnished with boiled potatoes.

Leipziger Allerlei: Leipzig Macedoine: diced root vegetables, green peas, diced green beans, asparagus tips and small morels, each vegetable cooked separately, mixed together, tossed in butter, bound with crayfish sauce; garnished with crayfish tails, small semolina dumplings shaped with a teaspoon, and fleurons. (German)

Lentilles: see lentils.

Lentils: F. Lentilles; G. Linsen: the mature seeds of a branching plant native of Southern Europe of which there are several varieties, the color is grey-green to light brown. Lentils must be soaked for several hours before they are cooked.
— **Bavarian Style:** à la bavaroise: cooked in fat pork stock, mixed with diced fried lean bacon, thickened with pale brown roux, seasoned with vinegar.
— **with Chipolatas:** aux chipolatas: cooked, drained, bound with butter, garnished with tiny fried pork sausages.
— **Creamed:** à la crème: cooked, finished off with butter, cream and chopped parsley.
— **Farmer Style:** à la paysanne: cooked, drained, mixed with glazed button onions, olive-shaped glazed carrots and diced ham, bound lightly with demi-glace.
— **French Style:** à la française: parboiled, simmered in red wine with diced fried lean bacon, bound with pale brown roux.
— **Little-Russian Style:** à la petite-russienne: cooked with a ham bone, larded onion, carrot and bunch of herbs;

Lentils

garnish removed, drained, simmered for a few minutes in butter with chopped fried onions, chopped parsley and demi-glace.

— **in Oil:** à l'huile: cooked, drained, served cold or luke warm mixed with oil, vinegar, chopped onions and seasoning.

— **with Ox Marrow:** à la moelle: cooked, bound with pale brown roux, served with sliced blanched ox marrow sprinkled with chopped parsley on top.

— **Provencal Style:** à la provençale: soaked, cooked in water with a pickled goose leg (oie confit), sliced onions, a clove of garlic, a bunch of herbs, seasoning and a little oil; when done bunch of herbs taken out, mixed with chopped parsley, bound with egg yolks mixed with oil, flavored with vinegar.

— **Russian Style:** à la russe: parboiled, simmered in butter with chopped onions and sour cream, mixed with chopped chives.

— **with Sausage:** au saucisson: cooked with a larded onion and ham bone, thickened with brown roux, served with slices of smoked sausage on top.

— **Specklinsen:** Lentils with Bacon: cooked with a larded onion and root vegetables; when done garnish removed, bound with pale brown roux, served covered with finely diced fried bacon. (German)

Lettuce: F. Laitue; G. Lattich, Kopfsalat: the name of several salad plants, chiefly the cabbage lettuce and the cos lettuce. Cabbage lettuce, of which there are many varieties, is also used as a vegetable.

— **Braised:** braisée: blanched, drained, water pressed out, cut in halves and folded, braised with sliced onion, carrots and bacon waste in fat bouillon; stock boiled up with demi-glace or meat glaze, strained and poured over the lettuce.

— **with Brown Butter:** au beurre noisette: braised, drained, covered with browned butter.

— **in Cream Sauce:** à la crème: blanched, cut lengthwise in halves or quarters according to size, braised, drained, covered with cream sauce.

— **Greek Style:** à la grecque: stuffed with rice prepared the Greek way, covered with thick veal gravy.

— **Judic:** braised halves, placed on slices of ox tongue, covered with thick meat gravy.

— **Old Fashioned Style:** à l'ancienne: large leaves scalded, filled with chopped spinach cooked in butter, mixed with chopped chives, chervil and mint, seasoned and bound with egg yolks, shaped into small balls and braised in fat stock; drained and served covered with bastard sauce.

— **with Ox Marrow:** à la moelle: braised, when done arranged in serving dish with blanched slices of ox marrow on top, covered with demi-glace or thick meat gravy, chopped parsley on top.

— **Stuffed:** farcie: same as braised but before folding stuffed with duxelles, chicken forcemeat or pork sausage meat.

— **Viennese Style:** à la viennoise: single leaves cooked in salt water, drained, chopped, heated up in butter, thickened with white roux, moistened with stock, seasoned with salt and nutmeg, boiled up, finished off with sour cream.

M

Macaroni: F. Macaroni; G. Makkaroni, Hohlnudel; I. Maccheroni: the best known of all Italian pastes. The best qualities are made of Durum wheat flour, semolina and farina thus containing little starch. They are of a creamy color and boil well. Macaroni must be cooked in plenty of boiling salt water "al dente", i. e. done but not soft. Plenty of butter and grated Parmesan cheese are essential.

— **with Anchovies:** aux anchois: cooked, drained, bound with butter, cream and grated Parmesan, mixed with chopped anchovy fillets.

— **Bayonne Style:** à la bayonnaise: cooked, mixed with diced ham, bound with demi-glace and served with grated Parmesan.

— **Black Friar's Style:** à la dominicaine: boiled, bound with butter, grated Parmesan and mushroom **purée**, mixed with chopped anchovy fillets.

— **Bologna Style:** à la bolognese: cooked, bound with butter and grated Parmesan, mixed with diced tenderloin of beef sautéd with chopped onions and braised in rich veal gravy.

— **with Breadcrumbs:** au mie-de-pain: cooked, drained, covered with breadcrumbs browned in a generous amount of butter.

— **alla calabrese:** 1. Calabrian Style: mixed with diced artichoke bottoms, simmered in oil, and Pecorino (a sort of ewe cheese). (Italian)
2. cooked, mixed with chopped ham, chopped fried onions and grated Parmesan, bound with tomato sauce flavored with garlic, a little hot oil poured on top.

— **Camerani:** cooked, bound with butter and grated Parmesan, mixed with diced sautéd eggplants, cockscombs and sliced mushrooms.

— **alla carbonara:** boiled, bound with butter, grated Parmesan and beaten eggs, mixed with diced ham and anchovy fillets. (Italian)

— **Citizen Style:** à la bourgeoise: same as Italian style.

— **with Cockscombs:** aux crêtes de coq: macaroni mixed with small cockscombs, sliced mushrooms and diced eggplants sautéd in butter, bound with demi-glace with tomato purée; filled in greased baking dish, sprinkled generously with grated Parmesan, butter dropped on top, gratinated in oven.

— **Croquettes:** cooked, drained, cut in small pieces, bound with thick Béchamel, grated Parmesan and egg yolks; cooled, shaped into small croquettes, dipped in egg and breadcrumbs, fried in deep fat.

— **Croquettes Milanese Style:** Croquettes à la milanaise: cooked, drained, cut in very small pieces, bound with thick Béchamel sauce, egg yolks and grated Parmesan,

Macaroni

mixed with finely diced mushrooms, truffles and ox tongue; allowed to cool, shaped into small croquettes, dipped in egg and breadcrumbs, fried in deep fat.

— **Cussy:** boiled, bound with butter and grated Parmesan, mixed with diced truffles and cockscombs.

— **English Style:** à l'anglaise: boiled, bound with thick veal gravy and grated Parmesan; filled in baking dish greased with butter, sprinkled with grated cheese and breadcrumbs, dotted with butter, gratinated.

— **Farmer Style:** à la paysanne: cooked, tossed in butter, mixed with tomatoes concassées and finely diced root vegetables simmered in butter; grated cheese served separately.

— **Garibaldi:** cooked, mixed with diced fried eggplants, bound with demi-glace; grated Parmesan served separately.

— **Genoese Style:** à la génoise: cooked, bound with Mornay sauce, mixed with sliced mushrooms; filled in greased baking dish, sprinkled with grated Parmesan, dotted with butter, gratinated.

— **German Style:** à l'allemande: cooked, drained, seasoned with salt, pepper and nutmeg, bound with butter, grated Parmesan and cream, served with fried ham.

— **Gratinated:** au gratin: prepared like Italian style with a little Béchamel sauce added; filled in greased baking dish, sprinkled with grated cheese, butter dropped on top, gratinated in oven.

— **with Gravy:** au jus: cooked and kept a little firm; cut in pieces and simmered in very rich beef gravy till the gravy is absorbed by the macaroni; grated Parmesan served separately.

— **Housekeeper Style:** à la ménagère: cooked, drained, bound with butter, grated Swiss cheese and cream, seasoned with nutmeg.

— **Hussar Style:** à la hussarde: cooked, bound with hussar sauce, chopped ham scattered on top; grated Parmesan served separately.

— **Italian Style:** à l'italienne: cooked, drained, sautéd with butter until macaroni is quite dry, seasoned with salt, pepper and nutmeg, bound with butter and half grated Parmesan and half Swiss cheese.

— **Levantine Style:** à la levantine: cooked, tossed in hot oil, bound with cream sauce mixed with tomato purée, grated Parmesan and diced ham.

— **Mariner Style:** à la marinière: bound with butter, grated cheese and mariner sauce, mixed with poached oysters mussels and shrimps.

— **Massimo:** cooked, drained, bound with butter, grated Parmesan and suprême sauce, mixed with chicken and mushroom strips.

— **Milanese Style:** à la milanaise: cooked, drained, cut in pieces, bound with grated Parmesan and demi-glace with tomato purée, mixed with julienne of ox tongue, mushrooms and truffles.

— **Montglas:** bound with Madeira sauce, mixed with strips of ox tongue, chicken, mushrooms and truffles; grated Parmesan served separately.

Macaroni

— **with Mussels:** aux moules; bound with butter and Norman sauce, mixed with very small poached and bearded mussels; grated Parmesan served separately.

— **Nantua:** cooked, drained, cut in pieces, bound with Nantua sauce, mixed with crayfish tails; grated Parmesan served separately.

— **Naples Style:** à la napolitaine: cooked, drained, cut in pieces, bound with butter and grated Parmesan; arranged in timbal dish alternately with beef braised in red wine and rich stock with tomatoes for about 10 hours or until the meat is cooked to a purée.

— **National Style:** à la nationale same as Italian style, tomatoes concassées and a little tomato sauce added.

— **Nice Style:** à la Niçoise: cooked, drained, mixed with tomatoes concassées with garlic and chopped onions, grated Parmesan sprinkled on top.

— **Nicotero:** boiled, drained, cut in pieces, bound with grated Parmesan, butter and Madeira sauce, mixed with hashed beef.

— **with Oysters:** aux huîtres: cooked, cut in pieces, tossed in butter, mixed with poached oysters and grated Parmesan, bound with cream sauce finished off with the oyster liquor.

— **Palermo Style:** à la palermitaine: cooked, drained, tossed in hot oil, bound with tomato sauce, mixed with chopped herbs.

— **Pie:** Pâté de macaroni: pie dish filled alternately with layers of macaroni mixed with butter and grated Parmesan, small slices of ox tongue, calf's sweetbread and chicken bound with Madeira sauce; covered with puff paste, brushed with egg yolk, baked in oven.

— **alla Principe di Napoli:** Prince of Naples: mixed with Mozzarella cheese, diced chicken and green peas, bound with rich thick beef gravy. (Italian)

— **Pudding American Style:** Pouding à l'américaine: baking dish greased with butter, filled alternately with layers of macaroni mixed with butter and grated Parmesan and hashed beef mixed with chopped green peppers; covered with chopped knob celery mixed with chopped peppers bound with demi-glace and cream, sprinkled with breadcrumbs and grated Parmesan, dotted with butter, gratinated in oven.

— **Queen Style:** à la reine: cooked, drained, mixed with chicken purée, bound with suprême sauce; filled in baking dish greased with butter, sprinkled with grated Parmesan, dotted with butter, gratinated in oven.

— **Rossini:** cooked, drained, cut in pieces, bound with butter and grated cheese, mixed with diced gooseliver and truffles, bordered with Madeira sauce.

— **Royal Style:** à la royale: bound with butter and grated Parmesan, mixed with sliced truffles, cooked in Madeira, and mushrooms.

— **Sicilian Style:** à la sicilienne: prepared like Italian style, velouté finished off with a purée of sautéd chicken livers added.

— **Venetian Style:** à la vénitienne bound with butter, grated Parmesan and velouté, mixed with julienne of mushrooms, truffles, chicken and ham.

Macaroni

— **alla vongole:** with Mussels: bound with butter and grated Parmesan, mixed with cooked mussels. (Italian)

— **with White Truffles:** aux truffles blanches: prepared like Italian style with white Piedmont truffles cut in very thin slices added.

Macedoine of Vegetables: Macédoine de légumes: root vegetables cut in small cubes, green peas, green beans cut in squares, asparagus tips cut in pieces, cauliflower sprigs and quartered morels, cooked separately, mixed, seasoned, tossed in butter or bound with cream sauce.

Mais: see corn, Indian.

Mange-tout: see sugar peas.

Mangold: F. Bette; G. Mangold, Mangel Wurzel: a field variety of the common beetroot. The leaves may be prepared like spinach, the stems like cardoon.

Marron: see chestnut.

Marrow, Small: F. Courgette; G. Kürbischen; I. Zucchetti: very small variety of vegetable marrow about the size of a small cucumber, cultivated chiefly in countries bordering the Mediterranean.

— **with Cheese:** au fromage: cut in slices, salted, allowed to stand for a while, sponged dry; put together in pairs filled with grated cheese mixed with beaten egg, dipped in frying batter, deep fried.

— **Creamed:** à la crème: peeled, shaped like large olives, scalded, simmered in butter, bound with light cream sauce.

— **English Style:** à l'anglaise: peeled, cut in small pieces, steamed or cooked in salt water, drained; melted butter served separately.

— **Fried:** frites: peeled, cut in not to thin slices, seasoned, coated with flour, fried in oil.

— **Fritters:** Beignets: cut in slices, salted, allowed to stand for a while, wiped dry, dipped in frying batter, deep fried.

— **Glazed:** glacées: peeled, cut lengthwise in quarters, quarters halved, cut like large olives, scalded, drained; cooked with butter, salt, a pinch of sugar and a few drops of water until they are done, the water evaporated and the marrow glazed.

— **Greek Style:** à la grecque: shaped like very large olives, but not peeled, cooked in marinade of white wine, vinegar, garlic, onions, fennel, peppercorns and dried orange peel; served cold in a part of the liquor.

— **Housekeeper Style:** à la ménagère: split lengthwise, hollowed out, filled with the chopped flesh mixed with hashed lamb, fried chopped onions, boiled rice, green peas, fried diced bacon, diced tomatoes and garlic; placed on greased baking dish with a little stock, sprinkled with breadcrumbs, dotted with butter, cooked and browned in slow oven.

— **Indian Style:** à l'indienne: prepared like glazed marrow sprinkled lightly with curry powder; a little thin Béchamel sauce poured on top at serving.

— **Menton Style:** à la mentonnaise: prepared like Nice style, stuffed with the chopped flesh mixed with chopped cooked spinach, grated Parmesan, parsley and garlic; sprinkled with breadcrumbs, oil dropped on top, gratinated in oven.

Marrow, Small

— **Nice Style:** à la niçoise: cut lengthwise, flesh scored in center and on the sides about 1/2 in. from edges, sprinkled with salt, allowed to rest for a while, moisture sponged off, cooked in oil but not browned; hollowed out without injuring the skin, flesh chopped, mixed with the double amount of risotto with grated Parmesan, crushed garlic and a soupspoon full of tomatoes concassées. Refilled in skin cupola-shaped, placed in greased baking dish, sprinkled with breadcrumbs, oil dropped on top, gratinated in slow oven; chopped parsley scattered on top and bordered with thick veal gravy.

— **Provencal Style:** à la provençale: cut in fairly thick slices but not peeled; salted, allowed to stand for a while, moisture sponged off, coated with flour, sautéd in hot oil; arranged in baking dish alternately with rice cooked in fat bouillon, diced tomatoes sautéd with chopped onions, parsley and garlic, sprinkled with grated Parmesan, gratinated in slow oven.

— **Roumanian Style:** à la roumaine: prepared like Nice style but with the chopped flesh mixed with plain boiled rice, diced tomatoes, chopped fried onions, parsley, garlic, oil and breadcrumbs; sprinkled with grated cheese, dotted with oil, gratinated in oven.

— **Sicilian Style:** à la sicilienne: cut in slices but not peeled; salted, allowed to stand for a while, sponged dry; put together in pairs filled with a mixture of sour cream, egg yolks, grated Parmesan and chopped chives seasoned with Cayenne pepper, dipped in egg and breadcrumbs, deep fried.

— **Spanish Style:** à l'espagnole: peeled, cut in slices, sautéd in oil and butter, arranged in greased baking dish alternately with diced tomatoes and sliced fried onions, seasoned with paprika, sprinkled with breadcrumbs, dotted with butter, gratinated in oven.

— **Turkish Style:** à la turque: prepared like Nice style, filled with the chopped flesh mixed with hashed mutton, boiled rice and eggs, flavored with garlic and marjoram; braised in oven in thin tomato sauce.

Marrow, Vegetable: F. Courge; G. Markkürbis: a kind of squash with a green to yellow mottled rind with light-colored flesh, very popular in the British isles. They are moist and tender when young, and dry and tough when old.

— **Baked:** peeled, cut in fairly large pieces, seeds removed, seasoned, covered with melted butter, baked in oven.

— **English Style:** à l'anglaise: peeled, cut in pieces, seeds removed, steamed or boiled, served covered with melted butter.

— **Mashed:** en purée: peeled, cut in pieces, steamed or boiled, mashed, seasoned, mixed with butter.

Millet: F. Millet; G. Hirse: a cereal — smallest of all grass grains — used for soups, puddings, bread and gruel.

— **Gruel:** Gruau: blanched, cooked in milk with a piece of butter seasoned with salt; served covered with browned butter.

— **Dumplings, Russian:** Pirogues de millet à la russe: blanched, cooked in milk, rubbed through a sieve, allowed to cool off; mixed with yeast and a little melted butter;

when it has risen well, mixed with flour, egg yolks, luke warm milk, salt and stiffly beaten egg whites shaped into round balls; flattened, stuffed with forcemeat, closed, brushed with milk, allowed to rise once more, baked and served hot with Russian soups.

Moelle de palmier: see palm shoots.

Monseta Catalana: navy beans cooked with a piece of lean bacon, drained, simmered in oil with chopped onions, garlic, the diced bacon and seasoning. (Spanish)

Morel: F. Morille; G. Morchel: fungus with a more or less conical or rounded cap, covered with ridges forming fairly deep pits like a honeycomb. The color varies from pale yellow to brown or black-brown. Being hollow they should be washed thoroughly in several changes of water to remove earth or grit sticking to them. Morels should not be eaten raw, they are perfectly harmless when cooked.

— **Andalusian Style:** à l'andalouse: sliced, simmered in oil with finely diced raw ham, chopped red peppers, moistened with demi-glace, flavored with Sherry; garnished with heart-shaped croûtons fried in oil.

— **Bordeaux Style:** à la bordelaise: sliced, sautéd in hot oil, seasoned, chopped shallots and parsley added, drained, flavored with lemon juice.

— **Chaumont Style:** à la Chaumont: quartered, sautéd in butter, sprinkled with flour, moistened with white stock, seasoned, cooked; thickened with egg yolks and cream, flavored with lemon juice.

— **Creamed:** à la crème: sliced, simmered in butter with chopped onions, cream added, seasoned, boiled down to the desired consistency.

— **d'Este:** simmered in butter with chopped onions, lemon juice and sour cream, seasoned, mixed with chopped herbs; served with a hard-boiled plovers egg on top.

— **with Fine Herbs:** aux fines herbes: sliced, sautéd in butter, seasoned, mixed shortly before serving with chopped herbs.

— **Forester Style:** à la forestière: blanched, filled with pork sausage meat mixed with the chopped stems and parsley; placed in well greased casserole, moistened with rich veal stock and braised; when done stock thickened and poured over the morels.

— **Poulette:** blanched, simmered with butter and lemon juice, bound with poulette sauce or finished off with velouté and cream.

— **Provencal Style:** à la provençale: prepared like Bordeaux style with garlic added.

— **Queen Style:** à la reine: washed, blanched briefly, filled through the stalk side with chicken forcemeat mixed with the finely chopped stalks; placed in a buttered sautoir, moistened with white stock and simmered in oven; stock reduced, mixed with suprême sauce and poured over the morels.

— **Spanish Style:** à l'espagnole: blanched, drained, sautéd in oil with chopped raw ham, deglaced with white wine, moistened with demi-glace, cooked, seasoned with paprika and lemon juice.

Morel

— **Toulouse Style:** à la toulousaine: cut in slices, sautéd in butter and oil with chopped onions, shallots and garlic, mixed with diced fried ham and tomatoes concassées.

— **Villeneuve:** creamed, served in pastry shell.

Morille: see morel.

Moussaka: eggplants split lengthwise, flesh scored, fried, hollowed out, the skins reserved. Flesh chopped, mixed with hashed mutton, chopped onions and mushrooms sweated in butter, chopped parsley and garlic; seasoned, bound with thick demi-glace, tomato purée and eggs. Greased charlotte mould lined with the skins, the dark side outside, filled alternately in layers with the forcemeat and sliced peeled eggplants fried in oil, closed with skins, covered with a greased paper and cooked in a water bath in oven for about an hour; allowed to stand for a few minutes, turned out on a round platter. (Roumanian)

Mousseron: see fairy ring mushroom.

Mushroom, Champignon: F. Champignon; G. Champignon, Edelpilz: fungus common on meadows and on downs where animals have grazed and also in gardens, known as field mushroom, champignon champêtre, but seldom marketed. Most mushrooms are now cultivated in quarries, cellars and sheds and are to be had at all times of the year. Cultivated mushrooms are sold as "buttons," young, round and unopened, or as caps.

— **Bordeaux Style:** à la bordelaise: 1. prepared like boletus. 2. cut in quarters, sautéd in butter with chopped shallots, bound with Bordeaux sauce, sprinkled with chopped parsley.

— **Burgundy Style:** à la bourguignonne: large caps, hollowed out, grilled, filled with snail butter.

— **Capuchin Style:** à la capucine: sautéd in oil with garlic and chopped parsley, mixed with chopped roasted pigeon meat, bound with German sauce.

— **Clain Valley:** à la vallée de Clain: caps of large field mushrooms, gills removed, stuffed with the chopped stems simmered in butter with chopped shallots and garlic, mixed with tomatoes concassées and chopped parsley; placed on greased baking sheet, sprinkled with breadcrumbs, mixed with chopped parsley, tarragon and chervil, and grated Parmesan, oil dropped on top, gratinated.

— **Creamed:** à la crème: cut in thick slices, simmered in butter with chopped shallots, seasoned, cooking finished in heavy cream.

— **Croquettes:** cooked, chopped, bound with thick Béchamel and egg yolks, seasoned, allowed to cool off; shaped into small cork-shaped croquettes, dipped in egg and breadcrumbs, deep fried.

— **Crust:** Croûte aux champignons: creamed mushrooms served in small round slices of bread, hollowed out and fried in butter.

— **with Fine Herbs:** aux fines herbes: cut in quarters or thick slices, sautéd in butter with chopped herbs.

— **in Glass Bell:** sous cloche: large caps, gills removed, seasoned with salt and pepper, lemon juice dropped on top, filled with herb butter, stood on head, cooked in

Mushroom
oven under glass cloche, brought to the table with the cover on.
— **Languedoc Style:** à la languedocienne: large caps, gills removed, stuffed with the stems simmered in butter and oil with the same amount of chopped shallots, seasoned with salt and nutmeg, chopped parsley added, sprinkled with breadcrumbs, oil dropped on top, browned in oven.
— **Livonian Style:** à la livonienne: button mushrooms cooked in oil, seasoned with salt, pepper and garlic, mixed with capers, sliced gherkins and small balls of cooked red beetroots, lemon juice added, served hot or cold.
— **Matinal:** small button mushrooms lightly fried in butter, diced tomatoes added, deglaced with Port, moistened with heavy cream and a little veal glace, cooked until done and the sauce reduced.
— **Perigord Style:** à la périgourdine: 1. large caps cut in slices, sautéd in oil with chopped shallots, mixed with slices of freshly cooked truffles, seasoned with salt, pepper and lemon juice, sprinkled with chopped parsley. 2. same as Bordeaux style with a generous amount of chopped truffles scattered on top.
— **Piedmont Style:** à la piémontaise: cut in thick slices, sautéd in oil with chopped shallots and chopped herbs, filled in greased baking dish, sprinkled with breadcrumbs and grated Parmesan, dotted with butter, gratinated in oven.
— **with Port:** au porto: small caps sweated in butter, seasoned, deglaced with Port, moistened with cream and cooked.
— **Poulette:** caps cooked in butter, lemon juice and a pinch of salt, bound with poulette sauce with the reduced mushroom stock added.
— **Provencal Style:** à la provençale: prepared like boletus.
— **Purée:** Purée de champignons: washed thoroughly, rubbed raw through a sieve, placed in stewpan with thick Béchamel and cooked until quite thick, seasoned with salt and pepper, finished off with heavy cream and butter.
— **Russian Style:** à la russe: prepared like boletus.
— **with Sherry:** au Xérès: prepared like with Port, taking Sherry instead of Port.
— **Soufflé:** Soufflé de champignons: white mushrooms washed thoroughly, drained, passed raw through a sieve, cooked in butter until all the moisture is evaporated, mixed with thick Béchamel and egg yolks, seasoned, stiffly beaten egg whites folded in, filled in greased soufflé dish, baked in oven.
— **Stuffed:** farcis: large caps, gills removed, stuffed with duxelles prepared with the stems, sprinkled with breadcrumbs dotted with butter, gratinated in oven.

N

Nalesniki: Polish Fritters: creamed cottage cheese mixed with butter and eggs, seasoned, wrapped in very thin unsweetened pancakes, dipped in egg and breadcrumbs or in frying batter, deep fried. (Polish)
Navet: see turnip.

Nettles: F. Orties; G. Brennesseln: commonly called stinging nettles. Wholesome and tasty as long as they are picked young. Prepared like spinach.

Nockerl: see noques.

Noodles: F. Nouilles; G. Nudeln: fairly hard dough made of wheat flour with egg yolks or eggs and yolks, salt and nutmeg (no water), allowed to rest for a while covered with a damp cloth, rolled out very thin, cut in thin long strips on a floured board and dried before cooking in salt water. They are then poured into a colander, refreshed with cold water and drained off. Also marketed in different grades.

— **Alsatian Style:** à l'alsacienne: same as with butter, a few uncooked noodles, broken into small pieces and fried brown in butter scattered on top.

— **Florence Style:** à la florentine: cooked, drained, mixed with butter and shredded spinach cooked in butter; filled in baking dish, veal gravy poured over the noodles, sprinkled with grated cheese, dotted with butter, gratinated in oven.

— **Grandmother Style: à la grand'mère:** mixed with butter and strips of fried bacon, arranged in timbale dish, very small croûtons fried in butter and chopped chives scattered on top.

— **Gratinated:** au gratin: mixed with Mornay sauce, filled in greased baking dish, sprinkled with grated Parmesan, dotted with butter, gratinated in oven.

— **Italian Style:** à l'italienne: cooked, drained, mixed with butter and grated Parmesan; bordered with tomato sauce or sauce served separately.

— **Pie:** Pâté de nouilles: cooked, drained, seasoned, mixed with butter, filled in greased pie or baking dish in layers alternately with ragoût of ham or chicken and mushrooms, covered with noodles, egg yolks mixed with cream and salt poured on top, baked in oven.

— **Polish Style:** à la polonaise: mixed with butter, seasoned, breadcrumbs browned in butter on top.

— **Swiss Style:** à la suisse: cooked, drained, seasoned, filled in greased baking dish, covered with hot cream, grated Parmesan sprinkled on top, baked in oven.

— **Westphalian Style:** à la westphalienne: mixed with strips of Westphalian ham, bound with thin Béchamel sauce, filled in greased baking dish, sprinkled with grated Parmesan, dotted with butter and gratinated in oven.

Noques, Nockerl, Nocken: small dumplings made of flour, eggs, milk, butter etc., shaped with a tea- or soupspoon and poached in salt water.

— **Czech:** à la tchèque: cream puff paste made with milk, shaped, poached in salt water, drained, covered with browned butter.

— **Flour: de farine: flour mixed with milk,** eggs and melted butter, seasoned, shaped, poached in salt water, drained and served covered with browned butter.

— **German:** à l'allemande: creamed butter mixed with egg yolks and flour, seasoned with salt and nutmeg, stiffly beaten egg whites folded in, shaped with a spoon, dropped in boiling salt water and poached.

Noodles

— **Polish:** polonaise: firm dough made of flour, eggs, melted butter, sour cream and salt, rolled out 1/2 in. thick, cut in small squares, poached in salt water; drained, arranged in timbale dish, covered with breadcrumbs browned in butter.

— **Semolina:** de semoule: semolina cooked in milk, seasoned, mixed with egg yolks, stiffly beaten egg whites folded in, shaped with a **spoon, poached, filled** in greased baking dish, sprinkled with grated Parmesan, dotted with butter, gratinated in oven.

— **Swiss:** à la suisse: cream puff paste shaped with two teaspoons, filled in greased baking dish, covered generously with grated Gruyère, melted butter dropped on top, baked in oven.

Nouillettes: especially thin, short noodles, prepared like noodles.

O

Occa, Oca, Oxalis; F. Oxalis; G. Oxalis, Sauerkleeknolle: a South American tuber somewhat resembling large walnuts with a yellow to red-brown skin and white floury flesh. Best when stale, the fresh tubers being a little acid. before being cooked they must be scraped, not peeled.

— **Creamed:** à la crème: boiled in salt water, drained, sliced, bound with thin Béchamel sauce, finished off with heavy cream.

— **Financier Style:** à la financière: cooked in white wine and white stock with seasoning in a stewpan with the cover on; drained, sliced and bound with Dutch sauce, to which the boiled down stock has been added; arranged in a timbale dish and served with chopped herbs on top.

— **Miller Style:** à la meunière: white and red occa boiled, cut in fairly thin slices, sautéd in butter until light brown; arranged in timbale dish, seasoned with salt, pepper and lemon juice, browned butter and chopped parsley on top.

— **Steward Style:** à la maître d'hôtel: cooked in white stock, drained, cut in slices; stock boiled down, thickened with white roux, seasoned, finished off with cream and chopped parsley, the slices bound carefully with this sauce.

Oignon: see onion.

Okra: see gombo.

Onion: F. Oignon; G. Zwiebel: a bulbous-rooted member of the lily family and the most valuable flavoring agent in cooking. There are many kinds of onions, viz:

— **Button or Pearl Onions** that are picked before they have reached full size and are used for garnishes and for pickling;

— **the Egyptian, Welsh and Rocambole** Onion or Sand Leek etc.

— **Spanish or Bermuda Onions,** the name given in the U. S. A. for all imported onions. They are milder than most of the other sorts because the acridity decreases in warm climes;
For serving whole, Spanish onions are chiefly used.

Onion

— **Boiled:** Bouilli: boiled carefully in half salted water and milk, drained and served covered with cream sauce.

— **Braised:** braisé: large onion, peeled, browned in butter, braised in stock; stock boiled down, mixed with demi-glace and poured over onion.

— **Fried:** frits: cut in round slices, coated with flour, fried in deep fat, seasoned with salt.

— **Glazed, Brown:** glacés à brun: button onions, peeled, dusted lightly with powder sugar, browned slowly in butter, moistened with brown stock, stock boiled down until onions are glazed.

— **Glazed, White:** glacés à blanc: button onions, peeled, moistened with white stock, butter added, cooked until done and the stock nearly evaporated, rolled to glaze them.

— **Gratinated:** au gratin: medium sized onions boiled, drained, placed in greased baking dish, seasoned, covered with cream sauce, sprinkled with grated cheese and breadcrumbs, dotted with butter, gratinated in oven.

— **Hungarian Style:** à la hongroise: large onions, boiled, drained, chopped coarsely, mixed with chopped green peppers simmered in butter, seasoned with salt and paprika, boiled up with cream.

— **Jewish Style:** à la juive: boiled, allowed to cool off, hollowed out, pulp chopped, mixed with chopped kale cooked in goose fat and filled in onion; sprinkled with breadcrumbs, goose fat dropped on top, gratinated in oven.

— **Lyonese Style:** à la lyonnaise: sliced, fried brown in butter, bound with a little meat glaze, seasoned with a dash of vinegar.

— **Marencic:** Spanish onion boiled, hollowed out, pulp chopped, mixed with spinach purée, covered with Mornay sauce, sprinkled with grated Parmesan, dotted with butter, gratinated in oven.

— **Purée:** Purée Soubise: cut in pieces, scalded, simmered in butter and white stock with rice, salt and pepper in the oven with the cover on, passed through a sieve, finished off with butter and cream. May also be prepared without the rice, boiled down until the moisture is evaporated, strained and mixed with thick Béchamel sáuce.

— **Stuffed:** farci: 1. boiled, allowed to cool off, hollowed out carefully, pulp chopped, mixed with chopped mushrooms and mirepoix bordelaise, filled in onion, sprinkled with breadcrumbs, melted butter dropped on top, gratinated in oven.

2. as above but pulp mixed with pork sausage meat, sprinkled with breadcrumbs, dotted with butter, cooking finished in oven.

— **Tart, Slavonian:** Tarte aux oignons à la slavonienne: onions, sliced, simmered in white stock and butter, allowed to cool off; mixed with raw beaten eggs and sour cream, seasoned with salt and crushed caraway seeds, spread thickly on round cake of yeast dough made with rye flour, diced salt pork scattered on top, allowed to raise, baked in oven.

— **Tartlets Mornay:** sliced, scalded, simmered in butter with a little white stock until done; bound with cream sauce, seasoned, filled in puff pastry tartlets baked light yellow, sprinkled with grated cheese, melted butter dropped on top, gratinated in the oven.

Orties: see nettles.

Oxalis: see Occa.

P

Palmist: F. Chou-palmiste; G. Palmkohl: the tightly rolled up last leaf of a palm tree, cut off before it has had the chance to open itself. Prepared like spring cabbage and eaten raw as a salad.

Palm Shoots: F. Moelle de palmier, Coeur de palmier; G. Palmenmark: the tender shoots of various palm trees used as a vegetable or salad. They are marketed canned.

— **with Butter:** au beurre: heated up, served with melted butter poured on top.

— **with Dutch Sauce:** à la sauce hollandaise: heated up, served on a folded napkin with Dutch sauce separately.

— **Florence Style:** à la florentine: filled with parboiled spinach coarsely chopped and bound with butter, egg yolks and cream, dipped in egg and breadcrumbs, deep fried; cream sauce served separately.

— **Italian Style:** à l'italienne: cut in pieces, simmered in butter with chopped shallots and lemon juice, seasoned, chopped parsley scattered on top.

— **Metropole:** placed in greased baking dish, covered with white onion purée, sprinkled with grated cheese and gratinated; garnished with cooked mushroom caps covered with demi-glace and chopped tarragon scattered on top.

— **Polish Style:** à la polonaise: served hot covered with breadcrumbs browned in plenty of butter.

Panais: see parsnip.

Papanasi cu Smantana: Cheese Cakes with Sour Cream: cottage cheese rubbed through a sieve, mixed with butter, eggs, egg yolks and thick cream, seasoned with salt, sugar and grated lemon peel; shaped into small round flat cakes, fried; sour cream served separately. (Roumanian)

Papaya, Tree Melon; F. Papaya; G. Baummelone, Papaya: the fruit of a tropical tree native of America and now cultivated extensively in Florida. Green unripe papayas are peeled, cut in halves, seeds removed, cut in regular pieces, blanched, simmered in milk and butter or in bouillon and served with butter. Papayas are also prepared like squash.

Parsnip: F. Panais; G. Pastinake: the white root of a plant of the parsley family, used for flavoring soups and as a vegetable. Prepared like knob celery.

Patate: see sweet potato.

Peas, Dried, Green or Yellow; F. Pois secs, jaunes ou verts; G. Trockenerbsen, grün oder gelb; both the green and the ripe yellow seeds are dried, green peas are better flavored. Split peas are marketed with the skin removed. Split and dried peas must be soaked before being boiled.

— **with Bacon:** au lard: boiled with an onion and a bunch of herbs; served covered with sliced fried onions and fried rashers of bacon.

Peas, Dried

— **Bohemian Style:** à la bohémienne: boiled, thickened with breadcrumbs, filled in baking dish greased with butter, sprinkled with breadcrumbs, butter dropped on top, browned in oven.

— **Erbsenmus:** Pease Pudding Austrian Style: soaked, boiled, thickened with pale yellow roux, rubbed through a sieve, served covered with fried onion rings. (Austrian)

— **Hessian Style:** à la hessoise: boiled, seasoned with vinegar and sugar, mixed with soaked raisins, thickened with cracker meal.

— **Pease Pudding:** Purée de pois secs à l'anglaise: soaked, boiled with a larded onion and a bunch of herbs; rubbed through a sieve, seasoned, mixed with beaten egg and butter.

Peas, Green Peas: F. Petit pois, Petit pois vert; G. Erbse, Grüne Erbse: one of the most important and popular vegetable of which there are innumerable varieties. The two main classes are the garden and the field pea.

— **Anna:** blanched, simmered in butter with shredded lettuce and chopped mint, mixed with glazed button onions.

— **with Butter:** au beurre: boiled, drained, bound with butter, seasoned with salt and a pinch of sugar.

— **with Crayfish Tails:** aux écrevisses: cooked, mixed with crayfish tails, bound with butter.

— **Dionysian Style:** à la dionysienne: boiled, drained, mixed with butter, chopped onions fried in butter, diced cooked carrots and potatoes and chopped chervil.

— **Dutch Style:** à la hollandaise: cooked, drained, bound with Dutch sauce.

— **English Style:** à l'anglaise: cooked, drained, served with a piece of fresh butter on top.

— **Farmer Style:** à la paysanne: mixed with shredded lettuce, an onion cut in quarters, butter, salt, a little sugar and water, cooked until done and thickened with butter paste.

— **Flemish Style:** à la flamande: small spring carrots and the same amount of cooked green peas mixed together and bound with butter.

— **Florence Style:** à la florentine: cooked, drained, mixed with chopped ham, chopped fried onions and chopped herbs, bound with tomato sauce.

— **French Way:** à la française: mixed with shredded lettuce, button onions, chopped chervil, butter, salt and a pinch of sugar, cooked with very little water; when done bound with butter paste.

— **German Style:** à l'allemande: boiled, drained, bound with German sauce.

— **Housekeeper Style:** à la ménagère: cooked, mixed with shredded lettuce and chopped onions simmered in butter.

— **Housewife Style:** à la bonne-femme: same as French way with diced blanched salt pork added.

— **with Lettuce:** aux laitues: cooked in the French way but with whole lettuce; when done lettuce cut in quarters, folded and placed on top of the peas.

— **Magdeburg Style:** à la magdebourgeoise: cooked, drained, tossed in butter, mixed with chopped parsley and breadcrumbs fried in butter.

Peas, Green

— **with Mint:** à la menthe: cooked with a bunch of mint, drained, tossed in butter, chopped mint on top.

— **Old Fashioned Style:** à l'ancienne: boiled in salt water with a bunch of herbs; drained, tossed in butter, seasoned, bound with egg yolks mixed with cream.

— **Parmentier:** cooked, mixed with diced boiled potatoes, thickened with butter paste.

— **Purée of:** Purée Saint-Germain: cooked, drained, rubbed through a sieve, finished off with butter and cream.

— **with Salt Pork:** au lard: diced salt pork fried lightly, sprinkled with flour, moistened with white stock, peas added, seasoned, cooked, served mixed with chopped parsley.

— **Saxon Style:** à la saxonne: cooked in white stock with butter, thickened with white roux, mixed with boiled flaked salt cod lightly fried in butter and chopped parsley.

— **Stewed: étuvées:** prepared in the French way in a fire-proof China or earthen pot hermetically closed.

— **with Stockfish:** au morue séché: cooked, mixed with flaked boiled stockfish, chopped parsley and butter.

— **Tenant Style:** à la fermière: small slices of onions, carrots, turnips and diced bacon simmered in butter, mixed with peas, moistened with white stock and stewed until done; thickened with butter paste, chopped parsley on top.

Peas, Sugar: Pois mange-tout: are different from the ordinary green peas lacking the parchement lining of the pod. Pod and peas may be cooked together and tossed in butter or served with a piece of fresh butter on top.

Peperoni: see peppers.

Peppers, Sweet Peppers, Pimiento, Fresh Paprika, Peperoni; F. Poivron doux; G. Paprikaschote, Pfefferschote: the mild flavored large fruit of a capsicum cultivated as vegetable. There are many different varieties, some a brilliant red, others green or yellow. They must be seeded and the filaments removed before being cooked. They are used as a vegetable, in salads, stews and as a garnish.

— **Boston Style:** à la bostonienne: very small peppers, blanched, peeled, seeds removed, filled with crabmeat, dipped in egg and breadcrumbs, moistened with melted butter, grilled slowly.

— **Creole Style:** à la créole: blanched, peeled, seeds removed, filled with creole rice, simmered in thin tomato sauce.

— **Gratinated:** au gratin: peeled, seeded, simmered in butter, placed in baking dish masked with Mornay sauce mixed with chopped cooked onions, covered with Mornay sauce, sprinkled with grated Parmesan, dotted with butter, gratinated in oven.

— **Housekeeper Style:** à la ménagère: blanched, seeds removed, stuffed with pork sausage meat mixed with the same amount of boiled rice, simmered in thin tomato sauce in oven.

— **Oriental Style:** à l'orientale: red peppers, peeled, seeds removed, cut in large squares, mixed with plenty of chopped onions sweated in oil beforehand, moistened with mutton stock, garlic added, simmered slowly until done.

— **Piedmont Style:** à la piémontaise: red peppers peeled, cut in halves, seeds removed, cooked in stock, drained;

Peppers
filled alternately in greased baking dish with risotto, sprinkled with grated Parmesan, melted butter dropped on top, gratinated in oven.
— **Purée of:** Purée de piements doux: blanched, seeds removed, cut in pieces, simmered in butter, mixed with rice cooked in bouillon, rubbed through a sieve, seasoned, finished off with butter.
— **Snagow Style:** à la Snagow: peeled, blanched, seeds removed, filled with saurkraut cooked beforehand in fat stock; placed in sautoir on sliced onions fried a pale yellow in oil, braised in light tomato sauce with diced tomatoes, when done seasoned with lemon juice; served hot or cold.
— **Spanish Style:** à l'espagnole: blanched, peeled, cut in halves or quarters, seeds removed, dipped in frying batter, deep fried.
— **Stuffed:** farcis: skinned, seeded, filled with risotto mixed with diced ham and mushrooms, simmered in thin tomato sauce.
— **Turkish Style:** à la turque: peeled, seeds removed, blanched, filled with two parts rice cooked in mutton stock and one part of cooked hashed mutton, seasoned with salt, pepper and garlic, bound with tomato purée; arranged on chopped onions sweated in oil, covered with thin tomato sauce, braised in oven.

Pétit Pois: see pea.

Pe-Tsai: Chinese Cabbage: a variety of cabbage resembling cos lettuce. A native of China but now grown in Europe chiefly in France. Prepared like Savoy cabbage.

Pieds de fenouil: see fennel.

Piment doux: see pimiento:

Pimiento: Piment doux: bright red variety of sweet peppers cultivated in Spain, used for stuffing olives, salads, stews, garnishes and as a vegetable. Marketed fresh and peeled and canned. See peppers.

Pissenlit: see dandelion.

Pizza: a sort of cake made of yeast dough or puff paste with tomatoes, cheese, olives, ham, anchovies etc., served hot. (Italian)
— **alla napoletana:** Naples Style: yeast dough made with lard rolled out to a thin round cake, brushed with olive oil, covered with slices of peeled and seeded tomatoes, a little Mozzarella cheese (cottage cheese will do) placed on top, seasoned with salt, pepper, majoran and thyme, a few chopped anchovy fillets scattered on the cheese, olive oil dropped on top, baked in oven. (Italian)

Podrida Créole: red haricot beans cooked in water with onions, garlic and a piece of lean bacon; thickened with butter paste, mixed with the diced bacon, served in a border of risotto without cheese, prepared with lard. (Spanish)

Pointes d'Amour: fancy name for green asparagus tips.

Poireau: see leek.

Poirée à carde: see chard.

Pois-chiches: see chick-peas.

Pois mange-tout: see sugar peas.

Pois secs: see peas, dried.

Poivron doux: see peppers.

Polenta: mush made of corn meal cooked in water with butter and salt, mixed with grated Parmesan.

— **Fried:** frit: cooked, spread on a baking sheet moistened lightly with water and allowed to cool off; cut in squares or lozenge-shaped, fried in butter, sprinkled with grated Parmesan, browned butter poured on top.

— **Piedmont Style:** à l'piémontaise: cooked in water with butter and salt, mixed with grated Parmesan, filled in greased mould and poached in water bath in oven; turned out on round platter, covered with tomato sauce, grated Parmesan served separately.

Pomme de terre: see potato.

Porridge: the meal of any kind of grain boiled with either water or milk and salt, usually cooked in a double boiler.

— **Oat-meal:** Bouillie d'avoine: oatmeal cooked in water and salt, served with sugar and cream as a breakfast dish.

Potato; F. Pomme de terre; G. Kartoffel, Erdäpfel: the most important of all vegetables, native of Peru. There are many varieties of potatoes, early and late, and hundreds of ways to prepare them. Potatoes with a waxy, rather yellowish pulp are best for frying and the whiter and softer ones for baking and boiling.

— **Aloo Madarasi:** chopped onions sweated in mustard oil, diced raw potatoes added, seasoned generously with curry powder, moistened with lentil stock, chopped lemon peel and a little cinnamon added and cooked, served with melted butter. (Indian)

— **Almond:** Pommes de terre amandines: croquette mixture with half their weight cream **puff paste,** shaped into croquettes of the desired shape, dipped in egg and slivered almonds, deep fried.

— **Alphonso:** Alphonse: boiled in the skin, peeled, sliced, mixed with herb butter, filled in greased baking dish, sprinkled with grated Gruyère, dotted with butter, gratinated.

— **Alsatian Style:** à l'alsacienne: small new potatoes, peeled, cooked in butter with diced bacon, chopped onions and herbs. Prepared out of season with large cubes of raw potatoes.

— **Ambassador Style:** à l'ambassadeur same as Voisin.

— **with Anchovies:** aux anchois: 1. raw slices simmered in butter with chopped onions, covered with sour cream, chopped anchovy fillets and parsley added, cooked until done.
2. German fried potatoes with chopped anchovy fillets and parsley added.

— **Anna:** cut into round slices, arranged in lavers in special mould or flat casserole containing clarified butter, baked in oven, turned out on round platter. For garnish use beaker moulds.

— **Ardennes Style:** à l'ardennaise: baked, hollowed out, filled with the mashed pulp mixed with butter, chicken purée, chopped ham and chives, sprinkled with grated cheese, browned in oven.

— **with Bacon:** au lard: button onions and diced bacon fried, chopped herbs and a little garlic added, dusted with flour, moistened with beef stock, olive-shaped raw potatoes added and cooked.

Potato

— **Baked:** au four: large mealy potatoes, baked in oven, split open, fresh butter inserted.

— **Baker Style: à la boulangère:** onions and potatoes cut in slices, onions sweated in butter, potatoes added, seasoned, baked in oven. Small potatoes may also be cut in quarters.

— **Bartholdy:** German fried potatoes tossed, when done, in butter and liquid meat glaze.

— **Basket:** Panier de pommes de terre: shoestring or straw potatoes fried between a special set of wire baskets in deep fat.

— **Bataillé:** cut in large cubes, blanched, deep fried.

— **Bénedictine:** cut with a spiral cutter, deep fried.

— **Berny:** croquette mixture with chopped truffle, apricot shaped, dipped in egg and chopped almonds, deep fried.

— **Berry Style:** à la berrichonne: shaped like castle potatoes, simmered in bouillon with diced lean bacon, chopped onions and herbs.

— **Biarritz: mashed** potatoes with finely diced ham, green peppers and chopped parsley added.

— **Bignon:** raw potatoes, peeled, shaped like small flat barrels, scooped out, filled with pork sausage meat; sprinkled with breadcrumbs, dotted with butter, cooked in slow oven, served with a border of Madeira sauce.

— **Bohemian Style:** à la bohémienne: baked in jacket, hollowed out, filled with the mashed pulp mixed with pork sausage meat, brushed with butter, cooked in oven.

— **Boiled:** à l'anglaise: peeled, boiled or steamed.

— **Bordeaux Style:** à la bordelaise: same as Parmentier with finely chopped garlic.

— **Brabant Style:** à la brabançonne: boiled, peeled, sliced, mixed with chopped shallots, parsley, butter and grated Parmesan; filled in Charlotte mould greased with butter, baked in oven, turned out.

— **Breton Style:** à la bretonne: cut in large cubes, cooked in consommé with chopped onions, crushed garlic and diced tomatoes.

— **Brioche:** duchess potato mixture shaped into small brioches, coated with egg yolks, baked in oven.

— **Brühkartoffeln:** Bouillon Potatoes: cut in large cubes, boiled in bouillon with crushed caraway seeds, finely diced root vegetables and chopped parsley. (German)

— **Bussy:** croquette mixture with chopped truffles, parsley and grated Parmesan, shaped like small cigars, dipped in egg and breadcrumbs, deep fried.

— **Byron:** baked, peeled, chopped with butter added, fried in tiny skillets, turned out; covered with cream, sprinkled with grated cheese, gratinated.

— **Carême:** mashed potatoes mixed with heavy cream and grated Parmesan, filled in greased scallop shells, sprinkled with grated cheese, butter dropped on top, gratinated.

— **with Caraway Seeds:** au cumin: peeled, boiled with caraway seeds added to water.

— **Castle:** Château: olive-shaped about the size of a pigeons egg, blanched, browned in butter, chopped parsley scattered on top.

— **Chambéry:** raw potatoes chopped coarsely, seasoned, mixed with butter and grated Parmesan, filled in greased

Potato

baking dish, sprinkled with Parmesan, dotted with butter, cooked in slow oven.

— **Chamonix:** same as Dauphine with grated cheese.

— **Champignol:** fondantes potatoes sprinkled with grated cheese and glazed.

— **Chancelor Style:** à la chancelière: cut out in ball shape, steamed or boiled, bound with light cream sauce blended with butter.

— **Chateaubriand:** olive-shaped, fried in butter, mixed with chopped herbs and veal glaze.

— **Chatouillard:** cut into long thin shavings, deep fried.

— **Chinese Style:** à la chinoise: raw potatoes, egg-shaped, hollowed out, filled with hashed beef mixed with chopped green peppers and spices; coated with melted butter, cooked in slow oven.

— **Chips:** same as Sarratoga chips.

— **Christie:** baked, hollowed out, stuffed with the mashed pulp mixed with purée of sautéd chicken livers and tomato purée.

— **Cocotte:** shaped like longish olives about a quarter of the size of castle potatoes, fried golden brown in clarified butter; sprinkled with chopped parsley at serving.

— **Colbert:** Parmentier tossed in butter, liquid meat glaze and chopped parsley.

— **Colombine:** à la colombine: peeled, cut in slices, sautéd with julienne of red or green peppers added.

— **Commander Style:** à la commodore: baked, hollowed out, pulp mashed, mixed with butter, spinach purée and chopped herbs; refilled in the skin, brushed with melted butter and pushed in the oven for a few minutes.

— **Continental Style:** à la continentale: cut in egg-shaped slices, fried in butter, served with coarse truffle julienne scattered on top.

— **Contrexville:** cut in quarters, fried in butter with diced bacon, chopped onions and chopped herbs.

— **Copeaux:** cut like wood shavings, deep fried.

— **Creamed:** à la crème: boiled in jacket, peeled, sliced, moistened with milk, butter and salt added, cooked, cream added when about to serve.

— **Creamed and Corn:** diced, cooked in milk and butter with sweet corn added, finished off with heavy cream.

— **Creamed, Hashed:** hachées à la crème: boiled, hashed, bound with thin cream sauce, filled in baking dish, sprinkled with breadcrumbs and grated cheese, dotted with butter, browned in oven.

— **Croquette:** Croquettes de pommes de terre: boiled, dried thoroughly, strained, mixed with butter and egg yolks, allowed to cool, shaped into croquettes, dipped in egg and breadcrumbs, deep fried.

— **Croquette Royal Style:** Croquettes de p. d. t. à la royale: croquette mixture with chopped truffles, shaped and fried as usual.

— **in Curry Sauce:** au currie: boiled in jacket, peeled, sliced, bound with light curry sauce.

— **Dauphine:** boiled, drained, strained, mixed with half as much unsweetened cream puff paste, shaped into croquettes or as desired, deep fried.

Potato

— **Dauphiné Style:** à la dauphinoise: sliced raw, placed in baking dish rubbed with garlic, seasoned, moistened with milk, sprinkled with grated Gruyère cheese, cooked and browned in oven.

— **Delmonico:** diced, cooked in milk with butter and seasoning, heavy cream and diced pimiento added, filled in baking dish greased with butter, sprinkled with breadcrumbs, dotted with butter, browned in oven.

— **Dietrich:** potato croquette mixture mixed with unsweetened cream puff paste, shaped into croquettes, dipped in egg and breadcrumbs, deep fried.

— **Dijon Style:** à la dijonaise: boiled, sliced, mixed with chopped ham, bound with thin mustard sauce prepared with Dijon mustard.

— **Dressel:** diced raw, cooked in milk, placed in baking dish, sprinkled with breadcrumbs and grated cheese, dotted with butter, browned in oven.

— **Duchess:** duchesse: peeled, boiled, strained, mixed with egg yolks and butter, seasoned; shaped into small cakes, with a piping bag into rosettes or any other fancy shape, brushed with melted butter, baked golden brown in oven.

— **Dutch Style:** à la hollandaise: 1. nicely shaped boiled potatoes covered with melted butter.
2. nicely shaped raw potatoes simmered in water and butter with button onions, seasoned with salt, pepper and vinegar.

— **Elisabeth:** dauphine potatoes stuffed with creamed spinach purée.

— **Farmer Style:** à la paysanne: cut in thick slices, simmered in butter and bouillon with a little garlic; when done mixed with shredded sorrel simmered in butter and chopped chervil.

— **Flemish Style:** à la flamande: shaped like small castle potatoes, simmered in butter and bouillon with button onions and olive-shaped carrots.

— **Florence Style:** à la florentine: well greased mould filled alternately with layers of sliced boiled potatoes and coarsely chopped spinach bound with cream sauce, butter poured on top, baked in oven; turned out on round flat baking dish, covered with cream, sprinkled with grated Parmesan, glazed.

— **Flower Villa:** Villa des fleurs: same as Delmonico with grated cheese.

— **Fondantes:** cut like castle potatoes but a little larger, blanched, cooked in butter without allowing them to brown, crushed lightly with a fork, fresh butter added until it is absorbed.

— **French Fried:** frites: cut into thick strips the length of a finger, deep fried.

— **Fried Dumplings:** Godard: dauphine potato mixture dropped with a teaspoon in deep fat and fried.

— **Frill: Collerette:** cut with a spiral cutter like frills, fried in deep fat.

— **Georgette:** baked, opened on one side, part of the pulp removed, filled with crayfish tails bound with Nantua sauce, served very hot on a napkin.

Potato

— **German Fried:** sautées à l'allemande: boiled in jacket, peeled, cut in rather thick slices, fried in butter golden brown.
— **Gilbertine:** raw round slices, blanched, cooked in veal gravy, thickened with cream; filled in greased baking dish, sprinkled with grated cheese, glazed.
— **Gourmet Style:** du gourmet: raw, cork-shaped, simmered in butter, when nearly done liquid meat glaze and chopped truffles added.
— **Gratinated:** au gratin: creamed potatoes filled in baking dish, sprinkled with grated cheese, dotted with butter, gratinated in oven.
— **Gratinated Mashed:** Purée de pommes de terre gratiné: mashed potatoes filled in greased baking dish, sprinkled with grated cheese, dotted with butter, gratinated in oven.
— **Hanoverian Style:** à la hannoverienne: peeled, nicely shaped, cooked in beef broth, served covered with flakes of fresh butter, sprinkled with chopped parsley.
— **Hashed Browned:** hachées brune: boiled, drained, chopped coarsely, mixed with butter and seasoning, fried on both sides in small frying pan like a pancake and turned out.
— **Heringskartoffeln:** Potatoes with Herring: sliced boiled potatoes and pieces of desalted herring fillets filled alternately in baking dish greased with butter, covered with sour cream, baked in oven. (German)
— **Housekeeper Style:** à la ménagère: baked, hollowed out, the pulp mashed with a fork, mixed with chopped ham, chopped fried onions, milk and seasoning; refilled in skin, sprinkled with grated cheese, dotted with butter, browned in oven.
— **Housewife Style:** à la bonne-femme: 1. raw, shaped like small castle potatoes, cooked together in butter with button onions browned lightly beforehand.
2. peeled, blanched for a few minutes, drained, chopped coarsely, simmered in butter and light cream with shredded lettuce, chopped parsley and seasoning.
— **Hungarian Style:** à la hongroise: sliced onions lightly fried in lard, sliced raw potatoes, diced tomatoes and paprika added, moistened with white stock and sour cream, cooked.
— **Ideal:** Idéale: croquette mixture with unsweetened cream puff paste mixed with short truffle strips, shaped into croquettes, dipped in egg and breadcrumbs, deep fried.
— **Irish:** à l'irlandaise: cut in longish ribbons, cooked in steam.
— **Italian Style:** à l'italienne: baked in oven, hollowed out, pulp mashed mixed with boiled rice, tomato purée and grated Parmesan; refilled in the skin, sprinkled with grated Parmesan, melted butter dropped on top, browned in oven.
— **in Jacket:** en robe de champs or en jaquette: boiled in the skin in salt water, drained and dried in oven for a few minutes.
— **Jackson:** baked, hollowed out, pulp mashed with a fork, seasoned, refilled in the skin, a generous amount of melted butter poured on top and pushed in the oven for a few minutes.

Potato

— **Kartoffelpuffer:** Potato Pancake: raw potatoes, peeled, grated, covered with water, pulp allowed to rest for a while, drained, squeezed perfectly dry, mixed with a little flour, egg yolks, sour cream, salt and stiffly beaten egg white; fried in small skillets as thin and as crisp as possible. (German)

— **Kartoffelspatzen:** cold boiled potatoes, grated, mixed with hot milk, butter, breadcrumbs, eggs, salt and pepper; shaped with two spoons, boiled, drained, covered with browned butter. (German)

— **Lafitte:** croquette mixture shaped like small cigars, dipped in egg and breadcrumbs, deep fried.

— **Lola Montez:** baked, hollowed out, pulp mashed, mixed with chopped peppers simmered in butter, chopped herbs and whipped unsweetened cream; refilled in jacket, pushed in the oven for a few minutes, glazed with butter.

— **Lorette:** dauphine potato mixture with grated Parmesan, shaped into small crescents, deep fried.

— **Lyonese Style:** à la lyonnaise: German fried potatoes mixed with fried sliced onions, chopped parsley scattered on top.

— **Macaire:** baked, hollowed out, pulp mashed lightly, seasoned, mixed with butter and fried in small frying-pan like a pancake.

— **Maire:** prepared like steward style but without parsley, a little cream added when about to serve them.

— **Majoran-Erdäpfel:** Marjoram Potatoes: boiled, cut in cubes, simmered in demiglace with chopped marjoram. (Austrian)

— **Maria:** croquette mixture with grated Parmesan, shaped into croquettes, dipped in egg and breadcrumbs, deep fried.

— **Marquise:** croquette mixture with butter and thick tomato purée, dressed on baking tin like meringues or round flat cakes, brushed with butter, browned in oven.

— **Mashed,** Purée of: Purée de pommes de terre: peeled mealy potatoes boiled or steamed, squeezed while hot through a ricer into a saucepan, fresh butter and hot milk or cream added and stirred lightly; salt added if necessary.

— **Match: allumettes:** cut match size from raw potatoes, soaked in water, dried perfectly, fried in deep fat, salted.

— **with Mint:** à la menthe: new potatoes boiled in the skin with a bunch of mint; peeled, rolled in butter, blanched mint leaves placed on top.

— **Mireille:** Anna potatoes with thin small slices of raw artichoke bottoms and truffles added.

— **with Mirepoix:** aux mirepoix: raw potatoes cut in cubes, browned in butter with very fine mirepoix.

— **Mirette:** cut in cubes, sautéd in butter, julienne of truffle added, tossed carefully in liquid meat glaze; filled in baking dish, sprinkled with grated Parmesan, glazed.

— **Monselet:** cut raw in thin slices, sautéd in butter, arranged like a ring with sautéd mushroom slices in center, truffle julienne scattered on top.

— **Mousseline:** mashed potatoes mixed with butter and whipped cream.

Potato

— **Mousseline, Gratinated:** Pommes de terre mousseline gratinées: mashed potatoes mixed with butter, egg yolks and whipped cream, filled in egg dish or pastry crust baked white, decorated with a part of the mixture with a star tube, melted butter dropped on top, baked in oven.

— **Nana:** dauphine potato mixture baked in beaker moulds greased with butter.

— **Nassau Style:** à la nassauvienne: baked in jacket, hollowed out, filled with the mashed pulp mixed with butter, cream, chopped chives and grated Parmesan; sprinkled with grated Parmesan, melted butter dropped on top, browned in oven.

— **New:** Pommes nouvelles: boiled in jacket, peeled, tossed in butter.

— **New, Roast:** Pommes nouvelles risolées: boiled in jacket, peeled, fried golden brown in butter in oven.

— **Ninette:** Anna potatoes mixed with grated Parmesan.

— **Norman Style:** à la normande: sliced raw, cooked in butter with chopped onions and leeks sweated in butter, dusted with flour, moistened with milk, seasoned, boiled up; filled in baking dish, sprinkled with grated cheese and gratinated.

— **Nostiz:** croquette mixture shaped into squares, dipped in melted butter and grated Parmesan, arranged on greased baking tin, sprinkled with breadcrumbs, crayfish butter dropped on top, baked in oven.

— **Nut:** noisettes: raw, cut with a vegetable borer in ball shape, browned in butter, chopped parsley sprinkled on top when about to serve.

— **O'Brien:** boiled, skinned, chopped coarsely, mixed with diced red peppers, browned in butter.

— **Pancake:** Galette de pommes de terre: raw potatoes, peeled, grated fine, pulp allowed to rest for a while, water drained thoroughly, mixed with beaten egg, a little flour, nutmeg and salt to make a thin batter; fried as thin and crisp as possible in a small skillet.

— **Parisian:** parisiennes: raw potatoes cut in ball shape, browned in butter, rolled in liquid meat glaze.

— **Parmentier:** raw, cut in cubes, browned in butter, sprinkled with chopped chives.

— **Parsley:** persilées: peeled, nicely shaped, boiled, rolled in melted butter, chopped parsley sprinkled on top.

— **Polish Style:** à la polonaise: boiled potatoes covered with breadcrumbs browned in butter.

— **Pont-neuf:** cut evenly the length and thickness of a thumb, deep fried.

— **Portuguese Style:** à la portugaise: diced raw, simmered in thin tomato sauce with garlic, chopped onions, thyme and bayleaf.

— **Provencal Style:** à la provençale: raw slices sautéd in oil with chopped garlic and herbs.

— **Puffed:** soufflées: large special potatoes cut evenly in round or square slices about 1/8 in. thick, perfectly dry when immersed in clean hot fat. Cooked in two or three stages each stage with increased heat; the final dip in very hot fat will puff up the potatoes in nicely-rounded cushions.

Potato

— **Riche:** raw potatoes cut lengthwise in quarters, blanched, browned in butter, mixed with chopped fried onions and chopped herbs.

— **Ritz:** raw potatoes cut in cubes, boiled, drained, mixed with chopped fried onions and diced red peppers simmered in butter.

— **Robert:** same as Macaire with beaten eggs, butter and chopped chives added to potato mixture.

— **Rosette:** duchess potato mixture mixed with tomato purée and kept fairly thick; when cold shaped into roses, dipped carefully in egg and breadcrumbs, deep fried.

— **Russian Style:** à la russe: 1. German fried potatoes, chopped ham and soft herring roes filled alternately in baking dish, covered with sour cream blended with egg yolks, sprinkled with grated Parmesan, dotted with butter baked in oven.
2. small potatoes, boiled, peeled, simmered in sour cream and butter.

— **Saint-Florentin:** croquette mixture with chopped ham, shaped as usual, dipped in egg and crushed noodles, deep fried.

— **Saratoga Chips:** round or oval, thinly sliced by machine or by hand, soaked in salt water, dried perfectly, deep fried, salted. Also sold commercially.

— **Sarlade Style:** à la sarladaise: cut raw in slices, mixed with a quarter of the amount of raw truffle slices, cooked and lightly browned in butter.

— **Savoy Style:** à la savoyarde: raw slices, filled in baking dish rubbed with garlic, covered with bouillon mixed with beaten eggs, sprinkled with grated Parmesan, dotted with butter, cooked in slow oven.

— **Schneider:** raw, fairly thick slices, cooked in beef stock and butter, finished off with meat glaze and chopped parsley.

— **Shoestring:** cordon de soulier: long potatoes cut in thin slices, half a dozen placed together, cut into even strips the longer the better, soaked in water, dried perfectly, fried quickly in deep fat, sprinkled with salt.

— **Snow:** en neige: boiled potatoes while still hot rubbed through a coarse sieve directly into serving dish.

— **Soufflé:** Soufflé de pommes de terre: mealy potatoes, boiled, mashed, mixed with butter, cream, egg yolks, seasoning, stiffly beaten egg whites added, filled in soufflé dish, sprinkled with grated cheese, dotted with butter, baked in oven.

— **Steamed:** à la vapeur: peeled, nicely shaped, cooked in steam.

— **Steward:** Maître d'hôtel: same as creamed potatoes with chopped parsley scattered on top.

— **Straw:** pailles: same as shoestrings but shorter.

— **Swabian Style:** à la souabe: raw potatoes cut lengthwise in quarters, cooked in beef stock and butter, served covered with chopped onions fried in a generous amount of butter.

— **Swiss Style:** à la suisse: raw slices cooked in milk with seasoning, placed in greased baking dish, sprinkled with grated Emmenthal or Gruyère cheese, gratinated in oven.

Potato

— **Surprise:** en surprise: baked in jacket, lid cut off, hollowed out, pulp mashed, mixed with butter, cream and chopped parsley, refilled in skin, lid put on, pushed in oven for a few minutes and served on folded napkin.

— **Suzette:** cut into egg shape, cooked in oven with butter, lid cut off, hollowed out carefully, pulp mashed, mixed with chopped ox tongue, chicken, mushrooms, butter and egg yolks, refilled into potato, lid put on, cooking finished off in oven; glazed with butter when about to serve.

— **Turkish Style:** à la turque: raw slices fried in oil, served on pilaf rice, covered with curry sauce.

— **with Turnips:** à la freneuse: mashed potatoes mixed with dixed turnips simmered in butter.

— **Vauban:** large cubes, blanched, drained, browned in butter.

— **Village Style:** à la villageoise: boiled, allowed to cool off, chopped coarsely, simmered in butter and cream.

— **Voisin:** prepared like Anna potatoes with grated Parmesan between the layers.

— **Warsovian Style:** à la varsovienne: cabbage leaves with the ribs removed, blanched, filled with croquette mixture, rolled together, simmered in butter and rich beef stock; served covered with the thickened gravy.

— **Westfälische Kartoffeln:** Westphalian Potatoes: mashed potatoes mixed with purée of sour apples and butter, covered with breadcrumbs browned in plenty of butter. (German)

Potiron: see pumpkin.

Pourpier: see purslane.

Pumpkin: F. Potiron; G. Kürbis: a large round kind of squash with a grooved surface and orange color. It is used for pies, pickled and as a winter vegetable.

— **Braised:** braisé: cut in cubes, scalded, browned in butter, braised with veal gravy.

— **German Style:** à l'allemande: cut in cubes, scalded, simmered in butter with chopped onions and diced bacon, moistened with demi-glace, cooked.

— **Hungarian Style:** à la hongroise: same as Kürbiskraut with paprika added.

— **Kürbiskraut:** cut in strips, salted, allowed to stand for a while, moisture squeezed out; strips mixed with fried sliced onions, dredged with flour, moistened with sour milk, seasoned with salt, pepper, aniseed and vinegar, stewed until done. (Austrian)

— **Mashed:** en purée: cooked, mashed, mixed with mashed freshly boiled potatoes, seasoned, finished off with butter and cream.

— **with Tomatoes:** à la tomate: chopped onions sweated in butter, diced tomatoes and diced pumpkin added, seasoned, simmered for a few minutes, moistened with tomato sauce, cooked, chopped parsley scattered on top.

Purée: vegetables cooked soft, strained, seasoned, finished off with butter, cream, milk, Béchamel sauce etc. as the case may warrant.

— **Argenteuil:** asparagus purée made with thick Béchamel sauce, butter and cream.

— **Brasilian:** brésilienne: purée of occa finished off with mashed potatoes, butter and cream.

Purée
— **Clamart:** purée of fresh green peas finished off with cream and butter.
— **Condé:** purée of red kidney beans cooked with red wine and lean bacon, finished off with butter.
— **Conti:** purée of lentils finished off with cream and butter.
— **Crécy:** mashed carrots mixed with rice purée, finished off with butter.
— **Dubarry:** purée of cauliflower mixed with potato purée, finished off with cream and butter.
— **Favorite:** purée of green beans thickened with Béchamel sauce, finished off with butter.
— **Flemish:** flamande: purée of Brussels sprouts mixed with potato purée.
— **Freneuse:** purée of turnips mixed with mashed potatoes and butter.
— **Musart:** purée of green haricot beans.
— **Palestine:** purée of Jerusalem artichokes mixed with the same amount of mashed potatoes, finished off with cream and butter.
— **Parmentier:** mashed potatoes.
— **Rachel:** purée of artichoke bottom with thick Béchamel, butter and cream.
— **Saxon:** saxonne: purée of turnips, potatoes and onions.
— **Soubise:** purée of onions cooked with rice.
— **Suzette:** purée of knob celery and potatoes, finished off with cream and butter.

Purslane F. Pourpier; G. Portulak: a garden plant with thick fleshy stalks and leaves used in salads and as a vegetable.
— **Brussels Style:** à la bruxelloise: leaves and stalks parboiled, chopped coarsely, simmered in oil with chopped parsley and garlic, seasoned with salt and nutmeg, mixed with bread, soaked in milk, and egg yolks; filled in greased baking dish, sprinkled with grated Parmesan, oil dropped on top, browned in oven.
— **Creamed:** à la crème: young leaves prepared like spinach purée, finished off with cream.
— **Dutch Style:** à la hollandaise: leaves blanched, chopped, simmered in butter, seasoned, bound with egg yolks and butter paste.
— **French Style:** à la française: parboiled stalks cooked in fat bouillon; drained, arranged in greased baking dish, sprinkled with grated Parmesan, dotted with butter and gratinated.
— **Fried:** frit: stalks cut into convenient pieces, cooked in salt water, drained, seasoned, dipped in frying batter, deep fried.
— **with Gravy:** au jus: stalks boiled in salt water, drained, simmered in butter, covered with thick veal gravy.

Q

Quenelle: see dumpling.

R

Radis: see radish.

Radish: F. Radis; G. Radieschen: the fleshy root of many radix plants, either round, oval, olive-shaped or tapering,

Radish
white, pink, scarlet or black in colour with a tangy peppery taste. Eaten with salt as an appetizer, in salads and as a vegetable when young.
— **Creamed:** à la crème: peeled, parboiled simmered in butter, finished off with cream or thin cream sauce.
— **Curried:** au curry: large radishes, sliced, blanched, simmered in butter with chopped onions, dusted with curry powder, cooked in thin cream sauce; served in border of plain boiled rice.
— **Glaced:** glacés: small radishes, peeled, blanched, cooked in veal stock and butter with a little sugar until moisture is completely evaporated and the radishes glazed.
— **Sautéd:** sauté: peeled, parboiled, sautéd in butter.

Rahalou: Vegetable Ragoût: blanched French beans, red peppers and eggplants, cut in large julienne, and okra, each part simmered for itself in oil with chopped shallots, seasoned with salt and paprika, bound with tomato sauce; served with pilaf rice.

Ravioli: dough of flour, eggs, luke warm water, oil and salt, prepared like noodle dough, rolled out very thin; stuffing prepared with chopped braised beef, calf's brains, cooked chopped spinach and anchovy fillets (optional), mixed with thick demi-glace, placed in small heaps at intervals; covered with another sheet of dough, cut out with a pastry wheel, cooked in salt water and allowed to draw for a few minutes. Drained, arranged in a timbale dish, covered with thick veal gravy, sprinkled with grated cheese, browned butter poured on top. (Italian)
— **Gratinated:** au gratin: cooked, drained, placed in greased baking dish covered with tomato sauce, sprinkled with grated Parmesan, melted butter poured on top, gratinated in oven.

Rhubarb: F. Rhubarbe; G. Rhabarber: plant of Asiatic origin cultivated for its fleshy leaf-stalks. Used for making pies and sometimes as a vegetable.
— **with browned Butter:** au beurre noisette: stalks peeled, cut in pieces of equal size, poached carefully in salt water, drained; arranged on platter and covered with breadcrumbs fried in a generous amount of butter.

Rice: F. riz; G. Reis; I. riso: a widely cultivated variety of grains, raised mainly in lands that can be flooded with water. Cultivated extensively in Asia and successfully in Italy, America and elsewhere. Patna, Carolina and Java rice are considered the best. Rice is used for risotto, pilaf, also pilaff, for curries, as a garnish, for sweets, stuffings etc.
— **Boiled**, Plain: nature: cooked quickly in salt water, refreshed in running cold water, drained, heated up. Rice must be done but firm and granular.
— **Creole Style:** à la créole: cooked in salt water, cooled quickly in running water, drained perfectly, spread in thin layer on tray or baking sheet, dried at low temperature in oven; should be granulated, loose and perfectly dry.
— **Croquettes:** Croquettes de riz: risotto bound with egg yolks, mixed with grated Parmesan and fresh butter,

Rice, Croquettes
spread on a baking sheet and allowed to cool off; shaped into croquettes of the desired shape, dipped in egg and breadcrumbs, deep fried; tomato sauce served separately (optional); risotto may be mixed with diced mushrooms, chicken, ham, chicken livers etc.
— **Fat:** au gras: cooked in fat bouillon until perfectly dry.
— **Greek Style:** à la grecque: pilaf rice mixed with fragments of pork sausage meat, shredded lettuce, green peas and diced red peppers.
— **Indian:** à l'indienne: same as Creole.
— **Montargis:** pilaf mixed with diced artichoke bottoms and truffles.
— **Palermo Style:** à la palermitaine: simmered in fat stock with diced tomatoes, mixed with chopped parsley and fresh butter; grated Parmesan served separately.
— **Parisian Style:** à la parisienne: pilaf mixed with diced mushrooms, grated Parmesan and tomato sauce.
— **Pilaf, Pilaff:** Pilaw, Pilaf: chopped onion sweated in butter with rice, moistened with the double amount of white stock, seasoned, cooked in oven with cover on without stirring. For Pilaf dishes see main course.
— **Risi Bisi,** Risi Pisi: fat rice mixed with a generous amount of fresh green peas.
— **Spanish Style:** à l'espagnole: sweated in butter with chopped onions, moistened with stock and a little tomato purée, diced ham and chopped sweet peppers added, cooked, seasoned with Cayenne pepper; when done mixed with fresh butter.
— **Valenciennes:** pilaf mixed with diced raw ham, diced tomatoes, diced sweet peppers and green peas.
— **White:** au blanc: cooked like plain rice, drained, spread on baking sheet, dried in slow oven, salted and mixed lightly with fresh butter; must be loose and granular.

Risotto, Italian Rice; F. Risotto; G. Käsereis, Risotto: chopped onion sweated in oil or butter, rice added and fried very lightly, filled up with bouillon — ratio of liquid to rice 3 : 1 —, boiled without stirring; when done grated Parmesan and flakes of butter added.
— **alla certosina:** prepared Italian style, served with ragoût of scampi, diced fish fillet, mushrooms and green peas bound with white wine sauce. (Italian)
— **Epicurean Style:** à l'épicurienne: risotto prepared with melted ox marrow, mixed with sliced fried pork sausage, filled in border mould; turned out, center filled with ragoût of calf's sweetbreads, cockscombs, cock's kidneys and truffles bound with demi-glace with tomato purée.
— **Fasten:** de carême: sweated in oil, moistened with fish stock; when done mixed with diced fish, lobster and shrimps.
— **Financier Style:** à la financière: served with financier garnish and sauce.
— **Florence Style:** à la florentine: onions and rice sweated with diced ox marrow; when done mixed with Parmesan, butter and diced tomatoes and truffles.
— **Gourmet Style:** du gourmet: risotto mixed with diced sautéd chicken livers, pressed in border mould and turned out; center filled with asparagus tips bound with cream sauce.

Rice

— **Italian Style:** à l'italienne: sweated in oil; when done mixed with butter and half grated Parmesan and half Gruyère.

— **Mariner Style:** à la marinière preapred like macaroni.

— **Matriciana:** prepared with diced salt pork, garlic and diced tomatoes. (Italian)

— **alla milanese:** garlic lightly fried in oil and diced ox marrow, taken out, rice sweated in the oil, moistened with broth, seasoned, colored with saffron; grated Parmesan served separately. (Italian)

— **Milanese Style:** à la milanaise: mixed with julienne of ox tongue, mushrooms, truffles, butter and grated Parmesan; served with tomato sauce.

— **Naples Style:** à la napolitaine: rice and onions sweated with diced salt pork, moistened with stock, seasoned, mixed with diced tomatoes; grated Parmesan served separately.

— **Parisian Style:** à la parisienne: mixed with diced mushrooms, tomato sauce and grated Parmesan.

— **Piedmont Style:** à la piémontaise: prepared with saffron, mixed with slices of white Italian truffles, grated Parmesan and butter.

— **Saint-Denis:** cooked with raw diced mushrooms; bordered with demi-glace, grated Parmesan served separately.

— **Turkish Style:** à la turque: prepared with saffron and diced tomatoes.

— **Valenciana:** prepared with diced fried ham and diced green peppers; bordered with demi-glace, grated Parmesan served separately.

— **Vengiana:** mixed with julienne of chicken, ham, mushrooms and truffles.

— **alle vongole:** with Mussels: prepared with fish stock, mussel stock and white wine, mixed with small bearded mussels. (Italian)

Riz: see rice.

Rutabaga: see swede.

S

Salsifis: see salsify.

Salsify: F. Salsifis; G. Schwarzwurzel: a long thin tapering root of which there are two different kinds: one with a black and the other with yellowish-white skin. Both have a pleasant taste and are used as a vegetable. Before further preparation the salsify is scraped and boiled in a blanc (water to which flour and raw kidney fat has been added).

— **Creamed:** à la crème: cut in small pieces, parboiled, simmered in butter, seasoned, cooking finished with cream.

— **Croquettes of:** Croquettes de salsifis: boiled, drained, chopped, bound with thick Béchamel and egg yolks, seasoned, allowed to cool off; shaped into croquettes, dipped in egg and breadcrumbs, fried in deep fat.

Salsify

— **Dutch Style:** à la hollandaise: cut in pieces about 5 in. long, boiled, drained, served with melted butter and boiled potatoes.

— **with Dutch Sauce:** à la sauce hollandaise: cut in pieces of about 5 in. long, boiled, drained, served on a napkin with Dutch sauce separately.

— **with Fine Herbs:** aux fines herbes: cooked, cut in pieces, sautéd in butter until pale brown, seasoned, served with chopped herbs scattered on top.

— **Fried:** frits: parboiled, drained, cut in pieces about 2 in. long, dipped in frying batter, deep fried.

— **Gratinated:** au gratin: large pieces, cooked, drained, arranged in greased baking dish masked with Mornay sauce, covered with Mornay sauce, sprinkled with grated cheese, dotted with butter, gratinated in oven.

— **Housewife Style:** à la bonne-femme: boiled, cut in pieces, simmered in butter sauce.

— **Polish Style:** à la polonaise: prepared like asparagus.

— **Poulette:** cut in pieces, parboiled, served in poulette sauce.

— **Royal Style:** à la royale: cut in pieces, cooked, bound with suprême sauce.

Saurkraut, Pickled Cabbage; F. Choucroute; G. Sauerkraut: white cabbage, shredded, pickled in barrels and fermented in its own juice.

— **with Champagne:** au champagne: braised in white wine and white stock with sliced onions and a piece of bacon; shortly before serving boiled up with a glass of champagne.

— **Creamed:** à la crème: cooked in white stock, drained, seasoned, mixed with butter, bound with cream mixed with egg yolks and paprika.

— **Dutch Style:** à la hollandaise: braised in white wine and white stock with sliced onions and apples, thickened with butter paste.

— **French Style:** à la française: cooked in white wine and fat stock with a larded onion, carrot and a few juniper berries.

— **Garnished:** garnie: braised in white stock and white wine with lard, smoked ribs of pork, sliced onions and whole carrots; when serving garnished with the carved pork, slices of ham, Frankfurters, the sliced carrots and boiled potatoes.

— **German Style:** à l'allemande: braised in white stock with sliced onions simmered in goose fat beforehand and with diced bacon.

— **Hungarian Style:** à la hongroise: braised in white wine with sliced onions lightly browned in butter, tomato purée, shredded red peppers, stock and a piece of smoked lean bacon.

— **with Oysters:** aux huitres: braised in white wine and white stock, served with poached oysters on top.

— **with Pineapple:** à l'ananas: braised in white stock and white wine with bacon, mixed with diced pineapple and pineapple juice, served in a hollowed out pineapple.

— **Russian Style:** à la russe: braised with chopped, lightly fried onions in white wine and water, finished off with sour cream.

Sea-Kale: F. Chou-marin; G. Meerkohl, Strandkohl: vegetable shoots that grow wild on the western coasts of Europe and are also culivated for the leaf-stalks which are bleached and forced. Used in salads and prepared like asparagus.

— **Braised:** braisé: cooked, chopped coarsely, stewed in mutton stock, thickened with pale brown roux.

— **in Cream Sauce:** à la sauce crème: cooked, covered with Béchamel sauce finished off with cream.

— **English Style:** à l'anglaise: cooked, served with butter sauce or with melted butter.

— **Dutch Style:** à la hollandaise: cooked, served with melted butter and boiled potatoes.

— **Milanese Style:** à la milanaise: cooked, well drained, arranged in layers, sprinkled with grated Parmesan, grated Parmesan also on top, covered generously with browned butter.

— **Polish Style:** à la polonaise: cooked, well drained, covered with breadcrumbs browned in a generous amount of butter.

— **Russian Style:** à la russe: parboiled, simmered in sour cream, grated horseradish and grated Parmesan added to sauce at serving.

Semolina: F. Semoule; G. Gries: the more or less coarsely ground gluten part of Durum or any other kind of hard wheat. Semolina is used to make gnocchi, for tartlets Chevreuse, for puddings and as a breakfast dish.

Semoule: see semolina.

Sorrel: F. Oseille; G. Sauerampfer: garden herb with erect stems used for flavoring soups and sauces, for salads and as a vegetable. The leaves have a pleasant acid taste. Prepared like spinach purée and served with lamb or as a stuffing for omelette.

Spaghetti: F. Spaghetti; G. Spaghetti: Italian paste somewhat like macaroni but thinner resembling long strings. Spaghetti is made of hard wheat and eggs and is cooked in fast boiling salt water "al dente", i. e. not to soft, well drained, mixed with butter, and prepared like macaroni.

— **with Anchovies:** aux anchois: prepared like macaroni.

— **Bordeaux Style:** à la bordelaise: prepared like macaroni.

— **Imperial Style:** à l'impériale: mixed with diced gooseliver, truffles and mushrooms, bound with Madeira sauce.

— **Milanese Style:** à la milanaise: prepared like macaroni.

— **Naples Style:** à la napolitaine: prepared like macaroni.

— **Piedmont Style:** à la piémontaise: mixed with butter, grated Parmesan and thin slices of Italian truffles; tomato sauce served separately.

— **Raguttati:** mixed with hashed braised beef, diced ham and sliced Mortadella sausage, bound with grated Parmesan and tomato sauce.

Spätzle: batter of flour, milk or water, eggs, salt and nutmeg, placed on a plank, scraped off with a knife in longish threads into boiling salt water (this is the original German way), or run through a coarse collander into boiling water. The threads or lumps are drained and tossed in butter or lightly fried in a skillet. (German)

Spinach: F. Epinards; G. Spinat: a leafy vegetable, native of Asia, now grown extensively all over the world and

Spinach
available pratically at all times of the year. Spinach is served in leaves (en branches) or puréed.

— **American Style:** à l'américaine: stewed in own juice, drained, chopped, simmered in butter, seasoned with salt and lemon juice; filled in timbale dish, garnished with sliced hard-boiled eggs.

— **Boats:** Barquettes d'épinards: pastry boats or boats made of duchess potato mixture filled with creamed purée, covered with Mornay sauce, sprinkled with grated cheese, melted butter dropped on top, browned rapidly.

— **with Boletus:** aux cèpes: whole leaves, boiled, drained, arranged in timbale dish, covered with sliced, sautéd boletus, sprinkled with grated Parmesan, melted butter poured on top.

— **Cakes:** Subrics: purée, simmered in butter until the moisture is evaporated, bound with thick Béchamel and beaten eggs, seasoned; spoonsfull dropped in hot clarified butter and fried, filled in timbale dish, cream sauce served separately.

— **Cavourma:** boiled, drained, chopped, mixed with chopped onions fried in butter and hashed mutton, a poached egg on top. (Turkish)

— **Countess Style:** à la comtesse: purée mixed with cream and chopped hard-boiled eggs.

— **Creamed:** à la crème: purée dried in browned butter until the moisture is evaporated, seasoned with salt and nutmeg, boiled up with heavy cream; filled in timbale dish, bordered with hot cream.

— **with Croûtons:** aux croûtons: creamed, garnished with cockscomb-shaped croûtons.

— **Cutlets:** Côtelettes d'épinards: purée mixed with thick Béchamel, egg yolks and Parmesan, seasoned, filled in greased cutlet moulds, poached in water bath in oven; turned out, allowed to cool off, dipped in egg and breadcrumbs, deep fried. May be served with tomato sauce separately.

— **with Eggs:** aux oeufs: creamed purée garnished with quartered hard-boiled eggs.

— **English Style:** à l'anglaise: whole leaves, boiled, drained well, served with fresh butter.

— **with Fleurons:** aux fleurons: same as creamed, garnished with fleurons.

— **Florence Style:** à la florentine: boiled whole leaves, well drained, filled in baking dish masked with Mornay sauce, covered with Mornay sauce, sprinkled with grated cheese and glazed.

— **with Garlic:** à l'ail: purée seasoned with salt and garlic, thickened with butterpaste.

— **German Style:** à l'allemande: boiled, drained, chopped, simmered in butter with chopped lightly fried onions and demi-glace, bound with breadcrumbs.

— **Gratinated:** au gratin: creamed purée filled in greased baking dish, sprinkled generously with grated Parmesan, dotted with butter, gratinated in oven.

— **Italian Style:** à l'italienne: 1. whole leaves, blanched, simmered in oil with chopped anchovy fillets and garlic, seasoned, a little gravy added.

Spinach

2. boiled, drained, chopped, simmered in butter with garlic and chopped anchovy fillets, filled in puff pastry shells, a little cream sauce on top.

— **Laubfrösche:** Tree frogs: large leaves, scalded, refreshed in cold water, well drained, four leaves filled with bread soaked in water, water squeezed out, mixed with chopped onions lightly fried in butter, scrambled eggs and chopped parsley, seasoned with salt, pepper and nutmeg, rolled together, simmered in bouillon; drained and bordered with cream sauce. (Swiss)

— **Nice Style:** à la niçoise: leaves, scalded, simmered in oil with chopped garlic, seasoned, mixed with raw eggs, filled in greased baking dish, sprinkled with breadcrumbs, dotted with butter, browned in oven.

— **Old Fashioned Style:** à l'ancienne: boiled, chopped, simmered in butter, seasoned with salt and nutmeg, finished off with cream.

— **Parmentier:** large baked potato, lid cut off, hollowed out, filled with creamed purée mixed with egg yolk, sprinkled with grated Parmesan, melted butter dropped on top, baked in oven.

— **Piedmont Style:** à la piémontaise: boiled, drained, chopped, mixed with crushed garlic, demi-glace and a little anchovy butter.

— **Purée:** Purée d'épinards: cooked, drained well, passed through a sieve, dried in casserole with butter, bound with thick Béchamel sauce or thickened with white roux, moistened with white stock and cooked in oven with the cover on.

— **Roman Style:** à la romaine: whole leaves simmered in butter, seasoned, mixed with diced anchovy fillets fried in butter.

— **Soufflé:** Soufflé d'épinards: purée mixed with the same amount of thick Béchamel, seasoned, egg yolks added, stiffly beaten egg whites folded in, filled in greased soufflé dish, sprinkled with grated Parmesan, melted butter dropped on top, baked in oven. Chopped anchovy fillets or truffle slices may be added.

— **Stuffed:** farcis: large leaves, scalded, refreshed in cold water, well drained, stuffed with veal forcemeat, rolled together, braised in light demi-glace.

— **Venetian Style:** à la venetienne: whole leaves, boiled, well drained, placed in timbale dish, covered with tomatoes concassées and anchovy strips, grated Parmesan sprinkled on top, covered with melted butter, gratinated in oven.

— **Viroflay:** cakes (subrics) filled in blanched leaves, arranged in a greased baking dish, sprinkled with grated Parmesan, dotted with butter, gratinated in oven.

Squash: F. Courge; G. Birnenkürbis: American name for many varieties of edible gourds, marrows and pumpkins of various sizes, shapes and colorings.

— **Candied:** glacée: peeled, seeds removed cut in small slices, seasoned, each slice dipped in powder sugar; placed in baking dish greased with butter, melted butter on top, baked in oven until brown.

— **Colache:** chopped onions lightly fried in butter, mixed with diced squash, diced tomatoes and fresh corn,

Squash
seasoned, stewed in slow oven without water with cover on. (Mexican)
— **Fried:** frite: cut in small slices, seasoned, dipped in egg and breadcrumbs deep fried.
— **Hungarian Style:** à la hongroise: diced, salted, drained; cooked slowly in lard with chopped onions, seasoned with salt and dusted generously with paprika, for a while, sour cream added and simmered until done.
— **Mashed:** en purée: peeled, cut in pieces, seeds removed, steamed, mashed, seasoned with salt and pepper, blended with butter.

Stachy, Chinese Artichoke, hedge-nettle; F. Crosne du Japon; G. Knollenziest: an Eastern perennial plant cultivated extensively in Europe and the U. S. A. for its underground rhizomes which are tender and taste faintly like artichokes. They must be thoroughly cleaned and well seasoned.
— **Boiled:** bouillis: boiled, drained, tossed in butter, seasoned with lemon juice.
— **Cardinal Style:** à la cardinale: parboiled, bound with crayfish sauce.
— **in Cream Sauce:** à la crème: parboiled, simmered in butter, heavy cream added and boiled down.
— **Croquettes:** Croquettes de crosnes: parboiled, chopped coarsely, bound with thick German sauce and egg yolk; allowed to cool off, shaped into croquettes, dipped in egg and breadcrumbs, deep fried.
— **Fritters:** Beignets: same preparation as croquettes, shaped, dipped in frying batter, deep fried.
— **Gratinated:** au gratin: boiled, drained, filled in greased baking dish, covered with Mornay sauce, sprinkled with grated cheese, dotted with butter, gratinated.
— **Italian Style:** à l'italienne: parboiled, simmered in Italian sauce.
— **Mashed:** en purée: boiled, strained, seasoned, finished off with cream and butter.
— **Milanese Style:** à la milanaise: boiled, drained, sprinkled with grated Parmesan, covered with browned butter.
— **Naples Style:** à la napolitaine: blanched, cooked in light tomato sauce, filled in baking dish, sprinkled with grated Parmesan, dotted with butter, browned in oven.
— **with Parsley Sauce:** au persil: blanched, simmered in butter, bound with parsley sauce.
— **Polish Style:** à la polonaise: boiled, drained, served covered with breadcrumbs browned in butter.
— **Sautéd:** sautés: parboiled, sautéd in butter.
— **in Velouté:** au velouté: blanched, simmered in butter, bound with velouté.

Succotash: cooked sweet corn and Lima beans, seasoned, buttered or creamed.

Swede, Swedish Turnip; F. Rutabaga; G. Kohlrübe: a turnip-rooted cabbage of the kohlrabi variety with orange-yellow flesh. Prepared like turnips.
— **Bohemian Style:** à la bohémienne: peeled, cut in strips, fried lightly in lard, moistened with half pale beer and half water, seasoned with sugar, pepper and salt, chopped fried onions added, cooked, thickened with brown roux.

Swede

— **Caramelised:** caramelisé: sugar burned with butter to a light brown color, swedes cut in thick strips or diced added, moistened with stock, seasoned, cooked, lightly thickened.

— **North German Style:** cut in thick strips, boiled with a piece of fat pork, diced potatoes added later on, thickened with butter paste, mixed with chopped parsley, served with the carved meat.

Sweet Potato, Batata; F. Patate; G. Batate, süße Kartoffel: a South American plant cultivated for its tubers. The flesh is tender and sweet, some sorts are dry and mealy when cooked or baked. Great favorite in the U. S. A. where it is sometimes called Long Potato. It is not related with the potato.

— **Algerian Style:** à l'algérienne: boiled, mashed, mixed with chestnut purée, bound with egg yolks; when cold shaped into croquettes, dipped in egg and breadcrumbs, deep fried.

— **Baked:** au four: baked in oven with the skin on.

— **Broiled:** grillés: boiled, peeled, cut in half, dipped in melted butter, broiled until light brown on both sides.

— **with Butter:** au beurre: boiled, peeled, sliced, fried lightly in butter.

— **Creole:** à la créole: boiled, peeled, cut lengthwise, placed in greased baking dish covered with sugar mixed with butter, grated orange peel, salt and mace; baked in oven until sugar and butter have formed a thick sirup.

— **French Fried:** frits: cut raw in strips, salted, dried, fried in deep fat.

— **Fried:** frits: boiled, peeled, dipped in frying batter, deep fried.

— **Glazed:** glacés: boiled, peeled, cut in halves, each half dipped in brown sugar boiled up with water; placed in greased baking dish, seasoned with salt and pepper, moistened with butter, baked until brown, basting occasionally.

— **Gratinated:** au gratin: boiled, peeled, sliced, mixed with cream sauce; filled in greased baking dish, sprinkled with grated Parmesan, dotted with butter, gratinated.

— **Griddled:** boiled, peeled, cut in thick slices or in halves, griddled.

— **Italian Style:** à l'italienne: boiled, peeled, sliced, placed in baking dish greased with butter, covered generously with grated Parmesan and melted butter, browned in oven.

— **Maple Candied:** glacés au sirop d'érable: boiled, peeled, sliced, placed in greased baking dish; covered with maple sirup boiled up with cider, water, butter and salt, baked in slow oven.

— **Southern Style:** à la méridionale: boiled, peeled, cut in thick slices, browned in butter; placed in greased baking dish, melted butter poured over, sprinkled generously with powder sugar, glazed in oven.

— **Stuffed with Chestnuts:** farcis aux marrons: baked, scooped out, filled with the mashed flesh mixed with chestnut purée and butter.

T

Tagliatelli: Italian paste in broad strips, prepared like macaroni.

Tarhonya: small barley-shaped Hungarian noodles made of hardwheat flour and eggs and dried. They are first fried lightly in lard, moistened with bouillon and cooked until the moisture is soaked up by the Tarhonya. Served with goulash and other Hungarian dishes. (Hungarian)

Teltower Rübchen: Teltow Turnips: a very small tasty kind of turnip grown in the vicinity of Berlin. (German)

— **Candied:** caramelisés: sugar burnt with butter to a light brown, moistened with brown stock and boiled up, the turnips added, seasoned, cooked until the moisture is nearly evaporated and the turnips brown and glazed.

Tomato: F. Tomate; G. Tomate: the fruit of a branching plant native of South America and now one of the most important of fruit-vegetables. Most tomatoes are bright red and round when ripe, others are oval or egg-shaped, some kinds are yellow. Used raw in appetizers, in salads, as a garnish and for soups and vegetables.

— **Algerian Style:** à l'algérienne: cut in halves, hollowed out, stuffed with chopped peeled tomatoes simmered in butter, mixed with chopped fried onions, garlic, breadcrumbs, beaten eggs, pepper and salt, sprinkled with breadcrumbs, oil dropped on top, baked in oven.

— **American Style:** à l'américaine: stuffed with creamed corn mixed with egg yolk, baked in oven.

— **Brasilian Style:** à la brésilienne: peeled, cut in quarters, seeds removed, fried in oil, mixed with cooked red kidney beans and diced bread fried in butter.

— **with Butter:** au beurre: small tomatoes, scored on top, simmered in butter.

— **Carolina Style:** à la caroline: stuffed with rice, dotted with butter, baked in oven; border of gravy poured around at serving.

— **with Chestnuts:** aux marrons: stuffed with crushed braised chestnuts, dotted with butter, cooked in oven, covered with Madeira sauce.

— **Concassées:** peeled, cut in halves, seeds removed, diced or chopped coarsely, filled in sautoir in which chopped onions have been sweated in butter, seasoned and cooked until the moisture is evaporated.

— **French Style:** à la française: stuffed with tomatoes concassées mixed with chopped parsley, tarragon, chives and garlic, sprinkled with breadcrumbs, dotted with butter, baked in oven.

— **Fried:** frites: 1. peeled, cut in thick slices, seasoned, dipped in frying batter, deep fried.
2. peeled, cut in thick slices, seasoned, turned in flour, dipped in egg and breadcrumbs, deep fried.

— **Geneva Style:** à la génevoise: stuffed with veal forcemeat mixed with chopped herbs, sprinkled with grated Parmesan, dotted with butter, baked in oven.

— **Gratinated:** au gratin: cut in thick slices, seasoned, filled in greased baking dish, sprinkled with breadcrumbs, dotted with butter, gratinated in oven.

Tomato

— **with Green Beans:** aux haricots verts: peeled, cut in quarters, seeds removed, seasoned, sautéd in butter, mixed with small green beans, seasoned, chopped parsley on top.

— **Grilled:** grillées: cut in halves, seasoned, brushed with oil, grilled.

— **Housewife Style:** à la bonne-femme: stuffed with pork sausage meat, mixed with chopped boiled cabbage, diced fried bacon and chopped fried onions, cooked covered with melted butter in oven.

— **Hussar Style:** à la hussarde: stuffed with salpicon of chopped red peppers, mushrooms, ox tongue and gherkins bound with Béchamel sauce, melted butter dropped on top, baked in oven.

— **Indian Style:** à l'indienne: stuffed with boiled rice mixed with curry sauce, fried in oil in oven.

— **Marianne:** greased baking dish filled alternately with layers of sliced tomatoes, strips of green peppers, sliced lightly fried onions and half-cooked rice, seasoned, tomatoe slices on top, sprinkled with breadcrumbs, dotted with butter, cooked in slow oven.

— **Marseille Style:** à la marseillaise: cut in halves, placed in greased baking dish, covered with mixture of chopped hard-boiled eggs, parsley, chervil and shallots, sprinkled with breadcrumbs mixed with chopped anchovies, dotted with oil, gratinated in oven.

— **Maryland:** slices filled in greased baking dish, seasoned, covered with melted butter, sprinkled with powder sugar, glazed in oven.

— **Navarrese Style:** à la navarraise: stuffed with mousseline chicken forcemeat mixed with diced chicken and truffle, poached in oven.

— **Old Fashioned Style:** à l'ancienne: stuffed with duxelles mixed with chopped ham and garlic, dotted with butter, baked in oven; bordered with demi-glace with tomato at serving.

— **Polish Style:** à la polonaise: stuffed with soaked bread mixed with butter, beaten eggs, chopped garlic and seasoning, baked in oven.

— **Portuguese Style:** à la portugaise: stuffed with risotto mixed with grated Parmesan and tomatoes concassées, cooked in oven, sprinkled with chopped parsley.

— **Provencal Style:** à la provençale: cut in halves, sprinkled with breadcrumbs mixed with chopped parsley and garlic, oil dropped on top, baked in oven.

— **Sautéd;** sautées: cut in slices, seasoned, coated with flour, sautéd in butter.

— **Stuffed:** farcies: stuffed with duxelles or with a meat stuffing, sprinkled with breadcrumbs, dotted with butter, baked in oven.

— **Turkish Style:** à la turque: stuffed with pilaf rice mixed with chopped fried onions and chopped fennel, fried in oil.

— **Virginia Style:** à la virginienne: peeled, seeds removed, cut in large cubes, seasoned, mixed with grated onions, filled in greased baking dish alternately with diced bread, sprinkled with breadcrumbs, melted butter poured on top, baked and gratinated in slow oven.

Tomato

— **White Friar's Style:** à la carmelite: lid cut off, hollowed out, stuffed with sole forcemeat mixed with sea hedgehog purée and chopped hard-boiled egg, lid replaced, poached in oven.

Tomate: see tomato.

Topinambour: see Jerusalem artichoke.

Truffe: see truffle.

Truffle: F. Truffe; G. Trüffel: an underground fungus growing only in certain parts of Europe. The best variety grows in the Périgord district of France. It is a black warty tuber, the size of a walnut to a small fist, highly aromatic, nearly black inside when fresh; canned truffle has lost much of its aroma. The truffles found in North Italy are white inside and the taste faintly resembling garlic. Fresh truffles are carefully brushed to remove the sand in the rough surface and simmered in rich stock with Madeira. Truffles are used for seasoning dishes, for patties, as a decoration for cold and hot dishes and as a vegetable.

— **Baked:** sous la cendre: seasoned, a few drops of brandy dropped on top, wrapped in pie dough and baked in oven about 30 minutes.

— **in Casserole:** en casserole: stewed in fireproof china casserole, hermetically closed, in oven with butter, mirepoix, Madeira and brandy. Served in the casserole and only opened at the table.

— **in Champagne:** au champagne: prepared like in Port.

— **Creamed:** à la crème: peeled, sliced, sweated in butter, seasoned, deglaced with brandy, cooked in cream, sauce reduced to the desired consistency.

— **Cussy:** cooked in Madeira, hollowed out, filled with quail purée mixed with the hollowed out pulp, covered with thick game gravy mixed with the reduced Madeira.

— **Grammont:** peeled raw, cut in slices, allowed to draw in butter, deglaced with Port, seasoned, cooked in cream and veal glace, served in vol-au-vent.

— **Italian Style:** à l'italienne: white Italian truffles, sliced, simmered in oil, deglaced with a few drops of white wine, chopped anchovy fillets and a little garlic added, cooked until done.

— **in Madeira:** au madère: seasoned, stewed in casserole with the cover on with mirepoix, Madeira and a little rich veal stock.

— **Métropole:** cooked in Madeira with mirepoix bordelaise, cut in dices, mixed with diced cooked ham sautéd in butter, bound with demi-glace mixed with the reduced and strained truffle stock; served in round, rather flat open puff pastry patty.

— **Piedmont Style:** à la piémontaise: cooked white truffles, sliced, bound with demi-glace finished off with anchovy butter, placed in greased baking dish, sprinkled with grated cheese, melted butter dropped on top, gratinated.

— **in Port:** au porto: large truffle cooked in a casserole with the cover on with mirepoix bordelaise and Port; when done filled in small silver or china container, the reduced stock boiled down with rich veal gravy, strained and poured over the truffle.

Truffle

— **Provence Style:** à la provençale: sliced raw, simmered in oil with Marsala, chopped shallots, anchovy butter and chopped parsley.

— **Rossini:** lid cut off, hollowed out, pulp chopped and cooked in butter and Madeira, mixed with chopped chicken breast and gooseliver poached in Port; truffle filled with the mixture, sprinkled with breadcrumbs, butter dotted on top, placed in small baking dish with a little thin Madeira sauce, cooked and gratinated in oven.

— **Talleyrand:** sliced, sweated in butter, deglaced with Madeira, cooked in rich thick veal gravy; served in a hollowed out brioche made of unsweatened yeast dough.

Turnip; F. Navet; G. weiße Rübe: plant of many varieties grown for its roots. The two main categories are the long and the round-rooted turnips of which the second is the tastiest. Turnips are used for flavoring stocks, in stews and as a vegetable. The „greens" or turnip tops are often cooked like spinach.

— **in Béchamel Sauce:** à la Béchamel: diced, boiled, simmered in butter, bound with thin Béchamel sauce.

— **Breton Style:** à la bretonne: boiled, bound with Breton sauce.

— **with Chestnuts:** aux marrons: cut in cubes, blanched, simmered in veal gravy, mixed with braised chestnuts.

— **Creamed:** à la crème: boiled, sliced, simmered in butter, mixed with light cream sauce.

— **Czech Style:** à la tchèque: cut in strips, cooked in pale beer, seasoned with salt, pepper and sugar, thickened with butter paste.

— **English Style:** à l'anglaise: cut in cubes, boiled, drained, seasoned, tossed in butter.

— **French Style:** à la française: cut in cubes, boiled, mixed with the same amount of boiled diced potatoes, bound with butter sauce seasoned with mustard.

— **Fried:** frits: cut in strips like French fried potatoes, parboiled, seasoned, turned in milk and flour, deep fried.

— **Glazed:** glacés: olive-shaped, simmered in white stock with butter, salt and a little sugar until the moisture is evaporated and the turnips are glazed.

— **with Gravy:** au jus: pealed, cut in quarters, parboiled, simmered in thick gravy.

— **Mashed:** en purée: boiled, puréed, seasoned, finished off with cream and butter.

— **Poulette:** boiled, sliced, bound with poulette sauce.

— **Pudding:** Pain de navets: boiled, mashed, bound with thick Béchamel sauce and egg yolks, seasoned, filled in greased pudding mould, placed in a water bath and poached in oven; turned out, covered with cream sauce.

— **Stewed:** étuvés: parboiled, simmered in butter.

— **Stuffed:** farcis: round turnips, boiled, lid cut off, hollowed out, pulp chopped, mixed with pork sausage meat, a little butter and cream, seasoned; refilled in the turnips, arranged in a baking dish, sprinkled with breadcrumbs, melted butter dropped on top, browned in oven.

W

Wareniki: sort of Russian ravioli made of noodle dough, stuffed with meat, cottage cheese, cabbage etc. and chiefly served covered with melted butter.
— **is kapussta:** with Saurkraut: noodle dough rolled out thin, cut out with a round cutter, filled with a small heap of saurkraut boiled in stock, drained, chopped, mixed with chopped fried onions and seasoned, covered with a second round piece of paste like ravioli; cooked in salt water, drained, filled in timbale dish, covered with sliced onions fried in plenty of butter. (Russian)
— **Litowski Wareniki:** chopped tenderloin and an equal amount of veal suet chopped finely, mixed with chopped onions sweated in butter, seasoned with salt, pepper and nutmeg, chopped parsley and very little Béchamel added; filled between two sheets of noodle dough rolled out thin and cut out with a round cutter, boiled in salt water, drained and served covered with melted butter. (Russian)

Watercress; F. Cresson, Cresson Alenois; G. Brunnenkresse: aquatic plant which grows freely in moist meadows and is extensively cultivated by market gardeners. Used for decorating dishes and for salad, seldom cooked.
— **Purée of:** Purée de cresson: boiled, drained, rubbed through a sieve, mixed with a little mashed potato, finished off with butter and cream.

Watruschki s tworogom: Cottage Cheese Patties: fresh cottage cheese strained, mixed with creamed butter, eggs and salt; rich unsweetened yeast dough rolled out thin, cut out fairly large with a round cutter, filled with the cheese mixture and folded crescent-shaped; brushed with egg yolk, allowed to rise, baked in hot oven, sour cream served separately. (Russian)

Winter Greens: same as kale.

Witloof: see French endive.

Yorkshire Pudding: batter of beaten eggs, flour, milk and salt, filled in skillet in which dripping has been heated, baked in oven; served cut in squares with roast beef.

Zucchetti: see marrow, small.

Salads

English: Salad
French: Salade
German: Salat
Italian: Insalata
Spanish: Ensalada

It is usual to differentiate between simple and combined salads. Simple salads are green, leaf and vegetable salads; combined salads may be made of fish, shell-fish, meat, game, poultry, fruit or a combination of these with vegetables or leaf salad. Leaf salads such as lettuce, cos lettuce, endive, chicory, escarole, Monk's beard etc. must be carefully washed, well drained, absolutely dry and crisp before serving. They are best prepared with French dressing to which chopped hard-boiled eggs, chopped herbs, mustard, cream or other condiments may be added.
Although all sorts of cooked vegetables may be used for salads, raw vegetables such as celery, knob celery, cucumbers, tomatoes, red and green peppers, carrots, artichoke bottoms etc. are most popular especially for people to whom a diet has been prescribed. The art of salad-making has been greatly promoted in America, and there seems to be no limit to what a good cook can do with food prepared in the form of salad.
Simple salads are chiefly served with roast or grilled meat, poultry and game, combined and American — the so-called first course — salads as an hors d'oeuvre. All salad ingredients must be of the very best quality, cut properly, never chopped beyond recognition and arranged neatly. Salad must be served very cold, a warm salad tastes insipid.
Leaf salads are best if prepared at the very last minute in the presence of the guest, and served, as in France, as an extra course.
For a good salad a good salad dressing is indispensable, only the finest oil and wine vinegar of a high standard ought to be used. The following is a selection of dressings:

1. Hard-boiled sieved egg yolk mixed with oil, vinegar, mustard, chopped tarragon and chopped shallots.
2. Hard-boiled sieved egg yolk, mustard, sugar, salt, pepper, chopped anchovies, capers, shallots, Cayenne pepper, sour cream and lemon juice.
3. Hard-boiled egg yolk, vinegar, oil, pepper, salt, Harvey sauce, catchup, heavy sweet cream and sugar.
4. Hard-boiled egg yolk, vinegar, salt, pepper, mustard, sugar, Cayenne pepper, oil and sour cream.
5. Hard-boiled egg yolk, oil, vinegar and salt.
6. Raw egg yolk, oil, vinegar and salt.
7. Chopped anchovy, mustard, oil, vinegar and garlic juice.
8. **French dressing, original:** one part vinegar, three parts oil, salt, pepper. Instead of the vinegar lemon juice may be used (especially for diet fare), mustard, hard-boiled chopped or crushed eggs or chopped herbs may be added as the case warrants.
9. **American French dressing:** $^2/_3$ of a gallon of vinegar, 2 cups paprika, salt, pepper, sugar, garlic powder well blended with 24 egg yolks, English mustard, Worcestershire sauce and 5 gallons of oil.

10. **Cream dressing:** heavy sweet cream seasoned with salt, pepper, lemon juice or vinegar.
11. **Sour cream dressing:** sour cream seasoned with salt and paprika.
12. **Mustard cream dressing:** heavy cream seasoned with mustard and a little lemon juice.
13. **Mayonnaise dressing:** mayonnaise thinned with a little cream.
14. **Fancy dressing:** hard-boiled sieved eggs, raw egg yolks beaten with oil, a little vinegar, mustard and red wine, seasoned with salt, pepper, mixed with chopped tarragon.
15. **Chatelaine dressing:** mayonnaise mixed with the same amount of whipped cream.
16. **Cheese dressing:** grated Parmesan cheese mixed with paprika, mayonnaise and celery salt.
17. **Chiffonade dressing:** original French dressing with chopped parsley, chopped hard-boiled eggs and red beetroots.
18. **Roquefort dressing:** sieved Roquefort mixed with original French dressing; the vinegar may be replaced by lemon or grapefruit juice.
19. **Escoffier dressing:** Escoffier sauce (commercial bottled sauce) mixed with thin mayonnaise, Chili sauce, lemon juice, Cayenne pepper and chopped chives.
20. **Lorenzo dressing:** original French dressing with Chili sauce and chopped hard-boiled eggs.
21. **St. Regis dressing:** original French dressing, English mustard, Worcestershire sauce and paprika.
22. **Plaza dressing:** 1. oil, tarragon vinegar, English mustard, Chili sauce and mushroom catchup;
    2. heavy cream mixed with red currant jelly (for fruit salads).
23. **Garlic dressing:** original French dressing with very small pieces of bread crust rubbed with garlic (for leaf salads only).
24. **Thousand Island dressing, original:** thin mayonnaise with Chili sauce and chopped red and green peppers.
25. **Thousand Island dressing, American:** American French dressing with variety of chopped green and red peppers, pickled relish, hard-boiled eggs and parsley.
26. **Russian dressing:** Thousand Island dressing Nr. 24 od 25 with chopped chives and caviar.
27. **Anchovy dressing:** anchovy paste mixed with sieved hard-boiled eggs, English mustard, oil, lemon juice, sugar and paprika. May also be made with sour cream.
28. **Special dressing:** Chatelaine dressing seasoned with tarragon vinegar, mixed with chopped chives.
29. **Deauville dressing à la Foulard:** 12 raw egg yolks, 1 cup honey, 1/4 cup vinegar, 1/2 cup dry mustard, 1 cup lemon juice, 2 cups wine vinegar, 1 tablespoon garlic powder, well blended wit 2,1/2 gallons of oil like mayonnaise, vinegar or water added if necessary.
30. **Fruit salad dressing:** heavy cream or mayonnaise mixed with red currant jelly and seasoned with lemon juice.

Original French dressing may also be variated with the addition of Harvey, Prince of Wales, O. K., Worcestershire or Chili sauce, tomato catchup, chopped capers, gherkins, shallots and many other ingredients.

A

Adelina: Adeline: small pieces of cooked salsify marinated in mayonnaise, garnished with sliced tomatoes and cucumbers.

Adlon: strips of cooked knob celery, red beetroots and potatoes mixed with strips of raw apples, served in a border of corn salad; original French dressing.

Aida: strips of artichoke bottoms, peeled tomatoes, green peppers and curly endives with chopped hard-boiled eggs on top; original French dressing with mustard.

Alexandra: diced grapefruit and hazelnut kernels placed on lettuce leaf, bordered with fresh stoned cherries and grapes; original French dressing.

Alexis: diced celery and chopped nuts placed on heart of lettuce; original or American French dressing.

Algerian: algerienne: diced cooked sweet potatoes, small marrows (courgettes) and raw diced tomatoes mixed with Mayonnaise flavored with garlic, bordered with white lettuce leaves with chicken julienne scattered on top.

Alhambra: shredded lettuce, diced artichoke bottoms and knob celery, slices of red beetroot mixed with mayonnaise.

Alice: 1. pieces of grapefruit, orange, apple slices, slivered nuts, diced red peppers and stoned morelos placed on lettuce leaves; original French dressing.
2. apple with the top cut off, hollowed out, filled with apple balls the size of peas, seeded red currants and slivered walnuts bound with lightly acidulated heavy cream, the top put back into position.

American: à l'américaine: slices of peeled tomatoes, celery julienne, onion rings, potato slices and halved hard-boiled eggs; original or American French dressing.

Andalusian: à l'andalouse: tomato quarters, julienne of green peppers, boiled rice, chopped onions and parsley, garlic; vinaigrette sauce.

Annette: potato slices, celery julienne and poached bearded mussels mixed with mayonnaise.

Apple: de pommes fruits: whole apples, cored, poached in light syrup, allowed to cool off, placed on lettuce leaf, covered with mayonnaise with whipped unsweetened cream folded in, grated grilled coconut scattered on top.

Archduke: à l'archiduc: strips of potatoes, red beetroots, French endives and truffles; original or American French dressing.

Arlesian: à l'arlesienne: diced fried eggplants, diced potatoes and tomatoes marinated in original French dressing with chopped parsley and garlic; garnished with onion rings.

of Artichoke Bottoms: de fonds d'artichauts: cold cooked artichoke bottoms diced; ravigote sauce.

Asparagus: d'asperges: cut in pieces, cooked, marinated in original French dressing or covered with mayonnaise.

Astor: sliced cucumber, julienne of red peppers, corn salad and watercress; sour cream and oil.

Astoria: diced grapefruit and pears, julienne of green and red peppers and slivered hazelnut placed on lettuce leaves; original French dressing.

Augustin: shredded cos lettuce, French beans, peeled quartered tomatoes, green peas and hard-boiled eggs cut in quarters; mayonnaise seasoned with Worcestershire sauce.

Avocado: kernels removed, sliced, placed on lettuce, chopped chervil scattered on top; French dressing.

B

Bagatelle: julienne of carrots and mushrooms, asparagus tips; original or American French dressing.

Bagration: julienne of celery, chicken, artichoke bottoms and macaroni cut in thin slices, bound with mayonnaise mixed with tomato purée; decorated with ox tongue, truffle, hard-boiled chopped egg yolk, julienne of hard-boiled egg white and chopped parsley.

Banana: de bananes: sliced, marinated in original French dressing or bound with mayonnaise.

Barcelona: à la barcelonnaise: julienne of red peppers, celery and mushrooms, diced truffle, sliced apples and shredded lettuce; original French dressing.

Basto: julienne of knob celery, apples, red peppers and shredded lettuce bordered with round apple and red beetroot slices; original French dressing.

Beatrix: julienne of chicken, potatoes and truffles, asparagus tips; mayonnaise with mustard powder.

Beaucaire: julienne of chicken, celery, knob celery, ham, mushrooms and sligthly sour apples bound with mayonnaise, chopped herbs scattered on top; garnished with round slices of potatoes and red beetroots.

Beetroot: de betteraves: 1. cooked, cut in julienne; original French dressing with mustard and chopped herbs or mayonnaise with mustard;
2. cooked or baked, peeled, sliced, mixed with diced apples, carraway seeds and grated horseradish, marinated in light wine vinegar for a few days.

Belle-Fermière: strips of boiled potatoes, celery, red beetroots and green peppers bound with mustard cream.

Belle de Nuit: crayfish tails and sliced truffles; original French dressing spiced sharply.

Bellevue: shredded lettuce, endives, chicory, celery and boiled Brussels sprouts bound with mayonnaise condimented with curry powder.

Berlin: à la berlinoise: diced knob celery bound with mayonnaise, bordered with corn salad with julienne of red beetroots on top.

Bermuda: julienne of red peppers and small French beans arranged on lettuce leaves; original or American French dressing.

Biarritz: diced knob celery and green peppers arranged on lettuce leaves, covered with mayonnaise.

Bismarck: shredded lettuce and red cabbage without hard ribs; French dressing with grated horseradish.

Bombay: plain boiled rice, diced mangoes and red peppers arranged on lettuce leaves; original French dressing.

Brasilian: à la brésilienne: cooked Lima beans, diced cooked knob celery, shredded green and red peppers; mayonnaise.

Bresse: à la bressanne: tomato slices, strips of artichoke bottoms and cooked navy beans; original French dressing.

Breton: à la bretonne: cooked navy beans, diced tomatoes and chopped onions; original or American French dressing with chopped herbs.

Bristol: julienne of apples, knob celery, gherkins, truffles, roasted chicken and tomatoes bound with mayonnaise.

Brunswick: shredded celery and diced artichoke bottoms; original or American French dressing.

Brussels: à la bruxelloise: shredded French endives, cooked Brussels sprouts and sliced potatoes arranged in bunches; original or American French dressing with chopped onions and herbs.

Buenos-Aires: sliced avocados, cucumbers, diced apples and green peppers and slivered Brasil nuts; original French dressing.

Byzantine: sliced apples and diced grapefruit arranged on salad leaves, covered with mayonnaise, chopped truffles and parsley scattered on top.

C

Californian: californienne: sliced pineapple, oranges, cauliflower sprigs and French beans arranged on lettuce leaves covered with mayonnaise.

Canaille: 1. diced artichoke bottoms, potatoes, mushrooms, truffles and sweet peppers, asparagus tips and shrimps; original or American French dressing seasoned with Cayenne pepper;
2. quarters of peeled tomatoes, julienne of celery, diced bananas, plain boiled rice and chopped onions; sour cream dressing.

Capricious: Caprice: julienne of ox tongue, ham, truffles, chicken and artichoke bottoms sliced raw; original or American French dressing with mustard or mayonnaise with mustard.

Carmen: grilled peeled red peppers and white chicken meat diced, plain boiled rice and green peas; original French dressing with mustard and chopped tarragon.

Caroline: sliced bananas and grapefruit arranged on lettuce leaves, chopped red and green peppers scattered on top; original French dressing.

Caruso: diced tomatoes and pineapple arranged on lettuce leaves; sour cream with lemon juice.

Casanova: julienne of truffles and celery bound with mayonnaise, sliced hard-boiled eggs on top, border of watercress.

Cauliflower: de choux-fleurs: sprigs, boiled, allowed to cool off, marinated in original or American French dressing, chopped chervil and parsley scattered on top.

Celery: de céleri: cut in julienne, marinated with salt and a little lemon juice, bound with mayonnaise.

Century's End: Fin de siècle: diced knob celery and artichoke bottoms and sliced French endives, asparagus tips and beans bound with mayonnaise, garnished with red beetroots, asparagus tips and sliced hard-boiled eggs.

20th Century: shredded celery and green peppers, sliced apples and hazelnut kernels bound with mayonnaise mixed with a little tomato purée.

Chambéry: large peeled tomato, hollowed out carefully, marinated inside with vinegar, filled with finely diced lobster, salmon, artichoke bottoms, green beans, gherkins and finely shredded lettuce bound with mayonnaise.

Charming Lady: dame charmante: half a baby melon scooped out, seeds and filaments removed, flesh diced and mixed with diced chicken breast, diced peeled tomatoes and orange fillets, bound with mayonnaise seasoned with tomato catsup and a little orange juice and mixed with chopped mustard fruit; filled high into the melon, very fine julienne of red peppers scattered on top.

Chatelaine: sliced hard-boiled eggs, truffles, artichoke bottoms and potatoes; original or American French dressing with chopped tarragon.

Chef salad: consists most times of varieties of different salads, including sliced red cabbage, white cabbage, tomatoes, shredded carrots etc. garnished with sliced hard-boiled eggs; original French dressing with chopped capers, chervil and tarragon.

Chevreuse: strips of French chicory, celery and truffles, garnished with sliced tomatoes; original or American French dressing.

Chicago: quarters of peeled tomatoes, julienne of carrots and mushrooms, asparagus tips, French beans and small slices of gooseliver; mayonnaise dressing.

Chief Ranger: grand-veneur: julienne of pheasant breast, raw mushrooms, celery and truffle bound with mayonnaise seasoned with mustard, grated horseradish and red currant jelly.

Chiffonade: shredded lettuce and French endives, julienne of red beetroots, knob celery and tomatoes and watercress; original or American French dressing with chopped chives.

Christmas: de noël: monk's beard, corn salad and julienne of truffle and celery arranged in bunches; original French dressing.

Cinderella: Cendrillon: coarse julienne of potatoes, truffles, artichoke bottoms and knob celery, apple slices and green asparagus tips; original or American French dressing.

Claire Fontaine: potato salad bordered with watercress, chopped herbs scattered on top, garnished with quarters of hard boiled eggs; original French dressing.

Club: du club: julienne of red peppers, celery and truffles arranged on lettuce leaves and covered with sliced apples; mayonnaise.

Cole Slaw: sliced cabbage, shredded carrots, green pepper, seasoned with salt, sugar and white pepper, bound with mayonnaise.

Comtoise: hearts of lettuce mixed when about to serve them with salt, pepper, vinegar and hot diced fried bacon.

Connaisseur: strips of chicken, celery and truffle bound with mayonnaise, garnished with green asparagus tips and tomato slices.

Corn or Lamb: de mâches: washed, drained; original French dressing.

Cos Lettuce: de romaine: cut in small pieces or shredded; original or American French dressing.

Countess': à la comtesse: diced knob celery, tomatoes and apples; mayonnaise.

Cremona: Crémone: stachy cooked in the Greek way, slices of peeled and seeded tomatoes garnished with anchovy fillets; original French dressing with mustard.

Creole: à la crèole: 1. small melon, top cut off, seeds removed, flesh diced, mixed with boiled rice, seasoned with salt and powdered ginger, bound with thick acidulated cream, refilled in melon, lid replaced, chilled;
2. boiled rice, julienne of celery and green peppers and shredded lettuce bound with mayonnaise.

Cressonnière: potato slices and watercress with chopped hard-boiled eggs and parsley on top; original French dressing.

Crispi: sliced avocados, oranges and grapefruit, stoned cherries and nut kernels bound with mayonnaise.

Cuban: cubaine: julienne of green peppers and peeled tomatoes, onion rings and celery; mayonnaise.

Cucumber: de concombres: sliced thinly, marinated with original French dressing, chopped chives or dill on top.

—, **American:** à l'américaine: peeled, seeds removed; cut in strips, chilled, arranged on lettuce leaves, covered with Tartar sauce.

—, **with Cream:** de concombres à la crème: peeled, sliced, bound with sour cream seasoned with salt, pepper, vinegar and chopped onions.

—, **Russian:** de concombres à la russe: peeled, sliced, bound with dressing prepared with strained cottage cheese mixed with sour cream and sour milk, seasoned with garlic, salt and pepper; chopped dill scattered on top.

Cultivator: cultivateur: corn salad and sliced green onions; original French dressing with chopped chervil and peppermint.

Cupido: shredded lettuce, cooked stachy, diced tomatoes and julienne of knob celery; original French dressing.

D

Dandelion: de dent de lion: only young bleached leaves should be used; original or American French dressing.

Danicheff: cooked knob celery cut in small slices, sliced potatoes, julienne of raw mushrooms and artichoke bottoms, white asparagus heads bound with mayonnaise, garnished with crayfish tails, truffle slices and quarters of hard-boiled eggs.

Danish: à la danoise: julienne of pickled cucumbers, red beetroots, knob celery, and smoked salmon marinated in French dressing with chopped onions, chives, chervil and tarragon, garnished with sliced hard-boiled eggs.

Delicous: délicieuse: orange pieces, diced pineapple and sliced tomatoes arranged on lettuce hearts; cream dressing seasoned with lemon juice.

Delmonico: diced apples and knob celery bound with mayonnaise finished off with heavy cream.

Del Monte: shredded green peppers and celery, sliced apples and diced pineapple bound with mayonnaise finished off with mustard and anchovy essence, arranged on lettuce leaves.

Demidoff: cooked crescent-shaped turnips, carrots, knob celery and small slices of green onions, crescent-shaped truffles scattered on top; original or American French dressing.

Diplomate: diced pineapple, celery and nut kernels bound with mayonnaise.

Divine: julienne of artichoke bottoms, celery, truffles and green asparagus tips marinated in vinegar, bound with heavy seasoned cream; garnished with shrimps.

Dixie: cooked sweet corn and diced tomatoes, arranged on salad leaves, covered with mayonnaise.

Don Carlos: diced tomatoes, artichoke bottoms and truffles, bordered with watercress with finely chopped onions and parsley on top; original French dressing.

Doria: round or olive-shaped cucumbers bound with mayonnaise finished off with cream, chopped chervil and tarragon.

Dumas: diced red beetroots, potatoes, cucumbers and tomatoes bound with mayonnaise flavored with anchovy essence; garnished with lettuce leaves, hard-boiled eggs cut in quarters and pickled cucumber slices, chopped chives, tarragon and chervil scattered on top.

Dutch: hollandaise: diced potatoes and smoked salmon, a little caviar and chopped onions; oil, lemon juice and chopped chive dressing.

Dyer: tomato slices arranged on lettuce hearts; original or American French dressing with Chili sauce.

E

Eddy: small slices of pineapple, grapefruit and apples, seeded grapes and slivered nuts bound with mayonnaise and arranged on lettuce leaves.

Egyptian: à l'egyptienne: cold pilaf rice mixed with diced sautéd chicken livers, diced ham, artichoke bottoms, mushrooms, green peas and lozenges of red peppers; original or American French dressing.

Elaine: sliced pears, pieces of grapefruit arranged on lettuce leaves, chopped red peppers on top; original French dressing.

Eleonore: cos lettuce hearts garnished with artichoke bottom alternately filled with green asparagus tips and poached eggs; mayonnaise.

Elisabeth: lettuce hearts with sour cream dressing.

Elsie: sliced avocados, pieces of grapefruit and peeled seeded grapes placed on white salad leaves, covered with mayonnaise, chopped nuts on top.

Emma: cucumber salad surrounded with tomato salad.

d'Estrées: julienne of raw truffles and celery bound with mayonnaise seasoned with mustard powder and Cayenne pepper.

Eugenie: shredded French endives, sliced cucumbers, diced knob celery and corn salad, garnished with sliced hard-boiled eggs; original or American French dressing.

Eve: 1. diced cooked knob celery, mushrooms, cucumbers, ham and apples; sour cream dressing;
2. apple, top cut off, hollowed out, filled with the finely diced pulp, bananas, pineapple and fresh peeled filberts; sour cream dressing with lemon juice.

Everard: red peppers, raw mushrooms and artichoke bottoms cut in strips, bound with mustard mayonnaise; julienne of truffle and celery scattered on top, bordered with tomato slices.

Excelsior: julienne of celery, red peppers and peeled tomatoes, arranged on lettuce leaves, covered with mayonnaise, chopped truffles scattered on top.

F

Fanchette: julienne of raw mushrooms, chicken meat, truffles and shredded lettuce or French endives; original or American French dressing.

Fancy: coarse julienne of pineapple, celery and red peppers, plain boiled rice and diced tomatoes; Escoffier dressing.

Farmer: paysanne: small slices of cooked carrots, turnips, knob celery and chopped onions in original or American French dressing, bordered with olive-shaped cooked potatoes marinated in oil and vinegar.

Favorite: chicken and truffle strips and green asparagus tips bound with creamed mayonnaise.

Fédora: sliced apples and oranges, shredded lettuce and knob celery julienne bound with mayonnaise.

Figaro: julienne of red ox tongue, celery, red beetroots and shredded lettuce, bound with mayonnaise mixed with a little tomato purée; garnished with anchovy fillets.

Flemish: à la flamande: potato and French endive julienne, diced desalted pickled herrings and onions baked in the skin, peeled and chopped when cold; original or American French dressing with chopped parsley and chervil.

Florence: florentine: julienne of red peppers and celery, shredded spinach and watercress; original French dressing.

Florida: 1. diced pineapple, grapefruit and bananas bound with creamed mayonnaise, chopped walnuts scattered on top; 2. peeled orange wedges arranged on lettuce hearts; cream dressing with lemon juice.

Four Seasons: quatre saisons: tomato, cucumber, lettuce and radish salads arranged in bunches.

Francillon: half poached mussels and half potato slices marinated in Chablis wine as long as they are warm, sliced truffles on top; vinaigrette sauce.

Frankfurt: francfortoise: diced red beetroots and potatoes, shredded red cabbage and sliced apples, garnished with sliced hard-boiled eggs; original French dressing.

French: à la française: shredded lettuce marinated in original or American French dressing with chopped herbs.
— **Endive:** de chicorée: cut in pieces, arranged in salad dish rubbed with garlic; original or American French dressing.

Fruit: de fruits: diced pears, apples, grapefruit, bananas and oranges, stoned cherries and grapes; Chatelaine dressing.

G

Gallati: white asparagus heads and button mushrooms; original or American French dressing.

Gambetta: sliced artichoke bottoms and truffles; mayonnaise dressing with chopped tarragon.

Garden Cress: de cresson alénois: washed, drained; original or American French dressing.

Gardener: à la jardinière: cooked diced root vegetables, green peas, diced green beans and cauliflower sprigs, garnished with a border of watercress, sliced hard-boiled eggs on top; original or American French dressing.

Garibaldi: course julienne of red peppers, celery and sliced apples, arranged on lettuce leaves, covered with mayonnaise.

Gaulish: à la gauloise: sliced truffles, mushrooms, potatoes and artichoke bottoms; mayonnaise dressing.

Georgette: diced red beetroots, artichoke bottoms, cucumbers, truffles and boiled rice bound with mayonnaise.

German: à l'allemande: diced apples, potatoes, pickled cucumbers and pickled desalted herrings, garnished with sliced beetroots, strips of desalted pickled herrings and hard-boiled egg whites; original French dressing with shopped onions, chopped hard-boiled eggs and mustard.

Globe: diced apples, pineapple, grapefruit and seedless tangerine wedges; original French dressing with chopped olives.

Goblin: des goblins: fancy sliced cooked potatoes, knob celery and truffles, raw sliced artichoke bottoms and mushrooms and green asparagus tips; mayonnaise with lemon juice and chopped tarragon.

Gourmet: du gourmet: coarse julienne of truffles, celery and cockscombs bound with mayonnaise blended with truffle essence, garnished with braised chestnuts and morels marinated in original French dressing with chopped herbs.

Gracia: julienne of red and green peppers, diced cooked knob celery and apple slices bound with mayonnaise.

Green Bean: de haricots verts: cut lozenge-shaped, cooked in boiling salt water, drained, chopped parsley scattered on top; original French dressing with chopped onions.

of Green Lima Beans: de flageolets: cooked, drained, when cold mixed with mayonnaise seasoned with mustard and mixed with chopped chives.

Grimod: diced red beetroots, green beans and cauliflower sprigs bound with mayonnaise, arranged on lettuce leaves.

H

Half-Mourning: Demi-deuil: julienne of potatoes and truffles bound with mustard cream, bordered with round truffle and potato slices.

Harvey: shredded lettuce, French endives and watercress; original or American French dressing seasoned with Harvey sauce.

Havana: à la havanaise: asparagus tips and shrimps placed on salad leaves, covered with mayonnaise finished off with cucumber purée.

Helena: Hélène: julienne of green peppers, asparagus tips, truffle slices and seeded tangerine wedges; original French dressing with a dash of brandy.

Henriette: cauliflower sprigs, carrots, turnips, navy beans and truffle slices; original French dressing with tarragon vinegar and chopped shallots.

Henry IV.: Henri IV.: diced artichoke bottoms and diced boiled potatoes mixed with chopped onions and chopped herbs arranged in bunches; original French dressing.

Hermine: julienne of chicken, inside stalks (hearts) of celery, French endives and potatoes; mayonnaise.

Herring with Apple: de hareng aux pommes: diced mellow apples and desalted pickled herring; original French dressing with chopped onions.

Humbert: tomatoes and sweet red peppers; original or American French dressing.

Hungarian: à la hongroise: 1. blanched shredded white cabbage, seasoned with salt, pepper, vinegar and very little oil, covered with diced fried bacon;
2. julienne of ox tongue, pickled cucumber, red peppers, French endives and truffle; original or American French dressing with paprika.

I

Imperial: à l'impériale: 1. strips of green beans, carrots, apples and truffles; original French dressing with chopped herbs;
2. French beans, white asparagus heads and truffle slices; original French dressing.

Indian: à l'indienne: 1. boiled rice, diced tomatoes, mangoes and chopped onions bound with mayonnaise seasoned with curry powder and mushroom catsup, julienne of red peppers on top.
2. rice, diced apples, julienne of red peppers and asparagus tips; curry cream.

Infante: white asparagus heads, and julienne of green and red peppers placed on salad leaves, covered with mayonnaise.

Irma: asparagus tips, cucumber slices, lozenges of green beans and cauliflower sprigs bound with creamed mayonnaise with chopped chervil and tarragon, arranged dome-shaped, shredded letuce and watercress scattered on top.

Isabella: sliced raw mushrooms, celery and truffle, sliced cooked artichoke bottoms and potatoes; original or American French dressing with chopped chervil.

Italian: à l'italienne: diced boiled potatoes, carrots, turnips, green beans and hard-boiled eggs, diced tomatoes, cooked green peas and diced salami (optional), bound with mayonnaise, garnished with stoned olives, anchovy fillets and capers.

J

Jamaica: Jamaïque: finely diced bananas, oranges, grapefruit, stoned cherries and chopped nuts, bound with mayonnaise, filled in banana skins, chopped grilled nuts on top.

Japanese: japonaise: same as Francillon.

Javanese: javanaise: orange pieces without skin or pips arranged on lettuce hearts, covered with cream seasoned with lemon juice, salt and horseradish, very fine julienne of orange peel scattered on top.

Jeanette: French beans, cauliflower sprigs and watercress; original or American French dressing, chopped herbs scattered on top.

Jefferson: shredded cos lettuce, coarse julienne of red peppers, celery and pineapple; Roquefort dressing.

Jockey Club: green asparagus tips and truffle julienne, each part marinated separately with vinegar and oil, bound with mayonnaise shortly before serving.

Joinville: salad of shrimps and diced truffles arranged on lettuce leaves, covered with mayonnaise.

Jolanda: diced carrots, sweet potatoes and celery; original French dressing mixed with grated red beetroots and chopped mint.

Judic: diced carrots, turnips, potatoes, green beans, red beetroots, cauliflower sprigs and Brussels sprouts, marinated in vinegar and oil, covered with ravigote sauce.

K

Khedive: sliced tomatoes, truffles and chopped onions, garnished with stuffed olives, chopped chives on top; original or American French dressing seasoned with Cayenne pepper.

Knickerbocker: slices of mellow apples, oranges and grapes arranged on lettuce leaves; original French dressing.

Knob Celery: de celeri-rave: boiled, peeled, sliced or cut in strips, marinated while still warm with original French dressing.

Kuroki: peeled orange pieces, julienne of green and red peppers arranged on lettuce leaves; original French dressing.

L

Lackmé: diced red peppers and peeled tomatoes, boiled rice and chopped onions; original French dressing seasoned with curry powder.

Lapérouse: quarters of peeled tomatoes, diced ham, French beans and sliced artichoke bottoms; sour cream dressing.

Laura: sliced peeled apples and julienne of green peppers bound with mayonnaise, arranged on salad leaves.

Lentil: de lentilles: soaked, cooked, drained, allowed to cool off; original or American French dressing with chopped onions.

Lettuce, Hearts of: Coeurs de laitue: white tender hearts split lengthwise; original or American French dressing or mixed with chopped herbs or chopped hard-boiled eggs, Chatelaine, Roquefort or Escoffier dressing, creamed mayonnaise or other dressing as desired.

Lorenzo: lettuce, corn salad, sliced red beetroots, pears and hard-boiled eggs; American or original French dressing with mustard and Chili sauce.

Lorette: Julienne of celery and beetroots in border of corn salad; original French dressing.

Louis: diced pineapple, celery and mellow apples bound with creamed mayonnaise flavored with Sherry.

Louise: pieces of grapefruit and seeded grapes placed on lettuce heart, covered with mayonnaise, chopped hazelnuts on top.

Louisette: cos lettuce heart, diced tomatoes, and peeled and seeded grapes; original or American French dressing.

Louisiana: slices of peeled and seeded tomatoes., blood oranges and bananas; dressing made of thick purée of raw tomatoes beaten with lemon juice and oil, seasoned with salt, sugar and pepper.

Luxor: julienne of knob celery, green beans, chicken breast, peeled tomatoes and red peppers; original French dressing made with lemon juice.

Lyonese: lyonnaise: cooked vegetable macedoine, anchovies, olives and capers bound with ravigote sauce.

M

Maintenon: Crabmeat, oysters and green asparagus tips bound with mayonnaise, truffle julienne scattered on top.

Majestic: diced mellow apples, green peppers and celery bound with mayonnaise.

Mandalay: boiled rice, diced peeled tomatoes, oranges, shredded green onions and red peppers; mayonnaise seasoned with curry powder, tomato catsup and mango chutney.

Mandragora: small pieces of cooked salsify, diced peeled tomatoes, bananas and green olives: Plaza dressing.

Manhattan: sliced apples, celery and julienne of red peppers bound with mayonnaise, decorated with nut kernels and green peppers, bordered with shredded lettuce.

Manon: pieces of grapefruit arranged on lettuce leaves; original French dressing with lemon juice and a pinch of sugar.

Margaret: Marguerite: diced potatoes, cucumbers, tomatoes and shrimps bound with mayonnaise.

Marianne: strips of knob celery, green peppers, truffle and red ox tongue bound with mayonnaise; garnished with sliced tomatoes and truffles.

Mariette: 1. diced pickles, pears and cucumbers bound with mayonnaise;
2. julienne of cooked carrots and orange wedges with blanched julienne of orange peel on top; original French dressing with orange juice.

Marquise: diced artichoke bottoms and cucumbers arranged on shredded lettuce, garnished with sliced hard-boiled eggs; mayonnaise.

of Baby Marrows: de courgettes: cut in strips, sautéd in oil, marinated while still hot with original French dressing; chopped chives scattered on top.

Martini: diced mellow apples, celery and peeled seeded grapes, bound with mayonnaise, filled in hollowed out orange, slivered nuts scattered on top.

Mary Louise: Marie Louise: sliced bananas, celery, apples and truffle bound with mayonnaise.

Mary Stuart: Marie Stuart: shredded lettuce, julienne of knob celery and truffles, bound with sour cream mixed with chopped chervil; garnished with sliced hard-boiled eggs.

Mascotte: 1. olive-shaped potatoes and truffles and diced artichoke bottoms; mayonnaise;
2. white asparagus heads, cooked plovers eggs, sliced cockscombs, crayfish tails and truffle slices; creamed mayonnaise.

Mazarin: julienne of celery, knob celery and truffle, vinaigrette with chopped herbs.

Mercedes: strips of endives, tomatoes, red peppers and truffles; mayonnaise with lemon juice.

Méronas: artichoke bottoms, potatoes and ham cut in strips, small pieces of spaghetti, green haricot beans and fresh filberts, marinated, bound with mayonnaise; garnished with slices of truffle cooked in red wine.

Merry Widow: endives, pieces of grapefruit and oranges, sliced apples and nut kernels bound with mayonnaise; julienne of red and green peppers on top.

Miami: tangerine wedges without seeds and sliced tomatoes placed on lettuce heart; original French dressing with lemon juice and a pinch of sugar.

Michelangelo: small pieces of salsify and diced cucumbers bound with mayonnaise, decorated with tomato quarters

Midinette: julienne of sour apples, knob celery, chicken breasts and Gruyère cheese bound with mayonnaise.

Mignon: diced artichoke bottoms and shrimps bound with creamed mayonnaise seasoned with Cayenne pepper, bordered with truffle slices.

Mignonne: diced potatoes, artichoke bottoms, knob celery, truffle and asparagus tips, marinated with original French dressing, covered with mayonnaise.

Mikado: 1. diced tomatoes, stachy and chopped onions, garnished with stuffed olives; French dressing;
2. celery julienne, diced potatoes, cooked stachy bound with mayonnaise;
3. cooked stachy, diced green beans and potatoes arranged on cos lettuce, covered with gribiche sauce.

Milliken: boiled rice, diced red peppers, truffles and avocados; original French dressing with grapefruit juice and chopped tarragon.

Millionaire's: du millionnaire: sliced avocados and truffles arranged on lettuce leaves, covered with mayonnaise with truffle essence, slivered almonds scattered on top.

Mimosa: 1. watercress garnished with hearts of lettuce, covered with chopped hard-boiled egg yolk; original or American French dressing.
2. lettuce hearts garnished with orange pieces, sliced bananas and peeled and seeded grapes; heavy cream seasoned with lemon juice.

Mirabeau: diced tomatoes and potatoes, sliced cucumbers, garnished with anchovy fillets; original French dressing with mustard.

Miss Helyett: asparagus tips, diced artichoke bottoms and potatoes; original French dressing.

Mixed: panachée: cooked navy beans, French beans, peas, cauliflower sprigs, mushrooms or other food, marinated in original French dressing, arranged in bunches, chopped parsley scattered on top.

Modern: julienne of celery, ham and truffle in mayonnaise, decorated with red beetroots, hard-boiled egg yolk and egg white and a little caviar.

Moldavian: moldavienne: salad of diced vegetable and truffle bound with jellied mayonnaise, filled in mould lined with aspic and decorated with truffle, sealed with aspic, chilled, turned out; garnished with fillets of smoked herring and caviar.

Monaco: à la monégasque: round potato slices, whitefish, artichoke bottoms cut in quarters, diced tomatoes and black olives; original French dressing finished off with mustard and anchovy purée.

Mona Lisa: strips of apples and truffle bound with mayonnaise with tomato catsup, arranged on heart of lettuce.

Monastry: du couvent: diced cucumbers and potatoes; French dressing.

Monk's Beard: Barbe de capucin: a special sort of bleached thin long chicory; American or original French dressing.

Montblanc: diced pineapple, grapefruit, julienne of green peppers and small strawberries marinated in original French dressing, covered with unsweetened whipped cream.

Monte Carlo: diced pineapple, oranges and grains of pomegranates, seasoned with lemon juice, salt and cream, filled in hollowed out órange, surrounded with shredded lettuce, chilled.

Monte Christo: diced lobster, potatoes, hard-boiled eggs and truffle, bound with mayonnaise seasoned with mustard, garnished with lettuce hearts.

Montgomery: diced potatoes, salsify, artichoke bottoms and hard-boiled eggs; original French dressing with chopped herbs.

Montmorency: julienne of celery and stoned cherries bound with horseradish cream seasoned with lemon juice.

in Mould: moulée: mould lined with aspic jelly, dicorated with hard-boiled egg white, truffle, blanched tarragon leaves, chervil etc., filled with vegetable, fish lobster, poultry or game salad, sealed with aspic jelly, chilled and turned out.

Muscovite: à la moscovite: Russian salad bound with jellied mayonnaise filled in parfait mould lined with aspic jelly, sealed with aspic jelly; chilled, turned out on round glass dish, garnished with tiny tartlets filled half with sharply seasoned sigui purée with caviar on top.

My Fancy: orange pieces and julienne of green peppers, arranged on lettuce hearts; original French dressing.

N

Nantese: nantaise: shrimps, smoked salmon strips and asparagus tips arranged on lettuce leaves, garnished with sliced hard-boiled eggs, chopped parsley sprinkled on top; original French dressing.

Naples: à la napolitaine: cooked spaghetti cut into small pieces, diced tomatoes and strips of Gruyère cheese; original French dressing flavored with garlic.

Nassau: sliced tomatoes, celery and strips of green and red peppers arranged on salad leaves; Chatelaine dressing.

of Navy Beans: de haricots blancs: cooked, allowed to cool off, drained; original French dressing with finely chopped onions and parsley.

Negresco: sliced avocados, truffles and slivered almonds bound with mayonnaise seasoned with truffle essence, arranged on lettuce leaves.

Nelusko: julienne of beetroots, cooked olive-shaped potatoes and asparagus tips; mayonnaise seasoned with Escoffier sauce.

Neptune: flaked cooked fish, marinated, covered with ravigote sauce, garnished with lettuce hearts.

Neva: lettuce heart with julienne of red beetroots, French endives and truffles; original or American French dressing.

New Orleans: diced grapefruit, bananas, oranges, avocados and grapes placed on lettuce leaves; original French dressing seasoned with Cayenne pepper.

New Year's: Bonne année: diced knob celery and red peppers bound with mayonnaise, arranged on lettuce leaves, capers scattered on top.

New York: diced mellow pears, oranges, apples and grapes arranged on lettuce leaf; original French dressing.
Nice: à la niçoise: French beans, quarters of peeled tomatoes and fancy shaped potatoes, garnished with anchovy fillets, olives and capers; original French dressing.
Nimrod: shredded lettuce, strips of game and red beetroots, decorated with sliced hard-boiled eggs; original French dressing.
Ninette: lettuce, haricot beans and diced potatoes; original French dressing with chopped tarragon.
Ninon: 1. quarters of lettuce with orange sections on top from which skin, pith and pips have been removed seasoned with lemon and orange juice, oil and salt; 2. diced artichoke bottoms, shrimps, truffles, oysters, cockcombs and cocks' kidneys; original French dressing.
Noémi: roast disjointed and boned squab chicken, crayfish tails and lettuce hearts; cream mixed with crayfish coulis, seasoned with lemon juice, salt and peppers as dressing; chervil leaves on top.
Norwegian: à la norvegienne: strips of boiled beef, smoked herring, potatoes, beetroots and apples garnished with anchovy fillets; original French dressing.
Nuns: des nonnes: boiled rice and julienne of chicken meat; American or original French dressing with mustard, chopped truffles scattered on top.

O

Olga: Strips of knob celery, red beetroots and French endives; original or American French dressing.
Onion, Swiss: d'oignons à la suisse: sliced fried onions marinated in wine vinegar, salt and pepper.
Opéra: julienne of chicken, ox tongue, celery, truffles and asparagus tips, bound with mayonnaise and arranged in bunches; decorated with sliced gherkins and cockcombs.
Oriental: à l'orientale: boiled rice, diced tomatoes, green and red peppers and green beans; American or original French dressing with garlic.
Orloff: diced melon and artichoke bottoms; original French dressing.
Otto: diced melon, mellow apples, pineapple, oranges and grapes bound with mayonnaise, arranged on shredded lettuce.
Oxford: diced chicken, gherkins, tomatoes and truffles arranged on lettuce leaves, garnished with sliced hard-boiled eggs, American or original French dressing with chopped tarragon.

P

Parisian: parisienne: mould lined with aspic jelly, decorated with thin crawfish slices surmounted with a truffle slice, filled with vegetable salad mixed with diced crawfish and lobster bound with jellied mayonnaise, sealed with aspic, chilled and turned out shortly before serving.
Parmentier: diced or olive-shaped boiled potatoes bound with white mayonnaise while still warm, sprinkled with chopped chervil.

Parsnip: de panais: boiled, peeled and cut in small thin slices; original French dressing.

Pascaline: cos lettuce, grapefruit quarters, sliced avocades and julienne of red peppers; original or American French dressing.

Pau: à la paloise: small pieces of cooked salsify, diced artichoke bottoms and asparagus tips; original or American French dressing.

Paulette: julienne of celery, cooked potatoes, raw truffles and green beans bound with mayonnaise.

Piedmont Style: à la piémontaise: 1. boiled rice, diced tomatoes and sliced Italian truffles; original French dressing flavored with garlic;
2. sliced boiled potatoes and Italian truffles decorated with anchovy fillets; mayonnaise.

Pieukerke: julienne of truffle and chicken, green peas and white asparagus heads bound with mayonnaise, julienne of red and green peppers scattered on top.

Pineapple and carrot: d'ananas et carottes: pineapple slice marinated in original French dressing with orange juice, covered with shredded lettuce, grated raw carrots on top.

Pissenlit: dent de lion: see dandelion.

Polish: polonaise: diced carrots, turnips, gherkins, pickled mushrooms, potatoes and pickled herring bound with mayonnaise, garnished with halved hardboiled egg filled with mayonnaise; chopped parsley and chervil on top.

Pompadour: cauliflower sprigs, diced cooked knob celery and potatoes; mayonnaise seasoned with mustard.

Portuguese: à la portugaise: diced tomatoes, sliced cooked mushrooms and potatoes marinated in white wine; original or American French dressing.

Potato: de pommes de terre: boiled in jacket, peeled, sliced, while hot mixed with bouillon, vinegar, oil, salt, pepper and chopped onions; chopped parsley scattered on top.

—, German Style: de pommes de terre à l'allemande: 1. same as potato salad with diced, peeled and cored mellow apples added.
2. boiled in jacket, peeled, sliced, while hot mixed with bouillon, vinegar and salt, bacon, onions and oil fried together and in some cases garnished with chopped scallion and parsley.

—, with Mayonnaise: de pommes de terre à la mayonnaise: boiled in jacket, peeled, sliced, marinated with vinegar, oil, salt and pepper, bound with mayonnaise.

Prince's: des princes: diced fresh cucumbers and truffles bound with remoulade sauce.

Provencal: à la provençale: artichoke quarters, sliced peeled and seeded tomatoes, coarse julienne of pumpkin blossoms and black stoned olives; original French dressing with chopped basil, anchovy purée and garlic.

Purslane: de pourpier: washed drained, shredded; original or American French dressing.

Q

Queen Isabella: Reine Isabelle: sliced lobster, shrimps, cooked salmon and chopped anchovy fillets, dressed on shredded lettuce, julienne of red peppers scattered on top; American or original French dressing.

Queen Madge: Reine Margot: large halved, peeled, tomatoes marinated with vinegar, scooped out, filled with shredded lettuce and shrimps bound with mayonnaise; garnished with watercress and radishes.

R

Rachel: julienne of celery, truffle, artichoke bottoms, boiled potatoes and green asparagus tips; light mayonnaise.

Radish: de radis: sliced, boiled, when cold mixed with original French dressing with chopped parsley and onions, dressed on lettuce leaves.

Regency: à la régence: thin truffle, cockscombs and cock's kidney slices, julienne of celery and green asparagus tips; French dressing with lemon juice.

Regent's: du régent: shredded cos lettuce bound with remoulade sauce, garnished with tomato and cauliflower salad.

Réjane: diced boiled potatoes, julienne of truffle and asparagus tips; original French dressing.

Rhenish: à la rhénane: diced ham, roast veal, smoked tongue, sausage, pickled herring, anchovy fillets, apples, pickled cucumbers, mushrooms and chopped onions, bound with mayonnaise finished off with purée of poached soft roes.

Rhubarb: de rhubarbe: peeled, cut in small pieces, cooked carefully; original French dressing.

Riviera: strips of pineapple and knob celery, shredded lettuce, tangerine and orange slices and small strawberries arranged on lettuce leaves, covered with mayonnaise mixed finely chopped green peppers.

Roosevelt: halved tomatoes, scooped out lightly, marinated with oil and lemon juice, filled with finely diced mushrooms, truffles, oranges and asparagus marinated in oil, lemon juice, salt and pepper.

Rose: sliced apples, red beetroots, carrots, asparagus tips and purslane; original French dressing.

Rosemonde: green asparagus tips and French beans cut into small pieces, marinated, bound with mayonnaise, small bunch of green asparagus tips marinated in original French dressing on top.

Russian: russe: diced carrots, turnips, green beans, truffles cooked mushrooms, lobster, ham, gherkins, ox tongue, sausage and anchovy fillets bound with mayonnaise, decorated with quarters of hard-boiled eggs, red beetroots, capers, caviar etc.

S

Saint-James: boiled rice, diced truffles and mushrooms; original French dressing with lemon juice instead of vinegar.

Saint-Jean: green beans cut in lozenges, green asparagus tips, green peas, sliced raw artichoke bottoms and fresh cucumbers bound with thin mayonnaise seasoned with lemon juice and mixed with chopped chervil; bordered with round slices of gherkins and hard-boiled eggs, blanched tarragon leaves on top.

Saint-Pierre: shredded celery, white asparagus heads, sliced potatoes, diced pineapple and grapefruit fillets; original French dressing with chopped mint.

Salisbury: garden cress, dandelion, endives, red beetroots and knob celery; original French dressing mixed with raw beetroot juice, chopped hard-boiled eggs scattered on top.

Salsify: de salsifis: cut in small pieces, cooked in a „blanc"; original French dressing.

Sarah Bernhardt: diced artichoke bottoms, green asparagus tips and quartered hard-boild eggs placed on salad leaves; original or American French dressing.

Saurkraut: de choucroûte: raw saurkraut chopped coarsely, mixed with original French dressing.

Scotch: écossaise: diced boiled potatoes, truffles and shredded lettuce marinated with original French dressing; decorated with anchovy fillets, chopped hard-boiled eggs scattered on top, bordered with mayonnaise seasoned with curry powder.

Sevilla: Séville: diced oranges and peeled seeded grapes placed on lettuce heart; original French dressing.

Sicilian: à la sicilienne: diced apples, tomatoes, cooked knob celery and artichoke bottoms; mayonnaise.

Signora: different kinds of diced fresh fruit placed on lettuce leaves; original French dressing.

Sommer: d'été: lettuce, watercress, cucumbers, red beetroots and sliced radishes arranged in bunches, garnished with halved hard-boiled eggs; original French dressing.

Sotteville: cos lettuce; cream dressing with lemon juice.

Spanish: espagnole: green beans, quarters of peeled and seeded tomatoes placed around, strips of red and green peppers on top of the beans, bordered with onion rings; American or original French dressing.

Sportsman: sprigs of cauliflower, red beetroots, watercress, smoked salmon strips and sliced hard-boiled eggs arranged in bunches: mustard cream.

Stanislaus: julienne of celery, grapefruit and grapes, arranged on lettuce leaves; original French dressing, chopped hazelnuts scattered on top.

Stroganoff: julienne of carrots and truffles, green peas and asparagus tips, bound with mayonnaise, chopped herbs scattered on top; garnished with hard-boiled plovers eggs cut in half.

Stuffed Tomato: de tomates farcies: large peeled tomatoes, hollowed out, stuffed with diced cucumbers and tomatoes marinated in original French dressing, placed on salad leaf, covered with mayonnaise.

Suburb: du faubourg: sliced cooked knob celery, potatoes and fried apples; original French dressing.

Surprise: peeled tomato, hollowed out, stuffed with finely diced apples, celery and chopped hazel nuts, bound with mayonnaise and placed on salad leaf.

Suzette: diced artichoke bottoms, truffles and green asparagus tips; American or original French dressing, chopped herbs scattered on top.

Swedish: à la suédoise: diced boiled beef, smoked herring, potatoes, pickled cucumbers, apples, stoned olives and capers; original French dressing with chopped herbs.

Swiss: à la suisse: diced cooked knob celery and red beetroots, bordered with corn salad; original or American French dressing.

T

Tanagra: julienne of celery, tomatoes and bananas; sour cream dressing.

Theresia: Thérèse: sliced cooked potatoes, knob celery and sliced apples bound with mayonnaise.

Tomato: de tomate: peeled, sliced, arranged in salad-bowl, original or American French dressing with finely chopped onions on top, besprinkled with chopped parsley.

Tosca: 1. julienne of chicken, ox tongue, artichoke bottoms and beetroots, bound with mayonnaise mixed with raw beetroot juice; decorated with sliced hard-boiled egg whites cut in shape of half-moons.
2. diced chicken, Italian truffles, celery and Parmesan bound with mayonnaise seasoned with mustard and anchovy purée.

Tours: à la tourangelle: cooked green Lima beans, julienne of cooked potatoes and green beans; creamed mayonnaise with chopped tarragon.

Trédern: crayfish tails cut lengthwise, poached and bearded oysters, green asparagus tips and thin truffle slices; creamed mayonnaise mixed with crayfish coulis.

Truffle: de truffles: thin raw truffle slices marinated with salt, lemon juice and oil, chopped herbs scattered on top.

Turenne: sliced cooked potatoes and knob celery, escarole and apple slices; original French dressing.

Turquoise: French endives, peeled and seeded tomato quarters, celery julienne and strips of red peppers; mayonnaise.

U

Uncle Sam: lettuce hearts covered with tartar sauce, chopped hard boiled eggs scattered on top.

Unequaled: nonpareille: julienne of cos lettuce, celery, peeled tomatoes and pineapple; thousand island dressing.

V

Vegetable: de légumes: any sort of diced or fancy shaped cooked vegetables, such as carrots, turnips, green beans, peas, cauliflower sprigs, asparagus tips etc. arranged in bunches on glass dish; French dressing, chopped parsley on top.
— **Gardner's** à la maraîchère: pieces of cooked salsify, knob celery, diced potatoes and red beetroots bound with mustard mayonnaise with grated horseradish, surrounded with corn salad.

Venetian: vénitienne: shredded celery, diced truffle, stoned olives and orange fillets; green mayonnaise mixed with purée of sautéd chicken livers.

Veronika: Véronique: julienne of celery, beetroots and shredded lettuce; American or original French dressing with diced fried bacon; garnished with sliced hard-boiled eggs.

Vicomte: diced ox tongue, green peppers, knob celery and asparagus tips; thick purée of raw tomatoes whipped with oil, lemon juice, salt and a pinch of sugar.

Victoria: diced crawfish, cucumbers, truffles and green asparagus tips, bound with mayonnaise mixed with purée made of the creamy parts of the crawfish; crawfish or lobster coral scattered on top.

Villeroi: julienne of celery and beetroot; original French dressing with mustard; garnished with sliced truffles.

Virginia: diced cooked knob celery, beetroots and potatoes; original French dressing.

W

Waldorf: 1. julienne of sour apples and knob celery bound with mayonnaise; slivered hazelnuts on top;
2. mellow apple, scooped out, filled with diced celery and apples, bound with mayonnaise, placed on lettuce leaf; chopped nuts on top.

Washington: small round slices of beetroot and sliced hard-boiled eggs arranged on lettuce leaves; original French dressing.

Westinghouse: sliced avocados, julienne of celery and grapes placed on lettuce leaves; original French dressing.

White Friar's: à la carmelite: diced potatoes, red beets, hard-boiled eggs, anchovy fillets and chopped onions; original French dressing.

Windsor: 1. large apple cut in halves, scooped out, filled with diced apples and pineapple bound with mayonnaise; placed on lettuce leaves, bordered with round pieces of peeled tomatoes,
2. julienne of knob celery, truffle, chicken, pickled cucumbers and mushrooms, bound with mayonnaise mixed with grated horseradish and seasoned with Worcestershire sauce; bordered with corn salad.

Winter: d'hiver: julienne of cooked knob celery, potatoes and beetroots; original French dressing with grated horse-radish.

Wladimir: diced sterlet, crayfish tails, smoked salmon, pickles, pickled cucumbers and mushrooms bound with mayonnaise with grated horseradish and mustard, garnished with hard-boiled lapwing eggs.

Yam-Yam: French beans, lettuce hearts cut in quarters, sliced cucumbers and julienne of knob celery; original or American French dressing.

Sweets

Hot and Cold Sweets, Gateaux, Pastries and Ices

French: Entremets de douceur, Glaces, Pâtisserie

German: Kalte und warme Süßspeisen, Eisspeisen und Gebäck

Basic Doughs and Mixtures

Puff Pastry: Feuilletage: 16 oz. flour, 16 oz. butter, 1/3 oz. salt, about 1 gill water. Dissolve salt in water, mix with the flour to make a semi-firm dough. Shape into a ball and allow to rest for 20 minutes. Roll out into a square and place butter, which must have the same firmness as the dough, in the center, fold ends towards center so as to enclose the dough. Roll out three times as long first in one and then the contrary direction, folding the dough towards the center twice between each turn. Allow to rest for half an hour and give two further double turns with a rest of half hour between them.

Short Pastry: **Pâte à foncer fine:** 16 oz. flour, 10 oz. butter, 2 oz. powder sugar, 1 egg, 1/3 oz. salt, 1 1/2 gills water. Place flour on table, make a bay, fill the other ingredients in the center and mix butter, egg, sugar and salt well before working in the flour. Shape into a ball, wrap in a cloth and place in the frig for further use.

Almond Short Pastry: Pâte à foncer amandinée: made like short paste with 10 oz. flour, 6 oz. ground almonds, 5 oz. sugar, 10 oz. butter, egg, a little lemon juice, 1 egg yolk.

Sugar Paste: Pâte sèche sucrée: 16 oz. flour, 7 oz. butter, 7 oz. sugar, 3 eggs, a little orange blossom water. Prepared like short paste.

Cream Puff Paste: Pâte à chou: 7 gills water, 7 oz. butter, 18 oz. flour, 16 eggs, 1/2 oz. salt. Boil water with butter and salt, add the sieved flour and stir until mixture does not adhere anymore on sides of saucepan; take off the stove and add eggs one by one stirring continuously.

Savarin Dough: Pâte à savarin: 16 oz. flour, 10 oz. butter, 8 eggs, 3/4 oz. yeast, 1/2 oz. salt, 2 oz. sugar, a little luke-warm water. Sieve flour in a bowl, make a bay in the center, add the yeast dissolved in the water, salt and eggs and work to a smooth dough by hand. Scrape dough from sides towards the center, place the softened butter in little lumps on top and allow to rise, add the sugar and beat thoroughly, by hand until butter and sugar are well blended.

Brioche Dough: Pâte à brioche: 18 oz. flour, 12 oz. butter, 1/2 oz. sugar, 1/2 oz. salt, 3/4 oz. yeast, 6 eggs, 3/4 gill luke-warm water. Dissolve yeast in luke-warm water, stir to preliminary dough with 6 oz. flour, allow to rise. Mix all the other ingredients with the melted butter, blend well with the yeast dough, dust with flour, cover with a cloth and allow to rise before further use.

Genoise Mixture: Pâte à genoise: 8 eggs, 8 oz. flour, 8 oz. sugar, 4 oz. butter, vanilla.
Whip eggs, sugar and vanilla in water bath until thick and foamy, then whip until cold. Take out the vanilla pod, fold in the flour and finally the melted but not hot butter. Fill in buttered and floured baking tin or mould, bake in moderate oven.

Savoy Sponge: Pâte à Biscuit de Savoie: 16 oz. sugar, 7 oz. flour, 7 oz. potato flour, 14 egg yolks, 14 egg whites, 1 tablespoon vanilla sugar. Egg yolks stirred with sugar to foam, the stiffly beaten egg whites, the sieved flour, potato flour and vanilla sugar folded in. Filled in greased moulds dusted with potato flour two thirds full, baked in moderate oven.

Frying Batter: Pâte à frire: 9 oz. flour, 1 oz. melted butter, 3/4 gill pale beer, 1 gill luke-warm water, pinch of salt, 2 stiffly beaten egg whites.
Mix flour, water, beer, butter and salt without stirring to much and fold eggs in shortly before use.

Meringue Mixture: Meringue ordinaire: 16 oz. sugar, 8 egg whites. Whip whites until quite stiff and fold in sugar. The number of whites may be augmented up to 12. Temperature of oven must be very low, meringues should be more dried then baked.

Italian Meringue Mixture: Meringue italienne: 16 oz sugar, 8 egg whites. 1. sugar and egg whites mixed in suitable copper or basin and whipped in water bath or on the oven until stiff and quite thick. 2. the sugar boiled to 40 deg. measured with the saccharometer and mixed boiling hot slowly with stiffly beaten egg whites.

Creams and Icings

Pastry Cream: Crème pâtissière: 16 oz. sugar, 1 quart milk, 12 egg yolks, 4 1/2 oz. flour, vanilla.
Yolks, sugar and flour stirred to foam, mixed slowly with the hot milk in which a vanilla pod has been infused, cooked for about two minutes after the mixture has come to a boil stirring all the time.

Saint-Honoré Cream: Crème à Saint-Honoré: same as pastry cream with 12 to 16 stiffly beaten egg whites folded in while the mixture is still boiling. If Saint-Honoré cream has to stand for a few hours it is best to add 4 leaves of dissolved gelatine, especially in summer.

Frangipane Cream: Crème frangipane: 7 oz. sugar, 7 oz. flour, 3 pints milk, 2 oz. crushed macararoons, 3 1/2 oz. butter, vanilla, pinch of salt, 4 eggs, 8 yolks.
Eggs yolks, sugar, flour and salt well mixed, boiled up with the milk and vanilla as for pastry cream, taken off the stove, butter and macaroons stirred in, filled in a basin and cover with greased paper.

English Cream or Vanilla Cream: Crème à l'anglaise: 16 oz. sugar, 16 egg yolks, 1 quart milk, vanilla or grated lemon peel.
Sugar and yolks stirred to foam, mixed with the milk boiled up with vanilla or lemon peel beforehand, whipped in water bath until mixture begins to thicken, taking care not to let it boil as the eggs would curdle. For sweet sauces only 10 yolks are taken.

Vanilla Butter Cream: Crème au beurre à la vanille: 16 oz. butter, 5—6 gills vanilla cream.
Cream butter and add the cold vanilla cream gradually. This is a basic butter cream and may be flavored with spirits, liqueurs, lemon, orange or other juices instead of the vanilla.

Fondant: 20 oz. loaf sugar, 4 gills water, a little lemon juice, 4 tablespoonfuls glucose.
Dissolve sugar with the water in a saucepan, add the other ingredients and cook, skimming frequently, until the sugar if a fork is dipped in can be blown away from the fork in little bubbles. Pour out on a marble moistened with very little water and let mixture cool off for a while until a sort of skin is formed. Work mixture continuously with a spatula forwards and backwards until it is hard and white. Keep for further use in a tin covered with a moistened cloth. Fondant may be flavored with spirits or liqueurs, coffee essence, dissolved chocolate etc.

Royal Icing: Glace royale: icing sugar mixed with egg white and a little lemon juice and stirred to the required consistency.

Pralin: 16 oz. sugar, 16 oz. peeled almonds or hazelnuts. Sugar boiled with very little water to brown caramel, mixed with the almonds or hazelnuts dried in the oven beforehand, placed on slightly oiled marble and allowed to cool. Pounded in mortar, sieved and filled in well closed tins dry and cool for further use.

Couverture: couverture is cut or chopped in small pieces and melted in water bath up to 86 to 91 deg. F. and stirred thoroughly before use. If it is hotter then 91 deg. or not stirred enough the effect will be a grey or spotty product. Couverture is used for icing gateaux, cakes, confectionary and for decorating sweets and cakes.

Sweets, Ices and Pastries

A

Abricot: see apricot.

Albuféras: small round cakes of short paste flavored with arrak, brushed with egg, chopped almonds scattered on top, baked; when cold iced with rum-flavored fondant.

Alligator Pear: see avocado.

Allumettes glacées: see puff pastry sticks.

Ananas: see pineapple.

Angel Cake: 1. stiffly whipped egg white mixed with sugar, flour, corn starch, salt, cream of tartar and vanilla flavor, filled in well-floured mould or baking sheet and baked; 2. stiffly beaten egg whites mixed with powder sugar, flour, grated lemon peel and vanilla, filled in mould with open center, baked; when cold coated with lemon icing.

Anis Cookies: stiffly beaten egg whites mixed with beaten egg yolks, flour, sugar and powdered anis, placed in small heaps on waxed baking sheet, baked.

Annona; F. Anone; G. Anona, Zimtapfel: name of a number of fleshy tropical fruits, especially the Cherimoya and the West Indian Custard Apple. The Cherimoya is a

Annona

native of Central and South America. The skin is a smooth brown-yellow, the white juicy pulp of delicious flavor; weight up to 15 lbs.

— **Brasilian Style:** à la brésilienne: cut in half and then in slices, peeled carefully, covered with hot syrup flavored with anisette and allowed to stand warm for a while; round flat deep fried croquettes of vanilla rice arranged on service dish, a drained annona slice on each, coated lightly with apricot sauce flavored with anisette; rest of the sauce served separately.

— **in Champagne:** au champagne: peeled, cut in slices, seeds removed, arranged on glass dish, served very cold with chilled champagne poured on top.

— **Fritters:** Beignets d'anone: fruit peeled carefully, sliced, seeds removed, sprinkled with sugar and allowed to stand for a while; dipped in frying batter, deep fried, served with powder sugar sprinkled on top.

Apple; F. Pomme; G. Apfel: a native of Europe and the most extensively cultivated of all fruit. At present more then 1500 varieties are grown in the temperate zones of the northern and southern hemispheres.

— **Adolf:** a lid cut off, cored, poached in white wine and sugar, allowed to cool; filled with vanilla rice flavored with kirsch and served with the lid replaced on top.

— **Andalusian Style:** à l'andalouse: peeled, cored, poached carefully, placed on base of vanilla rice, coated with meringue mixture, decorated with this mixture and baked; fruit syrup served separately.

— **Apfelschmarren:** diced apples mixed with pancake batter, rather thick pancakes baked; when brown on both sides torn in pieces with a fork, served dusted with powder sugar (Austrian)

— **Baked:** au four: cored, cavity filled with butter and sugar, placed on greased baking dish, baked in oven.

— **Bourdalou:** peeled, cored, cut in half, poached and drained; placed either in greased baking dish or on flat tart made of short paste and baked empty, covered with pastry cream mixed with crushed macaroons, sprinkled with sugar, melted butter dropped on top, glazed.

— **Brissac:** peeled, cored, poached in white wine, Madeira, sugar and vanilla and allowed to cool; drained, placed in glass dish, covered with vanilla cream mixed with whipped cream and stiffly beaten egg whites, flavored with arrack; crushed macaroons and chopped pistachios scattered on top, bordered with red currant jelly.

— **Bulgarian Style:** à la bulgarienne: core cut out, filled with pastry cream mixed with chopped grilled almonds, hazelnuts and Malaga grapes, cooked carefully in oven with butter and red wine; placed on tartlet of short pastry, covered with the boiled down wine mixed with red currant jelly.

— **with Butter:** au beurre: 1. peeled, cored, arranged on greased baking dish, opening filled with sugar and butter, cooked in oven in vanilla syrup, served covered with apricot sauce blended lightly with butter;
2. as above but placed on brioche slice, opening filled with butter, sugar and brandy stirred to foam.

Apple

— **Carignan:** peeled, cored, poached, placed on biscuit base, opening filled with chocolate ice, covered with vanilla syrup.

— **Cevennes Style:** à la cévénole: peeled, scooped out, poached, allowed to cool; filled with chestnut purée mixed with whipped cream.

— **Châtelaine:** peeled, cored, cooked in oven in butter and vanilla syrup; center filled with diced cherries bound with thick apricot sauce, covered with thin frangipane, crushed macaroons and powder sugar scattered on top, glazed in oven.

— **Chevreuse:** baking dish covered with semolina croquette mixture, peeled, quartered, poached apples arranged on top, the center filled with salpicon of fruit bound with apricot sauce; coated entirely with meringue mixture, decorated with this mixture, chopped pistachios scattered on top, baked in oven.

— **Condé:** prepared like pineapple.

— **Crownprince Style:** à la dauphine: peeled, cored, baked, when cold placed on vanilla rice, covered with cold apricot sauce flavored with kirsch.

— **Demidoff:** peeled, cored, poached, soaked with brandy and sugar, filled with apple purée mixed with sugar, vanilla, egg yolks and stiffly beaten egg whites and baked; whipped cream served separately.

— **Devil Style:** à la diable: peeled, poached in vanilla syrup, drained, covered quickly with Chantilly cream, bordered with kirsch, ignited and served burning.

— **in Dressing Gown:** en robe de chambre: peeled, cored, cavity filled with sugar, butter and currants, wrapped in puff paste, brushed with egg yolk, baked.

— **Eve:** peeled, cored, poached, placed in baking dish, cavity filled with soufflé mixture blended with apple purée and mixed with diced cherries and sponge soaked in anisette, baked in oven.

— **Favorite Style:** 1. peeled, cored, poached, allowed to cool, cavity filled with frangipane cream, dipped in frying batter and deep fried;
2. thick slices, core cut out, poached lightly, when cold coated with frangipane cream, dipped in egg and breadcrumbs, deep fried, dusted with sugar.

— **Florence Style:** à la florentine: peeled, cored, poached, allowed to cool; filled with cold vanilla rice, placed on tartlet filled with sweet chestnut purée, decorated with Chantilly cream.

— **Fool:** apple purée mixed with whipped cream.

— **Frédéric:** peeled, cored, poached, placed on base of genoise covered with rice; coated with meringue mixture, dusted with sugar, baked; bordered with sabayon or sabayon served separately.

— **Hélène:** peeled, cored, cut in half, poached and allowed to cool; dressed on vanilla ice, decorated with whipped cream and candied violets; hot or cold chocolate sauce served separately.

— **Housekeeper Style:** à la ménagère: cored but not peeled, cavity filled with butter and sugar, baked in oven; allowed to cool, cavity filled with red currant jelly, garnished with whipped cream.

Apple

— **Housewife Style:** bonne-femme: cored, scored all around, filled with butter and sugar, baked in oven, served hot or cold.

— **Irene:** peeled, cored, poached, allowed to cool; cavity filled with marzipan mixed with chopped pistachios and flavored with kirsch, placed on pistachio ice, covered with vanilla cream.

— **Jellied:** en gelée: peeled, cored, poached, allowed to cool; drained, cavity filled with stoned cherries bound with apple jelly, apple glazed with apple jelly.

— **Josephine:** peeled, cored, poached, allowed to cool, arranged on vanilla rice mixed with diced candied fruit and flavored with kirsch, cavity filled with pistachio cream, bordered with raspberry purée.

— **Little Duke:** à la petit-duc: 1. peeled, cored, poached; when cold cavity filled with pralin mixed with whipped cream, arranged on vanilla ice, covered with red currant jelly;
2. peeled, cored, cut in quarters, poached in white wine and lemon juice with sugar, allowed to cool, placed on glass dish covered with the reduced fond mixed with red currant jelly, topped with vanilla cream mixed with whipped cream flavored with arrack.

— **Lombard Style:** à la lombarde: peeled, cored, poached, allowed to cool; dressed on empress rice, decorated with Chantilly cream flavored with maraschino.

— **Mariette:** poached, dressed on chestnut purée, covered with apricot sauce flavored with rum.

— **Mary Stuart:** cored, peeled, poached, when cold cavity filled with pastry cream, wrapped in puff paste, brushed with egg, baked.

— **Meringuée:** whole or quartered peeled and cored apples, poached, arranged in baking dish on base of sweet rice, covered with meringue mixture, decorated with meringue, dusted with sugar, baked in oven.

— **Morgan:** mellow apple, a lid cut off, scooped out, filled with chopped pineapple mixed with jelly flavored with Danziger Goldwasser, lid replaced into position, apple glazed with jelly.

— **Muscovite:** moscovite: peeled and scooped out, poached in vanilla syrup, cavity filled with soufflé mixture with apple purée flavored with kümmel and baked.

— **Northern Style:** à la nordique: peeled, cored, poached, placed in greased baking dish, cavity filled with apple purée, covered with meringue mixture flavored with kümmel, baked in oven.

— **Norwegian Style:** à la norvégienne: 1. cold poached apple placed on vanilla ice, covered with lemon cream;
2. poached cold apple, cavity filled with fruit ice, covered with Italian meringue mixture flavored with rum, glazed rapidly.

— **Pie:** sliced apples mixed with sugar and grated lemon peel, filled high in pie dish, very little water added, closed with puff pastry or short pastry made with dripping, decorated with dough, brushed with egg yolk, baked; served hot or cold with custard or cream.

Apple

— **Pompadour:** peeled, scooped out, poached; when cold filled with hazelnut ice, placed on tartlet made of short paste, coated with meringue mixture and browned rapidly in oven.

— **Portuguese Style:** à la portugaise: peeled and scooped out, filled with salpicon of macaroons, oranges, currants and sultanas bound with frangipane cream; baked in oven, placed on semolina base, covered with red currant jelly mixed with blanched julienne of orange peel.

— **Richelieu:** peeled, cut in quarters, poached, when cold dressed in the center of a border of cold flummery, covered with whipped cream mixed with frangipane cream and crushed macaroons, decorated with Chantilly cream; apricot sauce flavored with kirsch served separately.

— **Slice:** Tranche aux pommes: puff pastry rolled out in strips, pastry edge made, center filled with cold sliced apples cooked in butter, mixed with currants and raisins, coated with light macaroon mixture, baked; cut in slices while still warm.

— **Swedish Style:** à la suédoise: peeled, scooped out, poached, allowed to cool; arranged on base of genoise masked with vanilla ice with apple purée, covered with red currant jelly, decorated with Chantilly cream.

— **Tart, Norman:** Tarte normande: flat flan ring lined with short pastry, masked with thick apple purée, covered with sliced apples, coated thinly with apple purée, dusted with sugar, baked in oven.

— —, **Russian:** tartelette de pommes à la russe, tartlet ring lined with short pastry, masked with thick apple purée, covered symmetrically with apple slices, baked; when done glazed with strained apricot marmelade; served hot or cold.

— **Tartlet:** tartlet mould lined with short paste, filled with thick apple purée mixed with chopped almonds, sugar and lemon juice, coated with meringue mixture, baked in slow oven.

— —, **Russian:** tartlette de pommes à la russe, tartlet mould lined with short paste and baked empty; when cold filled with thick sweetened apple purée flavored with kümmel, covered with strained thick apricot sauce, decorated with Chantilly cream, angelica leaves and a candied cherry in the center.

— **Tenant Style:** à la fermière: prepared as housewife style, dressed on brioche slice.

— **Van Dyck:** peeled, cored, poached, allowed to cool; placed on vanilla ice, covered with custard flavored with arrack.

Apricot; F. Abricot; G. Aprikose: fruit native of North China, introduced into Europe in the 4th Century B. C.; it is now grown in all countries of the temperate zones. Apricotes are marketed fresh and canned, the purée is valuable as a filling and for glazing cakes.

— **Aiglon:** poached, dressed on vanilla ice, candied violets scattered on top, covered with spun sugar.

— **Alexandra:** poached in vanilla syrup, placed on vanilla ice, covered with strawberry purée, crushed white and red candied rose petals scattered on top.

— **Andalusian Style:** prepared like pineapple.

Apricot

— **Aurora:** peeled, poached, when cold dressed on strawberry mousse.
— **Bourdalou:** prepared like apple.
— **Carmen Sylva:** peeled, poached, cut in quarters, macerated with maraschino; dressed in glass dish, covered with Chantilly cream, crushed macaroons scattered on top.
— **Colbert:** poached, stoned, cavity filled with vanilla rice, dipped in egg and breadcrumbs, deep fried; apricot sauce served separately.
— **Condé:** prepared like pineapple.
— **Creole Style:** prepared like pineapple.
— **Cussy:** round base of genoise, center filled with salpicon of fruit bound with thick apricot sauce, covered with half a poached apricot, coated with meringue, browned in oven; bordered with hot apricot sauce flavored with kirsch at serving.
— **Dreux:** flat brioche, hollowed out, filled with blancmanger, half a poached peeled apricot placed on top, covered with cold apricot sauce flavored with kirsch.
— **Duchess Style:** à la duchesse: tartlets of almond short paste filled with vanilla custard, half a cold poached apricot placed on top, covered with apricot purée, garnished with candied angelica, a cherry and Chantilly cream.
— **Femina:** peeled, poached in Curaçao syrup, served cold on orange ice.
— **Flambé:** peeled, poached, kirsch or any other desired spirit poured on top, ignited and served burning.
— **Fritters:** Beignets d'abricots: halves, peeled raw, macerated with sugar and kirsch, dipped in frying batter, deep fried; dusted with powder sugar, apricot sauce flavored with kirsch served separately.
— **Gratinated:** au gratin: 1. halves peeled and poached, dressed on thick apple purée filled in baking dish, covered with thin Condé pralin, dusted with sugar, glazed; 2. short paste tartlet half filled with pastry cream, half a poached apricot placed on top, covered with thin pastry cream, crushed macaroons and sugar sprinkled on top, glazed.
— **Imperial Style:** à l'impériale: cold poached half apricots arranged on empress rice, garnished with stoned cherries, covered with cold apricot sauce flavored with kirsch.
— **Jam:** Confiture d'abricots: peeled, stoned, cut in half, boiled up with the same weight of sugar cooked to the small thread, strained, the syrup boiled until quite thick, apricots and a few of the cracked and blanched kernels added, cooked until thick enough, filled in prewarmed pots or glasses and allowed to stand for a few days before tying them up.
— **Lombard Style:** à la lombarde: prepared like apple.
— **Madrid Style:** à la madriléne: half poached apricots placed on orange ice, decorated with Chantilly cream, garnished with peeled, quartered apples poached in Curaçao syrup.
— **Marquise:** two half apricots put together with marzipan cream, placed on vanilla rice finished off with whipped cream, covered with strawberry sauce, bordered with whipped cream blended with strawberry purée.
— **Meringuée:** prepared like pineapple.

Apricot

— **Mistral:** peeled raw, dusted with powder sugar, coated with wild strawberry purée, fresh slivered almonds scattered on top, covered entirely with Chantilly cream.

— **Negus:** peeled, poached, when cold arranged on chocolate ice, covered with cold apricot sauce, garnished with Chantilly cream.

— **in Nightdress:** en chemise: half apricots peeled raw, dusted with sugar, wrapped in puff pastry, brushed with egg yolk, baked; served dusted with powder sugar.

— **Polish Style:** à la polonaise: half poached apricots placed on base of vanilla-rice mixed with diced pineapple, covered with cold apricot sauce flavored with kirsch, slivered almonds scattered on top.

— **Sultan Style:** à la sultane: round base of genoise bordered with meringue mixture and browned in oven; center filled with sweet rice mixed with frangipane and slivered pistachios, half poached apricots placed on top, sprinkled with chopped pistachios; almond milk syrup whipped with butter served separately.

— **Victoria:** half poached apricots served on biscuit base or in tartlet, covered with apricot sauce flavored with kirsch, chopped pistachios scattered on top.

Avocado, Alligator Pear; F. Avocat; G. Avocatobirne: pear-shaped fleshy fruit of a tree native to tropical Africa but now grown in the U. S. A., Mexico, Central and South America and West Indies. It varies in weight according to the different varieties from 6 oz. up to 4 lbs., the tough skin is green to brown or purple, the flesh bright green to yellow and of an agreable taste.

— **Jaipure:** peeled, cut in halves, seed removed, cooked in white wine, sugar and lemon juice; when cold placed on base of vanilla rice, opening filled with Guava jelly, crushed macaroons scattered on top.

— **Louison:** ripe fruit peeled, split lengthwise, seeds removed, the two halves scooped out lightly and interior macerated with Anisette; placed on base of genoise soaked with Anisette syrup, opening filled with pralin ice, coated with Chantilly cream and sprinkled with ground pralin; served chilled with strawberry purée separate.

— **San Francisco:** peeled, sliced, seed removed, macerated in sugar and brandy; cold vanilla rice arranged in baking dish, covered with vanilla ice, the avocado slices placed on top, coated with meringue-mixture, decorated with meringue, dusted with sugar and browned rapidly.

— **Stewed:** en compôte: peeled, cut in quarters, seed removed, cooked in syrup flavored with ginger, served chilled.

Avocat: see avocado.

B

Baba with Rum: Baba au rhum: savarin dough mixed with raisins and currants, baked in baba mould, soaked while still hot with hot syrup flavored with rum; served with rum-flavored apricot sauce.

Badener Nocken: Baden Dumplings: butter creamed with egg yolks and sugar, flour, salt and stiffly beaten egg whites added, filled in well greased pan, covered with hot milk mixed with butter and sugar, baked in oven; served sprinkled with grated chocolate or sugar mixed with cinnamon. (Austrian)

Banana; F. Banane; G. Banane: the edible fruit of a large tree belonging to the family of the musaceae, a native of tropical Africa, now grown in most tropical and subtropical countries.

— **Bavarois:** peeled, mashed, mixed with sugar, lemon juice and melted gelatine, flavored with brandy, whipped cream folded in; filled in fancy mould, chilled, when set turned out.

— **Bourdalou:** prepared like apple.

— **with Chantilly Cream:** à la crème Chantilly: peeled, sliced, dusted with sugar, chilled, served covered with Chantilly cream.

— **Condé:** prepared like pineapple.

— **Copacabana:** small fruit peeled, cut in half, poached in brandy syrup, when cold arranged on vanilla ice, covered with cold chocolate sauce, grilled slivered almonds scattered on top.

— **Creole:** peeled, cut in halves, poached lightly in syrup flavored with rum, arranged on warm vanilla rice, covered with crushed macaroons, butter dropped on top, dusted with sugar, browned in oven; apricot sauce flavored with rum served separately.

— **flambées:** peeled, cut in halves, poached in kirsch syrup, placed in timbale or baking dish with a little syrup on top; sent hot into the dining room, warmed up kirsch or brandy poured on top and ignited in front of the guests.

— **Fritters:** Beignets de bananes: peeled, spit lengthwise, cut in half, macerated in brandy and sugar; dipped in frying batter, deep fried, dusted with sugar.

— **Hotelkeeper Style:** à la hôtelière: peeled, sliced, macerated with sugar, Maraschino and Curaçao, served chilled.

— **Meringuées:** peeled, split lengthwise and cut in halves, poached lightly, placed on vanilla rice masked with thick apricot sauce, covered and decorated with meringue mixture, dusted with sugar, browned in oven.

— **Meringuées with Chocolate:** meringuées au chocolat: bottom of baking dish masked with thick chocolate cream, peeled halved bananas placed on top, covered with meringue mixture, decorated, dusted with sugar, browned in oven.

— **Nice Style:** à la nicoise: split open lengthwise, pulp mashed, sugared and flavored with Maraschino, refilled in the shell, sprinkled with sugar, glazed.

— **Norwegian Style:** à la norvegienne: lid cut off, pulp removed, filled with banana ice, covered and decorated with meringue mixture, dusted with sugar, glazed rapidly under the salamander.

— **Oriental Style:** à l'orientale: peeled, cut in slices, poached lightly in lemon syrup, flavored with rose water; drained, arranged on almond ice, covered with English cream, garnished with Chantilly cream, chopped grilled almonds scattered on top.

Banana

— **Russian Style:** à la russe: lid cut off, scooped out, pulp mashed and mixed with soufflé mixture flavored with kümmel; refilled in the shell, dusted with sugar, baked like a soufflé.

— **Salad of, and oranges:** Salade de bananes and oranges: peeled, cut in oblique rather thick slices, arranged on glass dish alternately with orange fillets, dusted with powder sugar, flavored with rum.

— **with Strawberries:** aux fraises: split open lengthwise, flesh mashed, mixed with wild strawberries macerated in sugar and Curaçao, refilled in the skin, chopped pistachios scattered on top.

— **Swedish Style:** à la suédoise: peeled, diced, macerated with sugar and Swedish punch; filled in tartlet, covered with Chantilly cream flavored with Swedish punch.

Banane: see banana.

Bannock: fairly large round cake made of oatmeal, wheat, barley or pease meal according to the different localities.

Bavarian Cream: Bavarois: egg yolks, sugar, milk and vanilla stirred to a hot cream, soaked squeezed out gelatine added, allowed to cool until mixture shows signs of stiffening, whipped cream folded in, filled in prepared moulds and chilled in refrigerator before turning out. For fruit cream cold syrup of 30° is added to the same amount of fruit purée, flavored with lemon juice, soaked gelatine added and whipped cream is folded in.

— **Adelhaide:** orange flavored cream with Madeira.

— **Alexandria:** apricot cream decorated with Chantilly cream and half-stewed apricots.

— **Clermont:** vanilla cream with chestnut purée added, garnished with candied chestnuts.

— **Creole:** vanille cream mixed with sweet rice and diced pineapple, garnished with Chantilly cream and small pineapple slices.

— **Dalmatian:** dalmatienne: vanilla cream mixed with diced sponge and mixed fruit macerated in Maraschino.

— **Diplomat Style:** à la diplomate: mould lined with vanilla cream, filled with layers of chocolate and strawberry bavarois.

— **Empress Style:** à l'impératrice: mould lined with wine jelly, bottom decorated with cherries, filled with vanilla cream mixed with chopped pistachios.

— **Figaro:** cream of different colors and tastes, cut in dice when set, filled in mould, covered with wine jelly and chilled.

— **Florence Style:** à la florentine: almond cream, decorated with whipped cream flavored with kirsch, chopped pistachois scattered on the whipped cream.

— **Malakoff:** vanilla cream mixed with chopped almonds, currants and diced finger biscuits soaked in Maraschino.

— **Marie-Louise:** peach cream flavored with kirsch.

— **Mocha:** coffee cream.

— **Multicolored:** rubanée: mould filled with separate layers of almond, raspberry or strawberry and chocolate or coffee cream, lined with wine jelly beforehand.

— **My Queen:** mould lined with vanilla cream, filled with strawberry cream mixed with strawberries macerated in kirsch; when set turned out and garnished with strawberries macerated with kirsch.

Bavarian Cream

— **Nuns Style:** à la réligieuse: mould lined with chocolate cream, filled with vanilla cream.

— **Pompadour:** vanilla and chocolate cream in separate layers.

— **Regina:** mould filled separately with layers of vanilla and strawberry cream, garnished with strawberries macerated with Maraschino.

— **Richelieu:** mould lined with purée of prunes bound with gelatine and flavored with Prunelle, filled with vanilla cream.

— **Spanish:** à l'espagnole: orange cream garnished with orange fillets.

Bavarois: see Bavarian cream.

Beignets: see fritters.

Beignets soufflés: see cream puff paste fritters.

Berliner Luft: egg yolks creamed with sugar and lemon juice, grated lemon peel, soaked dissolved gelatine added, stiffly whipped egg whites folded in, filled in fancy mould and chilled; set turned out and served bordered with raspberry syrup. (German)

Berliner Torte: short paste flavored with cinnamon and grated lemon peel, mixed with grated hazelnuts, cut into four rounds and baked; when cold put together with red currant jelly and iced with vanilla fondant. (German)

Biscuits à la cuillière: see sponge fingers.

Biscuit glacé: see ice biscuit.

Blackberries; F. Baies de ronce; G. Brombeeren: name given to the fruit of a number of brambles, in America the Blackberry or Dewberry, in Europe to the Brambleberry. Blackberries are marketed fresh, frozen, canned and in syrup.

— **Astoria:** apple with a lid cut off, peeled, scooped out, poached carefully in syrup and lemon juice and allowed to cool; drained, coated with strained apricot jam, covered entirely with slivered roasted almonds, filled with poached and drained blackberries, bound with thick apricot sauce flavored with kirsch, slivered almonds scattered on top.

— **Bernese Style:** à la bernoise: macerated in maraschino and sugar, filled in tartlets baked empty, coated with strained red currant jelly, chopped pistachios scattered on top.

— **Pie:** pie dish filled with sugared blackberries flavored with grated lemon peel and a pinch of cinnamon, a few drops of water added, closed with puff pastry or pie dough, brushed with egg, baked; served hot or cold with cream or custard. (English)

— **and Apple Pie:** same as pie with sliced apples added. (English)

— **Pudding:** blackberries cooked in red wine with sugar, grated lemon peel and cinnamon; rubbed through a sieve, thickened with corn starch, stiffly beaten egg-whites and raw blackberries sugared beforehand, folded in and filled in charlotte mould; when cold and set turned out, served covered with vanilla sauce.

Blancmange: F. Blancmanger; G. Mandelsulz: a cold pudding made of almond milk, obtained by pounding almonds very finely with water and pressing the moisture out in

Blancmange

a cloth, sugar, gelatine and flavoring, filled in a cylindrical mould, chilled and turned out.

— **Chocolate:** au chocolat: basic mixture blended with dissolved chocolate.

— **Coffee:** au café: basic mixture flavored with strong coffee essence or soluble coffee powder.

— **Delmonico:** basic mixture blended with cherry jam and mixed with stoned cherries and diced angelica.

— **English:** à l'anglaise: English blancmange is made by boiling up sweetened milk, thickened with corn starch dissolved in cold milk, cooked, flavored with vanilla or according to taste, filled in mould and chilled.

— **with Hazelnuts:** aux avelines: basic mixture prepared with hazelnuts instead of almonds.

— **Maraschino:** au marasquin: basic mixture flavored with maraschino.

— **Pistachio:** aux pistaches: basic mixture prepared with half almonds and half bright green pistachios.

— **Strawberry:** aux fraises: strawberry purée mixed with the same quantity of basic mixture, thickened with gelatine.

— **Striped:** rubané: three or four different compositions, such as plain blancmange, basic mixture mixed with chocolate, coffee, strawberries or raspberries, filled alternately in mould.

Blazinde moldovenesti: Cottage cheese cakes: puff pastry rolled out thinly, cut in squares, center filled with a mixture of creamed cottage cheese, egg yolks, butter, sugar and salt, edges folded over on top, brushed with egg yolk, baked. (Roumanian)

Blueberries; F. Myrtilles; G. Blaubeeren, Heidelbeeren: berries of a number of different bushes widely distributed in Central Europe, Canada and the U.S.A.

— **Chantilly:** border mould lined with caramel, filled with royal, poached, allowed to cool; turned out, center filled with whipped cream mixed with blueberries sugared beforehand.

— **Swiss Style:** à la suisse: macerated in rum and vanilla sugar, filled in glasses, covered and decorated with Chantilly cream.

Böhmische Dalken: fermented dough made of flour, egg yolks, sugar, yeast, a little salt and stiffly beaten egg whites, rolled out, cut round with a cutter, allowed to rise, center indented with the fingers, baked; served hot with a little red currant jelly or plum jam in the indentation. (Austrian)

Bombe: see ice bombe.

Boulbett is tworog: dough made of creamed cottage cheese, egg yolks, sugar, flour and a pinch of salt, shaped into balls, baked; powder sugar and sour cream served separately. (Russian)

Buchteln, also Wuchteln: fermented dough made of egg yolks, flour, butter, sugar, yeast and a pinch of salt, rolled out thinly, cut into squares, center filled with apricot or plum jam, hazelnut or poppy cream, ends folded over, placed in greased pan, brushed with egg white, baked in oven; served hot or cold sprinkled with sugar. (Austrian)

C

Café glacé: see iced coffee.

Cassata: a kind of ice pudding of Italian origin filled in bombe mould lined with ice cream with two or three layers of bombe, mousse or ice biscuit mixture with plenty of diced fruit, macaroons, nuts etc.

— **Alhambra:** lined with vanilla ice, filled with whipped cream mixed with small strawberries macerated in crème de noyau liqueur.

— **Carmencita:** lined with raspberry cream ice, filled in layers with orange and vanilla ice mixed with blanched chopped candied orange peel macerated in kirsch.

— **Diplomate:** lined with vanilla ice, filled in layers with praliné ice, whipped cream mixed with poached chopped sour cherries macerated in brandy and sugar, and a third layer of praliné ice.

— **Naples Style:** à la napolitaine: lined with vanilla ice, filled with strawberry and praliné ice in layers containing crushed macaroons and diced candied fruit macerated in maraschino.

Cat's Tongues: Langues de chat: butter creamed with vanilla sugar, mixed with egg whites and flour, a little cream added; fingers piped on greased and lightly dusted baking sheet, baked in fairly hot oven.

Chamberlain Tartlet: wedged tartlet mould lined with puff pastry, brushed with apricot, filled with chopped apples mixed with breadcrumbs, sugar, cinnamon, grated lemon peel and a little rum, covered with puff paste, baked; when cold iced with vanilla fondant.

Champagne Fingers: sugar, eggs and egg yolks stirred to foam, sieved flour and starch flour folded in, piped into special finger moulds greased and dusted with flour and sugar beforehand; dried 3—4 hours, baked in moderate oven, shaked out of mould when done.

Charlotte; F. Charlotte; G. Krustenpudding, Charlotte: 1. a hot sweet with a framework of bread slices dipped in butter and a filling of apples or other fruit;
2. a mould lined with finger biscuits or strips of sponge cake etc., filled with Bavarian or other cream, jelly or ice.

— **Apple:** de pommes: bottom and sides of charlotte mould lined with not too thin strips of bread soaked in melted butter, filled with sliced apples cooked in butter until quite stiff, mixed with a little sugar and very thick apricot jam, covered with a round bread slice dipped in melted butter and baked; turned out, apricot sauce served separately.

— **Carmen:** mould lined with wafers, filled with a concoction of $^2/_3$ fresh tomato purée and $^1/_3$ pimiento purée mixed with diced ginger in syrup, syrup of 32 deg., melted gelatine and lemon juice, flavored with ginger powder and blended with whipped cream.

— **Chantilly:** charlotte made of sponge fingers, wafers or small cream puffs fixed directly on base of baked short paste with caramel or apricot jam boiled down to a thick paste, filled and decorated with Chantilly cream.

Charlotte

— **Florence Style:** à la florentine: mould lined with biscuit strips, filled with orange ice mixed with whipped cream; kept in deep freezer until required.

— **George Sand:** mould lined with small chocolate eclairs, filled with coffee cream ice, frozen, turned out, garnished with Chantilly cream, decorated with red currant jelly.

— **Harlequin:** à l'arlequin: lined with strips of sponge cake iced with chocolate, lemon and pistachio fondant, filled with cubes of different colored Bavarian cream, sealed with wine jelly; when set turned out, top decorated with glacé fruit.

— **Imperial Style:** à l'impériale: mould coated with maraschino jelly, lined with wafers, filled with vanilla Bavarian cream mixed with diced pears; when set turned out, garnished with small half poached pears, scooped out, filled with Chantilly cream, chopped angelica scattered on top.

— **Klondyke:** mould lined with small chocolate eclairs, filled with Chantilly cream thickened lightly with gelatine and flavored with Danziger Goldwasser; turned out when set and decorated on top with Chantilly cream.

— **with Madeira:** au madère: apple charlotte mixed with Malaga grapes; Madeira-flavored apricot sauce served separately.

— **Metternich:** mould lined with sponge fingers, filled with Chantilly cream blended with chestnut purée and lightly thickened with gelatine.

— **Montreuil:** mould lined with sponge fingers, filled with Bavarian cream with peach purée mixed with diced raw peaches.

— **Naples Style:** à la napolitaine: 1. lined with sponge strips, filled with Chantilly cream blended with chestnut purée, mixed with diced pineapple, candied lemon peel and raisins, thickened with gelatine;
2. genoise sponge baked in charlotte mould, when cold scooped out, filled with Chantilly cream blended with chestnut purée, top decorated with Chantilly cream and glacé fruit.

— **Norman Style:** à la normande: same as apple charlotte but apples flavored with Calvados (apple-jack); apricot sauce flavored with Calvados served separately.

— **Northern Style:** à la nordique: mould lined with strips of genoise sponge, filled with vanilla Bavarian cream flavored with kümmel and mixed with fruit salpicon.

— **Opéra:** mould lined with sugar wafers, filled with Bavarian cream mixed with a little purée of glacé chestnuts and salpicon of glacé fruits macerated in maraschino.

— **Parisian:** à la parisienne: lined with strips of genoise sponge coated with strained apricot jam and iced with pink fondant, filled with vanilla Bavarian cream.

— **Pear:** aux poires: prepared like apple charlotte with pears.

— **Pompadour:** mould lined with sponge strips, filled with pineapple Bavarian cream; when set turned out and bordered with puff pastry half-moons, cut open and filled alternately with chocolate and vanilla cream.

Charlotte

— **Renaissance:** mould lined with triangles of sponge cake iced with white and pink fondant, filled with vanilla Bavarian cream mixed with fruit salpicon; when set turned out, a round pineapple slice placed on top, decorated with glacé cherries and angelica.

— **Russian:** à la russe: bottom and sides of mould lined with sponge fingers, filled with vanilla Bavarian cream mixed with Chantilly cream. May also be filled with Bavarian cream of different flavors and then designated on menu as Russian orange cream, Russian chocolate cream etc.

Cherimoya: see annona.

Cherries; F. Cerises: G. Kirschen: fruit of the cherry tree with many varieties cultivated in all temperate climates. The two main categories are the sweet and the sour cherries. Cherries are marketed fresh, canned and frozen. For sweet dishes they must be stoned and are usually poached in light syrup.

— **in Claret:** au vin rouge: stoned, poached in red wine with sugar and cinnamon, drained, syrup boiled down, blended with red currant jelly and strained over the cherries; served cold with finger biscuits.

— **Dijon Style:** à la dijonnaise: poached in syrup flavored with black-currant liqueur, served in timbale dish with finger biscuits, a little kirsch poured on top.

— **Dubarry:** gateau ring lined with short paste, dusted with sugar, filled with stoned cherries, baked and allowed to cool; coated entirely with whipped cream mixed with macaroon crumbs and decorated with whipped cream.

— **Eldorado:** poached in vanilla syrup, drained, bound with brandy-flavored sabayon and served hot.

— **Frascati:** poached in kirsch-flavored syrup, served cold covered with Chantilly cream.

— **Henry IV.:** Henri IV.: puff paste tartlets lined with red currant jelly, half filled with almond ice, covered with poached cherries flavored with kirsch, masked and decorated with meringue mixture, browned in oven.

— **Jubilee:** Jubilée: poached, syrup mixed with red currant jelly and bound lightly with arrow-root, filled hot in small cocottes or silver containers, warm kirsch poured on top, served burning.

— **Tart:** Tarte aux cerises: butter creamed with sugar and egg yolks, mixed with ground almonds, grated lemon peel and flour, stiffly beaten egg whites folded in; gateau mould filled with half the mixture, covered generously with stoned cherries, coated with the remaining mixture, baked in moderate oven; when cold dusted with powder sugar.

— — **Sylvia:** tart ring lined with short pastry, filled with poached drained morellos, covered with sweet egg royal and baked in moderate oven; when cold iced with rum-flavored fondant.

— **Vacherin:** Vacherin aux cerises: sour cherries poached in vanilla syrup, drained and bound with red currant jelly; filled shortly before serving in nest-shaped vacherin, covered with a vacherin lid, decorated with Chantilly cream and served at once.

Cherries

— **Valéria:** tartlets half filled with red currant cream ice, cherries poached in sugared red wine on top, masked and decorated with Italian meringue mixture, browned rapidly, brushed lightly with dissolved red currant jelly, chopped pistachios scattered on top.

— **Van Dyck:** poached in white wine and sugar, dressed on vanilla ice, covered with arrak-flavored vanilla cream.

Chestnut; F. Marron; G. Edelkastanie: the nut or seed of all varieties of the chestnut tree, but chiefly of the Spanish or Sweet Chestnut cultivated in France and Italy. Marketed fresh, canned, in powder, preserved in vanilla syrup and glacé.

— **Chantilly:** purée of chestnuts cooked in vanilla syrup, arranged on sponge cake base soaked with kirsch syrup, covered and decorated with Chantilly cream, bordered with glacé chestnuts.

— **Croquettes:** chestnut purée thickened with egg yolks, sweetened, flavored with vanilla, shaped into croquettes, dipped in egg and breadcrumbs, deep fried; dusted with powder sugar, vanilla sauce served separately.

— **Montblanc:** Montblanc aux marrons: peeled, cooked in vanilla syrup, drained, rubbed through a sieve, when cold arranged like a small hill on a platter and covered entirely with Chantilly cream.

— **Slice:** two strips of sponge cake sandwiched with vanilla butter cream mixed with chestnut purée, coated with rum fondant, chopped almonds scattered on top, cut in slices.

Chocolat glacé: see iced chocolate.

Chworost: sort of noodle dough made of flour, eggs, very little water, sugar and rum, rolled out thin and cut into long strips; three strips twisted into tails, fried in clarified butter and served cold dusted with sugar and cinnamon. (Russian)

Compote: see fruit, stewed.

Coupe: see ice coupe.

Cream: Crème: 1. mixture of eggs, egg yolks, sugar and milk, with or without flour or cream powder stirred until the liqued binds to a cream;
2. mixture of egg, egg yolks, sugar and milk, filled in mould, poached in water bath;
3. mixture of wine or milk, egg yolks, sugar and gelatine with stiffly beaten egg whites or whipped cream;
4. whipped cream flavored with vanilla, fruit purée, chocolate, coffee etc.;
5. Bavarian cream (q. v.). Most creams are served cold, only very few warm. Creams are also used for filling cakes and pastries, especially pastry, frangipane and Saint-Honoré cream.

— **Brulée:** see burnt cream.

— **Burnt:** brulée: same as Viennese.

— **Caramel:** au caramel: prepared like royal in mould lined with caramel.

— **Chantilly:** whipped cream flavored with vanilla.

— **Chantilly with Fruit:** aux fruits: whipped cream mixed with a third of the amount purée of fruit such as strawberry, raspberry etc., filled in glasses, decorated with the fruit in question; sponge fingers served separately.

Cream

— **Chocolate:** au chocolat: prepared like vanilla cream with melted chocolate stirred in while still hot.

— **Diplomate:** English cream lightly jellied, mixed with whipped cream, flavored with brandy and maraschino, filled in layers with broken macaroons and sponge fingers or cubes of genoise; garnished with Chantilly cream and glacé cherries.

— **English:** anglaise: milk boiled up with vanilla, egg yolks stirred with sugar, the milk added and whipped in water bath until liquid binds to a cream. Served hot or cold as a sauce for sweets.

— **Florence:** florentine: royal cream mixed with ground pralin, filled in mould lined with a thin layer of caramel; when cold turned out, decorated with Chantilly cream flavored with kirsch, chopped pistachios scattered on top.

— **Frangipane:** prepared like pastry cream but finished off with butter and crushed macaroons.

— **Hazelnut:** aux noisettes: prepared like bavarois mixed with lightly grilled ground hazelnuts.

— **Mocha:** au moka: prepared like vanilla cream mixed with strong coffee essence or soluble powder; served when cold in glasses or glass dish, decorated with Chantilly cream and chocolate coffee beans.

— **Nesselrode:** Bavarian vanilla cream mixed with chestnut purée and finely diced candied cherries, lemon peel and sultanas soaked in Madeira beforehand; when set turned out, coated with thick chocolate sauce and decorated with whipped cream.

— **Opéra:** royal mixed with ground pralin poached in a border mould; when cold turned out, center filled with Chantilly cream mixed with crushed crystallized violets, bordered with strawberries macerated in kirsch and covered with spun sugar.

— **Orange:** à l'orange: prepared like pineapple cream, stiffly beaten egg whites may be added.

— **Pastry:** Crème pâtissière: milk boiled up with vanilla. stirred into egg yolks mixed with sugar and flour, cooked to a fairly thick cream. Cream powder may be used instead of yolks and flour. This cream is used for filling.

— **Pâtissière:** see pastry cream.

— **Pineapple:** à l'ananas: pineapple juice stirred with sugar, a little lemon juice and dissolved gelatine until mixture shows signs of stiffening, whipped cream added, filled in mould or glass dish and allowed to set before serving.

— **Queen Style:** à la reine: almonds pounded with a little cream and orange blossom water, rubbed through a sieve, mixed with whipped cream, lightly jellied, flavored with maraschino; filled in mould and turned out when set.

— **Regency:** régence: finger biscuits macerated in kirsch and maraschino, soaked in hot milk, rubbed through a fine sieve, mixed with whole eggs, egg yolks, sugar and a pinch of salt; filled in flat charlotte mould, poached, allowed to cool, turned out, covered with cold apricot syrup flavored with kirsch, bordered with half apricots decorated with a glacé cherry.

— **Royal:** royale ou crème renversée: whole eggs and egg yolks stirred with sugar, mixed gradually with hot milk in which vanilla has been infused, strained, filled in

Cream

greased mould, poached in water bath in oven with moderate temperature, turned out when quite cold.

— **Saint-Honoré:** same as pastry cream to which stiffly beaten egg whites have been added while still boiling hot.

— **Swedish:** à la suédoise: apple purée stirred with sugar, mixed with disolved gelatine, flavored with Swedish punch, whipped cream folded in, filled in fancy mould and allowed to set; turned out, garnished with small apple quarters poached in vanilla syrup, decorated with whipped cream.

— **Vanilla:** milk boiled up with vanilla pot; egg yolks mixed with sugar, the hot milk stirred in gradually, whipped in water bath until liquid binds to cream, served hot or cold; cold vanilla cream is usually decorated with whipped cream.

— **Viennese:** viennoise: prepared like caramel cream, not lined with caramel but the caramel dissolved in the milk.

— **Wine:** au vin: eggs and egg yolks mixed with sugar and a little lemon juice, whipped in water bath with good white wine until liquid binds to cream, soaked gelatine added; when mixture shows signs of stiffening, stiffly beaten egg whites folded in; filled in mould or served in glasses topped with whipped cream.

Cream Horns: Cornets à la crème: puff paste strips twisted in a spiral around tin or wooden horn moulds, brushed with egg, dipped on top in sugar, baked; removed from mould while hot, filled with vanilla or Chantilly cream when cold.

Cream Pots: Petits pots de crème: royal flavored with vanilla, coffee, chocolate, almonds, hazelnuts etc. filled in small heat-proof containers, egg-cocottes or China pots, poached in water bath in moderate oven; served cold decorated with whipped cream or to taste.

— **Arabian:** à l'arabe: coffee cream; chopped dates bound with thick apricot sauce flavored with orange blossom water on top, decorated with a rosette of Chantilly cream.

— **Banania:** vanilla cream; sliced bananas macerated in kirsch and bound with cold apricot sauce on top, small border of Chantilly cream.

— **Hélène:** vanilla pot with a round piece of poached pear on top covered with thick chocolate cream, bordered with Chantilly cream.

— **Mozart:** chocolate cream mixed with almond pralin, border of Chantilly cream with chopped grilled almonds scattered on top, a large chocolate truffle in the center.

— **Prince Nicolai:** vanilla cream mixed with ground pralin, coated lightly with apricot jelly, decorated with small strawberries soaked in green Chartreuse, bordered with Chantilly cream.

— **Queen Margot:** Reine Margot: almond cream, decorated with Chantilly cream with slivered pistachios scattered on top.

Cream Puff Paste Fritters: Beignet soufflés: cream puff paste divided into small round balls, fried in deep fat, filled with cream, jelly, jam etc.

Cream Puff Paste Fritters
- **with Bananas:** aux bananes: mixed with peeled bananas diced finely, divided into small pieces, deep fried, served powdered with vanilla sugar.
- **Dauphine:** filled with almond cream.
- **Nice Style:** à la niçoise: paste mixed with chopped Malaga grapes, candied fruit and apples, flavored with orange blossom water, deep fried, served powdered with sugar.
- **Viennese Style:** à la viennoise: cream puff paste made with milk, divided into small balls, deep fried, powdered with sugar; apricot sauce or raspberry syrup served separately.

Cream Puffs: Petits choux à la crème: small balls of cream puff paste piped on greased baking dish, brushed with egg, baked in moderate oven; when cold cut open, filled with Chantilly or vanilla cream, dusted with powder sugar.
- **Slice:** Gâteau millefeuilles; puff pastry rolled out thinly size of baking sheet, placed on sheet, punched with a fork, baked; cut in broad strips, coated with jellied pastry cream, 3 to 4 layers placed on top of each other. Top coated thinly with apricot or fruit jelly, iced with fondant, cut in pieces, placed on top of cream slices and these cut through.
- **Tartlet:** Tartelette à la crème: tartlet mould lined with short or puff pastry remnants, filled with plain pastry cream or cream flavored with almonds, hazelnuts or pralin with stiffly beaten egg whites folded in, baked in oven, served cold dusted with powder sugar.

Crème: see cream.

Crêpes: see pancakes.

Croquettes; F. Croquettes; G. Kroketten: concoction of rice semolina or fruit bound with frangipane cream etc., shaped, dipped in egg and breadcrumbs, deep fried and served with a sauce to taste.
- **Apricot:** d'abricots: sweet rice mixed with thick apricot jam and diced apricots, flavored with kirsch, shaped, dipped in egg and breadcrumbs, deep fried; apricot sauce flavored with kirsch served separately.
- **Massena:** sweet vanilla rice mixed with quince paste, shaped, dipped in egg and breadcrumbs, deep fried; Malaga sauce bound lightly with arrow-root served separately.
- **Nice Style:** à la niçoise: same as vanilla croquettes but rice mixed with fruit salpicon; apricot sauce flavored with maraschino served separately.
- **Orange:** à l'orange: sweet rice flavored with orange juice, mixed with diced orange sections, shaped into small balls, dipped in egg and breadcrumbs, deep fried; orange syrup flavored with Curaçao served separately.
- **Oriental:** à l'orientale: sweet vanilla rice flavored with ginger powder, mixed with diced ginger in syrup, shaped into half moons, dipped in egg and breadcrumbs, deep fried; lemon syrup or syrup flavored with rose water served separately.
- **Pineapple:** à l'ananas: sweet vanilla rice mixed with diced pinapple, dipped in egg and breadcrumbs, deep fried; pineapple syrup served separately.

Croquettes

— **Rice, with Almonds:** de riz aux amandes: same as vanilla croquettes but mixed with ground almonds.

— **Saint-Cloud:** semolina mixture blended with large seeded raisins, soaked in maraschino and chopped; fruit sauce served separately.

— **Semolina:** de semoule: semolina cooked in milk with butter, sugar and vanilla, bound with egg yolks blended with cream and allowed to cool; shaped into small balls, dipped in egg and breadcrumbs, deep fried; fruit syrup served separately.

— **Tutti-Frutti:** salpicon of fruit macerated in kirsch, bound with very thick frangipane cream, when cold cut out with a round cutter, dipped in egg and breadcrumbs, deep fried; maraschino-flavored apricot sauce served separately.

— **Vanilla:** du riz à la vanille: vanilla-flavored sweet rice bound with egg yolks and cream, shaped into croquettes, dipped in egg and breadcrumbs, deep fried; raspberry, strawberry or English sauce served separately.

Croûtes: see crusts.

Crumpets: milk warmed lightly with a little butter, mixed with beaten eggs, a pinch of salt, flour and yeast dissolved in luke warm milk to a not too soft dough and allowed to rise; rolled out, cut into thick round cakes about the size of a muffin, placed on a well greased baking sheet, allowed to rise once more, baked a light brown and served sliced and spread with butter or grilled. (English)

Crusts: Croûtes: slices of brioche, cake or bread fried crisp in butter or dried and glazed in oven, served garnished with fruit and coated with sauce.

— **with Bananas:** aux bananes: prepared like with pineapple, center filled with thick banana slices cooked in butter, covered with hot apricot sauce shortly before serving.

— **Golden:** Dorée: small slices of stale white bread or brioche soaked in cold sweetened milk flavored with vanilla, drained, dipped in lightly sweetened beaten egg, fried in clarified butter, dusted with vanilla sugar.

— **Lyonese:** à la lyonnaise: stale savarin cut into slices, placed on baking sheet, dusted with powder sugar, glazed in oven; arranged crown-fashion, decorated with glacé cherries and angelica leaves, center filled with quarters of stewed pears and apples, covered with kirsch-flavored apricot sauce at serving.

— **Madeira:** au madère: same as Lyonese, center filled with Malaga raisins, sultanas and currants, soaked in warm water, drained and bound with Madeira-flavored apricot sauce.

— **with Pineapple:** à l'ananas: bread slices fried in butter, arranged like a crown, garnished with a glacé cherry on each slice, center filled with hot poached pineapple slices, covered with hot apricot sauce shortly before serving.

Custard: egg yolks mixed with sugar and milk, flavored with vanilla or grated lemon peel, stirred in water bath until thick and creamy but not allowed to boil; served cold in glasses. Can also be made with cream powder.

Custard

— **Tart:** flan ring lined with puff pastry remnants, bottom masked with apricot jam, filled with custard cream, baked.

— **Tartlet:** Tartelettes à l'anglaise: prepared like tart but in small tartlet moulds, dusted with sugar, baked.

D

Dampfnudeln: plain yeast dough shaped into small round balls, placed in a greased baking pan with high bords in which a little luke warm milk has been poured; allowed to rise slowly, brushed with egg and baked in moderate oven; served hot with vanilla sauce. (German)

Darioles: dariole moulds lined with short paste, filled with sugar creamed with eggs, a little flour, milk and orange blossom water added, a little piece of butter placed on top, baked; turned out and dusted with icing sugar.

Dartois: strip of puff pastry rolled out about 1/8 in. thick and 4 in. wide, coated with almond cream, covered with a second strip, the edges pressed well on; division marked lightly with a knife, chequered with the point of a knife, baked; cut into pieces while still warm.

Date; F. Datte; G. Dattel: the fruit of an African and Asiatic palm tree now also grown in Southern Europe and California. There are several sorts of dates, the best ist the light brown Persian with soft sweet flesh. Dates are eaten fresh and dried; chiefly marketed dried.

— **Gateau:** Gâteau aux dattes: stiffly beaten egg whites mixed with sugar, egg yolks, stoned dates cut in strips, slivered almonds and chopped lemon peel, filled in greased and sugared gateau mould, baked in moderate oven; when cold turned out, served covered with whipped cream.

— **Queen Style:** à la reine: boiled up in sugar syrup flavored with Sherry, allowed to cool, stoned, center filled with marzipan, served cold with a litte of the syrup on top.

— **Stuffed:** farcies: 1. stoned, filled with marzipan flavored with maraschino, coated with dark couverture, when set striped with a thin piping tube;
2. stoned, stuffed with chopped hazelnuts boiled up with a little hony, rolled in coarse sugar;
3. stoned, filled with thick vanilla cream, dipped in egg and crushed macaroons, deep fried; vanilla sauce served separately.

— **Tartlet:** Tartelette aux dattes: egg yolks creamed with sugar, finely chopped dates and hazelnuts added, stiffly beaten egg whites folded in, filled in greased tartlet moulds, baked; served cold topped with Chantilly cream.

Datte: see date.

Devonshire Junket: sweet milk mixed with sugar and quickly turned by dissolved rennet tablets. Served cold sprinkled with a little grated nutmeg and garnished with whipped cream; stewed fruit is often served separately. Junket may also be flavored with lemon, vanilla, chocolate, cinnamon, Sherry etc.

E

Eaton Mess: crushed raw strawberries mixed with sweetened whipped cream.

Eclair: strips of cream puff paste dressed about 4 in. long and 3/4 in. thick on baking sheet, brushed with egg, baked until crisp; when cold filled with pastry cream of various flavors or whipped cream and iced with fondant.

— **Chocolate:** au chocolat: filled with Chantilly cream, iced with chocolate-fondant.

— **Maraschino:** au marasquin: filled with vanilla cream flavored with Maraschino, glazed with Maraschino-fondant.

— **Mocha:** Eclair au café: cut open at the side, filled with coffee-pastry cream or whipped cream, glaced with coffee-fondant.

— **Pistachio:** au pistaches: filled with vanilla or whipped cream mixed with pistachio purée, iced with pistachio fondant.

— **Victoria:** filled with orange cream, iced with fondant flavored with Curaçao.

F

Fanchonnettes: tartlet moulds lined with puff pastry, filled with almond cream, half baked, covered with meringue mixture, dusted with sugar and finished off in the oven; when cold garnished with red currant jelly.

Fennel Cake: sugar and egg yolks mixed, ground almonds, flour, a few fennel seeds added, stiffly beaten egg whites folded in, filled in greased and floured cake mould and baked.

Fig; F. Figue; G. Feige: the fruit of the fig tree, native of Asia minor, now cultivated all over the world in semi-tropical climates. Fresh mature figs are green, purple or black-violet. Figs are also marketed dried and canned.

— **Carlton:** ripe figs cut in quarters, covered with whipped cream blended with half the amount of raspberry purée, served chilled.

— **Chantilly:** cut in half, macerated in kirsch and sugar, served covered with Chantilly cream.

— **Eden:** glass dish half filled with lemon ice, besprinkled with crushed macaroons, fresh ripe figs cut in half and orange sections, macerated in kirsch and sugar, arranged on top, covered with whipped cream, crushed macaroons scattered on top.

— **Greek Style:** à la grecque: poached in white wine, lemon juice and sugar, served cold in the liquor.

— **Oriental Style:** à l'orientale: poached in lemon syrup, allowed to cool, served covered with sabayon.

— **in Port:** au porto: cut in halves, poached very shortly in syrup flavored strongly with Port and served cold in the syrup.

— **Salad:** cut in quarters, macerated in brandy and Curaçao with powder sugar, chilled; at serving a little Port poured on top.

Finger Biscuits: see sponge fingers.

Flamerie: see flummery.

Flan: large open tart or pie with a base and fluted border, baked in hoops either empty or filled with fresh fruit and baked with the fruit, sometimes covered with custard or glazed with thick syrup made of the fruit skins etc. or with strained apricot jam. The bottom of the paste, sugar or short pastry, must be pricked to prevent blistering. To prevent fruit soaking the base, ground hazelnuts or cake crumbs should be scattered on bottom of flan before placing fruit on top.

— **Apricot:** d'abricots: lined with short or sugar pastry, filled symmetrically with half apricots, baked, coated with thick strained apricot jam or glazed with apricot syrup.

— **Cherry:** aux cerises: baked empty to a pale yellow, filled with stoned cherries, covered with custard, baked; served dusted with powder sugar.

— **French Apple:** aux pommes à la française: lined with short pastry, dried rather than baked in oven, filled with very thick sweetened apple purée, covered symmetrically with thin apple slices, powdered with sugar, baked in oven; while still hot brushed lightly with thick strained hot apricot.

— **Orange:** à l'orange: baked empty, filled with orange sections without skin, pith or pips, covered and decorated with meringue mixture flavored with Curaçao, browned in oven.

— **Portuguese:** à la portugaise: lined with short pastry and baked a light yellow, filled with rice cooked in red wine, mixed with butter, sugar, egg yolks and stoned sour cherries, stiffly beaten egg whites folded in, baked, served cold.

— **Rice, with Meringue:** au riz meringué: baked empty, filled with sweet vanilla rice mixed with fruit salpicon, covered and decorated with meringue mixture, dusted with powder sugar, browned in oven.

— **with Strawberries:** aux fraises: baked empty, filled symmetrically with strawberries sugared beforehand, glazed with strained red currant jelly, slivered almonds or pistachios scattered on top.

Floating Island: stiffly whipped egg whites, sweetened with powder sugar, large spoonfuls poached in boiling milk flavored with vanilla and turned over to be done on both sides, drained; thin vanilla cream made with the milk, yolks and sugar, cream poured in glass dish with a heap of the cooked whites on top; served hot or cold.

Flummery; F. Flameri; G. Flammerie: a cold rice or semolina pudding made in many different ways and served with a cold fruit sauce or sabayon.

— **Chocolate:** au chocolat: prepared either in the French or the German way with semolina, mixed with grated chocolate and served with sabayon or with English sauce.

— **French Style:** à la francaise: semolina cooked in half white wine and half water; sugar, a pinch of salt and egg yolks added; stiffly beaten egg whites folded in, filled in fancy or border mould, poached in water bath and allowed to cool; turned out and served covered with raw fruit purée such as strawberry, raspberry, cherry etc.

— **German Style:** à l'allemande: semolina cooked in sweetened milk flavored with grated lemon peel; stiffly beaten egg whites folded in while still hot, filled in mould; when cold turned out and served with fruit syrup.

Flummery

— **Northern Style:** à la nordique: rice meal cooked to a thick mush, mixed with sugar, crushed macaroons, finely diced, blanched candied lemon peel and sultanas, stiffly beaten egg whites folded in, filled in mould; turned out and served cold with fruit syrup.

— **Rhubarb:** de rhubarbe: rhubarb cooked in very little water with sugar, lemon juice and cinnamon, strained, boiled with corn meal to flummery, stiffly beaten egg whites folded in, filled in mould; when cold turned out and served with sabayon.

— **Sour Cherry:** de griottes: purée of sour cherries, sugar and ground almonds cooked with rice meal to a fairly stiff mush, stiffly beaten egg whites folded in, filled in mould; served cold with sabayon.

Fraise: see strawberry.

Framboise: see raspberry.

Fritters: Beignets: fruit, thick creams, rice, semolina etc. dipped in frying batter, rolled in egg and bread or cake crumbs etc., deep fried and served with a wine or fruit sauce. See also cream puff paste fritters.

— **Apple:** de pommes: apples peeled and cored, cut in slices, macerated in kirsch and sugar, dipped in frying batter, deep fried, served dusted with powder sugar.

— **Apricot:** d'abricots: halved, dusted with sugar, dipped in frying batter, deep fried, sprinkled with granulated sugar, glazed; apricot sauce flavored with kirsch served separately.

— **Banana:** de bananes: peeled, cut in halves, macerated in sugar and kirsch or brandy, dipped in frying batter, deep fried, served dusted with powder sugar.

— **Grand-Marnier:** thick custard flavored with Grand-Marnier, allowed to cool, cut into rounds with a cutter, dipped in egg and bread or cake crumbs, deep fried; served dusted with sugar.

— **Grandmother Style:** Grand'mère: 1. fruit purée boiled down with sugar to a thick paste, allowed to cool, cut round or square, dipped in frying batter; deep fried, drained, sprinkled with sugar, glazed;
2. slice of brioche coated with jam, soaked lightly in kirsch syrup, dipped in frying batter and deep fried.

— **Harem:** cold vanilla rice flavored with rose water, shaped into small balls, dipped in egg and breadcrumbs, deep fried, served dusted with sugar and raspberry syrup.

— **Java:** à la javannaise: thick pastry cream mixed with diced bananas, allowed to cool, cut into small rounds, dipped in egg and breadcrumbs, deep fried; strawberry sauce served separately.

— **Mignon:** two soft macaroons scooped out lightly, sandwiched with apricot jam, soaked in kirsch-flavored syrup, dipped in egg and breadcrumbs, deep fried; served dusted with powder sugar.

— **Pineapple:** d'ananas: small slices poached in kirsch-flavored syrup, drained, dipped in frying batter, deep fried, covered with granulated sugar, glazed.

— **Pineapple Imperial Style:** d'ananas à l'impériale: two small slices of poached and drained pineapples with crushed macaroons soaked in maraschino-flavored syrup sandwiched in between, dipped in frying batter, deep fried, glazed.

Fritters

— **Polish:** à la polonaise: small very thin pancakes, spread with thick vanilla cream, rolled, cut in small pieces, dipped in egg and macaroon crumbs, deep fried; fruit syrup served separately.

— **Regina:** small round sponge biscuits, scooped out lightly, filled with apricot jam, soaked in cream, dipped in egg and breadcrumbs, deep fried; served dusted with powder sugar.

— **Spanish:** à l'espagnole: small round slices of white bread without the rind, soaked in sweetened milk, dipped in egg and breadcrumbs, deep fried, dusted with powder sugar and cinnamon; Malaga sabayon served separately.

— **Strawberry:** de fraises: macerated in kirsch and sugar, dipped in frying batter, deep fried; served dusted with powder sugar.

Fromage glacé: obsolete name for ice biscuit.

Fruit Bread: dried stewed pears, candied lemon peel and dried figs, minced, mixed with raisins, lightly roasted hazelnuts, ground almonds, grated lemon peel, ground cinnamon, cloves, nutmeg and sugar, moistened with a little rum and only enough wheatmeal bread dough added to bind the mixture; wrapped in a thin sheet of wheatmeal dough, allowed to rest before and after wrapping and baked.

Fruit Cake: Gateau aux fruits: butter, egg yolks and sugar stirred to foam, mixed with flour, blended with baking powder, diced candied orange and lemon peel, raisins, currants and sultanas macerated beforehand in rum, grated lemon peel and spices, stiffly beaten egg withes folded in lightly; filled in greased cake mould lined with greased paper; baked in slow oven.

Fruit Loaf: Pain aux fruits: mould lined with fruit jelly, filled with the same preparation as for fruit Bavarian cream but without adding whipped cream and with less gelatine, turned out when set.

— **George Sand:** lined with maraschino jelly, filled with peach mixture.

— **Parisian:** à la parisienne: lined with pineapple jelly mixed with chopped pistachios, filled with pineapple mixture flavored with orange juice.

— **Pineapple:** prepared with grated pineapple, lemon juice, and white wine, mixed with diced pineapple sugared beforehand, filled in mould lined with pineapple jelly.

— **Pompadour:** lined with anisette-flavored jelly, filled alternately with halved apricots, macerated in maraschino with slivered pistachios scattered on top, and apricot mixture; decorated with Chantilly cream and glacé chestnuts.

— **Richelieu:** apricot mixture filled in mould lined with blancmanger.

— **Strawberry:** aux fraises: strawberry mixture filled in mould lined with blancmanger or strawberry jelly.

— **Victoria:** mould filled alternately with strawberry mixture with crushed macaroons scattered on top and blancmanger.

Fruit Macedoine: Macédoine de fruits: large variety of fruits in season, small fruit left whole, large fruits such as pineapple, bananas, peaches, pears etc. cut in cubes, covered with cold vanilla syrup, flavored with liqueur to taste, served chilled in glass or crystal dish.

Fruit Salad: Salade de fruits: one or more kinds of fruit, left whole or sliced according to kind, covered lightly with syrup flavored with liqueur, served chilled in glass or crystal dish.

— **Banana and Orange:** de bananes et oranges: orange fillets and banana slices filled symmetrically in glass dish, covered lightly with rum-flavored syrup.

— **Chantilly:** any kind of fruit covered with kirsch-flavored syrup, coated and decorated with Chantilly cream.

— **Favorite Style:** à la favorite: bottom of glass dish filled with vanilla ice, covered with sponge fingers, diced fruit macerated in sugar and maraschino placed on top, coated with whipped cream, grated chocolate sprinkled on top.

— **with Kirsch:** au kirsch: any kind of fruit sliced or left whole according to kind, macerated with kirsch and sugar, served chilled.

— **Orange:** d'orange: orange sections without skin, pith or pips, covered with syrup flavored with Curaçao, Grand-Marnier or kirsch.

— **Peach:** de pêches: fresh mellow peaches peeled and stoned, sliced, lemon juice dropped on top, macerated in sugar and a little Cointreau.

Fruit, Stewed: Compote: stewed is a misnomer as fruit should always be poached carefully in hot syrup or, as in some cases, the boiling syrup only poured over the fruit.

— **Apples:** de pommes: peeled, cored, cut in quarters, poached in syrup to which a little lemon juice and white wine has been added.

— **Apricots:** d'abricots: peeled, halved, stoned, poached in vanilla syrup with a few of the peeled almonds added, when cold flavored with kirsch.

— **Bananas:** de bananes: peeled, cut in halves or in thick oblique slices, poached in vanilla syrup, when cold flavored with kirsch or rum.

— **Cherries:** de cerises: 1. stoned, poached in vanilla syrup; 2. stoned, poached in lightly sugared red wine with a small piece of cinnamon.

— **Figs:** de figues: fresh figs poached in vanilla syrup, when cold flavored with kirsch.

— **Peaches:** de pêches: prepared like apricots.

— **Pears:** de poires: peeled, cored, cut in halves, rubbed with lemon juice, poached in vanilla syrup with a little lemon juice added.

— **Pineapple:** d'ananas: peeled, cored, cut in slices, halved, poached in vanilla syrup.

— **Raspberries:** de framboises: prepared like strawberries.

— **Rhubarb:** de rhubarbe: peeled, cut in small pieces, poached in very little vanilla syrup.

— **Strawberries:** de fraises: covered with boiling vanilla syrup, allowed to cool off in the syrup; not boiled.

Fruit Tart: Tarte aux fruits: large open tart made of short pastry and baked empty, filled with fresh fruit and glazed with syrup made of the same fruit or strained apricot jam; sometimes filled and baked with the fruit and glazed while still hot.

G

Gateau; F. Gâteau; G. Torte: a rich large cake made in different ways, filled or not filled with cream, iced or not iced, often but not always decorated.

— **Apponyi:** stiffly beaten egg whites blended with sugar, ground hazelnuts, grated chocolate and a little flour, filled in round gateau tin and baked; when cold cut in slices and filled with chocolate butter cream, decorated with butter cream and with small round hippen (q. v.).

— **Chestnut:** Gâteau aux marrons: sponge cake, cut in three layers, filled with chestnut butter cream flavored with maraschino, glazed with couverture, decorated with triangles of nougat, a marzipan rose placed in the center, bordered with glacé chestnuts coated with couverture and placed in paper cases.

— **Dobos:** butter and sugar stirred to foam, eggs and flour added, layers spread on baking sheet, baked and cut immediately into round or oval slices; when cold put together with chocolate butter cream, top layer coated with caramelized sugar and marked with the cutting lines of the pieces of cake before being placed on top. (Hungarian)

— **Hazelnut:** aux noisettes: genoise mixed with ground hazelnuts baked in round or square mould; when cold cut in two or three slices, filled with butter cream mixed with lightly roasted and ground hazelnuts, sides and top coated thinly with the hazelnut butter cream and covered with chopped roasted hazelnuts, top dusted lightly with powder sugar.

— **Linz:** see Linzer Torte.

— **Manon:** brioche dough baked in charlotte mould; when cold cut in four slices and soaked lightly with kirsch syrup, replaced into position with the slices spread alternately with vanilla and chocolate pastry cream: the gateau is then brushed on sides and top with thick strained apricot jam, rolled in slivered roasted almonds and powdered with icing sugar.

— **Marignan:** round mould filled half full with savarin dough, allowed to rise, baked, soaked while still hot with hot rum or kirsch syrup; when cold a slice cut off on top, both sides lifted up at the end to imitate a basket and filled with a star tube with Italian meringue mixture or Chantilly cream, a thin strip of angelica stuck in the center to imitate the handle of the basket.

— **Mikado:** three thin rounds of meringue mixture and three round slices of genoise sponge spread with rum butter cream and placed alternately one on top of the other; top and sides coated thinly with rum butter cream and covered with chopped roasted almonds, powder sugar dusted on top.

— **Millefeuilles:** see cream slice.

— **Mocha:** Moka: round genoise cake cut in slices, put together with mocha butter cream, masked entirely with mocha butter cream, sides rolled in chopped roasted almonds, top decorated with a star tube with mocha butter cream.

Gateau

— **Paris-Brest:** thick crown of cream puff paste piped on greased baking sheet, baked; when cold cut open lengthwise, filled with St. Honoré cream mixed with ground and sieved pralin, top dusted with powder sugar.

— **Pithiviers:** round base made of puff pastry remnants, center filled with almond cream flavored with rum, edges of base moistened with water, a round sheet of puff paste placed on top, edges notched, top incised lightly with the point of a knife rosette-fashion, egg washed, baked; when nearly done dusted with powder sugar and glaced.

— **Prince:** du prince: genoise mixture baked in round mould; when cold cut into six slices, a little Madeira dropped on top, spread alternately with apricot jam and with raspberry jelly and put together again; coated and decorated entirely with meringue mixture, dusted with powder sugar and browned in oven.

— **Saint-Honoré:** round base of short pastry bordered with cream puff paste, baked, very small cream puffs glazed with caramel fixed on the border with caramel or thick apricot jam, center filled and decorated with Saint-Honoré cream (q. v.), glacé cherries and angelica. Center may also be filled with Chantilly, chocolate, coffee or other cream.

Gâteau glacé: see ice gateau.

Gelée: see jelly.

Genoise: see Vienna Cake.

Gingerbread: Pain d'épices: cake made of flour, eggs, butter and ginger powder sweetened with molasses. French gingerbread is made of flour mixed with honey, powder sugar, potash dissolved in a little milk, chopped almonds, candied orange and lemon peel, flavored with anise, cinnamon, powdered cloves, grated orange and lemon peel, baked in baking sheet with high border and brushed with syrup when done.

Glace simple: see ice cream.

Gooseberry; F. Groseille verte, groseille à maquereau; G. Stachelbeere: a fruit of the currant family, native of Southern Europe and North Africa, now grown in Europe and the U. S. A. There are different sorts of gooseberries, round, oval, red yellow or green, smooth or with a hairy prickly skin. Best picked green before they are fully ripe; used in different ways.

— **Cream, English:** Crème de groseilles vertes à l'anglaise: cooked with sugar and very little water, rubbed through a sieve, whipped with egg yolks, sugar and vanilla in water bath until mixture begins to thicken, then whipped cold and blended with whipped cream; served chilled in glasses with sponge fingers separately.

— **Fool:** cooked with a generous amount of sugar and vanilla, rubbed through a sieve, allowed to cool, blended with the same amount of whipped cream, served chilled in glasses. (English)

— **Tartlet Kempinski:** tartlet shells filled with cold gooseberries poached in heavy vanilla syrup and strained, covered with Chantilly cream mixed with macaroon crumbs.

Gooseberry
— **Trifle:** sponge fingers soaked in Sherry or Madeira, filled alternately in glass dish with sweetened gooseberry purée, coated with thick custard, garnished with whipped cream, crushed macaroons scattered on top.
— **Vacherin:** vacherins made of meringue mixture with a piped bord, filled with well drained cold gooseberries poached in vanilla syrup, garnished with Chantilly cream.

Götterspeise: Chantilly cream mixed with grated chocolate and pumpernickel. (German)

Gramolata: iced drink resembling sorbet served as a sweet or refreshment at parties. The basic mixture is usually a thin fruit syrup which should show 14 deg. when measured with the saccharometer. Gramolata ought to be lightly granulated after having been frozen. (Italian)
— **Almond:** aux amandes: blanched almonds with a few bitter ones added, ground or pounded finely, infused in syrup, strained, flavored with orange blossom water, frozen.
— **Lemon:** au citron: syrup in which lemon peel has been infused, mixed with lemon juice, strained and frozen.
— **Orange:** à l'orange: syrup in which grated orange peel has been infused, mixed with orange and a little lemon juice, strained and frozen.
— **Strawberry:** aux fraises: fresh strawberry purée mixed with fresh red currant juice, syrup and a little lemon juice, strained and frozen.

Granité: French name for gramolata (q. v.).

Grapefruit; F. Pamplemousse; G. Pampelmuse: large citrus fruit ranging in size from a large orange to a small melon with bright yellow skin, grown in the West Indies, South and North America and Israel. The pulp is slightly bitter and acid. Used as a breakfast fruit and for dessert.
— **American Style:** à l'américaine: cut in half, pulp scooped out, filled with sherbet made of the juice, garnished with grapefruit sections without skin, pith or pips, a little Sherry poured on top.
— **Californian Style:** à la californienne: cut in half, flesh scooped out, shells cleaned, filled with well chilled macedoine of grapefruit, melon and oranges macerated in sugar, maraschino and Curaçao, slivered walnuts scattered on top.
— **Florida:** small fruit, lid cut off, scooped out, filled with diced grapefruit, oranges, stoned cherries and small strawberries macerated with Sherry and sugar, covered with strawberry purée, slivered walnuts scattered on top.
— **Jeannine:** lid cut off of a small fruit, scooped out, filled with sherbet prepared with the pulp and pineapple juice, lid replaced into position, served at once.
— **Victoria Louise:** cut in half, scooped out, filled with water ice prepared with the juice mixed with orange juice and flavored with Curaçao; a rosette of Chantilly cream piped on top with a star tube, a glacé chestnut placed in the center.

Grießschmarrn: semolina cooked in milk to a rather thick mush, mixed with butter, eggs, sugar and a pinch of salt, baked in skillet like a pancake, torn into pieces with two forks, dusted with powder sugar; stewed plums served separately. (Austrian)

Groseilles vertes: see gooseberries.

Groseilles rouges: see red currants.

Guglhupf: dough made of yeast, flour and milk, enriched with eggs, butter and granulated sugar; mixed with seedless raisins, grated lemon peel and chopped almonds; filled in special guglhupf mould — greased with butter and coated with chopped almonds and breadcrumbs — about half full; allowed to rise in warm spot to about three-quarters full and baked; served dusted with powder sugar. (German)

Gurjeffski Kascha: semolina cooked in sweetened milk flavored with vanilla, mixed with butter and egg yolks; filled in greased baking dish alternately with fruit macedoine macerated in maraschino and the skim of milk or cream, gained from milk which has been placed in a moderate oven and taken off every time as soon as it is lightly browned; chopped almonds and sugar sprinkled on top, baked in oven; apricot sauce served separately. (Russian)

H

Harrogate Trifle: sponge cake baked in ring, when cold cut in three to four layers, each layer soaked with cherry-brandy-flavored syrup and spread with red currant jelly, sandwiched with thick custard, coated entirely with whipped cream, decorated with small macaroons. (English)

Hazelnut Roll: Roulade aux noisettes: sponge mixture blended with ground hazelnuts spread thin on baking sheet, baked in hot oven, taken off sheet immediately, dusted with sugar and kept in cold store over night to keep cake pliable; spread with vanilla butter cream flavored with kirsch and mixed with ground and sieved grilled hazelnuts, rolled together, glazed with kirsch-flavored fondant.

Hippen, Hohlhippen: almonds pounded with egg whites, sugar, stiffly beaten egg whites, a little flour and cinnamon added, spreach very thin on waxed baking sheets, baked in hot oven, taken off immediately and rolled around a rolling pin or thin round sticks; used as a garnish for gateau, ice coups etc. (German)

I

Ice Biscuit: Biscuit glacé: egg yolks mixed with sugar, whipped in water bath until the mixture has doubled in volume, whipped cold, blended with Italian meringue mixture, whipped cream and flavoring, placed in rectangular mould having several departments to hold various blends of ice, frozen in sharp freezing cabinet. After freezing cut in vertical slices and kept in deep freeze until required.

— **Bénedictine:** bottom of mould filled with strawberry mixture, center with Benedictine and top lined with violet mixture.

Ice Biscuit

— **Castle Garden:** Jardin du château: bottom lined with hazelnut mixture, center with genoise biscuit soaked in rum syrup, top with kirsch mixture; served covered with cold chocolate sauce.

— **Countess Style:** comtesse: Maraschino and strawberry mixture in four separate layers.

— **Marquise:** mould filled with kirsch and strawberry mixtures alternated twice.

— **Mexican Style:** à la mexicaine: bottom lined with banana mixture flavored with Curaçao, center filled with almond mixture with diced candied fruit, top with pineapple mixture.

— **Montblanc:** bottom lined with rum mixture, center with chestnut and top with vanilla mixture.

— **Naples Style:** à la napolitaine: bottom of mould vanilla, center strawberry and top pistachio mixture.

— **Nicolas:** bottom lined with praliné mixture, center with raspberry mixed with diced candied pineapple macerated in kirsch, top with chocolate mixture.

— **Queen Style:** à la reine: bottom lined with vanilla mixture, center with tangerine and top with chocolate mixture.

— **Regina:** vanilla and strawberry mixture in four separate layers.

— **Sigurd:** strawberry and pistachio, placed between two wafers of the same size.

Ice Bombe: Bombe: name of a special ice concoction moulded in a conical container and deep frozen. The mould is lined first with plain ice cream and the center filled with a bombe mixture of different flavor, to which may be added diced fruit and other ingredients. Fruit should be macerated in liqueur and sugar before being added to prevent it freezing too hard. Bombe mixture is made by whisking egg yolks with a syrup of 28. deg. first hot and then cold, blended with whipped cream and the desired flavor.

— **Aboukir:** lined with pistachio ice, filled with praliné bombe mixture with chopped pistachios.

— **African:** à l'africaine: lined with chocolate ice, filled with rum flavored apricot bombe mixture.

— **Aida:** lined with strawberry ice, center filled with kirsch flavored bombe mixture.

— **Aiglon:** lined with strawberry ice, filled with Chartreuse bombe mixture.

— **Aisha:** lined with strawberry ice, center filled with layers of pineapple and orange flavored bombe mixture.

— **Albuféra:** lined with vanilla ice, center filled with layers of bombe mixture flavored with anisette and mixed with strained cooked chestnuts.

— **Alexandra:** lined with vanilla ice, center filled with hazelnut bombe mixture.

— **Alhambra:** lined with vanilla ice, filled with strawberry bombe mixture; at serving bordered with strawberries macerated in kirsch.

— **Almeria:** lined with vanilla ice flavored with anisette, center filled with pomegranate flavored bombe mixture.

— **Alsatian:** alsacienne: lined with praliné ice, filled with layers of vanilla, pralin and chocolate bombe mixture.

— **Altenburg:** lined with chocolate ice, filled with Chantilly cream.

Ice Bombe

— **American:** à l'américaine: lined with strawberry ice, center filled with tangerine bombe mixture, decorated with pistachios.

— **Andalusian:** à l'andalouse: lined with apricot ice, center filled with vanilla bombe mixture.

— **Apricotine:** lined with apricot ice, center filled with layers of kirsch flavored bombe mixture with apricot jam in between.

— **Arabian:** arabe: lined with coffee ice, center filled with vanilla bombe mixture flavored with rum.

— **Archduke:** archiduc: 1. lined with strawberry ice, filled with vanilla praliné bombe mixture;
2. lined with strawberry ice, filled with almond-flavored bombe mixture.

— **Batava:** lined with pineapple ice, filled with strawberry bombe mixture with diced ginger in syrup.

— **Bismarck:** lined with vanilla ice mixed with ground almonds flavored with maraschino, center filled with apricot bombe mixture.

— **Bourdalou:** lined with vanilla ice, center filled with anisette-flavored bombe mixture, decorated with crystallized violets.

— **Braganza:** lined with lemon ice, center filled with layers of strawberry and rum bombe mixture.

— **Brasilian:** brésilienne: lined with pineapple ice, center filled with vanilla bombe mixture flavored with rum and mixed with diced pineapple.

— **Brides:** Petite mariée: lined with strawberry ice, filled with vanilla bombe mixture, covered at serving with spun sugar.

— **Camargo:** lined with coffee ice, filled with vanilla bombe mixture.

— **Cardinal:** 1. lined with raspberry and red currant ice, filled with vanilla bombe mixture with crystallized rose petals added;
2. lined with red currant ice, filled with maraschino-flavored vanilla bombe mixture.

— **Carmen:** lined with chocolat ice, filled with vanilla bombe mixture.

— **Carnot:** lined with raspberry ice, filled with maraschino bombe mixture; vanilla sabayon served separately.

— **Ceylon:** lined with tea ice, filled with rum-flavored bombe mixture.

— **Chantilly:** lined with chocolate ice, filled with layers of maraschino and kirsch-flavored bombe mixture; decorated with Chantilly cream.

— **Chateaubriand:** prepared like Andalusian.

— **Chinese:** chinoise: lined with tea ice, filled with maraschino-flavored vanilla bombe mixture.

— **Cleopatra:** lined with pistachio ice, filled with rum-flavored bombe mixture.

— **Columbia:** lined with kirsch ice, filled with pear bombe mixture, decorated with glacé cherries.

— **Coppelia:** lined with coffee ice, filled with praliné bombe mixture.

— **Countess Mary:** Comtesse Marie: lined with vanilla ice, filled with strawberry bombe mixture.

Ice Bombe

— **Creole:** 1. lined with pineapple ice, filled alternately with strawberry and pineapple bombe mixture;
2. lined with chocolate ice, filled with Curaçao-flavored bombe mixture.

— **Crownprince Style:** dauphin: lined with hazelnut ice, filled with kirsch-flavored bombe mixture.

— **Cyrano:** lined with praliné ice, filled with cherry bombe mixture flavored with kirsch.

— **Danitcheff:** lined with coffee ice, filled with kirsch-flavored bombe mixture.

— **Delicious:** délicieuse: lined with morello ice mixed with chopped almonds, filled with layers of strawberry and caramel bombe mixture.

— **Diplomate:** lined with vanilla ice, filled with maraschino-flavored bombe mixture with salpicon of candied fruit.

— **Duchess:** duchesse: lined with pineapple ice, filled with pear bombe mixture flavored with kirsch.

— **Dutch:** hollandaise: lined with orange ice, filled with Curaçao-flavored bombe mixture.

— **Edith:** lined with coffee ice, filled with kirsch-flavored bombe mixture.

— **Esterhazy:** lined with vanilla ice, filled with Chantilly cream mixed with diced candied fruit macerated in kirsch.

— **Excelsior:** lined with orange ice, filled with rum-flavored bombe mixture.

— **Falstaff:** 1. lined with praliné ice, filled with strawberry bombe mixture;
2. lined with hazelnut ice, filled with coffee-flavored bombe mixture.

— **Fanchon:** lined with hazelnut ice, filled with kirsch-flavored bombe mixture with small coffee sweets.

— **Farandole:** lined with tangerine ice, filled with hazelnut bombe mixture.

— **Fédora:** lined with orange ice, filled with praliné bombe mixture.

— **Fiametta:** lined with maraschino ice, filled with vanilla bombe mixture.

— **Florence:** florentine: lined with raspberry ice, filled with praliné bombe mixture.

— **Francillon:** lined with coffee ice, filled with cognac-flavored bombe mixture.

— **Frou-Frou:** lined with vanilla ice, filled with rum-flavored bombe mixture with salpicon of candied fruit.

— **Gabrielle:** 1. lined with peach ice, filled with vanilla bombe mixture;
2. lined with raspberry ice, filled with maraschino-flavored bombe mixture.

— **Georgette:** lined with hazelnut ice, filled with maraschino-flavored bombe mixture.

— **Ginger:** lined with orange ice, filled with vanilla bombe mixture blended with diced ginger in syrup.

— **Gismonda:** lined with hazelnut ice, filled with anisette-flavored bombe mixture with seeded white currants.

— **Gladstone:** lined with ginger ice, filled with genever-flavored bombe mixture with diced ginger in syrup.

— **Grand Duke:** grand duc: lined with orange ice, filled with Benédictine-flavored bombe mixture.

Ice Bombe

— **Havanna:** havanaise: lined with coffee ice, filled alternately with rum and vanilla bombe mixture.

— **Helen:** lined with hazelnut ice, filled with vanilla bombe mixture, served bordered with cold chocolate sauce.

— **Hilda:** lined with hazelnut ice, filled with Chartreuse-flavored bombe mixture with hazelnut pralin.

— **Ida:** lined with strawberry ice, filled with kirsch-flavored bombe mixture.

— **Illusion:** lined with coffee ice, filled with hazelnut bombe mixture.

— **Italian:** à l'italienne: lined with pistachio ice, filled in layers with strawberry and maraschino-flavored bombe mixture.

— **Jaffa:** lined with hazelnut ice, filled with orange-flavored bombe mixture.

— **Jamaica:** jamaique: 1. lined with rum-flavored pineapple ice, filled with tea-flavored bombe mixture;
2. lined with rum-flavored pineapple ice, filled with orange-flavored bombe mixture.

— **Japanese:** japonaise: lined with peach ice, filled with tea-flavored bombe mixture.

— **Jeanne d'Arc:** lined with vanilla ice, filled with chocolate bombe mixture praliné.

— **Jeritza:** lined with almond ice, filled with two layers of peach bombe mixture and two layers of whipped cream blended with raspberry purée.

— **Jocelyn:** lined with peach ice, filled with maraschino-flavored bombe mixture.

— **Joinville:** lined with chocolate ice with chopped almonds, filled with maraschino-flavored bombe mixture blended with salpicon of cherries.

— **Josephine:** lined with coffee ice, filled with pistachio bombe mixture.

— **Leopold:** lined with vanilla ice, filled with kirsch-flavored wild strawberry bombe mixture.

— **Little Duke:** petit-duc: lined with strawberry ice, filled with hazelnut bombe mixture with red currants.

— **Lyrical:** lyrique: lined with kirsch ice, filled with chocolate bombe mixture blended with fruit salpicon macerated in Cointreau; when turned out chequered with dark couverture and decorated with leaf gold; raspberry purée served separately.

— **Madeleine:** lined with almond ice, filled with kirsch-flavored vanilla bombe mixture blended with fruit salpicon.

— **Madrid:** Madriléne: lined with coffee ice, filled with vanilla bombe mixture.

— **Maharadja:** lined with pineapple ice finished off with champagne, filled with strawberry bombe mixture blended with small strawberries.

— **Maltese:** maltaise: lined with blood orange ice, filled with Chantilly cream flavored with tangerine juice.

— **Margot:** lined with almond ice, filled with pistachio bombe mixture.

— **Marie-Louise:** lined with chocolate ice, filled with vanilla bombe mixture.

— **Marquise:** lined with apricot ice, filled with champagne bombe mixture.

Ice Bombe

— **Marshall Style:** à la maréchale: lined with strawberry ice, filled alternately with layers of pistachio, vanilla and orange bombe mixture.

— **Mary Stuart:** Marie Stuart: lined with vanilla ice, filled with anisette-flavored bombe mixture blended with chopped poached cherries.

— **Mascot:** Mascotte: lined with peach ice, filled with kirsch-flavored bombe mixture.

— **Mathilda:** Mathilde: lined with coffee ice, filled with apricot bombe mixture.

— **Medicis:** lined with brandy ice, filled with raspberry bombe mixture.

— **Menelik:** lined with tangerine ice, filled with rum-flavored bombe mixture.

— **Mercedes:** lined with apricot ice, filled with Chartreuse-flavored bombe mixture.

— **Mignon:** lined with apricot ice, filled with praliné bombe mixture.

— **Mireille:** lined with red currant ice, filled with kirsch-flavored strawberry bombe mixture.

— **Moldavian:** moldave: lined with pineapple ice, filled with Curaçao-flavored bombe mixture.

— **Montblanc:** lined with vanilla ice, filled with layers of rum-flavored and chestnut bombe mixture.

— **Monte Carlo:** lined with tangerine ice, filled with anisette-flavored bombe mixture.

— **Monte Christo:** 1. lined with brandy ice, filled with strawberry bombe mixture;
2. lined with tangerine ice, filled with kirsch-flavored tangerine bombe mixture.

— **Montmorency:** lined with kirsch ice, filled with sour cherry bombe mixture.

— **Nabob:** lined with vanilla ice with chopped grilled almonds, filled with cognac-flavored bombe mixture blended with fruit salpicon.

— **Nelusko:** lined with hazelnut ice, filled with chocolate bombe mixture.

— **Nesselrode:** lined with vanilla ice, filled with Chantilly cream blended with crushed glacé chestnuts.

— **Northern:** nordique: lined with vanilla ice flavored with kümmel, filled with almond bombe mixture blended with fruit salpicon.

— **Odessa:** lined with apricot ice, filled with strawberry bombe mixture.

— **Odette:** lined with vanilla ice, filled with hazelnut bombe mixture.

— **Oriental:** à l'orientale: lined with ginger ice, filled with pistachio bombe mixture.

— **Otéro:** 1. lined with apricot ice, filled with kirsch-flavored bombe mixture;
2. lined with apricot ice, filled with cassis-flavored bombe mixture.

— **Othello:** lined with praliné ice, filled with peach bombe mixture.

— **Paradise:** lined with vanilla ice, filled with kirsch-flavored bombe mixture.

Ice Bombe

— **Parisian:** parisienne: 1. lined with pineapple ice, filled with chocolate bombe mixture with ground hazelnut pralin;
2. lined with strawberry ice, filled with hazelnut bombe mixture.

— **Pompadour:** lined with asparagus ice, filled with pomegranate bombe mixture.

— **Portuguese:** portugaise: lined with tangerine ice, filled with Curaçao-flavored bombe mixture.

— **Prince Pückler:** filled with layers of Chantilly cream flavored with maraschino and mixed with diced macaroons divided in three parts: one part left white, one part blended with strawberry purée and one part mixed with grated chocolate.

— **Princess:** lined with anisette ice, filled with vanilla bombe mixture.

— **Prophet:** prophète: lined with strawberry ice, filled with pineapple bombe mixture.

— **Queen Style:** à la reine: 1. lined with hazelnut ice, filled with strawberry bombe mixture.
2. lined with vanilla ice, filled with bombe mixture blended with crushed glacé chestnuts.

— **Queen Olga:** Reine Olga: lined with cherry ice finished off with champagne, filled with pineapple bombe mixture with diced **pineapple.**

— **Red Devil:** diable rose: lined with strawberry ice, filled with kirsch-flavored bombe mixture with glacé cherries.

— **Regenburg:** lined with pistachio ice, filled with almond bombe mixture.

— **Rosette:** lined with vanilla ice, filled with Chantilly cream and red currants.

— **Royal:** royale: lined with kirsch ice, filled with chocolate bombe mixture with ground pralin.

— **Saint-George:** lined with orange ice, filled with bombe mixture flavored with rum and Curaçao.

— **Sappho:** lined with strawberry ice, filled with vanilla bombe mixture with strawberries.

— **Sarasate:** lined with coffee ice, filled with vanilla bombe mixture with chopped grilled almonds.

— **Selika:** lined with praliné ice, filled with Curaçao-flavored bombe mixture.

— **Selma Kurz:** lined with strawberry ice, filled with whipped cream blended with raspberry purée and chopped grilled hazelnuts.

— **Sicilian:** sicilienne: lined with lemon ice, filled with vanilla bombe mixture with ground pralin.

— **Skobeleff:** lined with vodka ice, filled with Chantilly cream flavored with kummel.

— **Sovereign:** souverain: lined with chocolate ice, center filled with Chantilly cream.

— **Spanish:** espagnole: lined with coffee ice, filled with hazelnut bombe mixture.

— **Speranza:** lined with pistachio ice, filled with layers of maraschino-flavored and strawberry bombe mixture.

— **Succes:** succès: lined with apricot ice, filled with kirsch-flavored Chantilly cream blended with diced crystallized apricots.

Ice Bombe
— **Sultan:** sultane: lined with chocolate ice, filled with praliné bombe mixture.
— **Suzanne:** lined with rum ice, filled with vanilla bombe mixture with Bar-le-Duc red currants.
— **Swedish:** suédoise: lined with vanilla ice flavored with orange juice, filled with Chantilly cream mixed with fruit salpicon macerated in Swedish punch.
— **Theodora:** lined with kirsch ice, filled with vanilla bombe mixture.
— **Tortoni:** 1. lined with praliné ice, filled with coffee bombe mixture;
2. lined with almond ice, filled alternately with layers of apricot and coffee bombe mixture with ground grilled hazelnuts.
— **Tosca:** lined with apricot ice, filled with maraschino-flavored bombe mixture blended with fruit salpicon.
— **Trocadéro:** lined with orange ice, mixed with finely diced orange peel, filled with layers of Chantilly cream and genoise soaked with Curaçao, sprinkled with finely diced orange peel.
— **Trophy:** lined with kirsch ice, filled with tomato bombe mixture.
— **Tsar:** du tsar: lined with vanilla ice, filled with kümmel-flavored bombe mixture, decorated with crystallized violets.
— **Tutti-Frutti:** lined with strawberry ice, filled with lemon bombe mixture blended with fruit salpicon.
— **Valençay:** lined with almond ice, filled with whipped cream blended with raspberry purée flavored with maraschino.
— **Venetian:** vénitienne: lined with half vanilla and half strawberry ice, filled with maraschino-flavored bombe mixture.
— **Victoria:** 1. lined with strawberry ice, filled with Plombières mixture;
2. lined with strawberry ice, filled with bombe mixture with crushed glacé chestnuts and diced candied fruit;
3. lined with vanilla ice, filled with Chantilly cream with seeded red currants.
— **Westphalian:** westphalienne: lined with vanilla ice mixed with grated pumpernickel, filled with Chantilly cream blended with quartered fresh hazelnuts.
— **White Lady:** Dame Blanche: lined with vanilla ice, filled with bombe mixture with almond milk.
— **Zamora:** lined with coffee ice, filled with Curaçao-flavored bombe mixture.
— **Zanzibar:** lined with coffee ice: filled with Curaçao-flavored bombe mixture with ground almonds.

Ice Chocolate: Chocolat glacé: lightly frozen chocolate ice cream, filled in high goblet with Chantilly cream on top.

Ice Coffee: Café glacé: coffee ice frozen very lightly, filled in goblet with Chantilly cream on top.

Ice Coupe: Coupe: a combination of ice cream or different ices, fruit, liqueur, cream, whipped cream or other ingredients served in a glass or silver cup or goblet and nicely decorated.
— **Adelina:** chocolate ice on wild strawberries macerated in kirsch, garnished with Chantilly cream and a few wild strawberries on top.

Ice Coupe

— **Alexandra:** fruit macedoine with kirsch, covered with strawberry ice, garnished with strawberries.

— **American:** à l américaine: pineapple ice covered with pineapple salpicon and crushed macaroons, garnished with Chantilly cream, crystallized violets and a strawberry macerated with kirsch.

— **Andalusian:** à l'andalouse: orange sections macerated with maraschino, covered with lemon ice, garnished with whipped cream and orange sections.

— **Arlesian:** à l'arlésienne: vanilla ice mixed with salpicon of candied fruit macerated with kirsch, a small whole pear or a round piece poached in vanilla syrup placed on top and covered with cold apricot sauce.

— **Baby:** Bébé: half pineapple and half raspberry ice with small strawberries between the layers, decorated with Chantilly cream and crystallized violets.

— **Barbarina:** strawberry ice covered with a macaroon soaked in maraschino syrup, covered with thick chocolate cream, decorated with whipped cream and small pineapple pieces.

— **Brasilian:** à la brésilienne: diced fresh pineapple macerated with sugar and maraschino, covered with lemon ice.

— **Claire Dux:** fruit salpicon macerated with kirsch, round ball of hazelnut ice on top, covered with thick English cream, border of small strawberries.

— **Clo-Clo:** crushed remnants of glacé chestnuts soaked with maraschino, covered with vanilla ice, a glacé chestnut placed in the center, decorated with whipped cream mixed with strawberry purée.

— **Creole:** pineapple and banana salpicon macerated in kirsch, covered with lemon ice flavored with rum, decorated with whipped cream and fruit.

— **Denise:** coffee ice, liqueur pralinés on top, decorated with Chantilly cream.

— **Divine:** peach salpicon macerated in Cointreau, covered with chocolate ice, coated with English cream, decorated with Chantilly cream, crushed meringues and crystallized violets scattered on top.

— **Edna May:** vanilla ice covered with cherry compote coated with whipped cream blended with raspberry purée.

— **Elisabeth:** poached cherries macerated in kirsch and cherry brandy, covered and decorated with Chantilly cream, a little powdered cinnamon sprinkled on top.

— **Emma Calvé:** cup half filled with vanilla ice, covered with stoned poached cherries in kirsch, coated with raspberry purée.

— **Eugénie:** vanilla ice mixed with crushed glacé chestnuts flavored with maraschino, decorated with Chantilly cream and crystallized violets.

— **Favorite:** filled with half vanilla and half kirsch-maraschino ice, center of top filled with whipped cream mixed with strawberry purée, bordered with pineapple ice.

— **Forester Style:** à la forestière: woodruff ice mousse covered with wild strawberries in maraschino, garnished with whipped cream mixed with raspberry purée and wild strawberries.

— **Francis Joseph:** François-Joseph: diced pineapple in kirsch covered with orange ice, decorated with Chantilly cream.

Ice Coupe

— **Frou-Frou:** vanilla ice covered with peach salpicon, decorated with whipped cream and glacé cherries.

— **Helena:** Hélène: vanilla ice covered with diced pears macerated in kirsch, coated with thick cold chocolate sauce, crushed crystallized violets scattered on top.

— **Iris:** cherries poached in red wine with sugar and cinnamon, covered with strawberry ice mousse, decorated with Chantilly cream with chocolate chips on top.

— **Jacques:** fruit macedoine macerated with kirsch, covered with half lemon and half strawberry ice.

— **Jubilee:** Jubilé: salpicon of cherries in kirsch, covered with vanilla ice, decorated with Chantilly cream, chopped pistachios scattered on top.

— **King Style:** du roi: morello ice cream mixed with chopped morellos, covered and decorated with whipped cream, chopped pistachois scattered on top.

— **Little Duke:** Petit Duc: vanilla ice with half a poached peach on top, coated with red currant jelly, bordered with lemon ice.

— **Louis:** peach ice with a ripe abricot filled with marzipan on top, covered with whipped cream blended with strawberry purée.

— **Louis XV.:** strawberry ice mousse covered with stoned mirabelles, coated with peach jam, decorated with Chantilly cream.

— **Maharadja:** apricot ice mixed with chopped blanched almonds, covered with sliced mellow pears macerated in sugar and Benédictine, coated with red currant jelly, decorated with Chantilly cream with crushed ginger biscuits scattered on top.

— **Malmaison:** vanilla ice mixed with peeled seeded grapes, decorated with whipped cream, covered with spun sugar.

— **Medicis:** raspberry ice mousse mixed with wild strawberries, covered with raspberries macerated in maraschino, decorated with Chantilly cream and wild strawberries.

— **Melba:** peeled poached peach placed on vanilla ice, coated with purée of fresh raspberries, decorated with Chantilly cream.

— **Metternich:** salpicon of pineapple covered with raspberry ice, decorated with Chantilly cream flavored with vanilla liqeur.

— **Mexican:** à la mexicaine: tangerine ice mixed with diced pineapple.

— **Mireille:** glass filled half with vanilla and half with red currant cream ice, half a stoned nectarine placed on top, the cavity filled with white seeded currants, decorated with Chantilly cream, spun sugar on top (optional).

— **Mozart:** half vanilla and half almond ice with sliced peaches between the two, covered with raspberry syrup, decorated with Chantilly cream, grilled chopped almonds scattered on top.

— **Naples:** à la napolitaine: lemon ice covered with fruit macedoine flavored with liqueur, coated with apricot jelly, decorated with Chantilly cream.

Ice Coupe

— **Nice Style:** à la niçoise: 1. fruit macedoine macerated with Curaçao, covered with orange ice; 2. salpicon of peaches with maraschino covered with vanilla ice, decorated with Chantilly cream und glacé cherries.

— **Parisian:** à la parisienne: vanilla ice covered and decorated with Chantilly cream, decorated with small strawberries macerated in maraschino.

— **Portuguese:** portugaise: diced pineapple macerated in maraschino covered with orange ice, decorated with Chantilly cream and sour cherries.

— **Red Devil:** diable rouge: strawberry ice covered with stoned cherries poached in red wine, a little raspberry syrup poured on top, decorated with whipped cream mixed with strawberry purée.

— **Romanoff:** 1. vanilla ice covered with small strawberries soaked in orange juice and Curaçao, decorated with whipped cream; 2. vanilla ice covered with crushed strawberries topped with whipped cream; 3 vanilla ice covered with small strawberries soaked in Port, covered with heavy cream.

— **Royal:** à la royale: 1. vanilla ice mixed with wild strawberries macerated in kirsch, garnished with Chantilly cream. 2. fruit macedoine macerated in kirsch covered with vanilla ice.

— **Sahara:** vanilla ice with half a peeled and stoned peach macerated in kirsch filled with raspberry ice on top, decorated with whipped cream, triangles of pineapple and glacé cherries.

— **Saint-Martin:** macedoine of fruit with maraschino, covered with lemon and raspberry ice, decorated with Chantilly cream and strawberries.

— **Santa-Lucia:** vanilla ice covered with peeled and seeded grapes macerated in sugar and Benédictine, covered with cold chocolate sauce, crushed macaroons scattered on top, decorated with Chantilly cream with a little raspberry syrup dropped on top.

— **Savoy:** fruit macedoine macerated with anisette, covered with half coffee and half violet ice.

— **Singapore:** lemon ice covered with pineapple slices macerated in arrak, a macaroon soaked in arrak syrup placed on top.

— **Sublime:** vanilla ice covered with whipped cream mixed with sugar and grated pumpernickel, cocoa sprinkled on top.

— **Swedish:** suédoise: vanilla ice mixed with apple purée, half a cored and poached apple on top, covered with red currant jelly, decorated with Chantilly cream.

— **Sylvia:** diced bananas macerated in orange juice and kirsch, covered with hazelnut ice, decorated with Chantilly cream.

— **Thais:** 1. fruit macedoine and remnants of glacé chestnuts in kirsch, covered with vanilla ice, decorated with Chantilly cream; 2. vanilla ice with half a peach placed on top, bordered with Chantilly cream, cream covered with chocolate chips.

— **Tsarina:** à la tsarine: lemon ice covered with chopped cherries, decorated with Chantilly cream.

Ice Coupe
— **Tutti-Frutti:** filled alternately with strawberry, lemon and pineapple ice with salpicon of fruit macerated in kirsch between the layers.
— **Venus:** vanilla ice with a small poached peach surmounted with a large strawberry on tóp, bordered with Chantilly cream.
— **Vera Schwarz:** fruit salpicon macerated in maraschino, covered with raspberry ice, decorated with Chantilly cream, chopped pistachios scattered on top.
— **Victoria:** fruit macedoine macerated in fine champagne cognac, covered with half strawberry and half pistachio ice.
— **Walewska:** vanilla ice, sliced peaches macerated in kirsch, decorated with Chantilly cream and strawberries.
— **White Lady:** Dame Blanche: almond ice with half a poached peach filled with white currant jelly or seeded and jellied white currants on top, bordered with lemon ice.

Ice Cream: Glace simple: plain ice or ice cream may be divided into three basic compositions: 1. French type cream ice: sugar and egg yolks beaten with hot milk or cream or half and half, sugared and flavored, without allowing mixture to boil as boiling would curdle the yolks, and frozen; 2. fruit ice: fruit purée blended with the same quantity of syrup and a little lemon juice; 3. liqueur ice: cream or fruit ice flavored with liqueur American type ice cream is made of cream, milk or condensed milk thickened with gelatine, sugared and flavored and frozen in brine freezer; no eggs are used. Fruit ice prepared with red fruit purée is tastier and richer if a little raw cream is added when the ice is nearly frozen.
— **Almond ice cream:** Glace aux amandes: plain cream ice with finely ground sweet and a few bitter almonds infused in the milk beforehand.
— **Asparagus:** aux asperges: purée of blanched asparagus tips infused in the milk before preparing the basic cream.
— **Chocolate:** au chocolate: basic cream with a vanilla pod infused in the milk and grated chocolate added.
— **Coffee:** au café: basic cream mixture flavored strongly with coffee essence or soluble coffee powder.
— **Hazelnut:** aux avelines: lightly grilled hazelnuts pounded finely with a little milk and infused in milk before preparing the custard.
— **Pistachio:** aux pistaches: basic cream with 1/3 almonds and 2/3 pistachios ground finely and infused in the milk beforehand.
— **Praliné:** au praliné: basic mixture with finely pounded and strained almond pralin added.
— **Tea:** au thé: basic cream with a strong infusion of tea in the milk.
— **Vanilla:** à la vanille: basic mixture with a vanilla pod infused in the milk beforehand.

Ice Cream Apricot: Glace à l'apricot: apricot purée blended with syrup and a little lemon juice; sugar contents 18-19 deg. when measured with the saccharometer.
— **Banana:** aux bananes: banana purée infused beforehand in kirsch or maraschino syrup, lemon juice added; sugar contents 20-21 deg.

Ice cream.

— **Cherry:** aux cerises: stoned cherries and a few of the stones pounded in mortar, infused in kirsch syrup, strained and finished off with a little lemon juice; sugar contents 21 deg.

— **Lemon:** au citron: lemon peel infused in the syrup beforehand, lemon and a little orange juice added; sugar contents 22 deg.

— **Melon:** au melon: purée of very ripe melons blended with syrup, flavored with orange juice and orange blossom water; sugar contents 22 deg.

— **Orange:** à l'orange: grated orange peel infused in hot syrup, when cold orange and a little lemon juice added, strained; sugar contents 21 deg.

— **Peach:** aux pêches: prepared like apricot ice.

— **Pear:** aux poires: peeled and stoned mellow pears pounded with the same amount of sugar, rubbed through a sieve, juice of one lemon for each pound of pears and enough filtered water added to bring sugar contents to 22 deg. measured with the saccharometer.

— **Pineapple:** à l'ananas: grated pineapple infused in kirsch syrup and rubbed through a sieve; sugar contents 19 bis 20 deg.

— **Plum:** aux prunes: prepared like apricot ice.

— **Raspberry:** aux framboises: prepared like strawberry ice.

— **Red or White Currant:** à la groseille: half currant juice and half syrup, no lemon juice; sugar contents 20 deg.

— **Strawberry:** aux fraises: strawberry purée blended with syrup and the juice of lemon and orange; sugar contents 18 deg.

— **Tangerine:** aux mandarines: prepared like orange ice with tangerine juice.

Ice Gateau: Gâteau glace: an iced gateau is frozen in a round or square mould and consists of layers of different kinds of bombe mixture alternated or topped with light sponge cake usually soaked in liqueur flavored syrup, coated with whipped cream and decorated.

— **Brasilian:** brésilienne: square mould filled alternately with a thin slice of sponge cake soaked in Curaçao syrup, pineapple cream ice, sponge, chocolate bombe mixture covered with soaked sponge; when frozen turned out, coated and garnished with Chantilly cream, decorated with glacé pineapple.

— **Cédard:** bottom of round mould lined with a genoise slice soaked lightly in Curaçao syrup, filled with orange bombe mixture and frozen; covered with a round genoise slice of the same size iced with orange fondant and decorated with a star of orange glacé sections; sides of gateau garnished with Chantilly cream.

— **Dolores:** kirsch-flavored vanilla bombe mixture frozen in square mould; when frozen sides and top covered with chocolate chips, chopped pistachios scattered on top, lighly dusted with powder sugar; whipped cream served separately.

— **Japanese:** à la japonaise: tea bombe mixture blended with diced sponge finger soaked lightly in tangerine liqueur, filled in square mould; when frozen turned out, sides coated with chopped roasted almonds, top decorated

Ice Gateau
with whipped cream flavored with tangerine liqueur and garnished with half poached and well drained cold peaches.

— **Queen:** à la reine: round mould filled alternately with a slice of genoise soaked in kirsch syrup, a layer of almond bombe mixture, a layer of strawberry bombe mixture and a slice of soaked genoise on top; when frozen sides and top brushed with strained orange marmelade and coated with crushed macaroons, dusted on top with powder sugar.

— **Tortoni:** bottom of mould covered with thin round slice of genoise soaked lightly in maraschino syrup, filled with two layers of bombe praliné mixture with a thin soaked layer of genoise in between and covered with a third thin slice of genoise soaked in maraschino syrup; when frozen, coated on sides and top with whipped cream and covered with chopped roasted hazelnuts; dusted with powder sugar.

Ice Mousse or Foam: Mousse glacé: Italian meringue mixture blended with fruit purée, whipped cream folded in carefully; or thick English cream blended with fruit pulp, whipped cream folded in. For ice mousse on liqueur basis liqueur is used instead of the fruit pulp. Filled in fancy mould and frozen.

— **Absinth:** à l'absinthe: vanilla mixture flavored with absinth.

— **Apricot:** à l'abricot: basic mixture prepared with apricot pulp.

— **Chocolate:** au chocolat: basic mixture flavored with vanilla and mixed with dissolved chocolate.

— **Orange:** à l'orange: basic mixture prepared with orange juice and grated orange peel.

Ice Pudding: Pudding glacé: bombe or ice mousse mixture filled in pudding mould and frozen, served with a cold sauce.

— **Lyrical:** lyrique: vanilla bombe mixture blended with diced sponge fingers and pineapple glacé soaked in kirsch frozen; turned out, trellised with couverture, decorated with crystallized violets and leaf gold; fresh raspberry purée served separately.

— **Merville:** bombe mould lined with slices of Swiss roll filled with apricot jam, center filled with vanilla bombe mixture blended with chopped roasted hazelnuts and salpicon of candied fruits, frozen; turned out, covered with cold chocolate sauce.

— **Miramar:** charlotte mould filled alternately with sponge finger, strips of poached pineapple and tangerine sections macerated in kirsch, filled with pomegranate bombe mixture flavored with kirsch, frozen; chilled vanilla syrup served separately.

— **Nancy:** charlotte mould lined with sponge fingers lightly soaked in Grand-Marnier, filled with chocolate bombe mixture to which crushed macaroons have been added; frozen, served with cold vanilla sauce.

Ice Punch: Punch glacé: syrup of 22 deg. with an infusion of orange and lemon peel, blended with orange and lemon or other fruit juice and mixed with enough white wine or champagne to bring mixture to 18 deg. measured

Ice Punch
with the saccharometer; frozen rather stiff and mixed with a quarter of its amount with Italian meringue mixture and the desired flavor.

— **Cardinal:** pineapple ice punch flavored with Port and rum.

— **Favorite:** strawberry ice punch flavored with brandy.

— **Lucullus:** basic mixture prepared with pineapple juice and champagne, flavored with maraschino, kirsch and rum.

— **Roman:** à la romaine: basic mixture flavored with rum.

Ice Soufflé: Soufflé glacé: Basic mixtures: A. cream soufflé: same mixture as for ice mousse; B. fruit soufflé: fruit pulp mixed with an equal quantity of Italian meringue mixture and an equal amount of whipped cream. The mixture or mixtures are filled in a soufflé dish with a strip of stiff white paper placed around the inside edge of the dish and standing up about 2 in. above the edge. It is then placed in the deep freezer and frozen. Shortly before serving the top is dusted with a mixture of cocoa powder and icing sugar or with finely sieved pralin dusted lightly with icing sugar, and the paper is removed.

— **Bénedictine:** cream mixture flavored with Bénedictine, mixed with diced genoise or sponge finger lightly soaked with Bénedictine and brandy.

— **Cavalieri:** filled alternately with strawberry, chocolate and pineapple mixture with a thin slice of sponge soaked in kirsch syrup between the layers.

— **Elité:** filled with tangerine mixture; when nearly frozen, center scooped out, filled with diced candied oranges, pineapple and sponge finger soaked with brandy and Bénedictine, covered with tangerine mixture and frozen completely; at serving chequered with couverture and decorated with leaf gold.

— **Fédora:** filled alternately in layers with vanilla and hazelnut mixture.

— **Georgette:** fruit mixture prepared with pulp of morellos, alternated with vanilla mixture with diced genoise and candied cherries soaked in brandy.

— **Jamaica:** à la jamaique: basic mixture flavored with rum, mixed with diced sponge fingers soaked in rum syrup.

— **Margot:** almond mixture with small strawberries macerated in sugar and maraschino.

— **Miracle:** tangerine cream mixture with diced crushed macaroons and diced candied pineapple macerated in Grand-Marnier; lightly sugared wild strawberries served separately.

— **Montmorency:** basic mixture flavored with kirsch, mixed with chopped morellos macerated in sugar and kirsch.

— **Montrose:** vanilla mixture with diced pineapple macerated in sugar and maraschino; sugared wild strawberries served separately.

— **Nesselrode:** vanilla mixture with strained cooked chestnuts, decorated with small glacé chestnuts; cold chocolate sauce served separately (optional).

Ice Soufflé

— **Paquitta:** bottom of dish covered with a round genoise slice soaked with maraschino, alternated with a layer of strawberry or pineapple ice and diced pineapple, apricots, bananas and small strawberries macerated in sugar and maraschino; covered up to edge of paper strip with Chantilly cream and frozen; grated chocolate mixed with chopped pistachios sprinkled on top and lightly dusted with icing sugar.

— **Singhalese:** singalaise: layers of tea and banana cream mixture, sponge biscuits and diced pineapple soaked in maraschino between the layers.

— **Sylvia:** vanilla mixture with grated walnuts, mixed with diced candied apricots and sponge fingers soaked with kirsch.

— **Tortoni:** vanilla mixture with finely sieved pralin; when nearly frozen Chantilly cream piped on top with a thin tube like spaghetti and dusted with finely sieved grilled hazelnuts, freezing finished in deep freezer.

— **Yolanda:** raspberry fruit mixture with diced pineapple macerated in sugar and Curaçao.

Ischler Krapfen: butter creamed with sugar and egg yolks, ground almonds, cinnamon and grated lemon peel added, stiffly beaten egg whites folded in, small balls dressed on baking sheet and baked; when cold iced with fondant, decorated with angelica leaves and a glacé cherry. (Austrian)

J

Jalousies: puff pastry rolled out thin, cut into broad strips, center spread with vanilla-flavored almond cream, trellised with thin strips of puff pastry, baked, brushed with apricot jam, cut into regular pieces.

Jelly; F. Gelée; G. Gelee: jelly was formerly made chiefly of calf's feet but is now made with gelatine. The basic jelly is made of water, sugar, lemon peel and soaked gelatine, clarified with egg white whipped with white wine. Fortified wines, spirits or liqueurs are added after the jelly has been strained through a napkin and is cold; fruit jellies are made of half basic clarified jelly, with the double amount of gelatine, and half filtered fruit juice. If jelly is to be served in glasses or glass dishes it must be kept very light and only $^3/_4$ of the usual amount of gelatine added.

— **Apple:** de pommes: basic jelly mixed with filtered apple juice.

— **Carmen Sylva:** glass dish filled with a little strawberry jelly, when set covered with a layer of vanilla Bavarian cream, allowed to set, strawberries placed on top, sealed with light strawberry jelly; may also be filled in moulds.

— **Fruit, with Maraschino:** au marasquin et aux fruits: thin layer of maraschino-flavored jelly poured into mould, when set covered with fruit of different colors and kind, covered with jelly, allowed to set and filled in layers until mould is full.

— **Imperial:** à l'impériale: champagne jelly with poached pineapple cubes and slivered pistachios.

Jelly

— **Jubilee:** Jubilé: border mould filled with Port-flavored jelly; when set turned out, center filled with Chantilly cream.

— **Marbled:** marbrée: two or three jellies of different colors and flavors prepared the Russian way, mixed lightly and filled at once into a mould.

— **Muscovite:** jelly of any kind filled in cylindrical mould, placed in deep freezer just long enough to frost the outside lightly.

— **Northern Style:** à la nordique: wine jelly flavored with kümmel.

— **Orange:** à l'orange: very light orange flavored jelly filled alternately in glass dish with orange fillets.

— **Parisian:** à la parisienne: mould filled with alternate layers of strawberry and white wine jelly flavored with kirsch.

— **Pineapple:** d'ananas: fancy mould filled with pineapple jelly with layers of diced poached pineapple.

— **Royal:** à la royale: jelly prepared with pineapple juice and hock, when cold mixed with leaf gold and when it beginns to set with small cubes of poached pineapple; filled immediately in champagne glasses and served when completely set.

— **Russian:** à la russe: any kind of wine, liqueur or fruit jelly whipped to a foam when it begins to thicken and filled rapidly in mould.

— **Striped:** rubanée: mould lined in regular layers with jelly of different colors and flavors.

— **Sultans:** à la sultane: mould filled alternately with orange, lemon jelly and pistachio Bavarian cream, adorned with spun sugar.

— **Swedish:** Suédoise de fruits: wine jelly filled in layers in cylindrical mould with diced poached fresh fruit between the layers, allowed to set and turned out.

— **Vanilla:** à la vanille: basic jelly prepared with a vanilla pod, kept very light and flavored with kirsch; filled in champagne glass, garnished with Chantilly cream.

Junket: dessert made of sweet milk turned by dissolved rennet tablet, flavored with vanilla, chocolate, coffee, cinnamon, Sherry etc.

K

Kaiserschmarren: pancake batter made of butter creamed with egg yolks and sugar, flour, milk and raisins added, stiffly beaten egg whites folded in; baked into fairly thick pancakes, torn with two forks, dusted with sugar; stewed plums served separately. (Austrian)

Kaki: see Persimmon.

King Henry's Shoestrings: sponge cake made of egg yolks stirred to foam with sugar, mixed with flour, grated lemon peel, orange blossom water and a little lemon juice, stiffly beaten egg whites folded in, baked thin on greased and dusted baking sheet; cut into thin strips and dusted with powder sugar. (English)

Königskuchen: butter creamed with egg yolks, sugar and grated lemon peel, mixed with flour and stiffly beaten egg whites, filled in greased cake mould lined with greased and dusted paper, baked in moderate oven. (German)

L

Langues de chat: see cat's tongues.

Lemon Cheese Cakes: tartlet moulds lined with puff or short pastry, filled with lemon curd, dusted with powder sugar, baked.

— **Curd:** butter creamed with sugar and grated lemon peel, beaten eggs and lemon juice added, whipped in water bath like Dutch sauce.

Linzer Torte: butter creamed with sugar and eggs, mixed with ground almonds, flour and grated lemon peel to a smooth dough, allowed to rest and then rolled out rather thick; coated generously with red currant or raspberry jam, decorated crisscross with Linz dough over the whole surface and ring of dough placed around the edge; baked and dusted with powder sugar. (Austrian)

Liwanzen: dough made of flour, milk, butter, sugar, egg yolks and stiffly beaten egg-whites, shaped in small balls, placed on well greased dish, baked brown first on one and then the other side; served hot coated with thick prune jam, sugar mixed with cinnamon sprinkled on top. (Czecho-Slovakian)

M

Macaroons: ground almonds or almonds pounded in mortar, mixed with sugar, egg whites and vanilla to a rather soft paste, placed in small heaps on waxed baking sheet, brushed lightly with water, baked.

— **Hazelnut:** prepared like macaroons but made with hazelnuts roasted quite lightly and ground finely or pounded in the mortar.

Macédoine suédoise: see Swedish macedoine.

Madeleines: genoise sponge baked in small oval fluted moulds dusted with powder sugar when cold.

Mahalebi: Rose Cream: milk and sugar boiled up, mixed with rice starch dissolved in cold water, cooked to a thick mush, flavored with rose water, filled in a mould, chilled. (Turkish)

Mandarine: see tangerine.

Marillenknödel: rich yeast dough cut in squares, an apricot with a piece of sugar instead of the stone placed in the center, the ends of the dough folded over on top, closed and shaped into balls; allowed to rise, poached in boiling water, drained, covered generously with breadcrumbs browned in plenty of butter, dusted with powder sugar. (Austrian)

Marquise Alice: vanilla bavarois mixed with pounded sieved pralin and diced finger biscuits soaked in Anisette, filled in rather flat round mould and allowed to set; turned

Marquise Alice
out, masked entirely with Chantilly cream, decorated with lines of red currant jelly mottled with the point of a knife, base of cream garnished with very small triangular Condé cakes (q. v.).

Marron: see chestnut.

Marronier: round genoise sponge, cut in three slices, filled with chestnut butter cream flavored with vanilla, coated thinly with strained apricot jam, iced with chocolate fondant; the name „Marronnier" written with royal icing on top, decorated with royal icing.

Mascottes: genoise baked in baking tin with a high border; when cold cut open vertically, filled with praliné butter cream, cut into regular squares the size of a small gateau, top and sides coated thinly with praliné butter cream and covered with grilled slivered almonds.

Mecca Cakes: Pains de la Mecque: small egg-shaped cakes made of cream puff paste piped on greased baking sheet, brushed with egg, covered with coarse sugar and baked in moderate oven. May be cut open and filled with whipped cream blended with apricot purée or jam.

— **with Pistachios:** aux pistaches: filled with pistachio cream.

Melon: F. Melon; G. Melone: name of the fruit of a trailing plant. There are many kinds of melons in Europe and the U. S. A. of which the most popular are the Cantaloup, Persian, Honey Dew, Cassaba and Musk Melons.

— **Atlantic:** lid cut of, seeds removed, filled with melon ice, prepared with the flesh, mixed with diced bananas, garnished with Chantilly cream, chocolate chips scattered on top.

— **with Cognac:** au fine champagne: lid cut off, seeds removed, a little Cognac poured into the fruit, lid replaced, packed in ice and served chilled.

— **Creole Style:** à la créole: scooped out, flesh cut out in balls with a vegetable cutter, macerated in kirsch, maraschino and sugar, mixed with small strawberries, refilled in the melon, served chilled.

— **Marquise:** cut open in basket shape, seeds removed, flesh scooped out with a spoon and macerated with sugar and brandy, filled alternately with vanilla ice and the scooped out flesh, top garnished with whipped cream.

— **Mathis:** flesh scooped out, cut in small balls, macerated with sugar, brandy and champagne, refilled in melon alternately with vanilla ice, garnished with Benedictine-flavored whipped cream.

— **Modern Style:** filled alternately with almond ice, the diced flesh and wild strawberries macerated in sugar and maraschino.

— **Oriental Style:** à l'orientale: scooped out, filled with the diced flesh mixed with wild strawberries macerated in sugar and kirsch.

— **Surprise:** en surprise: flesh scooped out with a spoon, macerated with kirsch and sugar, bound generously with thick strawberry purée, chilled; placed in container with raw ice, covered and decorated with meringue mixture, dusted with powder sugar and browned.

— **Wilhelmine:** small melon, peeled, filled with vanilla cream, wrapped in puff pastry, brushed with egg, baked in oven.

Meringue: F. Meringue; G. Meringue, Baiser: egg whites beaten stiff with a pinch of salt, sifted sugar added, piped round, oval, in spirals or to any other desired shape on well floured baking sheets or on soft paper placed on a well soaped wooden board — this method keeps the inside soft which is easily scooped out — and baked very slowly without browning.

— **Chantilly:** two round or oval meringues filled and decorated with Chantilly cream.

— **Ice:** Meringue glacé: two oval meringues filled with vanilla or other ice cream decorated with whipped cream.

— **Ice-Wafer:** meringue mixture piped like square wafers, baked, both ends dipped in couverture; filled with ice cream to taste or topped with a thin slice of ice parfait, decorated with an ornament piped with couverture or with baked cream puff paste.

— **Mocha-Kirsch:** two spirals of meringue flavored with soluble coffee, brushed inside with couverture and base of each shell dipped in couverture; filled and put together with kirsch-flavored whipped cream, decorated on top with whipped cream, glacé cherries and an ornament made of couverture.

— **Strawberry:** aux fraises: two meringues piped in a spiral, scooped out, inside brushed with couverture; when set filled with diced strawberries macerated in brandy and mixed with whipped cream.

Meringue Tart: Tarte meringuée: two round layers of baked meringue, the top layer usually trellised, filled with ice-cream, whipped cream, fruit or other concoction.

— **Doris:** filled with vanilla ice cream mixed with diced pineapple macerated in Grand-Marnier, top decorated with Chantilly cream and candied pineapple.

— **Eribel:** filled with praliné ice cream mixed with salpicon of candied apricots macerated in Cointreau, covered lightly with Chantilly cream, top decorated with Chantilly cream trellised with red currant jelly with chopped pistachios in the openings.

— **Ravanola:** filled with Chantilly cream mixed with grated chocolate and crushed glacé chestnuts.

— **with Strawberries:** aux fraises: filled with Chantilly cream mixed with small strawberries macerated in kirsch and sugar.

Mince Pies: tartlet mould lined with puff pastry or puff pastry remnants, filled with mince meat, covered with puff pastry, baked, served hot dusted with icing-sugar. Mince meat: concoction of finely diced beef suet, roast tenderloin, currants, Malaga raisins, sultanas, diced candied orange, lemon peel and apples, grated orange and lemon peel, spices and sugar, macerated in brandy and Madeira at least a month before using.

Mirlitons: tartlet moulds lined with puff or short pastry, bottom masked with a thin apricot slice, filled with eggs stirred to a foam with sugar, coarsely crushed macaroons added, three half almonds placed on top, dusted generously with sugar, baked.

Mohnnudeln: Noodles with Poppy: noodle dough rolled out and cut into rather broad strips, cooked in boiling salt water and well drained; mixed with black poppy seeds finely ground, cooked in butter and milk, stirred with a little honey; granulated sugar sprinkled on top. (Austrian)

Mousse glacée: see ice mousse or foam.

Muffins: 1. dough made of flour, milk, butter, eggs, yeast and salt or only of flour, milk, yeast and salt, divided into small balls, flattened, filled in muffin rings, allowed to rise, baked without allowing the muffins to brown; served grilled, cut open and spread with butter. (English) 2. sugar creamed with butter and eggs, sifted flour and baking powder added, mixed with milk, flavored with vanilla, filled in muffin cups, baked slowly. (American)

— **Blueberry:** basic American mixture to which clean blueberries sprinkled with flour have been added.

— **Corn:** same mixture as American but made with half wheat flour and half yellow corn meal.

Mulberry: F. Mûre; G. Maulbeere: fruit of the mulberry tree, a native of Asia, now grown in Eastern Europe and the Southern U. S. A. Chiefly marketed fresh and eaten raw, as compote or in pies.

— **Pie:** prepared like blackberry pie.

— **Tart:** Tarte aux mûres: tart ring lined with short pastry, bottom covered lightly with cake meal or crumbs, filled with raw mulberries mixed with sugar and a little cinnamon, baked; when cold brushed over with red currant jelly or strained apricot jam.

Mûre: see mulberry.

Myrtilles: see blueberries.

N

Nelson Tartlets: tartlets moulds lined with short pastry, baked empty to a pale brown, brushed inside with apricot jam, filled with meringue mixture flavored with cinnamon and blended generously with slivered almonds, baked slowly in oven, served dusted with powder sugar.

Norman Apple Tartlets: Tartlettes aux pommes à la normande: tartlet lined with short pastry, baked empty, bottom covered with sweet vanilla rice, filled with sliced apples cooked in butter, coated with strained apricot jam.

Nürnberger Lebkuchen: Nürnberg Christmas Cakes: sugar stirred to a light foam with egg whites, a little dissolved vol and honey, ground almonds, spice, chopped candied orange peel and very little flour added; mixture spread thickly on thin round wafers, dried for two hours, baked and glazed with white, pink or chocolate icing. Will keep for months packed in cellophane or in tins. (German)

O

Omelette: F. Omelette; G. Omelette: for preparation see egg dishes. For sweet omelettes very little salt is used and a pinch of sugar added. For glazing or burning an electric rod is chiefly used nowadays instead of a red-hot poker.

— **with Bananas:** aux bananes: diced bananas fried in butter, omelette mixture poured over and prepared as usual.

Omelette

— **Célestine:** small omelette spread with jam, filled with a smaller one filled with jam, sprinkled with sugar, burnt symmetrically with red-hot poker.

— **Christmas:** de Noel: very light omelette filled with hot mincemeat, sprinkled with sugar, warm rum poured on top, served burning.

— **Claremont:** stuffed with thick apple purée, top sprinkled with sugar and burnt symmetrically with a red-hot poker or electric rod.

— **George Sand:** very light omelette filled with finely diced hot fruit and crushed candied chestnuts bound with thick apricot sauce, top brushed with butter, sprinkled with sugar and finely crushed and sieved macaroons, glazed rapidly under the salamander.

— **with Jam:** aux confitures: filled with jam or jelly, sprinkled with sugar burnt with red-hot poker.

— **with Kirsch:** au kirsch: light omelette dusted with sugar, warm kirsch poured on top, served burning.

— **Nero:** prepared like surprise but dressed to look like a volcano; when browned a marzipan cup placed in the crater, filled with warm rum or kirsch, lit up and served burning.

— **Norwegian:** norvégienne: prepared like surprise.

— **with Peaches:** aux pêches: filled with peach salpicon bound with apricot sauce flavored with kirsch, covered with apricot sauce flavored with kirsch.

— **with Rum:** au rhum: very light omelette, warm rum poured over, ignited at serving.

— **Soufflée:** egg yolks creamed with sugar, flavored with grated lemon, orange peel or vanilla, stiffly beaten egg whites folded in, preparation filled in oval greased baking dish, decorated with the same mixture with a star tube, baked, sprinkled with icing sugar, glazed and served at once.

— **Stephanie:** egg yolks creamed with sugar and vanilla, stiffly beaten egg whites folded in; preparation filled in omelette pan in which a little butter has been heated, when partly done finished off in not too hot oven; filled with small sugared strawberries or raspberries, folded together, dusted with sugar and served immediately.

— **Surprise:** en surprise: oval slice of genoise placed on greased oval baking dish, covered with ice cream, coated with omelette soufflée mixture or Italian meringue, decorated with the mixture, browned rapidly in oven.

— **Sylphs:** des sylphes: savarin soaked with maraschino syrup, thin slice of genoise placed on bottom of center, filled with strawberry mouse ice, covered with Italian meringue, decorated with the same mixture, browned rapidly in oven.

— **Vesuv:** prepared like surprise but round; when about to be served, a tiny nougat cup pressed into the crater, filled with warm rum and a piece of sugar, lit and served burning.

Orange: F. Orange; G. Apfelsine: a native of China and now grown in many different varieties in nearly all countries bordering the Mediterranean, in Israel, the

Orange

United States etc. The principal market varieties are the navels and Valencias; navels are round, thick skinned and seedless.

— **Bristol:** hollowed out and shaped like a basket, filled half with orange ice, covered with vanilla ice with diced pineapple bound with thick apricot sauce on top.

— **Côte d'Azur:** hollowed out and shaped like a small basket, filled with macedoine of fruit flavored with Curaçao, covered with orange ice.

— **with Curaçao:** peeled, sliced, pips removed, macerated on ice with sugar and Curaçao.

— **Gateau Montélimart:** flan ring lined with short paste, filled alternately with orange fillets and grated almonds, covered with orange soufflé mixture flavored with Curaçao, baked in slow oven; served cold with Chantilly cream.

— **Ilona:** hollowed out, half filled with chocolate ice mixed with finely diced candied ginger, covered with salpicon of orange bound with thick apricot sauce flavored with rum, garnished with a rosette of Chantilly cream with crushed strained pralin scattered on top.

— **Infant Style:** à l'infante: 1. hollowed out filled with orange ice, covered with meringue mixture, placed on crushed ice, browned rapidly.
2. hollowed out, half filled with strawberry ice, topped with orange soufflé mixture, baked rapidly.

— **Javanese Style:** à la javanaise: hollowed out, filled with orange ice mixed with finely diced candied ginger macerated with Curaçao, a little orange salad on top, coated with meringue, browned rapidly.

— **Madrid Style:** à la madriléne: filled with apricot ice covered with Chantilly cream, orange fillets macerated in sugar and Curaçao placed on top; border of cold apricot sauce.

— **Maltese Style:** à la maltaise: sweet rice mixed with salpicon of candied orange peel and juice of blood oranges, pressed in border mould, turned out, center filled with quarters of blood oranges, glazed with blood orange jelly.

— **Northern Style:** à la nordique: hollowed out, half filled with salpicon of orange flavored with kümmel, covered with vanilla ice.

— **Norwegian Style:** à la norvegienne: hollowed out, filled with orange ice mixed with diced pineapple, covered with meringue flavored with rum, browned rapidly.

— **Salad:** Salade d'oranges: peeled, cut in slices, pith and pips removed, filled in glass dish, macerated with sugar, Curaçao and kirsch; served chilled.

— **Sections:** Tranches d'oranges: lid cut off from large oranges, scooped out, cleaned, filled with orange jelly; when set cut in quarters or in eights.

— **Sevilla:** half oranges, hollowed out, filled with salpicon of oranges, bananas, pineapple, peaches and cherries soaked in peach brandy and sugar, glazed with jelly.

— **Slices:** butter creamed with sugar and grated orange peel, egg yolks and ground hazelnuts added, stiffly beaten egg whites folded in, baked in greased baking

Orange
sheet; when cold cut lengthwise in three, filled with orange butter cream and cut into strips of about 4 inches. Strips coated with orange fondant, garnished with orange fillets and cut in slices of about 1, 1/2 inches.
— **Soufflé:** fruit hollowed out, cleaned, filled with soufflé mixture prepared with the pulp, baked in oven.
— **Surprise:** hollowed out, filled with orange ice or orange jelly flavored with Curaçao, lid replaced on top, served on crushed ice.

P

Pain aux fruits: see fruit loaf.
Pain de semoule: see semolina loaf.
Palm Leaves: Palmiers: puff paste rolled out on granulated sugar, folded toward center twice from both sides, cut into thick slices, placed rather far apart on baking sheet, baked and caramelised.
Palmiers: see palm leaves.
Pamplemouse: see grapefruit.
Pancakes I: F. Crêpes; G. Eierkuchen: very thin small pancake, about 4 in. in diameter, made of eggs, flour, milk or cream, sugar and flavoring, sometimes a little melted butter added, baked brown on both sides in butter, folded or rolled, also stuffed, served dusted with powder sugar or glazed.
— **Cevennes Style:** à la cévenole: spread thinly with rum-flavored purée of glacé chestnuts, rolled up, dusted with icing sugar, glaced under the salamander.
— **with Chocolate:** au chocolat: baked, folded in four, dusted with powder sugar; sauce made of melted chocolate with a little cream and butter served separately.
— **Déjazet:** left open, coated with coffee cream, covered with meringue mixture, browned in oven; kirsch-flavored apricot sauce served separately.
— **Empire:** very thin pancakes spread thin with vanilla cream to which finely diced pineapple and crushed macaroons have been added; folded, dusted with powder sugar, a thin strip of red currant jelly piped across.
— **English:** à l'anglaise: made a little larger then usual, folded in four, dusted with sugar, served with lemon sections.
— **Gil Blas:** filled with butter creamed with sugar and a little lemon juice, mixed with ground hazelnuts and flavored with cognac; folded together and dusted with powder sugar.
— **Lemon, with Cointreau:** au citron à la Cointreau: material needed: thin small pancakes, butter creamed with grated lemon peel, sugar and lemon juice, glass of Cointreau. The pancakes are sent into the dining room where the waiter heats them up in a chafing dish and rolls them several times in the creamed butter until they are well soaked; they are then ignited with the Cointreau and served immediately on hot plates.
— **Monastery Style:** du couvent; pancake batter filled in skillet, finely diced mellow pears scattered on top, baked first on the one and then on the other side, served open dusted with powder sugar.

Pancakes I

— **Norman:** à la normande: 1. prepared the same way as Monastry style but with small thin slices of mellow apples;
2.very thin pancakes spread with thick apple purée mixed with finely diced apples cooked in butter, flavored with apple jack, rolled up, dusted with powder sugar.

— **with Orange:** à l'orange: filled with diced orange without skin, pith or pips bound with thick hot apricot jam flavored with Curaçao or Grand-Marnier, rolled together and dusted with powder sugar.

— **Russian:** à la russe: two thin pancakes sandwiched together with very thick apple purée mixed with diced poached pineapple, top dusted with powder sugar and glazed; sabayon flavored with allash served separately.

— **Suzette:** prepared like with Cointreau in a chafing dish in the dining room with butter creamed with grated orange peel, sugar, tangerine juice and Curaçao; batter also flavored with Curaçao and grated orange juice, a little melted butter added, sometimes flambéd.

— **Wilhelmine:** baked, a little cherry-brandy drippled on top, coated with vanilla soufflé mixture, browned in oven.

— **Yvonne:** two thin crêpes sandwiched with frangipane cream to which a little melted chocolate has been added, dusted with powder sugar, glazed.

Pancakes II: F. Pannequets; G. Pfannkuchen: pancakes made larger then crêpes, usually stuffed, rolled and cut in lozenge-shaped pieces.

— **Apple:** aux pommes: thin apple slices fried in butter, pancake batter poured on top, baked, served open dusted with sugar mixed with cinnamon.

— **with Cestnut Purée:** à la purée de marrons: stuffed with light purée of chestnuts cooked in vanilla-flavored syrup, rolled, cut in pieces, dusted with powder sugar, glazed.

— **with Chocolate Cream:** à la crème au chocolat: coated with pastry cream mixed with melted chocolate, rolled, cut in pieces, dusted with sugar, glazed.

— **with Cream:** à la crème: coated with pastry or frangipane cream, rolled, cut in pieces, dusted with sugar, glazed.

— **German:** à l'allemande: made with batter mixed with stiffly beaten egg whites, baked in oven with plenty of butter in large skillet, served open dusted with granulated sugar.

— **with Jam:** aux confitures: thin large pancakes coated with any kind of jam, rolled, cut in two lozenge-shaped pieces, dusted with powder sugar, glazed.

Pannequets: see pancakes II.

Parfait: egg yolks whipped first hot and then cold with sugar syrup of 28 deg., brandy, rum or other flavor added, whipped cream folded in, filled in special parfait mould and frozen. Parfaits are always prepared with one flavor only and the moulds are never lined with another kind of ice.

— **with brown Bread:** au pain bis: kirsch or vanilla-flavored parfait mixture blended with grated brown bread or pumpernickel.

— **with Chocolate:** au chocolat: parfait mixture blended with grated or dissolved chocolate.

Parfait

— **Coffee:** au café: parfait mixture blended with coffee essence or soluble coffee powder.

— **with Kirsch:** au kirsch: parfait mixture flavored with kirsch.

— **Marie Brizard:** parfait mixture flavored with anisette.

— **Praliné:** parfait mixture blended with ground and sieved hazelnut or almond pralin.

— **with Rum:** au rhum: parfait mixture flavored with rum.

— **with Tea:** au thé: parfait mixture blended with a strong extract of tea.

— **Vanilla:** à la vanille: parfait mixture flavored with vanilla.

Peach: F. Pêche; G. Pfirsich: one of the finest cultivated fruits, native of China or Persia, now grown in many varieties in Europe, America, Africa and Australia Marketed fresh, frozen, canned and dried in many grades.

— **Alexandra:** poached in vanilla syrup and allowed to cool; dressed on vanilla ice coated with strawberry purée, white and red crystallized rose petals scattered on top of the peaches.

— **Ambassador Style: à l'ambassadeur:** short pastry tartlet shell filled half full with almond cream, a small poached cold peach, of which the stone has been replaced by marzipan, placed on top, coated with wine jelly.

— **Andalusian Style:** à l'andalouse: poached, stoned, arranged on vanilla rice, covered and decorated with meringue mixture, browned in oven; hot apricot sauce served separately.

— **Aurora:** à l'aurore: poached in kirsch syrup and cooled, served in timbale dish on strawberry ice mousse, covered with cold Curaçao-flavored sabayon.

— **Bourdalou:** prepared like apricot.

— **Cardinal Style:** à la cardinale: prepared like pear.

— **Colbert:** poached in vanilla syrup, well drained, stone removed and replaced by vanilla rice, dipped in egg and breadcrumbs, deep fried; apricot sauce served separately.

— **Condé:** prepared like pineapple.

— **Cussy:** prepared like apricot.

— **Devil Style:** à la diable: placed on sponge base soaked with kirsch syrup, coated and decorated with meringue mixture mixed with chopped almonds, browned in oven; before serving warm kirsch poured on top and ignited.

— **Empress Style:** à l'impératrice: divided in half, poached in vanilla syrup, allowed to cool; drained, put together with vanilla ice, brushed rapidly with thick strained apricot jam, rolled in slivered roasted almonds; placed on sponge base soaked with kirsch and maraschino, peach covered with spun sugar.

— **Flambéd:** flambée: poached in vanilla syrup, peeled, syrup lightly thickened with arrow-root; peach placed in hot timbale dish with a little syrup, warm kirsch poured on top, ignited and served burning.

— **Greek Style:** à la greque: raw mellow peach, peeled, stoned, cut in half, macerated with kirsch and sugar, covered with purée of fresh figs blended with whipped cream and sugar, decorated with wild strawberries, slivered almonds scattered on top.

Peach

— **Henry:** Henri: placed on hazelnut ice, covered and garnished with Chantilly cream.
— **Hiller:** poached cold peach placed on almond ice, covered with maraschino-flavored whipped cream blended with strawberry puree, grated chocolate scattered on top.
— **Karputhala:** placed on peach ice, covered with Chantilly cream, garnished with red currants poached in honey.
— **Little Duke:** Petit-Duc: poached in vanilla syrup, when cold placed on vanilla ice covered with thin pineapple slices macerated in kirsch and maraschino, covered with red currant jelly.
— **Manuel:** peeled, divided in two, poached in vanilla syrup and allowed to cool; bottom of glass dish covered with champagne jelly mixed with leaf gold, when set peaches arranged on top, dish covered with same jelly when it starts thickening.
— **Marie:** mellow peach divides in two, stone removed and replaced by marzipan flavored with rum and cinnamon; peach wrapped in puff paste, eggwashed, baked; peach sauce served separately.
— **Melba:** poached in vanilla syrup and allowed to cool, drained, placed on vanilla ice, covered with raspberry purée.
— **Meringué:** placed on base of sweet rice, coated and dacorated with meringue mixture, browned in oven, small dots of red currant jelly on top.
— **Modern Style:** à la moderne: half poached peaches arranged on vanilla rice mixed with vanilla cream, covered and decorated with Chantilly cream, coarse macaroon crumbs scattered on top; cold peach sauce served separately.
— **Monte Carlo:** poached, arranged on peach ice, covered with raspberry purée.
— **Montreal:** halved poached peaches placed on large macaroons soaked with Benédictine, dusted with powder sugar, warm kirsch poured on top, ignited and served burning.
— **Montreuil:** poached, dressed on base of Condé rice, covered with peach syrup.
— **Montrose:** half a poached peach, the opening filled high with strawberry ice, placed on biscuit base soaked with kirsch syrup, coated entirely with Chantilly cream, garnished with Chantilly cream, angelica and glacé cherries.
— **Nassauer Hof:** poached, served on hazelnut ice, covered with cold chocolate sauce, garnished with whipped cream, chopped roasted almonds scattered on top.
— **Nelusko:** prepared like pear.
— **Northern Style:** à la nordique: prepared like pear.
— **Oriental Style:** prepared like pear.
— **Parisian Style:** prepared like pear.
— **Portuguese Style:** half poached peaches placed on base of cold vanilla rice mixed with diced pineapple, covered with thick kirsch-flavored cold apricot sauce, slivered roasted almonds scattered on top.
— **Queen Blanche:** Reine Blanche: peeled, poached in vanilla syrup, halved, placed on pineapple ice, covered with maraschino-flavored pineapple syrup.

Peach
— **Richelieu:** quartered peaches poached in vanilla syrup, allowed to cool, drained, dressed in the center of a cold flummery border decorated with glacé fruits, peaches coated with frangipane cream blended with whipped cream and macaroon crumbs, decorated with whipped cream; cold apricot sauce flavored with kirsch served separately.
— **Rose-Chéri:** poached in vanilla syrup, allowed to cool, drained, placed in timbale or glass dish, covered with pineapple purée diluted with champagne.
— **Sahara:** border mould lined with blancmange, filled with small half or quartered poached peaches, sealed with raspberry jelly; when set turned out, center filled with Chantilly cream blended with raspberry purée.
— **Salambo:** poached, dressed on orange ice, covered with cold almond cream, decorated with Chantilly cream, spun sugar on top.
— **Salisbury:** meringue vacherin with a piped border filled with pineapple ice, half a cold poached peach placed on top, coated with raspberry purée, decorated with Chantilly cream.
— **Stanislas:** poached, placed on raspberry ice, coated with red currant jelly, decorated with Chantilly cream flavored with anisette.
— **Sultan Style:** à la sultane: poached in vanilla syrup and allowed to cool, placed on pistachio ice, covered with chilled syrup thickened lightly with corn starch and flavored with rose water, adorned with spun sugar.
— **Vanderbilt:** border mould lined with champagne jelly, filled with small half or quartered cold peaches, cooled and drained, sealed with jelly flavored with Danzig Goldwasser; turned out when set, center filled with Chantilly cream.
— **White Lady:** Dame Blanche: poached, when cold dressed on vanilla ice covered with thin pineapple slices macerated in kirsch and maraschino; decorated with a star tube with Chantilly cream.
— **Wilhelma:** tartlet filled half full with sugared wild strawberries, half a poached peach placed on top, covered with cold vanilla cream blended with whipped cream, chopped pistachios scattered on top.

Pear: F. Poire; G. Birne: sweet, fragrant, soft, more or less juicy fruit of the pear tree cultivated all over the world in moderate climates. There are countless varieties of pears, most of them marketed fresh, some canned and dried.
— **Alma:** poached in Port, served cold decorated with Chantilly cream and grilled chopped almonds on top.
— **Andalusian Style:** à l'andalouse: prepared like pineapple.
— **Archduke Style:** à l'archiduc: poached halves placed on pineapple ice, covered with strawberry purée.
— **d'Aremberg:** peeled, cut in halves, scooped out lightly, poached; when cold opening filled with red currant jelly, placed on vanilla ice, covered with vanilla sauce, garnished with pistachios and crystalized violets.
— **Bar-le-Duc:** poached halves placed on red currant ice, covered with seeded red currants lightly bound with honey.
— **Bourdalou:** prepared like apple.

Pear

— **Bristol:** poached, placed on vanilla ice, covered with raspberry purée, decorated with dots of Chantilly cream with wild strawberries on top.

— **Cardinal Style:** cardinal: 1. poached, dressed on strawberry purée, slivered almonds scattered on top; 2. poached, dressed on vanilla ice, covered with strawberry purée, slivered almonds scattered on top.

— **Casanova:** poached halves placed on raspberry ice, covered with whipped cream flavored with Benedictine, grated chocolate scattered on top.

— **Condé:** prepared like pineapple.

— **Dreux:** prepared like apricot.

— **Edward:** Edouard: peeled, cored, poached in Maraschino syrup, placed on oval piece of genoise scooped out and filled with vanilla ice, covered with apricot jelly.

— **En Vogue:** poached, placed on vanilla rice, covered with hot red wine sauce, grilled slivered almond scattered on top, bordered with hot fruit macedoine.

— **Félicia:** halves poached, placed on base of Viennese cream, covered with Chantilly cream, crystallized rose petals scattered on top.

— **Flambée:** poached in kirsch syrup, syrup thickened lightly with corn starch, warm kirsch poured over, ignited and served burning.

— **Florence:** peeled, cored, diced, poached in vanilla syrup, drained, macerated with Curaçao, filled in glass dish, covered with light blancmanger, decorated with Chantilly cream.

— — **Style:** à la florentine: poached halves placed on base of cold semolina mush flavored with vanilla, covered with cold apricot sauce flavored with kirsch.

— **Gratinated:** au gratin: diced poached pears filled in tartlet shell masked with pastry cream, covered with pastry cream, crushed macaroons scattered on top, dusted with sugar, glazed.

— **Helena:** Hélène, also Belle Hélène: poached, dressed on vanilla ice, crystallized violets scattered on top; hot chocolate sauce served separately.

— **Hiller:** peeled, cored, diced raw, macerated in vanilla liqueur, filled in champagne glass, covered with whipped cream mixed with grated chocolate and crushed macaroons.

— **Imperial Style:** prepared like apricot.

— **Irene:** prepared like apple.

— **Kolschitzky:** puff pastry shell filled with vanilla cream, half a poached pear placed on top, covered with thick cold apricot sauce, grilled chopped hazelnuts scattered on top.

— **Lilly:** poached halves placed on vanilla ice, covered with cold chocolate sauce.

— **Little Duke:** petit-duc: pineapple slice macerated with kirsch and Maraschino, covered with cold vanilla rice, a half poached pear placed on top, covered with red currant jelly.

— **Lombard Style:** prepared like apple.

— **Louise:** small pear, peeled, cored, poached, center filled with cold almond cream, dipped in frying batter, deep fried, dusted with powder sugar.

— **Louis Philippe:** poached, placed on almond ice, covered with Maraschino syrup.

Pear

— **Majestic:** peeled, cored, halved, poached in white wine, sugar and butter, allowed to cool off, placed on slice of brioche, covered with persimmon purée..

— **Mary Garden:** peeled, poached, dressed on raspberry purée mixed with soaked glacé cherries, decorated with Chantilly cream.

— **Melba:** halves poached in vanilla syrup, arranged on vanilla ice, coated with purée of raw raspberries.

— **Menelik:** halves placed on pistachio ice, coated with cold chocolate sauce.

— **Mireille:** 1. soft raw pear peeled, cored, cut in half, dusted with vanilla sugar, covered with purée of wild strawberries, coated with Chantilly cream, crystallized violets and jasmin scattered on top; 2. halves placed on raspberry ice, covered with whipped cream flavored with rose liqueur.

— **Montrose:** peeled, poached, placed on chocolate ice, covered with cold chocolate sauce, chopped pralin scattered on top.

— **Negus:** peeled, poached, placed on chocolate ice, covered with cold apricot sauce, decorated with Chantilly cream.

— **Nelusco:** peeled, poached, placed on cold vanilla rice, covored with cold chocolate sauce.

— **Northern Style:** à la nordique: tartlet made of almond short paste filled with half a poached and trimmed pear, coated with thick cold apricot sauce flavored with kirsch.

— **Oriental Style:** à l'orientale: peeled, poached, placed on vanilla ice, covered cupola-shaped with Chantilly cream with red currant jelly on top, coated entirely with spun sugar.

— **Paillard:** poached halves dressed on cold vanilla rice, covered with vanilla cream, decorated with crystallized violets and angelica, bordered with vanilla syrup.

— **Parisian Style:** peeled, cored, cut in halves, poached, placed on base of genoise covered with hot vanilla rice, masked and garnished with Italian meringue mixture, decorated with glacé cherries, baked; hot apricot sauce served separately.

— **Richelieu:** prepared like pineapple.

— **Romanoff:** 1. mellow pears, peeled, cored, diced, macerated in Port, served in sherbet glass topped with Chantilly cream; 2. peeled halves poached in Curaçao syrup, allowed to cool, served covered with whipped cream flavored with kümmel.

— **Saint-Georges:** half a poached pear placed on brioche base, coated and decorated with meringue mixture, browned in oven; kirsch syrup served separately.

— **Salambo:** poached halves placed on orange ice, coated with almond cream, decorated with Chantilly cream, covered with spun sugar (optional).

— **Schouvaloff:** half a poached pear placed on genoise base, coated with meringue mixture, chequered with this mixture, browned in oven; decorated with red currant jelly and pistachios.

— **Sultan Style:** à la sultane: 1. peeled, poached, placed on pistachio ice, covered with syrup flavored with rose water, spun sugar on top; 2. placed on vanilla ice, coated with vanilla cream, chopped pistachios scattered on top, covered with spun sugar.

Pear

— **Swiss Style:** à la suisse: mellow pears peeled, cored, cut in quarters, macerated in kirsch and powder sugar, dipped in frying batter, fried in clarified butter.

— **Trocadero:** diced raw mellow pears and diced finger biscuits soaked in Curaçao, filled in glass or timbale dish, covered with Chantilly cream mixed with ground hazelnuts, grated chocolate scattered on top, dusted with powder sugar.

— **Van Dyck:** poached halves placed on genoise base, covered with thick cold chocolate sauce, crushed crystallized violets scattered on top.

— **White Lady:** Dame Blanche: poached in vanilla syrup, placed on vanilla ice, covered with thin pineapple slices macerated in kirsch and Marachino, decorated with Chantilly cream.

— **Zurich Style:** à la zurichoise: half a poached pear placed on oval vacherin filled with almond ice, covered with thick cold chocolate sauce, slivered grilled almonds scattered on top.

Pêche: see peach.

Persimmon: F. Kaki; G. Kaki: the small round fruit of two distinct species of the diospyrus tree grown in North America and Japan. Persimmons are very astringent when still green but sweet and of an agreeable taste when overripe or touched by frost.

— **Calcutta:** lid cut off, scooped out, filled with ice cream prepared with the flesh and puréed melon mixed with diced pineapple, covered and decorated with meringue mixture, placed on crushed ice, browned rapidly under the salamander.

— **Cyrill:** lid cut off, hollowed out, flesh diced and mixed with salpicon of bananas and pineapple, macerated with sugar and anisette, bound with thick apricot sauce, lid replaced served chilled.

— **Delmonico:** lid cut off, hollowed out, cream ice prepared with the flesh, filled into the fruit, decorated with Chantilly cream blended with chestnut purée, a candied hazelnut placed in the center.

— **Opera:** lid cut off, hollowed out, filled with a concoction of the puréed flesh mixed with banana purée, powder sugar and whipped cream, decorated with whipped cream, ground sieved pralin sprinkled on top, served well chilled.

— **Soufflé:** lemon-flavored soufflé, mixture blended with persimmon purée, filled in soufflé dish, baked; sabayon served separately.

Petits choux à la crème: see cream puffs.

Petits Fours: dainty small dry and glazed cakes of a great variety, of different shapes, various mixtures and fillings, decorated with taste and elegance such as tiny cream puffs filled with chocolate cream and iced with couverture; tiny round, square, oval or lozenge shaped genoise cakes stuffed with chocolate, coffee, almond, pralin, maraschino, Curaçao or other butter cream with an appropriate icing and decoration; candied fruit stuffed with marzipan; fancy boats filled with pineapple or other candied fruit bound with thick apricot jam flavored with kirsch and covered with chocolate fondant or almond butter cream; tiny stuffed meringues, sablés etc. etc.

Petits pots de crème: see cream pots.

Pie; F. Pâté; G. Pastete: the essential characteristics of a pie is that the food is cooked under a paste or crust in the pie-dish in which it is baked. The standard pie-dish is shallow and made of fireproof crockery or glass. These are called „deep-dish" pies in the U. S. A. Cream pies are usually open face pies, i. e. the bottom is partly or completely baked and then filled with cream or custard, covered with meringue mixture and baked. The dough is baked in round rather deep tins.

— **Apple and Cranberry:** sliced apples and cranberries filled in pie dish, sugar and very little water added, covered with puff pastry or pie dough, brushed with egg, baked; served cold with cream or custard. (English)

— **Cherry Meringue:** stoned cherries cooked in lemon-flavored syrup, thickened lightly with corn starch, filled in baked shell, covered and decorated with meringue mixture, browned in oven.

— **Coffee Chiffon:** cream made of strong coffee, sugar and egg yolks, thickened with gelatine, stiffly beaten egg whites folded in while still hot. Filled in baked pie shell, chopped nuts scattered on top, chilled and served dusted with powder sugar. (American)

— **Damson:** prepared like gooseberry pie with stoned damsons.

— **Gooseberry:** aux groseilles vertes: green gooseberries filled in pie dish, sugar and very little water added, covered with puff pastry or pie dough, baked; served cold with custard or cream.

— **Greengage:** aux reine-claudes: prepared like gooseberry pie.

— **Lemon Meringue:** custard made of eggs, lemon juice, a little water, sugar and cornstarch, filled in baked shell, covered and decorated with meringue mixture, baked. (American)

— **Peach:** aux pêches: made of half stoned and peeled peaches, sugar and very little water, filled in pie dish, covered with puff pastry, decorated to taste and baked; served with cream.

— **Plum:** prepared like damson pie.

— **Rhubarb:** rhubarb peeled, cut into small pieces, filled in pie dish with plenty of sugar, a little grated lemon peel and very little water, covered with puff pastry or pie dough, baked; served cold with cream or custard.

— **Strawberry Chiffon:** cream made of egg yolks, sugar and strawberry juice flavored with lemon juice, thickened with gelatine, stiffly beaten egg whites and crushed strawberries folded in; filled in baked shell and covered with whipped cream. (American)

Pineapple; F. Ananas; G. Ananas: fruit formed by the union of originally separate flowers which have become fleshy and consolidated into one pulpy mass. Native of tropical South America but now cultivated with great intensity in Hawai and in every tropical clime and subtropical country. It is marketed fresh, canned, frozen or as juice.

— **Aetna:** maraschino ice dressed on base of genoise sponge, covered with thin pineapple slices, coated evenly with meringue mixture and browned rapidly; small cup of pralin placed in center, filled with warm rum and ignited at serving.

Pineapple

— **Andalusian Style:** à l'andalouse: poached slices arranged on vanilla rice, coated with rose-colored meringue mixture, baked; pineapple syrup served separately.

— **Carlton Hotel:** round base of hazelnut parfait covered cupola-shaped with whipped cream mixed with diced pineapple macerated beforehand in maraschino and Grand-Marnier.

— **Caroline:** border of genoise glazed with rum fondant, center filled with vanilla rice, garnished with thin pineapple slices lightly covered with apricot.

— **Condé:** poached pineapple slices arranged on hot vanilla rice, coated with hot apricot sauce, decorated with angelica and cherries.

— **with whipped Cream:** à la crème Chantilly: thin slices arranged on glass dish, covered with whipped cream.

— **Cream Gateau:** cold baked genoise sponge cut into four layers, filled with cooked pineapple purée mixed with whipped cream and a little liquid gelantine, top and sides spread with cream; when set decorated with whipped cream and triangles of candied pineapple.

— **Creole:** poached slices dressed on vanilla rice mixed with diced candied fruit, covered with apricot sauce flavored with rum; served hot or cold.

— **Crust:** Croûte à l'ananas: stale baked savarin cut oblique in slices, slices browned in oven, arranged like a crown on round platter, center filled with diced pineapple bound with thick apricot sauce flavored with kirsch.

— **Curtet:** fancy mould lined with kirsch jelly, filled with diced poached pineapple, sealed with apricot jelly; chilled and turned out.

— **Cussy:** diced, poached, drained, bound with thick apricot purée, filled in large scooped out macaroon, coated with meringue mixture, baked; apricot sauce flavored with kirsch served separately.

— **Edward VII.:** whole pineapple, a lid cut off, scooped out, filled with vanilla ice mixed with the diced pulp and stoned cherries macerated in kirsch; served with the lid replaced on top.

— **Empress Style:** à l'imperatrice: thin pineapple slices arranged on cold vanilla rice mixed with diced candied fruit and flavored with maraschino, covered with raspberry purée.

— **Gastronomer Style:** à la gastronome: genoise sponge covered with banana ice flavored with maraschino, covered with poached pineapple slices, coated with vanilla souflé mixture; placed in container with crushed ice, baked rapidly in oven.

— **Gateau:** genoise mixture baked in round tin; when cold cut into two or three layers, filled with whipped cream mixed with grated pineapple; iced with pineapple fondant and eaten fresh.

— **Geisha:** tartlet filled with orange ice, covered with small slices of pineapple macerated with sugar, maraschino and kirsch, coated with pineapple syrup.

— **Georgette:** pineapple bavarois mixed with diced pineapple and salpicon of fruit macerated in kirsch and maraschino; filled in scooped out pineapple with the lid replaced.

Pineapple

— **Haroun-el-Rashid:** pineapple split lengthwise with the leaves and hollowed out, filled with pistachio ice, covered with thin pineapple slices macerated with kirsch, coated with thick raspberry purée, slivered pistachios scattered on top.

— **Jelly:** Gelée d'ananas: fancy mould lined with pineapple jelly, filled with cold, poached and diced pineapple, sealed with jelly, chilled and turned out.

— **Majestic:** whole pineapple, hollowed out, filled with vanilla bavarois mixed with the mashed pulp, served with the lid replaced on top.

— **Mascot:** Mascotte: round layers of genoise spread with apricot jam with pineapple slices of the same shape macerated in kirsch beforehand in between, coated with meringue mixture, chopped pistachios scattered on top, baked lightly; pineapple syrup served separately. Served hot or cold.

— **Master Joe:** thick slice soaked in sugar and kirsch or maraschino, covered with orange fillets and strawberries; cream served separately.

— **with Meringue:** meringué: slice placed on vanilla rice, covered with meringue mixture, dotted with red currant jelly, baked lightly.

— **Ninon:** pineapple slices arranged on vanilla ice filled in timbale dish, covered with wild strawberries, coated with rasberry purée, slivered pistachios scattered on top.

— **Orleans Style:** à la d'Orléans: slice soaked in sugar and kirsch placed on cold vanilla rice, decorated with whipped cream, candied cherries and angelica, bordered with cold apricot sauce flavored with kirsch.

— **Princess Style:** à la princesse: round genoise slice covered with thin pineapple slice soaked in kirsch syrup, a ball of strawberry ice placed in the center, bordered with whipped cream decorated with small strawberries macerated with maraschino.

— **Queen Style:** à la reine: border of baked genoise garnished with triangles of pineapple macerated in Cointreau, center filled with salpicon of cherries, apricots and pineapple bound with pineapple sauce.

— **Rich Style:** à la riche: tartlets of almond short paste filled with salpicon of pineapple mixed with whipped cream, a round slice of pineapple on top.

— **Royal Style:** à la royale: whole pineapple, lid cut of, scooped out, filled with the diced pulp mixed with salpicon of fruit macerated in maraschino and kirsch; lid replaced, bordered with peaches and strawberries macerated in kirsch.

— **Savoy:** pineapple slice placed on cold vanilla rice, half a poached peach on top, covered with strawberry purée, decorated with whipped cream.

— **Sovereign Style:** à la souveraine: round genoise slice soaked lightly with pineapple syrup, covered with pineapple slices macerated in maraschino and kirsch beforehand, coated with meringue mixture, slivered almonds scattered on top, baked lightly; bordered at serving with spun sugar. Apricot sauce served separately.

Pineapple

— **with Strawberries and whipped Cream:** whole pineapple, lid cut of, hollowed out, filled alternately with whipped cream and pineapple slices and strawberries soaked in kirsch, maraschino or Curaçao.

Tartlet: tartlet mould lined with short pastry and baked empty; when cold filled with pineapple butter cream, coated with pineapple fondant, a round pineapple slice placed on top.

— **Virginia:** whole fruit, hollowed out, filled with strawberry bavarois mixed with diced pineapple and wild strawberries.

Pischingerschnitten: Chocolate Wafers: six exceedingly thin hazelnut wafers sandwiched with butter creamed with sugar, egg yolks, grated chocolate and vanilla, coated with couverture or chocolate fondant. (Austrian)

Plazinde moldovenesti: see Blazinde moldovenesti

Plombière: vanilla ice cream mixed with salpicon of candied fruit macerated in kirsch, filled in parfait mould alternately with apricot jam.

Plum; F. Prune; G. Pflaume: tree stone fruit native of Asia, now cultivated in all countries with moderate climate in Europe and America. Plums are grouped by their color, the principal kinds are the domestic purple-blue plums, the yellow Egg-plums, the Green Gage, the Damson and the Mirabelle, all differing in size, color and flavor.

— **Canarian Style:** à la canarienne: large domestic plums peeled, stoned and poached in vanilla syrup; allowed to cool, drained, dressed on banana ice, garnished with whipped cream, short strips of ginger in syrup scattered on top.

— **Grandmother Style:** à la grand'mère: apricot plum or very large domestic plums, peeled, stoned and poached in vanilla syrup. Tartlets baked empty, filled 3/4 full with chestnut purée sweetened and mixed with whipped cream, half a plum placed on top, glazed with the cold syrup thickened with corn starch and flavored with rum.

— **Housewife Style:** à la bonne-femme: peeled, stoned and poached in vanilla syrup, dressed in a border of flummery, coated with the cold thickened syrup, slivered almonds scattered on top.

— **Lotharingian Style:** à la lorraine: greengages poached in vanilla syrup, drained, syrup thickened with arrow-root, flavored with quetch (a spirit distilled from plums) and poured cold over the greengages.

— **Martinique:** greengages poached in vanilla syrup, allowed to cool, stones removed; dressed on banana ice, covered with rum-flavored sabayon.

— **in Wine Jelly:** Reine-claudes en gelée: greengages poached carefully in vanilla syrup and allowed to cool; drained, arranged in glass dish and covered with very light wine jelly just as it starts thickening.

Plum Cake: butter and sugar stirred to foam, eggs added gradually and 2/3 of the flour mixed with sultanas, currants and diced candied lemon and orange peel, macerated beforehand with grated lemon peel and rum; finally the remaining flour mixed with baking powder added; filled in greased mould lined with greased and floured paper, baked in moderate oven. (English)

Poire: see pear.

Pomme: see apple.

Profiteroles: are small round cakes of cream puff paste piped on baking sheet, brushed with egg yolk, baked, hollowed out and filled with Chantilly or other creams.

— **with Chocolate:** au chocolat: filled when cold with very cold Chantilly cream, covered at serving with hot chocolate sauce.

— **with Strawberry Cream:** à la crème aux fraises: filled with Chantilly cream blended with strawberry purée, served in timbale dish on sabayon mixed with a little strawberry syrup.

— **Venetian Style:** à la vénitienne: filled with Chantilly cream, covered with cold purée of raw raspberries.

Prune: see plum.

Pudding; F. Pouding; G. Pudding: the term pudding covers a great number of different warm and cold desserts such as soufflé pudding made of cream puff paste with different flavors and stiffly beaten egg whites folded in, poached in water bath and served with an appropiate sauce; suet puddings, such as plum or roly poly; cereals cooked, combined with custard and baked in water bath in oven; various kinds of bread puddings etc.

— **Albemarle:** soufflé pudding mixture with ground almonds, baked, turned out and covered with English sauce.

— **Albuféra:** greased mould lined with macaroon crumbs, filled with semolina pudding mixture with raisins, baked, served with apricot sauce.

— **Apple, English:** de pommes à l'anglaise: greased pudding basin lined with suet dough, filled with thin apple slices mixed with sugar and grated lemon peel, covered with suet dough, covered with a napkin and tied fast with string; placed in boiling water, cooked about 2 hours and served in the basin. (English)

— **Bachelors:** à la bachelière: soufflé pudding mixed with diced apples and currants, served with sabayon.

— **Beaulieu:** mould filled in layers with vanilla and strawberry soufflé pudding mixture, baked, served with sabayon.

— **Bread and Butter:** small slices of bread without the crust, spread with butter, filled in greased pie dish, sultanas and currants soaked in luke-warm water and well drained scattered on top, dish filled with custard and baked. (English)

— **Bread, French:** de pain à la française: prepared like German bread pudding without cinnamon, the bread soaked in milk; served with English sauce, sabayon or fruit sauce.

— **Bread, German:** bread soaked in hock or Moselle wine, mixed with sugar and a pinch of cinnamon, rubbed through a sieve; mixed with egg and egg yolks, melted butter, stiffly beaten egg whites folded in, filled in pudding mould greased with butter and coated with breadcrumbs; poached in water bath in oven, served with raspberry syrup.

— **Cabinet:** greased charlotte mould filled alternately with pieces of sponge fingers and salpicon of candied fruit, raisins and currants, filled with custard (sweet royal), poached in water bath in moderate oven, turned out and served with sabayon.

Pudding

— **Cambacérès:** almond souflé pudding mixture with chopped angelica, baked, served with hazelnut-flavored custard.

— **Chestnut:** aux marrons: purée of chestnuts cooked in vanilla syrup, mixed with powder sugar and butter, dried on hot fire; mixed with egg yolks, stiffly beaten egg whites folded in, poached in water bath in oven filled in well greased mould; served with English sauce or apricot syrup flavored with vanilla.

— **Chevreuse:** semolina pudding served with kirsch-flavored sabayon.

— **Chinese:** à la chinoise: soufflé pudding mixed with diced crystallized ginger, served with apricot sauce flavored with ginger syrup.

— **Custard:** eggs beaten with sugar, mixed with hot milk flavored with vanilla or grated lemon peel, strained, filled in greased pie dish, poached in oven, dusted with powder sugar. (English)

— **Damson:** prepared like apple pudding with stoned damsons. (English)

— **Empress:** à l'impératrice (cold): border mould filled with champagne jelly, when set center filled with Bavarian cream mixed with diced peaches and crushed macaroons soaked in Madeira.

— **Figaro:** pudding soufflé mixture flavored with vanilla, mixed with melted chocolate and with strawberry purée, filled alternately in layers in pudding mould, baked, served with sabayon.

— **Fontainebleau** (cold): mould lined with Curaçao-flavored wine jelly, filled alternately with layers of Bavarian vanilla cream, chopped cherries and macaroons soaked in Curaçao syrup; allowed to set, turned out, served with Curaçao-flavored whipped cream.

— **Frankfurt:** de Francfort: almond soufflé pudding mixture made with ground almonds and grated rye bread, mixed with stoned cherries; baked, turned out, served with red wine sauce mixed with chopped cherries.

— **Franklin:** soufflé pudding mixture with fruit salpicon, served with almond sauce.

— **Harlequin:** à l'arlequin: soufflé pudding in four layers: vanilla, raspberry, pistachio and chocolate; served with sabayon.

— **Indian:** à l'indienne: soufflé pudding mixture flavored with ginger powder and mixed with diced crystallized ginger; English sauce flavored with ginger served separately.

— **Istrian:** almond soufflé pudding served with syrup flavored with orange blossom water.

— **Javanese:** à la javanaise: soufflé pudding mixture prepared with tea, mixed with chopped pistachios, baked; served with sabayon flavored with tea.

— **Lyonese:** lyonnaise: lemon flavored soufflé pudding served with sabayon.

— **Metternich:** chestnut pudding mixed with chocolate; chocolate sauce served separately.

— **Midland:** finely chopped suet mixed with breadcrumbs, sugar, eggs, chopped dried figs, milk, grated lemon peel, powdered cinnamon, cloves, nutmeg and salt, filled in

Pudding

greased pudding basin, tied with a buttered and floured napkin, boiled for 2—3 hours; served with apricot sauce. (English)

— **Mousseline:** butter creamed with sugar and egg yolks, whipped in water bath like Dutch sauce, stiffly beaten egg whites folded in; high border mould half filled with this concoction, poached in water bath in moderate oven, allowed to rest for a while before turning out; sabayon served separately.

— **Norman:** normande: basic soufflé pudding mixture with diced apples cooked in butter, baked, served with apricot sauce flavored with apple-jack.

— **Orange:** orange-flavored soufflé pudding mixture, baked, served with sabayon flavored with Curaçao.

— **Orléans:** soufflé pudding with crushed macaroons and Malaga grapes, served with sabayon made with Malaga.

— **Palmyra:** anisette-flavored souffle pudding, anisette-flavored and thickened syrup served separately.

— **Plum:** finely chopped beef suet, sultanas, currants, stoned prunes and raisins, diced candied orange and lemon peel, brown sugar, peeled and grated apples, breadcrumbs, flour and eggs kneaded to a homogenous mass with powdered cinnamon, ginger, nutmeg and rum as well as a little salt added, filled in greased pudding basin, tied in buttered and floured cloth and boiled for 6 hours; turned out, crushed lump sugar placed on top, rum poured over, served alight. (English)

— **Queens:** à la reine: greased cylindrical mould coated with chopped pistachios and macaroon crumbs, filled with vanilla pudding mixture alternately with crushed macaroons and chopped pistachios, baked; served with English sauce blended with pralin powder.

— **Regency:** régence: vanilla souflé pudding poached in mould lined with caramel; English sauce with caramel served separately.

— **Rice:** au riz: rice cooked in vanilla-flavored sweetened milk with a little butter, egg yolks added, stiffly beaten egg whites folded in, filled in greased mould coated with breadcrumbs, poached in water bath in oven; served with fruit or English sauce.

— **Rice, Creole:** riz à la créole: rice pudding in mould lined with caramel.

— **Rice, English:** de riz à l'anglaise: rice cooked in milk flavored with vanilla or grated lemon peel, sugar and butter added and kept a little liquid; bound with eggs, filled in greased pie dish, baked in oven, served dusted with powder sugar. (English)

— **Roly Poly:** suet dough rolled out thin, coated with jam, rolled up, tied in buttered and floured cloth, boiled for 2 hours; served with apricot or other fruit sauce corresponding to the filling.

— **Royal:** à la royale: greased charlotte mould lined with slices of Swiss roll, filled with vanilla pudding soufflé mixture, baked, served with Marsala-flavored apricot sauce.

— **Sans-Souci:** greased mould with currants scattered on bottom and sides, filled with soufflé pudding mixture with diced apples cooked in butter.

Pudding

— **Saxon:** saxonne: vanilla soufflé pudding served with vanilla sauce or sabayon.

— **Scotch:** à l'écossaise: French bread pudding mixed with sliced fruit in season, served with a purée of raspberries and red currants slightly thickened with arrow-root.

— **Semolina:** au semoule: prepared like tapioca pudding, filled in greased mould lined with semolina.

— **Slawjanski:** cabinet pudding, the custard mixed with grated chocolate, served with chocolate sauce.

— **Spotted Dick:** suet dough rolled out thin, covered generously with currants and sultanas, rolled up, tied in a buttered and floured napkin like a galantine, boiled for 2 hours; cut in thick slices and served with apricot or other hot fruit sauce.(English)

— **Tapioca:** de tapioca: tapioca cooked in milk with sugar and butter added, mixed with egg yolks, whipped egg whites folded in, filled in greased pudding mould, baked in water bath in oven; turned out and served with English or fruit sauce.

— **Tapioca, Brasilian:** de tapioca à la brésilienne: prepared like tapioca pudding but in moulds lined with caramel.

— **Vermicelli:** au vermicelle: vermicelli cooked in milk, mixed with beaten eggs and vanilla sugar, filled in pie dish, baked in moderate oven; served dusted with powder sugar.

— **Vesuv:** à la vésuvienne: basic pudding mixture blended with tomato jam, mixed with seedless Malaga raisins, filled in cylindrical mould, baked; at serving bordered with apricot sauce, warm rum poured into the opening, ignited and served burning.

— **Westphalian:** westphalienne: butter stirred to a foam with sugar, eggs, egg yolks and ground almonds, grated lemon peel, cinnamon, a little grated chocolate and grated pumpernickel added, stiffly beaten egg whites folded in, filled in greased mould, poached, served with red wine sauce or sabayon.

Pudding glacé: see ice pudding.

Puff Pastry Patty with Fruit: Vol-au-vent aux fruits: large puff pastry shell filled with macedoine of fruit bound with apricot flavored with kirsch.

Puff Pastry Sticks: Allumettes glacées: puff pastry rolled out thinly, cut in strips about 4, 1/2 in. wide, spread evenly with egg white mixed with powder sugar like thick cream, divided with a knife dipped in flour into pieces of about 1 in., placed on baking sheet, baked in hot oven.

Puits d'amour: puff pastry rolled out thin, cut out round with a cutter, edges brushed lightly with water, a ring of puff paste placed on each, brushed with egg, baked; when cold center filled with red currant jam or jelly.

Punch glacé: see ice punch.

Q

Quarktorte: Cottage Cheese Gateau: gateau mould lined with short pastry, filled with strained cottage cheese creamed with butter, sugar and egg yolks, flavored with grated lemon peel and cinnamon, mixed with currants, stiffly beaten egg whites folded in; baked in slow oven, served dusted with powder sugar when cold. (German)

R

Rahat-Loukoum: sugar boiled to the large thread, thickened with cornstarch, lemon juice and dissolved gum arabic added and cooked slowly; when thick enough slivered almonds, pistachios and hazelnuts added, flavored with rose water and filled in flat cake mould dusted generously with powder sugar to prevent sticking. When set cut in small cubes or sticks, rolled in powder sugar and stored dry. (Turkish)

Raspberry: F. Framboise; G. Himbeere: small fruit native of Europe and Northern Asia, now cultivated all over the world in moderate climates. Raspberries are cultivated in red, yellow and a few black varieties. Marketed fresh, frozen and canned.

— **Anita:** glass dish half filled with vanilla ice, sugared raspberries arranged on top, covered with pineapple ice, coated with raspberry purée, slivered pistachios scattered on top.

— **Erika:** macerated in apricot-brandy and sugar, placed in glass dish half filled with blancmanger, coated with red currant jelly, slivered almonds scattered on top; heavy cream served separately.

— **with Hazelnuts:** aux noisettes: dusted with sugar, chilled, arranged in glass dish or timbale, slivered fresh hazelnuts scattered on top.

— **Ninette:** dusted with powder sugar and chilled, placed on orange ice, covered with orange sabayon, slivered pistachios scattered on top.

— **with Orange Ice:** à la glace à l'orange: macerated in kirsch and powder sugar, placed on orange ice, covered with cold apricot sauce.

— **Pie:** pie dish filled with raspberries, sugared, covered with puff paste, decorated with puff paste, brushed with egg, baked; served hot or cold with cream.

Red Currants: F. Groseilles rouges; G. Johannisbeeren: the small rather acid fruit of wild and cultivated bushes, used chiefly for making jelly and juice.

— **Boats:** Barquettes aux groseilles: boat-shaped moulds filled with brioche dough, baked; when cold scooped out, filled with red currants poached in honey, coated and decorated with meringue mixture, browned in oven.

— **Pudding:** boiled with a little sugar, cinnamon and vanilla, strained, cooked to a mush with semolina, filled in mould and cooled; turned out and served covered with vanilla sauce.

— **Tartlets:** Tartelettes aux groseilles: tartlet moulds lined with short pastry and baked empty; when cold filled with sugared red currants, coated with red currant jelly.

— **Tenant Style:** à la fermière: strained cottage cheese flavored with cinnamon, sweetened, blended with whipped cream, mixed with stewed cold red currants; chilled, served in glasses decorated with whipped cream.

— **White Lady:** Dame Blanche: border mould filled with blancmanger, turned out when set, center filled with Chantilly cream mixed with red currants sugared beforehand.

Rhubarb: F. Rhubarbe; G. Rhabarber: large herbaceous plant, native of Asia, with thick stems and large leaves. The leaf-stalks are used for pies, compote etc. and are best young.

— **Flan:** Flan au rhubarbe: flan hoop lined with short paste, chopped hazelnuts and cake crumbs scattered on the bottom to soak excessive juice, filled with peeled rhubarb cut into small pieces, covered generously with sugar and baked; when half done custard (royal) poured over and when custard is set dusted with powder sugar and glazed.

— **Fool:** prepared like gooseberry fool.

— **Fried:** frit: peeled, cut in pieces, poached lightly in white wine and sugar, drained, rolled in granulated sugar, dipped in **frying batter**, deep fried; served dusted with powder sugar.

— **Mousse:** peeled, cooked in own juice with sugar vanilla, strained, flavored with kirsch, thickened with melted gelatine and allowed to cool; when beginning to set stiffly beaten egg whites folded in and filled in charlotte mould; turned out, garnished with Chantilly cream.

Rice: Riz: rice for sweet dishes, so-called Condé rice, must be thoroughly washed, blanched, washed in cold water again and cooked slowly in oven with the lid on, in sweetened, vanilla-flavored milk with a little butter added. Proportions: 1 quart milk, 18 oz rice, 10 oz sugar, 3, 1/2 oz butter, pinch of salt, vanilla or other flavoring. When rice is done 8 egg yolks added carefully.

— **Croquettes:** cold Condé rice shaped into small croquettes, dipped in egg and cake crumbs, deep baked; fruit sauce or syrup served separately.

— **Jackson:** parboiled, cooked in water, and white wine with lemon juice, grated lemon peel and sugar, mixed with sabayon slightly thickened with soaked gelatine, filled in fluted mould alternately with orange sections, without skin, pith or pips, macerated in sugar and kirsch: when set turned out and served with cold sabayon.

— **Empress:** à l'impératrice: Condé rice without yolks mixed with diced candied fruit macerated in kirsch and maraschino, blended with Bavarian vanilla cream, filled in high border mould of which the bottoms has been masked with raspberry jelly; chilled and turned out.

— **Lord Byron:** parboiled, cooked in water and white wine flavored with vanilla, sweetened, mixed with whipped cream slightly thickened with gelatine and diced pineapple macerated in Grand-Marnier; filled in fluted mould, allowed to set, served with cold pineapple syrup.

— **Maltese:** maltaise: mould lined with blood orange jelly, filled with Condé rice, without yolks, mixed with Bavarian orange cream made with blood oranges; allowed to set, turned out, garnished with orange sections.

— **Nesselrode:** Condé rice without eggs flavored with orange juice and maraschino, mixed with diced candied orange peel, pineapple and cherries, blended with chestnut purée and whipped cream slightly thickened with gelatine, filled in fluted mould; allowed to set, turned out and served with maraschino-flavored vanilla sauce.

— **Palermo:** palermitaine: border mould lined with blood orange jelly, filled with rice prepared as Empress rice, allowed to set; turned out, center garnished with Chan-

Rice
tilly cream and orange sections macerated in Curaçao and sugar.

— **Princess:** parboiled, cooked in half white wine and half water with sugar, vanilla, a pinch of salt and cinnamon; allowed to cool, filled like a cupola in glass dish, covered and garnished with Chantilly cream, bordered with thin pineapple slices.

— **Sicilian:** sicilienne: Empress rice in border mould; turned out when set, decorated with candied fruit, center filled with Plombière ice, garnished with strawberries.

— **Soufflé:** Soufflé au riz: Condé rice with stiffly beaten egg whites folded in, filled in greased soufflé dish, baked, when nearly done dusted with powder sugar and glazed; fruit sauce served separately.

— **Swiss:** suisse: mould lined with maraschino-flavored red currant jelly, filled with Empress rice without fruit; allowed to set, turned out, served bordered with red currant syrup.

— **Trauttmansdorf:** Condé rice without yolks mixed with diced fresh fruit, flavored with maraschino, blended with whipped cream slightly thickened with gelatine; filled in high fluted mould, allowed to set, served with strawberry or raspberry sauce or purée.

Rice Border with Fruit: Bordure Condé: hot Condé rice filled in greased border mould, turned out on round platter; center filled with hot fruit macédoine flavored with kirsch and bound with thick apricot sauce, border covered with kirsch-flavored apricot sauce.

— **Border Infant Style:** Bordure à l'infante: border of hot Condé rice, center filled with stoned cherries and peach quarters bound with thick hot apricot sauce.

— **Border Marquise:** Condé rice mixed with diced pears in border mould, center filled with small half or quartered pears, covered with hot Madeira-flavored apricot sauce.

— **Border Metropole:** border filled with Condé rice without eggs, blended with whipped cream, lightly thickened with gelatine; when set turned out, center filled with vanilla ice cream, garnished with whipped cream, small macaroons soaked in kirsch syrup and half a poached peach per person.

— **Border Sarah Bernhardt:** bottom of border mould masked with maraschino jelly with chopped pistachios scattered on top, filled with Condé rice mixed with whipped cream and a little gelatine, sealed with maraschino jelly; when set turned out, center filled with Chantilly cream garnished with wild strawberries.

— **Border Singapore:** Bordure de riz Singapoure: cold Condé rice flavored with maraschino, mixed with diced pineapple and filled in border mould; turned out and served with cold maraschino-flavored apricot sauce.

Richmond Maids of Honour: tartlet moulds lined with puff pastry, bottom masked with raspberry jam, filled with a concoction of ground almonds mixed with sugar, flavored with cinnamon and brandy, a little cream added and stiffly beaten egg whites folded in; dusted with powder sugar and baked. (English)

Riz: see rice.

Rocher de Glace: Ice Rock: four different kinds of ice cream, vanilla, pistachio, raspberry and chocolate, filled in high fancy mould, decorated with Chantilly cream to imitate a rock.

Rote Grütze: Red Gruel: red currants, raspberries, strawberries, blackberries or stoned cherries cooked with very little water, strained, sweetened, mixed with semolina, rice meal, sago or buckwheat flour, cooked to a rather thin mush, filled in glass bowls or moulds, turned out and served cold with cream, vanilla sauce or whipped cream. (German)

S

Sabayon: egg yolks stirred to foam with sugar, blended with white wine and whisked in water bath until the concoction is thick and foamy without allowing mixture to get too hot as the eggs would curdle. May be flavored with brandy, kirsch, rum etc. or lemon, orange, vanilla. Sabayon is also prepared with fortified wines such as Madeira, Port, Sherry, Malaga, Marsala or with fine Hock, Sauternes, Champagne etc. Sabayon is served cold in glasses as a sweet with sponge fingers, hot and cold as a sauce.

— **Frozen:** glacé: sabayon mixed with whipped cream, filled in mould, frozen and usually served, scooped out with a spoon dipped in hot water, in glasses chilled beforehand.

— **Frozen, Orange:** glacé à l'orange: prepared with orange juice and a little white wine, frozen and served in glasses with sponge fingers.

Sacher Torte: Austrian Chocolate Gateau: 8 oz. butter creamed with the same amount of sugar and a little vanilla, mixed gradually with 8 yolks and 7 oz. melted chocolate, 8 stiffly beaten eggs and 4 oz. flour folded in, filled in round mould and baked in moderate oven; when cold coated thinly with apricot and iced with chocolate fondant; always served with whipped cream. (Austrian)

Salade de fruits: see fruit salad.

Salambos: very short, rather thick eclairs, stuffed with vanilla pastry cream, top dipped in sugar cooked to the crack and besprinkled with chopped pistachios before the sugar gets cold.

Salzburger Nockerl: butter creamed with sugar and egg yolks, a little flour added, stiffly beaten egg whites folded in; pan with a high border greased with butter, bottom covered with milk, filled with the dough shaped like dumplings with two spoons, baked in oven; served covered with hot vanilla sauce or sauce served separately. (Austrian)

Sauces et sirops pour entremets: see sweet sauces.

Savarin: savarin dough filled in savarin mould, allowed to rise, baked, soaked while still hot in syrup, served hot or cold.

— **Cardinal:** cold savarin soaked in maraschino syrup, center filled with quarters or half poached and drained peaches; covered with thick strawberry purée, slivered almonds scattered on top.

— **Cédard:** soaked with orange syrup flavored with Curaçao; when cold cut carefully in vertical slices, slices coated with orange butter cream flavored with Curaçao, put back, savarin coated thinly with apricot jam and iced

Savarin

with Curaçao-flavored fondant; placed on round platter, center filled with orange sections macerated in Curaçao and sugar, garnished with Chantilly cream; Curaçao-sabayon served separately.

— **Chantilly:** cold savarin soaked with kirsch-flavored syrup, center filled high up with Chantilly cream.

— **Creole:** cold savarin soaked in rum-flavored syrup, coated with thick apricot jam, garnished with angelica leaves and glacé cherries; center filled with cold Condé rice (without yolks) mixed with a generous amount of diced bananas and blended with whipped cream, covered with thin pineapple slices glaced with thick apricot jam; cold apricot sauce flavored with rum served separately.

— **with Fruit:** aux fruits: soaked in kirsch-flavored syrup, served hot with fruit macedoine bound with thick kirsch-flavored apricot sauce filled in center.

— **Medicis:** cold savarin soaked in maraschino-flavored syrup, center filled with almond cream, garnished with Chantilly cream.

— **Montmorency:** hot savarin soaked in kirsch-flavored syrup, center filled with stoned cherries bound with thick kirsch-flavored apricot sauce; cherry syrup bound slightly with arrow-root served separately. May also be served cold.

— **Orange:** à l'orange: soaked in orange-flavored syrup, coated with thick Curaçao-flavored apricot jam; when cold center filled with orange cream, garnished with candied orange sections.

— **Peter the Great:** Pierre le Grand: soaked in kirsch-flavored syrup, allowed to cool, coated with thick apricot and covered with chopped almonds and pistachios, center filled high with Chantilly cream.

— **with Strawberries:** aux fraises: cold savarin soaked in vanilla syrup, center filled with Chantilly cream mixed with small strawberries macerated in maraschino and sugar.

Schwarzwälder Eierküchlein: Black Forest Pancakes: pancake batter flavored with kirsch, thin pancakes baked, filled with sugar creamed with butter, mixed with finely chopped cooked and drained sour cherries flavored with kirsch; rolled up, dusted with sugar, a little warm kirsch poured on top, served burning. (German)

— **Kirschtorte:** Black Forest Gateau: three round layers are needed: a thin base of short paste, a layer of genoise sponge and layer of chocolate sponge. Base coated with red currant jelly, chocolate sponge placed on top, covered with well drained cherries bound with kirsch-flavored whipped cream lightly thickened with gelatine, layer of genoise sponge on top, pressed down slightly and masked thickly with slightly thickened whipped cream blended with melted chocolate. Top and sides smoothed with a palette, gateau placed in frig for an hour, top decorated with whipped cream, stoned, well drained cherries and chocolate chips. (German)

Schlosserbuben: large prunes soaked in water, cooked in lemon-flavored syrup and allowed to cool; drained, stones removed and replaced by a peeled almond, dipped in frying batter prepared with white wine, deep fried, rolled in grated chocolate and served dusted with powder sugar. (Austrian)

Semelles: see shoe soles.

Semolina: F. Semoule; G. Griess: the gluten part of durum wheat ground more or less finely.

— **Loaf:** Pain de semoule: semolina cooked in sweet vanilla-flavored milk to light mush, mixed with vanilla cream and whipped cream, filled in mould and allowed to cool; served with fruit syrup.

— **Oriental Style:** à l'orientale: mould lined with jelly flavored with rose water, filled with semolina mixture, turned out, served bordered with syrup blended with pistachio purée.

— **Pudding:** Pouding au semoule: cooked in milk boiled up with a little butter, mixed with egg yolks, sugar, grated lemon peel and ground almonds, stiffly beaten egg whites folded in, filled in greased pudding mould, baked in water bath in oven; turned out, served with fruit, vanilla or chocolate sauce.

— **Soufflé:** cooked in milk, mixed with butter, sugar, egg yolks and vanilla or grated lemon peel, stiffly beaten egg whites folded in, filled in greased soufflé dish, baked; raspberry syrup served separately.

Sfogliatelle: strips or triangles of puff pastry filled with rum-flavored vanilla pastry cream blended with whipped cream or cottage cheese creamed and mixed with diced candied orange peel, vanilla, cinnamon and whipped cream, filled also with chocolate cream, jam etc. (Italian)

Sherbet: Sorbet: a rather liquid kind of ice made with fruit juice, syrup and lemon juice or syrup flavored with lemon juice and fortified wine or liqueur, mixed when frozen with a quarter of the amount Italian meringue mixture or whipped cream, served in glasses chilled beforehand. Sugar contents of sherbet: 15 deg. measured with the saccharometer.

— **Kirsch, Rum or Brandy:** syrup of 18 deg. mixed with enough spirits to bring sugar contents to 15 deg.

— **Pineapple:** à l'ananas: syrup of 22 degrees blended with pineapple, a little lemon juice and white wine, frozen and mixed with Italian meringue mixture.

— **Port:** au porto: juice of 2 lemons and 1 orange, 2 gills Port and enough syrup of 22 deg. to bring sugar contents of sherbet to 15 deg.

— **Strawberry:** strawberry juice seasoned with a little lemon juice, mixed with white wine and brought to 15 deg., frozen, mixed with Italian meringue mixture.

— **Woodruff:** à l'asperule: Moselle wine in which woodruff has been infused mixed with syrup of 22 deg. and a little lemon juice to 15 deg., frozen, mixed with Italian meringue mixture.

Shoe Soles: Semelles: **puff pastry rolled out on granulated sugar, cut out round and each piece rolled separately on sugar to longish shape, baked and caramelised.**

Shortbread or Cake: round cake made of short paste enriched with more than the usual amount of butter, flavored with vanilla or grated lemon peel.

Sirne Paska: Easter Cheese: very dry cottage cheese strained, creamed with butter, slightly sweetened, mixed with thick sour cream and flavored to taste; filled in a wooden or other mould lined with a mousseline cloth, covered with a lid of wood and pressed lightly to allow the moisture to escape for 24 hours, turned out and served chilled. Sirne Paska is usually filled in a wooden mould in which the Greek Orthodox cross has been carved. If not available, garnish with currants or raisins with the sign X (Christ is risen). (Russian)

Snow Eggs: Oeufs à la neige: stiffly beaten egg whites with sugar folded in, dropped with a spoon or piped round or oval on greased pan with high border and covered with hot, sweetened, vanilla-flavored milk, poached, taken out and strained, allowed to cool; served covered with cold vanilla sauce prepared with the milk.

— **Chocolate:** à la chocolat: served covered with cold chocolate sauce blended with whipped cream.

— **Nignon:** custard poached in border mould and turned out, center filled high with snow eggs prepared with grated chocolate in the meringue mixture, plain snow eggs placed on border; chocolate snow eggs coated with thick cold vanilla sauce and plain snow eggs with cold chocolate sauce; both sauces also served separately.

— **Raspberry:** à la framboise: served covered with slightly sweetened purée of raw raspberries.

Sorbet: see sherbet.

Soufflé: F. Soufflé; G. Auflauf: very light hot sweet filled in greased soufflé dish, baked in moderate oven; shortly before soufflé is done dusted with sugar and glazed. Basic recipes: 1. cream soufflé, proportions for 12 persons: 9 oz. sugar mixed with 2 whole eggs and 8 yolks, 8 oz. flour added, diluted with 1 quart of warm milk and cooked like pastry cream; when lightly cooled off 4 oz. butter added and 12 stiffly beaten egg whites folded in. 2. fruit soufflé, proportions for 10 persons: 18 oz. sugar cooked to the large crack, mixed with 15 oz. purée of the desired fruit, poured over 10 stiffly beaten egg whites and folded in lightly.

— **with Absinth:** à l'absinthe: flavored with absinth.

— **Aida:** orange flavor, mixed with salpicon of fruit soaked in Curaçao.

— **Almond:** aux amandes: basic recipe mixed with finely ground almonds, flavored with kirsch.

— **Apple:** de pommes: fruit mixture prepared with apple purée, flavored with kirsch.

— **Apricot:** d'abricots: fruit mixture prepared with apricot purée.

— **Banana:** de bananes: vanilla cream mixture with diced bananas macerated in kirsch beforehand.

— **Camargo:** $^1/_2$ hazelnut and $^1/_2$ tangerine cream mixture prepared with grated tangerine peel and juice instead of milk; sponge fingers soaked with Curaçao between the layers.

— **Cavalieri:** basic cream recipe mixed with banana slices macerated in kirsch beforehand.

— **Charterhouse:** à la chartreuse: vanilla mixture flavored strongly with Chartreuse liqueur.

Soufflé

— **Cherry:** aux cerises: basic recipe prepared with juice of sour cherries, mixed with stoned poached cherries, drained and macerated in kirsch beforhand.
— **Chocolate:** au chocolat: basic recipe with chocolate dissolved in the milk added.
— **Coffee:** au café: basic recipe prepared with strong coffee instead of milk.
— **Elisabeth:** vanilla mixture with diced macaroons, soaked with kirsch and maraschino, and crushed crystallized violets.
— **Florida:** vanilla mixed with apple purée, flavored with arrack.
— **Grand-Marnier:** basic mixture flavored with Grand-Marnier.
— **Harlequin:** à l'arlequin: soufflé dish filled $^1/_2$ with vanilla and $^1/_2$ with vanilla mixture with grated chocolate.
— **Idéal:** vanilla mixture with ground pralin and crushed macaroons soaked with noyaux liqueur.
— **Indian:** à l'indienne: vanilla mixture with diced candied ginger.
— **Javanese:** javanaise: basic mixture prepared with tea instead of milk, mixed with chopped pistachios.
— **Lemon:** au citron: basic mixture flavored with lemon juice and grated lemon peel.
— **Lucullus:** fruit or vanilla mixture filled in the opening of a savarin soaked with kirsch syrup; savarin surrounded with a greased paper to bake soufflé and taken off at serving.
— **Maltese:** maltaise: basic recipe prepared with the juice of blood oranges and flavored with Curaçao.
— **Mercedes:** basic recipe mixed with fruit salpicon soaked in kirsch and maraschino.
— **Milanese:** à la milanaise: basic recipe mixed with grated lemon peel and crushed macaroons soaked with maraschino.
— **Montmorency:** prepared like cherry soufflé, cherries macerated in cherry-brandy.
— **Northern Style:** à la nordique: vanilla mixture flavored with kümmel.
— **Orange:** basic cream recipe with grated orange peel and orange juice instead of milk.
— **Oriental** à l'orientale: 1. vanilla mixed with chopped pistachios;
2. mocha mixed with coarsely grated chocolate.
— **Orléans:** basic recipe mixed with diced finger biscuits, fruit and angelica salpicon flavored with peach-brandy and kirsch.
— **Palmyra:** vanilla mixture placed in soufflé dish alternately with sponge fingers soaked in anisette.
— **Paulette:** vanilla mixture with firm strawberry pulp; fresh strawberries served separately.
— **Persimmon:** de kaki: vanilla mixture with purée of ripe persimmons and lemon juice added.
— **Pineapple:** d'ananas: vanilla cream mixture with diced pineapple macerated in kirsch.
— **Rachel:** $^1/_2$ vanilla and $^1/_2$ pistachio mixture.
— **Raspberry:** de framboises: fruit mixture prepared with mashed raspberries.

Soufflé

— **Rothomago:** half filled with diced fruit macerated with kirsch, covered with vanilla mixture flavored with kirsch.

— **Rothschild:** 1. vanilla soufflé mixed with fruit salpicon macerated in Danzig Goldwasser, surrounded with strawberries at serving;
2. soufflé dish filled ⅓ with vanilla ice, topped with fruit salpicon macerated in kirsch, covered with vanilla soufflé mixture; soufflé dish placed on crushed ice, baked rapidly.

— **Royal:** à la royale: basic mixture with fruit salpicon and diced sponge fingers soaked with kirsch.

— **Sicilian:** sicilienne: orange soufflé mixed with ground pralin and diced oranges.

— **Skobeleff:** vanilla mixture with ground pralin, finger biscuits soaked in anisette and seeded red currants.

— **Strawberry:** aux fraises: fruit mixture with strawberry purée.

— **Tangerine:** à la mandarine: prepared like orange soufflé with tangerines.

— **Vanilla:** à la vanille: basic mixture flavored with vanilla.

— **Violet:** à la violette: vanilla mixture with crushed crystallized violets, garnished with crystallized violets.

Soufflé glacé: see ice soufflé.

Sponge Fingers: Finger Biscuits: Biscuits à la cuillière: egg yolks and sugar stirred to foam, egg whites stiffly beaten with sugar and sieved flour folded in, piped on waxed baking sheets, dredged with dry sugar, baked.

Spoom: prepared like iced punch but with the double amount of Italian meringue mixture.

Strawberry: F. Fraise; G. Erdbeere: fruit of small plants of various species growing wild and cultivated in moderate climes. The wild strawberry is much smaller but more fragrant than the cultivated sorts. Strawberries are available either fresh, canned or frozen all the year round.

— **Arlesian Style:** à l'arlésienne: tartlet half filled with vanilla ice mixed with fruit salpicon, topped with strawberries macerated in kirsch, covered with apricot sauce flavored with kirsch.

— **Baby's Dream:** Rêve de Bébé: pineapple scooped out, placed on base of genoise biscuit iced with fondant icing, filled alternately with small thin pineapple slices macerated in kirsch and wild strawberries macerated in pineapple juice and maraschino, Chantilly cream between the layers.

— **Barquettes:** boat-shaped mould lined with almond-short paste, baked empty, when cold filled with whipped cream blended with strawberry purée, small strawberries placed on top, coated with red currant jelly.

— **Bristol:** placed on vanilla ice, covered with purée of raw strawberries.

— **Cardinal:** served on vanilla ice, covered with raspberry purée, slivered almonds scattered on top.

or **cil:** macerated in sugar and orange juice, served
the red with Chantilly cream.

— **Cava** **Champagne:** au champagne: sugared, macerated in
mac pagne, served covered with champagne sorbet.

— **Ch ar tilly:** sugared, served chilled covered with Chantilly
st n.

Strawberry

— **Charterhouse Style:** à la chartreuse: border mould lined with wine jelly, filled with small strawberries and diced pineapple macerated in maraschino, sealed with wine jelly; when set turned out, center filled with Chantilly cream mixed with fruit salpicon.

— **Chilled:** rafraichies: macerated in sugar, kirsch and maraschino, served well chilled in crystal or glass dish.

— **Creole Style:** à la créole: half strawberries and half diced fresh pineapple macerated in kirsch and sugar, arranged on thin pineapple slices macerated in kirsch, covered lightly with kirsch syrup.

— **Femina:** large strawberries macerated in sugar and Grand-Marnier, served on orange ice.

— **Fritters:** Beignets aux fraises: small strawberries or wild strawberries macerated in sugar and kirsch, rolled in very thin pancake, cut in small pieces, dipped in frying batter, deep fried, served dusted with sugar.

— **Gourmand:** lid of a small melon cut off, seeds and filaments removed, filled with the diced flesh mixed with small garden and wild strawberries macerated in sugar and kirsch, lid replaced into position.

— **Lacroix:** macerated in Grand-Marnier and cognac, arranged on almond ice, covered with orange sabayon, crushed crystallized violets scattered on top.

— **Margarite:** Marguerite: wild strawberries macerated in kirsch and maraschino, mixed with pomegranate sorbet, filled in chilled glass or timbale dish, covered and decorated with maraschino-flavored whipped cream.

— **Marquise:** macerated in kirsch and rolled in coarse sugar, served in bowl on whipped cream blended with strawberry purée.

— **Melba:** served on vanilla ice, covered with raspberry purée.

— **with Meringue:** meringués: macerated in maraschino, mixed with meringue mixture, filled cupola-shaped in baking dish, powdered with icing-sugar- browned in oven.

— **Modern Style:** à la moderne: fancy mould lined with champagne jelly, filled with strawberry Bavarian cream; when set turned out and served bordered with strawberries macerated in maraschino.

— **Monte Carlo:** macerated in sugar with brandy and Benédictine, served covered with Chantilly cream.

— **Nina:** macerated in kirsch and maraschino, served on pineapple ice, covered with whipped cream blended with strawberry purée.

— **Ninon:** vanilla ice filled in timbale dish with a cavity left open in the center, cavity filled with sugared wild strawberries covered with raspberry purée, chopped pistachios scattered on top, strawberries bordered with small thin pineapple slices.

— **Parisian Style:** macerated in sugar, lemon juice and maraschino, served covered with whipped cream blended with strawberry purée.

— **Patti:** macerated in kirsch, served on chocolate ice, covered and decorated with Chantilly cream.

Strawberry

— **Pharao:** tartlet of almond short paste half filled with strawberry ice, covered with Chantilly cream, small strawberries macerated in kirsch and maraschino arranged on top.

— **in Red Wine:** au vin rouge: small strawberries, sugared, served covered with Burgundy cool but not chilled.

— **Renaissance:** macerated in sugar and kümmel, arranged on pinapple ice mousse, covered with English sauce flavored with kirsch, decorated with Chantilly cream.

— **Ritz:** sugared, served covered with whipped cream mixed with half wild strawberry and half raspberry purée.

— **Roman Style:** à la romaine: small strawberries macerated in sugar, lemon juice and Curaçao.

— **Romanoff:** 1. macerated in Port, filled in high goblet, covered with whipped cream, a strawberry in the center; 2. macerated in Curaçao, filled in high goblet with Chantilly cream on top.

— **Sarah Bernhardt:** macerated in cognac and Curaçao, placed on pineapple ice, covered with strawberry purée mixed with whipped cream and flavored with Curaçao.

— **Shortcake:** round sponge cake topped with sugared strawberries, covered thickly with Chantilly cream, cut into portions at serving.

— **Supreme of:** Suprême de fraises: border mould lined with strawberry Bavarian cream, filled with small strawberries macerated in kirsch, sealed with strawberry cream; when set turned out, center filled with Chantilly cream and decorated with strawberries.

— **Tart:** Tarte aux fraises: flan mould lined with puff pastry or puff pastry remnants, baked empty to a light color, filled with strawberries lightly crushed and blended with meringue mixture, dusted with icing sugar, browned in oven.

— **Tivoli of:** Tivolis aux fraises: fancy mould lined with kirsch-flavored jelly, filled with Bavarian cream mixed with strawberry purée; when set turned out and garnished with diced kirsch jelly.

— **Victoria:** wild strawberries covered with hot Curaçao-flavored syrup, allowed to cool, served in glass covered with Chantilly cream mixed with diced pineapple.

— **Wilhelma:** soaked in orange juice, and kirsch, served in glass covered with Chantilly cream, decorated with a glacé cherry.

— **Zelma Kuntz:** sugared, chilled, served in timbale dish covered with whipped cream blended with raspberry purée, hazelnut pralin scattered on top.

Streuselkuchen: fermented yeast dough rolled out thin, placed on greased baking sheet, covered generously with melted butter mixed with flour, sugar and a little cinnamon, rubbed by hand into very small lumps, allowed to rise, baked. (German)

Strudel: Austrian speciality made of strudel dough drawn out by hand on a floured table cloth as thin as a sheet of paper, apple or other filling placed on top, rolled up like a long Swiss roll, brushed with butter, baked slowly on greased baking dish, served hot or cold dusted with powder sugar. Strudel dough is made similar to noodle

Strudel
dough with flour, pinch of salt, an egg, a tablespoon of oil or lard, a few drops of vinegar and lukewarm water, worked well, covered and allowed to rest at least 1 hour before drawing out.

— **Apfel:** apple: dough drawn out thin, finely sliced apples, croûtons fried in butter, a few currant, sultanas and chopped almonds scattered on top, besprinkled with granulated sugar and a little cinnamon, rolled up, brushed generously with butter, baked in moderate oven; served hot or cold with whipped cream. (Austrian)

— **Kirschen:** Cherry: made like apple strudel with stoned cherries with more croûtons scattered on the dough to soak up the cherry juice, sugar and grated lemon peel. (Austrian)

— **Mohn:** Poppy: crushed black poppy seeds pounded in mortar, mixed with sugar and red wine, allowed to soak for an hour, melted butter, egg yolks, a little honey and apricot jam, grated lemon peel, chopped raisins and vanilla added; strudel dough spread with this mixture, rolled up and baked like apple strudel. (Austrian)

— **Nuss:** Hazelnut: butter creamed with eggs, sugar and ground hazelnuts, flavored with cinnamon, spread thin on the strudel dough, rolled up, baked, served cold. (Austrian)

— **Topfen:** Cottage Cheese: cottage cheese, strained, creamed with egg yolks, sugar and vanilla, stiffly beaten egg whites folded in, spread on the strudel dough and prepared like apple strudel. (Austrian)

Suédoise de fruits: see jelly, Swedish.

— **de pommes:** see Swedish apple jelly.

Swedish Apple Jelly: Suédoise de pommes: mould lined with apple jelly, filled alternately with small cold apple balls cut out with a vegetable borer, one part poached in syrup flavored with kirsch and the other part in raspberry syrup and well strained, sealed with apple jelly, allowed to set, turned out.

— **Macedoine:** Macédoine à la suédoise: fresh fruit of all kinds, diced, macerated in Swedish Punch — or if not available in kirsch and maraschino —, chilled, filled in high glasses, covered with fresh cream.

Swiss Roll: Roulade: sponge mixture spread thin on greased and floured paper on baking sheet, baked, removed from sheet at once, filled immediately with jam or butter cream, rolled together, dusted with powder sugar or coated with fondant icing of different colors and tastes, cut in suitable pieces.

T

Tailli Kataif: noodles cooked in sweetened milk, served covered with raisin syrup. (Turkish)

Tangerine: F. Mandarine; G. Mandarine: small citrus fruit of the orange family with a loose very fragrant peel and a sweet and mild flavor. Chiefly marketed fresh.

— **Almina:** lid cut off, hollowed out, filled with Bavarian cream prepared with the fruit juice, flavored with kirsch and mixed with crushed crystallized violets; rosette of Chantilly cream and crushed violets on top

Tangerine

— **Côte d'Azur:** cut open like a small basket, hollowed out, filled with fruit macédoine with a generous amount of tangerine macerated in Curaçao, covered with tangerine ice.

— **Frosted:** givrée: lid cut off, hollowed out, filled with tangerine ice cream, lid replaced, besprinkled lightly with water, placed in deep freezer just until the fruit is lightly frosted outside.

— **Norwegian Style:** à la norvégienne: lid cut off, hollowed out, filled with tangerine ice, covered and decorated with rum-flavored meringue mixture, dusted with sugar, placed on raw ice, browned rapidly in oven.

— **Portuguese Style:** à la portugaise: lid cut off, hollowed out, filled with Condé rice without yolks flavored with tangerine juice, mixed with tangerine fillets and blended with whipped cream; garnished with tangerine fillets, glazed with tangerine jelly.

— **Surprise:** en surprise: lid cut off, hollowed out, filled with tangerine-flavored soufflé mixture, baked and served at once.

— **Swedish Style:** à la suédoise: lid cut off, hollowed out, filled with tangerine-flavored Bavarian cream, lid replaced with imitation leaves made of greencolored marzipan.

Tarte meringuée: see meringue tart.

Tartelette: see tartlet.

Tartlet: F. Tartelette; Gr. Törtchen: fruit tartlets are a great favorite for dessert. Plain or fluted, flat or high tartlet moulds lined with short, almond or puff pastry and baked empty, filled with cream, fruit or both, usually coated with thick strained apricot jam or some kind of jelly. Fruit barquettes or boats filled with fruit are made the same way in boat moulds.

— **Apple:** aux pommes: diced apples cooked in butter, bound with pastry cream, filled in short paste tartlet, covered with round poached apple slice, coated with apricot jam.

— **Apple, French:** aux pommes à la française: mould lined with puff pastry remnants, baked very lightly, filled with thick apple purée, covered symmetrically with very thin apple slices, baked; coated while still hot with strained apricot jam.

— **Apple, Russian:** aux pommes à la russe: short paste tartlet baked empty, filled with thick apple purée flavored with kummel, a small round slice of pinapple placed on top, coated with apricot jam.

— **Apricot:** à l'abricot: tartlet shells baked empty, brushed inside with couverture, bottom masked with vanilla cream, three small half apricots, peeled, poached in vanilla syrup and well drained, placed on top, coated with wine jelly or apricot, chopped almonds scattered in the center.

— **Cherry and Banana:** de cerises et banane: short paste tartlets filled with stoned stewed cherries bound with the thickened syrup, a crown of thin banana slices placed on top, covered with apricot jam.

— **Cottage Cheese and Strawberry:** cottage cheese creamed with sugar, egg yolks and vanilla, blended with whipped cream a little melted gelatine and small strawberries, filled in high fluted tartlet moulds and allowed to set; garnished with Chantilly cream.

Tartlet

— **Fruit:** short pastry tartlets filled with small fruit macedoine bound with thick apricot jam, a rosette of Chantilly cream in center, edges bordered with chopped pistachios.

— **Grape:** aux raisins: puff pastry tartlet baked empty, bottom masked with pastry cream, filled with peeled and seeded grapes mixed with meringue mixture, dusted with powder sugar, browned in oven.

— **Nut:** noisette: mould lined with short pastry, bottom of mould masked with jam, filled with paste made of ground hazelnuts mixed with sugar, very little flour and water, stiffly beaten egg whites folded in, flavored with vanilla or kirsch, dusted with sugar, baked.

— **Orange:** short pastry tartlets masked with a little orange cream, filled with diced oranges without pith, skin or pips, bound with orange syrup thickened with cornstarch, an orange section placed on top, glazed with orange syrup, chopped almonds scattered around the edge.

— **Pineapple:** à l'ananas: short pastry tartlets filled with poached diced pineapple bound with thick apricot jam, decorated with Chantilly cream.

— **Strawberry:** aux fraises: 1. short pastry tartlets filled with very small strawberries dusted with sugar, garnished with Chantilly cream;
2. short pastry tartlet filled with meringue mixture blended with small strawberries, dusted with sugar, browned in oven, served cold;
3. high fluted tartlet mould lined with almond short pastry, filled with butter creamed with egg yolks, sugar and ground almonds, flavored with vanilla, mixed with large cubes of strawberries and baked; when cold glazed with kirsch-flavored fondant.

Thousand Leaves Cake: see cream slice.

Timbale: genoise, brioche, baba or other dough baked in a round or half-conical tin mould, hollowed out and filled, or mould lined with short or other paste, baked empty and filled when cold.

— **d'Aremberg:** charlotte mould lined with rather firm brioche dough, filled with quartered pears poached in vanilly syrup alternated with apricot jam, closed with brioche dough with a little hole in the center to allow the steam to escape; baked in moderate oven, turned out and served covered with maraschino-flavored apricot sauce.

— **Bourdalou:** timbale mould lined with almond short paste, filled alternately with fruit macedoine and frangipane cream, closed with short pastry and baked in moderate oven; turned out and served covered with vanilla-flavored apricot syrup.

— **Chantilly:** Savarin dough baked in charlotte mould, when cold hollowed out, soaked with kirsch syrup, filled alternately with Chantilly cream and fruit macedoine, decorated with Chantilly cream.

— **Condé:** charlotte mould lined with short pastry and baked empty; filled alternately with vanilla rice blended with whipped cream and half stewed apricots, when set turned out and served covered with apricot sauce.

Timbale

— **Duchess:** rather flat round timbale made of short pastry, filled with diced poached apples mixed with raisins and bound with thick kirsch-flavored apricot sauce.

— **Louis Napoleon:** brioche dough baked in charlotte mould, hollowed out carefully, filled with fruit macedoine bound with thick apricot sauce, coated and decorated with meringue mixture, dusted with powder sugar, browned in oven.

— **Marie Louise:** stale genoise baked in timbale mould, hollowed out in one piece and cut in slices, each slice masked with Italian meringue mixture with salpicon of peaches, cherries and pineapple scattered on top, replaced; genoise masked and decorated with Italian meringue mixture, a turban of half peaches placed on top with dots of meringue mixture in between, browned in slow oven; kirsch-flavored peach sauce served separately.

— **Parisian:** à la parisienne: brioche dough baked in charlotte mould, allowed to cool and scooped out; filled with peeled and quartered pears and apples, halved peaches and apricots poached in vanilla syrup, pineapple cut in cubes, lozenge-shaped angelica, seeded and peeled grapes and raisins soaked in lukewarm water bound with kirsch flavored apricot purée.

— **Sicilian:** à la sicilienne: brioche dough baked in charlotte mould, when cold hollowed out and brushed inside with strained apricot jam; filled with orange fillets, lemon jelly poured over just before it begins to set, decorated with orange fillets.

Topfengolatschen: puff pastry rolled out thin, cut in squares, center filled with butter creamed with sugar, cottage cheese, eggs, vanilla and grated lemon peel, a few currants added; ends folded over on top, brushed with egg, baked. (Austrian)

Topfenknödel: butter creamed with sugar, whole eggs and cottage cheese, a pinch of salt and very little flour added, shaped into dumplings, poached in boiling lightly salted water; drained, covered with breadcrumbs browned in a generous amount of butter; plum compote served separately. (Austrian)

Topfenpalatschinken: Cottage Cheese Pancakes: large thin pancakes filled with a mixture of strained cottage cheese creamed with sugar, egg yolks and grated lemon peel, mixed with currants, stiffly beaten egg whites folded in, rolled, cut in pieces, filled in greased soufflé dish, covered with sweet custard (royal) and baked; shortly before they are done dusted with powder sugar and glazed. (Hungarian)

Trifle: sponge cake sliced, spread with raspberry jam, placed in glass dish, soaked lightly with Sherry, covered with fruit salad and jelly made with the fruit juice, as soon as it begins to thicken, coated with thick custard, decorated generously with whipped cream and garnished with glacé or fresh fruit. (English)

V

Vacherin: small round base of meringue mixture piped in consecutive circles on greased and floured baking sheet with a ring piped with round tube on the edge, and a second circle with a round edge, filled with piped lattice

Vacherin
work, both only large enough for one portion, dried rather than baked in oven. Bottom base filled with whipped cream or ice, covered with the second circle, garnished with whipped cream, fruit, chocolate chips etc.
— **Berolina:** filled with whipped cream blended with raspberry purée, garnished with whipped cream with lattice work piped with red currant jelly and hippen leaves.
— **Chantilly:** filled with Chantilly cream, garnished with Chantilly cream, angelica leaves and glacé cherries.
— **Iced:** glacé: filled with ice cream, garnished with Chantilly cream.
— **Nignon:** base filled with whipped cream flavored with kirsch, mixed with grated chocolate and crushed glacé chestnuts; garnished with Chantilly cream, a glacé chestnut and chocolate chips.

Vol-au-vent aux fruits: see puff pastry patty with fruit.

W

Wariniki Mallorussiski: noodle dough rolled out thin, cut in squares or round with a cutter, center filled with butter creamed with egg yolks, sugar, strained cottage cheese and grated lemon peel, edges moistened with water, a second layer of noodle dough placed on top and the edges pressed on firmly; cooked in salt water, drained, covered with sugar and melted butter, sour cream served separately. (Russian)

Wiener Krapfen: Viennese Doughnuts: rich fermented dough made of flour, eggs, butter, yeast, milk, grated lemon peel and sugar, rolled out thin, cut out round with a cutter, filled with apricot, raspberry or pineapple jam, covered with a second round of dough and allowed to rise; fried in deep fat — not too many at the same time, or they will not be able to rise properly — and turned two or three times; when done dusted with icing sugar. (Austrian)

Z

Zabaglione: see sabayon.

Zwetschenknödel: Plum Dumplings: plain fermented dough rolled out thin, cut in squares, filled with a plum the stone of which has been replaced by a lump of sugar; the ends of dough folded over on top and closed, allowed to rise, cooked in slightly salted water and well drained; served covered with breadcrumbs browned in a generous amount of butter and sugar. (Austrian)

Sweet Sauces and Syrups

Sauces et syrups pour entremets: foundation of sweet sauces for hot or cold desserts are either light vanilla cream (English sauce), fruit jam, marmelade, syrup or a sabayon (q. v.). Syrups are usually slightly thickened with corn starch and may be flavored with spirits or liqueurs.

Almond Milk: au lait d'amandes: ground sweet and a few bitter almonds pounded in mortar with a little syrup, pressed out in a cloth, prepared like English sauce or mixed with syrup slightly thickened with rice starch, flavored with orange blossom water.

Apricot: abricot: dried or fresh apricots cooked with very little water, rubbed through a sieve, boiled up with slightly thickened syrup flavored with vanilla, strained.

— **Syrup:** Sirop d'abricots: purée of raw, very ripe apricots blended with thickened syrup to which one or two crushed almonds have been added before straining.

Arrack: apricot sauce flavored with arrack.

Brandy: syrup of 15 deg. thickened with arrow-root or English sauce flavored with brandy.

Caramel: made like English sauce with the sugar burnt to caramel or thickened syrup mixed with caramel. boiled up with a little cream and butter.

Cherry: aux cerises: cherries cooked as compote, rubbed through a sieve, mixed with the reduced syrup and the same amount of red currant jelly, flavored with kirsch.

Chocolate: au chocolat: chocolate dissolved with water, a little vanilla sugar added, cooked, finished off before serving with cream and a small piece of butter.

English: Crème ou Sauce à l'anglaise: custard made of powder sugar stirred with egg yolks, cooked in double boiler or beaten in water bath with scalded milk flavored with vanilla or lemon zest until it begins to thicken, strained, used hot or cold.

Hard: butter creamed with sugar, a little cream added, flavored generously with brandy. Hard sauce is served chiefly for plum or similar puddings.

Orange: strained orange marmelade mixed with orange syrup, flavored with Curaçao.

— **Syrup:** Sirop d'orange: plain syrup flavored with orange and lemon peel, slightly thickened, blended with orange juice.

Praliné: English sauce mixed with very finely ground pralin and a little vanilla sugar.

Raspberry: aux framboises: prepared like cherry or strawberry sauce.

Red Currant: aux groseilles: dissolved red currant jelly mixed with a little syrup, thickened very lightly with arrow-root, flavored with kirsch.

Richelieu: vanilla syrup thickened with arrow-root, flavored with kirsch, mixed with julienne of cherries.

Strawberry: strawberry jam rubbed through a sieve, mixed with syrup, flavored with kirsch.

— **Syrup:** Sirop de fraises: syrup mixed with raw strawberry purée, thickened, strained; may be flavored with a little kirsch.

Syrup: sirop: simple syrup is ordinary sugar boiled up with water measuring about 15 to 18 deg read on the saccharometer. For desserts it is slightly thickened with arrow-root or cornstarch, boiled up, strained, mixed with pure fruit juice or flavored with spirits or liqueurs. Commercial fruit syrups are the juice of fresh fruit heavily sweetened and concentrated.

Vanilla: vanille: same as English sauce.

Wine: see sabayon.

The Bill of Fare

The bill of fare or menu; F. Carte, carte du jour, menu; G. Speisekarte, Tageskarte, Menü, is a list of the dishes served at a meal. There are two different sorts of bills of fare:

1. The standard or à la carte bill of fare — Carte du jour —, a complete list of all food served, showing the price of each dish;
2. The fixed price or "table d'hôte" bill of fare — Menu à prix-fixe —, a selection of foods for a complete meal, either breakfast, luncheon or dinner sold at a fixed price. The price of banquets or parties are usually calculated separately as the case may warrant.

The word "menu" is derived from the French "minute" and means small, a small list, but in commercial places the list of dishes is very seldom small, they seem to have a tendency to get longer and longer every day. But large menus are expensive and wasteful; they necessitate a large supply of food, a large brigade of cooks to prepare it, and result in over production, leftovers are not to be avoided and cannot always be used up in a rational way.

The object of restaurant menus is to attract the attention of prospective customers. The standard bill of fare should, therefore, show a selection of seasonal food, a variety of dishes featured in the gastronomical order showing prices plainly, as prices are noticed by guests first. Some restaurants have specialities which are repeated nearly every day, while others change their bill of fare daily. The bills of fare of the very best restaurants in Europe are usually very small, the seasonable dishes and specialities are listed on a special carte du jour.

It goes without saying that all English and foreign names must be spelled correctly. Unnecessary adjectives, embellishments and foreign language terms should be avoided as far as possible. Garnishes and culinary terms not generally known must be explained. Above all it must not be fortgotten that a bill of fare is not a catalogue, and that a great number of dishes of the same category exasperate the guest who ist not able to find what he wants.

Every bill of fare is the visiting card of the house It must be printed on fine paper with a cover that is not easily soiled. The lay-out displaying specialities and the type used for printing are of the same importance as visibility for quick reading. Taste, originality and new ideas in the make-up and illustration of the bill of fare are characteristics that ought to be observed.

The custom of naming dishes is very old and was known already in Roman times. Although it is difficult to trace the origin of all terms, many dishes plainly point to countries, cities and trades, while others are named in honor of

historical or other more or less famous persons. Regional dishes are also well represented on the bill of fare, emperors, kings and princes are especially numerous.

Menu-making is an art. The chef who is responsible for setting up the bill of fare must not only be an experienced cook, he ought also be a good salesman, able to calculate the price of food correctly so as to realize a fair margin of profit. He must also have a good knowledge of the science and developement of nutrition and to be able to fix the caloric values as well as the vitamin and mineral contents of food.

The selection of food for a banquet or dinner party must be especially well studied. General rules are:

1. No kind of food, whether fish, meat, poultry, game, vegetables or fruit should appear twice on the same menu. If, for instance, a cream of chicken is served as a soup, chicken must not be served as a main dish.
2. Color of food must change. White meat must not be served after a white fish.
3. The serving of similar sauces must be avoided. If a sauce Béarnaise is served with the meat, Dutch sauce (Hollandaise) must be avoided for fish or vegetables.
4. Never serve two courses fried in deep fat in one menu, such as a fried fish and potato croquettes as a garnish or fritters as a sweet.
5. If a thick white soup is served it may be followed by a white fish if the fish is breadcrumbed and fried, grilled or served with a red wine or other dark sauce. After a thick chicken soup only meat or game are permitted as a main dish.
6. If a combined fruit salad is served with the main dish, fruit must be avoided as a sweet; candied fruit in ice or creams is not considered as fruit.
7. Generous vegetable garnishes for the main dish ought to be served separately on a dish. A tenderloin "jardinière or bouquetière" looks wonderful when presented to the guests, but after the third guest has been served it is usually a sad sight. Besides that vegetables can be served much hotter and quicker if arranged on a separate platter.

During the middle ages a banquet was a very lavish affair and an endless number of dishes were placed on the table. Up to the end of the nineteenth century the so-called classical menu was de rigueur at all official banquets. A classical menu comprized at least twelve courses, viz.:

Cold side dishes	**Hors-d'oeuvre froid**
Soup	Potage
Hot side dishes	**Hors-d'oeuvre chaud ou** Entrée volante
Fish	Poisson
Main dish or remove	Relevé ou Pièce de résistance
Hot Entrée	Entrée chaude
Cold Entrée	Entrée froide
Sherbet	Sorbet
Roast, Salad	Rôti, salade
Vegetable	Légume

Hot Sweet	Entremet de douceur chaud
Cold Sweet or Ice	Entremet de douceur froid ou glace
Cheese	Fromage
Dessert	Dessert

Shortly before the first world war these menus were greatly curtailed, and it was not usual to serve more then

Hors-d'oeuvre
Soup
Fish or Shellfish
Main dish
Hot or cold entrée
Sherbet
Roast, salad
Vegetable
Hot Sweet
Cold Sweet or ice
Dessert

Apart from food shortage, the science of nutrition has made tremendous progress between and after the world wars, so that people have accustomed themselves to eating much less than before. Banquets or dinner parties of more than seven courses at the upmost are seldom served, five courses being practically the rule. A banquet or dinner party nowadays comprizes:

Hors-d'oeuvre	Iced melon, caviar, oysters, smoked salmon or gooseliver patty etc. but no mixed side dishes or appetizers.
Soup	Consommé or very light thick soup
Fish	which may be replaced by a hot dish of shellfish
Main dish	either meat, poultry or game served with vegetables and a suitable salad
Light sweet or ice	a combination of ice cream and fresh fruit is a great favorite
Cheese and dessert	or only dessert

Instead of the hors d'oeuvre a cold entrée such as lobster en bellevue or a gooseliver parfait or patty may be served after the main dish, shellfish only if it has not been served for the fish course. Vegetables are nearly always served with the main dish, except when they replace another course. What a tremendous quantity of food was eaten formerly is shown by the following historical menus:

BANCQUET
du Roy de France Charles V.
et du Jehan de Lorraine

ES PREMIER MESTZ:
Venoison de sanglier en souppes
Sabouret de poussin
Boussac de lièvres Oyes a la trayson

SECOND MESTZ:
Cines Hayroos Heron Faisons
Paons Trimolecte de perdrix

TIERS MESTZ:
Most Jehan Paste de merles
Pysons au sucre

LE QUART MESTZ:
Darioles de çresme fricts
Paste de poyres

QUINT MESTZ:
Amendes nosilles Poyres crues
Jonchees

This Banquet was served to the king about 1373, it was supervised by the royal master chef Taillevent, the first French chef of which we have any knowledge, who was also the author of one of the first cookery books "Le Viandier". The Sabourat on this menu was a sort of ragout, the Trimolecte a salmi of partridges, the Boussac some kind of jugged hare. Cines are swans and Paons peacock.
A royal banquet served at the court of Louis XVIII. on the 6 th of January 1820 comprized not less then 2 soups, 4 grosses pièces, 16 entrées, 4 other grosses pièces, 4 roasts, 16 entrements of vegetables, farinaceous dishes and sweets as well as 16 baskets with dessert. A family dinner given by his predecessor, Napoleon I., was much less lavish. Here the menu:

Aux Tuileries 1811
(Samedi saint)

2 Potages:
Au macaroni et à la purée de marrons

2 relevés:
Pièce de boeuf bouilli garnie aux legumes
Brochet à la Chambord

4 entrées:
Côtelettes de mouton à la Soubise
Perdreaux à la Montglas
Fricassée de poulets à la chevalier
Filets de canards au fumet

2 rôtis:
Chapon au cresson
Gigot d'agneau

2 plats de légumes:
Choux-fleurs au gratin
Céleri-navet au jus

4 entremets au sucre:
Crème au café
Gelée d'orange
Génoise décorée
Gaufres à l'allemande

This is almost a modern menu as chiefly only one dish of each course was eaten.
To show the difference between then and now, here is an example of a modern banquet:

The Dorchester, Park Lane, LONDON

MENU

La Goutte d'Or au Fumet de Cailles

*

La Mousseline de Coquilles St. Jacques «Centenaire»

*

La Coeur de Filet de Boeuf «Caterer and Hotelkeeper»
La Sauce Ratafia
Les Délices des Belles Forêts aux Herbes
Les Pommes de Jersey rissolées au Four

*

Les Asperges Tièdes
Le Beurre Fondu

*

Les Fromages d'Angleterre
Le Céleri Cru

*

La Crêpe Sans Rival
Le Rocher Vanille

*

Le Café
Mignardises

WINES

Perrier-Jouet Finest Quality (Reception)
Grand Brut

La Reina Verdelho

Eitelsbacher Marienholz Auslese 1971
Estate Bottled

Château Gruaud Larose St. Julien 1962

Beaune, Les Bressandes Tastevin Chanson 1967

Delamain Pale and Dry

*

Occasion: The **Caterer and Hotelkeeper** Centenary Dinner
Covers: 300
Date: 23rd March 1978
Managing Director: A. J. Ruault
Maître chef des cuisines: A. Mosimann

Table Service

For every catering establishment good organization is essential. Correct table service is of the greatest importance, as the art of the chef can easily be spoiled by mistakes or careless service. There are hard and fast rules that must be learned by every waiter or waitress. Catering establishments differentiating in size and class, the following directions are given for a first class house.

Restaurant Service

When a table is laid for four persons, for instance, two places are always laid opposite one another. The table cloth, protected by an underfelt, is laid with the central fold directly in the center of the table, so that it can fall down evenly on all sides. Cruets and the bill of fare are placed on the table for luncheon and dinner, the wine list is usually presented to the guest by the waiter. A service plate with a small knife and fork for the hors d'oeuvre, covered with a folded napkin, is set for each cover. On the left of the plate a large fork and a fish fork, and on the right a large knife, a fish knife and a soup spoon are laid. The dessert cutlery is placed on the top side of the plate, the fork with the tines pointing to the right inside and the spoon pointing in the opposite direction on the outside. If a dessert knife is necessary it is brought by the waiter later on. A bread plate with a butter knife is placed to the left of the service plate next to the fish fork. In some countries wine glasses are set, in others they are first placed on the table when wine is ordered by the guest. An ashtray on each table is obligatory and only removed at the guest's request.

Bread and butter is served with the hors-d'oeuvre, the waiter placing a pat of butter and a small roll on the bread plate. If French bread is offered, it is rolled partly in a napkin, the waiter cuts a piece off and offers it to the guest. After the hors d'oeuvre has been removed soup is served. The soup plate is always placed on a flat plate if the service plate has been taken away. If the soup is served in cups, the cup must stand on a saucer with the handle on the guest's left, the saucer placed on a dessert plate. The soup spoon is then replaced by a dessert spoon. The fish dish is shown to the guest first and then served on a plate from the serving table. Dishes can, of course, be handed around, so that the guest can serve himself, but this is only customary at banquets or dinner parties. When serving the main dish, the meat ist placed at the bottom of the plate close to the guest, covered lightly with sauce, potatoes and vegetables on one side. A plate should never be filled so full that the edge is covered with food, overfilled plates are unappetizing. It is better to serve a smaller portion and give a second helping. If salad is served at the same time, the plate is placed on the left side of the guest. In first class houses green salads are prepared by the waiter at the service table, asking the guest how he would like the dressing. After the sweet has been served — hot sweets on hot and cold sweets or ice on cold plates — but no cheese, butter plates and the cruet are removed and the table is wiped with a napkin to free it from crumbs. Used cutlery is, of course, removed with each course. An ashtray and matches are placed in front of each guest at the end of the meal. It goes without saying that food is always served from the left side of the guest and wine is poured into the glass from the right side. Floral decorations must be kept low, white flowers show off badly on a white table cloth.

Wine Service

Wine ought to be served by waiters qualified to do so. Every good waiter ought to have some knowledge of wine, how to serve it and of the right temperature for the different kinds of wine. In France a special waiter, the sommelier, is responsible for the wine service. First class wines are always opened in front of the guest. If the bottle has a tin foil, this is cut off first a little below the top of the neck before the bottle is opened with a cork screw. After the cork has been drawn out the opening is wiped with a clean napkin. The bottle is then presented to the guest who has ordered it with the label turned towards him, so that he can see if it is the right wine that he has ordered. A little wine is poured into the glass for him to taste. If it has found his approval, ladies — if there are any present — are served first and then the gentlemen; elder people are served before the younger ones. If a bottle of white wine or champagne is served in an ice bucket a napkin is placed around the bottle neck. Red wine served in a basket ought to have a napkin placed under the neck to prevent straining the table cloth. The bottles are always placed on the right side the guest who ordered them or on the serving table so that the waiter can refill the glasses.

Breakfast Service

Anglo-American Breakfast

An American breakfast usually consists of strong coffee and cream, chilled fruit juice, hot fresh toast, rolls or muffins and butter, jam or marmelade or honey. A number of dishes are served to the guests order, such as cereals with cream, an egg dish, Finnan Haddie or kippered herrings or other fried or grilled fish, broiled ham or bacon, a chop etc. Iced water is indispensible.

In England tea is mostly served, sometimes coffee or cocoa, marmelade, honey, hot fresh toast or rolls and butter, and to order porridge with cream and sugar separately, boiled or fried eggs, eggs and bacon or ham, haddock, kippers, fried sausages and tomatoes or bacon, a mutton chop or cold meat etc.

European Breakfast

This is much plainer than the Anglo-American breakfast. It consists of coffee and milk, tea or chocolate, different sorts of bread, rolls and rusks, butter, jam, honey, and to order a boiled or fried egg or other egg dish, cold meat or cheese.

Fruit juice is now often in demand and cereals are also getting popular.
Breakfast tables are usually laid the evening before without cups which are brought warmed up to the table with the order. A breakfast plate with a folded napkin on top is laid for each cover with a small knife on the right side, for the Anglo-American breakfast often a knife and spoon, sometimes a fish knife and fork and a jam spoon. The saucer is placed on the right side of the plate, when the cup is brought in it is placed on the saucer with the handle to the right and the spoon parallel to the handle. The tea or coffee pot is placed on the right a little higher than the cup and above this the cream and the water jug. Marmelade, jam or honey, butter, sugar and salt may be placed immediately behind the cover and rolls in the center of the table. Toast or griddle cakes are brought in fresh on demand, and hot breakfast dishes are best served directly on hot plates and not on a dish. After the breakfast plates have been removed, an ashtray is placed in front of the guests who would like to smoke.

Afternoon Tea

For afternoon tea the table is laid in the same way as for breakfast, often with a colored table cloth and napkins. Instead of bread and rolls sandwiches, cake and pastries are served. In this case a pastry fork is laid on the napkin. For toast and muffins and butter a small knife is also necessary. An ashtray is always placed on the tea table.

Banquet Service

As soon as the menu has been chosen and the date and the number of guests are fixed, arrangements can be made for setting the table. Special attention must be paid to suitable floral decorations. The shape of the table depends upon the size of the room, it may be T —, round, oval, horseshoe or block-shaped. For a banquet consisting for instance of hors d'oeuvre, clear soup, fish, a main dish with vegetables and salad, ice biscuit and coffee each cover is laid with a large service plate, a large knife and fork, a dessert spoon for the soup, fish and dessert knives and forks, a bread plate with a small knife, a water, a wine and a champagne glass. Formerly it was customary to place five glasses on the table at banquets, now the glasses are changed if more than one wine is served. Plates for the hors d'oeuvre are laid, cups for the soup and plates for the fish and the main dish are kept in the hot cupboard ready for use. A soup ladle, saucers for the soup, plates to place under the saucers and dessert plates are kept ready for use on a separate service table.
Cocktails or a glass of champagne are usually served in the lounge before the start of the banquet. If a fortified wine such as Port, Sherry or Madeira is served with an hors d'oeuvre, gooseliver patty or parfait for instance, southern wine glasses must be set.
At a wedding the service always starts from the center with the bridal couple, at banquets the most important guest is served first. The first course is served from right to left, the second from left to right. the other courses alternately. If ladies are present they ought to be served first, but this is

not customary everywhere. For a banquet service one waiter is usually alloted for eight persons and one wine waiter for twelve to sixteen persons. After the meal coffee and liqueurs are usually served at small tables in a separate lounge.

Cold Buffets

Cold buffets are arranged for receptions, weddings, dances and other festive occasions. They are set up on large special tables where the guests can choose what they want. An aperitif, a hot consommé in winter and a cold soup in summer are often served first. Guests can sit down at small tables after having chosen. Formerly guests used to help themselves but it is now usual for one or more cooks in immaculate white to serve the guests. Plates and cutlery are put at the cooks place. The cook takes the plate, fills it with the food selected by the guest and places a knife on the right and a fork on the left side of the plate. Plates and cutlery are always changed for dessert. It is, however, much more convenient, if the cutlery is arranged on the front side of the buffet table for the guests to take it themselves. Napkins, rolls, cruets and sugar are placed on a separate table next to the buffet.

American Meat Cuts

Beef Chart

Veal Chart

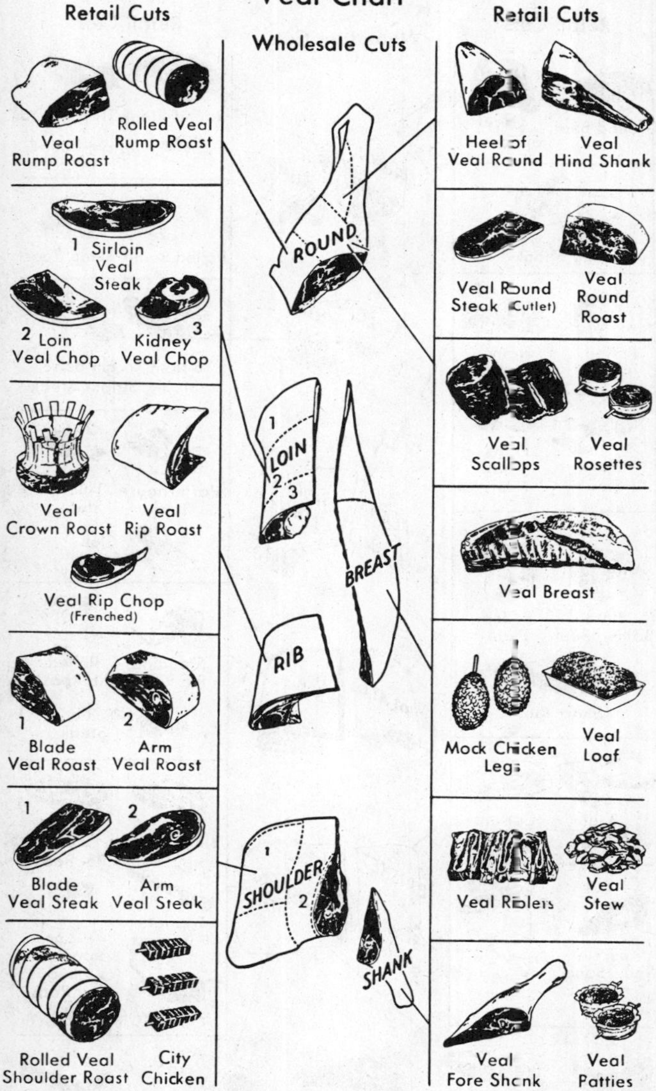

Retail Cuts
Wholesale Cuts
Retail Cuts
Veal Rump Roast
Rolled Veal Rump Roast
1 Sirloin Veal Steak
2 Loin Veal Chop
3 Kidney Veal Chop
Veal Crown Roast
Veal Rip Roast
Veal Rip Chop (Frenched)
1 Blade Veal Roast
2 Arm Veal Roast
1 Blade Veal Steak
2 Arm Veal Steak
Rolled Veal Shoulder Roast
City Chicken
ROUND
LOIN
RIB
BREAST
SHOULDER
SHANK
Heel of Veal Round
Veal Hind Shank
Veal Round Steak (Cutlet)
Veal Round Roast
Veal Scallops
Veal Rosettes
Veal Breast
Mock Chicken Legs
Veal Loaf
Veal Riblets
Veal Stew
Veal Fore Shank
Veal Patties

Lamb Chart

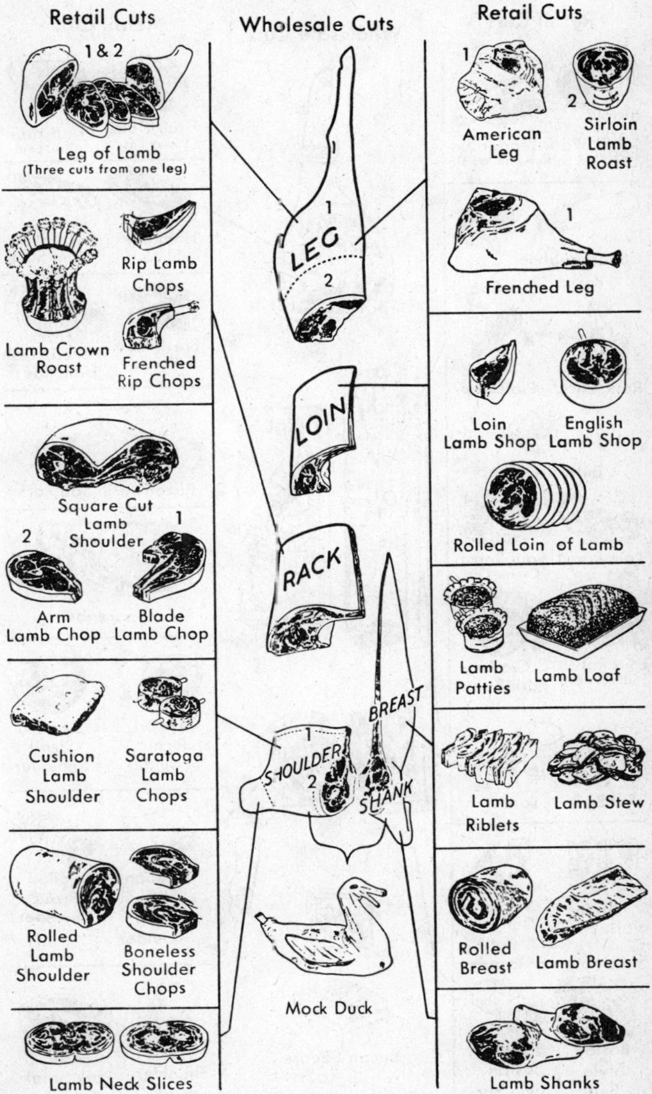

Retail Cuts
Wholesale Cuts
Retail Cuts
1 & 2
Leg of Lamb
(Three cuts from one leg)
Lamb Crown Roast
Rip Lamb Chops
Frenched Rip Chops
Square Cut Lamb Shoulder
2
1
Arm Lamb Chop
Blade Lamb Chop
Cushion Lamb Shoulder
Saratoga Lamb Chops
Rolled Lamb Shoulder
Boneless Shoulder Chops
Lamb Neck Slices
1
1
LEG
2
LOIN
RACK
BREAST
1
SHOULDER
2
SHANK
Mock Duck
1
American Leg
2
Sirloin Lamb Roast
1
Frenched Leg
Loin Lamb Shop
English Lamb Shop
Rolled Loin of Lamb
Lamb Patties
Lamb Loaf
Lamb Riblets
Lamb Stew
Rolled Breast
Lamb Breast
Lamb Shanks

Pork Chart

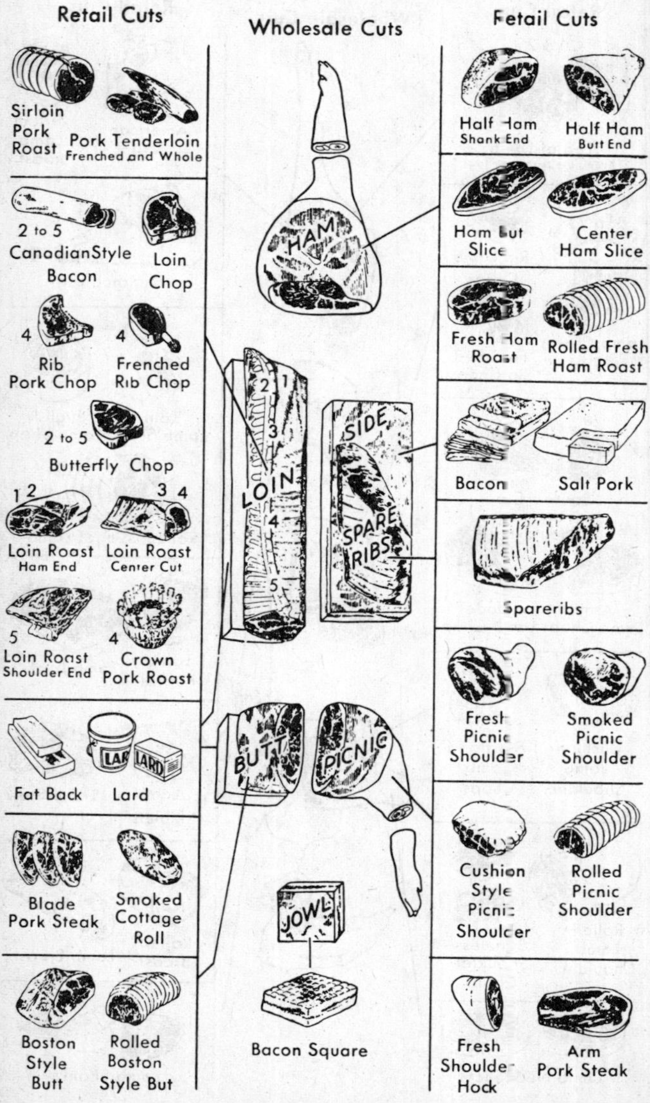
Retail Cuts
Wholesale Cuts
Retail Cuts
Sirloin Pork Roast
Pork Tenderloin
Frenched and Whole
2 to 5
Canadian Style Bacon
Loin Chop
4
Rib Pork Chop
4
Frenched Rib Chop
2 to 5
Butterfly Chop
1 2
3 4
Loin Roast
Ham End
Loin Roast
Center Cut
5
Loin Roast
Shoulder End
4
Crown Pork Roast
LARD
LARD
Fat Back
Lard
Blade Pork Steak
Smoked Cottage Roll
Boston Style Butt
Rolled Boston Style Butt
HAM
2
1
3
LOIN
4
5
SIDE
SPARE RIBS
BUTT
PICNIC
JOWL
Bacon Square
Half Ham
Shank End
Half Ham
Butt End
Ham Butt Slice
Center Ham Slice
Fresh Ham Roast
Rolled Fresh Ham Roast
Bacon
Salt Pork
Spareribs
Fresh Picnic Shoulder
Smoked Picnic Shoulder
Cushion Style Picnic Shoulder
Rolled Picnic Shoulder
Fresh Shoulder Hock
Arm Pork Steak

Carving

Carving is an ancient art, and it is well known that wealthy Romans already employed special carvers, the so-called scissores. During the middle ages carving was considered a fine art which every nobleman ought to understand as well as fencing, dancing and riding. At court the carver or ecuyer tranchant was usually a nobleman of ancient lineage. One of the first books on the art of carving is "Il Trinciante" by Vincenzio Cervio, that was published in Venice 1581.
Although this is not a textbook on carving, we believe that every accomplished waiter ought to have more than a smattering of carving, to be able to carve in front of the guest. Good carving requires practise, knowledge of the anatomy of the different joints and patience. For carving in front of the guest following utensils are needed:

1. A square or round carving board with a groove around the edge to prevent the juice from running over the table cloth;
2. Three knives: a long thin knife, the so-called tranchelard, a strong pointed knife about 8 in. long and an smaller sharp broad knife. A fish and a table knife are very useful and a carving steel, a carving and an ordinarv table fork are also necessary. Note that knives should never be sharpened before the guests in the dining room.
3. A hot-plate (rechaud), hot plates, a napkin and, if cold salmon is carved, a jug of hot water to dip in the knife.

In carving, slices should not be too large or too small. The knife must be guided with very light pressure, slices should have a smooth surface and must be equally thick everywhere.

Carving of Fish

Sole or other small flatfish, fried, grilled or poached: the small bones along the edge are removed first with help of a fish knife. The fish is then divided in half along the back.

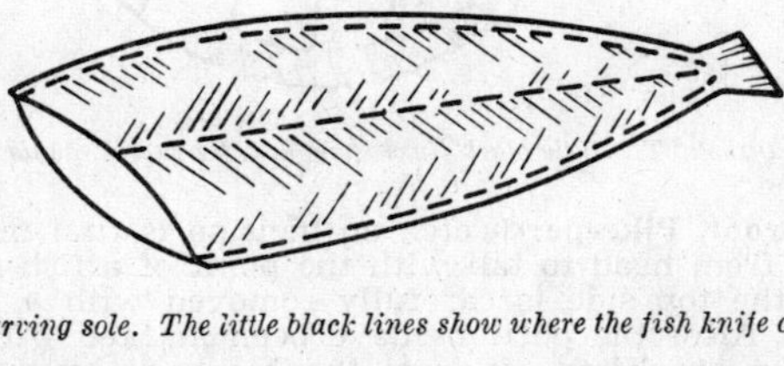

Carving sole. The little black lines show where the fish knife cuts

The two fillets are pushed sideways from the backbone with two forks, placed on a hot plate or silver dish and kept hot on the rechaud until the whole fish is carved. The backbone is lifted off with the head, the edge bones of the lower fillets removed and the two fillets are separated.

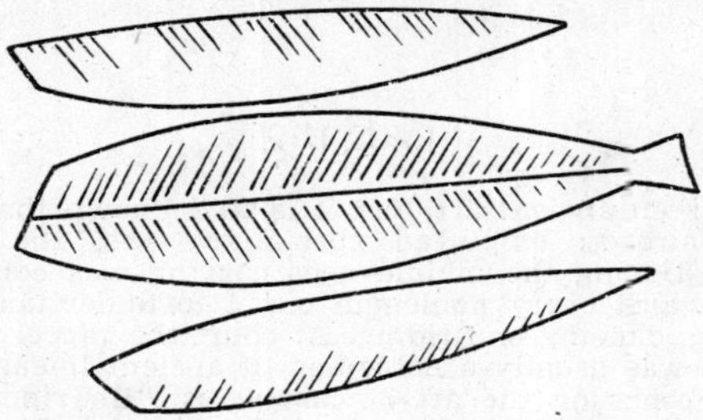

The fillets are pushed away from the backbone

Turbot or Brill: first of all the bones are removed from the edge. The fish is cut down the back with a sharp knife from head to tail. It is then carved, in the opposite direction, from the belly side into fairly thick slices, and these can be lifted off with a fish knife and fork or a flat fish ladle. The slices on the belly side should be cut larger because of the abdominal cavity. After the top side has been carved, the back bone is cut through at two or three places with a sharp knife and removed. The lower side of the fish is carved in the same way as the top side. The skin is always removed before the cuts are placed on hot plates.

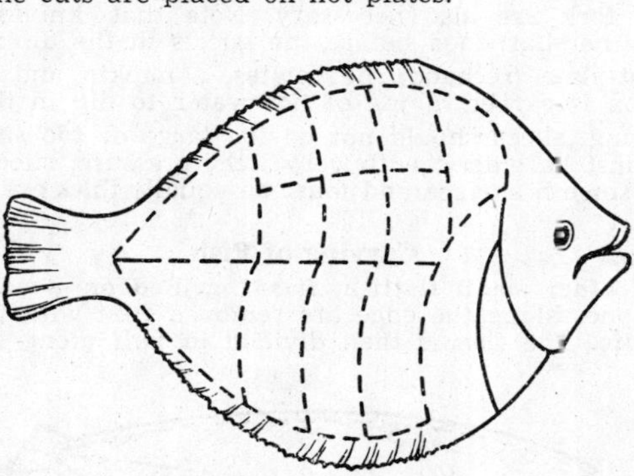

Carving turbot. The little black lines show how the turbot should be carved

Salmon-trout, Pike-perch etc.: an incision is first made along the back from head to tail with the point of a fish knife. The skin on the top side is carefully removed with a fish knife and fork. After the portions have been marked with a sharp knife, they are lifted off from the backbone by pushing the fish knife along the bone to loosen them, starting directly behind the head. Head and backbone are removed in the same way and the lower part divided into portions.
Salmon: broad incisions are first made with the point of a sharp knife from the middle of the back towards the belly.

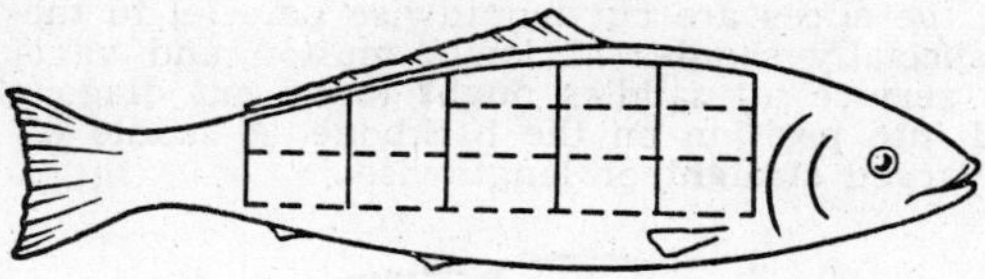

Salmon. The little black lines show the different cuts

With the point of the knife one or more lines are now drawn from head to tail and the skin is removed; the number of lines depends upon the size of the salmon, the difference between these lines and the incisions from the back towards the belly should show the size of each portion. The skin is removed from this side and the slices are cut off, starting either at the tail or head end. After one side has been carved, the other side is divided into portions in the same way. In carving cold salmon, cuts are smoother if the knife is dipped each time in a jug of hot water. The belly, being most difficult to carve into good portions, is not served in first class houses and is sent back to the kitchen to be used otherwise.

Lobster or Crawfish (spiny lobster): this is very easy to carve. The lobster is held down firmly by the head with a napkin and pierced vertically with a short strong knife from head to tail and cut with a levering motion. The shell is held down with a spoon, the meat lifted out with a fork and cut diagonally after the intestines have been removed. The claws are severed from the body beforehand, cracked open with a strong knife and the meat removed with a fork.

Carving of Meat

Saddle of veal, mutton or venison: an incision is made right and left of the centerbone right down to the backbone and with a slanting cut along the center and backbone the meat is lifted from the bones. It is carved in not too thin diagonal slices and placed at once on hot plates; for banquet service it ist replaced into position on the backbone. For saddles of mutton, lamb or venison the slices may also be cut straight.

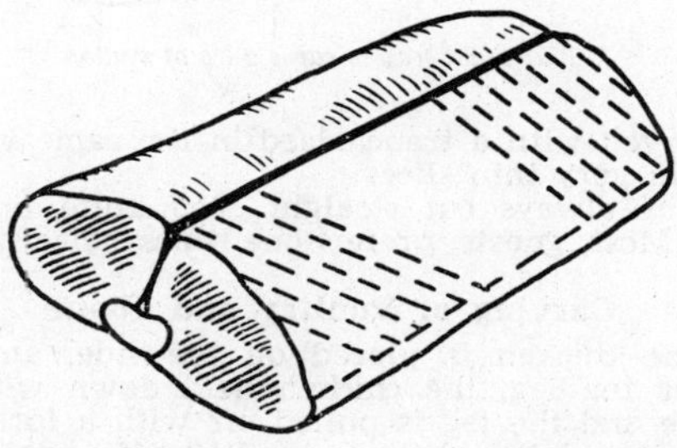

Carving saddles of veal, mutton or venison. The meat may be carved in diagonal or straight slices

American and English guests prefer the so called English cut, i. e. the slices are cut lengthwise parallel to the center-bone, especially saddles of lamb, mutton and venison. For banquet service all saddles ought to be cut diagonally and replaced into position on the backbone. A saddle of hare is always carved straight or lengthwise.

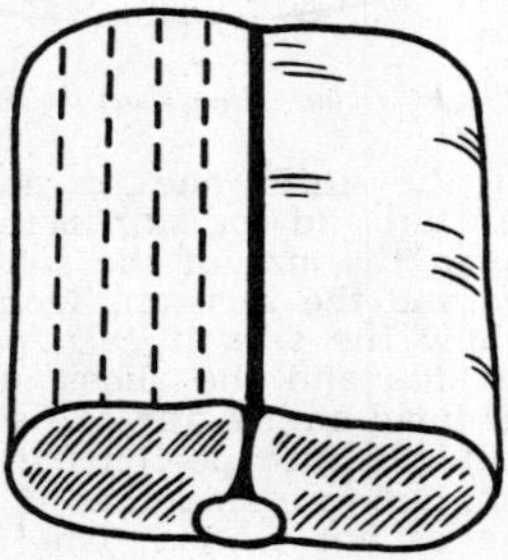

The so-called "English cut". The slices are carved parallel to the center-bone

Leg of mutton: first of all an incision is made at the knee cap and a few small slices are cut off against the bone being held with a napkin or a special holder. Long thin and somewhat slanting slices may then be easily cut as far as the bone, and after the top side has been carved, the leg is turned round and the other side carved in the same way. As a rule the carver cuts slices of equal size and thickness from right to left towards himself.

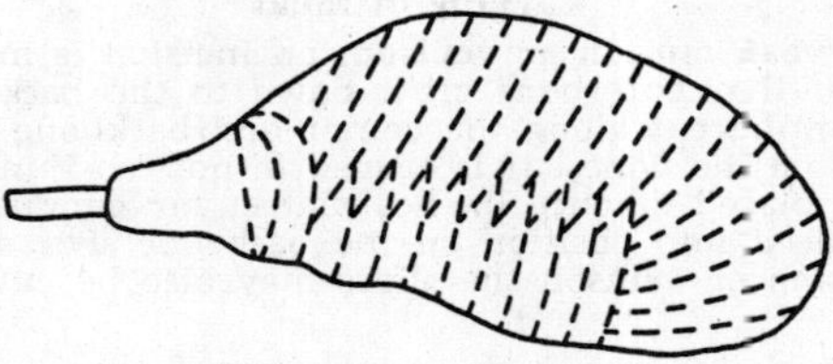

This is the way to carve a leg of mutton

Ham: is carved with a tranchelard in the same way as a leg of mutton in very thin slices.
Roastbeef: is always cut straight. The knife must be held vertically. Most guests prefer one thick slice to two thin ones.

Carving of Poultry and Game

Chicken: the chicken is placed on the side, an incision is made under the leg, the chicken held down with the back of the knife and the leg is pulled off with a fork. It is then turned round and the other leg pulled off in the same way. The chicken is now placed on the back and the wings on each side with a small part of the breast cut off, cutting through the wing joint. A sharp knife is now passed along the back bone from the point of the breast, the carcass held with a fork and the breast is cut off with a cut following the bone. The breast ist either left whole or divided into two parts according to size. The legs are halved at the joint with a sharp knife, held down with the fork stuck into the lower leg. There are several ways to carve chicken but this is the easiest.

Poularde and Turkey: are always begun at the wings. Thin slices are made parallel to the center breastbone, down to the very bone. The legs are pulled off in the same way as chicken. In serving turkey the legs are sliced, dark meat is first placed on the plate with a nice slice of white meat on top.

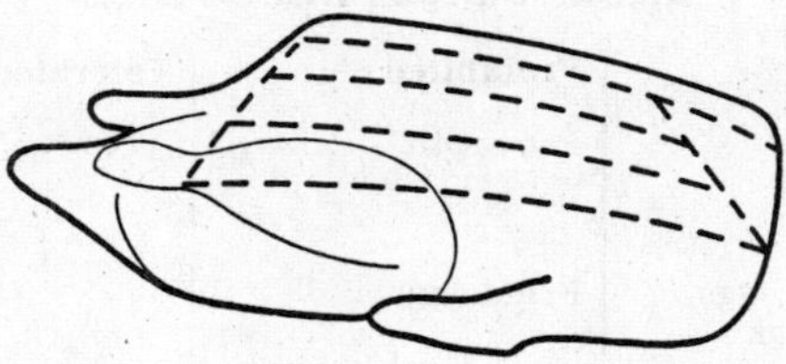

How to carve a duck

Duck: the duck is placed first on one and then on the other side and the legs are pulled off as chicken. The duck is then laid on the back, a fork is pushed in the left side of the breast and the right wing cut off cutting through the joint. The left wing is severed in the same way. Now the two breast halves are loosened carefully by passing a sharp knife along the center bone and then along the back and lifted off with a fork. Both halves are cut into thin fillets along the whole length from back to front. The legs are divided in the same way as chicken.

Pheasant: is carved like chicken. After the legs have been removed the breast is best carved in flat and not too thin slices with a very sharp knife.

Partridge, Squab chicken, Pigeon: all smaller birds are simply held down on the carving board and cut in half lengthwise with a sharp knife.

Before carving the whole piece or roast must be shown to the guest. After a piece has been carved, a saddle of venison, lamb etc. it must be possible to put it together again. That means that everything must be carved without being damaged when cut. Carving must be accomplished quickly and with accuracy, so as to serve everything hot. If a chicken is carved, for instance, the parts cut off are placed at once on a dish on at hot plate, to keep them hot until the whole bird has been carved. A fork must never be stuck into underdone meat, otherwise the juice will run out.

Dietaries

Dietaries can not be applied generally, they must be prescribed individually for each patient by the physician. The following dietaries are only general rules and may be altered or modified by the physician when necessary.

Digestive Organ Disease Diets

Permitted	**Prohibited**	**Tolerated**
Gruel Milk Soups Thick Soups	Fat broth	
Soft boiled eggs Poached eggs	Fried eggs	
Trout Tench Sole Turbot	Lobster, Crayfish, Smoked Fish, Sardines in oil	
Veal and Lamb Chicken, lean, Pigeon Brain, Sweetbread Tongue,Minced veal Tenderloin roasted medium Raw chopped beef (Tartar) Sausage without fat Lachsschinken (lean smoked fillets of ham)	All fat meat, Goose, Duck, Game, Smoked meat, fat sauces	
Boiled and mashed potatoes, buttered rice, noodles Carrots, Asparagus, Spinach, Mangold, Lettuce, French beans, Celery, Young tender cabbage-turnips, Salsify	German,French and all fried potatoes, all kinds of cabbage, Onions, Mushrooms	
Gervais, Cottage cheese, Cream cheese	Gorgonzola, Stilton, Roquefort, Camembert, Parmesan cheese	

Permitted	Prohibited	Tolerated
Oranges, mellow apples, bananas, lemons	all other fruit	
Stewed fruit with very little sugar	compote of stone fruit	
Whipped cream, Joghourt, Buttermilk		
Thin black tea, Infusions, Mineral waters, Milk	Coffee, Beer, Wine, carbonated Water	
White Bread, Toast, Graham Bread, Rusks		
Butter, Cream	Bacon, Lard, hardened Fats	
Nutmeg, Bay leaves, very little Salt	all other Spices	

Diabetes Mellitus Diets

Permitted	Prohibited	Tolerated
Broth without fat garnished with vegetables	Thick Soups	
Eggs		
Lean meat, Game, Poultry	Liver	Liver sausage
Fish		
Caviar		
All vegetables	Leguminous plants, Fennel, Salsify, Flour, Meals, Tapicca	Carrots, red Beetroots
Sweets, without sugar or flour, made with gelatine	Sugar, Honey, Jam, Marmelade	
Saccharine, Sionon, Sucrinettes		
Apples, Oranges *	all other fruit	

* Only the exact amount prescribed by the physician.

Permitted	Prohibited	Tolerated
Sour Stonefruit, Grapefruit, Lemons, Nuts, Almonds		
Cheese		
Mineral Waters, Dry Wines, Cognac	Liqueurs, Beer, Champagne	
Butter, Oil, Lard (very little)		
Whole-meal Bread* Graham Bread, Swedish Health Bread	Cakes, Pastries etc.	
Coffee, Tea, Butter-milk, Joghourt		Milk
Potatoes *		

Heart and Artery Disease Diets

Permitted	Prohibited	Tolerated
Raw Vegetables and Salads (Crudités)	Soups	
All kinds of Spices Monosodium Glutamate (MSG) instead of Salt	Salt	
Lean Meat in small quantities	Fat Meat and Poultry, Pork, Pickled and Smoked Meat, Smoked Fish, Fish preserved in brine, Preserved fish	
Fresh Fish		
Any amount of vegetables	Flatulent vegetables (Cabbage, Onions etc.)	
Butter, Cream (very little), Oil		
Potatoes	German, French and all other fried potatoes	

* Only the exact amount prescribed by the physician.

Permitted	Prohibited	Tolerated
Any amount of honey, Sugar, Sweet Desserts		
Fruit	Stone-fruit	
Stewed Fruit		
Malt-coffee, very little, Very little liquid	Coffee, all Alcoholic Beverages	
Cottage Cheese	all Salted Cheeses	
Saltless Bread	all Bread seasoned with Salt	

Kidney and Urinary Tract Diets

Permitted	Prohibited	Tolerated
Raw Vegetables and Salads (Crudités)	Soups	
Monosodium Glutamate instead of Salt	Salt	
All NaCl-free Spices		
All and any amount of Vegetables		Spinach, Tomatoes, Asparagus, Rhubarb *
Very little Meat	Smoked or Pickled Food, Sausages Saltwater Fish	
Freshwater Fish		
Sweet Desserts, Pastries		
Permitted Food fried in deep fat		
Saltless Butter, Oil and Palm fat	Bacon, Salt Pork, Lard	
Chocolate	Alcoholic Beverages	
Italian Pastes, Rice	Bread seasoned with Salt	
	Cheese	Cottage Cheese *

* Only with special permission of the physician.

Glossary of Culinary Terms, Expressions and General Hints

Agar Agar: product of edible seaweeds and other species of algae used instead of gelatine. The jellying power is much greater than that of gelatine.

Aiguillettes: thin long strips, vertically cut, principally of breast of duck and other poultry.

Aile: wing of poultry or game; aileron: wing tip.

Angelica: Angélique; a plant of the Umbelliferae family. The young green leaf stalks are candied and used for pastries, sweets and confectionary.

Annoncer: to call out orders, to announce.

Appareil: culinary term for a prepared mixture, for instance bombe appareil, croquette appareil etc.

Apricoter: to coat with strained and reduced apricot jam.

Aromates: vegetables and herbs used for flavoring.

Arrow-Root: starch obtained from the root of the tropical Maranta plant. Used for thickening, in milk, puddings, as a diet for invalids etc.

Assaisonner: to season.

Bain-marie: water bath: a receptacle filled partly with water to keep soups, sauces etc warm.

Barder: to bard: to cover poultry or feathered game with thin slices of fat bacon.

Baron d'agneau: Baron of Lamb: the saddle and legs of lamb in one piece. Expression used also for mutton.

— **of Beef:** a double loin of beef in one piece.

Beurre pour les escargots: see snail butter.

— **manié:** see butterpaste.

Birds Nests: Nids de hirondelles: the gelatinous muceous nests of a South Asian swift that form their nests on the coast cliffs. They are used for soup and swell up when soaked in water.

Bisque: name of certain shellfish soups thickened with rice. They were originally prepared with army biscuits or breadcrusts, therefore the name bisque.

Blancher: to blanche, to scald or to whiten food in boiling liquid.

Bombay Ducks: canned, smoked and especially dried bummaloe fish imported from India and served with curry dishes.

Bouquet garni: bunch of herbs tied together: parsley stalks, thyme, bayleaf etc., or bunch of vegetables: leeks, celery, carrots.

Brider: to truss poultry or feathered game.

Brigade: crew, team, culinary term used for the cooks of a kitchen if at least five are employed.

Brunoise: vegetables cut into very small cubes, also a garnish for consommé.

Butterpaste: Beurre manié: butter and flour kneaded together. Used as a thickening.

Canapé: small slice of bread cut into various shapes, plain, toasted or fried, spread and garnished, served as an appetizer or cocktail snack.
Caramel Color: burnt sugar dissolved in water, used for coloring liquids. Commonly known as "monkey" or "black Jack".
Cassolette: small china container or pot, usually heatproof, used for serving one portion of fine ragouts, eggs etc.
Chemiser: to line a mould with jelly, ice cream, forcemeat etc.
Chicken Essence: Essence de volaille: very strong fairly saltless chicken stock boiled down or chicken trimmings sweated in butter with mushroom waste etc. covered with chicken stock and boiled slowly for at least an hour.
Chiffonade: leaf vegetables or salads cut in fine shreds.
Chorizo: a sharply seasoned Spanish sausage flavored with garlic.
Cimier: a saddle of venison, mainly of stag.
Ciseler: to score, to incise, to make small cuts on both sides of small fish to allow the heat to penetrate quicker.
Cloche: Bell: a round silver, metal or glass cover to keep food hot. Glass bells are also used for serving champignons sous cloche.
Cockscombs: Crêtes de coq; cockscombs are a delicacy and should not be discarded. To keep them white they are first steeped in cold water and heated gently only enough to be able to strip the thin skin off. They are kept in cold water until all the blood is drained out and then stewed in lemon juice and butter or white stock.
Cocotte: either a small individual china or earthenware fireproof pot for eggs, ragoûts etc. or a larger oval one with a lid for cooking such dishes as poulet or poussin en cocotte etc.
Condimenter: to season with condiments.
Couronne, en couronne: to arrange and serve food in shape of a crown.
Crépine: see pig's caul.
Crêtes de coq: see cockscombs.
Croûton: small cubes of fried bread for soups, bread cut in heart or other fancy shapes used for garnishing all kinds of dishes.
Dariole: small beaker mould.
Darne: middle section of fish, especially salmon.
Dégraiser: to degrease, to skim off fat on stocks, soups, sauces etc.
Dégraissis: the fat skimmed off on stocks, soups etc., often used for cooking vegetables after having been clarified.
Désosser: to bone, to remove bones from meat, poultry etc.
Double de mouton: double d'agneau: the two legs of mutton or lamb in one piece, not divided.
Dresser: to dress, to arrange, to garnish.
Duxelles, Dry: Duxelles sèche: chopped onions and shallots sweated in half oil and half butter, ten times as much finely chopped mushroom stems and peels pressed out beforehand added and simmered until perfectly dry. Chopped parsley, salt and pepper added, when cold filled in basin and covered with greased paper. Used for sauces etc.

Duxelles
— **for stuffing vegetables:** Duxelles pour de légumes farcis: dry duxelles boiled up with white wine until the wine is completely reduced, demi-glace with tomato, a little bit of crushed garlic and breadcrumbs added and simmered until thick enough to stuff vegetables.
Egg Whites, To Whisk stiff: egg whites must be absolutely free from yolk to get stiff properly. They must be whisked slowly first and then quicker as soon as they show signs of stiffening. To prevent them from turning a pinch of salt is added, and if they destined for sweets a little finely granulated sugar.
Escalope: collop, thin pared slice of meat.
Essence de champignons: see mushroom essence.
— **de gibier:** see game essence.
— **de poisson:** see fish essence.
— **de truffes:** see truffle essence.
— **de volaille:** see chicken essence.
Etamine: a cloth for straining soups, sauces and other fluids.
Étuver: to stew or steam in very little liquid.
Farce: see forcemeat.
— **à gratin:** see gratin forcemeat.
Farcir: to stuff or fill.
Fillet (in connection with citrus fruit) the flesh cut out in sections without skin, pith or pips.
Fish Essence: fish bones and heads, sliced onions, mushroom waste and parsley stalks sweated in butter, covered with half fish stock and half white wine, cooked slowly for 20 minutes, finished off with a little lemon juice, strained.
Flamber: to flame: to singe poultry or game or to pour spirits or liqueur over a dish and to serve it burning.
Fleurons: puff pastry rolled out rather thin, cut in shape of crescents or half-moons, brushed with egg, baked in hot oven. Used as a garnish.
Fond: basic stock.
Forcemeat: Farce: meat, poultry, fish, game etc. pounded in a mortar or passed several times through the maschine, rubbed through a sieve, mixed with eggs or panade, seasoned and used for stuffing. Mousseline forcemeat is made of meat, fish, poultry or game, rubbed through a sieve, seasoned, mixed with egg whites to a paste and with cream until light and fluffy. Mousseline forcemeat must be very light and is tested by poaching a small spoonful in boiling hot water.
Frapper: to chill.
Friture: frying fat, also the name of the food fried in the fat.
Froth: Mousse: either a very light and fluffy cold or hot forcemeat preparation or a light ice or cream.
Fumet: essence, chiefly of fish or game.
Game Essence: Essence de gibier: game trimmings and waste chopped into small pieces, browned in butter, sliced onions and mushroom waste added, allowed to draw, barely covered with water and cooked for two hours, strained.
Glace de gibier: see glaze.
— **de poisson:** see glaze.
— **de viande:** see glaze.
— **de volaille:** see glaze.

Glacer, to glaze: to brown dishes covered with a strongly buttered sauce rapidly under a salamander or in a hot oven; to glaze meat by basting it often with its own fat; to brush meat etc. with liquid meat glaze; to cover cold food with jelly; to glaze cakes or pastries with strained apricot jam or with icing.

Glacier: ice cream maker, pastry cook specialized in ice cream.

Glaze, Meat Glaze: Glace de viande: boiled down strong, saltless stock, reduced to the thickness of jelly, used for glazing cooked meat etc. or for strengthening soups and sauces. Glaze is also made of fish, chicken or game stock.

Gratin: a gratinated dish. Applied to dishes covered with breadcrumbs, grated cheese, butter etc. browned in the oven or under a salamander.

— **Forcemeat:** Farce à gratin: forcemeat made of equal amounts of bacon from breast, veal and veal liver, butter, mushrooms waste, truffle peels, egg yolks, seasoning, a little Madeira and reduced demi-glace, liver, veal and bacon diced and sautéd lightly beforehand.

Green Vegetable Color: well washed and drained spinach pounded in a mortar, the juice pressed out in a cloth. This juice is lightly heated on top of a saucepan with hot water until the green part has set on the bottom of the receptacle used. The clear fluid on top is poured away, the green residue rubbed through a fine sieve and used as a coloring.

Hermetical Sealing: in fine cookery the closing of a cocotte or other receptacle with bread dough or only flour mixed with water to prevent the escape of aroma.

Historier: to decorate, to embellish.

Hure: head of boar or pig. Hure de sanglier, wild boar's head.

Julienne: vegetables or other food cut into fine shreds.

Kwas: drink made by fermenting rye flour, sugar, yeast, malt and water. (Russian)

Lardons: small strips of bacon.

Macérer: to macerate: to soak or steep in sugar and spirits or liqueur; to pickle briefly.

Marzipan: Massepain: a paste made of blanched ground almonds and sugar.

Masquer: to mask: to coat, to cover any kind of hot or cold food with sauce or jelly or to cover the bottom of a dish or mould with sauce, jelly etc.

Matignon: the red part of carrots, an equal amount of onions and raw ham and a third as much celery cut into very small exceedingly thin slices, simmered in butter with a small bayleaf and a sprig of thyme, deglaced with Madeira.

Mie-de-pain: fresh breadcrumbs, white bread a few days old with the rind cut off, rubbed through a coarse sieve and used together with eggs as a coating for fish, meat etc.

Mirepoix: carrots and an equal amount of onions and lean bacon and a third of the amount celery cut into more or less large dice according to use, a sprig of thyme and a small bayleaf sweated in butter.

— **Bordelaise:** carrots and the same amount of onions and a few parsley stalks cut like brunoise, a pinch of thyme and powdered bayleaves added, stewed slowly in butter until the moisture is completely evaporated. Is used chiefly for hot lobster or other shellfish dishes.

Monter: to whip eggs or egg whites, to whip butter in a sauce etc.

Mousse: see froth.

Mushroom Essence: Essence de champignons the short fond in which mushrooms have been poached reduced.

— **Powder:** dried mushrooms or fresh mushrooms cut in slices and dried in a warm cupboard, pounded in mortar until quite fine, dried again, sieved, mixed with a little salt and pepper and kept in well closed tins in a dry place. Useful for flavoring soups and sauces

Panaché: mixed, multi-colored, mixed ice, cream or jelly in a mould, mixed fruit or vegetables.

Panade: 1. bread soaked in milk seasoned lightly with salt and dried stirring continously until the paste does not adhere any more on the spoon. Used for fish forcemeat;
2. Panade à la farine: water boiled up with butter and a pinch of salt, taken off the stove, sieved flour added and dried on the stove like cream puff paste (q. v.). Used for all sorts of forcemeat.
3. Panade frangipane: egg yolks and flour stirred together, melted butter, salt, pepper and grated nutmeg added, mixed gradually with hot milk, stirred on the fire with a whisk like very thick cream. Used for fish and chicken forcemeat.
All panades are cleared off in a bassin greased with butter for further use.

Panne: leaf lard, green lard, used largely for forcemeat, galantines etc.

Pese-sirop: saccharometer, sugar scales.

Pig's Caul: Crépine: a membrane in the shape of a net covering the lower part of the pig's bowels.

Plat russe: Russian dish: oval baking dish of fireproof china with a rather low border in various sizes for serving hot or cold food.

Pralin à Condé: egg white stirred with powder sugar to foam, mixed with more or less large amount of chopped almonds according to use. Used for pastries and sweets.

Primeurs: early or forced fruit or vegetables, the first in season are generally classed under this name.

Ragoût: a rich seasoned stew either brown or white.

Réduire: to reduce, to boil down a liquid to the desired consistency.

Remouillage: bones boiled up again with fresh water after the stock has been poured off once.

Renverser: to unmold, to turn food out on a dish.

Rissoler: to bake or fry sharply to brown color in the hot oven. Pommes rissolées, browned potatoes.

Roux, Blonde: 10 oz. flour cooked in 8 oz. of clarified butter to a light yellow color.

— **Brown:** Roux brun: 10. oz. flour browned very slowly in 8 oz. of clarified butter or excellent clarified dripping. Used for brown sauces.

— **White:** Rout blanc: 10 oz. flour cooked slowly in 8 oz. clarified butter, stirred continously and kept white. Used for white sauces and soups.

Salpicon: meat, poultry, fish etc. cut into very small cubes for small ragoûts, also finely diced fruit etc. for sweets.

Sauter: a quick cooking process, to brown rapidly in a sauté pan, to toss in hot fat over a sharp fire anything that needs quick cooking.

Snail Butter: beurre pour les escargots: butter creamed, mixed with finely chopped shallots, very little finely crushed garlic, chopped parsley, salt and pepper.

Tamis: tammy, a hair sieve for straining food.

Tapioca: starch obtained from the root of the cassava plant which grows in the tropics. It is marketed as flaked, pearl and granulated tapioca and in the form of flour.

Timbale: a half-conical mould of tin in various sizes; a kind of hot meat loaf; a half-conical silver dish with a flat bottom for serving fine dishes and vegetables.

Trancher: to carve; tranche: slice.

Truffle Essence: the short stock in which truffles have been cooked boiled down.

Verjus: the juice of unripe fruit especially sour grapes.

Vesiga: jelly-like substance found around the spinal marrow of the great sturgeon, marketed dry. Swells to five times its volume when soaked. Used for culibijaka and other Russian patties.

Zeste: the outside skin of lemons, oranges etc. peeled off finely.

Wine

Wine is the pure, naturally fermented juice of fresh ripe grapes. The alcohol in wine is nature's means of preserving the juice of the grape. It is the only fruit that will naturally preserve itself, without anything being added or taken away. Wine is also made from other fruits, such as blackberries, red currants etc. In this case it must be called by the name the respective fruit.
In aging wine develops smoothness, mellowness and character. Most wines, however, complete their aging fairly early and lose quality with further storage. Age is, therefore, not a positive guide to quality. Good wines are bottled after having been aged in the cask as long as necessary. The time required after bottling depends upon the kind of wine. Some wines reach their maturity in a few months, others are best after two to four years and great wines may be found in perfect condition after half a century.
Generally speaking there are five classes of wine: Appetizer wines, red wines, white wines, dessert and sparkling wines.
Serving one wine at a meal is the most usual procedure. For dinner parties or other festive occasions three or more wines are often served. More than three glasses should never be placed on the table even for a most elaborate dinner: a white wine, a red wine and a champagne glass. Additional glasses are brought in at the proper time.

Hints on Wine Serving

There are traditional gastronomic rules that should be adhered to:

For Appetizers and Soups	Sherry or dry Madeira
For white Fish	a dry white wine
For dark or fat Fish (salmon, salmon trout carp etc.)	a pink wine (Vin rosé, Schillerwein), Claret or another light red wine
Main dish, roasts etc. other than game	a fine Bordeaux or Burgundy
Entrées	Haute-Sauternes, a fine wine of the Rhinegau, Palatinate or Rhenish Hesse
Game	a rich Burgundy
Sweets	Champagne, sparkling Hock or sparkling Burgundy
Dessert, Nuts, Fruit, Cakes	Port, white Port, Tokay, Muscatel
Cheese	Burgundy, Bordeaux or some other rich red wine

These are the wines that go best with the respective food. Three wines however, are nearly always enough, even for a formal diner party: a red, a white and a sparkling wine, especially if an Apéritif or a Cocktail has been served before dinner.
A good wine deserves a good glass. There are standard glasses for each kind of wine, but a tulip-shaped wine glass of

5- to 8 ounce capacity is suitable for red and white table wines.
Regardless of tradition, the best rule for the choice of wine is the kind which is most pleasant to him who drinks it.
Wine must be served at the right temperature. Red wines are always served at room temperature, pink wines should be cool and white wines ought to be chilled according to kind. If they are too cold the fine bouquet will suffer. Champagne and sparkling Hock etc. is chilled at 44° F.

How to read Label on the Wine Bottle

You can tell exactly from which grapes the wine is made, where it comes from, from which vineyard, how old it is etc. by the labels of French, German and most other foreign wines.
The finest growths of France are classified as far as white and red Bordeaux is concerned. The general terms are:

1 er cru or 1 er grand cru classé	First Growth classified or first grand growth
2 em cru	Second Growth
3 em cru	Third Growth
4 em cru	Fourth Growth
5 em cru	Fifth Growth

These are the finest Bordeaux wines (Clarets) and may be found either in the districts of Médoc, Graves, Sauternes and Saint-Emilion. A cru Bourgeois is a good wine but not up to the standard of the classified growths, a Grand Cru is the best of all growths and means a superlative wine.
A bottle of Bordeaux bearing the following text on the label

Château Haut-Brion
Premier Grand Cru Classé
Appélation Graves Contrôlée
1949
Mise en Bouteilles au Château

shows that this wine is the first and finest of classified growths made of grapes from the vineyards of Haut-Brion in the district of Graves 1949, bottled at the Château, and that it has been officially controlled as correct.
Burgundies are not classified as growths but known as Tête de Cuvée or as Premières Cuvées.
New regulations for German wines. The different kinds of grapes commonly used in making wine are numerous. According to the regulations fixed by the E. E. C. (Common Market) 1971 the following specification for German wines have been legally sanctioned by the Federal Government:

1. Table-wine (Tafelwein)

For this wine the label on the bottle is allowed to name the district, the community or the locality of the vineyard.

2. High-grade wine (Qualitätswein)

a) High-grade wine
b) High-grade wine with a predicate (guarantee): Qualitätswein mit Prädikat.

High-grade wine (Qualitätswein) may only be produced of grapes grown, gathered and processed from particuclar defined vineyards.
For high-grade wine with a predicate (Qualitätswein mit Prädikat) the grapes must be the product of one sole domain or district recorded in the official list of vineyards. These wines are not allowed to be improved in any way or deprived of their natural acidity.
High-grade wines with a predicate include such with the specification „Auslese" or „feinste Auslese", meaning that the grapes have been selected after the general harvest. „Trockenbeeren-Auslese" signifies that the wine is made of grapes that have been left on the vine until the „noble rot" causes them to shrink, thus concentrating the sugar juices, bouquet and aromatic substances, and Kabinett.
The classification of high-grade wine with or without a predicate is subject to an official test and an ordonance that the wine has received a test-number.

Wine Dictionary

A

Ackermann: the chief wine-producing district of Bessarabia.
Aescher: red wine of the Canton Basel.
Affenthaler: fine red wine, Baden, Germany.
Ahrweiler: red wine of the Ahr Vally, Germany: Ahrweiler Berg, Kalvarienberg, Rosenthal, Taubhaus etc.
Alba Flora: white wine of the island Majorca made from Malvasia grapes.
Albana: dry Emilian white wine.
Aldeno: red and white Tyrolian wines from the district of Nogaredo.
Aleatico di Portoferraio: sweet red Tuscan wine.
Alicante: Spanish red and white wines: Alicante Alaque and Fondillon.
Almissa: sweet red dessert wine of Dalmatia.
Aloxe-Corton: Côte de Beaune, Burgundy, excellent red and white wines.
Also: red and white Hungarian wines: Also-Dergicse, Also-Galla, Also-Homorod, Also Némedi and Also-Raks.
Altesses, Vin des: one of the best white wines of French Savoy.
Alzeyer: white wines (Hock) of Rhenish Hesse: Alzeyer Backem, Geierstein, Hühnerberg, Kesselring
Amontillado: popular type of Sherry, Fino or Vino de pasto, neither very dry nor sweet.
Amoroso: full-bodied Sherry, sweeter and darker than Amontillado.
Amoureuses, Les: red Burgundy of the commune Chambolle-Musigny.
Andelfingen: Swiss red wine of the Canton Zurich.
Anglade, Château d': red wine (Claret) of the Médoc.
Angludet, Château: a fair red wine of the Médoc.
Anseillan, Château d': a Bourgeois growth of the Médoc, commune Pauillac.
Anthosmias: golden-colored Greek wine.
Arader: Hungarian wines from the Arad vineyards: Bakator (white), Kadarka (red).

Arbanats, Château d': white Graves wine of Bordeaux.
Arche, Château d': rich golden white wine, one of the second Growths of Sauternes.
Arcins, Château d': Bourgeois Growth of the Listrac district, Bordeaux.
Arlesheimer: Swiss red wine of the Canton Basel.
Aromatico di Chiavenna: sweet red and white dessert wines of the Lombardy.
Arsac, Château d': claret and white Bordeaux of the Médoc near Margaux.
Arzheimer: red Rhine wine.
Assmanshäuser: Rhenish wine: Bingerloch, white, Bohren, red, Eckerstein, red, Frankenthal, red, Hinterkirch, red, Kessrich, white, Silberberg, white.
Astheimer: red table wine of Franconia.
Aszu: sweet Hungarian wine of the Tokay type.
Auggener Markgräfler: white table wine from the vineyards of Auggen in Baden, Germany.
Aulhausener: white Rhenish table wine (Hock).
Auvernier: red wine from the Swiss Canton Neuchatel.
Ayler: a good white wine of the Saar Valley in the Sarburg district. The best are Ayler Kupp and Herrenberg.

B

Badacsony: Hungary: white wines: Auvergnas gris, Keknyelü, Rizling; dessert wine, Badacsony Szürkebarát.
Baden: Canton Argau, Switzerland, white and red wines: Gaisberger, Goldwändler.
Bagneux: a pink Anjou wine.
Balac, Château: Bourgeois Growth of the Médoc, red Bordeaux.
Balcik: a white Bulgarian wine.
Banat: Jugo-Slavia, red and white wine.
Banyuls: Sweet dessert wine from the vineyards of Roussillon.
Barateau, Château: Bourgeois growth of the Médoc, red Bordeaux.
Bardolino: red Venetian wine.
Barka: red wine of Tripolis.
Barra-a-Barra: red and white Portuguese wines.
Basque, Le: red Bordeaux, Graves.
— **Château le:** red Bordeaux, St. Emilion.
Batalley, Château: red Bordeaux, a fifth growth of the Médoc, Pauillac.
Batard-Montrachet: fine white wine of the Côte d'Or, commune Puligny-Montrachet.
Beauclair Johannisberger Riesling: dry American white wine.
Beaumont: dry American red wine.
— **Château:** red Bordeaux, a Bourgeois growth of the Médoc.
Beauregard, Château: red Bordeaux, one of the first growths of Pomerol.
Beaurose Burgundy: dry American wine.
Beau-Site, Château: red Bordeaux, a Bourgeois growth of the Médoc, community St. Estèphe.
Bel-Air, Château: red Bordeaux, one of the first growths of St. Emilion.
Belgrave, Château: red Bordeaux, a fifth growth of the Médoc.
Belleville: red and white wines of Lorraine.
Bellevue, Château: red Bordeaux, a first growth of St. Emilion.

Benicarlo: a very dark full Spanish red wine.
Bensenello: white and red Tyrolian wines from the district Roveretto.
Bergheimer: Alsatian white wines: Altenberg and Kanzelberg.
Berliquet, Château: red Bordeaux, one of the first growths of St. Emilion.
Bernkastler: very fine white Moselle wines: Bacestube, Doktor, Graben, Pfaffenberg, Rosenberg, Schloss, Schwanen, Spitz.
Besigheimer: red and white wines of Wurtemberg.
Beychevelle, Château: red Bordeaux, a fourth growth of the Médoc, commune St. Julien.
Beze, Clos de: one of the best Burgundies of the commune of Gevrey Chambertin.
Bianco dell'Elba: soft white Tuscan wine.
Bieler See: Switzerland, Canton Bern, white and red wines: Twamm, Schafis, Biel, Wingreis etc.
Binger: white wines of Rhenish Hesse (Hocks): Eisel, Gänsberg, Hungerborn, Kempfnerberg, Mittelpfad, Rochusberg etc.
Birle Duchan: Caucasian white wine.
Bisager: Croatian white wines: Alodial, Kraljevina, Zierfahndler.
Bischoffinger: Baden, white wine.
Bischoffsheimer: red and white Alsatian wines.
Blanc de Blanc: name of a still wine made exclusively from white grapes from Champagne vineyards.
Blockersberg: red table wine of Adlersberg, Hungary.
Bockelheimer, Schloss: one of the finest white wines of the Nahe Valley.
Bodendorfer: red wine of the Ahr Valley.
Bodenheimer: the white wine of the vineyards of Bodenheim, Rhenish Hesse: Ahländer, Hoch, Kahlenberg, Kapellenberg, Leiseberg etc.
Bonnezeaux: a rich sweet white Anjou wine of the Côteaux du Layon.
Bopparder: white Rhine wine (Hock): Hamm, Oberspray etc.
Bouscaut, Château du: red Bordeaux, Graves, and white Bordeaux, Graves.
Bouzy: white and red still wines of the Champagne.
Boyd-Cantenac: red Bordeaux, one of the third growths of the Médoc, commune of Margaux.
Branaire-Ducru, Château: red Bordeaux, one of the fourth growths of the Médoc, commune St. Julien.
Brane-Cantenac, Château: red Bordeaux, one of the second growths of the Médoc.
Brauneberger: one of the best Moselle wines: Falkenberg, Hasenläufer, Juffer, Lei and Nonnenfels.
Brillette, Château: a Bourgeois growth of the Médoc, red Bordeaux.
Broustet Nairac, Château: white Sauternes wine, commune of Barsac.
Büdesheimer: table wines from the vineyards of Büdesheim, Rhenish Hesse: Sazflecken (red), Scharlachberger and Setzling (white).
Bühlerthaler: white table wine of Baden, Germany.
Burignon: Swiss white wine of the Canton of Vaud.
Buttafuoco: red Lombard wine, tart.

C

Cabeceiras de Basto: a red Portuguese table wine.
Cach, Château: red Bordeaux, a Bourgeois growth of the Médoc.
Cadet, Château: red Bordeaux of the St. Emilion district.
Caillou, Château: white Bordeaux, one of the second growths of Sauternes, commune of Barsac.
Caldaro: Tridentine red wine.
Callao: a fortified Peruvian wine.
Calon-Segur: red Bordeaux, one of the third growths of the Médoc, commune of St. Estèphe.
Camarite: a light red Greek table wine.
Camensac, Château: red Bordeaux, one of the fifth growths of the Médoc.
Campoloro: red and white table wines of the Island of Corsica.
Cannstätter: red and white wines of Wurtemberg: Berg, Halden, Steinhalden etc.
Canon, Château: red Bordeaux, one of the first growths of St. Emilion.
Canon-La-Gaffeliére: red Bordeaux, one of the first growths of St. Emilion.
Cantegril, Château: white Bordeaux, one of the second growths of the Sauternes district, comune Barsac.
Canteloup, Château: red Bordeaux, a Bourgeois growth of the Médoc.
Cantemerle, Château: red Bordeaux, one of the fifth growths of the Médoc.
Cantenac-Brown, Château: red Bordeaux, one of the third growths of the Médoc.
Cape Burgundy: red wine of the Burgundy type of the Cape Colony.
— **Madeira:** a fortified wine of the Madeira type of the Cape colony.
Caseler: an excellent white wine of the Ruwer Valley.
Castelli Romani: red table wines from the vineyards near Rome.
Castello Branco: a red Portuguese table wine.
Castera, Château du: red Bordeaux, a Bourgeois growth of the Médoc, also a white Bordeaux.
Cavaleser: red and white Tyrolian wines:
Cerasolo: very soft Abruzzian red wine.
Cerasulo di Vittoria: very full Sicilian red wine.
Certan, Château: red Bordeaux, one of the first growths of Pomerol.
Chablais: Swiss white wines of the Canton of Vaud: Aigle, Yvorne and Villeneuve.
Chablis: white wine from the vineyards of Chablis, Dép. Yonne: Clos, Valmur, Vaudésir, Grenouille, Blanchot, Preuze, Mont de Milieu, Vaulorent etc.
Chambertin: one of the most famous red wines of Burgundy, commune Gevrey-Chambertin.
Chambolle-Musigny: commune of the Côte d'Or famous for its red wines: Les Musigny, Les Amoureuses, Les Bonnes Mares and Les Charmes.
Champagne: name of the sparkling wines made from the grapes grown in the vineyards of the former Province of

Champagne. There are also excellent still wines made in Champagne.

Chante-Alouette: white table wine of Hermitage (Côtes du Rhône).

Chasse-Spleen: red Bordeaux, a Bourgeois growth of the Médoc.

Château Beulieu: dry American white wine.

— **Chalon:** very fine white wine, like a dry Sherry, made in the communes of L'Etoile, Voiteur and Ménétrue, Dép, Jura.

— **Martin:** red American Burgundy.

— **Masson:** red Californian wine of the Burgundy type.

Châteaumeillant: fine red table wine of the Berry.

Châteauneuf-Du-Pape: one of the best red wines of the Rhône Valley near Avignon.

Château-Salins: a good red table wine of Lorraine.

Chatolle, Cru de la: red Bordeaux, one of the first growths of the Médoc.

Cheval Blanc, Château: red Bordeaux, the first growth of the Graves, St. Emilion.

Chevalier-Montrachet: one of the best white Burgundies of the Dép. Côte d'Or.

Chianti: rather tart Tuscan red wine.

Chiaramonte: a red table wine of Sicily.

Chiaretto-Bonarda: pink Lombard wine.

Chichée: white wine of the commune of Chichée, Dép. Yonne.

Chilean Wines: red and white wines, the best are those from the Maipo district.

Cissac, Château: red Bordeaux, one of the Bourgeois growths of the Médoc.

Citran, Château: red Bordeaux of the Médoc.

Cairettede Dié: a red semi-sparkling wine from Die, Dep. Drôme.

— **de Gaillac:** a semi-sparkling pink wine of the Dép. Tarn.

Clarke, Château: red Bordeaux, a Bourgeois growth of the Médoc.

Clerc-Milon, Château: red Bordeaux, one of the fifth growths of the Médoc, commune Pauillac.

Clinet, Château: red Bordeaux, one of the first growths of Pomerol.

Clos de l'Angelus: red Bordeaux, one of the first growths of St. Emilion.

— **Arlots:** red Burgundy of the Dép. Côte d'Or.

— **du Barrail:** red Bordeaux.

— **de Bèze:** excellent red wine of the commune Gevrey-Chambertin, Dép. Côte d'Or.

— **Blanc:** red Burgundy, commune of Pommard.

— **du Cardinal:** white Bordeaux of the Médoc.

— **Fourtet:** red Bordeaux, first growth of St. Emilion.

— **du Clocher:** red Bordeaux, a Bourgeois growth of the Médoc.

— **des Lambrays:** excellent red Burgundy of the Dép. Côte d'Or.

— **des Mouches:** red Burgundy wine of the commune of Beaune.

— **du Moulin:** white Alsatian wine of the commune of Riquewhir.

— **du Roi:** fine red Burgundy of the commune Aloxe-Corton, Dép. Côte d'Or.

Clos de l'Angelus
— **Saint-Jean:** red Burgundy wine, commune Chassagne, Dép. Cote d'Or.
— **Sainte-Odile:** white Alsatian wine.
— **de Vougeot:** red Burgundy, commune Vougeot, Dép. Côte d'Or.
Closerie, La: red Bordeaux, a Bourgeois growth of the Médoc.
Collares: red wines from Cintra near Lisbon, Portugal.
Collio Friulano: Italian white wine from Venezia Giulia.
Constantia: South African dessert wine made from small muscat grapes.
Conthey, Château de: white wine of the Canton Valais, Switzerland.
Corbin, Château: red Bordeaux, one of first growths of the Graves, St. Emilion.
Coronata: dry white Ligurian wine.
Cortaillod: Swiss red wine of the Canton Neuchatel.
Corvo di Casteldaccia: dry Sicilian white wine.
Cos d'Estournel, Château: red Bordeaux one of the second growths of the Médoc.
— **Labory:** red Bordeaux, a fifth growth of the Médoc. St. Estèphe.
Côte Rôtie: red wine, commune of Ambuis in the Rhône valley.
Coulée de Sarrant: sweet white wine of the Côteaux de la Loire, Anjou.
Coutet, Château: white Sauternes wine of the commune of Barsac.
Couvent, Clos du: red Bordeaux, one of the first growths of St. Emilion.
Crest Blanca: white sparkling American wine of the Champagne type.
Crimea: Russia, excellent red, white and sparkling wine.
Crock, Château Le: red Bordeaux, a Bourgeois growth of the Médoc, St. Estèphe.
Croix, Château La: 1. red Bordeaux, one of the first growths of Pomerol;
2. red Bordeaux, district Entre-deux-Mers, Gironde.
Croix-Blanche, La: white Bordeaux, a „vin ordinaire", commune of Ludon, Médoc.
Croix-de-Merlet: white wine of Blayais Dép. Gironde.
Croix-Noires, Les: red Burgundy wine, commune Pommard, Côte d'Or.
Croizet-Bages, Château: red Bordeaux, one of the fifth growths of the Médoc.
Cure-Bon-La-Madeleine, Château: red Bordeaux, one of the first growths of St. Emilion.
Cyprus: wines of the Malvasia type: Limassol, Nicosia, Paphos, Larnaca and Famagusta.
Czegleder: a white Hungarian table wine.

D

Dalmatiner: red and white wine, Dalmatia, Jugo-Slavia.
Damascus Muscat: a red wine of Syria.
Dampierre: a good pink wine of Anjou.
Dante Malvasia: a dessert wine of the Canaries.
D'Arche, Château: white Bordeaux, one of the second growths of Sauternes.

Dargagny: Swiss white wine of the Canton Genève.
Daugay, Château: red Bordeaux, a second growth of St. Emilion.
Dauzac, Château: red Bordeaux, a fifth growth of the Médoc.
Dealu mare: a fairly strong Roumanian white wine.
Deidesheimer: the white wine of some of the best vineyards of the Palatinate: Bischofsberg, Erdner, Fleckinger, Grein, Kalkofen, Kieselberg, Kränzler, Nonnenstück, Petershöhe etc.
Dernauer: red table wine of the Ahr Valley (Germany).
Desmirail, Château: red Bordeaux, one of the third growths of the Médoc.
Dettelbacher: a white table wine of Franconia.
Detzemer: white Moselle wine.
Deutsch-Landsberg: white wines, Transylvania, Roumania: Blumegg, Eibiswald, Stainz.
Dézaley: excellent Swiss white table wine of the Canton of Vaud.
Dhroner: white Moselle wine.
Dillon, Château: red Bordeaux, a Bourgeois growth of the Médoc.
Dolceaqua: red Ligurian wine.
Dole de Sion: red wine of the Swiss Canton of Valais.
Domenique, La: red Bordeaux, one of the first growths of the Graves, St. Emilion.
Döttinger: Swiss red wine of the Canton Aargau
Doumens, Château: red Bordeaux, a Bourgeois growth of the Médoc, commune Margaux.
Dragasani: red and white Roumanian table wines.
Drakenstein: one of the best white wines of the Cape Province.
Dromersheimer: white wine of Rhenish Hesse (Hock): Hütte, Mainzer Weg, Professor, Bochusberg.
Duc d'Epernon, Château: white Bordeaux wine, Graves.
Ducru-Beaucaillou, Château: red Bordeaux, one of the second growths of the Médoc, St. Julien.
Ducru-Ravez, Château: red Bordeaux, Médoc.
Duhart-Milon, Château: red Bordeaux, a fourth growth of the Médoc, commune of Pauillac.
Duprina: red Bulgarian table wine.
Durbach: Baden: Bühl, Binsenloch, Staufenberg.
Durfort-Vivens, Château: red Bordeaux, one of the second growths of the Médoc, commune of Margaux.
Dürkheimer: white wine (Hock) and red wines of the Dürkheim vineyards of the Palatinate: Feuerberg, Forst, St. Michaelsberg, Spielberg.

E

Eberstadt: Wurtemberg, red and white wine.
Edenkobener: Heide, Kieferberg, Klostergarten, Letten, white and red wine, Rhenish Palatinate.
Edesheimer: Forst, Gereckt, Weyherweg, white wine, Rhenish Palatinate.
Efringen: white wine of Baden, Germany.
Egri Bikaver: red Hungarian table wine.
— **Kadarka:** red Hungarian table wine.
Ehrenstädter: a white wine of Baden, Germany.
Einersheimer: a white Franconian table wine.
Eitelbacher: one of the finest white wines of the Ruwer Valley, the best vineyard is the Karthäuserhofberg.

El Kseur: Algerian red wine.
Ellerstadt: Rhenish Palatinate, white and red wines.
Elsheim: Rhenish Hesse, white wine.
Endingen: Baden, white wine.
Erbacher: one of the best white wines (Hock) of the Rhinegau, especially: Herrenberg, Schloss, Honigberg, Klostergarten, Langenmorgen and Wormloch.
Erdener: one of the good Moselle wines: Treppchen and Lösenicher.
Ergersheimer: a white Franconian table wine.
Erlau: red and white Hungarian wine.
Essenheim: Rhenish Hesse, white and red wine.
Est' Est' Est' (Montefiascone): fragrant white wine from Latium.
Estournel, Cos d': red Bordeaux, one of the second growths of the Médoc, St. Estèphe.
Ettenheim: Baden, white wine.
Euböa: Greek island wine, red and white.

F

Falerno: red and white wine from Latium.
Fatin, Château: red Bordeaux, Bourgeois growth of the Médoc, St. Estèphe.
Faye-sur-Layon: white wines of the Côteaux du Layon, Anjou.
Feldbach: Austria: Blumau, Edelsbach, Muggendorf, Zerlach, white and pink wines.
Fellbach: Wurtemberg: Lämmler, Hint, Berg, Staig, Raise, white and red wines.
Felsoer: Hungarian red and white wines: Almas, Balog, Csany, Habot, Ludany, Novaj, Bajk etc.
Fendant: Swiss white wines of the Canton Valais: Fendant de Sion, Chamosons, Laytron and Fuilly.
Fernand-Vegelesses: red Burgundy of the Côte d'Or.
Ferrande, Château: a white Bordeaux wine, Graves.
Ferrant, Château: red Bordeaux, one of the second growths of the St. Emilion.
Feuerbach: Wurtemberg: Lemberg, Hohenwarte, Schloss etc., red wines.
Feuerthaler: a good Franconian white wine.
Fiano de Avellino: dry Campanian white wine.
Figeac, Château: red Bordeaux, one of the first growths of the Graves of St. Emilion.
Figueira: a Portuguese red wine.
Filzener: delicate white wine from Filzen, Saar.
Flein: Wurtemberg: Altenberg, Grafenberg, Fuchssprung, Sandberg, white and red wines.
Fior di California: red Californian table wine.
Forchheimer: a white Franconian wine.
Forster: one of the finest growths of white wines (Hock) of the Palatinate: Ungeheuer, Hölle, Freundstück, Jesuitengarten, Kirchenstück, Stift, Ziegler etc.
Fourcas-Dupre, Château: red Bordeaux, a Bourgeois growth of the Médoc.
Fourtet, Clos: red Bordeaux, one of the first growths of the St. Emilion.
Franciacorta: red wine, Lombardy.
Frascati: white wine from the vineyards of Frascati in the Latium.

Freccia Rossa di Casteggio: dry white Lombard wine.
Freinsheim: Rhenish Palatinate, Oschelskopf, Hahnen, white and red wines.
Frickenhausen: Franconia: Berg, Fischler etc., white and red wines.
Friesenheimer: white wine (Hock) of Rhenish Hesse: Basemer Auslese, Goldgrub, Hollerheck, Sott.
Fünfkirchner: white and red Hungarian wines: Deindol, Kalvarienberg etc.
Furmint Edes: white wine of the Kecskemet districts of Hungary.

G

Gachnang: Canton Thurgau, Switzerland: Gerlikon Islikon, Niederweil, Oberweil etc., white and red wines.
Gallais, Château: red Bordeaux, a bourgeois growth of the Médoc.
Garganega di Cambellara: white Venetian wine
Gaualgesheimer: the white wine (Hock) from the vineyards of Gaualgesheim, Rhenish Hesse: Berg, Frohnpfad, Hasensprung, Honiggarten, Kreuz.
Gau-Bickelheimer: white wine of the Oppenheim district of Rhenish Hesse.
Gay, Château le: red Bordeaux, one of the first growths of Pomerol.
Gazin, Château: red Bordeaux, commune of Pomerol.
Gebweiler: white Alsatian wine: Kitterle Wanne etc.
Geisenheimer: one of the best white wines (Hock) of the Rhinegau: Altbaum, Fuchsberg, Kapellenberg Katzenloch, Kirchgrube, Kläuserweg, Mäuerchen, Steinacker etc.
Geneste, Château: red Bordeaux, Graves.
Giovo: Tyrolian red and white wines of the district Lavis.
Gironville, Château: red Bordeaux of the Médoc.
Giscours, Château: red Bordeaux, one of the third growths of the Médoc, commune Labarde.
Givry: red Burgundy of the Côte Chalonaise.
Godramersteiner: Rhenish Palatinate, red and white wine.
Gombasser: Transylvanian red wine: Carbenet, Merlot.
Graascher: one of the best of white Moselle wines: Abtsberg, Domprobst, Goldtröpfchen, Goldwingert, Himmelreich, Hochstück, Josephshöfer, Münzlei.
Gran Caruso di Ravello: pink wine from Campania.
Granada: Spain: Albunol, Baza, Guadix, red and white wine.
Grand-Puy-Lacoste, Château: red Bordeaux of the Médoc, commune Pauillac.
Graz: Austria, Aichegg, Gasselberg, Ligist, Reiteregg, white and red wines.
Greco di Gerace: dry Apulian white wine.
— **Todi:** white Umbrian wine.
— **Tufo:** sparkling Campanian white wine.
Grénache Rose: dry American red wine.
Grigioni: dry red Lombard wine.
Grinzing: Austria, white wine.
Gruaud-Larose-Faure, Château: a second growth of the Médoc, commune St. Julien, red Bordeaux.
Gruaud-Larose-Sarget, Château: red Bordeaux, one of the second growths of the Médoc, St. Julien.

Grumello: dry red Lombard wine.
Grünhäuser: one of the finest white wines of the Ruwer Valley, the best is from the vineyard of Herrenberg: Maximin Grünhäuser Herrenberg.
Guanajuata: red and white Mexican wines.
Guiraud, Château: one of the first growths of Sauternes wines, white Bordeaux.
Gumpolskirchen: Austria, white and red wine.
Guncinà: Tridentine red wine.
Guntersblumer: Rhenish Hesse, red and white wine.
Gyüd (Baranya), Hungary, red and white wine.

H

Haardter: white wine of the Palatinate: Guckinsland, Pfad, Schlossberg.
Hainfeld: Franconia: Letten, An der Kapelle, Fröhnbühl etc., white wine.
Hallburger Riesling: a white Franconian wine.
Hallgartener: one of the best white wines (Hock) of the Rhinegau: Biegels, Deutelberg, Hasenlauf, Kirchgarten, Kirschenacker, Sandgrube.
Hambach: Rhenish Palatinate: Kaiserstuhl, Hörst, Sommerhalde etc., white and red wine.
Hammelburg: Franconia: Leisten, Liebenthal, Geilesberg, Frohnbühl, white and red wine.
Hattenheimer: one of the finest white wines (Hock) of the Rhinegau, especially those of the vineyards of Schloss Reinhardtshausen, Berg, Boxberg, Deutelsberg, Gassenweg und Heiligenweg.
Haut Bailly, Château: red Bordeaux of the Graves, Léognan.
Haut-Barsac: one of the good white Sauternes wines of the commune Barsac.
Haut-Bergey, Château: red Bordeaux of the Graves, commune of Léognan.
Haut Brion, Château: the most famous of the Graves wines, commune of Pessac, red Bordeaux, first growth.
Haut-Brion Larrivet, Château: famous red Bordeaux, Graves district.
Haut-Lafite, Château: famous red Bordeaux, Graves.
Hauterive, Château: red Bordeaux, one of the Bourgeois growths of the Médoc.
Haut-Peyraguey, Clos: famous white Sauternes wine, commune of Bommes.
Haut-Simard, Château: red Bordeaux, one of the second growths of St. Emilion.
Hebron: a Syrian red wine.
Hegener Seewein: red wine of Baden, Germany.
Heilbronn: Wurtemberg: Buchern, Hundsberg, Halden, Lerchenberg, Stauffenberg, white and red wine.
Heiligensteiner: Alsatian white wine.
Heimersheimer: red table wine of the Ahr Valley.
Hemigkofener: white and red Wines of Wurtemberg: Bergerhalde, Ettanberg, Nunzenberg, Sonnenhalde etc.
Heppenheimer: white wine (Hock) of Rhenish Hesse: Bergstraße, Schloßberg, Steinkopf.
Hermitage, Vins de l': red and white table wines from the vineyards around Tain, Dép. Drôme.

Hernals: Lower Austria: Altenberg, Dornach, Grinzing, Nussdorf, Weidling, white and red wine.
Herrschäftler: Maienfeld, Malans, Jennins, Fläsch, red wines of the Swiss Canton Zurich.
Herxheim: Rhenish Palatinate: Himmelreich, Felsenberg, Sommerseite, white and red wine.
Hesslocher: white wine (Hock) of Hessloch, Rhenish Hesse: Aupern, Obere and Untere Blende, Steckweiler, Felsenwein.
Heubacher: a white Franconian wine.
Hochheimer: the white wine (Hock) from the vineyards of Hochheim, Rhinegau. The best are: Domdechanei, Kirchenstück, Im Stein, Berg, Daubhaus, Im Bangert etc.
Hollenburg: Austrian white wines from the vineyards of Johannesberg, Prechte, Röhrendorfer, Steinbiegl, Schiefer.
Homburger: white wine of Franconia.
Hospices de Beaune: excellent red Burgundies of the commune of Pommard, especially: Cuvées Billarded and Dames de la Charité.

I

Ihringer Kaiserstuhler: red and white wines of Baden, Germany.
Ilbesheim: Rhenish Palatinate: Kirchberg, Rittersberg, Westerberg, white and red wines.
Inferno: red tart Italian wine from Lombardy.
Ingelfinger: white and red wines of Wurtemberg: Belsenbergerweg, Bühn, Goldberg, Hofäckerle, Krumme Stein, Neuweg.
Iphofen: Franconia: Apfelsteingrund, Berg, Buchen, Flösslein, Sandgrube, white wine.
Irouleguy: red table wines of the Basque country.
Isle St. George Haute-Sauterne: American wine of the Sauternes type.
Jean Latour: New York State champagne.
Jerusalemer: Austrian red and white wines of Styria.
Johannisberg: excellent Swiss white wine of the Canton Valais.
Johannisberger: one of the most famous growths of the Rhinegau (Hock). The best are Schloss and Klauss, after that Bangert, Bein, Fischerhöll, Goldatzel, Hölenkopf, Nonnenhöll, Steinäcker etc.
Jugendheimer: white wine (Hock) from the vineyards of Jugenheim, Rhenish Hesse.
Julienas: red wine, Beaujolais.
Jurancon: orange-colored dessert wine from the grapes of the vineyards near Pau.

K

Kaiserstuhler: white wines of the vineyards of Baden, Germany: Bickensohler, Bötzinger, Eckardsberger, Eichstettener, Föhrenberger, Küchlingsbergener etc.
Kaltererseewein: a good Tyrolean red wine.
Karthauser: red table wine of the Swiss Canton Thurgau.
— **Hofberg:** the finest white wine of the Eitelsbach vineyard in the Ruwer Valley.

Kauber: white wine (Hock) of the vineyards of Allenfels, Bacherweg, Backofen, Hutsberg, Lange Treppe, Schloßberg, Rheingräbe, Scheib etc. in Rhinegau.
Kauschauer: Roumanian red wine.
Kerschbacher: Austrian white wine of Styria.
Kiedricher: white Rhine wine (Hock) from the vineyards of Bein, Berg, Brücke, Gräfenberg, Langenberg, Oberberg, Turmberg, Weiberpfad etc.
Kippenheimer: red wine of Baden, Germany.
Kirchener Markgräfler: white wine of Baden, Germany.
Kirchhofen: Baden, Germany, white wine.
Kitzinger: white wine of Franconia.
Klein- & Grossbockenheim: Rhenish Palatinate: Berg, Halde, Dom, Erbacher, Goldgrube, Mulde white and red wine.
Klettgauer: Swiss red wines of the Canton Schaffhausen: Hallau, Wilchingen, Trasadingen.
Klosterneuburger: red and white Austrian wines.
Knipperle: Alsatian white wine.
Königsbacher: very fine wines of the Palatinate: Schloß and Idig (white), Jungfernwein (red).
Königswinter: red Rhenish wines: Drachenblut, Drachenfels, Rheinbleichart.
Korbel Rouge: sparkling American Burgundy.
Kornneuburger: Lower Austria: Bisamberg, Grafendorf, Hausleiten, Obersdorf, white and red wine.
Kovaszinc: Hungary, white and red wine.
Kövesder: white Hungarian table wine.
Krajin: Jugo-Slavia, white and red wine.
Krems: Lower Austria: Absdorf, Engabrunn, Furth, Gösing, Kammern, white and red wine.
Kreuznacher: white and red wines of the Nahe Valley: Belz, Breitweg, Hinkelstein, Kahlenberg, Klosterberg etc.
Kreuzwertheimer: white wine of Franconia.
Kymi: red wine of the Greek island Eubea.

L

Laacher: red wine from the Ahr Valley: Berg, Sonnenscheide.
Labegorce, Château: red Bordeaux, a Bourgeois of the Médoc, commune Margaux.
La Cabanne, Château: red Bordeaux, one of the first growths of Pomerol.
Lacaussade-Milon, Château: red Bordeaux, a Bourgeois growth of the Médoc, Pauillac.
La Côte: Swiss white wine of the Canton of Vaud: La Côte Luins, Mont, Fecky etc.
Lacrima di Castrovillari: dry Calabrian white wine.
Lacryma Christi: dry white wine from Campania.
La Dominique: red Bordeaux, one of the first growths of the Graves of St. Emilon.
Lafaurie Peyraguey, Château: white wine, one of the first growths of Sauternes, commune Bommes.
Lafite-Canteloup, Château: red Bordeaux, a Bourgeois supérieure growth of the Médoc.
Lafite-Rothschild, Château: red Bordeaux, Pauillac, first growth Médoc.
Lafitte, Château: Commune of Yvrac, Entre-deux-mers, red and white Bordeaux.

Lafitte-St. Estèphe, Château: red Bordeaux, one of the Bourgeois growths of the Médoc.
La Fleur, Château: red Bordeaux, one of the first growths of Pomerol.
La Fleur-Milon, Château: red Bordeaux, a Bourgeois growth of the Médoc, Pauillac.
Lafonta, Château: red and white Bordeaux.
La Gaffelière-Naudes, Château: red Bordeaux, one of the first growths of St. Emilion.
Lagarde, Domaine de: red Bordeaux, Graves, commune of Martillac.
La Gaude: red table wine of La Gaude, Dép. Var.
Lagrange, Château: red Bordeaux, one of the third growths of the Médoc, commune St. Julien.
Lagrime di S. Maddalena: Tridentine red wine.
La Lagune, Château: red Bordeaux, one of the third growths of the Médoc, commune of Ludon.
Lalande, Château: red Bordeaux, a Bourgeois growth of the Médoc, St. Estèphe.
Lamarque, Château: red Bordeaux, one of the Bourgeois growths of the Médoc.
La Marzelle-Figeac, Château: red Bordeaux, one of the first growths of the Graves of St. Emilion.
Lambrusco: tart Emilian red wine.
La Montagne, Château: white Bordeaux, one of the second growths of Sauternes commune Preignac.
Lamothe-Bouscaut, Cru: red Bordeaux, Graves, commune Cadaujac.
Lamothe-De-Bergeron, Château: red Bordeaux, a Bourgeois growth of the Médoc, commune Cussac.
Lamplberger: red and white Austrian wines.
Lanessan, Château: red Bordeaux, a Bourgeois growth of the Médoc, commune Cussac.
Langheimer: a white Franconian wine.
Langenlonsheim: Nahe, Rhineland: Borngraben, Epfenpfad, Hinterbergen, white wine.
Langoa-Barton, Château: red Bordeaux, a third growth of the Médoc, St. Julien.
Larose-Perganson, Château: red Bordeaux, a Bourgeois growth of the Médoc.
La Rue: sparkling American Burgundy.
Lascombes, Château de: red Bordeaux, one of the second growths of the Médoc, Margaux.
Latour, Château: one of the three first growths of the Médoc, commune of Pauillac.
La Tour-Blanche, Château: one of the first growths of Sauternes, white Bordeaux, commune of Bommes.
La Tour-Carnet, Château: red Bordeaux, a fourth growth of the Médoc.
La Tertre, Château: red Bordeaux, one of the fifth growths of the Médoc, commune of Arsac.
Laubenheimer: fine white wines (Hock) of Rhenish Hesse: Ay, Daubenberg, Distelfink, Häuschen, Steig, Steinkreuz.
Laudenbacher: white wine of Baden, Germany.
Laufener Markgräfler: white table wine of Baden, Germany.
Lauffen: Wurtemberg, red and white wines: Aier, Baumgarten, Dornhalden, Jungfrau.
Lavaux: Canton Vaud, Switzerland: Châtelard, Grandvaux, Epesses, Dézaley, Montreux, white and red wine.

Leanika: Hungarian white wine of the Kecskemet district.
Le Boscq, Château: red Bordeaux, a Bourgeois growth of the Médoc, St. Estèphe.
Le Crock, Château: red Bordeaux, a Bourgeois growth of the Médoc, St. Estèphe.
Leibnitz: Lower Austria: Altenbach, Ehrenhausen, Flamsberg, Gamlitz, white and red wine.
Leistadt: Rhenish Palatinate: Feldenberger, Hang, Kessler, white and red wine.
Leoville-Lascasses, Château: red Bordeaux, a second growth of the Médoc, St. Julien.
Lesbian Wine: Greek wine of the island of Lesbos.
Les Côtes de l'Orbe: white and red wines Canton Vaud, Switzerland.
Limoux, Blanquette de: semi-sparkling white wine from Limoux, Dép. Aude.
Lindauer Seewein: white wines from the vineyards around the Lake of Constance.
Lorcher: white wines (Hock) of the Rhinegau: Bodenthaler, Geisberger, Kappenberg, Niederflur, Pfaffenwiese.
Lorchhausener: white wines (Hock) of the Rhinegau: Hohberg, Laute, Sandmorgen, Fliesserstiel.
Loudenne, Château: red Bordeaux, a Bourgeois growth of the Médoc, commune of St. Yzans.
Louvière, Château la: red Bordeaux, Graves.
Lugana: red and white wine from Lombardy.
Luttenberger: Austrian red and white wines of Styria: Altenberg, Nachtigall, Eisenthürer.

M

Madeira: name of a number of sweet fortified wines from the Island of Madeira: Madeira Malvazia, Batardo, Calheta, Estrato, Oliveiras etc.
Madère, Château de: white Bordeaux wine, Graves, commune of Podensac.
Madrigal: Spanish white wine.
Maikammer: Rhenish Palatinate: Vogelsang, Spielfeld, Mandelacker, Kalkofen, white and red wines.
Malaga: one of the best dessert wines of Spain: Guinola, Lagrimas, Pedro Jimenez, Velez, seco, Vino tierno.
Malartic-Lagravière, Château: red Bordeaux, Graves, commune of Léognan.
Malescot-Saint-Exuperey, Château: red Bordeaux, one of the third growths of the Médoc, commune of Margaux.
Malle, Château de: white Bordeaux, Sauternes, commune of Preignac.
Malmsey: sée Malvasia.
Malvasia; Malmsey: a sweet dessert wine made of the Malvasia grape in Cyprus, Madeira, the Canary Islands, Italy and elsewhere.
Malvasia di Brindisi: sweet Apulian white wine.
— **Lipari:** sweet Sicilian white wine.
— **Lucania:** fragrant white wine from Basilicata.
— **Malatico:** sweet Emilian dessert wine.
Mangualde: Portuguese red wine.
Manzanilla: a pale dry Sherry.
Marburger: red Austrian wine of Styria.

Marbuzet, Château de: red Bordeaux, a Bourgeois growth of the Médoc, commune of St. Estèphe.
Marconnets, Les: red Burgundy from the vineyards of Beaune.
Marechaudes: red Burgundy from the vineyards of Aloxe-Corton.
Margaux, Château: red Bordeaux, first growth of the Médoc.
Markgräfler: white wine from the vineyards of Baden: Etringer, Kirchener, Laufener, Lörracher, Mühlheimer.
Markobrunner: white Hock, one of the best growths of the Rhinegau: Markobrunner Auslese, Kabinet, Schönborn.
Marquis d'Alesme-Becker, Château: red Bordeaux, a third growth of the Médoc, Margaux.
Marquis-de-Terme, Château: one of the fourth growths of the Médoc, Margaux.
Marsala: the best of Italian dessert wines made of grapes grown in Sicily: Inghilterra, Doppia, Concia, Italia, Concia Italia, Vergine.
Mascara: Algerian red wine.
Mavrodaphne: a very sweet red dessert wine from the vineyards of Patras, Greece.
Maximiner Grünhauser: one of the finest white wines of the Ruwer Valley, Germany.
Meersburger Seewein: red table wine from the vineyards near the Lake of Constance.
Mendoza: Argentine red wine.
Mercurey: red Burgundy of the Côte Chalonnaise.
Mergentheimer: white and red wines of Wurtemberg: Arkau, Elfenberg, Häsle, Kötter etc.
Merlot: Swiss red wine of the Canton Tessin.
Merziger: white wine of the Saar Valley.
Mettenheim: Rhine Hesse: Platte, Schloßberg, Herrengarten, Nordrieth, white wine.
Meursault: commune of the Côte de Beaune producing good white wine: Meursault Les Perrières, Les Charmes, La Goutte d'Or etc.
Michelbach: Wurtemberg, red wine.
Midi, Vins du: table wines of the vineyards of the Hérault, Gard and Dép. Aude.
Migraine: red wine of the vineyards of Auxerre, Dép. Yonne.
Millet, Château: red Bordeaux, Graves, commune of Portet.
Miltenberg: Franconia, white wine.
Minervois: one of the best pink wines of the Languedoc.
Mitidja: red and white Algerian wines.
Mittelheimer: white wines (Hock) of the Rhine: Edelmann, Glockerstrang, Grasswald, Lett etc.
Mölsheimer: white wines (Hock) of Rhenish Hesse: Hengstgewann, Hinter dem Kirchhof, Rothenbusch, Silberberg.
Mönchhofer: Austrian white wine of the Burgenland.
Moncorvo: Portuguese white wine.
Mònica: fortified Sardinian red wine.
Montagne, Château: red Bordeaux, a Bourgeois growth of the St. Emilionais.
Montagne, Château la: white Bordeaux, a second growth of Sauternes.
Montagny: an excellent white Burgundy of the Côte Chalonnaise.
Montalbano: red Tuscan wine.
Montbazillac: a rich golden-colored dessert wine from the vineyards of Montbazillac, Dép. Dordogne.
Mont d'Or: Swiss white wine of the Johannisberg type from Cully, Canton Vaud.

Monte Carlo: red and white Tuscan wine.

Montilla: a dry nutty Sherry from Montilla, region of Cordoba.

Montlouis: a red Touraine wine of the Loire Valley.

Montrachet Le: the finest white Burgundy from the vineyards of Le Montrachet, commune Puligny-Montrachet.

Montrose, Château: red Bordeaux, a second growth of the Médoc, St. Estèphe.

Mor: white Hungarian wine.

Morey-Saint-Denis: commune of the Côte de Nuits noted for its red wine. The best are: Clos de Tart, Clos de la Roche and Clos des Lambrays.

Morgon: excellent Beaujolais of the commune of Villie-Morgon.

Morin, Château: red Bordeaux, a Bourgeois growth of the Médoc, commune St. Estèphe.

Moscatel: name given to all wines made of muscat grapes in Spain and the Argentine.

— **de Setubal:** Portuguese white wine made of muscat grapes.

Moscato Atesino: sweet white Tridentine muscat wine.

— **di Capestrano Atesino:** sweet Abruzzian muscat wine.

— **die Casteggio:** white sweet muscat wine from Lombardy.

— **di Cosenza:** white, very sweet Calabrian muscat wine.

— **die Lucania:** white muscat wine from Basilicata.

— **di Montalcino:** sweet white Tuscan wine.

— **die Pantelleria:** white sweet Sicilian muscat wine.

— **di Stromboli:** red wine of Sicily.

— **die Tempio:** sweet Sardinian muscat wine.

— **di Trani:** very sweet white Apulian wine.

Moulin-à-Vent: the best red wine of the Beaujolais from the vineyards of the communes of Chénas and Romanèche-Thorins.

— **-du-Bourg, Domaine du:** red Bordeaux, one of the Bourgeois growths of the Mèdoc, commune of Listrac.

— **-du-Cadet:** red Bordeaux, one of the first growths of St. Emilion.

— **-Saint-Georges:** red Bordeaux, one of the first growths of St. Emilion.

Mouton d'Armailhacq, Château: red Bordeaux, one of the fifth growths of the Médoc, commune Pauillac.

Mouton-Rothschild, Château: red Bordeaux, the first of the second growths of the Médoc, commune Pauillac.

Münsterer: the white wine (Hock) of the vineyards of Münster, Nahe Valley: Kapellenberg, Langenberg.

Muscat de Frontignan: sweet Californian wine.

Muscadet: white wine from the vineyards of the Lower Loire.

Muscatel: one of the sweet fortified wines of California.

Musigny, Les: famous red Burgundy from the vineyards of Chambolle-Musigny, Dép. Côte d'Or.

Muskotaly: fine white muscat wine from the Villany vineyards, Hungary.

Mussbach: Rhenish Palatinate: Stecken, Pabst, Lauterbach, Spiegel, white and red wines.

N

Nackenheimer: one of the best white wines (Hock) of Rhenish Hesse: Engelsberg, Riesling, Rothenberg etc.
Napa Valley: wine-producing district of California which produces some of the best red and white wines.
Nebouana: one of the best red table wines of Roumania.
Nemes Kadarka: red table wine from the Kadar vineyards, Hungary.
Nenin, Château: red Bordeaux, one of the first growths of Pomerol.
Neszmély: Hungarian white and red wine.
Neuberger: Austrian red and white wines of Styria.
Neustädter: white wine (Hock) from different vineyards of the Palatinate: Berg, Böhl, Haardt, Hüttbaum, Klausenberg, Vogelsang etc.
Nieder-Ingelheim: Rhenish Hesse: Bruderweg, Flecht, Horn, Steinacker.
Niedermenniger: white wine of the Saar Valley: Euchariusberg, Herrenberg, Sonnenberg.
Niersteiner: white wines (Hock) of excellent quality from the vineyards of Rhenish Hesse: Auflangen, Domthal, Glöck, Hipping, Rehbach, Rohr, Thal etc.
Norheimer: white wine (Hock) from the Nahe Valley: Hasselberg, Hinterberg.
Nuits-Saint-Georges: very fine red Burgundy from the commune Nuits-Saint-Georges, Dép. Côte d'Or. Best vineyards: Les Saint-Georges, Aux Cailles, Les Prulièrs, Les Murgers and Les Vaucrains.
Nussdorfer: Austrian white wines: Nussberger, Prälatenwein etc.

O

Oberemmeler: fine white wines from the vineyards of Oberemmel in the Saar Valley: Agritiusberg, Rauler, Rosenberg.
Ober-Hollabrunn: Lower Austria: Alberndorf, Braunsdorf, Frauendorf, white and red wine.
Ober-Ingelheimer: Rhenish Hesse: Atzel, Bellen, Heerweg, Kirchenstück white and red wine.
Oberlahnsteiner: white Rhenish wine (Hock) from the vineyards of Oberlahnstein: Bauernthal, Leimgrube, Hasenberg, Mainzberg, Helmesthal.
Ockenheimer: white wines (Hock) of Rhenish Hesse: Bürgerweg, Füllkopf, Hölle, Jakobsberg, Kuhweg.
Ockfener: one of the best white wines of the Saar. The best vineyards are: Bockstein, Herrenberg, Geisberg Neuwies and Heppenstein.
Odopesti: Roumania, white and red wine.
Oestricher: one of the finest white wines (Hock) of the Rhinegau from the vineyards of Doosberg, Klostergarten, Eisenweg, Kellerberg, Neuberg etc.
Ofener: red and white Hungarian wines: Adlersberg, Blocksberg, Gellerthegyi, Türkenblut.
Ohio State Port: American wine of the Port type.
Olivier, Château: red Bordeaux, Graves commune of Léognan.
Oloroso: a dark rich and popular type of Sherry.

Oppenheimer: the white wines (Hock) from the vineyards of Oppenheim, Rhenish Hesse: Sackträger, Herrenberg, Kreuz, Krötenbrunnen, Daubhaus etc.
Orbe: Canton Vaud: La Sarraz, Arnex, Valeyres, Champvent, white wine.
Orvieto: sweet white Umbrian wine.
Osthofener: white wines (Hock) of Rhenish Hesse: Goldberg, Hasenbiss, Hinter der Kirche etc.
Ottweiler: red and white Alsatian wines.

P, Q

Paceta: red table wine of Rioja, Spain.
Palestro: Algerian red wine.
Palmer, Château: red Bordeaux, one of the third growths of the Médoc.
Pape-Clement, Château: red Bordeaux, Graves commune Pessac.
Parnay, Château de: famous white wine of the Saumur district of Anjou.
Passe-Tous-Grains: a red wine made in Burgundy from Pinot and Gamay grapes mixed.
Pavie, Château: red Bordeaux, a first growth of St. Emilion.
Pelletan, Château: red Bordeaux, one of the first growths of St. Emilion.
Peralta: a sweet, Tawny fortified wine of Navarre.
Pergos: a red table wine of Morea, Greece.
Perrières, Les: excellent white Burgundy of the commune of Meursault, Dép. Côte d'Or.
Peruvian Wine: these are grown chiefly in the regions of Ica, Lima, Pisco and Sicamba.
Petit-Faurie-de-Soutard, Château: red Bordeaux, one of the first growths of St. Emilion.
Petit-Moulinet: red Bordeaux, a second growth of Pomerol.
Petit Village, Château: red Bordeaux, one of the first growths of Pomerol.
Pfaffstättener: Austrian red and white wines: Tavlsteiner, Zirnberger (white), Höll (white and red).
Pfullinger: white and red wines from Wurtemberg: Katzenbohl, In Linden, Raith, Wagenrieth.
Phelan-Ségur, Château: red Bordeaux, one of the Bourgeois growths of the Médoc, St. Estèphe.
Piada, Château: white Bordeaux, a second growth of Sauternes.
Picard. Canteloup, Château: red Bordeaux, a Bourgeois growth of the Médoc, St. Estèphe.
Piccoli: sweet Italian white wine from Venezia Giulia.
Pichon-Longueville, Château: red Bordeaux, a second growth of the Médoc commune Pauillac.
Piesporter: one of the best white wines of the Moselle: Goldtröpfchen, Falkenberg, Lay, Taubengarten.
Pinot: red and white Italian wine from Venezia Giulia.
Polcevera: dry white Ligurian wine.
Pomal: a red table wine of Rioja, Spain.
Pontac-Lynch, Château: red Bordeaux, one of the Bourgeois growths of the Médoc, commune of Cantenac.
Pontet-Canet, Château: red Bordeaux, the first of the fifth growths of the Médoc, Pauillac.

Port: a fortified wine made from grapes grown in the valley of the upper Douro.
Port-Ludon: red Bordeaux of the Médoc.
Pouilly-Fumé: white wine of the vineyards of Pouilly-sur-Loire, Dép. Nièvre.
Pouilly-Fuissé: white wine of the communes Pouilly and Fuissé, Dép. Saône-et-Loire.
Poujeaux, Château: red Bordeaux, a Bourgeois growth of the Médoc, commune Moulis.
Praminer: dry white Italian wine from Venezia Giulia.
Priban, Château: red Bordeaux, one of the Bourgois growths of the Médoc.
Priorato: red Catalane wine.
Prosecco: white Italian wine from Venezia Giulia.
Prosecco: white dry Venetian wine.
Purkaer: red Roumanian table wine.
Quart de Chaume, Le: white Anjou wine.

R

Rabaud-Promis, Château: white Bordeaux, one of the first growths of the Sauternes, commune de Bommes.
Radolfzeller: red wine from the vineyards near the Lake of Constance.
Ramandolo: very sweet yellow Venetian wine.
Randersacker: one of the best Franconian white wines of the Würzburg district known as Steinwein: Lämmerberg, Marsberg, Pfülben, Spielberg.
Rappoltsweiler: red an white Alsatian wines.
Ratscher: white wine from Styria: Austria.
Recioto: red Venetian wine.
Remicher: a white wine from the Remich vineyards of the Grand Duchy of Luxembourg.
Reutlinger: white and red wines from the vineyards of Reutlingen, Wurtemberg.
Rhauenthaler: one of the finest of white wines (Hock) from the Rhinegau. The best vineyards are: Langenstück, Pfaffenberg, Alzern, Bienengarten, Roseneck, Taubenberg, Geishorn, Geierstein.
Rheinau: Swiss red wine of the Canton Zurich.
Rhenser: white Rhine wine (Hock) from the vineyards of Alber, Corneliusgraben, Gassenberg, Geissener Berg, Königstuhl etc.
Ribolla: sweet Italian white wine from Venezia Giulia.
Richebourg: a superlative red Burgundy from a vineyard of the commune Vosne-Romanée.
Riesling: white Italian wine from Venezia Giulia.
Rieussec, Château: white Bordeaux, one of the first growths of Sauternes, commune Fargues.
Rioja: red and white wines of the Ebro Valley, Spain.
Riquewihr: fine Alsatian white wine.
Rivesaltes: sweet dessert wine made from muscat grapes in the French Pyrenees.
Roboso: red Venetian wine, tart.
Rochet, Château: red Bordeaux, one of the fourth growths of the Médoc, St. Estèphe.
Rödelseer: white wine of Franconia: Pfülben, Rothenfels.
Romaneche-Thorins: a well-known growth of the Beaujolais, red Burgundy.

Romanée-Conti: one of the finest of red Burgundies, commune Vosne-Romanée, Côte de Nuits.
Rossese: red Ligurian wine.
Roussette: a popular white wine from the vineyards of Seyssel, Dép. Ain.
Ruedesheimer: one of the best known white wines (Hock) from the vineyards of the Rhinegau: Berg, Brunnen, Berg Rosenberg, Schlossberg, Bienengarten, Ehrenfels, Kirchweg, Rosengarten etc.
Rùfina: a Tuscan red wine.
Ruppertsberger: one of the finest white wines (Hock) of the Palatinate. The best vineyards are: Gaisböhl, Hofstück, Hausbrunnen, Reiterpfad, Achtmorgen, Kieselberg etc.
Russin: Swiss white wine of the Canton Genève.
Ruszter: white and red Hungarian wines.

S

Saalecker: white wine of Franconia.
Sacrantino: fragrant Umbrian red wine.
Sagunta: red Spanish table wine.
Saint-Estèphe, Château: red Bordeaux, one of the Bourgeois growths of St. Estèphe.
Saint-Georges, Les: red Burgundy, the best of the vineyards of Nuits-Saint-Georges, Dép. Côte d'Or.
Saint-Peray: a famous sparkling white wine produced in the communes of the Ardèche, Rhône Valley.
Saint-Pourcain: a famous still white wine of the commune Allier, Loire Valley.
Saint-Satur: excellent white wine from the Sancerre district, Berry.
Salta: red and white Argentine wines.
Salurner: red Tyrolian wine from the vineyards near Bozen.
Sambatella: red table wine of Calabria.
Samos: a sweet Greek dessert wine from the vineyards of Samos.
Sancerre, Château de: a white wine from the vineyards of Sancerre, Dép. Cher.
San Gimignanao: a good red table wine of the Chianti district, Italy.
Sanglovese: red Emilian wine.
Sangue di Drago-Meranese di collina: dry Tridentine red wine.
— **Giuda:** dry red Lombard wine.
Sankt Galler Oberländer: Swiss red wines of the Canton Zurich: Sargans, Mels and Wellenstädt.
— **Rheintaler:** Swiss red wines of the Canton Zurich: Berneck, Altstätten, Rebstein, Balgach.
— **Louis:** red wine of Lorraine.
— **Magdalener:** the best red wine of Saint-Magdalen, Bozen in Tyrol.
Sansella: red dry Lombard wine.
Santa Catharina: white Brasilian wine.
— **Giustina:** Tridentine red wine.
— **Magdalena:** Tridentine red wine.
Sante-Stefano: red table wine from Tuscany.
— **di Cerignola:** red, rather tart Apulian wine.
Saragossa: red Spanish wine.
Sarganzer: Swiss red and white wines: Buel, Ackeren, Hinterschloss, Ratell, Sandgrub etc.

Satigny: Swiss white wine of the Canton of Genève.
Sauerschwabenheimer: red and white wines of Rhenish Hesse: Dreimorgen, Geissberg, Häuserweg, Hochstaffel.
Saulnes: red and white wines of Lorraine.
Sauvignon: white Italian wine from Venezia Giulia.
Scharlachberger: one of the finest white wines (Hock) of Rhenish Hesse: Rochusberg, Steinkantweg etc
Schiersteiner: fine white wine of the Rhine: Berg, Dachsberg, Hölle, Höllberg, Sonnenberg, Zäumchen.
Schloß Johannisberger: very fine white wine (Hock) of the Rhinegau: Nonnenhöll, Kehr, Oberberg, Osterweinberg, Rothsang, Langenberg, Kippelacker.
Schodener: white wine of the Saar Valley: Bockstein, Geisberg.
Schönnaer: Tyrolian red wine from the district Meran: Schloßgut Goyen, Schloßgut Vernau.
Semillon Riesling: dry American white wine.
Sercial: one of the most distinctive dry wines of the island of Madeira.
Serrigny: a red Burgundy of the Côte d'Or.
Sherry: a fortified wine made from white grapes grown in the Jerez district of South Spain.
Siblinger: a fine white wine of the canton of Schaffhausen, Switzerland.
Sidra: dessert wine of Tripolis.
Sigalas-Rabaud, Château: white Bordeaux, one of the first growths of Sauternes, commune of Bommes.
Sistov: Bulgarian white wine.
Smith-Haut-Lafite, Château: red Bordeaux, one of the best growths of the Graves, comune Martillac.
Soave: half sweet white Venetian wine.
Soleil de Sierre: a golden wine from the wineyards of Sierre, Canton Valais.
Somlauer Auslese: a fine white table wine from the vineyards of Somlyo in Hungary.
Sopron: Hungary, white and red wine.
Sparkling Catawba: Ohio State wine of the Champagne type.
Spumanti dell'Elba: sparkling Tuscan wine.
Staffelberger: red and white wines of Franconia.
Staffelsteiner: white wine of Franconia.
Staufener: white wine of Baden from the vineyards of Burghalden, Schloßberg.
Steinberger: one of the finest white wines (Hock) of the Rhinegau: Rosengarten, Kabinett, Goldener Becher, Neuweg, Oberhöhe, Hühnerschritt, Pflänzer, Zehntstück.
Steiniger: dessert wine of Transylvania.
Suduiraud, Château: white Bordeaux, one of the first growths of Sauternes, commune of Preignac.
Supreme Pale Dry Sherry: Sweet Californian dessert wine.
Syracuse: a red dessert wine made mostly of muscat grapes in Sicily.
Szeksard: red table wine from the vineyards of Tolna, Hungary.
Szökefalvaer: white Transylvanian wines: Leanyka, Sauvignon, Som.
Szomerodny: one of the best white table wines of Hungary.

T

Talbot, Château: red Bordeaux, one of the fourth growths of the Médoc, St. Julien.
Talyaer: a fortified Hungarian wine.
Tarragona: e sweet fortified wine from the vineyards of Tarragona in Spain.
Tarrasa: Spanish dessert wine.
Tauberwein: red and white wine of Baden, Germany.
Tavel: one of the best pink wines from the vineyards of Lirac, Rhône.
Tawny Port: a blend of wines of a number of years kept at Oporto for many years and matured in wood.
Teciuci: white and red Roumanian wine.
Terezovac: Bosnian wine.
Terlaner: Tyrolian white wine.
Terlaner-Verduzzo: dry white Italian wine from Venezia Giulia.
Termano: Tridentine dry white wine.
Termo: a white Portuguese wine made of grapes grown in the Lisbon region.
Teroldego: Tridentine red wine.
Terrano: Italian red wine from Venezia Giulia.
Tertre, Château du: red Bordeaux, one of the fifth growths of the Médoc, commune of Arsac.
Thiaucourt: red and white wine of Lorraine.
Tifliser Riesling: red and white Caucasian wine.
Tinto do Bocca de Mina: red Portuguese wine.
Tokai: white Italian wine from Venezia Giulia.
Tokay: name of the wines grown in the vineyards of the Hegyalda district in Hungary. The best known are: Tokaij Essencia, Tokaij aszu and Tokaij Szamarodner.
Tokay-Ausbruch: one of the good Hungarian golden-colored wines.
Tomina: red Bolivian wine.
Torcolato di Braganze: dry white Venetian wine.
Tordaer: red and white wine of Transylvania.
Torres Vedra: red and white wines grown in the vineyards of the Tagus Valley near Lisbon.
Trabacher: a fine white wine of the Moselle: Schlossberg, Ungsberg etc.
Trabener: a fine delicately flavored wine of the Moselle. The best vineyards are: Würzgarten, Kräuterhaus, Rickerlsberg.
Travel: a good pink wine from the Rhône Valley.
Trebbiano: Abbruzzian wine, white, dry.
— white Emilian wine.
Trierer: white wine of the Moselle: Grünhäuser, Avelsbacher, Tiergärtner.
Trittenheimer: one of the best white wines of the Moselle: Laurentiusberg, Falkenberg, Apotheke.
Troplong-Mondot, Château: red Bordeaux, one of the first growths of the St. Emilion.
Türkheimer: red and white Alsatian wines.
Twann: deep golden wine from the vineyards of Sienne in the Swiss Canton Berne.

U

Uerziger: white wine of the Moselle. The best vineyards are Kranklay, Schwarzlay, Würzgarten, Herzlei.
Uffenheimer: white wine of Franconia.
Uhla: Syrian dessert wine.
Ungsteiner: white wine of the Palatinate: Brenner, Edelknecht, Feuerberg, Herrenberg, Kreuz etc.
Untertürkheimer: red and white wines of Wurtemberg: Altenberg, Blick, Deukenklinge, Galgenberg, Möchberg.

V

Vachery: Caucasian red wine.
Valdepenas: red Spanish table wine.
Valencia: dark red wine from the Province of Levante, Spain.
Valgella: dry red Lombard wine.
Valpantena: very soft red Venetian wine.
Valpolicella: red Venetian wine.
Vedrines, Château: white Bordeaux, one of the second growths of Sautnernes, commune of Barsac.
Verdiso: white dry Venetian wine.
Verduzzo: white Lombard wine.
Vermentino: dry white Ligurian wine.
— di Gallura: dry Sardinian white wine.
Vernaccia: very dry Sardinian white wine.
— di S. Gimignano: dry white wine form Tuscany.
Vianna do Castello: red Portuguese wine.
Villemaurine, Château: red Bordeaux, one of the first growths of St. Emilion.
Villinger: Swiss red wine of the Canton Aargau.
Vin nobile di Montepulciano: slightly bitterish Tuscan red wine.
Vino Gerapigo: red Portuguese wine.
— die Bacco: red Greek wine.
— delle Cinque Terre: very sweet white Ligurian wine.
— santo: a dark brown Greek dessert wine.
Virginia Dare: pink Californian wine.
Vollradser: one of the best white wines (Hock) of the Rhinegau.
Volnay: fine red Burgundy of the Côte de Beaune, Dép. Côte d'Or.
Vöslauer: red and white Austrian wines: Goldeck, Gradenthaler, Oberkirchner.
Vouvray: the chief wine-producing center for sparkling and still white wine in the Touraine country.

W

Wachenheimer: the finest white wine of the Palatinate: Altenberg, Bächel, Dürkheimer Weg. Schenkenböhl, Gerichtspfad etc.
Wachenheimer: excellent white wine of Rhenish Hesse: Held, Rothenbusch.
Walporzheimer: red wine of the Ahr Valley: Domdechanei, Beatrixberg, Domlei, Klosterlei.

Wehlener: fine white wine of the Moselle: Münzlei, Nonnenberg.

Weinheimer: red and white wines of Baden, Germany.

Wiltinger: fine white wine of the Saar Valley: Rosenberg, Schlossgarten, Braunfels, Kupp, Scharzberger, Scharzhofberger.

Winkeler: fine white wine (Hock) of the Rhinegau. The best vineyards are: Bienenberg, Jesuitengarten, Hasensprung, Dachsberg, Honigsberg, Kreuzweg, Neuberg.

Winterthurer: Swiss red wines: Brühlberg, Fuchslisbrunnen, Rappenhalden, Veltheim, Stadtberg.

Winzenheimer: white wine of the Nahe Valley: Berg, Brauen, Metzler, Setzling.

Wormser: white wine (Hock) of Rhenish Hesse: Liebfraumilch, Kapuzinergarten, Luginsland.

Würzburger: the fine white wines of the Palatinate from the vineyards of Würzburg and nearby vineyards of Franconia; the best are: Schlossberg, Pfaffenberg, Abtsleite, Felsenleiste, Gutenthal, Harfe, Heiligengeistwein, Schalksberg.

Y

Yquem, Château d': white Bordeaux, the finest growth of Sauternes.

Yvorne: Swiss white wine: Bezencenet, Clos de la George, Clos du Rocher, Maison Blanche.

Z

Zeller: red wine of Baden, Germany.

Zeltenberger: white Alsatian wine.

Zeltinger: white wine of the Moselle. The best vineyards are: Stefanslay, Kirchenpfad, Schlossberg, Sonnenuhr, Himmelreich, Rotlay.

Zomborer: white Hungarian wine.

Zwölfmalgreiener: white and red Tyrolian wines: Hörtenberger, Justina, Laifacher.

Spirits, Liqueurs, Bitters etc.

Absinth: elixir distilled with wormwood, anise, fennel, balm and hyssop, about 50 % alcohol, forbidden in many countries because of its injurious effect on the nervous system. It is now exported from France under the name Pernod, a substitute without wormwood.

Advocaat: a Dutch liqueur the base of which is brandy and egg yolks.

Allasch: a highly rectified kummel strongly flavored with caraway seeds, originally made in Allasch near Riga but now also made in Germany and elsewhere.

Amer Picon: one of the most popular of French bitters.

Angostura Bitters: the most renowned brand of bitters named after the town of Angostura in Venezuela where a German physician, Dr. Siegert, first made it for his own use. It is a compound from the bitter aromatic bark of the Casparia tree and a number of herbs and spices.

Anisette: a sweet French liqueur flavored with anise and coriander.

Apple Jack: name of a spirit extracted from cider frozen solid and left out-of-doors during the winter months.

Apricot Brandy, Abricotine: a cordial, the base of which should be brandy, made with fresh or dried apricots and sweetened.

Apry: an excellent very sweet apricot-flavored liqueur with grape-brandy base.

Aquavit: a highly rectified colorless Scandinavian spirit distilled from potatoes or grain, flavored with caraway seeds.

Armagnac: name of the brandy distilled from grapes in the Departement Gers in France. The main qualities are: Grand, Fin and Petit Armagnac. The flavor of Armagnac differs from Cognac and is prized by connoisseurs.

Arrack, Arack, Arrak: a fiery spirit distilled in India from rice. Batavia Arrack is distilled from molasses and rice in Indonesia.

Baccardi: a popular very light brand of rum.

Barack Pálinka: a dry fiery brandy distilled from fresh ripe apricots in Hungary.

Benedictine: a pale green herb cordial, sweet and highly aromatized, formerly made by monks of the Benedictine order in Fécamp in Normandy, and since the French revolution commercially by a company. The components are a trade secret. One of the finest of French liqueurs.

Blackberry Brandy: a spiced blackberry cordial with a brandy base.

— **Liqueur:** a blackberry-flavored liqueur made from blackberry brandy with a certain percentage of red wine.

Boonekamp: an excellent bitters containing cloves, fennel, coriander, gentian, liquorice, Curaçao peels and other flavoring agents.

Bourbon Whisky: whisky made from the fermented mash of grain of which 51 % must be maize.

Brandy: F. Eau de vie; G. Weinbrand: spirits distilled from the fermented juice of fruit, particularly from grapes.

Calvados: a pale brandy distilled from sound but not overripe partly sweet and partly sour apples in Normandy aged in wood like other brandies.

Cassis, Crème de cassis: a cordial made of black currants, also black currant syrup.

Certosa: an Italian liqueur resembling Chartreuse made in different colors and flavors.

Chartreuse: famous liqueur made of herbs and spices originally by Carthusian monks at the monastry of La Grande Chartreuse in France. It is made in green and yellow. Formerly there was also a third white elixir which was the most alcoholic of all three.

Cherry Brandy: a sweet cordial made on brandy base with the juice of ripe cherries and some of the crushed stones. Kirsch (q. v.) is a pure white unsweetened distilled cherry brandy.

— **Liqueur:** rich heavy liqueur made of wild cherries with a base of brandy. Popular brands are Cherry Rocher and Cherry Heering.

Cognac: brandy distilled from the wine made in the Departement Charente in France of which Cognac is the capital and should be applied to brandies of this departement only. The finest cognacs are distilled in the Grande Champagne, Fine Champagne and Borderies districts, other vineyards are Fin Bois and Bon Bois. In practice Cognac is a blend of the different kinds of brandies distilled from these districts. The French taste in brandies not being the same as in America, Great Britan, Germany etc. Cognac is blended specially for various other countries. The significance of letters on Cognac bottles are:

E — extra or special	P — pale
F — fine	S — superior
M — mellow	V — very
O — old	X — extra

V. S. O. P. for instance means very soft old pale.

Cointreau: one of the best white French liqueurs flavored with the peel of Curaçao and other oranges.

Cordial Medoc: a liqueur made of orange Curaçao, cognac and dessert wine.

Crème: name of a number of very sweet French liqueurs made with fruit or other flavor, such as:

Crème d'ananas	=	pineapple
Crème de bananes	=	banana
Crème de cacao	=	chocolate
Crème de cassis	=	black currant
Crème de fraises	=	strawberries
Crème de menthe	=	peppermint
Crème de moka	=	coffee
Crème de noyau	=	cherries and cherry stones
Crème de Prunelle	=	sloes
Crème de vanille	=	vanilla.

Curaçao: an orange-flavored liqueur made originally in Holland from green Curaçao oranges, cane sugar and brandy, now also made in other countries on the base of brandy, gin or other spirits flavored with the peel of Curaçao oranges, as yellow, white or green Curaçao. Made in three grades: sec, double sec and triple sec.

Danziger Goldwasser: a highly rectified spirit flavored with cinnamon, coriander, herbs and spices, lightly sweetened, containing a large number of pieces of gold leaf originally distilled in Danzig but now made elsewhere as well.

Drambui: the only liqueur made from Scotch whisky, honey, herbs and spices.

Eau de vie de marc: a spirit distilled from the husks of grapes which have been pressed to make wine.

Enzian: a spirit distilled from the roots of gentian found in the European alps and the Pyrenees, made chiefly in Germany and Switzerland.

Forbidden Fruit: a sweet citrus liqueur made of West Indies grapefruit, brandy and other flavoring agents.

Genever: Dutch Gin: a spirit distilled from grain and malt flavored with juniper berries.

Gin: a distillate of grain spirits with juniper berries, herbs and flavors according to the taste of the distillers. There are two types of London gin, dry and sweet.

Grand-Marnier: very fine French liqueur with a brandy base flavored with orange.

Grappa: an Italian spirit corresponding to the French eau-de-vie de marc.

Grenadine: a very sweet reddish, non-alcoholic syrup flavored with pomegranates, used for drinks and cocktails.

Halv om Halv: a bitter liqueur made from Curaçao orange peels and other flavoring agents.

Kirsch: F. Kirsch; G. Kirschwasser: a pure white brandy distilled from the juice of very small, juicy black cherries in the Black Forest in Germany, the Vosges and Switzerland. The Black Forest Schwarzwälder Kirschwasser is considered the best.

Kornbranntwein: a spirit distilled from rye, wheat, buckwheat, oats or barley in Germany.

Kummel, Kümmel: a popular liqueur distilled from grain, flavored with caraway seeds, cumin and sometimes anise, not colored. Made in Berlin, Holland and formerly in Riga.

Liqueur d'Or: a colorless, lemon-flavored imitation of Danziger Goldwasser.

Mandarine, Mandarinette: liqueur flavored with tangerine.

Maraschino: Marasquin: liqueur distilled from marasca cherries in Dalmatia and exported from Zara in straw-covered bottles.

Marc de Bourgogne: a spirit distilled from the husks of Burgundy grapes which have been pressed to make wine.

— **de Champagne:** spirit distilled from the husks of the grapes grown in the Champagne district which have been pressed to make wine.

Peach Brandy: various spirits, mostly brandy, sweetened and flavored with fresh or dried peaches.

Prunelle: a French liqueur made of fresh sloes.

Quetsch: a pure white spirit distilled chiefly in Alsace from the fermented juice of plums.

Raspberry Brandy: F. Framboise; G. Himbeergeist: a dry fiery pure white brandy distilled from raspberries in Germany, Alsace and Switzerland.

Rum: Rhum: spirits made of the fermented juice of the sugar cane, for the most part of the molasses with an addition of the residue of previous distillations. There are four types: 1. Cuban rum, either white or gold; 2. Jamaica rum, dark and rather pungent; 3. Barbados, New England, Mexican and Puerto Rican rums, which are not quite as good as the former; 4. rum distilled in the Southern Caribbean isles.

Slivowitz: a very fine plum brandy distilled with a part of the crushed plum kernels in Yugoslavia, Hungary and Roumania.

Steinhäger: a highly rectified white grain brandy flavored with juniper berries and other flavoring agents made in Germany.

Swedish or Caloric Punch: a highly alcoholic compound with a basis of rum or arrack flavored with spices and other flavouring agents, served neat or with hot water in winter.

Tafia: name of a spirit distilled from molasses in the West Indies.

Vieille Cure: a fine green-colored French liqueur flavored with herbs and other ingredients.

Vodka: spirits distilled from rye or wheat (sometimes potatoes) with a small amount of malt in Russia. It is not aged and must be served very cold.

Whisky, Whiskey: spirits obtained by the distillation of grain, rye, corn, barley, wheat etc. Scotch and Irish whiskies are made primarily from barley, American and Canadian rye whiskies from rye and bourbon whisky from corn, all contain a certain amount of barley malt. Scotch and Irish whiskies contain as much as 40 % barley malt. In Scotland the barley malt is dried in kilns above peat fire thus giving the smoky taste.

Bar Drinks

Cobbler: name of an iced and sweetened „long" drink made with various wines and spirits, shaved ice and fruit or foliage as decoration.

Cocktail: a short drink, cold and hard, chiefly alcoholic, made by mixing two, three or more ingredients in a shaker with shaved ice, served in small glasses with or without a spiral of lemon peel.

Cooler: a long drink served in a tall glass with a lump of ice, filled up with carbonated water, ginger ale etc.

Crusta: name of an elaborate cocktail now somewhat demoded. For crustas the rim of the glass is usually moistened with lemon juice and then dipped in granulated sugar.

Daisy: an elaborate kind of cooler strained into a small highball glass or a goblet and decorated with fruit, flowers or a sprig of mint.

Fizz: a thoroughly mixed and frappéed drink: strained into a 6- to 8 ounce glass and fizzed by adding charged water in a fine stream; it should be served foaming.

Flip: wine or liquor shaken with sugar or sugar syrup and cracked ice, a whole egg added, strained into a 3-to 4 ounce glass with a dash of grated nutmeg on top.

Highball: any tall iced drink consisting of a base liquid, alcoholic or non-alholic with or without flavoring agents and charged water, but without citrus juices.

Julep: a long drink made of whisky, brandy, rum etc., cracked ice, green mint and sugar or sugar syrup.

Sangaree: chilled and sweetened wine, beer or liquor served in a highball glass dusted with grated nutmeg.

Sling: a mixture made with lemon and either sugar or a sweet liqueur, served hot or cold. Cold slings are finished off with charged water.

Smash: a long drink with plenty of ice, more or less spirits and mint as a flavoring agent.

Sour: a long drink with a brandy, whisky, gin or apple-jack basis with plenty of ice and some citrus juice.

Swizzle: a kind of cocktail mixed with a swizzle stick used as a whisk, instead of being shaken in a shaker.

Toddy: 1. a hot drink made with spirits, hot water, sugar and lemon. 2. a long drink similar to sling but made with plain water.

A

Absinth Cocktail: 3 parts Absinth, 2 parts water, 1 teaspoonful sugar syrup, a dash of anisette, 4 dashes Angostura, a twist of lemon over each cocktail.

Ale Egg Nog: egg yolk, sugar and a pinch of sugar whisked with hot ale.

— **Flip:** egg, sugar, syrup, cracked ice and ale mixed in a shaker, strained into a small sour glass, a pinch of grated nutmeg on top.

1. *Bar glass*
2. *Strainer*
3. *Shaker*
4. *Squirter*
5. *Electric shaker*
6. *Siphon*
7. *Ice pick*
8. *Strainer for fruit juice*
9. *Handpress for fruit juice*

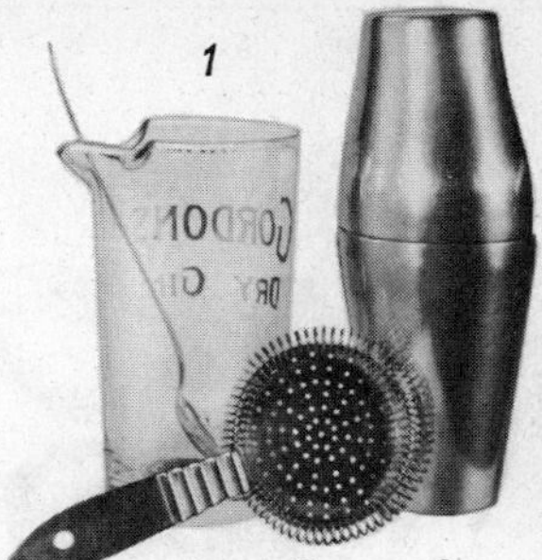

1 2 3

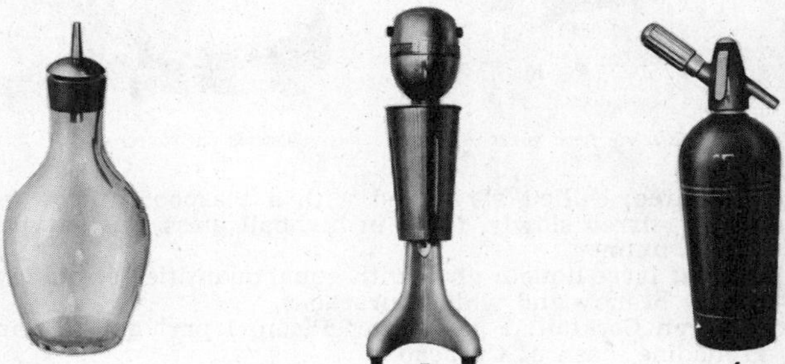

4 5 6

7 8 9

1. Collins glass. 2. Fizz glass, 3. Small cocktail glass, 4. Large cocktail glass 5. Whisky or Highball glass. 6. Old-fashioned glass, 7. Sour or Julep glass

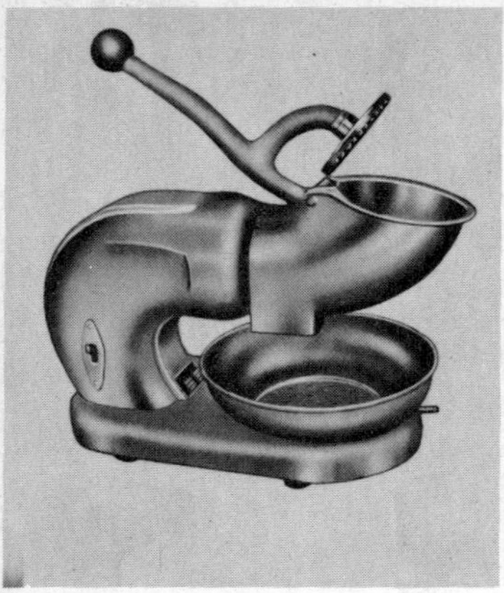

Electric fruit press

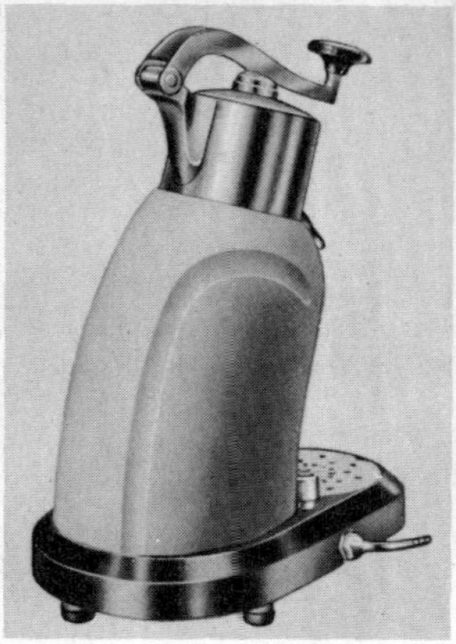

Electric ice shaver

Ale Sangaree: chilled ale mixed with a teaspoonful powder sugar, stirred slowly, filled in highball glass, dusted with grated nutmeg.

Allemania: large liqueur glass with equal quantities of brandy, cherry brandy and white Curaçao.

Amer Picon Cocktail: 1 part Amer Picon, 1 part gin, $^1/_4$ part grenadine, dash of Curaçao.

American Beauty Cocktail: 1 part orange juice, 1 part grenadine, 1 part brandy, 1 part French vermouth, dash of Crème de menthe, topped with a little Port.

— **Flip:** same as brandy flip made with rye whisky.

— **Glory:** lump of ice in champagne glass, juice of half an orange, 2 dashes of sugar syrup, filled with 2 parts champagne and 1 part charged water.

Angel's Wing: pony glass filled $^2/_3$ with apricot-brandy, covered with whipped cream.

Apple Blossom: applejack Manhattan with 2 dashes grenadine and 2 dashes pineapple juice, stirred.

Applejack Toddy: 1 part sugar syrup, 3 parts applejack, 2 cloves, 1 thin slice lemon, 1 pinch of ground cinnamon and 1 of nutmeg, combined in goblet or highball glass, filled with hot or cold water.

B

Bacardi Cocktail: teaspoon grenadine, $^1/_3$ gin, $^2/_3$ Bacardi rum, juice $^1/_2$ small lime, cracked ice, strained.

Bachelor's Cocktail: 1 part Crème de cacao, 1 part brandy, $^1/_2$ part fresh milk, cracked ice, shaked, strained.

Baltimore Egg Nog: egg yolk beaten to foam with a teaspoonful sugar, a liqueur glass brandy, rum and peach brandy added stirring constantly, milk and cream added, the stiffly beaten egg white folded in.

Belfast Cooler: lump of ice and lemon juice in tall glass, filled with ginger ale.

Bénédictine glacé: pony glass half filled with cracked ice, filled up with Bénédictine, serve with straws.

Black Stripes: 1 part water, 1 part molasses, 3 parts Jamaica rum, shaken vigorously with ice.

Black Thorn: 1 part Italian vermouth, 1 part Irish whisky, 4 dashes absinth, 4 dashes orange bitters, a cherry.

Bobsleigh Cocktail: 1 part gin, 1 part noyeau, 5 dashes Angostura, a spiral of lemon peel and a cherry.

Bodega Cobbler: 1 part each Sherry, Port and brandy, cracked ice, 1 teaspoonful sugar syrup, 5 dashes absinth, glass filled with charged water.

Bombay Cocktail: 1 part French vermouth, 2 parts brandy, 3 dashes Curaçao and Angostura, lemon slice.

Bossom Caresser: 1. cracked ice, 1 egg yolk, 1 pony rapsberry syrup, 1 pony brand, 2 pony milk, shaken vigourously, strained.

2. cracked ice, 1 egg yolk, 1 teaspoon grenadine, 1 dash marachino, 1 dash brandy, 2 pony Sherry, strained.

Boston Cooler: tall glass, lump of ice, rum, tablespoon sugar syrup, juice of half a lemon, filled with charged water, a lemon spiral hung over the edge of the glass.

Brandy Cobbler: glass with shaved ice, 2 teaspoons sugar syrup, filled to within 1/2 an inch of the rim with brandy, twist of lemon peel.

— **Cocktail:** 1. in a mixing glass place 2/3 brandy, 1 teaspoon gum syrup, juice 1/2 lemon, cracked ice, stir and strain; 2. cracked ice, brandy, 1 dash Curaçao, 2 dashes orange bitters, strained, a cherry and a lemon spiral.

— **Crusta:** shaker half filled with cracked ice, juice of 1/2 lemon, teaspoon sugar syrup, jigger of brandy, well shaken, strained into the prepared glass.

— **Flip:** cracked ice, egg yolk, 1 teaspoon powdered sugar, jigger of brandy, strained, dusted, with ground nutmeg.

— **Highball:** 2 cubes of ice in 8 oz-glass, 2 oz brandy, filled with charged water, stirred.

— **Julep:** 1/2 teaspoon powdered sugar and 4 sprigs of mint mashed in mixing glass, turned into a goblet or glass, 1 jigger brandy, a few drops orange bitters added, half filled with plain water, filled with ice, decorated with fruit in season and mint.

— **Punch:** 1. 1/2 part each sugar syrup and Curaçao, 1 part each lemon and orange juice, 1/8 part grenadine, 2 parts brandy, blend well, chill and add 3 parts soda water at serving.

2. 3 lumps of sugar in tall glass, 1 tablespoon lemon juice, 2 jiggers brandy, lemon slice, glass filled with hot water.

— **Sling:** 1 lump of sugar in tall glass, 1 jigger brandy, twisted lemon peel, 1 teaspoon lemon juice, 4 dashes Angostura added, filled with hot water, stirred, served with a spoon.

— **Smash:** 1/2 teaspoon powdered sugar, 3 sprigs of mint and 1 teaspoon of cold water mashed to a pulp, small wine glass brandy and two tablespoons ice added, well shaken, strained into a tumbler, garnished with fruit in season and mint sprigs, served at once.

— **Sour:** 1 jigger brandy, juice of 1/2 small lemon and ice placed in shaker, shaken vigorously, strained into a tumbler, filled with carbonated water, garnished with thin lemon slice.

— **Split:** brandy served with lumps of ice and a small bottle of soda water, guest serves himself.

Brandy

— **Toddy:** 1. place 1 teaspoon powder sugar, 1 jigger brandy and 3 drops Angostura in mixing glass, add cracked ice, stir well, strain into tall tumbler, serve with lemon or orange slice on top and straws;
2. same as above substituting warm water for ice.

Bronx Cocktail: 1. in shaker $^1/_4$ Italian vermouth, $^1/_4$ French vermouth, $^1/_2$ part gin, shake with ice, strain and add thin slice of orange;
2. 1 part French vermouth, 1 part Italian vermouth, 1 part orange juice, 6 parts gin, shake with ice, drop a twist of lemon peel into each glass.

Brunswick Cooler: lump of ice, 2 teaspoons sugar syrup, $^1/_2$ juice of large lemon, filled with ginger ale, garnished with lemon slice and fruit, served with straws.

Byrrh-Citron: 1 pony lemon syrup, a jigger Byrrh, a large cube of ice.

C

California Cobbler: goblet filled with shaved ice, 1 teaspoon sugar syrup, orange juice and Curaçao added, filled with Californian white wine, stirred, a few drops of Port on top, served with straws.

Calvados Cocktail: $^1/_4$ Curaçao, $^3/_4$ Calvados, 2 dashes Angostura, 3 drops gum syrup, cracked ice, strained, served with twisted lemon peel.

Champagne Bowl: orange and lemon slices, diced peaches and fresh pineapple dusted with powdered sugar, a pony brandy poured on top, macerated for a couple of hours, filled up with champagne and stirred lightly, served well chilled.

— **Cobbler:** shaved ice, teaspoon sugar syrup, a few dashes lemon juice, filled up with champagne, garnished with a twist of lemon and orange peel.

Champagne Cocktail: place lump of sugar in champagne glass, add 2 dashes Angostura, fill glass with chilled champagne, do not stir so as not to dissolve the sugar.

Cherry Blossom: 1 part Curaçao, 1 part grenadine, 2 parts lemon juice, 3 parts cognac, 3 parts kirsch shaken with ice, decorated with a cherry.

Chicago: place in bar glass 2 cubes cracked ice, 1 jigger cognac, 1 dash Angostura, 3 dashes Curaçao, stir, strain into a chilled champagne glass, fill glass with champagne.

Chinese: 2 dashes each Angostura, marachino, grenadine and Curaçao and 1 jigger medium-type rum, shake with ice, strain, a twist of lemon over each glass, decorate with a cherry.

Cincinnati: in tumbler half chilled ale and half ginger ale.

Claret Cup: dissolve 2 tablespoons granulated sugar with very little water in punch bowl, add one sliced lemon, juice of one orange, $^1/_2$ jigger rum, 1 bottle claret, 1 bottle champagne and a large chunk of ice, stir until well chilled, remove ice, garnish with strawberries or raspberries, serve at once.

— **Flip:** 1 whole egg, 1 teaspoon sugar, 2 oz. claret, shake with ice, strain, dust with ground nutmeg.

— **Lemonade:** 1 teaspoon sugar syrup, 6 dashes lemon juice, lumps of ice, filled with claret, served with straws.

Club Cocktail: $^1/_3$ Italian vermouth, $^1/_3$ gin, 2 dashes orange bitters, 1 teaspoon sugar syrup, $^1/_6$ yellow Chartreuse, shaved ice, shaken, strained in cocktail glass.

Coaxer: 1 teaspoon sugar syrup, 2 dashes lemon juice, 1 egg white, 2 jiggers Scotch whisky, well shaken with ice, strained.

Coffee Cobbler: 1 teaspoon sugar syrup, 1 pony each brandy and crème de café, filled in glass with cracked ice, cold strong coffee poured in up to $^3/_8$ of an inch from the rim, stirred, served with straws.

— **Cocktail:** 1 part sugar syrup, 4 parts Port, 4 parts brandy, 1 whole egg for four drinks, shake with cracked ice, strain.

— **Flip:** 1. made like brandy flip with equal parts brandy and Port;
2. made like brandy flip with Crème de café.

Columbia Skin: 1 teaspoon sugar, 2 dashes lemon juice, 2 jiggers rum, shaken with crushed ice, strained, a twisted lemon peel on top.

Continental Cocktail: 1. shaved ice, juice of $^1/_2$ lime, $^3/_4$ teaspoon powdered sugar, 1 teaspoon Crème de menthe, 1 jigger Jamaica rum, shake well, strain.
2. cracked ice in shaker, 2 dashes each Angostura, Curaçao, orange bitters and maraschino, 3 dashes each French and Italian vermouth, strained in champagne glass, glass filled with champagne.

Cooper: half porter and half stout.

Corpse Reviver: equal parts of grenadine, anisette, strawberry liqueur, green Chartreuse, cherry-brandy, vanilla liqueur, kirsch and brandy filled in tall liqueur glass without mixing.

Cuban Cocktail: $^2/_3$ brandy, $^1/_3$ apricot brandy, juice of $^1/_2$ lemon, dash of orange bitters.

Curaçao Punch: place in shaker cracked ice, 1 teaspoon sugar syrup, 2 dashes lemon juice, $^1/_4$ part each brandy and rum and 1 part Curaçao, shake, strain, garnish with orange slice and fruit, serve with straws.

D

Daiquri: 1. cracked ice, $^1/_2$ teaspoon sugar, juice of half a lime, 1 jigger white label rum;
2. Juice of $^1/_2$ lime, $^1/_2$ teaspoon powdered sugar, $^2/_3$ Bacardi rum, $^1/_6$ grenadine;
3. 1 part Crème d'ananas, 2 parts citrus juice, 8 parts Cuban rum.

Delaware Punch: tumbler half full of cracked ice, 2 teaspoons sugar syrup, 1 jigger brandy, 2 jiggers rum, 2 dashes lemon juice, garnished with fruit in season, served with straws.

Denver Cocktail: shaved ice, $^2/_3$ whisky, $^1/_3$ rum, dash of orange bitters, twist of lemon peel on top.

Derby Cocktail: shaved ice, 2 dashes peach bitters, jigger of gin, 1 sprig of fresh mint, strained, served with an olive.

— **Sour:** tall glass with shaved ice, 1 jigger Curaçao, 1 jigger rye whisky, 2 spoons lemon juice, garnished with fruit, served with straws.

Devil Cocktail: shaved ice, $^1/_4$ teaspoon each green peppermint liqueur and maraschino, $^1/_2$ jigger brandy, pinch of Cayenne pepper, strained, served with a lemon slice.

Dogs Nose: glass of porter beer with a few dashes of gin.

Dubonnet Cocktail: shaved ice, 1/2 Dubonnet, 1/2 gin, 3 dashes Angostura.

Dubonnet-Citron: same as Byrrh-Citron made with Dubonnet.

Dutch Punch: hot tea flavored strongly with rum and sweetened with lump sugar on which orange peel has been rubbed.

E

East India Cocktail: cracked ice, 1 dash each Curaçao and maraschino, 2 dashes Angostura, 1 teaspoon pineapple juice, 1 jigger brandy, strained, decorated with twist of lemon and a cherry.

Egg Flip: cracked ice, 1 egg yolk, 2 dashes each Curaçao and noyau, 2 teaspoons sugar syrup, one pony each brandy and Sherry, vigorously shaken, strained, a little ground nutmeg dusted on top.

— **Nog:** place 2 teaspoons granulated sugar in large tumbler, dissolve with a little water, add 1 whole egg, 2 tablespoons rum, 2 jiggers brandy; turn mixture in shaker with 4 tablespoons finely cracked ice, fill with rich milk, shake vigorously, strain in clean tumbler, serve with a little ground nutmeg on top. May be made with whisky, applejack, kirsch etc. instead of brandy.

— **Nog Hot:** 1 egg yolk, 1 teaspoon powdered sugar and a small glass of milk whisked on the fire until thick, a pony of rum added, strained into a punch glass, a little ground nutmeg dusted on top. May be made with rum or whisky.

Encore: pour into tall liqueur glass 1 part maraschino, 1 part Curaçao and 1 part brandy without mixing and serve burning.

Eye Opener: 1. cracked ice, a whole egg, 1 teaspoon powdered sugar, 1 jigger each rum and brandy, shake vigorously, strain;
2. 1 egg white, 2 dashes whisky, 1 pony absinth, shake vigorously, strain into whisky glass and fill with carbonated water.

F

Fancy Brandy Cocktail: cracked ice, 2 dashes orange bitters, 1 dash Angostura, 1 teaspoon sugar syrup, 1 pony brandy, strained in a champagne glass, filled with champagne, a twist of lemon and a cherry on top.

— **Whisky Smash:** cracked ice, 3 mashed mint sprigs, 1 teaspoon sugar syrup, 3 dashes noyau, 1 jigger whisky, strained into a tall glass, garnished with fruit and mint, served with straws.

Fernet Branca Cocktail: 1 part Fernet Branca, 1 part cognac, 3 dashes each sugar syrup and Angostura, served with an orange twist.

Forbidden Fruit Cocktail: 1 part each French vermouth, gin and Forbidden Fruit shaken with cracked ice.

Friar's Cocktail: equal parts of French vermouth, gin and pineapple juice, shaken with ice until frothy, strained and served at once.

G

Gin and Bitters: glass rinsed with Angostura or other bitters, the excess shaken out, filled with iced gin.

— **Cobbler:** shaved ice in tall glass, 2 teaspoons sugar syrup added and a dash of pinapple syrup, filled to within half an inch of the rim with gin, garnished with mint and fruit, served with straws.

— **Cocktail:** same as brandy cocktail with gin instead of brandy.

— **Daisy:** same as brandy daisy using gin instead of brandy.

— **Fix:** place in mixing glas 1 teaspoon powdered sugar, 3 dashes Angostura bitters, 3 drops of Curaçao, 1 pony gin and cracked ice, stir well, strain into tumbler, fill with carbonated water, a slice of lemon on top.

— **Fizz:** 1 tablespoon sugar syrup, juice of 1 medium sized lemon, 1, 1/2 jiggers gin, shaken with crushed ice, strained, filled in tall glass, fizzed up with carbonated water stirring constantly.

— **Flip:** same as brandy flip substituting gin for brandy.

— **Grog:** 1 teaspoon sugar dissolved with a little warm water in tall glass, filled 2/3 with hot water or tea, a generous jigger of gin added, a slice of lemon on top.

— **and It:** 1 part Italian vermouth and 3 parts gin, chilled, in America; in Europe the proportions are usually half French vermouth and half gin.

— **Julep:** prepared like brandy julep substituting gin for brandy.

— **on the Rocks:** London gin poured over ice cubes in old-fashioned or sour glass.

— **Sangaree:** made like brandy sangaree with gin instead of brandy.

— **Sling:** same as brandy sling substituting gin for brandy.

— **Smash:** same as brandy smash substituting gin for brandy.

— **Sour:** same as brandy sour substituting gin for brandy.

Gloom Lifter: 1 part sugar syrup, 2 parts lemon juice, 6 parts Irish whisky, 1 egg white for 2 drinks, shaken vigorously with cracked ice.

Golden Slipper: place in tall liqueur glass without mixing 1/3 yellow Chartreuse, an egg yolk on the Chartreuse, fill to within 3/8 of an inch from the rim with Danziger Goldwasser.

Golf Cocktail: cracked ice, 2 dashes orange bitters, 1 part French vermouth, 1/2 part gin, strained, served with an olive.

Gordon Cocktail: 1 part Amontillado Sherry, 5 parts Gordon gin, stirred with ice and filled in cocktail glass with an olive.

Grande Duchesse: 1 part grenadine, 2 parts lime juice, 2 parts Jamaica rum, 4 parts vodka, shaken with crushed ice.

Grasshopper: half Crème de cacao and half green peppermint liqueur served in liqueur glass without mixing.

Grenadier Cocktail: 2/3 brandy, 1/3 ginger brandy, a dash of Jamaica ginger, 1 teaspoon sugar syrup, shaken with ice, strained.

H

Half and Half: chilled goblet filled with half lager and half porter beer.

Hawaiian Gin Cocktail: 3/4 gin, 1/4 pineapple juice, 2 dashes of grenadine, shaken with ice and strained.

High Life: a tall glass half full of crushed ice, filled with a Sherry glassful brandy, 1 teaspoon sugar syrup, 3 dashes lemon juice and carbonated water.

Hock Cobbler: fill in tall tumbler 1 level tablespoon powdered sugar and a little water until sugar is dissolved, add 2 wineglasses Rhine wine, fill with shaved ice and garnish with fruit in season.

Hoppel Poppel, Cold: 3 egg yolks stirred to foam with 2 teaspoons powdered sugar and a little ground nutmeg, a cup of heavy cream added gradually; best made in rotary beater;
2. two egg yolks stirred to foam with 2 teaspoons vanilla sugar and grated lemon peel, a jigger of rum added, whisked with 1/2 cup milk until frothy and served in tall glass.

Hoppel Poppel, Hot: scald 3/4 cup heavy cream or half cream and milk, sweeten with 1 teaspoon powdered sugar, pour gradually over 2 egg yolks stirring rapidly add 1/2 jigger rum and serve very hot.

Horse's Neck, Plain: peel a lemon in a continuous spiral and hang inside over edge of glass, place 3 cubes of ice in tall glass and fill with ginger ale.

— — **with a Kick:** same as before with a jigger rum, brandy, whisky, gin or applejack added.

Hurricane: 1 part vodka, 2 parts brandy, 1 teaspoon absinth, shaken with ice and strained into cocktail glass.

I

Ice Cream Kirsch Cooler: place in shaker 1 small dip vanilla ice cream, 1 egg yolk, 2 tablespoons cracked ice, 2 tablespoons kirsch, 4 dashes Curaçao, shake well, strain in tall tumbler, fill with soda water, a little ground nutmeg dusted on top.

Ice Cream Soda: large spoon ice cream in tall glass, 1 tablespoon fruit syrup added, filled with carbonated water, stirred, served with spoon and straws.

Iced Coffee: 1. crushed ice in shaker with 2 dashes noyau, 1 teaspoon sugar syrup, 1 pony brandy and 1/2 cup strong cold coffee, shaken, drained, served with straws;
2. tablespoon coffee ice cream in delmonico glass, filled 3/4 full with strong cold coffee, topped with whipped cream.

— **Tea:** shaker with crushed ice, 2 dashes of noyau, 1 teaspoon sugar syrup, 1 pony rum and 1/2 cup tea, shaken, drained in Delmonico glass and served with straws.

Ideal Cocktail: 1/2 part sugar syrup, 1 part each grapefruit juice and French vermouth, 2 parts gin, shaken with cracked ice and strained.

Imperial Fizz: same as gin fizz using a squirt of champagne instead of carbonated water.

International Cocktail: cracked ice, 1/4 part yellow Chartreuse and 1 part brandy, a dash of pineapple syrup, shaken strained and served with a lemon slice.

Irish Cocktail: shaved ice, 2 dashes each anisette and Curaçao, 1 dash each maraschino and Angostura bitters, 3/4 Irish whisky, strained, served with a twist of lemon peel and an olive.

— **Coffee:** a cup of strong hot coffee with a pony Irish whisky topped with whipped or heavy cream.

— **Collins:** 1 tablespoon sugar syrup, juice of a medium-sized lemon, 2 jiggers Irish whisky, 4 ice cubes added, filled with charged water and stirred; served in a Collins glass.

J

Japanese Cocktail: 1. cracked ice, 1 part orgeat, 8 parts cognac, 1 dash Angostura;
2. 1 teaspoon sugar syrup, 3 dashes Angostura, 2 dashes maraschino, Sherry glass Eau céleste, cracked ice, strained, served with a lemon spiral, an olive and straws.

Jersey City: 1/2 part each sugar syrup and lemon juice, 3 parts apple brandy, 1 dash Angostura, a lemon spiral on each glass.

— **Cocktail:** cracked ice, 1 teaspoon sugar syrup, 3 dashes Angostura, 1 Sherry glass apple cider, shaken and strained in a Sherry glass.

— **Lily:** half brandy and half green Chartreuse in tall liqueur glass without mixing.

Jockey Club Cocktail: shaved ice, 1/2 Italian vermouth. 1/2 rye whisky, 2 dashes maraschino, served with twist of orange peel.

John Collins: 1 tablespoon sugar syrup, juice of a medium-sized lemon, 2 jiggers dry London gin, stirred together in Collins glass, 3 ice cubes added, filled with charged water and stirred again.

K

Kikiriki: tall glass half filled with ice, 1 jigger each Moselle wine, Port and soda water added, served with straws.

Kilrain Punch: cracked ice in shaker with 3 crushed mint leaves, 1 teaspoon sugar syrup, 2 teaspoons raspberry syrup, 1/2 pony rum, shaken, strained, filled in middle-sized glass, filled with water, garnished with fruit; straws.

Kirsch Crusta: shaker half filled with shaved ice, 1 chunk of pineapple, 1 teaspoon gum syrup, 3 dashes Angostura, 3 dashed orange bitters, 1/2 lime juice, 1 1/2 jiggers kirsch, well shaken and strained into prepared glass.

Kiss me: 1 part maraschino and 1 part vanilla liqueur filled into a tall liqueur glass without mixing.

— — **quick:** cracked ice in shaker, 2 dashes Angostura, 4 dashes Curaçao, 2 dashes absinth, shaken and strained in middle-sized glass, filled with carbonated water.

Klondyke Cocktail: cracked ice, 4 dashes orange bitters, 2 dashes apple cider, 1 teaspoon sugar syrup, 1 jigger Italian vermouth, shaken, strained in large cocktail glass, garnished with an olive and a lemon twist.

Knickebein: high liqueur glass with a heavy liqueur such as Chartreuse, Bénédictine etc at the bottom, an unbroken egg yolk floating on top, covered with brandy or other spirits or light liqueur.

Knickerbocker: cracked ice, 1 dash lemon juice, 4 dashes Curaçao, 2 teaspoons raspberry syrup, 2 jiggers rum, shaken, strained in middle-sized glass, garnished with fruit, served with straws.

Knock out: shaker with cracked ice, 1 teaspoon sugar, 1 egg yolk, 1 pony each rye whisky and Madeira, shaken strained into a punch glass, filled with chilled champagne, garnished with fruit; straws.

L

Ladies Blush: cracked ice, 1 pony anisette, 2 dashes Curaçao, 1/2 pony absinth, well shaken, strained into small tumbler, filled with 1/2 a wine of glass water.

— **Cocktail:** cracked, ice, 1 teaspoon sugar syrup, 3 dashes peppermint, 3 dashes Curaçao, 1 pony kirsch, shaken strained, served with an orange slice.

Lamb's Wool: 1 cup milk boiled up with 1 tablespoon oatmeal, strained, mixed with a teaspoon sugar and 1 jigger rum, served hot.

Leave it to me: 1 teaspoon sugar syrup, 1 tablespoon lemon juice, 1 dash each raspberry syrup and maraschino, 1 jigger gin, shaken with ice, strained, served with lemon slice and straws.

Lemon and Dash: chunk of ice in a tumbler, filled with equal parts of pale ale and lemonade.

Little Devil: shaved ice in shaker, 1/3 dry gin, 1/3 rum, 1/6 Cointreau, 1/6 lime juice.

London Cocktail: 1. shaker with shaved ice, 1/3 pineapple juice, 1/3 French vermouth, 1/3 dry gin, garnished with an olive; 2. 3 dashes orange bitters, 2 dashes Curaçao, 1 dash Oxgène-Cusinier, 1 jigger dry gin, strained, served garnished with fruit and sraws.

Louisa Cocktail: 1/3 each Italian vermouth, dry gin and Calvados, 1 teaspoon yellow Chartreuse, shaken with ice, served strained with a twist of orange peel.

Love Reviver: egg yolk in a Sherry glass filled with 1/3 part each brandy, kirsch and maraschino, served with a spoon.

Lover's Delight: 1 part Cointreau, 1 part Forbidden Fruit, 1 part cognac, 3 dashes lemon juice, shaken with ice and strained.

M

Madeira Cobbler: 1 teaspoon powdered sugar dissolved in a tablespoon water in tall glass, stirred until melted, 1 1/2 wine glasses Madeira added, glass filled with shaved ice, garnished with fresh fruit including a sliver of pineapple.

Maiden's Blush: shaved ice in shaker, 2/3 gin, 1/3 anisette, 1 teaspoon grenadine, shaken and strained.

Manhattan, Dry: 1 part French vermouth, 2 parts whisky, 1 dash of Angostura.

— **Sweet:** 1 part Italian vermouth, 2 parts whisky, 1 dash of Angostura.
A cherry in each glass for all Manhattans.

— **Lemonade:** tall glass with a chunk of ice, 1 teaspoon sugar syrup, 1 Sherry glass Italian vermouth, 1 dash of Angostura, filled up with carbonated water, garnished with fruit.

Marquise: tall glass half full of shaved ice, wine glass Hock, 2 tablespoons pineapple syrup, filled with carbonated water, garnished with fruit, served with straws.

Martini, Dry: 1 part French vermouth, 2 parts gin, 2 dashes orange bitters.

— **Medium:** 1/2 part each French and Italian vermouth, 2 parts gin, 1 dash each orange bitters and Angostura.

— **Sweet:** 1 part Italian vermouth, 1 part gin, 1 dash Angostura.

All Martinis are garnished with an olive.

Mayfair Cocktail: shaved ice in shaker, 1/2 gin, 1/2 orange juice, 3 dashes apricot syrup, 1 dash clove syrup, shaken and strained.

Medford Rum Sour: shaker with cracked ice, 1 tablespoon sugar syrup, juice of half a lemon, 1 jigger rum, shaken, strained, garnished with a small slice of lemon and orange and a pineapple sliver, served with straws.

Menthe glacée: high liqueur glass 3/4 full of shaved ice, 1 pony peppermint.

Mikado Cocktail: 1 jigger cognac, 2 dashes each orgeat, Curaçao and noyau, shaken with cracked ice, strained, garnished with a cherry and a lemon twist.

Milk and Soda: tumbler half full of cold milk filled up with soda water. A tablespoon or two of raspberry, strawberry, black currant, ginger or other syrup may be added.

— **Punch, Hot:** 1 tablespoon sugar, 1 pony brandy and 1 of rum in a punch cup, filled with hot milk, stirred, a little ground nutmeg dusted on top.

Mint Julep: same as brandy julep substituting gin for brandy.

Mississippi Punch: 1 part sugar syrup, 1 part brandy, 2 parts lemon juice and 3 parts Bourbon whisky stirred with crushed ice in mixing glass, strained in a Collins glass packed with crushed ice, filled to 1/2 inch of the rim with charged water, a tablespoon of Jamaica rum and fruit on top, served with straws.

Morning Call: shaker with cracked ice, 1 part Curaçao, 1 part rum, 4 dashes Angostura, shaken and strained, served with a lemon twist.

Mulled Ale or Beer: 1 clove, a tiny bit of cinnamon, a little grated nutmeg and sugar to taste infused in 1 cup of water for 5 minutes, strained, 1 pint heated — not boiled — ale or beer added, strained, served in hot mugs or punch glasses.

— **Claret:** 1 bottle claret flavored with 2 cloves, 1/8 grated nutmeg and 1/3 cup sugar heated until a little foam rises on the surface, strained, beaten on the fire with 4 egg yolks until thick, but not boiled as the yolks would curdle, served in prewarmed mugs or punch glasses.

N

Napoleon Cocktail: 1 teaspoon sugar syrup, 2 dashes lemon juice, 1 part each gin and whisky, shaken with ice, strained, a lemon twist on top.

National: shaker with cracked ice, juice of 1/2 lime and the same quantity pineapple juice, 1 teaspoon powdered sugar, 1 jigger rum, shaken and strained into a champagne glass.

Nectar: thin apple slices and the thin peel of a lemon sprinkled with powdered sugar and infused for 6 hours in a punch bowl, filled with half Hock or Moselle and half champagne.

Negus Punch: lump of sugar rubbed with lemon, 2 teaspoons lemon juice and 1/2 cup Sherry in punch glass, filled with hot water, a little grated nutmeg on top.

Nevada Cocktail: 1 teaspoon sugar syrup, 2 teaspoons grape-juice, 2 teaspoons lime juice, 1 jigger white label rum, shaken with cracked ice and strained.

New Orleans Fizz: a little cracked ice in shaker, 3 drops orange flower water, juice of 1/2 a lemon and 1/2 a lime, 1/2 jigger of gin and 1/2 of milk, shaken until creamy, strained into a tumbler and filled with seltzer.

O

Old Chums Reviver: shaker with cracked ice, juice of 1/2 lemon, 1 teaspoon sugar, 1/2 pony raspberry syrup, 1 generous jigger brandy, shaken, strained into a highball glass, filled with carbonated water, served with a cherry and straws.

Old-Fashioned Cocktail: 2 cubes cracked ice in glass, 1 teaspoon sugar syrup, 3 dashes Angostura, 1 pony whisky, stirred, drop of lemon peel, a lemon twist and a cherry on top.

— **Gin and Bitters:** 4 dashes Angostura, 3/4 jigger gin and cracked ice in shaker, shaken, strained in cocktail glass, served with a twist of lemon.

Olympia Cooler: Collins glass half full of shaved ice, juice of half a lemon, 1 generous jigger Scotch whisky, filled with ginger ale.

Opera Cocktail: cracked ice in shaker, 1 part each Dubonnet and white label rum, a dash of lemon juice, strained, a twist of orange peel.

Orange Blossom Cocktail: shaker half filled with shaved ice, 1/4 rum, 1/4 Cointreau, 1/2 orange juice, well shaken and strained.

— **Lemonade:** tumbler with a cube or two of ice, 1 teaspoon sugar syrup, a dash of lemon juice, juice of 1 orange, filled up with plain or carbonated water.

Orgeat: sweet almonds pounded in mortar, steeped in hot milk, slightly sweetened, pressed through a cloth, flavored with orange blossom water.

— **Punch:** punch glass half full of shaved ice, a teaspoon sugar syrup, 2 dashes novau, 1 generous pony brandy, filled with orgeat, a few drops of red wine, fruit and a lemon slice on top, served with straws.

P

Panaché: tumbler filled with half lager beer and half lemonade.

Parisian Cocktail: 1/3 dry Italian vermouth, 1/3 crème de cassis and 1/3 gin shaken with cracked ice.

— **Pousse-Café:** tall liqueur glass with equal quantities of green Chartreuse, orange Curaçao, kirsch and cognac without mixing.

Peppermint Lemonade: 2 cubes of ice in tumbler, 2 teaspoons lemon juice, 1 pony peppermint, filled with carbonated water.

Pick-me-up: 1. equal parts of anisette and Italian vermouth, juice of 1/2 small lime, shaken with ice and strained; 2. shaker with crushed ice, 1 dash lemon juice, 1 teaspoon grenadine, 1 dash kirsch, shaken, strained in champagne glass, filled up with champagne.

Picon-Citron: same as Byrrh-Citron but made with Amer Picon.

Pineapple Bowl: peeled pineapple cut into small slices, placed in a glass bowl sprinkled generously with sugar, half a bottle Rhine wine added, covered and allowed to stand for 2—3 hours on ice. Stirred, half Rhine and Half Moselle wine added to bring total quantity up to about 5 quarts. Served chilled with 1 or 2 small slices pineapple in bowl glasses.

— **Cobbler:** glass half filled with cracked ice, tablespoonful pineapple syrup, filled with white wine, garnished with pineapple.

— **Fizz:** a rum fizz with pineapple juice instead of lemon juice.

— **Punch:** glass half filled with cracked ice, one liqueur glass brandy, pineapple juice and pineapple liqueur, filled with charged water, garnished with a slice of pineapple and a cherry.

Port Cocktail: cracked ice in shaker, 3 dashes Angostura, 1/4 maraschino, 3/4 Port, shaken and strained.

— **Flip:** shaker with very little crushed ice, 1 egg yolk, 1 level teaspoon sugar, 1 wineglass Port, shaken vigorously, strained into a small tumbler, grated nutmeg dusted on top.

— **Sangaree:** 2 teaspoons sugar syrup in highball glass with 3 or 4 small ice cubes, 1 wineglass Port added, stirred until glass is frosted, strained into a tumbler, filled with water, grated nutmeg dusted on top.

Prairie Oyster: 1. mix together in old-fashioned glass 1 pony brandy, 1 tablespoon of vinegar and 1 of Worcestershire sauce, 1 teaspoon of catsup and 1 of Angostura, drop in an egg yolk, a dash of Cayenne pepper on top; 2. 1 teaspoon of cold tomato sauce, Worcestershire sauce and 1 of vinegar, a pinch of pepper and salt, a pony Sherry and an egg yolk.

Prince of Wales: tall glass half full of shaved ice, 3 dashes Angostura, 1 wineglass champagne, filled with Apollinaris water, served with a lemon slice and straws.

Princess Mary: shaker with shaved ice, 1/3 gin, 1/3 crème de cacao and 1/3 heavy cream, shaken vigorously and strained.

Q

Queen Cocktail: 1. shaved ice in shaker, 2 parts vodka, 1 part Cointreau, 1 dash orange bitters, shaken and strained; 2. 2 dashes sugar syrup, 2 dashes Curaçao, 5 dashes noyau, 1 dash peppermint and 1 pony brandy shaken with ice and strained.

Queen Charlotte: small tumbler half full of shaved ice, 2 dashes lemon juice and a wineglass orgeat, filled with soda water.

R

Rainbow: equal parts of maraschino, peppermint, apricotine, Curaçao, kirsch and brandy in tall liqeur glass, not mixed.

Raspberry Punch: punch glass half full of shaved ice, 2 dashes maraschino, brandy and lemon juice, pony raspberry syrup, filled with champagne, garnished with fresh raspberries.

Remsen Cooler: a Collins glass with a long lemon spiral, 3 ice cubes, 2 jiggers Scotch whisky, glass filled with charged water.

Rose Cocktail: 1 part kirsch, 2 parts Noilly-Prat vermouth, 1 teaspoon raspberry syrup, shaken with ice and strained.

Rum Cocktail: shaker with cracked ice, 2 dashes Cointreau, 1 jigger rum, 1/4 teaspoon each sugar and lemon juice, 1/2 jigger French vermouth, shaken and strained, twisted lemon peel on top.

— **Crusta:** shaker with crushed ice, 1/4 liqueur glass gum syrup, 3 drops orange bitters, 3 drops Curaçao, juice of 1/2 lemon, 1 1/2 jiggers rum, shaken and strained in prepared glass.

— **Punch:** half rum and half hot water in punch glass, 1 teaspoon sugar syrup, a slice of lemon on top.

Rumba Cocktail: 1 part gin, 2 parts Jamaica rum, 2 dashes grenadine, shaken with crushed ice and strained.

S

Sam Ward: chilled cocktail glass with shaved ice, spiral of lemon peel around the edge, filled with yellow Chartreuse, served with a straw.

Saratoga Cocktail: cracked ice in shaker, 1 teaspoon pineapple syrup, 2 dashes of orange bitters and 2 of maraschino, 1 pony brandy, strained into wineglass, filled with champagne, fresh fruit on top.

— **Cooler:** half and half sarsaparilla and ginger ale.

Schorle Morle: half hock or moselle wine and half soda water.

Scotch Whisky Cocktail: cracked ice in shaker, 2/3 Scotch whisky, 1/3 Italian vermouth, 3 dashes Angostura, shaken and strained, a curl of lemon peel added.

Shandy Gaff: half ale and half ginger ale stirred quickly with bar spoon.

Sherry and Bitters: 3 dashes Angostura in wine glass, filled with Sherry.

— **Cobbler:** tall glass filled to with shaved ice, 2 teaspoons Curaçao added, filled with a wineglass Sherry, garnished with fruit and an orange slice, served with straws.

— **Flip:** cracked ice in shaker, 1 egg yolk, 1 teaspoon powdered sugar, 1 wineglass Sherry, shaken vigorously, strained into a tumbler, dusted with ground nutmeg.

Side Car Cocktail: 1. 1/3 Cointreau, 1/3 brandy and 1/3 lemon juice in shaker with ice, strained;
2. 1/4 Cointreau, 1/2 lemon juice, 2 parts cognac.

Silver Fizz: shaker with cracked ice, 1 level teaspoon powdered sugar, juice of 1/2 lemon, 1 egg white and 1 jigger gin, shaken vigorously, strained into a medium-sized tumbler, a squirt of seltzer added.

— **Streak:** shaker with cracked ice, 1/2 kummel and 1/2 gin, shaken and strained.

Sleeper: 1 egg yolk stirred to foam with 1 teaspoon of sugar and 1 of lemon juice in punch glass, 1/2 jiggers rum added, filled with hot water.

Snow Ball: a silver fizz with whisky instead of gin and ginger ale instead of the charged water.

Stone Fence: same as Remsen cooler using hard cider instead of the carbonated water.

Strawberry Lemonade: tumbler or highball glass with a large lump of ice, small glass of lemon and one of strawberry syrup, filled with carbonated water, served with straws.

Swedish Punch: punch glass 3/4 full of shaved ice, filled with caloric punch.

T

Tango Cocktail: shaker with cracked ice, 1/6 Curaçao, 1/6 orange juice, 1/3 Italian vermouth and 1/3 gin, shaken and strained.

The Real Thing: lump of sugar in champagne glass, 1 pony cognac, filled up with champagne.

Tipperary: 1 sprig mint crushed with 1 teaspoon grenadine and orange juice, 1 part French vermouth, 3 parts gin, shaken with cracked ice, strained.

Tip Top Punch: punch glass half filled with shaved ice, 2 dashes lemon juice, 2 teaspoons sugar syrup, 1 1/2 jiggers gin, filled with carbonated water.

Tom Collins: 1 tablespoon sugar syrup, juice of a medium-sized lemon, 2 jiggers gin, stirred in Collins glass with 4 cubes of ice, glass filled with charged water.

Trinity: a dry Manhattan made with Scotch whisky and a dash of orange bitters, apricot brandy and white crème de menthe.

Tuxedo: shaker with cracked ice, 1 dash of maraschino and another of anisette, 2 dashes orange bitters, 1 part French vermouth and 1 part gin, shaken, strained, garnished with a cherry and a twisted lemon peel.

V

Vermouth Cocktail: 1. cracked ice in shaker, 1 cocktail glass Italian vermouth, 3 dashes of Fernet Branca, shaken strained;
2. 2 dashes Angostura, 3 dashes noyau, 3 dashes Curaçao, 1 cocktail glass Italian vermouth, shaken with ice and strained.

— **frappé:** saucer champagne glass with shaved ice, filled with vermouth, served with a straw.

Volga Cocktail: shaken with cracked ice, 2 dashes of grenadine and 2 of Angostura, 2 parts vodka, 1 part orange juice, 1 part lemon juice, strained.

W

Wedding Night: pour into tall liqueur glass without mixing equal parts Parfait d'amour, peppermint and cherry-brandy.

Whisky Cobbler: same as brandy cobbler substituting whisky for brandy.

— **Cocktail:** made like brandy cocktail using whisky instead of brandy.

— **Crusta:** made like brandy crusta substituting whisky for brandy.

Whisky

— **Daisy:** made like brandy daisy with whisky instead of brandy.

— **Fix:** same as gin fix substituting whisky for brandy.

— **Fizz:** made like gin fizz using whisky instead of gin.

— **Flash:** shaker with cracked ice, 1 dash lemon juice, 2 dashes pineapple syrup, 1 1/2 jiggers whisky, strained in cocktail glass with the rim dipped in sugar.

— **Grog:** 1 teaspoon sugar in tall glass, filled 2/3 with hot water or tea leaving the spoon in, 1 1/2 jiggers whisky and hot water or tea leaving the spoon in, 1 1/2 jiggers whisky and a slice of lemon added.

— **Julep:** same as brandy julep with whisky instead of brandy.

— **Snapper:** tumbler half full of shaved ice, 1 teaspoon powdered sugar, 4 dashes lemon juice, 2 dashes raspberry syrup, 1 teaspoon honey, 2 jiggers whisky, filled with carbonated water, served with a lemon slice and straws.

— **Spider:** small tumbler half full of shaved ice, 3 dashes Angostura, 2 jigger whisky, filled with ginger ale.

— **Squirt:** half a crushed peach, 1 table spoon sugar syrup, 1 teaspoon Curaçao, 1 jigger whisky shaken with crushed ice, poured in a highball glass and filled with charged water.

— **Sour:** same as brandy sour substituing whisky for brandy.

White cocktail: 1 part anisette, 5 parts gin, 1 dash orange bitters, shaken with ice and strained, twist of lemon peel on top.

— **Lady:** 1/4 Cointreau, 1/2 lemon juice, 2 parts gin, 1 egg white, shaken vigorously with ice until creamy, strained in coktail glass.

Widows Kiss: tall liqueur glass filled with equal parts green Chartreuse with an egg yolk floating on top, maraschino and Bénédictine without mixing.

Y

Yacht Club: 1 part Italian vermouth, 3 parts gold label rum, 1 dash apricot liqueur.

Yale Club Cocktail: place in old-fashioned glass 1 ice cube cracked in 3 pieces, 1 lump of sugar doused with orange bitters, 1 slice of lemon, 1 twisted lemon peel and 1 maraschino cherry, fill with 1 jigger Bourbon whisky and stir gently.

You and I: a whisky sour substituting orange Curaçao for sugar syrup.

Coffee and Tea

All guests appreciate a good cup of coffee, but good coffee depends upon many things besides the actual making. Good coffee should be clear and of fine flavor.

There are many different ways of making coffee. After years of experience the filtration method has been recognized as the best.

Sparkling fresh water should always be used for the different methods: 1. Pot method; 2. Vacuum method; 3. Percolator method; 4. Drip pot method. Coffee should be ground coarse for the pot method, very fine but not pulverized for the vacuum method, medium for the percolator and fine for the drip pot method.

Hints on Coffee Making

1. Always use the best coffee possible.
2. Be sure that your coffee is ground exactly as fine as you need it.
3. Be accurate in measuring dry coffee and water.
4. Be sure that water is always boiling at a gallop.
5. Water must be boiled fresh. If it boils too long before being used it becomes stale and the flavor of your coffee will suffer.
6. Water must never be taken from the hot water system.
7. Be sure that the coffee maker or machine is absolutely clean.
8. Use 8 level tablespoons of coffee for each quart of water, more if a stronger coffee is required. Longer brewing or over-percolating will not make it stronger without impairing in flavor.
9. Fresh grinding is the secret of good coffee.
10. Unroasted coffee beans will keep almost indefinitely, but roasted coffee starts deteriorating soon after roasting.
11. Do not buy more coffee than can be consumed in a week and keep it in a well closed tin.
12. Remember that coffee loses its flavor if exposed to the air.
13. Do not keep coffee in a warm place because it will lose flavor through oxidation of the fat in the coffee.
14. Cups should be hot when you serve coffee.
15. Cream must not be served cold from the refrigerator. It must not be exposed to foreign flavors.
16. Remember that coffee must never be reheated and that boiled coffee is spoiled.
17. Serve coffee as soon as possible after it has been made.

Hints on Tea Making

1. Never make tea in a metal tea pot.
2. Never boil tea.
3. Heat your tea pot with fresh hot water before putting in the tea.
4. Be sure that the water is boiling at a gallop before it is poured over the tea.

5. Use fresh water drawn from the cold water faucet and pour it over the leaves as soon as it starts boiling at a gallop.
6. Use one rounded teaspoon for each cup and an additional spoonful for 6 to 8 cups.
7. Let the tea steep in a covered pot for 3 minutes and pour it off in another hot pot so that the leaves will not instil bitterness.
8. Never use tea leaves twice.
9. Cups should be warmed before they are filled.
10. Serve fresh, not too heavy cream, fresh milk or sliced lemon and sugar for tea.
11. Never serve hot or boiled milk because it spoils the flavor of tea.
12. Buy the best quality tea only and remember that China tea produces a light straw or amber tint and black tea makes an infusion which is copper in tone.

Vocabulary

English	French	German	Italian	Spanish
		— A —		
Alcohol	Alcool	Alkohol	Alcoole	Alcohol
Almond	Amande	Mandel	Mandorla	Almendra
Almond-milk	Orgeat	Mandelmilch	Mandorlato	Horchata de almendras
Alum	Alun	Alaun	Allume	Alumbre
Anchovy	Anchois	Sardelle	Acciuga	Anchoa
Angelica	Angélique	Engelswurz	Angelica	Angelica
Aniseed	Anis	Anis	Anice	Anis
Appetite	Appétit	Appetit	Appetito	Apetito
Apple	Pomme	Apfel	Mela	Manzana
Apple-cider	Cidre	Apfelwein	Sidro	Sidra
Apricot	Abricot	Aprikose	Albicocca	Albaricoque
Artichoke	Artichaut	Artischocke	Carciofo	Alcachofa
Aroma	Arome	Duft, Aroma	Aroma	Aroma
aromatic	aromatique	aromatisch	aromatico	aromatico
Ashes	Cendres	Asche	Ceneri	Ceniza
Asparagus	Asperges	Spargel	Asparago	Espárrago
		— B —		
Baby Chicken Squab Chicken	Poussin	Kücken	Pulcino	Pollito
Bacon	Lard	Speck	Lardo	Lardo
Baker	Boulanger	Bäcker	Fornaio	Panadero
Banana	Banane	Banane	Banana	Platano
Banquet	Banquet	Festessen	Banchetto	Festin
Barley	Orge	Gerste	Orzo	Cebada
Basil	Basilic	Basilikum	Basilico	Basilico
Bass	Bar	Barsch	Pesce	Lubina
Bay-leaf	Laurier	Lorbeerblatt	Alloro	Laurel
Beef	Boeuf	Ochsenfleisch	Manzo	Carne de vaca
Beef-tea	Jus de viande	Fleischtee	Sugo di carne	Jugo de carne
Beer	Bière	Bier	Birra	Cerveza
Beet-root	Betterave	Rote Rüben	Barbabietola	Remolacha
Bell	Cloche	Glocke	Campana	Campana
Belly	Ventre	Bauch	Pancia	Vientre
Bill	Addition	Rechnung	Conto	Cuenta
Bill of fare	Carte de mets Carte du jour	Speisekarte Tageskarte	Lista delle Vivande Carta del Giorno	Lista de platos Platos del dia
Biscuit	Biscuit	Biskuit	Biscotto	Bizcocho
bitter	amer	bitter	amaro	amargo
black	noir	schwarz	nero	negro
Black coffee	Café noir	Schwarzer Kaffee	Caffè nero	Café negro
Black currants	Cassis	Johannisbeeren, schwarze	More	Grosellas

English	French	German	Italian	Spanish
Black-pudding	Boudin noir	Blutwurst	Sanguinaccio	Morcilla
Blood	Sang	Blut	Sangue	Sangre
Boarding-house	Pension	Fremden-heim	Pensione	Casa de huespes
Blueberry	Myrtille	Heidelbeere	Mirtillo	Arandano
Bone	Os	Knochen	Osso	Hueso
Border	Bordure	Rand	Bordo	Borde
Bottle	Bouteille	Flasche	Bottiglia	Botella
Brains	Cervelle	Hirn	Cervella	Sesos
Braised meat	Viande braisé	Schmor-fleisch	(Manzo, Vitello) Brasato	Carne estofado
Brandy	Eau de vie	Branntwein	Acquavite	Aguardiente
Bread	Pain	Brot	Pane	Pan
Bread-crumbs	Chapelure	Reibbrot	Pane grattugiato	Pan rallado
Breakfast	Petit-déjeuner	Erstes Frühstück	Prima Colazione	Desayuno
Breast Brisket	Poitrine	Brust	Petto	Pecho
Breast of veal	Poitrine de veau	Kalbsbrust	Petto di vitello	Pecho de ternera
Brewery	Brasserie	Brauerei	Birreria	Cerveceria
Brisket of beef	Poitrine de boeuf	Rinderbrust	Petto di manzo	Pecho de vaca
Broad bean	Féve	Saubohne	Fave	Habas
Bucket, Pail	Bidon	Eimer	Secchia	Cubo
Buckwheat	Sarrasin	Buchweizen	Grano saraceno	Trigo saraceno
Butcher	Boucher	Fleischer	Macellaio	Carnicero
Butler	Maître d'hotel	Haushof-meister	Maggior-domo	Maitre de hotel
Butter	Beurre	Butter	Burro	Mantequilla
Buttermilk	Petit-lait	Buttermilch	Siero	Suero
buy	acheter	kaufen	comprare	comprar

— C —

English	French	German	Italian	Spanish
Cabbage	Chou	Kohl	Cavolo	Col
Cake	Gâteau	Kuchen	Pasticceria	Pastel
Calf's feet	Pieds de veau	Kalbsfüße	Zempetto di vitello	Manos de ternera
Calf's head	Tête de veau	Kalbskopf	Testina di vitello	Cabeza de ternera
Calf's liver	Foi de veau	Kalbsleber	Fegato di vitello	Higado de ternera
Calf's pluck	Fraise de veau	Kalbs-gekröse	Rete di vitello	Asa lura de ternera
Calf's Sweet-bread	Ris de veau	Kalbsmilch	Animelle di vitello	Molleja de ternera
Can	Boîte	Dose	Scatola	Lata
Capers	Câpres	Kapern	Capperi	Alcaparra
Capon	Chapon	Kapaun	Cappone	Alcarab
Caramel	Caramel	Karamel	Caramello	Caramelo
Caraway-seeds	Cumin	Kümmel	Cumino	Comino
Carcass	Carcasse	Gerippe	Carcassa	Esqueleto
Cardoon	Cardon	Karde	Cardo	Cardon
Carp	Carpe	Karpfen	Carpione	Carpa
Carrot	Carotte	Mohrrübe, Karotte	Carote	Zanahorie
Cauliflower	Choufleur	Blumenkohl	Cavolfiori	Coliflor
Caviar	Caviar	Kaviar	Caviale	Cavial

English	French	German	Italian	Spanish
Cayenne pepper	Poivre de Cayenne	Cayenne-pfeffer	Pepe di Caienna	Pimienta de Cayenne
Celeriac, Knob Celery	Celeri-rave	Knollen-sellerie	Sedano rapa	Apio
Cellar	Cave	Keller	Cantina	Cueva
Champagne	Champagne	Schaumwein	Vino Spumante	Champañ
Cheese	Fromage	Käse	Formaggio	Queso
Cherry	Cerise	Kirsche	Ciliegia	Cereza
Chervil	Cerfeuil	Kerbel	Cerfoglio	Perifollo
Chestnut	Marron	Kastanie	Marroni	Castaña
Chick-pea	Pois chiche	Kichererbse	Ceci	Garbanzos
Chicken	Poulet	Huhn	Pollo	Pollo
Chicken liver	Foie de volaille	Hühner-leber	Fegato di pollo	Higado de pollo
Chicory	Chicorée	Chicoree	Cicoria	Achicoria
Chicory, French or Belgian	Endive	Endivie	Endivia	Escarola
China, Porcelain	Porcelaine	Porzellan	Porcellana	Porcelana
Chitterlings, Pluck	Fraise, Fressure	Gekröse	Trippa	Asadura
Chive	Ciboulette	Schnittlauch	Porrino	Cebolleta
Chocolate	Chocolat	Schokolade	Cioccolata	Chocolate
Cider	Cidre	Apfelwein	Sidro	Sidra
Cigar	Cigare	Zigarre	Sigaro	Cigarro
Cigarette	Cigarette	Zigarette	Sigaretta	Cigarrillo, pitillo
Cinnamon	Cannelle	Zimt	Cannella	Canela
Clams	Clovisses	Venus-muscheln	Conchiglie	Coquillas
Claret, red wine	Vin rouge	Rotwein	Vino rosso	Vino tinto
clean	propre	rein	puro	limpio, puro
clear	clair	klar	chiaro	claro
Clear soup	Consommé	Fleisch-brühe	Brodo	Caldo
Cloves	Girofles	Gewürz-nelken	Chiodi di Garofani	Clavos
Cocoa	Cacao	Kakao	Cacao	Cacao
Coco-nut	Noix de coco	Kokosnuß	Cocco	Coco
Cod	Cabillaud	Kabeljau	Merluzzo fresco	Bacalao fresco
Coffee	Café	Kaffee	Caffè	Café
Coffee-pot	Cafetière	Kaffee-kanne	Caffettiera	Cafétera
Coffee with milk	Café au lait	Kaffee mit Milch	Caffè con latte	Café con leche
cold	froid	kalt	freddo	frío
Cold meat	Viande froide	Aufschnitt	Carne fredda	Fiambres
Collop	Escalope	Schnitzel	Braciola	Escalopin
coagulated	caillé	geronnen	coagulato	coujarse
Cook	Cuisinier	Koch	Cuoco	Cocinero
cook, boil	cuire	kochen	cucinare	cocer
Cork	Bouchon	Korken	Turacciolo	Corcho
cold, fresh	frais, fraiche	frisch, kühl	fresco	fresco
cool, to	rafraîchir	kaltmachen	raffreddare	refrescar
Cork screw	Tire-bouchon	Korken-zieher	Cava-turaccioli	Sacacorchos
Corn flour, Corn starch	Farine de maïs	Maismehl	Farina di grano turco	Harina de maiz

English	French	German	Italian	Spanish
Corn salad Lamb salad	Salade de mâche	Rapunzel-salat	Insalata di Raperonzoli	Collejas
Cos lettuce	Laitue romaine	Bundsalat, römischer Salat	Lattuga romana	Ensalada romano
Cover	Couvert	Gedeck	Coperto	Cubierto
Crab	Crabe	Krabbe	Granchio	Camarones
Cranberries	Airelles rouges	Preisel-beeren	Mirtillo rosso	Arandano
Crayfish	Écrevisse	Krebs	Gambero	Cangrejo
Cream	Crème	Rahm, Sahne	Panna	Crema
Crust	Croûte	Kruste	Crosta	Costra
Cucumber	Concombre	Gurke	Cetriolo	Pepino
Cup	Bol	Bowle	Bacinella	Kaps
Cottage cheese	Fromage blanc	Quark	Cacio bianco	Cuajada
Currants	Raisins de Corinthe	Korinthen	Uva di Corintc	Pasa di Corintc
Curry	Currie	Curry	Curry	Curry
Cutlet, chop	Côtelette	Kotelette, Rippe	Costoletta	Chuleta

— D —

English	French	German	Italian	Spanish
Dandelion	Pissenlit, Dent-de-lion	Löwenzahn	Dente di leone	Diente de león
Date	Datte	Dattel	Dattero	Dátil
Decanter	Carafe	Karaffe	Caraffa	Garrafa
Deer	Cerf	Hirsch	Cervo	Ciervo
Delicious	délicieux	geschmack-voll	elegante	de muy buen gusto
different	divers	verschieden	diverso	diferente
Dining-room	Salle à manger	Speisesaal	Sala da pranzo	Comedor
Dinner	Diner	Mittagessen	Colazione	Comida
Dish	Plat	Gericht, Schüssel	Piatto	Manjar, Fuente
Dough, Paste	Pâte	Teig	Pasta	Pasta
Drink	Boisson	Getränk	Bibita	Bebida
drink	boire	trinken	bere	beber
Drop	Goutte	Tropfen	Goccia	Gota
dry	sec	trocken	secco	seco
Duck	Canard	Ente	Anitra	Pato
Dumpling	Quenelle	Kloß	Polpette, Gnochi	Albondigas

— E —

English	French	German	Italian	Spanish
eat	manger	essen	mangiare	comer
edible	mangeable	eßbar	mangiabile	comestible
Eel	Anguille	Aal	Anguilla	Anguila
Eel-pout	Lotte	Aalraupe, Quappe	Lasca	Lota
Egg	Oeuf	Ei	Uova	Huevo
Egg yolk	Jaune d'oeuf	Eigelb	Tuorlo (d'uovo)	Yema de huevo
Egg white	Blanc d'oeuf	Eiweiß	Albume	Clara de Huevo
empty	vide	leer	vuoto	vacio
Essence, Extract	Extrait, Essence	Auszug	Essenza	Extracto

English	French	German	Italian	Spanish
— F —				
fat	graisse	fett	grasso	graso
Fattened chicken, Poularde	Poularde	Masthuhn, Poularde	Pollastra	Pollo
Fennel	Fenouil	Fenchel	Finocchio	Hinojo
Festival, Feast	Fête	Fest	Festa	Fiesta
Field-fare	Grive	Krammets-vogel	Tordo	Tordo
Fig	Figue	Feige	Fico	Higo
Fig-pecker	Bec-figue	Feigen-drossel	Beccafico	Papafigo
Fillet of beef, Tenderloin	Filet de boeuf	Lenden-braten	Filetto di bue	Lomo
fine	fin, fine	fein	fino, delicato	fino
Fire	Feu	Feuer	Fuoco	Fuego
Fire-place, Stove	Fourneau	Herd	Focolare	Fogon
First	Premier	der Erste	Primo	Primero
Fish	Poisson	Fisch	Pesce	Pescado
Fish-bone	Arête	Gräte	Lisca	Espina
Fish-market	Marché aux poissons	Fischmarkt	Pescheria	Mercado de pescado
Flounder	Flet	Flunder	Passera	—
Flour	Farine	Mehl	Farina	Harina
Foam, Froth	Mousse	Schaum	Spuma	Espuma
Forced fruit or vegetable	Primeur	Frühobst Früh-gemüse	Primizie	Temprano
Forcemeat	Farce	Füllsel, Farce	Ripieno	Relleno
Fork	Fourchette	Gabel	Forchetta	Tenedor
Fowls	Volaille	Geflügel	Pollame	Aves de corral
French beans	Haricots verts	Bohnen, grüne	Fagiolini	Judia verde
Fresh haddock	Aiglefin	Schellfisch	Nasello	Besugo
Fried egg	Oeuf au miroir, sur le plat	Spiegeleier	Uova al tegame	Huevos al plato
Fritters	Beignets	Krapfen	Frittelle	Buñuelo
Frog	Grenouille	Frosch	Rana	Rana
frozen	glacé	gefroren	gelato	helarce
Fruit	Fruit	Obst	Frutta	Fruta
Fruit, dried	Fruits sechés	Dörrobst	Frutta secca	Fruta seca
Fruit plate	Compotière	Frucht-schüssel	Recipiente per Frutta	Compotera
Frying-pan, Skillet	Poêle à frire	Bratpfanne	Padella	Sartén
— G —				
Garlic	Ail	Knoblauch	Aglio	Ajo
Garnish	Garniture	Garnitur	Guarnitura	Guanicón
Gastro-nomer	Gastronome	Fein-schmek-ker, Ga-stronom	Buongustaio	Gastrónomo
Gherkins	Cornichons	Essiggurken	Cetriolini	Pepinillos
Giblets	Abats de volaille	Geflügel-klein	Frattaglie	Memudillos

English	French	German	Italian	Spanish
Ginger	Gingembre	Ingwer	Zenzero	Jengibre
Ginger-bread	Pain d'épice	Lebkuchen	Pan pepatc	Alfajor
good	bon, bonne	gut	buono	bueno
Goose	Oie	Gans	Oca	Ganso, Oca
Gooseberry	Groseille verte	Stachel-beere	Uva spina	Grosella
Gooseliver	Foie gras	Gänseleber	Fegato d'oca	Higado de oca
Grapes	Raisins	Wein-trauben	Uva	Uvas
Gravy, Juice	Jus, Suc	Saft	Sugo	Jugo
green	vert	grün	verde	verde
Green cabbage	Chou vert	Grünkohl	verza	Repollo
grey	gris	grau	grigio	gris
Grill	Gril	Rost	Gratella	Parilla
Gristle	Tendron	Knorpel	Cartilagine	Cartilago
Grits	Gruau	Grütze	Orzo	Engrudo
Gruel, Barley	Crème d'orge	Gersten-schleim	Orzo perlato	Cerveza
Gudgeon	Goujon	Gründling	Ghiozzo	Gobio
Guinea fowl	Pintade	Perlhuhn	Gallina faraona	Pintada

— H —

English	French	German	Italian	Spanish
Ham	Jambon	Schinken	Prosciutto	Jamón
Hare	Lièvre	Hase	Lepre	Liebre
Hash	Hachis	Gehäck	Trito, Carne tritata	Salpicón
hashed, minced	haché	gehackt	Tritato	piqué
Haunch	Cuissot	Wildkeule	Coscia	Pernil
Haunch of venison (roe)	Gigot de chevreuil	Rehkeule	Coscia di capriolo	Asada de corzo
Hazel-hen	Gelinotte	Haselhuhn	Gallina regina	Gallina
Hazelnut	Noisette	Haselnuß	Nocciola	Avellana
Head	Tête	Kopf	Testa	Cabeza
Head-chef	Chef de cuisine	Küchen-meister	Capo cuoco	Jefe de la Cocina
Head-waiter	Maître d'hotel	Ober-kellner	Primo cameriere	Jefe de Camareros
Heat	Chaleur	Hitze	Calore	Calor
Heath-cock	Coq de Bruyère	Auerhahn	Urogallo	Urogallo
Herbs	Herbes	Kräuter	Erbe	Hierbe
Herring	Hareng	Hering	Aringa	Arenque
Hip. Haw	Eglantine	Hagebutte	Rosa canina	Escaromujo
Hock, Rhenish wine	Vin du rhin	Rheinwein	Vino del Reno	Vino del Rin
Honey	Miel	Honig	Miele	Miel
Hops	Houblon	Hopfen	Luppolo	Lubulo
Horseradish	Raifort	Meerrettich	Rafano	Rábeno
hot	chaud	heiß	caldo	caliente
Hotel	Hôtel	Gasthof, Hotel	Albergo	Hotel
Household bread	Pain de ménage	Hausbrot	Pane caserellio	Pan casero
Hunger	Faim	Hunger	Appetito	Hambre

English	French	German	Italian	Spanish
— I —				
Ice	Glace	Eis	Ghiaccio	Hielo
Ice-cream	Glace	Gefrorenes, Eiscreme	Gelato	Helado
Icing	Glace royale	Zuckerguß	Chiaccia Reale	Bano de azúcar
Infusion	Infusion	Aufguß	Infusione	Infusión
Indian Corn	Maïs	Mais, Kukuruz	Grano turco	Maiz
— J —				
Jam	Confiture	Konfitüre	Marmellata	Mermelada
Jelly	Gelée	Gelee	Gelatina di frutta	Salmuera
Jug, pitcher	Crûche	Krug	Brocca	Jarro
— K —				
Kernel	Noyau	Kern	Nócciolo	Hueso
Kidney	Rognon	Niere	Rognone	Riñones
Kitchen	Cuisine	Küche	Cucina	Cocina
Knife	Couteau	Messer	Coltello	Cuchillo
— L —				
Lamb	Agneau	Lamm	Agnello	Cordero
Lamb cutlet	Côte d'agneau	Lamm-rippchen	Costolette di agnello	Costillas di cordero
Lard	Saindoux	Schweine-fett	Sugna	Manteca
Lark	Mauviette	Lerche	Allodola	Alondra
lean	maigre	mager	magro	flaco
Leek	Poireau	Lauch, Porree	Porro	Puerro
Leg	Gigot	Keule	Cosciotto	Oierna
Leg of lamb	Gigot d'agneau	Lammkeule	Coscia d'agnello	Pierma di cordero
Leg of mutton	Gigot de mouton	Hammel-keule	Cosciotto di castrato	Pierna di carnero
Leg of veal	Cuisseau de veau	Kalbskeule	Coscia di vitello	Maza de ternera
Lemon	Citron	Zitrone	Limone	Limón
Lemonade	Limonade	Limonade	Limonata	Limonada
Lemon juice	Jus de citron	Zitronen-saft	Sugo di limone	Jogo de limón
Lentil	Lentille	Linse	Lenticchie	Lenteja
Lettuce	Laitue	Lattich, Kopfsalat	Lattuga	Lechuga
Light	Lumière	Licht	Luce	Claridad
Lungs, Lights	Mou	Lunge	Polmone	Pulmón
Lime-blos-som tea	Tilleul	Linden-blütentee	Tiglio	Tild
Linseed oil	Huile de lin	Leinöl	Olio di lino	Aceite de linaza
Liquor	Liqueur	Likör	Liquore	Licor
Liter	Litre	Liter	Litro	Litro
Liver	Foie	Leber	Fegato	Higado
Lobster	Homard	Hummer	Astice	Langosta
living. alive	vif. vivant	lebend	vivo	viviente
Loin of veal	Longe de veau	Kalbsnie-renbraten	Lombata di vitello	Riñonada de ternera
lukewarm	tiède	lauwarm	tiepido	tibia
Lunch	Déjeuner à la fourchette	Gabel-frühstück	Colazione	Almuerzo

English	French	German	Italian	Spanish
— M —				
Macaroni	Macaroni	Makkaroni	Maccheroni	Macarrones
macerate	macérer	beizen, macerieren	marcerare	ablander
Mackerel	Maquereau	Makrele	Sgómbro	Verdel
Malt	Malt	Malz	Malto	Malta
Management	Administration	Leitung, Direktion	Amministrazione	Dirección
Manager	Directeur, Gérant	Leiter, Direktor	Direttore	Gerente
Marchpane, Marzipan	Massepain	Marzipan	Marzapane	Mazepán
Margarine	Margarine	Margarine	Margarina	Manteca vegetal
Marjoram	Marjolaine	Majoran	Maggiorana	Mejorana
Market	Marché	Markt	Fiera	Feria
Marmelade	Marmelade	Marmelade	Marmellata	Marmelada
Marrow	Moelle	Mark	Midollo	Tuetano
Mash	Purée	Mus	Purea, Passato di	Puré
Mashed potatos	Purée de pommes de terre	Kartoffelmus	Passato di patate Purea di patate	Puré de patatas
Matches	Allumettes	Zündhölzer, Streichhölzer	Fiamifferi	Fósfori
Meal	Répas	Mahlzeit	Pasto	Comida
Meat	Viande	Fleisch	Carne	Carne
Medlars	Nefles	Mispeln	Nespola	Nispole
Melon	Melon	Melone	Mellone	Melón
Menu	Menu	Menü	Minuta, Lista delle Vivande	Menu
Milk	Lait	Milch	Latte	Leche
Millet	Millet	Hirse	Miglio	Mijo
Mince, Hash	Hachis	Hackfleisch	Carne tritata	Picadillo
Mint	Menthe	Minze	Menta	Menta
mix	mêler,	mischen	mescolare	mezclar
mixed	mêlé mélanger	gemischt	misto	amalgamata
Mixed fruit	Fruits panachés	Gemischtes Obst	Frutta mista	Frutas varidas
mock, false	faux, fausse	falsch	falso	falso
Morello	Griotte	Sauerkirsche	Marasche	Guindilla
Morils	Morilles	Morcheln	Spugnole	Colmenillas
Mould	Moule	Form	Forma, Stampo	Molde
Mulberries	Mûres	Maulbeeren	More	Moras
Mulled Claret	Vin brulé	Glühwein	Vino brulé	Vino caliente
Mushroom	Champignon	Champignon	Funghi	Champignon
Mussel	Moule	Miesmuschel	Mítili, Muscoli	Almejas
Must	Moût	Most	Mosto	Mosto
Mustard	Moutarde	Senf, Mostrich	Senape	Mostaza
Mutton	Mouton	Hammel	Montone	cordero
Mutton cutlet	Côte de mouton	Hammelrippe	Braciola di Montone	Chuletas de cordero

English	French	German	Italian	Spanish
— N —				
Napkin	Serviette	Mundtuch	Tovagliolo	Servilleta
Nettles	Orties	Brennessel	Ortiche	Ortiga
Noodles	Nouilles	Nudeln	Tagliarini	Fideos
Nut	Noix	Nuß	Noce	Nuez
Nutmeg	Muscade	Muskat	Noce-Moscata	Nuez Moscada
— O —				
Oats	Avoine	Hafer	Avena	Avena
Oil	Huile	Oel	Olio	Aceite
old	vieux, vieille	alt	vecchio	viejo
Olive	Olive	Olive	Oliva	Aceituna
Omelette	Omelette	Omelette	Frittata	Tortilla
Onion	Oignon	Zwiebel	Cipolla	Cebolla
Orange	Orange	Apfelsine	Arancia	Naranja
Ortolan	Ortolan	Fettammer	Ortolano	Vérderon
Ox-cheek, muzzle	Museau de boeuf	Ochsenmaul	Muso di bue	Hocico de vaca
Ox-tail	Queue de boeuf	Ochsen-schwanz	Coda di bue	Rabo de vaca
Ox-tongue	Langue de boeuf	Ochsen-zunge, Rinder-zunge	Lingua di bue	Lengua de vaca
Oyster	Huître	Auster	Ostriche	Ostra
— P —				
Palate	Palais	Gaumen	Palato	Paladar
Pancake	Pannequet	Pfann-kuchen	Frittella	Tortilla
Parings	Parures	Abfälle	Ritagli	Despojos
Parsley	Persil	Petersilie	Prezzemolo	Perejil
Parsnip	Panais	Pastinake	Pastinaca	Pastinaca
Partridge	Perdreau	Rebhuhn	Pernice	Perdix
Pastry	Pâtisserie	Backwerk	Pasticceria	Pasteleria
Pastry-cook	Pâtissier	Konditor	Pasticciere	Confitero
Peach	Pêche	Pfirsich	Pesca	Alberchigo
Peacock	Paon	Pfau	Pavone	Pavo real
Pear	Poire	Birne	Pera	Pera
Pearl barley	Orge perlé	Perlgerste	Orzo brillato	Cebada
Peas	Petits pois	Erbsen	Piselli	Guisantes
Peel, Skin	Écorce, Pelure	Rinde, Schale, Haut	Scorza Peluria	Corteza Cáscava Pellejo
Pepper	Poivre	Pfeffer	Pepe	Pimienta
Pepper-box	Poivrier	Pfeffer-büchse	Macinino del Pepe	Pimentero
Peppers, Sweet	Poivron doux	Paprika-schote	Peperoni	Pimiento
Perch-pike	Sandre	Zander	Luccioperca	Lucio
Pheasant	Faisan	Fasan	Fagiano	Faisán
Pickle	Marinade	Beize	Marinata	Cáustico
Pickled cabbage, Sauer-kraut	Choucroute	Sauerkraut	Crauti	Berzas
Pie	Pâté	Pastete	Pasticcio	Pastel
Pigeon	Pigeon	Taube	Piccione	Paloma
Pike	Brochet	Hecht	Luccio	Lucio
Piment, Allspice	Piment	Piment	Paprika	Pimienta

English	French	German	Italian	Spanish
Pine-apple	Ananas	Ananas	Ananasso	Piña Tropical
Pistachios	Pistaches	Pistazien	Pistacchio	Pistachos
Plate	Assiette	Teller	Piatto	Plato
Plover	Vanneau	Kiebitz	Vannello	Avefria
Plover's eggs	Oeufs de vanneau	Kiebitzeier	Uova di vannello	Huevos di avefria
Plum	Prune	Pflaume	Prugna	Ciruela
Pudding	Pouding	Pudding	Budino	Pudin
Pumpkin	Potiron	Kürbis	Zucca	Calabaza
Punch	Ponche	Punsch	Ponce	Ponche
Pomegranate	Grenade	Granatapfel	Mela grana	Granada
Poppy	Pavot	Mohn	Papavero	Adormidera
Pork	Cochon, Porc	Schwein	Porco, Maiale	Cerdo
Pork cutlet, chop	Côte de porc	Schweinsrippe	Costolette di maiale	Chuleta de cerdo
Pork-trotters	Pieds de porc	Schweinsfüße	Zampetti di porco	Manos de cerdo
Port	Porto	Portwein	Vino d'Oporto	Oporto
Pot	Pot	Topf	Pentola	Tarro
Potato	Pomme te terre	Kartoffel	Patata	Patata
pound	piler	stoßen	pilare	Machacar
Powder-sugar	Sucre en poudre	Puderzucker	Zucchero fino	Azúcar cande
Preserve	Conserve	Konserve	Conserva	Conserva

— Q —

Quail	Caille	Wachtel	Quaglia	Codorniz
Quince	Coing	Quitte	Cotogna	Membrillo

— R —

Rabbit	Lapin	Kaninchen	Coniglio	Conejo
Radish	Radis	Radieschen	Rapanello	Rabaníto
Raspberry	Framboise	Himbeere	Lampone	Frambuesa
rasped, grated	rapé	gerieben	grattugiato	rallado
raw	cru	roh	crudo	crudo
Red currant	Groseille rouge, de Bar	Johannisbeere, rote	Ribes rosso	Grosella
Red mullet	Rouget	Rotbarbe	Triglia	Salmonete
Restaurant	Restaurant	Gaststätte, Restaurant	Ristorante	Restaurante Fonda
Rhubarb	Rhubarbe	Rhabarber	Rabarbaro	Ruibarbo
Rice	Riz	Reis	Riso	Arroz
ripe	mûr	reif	maturo	maduro
roast	rôtir	braten	arrostire	asar
Roast pork	Porc rôti	Schweinebraten	Arrosto di maiale	Asado de cerdo
Roast loin of veal	Longe de veau rôtie	Kalbsnierenbraten	Lombata di vitello	Asado de ternera de riñones
Roast	Rôtis, rôts	Braten	Arrosto	Asado
Roebuck	Chevreuil	Reh	Capriolo	Corzo
Rolls	Petit pain blanc	Weißbrötchen	Panini bianchi	Pan blanco
Rum	Rhum	Rum	Rhum	Ron
Rye bread	Pain de seigle	Roggenbrot	Pane nero	Pan moreno

English	French	German	Italian	Spanish
		— S —		
Saddle	Selle	Rücken	Schiena	Lomo
Saddle of venison (roe)	Selle de chevreuil	Rehrücken	Lombo di capriolo	Lomo de corzo
Saffron	Safran	Safran	Zafferano	Azafran
Sage	Sauge	Salbei	Salvia	Salvia
Salad	Salade	Salat	Insalata	Ensalada
Salad-dish	Saladier	Salat-schüssel	Insalatiera	Ensaladera
Salmon	Saumon	Lachs, Salm	Salmone	Salmón
Salt	Sel	Salz	Sale	Sal
Sandwich	Sandwich	Belegtes Brot	Panini imbottiti	Pan cecina
Sardine	Sardine	Sardine	Sardine	Cerdeña
Sauce	Sauce	Sauce, Tunke	Salsa	Salsa
Sausage	Saucisse	Würstchen	Salsiccia	Salchichón
Season	Saison	Jahreszeit	Stagione	Estación
Celery	Céleri	Sellerie	Sedano	Apio
Semolina	Semoule	Grieß	Semolino	Semola
sharpen	aiguiser	schleifen	affilare	aguzar
Sherry	Xerès	Sherry	Sherry	Jerez
Shin, Knuckle	Jarret	Hesse	Garetto	Carvejón
Shoulder	Épaule	Schulter	Spalla	Hombro
Side-dish, Appetizer	Hors d'oeuvre	Vorspeise	Antipasti	Entremeses
Sieve	Passoire	Sieb	Staccio	Tamiz
Skate	Raie	Rochen	Razza	Raya
Skin	Peau	Haut	Pelle	Piel
Slice	Tranche	Scheibe	Fetta	Loncha
small	petit	klein	piccolo	pequeño
Smell	Odeur	Geruch	Odore	Olor
smoke	fumer	rauchen	fumare	humear
Smoked beef	Boeuf fumé	Rauch-fleisch	Carne affumicata	Carne ahumado
smoked	fumé	geräuchert	affumicato	ahumado
Snail	Escargot	Schnecke	Lumache	Caracole
Snipe	Bécasse	Schnepfe	Beccaccia	Becada
soft	mou	weich	morbido	blando
Soft roe	Laitance	Fischmilch	Laitances	Huevas de pescado
Sole	Sole	Seezunge	Sogliola	Lenguado
Sorrel	Oseille	Sauer-ampfer	Acetosella	Acedera
Soup	Potage	Suppe	Minestra	Sopa
sour	aigre	sauer	acido	acido
sparkling	mousseux	schäumend	spumante	espumoso
Spices	Epices	Gewürze	Spezie	Especie
spicy	piquant	scharf, pikant	piccante	Picante
Spinach	Epinards	Spinat	Spinaci	Espinaca
Spit	Brôche	Spieß	Spiedo	Pica
Spoon	Cuillière	Löffel	Cucchiaio	Cuchara
Stew, Ragout	Ragoût	Würzfleisch	Intingolo	Guisado
Stewed fruit	Compôte	Dunstobst, Kompott	Composta di frutta	Compota
Stomach	Estomac	Magen	Stomace	Estómago
Strawberry	Fraise	Erdbeere	Fragole	Fresa
stuffed	farci	gefüllt	farcite	relleno
Sturgeon	Esturgeon	Stör	Storione	Esturión
Sugar	Sucre	Zucker	Zucchero	Azúcar
Supper	Souper	Abendessen	Cena	Cena
sweetened	sucré	süß	zuccherato	dulce

English	French	German	Italian	Spanish
Sweetmeats	Bonbons	Bonbons	Confetti	Bombon
Sweets	Entremet sucré	Süßspeise	Tramessi zuccherat:	Postre
Syrup	Sirop	Sirup	Sciroppo	Jarabe
— T —				
Table	Table	Tisch	Tavola	Mesa
Table-cloth	Nappe	Tischtuch	Tovaglia	Mantel
Tail	Queue	Schwanz	Coda	Rabo
Tangarine	Mandarine	Mandarine Zwerg-apfelsine	Mandarino	Mendarina
Tarragon	Estragon	Estragon, Bertram	Serpentaria	Estragon
Taste	Goût	Geschmack	Gusto	Gusto
taste	goûter	kosten	gustare	costar
tasteless, insipid	fade, insipide	geschmack-los	insipido	insipidez
Tavern	Taverne	Kneipe	Taverna	Taberna
Tea	Thé	Tee	Thè	Té
Teal	Sarcelle	Knäckente	Arzavola	Cerceta
tender	tendre	zart, mürbe	tenero	tierno
Thick soup	Potage lié	dicke Suppe	Minestrone	Sopa
Thyme	Thym	Thymian	Timo	Tomillo
Toast	Pain grillé	Röstbrot	Pane tostato	Pan tostado
Tomato	Tomate	Tomate	Pomodoro	Tomate
tough	dur	hart, zähe	duro	duro
Trails	Intestins	Eingeweide	Intestino	Intestinos
Tray	Plateau	Tablett	Vassoio	Bandeja
Trout	Truite	Forelle	Trota	Trucha
Truffle	Truffle	Trüffel	Tartufi	Trufa
Tumbler	Gobelet	Becher	Calice, coppa	Copa
Tunny-fish	Thon	Thunfisch	Tonno	Atún
Turbot	Turbot	Steinbutt	Rombo	Rodaballo
Turkey	Dinde	Pute, Indian	Tacchino	Pava
Turnips	Navets	Weiße Rüben	Navone	Nabos
Turtle	Tortue	Schildkröte	Tartaruga	Tortuga
— U —				
underdone, rare	saignant	blutig	sanguinante	sangrante
— V —				
Vanilla	Vanille	Vanille	Vaniglia	Vainilla
Veal, Calf	Veau	Kalb	Vitello	Ternera
Veal cutlet, veal chop	Côte de veau	Kalbsrippe	Costolette di vitello	Costila de ternera
Vegetables	Légumes	Gemüse	Legumi	Legumbre
Venison, Game	Gibier	Wild	Selvaggina	Caza
Vermicelli	Vermicelle	Faden-nudeln	Vermicelli	Fideos
Vermouth	Vermouth	Wermut	Vermuth	Vermut
Vinegar	Vinaigre	Essig	Aceto	Vinagre
— W —				
Waiter	Garçon, Sommelier	Kellner	Cameriere	Camarero
to warm-up	rechauffer	aufwärmen	riscaldare	calentar
Water	Eau	Wasser	Acqua	Agua

English	French	German	Italian	Spanish
Water bath	Bain-marie	Wasserbad	Bagno-Maria	Baño Maria
Water-cress	Cresson	Brunnen-kresse	Crescione	Berros
Watermelon	Pastèque	Wasser-melone	Cocomero	Sandía
well-done	bien cuit	durch-gebraten	ben cotto	Bien asado
Whipped cream	Crème fouettée, Crème Chantilly	Schlagsahne	Panna montata	Nata batida
White wine	Vin blanc	Weißwein	Vino bianco	Vino blanco
Whole	entier	ganz	completo	entero
Wild-boar	Sanglier	Wild-schwein	Cinghiale	Jabali
Wine	Vin	Wein	Vino	Vino
Wing	Aile	Flügel	Ali	Ala
Wing of chicken	Aile de poulet	Hühner-flügel	Ala di pollo	Ala de pollo
Woodcock	Bécasse	Wald-schnepfe	Beccaccia	Becada
Woodruff	Asperule	Wald-meister	Mughetto	Asperula

— Y —

Yeast	Levure	Hefe	Lievito	Levadura
yellow	jaune	gelb	giallo	amarillo
young	jeune	jung	giovane	joven
Young wild boar	Marcassin	Frischling	Cinghialetto	Jabato

English Index

D

French Index

Index of National and Regional Dishes